WILLIAM WORDSWORTH

THE CRITICAL HERITAGE

Volume I 1793–1820

Edited by
ROBERT WOOF

London and New York

First published 2001
by Routledge
11 New Fetter Lane, London EC4P 4EE

Simultaneously published in the USA and Canada
by Routledge
29 West 35th Street, New York, NY 10001

Routledge is an imprint of the Taylor & Francis Group

Typeset in Adobe Caslon by
RefineCatch Limited, Bungay, Suffolk
Printed and bound in Great Britain by
TJ International Ltd, Padstow, Cornwall

British Library Cataloguing in Publication Data
A catalogue record for this book is available from the British Library

Library of Congress Cataloging in Publication Data
William Wordsworth / [compiled by] Robert Woof.
p.   cm. – (Critical heritage series)
Includes bibliographical references and index.
1. Wordsworth, William, 1770–1850 – Criticism and interpretation.
I. Woof, Robert.   II. Series.
PR5888 .W44   2001
821'.7 – dc21   00–045941

ISBN 0–415–03441–8

WILLIAM WORDSWORTH: THE CRITICAL HERITAGE

Volume I 1793–1820

THE CRITICAL HERITAGE SERIES

GENERAL EDITOR: B. C. SOUTHAM, M.A., B.LITT. (OXON)
Formerly Department of English, Westfield College,
University of London

The Critical Heritage series collects together a large body of criticism on major figures in literature. Each volume presents the contemporary responses to a particular writer, enabling the student to follow the formation of critical attitudes to the writer's work and its place within a literary tradition.

The carefully selected sources range from landmark essays in the history of criticism to fragments of contemporary opinion and little published documentary material, such as letters and diaries.

Significant pieces of criticism from later periods are also included in order to demonstrate fluctuations in reputation following the writer's death.

For a list of volumes in the series, see the end of the book.

General Editor's Preface

The reception given to a writer by his contemporaries and near-contemporaries is evidence of considerable value to the student of literature. On the one side we learn a great deal about the state of criticism at large and in particular about the development of critical attitudes towards a single writer; at the same time, through private comments in letters, journals or marginalia, we gain an insight upon the tastes and literary thought of individual readers of the period. Evidence of this kind helps us to understand the writer's historical situation, the nature of his immediate reading public, and his response to these pressures.

The separate volumes in the Critical Heritage series present a record of this early criticism. In each volume the documents are headed by an Introduction, discussing the material assembled and relating the early stages of the author's reception to what we have come to identify as the critical tradition. The volumes make available much material that would otherwise be difficult of access and present-day readers will be in a position to arrive at an informed understanding of the ways in which literature has been read and judged.

Dr Woof's first *Wordsworth* volume, running from the earliest reviews of 1793 to *The River Duddon* volume of 1820, treats a vast body of criticism, including journal reviews, satires, parodies and imitations, together with fugitive comments in private letters and journals, some of which material has not been seen in print before.

The strict chronological arrangement of the material, together with Dr Woof's illuminating Introduction and the extensive headnotes, provide us with an invaluable perspective on Wordsworth's towering presence amongst his contemporaries and enable us to follow the stages of his poetic growth and change over the years.

BCS

Contents

II *LYRICAL BALLADS*: OPINIONS, NOVEMBER 1798–JULY 1800

III *LYRICAL BALLADS*: REVIEWS, OCTOBER 1798–APRIL 1800

IV *LYRICAL BALLADS*: OPINIONS, AUGUST 1800–FEBRUARY 1801

V *LYRICAL BALLADS*: REVIEWS, FEBRUARY 1801–APRIL 1804

VI *POEMS, 1807*: REVIEWS, 1807–1811

VII *POEMS, 1807*: OPINIONS, 1806–1814

VIII *CONVENTION OF CINTRA*: REVIEWS AND OPINIONS, 1809–1833

IX *THE EXCURSION*: REVIEWS, 1814–1820

X *THE EXCURSION*: SOME OPINIONS, 1812–1818

XI *POEMS*, 1815 and THE WHITE DOE OF RYLSTONE: REVIEWS AND OPINIONS, 1808–1820

CONTENTS

XII LETTER TO A FRIEND OF ROBERT BURNS: REVIEWS AND OPINIONS, 1816–1817

XIII 'THANKSGIVING ODE': REVIEWS AND OPINIONS, 1816–1817

XIV 'PETER BELL' AND 'THE WAGGONER':
REVIEWS AND OPINIONS, 1819

Acknowledgements

I would like to thank the many librarians over many years who have given me access to their collections, both of periodicals and of archives. The biggest debts are to the British Library and to the Wordsworth Library, but, as will be evident from the sources cited, private owners were always generous. I would like to acknowledge the assistance I received from the University of Newcastle upon Tyne and the Leverhulme Trust in making research possible over the years.

I would like to thank Sally Woodhead for her accurate and thoughtful typing of the text; Peter Regan for encouraging me to think that the book might be a finishable project; Alan Beale for translating and identifying foreign quotations; and my wife, Pamela, who, thirty years ago, thought the project an excellent idea. It is, and always was, her book.

Abbreviations and Note on References

Abbreviations have been kept to a minimum. Whenever possible, full references are given with each of the extracts.

Wordsworth's texts are difficult to cite. There has been no complete edition of his poems since the work of Ernest de Selincourt and Helen Darbishire in the mid-twentieth century. The admirable Cornell's *Wordsworth*, general editor Stephen Parrish, will be the basis of a future edition.

After the name of the poem, the reader is referred to the de Selincourt/Darbishire text. Because the revisions are particularly radical in Wordsworth's early work, such as *Lyrical Ballads*, 1798 and 1800, and *Poems 1807*, additional references are given to those volumes.

LB (1798) & *LB (1800)*	*Lyrical Ballads: Wordsworth and Coleridge. The text of the* 1798 *edition with the additional* 1800 *poems and the Prefaces edited with introduction, notes and appendices,* R. L. Brett and A. R. Jones (London, Methuen and Co. Ltd, 1963).
Poems 1807	*Wordsworth: Poems in Two Volumes, 1807*, ed. Helen Darbishire (Oxford, Clarendon Press, 1914).
PW	*The Poetical Works of William Wordsworth*, ed. Ernest de Selincourt, volumes I–V, 1940–9. Second edition (of Vols. I–III), ed. Helen Darbishire, 1952–4).
PW, I	Volume I, ed. Ernest de Selincourt, 1940, revised by Helen Darbishire, 1952.
PW, II	Volume II, ed. Ernest de Selincourt, 1944, revised by Helen Darbishire, 1952.
PW, III	Volume III, ed. Ernest de Selincourt, 1946, revised by Helen Darbishire, 1954.
PW, IV	Volume IV, ed. Ernest de Selincourt and Helen Darbishire, 1947.
PW, V	Volume V, ed. Ernest de Selincourt and Helen Darbishire, 1949.

Introduction with Select Bibliography

'He strides on so far before you he dwindles in the distance.'

This was Coleridge's explanation for the failure of intelligent men, in this case his patron, Tom Wedgwood, and the Whig and one-time radical, James Mackintosh, to recognise Wordsworth's power. It was Coleridge who enunciated the principle (one also shared by Wordsworth) which later defended Wordsworth from the attacks of his earliest critics: 'every great and original writer, in proportion as he is great or original, must create the taste by which he is to be relished; he must teach the art by which he is to be seen.' Much of our understanding of Wordsworth springs from Coleridge, but, perhaps to a surprising extent, it depends also on what Wordsworth himself has told us about his art. His prefaces and essays, his letters, his dictated notes, records of his conversation, his sister Dorothy's Journals, have all been potent in elucidating the nature of his poetry: of course, intentions are no substitute for great poetry, but if the poet is indeed as great as Wordsworth was, his insights about his own work cannot be ignored.

Yet it is still a valid question whether or not Wordsworth's published writings about his verse were a help or a hindrance to the growth of his reputation during his lifetime. The seminal Preface to *Lyrical Ballads*, 1800, has insights which scholars and poets still delight to debate, and Wordsworth himself came to see that it was sometimes difficult for his contemporaries to understand his new emphasis on a poetry that was true to the very nuance of human feelings. About Coleridge's remark in the *Biographia Literaria*, 1817, that the theory had been the first object of the critics' attack and had got in the way of the poetry, he commented wryly:

In [the *Biographia*] there is frequent reference to what is called Mr. W's theory & his Preface. I will mention that I never cared a straw about the theory – & the Preface was written at the request of Mr. Coleridge out of sheer good nature. I recollect the very spot, a deserted Quarry in the Vale of Grasmere where he pressed the thing upon me, & but for that it would never have been thought of.

(Marginalia in Barron Field's Memoirs of Wordsworth, 1839,
ed. Geoffrey Little, Sidney, 1975, 62)

There is truth in the notion that some critics did see the Preface as a stick with which to beat the poet – not, one notes, immediately after publication but over the next few years, when it had settled, after revisions in 1802 and 1805, upon its revolutionary foundations. Indeed, there were few immediate reviews of *Lyrical Ballads* with its Preface (1800); the edition was generally regarded as a re-issue of the 1798 volume, an old publication.

In these early years there was a special vital audience which nurtured Wordsworth – a fit audience but few – which consisted of his family – Dorothy and Christopher in particular, but also his sailor-brother John with his future wife Mary and her sister Sara Hutchinson adding their voices. There was also Elizabeth Threlkeld, later Elizabeth Rawson, whose letters through fragmentary comments show how the Wordsworth cousins were taking a warm interest. And then, outside the immediate family, was the acquired 'family' – friends such as the young Pinneys, sons of a Bristol sugar merchant; Francis Wrangham, Wordsworth's co-author in an imitation of Juvenal's Eighth Satire; Basil Montagu, whose child Wordsworth and Dorothy looked after. By 1797/8, the Bristol circle had enlarged to include some who were better known to Coleridge than to Wordsworth – Joseph Cottle, Thomas Poole, James Tobin, John Estlin and James Losh and his clerical friend, Richard Warner, who were settled at Bath, the former suffering from ill health. Losh in 1798 lent his fellow Cumbrian his cottage at Shirehampton and not only sent Wordsworth new books but was one of the earliest to listen to Wordsworth reading his new poems aloud. John Thelwall was a more notorious figure, whose retirement to the Wye Valley, by way of a visit to Alfoxden in 1797, simply reminds us of the network of support Wordsworth and Coleridge possessed. Thelwall was a weakish poet, and only with exaggeration could he be called a fellow writer: still, his letters written from the Wye Valley in 1798 – (see *Towards Tintern Abbey*, Grasmere, 1998, 80–2), express sympathies for the teaching power of nature some four months before Wordsworth wrote 'Tintern Abbey'. Even William Godwin, the radical philosopher in London, thought in 1797 of recommending the two poets to the Wedgwoods as possible researchers for a proposed education project. There were other lively figures – such as Dr Thomas Beddoes and his brilliant young assistant,

2

Humphry Davy; Davies Giddy, Cornish MP and patron to both Davy and Thomasina Dennis, the latter a young writer who became governess to the family of the second Josiah Wedgwood; Thomas, Josiah's philosophically-minded brother; and the Allen family who linked the Wedgwoods and Sir James Mackintosh, since the second Josiah and Mackintosh married sisters. A key London friend was Charles Lamb who, from 1797, became one of those lifetime presences, attentive to Wordsworth's authorship through the years. A year later the young Hazlitt was to journey to Alfoxden and Nether Stowey from Shropshire: he was to brood for seventeen years before publishing the first of his commentaries and a further eight before he published the scintillating *On My First Acquaintance with Poets* in Leigh Hunt's *The Liberal*, 1823. Hazlitt's future brother-in-law, John Stoddart (the future editor of *The Times*, ruthlessly satirised as Doctor Slop by William Hone), was a cold-hearted Godwinian rationalist (according to Lamb) who typified one group of reviewers – lawyers who took time off their legal studies to appraise and often roast a poet. Denman, Lockhart, John Taylor Coleridge and the redoubtable Francis Jeffrey were all practising lawyers.

It was one of those lucky/unlucky chances that Wordsworth persuaded his London friend, John Stoddart, staying at Grasmere on his way to Scotland (where he was courting Isabella Moncrieff), to review *Lyrical Ballads* for the *British Critic* (1802). Stoddart had become (after severe initial doubts) somewhat intemperate in his advocacy of his Lake friends, both in print and in conversation, and seems to have irritated a group of young Edinburgh Whigs about to begin a new quarterly, the *Edinburgh Review*: Francis Jeffrey became their leader, but the circle included Mackintosh, Sydney Smith and Francis Horner.

Wordsworth and Coleridge put on the title-page of the 1800 *Lyrical Ballads* the Latin motto, 'Quam nihil ad genium, Papiniane, tuum!', which means 'not exactly to your taste, o lawyers', and this carried an implicit challenge to the reviewers who were indeed lawyers hoping to gain an extra penny to their often scanty purses. They took on a review of books, often in bulk, rather as if they were taking on a brief. They were cutting, scathing and entertaining. Francis Jeffrey, whose first reaction to the anonymous 1798 *Lyrical Ballads* was favourable, was, from 1802, to make Wordsworth's poetry the subject of some powerful attacks. There is a spurious reasonableness and liveliness about Jeffrey's essays that sweep a reader on, and yet, when Jeffrey was faced with the 'Ode: Intimations of Immortality', he can only dismiss it in 1807 as 'the most

3

illegible and unintelligible part of the publication'. And *The Excursion* in 1814 was received by Jeffrey with a contempt of celebrated proportions: 'This will never do'; in this way Jeffrey buried in his ironic manner even the small vestiges of praise that he allowed the poem. Two years later his review of *The White Doe of Rylstone* began,

This we think has the merit of being the very worst poem we ever saw imprinted in a quarto volume.

Jeffrey fought his way against Wordsworth by means of these essays, and such opening sentences declared the tone. Robert Southey observed that Jeffrey could not spoil the laurels of Wordsworth and Coleridge and himself, though he might mildew their corn. Whatever the effect on Southey's corn, Wordsworth's sales were slow, and undoubtedly Jeffrey was in some measure responsible. Southey, the weakest of the three poets, was himself perhaps one whose presence among the Lake poets veiled Wordsworth's excellence and originality from his readers. Francis Jeffrey found that by attacking the Lake poets as a school, he could sweep all their separate faults together and so tar and ridicule their reputations. Wordsworth and Coleridge in fact were different enough, and Southey was never a serious party to their collaborations. Arguably, Wordsworth never accepted Southey as a major poet, though he did admire him as a good man and as a neighbour. Coleridge thought of Southey as a prose writer, and his late comment in *Table-Talk* (in manuscript but never published by him) that Southey's poetry had as much relation to poetry as dumb-bells do to music echoes that undercurrent of distress that both Wordsworth and Coleridge always felt about Southey's poetry: even as early as March 1796 Wordsworth declares Southey's poetry to be the work of a coxcomb.

But it is not just that Stoddart, by his extravagant praise, poisoned the water between the Lake poets and the Scottish reviewers – he probably had a positive effect and laid the basis for the more favourable appreciation that Wordsworth received from Walter Scott. Wordsworth's friendship with Scott was established by William and Dorothy's tour to Scotland in the late summer of 1803. Scott is one example of an individual reaction. Much of the commentary that follows comes from domestic or private views and these complement those in the public magazines. Unpublished letters and journals have been searched out; commentary often comes from writers who might, in the first instance, have seen Wordsworth and Coleridge as possible rivals: most of them became admirers. Indeed, most of the truly great writers of

Wordsworth's age saw him clearly and saw him whole. Coleridge was the closest – and perhaps significantly, one must apologise that the one great work that is not included in these volumes is Coleridge's *Biographia Literaria*, 1817; this is the most systematic appreciation of Wordsworth's work, setting it in the context of Coleridge's own difficult philosophical move from Locke to the German transcendentalists; Wordsworth was presented in the *Biographia* as one who showed the organic power of the faculty of the Imagination; and Wordsworth's position is not the less enhanced by his being placed beside only one other poet, and that is Shakespeare. Although Wordsworth's defects are acknowledged, his quintessential originality is insisted upon. The impact of Coleridge's commentary can be detected in the increasing interest within the universities – William Whewell, for instance, the future Master of Trinity, was forced to reconsider Wordsworth's poetry in the light of Coleridge's remarks. Again, Coleridge's impact comes through members of his family, such as his nephew, the lawyer John Taylor Coleridge, and later his brilliant daughter, Sara, who was to take up her father's torch and place Wordsworth's pre-eminence before the reader.

Interestingly, what both Wordsworth and Coleridge especially seemed to fear was the parodist and the satirist. They were aware of the impact that William Gifford's sniping *Baviad* had had in the 1790s. When Peter Bayley published in 1803 some fairly modest parodies, the poets took extreme action to try to get him attacked in the press. Parodists and satirists were, from time to time, to produce, and even orchestrate, wintry responses to Wordsworth. Clearly, some of it derived from Jeffrey's mocking superiority, which can seem to be an attitude rather than an argument; in truth, Jeffrey's argument from decorum had a sociological basis in that he felt that Wordsworth took up unsuitable subjects for one who had aspiration to be a great poet. Jeffrey could not stand the new sympathy for the weak, the poor, the oppressed; not for him the revolutionary and democratic idea that Wordsworth expressed in his letter to Charles James Fox, January 1801, when he declared that he wanted to show that 'men who do not wear fine cloaths can feel deeply'. Jeffrey's attitude was to lead to Byron's *English Bards and Scotch Reviewers* (1808) – a work in which Byron took up the same cudgels, not because he had read Wordsworth closely, but because it was more fun to imitate Jeffrey's and Gifford's bravado attacks. Byron's style here is that of an irritated superiority, touched by a sense of aristocracy, and has few fine perceptions. Byron was aware of the opinions of his radical acquaintance, Leigh Hunt, whose *Feast of Poets* (first published in 1811 but frequently revised), presented Wordsworth and his friends scornfully expelled from the Feast by Apollo himself. However, part of the turbulence that Wordsworth caused in critical circles is illustrated by Hunt's being forced to see Wordsworth for himself, rather than through the window of Jeffrey's mind. Thomas Barnes, the great and future editor of *The Times*, had instructed Hunt (while the latter was in gaol for libelling the Prince Regent) on Wordsworth's excellencies; thereafter, Hunt spoke more appreciatively of Wordsworth in successive editions of *The Feast of Poets*, 1814 and 1815. Hunt progressively revised his poem until Wordsworth was not only accepted but elevated – to Byron's disgust – to be 'the prince of the bards of his time'. Byron became himself the true heir to Jeffrey's tradition, so that he not only attacked Wordsworth in imitation of Jeffrey, but brought into play his own sense of the absurdity of the Lake poets' claims. As well as pointing out that Coleridge had taught metaphysics to the nation, and wishing that he would 'explain his explanation', Byron fell upon Wordsworth's *Excursion*:

> Wordsworth's last quarto, by the way, is bigger
> Than any since the birthday of typography;
> A drowsy frowzy poem called the 'Excursion,'
> Writ in a manner which is my aversion.
> (*Don Juan*, III, 845–8)

But, as Macaulay observed, 'though always sneering at Mr Wordsworth, he [Byron] was yet, though perhaps unconsciously, the interpreter between Mr Wordsworth and the multitude. . . . What Mr Wordsworth had said like a recluse, Lord Byron said like a man of the world.' Certainly parts of the popular *Childe Harold*, III (1816), were a direct result of Shelley's persuading Byron to read Wordsworth for himself; it was a temporary phase for Byron, but many readers notice the 'plagiarisms' from Wordsworth – low-keyed and inadequately explored as some of them are. Byron may have stolen his enemy's clothes and, having tried them on, decided to reject them, but his very concern with Wordsworth, even to attack him, seems to have done Wordsworth no harm.

Wordsworth knew that the attackers, the parodists and the plagiarists could be useful as well as dangerous. There must have been some core of significant truth in Wordsworth's news and advice in 1817 to his friend Samuel Rogers: 'Why don't you hire somebody to abuse you? . . . For myself, I begin to fear that I should soon be forgotten if it were not for my enemies'. Whether Wordsworth was exactly pleased that he should be attacked anonymously by John Hamilton Reynolds with his witty

'*Peter Bell: A Lyrical Ballad*', in 1819, is not recorded. But Reynolds was one who, some five years before, had sought Wordsworth's approval by sending him his poems; he had received Wordsworth's sensible criticisms with disappointment, and turned his real understanding of the poet to comic effect. In this he resembles James Hogg, whose *Poetic Mirror* (1816) provides blank-verse tales written in the manner of *The Excursion*: the parodia, or imitation, is so good that the necessary bathos for comic effect is extraordinarily minimal. Shelley's *Peter Bell the Third* (1819), posthumously published in 1839, is more an essay on the poet than a parody of the poem (which Shelley in Italy had only read about in Leigh Hunt's review in the *Examiner*).

All the controversy about Wordsworth's theories and his supposed application of them had sparked off a great critical debate; and the impressive thing about the criticism of Wordsworth in his own lifetime, despite the many baffled responses, is the way that the major writers rose to the challenge he presented.

Coleridge, as we have noted, was the greatest to illuminate his contemporaries about Wordsworth's powers: his *Biographia* (1817) is a treatment not only of himself but also of the nature of poetry and of Wordsworth's work as an illustration of that theory. More, and this we are able to show in the following pages, in his letters and conversations, Coleridge worked like a secret agent to further Wordsworth's fame. And so, too, did others, though on a different intellectual level. Lady Beaumont, the blue-stocking wife of the painter, Sir George, could embarrass her husband (and the poet) with her fervent advocacy. Henry Crabb Robinson, indefatigable diarist, though he published little, ministered remarkably to Wordsworth's cause; in coach or in drawing-room, in London, the provinces or in Germany, he would draw out a copy of the poems and read aloud. Charles Lamb published a favourable review of *The Excursion* in the *Quarterly Review* of 1814 (alas, sadly mutilated by the editor) but he also constantly recorded a bold and detailed response to Wordsworth in his letters. William Hazlitt stands out as one of the most interesting of Wordsworth's public advocates. He shared with Hunt (and Byron and Shelley) an aversion to Wordsworth's later politics and had little liking for him as a man. And yet, throughout Hazlitt's writing, there is a shrewd apprehension of the great Wordsworth, warts and all:

He sees nothing loftier than human hopes; nothing deeper than the human heart. This he probes, this he tampers with, this he poises with all its incalculable weight of thought and feeling, in his hands; and at the same time calms the throbbing pulses of his own heart, by keeping his eye ever fixed on the face of nature.

(from The Spirit of the Age, 1825)

So, armed with instinct, commonsense and a certain hostility, Hazlitt teases out the significance of Wordsworth, and if there is no point of rest in Hazlitt's thinking, it is because Wordsworth cannot be dismissed or categorised; there is no magic, as Rumpelstiltskin discovered, when a thing can be precisely named. Hazlitt's criticisms were to fall on the receptive ears of John Keats: but Keats's intelligence is sufficiently independent and his commentary is part of a larger concern with his poetical identity. But for all the creative writers – Lamb, Walter Scott, De Quincey, Shelley, Keats, even Clare, the late Blake and the early Tennyson – Wordsworth had become one of those mountains which had to be climbed because it became increasingly impossible to go round him. This was even to be the situation of lesser poets who might be described as literary journalists: the fair-minded non-conformist James Montgomery, who was both a reviewer and a rhetorical verse-writer, and, again, the more talented but, to Wordsworth, the unreliable figure of Leigh Hunt.

There was enough written on Wordsworth's behalf during his own lifetime to fill several feet of library shelves. Leisurely articles, long and often anonymous, appeared in periodicals by such minor writers as John Scott, the editor of the *Champion* and the *London Magazine*; Thomas Noon Talfourd, lawyer and poet; Thomas de Quincey and John Wilson (from 1820 Professor of Moral Philosophy at Edinburgh University), not to mention the growing fullness of American admiration – the painter Washington Allston, the Unitarian W. E. Channing, the young Harvard professor George Ticknor, prelude to editors such as Henry Reed; another powerful voice, as yet confined to a personal journal, was Emerson's, who had aspirations to be a great poet. It was this massing of many recognitions that led, eventually, to Wordsworth's becoming Poet Laureate in 1843 on the death of his neighbour, Robert Southey. The enterprising new University of Durham had, in 1838, noted that he was in the area and promptly gave him his first Honorary Doctorate, but it was one year later, on 12 June 1839, at a great reception at the Sheldonian Theatre in Oxford, when Isabella Fenwick, the friend of his later years, and the recorder of all his own notes on his poems in the 1840s, recorded in her letters:

No such acclamations had been heard excepting on the appearance of the Duke of Wellington – these however did not much move him – but when the public

Orator spoke of him as the Poet of humanity – and as having through the power of love & genius – made us feel as nothing the artificial distinctions which separate the different classes of society and that 'we have all one common heart' – then he felt understood & recognised – & was thankful.

(Ms. Wordsworth Trust)

Robert Browning's melancholy view of Wordsworth in 'The Lost Leader' (1845) owes something to the paranoid (and sometimes brilliant) comments by the painter Benjamin Robert Haydon, and to Elizabeth Barrett (see my essay in *Benjamin Robert Haydon*, Grasmere, 1996). Certainly, Browning's view of Wordsworth contrasted with that of the ardent John Ruskin who, on the same day, was awarded the Newdigate Prize for Poetry. Browning's dramatised portrait, for which he later apologised, has also some of its origins in what Browning discovered of Shelley's disappointment with Wordsworth. The critiques of Browning and Shelley, both written in verse, represent one of the real difficulties for a volume concerned with this poet's critical heritage: for when a poet has absorbed a great writer from his own or from a previous generation, the very admiration that the younger poet feels will also be tinctured by the deepest level of rivalry and criticism which affects the whole of the young poet's work. If, for instance, one were to consider *Alastor* (1816), a poem in which Shelley was becoming for the first time the master of his own voice, one would find there a wonderful presentation of a Wordsworthian kind of poet, one who certainly has failed in his mission but whose failure is both honourable and heroic. Shelley famously cites Wordsworth's own lines as an epigraph to *Alastor* – 'The good die first, / And those whose hearts are dry as summer's dust, / Burn to the socket'. [*The Excursion*, I, 500-2]. Shelley was rightly sceptical that an early death proved moral worth.

But the full nineteenth-century story will have to be the work of a volume other than this publication, which concludes in 1820. This avoids the massive reviews of *Ecclesiastical Sonnets* and *Memorial of a Tour of the Continent 1820*, published 1822, which assured us that Wordsworth had, with this least memorable of his poetry, found a rather drear coincidence of taste with the reviewers and reading public. Wordsworth in his later poetry became a muted spokesman for the Church of England. He had been confronted by niggling critics such as John Wilson ('Christopher North') or his own nephews about possible heretical touches in his notion of pre-existence in the 'Ode: Intimations of Immortality'. He had stiffened some of the theological and religious references in his revisions of *The Prelude* before its posthumous

9

publication, but it would seem that one of the triumphs of his poetry was that it would provide for many readers of different beliefs, as it did for Mill, a near-religious experience: the American Unitarian, W. E. Channing, used Wordsworth along with the Bible as a spiritual source. The Quakers, influenced by Thomas Clarkson's *Portraiture of Quakerism* (1806), found Wordsworth a moral teacher. John Sterling, the friend of Carlyle and of Mill, was to recommend Wordsworth's poetry as softening the 'dry hard spirit of modern unitarianism'. People were to catch sight of Wordsworth's wish to show, as he had put it to Charles James Fox, 'that men who do not wear fine cloaths can feel deeply'; or, as he put it in 'The Cumberland Beggar': 'we have all of us one human heart'. John Keble was to claim that Wordsworth, 'whether he discoursed on man or nature, failed not to lift up the heart to holy things, tired not of maintaining the cause of the poor and simple, and so, in perilous times was raised up to be a chief minister not only of noblest poesy but of high and sacred truth . . .'. But beyond such democratic and humane sentiments, tribute should be paid to Wordsworth's capacity to construct a language, newly coined, whereby to express his natural theology: phrases such as 'something far more deeply interfused', 'soul of all my moral being', 'Wisdom and spirit of the universe', 'Presences of nature', or, not least, 'The mind of man . . . married to this goodly universe' were to have far-reaching reverberations. Religious commentators of quite different persuasions did not find Wordsworth too difficult to fit into their own organised systems of belief. Here, perhaps, lay, and still remains, Wordsworth's importance: that somewhere along the line of people's belief, he touches, develops, enlivens their consciousness of things as they are, and not always in expected ways. His very research into the way people live (an element emphasised by Dorothy's Grasmere Journals, 1800–1803) marks him as a writer with a novelist's sensibility, even though that is to name only one aspect of his poetry. His matter-of-factness is combined with a capacity to generalise, as if, out of his practice of keeping his eye on both people and nature, he earned the right to give intimations of human order; even of immortality.

At his death, the obituaries, the reviews of *The Prelude* (1850) and of *Memoirs of William Wordsworth* (1851) by his nephew, Christopher Wordsworth, politely crowded in; but no great critic emerged at this point. Most unusually, Emerson spoke of Wordsworth's 'oriental abstraction', thus suggesting in a phrase Wordsworth's massive capacity for significant meditation. Emerson indeed sent a private letter to Henry Reed who had asked for his 'opinion of Mr. Wordsworth's Genius':

. . . I have been in New York two days, & there is no time in Philadelphia, I find, for a stranger; – no time there to sit & sum his obligations to the solitariest & wisest of poets, I do not know but I must defer it altogether to a silent hour, by & by, far from cities. It is very easy to see, that to act so powerfully on this practical age, he needed, with all his oriental abstraction, the indomitable vigor rooted in animal constitution, for which country men are marked. Otherwise he could not have resisted the deluge-streams of their opinion with success. One would say, he is the only man among them who has not in any point succumbed to their ways of thinking, & has prevailed. I mean, not consciously consented, – for his Church and State, though genuine enough in him, I look upon as the limitations & not the excellence of his genius.

Rather than not write, I will send this rude note, reserving my right to communicate a more considered ballot, as soon as I find a quiet halfhour to rejoice in my remembrances of this old benefactor.
(Ms. The Wordsworth Library, dated 1 January 1854: see also *Transactions of Wordsworth Society*, 1883, V, 124.)

But *The Prelude* was largely mistaken for a repetition of *The Excursion*, and its appearance was muffled by the publication of *In Memoriam*, the work of Tennyson, the rising star, soon to be the next Poet Laureate. Wordsworth's presence was felt by Tennyson and, interestingly, was promoted by Tennyson in helping Francis Palgrave to make a selection of Wordsworth's lyrics in *The Golden Treasury* (1861): 'You will see', Palgrave told Christopher Wordsworth, 'that WW. has given us more numerically & quantitively than any other poet'.

Stephen Gill's admirable *Wordsworth and the Victorians* (1998) rightly points to the 1870s as the moment when Wordsworth's reputation and achievement become the subject of serious debate. It is at this point that John Stuart Mill publishes his *Autobiography* (1873), an impressive personal testimony to the kind of power that Wordsworth's poetry could have, a power which Matthew Arnold had already named a healing power in his 'Memorial Verses', his elegy on the death of Wordsworth in 1850. Mill explains that in 1828 he had experienced 'a crisis in my mental history'. It was then that he discovered the healing power of Wordsworth:

. . . Wordsworth would never have had any great effect on me, if he had merely placed before me beautiful pictures of natural scenery. Scott does this still better than Wordsworth, and a very second-rate landscape does it more effectually than any poet. What made Wordsworth's poems a medicine for my state of mind, was that they expressed, not mere outward beauty, but states of feeling, and of thought coloured by feeling, under the excitement of beauty. They seemed to be the very culture of the feelings, which I was in quest of.

This is the account of a writer outside the Christian tradition and, indeed, the very phrase, 'a medicine for my state of mind', echoes a line from the madman's speech in Shelley's *Julian and Maddalo* (1. 355): gone is the context of suffering and humiliation of Shelley's madman; in Mill's world the medicine for his mind is the Wordsworthian world of internal feelings influenced by beauty.

Along with Mill's *Autobiography* there is the subtle essay by R. H. Hutton, originally published in 1857 but collected in 1871 as 'Wordsworth and His Genius'; Walter Pater's 'On Wordsworth' (1874) wonderfully presents Wordsworth's coherence in his capacity to convey the true voice of feeling; and, differently, the sceptic Leslie Stephen, in contrast to, say, Matthew Arnold, determined to show that he could explicate 'Wordsworth's Ethics', and did so in the *Cornhill Magazine*, 1876. Arnold was to provoke passionate responses by concluding his essay on Byron by stating that 'Wordsworth and Byron stand out by themselves. When the year 1900 is turned, and our nation comes to recount her poetic glories in the century which has then just ended, the first names with her will be these.' Swinburne, who much preferred Coleridge and Shelley, would have none of this (see 'Wordsworth and Byron', *Nineteenth Century*, 15, April and May, 1884). Alfred Austin, the future Poet Laureate, had found Wordsworth as presented by Arnold to possess little achievement as a poet, since Wordsworth 'does not treat Great material and he totally lacks Character, Action, Invention and Situation' (see Gill, 1998, 218).

The public discussions in the 1870s and 1880s interestingly still included the leading writers of that time: but, significantly, the new approaches of textual scholarship and of biographical research were at hand. William Knight – the first Secretary of the Wordsworth Society, founded in 1884 – later was to have his work mockingly characterised by his twentieth-century successor, Ernest de Selincourt, as 'the reign of chaos and old night'. Yet it was William Knight, along with Ernest Dowden, who was to lay the foundations for the exacting editorial approach made possible by access to Wordsworth's worked, and re-worked, manuscripts. Readers had to wait for Emile Legouis' *The Early Life of William Wordsworth 1770–1798* (1896), nearly half a century after Wordsworth's death, to be taught the taste by which *The Prelude* was to be enjoyed. Despite these explorations and several fine Victorian essays from Pater, Leslie Stephen and Matthew Arnold, the twentieth and twenty-first centuries – with their great tide of interpreters, editors, historians of ideas – still reach forward, still find Wordsworth ahead.

SELECT BIBLIOGRAPHY

Coleridge, Samuel Taylor (1912), *The Complete Poetical Works of Samuel Taylor Coleridge*, ed. E. H. Coleridge, 2 vols, Oxford.

—— (1956–71), *Collected Letters of Samuel Coleridge*, ed. E. L. Griggs, 6 vols, Oxford.

—— (1969), *The Friend*, ed. Barbara E. Rooke, 2 vols, Princeton.

—— (1983), *Biographia Literaria*, eds. James Engell and W. J. Bate, 2 vols, Princeton.

Gill, Stephen (1989), *William Wordsworth: A Life*, Oxford.

—— (1998), *Wordsworth and the Victorians*, Oxford.

Moorman, Mary (1965), *William Wordsworth: A Biography*, 2 vols, Oxford.

Owen, W. J. B. (1957), 'Costs, Sales, and Profits of Longman's Editions of Wordsworth', *Library*, 5th ser. 12, 93–107.

Peacock, Markham L. (1950), *The Critical Opinions of William Wordsworth*, Baltimore.

Reed, Mark (1967), *Wordsworth: The Chronology of the Early Years, 1770–1799*, Cambridge, Mass.

—— (1975), *Wordsworth: The Chronology of the Middle Years, 1800–1815*, Cambridge, Mass.

Reiman, Donald, ed. (1972), *The Romantics Reviewed. Part A: The Lake Poets*, 2 vols, New York.

Smith, Elsie (1932), *An Estimate of William Wordsworth by His Contemporaries 1793–1822*, Oxford.

Woof, Robert (1962a), 'Coleridge and Thomasina Dennis', *University of Toronto Quarterly*, 32, 37–54.

—— (1962b), 'Wordsworth's Poetry and Stuart's Newspapers: 1797–1803', *Studies in Bibliography*, XV, 149–89.

—— (1970a), 'John Stoddart, "Michael", and *Lyrical Ballads*', *Ariel*, University of Calgary, I, April, 7–22.

—— (1970b), 'Wordsworth and Coleridge: Some Early Matters', *Bicentenary Wordsworth Studies in Memory of John Alban Finch*, eds. Jonathan Wordsworth and B. Darlington, Ithaca, NY, 76–91.

—— (1984), 'John and Sarah Stoddart: Friends of the Lambs', *The Charles Lamb Bulletin*, January, 93–109.

—— (1986), 'The Matter-of-Fact Paradise', *The Lake District: A Sort of National Property*, ed. John Murdoch, London, 9–28.

—— (1995), 'The Presentation of the Self in the Composition of *The Prelude*', in *Presenting Poetry*, eds Howard Erskine-Hill and Richard A. McCabe, Cambridge.

Wordsworth, Dorothy, (1941), *Journals of Dorothy Wordsworth*, ed. Ernest de Selincourt, 2 vols, London.

—— (1971), *Journals of Dorothy Wordsworth: The Alfoxden Journal, 1798; The*

Grasmere Journals, 1800–1803, with an introduction by Helen Darbishire, ed. Mary Moorman, 2nd edn, Oxford.

—— (1991), *The Grasmere Journals*, ed. Pamela Woof, Oxford.

Wordsworth, William, *The Poetical Works of William Wordsworth*, ed. Thomas Hutchinson, Oxford and London: 1895.

—— *The Prose of William Wordsworth*, ed. Alexander B. Grosart, 3 vols, London, 1876.

—— *The Letters of William and Dorothy Wordsworth*, ed. Ernest de Selincourt, 6 vols, Oxford, 1935–9, rev. Alan G. Hill, 8 vols., Oxford, 1967–93.

—— *The Poetical Works of William Wordsworth*, ed. Ernest de Selincourt and Helen Darbishire, 5 vols, Oxford 1941–9; rev. edn 1952–9.

—— *Wordsworth and Coleridge, Lyrical Ballads, 1798*, ed. W. J. B. Owen, 2nd edn, 1969.

—— *The Prose Works of William Wordsworth*, eds W. J. B.Owen and Jane Worthington Smyser, 3 vols, Oxford, 1974.

—— *The Fenwick Notes of William Wordsworth*, ed. Jared Curtis, London, 1993.

I

Early notices and opinions, 1793–1801

1. Dorothy Wordsworth (1771–1855)

From a letter to Jane Pollard (1771–1847), 16 February 1793

By this Time, you have doubtless seen my Brother William's Poems, and they have already suffered the Lash of your Criticisms. I should be very glad if you would give me your opinion of them with the same Frankness with which I am going to give you mine. The Scenes which he describes have been viewed with a Poet's eye and are pourtrayed with a Poet's pencil; and the Poems contain many passages exquisitely beautiful, but they also contain many Faults, the chief of which are Obscurity, and a too frequent use of some particular expressions and uncommon words, for instance *moveless*, which he applies in a sense if not new, at least different from its ordinary one; by moveless when applied to the Swan he means that sort of motion which is smooth without agitation; it is a very beautiful epithet but ought to have been cautiously used, he ought at any rate only to have hazarded it once, instead of which it occurs three or four times.[1] The word *viewless*, also, is introduced far too often, this, though not so uncommon a word as the former ought not to have been made use of more than once or twice – I regret exceedingly that he did not submit the works to the inspection of some Friend before their Publication, and he also joins with me in this Regret. Their Faults are such as a young Poet was most likely to fall into and least likely to discover, and what the Suggestions of a Friend would easily have made him see and at once correct. It is however an error he will never fall into again, as he is well aware that he would have gained considerably more credit if the Blemishes of which I speak had been corrected. My Brother Kitt and I, while he was at Forncett, amused ourselves by analysing every line and prepared a very bulky Criticism, which he was to transmit to William as soon as he should have [ad]ded to it the [remarks] of his Cambridge Friends. At the conclusion of the [E]vening Walk, I think you would be pleased with those lines, 'Thus hope first pouring from her blessed Horn' &c.&c.[2] You would espy the little gilded Cottage in the Horizon, but perhaps your less gloomy Imagination and your anxiety to see your Friend placed in that happy Habitation might make you overlook the dark and broad Gulph between. If you have not yet seen the Poems pray do not make known my opinion of them – let them pass the fiery ordeal.

(*EY*, 88–9)

EDITOR'S NOTES

1. The word, 'moveless', occurs in *Evening Walk* (1793) ll. 104 and 206 where it is 'applied to the Swan', and in *Descriptive Sketches* l. 206; 'viewless' occurs in *Evening Walk* (1793) l. 148, and in *Descriptive Sketches* (1793) ll. 36, 92, 227, 548, 648; in l. 36 it was changed to 'sightless' in 1794. These words were all removed in later editions, as were 'breathless', 'shadeless', 'harmless', 'roofless', 'cloudless', 'bottomless', 'hopeless', 'weedless', 'pulseless'.
2. *Evening Walk* (1793), l. 407. The longed-for cottage retreat is seen in the distance, though 'dark and broad the gulph of time between' (l. 414).

2.

Unsigned review, *Analytical Review*, March 1793, XV, 294–7

Joseph Johnson published this periodical as well as *Descriptive Sketches* and *Evening Walk* (both 1793) and there is inevitably a touch of advertisement about the reviews. This early review was rendered doubly effective for Wordsworth since the long extract from *Descriptive Sketches* was reprinted in a major provincial newspaper, the weekly supplement to the *Sherborne Advertiser*. The extract appeared in the *Weekly Entertainer* 22 (30 September 1793), 334–5 under the heading, 'From Descriptive Sketches of the Alps, by V. Wordsworth [*sic*]', with the misprint of 'shed' for 'shade'. The *Analytical Review* notices of the two poems are usefully placed as far as Wordsworth is concerned: they come immediately after a long review of Erasmus Darwin's much-heralded *Botanic Garden* (1791), and this juxtaposition might account for the fact that Wordsworth's poems were known at this early date at Derby, the home of Darwin, and at Exeter (see Christopher Wordsworth's diary).

a. *Descriptive Sketches*

CERTAINLY nothing can be conceived better adapted to inspire sublime conceptions, and to enrich the fancy with poetical imagery, than a tour to the Alps. The present poem, as we learn from the dedication, is the result of such a tour, made by the author with a single companion on foot: and our traveller has not been an indolent spectator of the magnificent and varied scenes through which he has passed. The diversified pictures of nature which are sketched in this poem, could only have been produced by a lively imagination, furnished by actual and attentive observation with an abundant store of materials. The majestic grandeur of mountains, the rich and varied scenery of lakes and vallies, the solemn gloom of ruined monasteries and abbeys, and the different aspect of Alpine scenes in the morning and evening, during a storm, and in other atmospherical changes, are described with studied variety of imagery; the piece is occasionally enlivened with human figures, and the whole is rendered instructive by the frequent introduction of moral reflections. At the same time we must own, that this poem is on the whole less interesting than the subject led us to expect; owing in part, we believe, to the want of a general thread of narrative to connect the several descriptions, or of some episodical tale, to vary the impression; and in part also to a certain laboured and artificial cast of expression, which often involves the poet's meaning in obscurity. But our readers will be best able to judge of the nature of this performance, and the degree of entertainment it is likely to afford them, from a specimen. We shall select the description of the lake of Uri, and a stormy sunset.

[Quotes *Descriptive Sketches* (1793), ll. 284–347:

> Lo! Fear looks silent down on Uri's lake . . .
> The mountains, glowing hot, like coals of fire.]

We fancy there are few readers, whose imagination will be sufficiently glowing, to bear this last image, without pronouncing it extravagant. Perhaps too, some others may be disposed to censure, as degrading the subject to which it is applied, the image of the sun 'shaking his flashing shield from behind the clouds.' But it will not be denied, that the scenery of the hermit's hut is well conceived and described, and that Freedom is poetically exhibited as an allegorical person. The subject of freedom the poet afterwards resumes, in the following pleasing lines:

[Quotes *Descriptive Sketches* (1793), ll, 719–39:

> In the wide range of many a weary round . . .
> And whiter is the hospital bed.]

b. *Evening Walk*

THIS descriptive poem is so nearly of the same character with the preceding, that it is only necessary to remark in general, that it affords distinct and circumstantial views of nature, both inanimate and animate, which discover the eye of a diligent observer, and the hand of an able copyist of nature. We give the following picturesque passage.
[Quotes *Evening Walk* (1793), ll. 301–28;

> Sweet are the sounds that mingle from afar . . .
> Tune in the mountain dells their water lyres.]

3.

Unsigned review, *Critical Review*, July 1793, VIII, 347–8

Our northern lakes have of late years attracted the attention of the public in a variety of ways. They have been visited by the idle, described by the curious, and delineated by the artist; their beauties, however, are not exhausted, and this little poem is a proof of it. Local description is seldom without a degree of obscurity, which is here increased by a harshness both in the construction and the versification; but we are compensated by that merit which a poetical taste most values, new and picturesque imagery. There are many touches of this kind, which would not disgrace our best descriptive poets. The sun-set, an appearance so often described, has strokes perfectly new:

> A long blue bar its ægis orb divides,
> And breaks the spreading of its golden tides.
> [*Evening Walk* (1793), ll. 153–4]

The heron that

> Springs upward, darting his long neck before,
> [*Ibid.*, l. 308]

> The char, that for the May-fly leaps,
> And breaks the mirror of the circling deeps,
> [*Ibid.*, ll. 311–12]

are equally happy; but we were particularly pleased with the following description of the swan:
[Quotes *ibid*. ll. 195, 199–218:

> I love – – – – – – – – – – – – – – – – – – –
> Along the 'wild meand'ring shore' to view . . .
> Close by her mantling wings' embraces prest.]

The beauty of *the moveless form of snow*, need not be pointed out to a lover of poetry. – The *beggar*, whose babes are starved to death with cold, is affecting, though it has not equal strength with the soldier's wife in *Langhorne's Country Justice*, which seems in some measure to have suggested the idea.

We doubt whether *atop*, for on the top, is not a contraction too barbarous, and *sugh*, though an expressive word, too local to be used in any species of elegant writing.

4.

Unsigned review, *Critical Review*, August 1793, VIII, 472–4

The wild, romantic scenes of Switzerland have not yet been celebrated by an English poet; and its uncultivated beauties, which of themselves inspire the most sublime and poetical ideas, which suggest the terrible graces of rude rocks, majestic waterfalls, the abrupt cleft, and the seeming tempestuous sea arrested by the torpifying power of frost into the bold glaciere, seem to have been surveyed by few of the poetic race,

> ——Cui mens divinior atque os
> Magna sonaturam.[1]

The objection is scarcely removed. Mr. Wordsworth has caught few sparks from these glowing scenes. His lines are often harsh and prosaic, his images ill-chosen, and his descriptions feeble and insipid.

The Introduction is almost unintelligible, or, if intelligible, conveys only a vague, seemingly an inaccurate idea.
[Quotes *Descriptive Sketches* (1793), ll. 1–12:

> Were there, below, a spot of holy ground . . .
> In cataracts, or sleeps in quiet lakes.]

21

The following description of the Lake Como is in our author's best style; yet it has many of the faults already mentioned:
[Quotes *ibid.* (1793), ll. 80–105:

> More pleas'd my foot the hidden margin roves . . .
> As up th' opposing hills, with tortoise foot, they creep.]

The next passage we shall select is more characteristic of the author's general manner.
[Quotes *ibid.* (1793), ll. 201–14:

> A giant moan along the forest swells . . .
> And the bridge vibrates, tottering to its fall.]

We have not room for numerous extracts, and shall therefore conclude with some lines, which possess both the merit of glowing, but incorrect description, and the harshness, which is too prevalent through the whole poem.
[Quotes *ibid.* (1793), ll. 317–29:

> Mid stormy vapours ever driving by . . .
> Strange 'weeds' and alpine plants her helm entwine.]

EDITOR'S NOTE

1. Horace, *Satires* 1.4.43–45. 'sonaturam' should read 'sonaturum': 'who has a more divine soul and a tongue of noble utterance'.

5.

Unsigned review, *European Magazine*, September 1793, XXIV, 192–3

A living poetical writer has observed.

> That which was formed to captivate the eye,
> The ear must coldly taste; description's weak,
> And the Muse falters in the vain attempt.

To the truth of this remark we cannot refuse our assent, after comparing some of the best descriptions given by our greatest writers with the objects described. Perhaps of all the scenes which Great Britain can boast as possessing superior beauty and grandeur, none exceed the English Alps in the northern parts of this island; but of the various descriptions which have been from time to time given of them, how inadequate have the best of them been, and how little satisfaction have they afforded to the reader, when compared with the sensations produced by the beautiful originals. Mr. Wordsworth's paintings, however, do not want force or effect, and read on the spot, we are convinced would receive additional advantages from the minuteness and accuracy of his pencil. His description of the fate of the Beggar and her Children is very pathetically delineated, and other parts of the poem are intitled to praise. As a specimen we shall select the following lines:

[Quotes *Evening Walk* (1793), ll. 191–240:

> Now while the solemn evening shadows fail . . .
> Your young on winter's winding-sheet of snow.]

6. Thomas Holcroft (1749–1809)

Unsigned review, *Monthly Review*, October 1793, XII, 216–18

Wordsworth's poems no doubt suffer at Holcroft's hands as the review of them is seen to be part of a substantial attack on descriptive poetry which Holcroft launches in this issue. Holcroft's reference in the first line '(See page 166, &c.)', takes his reader to the more substantial review of *The South Downs* an anonymous descriptive poem, which attacks the whole genre:

Let [the poet] therefore consider, first, whether the descriptive poem be not in itself a bad species of poetry. The subjects selected are necessarily miscellaneous, and may be supposed well or ill chosen, according to the varying judgement of each reader. Will such subjects admit of that delightful unity, that attractive pathos, which the interest excited for some person or some event is capable of producing? Are not the episodes, without which Descriptive Poetry perhaps could not exist, each and all of them blemishes? Throughout the whole of this long poem, how often do we recollect the subject of it, namely, the Downs? Let the author cast his eye over his own table of contents, and try the question. If he be impartial, he will confess to himself that, even while speaking of his mowers, reapers, and shepherds, – though they be actually on the spot, – the Downs are forgotten.

Again on page 221 of the same issue, Holcroft began a review of George Cumberland's *A Poem on the Landscapes of Great Britain* in like irritation, 'Thirty-six pages more of descriptive poetry!' (See B. C. Nangle, *Monthly Review, Second Series*, Oxford, 1955, 31–2 and 243; Holcroft is shown to have been a frequent reviewer.)

---

a. *Descriptive Sketches*

More descriptive poetry! (See page 166, &c.) Have we not yet enough? Must eternal changes be rung on uplands and lowlands, and nodding forests, and brooding clouds, and cells, and dells, and dingles?

Yes; more, and yet more: so it is decreed.

Mr. Wordsworth begins his descriptive sketches with the following exordium:

> Were there, below, a spot of holy ground,
> By Pain and her sad family *un*found,
> Sure, Nature's God that spot to man had giv'n,
> Where murmuring *rivers join* the song of *ev'n!*
> Where *falls* the purple morning far and wide
> *In flakes* of light upon the mountain side;
> Where summer suns in ocean sink to rest,
> Or moonlight upland lifts her hoary breast;
> Where Silence, on her night of wing, o'er-broods
> Unfathom'd dells and undiscover'd woods;
> Where rocks and groves the *power* of waters *shakes*
> In cataracts, or sleeps in quiet lakes.
>
> [*Descriptive Sketches* (1793), ll. 1–12]

May we ask, how it is that rivers join the song of ev'n? or, in plain prose, the evening! but, if they do, is it not true that they equally join the song of morning, noon, and night? The *purple morning falling in flakes* of light is a bold figure: but we are told, it falls far and wide – Where? – On the mountain's *side*. We are sorry to see the purple morning confined so like a maniac in a straight waistcoat. What the night of wing of silence is, we are unable to comprehend: but the climax of the passage is, that, were there such a spot of holy ground as is here so sublimely described, *unfound* by Pain and her sad family, Nature's God had surely given that spot to man, though its *woods* were *undiscovered*.

Let us proceed,

> But *doubly* pitying Nature loves to show'r
> Soft on his *wounded heart* her healing pow'r,
> Who *plods* o'er hills and vales his road *forlorn*,
> Wooing her varying charms from eve to morn,
> *No sad vacuities* his heart *annoy,*
> *Blows* not a Zephyr but it *whispers joy*;
> For him *lost* flowers their *idle* sweets *exhale*;
> He *tastes* the meanest *note* that swells the gale;
> For him sod-seats the cottage-door adorn,
> And *peeps* the far-off *spire*, his evening bourn!
> Dear is the forest *frowning* o'er his head,
> And dear the green-sward to his *velvet tread*;
> Moves there a *cloud* o'er mid-day's flaming eye?
> Upwards he looks – and calls it luxury;
> Kind Nature's *charities* his steps attend,
> In every babbling brook he finds a friend.
>
> [*Ibid.*, ll. 13–28]

Here we find that *doubly* pitying Nature is very kind to the traveller, but that this traveller has a *wounded heart* and *plods* his road *forlorn*. In the next line but one we discover that –

> No *sad vacuities* his heart *annoy*;
> Blows not a Zephyr but it whispers *joy.*

The flowers, though they have lost themselves, or are lost, exhale their idle sweets for him; the *spire peeps* for him; sod-seats, forests, clouds, nature's charities, and babbling brooks, all are to him luxury and friendship. He is the happiest of mortals, and plods, is forlorn, and has a wounded heart. How often shall we in vain advise those, who are so delighted with their own thoughts that they cannot forbear from putting them into ryhme, to examine those thoughts till they themselves understand them? No man will ever be a poet, till his mind be sufficiently powerful to sustain this labour.

b. *Evening Walk*

In this Epistle, the subject and the manner of treating it vary but little from the former poem. We will quote four lines from a passage which the author very sorrowfully apologizes for having omitted:

Return delights! with whom my road beg*un*,
When *Life-rear'd* laughing *up her* morning *sun*;
When Transport kiss'd away my April tear,
"Rocking as in a dream the tedious year."

[*Evening Walk* (1793), ll. 27–30]

Life *rearing* up the sun! Transport kissing away an *April* tear and *rocking* the year as in a dream! Would the cradle had been specified! Seriously, these are figures which no poetical licence can justify. If they can possibly give pleasure, it must be to readers whose habits of thinking are totally different from ours. Mr. Wordsworth is a scholar, and, no doubt, when reading the works of others, a critic. There are passages in his poems which display imagination, and which afford hope for the future: but, if he can divest himself of all partiality, and will critically question every line that he has written, he will find many which, he must allow, call loudly for amendment.

7. Christopher Wordsworth (1774–1846)

Extract from his diary, 1793

This diary records Christopher Wordsworth's second year at Trinity College, Cambridge. Several of the undergraduates (apart from Coleridge) who discussed Wordsworth with Christopher were themselves to attempt poetical composition: Dewhurst Bilsborrow from Derby contributed panegyrical verses to Darwin's *Zoonomia* (1794); C. V. LeGrice (1773–1858), schoolfellow of Coleridge, admirer late in life of Wordsworth, was a reviewer and writer of verses; William Rough (1772–1838), editor of the short-lived *University Magazine* (1795) and author of *Lorenzino di Medici* (1797), a poor poem, became a London lawyer and finally Chief Justice of Ceylon. The two members of the Literary Society at Exeter, where, according to Coleridge, Wordsworth was esteemed, were Dr. Hugh Downham (1740–1809) and Richard Hole (1746–1803), poet and antiquary. Christopher Wordsworth's diary reads:

a. Tuesday, 5 [November 1793]

. . was to have gone to Coleridge's to wine, to consult on ye. plan [to form a literary society] had I not been engaged at home with ye. Howeses &

Strickland. Went with them to ye. Coffee house. On my going out met Bilsborrow. returned back with him. Soon after came in Le Grice, Coleridge & Rough. Got all together in a box (& having met with ye. monthly review of my Brs. Poems) entered into a good deal of literary & critical conversation on Dr. Darwin. Miss Seward. Mrs. Smith. Bowles. and my Br. Coleridge spoke of the esteem in wch. my Br. was holden by a society at Exeter. of wch. Downham & Hole were members as did Bilsborrow (wch. he had before told me) of his repute with Dr. D. Miss Seward &c &c at Derby . . .

b. Saturday 9 [November 1793]

No author ought I think, without he enters ye. world with considerable advantages, to begin with publishing a very elaborate work: however, not a work upon wch. tastes may very considerably vary. e.g. my Brs. Poems. If *he* had had his reputn. raised by some less important & more *popular* poem, it would have ensured from petty critics a diffn. reception to his 'Descrpve. Sketches' & 'Evening Walk' – Chapel.

(*Social Life at the English Universities in the Eighteenth Century*, C. Wordsworth, 1874, 589–90, corrected from Ms. at Trinity College, Cambridge.)

8.

Unsigned notice, *English Review*, 1793, XXII, 388

This notice was later reprinted in the *Scots Magazine*, 1793, LVI, 24.

a. *Descriptive Sketches*

The romantic scenes in the Alps have been celebrated by numerous travellers, and are described by the present author in an animated strain of poetry. If he rises not to a sublimity proportionable to the most magnificent objects of nature, he at least seems to catch from them a degree of poetical enthusiasm.

b. *Evening Walk*

This Epistle is the production of the author of the preceding Sketches. It presents us with a series of natural imagery, which, being drawn from rural life, affords a soothing pleasure to the fancy. The versification is easy, and corresponds with the agreeable simplicity of the subject.

9.

Review signed 'Peregrinator', *Gentleman's Magazine*,
March 1794, LXIV, 252–3

Reviewed by a Travelling Correspondent.

Mr. URBAN, *Penrith, Sept. 6.* [1793]

On my arrival at this place, after having just compleated a tour of the Lakes, I chanced yesterday to meet with Mr. Wordsworth's poem. I have read it through carefully more than once; and, finding myself much pleased with it, not only as a poem in the abstract, but more particularly as a companion of the traveller who knows how to feel and estimate the real beauties of Nature, and, at the same time, is not averse to the children of the Muse; I know not how I can better repay to these delightful vales the very large debt of pleasure I owe them, than by attempting farther to extend the prevalence of their charms, by recommending this poem to the attention of their several visitants.

Of the author of this poem the only knowledge I can boast is that of having seen him once or twice while I was his contemporary at Cambridge. The only time. indeed, that I have a clear recollection of having met him, I remember his speaking very highly in praise of the beauties of the North; with a warmth indeed which, at that time, appeared to me hardly short of enthusiasm. He mentioned too, which appears also from the present poem, that he had received the whole of his education in the very bosom of the Lakes, at a small seminary, which has produced of late years in our University several names which have done it very considerable credit.

After giving a short characteristic sketch of the principal Lakes, he concludes the enumeration with that of Esthwaite, the name of the one which adorns the sweet vale,

> where *he* taught, a happy child,
> The echoes of the rocks *his* carols wild.
>
> [*Evening Walk* (1793), ll. 19–20]

After some beautiful and pathetic lines which contrast his present with his former wanderings.

> When link'd with thoughtless mirth he cours'd the plain,
> And hope itself was all *he* knew of pain,
>
> > [*Ibid.* ll. 31–2]

he checks his complaints, and proceeds thus,

> > Say, will my friend, with soft affection's ear
> > The hist'ry of a poet's evening hear?
> >
> > > [*Ibid.* ll. 51–52]

Afterwards succeeds a very accurate and well-marked description of a sultry summer's noon, and a waterfall, which, as a note informs us, is meant to convey the features of that delicious little scene, the lower cascade at Rydal, where he hides himself

> > Till eve's mild hour invites his steps abroad.
> >
> > > [*Ibid.* l. 88]

Among the several particulars of his Walk your readers will admire the following description of a slate quarry:
[Quotes *Evening Walk* (1793), ll. 139–50:

> > Bright'ning the cliffs between where sombrous pine, . . .
> > Glad from their airy baskets hang and sing.]

I am unwilling to trouble you much with quotations, otherwise I should be tempted to transcribe Mr. Wordsworth's spirited description of the cock, or his very elegant one of the swan, and the tale of the beggar which succeeds it. You will excuse me, however, if, farther to justify the good opinion I have conceived of this poem, I request your insertion of the following description of the Northern lights, and that of night which succeeds it:
[Quotes *ibid.* (1793), ll. 339–88

> > Mid the dark steeps repose the shadowy streams . . .
> > Still the cold cheek its shudd'ring tear retains.]

Of this poem I have yet seen no review. I wish the pleasure, which I myself have received from it, to be imparted to others who shall have to make, or who have already made, the same tour. Lest, however, any one should be tempted to look into this poem by my recommendation and find himself disappointed, I must forewarn your readers that no description of particular spots is here aimed at; such an attempt in poetry could have been productive of little but vague, uninteresting description, and tiresome repetition: they will find, however, the general imagery of the country enumerated and described with a spirit and elegance which prove that the author has viewed nature with the attentive and warm regard of a true poet. Feeling for the credit of my own University, I think we have reason to expect much from this, I suppose, first production (though by no means a faultless one) of Mr. W's muse; I trust he will restore to us that laurel to which, since Gray laid down 'his head upon the lap of earth,' and Mason 'declined into the vale of years,' we have had so slight pretensions. From the concluding page of this poem I am glad to find it is not the only offspring of Mr. Wordsworth's pen; he there advertises 'Descriptive Sketches taken during a pedestrian Tour in the Alps.'

10.

Unsigned notice, *New Annual Register 1793*, 1794

This notice was published in the anonymous *Biographical Anecdotes and Characters*, 1794.

In December 1798 the *Anti-Jacobin Review and Magazine* I, 700 complained that the reviewing of Domestic Literature in the *New Annual Register*,

> if executed with impartiality, might be a useful epitome of all the publications of the year; but as it is managed at present, it is only a re-echo of the Monthly, Critical, and Analytical Reviews. The same opinions, the same characters, the same factitious views point out the prototypes.

Mr. Wordsworth's 'Descriptive Sketches in Verse, . . .' among many harsh lines, obscure expressions, and incorrect imagery, offer to the reader many beautiful pictures, which shew that he was not an inattentive or insensible spectator of the rich scenes which he visited; and that he possesses a lively and fertile imagination. With a chastised taste, and the deliberate exercise of that good sense in which he certainly is not defective, he might render his poetry a pleasing companion to the traveller among those interesting scenes.

The same remarks apply to 'An Evening Walk . . .' by the same author.

11. Samuel Taylor Coleridge (1772–1834)

A note to his poem, 'Lines written at Shurton Bars', 1795/6

Written between September 1795 when the poem was composed and March 1796 when the notes for *Poems* (1796) were written out for the printer, this is Coleridge's first written comment on Wordsworth. Though he refers to Wordsworth's published poems, he would at least have heard Wordsworth recite the unpublished *Salisbury Plain*. Only the first sentence of the note was published; Coleridge's irritable commands on the manuscript that the note be printed in full were ignored by Cottle in both 1796 and 1797. (See R. S. Woof, 'Wordsworth and Coleridge: Some Early Matters', *Bicentenary Wordsworth Studies*, Cornell, 1970, 76–91 for a full discussion).

– The expression 'green Radiance' is borrowed [from a poem *deleted*] of Mr. Wordsworth [*Evening Walk* (1793), l. 278] a Poet whose versification is occasionally harsh and his diction too frequently obscure: but whom I deem unrivalled among the writers of the present day in [strong conceptions *deleted*] manly sentiment, novel imagery, and vivid colouring. – His chief work is a Poem entitled 'Descriptive Sketches of the Alps'. The Reviewers have spoken with contempt of it. In the style of Fable, which makes the inanimate 'instinct with thought', suppose, that a small hollow Cylinder, [thrown into the midst *deleted*] which had been fixed into the channel of a mighty stream, should judge of the torrent by the Quantity of Water which passed through itself – Should we wonder that the Cylinder should [speak *deleted*] think contemptuously of the Torrent? – A Gentleman near Bristol [has made *deleted*] makes it an invariable rule to [publish *deleted*] purchase every work that is violently abused by the Reviewers: and with a very few exceptions I never saw a more judicious collection of recent Compositions, both in prose and verse.

12. Anna Seward (1747–1809)

From a letter to Rev. H. F. Cary, dated 'Lichfield, March 4, 1798'

J. L. Clifford ('The Authenticity of Anna Seward's Published Correspondence', *Modern Philology* xxxix, 113–22) points out that dates must be regarded as only approximately correct, since Anna Seward in later life prepared her letters for publication from her own copies and considerably revised them. The context of the comment on Wordsworth is a discussion of Coleridge's *Poems* (1797). The remark that she had never before heard of Wordsworth is surprisingly inconsistent with the statement by Bilsborrow in 1793 (see entry 7a).

[Coleridge's] assertion, in a note, page 88, of the unrivalled powers, among the poets of the present day, of Wordsworth's muse in poetic essentialities, induced me instantly to send for his poems. I was extremely surprised, for it was a name I had not once heard of, though I find his poems had been published some time. This superiority which Coleridge assigns to them, is just as founded as the asserted superiority of Schiller to Shakespeare. Wordsworth has genius – but his poetry is harsh, turgid, and obscure. He is chiefly a poetic landscape painter – but his pictures want distinctness. It is strange that Mr C. should, in that note, attribute originality to Wordsworth's expression *green* radiance, for the light of the glow-worm.[1] That light is perfectly stellar, and Ossian calls the stars green in twenty parts of his poetry, translated and published, before Wordsworth, who is a very young man, was in existence.

I who had always, since I first in childhood began to observe the characteristic appearances of the objects of nature, seen the stars and the glow-worm effusing greenish beams, wondered, on my introduction to the muses, to find none of their votaries pointing out that tinge in the lustre of some of the largest and brightest, and in the light of the glow-worm. When Ossian came out, in my early youth, I was charmed to find him confirming, by his epithet *green* for the stars, the accuracy of my visual perception. The following lines are in my Langollen Vale:

> While glow-worm lamps effuse a pale green light,
> Such as in mossy lanes illume the starless night.

(*Letters of Anna Seward*, ed. Walter Scott, 1811, v. 60–2)

Publication that he can secure you from every Expense, without risque to himself, and you will receive the profits that may arise after the expenses are paid. He recommends having 500 copies struck off instead of 250 – He is now engaged in his weekly publication called Watchman, the method he intends to adopt in the sale of your Work is, to persuade his Bookseller to get the People that sell the Watchman to take a few copies of your Poem, by which means he can ascertain how far it can be practicable to publish it without hazard to any party –

(R.S. Woof, 'Wordsworth and Coleridge: Some Early Matters', *Bicentenary Wordsworth Studies*, Cornell, 1970, 90)

b. From a letter to James Tobin, 12 April 1796

James Tobin was the near-blind brother of John, the dramatist.

... I remained three Weeks with Wordsworth at Race-down, who desired me to say, how happy it will make him to see you there – but not to expect any thing more than democratic fair [*sic*] – His Salisbury Plain is so much altered that I think it may in truth be called a new Poem – I doubt not but you will see it in Print within the duration of a few Weeks – While we were with him he relaxed the rigour of his philosophic Nerves so much as to go a Coursing several times, and I assure you did not eat the unfortunate Hares with less relish because he heard them heave their death groans, and saw their Eyes directed towards Heaven with that glare of vacant sadness which belongs to the expiring creature – for his usual Appetite shewed itself at the dining Table – Miss Wordsworth has undoubted claim to good humour, but does not possess in my opinion, that je ne sais quoi, so necessary to sweeten the sour draught of human misfortune and smooth the ruged [*sic*] road of this Life's passage ...

(Ms. Pinney Papers, University of Bristol)

16. Charles Lamb (1775–1834)
From a letter to Coleridge, late May 1796

The poem is the manuscript of 'Salisbury Plain'.

Wordsworth's poem I have hurried thro' not without delight.

(*The Letters of Charles and Mary Lamb*, ed. E. V. Lucas, 1935, I, 9)

17. Samuel Taylor Coleridge
From letters, 1796–1798

a. From a letter to John Thelwall, 13 May 1796

The poem under discussion is Coleridge's 'Religious Musings'.

A very dear friend of mine, who is in my opinion the best poet of the age (I will send you his Poem when published) thinks that the lines from 364 to 375 & from 403 to 428 are the best in the Volume – indeed worth all the rest – And this man is a Republican & at least a *Semi*-atheist.

(*Collected Letters of Samuel Coleridge*, ed. E. L. Griggs, Oxford, 1956–71, I, 215–6)

b. To John Prior Estlin, 10 June 1797

This is a lovely country – & Wordsworth is a great man. – He admires your sermon against Payne much more than your last – I suppose because he is more inclined to Christianity than to Theism, simply considered . . .

(*Ibid.*, i, 327)

c. To Robert Southey, 17 July 1797

Wordsworth is a very great man – the only man, to whom *at all times* & in *all modes of excellence* I feel myself inferior – the only one, I mean, whom I *have yet met with* – for the London Literati appear to me to be very much like little Potatoes – i.e. *no great Things*! – a compost of Nullity & Dullity.

(*Ibid.*, i, 334)

d. To Joseph Cottle, 7 March 1798

– The Giant Wordsworth – God love him! even when I speak in the terms of admiration due to his intellect, I fear lest those terms should keep out of sight the amiableness of his manners – he has written near 1200 lines of a blank verse,[1] superior, I hesitate not to aver, to any thing in our language which any way resembles it. Poole (whom I feel so consolidated with myself that I seem to have no occasion to speak of him out of myself) thinks of it as likely to benefit mankind much more than any thing, Wordsworth has yet written.

(*Ibid.*, i, 391)

e. To John Prior Estlin, 18 May 1798

I have now known him [Wordsworth] a year & some months, and my admiration, I might say, my awe of his intellectual powers has increased even to this hour – & (what is of more importance) he is a tried good man. – On one subject we are habitually silent – we found our data dissimiliar, & never renewed the subject/It is his practice and almost his nature to convey all the truth he knows without any attack on what he supposes falsehood, if that falsehood be interwoven with virtues or happiness – he loves & venerates Christ & Christianity – I wish, he did more – but it were wrong indeed, if an incoincidence with one of our wishes altered our respect & affection to a man, whom we are as it were instructed by our great master to say that not being against us he is for us. – His genius is most *apparent* in poetry – and rarely, except to me in tête à tête, breaks forth in conversational eloquence.

(*Ibid.*, i, 410)

EDITOR'S NOTE

1. Mainly, one presumes, 'The Ruined Cottage' Ms. B. (*PW*, V, 379–99).

'THE BORDERERS'

18. Samuel Taylor Coleridge

From letters, 1797

a. To Joseph Cottle, 8 June 1797

– Wordsworth admires my Tragedy – which gives me great hopes. Wordsworth has written a Tragedy himself. I speak with heart-felt sincerity & (I think) unblinded judgement, when I tell you, that I feel myself a *little man by his* side; & yet do not think myself the less man, than I formerly thought myself. – His Drama is absolutely wonderful. You know, I do not commonly speak in such abrupt & unmingled phrases – & therefore will the more readily believe me. – There are in the piece those *profound* touches of the human heart, which I find three or four times in 'The Robbers' of Schiller, & often in Shakespere – but in Wordsworth there are no *inequalities*. T. Poole's[1] opinion of Wordsworth is – that he is the greatest Man, he ever knew – 'I coincide. –

(*Collected Letters of Samuel Coleridge*, ed. E. L. Griggs, Oxford, 1956–71, i, 325)

b. To John Prior Estlin, 9 June 1797

I am at present sojourning for a few days with Wordsworth, at Racedown Lodge, near Crewkherne: & finishing my Tragedy. Wordsworth, who is a strict and almost severe critic, thinks very highly of it – which gives me great hopes . . .

(*Ibid.*, i, 326)

EDITOR'S NOTE

1. Wordsworth met Poole probably in early April, at Nether Stowey.

19. Robert Southey (1774–1843)

From a letter to C. W. Williams Wynn, 22 September 1797

Coleridge has written a tragedy – by request of Sheridan. It is uncommonly fine – the very character appears to me to possess qualities which can not possibly exist in the same mind. But there is a man, whose name is not known in the world – Wordsworth – who has written great part of a tragedy, upon a very strange and unpleasant subject – but it is equal to any dramatic pieces which I have ever seen.

(*New Letters of Robert Southey*, ed. Kenneth Curry, 1965, I, 148)

20. Edward Ferguson (1764–1843)

From a letter to his brother Samuel, 13 February 1798

From the death of their mother in 1773, both Edward and Samuel had been brought up at Halifax by their Aunt, Elizabeth Rawson (née Threlkeld). In 1778, on the death of her mother, Dorothy Wordsworth joined this Threlkeld/Ferguson household, staying for nine years. Samuel had emigrated to Philadelphia in 1790.

Dorothy and Wm Wordsworth have been in London in order to get a Play they have been writing on the Stage but it has been refus'd at Covent Garden where their Friends were though from all accounts it was Masterly performance – a Tragedy of a very uncommon Sort – beautiful language – and universally admir'd by all who read it – they think the refusal is owing to the deprav'd State of the Stage at present and are undetermin'd whether to wait till a change takes place or publish it if the latter we shall have copies immediately – and will send you.

(*EY* 197, footnote 1)

21. Elizabeth Rawson (née Threlkeld) (1774–1827)

From a letter to her nephew Samuel Ferguson, 14 February 1798

Elizabeth Threlkeld was first cousin of the Wordsworths' mother with whom Dorothy had lived for nine years at Halifax.

Dorothy and William Wordsworth have been in London, and at Mr Nicholsons the motive of their Journey was to offer a Tragedy for the inspection of the Manager at Covent Garden theatre which they were induced to believe he would accept and that it would have a prodigious run. They had planned many schemes to follow if it succeeded, one of which was a pedestrian tour through Wales and by Yorkshire into Cumberland. This would *by many* be thought rather a *wildish* scheme, but by them it was thought very practicable and would certainly have been put into execution, had not the Play been unfortunately rejected. I received a very entertaining letter from Dorothy on the occasion, she says they are not disappointed with its rejection, but I cannot give implicit credit to her assertion. William is not determined whether he shall publish it or no, he expects a reform to take place in the Stage, and then it may be brought forward to great advantage. These are visionary plans the distant prospect of which may be very pleasant, but which on a nearer view, almost always disappoint one. However they are happy in having very fertile imaginings which are a continual source of entertainment to them, and serve to enliven many of their solitary hours. I believe Williams Play has very great merit; the language is beautiful, and it is uncommonly interesting Miss Nicholson tells me; but the Metaphysical obscurity of one character was the great reason for its rejection. I wish we could send you a copy of it, for I dare say you will be as anxious as we are, to read the performance of our relation, and that of so excentric a young man.

(*EY* 197, footnote 1)

22. Samuel Taylor Coleridge

From a letter to Joseph Cottle, early April 1798

My Tragedy employed and strained all my thoughts and faculties for six or seven months: Wordsworth consumed far more time, and far more thought, and far more genius.

(*Collected Letters of Samuel Taylor Coleridge*, ed. E. L. Griggs, Oxford, 1956–71, i, 402)

23. William Hazlitt (1778–1830)

Reminiscences of Wordsworth and Coleridge in 1798, recollected after 25 years; extracts from 'My First Acquaintance with Poets', *The Liberal*, April 1823

When Barron Field quoted extracts from this essay in his unpublished study of Wordsworth (1839), he noted that Hazlitt was 'a reformer to the last'; Wordsworth annotated Field's manuscript in 1840: 'This implies that I was not a reformer to the last – only my views of reform differ greatly from Mr. Hazlitt's &c. &c.' (Ms. British Museum).

a. Account of Coleridge's conversation at Wem in Shropshire, January 1798

Coleridge added that Mackintosh and Tom Wedgwood (of whom, however, he spoke highly) had expressed a very indifferent opinion of his friend Mr. Wordsworth, on which he remarked to them:

He strides on so far before you, that he dwindles in the distance.

b. Account of a visit to Coleridge and Wordsworth, late May–early June 1798

In the afternoon, Coleridge took me over to All-Foxden, a romantic old family-mansion of the St. Aubins, where Wordsworth lived . . . Wordsworth himself was from home, but his sister kept house, and set before us a frugal repast; and we had free access to her brother's poems, the *Lyrical Ballads*, which were still in manuscript, or in the form of *Sybilline Leaves*. I dipped into a few of these with great satisfaction, and with the faith of a novice . . .

[The following] morning, as soon as breakfast was over, we strolled out into the park, and seating ourselves on the trunk of an old ash-tree that stretched along the ground, Coleridge read aloud with a sonorous and musical voice, the ballad of *Betty Foy*. I was not critically or sceptically inclined. I saw touches of truth and nature, and took the rest for granted. But in the *Thorn*, the *Mad Mother*, and the *Complaint of a Poor Indian Woman*, I felt that deeper power and pathos which have been since acknowledged,

'In spite of pride, in erring reason's spite,'

as the characteristics of this author; and the sense of a new style and a new spirit in poetry came over me . . .

Coleridge lamented that Wordsworth was not prone enough to believe in the traditional superstitions of the place, and that there was a something corporeal, a *matter-of-fact-ness*, a clinging to the palpable, or often to the petty, in his poetry, in consequence. His genius was not a spirit that descended to him through the air; it sprung out of the ground like a flower, or unfolded itself from a green spray, on which the gold-finch sang. He said, however (if I remember right), that this objection must be confined to his descriptive pieces, that his philosophic poetry had a grand and comprehensive spirit in it, so that his soul seemed to inhabit the universe like a palace, and to discover truth by intuition, rather than by deduction. The next day Wordsworth arrived from Bristol at Coleridge's cottage. I think I see him now. He answered in some degree to his friend's description of him, but was more gaunt and Don Quixote-like. He was quaintly dressed (according to the *costume* of that unconstrained period) in a brown fustian jacket and striped pantaloons. There was something of a roll, a lounge in his gait, not unlike his own Peter Bell. There was a severe, worn pressure of thought about his temples, a fire in his eye (as if he saw something in objects more than the outward appearance), an intense high narrow forehead, a Roman nose, cheeks furrowed by strong purpose and feeling, and a convulsive inclin-ation to laughter about the mouth, a good deal at variance with the solemn, stately expression of the rest of his face. . . .

He sat down and talked very naturally and freely, with a mixture of clear gushing accents in his voice, a deep guttural intonation, and a strong tincture of the northern *burr*, like the crust on wine. He instantly began to make havoc of the half of a Cheshire cheese on the table, and said triumphantly that 'his marriage with experience had not been so unproductive as Mr. Southey's in teaching him a knowledge of the good things of this life.' He had been to see the *Castle Spectre* by Monk Lewis, while at Bristol, and described it very well. He said 'it fitted the taste of the audience like a glove.' This *ad captandum*[1] merit was however by no means a recommendation of it, according to the severe principles of the new school, which reject rather than court popular effect. . . .

We went over to All-Foxden again the day following, and Wordsworth read us the story of Peter Bell in the open air; and the comment made upon it by his face and voice was very different from that of some later critics! Whatever might be thought of the poem, 'his face was as a book where men might read strange matters,' and he announced the fate of his hero in prophetic tones. There is a *chaunt* in the recitation both of Coleridge and Wordsworth, which acts as a spell upon the hearer, and disarms the judgment. Perhaps they have deceived themselves by making habitual use of this ambiguous accompaniment. Coleridge's manner is more full, animated, and varied; Wordsworth's more equable, sustained, and internal. The one might be termed more *dramatic*, the other more *lyrical*. Coleridge has told me that he himself liked to compose in walking over uneven ground, or breaking through the straggling branches of a copse-wood; whereas Wordsworth always wrote (if he could) walking up and down a straight gravel-walk, or in some spot where the continuity of his verse met with no collateral interruption. Returning that same evening, I got into a metaphysical argument with Wordsworth, while Coleridge was explaining the different notes of the nightingale to his sister, in which we neither of us succeeded in making ourselves perfectly clear and intelligible.

. . . He [Coleridge], said the *Lyrical Ballads* were an experiment about to be tried by him and Wordsworth, to see how far the public taste would endure poetry written in a more natural and simple style than had hitherto been attempted; totally discarding the artifices of poetical diction, and making use only of such words as had probably been common in the most ordinary language since the days of Henry II.

('My First Acquaintance with Poets', *The Complete Works of William Hazlitt*, ed. P. P. Howe, 1930, XVII, 116–20)

c. Account of discussion with Wordsworth on 'The Poems on the Naming of Places', which must have taken place late in 1803

I once hinted to Wordsworth, as we were sailing in his boat on Grasmere lake, that I thought he had borrowed the idea of his *Poems on the Naming of Places* from the local inscriptions of the same kind in Paul and Virginia. He did not own the obligation, and stated some distinction without a difference, in defence of his claim to originality. Any the slightest variation would be sufficient for this purpose in his mind; for whatever *he* added or omitted would inevitably be worth all that any one else had done, and contain the marrow of the sentiment.

(*Ibid.*, 115–16)

EDITOR'S NOTE

1. (intended) to win the approval (of the crowd).

24. Thomasina Dennis (1771–1809)

From a letter to Davies Giddy (1767–1839), 4 October 1798 and his reply, 17 November 1798

Thomasina Dennis was governess in the Wedgwood family, 1798–1800. The 'unlucky Tragedy' discussed in the letters is *The Borderers*.

I have seen a little Volume of Wordsworth's lately published entitled Lyrical Ballads, which gave me a rather favourable opinion of his talents, till he lent Mr. Wedgwood an unlucky Tragedy which I wish you could see. Mr. Wordsworth has taken great pains in a long unintelligible preface to delineate a most infernal Character, yet the Hero of his play is no more than a common Vilain – his name is Rivers, having drowned a *Dog* for pure mischief, he affects to be witty upon it, and this is the only *heroic action* perform'd by him – Mortimer, another Personage, in a paroxysm of grief exclaims

> 'Tis plain as day that eyes were made
> For a wise purpose, verily to weep with

44

(then looking round he adds)

> A pretty prospect this, a Masterpiece of Nature!
> (to Herbert)   My ancient have you ever practised farming
> Pray tell me what this land is worth by the Acre?

Did ever any body grieve with so much sang froid? yet this is as good sense and the language as elegant as in any part of the Play – The rest of the Dramatis Personae are, a blind old Man, led by his Daughter, who when told by Mortimer that he has killed her Father, clasps *him* (Mortimer) in her arms and protests that he is innocent!! A gang of Robbers, the most virtuous men imaginable, and an old Beggar Woman scolding crying and swearing compose this respectable group – He offered this play to the Manager of Drury lane – it was returned with a simple refusal, Wordsworth said he might be mistaken, but he thought there was a good deal of genius in it –

In Practical Education there is a translation of Ovid's House of Sleep, by Sneyd Edgworth, a little Boy

> Far in a vale there lies a cave forlorn
> Which Phoebus never enters eve or morn
> The misty clouds inhale the pitchey ground
> And twilight lingers all the vale around.
> No watchful cocks Aurora's beam invite
> No dogs nor geese the guardians of the night
> No flocks nor herds disturb the Silent plains
> Within the sacred walls mute quiet reigns
> And murmuring Lethe soothing sleep invites:
> In *dreams again* the flying past delights

(I admire the thought contained in this line)

> From milky flowers that near the cavern grow
> Night scatters the collected sleep below —

You will hardly believe that the author of the despicable Tragedy just quoted had the impudence to say that he wrote better verses than these at ten years old —

Davies Giddy's reply:

Mr Wordsworth I have frequently heard of: but I do not recollect to have seen any other specimens of his poems than the extracts in the Reviews. To succeed in writing a good Tragedy has ever been held a task of

45

extreme difficulty only yielding to the Epic on account of its greater length. Yet mediocrity one should think might be attain'd in this as in everything else by moderate abilities & considerable exersion. Mr Wordsworth & Mr Coleridge seem however strong instances to the contrary – perhaps the passage 'Tis plain that Eyes etc may be an extremely bad imitation of some scene describing the first stage of Grief, when the sufferer for a short time forces his attention from the object really occupying his Mind, and by the effort, destroying his accustom'd Train of Thoughts appears to wander from subject to subject with the levity of an Idiot – Sneyd Edgeworth's translation of the House of Sleep most certainly does great credit to himself & his instructors –

(R. S. Woof, 'Coleridge and Thomasina Dennis', *University of Toronto Quarterly*, XXXII, 1962, 44–6)

25. Charles Lloyd (1775–1839)

From a letter to Thomas Manning, 28 December 1798

Charles Lloyd was a minor poet, brother of Priscilla who married Christopher Wordsworth. He probably had the advantage of hearing Wordsworth read *The Borderers* at Alfoxden, 15 September 1797 (*Collected Letters of Samuel Taylor Coleridge*, ed. E. L. Griggs, Oxford, 1956–71, i, 345–6). (See also entry 58.)

We [himself and Christopher Wordsworth] have Wordsworth's play here [Birmingham] – & have read it over again – I cannot agree with you in opinion about it –

(*Lloyd-Manning Letters*, ed. F. L. Beaty, Indiana, 1957, 17)

For Manning's low opinion of Wordsworth's poetry in general see entry 63:
　　Although Lloyd, after 1800 when he lived in the Lake District with his family, is a neighbourly presence in the Wordsworths' domestic life, he was not highly regarded: 'I know too well that both Wordsworth and Coleridge entertain a profound contempt for my poor Charles', his wife Sophia Pemberton told De Quincey (*Recollections of the Lakes and the Lake Poets*, ed. David Wright, 1970, 323). De Quincey's accounts of Lloyd are touched with a fine gothic power (*ibid.*, 313, 333, and *Confessions of an English Opium-Eater . . . With notes of De*

Quincey's Conversation by Richard Woodhouse, and other editions, ed. Richard Garnett, 1885, 200–2). Woodhouse records De Quincey's opinion 3 November 1821: 'He is . . . the very worst possible writer, though a man of talent in a particular way, in every style except one – that of a sort of Rousseauish feeling and sentiment. His novels are full of it. [John] Taylor [editor of the *London Magazine*] mentioned that he had some MS. Novels in verse of his, which were all of that class and would not do for the magazine, for which purpose they were offered.' It was at this point that Lloyd published 'Poetical Essays on the Character of Pope as a Poet and Moralist'; and 'On the Language and Objects most fit for Poetry'. The second of these verse-essays was a reply to Wordsworth's Preface to *Lyrical Ballads*. Lloyd argues that town life and men of affairs are just as likely, and perhaps more likely, to provide the appropriate subject matter for poetry as rural life and country people. 'How little theoretic errors can / A native glory dim, – how in the ban / Of his own errors god-like he doth fare:'

> Before he rose, there were, for every theme,
>   Many prescriptive phrases, all inane,
> Since all bombastic; and with these did teem
>   And with their misplac'd ornaments and vain,
>   Whate'er profess'd to be poetic strain:
> These, universal, e'er he 'gan his task,
>   He hath quite banish'd from the bard's domain;
> We thank him, poesy, that we may bask
> In light of thy clear face, from whence he tore the mask!

Lloyd concludes with Wordsworth's *The White Doe*, 1816:

> And let us add, that in the magic page
>   Of legendary law, wherein "the fate
> O'the Nortons," he our pity would engage,
>   A glorious monument he doth create,
>   Where on his theme all accessories wait,
> Pomp, superstition, mystery, pride of name!
>   There let the scoffer turn; there consecrate
> Will he behold, to illegitimate fame,
> All that which may confirm the bard's immortal claim.
>
>   (*Poetical Essays*, 1821, 66–7)

Lloyd thought his remarks had caused offence but Wordsworth replied that he had not read Lloyd's book: 'I am sorry you should have imagined that anything connected with myself as a literary person, could have given me offence. This is not an age, which will allow an author's feelings to be in that state without disgrace to his philosophy' (20 February 1822, *LY*, I, 106). Wordsworth then explains how he was offended that Lloyd had gossiped to Hazlitt, allowing Hazlitt, with satirical glee, to attack Wordsworth in the third volume of the

London Magazine for inconsistency in political opinions. Hazlitt speaks of Wordsworth's being 'smit with the love of simplicity and equality' when Wordsworth first knew Lloyd in the north in 1800: Wordsworth would visit Lloyd at Brathay and 'used to come in, and without ceremony snuff one of [two candles] out, saying, it was a shame to indulge in such extravagance, while many a poor cottager had not even a rushlight to see to do their evening's work by. . . . In 1816 (oh! fearful lapse of time, pregnant with strange mutability), the same enthusiastic lover of economy, and hater of luxury, asked his thoughtless friend to dine with him in company with a certain lord, and to lend him his man-servant to wait at table; and just before they were sitting down to dinner, he heard him say to the servant in a sonorous whisper – "and be sure you don't forget to have six candles on the table!"' (*The Collected Works of Hazlitt*, ed. P. P. Howe, XVII, 26–7).

The essential untruth of Lloyd's gossip to Hazlitt, which must have been after Lloyd arrived in London, June 1819, is indicated in *Letters of Mary Wordsworth*, ed. M. Burton, 1958. 84, and in De Quincey's remarks recorded in Woodhouse's diary, cited above. The date of Lloyd's joining Lord Lowther at Rydal Mount for dinner must be late 1818 or early 1819 when Lloyd was living with his man-servant in Ambleside, after having escaped from a mad-house in York.

'LINES LEFT UPON A SEAT IN A YEW-TREE'

26. Charles Lamb

From a letter to Coleridge, 19 or 26 July 1797

Lamb had visited Coleridge at Nether Stowey, early July 1797, and must have either heard or read there Wordsworth's poem, 'Lines Left upon a Seat in a Yew-tree'.

You would make me very happy, if you think W. has no objection, by transcribing for me that inscription of his. I have some scattered sentences ever floating on my memory, teasing me that I cannot remember more of it. You may believe that I will make no improper use of it. . . . But above all, *that Inscription*! – it will recall to me the tones of all your voices –

(*The Letters of Charles and Mary Lamb*, ed. E. V. Lucas, 1935, i, 117)

27. Thomas Wedgwood (1771–1805)

From a letter to William Godwin (1756–1836) 31 July 1797

Wedgwood wished to initiate research into the education of genius 'which should anticipate a century or two'. He wanted 'superintendents for the practical part' of the educational experiment. His notion of Wordsworth must have come from Godwin and Basil Montagu.

The only persons that I know of as at all likely for this purpose, are Wordsworth & Coleridge. I never saw or had any communication with either of them. Wordsworth, I understand to have many of the requisite qualities & from what I hear of him, he has only to be convinced that this is the most promising mode of benefiting society, to engage him to come forward with alacrity. The talents of Coleridge I suppose are considerable &, like Wordsworths, quite disengaged. I am only afraid that the former [i.e. Coleridge] may be too much a poet & religionist to suit our views. The superintendents should assist in the prelim[y]. discussions.

('Coleridge, Wordsworth, and the Wedgwood Fund', David V. Erdman, *Bulletin of the New York Public Library*, vol. 60 no. 9 September 1956, 431.)

28. Elizabeth Rawson (née Threlkeld)

From a letter to Samuel Ferguson, 31 March 1799

I do not wonder at your sentiments on Wm Wordsworth's poems but lament that he is spending his youth in so unprofitable a way.

(*EY* 254, footnote 2)

29. Joanna Hutchinson (1780–1841)

From a letter to John Monkhouse, 18 May 1799

Joanna Hutchinson was Wordsworth's sister-in-law.

I dare say you will be surprized when I tell you William and Dolly Wordsworth are arrived at Sockburne. I cannot help telling you how genteely your *Pappa* and Poet George behaved – You must know your farther got a fall from his Horse and got very much wet so much as to be fors'd to have his *Britches* change, as soon as he herd William and Dolly was coming he said he must be off – and that he would not have time to come back to Sockburne but upon examination his small close was so wet he could not possibly put them on therefore he was obliged to stay: However he and George sat all the afternoon in the Kitchen enjoying the company of the Blacksmith and Tailor, at last however they were prevailed on to go into the Parlor and upon Mary asking them where they had been Geo: reply'd why you would not have had us so unmannerly as to have left the Tailor and the Smith. This you may be sure rais'd a laugh. –

don't you think they behaved elegantly

However both your father and George was so much pleased with there company that I dare say they now think the time very ill spent that was bestowed upon the Blacksmith and his companion –

(Ms. The Wordsworth Library; printed R. S. Woof, 'Wordsworth in the North-East', *Inward Eye*, 1970, 28–9)

30. Samuel Taylor Coleridge

From a letter to Poole, 21 March 1800

I would to God, I could get Wordsworth to re-take Alfoxden – the Society of so great a Being is of priceless Value – but he will never quit the North of England – his habits are more assimilated with the Inhabitants there – there he & his Sister are exceedingly beloved, enthusiastically. Such difference do small Sympathies make – such as Voice, Pronunciation, &c. – for from what other Cause can I account for it –. Certainly, no one, neither you, or the Wedgewoods, altho' you far more than any one else, ever entered into the feeling due to a man like Wordsworth – of whom I do not hesitate in saying, that since Milton no man has *manifested* himself equal to him.

(*Collected Letters of Samuel Taylor Coleridge*, ed. E. L. Griggs, Oxford, 1956–71, i, 582)

31. James Losh (1763–1833)

From his diary, 1798–1801

A nervous illness made Losh retire from a promising law career in London to Bath in 1796. He then translated, wrote modest contributions to periodicals, married and finally resumed his legal career in Newcastle upon Tyne in 1800. Wordsworth stayed with his fellow Cumbrian in Bath, 12–15 June 1798, and again, with Dorothy, 8–9 July. He and Losh remained on friendly terms throughout life, despite political differences in later years, Losh, unlike Wordsworth, continuing to advocate parliamentary reform. It is important to note that Losh's experience of Wordsworth's early poetry was that of hearing it or reading it aloud.

a. June–September 1798

12 June 1798 . . . Supper, Wordsworth & Mr. A. Cottle, a very fine day. Wordsworth pleasant and clear, but too ernest and *emphatic* in his manner of *speaking in conversation*.

15 June . . . Conversation with Wordsworth, hearing his poems &c. walks.

19 September . . . Dinner, Tea &c. Warner, Coleridge and Wordsworth poems [presumably *Lyrical Ballads*] aloud.

(Ms. Carlisle City Library)

b. September 1800

Dorothy Wordsworth wryly records in her *Journal*, 31 August 1800, 'Losh's opinion of Southey – the first of poets'. Coleridge was at Grasmere on that day

51

and would know Losh's estimate. When Losh came to see him at Keswick on 4 September, he perhaps persuaded him to a somewhat different view of Southey and Wordsworth. Certainly Losh took good note of Coleridge's opinion: the two men talked about Southey, and Losh wrote on 4 September:

> Southey about two years [ago] showed me two books of this poem [Madoc] which I admired but thought deficient in *dignity of sentiment and style* – Coleridge agrees with me in this but says that those books have been entirely rewritten – Wordsworth (whom Coleridge considers as the first Poet now living) is about to publish another vol. of his Lyrical Ballads which have had great success – he is also engaged in a great moral work in verse.

(*Ibid.*)

c. April 1801

11 April 1801 . . . Wordsworth's poems 2 [hours].
12 April 1801 . . . Wordsworth's poems 2. Walks with Celia [his wife] 2. Sermon and prayers 1. Wordsworth's poems another hour and finished – this is the 2^d. vol: of his Lyrical Ballads, and its contents are in my opinion very superior to the [*sic*] those of the first – There is much genuine poetry & accurate knowledge of nature in these poems, and some of them are happily expressed such as 'Michael', those 'on naming places', 'the Cumberland beggar', and some others – Wordsworth is however too often defective in elegance of language, and clearness of arrangement – he will notwithstanding, some day, be a great Poet.

(*Ibid.*)

II

Lyrical Ballads: opinions,
November 1798–July 1800

32. Christopher Wordsworth

From a letter 3 November 1798 to Jonathan Walton (1774–1846),
his contemporary at Trinity, Cambridge

Have you yet read the Lyrical Ballads & how do you like them? They are
reviewed in the Critical of last month and are, or rather perhaps their
author is, very highly spoken of. I say their author, for the Reviewer,
though he thinks the work displays the highest genius, is not pleased wth.
the subjects on which he has chosen to write – and the manner (experimental) in which most of them are treated. The Reviewer is no doubt
Southey – and perhaps one may see something of his enmity to
Coleridge in the manner in wh. he speaks of the 'Ancient Marinere'. For
my own part the Ballads now (at first I thought them strange) please me
by far the most – particularly the 'Idiot Boy' – the 'Thorn' and the 'We
are Seven'. Lloyd thinks the ballads too bare of ornament – I confess I do
not – I feel them I think more strongly for the want of it.

(Ms. The Wordsworth Library)

33. Charles Lamb

From a letter to Robert Southey, 8 November 1798

Lamb both praises 'Tintern Abbey' and defends 'The Ancient Mariner'
against Southey's disapproving comments on that poem in the *Critical
Review*.

'The Ancient Marinere' plays more tricks with the mind than that last
poem 'Tintern Abbey', which is yet one of the finest written.

(*Collected Letters of Samuel Taylor Coleridge*, ed. C. L. Griggs, Oxford, 1956–71,
i, 137)

34. Thomas Denman (1779–1854)

From a letter to his sister Sophia, Mrs. Matthew Baillie, November 1798[1]

Denman was then an undergraduate at St John's College, Cambridge (where his great friend was J. H. Merivale – see entry 152), and he thought at that time that the probable author of *Lyrical Ballads* was Coleridge. His admiration lasted; his daughter remembered hearing '"The Idiot Boy", bits of Shakespeare, Milton, &c., all read in his deep sonorous voice, with dramatic effect'. (J. Arnould, *Memoir of Lord Denman*, 1873, i. 77). Despite this, there was one poem, 'A Poet's Epitaph', first published in *Lyrical Ballads* 1800, that could always rouse Denman to irritation. He recalled to J.T. Coleridge in 1837 when he was Lord Chief Justice that Wordsworth's stanza, 'A lawyer art thou? draw not nigh . . . The hardness of that sallow face', 'made me so sore, five-and-thirty years ago, that I followed out his attack on professions by a parody running through all walks of life' (*ibid.*, ii. 86). Denman visited Wordsworth at Rydal Mount in August 1841.

Have you yet met with 'Lyrical Ballads,' from which 'Goody Blake' is taken. They would, I think, delight you extremely; they consist of very pleasing tales and reflections, which are made doubly interesting by a simplicity of style, at once dignified and impressive. I can hardly help copying out two or three short passages for you, but you must buy the book.

(J. Arnould, *Memoir of Lord Denman*, 1873, i, 23)

EDITOR'S NOTE

1. Sophia's sister-in-law was Scottish playwright Joanna Baillie (see entry 116).

35. Robert Southey

From a letter to C. W. W. Wynn, 17 December 1798

The *Lyrical Ballads* are by Coleridge and Wordsworth. The Night [ing] ale, the Dungeon, the Foster Mothers Tale, and the long ballad of the Old Mariner are all that were written by Coleridge. The ballad I think nonsense, the nightingale tolerable. The other two are pieces of his tragedy. For Wordsworths poems, the last ['Tintern Abbey'] pleased me best, and tho the Idiot Boy is sadly dilated, it is very well done. I reviewed them two months ago [see entry 47].

(*New Letters of Robert Southey*, ed. Kenneth Curry, I, 176–7)

36. Hannah More (1745–1833)

Joseph Cottle recalls her comments on first reading *Lyrical Ballads*, probably late 1798

It reflects credit on Hannah More, to whom I had presented the first volume, that she immediately perceived the merits of the 'Lyrical Ballads.' On my visiting Barley Wood soon after, she said to me, 'Your young friend Wordsworth, surpasses all your other young friends,' when producing the book, she requested me to read several of the poems, which I did, to the great amusement of the ladies. On concluding, she said, 'I must hear "Harry Gill," once more.' On coming to the words, 'O, may he never more be warm!' she lifted up her hands, in smiling horror.

(Joseph Cottle, *Reminiscences of Coleridge and Southey*, 1847, 260)

37. Sara Coleridge (1770–1845)

From a letter to Thomas Poole, March 1799

Sara was the wife of Samuel Taylor Coleridge.

The Lyrical Ballads are laughed at and disliked by all with very few excepted.

(*Minnow among Tritons*, ed. Stephen Potter, 1934, 4)

38. Francis Jeffrey (1773–1850)

From a letter to Robert Morehead, 21 March 1799

Francis Jeffrey was to become from 1802 the most influential of Wordsworth's hostile critics. His private comments, however, tend to sound a more positive note.

Then I have been enchanted with a little volume of poems, lately published, called 'Lyrical Ballads,' and without any author's name. [Comments particularly on Coleridge's *The Ancient Mariner*.]

(*Memorials of the Life and Writings of the Rev. Robert Morehead, D.D.*, ed. Charles Morehead, Edinburgh, 1875, 102)

39. Robert Southey

From a letter to his wife Edith, 9 May 1799

I then went to Arch's, a pleasant place for half an hour's book news: you know he purchased the edition of the Lyrical Ballads; he told me he believed he should lose by them, as they sold very heavily. . . . My books sell very well.

(*Life and Correspondence of Robert Southey*, ed. C. C. Southey, 1849, II, 16)

40. Mary Spedding (1768–1828)

From a letter to her brother William in India, 22 November 1799

Mary Spedding was the sister of the three Spedding boys who had been contemporaries of the Wordsworth boys at Hawkshead Grammar School. She and her sister Margaret were living with the eldest brother John Spedding who, since his marriage to Sara Gibson of Newcastle upon Tyne in autumn 1799, had moved to Governor's House, Keswick. It must have been here that Wordsworth and Coleridge dined on 9 or 10 November 1799. The letter is written from Newcastle where the Speddings went for an extended stay on 12 November, and there, Mary paid a visit of a few days to James Losh of Jesmond, Newcastle. It was doubtless Losh's copy of *Lyrical Ballads* that she read.

. . . talking of Germany, we the other day, saw William Wordsworth who has been there – he came to Keswick with Coleridge the Poet, & dined with us – [expresses regret at not seeing John Wordsworth who had met William Spedding in India and had introduced him to Wordsworth's cousin, Thomas Myers, Receiver General for Bengal.] I do not think that Wordsworth seems to be making much out in the way of literature – there was a volume of poems, called 'Lyrical Ballads' published the other day by him & the above mentioned Coleridge – by way of making forty pounds for their tour to the Continent – they are really such queer odd sort of things that if everybody was of my mind, the profits would not answer for a journey – he was however we all thought greatly improved in manners & extremely agreeable.

(Ms. Spedding Papers, The Wordsworth Library)

41. Henry Crabb Robinson (1775–1867)

From his résumé of the events of 1799

I was under great obligation to Hazlitt as the director of my taste. It was he who first made me acquainted with the *Lyrical Ballads* and the poems generally of Wordsworth, Coleridge, Lamb, and Southey, . . .

(*Henry Crabb Robinson on Books and their Writers*, ed. Edith J. Morley, 1938, I. 6)

42. Robert Southey

From a letter to Coleridge, 1 April 1800

I take with me for the voyage your poems, the Lyrics, the Lyrical Ballads, and Gebir; and, except a few books designed for presents, these make all my library.

(*Life and Correspondence of Robert Southey*, ed. C. C. Southey, 1849, II, 56)

43. Samuel Taylor Coleridge

From a letter to Humphry Davy, 25 July 1800

At this time Davy was in Bristol seeing the 1800 edition of *Lyrical Ballads* through the press.

At all event those poems must not as yet be delivered up to them [the printers]; because that beautiful Poem, the Brothers, which I read to you in Paul Street, I neglected to deliver to you – & that must begin the Volume.

(*Collected Letters of Samuel Taylor Coleridge*, ed. E. L. Griggs, Oxford, 1956–71, 611)

'THERE WAS A BOY'

44. Samuel Taylor Coleridge

From a letter from Ratzeburg, Germany, to Wordsworth, 10 December 1799

... The blank lines gave me as much direct pleasure as was possible in the general bustle of pleasure with which I received and read your letter. I observed, I remember, that the 'fingers woven',[1] &c., only puzzled me; and though I liked the twelve or fourteen first lines very well, yet I like the remainder much better. Well, now I have read them again, they are very beautiful, and leave an affecting impression. That

> Uncertain heaven received
> Into the bosom of the steady lake,[2]

I should have recognised any where; and had I met these lines running wild in the deserts of Arabia, I should have instantly screamed out 'Wordsworth!' ...

(*Collected Letters of Samuel Taylor Coleridge*, ed. E. L. Griggs, Oxford, 1956–71, I, 452–3)

EDITOR'S NOTES

1. 'There was a Boy', l. 7.
2. *Ibid.*, ll. 24–5.

'A SLUMBER DID MY SPIRIT SEAL'

45. Samuel Taylor Coleridge
From a letter to Thomas Poole, 6 April 1799

The Epitaph is 'A slumber did my spirit seal'.

Some months ago Wordsworth transmitted to me a most sublime Epitaph whether it had any reality, I cannot say. – Most probably, in some gloomier moment he had fancied the moment in which his Sister might die.

(*Collected Letters of Samuel Taylor Coleridge*, ed. E. L. Griggs, Oxford, 1956–71, I, 479)

III

Lyrical Ballads: reviews,
October 1798–April 1800

46.

Unsigned review, *Monthly Mirror*, October 1798, vi, 224–5

The contents of this little volume were 'written chiefly with a view to ascertain how far the language of conversation is adapted to the purposes of poetic pleasure.' The author has certainly accomplished his purpose, and instead of the pompous and high-sounding phraseology of the *Della Cruscan school*, has produced sentiments of feeling and sensibility, expressed without affectation, and in the language of nature. If this style were more generally adopted, it would tend to correct that depraved taste, occasioned by an incessant *importation* from the press of *sonnets* and other poems, which has already made considerable inroads upon the judgment. We extract the following as a specimen of the author's talents. [Quotes 'Lines left upon a Seat in a Yew-tree'.]

47. Robert Southey

Unsigned review, *Critical Review*, October 1798, xxiv, 197–204

When he returned from Germany in 1799 Wordsworth wrote to Cottle expressing his disappointment in Southey's review:

... Southey's review I have seen. He knew that I published those poems for money and money alone. He knew that money was of importance to me. If he could not conscientiously have spoken differently of the volume, he ought to have declined the task of reviewing it.

The bulk of the poems he has described as destitute of merit. Am I recompensed for this by vague praises of my talents? I care little for the praise of any other professional critic, but as it may help me to pudding . . .'

(*EY*, 267–8)

THE majority of these poems, we are informed in the advertisement, are to be considered as experiments.

'They were written chiefly with a view to ascertain how far the language of conversation in the middle and lower classes of society is adapted to the purposes of poetic pleasure.' r.i.

Of these experimental poems, the most important is the Idiot Boy, the story of which is simply this. Betty Foy's neighbour Susan Gale is indisposed; and no one can conveniently be sent for the doctor but Betty's idiot boy. She therefore puts him upon her poney, at eight o'clock in the evening, gives him proper directions, and returns to take care of her sick neighbour. Johnny is expected with the doctor by eleven; but the clock strikes eleven, and twelve, and one, without the appearance either of Johnny or the doctor. Betty's restless fears become insupportable; and she now leaves her friend to look for her idiot son. She goes to the doctor's house, but hears nothing of Johnny. About five o'clock, however, she finds him sitting quietly upon his feeding poney. As they go home they meet old Susan, whose apprehensions have cured her, and brought her out to seek them; and they all return merrily together.

Upon this subject the author has written nearly five hundred lines. With what spirit the story is told, our extract will evince.
[Quotes 'The Idiot Boy', *PW*, II, pp. 76–8, ll. 312–91; *LB (1798)*, pp. 96–9, ll. 322–401:

> Oh reader! now that I might tell . . .
> Her limbs are all alive with joy.]

No tale less deserved the labour that appears to have been bestowed upon this. It resembles a Flemish picture in the worthlessness of its design and the excellence of its execution. From Flemish artists we are satisfied with such pieces: who would not have lamented, if Corregio or Rafaelle had wasted their talents in painting Dutch boors or the humours of a Flemish wake?

The other ballads of this kind are as bald in story, and are not so highly embellished in narration. With that which is entitled the Thorn, we were altogether displeased. The advertisement says, it is not told in the person of the author, but in that of some loquacious narrator. The author should have recollected that he who personates tiresome loquacity, becomes tiresome himself. The story of a man who suffers the perpetual pain of cold, because an old woman prayed that he never might be warm, is perhaps a good story for a ballad, because it is a well-known tale: but is the author certain that it is '*well authenticated?*' and does not such an assertion promote the popular supersitition of witchcraft?

In a very different style of poetry, is the Rime of the Ancyent

Marinere; a ballad – (says the advertisement) 'professedly written in imitation of the *style*, as well as of the spirit of the elder poets.' We are tolerably conversant with the early English poets; and can discover no resemblance whatever, except in antiquated spelling and a few obsolete words. This piece appears to us perfectly original in style as well as in story. Many of the stanzas are laboriously beautiful; but in connection they are absurd or unintelligible. Our readers may exercise their ingenuity in attempting to unriddle what follows.

[Quotes Coleridge's 'Ancient Mariner' ll. 301–22:

> The roaring wind! it roar'd far off . . .
> The dead men gave a groan.]

We do not sufficiently understand the story to analyse it. It is a Dutch attempt at German sublimity. Genius has here been employed in producing a poem of little merit.

With pleasure we turn to the serious pieces, the better part of the volume. The Foster-Mother's Tale is in the best style of dramatic narrative. The Dungeon, and the Lines upon the Yew-tree Seat, are beautiful. The Tale of the Female Vagrant is written in the stanza, not the style, of Spenser. We extract a part of this poem.

[Quotes 'The Female Vagrant', *PW*, I, pp. 110–14, ll. 271–369; *LB (1798)*, pp. 47–51, ll. 91–180:

> 'Twas a hard change, an evil time was come . . .
> And near a thousand tables pined, and wanted food.]

Admirable as this poem is, the author seems to discover still superior powers in the Lines written near Tintern Abbey. On reading this production, it is impossible not to lament that he should ever have condescended to write such pieces as the Last of the Flock, the Convict, and most of the ballads. In the whole range of English poetry, we scarcely recollect any thing superior to a part of the following passage.

[Quotes 'Tintern Abbey', *PW*, II, pp. 261–2, ll. 65–111; *LB (1798)*, pp. 113–5, ll. 66–112:

> So I dare to hope
> Though changed, no doubt, from what I was . . .
> The guide, the guardian of my heart, and soul
> Of all my moral being.]

The 'experiment,' we think, has failed, not because the language of conversation is little adapted to 'the purposes of poetic pleasure,' but because it has been tried upon uninteresting subjects. Yet every piece discovers genius; and, ill as the author has frequently employed his talents, they certainly rank him with the best of living poets.

48.

Unsigned review, *Analytical Review*, December 1798, xxviii, 583–7

'It is the honourable characteristic of poetry,' says the author of these ballads, in the advertisement which is prefixed to them (p. i), 'that its materials, are to be found in every subject which can interest the human mind. The evidence of this fact is to be sought, not in the writings of critics, but in those of poets themselves.

'The majority of the following poems are to be considered as experiments. They were written chiefly with a view to ascertain how far the language of conversation in the middle and lower classes of society is adapted to the purposes of poetic pleasure. Readers accustomed to the gaudiness and inane phraseology of many modern writers, if they persist in reading this book to its conclusion, will perhaps frequently have to struggle with feelings of strangeness and awkwardness: they will look round for poetry, and will be induced to enquire by what species of courtesy these attempts can be permitted to assume that title. It is desirable that such readers, for their own sakes, should not suffer the solitary word poetry, a word of very disputed meaning, to stand in the way of their gratification; but that, while they are perusing this book, they should ask themselves if it contains a natural delineation of human passions, human characters, and human incidents; and if the answer be favorable to the author's wishes, that they should consent to be pleased in spite of that most dreadful enemy to our pleasures, our own pre-established codes of decision.'

There is something sensible in these remarks, and they certainly serve as a very pertinent introduction to the studied simplicity, which pervades many of the poems. The 'Rime of the ancyent Marinere,' a ballad in seven parts, is written professedly in imitation of the style as well as of the spirit of the ancient poets. We are not pleased with it; in our opinion it has more of the extravagance of a mad german poet, than of the simplicity of our ancient ballad writers.

Some of our young rhymesters and blank-verse-men, highly delighted with the delicacy of their own moral feelings, affect to look down on every thing human with an eye of pity. To them the face of nature is eternally shaded with a funereal gloom, and they are never happy but when their affections, to use the words of Sterne are fixed upon some melancholy cypress. We are happy to conjecture, from some passages in these poems, that the author of them classes not with these sable songsters; in his ode to the nightingale he says,

[Quotes Coleridge's 'Nightingale', ll. 7–23:

All is still,
A balmy night! . . .
And many a poet echoes the conceit.]

Among the poems which particularly pleased us from their character either of simplicity or tenderness, or both, are, that from which we have made the preceding extract, 'The Thorn,' 'The Mad Mother,' 'The Idiot Boy,' and that with which we shall present our readers, the tale of 'Goody Blake and Harry Gill:' a tale founded on a well authenticated fact, which happened in Warwickshire. Dr. Darwin relates it among other curious instances of maniacal hallucination in the second volume of his Zoonomia.

[Quotes 'Goody Blake and Harry Gill', *PW*, IV, p. 173; *LB (1798)*, p. 54]

49.

Unsigned notice, *Monthly Magazine*, supplement: 15 January 1799,
vi. 514

The author of '*Lyrical Ballads*', has attempted to imitate the style of our old English versifiers, with unusual success; '*The Auncient Mariners*', however, on which he particularly prides himself, is in our opinion, a particular exception; some of his pieces are beautiful, but others are stiff and laboured.

50.

Unsigned notice, *New Annual Register 1798*, 1799, 200–3

The 'Lyrical Ballads, with a few other Poems,' are the productions of an author of considerable talents, 'written chiefly with a view to ascertain how far the language of conversation in the middle and lower classes of society, is adapted to the purposes of poetical pleasure.' Many of the ballads are distinguished by great simplicity and tenderness, and contain a very 'natural delineation of human passions, human characters, and human incidents.' With others we have been less satisfied, considering them to be unfortunate experiments, on which genius and labour have been misemployed. Of the remaining pieces some are highly beautiful and pleasing, and present us with passages which entitle the author to a very respectable rank among modern poets.

[Quotes 'Goody Blake and Harry Gill', *PW*, IV, p. 173; *LB (1798)*, p. 54]

51.

Unsigned review, *New London Review*, January 1799, 33–5

It is possible that the author of this review was Robert Heron (1764–1807), as he is one of the two known reviewers for this short-lived periodical, edited by Vernor and Hood. The other known contributor of reviews, also a Scot, was John Leyden, who, in a letter of December 1799 to James Brown, lists his own reviews and states that he 'renounced all engagements with the Editors' of the *New London Review*, 'As my personal enemy Heron was employed in the work and as I thought the character of my coadjutors very contemptible' (Ms. University of Newcastle upon Tyne.)

As this volume has some pretension to originality, it is peculiarly an object of critical examination; the writer professes that 'the majority of the poems are to be considered as *experiments*.' It is our duty to state his views, and to estimate his execution.

He says 'these poems were written chiefly with a view to ascertain how far *the language of conversation*, in the *middle* and *lower* classes of society, is adapted to the purposes of poetic pleasure.' That there should ever have been a doubt upon this subject in the mind of a man of taste, is not a little surprizing. The language of *conversation*, and that too of the *lower classes*, can never be considered as the language of *poetry*. What is to affect the imagination, must at least address itself to the imagination; and the imagination has its peculiar style. It is chiefly objected to French poetry, that in general, it is the language of conversation; this is not strictly true; but because it is frequently nothing more than elegant; because it is at times divested of poetical diction; of the colourings, the freshness, and the graces of poetry; men of taste in Europe, have universally depreciated its claim to the honours of genuine poetry.

Our author, conscious of his paradox, and of the feelings of his readers, adds that 'they will often look round for poetry, and enqire by what species of courtesy these attempts can be permitted to assume that title.' We really sympathise with the forlorn reader; but our author, to moderate his despair, offers a singular consolation; he assures us, that we have no settled notion of what poetry is. These are his words, 'It is desirable that they should not suffer the *solitary word*, poetry, *a word* of very *disputed meaning*, to stand in the way of their gratification.' Nothing can be more ludicrous than this ingenious request of our author, excepting its grave refutation. If the writer of these poems, will for a moment, dismiss his jocular paradox (and we almost suspect that some of these poems were intended merely as lusory effusions) we trust to his cultivated taste, and his poetical acquirements, to tell us *what is poetry*. He will find no difficulty in resolving the question, by comparing Dryden with D'Urfey, Pope with Pomfret, and Waller with Walsh.

Our author must have had very unsettled notions of what we are to understand by the term poetical SIMPLICITY. He is not singular in this unhappy indecision of taste; we have had a multitude of rhimers who have looked into the earliest efforts of the art, for their models; and seem to have thought, that rudeness was synonimous to simplicity. Bishop Percy's publication of the Reliques of Ancient Poetry, has been the fertile mother of a numerous and meagre race of *stanza-enditers*.

We may distinguish a *simple* style from a style of *simplicity*. By a simple style we may suppose a colloquial diction, debased by inelegance, and gross by familiarity. Simplicity is a manner of expression, facile, pure, and always elegant. Simplicity, will not detract from the elevation of the thoughts, nor injure the beauty of the composition. The arch-critic of France, felt and marked the distinction, in these happy lines.

71

Quoique vous ecrivez, evitez la BASSESSE,[1]
Le *stile le moins noble*, a pourtant sa *noblesse*.

ART. PORT. C.I.

The simple style has all the squalid nakedness of a BEGGAR, and simplicity, the lovely nudity of a GRACE.

Thoughtless of beauty she is BEAUTY'S SELF!

THOMSON.

Our criticism is so just, that our poet seems to have felt its truth, while he was employed in its violation; and so far from these poems being entirely written in the eccentric principle he proposes, we shall find, that he has many exquisite thoughts exquisitely expressed. If ever he disgusts by the meagreness and poverty of his composition, it is precisely where, aiming at simplicity, he copies the rudest effusions of our vulgar ballads. So far indeed from obtaining that simplicity to which he pretends, we, at times, have wished that he were somewhat *more* simple. Among his irregular verses, we are often surprised with beautiful expression, and sometimes displeased with a turgid obscurity, which evidently shews, that our poet found it impossible to keep the imagination alive, in the creeping measures of *conversation verses*. In the first ballad, entitled 'The Rime of the Ancyent Marinere,' the following stanza is a dark enigma. It is a moonlight scene, where the inimitable expression of Shakespeare, was floating in the recollection of the writer.

> The rock shone bright, the kirk no less
> That stands above the rock;
> The moon-light *steeped in silentness*
> The steady weather-cock.

Our poet more happily describes the morning sun, at sea, in the 'Female Vagrant.'

> In the calm sunshine slept the glittering main;
> The very ocean has its hour of rest,
> That comes not to the human mourner's breast.
> Remote from man, and storms of mortal care,
> A heavenly silence did the waves invest;
> I looked and looked along the silent air,
> Until it seemed to bring, a joy to my despair.

[*LB* (1798), pp. 49, ll. 138–49]

This is a very elegant passage, and there are many such, but while the reader will admire these, he cannot but smile, as he perceives how easily the poet forgets the principle he lays down in his preface.

Our limits will not permit us to offer the reader many specimens of that simplicity, in which, in our opinion, the author has egregiously failed. If such passages as the following find admirers, the writer is fortunate; for they never cost him any labour in the composition.

Of an old woman, we are told,

> This woman dwelt in Dorsetshire,
> Her hut was on a cold hill side;
> And in that country coals are dear,
> For they come far by wind and tide.
>
> Her evenings then were dull and dead,
> Sad case it was, as you may think:
> For very cold to go to bed,
> And then for cold not sleep a wink.

[Quotes 'Goody Blake and Harry Gill', (revised 1837), *PW*, IV,. pp. 173–4 ll. 29–32 and ll. 45–8 (see footnotes); *LB (1798)*, pp. 55–6, ll. 29–32, and ll. 45–8.]

The greater part of this volume is not composed in this inartificial and anti-poetical manner. Some of the poems are so far removed from the rudeness they affect, that their entire texture is brilliant and rich, and there are many passages of perfect beauty. Our poet seems to want nothing, but more fortunate topics than those he has, at times, unhappily selected. We hope, that by this time, he is convinced of the failure of these '*Experiments*;' but we recommend them to the curious, as the failures of a man of genius. We take our leave of the writer, in the words of Boileau.

> Prenez mieux votre ton. Soyez SIMPLE AVEC ART,
> Sublime sans orgueil, agreeable sans fard.[2]

EDITOR'S NOTES

1. Whatever you write, avoid vulgarity,
    A less noble style, nevertheless has its own nobility.

2. Choose your tone better, be uncomplicated with Art,
    Sublime but not arrogant, pleasant but not cosmeticised.

52. Dr Charles Burney (1726–1814)

Unsigned review, *Monthly Review*, June 1799, xxix. 202–10

The eighteenth-century meaning of the word, 'lyrical' (Dr Johnson defines it as 'poetry sung to a harp'), possibly lies behind Burney's reviewing of this volume: more than half the volumes he covered for the *Monthly Review* were on musical subjects. He was a friend of Johnson; a music historian; and the father of Fanny (see B. C. Nangle, *Monthly Review, Second Series*, Oxford, 1955, 9, 159). He was also a friend of George Dyer; he possessed, 'from the author', Dyer's *The Poet's Fate*, where Wordsworth is favourably mentioned.

The author of these ingenious compositions presents the major part of them to the public as *experiments*; since they were written, as he informs us in the *advertisement* prefixed, 'chiefly with a view to ascertain how far the language of conversation in the middle and lower classes of society is adapted to the purposes of poetic pleasure.'

Though we have been extremely entertained with the fancy, the facility, and (in general) the sentiments, of these pieces, we cannot regard them as *poetry*, of a class to be cultivated at the expence of a higher species of versification, unknown in our language at the time when our elder writers, whom this author condescends to imitate, wrote their ballads. – Would it not be degrading poetry, as well as the English language, to go back to the barbarous and uncouth numbers of Chaucer? Suppose, instead of modernizing the old bard, that the sweet and polished measures, on lofty subjects, of Dryden, Pope, and Gray, were to be transmuted into the dialect and versification of the xivth century? Should we be gainers by the retrogradation? *Rust* is a necessary quality to a counterfeit old medal: but, to give artifical rust to modern poetry, in order to render it similar to that of three or four hundred years ago, can have no better title to merit and admiration than may be claimed by any ingenious forgery. None but savages have submitted to eat acorns after corn was found. – We will allow that the author before us has the art of cooking his acorns well, and that he makes a very palatable dish of them for *jours maigres*: but, for festivals and *gala* days,

> *Multos castra juvant, & litu o tubae*
> *Permistus sonitus.*[1]

We have had pleasure in reading the *reliques of antient poetry*, because it was antient; and because we were surprised to find so many beautiful thoughts in the rude numbers of barbarous times. These reasons will not apply to *imitations* of antique versification. – We will not, however, dispute any longer about names; the author shall style his rustic delineations of low-life, *poetry*, if he pleases, on the same principle on which Butler is called a poet, and Teniers a painter: but are the doggrel verses of the one equal to the sublime numbers of a Milton, or are the Dutch boors of the other to be compared with the angels of Raphael or Guido? – When we confess that our author has had the art of pleasing and interesting in no common way by his natural delineation of human passions, human characters, and human incidents, we must add that these effects were not produced by the *poetry*: – we have been as much affected by pictures of misery and unmerited distress, in *prose*. The elevation of soul, when it is lifted into the higher regions of imagination, affords us a delight of a different kind from the sensation which is produced by the detail of common incidents. For this fact, we have better authority than is to be found in the writings of most critics: we have it in a poet himself, whose award was never (till now) disputed:

> The poet's eye, in a fine frenzy rolling,
> Doth glance from heaven to earth, from earth to heav'n;
> And, as imagination bodies forth
> The forms of things unknown, the poet's pen
> Turns them to shape, and gives to aiery nothing
> A local habitation and a name.
>
> SHAKSPEARE [*Midsummer Night's Dream*, V.i.12–17]

Having said thus much on the *genus*, we now come more particularly to the *species*.

The author's first piece, the *Rime of the ancyent marinere*, in imitation of the *style* as well as of the spirit of the elder poets, is the strangest story of a cock and a bull that we ever saw on paper: yet, though it seems a rhapsody of unintelligible wildness and incoherence, (of which we do not perceive the drift, unless the joke lies in depriving the wedding guest of his share of the feast,) there are in it poetical touches of an exquisite kind.

The Dramatic Fragment, if it intends anything, seems meant to throw disgrace on the savage liberty preached by some modern *philosophes*.

The *Yew-Tree* seems a seat for *Jean Jaques*: while the reflections on the subject appear to flow from a more pious pen.

The Nightingale sings a strain of true and beautiful poetry; – Miltonic, yet original; reflective, and interesting, in an uncommon degree.
[Quotes Coleridge's 'Nightingale' except for the subtitle, 'A Conversational Poem, Written in April, 1798'.]
The Female Vagrant is an agonizing tale of individual wretchedness; highly coloured, though, alas! but too probable. Yet, as it seems to stamp a general stigma on all military transactions, which were never more important in free countries than at the present period, it will perhaps be asked whether the hardships described never happen during revolution, or in a nation subdued? The sufferings of individuals during war are dreadful: but is it not better to try to prevent them from becoming general, or to render them transient by heroic and patriotic efforts, than to fly to them for ever?

Distress from poverty and want is admirably described, in the '*true story of Goody Blake, and Harry Gill*;' but are we to imagine that Harry was bewitched by Goody Blake? The hardest heart must be softened into pity for the poor old woman; – and yet, if all the poor are to help themselves, and supply their wants from the possessions of their neighbours, what imaginary wants and real anarchy would it not create? Goody Blake should have been relieved out of the *two millions* annually allowed by the state to the poor of this country, not by the plunder of an individual.

Lines on the first mild day of March abound with beautiful sentiments from a polished mind.

Simon Lee, the old Huntsman, is the portrait, admirably painted, of every huntsman who, by toil, age, and infirmities, is rendered unable to guide and govern his canine family.

Anecdote for Fathers. Of this the dialogue is ingenious and natural: but the object of the child's choice, and the inferences, are not quite obvious.

We are seven: – innocent and pretty infantine prattle.

On an *early Spring*. The first stanza of this little poem seems unworthy of the rest, which contain reflections truly pious and philosophical.

The Thorn. All our author's pictures, in colouring, are dark as those of Rembrandt or Spanioletto.

The last of the Flock is more gloomy than the rest. We are not told how the wretched hero of this piece became so poor. He had, indeed, ten children: but so have many cottagers; and ere the tenth child is born, the eldest begin to work, and help, at least, to maintain themselves. No oppression is pointed out; nor are any means suggested for his relief. If the author be a wealthy man, he ought not to have suffered this poor peasant to part with *the last of the flock*. What but an Agrarian law can prevent poverty from visiting the door of the indolent, injudicious, extravagant, and, perhaps, vicious? and is it certain that rigid equality of property as well as of laws could remedy this evil?

The Dungeon. Here candour and tenderness for criminals seem pushed to excess. Have not jails been built on the humane Mr. Howard's plan, which have almost ruined some counties, and which look more like palaces than habitations for the perpetrators of crimes? Yet, have fewer crimes been committed in consequence of the erection of those magnificent structures, at an expence which would have maintained many in innocence and comfort out of a jail, if they have been driven to theft by want?

The mad Mother; admirable painting! in Michael Angelo's bold and masterly manner.

The Idiot Boy leads the reader on from anxiety to distress, and from distress to terror, by incidents and alarms which, though of the most mean and ignoble kind, interest, frighten, and terrify, almost to torture, during the perusal of more than a hundred stanzas.

Lines written near Richmond – literally '*most musical, most melancholy!*'

Expostulation and Reply. The author tells us that 'these lines, and those which follow, arose out of conversation with a friend who was somewhat unreasonably attached to modern books of moral philosophy.' These two pieces will afford our readers an opportunity of judging of the author's poetical talents, in a more modern and less gloomy style than his Ballads:

[Quotes 'Expostulation and Reply', *PW*, IV, p. 56; *LB (1798)*, p. 103. and 'The Tables Turned', *PW*, IV, p. 57; *LB (1798)*, p. 104.]

The Old Man travelling, a Sketch, finely drawn: but the termination seems pointed against the war; from which, however, we are now no more able to separate ourselves, than Hercules was to free himself from the shirt of Nessus. The old traveller's son might have died by disease.

Each ballad is a tale of woe. The style and versification are those of our antient ditties: but much polished, and more constantly excellent. In old songs, we have only a fine line or stanza now and then; here we meet with few that are feeble: – but it is *poesie larmoiante*. The author is more plaintive than Gray himself.

The Complaint of a forsaken Indian Woman: another tale of woe! of the most afflicting and harrowing kind. The want of humanity here falls not on wicked Europeans, but on the innocent Indian savages, who enjoy unlimited freedom and liberty, unbridled by kings, magistrates, or laws.

The Convict. What a description! and what misplaced commiseration, on one condemned by the laws of his country, which he had confessedly violated! We do not comprehend the drift of lavishing that tenderness and compassion on a criminal, which should be reserved for virtue in unmerited misery and distress, suffering untimely death from accident, injustice, or disease.

Lines written near Tintern Abbey. – The reflections of no common mind; poetical, beautiful, and philosophical: but somewhat tinctured with gloomy, narrow, and unsociable ideas of seclusion from the commerce of the world: as if men were born to live in woods and wilds, unconnected with each other! Is it not to education and the culture of the mind that we owe the raptures which the author so well describes, as arising from the view of beautiful scenery, and sublime objects of nature enjoyed in tranquillity, when contrasted with the artificial machinery and 'busy hum of men' in a city? The savage sees none of the beauties which this author describes. The convenience of food and shelter, which vegetation affords him, is all his concern; he thinks not of its picturesque beauties, the course of rivers, the height of mountains, &c. He has no *dizzy raptures* in youth; nor does he listen in maturer age 'to the still sad music of humanity.'

So much genius and originality are discovered in this publication, that we wish to see another from the same hand, written on more elevated subjects and in a more cheerful disposition.

EDITOR'S NOTE

1. Horace, *Odes*, I, i, 23–4: 'Military life and the blast of the trumpet mixed with that of the clarion please many people'.

53.

Unsigned review, *British Critic*, October 1799, XIV, 364–9

Sometimes attributed to Wrangham, but there is no evidence for it. John Stoddart (1773–1856) is the probable author, for he wrote the review of the second edition (see entry 84). The two reviews dovetail so well, and even repeat the same phrasing against Erasmus Darwin. Stoddart's letter of 1 January 1800 indicates that he had not reviewed for three months and that to be an occasional writer in the *British Critic* was all he could expect (see entry 84). This review alone names Coleridge and hints that there may be more than one author. Stoddart first met Wordsworth when he was sharing rooms with Montagu in the summer of 1796; Godwin, the Pinneys and Wrangham were other mutual friends. Against Stoddart's authorship is the report of his 'disgust' on reading 'The Idiot Boy' (see entry 64).

The attempt made in this little volume is one that meets our cordial approbation; and it is an attempt by no means unsuccessful. The endeavour of the author is to recall our poetry, from the fantastical excess of refinement, to simplicity and nature. The account of this design, and its probable effects upon modern readers, is so very sensibly given in the Introduction, that we shall insert the passage at large.

[Quotes the first four paragraphs of the Advertisement:

> It is the honourable characteristic of poetry . . .
> in many cases it necessarily will be so.]

We fully agree with the author, that the true notion of poetry must be sought among the poets, rather than the critics; and we will add that, unless a critic is a poet also, he will generally make but indifferent work in judging of the effusions of Genius. In the collection of poems subjoined to this introduction, we do not often find expressions that we esteem too familiar, or deficient in dignity; on the contrary, we think that in general the author has succeeded in attaining that judicious degree of simplicity, which accommodates itself with ease even to the sublime. It is not by pomp of words, but by energy of thought, that sublimity is most successfully achieved; and we infinitely prefer the simplicity, even of the most unadorned tale, in this volume, to all the meretricious frippery of the *Darwinian* taste.

The Poem of 'the Ancyent Marinere,' with which the collection opens, has many excellencies, and many faults; the beginning and the end are striking and well-conducted; but the intermediate part is too long, and has, in some places, a kind of confusion of images, which loses all effect, from not being quite intelligible. The author, who is confidently said to be Mr. Coleridge, is not correctly versed in the old language, which he undertakes to employ. 'Noises of a *swound*,' p. 9, and 'broad as a *west*,' p. 11, are both nonsensical; but the ancient style is so well imitated, while the antiquated words are so very few, that the latter might with advantage be entirely removed without any detriment to the effect of the Poem. The opening of the Poem is admirably calculated to arrest the reader's attention, by the well-imagined idea of the Wedding Guest, who is held to hear the tale, in spite of his efforts to escape. The beginning of the second canto, or fit, has much merit, if we except the very unwarrantable comparison of the Sun to that which no man can conceive: – 'like God's own head,' a simile which makes a reader shudder; not with poetic feeling, but with religious disapprobation. The following passage is eminently good.

[Quotes Coleridge's 'Ancient Mariner':

> The breezes blew, the white foam flew . . .
> Ne any drop to drink.]

The conclusion, as we remarked before, is very good, particularly the idea that the Marinere has periodical fits of agony, which oblige him to relate his marvellous adventure; and this,

> I pass, like night, from land to land,
> I have strange power of speech;
> The moment that his face I see,
> I know the man that must hear me;
> To him my tale I teach.

Whether the remaining poems of the volume are by Mr. Coleridge, we have not been informed; but they seem to proceed from the same mind; and in the Advertisement, the writer speaks of himself as of a single person accountable for the whole. It is therefore reasonable to conclude, that this is the fact. They all have merit, and many among them a very high rank of merit, which our feelings respecting some parts of the supposed author's character do not authorize or incline us to deny. The Poem on the Nightingale, which is there styled *a conversational Poem*, is very good; but we do not perceive it to be more conversational than Cowper's Task, which is the best poem in that style that our language possesses. 'The Female Vagrant,' is a composition of exquisite beauty, nor is the combination of events, related in it, out of the compass of possibility; yet we perceive, with regret, the drift of the author in composing it; which is to show the worst side of civilized society, and thus to form a satire against it. But let fanciful men rail as they will at the evils which no care can always prevent, they can have no dream more wild than the supposition, that any human wisdom can possibly exclude all evils from a state which divine Providence has decreed, for reasons the most wise, to be a state of suffering and of trial. The sufferers may be changed, by infinite revolutions, but sufferers there will be, till Heaven shall interfere to change the nature of our tenure upon earth. From this beautiful Poem, partly on account of its apparent design, and partly because the loss of the connection would destroy much of its effect, we shall make no extract.

The story of 'Goody Blake and Harry Gill,' is founded, the Introduction tells us, 'on a well-authenticated fact which happened in Warwickshire.' Yet it is a miracle; and modern miracles can seldom be admitted, without some degree of credulity, or a very uncommon weight of evidence. One of the simplest stories in the book, is that entitled 'We are Seven;' yet he must be a very fastidious reader who will deny that it has great beauty and feeling.

The tale of 'the Thorn' has many beauties; nor can we pass without notice 'the Mad Mother,' or the long and familiar tale of 'the Idiot Boy,' which, though it descends quite to common life, is animated by much interest, and told with singular felicity. One more Poem we shall particularly notice for its pathos, and shall indeed insert the whole. The imagery of it is in many instances new, and is introduced with admirable effect.

[Quotes 'The Complaint of a Forsaken Indian Woman', *PW*, II, p. 40; *LB (1798)*, p. 106.]

The purchasers of this little volume will find that, after all we have said, there are poems, and passages of poems, which we have been obliged to pass over, that well deserve attention and commendation; nor does there appear any offensive mixture of enmity to present institutions, except in one or two instances, which are so unobtrusive as hardly to deserve notice.

At the end of the year the review was summarised and a sentence appears in the same volume (XIV–XV):

> . . . The work entitled *Lyrical Ballads*, contains many specimens of original and animated poetry, nor does the author so often descend to the flat ground of mere conversation in rhyme, as he seems to threaten in his Preface [i.e. Advertisement].

54.

Unsigned review, *Naval Chronicle*, October, November 1799, II, 328–30, 418–20

The *Naval Chronicle* was edited by Rev. James Stanier Clarke (1765–1834) (famous as a correspondent of Jane Austen) and John McArthur (1755–1840); they were probably responsible for the book notices. This review perhaps explains Coleridge's anecdote reported in *Letters, Conversations and Recollections of S. T. Coleridge* (ed. Thomas Allsop, 2nd edn. 1858, 128):

> I was told by Longmans that the greater part of the Lyrical Ballads had been sold to seafaring men, who having heard of the Ancient Mariner, concluded that it was a naval song-book, or, at all events, that it had some relation to nautical matters.

The author[1] of these admirable Poems informs us in the advertisement, that the majority of them were written chiefly with a view to ascertain how far the language of conversation in the middle and lower classes of Society is adapted to the purposes of Poetry.

The Rime of the Ancyent Marinere, which consists of seven ballads, is written in the Style, as well as in the Spirit, of our early poets. – The argument is as follows . . .

To an accurate observer, Superstition will generally be seen more or less prevalent in our character: it is the Weed of a religious Mind; and though it must ever wither before the clear light of reason, yet so great is our predeliction for supernatural agency, that whatever has a tendency to the marvellous is readily received and liberally encouraged.

The *Lyrical Ballads* powerfully awaken this too prevailing passion, and possess a very uncommon, and singular degree of merit. We trust the author will ere long gratify the public with his name, since he promises to rank amongst the first of our poets; not only for the various harmony of Rhythm, but also for the bold efforts of a mind that has dared to think for itself – yet pourtrays with diffidence its own original impressions in quaint but simple language. We have selected the first and fourth parts of The Ancyent Marinere . . .

EDITOR'S NOTE

1. By January 1800, the author was known to the editors of the *Naval Chronicle*; they comment in their Preface (vi):

> A Cambridge Correspondent, on whom our readers may rely, informs us, that "The Rime of the Ancyent Mariner," is undoubtedly the composition of Mr. Coleridge of Jesus College: we particularly recommend the perusal of the whole to our Professional Correspondents, who must not complain of a dearth of Poetic Genius, when such compositions appear.

54a. Alexander Thomson (1763–1803)

From *The British Parnassus at the Close of the Eighteenth Century*,
Edinburgh, 1801, 36–37

Edinburgh author and translator from German. The style here is not so much satirical as humorous. He surveys all recent publications and here comments on *Lyrical Ballads*, 1798, suspecting that although the author is rumoured to be Coleridge, more than one writer may be involved.

There is COLERIDGE, whose flights no restriction can fetter,
Who has peopled the whole of his Old Navigator*
With extravagant shapes, both of Horror and Fear,
But for what end collected, is not quite so clear:
His too are perhaps those eccentric designs,
Where whimsical fancy with Ridicule joins;
Like the comfortless state of bewitch'd HARRY GILL†
When with ten waistcoats cover'd, his teeth chatter'd still.

---

* The Ancient Marynere, is the first article among the Lyrical Ballads, and report has in general given it to Coleridge. Its merit, in the fanciful style, is great, but there is no piece of Poetry which I at present recollect, to which the question of Cui Bono applies with so much propriety and force.

† This is the sixth Article in the Lyrical Ballads, and of the same style is the sixteenth, called the Idiot Boy; whether either of them belong to Coleridge, is hitherto a question that has not been decided.

55. W. Heath (1749–1852)

Unsigned notice, *Anti-Jacobin Review*, April 1800, V, 434 [misprinted as 334]

Because Coleridge and Wordsworth had insisted that *Lyrical Ballads* should be published anonymously (28 May 1798, *Coleridge Letters*, ed. E. L. Griggs, 1956, I, 412), this generous reviewer was ignorant that Coleridge had been attacked by George Canning in his verses in the *Anti-Jacobin; or Weekly Examiner*, Monday, 9 July 1798, 286; indeed, Canning's poem was the inspiration for Gilray's great cartoon prepared to launch the successor publication: *Anti-Jacobin Review and Magazine*, 1 August 1798. The recognition that their names might hinder the publication ('Wordsworth's name is nothing – to a large number of persons mine *stinks*') says much for the two poets' political and publishing acumen.

This is a volume of a very different description from the above [R. J. Thorne's *Lodon and Miranda*]. It has genius, taste, elegance, wit, and imagery of the most beautiful kind. 'The ancyent Marinere' is an admirable 'imitation of the style as well as of the spirit of the elder poets.' 'The foster Mothers Tale' is pathetic, and pleasing in the extreme – 'Simon Lee the old Huntsman' – 'The idiot Boy,' and the Tale of 'Goody Blake, and Harry Gill' are all beautiful in their kind; indeed the whole volume convinces us that the author possesses a mind at once classic and accomplished, and we, with pleasure, recommend it to the notice of our readers as a production of no ordinary merit.

56. Daniel Stuart (1766–1846)

Reviews and Comments in the *Morning Post* and the *Courier*, April and June 1800

Stuart was editor and proprietor of both papers and in April 1800 began a short campaign on behalf of *Lyrical Ballads*, though without naming the authors. This did not go unnoticed in Grasmere; Coleridge wrote to Stuart on 15 July 1800:

Wordsworth requests me to be very express in the communication of his sincere thanks to you, for the interest which you have been so kind to take in his poems. We are convinced that you have been of great service to the sale.

a. *Morning Post*, 2 April 1800

It has been the habit of our Paper to present our Readers with none but Original Poetry; but we have been so much captivated with the following beautiful Piece, which appears in a small volume entitled LYRICAL BALLADS, that we are tempted to transgress the rule we have laid down for ourselves. Indeed, the whole Collection, with the exception of the first Piece, which appears manifestly to have been written by a different hand, is a tribute to genuine nature.

[Reprints 'The Mad Mother', *PW*, II, p. 107; *LB (1798,) p. 82*]

(R. S. Woof, 'Wordsworth's Poetry and Stuart's Newspapers: 1797–1803', *Studies in Bibliography*, XV, 1962, 172–3)

This produced a wry, even negative response from Thomasina Dennis who wrote to Davies Giddy on 9 April:

Mr Coleridge is still in London writing for the Morning Post – his style continues as stiff and affected as ever – you know how he professes no very high respect for the Greek or Latin poets – I could but smile to see in the morning Post a very warm panegyric on a little poem of Wordsworth's called the Mad Mother, in which are these lines.

> I'll teach my babe the *sweetest things*
> I'll teach him how the *Owlet sings*

A little before, she says she has her babe with her, or else she were alone – In plain prose she has company, or else she had been by herself.

(R. S. Woof, 'Coleridge and Thomasina Dennis', *University of Toronto Quarterly*, xxxii, 1962, 49–50)

b. *Courier*, 7 April 1800

The following beautiful piece of poetry is taken from a small collection called *Lyrical Ballads*. We do not hesitate to pronounce the author to be one of the first poets of the age, and we earnestly recommend them to the earnest perusal of all our readers.

[Reprints 'We are Seven', *PW*, I, p. 236; *LB (1798)*, p. 66.]

(*Ibid.*)

c. *Courier*, 9 April 1800

[Reprints 'The Last of the Flock']

(*Ibid.*)

d. *Courier*, 19 April 1800

The Female Vagrant is extracted from the *Lyrical Ballads*, which we cannot too often and too warmly recommend to our Readers. The excellence of the following piece renders it totally unnecessary for us to make any apology for the length of space it occupies [Three newspaper columns].

(*Ibid.*)

e. *Morning Post*, 21 June 1800

TO CORRESPONDENTS. It has been repeatedly asked why we have published no further extracts from the Lyrical Ballads, from which we some time ago took the beautiful Poem of The Mad Mother. We would continue those extracts, if it were not the rule of this Paper to give none but Original Poetry, and if the volume of Lyrical Ballads were not already in the hands of everyone who has a taste for Poetry. It is to be had [sic] the corner of Lombard and Gracechurch-streets.

(*Ibid.*)

IV

Lyrical Ballads: opinions,
August 1800–February 1801

57. Samuel Taylor Coleridge

From letters, 1800–1801

a. To James Tobin, 17 September 1800

I abandon Poetry altogether – I leave the higher & deeper kinds to Wordsworth, the delightful, popular & simply dignified to Southey; & reserve for myself the honorable attempt to make others feel and understand their writings, as they deserve to be felt and understood. . . . Does not Davy admire Wordsworth's RUTH? I think it the finest poem in the collection.[1]

(*Collected Letters of Samuel Taylor Coleridge*, ed. E. L. Griggs, Oxford, 1956–71, I, 623)

b. To Humphry Davy, 9 October 1800

I would rather have written Ruth, and Nature's Lady ['Three years she grew . . .'] than a million such poems as ['Christabel']

(*Ibid.*, I, 632)

c. Again to Humphry Davy, 2 December 1800

Wordsworth has nearly finished the concluding poem ['Michael']. It is of a mild unimposing character; but full of beauties to those short-necked men who have their hearts sufficiently near their heads –

(*Ibid.*, I, 649)

d. To William Godwin, 6 December 1800

For myself, I would rather have written the Mad Mother, than all the works of all the Bolinbrokes & Sheridans, & their Brother Meteors . . .

(*Ibid.*, I, 652)

e. To Humphry Davy, 11 January 1801

You say W.'s 'last poem is full of jus[t] pictures of what human life ought to be' – believe me, that such scenes & such char[acters] really exist in this county – the superiority of the small Estates-man, such as W. pain[ts] in old Michael, is a God compared to our Peasants and small Farmers in the South: & furnishes important documents of the kindly ministrations of local attachment & hereditary descent –

(*Ibid.*, II, 663)

f. To Thomas Poole, 16 March 1801

You have seen, I hope, the lyrical Ballads – In the divine Poem called Michael, by an infamous blunder of the Printer near 20 lines are omitted in page 210,[2] which makes it nearly unintelligible – Wordsworth means to write to you & to send them together with a list of the numerous Errata. The character of the Lyrical Ballads is very great, & will increase daily. They have *extolled* them in the British Critic.

(*Ibid.*, II, 707)

g. To William Godwin, 25 March 1801

Have you seen the second Volume of the Lyrical Ballads, & the Preface prefixed to the First? – I should judge of a man's Heart, and Intellect precisely according to the degree & intensity of the admiration, with which he read those poems – Perhaps, instead of Heart I should have said Taste, but when I think of The Brothers, of Ruth, and of Michael, I recur to the expression, & am enforced to say *Heart*. If I die, and the Booksellers will give you any thing for my Life, be sure to say – 'Wordsworth descended on him, like the Γνῶθι σεαυτόν[3] from Heaven; by shewing to him what true Poetry was, he made him know, that he himself was no Poet.'

(*Ibid.*, II, 714)

h. To William Godwin, 23 June 1801

Yet *seriously* I should have small fellow-feeling with a man who could read 'the Brothers' & 'Michael' with indifference, or (as some have done) with merriment – & I must add too (in proof of a favorite opinion of my own, viz. that where the Temper permits a *sneer*, the Understanding most frequently makes a blunder) that . . . [and Coleridge goes on to develop the notion that 'the works of a contemporary writer hitherto without fame or rank' can be used 'as a *touchstone* by which to come at a decision in my own mind concerning a Man's Taste & Judgement'.]

(*Ibid.*, II, 738)

EDITOR'S NOTE

1. See entry 736 for Coleridge's distress at Wordsworth's revisions of 1802.
2. ll. 191–206. For a full discussion of Wordsworth's typographical intentions for 'Michael', and thus the thematic importance of these lines, see R. S. Woof, 'John Stoddart, "Michael" and *Lyrical Ballads*', *Ariel* (April 1970), i. 2, 7–22.
3. 'Know thyself'.

58. Charles Lloyd

From letters, 1801

a. To Thomas Manning, 26 January 1801

We have not any society except the Wordsworth's – they are very unusual characters – indeed Miss Wordsworth I much like – but her Brother is not a man after my own heart – I always feel myself depressed in his society –

(*Lloyd–Manning Letters*, ed. F. L. Beaty, Indiana University Press, 1957, 61)

b. To Thomas Manning, 31 March 1801

With regard to the second volume of the lyrical ballads I think you considerably underrate it – though, to confess the truth, I have felt myself disappointed in the perusal of its contents – I admire the simplicity, the pure feelings, & the delicate discrimination of natural objects, which is to be found in some of them – but their total [want absence *deleted*] nakedness in point of imagination – their puerile minuteness – their cold accuracy, (unillumed & uninvigorated by the deliciously blending light & shades of poetic feelings,) disgust, & weary me – . . .

[Mr. and Mrs. Clarkson had been, and their visit, he claimed, had ill fitted him] for passing a judgment on compositions whose only claim to merit, is their power of exciting sympathy; & sympathy of no ordinary or obtrusive kind – I [like *deleted*] am pleased with 'the Brothers' – 'Ruth' – 'the two April mornings' 'Nutting' & 'Three years she grew in sun & shower' these are they which have hitherto alone impressed me – but not one of them, except the Brothers, has excited a strong emotion – I quite agree with you that inanimate nature owes its chief value to its associations with animate – & I think it a perversion of the human mind to cultivate a love for it as a primary object – I class it among a number of tastes which an elegant mind *may* pursue – but always to be held subordinate to [many *deleted*] others – . . .

A poet, I think, always ought to compliment a reader [on the *deleted*] with the supposition of his possessing [of *deleted*] some of his [of *deleted*] own imagination – he should rather touch a train of known associations happily & lightly – than enter into minute analysis – Burns's address of his genius in 'The vision' beginning at these lines 'of these am I Coila my name' to the end of the poem is an instance of the former – W[ordsworth] I think is to be blamed for the latter – . . .

(*Ibid.*, pp. 66–7)

59. Thomas Clarkson (1760–1846) and Catherine Clarkson (1772–1856)

From letters and writings, 1800–1806

In 1794, Thomas Clarkson built Eusemere, a house at the north end of Ullswater. His health had broken down after some seven years of unremitting work, gathering evidence against the Slave Trade. On 19 January 1796 he married Catherine Buck, and to their house on 17 November 1799, Wordsworth brought Coleridge. Within fifteen months, the Clarksons were among the closest of the Wordsworths' friends. Wordsworth's own sympathy with negroes was to find expression in two of his finest sonnets: 'The Banished Negroes: 1st. September 1802' and 'To Toussaint L'Ouverture' (1802). While his *Poems* (1807) were in the press, he added a celebratory sonnet: 'To Thomas Clarkson, on the first passing of the Bill for the abolition of the Slave Trade, March 1807'.

a. Catherine Clarkson. From a letter to Priscilla Lloyd, 12 January 1800

Priscilla Lloyd was soon to marry Wordsworth's brother, Christopher.

I must tell you that we [had] a Visit from Coleridge and W. Wordsworth who spent a whole day with us. C was in high Spirits & talk'd a great

92

deal. W. was more reserved but there was neither hauteur nor moroseness in his Reserve. He has a fine commanding figure is rather handsome & looks as if he was born to be a great Prince or a great General. He seems very fond of C. laughing at all his Jokes & taking all opportunities of shewing him off & to crown all he has the manners of a Gentleman.

(*Wordsworth Chronology 1770–99*, Mark Reed, 1967, 280–1)

b. Catherine Clarkson. From letters to Rev. R. E. Garnham, 1801–2

R. E. Garnham was a Fellow of Trinity College, Cambridge.

12 February 1801
. . . I think I told you in my last that I expected Wordsworth & his Sister to visit us. Well – they have been here & staid more than three weeks & have left us with a very favourable opinion of them – You must buy W— — two volumes of Lyrical Ballads & tell me what you think of them. We have not got them yet. I am fully convinced that Wordsworths Genius is equal to the Production of something very great, & I have no doubt but he will produce '*something that Posterity will not willingly let die*', if he lives ten or twenty years longer. – I was very much affected by '*the Brothers*' when I saw it in manuscript – pray tell me how it affects you, & any body else whom you may happen to converse with who has read it – I want to ascertain how much of the feeling w^h it excited in me, was occasion'd by the Knowledge I have of the country & the manners of the Inhabitants – The Brothers, Lucy Gray, poor Susan, Timothy & the Poem where Bewick is praised are all that I have seen of the second Volume – Lucy Gray is I think inimitable.

(*Correspondence of Henry Crabb Robinson with the Wordsworth Circle*, ed. E. J. Morley, 1927, i, 41)

20 May 1802
Note here Catherine Clarkson's immediate recognition of the private nature of the poems of 1802. These poems when published in *Poems* (1807) were particularly attacked for triviality.

I am glad that you are so pleased with my friends W[ordsworth] & his Sister. I am sure that if you knew them you would love them as I do & that is with all the Heart – they love me too – not quite so much as you do perhaps but very much – I assure you I am not a little elevated in my own estimation by the regard they have for me – They have both been here since I wrote to you last – W— has lately written a number of the most beautiful little Poems many of wh. I daresay will never meet the publick Eye at least not during his own & his Sister's Lives –

(Ms. Dr. Williams' Library)

c. Thomas Clarkson, extract from *A Portraiture of Quakerism*, 1806, II, 146–50

Clarkson, though himself not a Quaker, was the first to connect Wordsworth's poetry with Quaker thought. This was a notion that later found favour with Charles Lamb (review of the *Excursion*, 1814) and William Howitt, more extravagantly (*Homes and Haunts*, 1847). Clarkson's chapter heading, in italics, summarises his argument.

The Spirit of God, which has been thus given to man in different degrees, was given to him as a spiritual teacher or guide in his spiritual concerns – It performs this office, the Quakers say, by internal monitions . . . if encouraged, it teaches even by the external objects of the Creation – William Wordsworth.

But this Spirit is considered by the Society, not only as teaching by inward breathings as it were, made immediately and directly upon the heart, without the intervention of outward circumstances, but as making the material objects of the universe, and many of the occurrences of life, if it be properly attended to, subservient to the instruction of man; and as enlarging the sphere of his instruction in this manner in proportion as it is received and encouraged. Thus, the man, who is attentive to these divine notices, sees the animal, the vegetable, and the planetary world with spiritual eyes. He cannot stir abroad, but he is taught in his own feelings, without any motion of his will, some lesson for his spiritual advantage; or he perceives so vitally some of the attributes of the Divine Being, that he is called upon to offer some spiritual incense to his Maker. If the lamb frolics and gambols in his presence as he walks along, he may be made spiritually to see the beauty and happiness of innocence. If he finds the stately oak laid prostrate by the wind, he may be spiritually taught to discern the emptiness of human power; while the same Spirit may teach him inwardly the advantage of humility, when he looks at the little hawthorn, which has survived the storm. When he sees the change and the fall of the autumnal leaf, he may be spiritually admonished of his own change and dissolution, and of the necessity of a holy life. Thus, the Spirit of God may teach men by outward objects and occurrences in the world. But where this Spirit is away, or rather where it is not attended to, no such lesson can be taught. Natural objects of themselves can excite only natural ideas; and the natural man, looking at them, can derive only natural pleasure or draw natural conclusions from them. In looking at the sun he may be pleased with its warmth, and anticipate its advantage to the vegetable world. In plucking and examining a flower, he may be struck with its beauty, its mechanism, and its fragrant smell. In observing the butterfly, as it wings its way before him, he may smile at its short journeys from place to place, and admire the splendour upon its wings. But the beauty of creation is dead to him, as far as it depends upon connecting it spiritually with the character of God; for no spiritual impression can arise from any natural objects, so that these should be sanctified to him, but through the intervention of the Spirit of God.

William Wordsworth, in his instructive Poems, has described this teaching by external objects in consequence of impressions from a higher power, as differing from any teaching by books or by the human understanding, and as arising without any motion of the will of man, in so beautiful and simple a manner, that I cannot do otherwise than make an extract from them in this place. Lively as the poem is, to which I allude, I conceive it will not lower the dignity of the subject. It is called 'Expostulation and Reply,'[1] and is as follows: [Quotes the poem].

EDITOR'S NOTE

1. In the editions of *Lyrical Ballads*, 1800, 1802 and 1805, 'Expostulation and Reply' replaced 'The Ancient Mariner' as the opening poem.

60. John Wordsworth (1772–1805)

From letters, 1801

a. To Wordsworth, 28 January 1801

John reports he has delivered to Longman the letters which were to accompany the complimentary copies to be sent 'to the great men & women'. Coleridge wrote the letters to Mrs Jordan, Mrs Barbauld, William Wilberforce, the Duchess of Devonshire and Sir Bland

Burgess. Wordsworth wrote to Charles James Fox 14 January 1801 (see *EY* 312–15).

I was much pleased with your letter to Mr Fox & with the others of course in a smaller degree indeed I should have been much disappointed if I had not seen them – now I do request that if they answer these letters you will have the goodness to [send *deleted*] let me know what they say – I cannot express how much everyone that I have seen appears to be delighted with some *one* of your poems & more particularly the Brothers – I have seen Stoddart's review but I thought it too flattering, I mean too much of a panegyric they will see immediately that it has been written by a Friend – & it is to be submitted to the perusal of the *Reviewers*. Pinney was much delighted with the Brothers & with the Song 'She dwelt among' the rest he seem'd to think highly of – John Myers[1] was very [deeply *deleted*] much indeed affected by the Brothers & some of my friends that you are not acquainted with have spoken in the most high terms of your poems – Longman who by the way is a most damnable Jew could not help expressing how high Mr. W's character stood in the poetical department & show'd by his looks that he expected to gain a great deal by the Book – . . . I have been exceedingly pleased with the poem of the C. beggar I was at the first reading disappointed with Michael at the second reading I was a [little *deleted*] not a little pleased – but latterly I have been excessively delighted with it. when I first read it I thought the circumstances too minute & the language too low for a blank verse poems [*sic*], & from what Stoddart had told me I thought it would have been a poem in rhyme[2] but now think it most interesting & particularly to those who are acquainted & have liv'd in Cumbd. – . . . I think Stoddart a very poor Judge of Poetry

(Ms. The Wordsworth Library; also printed in *Letters of John Wordsworth*, ed. Carl Ketcham, Cornell, 1970, 82–3)

b. To Wordsworth, 6 February 1801

John is commenting on three of the poems in the sequence *Poems on the Naming of Places*: ii, 'To Joanna', 'Amid the smoke of cities . . .'; iv ['Point Rash Judgement'] 'A narrow girdle of rough stones . . .'; v, 'To M. H.', 'Our walk was far among the ancient trees'.

. . . I did not like your poem of point rash judgement when I first read it – but I have since been excessively pleased with parts of it – & particularly with this part – 'That was its horse, its Chariot &c. & the whole of that Description – & also of the one that follows but Joanna is my favourite poem.

(*Ibid.*, 87)

c. To Dorothy Wordsworth, 21 February 1801

Arch has had a great sale of the 2nd. Vol tho I was surprised to find he had sold but a very few of the 2nd. edition – he said his customers complain'd of being cheated out of a preface –

(*Ibid.*, 92)

d. To Mary Hutchinson, 24 February 1801

– You must know then that P. R. Judgement is not a particular favourite there are some parts of it that in my opinion are written in the true stile of poetry – I like much the description of the thistles beard having noticed it myself – but the latter part I have thought *too quaint* – Yet I am sure it is a poem that will please many people –

(*Ibid.*, 93–4)

e. To Mary Hutchinson, 25–26 February 1801

– Cottle had no *hand* in the correction of the proofs it was intrusted to Mr Davy whom I suppose you must have heard of he is a great Chemist at Bristol – I like your criticism of Michael & except the language which you do not mention it has the same effect upon me –

the Danish Boy does not at all interest me it is meant as a *wild* story and dream of Fancy – You ask me what impression these vols. have made the fact is everyone is so full of his own business that *even I* scarce hear them mentioned except I leg them in myself – when the Reviews come out we shall know more abt. them – I was with Stoddart this morning who is writing in a *friendly* way for the British Critic. I saw the Review of them which he had written[3] & it did not please me I thought it too indiscriminately flattering he says he has shown it to the Reviewers & they approve of his review – but will make some small alterations – I think in time they will become popular but it will be by degrees – the fact is there are not a great many that will be pleased with the poems but those that are pleased will be pleased in a high degree & they *will be people of sense* this will have weight – & people who neither understand

97

or wish to understand will buy & praise them – Longman is a vile abominable and impudent Jew[4] for only giving Wm 80£ for the 2 Editions he will clear at least 400£ or perhaps 500£ – they are sure of a good and steady sale – Wm says that the nutting and Joanna shew the greatest genious [*sic*] of any poems in the 2d Vol Joanna is indeed a most delightful poem it is my greatest favourite it is a perfect poem has a beginning middle – and end – Kitt is very much pleased with the poems.

(*Ibid.*, 95–6)

f. To Mary Hutchinson, 9–10 March 1801

I do not think that W[s] poetry will become popular for some time to come it certainly does not suit the present taste I was in the company the other evening with a gentleman[5] he read the [Cumberland] Beggar 'Why says he this is very pretty but you may call it any but poetry – I like the description but still it is very different to what I should conceive poetry to be ['] – I said it might be true (for I like to give people their own way) & that perhaps from local circumstances I might be more interested in it than it deserved – the truth is there are few people that like, or read, poetry many who buy it – buy it for the name – read about twenty [lines] the language is very fine, They are content with praising extravagantly the whole poem. Most of W[s] poetry improves upon 2[d] 3 or 4th reading now people in general are not sufficiently interested with the first reading to induce them to try a 2[d].

(*Ibid.*, 103)

EDITOR'S NOTES

1. A lawyer cousin, with whom Wordsworth went to Cambridge in 1787.
2. Wordsworth indeed wrote a rhymed poem, 'The Sheepfold', an earlier version of 'Michael', in October–November 1800; he burnt this composition on 9 November, just after Stoddart had visited him at Grasmere. For some of the text of the fragment that remains and a discussion of the composition of 'Michael' see my *Ariel* article, cited earlier, p. 91.
3. See entry 84 for Stoddart's review.
4. There is no evidence that Wordsworth shared his brother's casual antisemitic view.
5. Later in the letter John identifies the man: 'he is of the class of Loshs's of Carlisle if you ever heard of them – Indeed my brother's poetry has a great

deal to struggle [against] but I hope it will overcome all – it is certainly founded upon nature – & that is the best foundation – Mr Losh is a great favourite with my brother but that do not hit upon this point –' (*ibid.*, 105). John had gone to Hawkshead School with William and George Losh, younger brothers of James [see entry 31], the 'great favourite with my brother'. That the 'gentleman' is 'of the class of Loshs's of Carlisle' suggests one of their circle, such as Losh's brother-in-law, John Baldwin, in whose lodgings Wordsworth stayed in Hamburg, 1798.

61. Charles Lamb

From letters, 1801

a. To Wordsworth, 30 January 1801

On 6 August 1800 Lamb had asked Coleridge to get him the new second volume; Wordsworth sent him the two volumes of *Lyrical Ballads* (1800), and they were debited to Wordsworth's account at Longman's on 29 January 1801:

Thanks for your Letter and Present. I had already borrowed your second volume. What most please me are, the Song of Lucy . . . ['She dwelt among the untrodden ways']. *Simon's sickly daughter* in the Sexton made me *cry*. Next to these are the description of the continuous Echoes in the story of Joanna's laugh, where the mountains and all the scenery absolutely seem alive – and that fine Shakesperian character of the Happy Man, in the Brothers,

> — that creeps about the fields,
> Following his fancies by the hour, to bring
> Tears down his cheek, or solitary smiles
> Into his face, *until the Setting Sun*
> *Write Fool upon his forehead.*
> ['The Brothers', *PW*, II. p. 4, ll. 108–12;
> *LB (1800)*, p. 136, ll. 106–10.]

I will mention one more: the delicate and curious feeling in the wish for the Cumberland Beggar, that he may have about him the melody of Birds, altho' he hear them not. Here the mind knowingly passes a fiction upon herself, first substituting her own feelings for the Beggar's, and, in the same breath detecting the fallacy, will not part with the wish. – The

99

Poet's Epitaph is disfigured, to my taste by the vulgar satire upon parsons and lawyers in the beginning, and the coarse epithet of pin point in the 6th stanza. All the rest is eminently good, and your own. I will just add that it appears to me a fault in the Beggar, that the instructions conveyed in it are too direct and like a lecture: they don't slide into the mind of the reader, while he is imagining no such matter. An intelligent reader finds a sort of insult in being told, I will teach you how to think upon this subject. This fault, if I am right, is in a ten-thousandth worse degree to be found in Sterne and many many novelists & modern poets, who continually put a sign post up to shew where you are to feel. They set out with assuming their readers to be stupid.

(*The Letters of Charles and Mary Lamb*, ed. E. V. Lucas, 1935, I, 239)

b. To Robert Lloyd, 7 February 1801

Wordsworth has published a second vol. – 'Lyrical Ballads.' Most of them are very good, but not so good as first vol.

(*Ibid.*, I. 245)

c. To Manning, 15 February 1801

I had need be cautious henceforward what opinion I give of the 'Lyrical Ballads.' All the North of England are in a turmoil. Cumberland and Westmoreland have already declared a state of war. I lately received from Wordsworth a copy of the second volume, accompanied by an acknowledgement of having received from me many months since a copy of a certain Tragedy, with excuses for not having made any acknowledgement sooner, it being owing to an 'almost insurmountable aversion from Letter-writing.' This letter I answered in due form and time, and enumerated several of the passages which had most affected me, adding, unfortunately, that no single piece had moved me so forcibly as the *Ancient Mariner*, *The Mad Mother*, or the *Lines at Tintern Abbey*. The Post did not sleep a moment. I received almost instantaneously a long letter of four sweating pages from my Reluctant Letter-Writer, the purport of which was, that he was sorry his 2d vol. had not given me more pleasure (Devil a hint did I give that it had *not pleased me*), and 'was compelled to wish that my range of sensibility was more extended, being obliged to believe that I should receive large influxes of happiness and happy Thoughts' (I suppose from the L. B.) – With a deal of stuff about a certain Union of Tenderness and Imagination, which in the sense he used Imagination was not the characteristic of Shakspeare, but which Milton possessed in a degree far exceeding other Poets: which Union, as the highest species of Poetry, and chiefly deserving that name, 'He was most proud to aspire to'; then illustrating the said Union by two quotations from his own 2d vol. (which I had been so unfortunate as to miss). 1st Specimen – a father addresses his son:

> When thou
> First camest into the World, as it befalls
> To new-born Infants, thou didst sleep away
> Two days: and *Blessings from Thy father's Tongue*
> *Then fell upon thee.*

['Michael', *PW*, II, p. 90, ll. 339–43; *LB (1800)*, p. 230. ll. 339–43.]

The lines were thus undermarked, and then followed 'This Passage, as combining in an extraordinary degree that Union of Imagination and Tenderness which I am speaking of, I consider as one of the Best I ever wrote!'

2d Specimen. – A youth, after years of absence, revisits his native place, and thinks (as most people do) that there has been strange alteration in his absence: –

> And that the rocks
> And everlasting Hills themselves were changed.

['The Brothers', *PW*, II, p. 3, ll. 98–9; *LB (1800)*, p. 136, ll. 96–7; oddly, Lamb here misquotes, anticipating Wordsworth's later revision, 'everlasting hills' for 'the eternal hills']

You see both these are good Poetry: but after one has been reading Shakspeare twenty of the best years of one's life, to have a fellow start up, and prate about some unknown quality, which Shakspeare possessed in a degree inferior to Milton and *somebody else!!* This was not to be *all* my castigation. Coleridge, who had not written to me some months before, starts up from his bed of sickness to reprove me for my hardy presumption: four long pages, equally sweaty and more tedious, came from him; assuring me that, when the works of a man of true genius such as W. undoubtedly was, do not please me at first sight, I should suspect the fault to lie "in me and not in them," etc. etc. etc. etc. etc. What am I to do with such people? I certainly shall write them a very merry Letter. Writing to *you*, I may say that the 2d vol. has no such pieces as the three I enumerated. It is full of original thinking and an observing mind, but it does not often make you laugh or cry. – It too artfully aims at simplicity of expression. And you sometimes doubt if Simplicity be not a cover for Poverty. The best Piece in it I will send you, being *short*. I have grievously offended my friends in the North by declaring my undue preference; but I need not fear you: –

[Quotes 'She dwelt among the untrodden ways'.]

This is choice and genuine, and so are many, many more. But one does not like to have 'em rammed down one's throat. 'Pray, take it – it's very good – let me help you – eat faster.'

(*Ibid.*, I, 246–7)

d. To Manning, late February 1801

So, you don't think there's a Word's-worth of good poetry in the treat L.B.! I daren't put the dreaded syllables at their just length, for my back tingles from the northern castigation. . . .

'Tis half-past twelve o'clock, and all sober people ought to be a-bed. Between you and me, the *Lyrical Ballads* are but drowsy performances.

(*Ibid.*, I, 251)

62. Christopher Wordsworth

Extracts from letters to Rev. Jonathan Walton, 1801

a. 16 February 1801

I have lately received a second vol: of the Lyrical Ballads. You must send for it. There is a new Edition of the 1st. Vol: with a new preface – but in other respects it has not any very important alterations except indeed a new poem by Coleridge. The whole of the second vol: is very valuable – several of the poems are exquisitely beautiful. They are of a much humaner and gentler cast than the first volume and consequently much better calculated for general favour. Indeed the second vol: ought to be read before the first. I have no doubt of their being exceedingly popular. Nor do I think that I am mistaken in saying that they mark out my Brother as decidedly the first of living English Poets.

(*William Wordsworth*, Elizabeth Wordsworth, 1891, 79; punctuation corrected from the Ms. Wordsworth Library)

b. 15 April 1801

Have you read the Lyrical Ballads? I shall be glad to hear that you have read them with pleasure. The Michael, the Brothers, Ruth the Cumberland Beggar, Joanna &c &c all seem to me exquisitely beautiful, and of very great moral value. 'There was a boy', Nutting, the Childless Father, and the Poems about Matthew I also like exceedingly.

(*Ibid.*, 79)[1]

EDITOR'S NOTE

1. Elizabeth Wordsworth mistakenly dates the letter 16 April, and heads it as from Cambridge, whereas it is written from Forncett.

63. Thomas Manning (1772–1840)

From letters to Charles Lamb, February–March 1801

Manning was a mathematician and private tutor to, among others, Charles Lloyd, at Cambridge. He went on to become a traveller and student in China.

a. Postmark 25 February 1801

I have not time to give you my opinion of the 2^d Vol of Ly^l Ballads, except that I think tis utterly absurd from one end to the other. *You* tell me tis good poetry – if you mean that there is nothing puerile, nothing bombast or conceited, or any thing else that is so often found to disfigure *poetry*, I agree, but will you read it over & over again? Answer me that, Master Lamb. Xtover Wordsworth has the most exalted idea of it you can imagine – for my part I had rather sit spinning all day than prosing over such uninteresting accounts of uninteresting things.

(*Letters of Thomas Manning to Charles Lamb*, ed. Gerturde A. Anderson, 1925, 52)

b. **Postmark 14 March 1801**

I perused the Colerigian & Wordsworthian letters. Sheer nonsense, by
God. I wonder Coleridge (who I know is a poet – I don't know that W. is
not, but I'll be damned if *that* be poetry he has passed [?] upon us in the
2ᵈ Vol.) – I say I wonder Coleridge can be taken in by such foolish stuff.
By habit one may learn to be excited by any thing – one may live so long
with sheep & silly shepperds as to take the Baaing of a Lamb for poetry
– but what is that to the purpose – would Shakespear have taken it for
poetry? Oh! but *he*'s no judge perhaps – would Milton then? To *gravely*,
mind that, *gravely* tell us of a sheep drawn out of a hole, & chronicle the
beggar's two penny mishap – who is it, Pope or Swift that ridicules the
poets who chronicle small beer? No, no, I believe tis the Huswifes. Well, I
can't spend any more time about an old woman's Gossip.

(*Ibid.*, 54–5)

64. William Wordsworth

Wordsworth notes his critics: from a letter to Sara Hutchinson, late
February–early March 1801

For Coleridges entertainment I send the following harmonies of
criticism –

Nutting	Nutting
Mr C. Wordsworth worth its weight in gold	Mr Stoddart can make neither head nor tail of it.
Joanna	Joanna
Mr John Wordsworth the finest poem of its length you have written	Mr Stoddart takes the description of the echoes as a thing regularly and permanently believed of course can make nothing of the poem.
Poet's Epitaph	Poet's Epitaph
Mr. Charles Lamb the latter part eminently good and your own	Mr Stoddart The latter part I dont like, it is very ill written.

Cumberland Beggar

Mr John Wordsworth
Indeed every body seems
delighted with Cumberland beggar.

Mr Charles Lamb
The instructions too direct You
seem to presume your readers are
stupid &c. &c.

Idiot Boy

Mr John Wordsworth
To a Lady a friend of mine I gave
the 2 vol: they were both new to
her. The idiot Boy of all the poems
her delight; could talk of no thing
else.
But here comes the Waggon!

Idiot Boy

Mr Stoddart
Thrown into a *fit* almost with
disgust, cannot *possibly* read it.

(*EY*, 319–21)

65. Joanna Hutchinson (1780–1841)

From a letter to John Monkhouse, 2 May 1801

. . . have you seen the Lyrical Ballads – what do you think of them, are
they not *most* beautiful – that Poem to Mary H – is beyond everything –
the Brothers, the female Vagrant, and ruth – the Nightingale, lines on
revisiting the banks of the Wye &c &c – are my greatest favorites – what
do you think of the *fair* Joanna – it is thought a very capital one – but I
like any of them, as well – The female Vagrant – I could read for ever,
and always find something new – I shall I am afraid neither see, nor hear
anything of the Wordsworth's now Sara is gone – they are very nice folks
– I love them dearly – I don't admire Mr Coleridge half so much as
William Wordsworth Sara thought I would have liked him better he
is not half so *canny* a *man*, Dorothy is a *sweet* woman – is not handsome
but has uncommon good countenance – and is very lively.

(Ms. Wordsworth Library)

66. Charles James Fox (1749–1806)

Letter to Wordsworth, 25 May 1801

Sir, I owe you many apologies for having so long deferred thanking you for your Poems and your obliging letter accompanying them, which I received early in March. – The Poems have given me the greatest pleasure and if I were obliged to choose out of them, I do not know whether I should not say that Harry Gill, We are Seven, the Mad Mother, and the Idiot, are my favourites. I read with particular attention the two you pointed out, but whether it be from my early prepossessions, or whatever other cause, I am no great friend to blank verse for subjects which are to be treated of with simplicity. You will excuse my stating to you my opinion so freely, which I should not do if I did not really admire many of the Poems in the Collection, and many parts even of these in blank Verse. Of the Poems which you state not to be yours, that entitled *Love* appears to me to be the best, and I do not know who is the Author. The Nightingale I understand to be Mr. Coleridge's, who combats I think very successfully the mistaken prejudice of the nightingale's note being melancholy. I am, with great truth, Sir, Your most obedient servant,

(*The Prose Works of William Wordsworth*, ed. Alexander B. Grosart, 1876, II, 205–6; corrected from Wordsworth Library Ms.)

67. George Bellas Greenough (1778–1855)

From his diary, 22 September 1801

Greenough was a companion of Coleridge at Göttingen. He missed the Wordsworths when they visited Göttingen in April 1799. On his return to England he went to the Lakes with another Göttingen companion, Clement Carlyon, and there, probably in late May or early June 1801, he met and talked with the Wordsworths. During August and September 1801 Greenough visited Carlyon at his home in Truro.

I procured from the library Wordsworth's lyrical Ballads: I think them in general superior to those of Coleridge's with which they are interspersed.

(Ms. University College, London)

68. Dorothy Wordsworth

Journal extract, 28 December 1801

Wordsworth was invited by his brother Richard's friend Joshua Lucock Wilkinson, a London solicitor, to sup with him at the Keswick inn, The Royal Oak. There he also met John Hope Johnstone (1765–1843), later the fourth Earl of Hopetown. 'Johnston' never took the title of Marquis, which had been claimed by his father, on inheriting the estates and fortune of George Johnstone, the last Marquis of Annandale (died 1792). Mrs William Harcourt was in the Court circle. Her husband became the third Earl of Harcourt in 1809 and deputy keeper of Windsor Castle.

. . . met a young man (a predestined Marquis) called Johnston – he spoke to him [Wordsworth] familiarly of the LB – he had seen a copy presented by the Queen to Mrs Harcourt – said he saw them everywhere & wondered they did not sell.

69. Robert Southey

From letters, 1801–1802

a. To Samuel Taylor Coleridge, 11 July 1801 (Southey had returned from Portugal in June)

I feel here [Bristol] as a stranger; somewhat of Leonard's feeling. God bless Wordsworth for that poem [i.e. 'The Brothers'].

(*Life and Correspondence of Robert Southey*, ed. C. C. Southey, 1849, II, 249)

b. To Grosvenor C. Bedford (1773–1839), 19 August 1801

Bedford was Southey's schoolfriend and life-long correspondent; he held a treasury post.

If you have not seen the second volume of Wordsworth's Lyrical Ballads, I counsel you to buy them, and read *aloud* the poems entitled The Brothers, and Michael; which, especially the first, are, to my taste, excellent. I have never been so much affected, and so *well*, as by some passages there.

(*Ibid.*, II, 160)

c. To Coleridge, 4 August 1802

We shall probably agree altogether some day upon Wordsworth's Lyrical Poems. Does he not associate more feeling with particular phrases, and you also with him, than those phrases can convey to any one else? This I suspect. Who would part with a ring of a dead friend's hair? and yet a jeweller will give for it only the value of the gold: and so must words pass for their current value.

(*Ibid.*, II, 191)

70. John Wilson ('Christopher North') (1785–1854)

From a letter to Wordsworth, 1802

John Wilson became first a poetic disciple of Wordsworth and then his maverick critic. Wilson's daughter, Mary Gordon, in her *Memoir of Christopher North*, Edinburgh, 1862, I. 39, described him among his student companions at Glasgow:

> With these young men poetry was a frequent subject of discussion, and there was one poet viz., William Wordsworth, on whose merits, then but little recognised, they found themselves unanimous.

Among these young men was Alexander Blair (*fl.* 1790–1836), always Wilson's intellectual mentor. Together they wrote in Coleridge's *The Friend*, 1809–1810, under the name 'Mathetes' from the Greek meaning 'pupil' or 'disciple', a signature suggested by De Quincey. Wordsworth side-stepped their implicit invitation that he should be their teacher in a degenerate age. Much earlier, on 7 June 1802 (*EY*, 352–8) Wordsworth, replying to the precocious 17-year-old Wilson, did indeed teach, producing for Wilson one of the most helpful expositions of his poetic art. The manuscript of Wilson's letter is in the Wordsworth Library and is the source of the following text, hitherto slightly misprinted in Mary Gordon's *Memoir of Christopher North*, I, 40ff. The letter is addressed to Wordworth at 'Ambleside, Westmoreland, England', the hand probably secretarial.

My Dear Sir

You may perhaps be surprised to see yourself addressed in this manner by one who never had the happiness of being in company with you, and whose knowledge of your Character is drawn solely from the perusal of your Poems. But Sir, though I am not personally acquainted with you, I may almost venture to affirm that the qualities of your Soul are not unknown to me. In your Poems I discovered such marks of delicate feeling, such benevolence of disposition, and such knowledge of human nature, as made an impression on my mind that nothing will ever efface – and while I felt my Soul refined by the Sentiments contained in them, and filled with those delightful emotions which it would be almost impossible to describe, I entertained for you an attachment made up of Love, and admiration. Reflection upon that delight which I enjoyed from reading your Poems, will ever make me regard you with gratitude, and the consciousness of feeling those emotions you delineate, makes me proud to regard your character with esteem and admiration. In whatever view you regard my behaviour in writing this letter, whether you consider it as the effect of ignorance and conceit, or correct taste and refined feeling, I will in my own mind be satisfied with your opinion. To receive a letter from you would afford me more happiness than any occurrence in this world, save the happiness of my friends – and greatly enhance the pleasure I receive from reading your Lyrical ballads. Your silence would certainly distress me – but still I would have the happiness to think, that the neglect even of the virtuous cannot extinguish the sparks of sensibility, or diminish the luxury arising from refined emotions. That luxury, Sir, I have enjoyed – that luxury your Poems have afforded me – and for this reason do I now address you. Accept my thanks for the raptures you have occasioned me – and however much you may be inclined to despise me, know at least that these thanks are sincere & fervent.

109

To you Sir, Mankind are indebted for a species of Poetry, which will continue to afford pleasure, while respect is paid to virtuous feelings – and while sensibility continues to pour forth tears of rapture. The flimsy ornaments of language used to conceal meaness of thought, and want of feeling, may captivate for a short time the ignorant and the unwary – but true taste will discover the imposture and expose the authors of it to merited contempt. The real feelings of human nature, expressed in simple *and* forcible language, will on the contrary, please those only who are capable of entertaining them – and in proportion to the attention which we pay to the faithful delineation of such feelings, will be the enjoyment derived from them. That Poetry therefore which is the language of Nature, is certain of immortality, provided circumstances do not occur, to pervert the feelings of humanity, and occasion a complete revolution in the government of the Mind. That your Poetry is the language of Nature, in my opinion, admits of no doubt. Both the thoughts and expressions may be tried by that Standard. You have seized upon those feelings that most deeply interest the heart – and that also come within the Sphere of common observation. You do not write merely for the pleasure, of philosophers and men of improved taste, but for all who think, – for all who feel. If we have ever known the happiness arising from parental or fraternal love – if we have ever known that delightful sympathy of Souls connecting persons of different Sexes, – if we have ever dropped a tear at the death of friends, – or grieved for the misfortunes of others – if in short we have ever felt the more amiable emotions of human nature – it is impossible to read your Poems without being greatly interested, and frequently in raptures. Your sentiments, feelings and thoughts are therefore exactly such as ought to constitute the subject of Poetry and cannot fail of exciting interest in every heart.

But Sir, your merit does not solely consist in delineating the real features of the human mind, under those different aspects it assumes when under the influence of various passions, and feelings – you have in a manner truly admirable, explained a circumstance very important in its effects upon the Soul when agitated, that has indeed been frequently alluded to, but never generally adopted by any Author, in tracing the progress of emotions. – I mean that wonderful effect which the appearances of external nature, have upon the mind when in a State of strong feeling. We must all have been sensible, that when under the influence of grief, nature when arrayed in her gayest attire, appears to us dull and gloomy – and that when our hearts bound with joy, her most deformed prospects seldom fail of pleasing. This disposition of the mind to assimilate the appearances of external nature to its own situation is a fine subject for poetical allusion, and in several Poems you have employed it with a most electrifying Effect. But you have not stopped here. You have shown the effect which the qualities of external nature have, in forming the human mind – and have presented us with several characters whose particular biass [*sic*] arose from that situation in which they were placed with respect to the Scenery of nature. This Idea is inexpressibly beautiful, and though I confess that to me it appeared to border upon fiction when I first considered it, yet at this moment *I* am convinced of its foundation on nature, and its great importance in accounting for various phenonema in the human Mind. It serves to explain those diversities in the structure of the mind which have baffled all the ingenuity of philosophers to account for. It serves to overturn the Theories of men who have attempted to write on human nature, without a knowledge of the causes that affect it, and who have discovered greater eagerness to show their own subtlety than arrive at the acquisition of truth. May not the face of external nature through different quarters of the globe, account for the dispositions of different nations? May not mountains, forests, plains, groves, and lakes, as much as the temperature of the Atmosphere, or the form of government, produce important effects upon the human Soul, and may not the difference subsisting between the former of these in different countries, produce as much diversity among the inhabitants as any varieties among the latter? The effect you have shown to take place in particular cases so much to my satisfaction most certainly may be extended so far as to authorise general inferences. This Idea has no doubt struck you – and I trust that if it be founded on nature, your mind so long accustomed to philosophical investigation will perceive how far it may be carried, and what con-sequences are likely to result from it. – Your Poems, Sir, are of very great advantage to the world, from containing in them a system of philosophy, that regards one of the most curious subjects of investigation – and at the same time one of the most important. But your Poems may not be considered merely in a philosophical light, or even as containing refined and natural feelings – they present us with a body of morality of the purest kind. They represent the enjoyment resulting from the cultivation of the social affections of our nature; – they inculcate a conscientious regard to the rights of our fellow men; – they show that every creature on the face of the Earth is entitled in some measure to our kindness; – they prove that in every mind however depraved there exist some qualities deserving our esteem – they point out the proper way to happiness – they show that such a thing as perfect misery does not exist – they flash on our Souls conviction of immortality – Considered therefore in this view, Lyrical ballads is, to use your own words, the book which I value next to my bible – and though I may perhaps never have the happiness of seeing you, yet I will always consider you as a friend who has by his instructions done me a Service which it never can be in my power to repay. Your instructions have afforded me inexpressible pleasure, – it will be my own fault if I do not reap from them much advantage.

I have said, Sir, that in all your Poems you have adhered strictly to natural feelings, and described what comes within the range of every persons' observation. It is from following out this plan that in my estimation you have surpassed every Poet both of ancient and modern times. But to me it appears that in the execution of this design, you have inadvertently fallen into an Error, the effects of which are however exceedingly trivial. No feeling, no State of mind, ought in my opinion to become the Subject of Poetry, that does not please. Pleasure may indeed be produced in many ways, and by means that at first sight appear calculated, to accomplish a very different end. Tragedy of the deepest kind produces pleasure of a high Nature. To point out the causes of this would be foreign to the purpose. But we may lay this down as a general rule, that no description can please, where the Sympathies of our Soul are not excited, and no narration interest, where we do not enter into the feelings of some of the parties concerned. On this principle many feelings which are undoubtedly natural, are improper subjects of Poetry, and many situations no less natural, incapable of being described so as to produce the grand effect of poetical composition. This, Sir, I would apprehend is reasonable – and founded on the constitution of the human mind. There are a thousand occurrences happening every day, which do not in the least interest an unconcerned Spectator – though they no doubt occasion various emotions in the breast of those to whom they immediately relate. To describe these in poetry would be improper. – Now Sir, I think that in several cases you have fallen into this Error. You have described feelings with which I cannot sympathise – and situations in which I take no interest. I know that I can relish your beauties – and that makes me think that I can also perceive your faults. But in this matter I have not trusted wholly to my own Judgement, but heard the sentiments of men whose feelings I admired and whose understanding I respected. In a few cases then, I think that even you have failed to excite interest. – In the poem entitled the Idiot boy, your intention, as you inform us in your preface, was to trace the maternal passion through its more subtle windings. This design is no doubt accompanied with much difficulty, – but if properly executed, cannot fail of interesting the heart. But Sir in my opinion, the manner in which you have executed the plan, has frustrated the end you intended to produce by it. The affection of Betty Foy, has nothing in it, to excite interest. It exhibits merely the effects of that instinctive feeling inherent in the constitution of every animal. The excessive fondness of the mother disgusts us – and prevents us from sympathising with her. We are unable to enter into her feelings – we cannot conceive ourselves actuated by the same feelings, and consequently take little or no interest in her Situation. The object of her affection is indeed her Son – and in that relation much consists – but then he is represented as totally destitute of any attachment towards her – the State of his mind is represented as perfectly deplorable – and in short to me it appears almost unnatural that a person in a State of complete ideotism [sic], should excite the warmest feelings of attachment in the breast even of his Mother. This much I know, that among all the people I ever knew to have read this poem, I never met one who did not rise rather displeased from the perusal of it – and the only cause I could assign for it was the one now mentioned. This inability to receive pleasure from descriptions such as that of the Idiot boy, is I am convinced founded upon established feelings of human nature; and the principle of it constitutes as I daresay you recollect, the leading feature of Smiths Theory of moral Sentiments. I therefore think that in the choice of this Subject, you have committed an Error. You never deviate from Nature, – in you that it [sic] would be impossible but in this case you have delineated feelings which though natural do not please – but which create a certain degree of disgust and contempt. With regard to the manner in which you have executed your plan, I think too great praise cannot be bestowed upon your talents. You have most admirably delineated the ideotism of the boy's mind – and the situations in which you place him are perfectly calculated to display it. The various thoughts that pass through the mothers mind; are highly descriptive of her foolish fondness – her extravagant fears – and her ardent hopes. The manner in which you show how bodily sufferings are frequently removed by mental anxieties or pleasures, in the description of the cure of Betty Foy's female friend, is excessively well managed – and serves to establish a very curious and important Truth. In short every thing you proposed to execute has been executed in a masterly manner. The fault, if there be one, lies in the plan, not in the execution. This poem I have heard recommended as one in your best manner, and accordingly it is frequently read under this belief. The judgement formed of it, is consequently erroneous. Many people are displeased with the performance – but they are not careful to distinguish faults in the plan, from faults in the execution – and the consequence is that they form an improper opinion of your genius. In reading any composition, most certainly the pleasure we receive arises almost wholly from the Sentiments, thoughts, & descriptions contained in it. A secondary pleasure arises from admiration of those talents requisite to the production of it. In reading the Idiot boy, all persons who allow themselves to think must admire your talents – But they regret that they have been so employed – and while they esteem the Author, they cannot help being displeased with his performance. I have seen a most excellent painting of an Ideot [*sic*] – but it created in me inexpressible disgust. I was struck with the excellence of the picture – I admired the talents of the artist – but I had no other source of pleasure. The Poem of the Ideot boy produced upon me an effect in every respect similar. I find that my remarks upon several of your other Poems must be reserved for another Letter. If you think this one deserves an answer – a letter from Wordsworth would be to me a treasure. If your silence tells me that my letter was beneath your notice, you will never again be troubled by one whom you consider as an ignorant admirer. But if your mind be as amiable as it is reflected in your Poems – you will make allowance for defects that age may supply and make a fellow creature happy, by dedicating a few moments to the instructions of an admirer and sincere friend

John Wilson
Professor Jardines, College, Glasgow,
May 24. 1802

71. Dr Alexander Carlyle (1722–1805)

From a letter to Miss Mitchelson, *c.* 1802

Carlyle was a Scotch divine with literary friendships including Smollett, John Home, Robertson, John Armstrong and Adam Smith. In this letter of around 1802, addressed to Miss Mitchelson, he shows a remarkably sensitive early reading of 'The Brothers' and 'The Idiot Boy'.

I must tell you, who I know will sympathise with me, that I was very much delighted indeed, on the first sight of a new species of poetry, in

'The Brothers,' and 'The Idiot Boy,' which were pointed out to me by Carlyle Bell, as chiefly worthy of admiration. I read them with attention and was much struck. As I call every man a philosopher, who has sense and observation enough to add one fact relating either to mind or body, to the mass of human knowledge, so I call every man a poet, whose composition pleases at once the imagination and affects the heart. On reading 'The Brothers,' I was surprised at first with its simplicity, or rather flatness. But when I got a little on, I found it not only raised my curiosity, but moved me into sympathy, and at last into a tender approbation of the surviving brother, who had discovered such virtuous feelings, and who, by his dignified and silent departure, approached the sublime. After being so affected, could I deny that this was poetry, however simply expressed? Nay, I go farther, and aver that, if the narration had been dressed in a more artificial style, it would hardly have moved me at all.

When I first read 'The Idiot Boy,' I must confess I was alarmed at the term as well as the subject, and suspected that it would not please, but disgust. But when I read on, and found that the author had so finely selected every circumstance that could set off the mother's feelings and character, in the display of the various passions of joy and anxiety, and suspense and despair, and revived hope and returning joy, through all their changes, I lost sight of the term *Idiot*, and offered my thanks to the God of Poets for having inspired one of his sons·with a new species of poetry, and for having pointed out a subject on which the author has done more to move the human heart to tenderness for the most unfortunate of our species, than has ever been done before. He has not only made his Idiot Boy an object of pity, but even of love. He has done more, for he has restored him to his place among the household gods whom the ancients worshipped.

(*Autobiography*, ed. J. H. Burton, London 1910, pp. 593–4)

72. Richard Warner (1763–1857)

From *Tour Through the Northern Counties of England*, 1802

Warner was a clergyman at Bath and friend of James Losh (see entry 31). He was the author of several tours, perhaps a habit he caught from

William Gilpin for whom he was once curate. Wordsworth and Coleridge would hardly thank him for his extravagant and absurd espousal of their cause. His account is dated 'Ambleside, July 13th [1801]'.

The animated, enthusiastic, and accomplished Coleridge, whose residence at Keswick gives additional charms and interest to its impressive scenery, inspired us with terror, whilst he described the universal uproar that was awakened through the mountains by a sudden burst of involuntary laughter in the heart of their precipices; an incident which a kindred intellect, his friend and neighbour at Grasmere, Wordsworth, (whose 'Lyrical Ballads,' exclusively almost of all modern compositions, breathe the true, nervous, and simple spirit of poetry) has worked up into the following admirable effusion: [quotes 'Joanna', ll. 38–76].

(*Tour through the Northern Counties of England*, 1802, 100–2)

Coleridge, in a letter of 27 July 1802, commented to Sara Hutchinson:

> Could you believe now, that the Rogue made up all this out of my telling him, that Wordsworth's Echo, tho' purposely beyond Nature, was yet only an *exaggeration* of what really would happen – for that I myself with John Wordsworth & William had laughed aloud at Stickle Tarn in Langdale, & that the effect was quite enough to justify the Poem from being more extravagant, than it was it's purpose to be . . . From foolish men, that write Books, Lord deliver me!

73. Samuel Taylor Coleridge

From letters, 1802

a. To William Sotheby, 13 July 1802

Here, for the first time, Coleridge indicates that differences have emerged in the critical opinions of himself and Wordsworth.

[I must] set you right with regard to my perfect coinc[idence with] his [Wordsworth's] poetic Creed. It is most certain, that that P[reface arose from] the heads of our mutual Conversations &c – & the f[irst pass]ages were indeed partly taken from notes of mine / for it was at first intended, that the Preface should be written by me – and it is likewise true, that I warmly accord with W. in his abhorrence of these poetic Licences, as they are called, which are indeed mere tricks of Convenience & Laziness. *Exemp. Grat.* Drayton has these Lines –

> Ouse having Ouleney past, as she were waxed mad,
> From her first stayder Course immediately doth gad,
> And in meandred Gyres doth whirl herself about,
> *That, this* way, here and there, back, forward, in and out,
> And like a wanton Girl oft doubling in her Gait
> In labyrinthine Turns & Twinings Intricate &c &c –[1]

the first poets observing such a stream as this, would say with truth & beauty – it *strays* – & now every stream shall *stray* wherever it prattles on it's pebbled *way* – instead of it's bed or channel /. I have taken the instance from a Poet, from whom as few Instances of this vile common-place trashy Style could be taken as from any writer ... – In my opinion every phrase, every metaphor, every personification, should have it's justifying cause in some *passion* either of the Poet's mind, or of the Characters described by the poet – But *metre itself* implies a *passion*, i.e. a state of excitement, both in the Poet's mind, & is expected in that of the Reader – and tho' I stated this to Wordsworth, & he has in some sort stated it in his preface, yet he has [not] done justice to it, nor has he in my opinion sufficiently answered it. In my opinion, Poetry justifies, as *Poetry* independent of any other Passion, some new combinations of Language, & *commands* the omission of many others allowable in other compositions / Now Wordsworth, me saltem judice, has in his system not sufficiently admitted the former, & in his practice has too frequently sinned against the latter. – Indeed, we have had lately some little contro-versy on this subject – & we begin to suspect, that there is, somewhere or other, a *radical* Difference [in our] opinions ...

(*Collected letters of Samuel Taylor Coleridge*, ed. E. L. Griggs, Oxford, 1956–71, II, 812)

b. To Southey, 29 July 1802

Of course, Darwin & Wordsworth having given each a defence of *their* mode of Poetry, & a disquisition on the nature & essence of Poetry in general, I shall necessarily be led rather deeper – and these I shall treat of either first or last / But I will apprize you of one thing, that altho' Wordsworth's Preface is half a child of my own Brain / & so arose out of Conversations, so frequent, that with few exceptions we could scarcely either of us perhaps positively say, which first started any particular Thought – I am speaking of the Preface as it stood in the second Volume [edition?] – yet I am far from going all lengths with Wordsworth / He has written lately a number of Poems (32 in all) some of them of considerable Length / (the longest 160 Lines) the greater number of these to my feelings very excellent Compositions / but here & there a daring Humbleness of Language & Versification, and a strict adherence to matter of fact, even to prolixity, that startled me / his alterations likewise in Ruth perplexed me / and I have thought & thought again / & have not had my doubts solved by Wordsworth / On the contrary, I rather suspect that some where or other there is a radical Difference in our theoretical opinions respecting Poetry – / this I shall endeavor to go to the Bottom of – and acting the arbitrator between the old School & the New School hope to lay down some plain, & perspicuous, tho' not superficial, Canons of Criticism respecting Poetry. – What an admirable Definition Milton gives quite in an obiter way – when he says of Poetry – that it is '*simple, sensuous, passionate.*'! – It truly comprizes the whole, that can be said on the subject. In the new Edition of the L. Ballads there is a valuable appendix, which I am sure you must like / & in the Preface itself considerable additions, one on the Dignity & nature of the office & character of a Poet, that is very grand, & of a sort of Verulamian Power & Majesty – but it is, in parts, (and this is the fault, me judice, of all the latter half of that Preface) obscure beyond any necessity – & the extreme elaboration & almost constrainedness of the Diction contrasted (to my feelings) somewhat harshly with the general style of the Poems, to which the Preface is an Introduction . . . Sara said with some acuteness, that she wished all that Part of the Preface to have been in Blank Verse – & vice versa &c – However, I need not say, that any diversity of opinion on the subject between you & myself, or Wordsworth and myself, can only be small, taken in a *practical* point of view.

(*Ibid.*, II, 830–1)

c. To Sotheby, 19 September 1802

Did you see a very fine Sonnet on Buonaparte 'I grieved for Buonaparte' in the Morning Post of Wednesday or Thursday last – ? It was written by Wordsworth – & comes upon my Feelings, as in the spirit of the best of Milton's Sonnets.

(*Ibid.*, II, 869)

EDITOR'S NOTE

1. *Poly-Olbion*, 22, ll. 17–22.

74. Thomas Twining (1735–1804)

From a letter to his half-brother, Richard, 3 November 1802

The Twinings were friends of Dr William Cookson, Wordsworth's uncle. Thomas was the translator of Aristotle's *Poetics* (1789). Richard (1749–1824), the tea merchant (not his son Richard as Reed p. 81 has it), had called at Dove Cottage, 23 August 1800, 'So M^r. W^m. Wordsworth is married! To some wood-nymph wild, or to some mountain nymph, I warrant you!' Thomas's reply follows.

. . . By all means some time or other, read Adam Smith's Theory of Moral Sentiments. I am pretty sure you will be pleased with it. . . . The name of the Wood nymph that Mr Wordsworth is said to have married is Hutchinson, of Wykeham near Scarborough. From his poetry, I like the man & wish him happy. It would be very easy to write something *like* his poetry, in *ridicule* of his poetry. But the poetry itself is in my opinion (at least the best of it) such as few men, very few poetical men, could write. But, pray, now don't take him up after Adam Smith. Commerce & sentiment, reasoning & description, matter of fact & matter of fancy will not go well cheek by jowl together.

(Ms. British Museum)

75. Fanny Allen (1781–1875)

A reminiscence recorded by her niece, Elizabeth Wedgwood, 1802

This piece concerns a visit by Coleridge to the Allens at Cresselly, late November–December 1802. Fanny (sister-in-law to Josiah Wedgwood) was not alone in having difficulties with the first, no longer surviving, version of 'Resolution and Independence'; it is clear from Wordsworth's defensive letter of 14 June 1802 that Sara Hutchinson had not been able to respond as Wordsworth wished to the figure of the Leech-gatherer.

Another day at Cresselly, Coleridge, who was fond of reading MS. poems of Wordsworth's, asked Fanny whether she liked poetry, and when she said she did, came and sat by her on the sofa, and began to read the *Leechgatherer*. When he came to the passage, now I believe omitted, about his skin being so old and dry that the leeches wouldn't stick, it set Fanny a-laughing. That frightened her, and she got into a convulsive fit of laughter that shook Coleridge, who was sitting close to her, looking very angry. He put up his MS., saying he ought to ask her pardon, for perhaps to a person who had not genius (Fanny cannot exactly remember the expression) the poem might seem absurd. F. sat in a dreadful fright, everybody looking amazed, Sarah looking angry; and she almost expected her father would turn her out of the room, but Uncle Tom came to her rescue. 'Well, Coleridge, one must confess that it is not quite a subject for a poem.' Coleridge did not forgive Fanny for some days, putting by his reading aloud if she came in. But afterwards he was very good friends with her, and one day in particular gave her all his history, amongst other things, 'and there I had the misfortune to meet with my wife.'

(R. B. Litchfield, *Tom Wedgwood: the First Photographer*, 1903, 125–6)

76. Robert Southey

From letters, 1802–1803

a. To C. W. W. Wynn, 22 December 1802

Vidi the Review of Edinburgh.[1] The first part is designed evidently as an answer to Wordsworth's Preface to the second edition of the Lyrical Ballads; and, however relevant to me, *quoad* Robert Southey, is certainly utterly irrelevant to Thalaba.

(*Life and Correspondence of Robert Southey*, ed. C. C. Southey, 1849, II, 196)

b. To John May, *c.* 29 January 1803

With regard to that part of the review[2] which relates to Wordsworth, it has obviously no relation whatever to 'Thalaba,' nor can there be a stronger proof of want of discernment, or want of candour, than in grouping together three men so different in style as Wordsworth, Coleridge, and myself, under one head. The fault of Coleridge has been a too-swelling diction; you who know his poems know whether they ought to be abused for mean language. Of 'Thalaba,' the language rises and falls with the subject, and is always in a high key. I wish you would read the Lyrical Ballads of Wordsworth; some of them are very faulty; but, indeed, I would risk my whole future fame on the assertion that they will one day be regarded as the finest poems in our language. I refer you particularly to 'The Brothers,' a poem on 'Tintern Abbey,' and 'Michael.' Now, with Wordsworth I have no intimacy; scarcely any acquaintance. In whatever we resemble each other, the resemblance has sprung, not, I believe, from chance, but because we have both studied poetry – and indeed it is no light or easy study – in the same school, – in the works of nature, and in the heart of man.

(*A Selection from the Letters of Robert Southey*, ed. J. W. Warter, 1856, 214)[3]

EDITOR'S NOTES

1. See entry 89.
2. See *ibid.*
3. Here the letter is dated 'Bristol 1803'; the Ms. in Boston Public Library, however, shows the London postmark, 31 January.)

77. Thomas De Quincey (1785–1869)

From letters, 1803–1804

These letters were written before De Quincey ever met Wordsworth. He was not to meet him until 4 November 1807.

a. 31 May 1803

I suppose that most men would think what I am going to say – strange at least or rude: but I am bold enough to imagine that, as you are not yourself 'in the roll of common men,' you may be willing to excuse anything uncommon in the liberty I am now taking.

My object in troubling you, Sir, is that hereafter I may have the satisfaction of recollecting that I made one effort at least for obtaining your [friendship *scratched out*] notice – and that I did not, through any want of exertion on my own part, miss that without which what good can my life do me? I have no other motive for soliciting your friendship than what (I should think) every man, who has read and felt the 'Lyrical Ballads,' must have in common with me. There is no need that I should express my admiration and love for those delightful poems; nor is it possible that I should do so. Besides, I am persuaded that the dignity of your moral character sets you as far above the littleness of any vanity which could be soothed by applause feeble and insignificant as mine – as the transcendency of your genius makes all applause fall beneath it. But I may say in general, without the smallest exaggeration, that the whole aggregate of pleasure I have received from some eight or nine other poets that I have been able to find since the world began – falls infinitely short of what those two enchanting volumes have singly afforded me; – that your name is with me for ever linked to the lovely scenes of nature; – and that not yourself only but that each place and object you have mentioned – and all the souls in that delightful community of your's – to me

'Are dearer than the sun!'

With such opinions, it is not surprising that I should so earnestly and humbly sue for your friendship; – it is not surprising that the hope of that friendship should have sustained me through two years of a life passed partially in the world – and therefore not passed in happiness; – that I should have breathed forth my morning and my evening orisons for the accomplishment of that hope; – that I should now consider it as the only object worthy of my nature or capable of rewarding my pains. Sometimes indeed, in the sad and dreary vacuity of worldly intercourse, this hope will touch those chords that have power to rouse me from the lethargy of despair; and sometimes, from many painful circumstances – many many bitter recollections, it is my only refuge.

(*Letters: De Quincey to Wordsworth*, ed. John E. Jordan, Berkeley and Los Angeles 1962, 30–1)

b. 14 March 1804

Some years ago spending my holidays at Bath I was shewn the poem of We are Seven which was handed about in manuscript. Between this period & that when I afterwards discovered the volume from which it was taken a long time intervened. During this interval I gradually came under the dominion of my passions, & from frequent meditation on some characters of our own, & some of ancient story, & afterwards on some of the German Drama, I began to model my conduct & my aims on theirs: by degrees, being dazzled by the glory thrown on such objects by the voice of the people, & miserably deluding myself with the thought that I was led on by high aims, & such as were most worthy of my nature I daily intoxicated myself more & more with that delirious & lawless pleasure which I drew from the hope of elevating my name in authority & kingly splendour above every name that is named upon earth. For I felt myself unable to live in the pursuit of common objects, & unfettered by any ties of common restraint – & I felt, too, or imagined myself able to compass any plans capable of gratifying that stimulating class of desires which I then thought ebullitions of the highest state of moral improvement, but which I now consider as only a less degrading species of sensualism. Yet admidst all these feverish & turbulent dreams of meditation, it was not possible that I, maintained from my infancy in the Love of Nature, should not, at times relent & resign myself to a confused feeling of purer & more permanent pleasure flowing from other sources – therefore during my long & lonely rambles through many beautiful scenes sometimes in the stillness & silence of surrounding nature, & sometimes in her merest sights & sounds I felt her mild reproach, and so, gradually prepared for being weaned from my temporary frenzy, I looked round for some guide who might assist to develope & to tutor my new feelings, & then it was that from a recollection of the deep impression made on me by the short poem I have mentioned I knew where to seek that guidance, & where I sought, I found it.

(*Ibid.*, 36–7)

78. Samuel Taylor Coleridge

From letters, 1803–1804

a. To Wordsworth, 23 July 1803

– Sir G. & Lady B[eaumont], who are half-mad to see you – (Lady B. told me, that the night before last as she was reading your Poem on Cape RASH JUDGEMENT, had you entered the room, she believes she should have fallen at your feet) Sir G. & his wife both say, that the Picture[1] gives them an idea of you as a profound strong-minded Philosopher, not as a Poet – I answered (& I believe, truly –) that so it must needs do, if it were a good Portrait – for that you were a great Poet by inspirations, & in the Moments of revelation, but that you were a thinking feeling Philosopher habitually – that your Poetry was your Philosophy under the action of strong winds of Feeling – a sea rolling high. –

(*Collected Letters of Samuel Taylor Coleridge*, ed. E. L. Griggs, Oxford, 1956–71, II, 957)

b. To Thomas Poole, 14 October 1803

I saw him [Wordsworth] more & more benetted in hypochondriacal Fancies, living wholly among *Devotees* – having every the minutest Thing, almost his very Eating & Drinking, done for him by his Sister, or Wife – & I trembled, lest a Film should rise, and thicken on his moral Eye. – The habit too of writing such a multitude of small Poems was in this instance hurtful to him – such Things as that Sonnet of his in Monday's Morning Post, about Simonides & the Ghost[2] – / I rejoice therefore with a deep & true Joy, that he has at length yielded to my urgent & repeated – almost unremitting – requests & remonstrances – & will go on with the Recluse exclusively. – A Great Work, in which he will sail; on an open Ocean, & a steady wind; unfretted by short tacks, reefing, & hawling & disentangling the ropes – great work necessarily comprehending his attention & Feelings within the circle of great objects & elevated Conceptions – this is his natural Element – the having been out of it has been his Disease – to return into it is the specific Remedy, both Remedy & Health. It is what Food is to Famine. I have seen enough, positively to give me feelings of hostility towards the plan of several of the Poems in the L. Ballads: & I really consider it as a misfortune, that Wordsworth ever deserted his former mountain Track to wander in

Lanes & allies; tho'in the event it may prove to have been a great Benefit to him. He will steer, I trust, the middle course. – But he found himself to be, or rather to be called, the Head & founder of a *Sect* in Poetry: & assuredly he has written – & published in the M. Post, as W. L. D. & sometimes with no signature – poems written with a *sectarian* spirit, & in a sort of Bravado. – I know, my dear Poole, that you are in the habit of keeping my Letters; but I must request of you, & do *rely* on it, that you will be so good as to destroy this Letter –

(*Ibid.*, II, 1013)

c. To Richard Sharp, 15 January 1804

Wordsworth is a Poet, a most original Poet – he no more resembles Milton than Milton resembles Shakespere – no more resembles Shakespere than Shakespere resembles Milton – he is himself: and I dare affirm that he will hereafter be admitted as the first & greatest philosophical Poet – the only man who has effected a compleat and constant synthesis of Thought & Feeling and combined them with Poetic Forms, with the music of pleasurable passion and with Imagination or the *modifying* Power in that highest sense of the word in which I have ventured to oppose it to Fancy, or the *aggregating* power – in that sense in which it is a dim Analogue of Creation, not all that we can *believe* but all that we can *conceive* of creation. Wordsworth is a Poet, and I feel myself a better Poet, in knowing how to honour *him*, than in all my own poetic Compositions, all I have done or hope to do – and I prophesy immortality to his *Recluse*, as the first & finest philosophical Poem, if only it be (as it undoubtedly will be) a Faithful Transcript of his own most august & innocent Life, of his own habitual Feelings & Modes of seeing and hearing.

(*Ibid.*, II, 1034)

EDITOR'S NOTES

1. Probably a portrait by Hazlitt which has not survived.
2. The Sonnet, 'I find it written of Simonides' was published in the newspaper on 10 October, but never reprinted by Wordsworth. *PW*, III, 408.

79. Sir George Beaumont (1753–1827)

From letters, 1803–1806

The painter Beaumont had met Coleridge at Sotheby's house in London and disliked him, but in July 1803 the Beaumonts, staying in the half of Greta Hall, Keswick, not occupied by Coleridge, grew to like him, and so began their friendship with both Coleridge and Wordsworth.

a. From a letter to Coleridge, *c.* 15 August 1803

On 13 August 1803, Coleridge had sent Beaumont, now staying at Lowther Castle, a copy of the revised 'Leech Gatherer' ('Resolution and Independence'). Beaumont gave Wordsworth (whom he had not then met) a piece of land near Keswick so that it would be possible for the two poets to live closer to each other.

I more & more admire the beginning of the Leech gatherer improved . . . long very long may you live in that blessed vale together.

(Ms. Pierpont Morgan Library)

b. From a letter to Wordsworth, 25 November 1805

The Highland Lass [i.e. 'Solitary Reaper'] is delightful, when all is so exquisite & highly finished, perhaps I should not select any particular passage, but I was [Ms. incomplete]

(Ms. The Wordsworth Library)

c. From a letter to Wordsworth, late August/early September 1806

I know it will be a pleasure to you to hear when I am oppressed by that morbid dejection your works are a balm to my mind. Lady B. has several times read over to me lately the lines on Nelson [i.e. 'Character of the Happy Warrior'] & I like them better & better every time I hear them – this is certainly the test of excellence – but why should I mention those lines in particular except that the doctrine in them is congenial with the present state of my mind.

(Ms. The Wordsworth Library)

80. John Rickman (1771–1840)

From a letter to Southey, 26 March 1804

Rickman is commenting on Coleridge who was about to sail to Malta.

If he dies, it will be from a sulky imagination, produced from the general cause of such things; i.e. want of regular work or application: which is great pity. Happening to look into the Lyrical Ballads the other day, there was (under the title 'Lines left on Seat under a Yew Tree') an account of somebody so written as to be very evidently a *self-portrait* – Wordsworth's I believe; and the same would not be very un-true of Coleridge. It is certainly to admire Nature in the country too much, when it leads us into final Evil, and self-discontent, so founded as those lines demonstrate to be felt, and *justly* felt, can hardly be denied. Why should not the beauties of Nature be to a grown thinking man, what play hours are at school? Then no harm would be done, and the world would not lose men capable of being the most usefull members of society.

(*Life and Letters of John Rickman*, Orlo Williams, 1912, 108)

81. Francis Jeffrey and Francis Horner (1778–1817)

An exchange, July–September 1804

Francis Horner, lawyer and Whig, left Edinburgh to live in London, and in April 1804 was visited by his friend, Jeffrey, when apparently they enjoyed reading *Lyrical Ballads*. Horner therefore was surprised at Jeffrey's tone.

a. Jeffrey. Unsigned review of *Popular Tales* by Maria Edgeworth, *Edinburgh Review*, July, 1804, VIII, 330

This is an attempt, we think, somewhat superior in genius, as well as utility, to the laudable exertions of Mr. Thomas Paine to bring disaffection and infidelity within the comprehension of the common people, or the charitable endeavors of Messrs Wirdsworth & Co. [*sic*] to accommodate them with an appropriate vein of poetry. Both these were superfluities which they might have done very tolerably without; but Miss Edgeworth has undertaken to improve, as well as to amuse them, and to bring them back from an admiration of pernicious absurdities, to a relish for the images of those things which must make the happiness of their actual existence.

b. Horner. Letter to Jeffrey, 13 August 1804

Southey's Madoc is in the Press, I understand, and will make its appearance the beginning of winter: Wordsworth's poems, for he has two great ones, that is, long ones, will not be published so soon. One of these is to be called the Recluse, and the other is to be a history of himself & his thoughts; this philosophy of egotism & shadowy refinements really spoils a great genius for poetry – We shall have a few exquisite gleams of natural feeling, sunk in a dull ugly ground of trash & affectation. I cannot forgive your expression, Wordsworth & Co.; he merits criticism, but surely not contempt; to class him with his imitators is the greatest of all contempt. I thought our perusal of the Lyrical Ballads [in] the Temple w^d have prevented this; we found much to admire, but you will not admire. Sharp is however at the other extreme, I admit: but I insist it is the better of the two: he has been living at the lakes with these crazed poets, Wordsworth read him some thousand lines, & he repeated to me a few of these one day which I could not worship as he wished me.

(Ms. London School of Economics)

c. Jeffrey. Reply to Horner, 3 September 1804

I am almost as great an admirer as Sharpe. The only difference is, that I have a sort of consciousness that admirers are ridiculous, and therefore I laugh at almost everything I admire, or at least let people laugh at it without contradiction. You must be in earnest when you approve, and have yet to learn that everything has a respectable, and a deridable, aspect. I meant no contempt for Wordsworth by putting him at the head of the poetical firm. I classed him with Southey and Coleridge who were partners once, and have never advertised their secession.

(Henry Thomas, Lord Cockburn, *Life of Lord Jeffrey*, 1852, II, 91)

82. Anna Seward

From a letter to Rev. Robert Fellowes, 31 May 1806

Mr Wordsworth has undoubtedly genius, and charming passages are to be found in his verse; but on the whole, it is not first rate; often meanly familiar, and almost as often turgid and obscure; therefore I cannot think his judgment and decisions should be implicitly received. He is right in observing, that the use of common life simple language in verse, is frequently a beauty, but not right in extending that use to all modes of phraseology within the limits of the immodest, the disgusting, and the ungrammatic. A thousand instances might be brought where neither decency or grammar are violated, and yet where a low and ludicrous effect is produced in verse by habits of expression which even polite conversation might not refuse to tolerate; [rather inconsequentially quotes examples from Dryden, Shakespeare and Hayley, who has been 'deplorably infected by Wordsworth's system'].

Mr Wordsworth's rule is vague, indiscriminate, and dangerous as a guide to the poetic student. If the composition be light and trivial, so much the more does it require a polished elegance in the manner of giving it; [continues to condemn Wordsworth's theory in the light of Dr. Johnson's criticism]

(*Letters of Anna Seward*, 1811, ed. Walter Scott, vi, 258–61)

83. Joseph Farington (1747–1821)

From his diary, 1806

Farington, painter and diarist, and, as early as 1779, a friend of Wordsworth's uncle, William Cookson. It was Cookson who, in December 1784, wrote the brief prose descriptions for Farington's *Views of the Lakes in Cumberland and Westmorland*, published in parts, and completed 1789.

a. 21 March 1804

Sir George [Beaumont] spoke of Coleridge having been with him at Dunmow, – He went for 2 days and stayed 10.

Wordsworth continues in Westmorland. He has just chosen to forego professional views, preferring retirement upon something more than £100 a year with the gratification of his indulging his imagination to any worldly advantages. – He has long been what He calls idle, *not writing*, finding it affected His nerves: but He is now engaged on a more considerable work than any of his former ones which he calls '*The Recluse*'. – Sir George read part of a Poem by Him called 'Tintern abbey', which He thinks exquisite, & has read it 100 times. – He also read 'the Beggar' ['The Old Cumberland Beggar'] – Those were published with others by him & Coleridge by Longman the Bookseller in 1800 [1798]. – Sir George said he was infinitely indebted to Wordsworth for the good He had recd. from His poetry which had benefitted Him more, had more purified his mind than any Sermons had done. – Coleridge has more learning, – more reading, than Wordsworth, but Sir George thinks Him not equal in poetical power.

(*The Diary of Joseph Farington*, ed. Kenneth Garlick and Angus MacIntyre, Yale University Press, New Haven and London, 1979, VI, 2270–1)

b. 21 April 1804

Dr. Cookson called. He talked of His nephew, Wordworth, the Poet, who for a time had been a great supporter of French principles,[1] which caused a coolness between them. – Since the death of Lord Lonsdale, the affairs which the late Mr. Wordsworth left unsettled have been arranged, & Lord Lowther has paid to the Children of Mr. Wordsworth £9000. There are 4 Brothers and a Sister, One in the Church,[2] who has distinguished himself by his writings, – & another in the India service.[3]

(*Ibid.*, VI, 2303)

c. 17 June 1806

Wordsworth dined with Taylor[4] while He was in London. – Taylor found Him strongly disposed towards Republicanism. His notions are that it is the duty of every Administration to do as much as possible to give consideration to the people at large, and to have *equality* always in view; which though not perfectly attainable, yet much has been gained towards it and more may be. – Taylor thinks Wordsworth much superior as a Poet to Coleridge & Southey; but that all of them affecting to be simple and natural, they frequently reduce their expressions to what may almost be called *clownish*. He said Jerningham[5] had told Him that the Bishop of London,[6] speaking of their works said, 'Whatever merit there might be in them it was not *legitimate Poetry*'.

Northcote[7] had met Wordsworth at *Godwins*, who in speaking of Coleridge & Wordsworth said, He preferred the *conversation of the former*, – and the *Poetry of the latter*.

(*The Farington Diary*, ed. Kathryn Cave, VII, 1982, 2785)

d. 20 July 1806

The conversation during dinner time[8] was chiefly respecting Cowper and his works. . . .

Dr. Johnson was mentioned. – Wilberforce regretted that He had never seen Him. – Of Cowper He sd. that what He produced, as an Author, appeared to have flowed naturally from Him on some occasion that affected His mind. – 'So, He added, He thought it should always be. He would have men act only from the impulse of nature & feeling. Wordsworth, on the contrary, lives to make verses'.

(*Ibid.*, VIII, 2825 & 2827)

e. 7 November 1806

After tea Lady Beaumont read some poetical compositions of Burns – & Wordsworth. – The Latter is now with His family in Sir George's farm house at Cole Orton. – Wordsworth's House at Grassmere is too small for his family & too cold in the winter. He is employed on a Poem – the *progress of His own mind*, viz: How He was affected by objects & circumstances as He advanced in life. – This work He proposes to delay publishing till He shall have made Himself more important & cause what respects Him [to be] more interesting, by some production of a different kind.

(*Ibid.*, VIII, 2898–9)

f. 17 February 1807

Dance[9] I dined with. . . . We had much conversation on Poetry. Smirke[10] expressed Himself strongly on the great excellence of Wordsworth's Poetry, and said while reading some of his poetical productions He had been quite overcome. – Dance also appeared to be much delighted with them. Both scouted mere versification, which is too often admired. Dance sd. that alone is true poetry, which expresses the strong feelings of the mind of the Author so as to cause the heart of the reader to vibrate in unison with those feelings. – He said that He had never been affected by the works of *Dryden*, so as to acknowledge Him to have been a great Poet. –

(*Ibid.*, VIII, 2970–1)

EDITOR'S NOTES

1. Wordsworth's reputation as a radical continued until at least 1809 when Sir George Beaumont warned Haydon and David Wilkie: 'I caution you against his terrific democratic notions' (B. R. Haydon, *Autobiography*, ed. Tom Taylor, introduction by Edmund Blunden, Oxford, 1927, 126).
2. Christopher Wordsworth, the poet's younger brother.
3. John Wordsworth, who was to die a year later as Captain of the *Earl of Abergavenny*, sunk off the Dorset coast in February 1805.
4. John Taylor (1755–1832), journalist (and Royal Oculist), some time in Tory pay and involved with the Tory newspapers, *The True Briton* (morning) and *The Sun* (evening); part owner of this last from 1805. In 1801, Wordsworth, consciously trying to cultivate some Tory press support, sent *Lyrical Ballads* to Taylor (and to Sir Bland Burgess). In his letter on that occasion (9 April 1801), Wordsworth made it clear that he and Coleridge were opposed to 'jacobinical pathos', and sought rather a non-party 'pathos of humanity'. Farington's report suggests that Wordsworth has not properly won Taylor to either his poetry or his politics.
5. Edward Jerningham (1737–1812), poetaster.
6. Dr Beilby Porteus (1731–1808).
7. James Northcote (1746–1831), painter and author, does not seem to have been a determined admirer of Wordsworth's poetry: Hazlitt records his conversation, *c*1829:

   > when G[odwin] plagues me about my not having sufficient admiration of W[ordsworth]'s poetry, the answer I give is, that it is not my fault, for I have utterly forgotten it; it seemed to me like the ravelings of poetry.
   >
   > (*Hazlitt*, ed. P. P. Howe, XI, 311)

8. W. W. Bowdler, a young lawyer from Yorkshire, was also present.
9. George Dance, R. A. (1741–1825), architect, portrait artist and a close friend to Sir George Beaumont, whose house, Coleorton, Dance redesigned. Farington's Diary shows that Dance sat at the head of the table, Farington on his right, Smirke on his left. The three other diners were the artists Thomas and William Daniel and Dance's son Charles, the playwright.

10. Robert Smirke, R. A. (1752–1845); George III refused to appoint him as Keeper of the Academy because of his pronounced Revolutionary principles; Smirke's enthusiasm for Wordsworth might stem in part from his being a Cumbrian, born near Wigton, Carlisle.

V

Lyrical Ballads: reviews,
February 1801–April 1804

84. John Stoddart (1773–1856)

Letter and unsigned review, 1801

Stoddart's original opinions of Wordsworth's poetry were probably not dissimilar to those adverse ones which Wordsworth himself entertainingly formulates (see entry 64), but his stay in the Lakes with Wordsworth and Coleridge in October and November 1800 (see entry 53) had probably prepared him to be at least a considerate critic.

a. From a letter to Coleridge, 1 January 1801

I find here a letter from Wordsworth recommending me to enlist in the Monthly Fencibles but little know I of their soft phrase, for till now some 3 moons wasted I never dreamt of criticising & know not one of that Corps – If my literary Talents entitle me to become 'an occasional Writer in the British Critic' tis all I can hope – the Christian humility of Dr. Parr aspired no higher, & shall I who am nothing to that great man lift myself into a loftier pulpit – Yet if I can contrive to creep into the Monthly I will – but as I said before pressus nihil sum,[1] by the favor of Dr. Shaw I may be introduced into the Antichamber of Poeticide in the British Critic, but who shall say unto Griffiths enroll him among the Elders of your venerable bench. Perhaps if you were to come to town & take me by the hand even Phillips might suppose me in the way of being a great literary character –

(R. S. Woof, 'John Stoddart, "Michael" and *Lyrical Ballads*', *Ariel* (April 1970), i. 18–19)

Clearly Stoddart would prefer to write for Griffiths in the *Monthly Review* or Phillips in the *Monthly Magazine*. As his 'poeticide' suggests, the reputation of the *British Critic* as an organ for poetry reviews was not high; Anna Seward (*Letters*, v. 340–41) in a letter of 5 January 1801 demonstrates that Nares, one of the *British Critic* editors, gave poetry little attention. Stoddart's review in draft form was seen by John Wordsworth before 28 January 1801 (see entry 60e); it then went to the 'Reviewers', the editors presumably, who made some revisions (letter of John Wordsworth to Mary Hutchinson, 27 February 1801). What these revisions were we do not know, but John Wordsworth apparently thought that the last paragraph of Stoddart's review was not Stoddart's work (letter of

John to Dorothy Wordsworth, 2 March 1801, when the February *British Critic* was actually published).

b. Unsigned review, *British Critic*, February 1801, xvii, 125–31

Stoddart's review was partially reprinted – and as such was Wordsworth's first in America – by John Dennie in Philadelphia (*Portfolio*, 13 June 1801, I. 188–9).

In our Review for October, 1799, we noticed, with considerable satisfaction, the first edition of this work, then comprised in one anonymous volume. It is now extended, by the addition of another volume; and the author has given his name to it, with the exception of the *Ancient Mariner*, the *Foster Mother's Tale*, the *Nightingale*, the *Dungeon*, and the poem entitled *Love*; all of which, as he informs us, are furnished by a friend, whose opinions on the subject of Poetry agree almost entirely with his own. From this similarity of mind, and from some expressions in the Advertisement prefixed to the first edition, we were then led to attribute the whole to Mr. Coleridge, the supposed author of the Ancient Mariner: we now, therefore, add to the list of our Poets another name, no less likely to do it honour. Mr. Wordsworth has, indeed, appeared before the public some years ago, as author of Descriptive Sketches in Verse, and of an Evening Walk; compositions, in which were discoverable the fire and fancy of a true poet, though obscured by diction, often and intentionally inflated. His style is now wholly changed, and he has adopted a purity of expression, which, to the fastidious ear, may sometimes perhaps sound poor and low, but which is infinitely more correspondent with true feeling than what, by the courtesy of the day, is usually called poetical language.

Whatever may be thought of these Poems, it is evident that they are not to be confounded with the flood of poetry, which is poured forth in such profusion by the modern Bards of Science, or their brethren, the Bards of Insipidity. The author has thought for himself; he has deeply studied human nature, in the book of human action; and he has adopted his language from the same sources as his feelings. Aware that 'his Poems are so materially different from those upon which general approbation is at present bestowed,' he has now defended them in a Preface of some length; not with the foolish hope of reasoning his

138

readers into the approbation of these particular Poems, but as a necessary justification of the species of poetry to which they belong. This Preface, though written in some parts with a degree of metaphysical obscurity, conveys much penetrating and judicious observation, important at all times, but especially when, as it is well observed, 'the invaluable works of our elder writers are driven into neglect by frantic novels, sickly and stupid German tragedies, and deluges of idle and extravagant stories in verse.' Perhaps it would be expecting too much from any one but Shakspeare, were we to demand that he should be the Poet of human nature. It would be no mean, it would indeed be a very lofty praise, to assert of a writer, that he is able to pour into other bosoms powerful feelings of a particular class, or belonging to a particular order of men. To this praise, Mr. Wordsworth lays a well-supported claim. He declares himself the Poet chiefly of low and rustic life (some specimens of ability he has given in other lines, but this is evidently his excellence) and he pourtrays it, not under its disgusting forms, but in situations affording, as he thinks, the best foil for the essential passions of the heart, incorporated with an elementary and durable state of manners, and with the beautiful and permanent forms of nature.*

Each separate Poem has, as its distinct *purpose*, the development of a feeling, which gives importance to the action and situation, and not the action or situation to the feeling. Whether the particular purpose is, in every case, *worthy* of a Poet, will perhaps admit of some doubt. We have no hesitation in saying, that it is generally interesting, often invaluable; but on these points the author shall speak for himself.

[Quotes from *para*. 7 of the Preface:

> This object I have endeavoured in these short Essays ... may be distinctly and profitably contemplated.]

Of the judicious degree of simplicity in language which the author attained in his first volume, we formerly expressed our approbation. The second is written with equal felicity, being alike grounded upon an accurate and attentive observation of those modes of speech, which are

---

* Mr. Wordsworth seems to be peculiarly well situated for the subjects of such a study. The vicinity of the Lakes in Cumberland and Westmoreland (the scene of most of his Poems) is chiefly inhabited by an order of men nearly extinct in other parts of England. These are small farmers, called in that part of the country '*Statesmen*', who, cultivating their own little property, are raised above the immediate pressure of want, with very few opportunities of acquiring wealth. They are a mild, hospitable people, with some turn for reading; and their personal appearance is, for the most part, interesting.

prompted by the natural flow of passion. Where the subjects are supplied by rustic life, the language of rustics, purified only from accidental associations of disgust, is also adopted, and for this simple and weighty reason; because,

such a language, arising out of repeated experience and regular feelings, is a more permanent, and a far more philosophical, language, than that which is frequently substituted for it by poets, who think that they are conferring honour upon themselves and their art, in proportion as they separate themselves from the sympathies of men, and indulge in arbitrary and capricious habits of expression, in order to furnish food for fickle tastes, and fickle appetites, of their own creation.

The author has argued with great ingenuity, and at some length, on the absurdity of the distinction frequently made between the appropriate language of prose, and that of metrical composition. He has shown, that the two species of writing may be wholly similar in every thing but metre; and that neither of them can be dignified by any other means than energy and loftiness of thought. A great part of this argument would appear useless, had we not unhappily witnessed, in some striking instances, how much the public taste may be misled by affected pomp and false glitter of language. We cannot too often repeat, that the frippery and fustian of the Darwinian phraseology, is no more compatible with a just classical taste, than the heterogeneous mixture of science and fancy is allowable in a poetical subject. The faults of this kind, in the second volume, are so very few, as to deserve no notice, in comparison with the general purity of the style. As to the subjects, it must be owned that their worth does not always appear at first sight; but, judging from our own feelings, we must assert, that it generally grows upon the reader by subsequent perusal. The following remarks may, perhaps, illustrate the cause of this improving interest.

1. It is not requisite that the poetic feeling should be strictly referable to any of those known and powerful classes, called the sublime, the terrible, the pathetic, &c. It may sometimes consist in a gentle agitation of the contending emotions, from which a preponderance of pleasure is ultimately produced, as from the melancholy recollections of a cheerful old man, in the *Two April Mornings*, and the *Fountain*; sometimes it may arise from the mixture of lively imagery with various feelings, as with exultation and pity, in the two parts of *Hartleap Well*; sometimes it may be founded on the soft, and almost insensible affections which we receive from natural scenery, aided, perhaps, by some accidental association in

our own minds. Of this kind are the different Poems on the *Naming of Places*, *Lines written with a Slate Pencil*, *&c. Rural Architecture*, and some others.

2. Even where the feeling intended to be called forth is of a rich and noble character, such as we may recur to, and feed upon, it may yet be wrought up so gradually, including so many preparatory circumstances of appropriate manners, of local description, of actual events, &c. that the subtle uniting thread will be lost, without a persevering effort toward attention on the part of the reader. Who, that has studied Shakspeare, must not be conscious how often the connection of minute and trifling incidents with the main story has eluded his observation, until after repeated perusals? Something of this kind will probably occur to the readers of the *Brothers*, the *Cumberland Beggar*, and more particularly of the Poem, entitled *Michael*; yet these three are of the highest order of Poems in the volume. The interest, especially of the first, is so dramatically wrought up, the minute touches are so accurately studied, the general effect is so insensibly produced, and appeals so forcibly to the heart, as to rank its author far beyond the reach of common-place praise or censure.

3. There is a third class of Poems possessing a strong effect, which results equally from the power of imagination and of feeling; in these, the prominent features of the story are all along attended with a concurring splendour of poetic ornament, and the combined influence of these agents pervades every part of the composition. This is greatly the case in the Poem of *Ruth*, and in that of *Ellen Irwin*, of which the latter is merely narrative; the former intermixes much of deep and interesting speculation: to this class also may be referred *Lucy Gray* and *Poor Susan*, with several beautiful specimens in the second volume.

4. Other small pieces have different characteristics. The *Fragment* of the Danish Boy is a mere creation of fancy; the *Pet Lamb* presents a portraiture of infantine simplicity; and the lines in pages 50 and 53,[2] are masterly sketches of those 'strange fits of passion,' which sometimes unaccountably flash across a poetical mind.

From the longer Poems it is almost impossible to select any passage without injury to its effect, owing to a want of that interest which the context supplies. We shall, however, venture to cite the following tender touches from the *Brothers*.

[Quotes 'The Brothers', *PW*, II, p. 7, ll. 227–35; *LB* (*1800*), pp. 140–1, ll. 231–9:

> —though their parents
> Lay buried side by side, as now they lie,
> The old man was a father to the boys,
> Two fathers in one father: and if tears
> Shed, when he talk'd of them where they were not,
> And hauntings from the infirmity of love
> Are ought of what makes up a mother's heart,
> This old man, in the day of his old age,
> Was half a mother to them.]

In the *Poet's Epitaph*, an effusion of good-humoured satire, is succeeded by this picture of animated and engaging sensibility;

> [Quotes 'A Poet's Epitaph', *PW*, IV, pp. 66–7, ll. 37–60; *LB* (*1800*), pp. 207–8, ll. 37–60:
>
> > But who is he with modest looks . . .
> > Or build thy house upon this grave.]

Perhaps the English language can boast few instances of descriptive poetry, enlivened with a happier variety of imagery, than the fanciful echo in the Poem inscribed to *Joanna*. The lady's laugh, to be sure, is loud, but it is not unpleasing.

> [Quotes 'Poems on the Naming of Places: To Joanna', *PW*, II, p. 113–4, ll. 51–65; *LB* (*1800*), p. 215, ll. 51–65:
>
> > When I had gazed perhaps two minutes' space . . .
> > And Kirkstone tossed it from his misty head.]

But the most singular specimens of unpretending, yet irresistible pathos, are the two *Songs*, p. 50 and 52. In artlessness, they strongly remind us of Burns; but perhaps go beyond him in delicacy. As they have a secret connection, we shall insert both.

> [Quotes 'Strange fits of passion have I known', *PW*, II, p. 29; *LB* (*1800*), p. 150 and 'She dwelt among th' untrodden ways', *PW*, II, p. 30; *LB* (*1800*), p. 151]

When the art of poetry has been long cultivated among polished people, and brought to a state of great refinement, the natural operation of an ill-judged ambition, to excel even those who have most successfully adorned the language, leads writers either to employ an affected and over-laboured style, or, at least, to keep always upon the high stilts of elegance, to the exclusion of Nature and Simplicity. In such a state of the poetic art, that man may be considered as a public benefactor, who, with talents equal to the task, which is arduous, recals attention to the more natural style, and shows what may be effected by simple language, expressive of human passions, and genuine, not artificial feelings. In this character, Mr. Wordsworth appears; and appears with a success, to which we could by no means refuse our approbation. We will not deny that sometimes he goes so far in his pursuit of simplicity, as to become flat or weak; but, in general, he sets an example which the full-dressed poet of affectation might wish, but with in vain, to follow.* He would correct Mr. W. as the dancing-master of Hogarth would correct the attitude of Antinous.

EDITOR'S NOTES

1. 'I am under no pressure'.
2. 'Strange fits of passion have I known' and 'A slumber did my spirit seal'.

85.

Editorial notice, *British Critic*, June 1801, XVII, p. xiii of the Preface

---

Brief book notices, such as this, appeared in the six-monthly retrospective Preface.

Other poetical works, of various talent, still claim our attention. Among these, we must by no means omit to notice the *Lyrical Ballads*, now avowed to be the work of *Mr. Wordsworth*; assisted by a very few contributions from his friends. Though the style of simplicity, professedly adopted in these poems, may sometimes disappoint the reader, yet the principle of preferring the value of ideas to the sound of words, and the truth of nature and passion to the splendour of ornament, is so very salutary in the present state of public taste, that we cannot feel a critical duty more strong, than that of recommending it by every favourable example; and many such will certainly be found in Mr. W.'s volumes.

---

* The title of the Poems is, in some degree, objectionable; for what Ballads are not *Lyrical?* Besides, there are many compositions in blank verse, not at all Lyrical.

86.

Unsigned review, *Monthly Mirror*, June 1801, XI, 389–92

Though the new school of philosophy, to which we are utterly averse, has introduced a new school of poetry, which we do not altogether admire; yet, from Mr. Wordsworth, who may be regarded as the senior professor in this Parnassian college, we wish not to withhold our warm eulogium. Energy of thought, pathos of sentiment, and exquisite discrimination in selecting whatever is picturesque in imagery, or interesting in nature, are the distinguishing characteristics of these poems: yet an obscurity too often arises, from a romantic search after simplicity, and there is a studied abruptness in the commencement and termination of several pieces, which makes them assume an appearance of mere fragments. Where we meet with a complete poem, like that entitled 'The Brothers,' our gratification is proportionably complete. We regret, however, that these volumes are marked by a querulous monotony of woe, which we cannot applaud: for a wayward spirit of discontent has lately been let loose upon the world, and seems calculated to diffuse the seeds of general dissatisfaction, by libelling all mankind. These well-told tales are mostly tales of sorrow, and this sorrow takes its root from the hollow-heartedness of human beings, or the calamities incident to human life. The vista is dreary, and the objects which present themselves at its extremity are involved 'in gloomiest shade.'

From the sombre colouring spread over several pieces in this collection, against which the social principle has led us to complain, we are zealous to except the following sweetly-simple dialogue; and to let our readers partake in the tearful delight we have experienced from its perusal. It is designed to shew the perplexity and obscurity which, in childhood, attend our notion of death, or rather our utter inability to admit that notion.

[Quotes 'We are Seven', *PW*, I, p. 236; *LB* (*1798*), p. 66.]

Mr. Wordsworth is not unaware that, in some instances, sensations even of the ludicrous may be given to his readers by expressions which appeared to himself tender and pathetic. We are apprehensive that certain phrases and epithets in the preceding stanzas will be liable to this unfortunate perversion, with those whose mental associations may carry them back to the nursery, who cherish fancy more than feeling, and prefer a witless parody to a composition that meliorates the heart.

The following reflections, which occur in 'A Description of the old Cumberland Beggar,' are admirable, as are many others in this most fascinating publication.
[Quotes 'The Old Cumberland Beggar', *PW*, IV, pp. 236–7 ll. 73–105; *LB* (*1800*), p. 202, ll. 73–97:

> —'Tis Nature's law
> That none, the meanest of created things . . .
> Doth find itself insensibly dispos'd
> To virtue and true goodness.]

There is all the moral pith and nervous force of Cowper in this paragraph, without any semblance of imitation; and if Mr. W. should proceed to poetic flights of equal altitude, and should soar as long upon the wing, we doubt not that he will obtain a niche near the author of the Task, in the temple of 'aye enduring Fame.'

87.

Unsigned notice, *Monthly Review*, June 1802, XXXVIII, 209

This piece was reprinted exactly, and without acknowledgement, in the *Literary and Masonic Magazine*, I, 462, September 1802.

In our xxixth Vol. N. S. we gave an account of the first part of these *Lyrical Ballads*; which appeared without the Poet's name. As we then paid a particular attention to the style and manner of the unknown writer, we think it unnecessary to enlarge with critical discrimination on the character and merits of the poems now before us. Suffice it, therefore, to observe that we deem the present publication not inferior to its precursor; and to express our hope that this will not prove the last time of our meeting this natural, easy, sentimental Bard, in his pensive rambles through the wilds and groves of his truly poetic, though somewhat peculiar, imagination.

88.

American notices, 1799–1810

The first American notices come from Joseph Dennie (1768–1812) who would appear to have had a volume of 1798 *Lyrical Ballads* by 13 June 1801: he could have printed 'Goody Blake and Harry Gill' from the *New Annual Register* (see entry 50) and 'We are Seven' from the *Courier*, 7 April 1800 (see entry 56b). David Simpson in 'Wordsworth in America', *The Age of William Wordsworth: Critical Essays on the Romantic Tradition*, (ed. Kenneth R. Johnston and Gene W. Ruoff, 1987, Rutgers, 278), notes that 'Dennie seems not to have picked up any radical or Jacobin signals from them as both Wordsworth and Coleridge had hoped that by not putting their names on the 1798 *Lyrical Ballads*, political attacks had been avoided'. Joseph Dennie, as editor of the *Portfolio*, was a federalist and a conservative in political matters. It was fortunate for James Humphreys as Wordsworth's first American editor that he got the support of Dennie when *Lyrical Ballads* appeared in 1802. R. H. Rose's parodies in 1804 keep Wordsworth's name before the public, but three notices of 1807 to 1810 suggest that the English reviews had had their negative effect. There was to be no new American edition of Wordsworth until 1824. His reputation was nevertheless fostered by Washington Allston, William Channing, George Ticknor and Richard Dana, particularly after 1815 and the end of the Napoleonic Wars.

a. 2 September 1799

'Goody Blake and Harry Gill' reprinted in *The Farmer's Museum*, Walpole, New Hampshire, edited by Joseph Dennie (1768–1812). Possibly reprinted from the *New Annual Register, or General Repository, Politics and Literature for the year 1798*, London, 1799 [201–3].

b. 9 August 1800

'We are Seven' reprinted in Philadelphia in John Ward Fenno's *United States Gazette*, editor Joseph Dennie. Its 'inimitable simplicity and tenderness' was praised, Coleridge being the supposed author.

c. 17 January 1801

'Simon Lee' reprinted in the *Portfolio*, I, no. 3, 24, Philadelphia, also edited by Joseph Dennie, circulation 2,000.

The Public may remember reading in some of our news papers the interesting little ballads of 'We are Seven' and 'Goody Blake and Harry Gill.' They were extracted from LYRICAL BALLADS, a collection remarkable for originality, simplicity and nature, to which Mr. Wordsworth of St. John's College, Oxford, is a principal contributor.

d. 21 March 1801

'The Thorn' reprinted, *Portfolio*, I, 12, 94–5.

e. 13 June 1801

Portfolio, I, no. 24, 191.

We have had frequent occasion in the course of our literary selections, to express the warmest admiration of the genius, spirit and simplicity of 'Lyrical Ballads,' a volume which contains more genuine poetry than is to be found, except in the volumes of SHAKESPEARE and CHATTERTON – The 'LITERARY' article, borrowed from the British Critic[1], and inserted in our front pages, corroborates the partiality of the editor for the talents of Mr. Wordsworth. The second volume of these 'Ballads' has been ordered from England, and when the editor shall have received a copy, it will be in his power to adorn his pages with *gems* of a soft and permanent lustre.

f. 18 July 1801

'Anecdote for Fathers' and 'The Mad Mother' both 'From Lyrical Ballads', *Portfolio*, I, 29, 232.

g. 5 December 1801

'Ellen Irwin' and 'Strange Fits of Passion', *Portfolio*, I, 49, 391–2.

h. 19 December 1801

From the *Portfolio*, I, 51, 407–8.

Mr. James Humphreys, of this city, will shortly publish a very neat, convenient, and cheap edition of the delightful ballads of WORDS-WORTH, of which some exquisite specimens may be found in the poetical department of the Port Folio. If these little poems, simple, natural, and pathetic, be generally read, with the same delights, which they afforded the writer of this article, the sale would be a mine to the bookseller.

The following delightful fable ['The Waterfall and the Eglantine'], and the subsequent poems ['Lucy Gray' and 'Andrew Jones'], are from the magical pen of WILLIAM WORDSWORTH, a genuine poet, who judiciously employs the language of simplicity and NATURE, to express the tones of passion; who has forsaken the necromantic realms of German extravagance, and the torrid zone of Della Cruscan ardour, and has recalled erring readers 'from sounds to things, from fancy to the heart.'

i. January 1802

Unsigned notice in the *American Review and Literary Journal*, II, 118–9. The writer of this notice was possibly Charles Brockden Brown (1771–1810), the novelist and editor of the magazine. The first American edition of *Lyrical Ballads* was advertised on 15 January 1802 in the *Gazette of the United States*, along with reprinted sections of Stoddart's *British Critic* review. The American edition was put together from both the English 1798 and 1800 volumes: for notes on the edition see J. D. Campbell, *Athenaeum*, 17 February 1894, and L. A. Fisher, *Modern Language Notes*, February 1900, 77–84. Both miss J. R. Lowell's note: James Humphreys had been 'encouraged by a sufficient *list of subscribers* to reprint the full edition of *Lyrical Ballads*,' 1798 but the 1800 volumes arrived before he completed his reprinting (*The Writings of J. R. Lowell*, 'Literary Essays', 1890, IV, 38). The subscription list has not survived.

'Lyrical Ballads,' with other Poems, by *W. Wordsworth*, have been reprinted by *James Humphreys*, of Philadelphia, two volumes 12mo. in one. This edition contains a long, but ingenious and well written preface, by the author, in which he examines the properties of prose and verse, and which should be read by all who wish to enter into the spirit of these ballads. Mr. W. endeavours to maintain, that between poetry and prose there neither is nor can be any essential difference; that some of the most interesting parts of the best poems will be found to be strictly the language of prose when prose is well written; and he incidentally remarks, that much confusion has been introduced into criticism by contra-distinguishing poetry and prose instead of poetry and science, for that the strict antithesis is prose and metre. He considers the music of verse, arising from a certain artificial arrangement of words, and coincidence of sounds, as the only quality necessary to form the contrast and antithesis of prose. To prove the truth of this theory by his own practice, the author excludes from his poetry all personifications of abstract ideas, as not making any regular or natural part of the language of men, and for the same reason he employs very little of what is called *poetic diction*, consisting of phrases and figures of speech, which, he observes; 'from father to son have been regarded as the common inheritance of poets.' This is indeed stripping poetry at once of half her plumage, and condemning her to skim along the vale, without daring to soar into the sublime regions of fancy. The laws prescribed by Mr. W. may suit a particular species of poetry like his own, but we apprehend that their authority will not be acknowledged by the lovers of poetry in general.

As the author has drawn his subjects from the incidents of common life, for the purpose of tracing in them without ostentation the primary laws of our nature, he has chosen a style imitative of the language of ordinary conversation in the middle classes of society. On this plan we think he has made some successful experiments. As the poems are almost entirely free from intricacy of thought or expression, they may be read by the simplest swain without difficulty. Some of them appear to us too humble both in style and sentiment to be generally interesting. Many of the pieces display a lively sensibility to the beauties of rural scenery; but they are particularly distinguished for the delicate and affecting manner of pourtraying the sensations of the mind, when agitated, as the author expresses it, by the great and simple affections of our nature; – of nature, however, as she appears in the walks of low and rustic life.

j. 27 February 1802

From the *Portfolio*, II, VIII, 62

The popularity of Wordsworth's Ballads increases every hour. We are confident, that Messrs. Humphreys and Groff, the praise-worthy publishers of poetry, not unworthy the muse of CHATTERTON, will be amply remunerated for their care and expense in publishing a complete and neat edition of verses, which will *outlive their century.*

k. 3 September 1803

'The Fountain', *Portfolio*, III, 36, 238

Wordsworth seems to follow Goldsmith in the easy and agreeable track of simplicity. I know not with what emotion the lovers of the tumid style will peruse the following, but he among my readers who laughs at Blackmore and Della Crusca, will approve it.

l. 10 September 1803

'Song For the Wandering Jew', *Portfolio*, III, 37, 296

On a well-known tradition of morbid restlessness and abhorred longevity of a certain imaginary personage, supposed to have been cursed at the crucifixion, the ensuing song has been founded by the fruitful genius of Mr. Wordsworth.

m. 1 October 1803

'A Whirl-blast from behind the Hill', *Portfolio*, III, no. 40, 320

Mr. Wordsworth has a rare talent of remarking many of the minuter operations of nature, and of describing them at once in the simplest, and yet most interesting manner. The use that he derives from his observation of rural circumstance is a great lesson to those who walk in the forest.

n. 24 March 1803

'The Oak and the Broom', *Portfolio*, IV, 12, 96

We are very enthusiastic admirers of the genius of Mr. Wordsworth, an Oxford scholar, an original poet, and, as it appears, an amiable and humane man. He seems to have found or made a new walk in poetry, and we doubt not he will have many admiring followers. We cannot refrain from adding, that his Lyrical Ballads have reached the *third* edition in a very short period, and that a majority of critics, as well as readers of taste, have agreed that he has, like Gay, discovered the secret of exhibiting the most pleasing and most interesting thoughts in the simplest expression.

o. 18 August 1804

The *Portfolio*, IV, 33, 257–8, published a parody by R. H. Rose, writing under the name 'R. Shallow'; this 'Lyrical Ballad' had twenty-nine quatrains and elaborate notes, quoting from the poems parodied. For Peter Bayley's influence, see entry 93.

'The Idiot Boy,' 'We are Seven,' 'Lines written in Early Spring,' 'Anecdote for Fathers,' 'Goody Blake,' 'The Thorn,' 'Strange Fits of Passion,' 'Tintern Abbey,' 'Heartleap Well,' 'The Mad Mother,' 'It was an April Morning,' 'Ruth,' and 'Joanna.'

The parody, somewhat revised, was republished by Dennie in R. H. R.'s *Sketches in Verse*, 1810, 58–73.

p. 27 October 1804

The *Portfolio*, IV, 43, 342–3, published another parody by R. H. Rose of Wordsworth's 'Written in Germany, on one of the coldest days of the century'; this time there was no introductory note or footnotes, but Wordsworth's poem was also printed in full.

q. 14 November 1807

Dennie's comment in the *Portfolio*, IV, 20, 308, suggests that he has been influenced against Wordsworth by the adverse English reviews.

Wm. Wordsworth has published two volumes of poems. We hope that he does not *continue to strike the very base string of humility.*

r. March 1809

Portfolio, II, N.S., 1, 256.

William Wordsworth stands among the foremost of those English bards, who have mistaken silliness for simplicity; and with a false and affected taste, filled their pages with the language of children and clowns.

s. May 1810

In *Portfolio*, III, N.S., 438, the comment now seems so slight that it is even doubtful whether Dennie actually read Wordsworth's *Poems* (1807).

Some of Mr. Wordsworth's earlier effusions of poetical genius were certainly not unworthy of the muse. But, of late, he has extended so far his theory of simplicity in writing that it degenerates into burlesque and puerility.

EDITOR'S NOTE

1. Stoddart's review from the *British Critic* (see entry 138b) was reprinted on pp. 188–9.

89. Francis Jeffrey

Unsigned review of Southey's *Thalaba, Edinburgh Review*, October
1802, I, 63–83

Thalaba provides Jeffrey with the excuse to condemn the poetic theories of
Wordsworth, named for the first time here as the head of a 'sect'. His tone
is quite different from that of his other notice of *Thalaba* a month later in
the *Monthly Review* for November 1802 where he gives a traditional
summary with comment. The review in the *Edinburgh* is more firmly in
line with the principles of that magazine's first editor, Sydney Smith: 'If
any writing friends have a mind to barbecue a poet or two or strangle a
metaphysician or do any other act of cruelty to the dull men of the Earth,
we are in hopes they will make our journal the receptacle of their exploits
– one shall make it a point of honour neither to mutilate contributions, or
to reveal the names of contributors.' For Southey's comment on this
review, see entry 76.

Poetry has this much, at least, in common with religion, that its
standards were fixed long ago, by certain inspired writers, whose authority it is no longer lawful to call in question; and that many profess to be
entirely devoted to it, who have no *good works* to produce in support of
their pretensions. The catholic poetical church, too, has worked but few
miracles since the first ages of its establishment; and has been more
prolific, for a long time, of Doctors, than of Saints: it has had its corruptions and reformation also, and has given birth to an infinite variety of
heresies and errors, the followers of which have hated and persecuted
each other as cordially as other bigots.

The author who is now before us, belongs to a *sect* of poets, that has
established itself in this country within these ten or twelve years, and is
looked upon, we believe, as one of its chief champions and apostles. The
peculiar doctrines of this sect, it would not, perhaps, be very easy to
explain; but, that they are *dissenters* from the established systems in
poetry and criticism, is admitted, and proved indeed, by the whole tenor
of their compositions. Though they lay claim, we believe, to a creed and a
revelation of their own, there can be little doubt, that their doctrines are
of *German* origin, and have been derived from some of the great modern
reformers in that country. Some of their leading principles, indeed, are
probably of an earlier date, and seem to have been borrowed from the

great apostle of Geneva. As Mr Southey is the first author, of this persuasion, that has yet been brought before us for judgment, we cannot discharge our inquisitorial office conscientiously, without premising a few words upon the nature and tendency of the tenets he has helped to promulgate.

The disciples of this school boast much of its originality, and seem to value themselves very highly, for having broken loose from the bondage of ancient authority, and re-asserted the independence of genius. Originality, however, we are persuaded, is rarer than mere alteration; and a man may change a good master for a bad one, without finding himself at all nearer to independence. That our new poets have abandoned the old models, may certainly be admitted; but we have not been able to discover that they have yet created any models of their own; and are very much inclined to call in question the worthiness of those to which they have transferred their admiration. The productions of this school, we conceive, are so far from being entitled to the praise of originality, that they cannot be better characterised, than by an enumeration of the sources from which their materials have been derived. The greater part of them, we apprehend, will be found to be composed of the following elements: 1. The antisocial principles, and distempered sensibility of Rousseau – his discontent with the present constitution of society – his paradoxical morality, and his perpetual hankerings after some unattainable state of voluptuous virtue and perfection. 2. The simplicity and energy (*horresco referens*)[1] of Kotzebue and Schiller. 3. The homeliness and harshness of some of Cowper's language and versification, interchanged occasionally with the *innocence* of Ambrose Philips, or the quaintness of Quarles and Dr Donne. From the diligent study of these few originals, we have no doubt that an entire art of poetry may be collected, by the assistance of which, the very *gentlest* of our readers may soon be qualified to compose a poem as correctly versified as Thalaba, and to deal out sentiment and description, with all the sweetness of Lambe, and all the magnificence of Coleridge.

The authors, of whom we are now speaking, have, among them, unquestionably, a very considerable portion of poetical talent, and have, consequently, been enabled to seduce many into an admiration of the false taste (as it appears to us) in which most of their productions are composed. They constitute, at present, the most formidable conspiracy that has lately been formed against sound judgment in matters poetical; and are entitled to a larger share of our censorial notice, than could be spared for an individual delinquent. We shall hope for the indulgence of our readers, therefore, in taking this opportunity to inquire a little more particularly into their merits, and to make a few remarks upon those peculiarities which seem to be regarded by their admirers as the surest proofs of their excellence.

Their most distinguishing symbol, is undoubtedly an affectation of great simplicity and familiarity of language. They disdain to make use of the common poetical phraseology, or to ennoble their diction by a selection of fine or dignified expressions. There would be too much *art* in this, for that great love of nature with which they are all of them inspired; and their sentiments, they are determined shall be indebted, for their effect, to nothing but their intrinsic tenderness or elevation. There is something very noble and conscientious, we will confess, in this plan of composition; but the misfortune is, that there are passages in all poems, that can neither be pathetic nor sublime; and that, on these occasions, a neglect of the embellishments of language is very apt to produce absolute meanness and insipidity. The language of passion, indeed, can scarcely be deficient in elevation; and when an author is wanting in that particular, he may commonly be presumed to have failed in the truth, as well as in the dignity of his expression. The case, however, is extremely different with the subordinate parts of a composition; with the narrative and description, that are necessary to preserve its connection; and the explanation, that must frequently prepare us for the great scenes and splendid passages. In these, all the requisite ideas may be conveyed, with sufficient clearness, by the meanest and most negligent expressions; and if magnificence or beauty is ever to be observed in them, it must have been introduced from some other motive than that of adapting the style to the subject. It is in such passages, accordingly, that we are most frequently offended with low and inelegant expressions; and that the language, which was intended to be simple and natural, is found oftenest to degenerate into mere slovenliness and vulgarity. It is in vain, too, to expect that the meanness of those parts may be redeemed by the excellence of others. A poet, who aims at all at sublimity or pathos, is like an actor in a high tragic character, and must sustain his dignity throughout, or become altogether ridiculous. We are apt enough to laugh at the mock-majesty of those whom we know to be but common mortals in private; and cannot permit Hamlet to make use of a single provincial intonation, although it should only be in his conversation with the grave-diggers.

The followers of simplicity are, therefore, at all times in danger of occasional degradation; but the simplicity of this new school seems intended to ensure it. *Their* simplicity does not consist, by any means, in the rejection of glaring or superfluous ornament, – in the substitution of elegance to splendour, or in that refinement of art which seeks concealment in its own perfection. It consists, on the contrary, in a very great degree, in the positive and *bona fide* rejection of art altogether, and in the bold use of those rude and negligent expressions, which would be banished by a little discrimination. One of their own authors, indeed, has very ingeniously set forth, (in a kind of manifesto that preceded one of their most flagrant acts of hostility), that it was their capital object 'to adapt to the uses of poetry, the ordinary language of conversation among the middling and lower orders of the people.' What advantages are to be gained by the success of this project, we confess ourselves unable to conjecture. The language of the higher and more cultivated orders may fairly be presumed to be better than that of their inferiors: at any rate, it has all those associations in its favour, by means of which, a style can never appear beautiful or exalted, and is adapted to the purposes of poetry, by having been long consecrated to its use. The language of the vulgar, on the other hand, has all the opposite associations to contend with; and must seem unfit for poetry, (if there were no other reason), merely because it has scarcely ever been employed in it. A great genius may indeed overcome these disadvantages; but we can scarcely conceive that he should court them. We may excuse a certain homeliness of language in the productions of a ploughman or a milkwoman; but we cannot bring ourselves to admire it in an author, who has had occasion to indite odes to his college bell, and inscribe hymns to the Penates.

But the mischief of this new system is not confined to the depravation of language only; it extends to the sentiments and emotions, and leads to the debasement of all those feelings which poetry is designed to communicate. It is absurd to suppose, that an author should make use of the language of the vulgar, to express the sentiments of the refined. His professed object, in employing that language, is to bring his compositions nearer to the true standard of nature; and his intention to copy the sentiments of the lower orders, is implied in his resolution to make use of their style. Now, the different classes of society have each of them a distinct character, as well as a separate idiom; and the names of the various passions to which they are subject respectively, have a signification that varies essentially according to the condition of the persons to whom they are applied. The love, or grief, or indignation of an enlightened and refined character, is not only expressed in a different language, but is in itself a different emotion from the love, or grief, or anger, of a clown, a tradesman, or a market-wench. The things themselves are radically and obviously distinct: and the representation of them is calculated to convey a very different train of sympathies and sensations to the mind. The question, therefore, comes simply to be – which of them is the most proper object for poetical imitation? It is needless for us to answer a question, which the practice of all the world has long ago decided irrevocably. The poor and vulgar may interest us, in poetry, by their *situation*; but never, we apprehend, by any sentiments that are peculiar to their condition, and still less by any language that is characteristic of it. The truth is, that it is impossible to copy their diction or their sentiments correctly, in a serious composition; and this, not merely because poverty makes men ridiculous, but because just taste and refined sentiment are rarely to be met with among the uncultivated part of mankind; and a language, fitted for their expression, can still more rarely form any part of their 'ordinary conversation'.

The low-bred heroes, and interesting rustics of poetry, have no sort of affinity to the real vulgar of this world; they are imaginary beings, whose characters and language are in contrast with their situation; and please those who can be pleased with them, by the marvellous, and not by the nature of such a combination. In serious poetry, a man of the middling or lower order *must necessarily* lay aside a great deal of his ordinary language; he must avoid errors in grammar and orthography; and steer clear of the cant of particular professions, and of every impropriety that is ludicrous or disgusting: nay, he must speak in good verse, and observe all the graces in prosody and collocation. After all this, it may not be very easy to say how we are to find him out to be a low man, or what marks can remain of the ordinary language of conversation in the inferior orders of society. If there be any phrases that are not used in good society, they will appear as blemishes in the composition, no less palpably, than errors in syntax or quantity; and, if there be no such phrases, the style cannot be characteristic of that condition of life, the language of which it professes to have adopted. All approximation to that language, in the same manner, implies a deviation from that purity and precision, which no one, we believe, ever violated spontaneously.

It has been argued, indeed, (for men will argue in support of what they do not venture to practise), that as the middling and lower orders of society constitute by far the greater part of mankind, so, their feelings and expressions should interest more extensively, and may be taken, more fairly than any other, for the standards of what is natural and true. To this, it seems obvious to answer, that the arts that aim at exciting admiration and delight, do not take their models from what is ordinary, but from what is excellent; and that our interest in the representation of any event, does not depend upon our familiarity with the original, but on its intrinsic importance, and the celebrity of the parties it concerns. The sculptor employs his art in delineating the graces of Antinous or Apollo, and not in the representation of those ordinary forms that belong to the crowd of his admirers. When a chieftain perishes in battle, his followers mourn more for him, than for thousands of their equals that may have fallen around him.

After all, it must be admitted, that there is a class of persons (we are afraid they cannot be called *readers*), to whom the representation of vulgar manners, in vulgar language, will afford much entertainment. We are afraid, however, that the ingenious writers who supply the hawkers and ballad-singers, have very nearly monopolized that department, and are probably better qualified to hit the taste of their customers, than Mr Southey, or any of his brethren, can yet pretend to be. To fit them for the higher task of original composition, it would not be amiss if they were to undertake a translation of Pope or Milton into the vulgar tongue, for the benefit of those children of nature.

There is another disagreeable effect of this affected simplicity, which, though of less importance than those which have been already noticed, it may yet be worth while to mention: This is, the extreme difficulty of supporting the same low tone of expression throughout, and the inequality that is consequently introduced into the texture of the composition. To an author of reading and education, it is a style that must always be assumed and unnatural, and one from which he will be perpetually tempted to deviate. He will rise, therefore, every now and then, above the level to which he has professedly degraded himself; and make amends for that transgression, by a fresh effort of descension. His composition, in short, will be like that of a person who is attempting to speak in an obsolete or provincial dialect; he will betray himself by expressions of occasional purity and elegance, and exert himself to efface that impression, by passages of unnatural meanness or absurdity.

In making these strictures on the perverted taste for simplicity, that seems to distinguish our modern school of poetry, we have no particular allusion to Mr Southey, or the production now before us: On the contrary, he appears to us, to be less addicted to this fault than most of his fraternity; and if we were in want of examples to illustrate the preceding observations, we should certainly look for them in the effusions of that poet who commemorates, with so much effect, the chattering of Harry

Gill's teeth, tells the tale of the one-eyed huntsman 'who had a cheek like a cherry,' and beautifully warns his studious friend of the risk he ran of 'growing double.' . . .

1. 'I shudder to relate' (*Aeneid*, 2, 204).

90. Daniel Stuart (1766–1846)

Notices in the *Morning Post*, 1803

Daniel Stuart was editor of the *Morning Post* at this time.

a. 13 January 1803

The following beautiful lines, never before published, were written by one of the first poets of the present day; and we call attention to them the more particularly, as the sentiments they express so closely agree with those of this Paper:
[Quotes 'Is it a reed that's shaken by the wind'.]

b. 29 January 1803

We have been favoured with a dozen Sonnets[1] of a Political nature, which are not only written by one of the first Poets of the age, but are among his best productions. Each forms a little Political Essay, on some recent proceeding. As we wish to publish them in connection with each other we now Reprint No. I. and No. II. the first from the Paper of September last; the second from our Paper of the present month. The other Numbers shall follow in succession.
[Quotes 'Is it a reed . . .' and 'I griev'd for Bonaparte'.]

1. Seven, not twelve, sonnets appeared; see R. S. Woof, 'Wordsworth's Poetry and Stuart's Newspapers: 1797–1803', *Studies in Bibliography*, 1962, XV, 184–5.

91.

Form an unsigned review of *Remarks on Scotland* by John Stoddart, *Anti-Jacobin Review*, February 1803, XIV, 153–62

Possibly the work of Robert Heron who is known to have reviewed for the *Anti-Jacobin* and who had himself published in 1793 *Journey through a Part of Scotland*.

Our author [Stoddart] launches out into the most indiscriminate and extravagant praise of the poets, *Burns* and *Wordsworth*, the former of whom he regards as the first of poets, and the latter as the genuine poet of nature. His incessant allusion to them is not less offensive than his unqualified praise. He may certainly be allowed to retain his own opinion of their merits, but he should not attempt, so dogmatically, to impose it upon others.

(p. 157.)

92.

Essay, signed 'T.N.', 'On the Corruptions of Literature', *Edinburgh Magazine* July 1803, xxii, 26–7

T. N.'s phrasing, 'Southey, Coleridge, Wordsworth, Loyd and Co.', recalls the satirical verse in the first number of the *Anti-Jacobin*, July 1798: 'C—DGE and S—TH-Y, L—D, and L—BE, and Co.' He follows Jeffrey (*Edinburgh Review*, October 1802) in including Wordsworth, and his essay is another example of the unfairness of treating the poets as a group.

The miscellaneous poetry of the present day, with some exceptions, to the readers of Shakespeare and Milton, is puerile and conceited. The querelous woe-begone strains of Southey, Coleridge, Wordsworth, Loyd and Co., exclusive of their sceptical character, tend to excite the restless and uneasy feelings of the mind, and render it discontented with the allotments of Providence. Sometimes the tales of the nursery, of the blue-beards and hobgoblins of Germany, dressed up in baby language, are thrown upon the world in expectation of praise and patronage. Some of their effusions are distinguished for the most unbounded benevolence. Mr Coleridge, who has attained great celebrity among modern poets, has written an ode to the young foal of an ass, and in his pathetic address to this meek child of nature, he exclaims, 'spite of the fool's scorn, I hail thee brother.'

It is a melancholy thought, that men can be found who so strenuously endeavour to lessen that small portion of good which is allotted to this life, that they should employ those means which are eminently calculated to refine, instruct, and elevate the mind, to effect its degradation and corruption. Yet, it is too well known, that, for the attainment of these objects, they have laboured with a perseverance unwearied as the wing of time, and with an appetite keen as the grave. They have explored every avenue to the human mind, and availed themselves of its weaknesses, its passions, and its prejudices. They have adapted themselves to the capacities of every class of men, to extend their influence and increase the number of their proselytes. Their principles have been diffused through the whole mass of human science, from sober treatises on morals and philosophy, down to penny sheets and ballads for the information of children . . .

93. Robert Southey (with Wordsworth and Coleridge)

Unsigned Review of *Poems* by Peter Bayley, *Annual Review 1803*, published May 1804, preface dated 25 April 1804

Poems was published in London in 1803 and in Philadelphia the following year. The American edition prompted some of R. H. Rose's parodies. The extracts quoted by Southey seem sufficiently representative of Peter Bayley's (1778–1823) parodies and indicate that the poems in themselves are not of importance, but only, as the three poets suspected, as they contributed to a spirit of ridicule. Wordsworth, Coleridge and Southey fed each other's indignation over Bayley's *Poems*, a mixture of talent, plagiarism and timid parody. As early as 16 October 1803 Wordsworth told Scott that Southey was:

> to review a Vol. of Poems by a somebody Bayley Esqr which contains a long dull Poem in ridicule of the Idiot Boy, and in which Squire Bayley has mentioned by name "Mr Wordsworth that most simple of all simple Poets", so no mercy for Squire Bayley.
>
> (*EY*, 413)

On 9 December Wordsworth sent Coleridge several comments on Bayley's *Poems* and these Southey incorporated into the review. In November Coleridge wondered whether to 'expose' Bayley in the *Morning Post* (*Coleridge Notebooks*, ed. Kathleen Coburn, I, entry 1673), and used the phrase with which Southey was to begin his review, 'Stop thief!' Like Southey, Coleridge thought that 'Peter Bayley' was probably a pseudonym, perhaps, for Canning, who had written parodies (though not of Wordsworth) in the *Anti-Jacobin Review* of 1798. John Ferriar (1761–1815) reviewed Bayley favourably in the *Monthly Review*, September 1803, xlii, 157–63. He suggested that 'the name that stands on the title page . . . is only a *nom de guerre*; and that a former acquaintance amuses himself with our perplexity. . . . ' This false scent probably led the poets to overestimate the importance and insidiousness of Bayley's attack. Southey mentioned no candidates for the identity of Peter Bayley: he wrote on 19 November 1803 of:

> some fellow, who writes under the assumed name of Peter Bayley, Jun., Esq. He has stolen from Wordsworth in the most wholesale way and most artfully, and then at the end of his book thinks proper to abuse Wordsworth by name. I mean to prove his thefts one by one, and then call him rascal.
>
> (*A selection from the Letters of Robert Southey*, ed. J. W. Warter, 1856, I, 245)

The review was soon written and sent off, along with Southey's other notices for the *Annual Review*, by the end of January 1804. The abuse of Wordsworth by name that both Wordsworth and Southey mention is in a note appended by Peter Bayley to a verse near the end of his 'Fisherman's Wife. Dedicated to all admirers of the familiar style of tale-writing, so popular in 1800.' It is worth quoting two stanzas of the parody:

> Mother! dear Mother! cease to weep!
> My father will return anon,
> At eve he'll come: beyond the lake
> He waits secure, or else to take
> His fish to market he is gone.

> Oh, comfort is a blessed thing!
> It falls upon the mind like dew;
> This simple speech of little Jane
> Gave peace to Rachel's tortur'd brain,
> And bade her smile serene anew.

The note on this first stanza is:

> The simplicity of that most simple of all poets, Mr. Wordsworth him-
> self, is scarcely more simple than the language of this stanza. Absit
> invidia dicto. [May envy be far from my saying]

STOP thief! Mr. Peter Bayley, jun. is a literary sharper, who has obtained credit upon false pretences, and made his way into good company by wearing stolen clothes. Without farther preamble we shall proceed to convict this gentleman of plagiarisms as artful, as dishonourable and as dishonest, as have ever stamped any pretender with infamy.

The poem entitled an Evening in the Vale of Festiniog, is made up from the Lyrical Ballads of Mr. Wordsworth.

> It is a blessed scene, and I rejoice
> That I have felt inweve into my being
> A love of the green fields, and azure sky,
> Mountains, and all the multitudinous throng
> Of waves that sound along the rocky shore.
> And therefore (for this never-dying passion,
> This craving appetite, has led me on,
> As though possess'd with moody thoughts, and fed
> With wayward fancies) – therefore have I roam'd
> Through devious wilds, through pathless glens, and climb'd
> The tall cliff's topmost crag, and therefore bar'd
> To the sharp mountain-blast my glowing breast.
> Nor nursing other feelings have I sought
> The savage grandeur of yon wilds sublime,
> The foaming cat'ract, or the softer voice
> Of bub'ling hill-streams – To this place I come
> Led by the self-same impulse.
>   This hoar stone,
> Studded with moss, with green and fringed moss,
> With crimson fret-work, and bright cups of gold,
> And all emboss'd with curled knots, and tufts
> Of lichens – this hoar stone shall be my seat.

These lines are botched up from the following passages of the Wye and the Thorn.

[Quotes 'Tintern Abbey' *PW*, II, pp. 261–2, ll. 65–88, 136–7, 102–5, and 'The Thorn' *PW*, II, pp. 241–2, ll. 12–3, 38–40, 43–4.]

The next instance is more obvious and more offensive, as it is a base and unfeeling parody upon what we shall not scruple to call one of the finest passages that ever was or can be written.

> Who so unbless'd as to lock up his heart
> Against the soothing power and sweet illapse
> Of Nature's voice! – For sure there dwells a voice,
> A moving spirit, and a speaking tongue,
> In the loud waters, and the nimble air,
> And the still moonbeam, and the living light
> Of suns, resplendent in their mid career.

[Quotes 'Tintern Abbey' *PW*, II, pp. 261–2, ll. 93–102; *LB* (*1798*), p. 114, ll. 94–103:

> And I have felt . . .
> And rolls through all things.]

Mr. Peter Bayley, aware that so remarkable a passage as this would be recognised, has affected in one part to imitate Petrarch, and for 'the living light of suns' has quoted *un vivo sole*[1]. A knave is never so knavish as when he affects honesty. Unfortunately for this gentleman, we also understand Italian, and we know that the phrase 'un vivo sole' is one of the metaphors common to all rhymers, one of the slang compliments of the Italian poets to their mistresses.

[Develops this Italian point as outlined in Wordsworth's letter to Coleridge (*EY*, 424–6.); and attacks Bayley's plagiarisms, both from *Lyrical Ballads* and from other works.]

Pilfering Peter Bayley perhaps supposes, that he has made the thoughts of others his own by his manner of remodelling them. There is a passage in one of Donne's Satires which will fit this gentleman.

> But he is worst who, beggarly doth chaw
> Others wits fruits, and in his rav'nous maw
> Rankly digested, doth those things out-spue
> As his own things; and they're his own 'tis true:
> For if one eat my meat, tho' it be known
> The meat was mine,——

Old Donne is somewhat coarse in his expression; but Mr. Bayley may turn to the thirtieth line of his second satire, to see how such gentlemen as himself appropriate their neighbours meat. *But enough of versifying rogues.* It is sufficient to add, that Mr. Peter Bayley has pillaged Akenside as he has Mr. Bowles and Mr. Wordsworth; that he may be tracked to Cowper and to Charlotte Smith; in short, that his whole volume is one mass of patchwork. *Enough of versifying rogues!* We have a heavier charge than that of simple roguery to bring against this dishonest man.

That Mr. Bayley should never praise, never refer to the authors whom he has plundered, was to be expected; to have so named them would have been giving a hint to his detection. This is the common trick of plagiarists; but Mr. Bayley is no common plagiarist, and he has advanced one step farther in meanness. After having made up his own poems by scraps from Mr. Wordsworth's, he has had the baseness to attempt to ridicule Mr. Wordsworth, and has sneered at him by name; in the hope, that those of his readers who have never read the Lyrical Ballads, may be prevented from reading them by the contempt which he has thus expressed. The miserable vanity which tempted this gentleman to build his own fame upon another's merits, to pilfer the reputation of a contemporary, to plume his own magpye tail with the feathers of the bird of paradise, this wretched craving for notoriety would have deserved no heavier punishment than the contempt and scorn which necessarily would follow detection; but this other offence is of a deeper die. Like a loathsome reptile, it is not enough for him to feed and fatten, but he must endeavour to sting and to stain with his pollutions. The moral turpitude of this action excites our wonder and indignation. We know not the name which is hidden under this *alias* of Peter Bayley; and happy it is for him, that he can be thus concealed; but be he whom he may, this we shall say of him –

Hic niger est, hunc tu Romane caveto![2]

EDITOR'S NOTES

1. 'a bright sun'.
2. 'This man is black (wicked); Roman, beware of this man' (Horace, *Satires*, I, 4, 85).

VI

Poems, 1807: reviews, 1807–1811

94. Byron (1788–1824)

Unsigned review, *Monthly Literary Recreations*, July 1807, iii, 65–6

Byron did not know Eugenius Roche, the editor of this short-lived periodical (three issues, 1806–7). Byron's letter, 21 July 1807, to Ben Crosby, the
publisher both of Byron's poems and of the periodical, allows the editor a
free hand with the article on Wordsworth; whether changed or not, on 2
August Byron acknowledges the printed version as his (*Byron's Letters and
Journals, 1814–1815*, ed. Leslie A. Marchand, 1973, I, 150).

Byron responds to Wordsworth's patriotic sonnets but not to the section entitled 'Moods of My Own Mind'; his dismissal of 'INNOCENT
ODES' appears to be a reference to 'Ode: Intimations of Immortality',
for he also refers to the Latin motto Wordsworth attached to that poem.
'Ode to Duty', the only other ode in the volumes, has nothing of the free
stanzaic form shared by 'The Ode: Intimations . . . ' and the poems in
'Moods of My Own Mind', which Byron disliked. Further, Wordsworth's
use of the word 'innocent' is only found at the conclusion of 'The Ode:
Intimations . . . ': 'The innocent brightness of a new-born Day/Is lovely
yet.'

The volumes before us are by the author of Lyrical Ballads, a collection
which has not undeservedly met with a considerable share of public
applause. The characteristics of Mr. W.'s muse are simple and flowing,
though occasionally inharmonious verse, strong, and sometimes irresistible appeals to the feelings, with unexceptionable sentiments. Though
the present work may not equal his former efforts, many of the poems
possess a native elegance, natural and unaffected, totally devoid of the
tinsel embellishments and abstract hyperboles of several contemporary
sonneteers. The last sonnet in the first volume, is perhaps the best, without any novelty in the sentiments, which we hope are common to every
Briton at the present crisis; the force and expression is that of a genuine
poet, feeling as he writes:

[Quotes sonnet, 'November 1806' ('Another year! another deadly blow!')
PW, III, p. 122; *Poems 1807*, p. 160.]

The song at the Feast of Brougham Castle, the Seven Sisters, the Affliction of Margaret —— of —— possess all the beauties, and few of the
defects of this writer: the following lines from the last are in his first style.

[Quotes 'The Affliction of Margaret—of—', *PW*, II, p. 48, ll. 22–8; *Poems 1807*, pp. 54–5, ll. 22–8:

> Ah! little doth the young one dream . . .
> But do not make her love the less.]

The pieces least worthy of the author are those entitled 'Moods of my own Mind,' we certainly wish these 'Moods' had been less frequent, or not permitted to occupy a place near works, which only make their deformity more obvious; when Mr. W. ceases to please, it is by 'abandoning' his mind to the most common-place ideas, at the same time clothing them in language not simple, but puerile: what will any reader or auditor, out of the nursery, say to such namby-pamby as 'Lines written at the foot of Brother's Bridge.'

[Quotes 'The cock is crowing', *PW*, II, p. 220; *Poems 1807*, p. 219.]

'The plough-boy is whooping anon, anon,' &c. &c. is in the same exquisite measure; this appears to us neither more or less than an imitation of such minstrelsy as soothed our cries in the cradle, with the shrill ditty of

> Hey de diddle,
> The cat and the fiddle:
> The cow jump'd over the moon,
> The little dog laugh'd to see such sport,
> And the dish ran away with the spoon.

On the whole, however, with the exception of the above, and other INNOCENT odes of the same cast, we think these volumes display a genius worthy of higher pursuits, and regret that Mr. W. confines his muse to such trifling subjects; we trust his motto will be in future, 'Paulo majora canamus.' Many, with inferior abilities, have acquired a loftier seat on Parnassus, merely by attempting strains in which Mr. W. is more qualified to excel.

95.

Unsigned review, *Critical Review*, August 1807, XI, third series, 399–403

Wordsworth, informed by Southey of C.V. le Grice's supposed malice towards Coleridge and all Coleridge's friends (he had adversely reviewed Southey's *Madoc*), wrote to Wrangham on 12 July 1807 asking him to use his influence with the publisher of the *Critical*, Mawman, to ensure that the poems were not reviewed by le Grice. Montagu, a friend of Wrangham, Wordsworth and Mawman, appears to have helped: 'but alas!' wrote Wordsworth to Wrangham on 4 November 1807, 'either for me, or for the Critical Review, or both! it has been out of the frying-pan into the fire' (*MY*, I, 173.)

Possibly the author of the review was the unidentified attorney's clerk, not 20 years old, who told Mrs. Montagu that he would give Wordsworth 'a glorious trimming' (see entry 110).

It is just possible the author was J. H. Merivale (see entry 152), a young lawyer and a newcomer to the *Critical Review*, who, on 11 January 1808, wrote to his mother: 'My connection with the Critical is really a source of great amusement, and, (if not too much divulged,) I am confident of advantage to me also. It keeps me actively employed, prevents me from growing melancholy on occasional deficiencies of business, gives me a great deal of useful information, and habituates me to a freedom and ease of expression. It has become more pleasant to me of late from a circumstance that [Thomas] Denman has also engaged in it, and pursues it with great spirit'. Denman had engaged 'to furnish all Political articles ... I have undertaken myself the departments of modern history, romance, and occasional antiquarian researches and belles lettres ... in the last two months that I have been in town, I have already written enough to produce very near thirty pounds, and this with so much ease to myself' (see *Family Memorials, Compiled by Anna W. Merivale*, 1884, 161–2). In 1819 Merivale records of the Italian poet Foscolo: 'He is as much wrappped up in himself as Wordsworth' (*ibid.*, 204). Wordsworth told Francis Wrangham that he had not read this review: 'But from what I have heard of the contents of this precious piece, I feel not so much inclined to accuse the author of malice as of sheer, honest insensibility, and stupidity' (*MY*, I, 174).

A SILLY book, is a serious evil; but it becomes absolutely insupportable when written by a man of sense. A fool may scribble without giving any great offence to society, his 'Daisies,' 'Cuckoos', 'green Linnets', and 'falling Leaves,' are as innocent as the 'lovely creatures' to which they are addressed; but we cannot see real talents and genius squandered away on uses

> So weary, stale, flat, and unprofitable,

as those which Mr. W. selects for the subjects of his muse; without sentiments too lively for indifference, and not quite gentle enough for mere compassion.

We have, at different times, employed ridicule with a view of making this gentleman ashamed of himself, and bringing him back to his senses. But, unfortunately, he is only one of a tribe who keep each other in countenance by mutual applause and flattery, and who having dubbed themselves by the name of poets, imagine they have a right to direct the taste of the nation, and thus, infinitely to their own satisfaction, abuse the good sense and weary out the patience of mankind with their fantastic mummeries. We have now done with laughing, and earnestly entreat Mr. W. (if his feelings are not *too fine* to allow of his holding converse with minds of our gross unsentimental texture) when he takes up this Review, to carry it into his closet with him, banishing himself for a quarter of an hour from the company of Messrs. —— and —— and —— and, if possible, from 'the moods of his own mind' also, and consider seriously the few words we have to say to him.

As the tone of the stomach is injured and at last ruined by the perpetual irritation of strong liquors; as sensual indulgence gradually weakens and confounds, and, in the end, annihilates every finer feeling and nobler power of the soul; and as these causes necessarily and invariably tend to the production of those effects; so, with equal certainty, and equally in the common course of nature, does the unlimited gratification of vicious sensibility pervert the imagination, corrupt the taste, and finally destroy the power of just descrimination [*sic*] and all the natural energy of genius.

Had Mr. Wordsworth set any bounds whatever to the excesses of sentiment, had he given any admission to the suggestions of reason and experience, had he resisted the over-weening impulses of vanity, and estimated properly the poor and wretched affectation of singularity, he had that within him which might have insured him a high and distinguished literary reputation. He is gifted by nature with pure and noble feelings, with a mind capable of admiring and enjoying all her charms, and a heart alive to the impressions of benevolence and virtue. He has acquired the command of language and the power of harmony. He possesses a warm imagination, and all the enthusiasm of genuine poetry.

We are not among the number of his injudicious friends and flatterers; yet our memory has often dwelt with delight on his 'Tintern Abbey,' his 'Evening sail to Richmond,' his 'Michael,' and a few more of the pieces contained in his first publication of Lyrical Ballads. Even in our magisterial chair we are not ashamed to confess that he has had the power to draw 'iron tears' from our stony hearts. We wish that we could say as much of any one of the numerous specimens now before us. But alas! we fear that the mind of Mr. W. has been too long accustomed to the enervating debauchery of taste for us to entertain much hope of his recovery. He must endure self-denial, practise much ungrateful humility, and absent himself from much of that society which is so dear to his vanity; he must wean himself from his vain and fantastic feeding, must

> Dine on sweet thoughts, and sup on sentiment;

He must undergo a certain term of rigid penance and inward mortification; before he can become what he once promised to be, the poet of the heart: and not the capricious minion of a debasing affectation.

But when the man to whom, in early youth, nature

> 'Was all in all' – who 'cannot paint
> What then he was – the sounding cataract
> Haunted him like a passion; the tall rock,
> The mountain, and the deep and gloomy wood,
> Their colours and their forms, were then to him
> An appetite; a feeling and a love
> That had no need of a remoter charm
> By thought supplied, or any interest
> Unborrowed from the eye;'
> ['Tintern Abbey', *PW*, II, p 261, ll. 75–83;
> *LB (1798)*, p. 114, ll. 76–84]

When that man is found, in his riper years, drivelling to a red-breast in such mock-verses as

> Art thou the bird whom man loves best,
> The pious bird with the scarlet breast,
> Our little English robin;
> The bird that comes about our doors
> When autumn winds are sobbing?
> Art thou the Peter of Norway Boors?
> Their Thomas in Finland,
> And Russia far inland?
> ['The Redbreast and the Butterfly', *PW*, II,
> p. 149 ll. 1–8; *Poems 1807*, p. 24, ll. 1–8]

And thus to a common pile-wort,

Pansies, lilies, kingcups, daisies,
Let them live upon their praises;
Long as there's a sun that sets
Primroses will have their glory;
Long as there are violets,
They will have a place in story;
There's a flower that shall be mine,
'Tis the little Celandine.
Eyes of some men travel far
For the finding of a star;
Up and down the heavens they go,
Men that keep a mighty rout!
I'm as great as they, I trow,
Since the day I found thee out,
Little flower! – I'll make a stir
Like a great astronomer . . .

['To the Small Celandine', *PW*, II pp. 142–3, ll. 1–16;
Poems 1807, pp. 30–1, ll. 1–16]

And thus to a little baby:

That way look, my infant, lo!
What a pretty baby show!
See the kitten on the wall,
Sporting with the leaves that fall,
Wither'd leaves, one, two, and three,
From the lofty elder-tree!

['The Kitten and the Falling Leaves', *PW*, II, p. 170,
ll. 1–6; *Poems 1807*, p. 58, ll. 1–6]

And again:

'Tis a pretty baby-treat;
Nor, I deem, for me unmeet;

[*Ibid.*, *PW*, II, p. 171, ll. 41–2; *Poems 1807*,
p. 60 ll. 41–2]

And thus to his mistress:

I led my Lucy to the spot, 'Look here!'
Oh! joy it was for her, and joy for me!

['Among all lovely things my Love had been', *PW*, II,
p. 466, ll. 19–20; *Poems 1807*, p. 75, ll.19–20]

174

And thus to a sky-lark:

> Drunken lark! thou would'st be loth
> To be such a traveller as I.
> Happy, happy liver!
> With a soul as strong as a mountain river,
> Pouring out praise to the Almighty Giver,
> Joy and jollity be with us both!
> Hearing thee, or else some other,
> As merry a brother,
> I on the earth will go plodding on,
> By myself, chearfully, till the day is done.
>> ['To a Sky-Lark', *PW*, II, p. 142, ll. 20–31; *Poems 1807*,
>> pp. 89–90, ll. 20–9]

And thus to Alice Fell,

> 'And whither are you going, child.
> To night along these lonesome ways?'
> 'To Durham' answer'd she half wild –
> 'Then come with me into the chaise.'
>> ['Alice Fell', *PW*, I, p. 233, ll. 33–6; *Poems 1807*,
>> p. 94, ll. 33–6]

and thus to two well-dressed women, by way of greeting:

> 'What you are stepping westward?' – 'Yea.'
>> ['Stepping Westward', *PW*, III, p. 76 l. 1; *Poems 1807*,
>> p. 188, l. 1]

And thus to a butterfly,

> Little butterfly! indeed
> I know not if you sleep, or feed:
>> ['To a Butterfly', *PW*, II, p. 22, ll. 3–4; *Poems 1807*,
>> p. 234, ll. 3–4]

How can we sufficiently lament the infatuation of self-conceit and our own disappointed hopes!

Is it possible for Mr. W. not to feel that, while he is pouring out his nauseous and nauseating sensibilities to weeds and insects, he debases himself to a level with his own 'ideot-boy,' infinitely below his 'pretty Celandine' and 'little butterfly?'

Above all things we would intreat Mr. W. to spend more time in his library and less in company with the 'moods of his own mind.' If he is not too proud to be taught, he may yet derive instruction and amendment from books; but, in his present diseased state, he is the very worst companion for himself.

We have said that the present volumes contain no poems which will bear a comparison with the best of his Lyrical Ballads. Yet there are a few, which though not free from affectation would do credit to a poet of less acknowledged abilities. We here and there discover symptoms of reason and judgment, which we gladly hail as a proof that his mind is not yet irrecoverably lost in the vortex of false taste and puerile conceit.

96.

Unsigned review, *Records of Literature*, October 1807, i, 468–9

As neither preface, address, or advertisement informs us why these poems are published, we are unable to inform our readers of the author's design in so doing.

The first volume contains twenty-two poems and forty-seven sonnets – The second, thirty-four poems, and twelve pieces which the author names 'Moods of my own Mind' – This term also is unexplained, altho' each volume is concluded by 'Notes.'

Walter Scott's *Hellvellyn* has given occasion for a poem by Mr. W. of which we insert two stanzas. As our space is so confined, that we have not room to insert it in regular lines, we shall leave it to the reader's discernment to cut it into lengths. A Shepherd is supposed to hear the barking of the animal immortalized by Mr. S.

[Quotes 'Fidelity', *PW*, IV, pp. 81–2, ll. 34–49; *Poems 1807*, pp. 19–20, ll. 34–49.]

Not knowing what to think, a while the Shepherd stood: then makes his way towards the Dog, o'er rocks and stones, as quickly as he may, nor far had gone before he found a human skeleton on the ground, sad sight! the shepherd with a sigh looks round to learn the history. From those abrupt and perilous rocks, the man had fallen, that place of fear! at length upon the shepherd's mind it breaks, and all is clear: he instantly recalled the name, and who he was and whence he came; remembered too the very day on which the traveller passed this way.

We cannot determine whether this poem is an imitation of, or a parody on that of Walter Scott.

[Scott's 'Hellvellyn' was based on the same story, but independent of Wordsworth's 'Fidelity'.]

Mr. W. thus pathetically and movingly expresses, or rather obscurely hints, at his apprehensions of Bonaparte's unfitness for the imperial dignity. This also is poetry.

[Quotes sonnet 'I griev'd for Buonaparte' as a passage of prose. *PW*, III, p. 110; *Poems 1807*, p. 138.]

We have searched in vain among the notes for an explanation of the term 'The blood of a man's mind' [misquoting 'the vital blood / Of that Man's mind what can it be?'].

97.

Unsigned review, *Le Beau Monde, or, Literary and Fashionable Magazine*, October 1807, II, 138–42

MR. WORDSWORTH, in those poems which he is here pleased to call κατ᾽ ἐξοχγν̕,[1] by way of pre-eminence, *the* Lyrical Ballads, gave considerable testimony of strong feeling and poetic powers, although like a histerical school-girl he had a knack of feeling about subjects with which feeling had no proper concern: Feeling and nature are two very pretty words, and much in use with the philosophical and *simple* poets, among whom Mr. Wordsworth is ambitious to be enrolled: but the descriptions of feeling and nature are not necessarily valuable in all their shapes, and that affection of the mind which employed on a great or universally interesting topic would inspire our general sympathy, is most likely, when exercised upon a mean object, or a chimerical idea, to excite no emotion but laughter. In the Lyrical Ballads before mentioned, something was good, much tolerable, and a vast deal ridiculous. In the present volumes, the good is, as Shakspeare says of Gratiano's reasons, like a grain of wheat hidden in a bushel of chaff, for which we may long labouriously seek, and which, when we have found it, is not worth the search. We really begin to think that the new school of poets, as they think fit to call themselves, suppose folly to be feeling, and consider nature as synonymous with nonsense. After reading the poems before us, we were, and still are, inclined to doubt the fulfilment of the motto which stands prefixed,[2] and which implies the possession of strong faculties:

> *Posterius graviore sono tibi musa loquetur*
> *Nostra: dabunt cum securos mihi tempera 'fructus,'*

> Hereafter, at better opportunity, our muse
> shall speak to you in a more impressive tone.

But this muse really seems to be in her dotage. We hoped that the childish effusions that were mixed among the poems in the former work, were the errors of a mind then in its poetical dawn, and that a more mature experience would wipe away the morning dew, and leave the flower untarnished and fair. But we now apprehend that this nurse, at the time she produced Lyrical Ballads, was not the whining scholar, but the lean and slippered eld, and that she now has shifted into that second childhood, in which, though *sans* eyes, *sans* ears, and *sans* teeth, she unluckily is not *sans* tongue. Accordingly, through two duo-decimo volumes, she drivels out her puerilities, almost unassisted by any tokens of the genius which once seemed to be sprouting within her. Wherever those do occur we will point them out with all possible candour.

The first poem is by no means the worst – but we will begin fairly:

> TO THE DAISY.
> In youth from rock to rock I went,
> From hill to hill, in *discontent*,
> *Of pleasure high and turbulent*,
> *Most pleased when most uneasy.*

> *Quere* – What this means, or how it can be?

> But now my own delights I make,
> My thirst at every rill can slake,
> *And gladly nature's love partake*
> *Of thee, sweet daisy*

We repeat the foregoing *quere*.
The next verse is intelligible:

> When soothed a while by milder airs
> Thee winter in the garland wears,
> That thinly shades his few grey hairs;
> Spring cannot shun thee;

178

> Whole summer fields are thine by right;
> And autumn, melancholy wight!
> Doth in thy crimson head delight
>> When rains are on thee.
>
> In shoals and bands, a morrice train,
> Thou greet'st the traveller in the lane;
> *If welcome once thou count'st it gain.*

How so?

>> Thou art not daunted,
>> Nor car'st if thou be set at naught;
>> And oft alone in nooks remote
>> We meet thee, *like a pleasant thought,*
>>> When such are wanted.

Where is the resemblance between the pleasant thought and this daisy?

>> Be violets in their secret mews
>> The flowers the wanton zephyrs chuse;
>> Proud be the rose, with rains and dews
>>> Her head impearling;
>> Thou liv'st with less ambitious aim –

The daisies on Mr. Wordsworth's estate, have not, we conclude, in common with violets and roses, the advantages of wind, rain, and dew.

>> Thou liv'st with less ambitious aim,
>> Yet hast not gone without thy fame;
>> Thou art indeed by many a claim
>>> The poet's darling.

It will be difficult to discover why the daisy, above every other humble flower of the field, should have such special claims to poetic favour.

>> If to a rock from rains he fly,
>> Or, some bright day of April sky,
>> Imprisoned by hot sunshine lie
>>> Near the green holly,
>> And wearily at length should fare;
>> He need but look about, and there
>> Thou art! a friend at hand, to scare
>>> His melancholy.

A very new prescription for the cure of hypochondria!

> A hundred times, by rock or bower,
> Ere thus I have lain couch'd an hour,
> Have I derived from thy sweet power
>   Some apprehension;
> Some steady love; some brief delight;
> Some memory that had taken flight;
> Some chime of fancy wrong or right;
>   Or stray invention.

Let Dr. Rees[3] take care: if this idea be prosecuted, who knows but the daisy may some day or other, by the amplitude of its information, supercede the necessity of an Encyclopædia?

It also performs the functions of a Bible, at least if we conjecture rightly, as to the sense of the following very cabalistic passage:

> If stately passions in me burn.
> And one chance look to thee should turn,
> I drink *out of an humbler urn*
>   *A lowlier pleasure;*
> The homely sympathy that heeds
> The common life, our nature breeds;
> A wisdom fitted to the needs
>   Of hearts at leisure.
> When, smitten by the morning ray,
> I see thee rise alert and gay,
> Then cheerful flow'r! my spirits play
>   With kindred motion:
> At dusk, I've seldom marked thee press
> The ground, *as if in thankfulness*
> Without some feeling, *more or less*,
>   Of true devotion.

Here's emblematical piety with a vengeance! Next observe the daisy acting as a ledger, keeping accounts of some out-of-the-way debts, and entering itself as creditor:

> And all day long I number yet,
> All seasons through another debt
> Which I, wherever thou art met,
>   To thee am owing:

An instinct call it, a blind sense;
A happy, genial influence,
Coming, one knows not how nor whence,
 Nor whither going.

True – 'one knows not,' one understands not, and one cares not.

The next and last stanza contains four very bold and poetical figures, if we may so call them, apostrophe, simile, prophecy, and panegyric: all of them to us equally unintelligible.

Child of the year! that round dost run
Thy course, bold lover of the sun,
And cheerful, when the day's begun,
 As morning Leveret,
Thou long the poet's praise shalt gain:
Thou will be more beloved by men
In times to come; thou not in vain
 Art nature's favourite.

When Burns had written so sweetly to the daisy, it was ill-judged in Mr. Wordsworth to select such a subject.

The second sonnet goes only to express a desire of kissing a lady called Louisa. Is not this rather incorrect for a married man?

The third is a bald history of the traveller who perished on Helvellyn: unluckily for Mr. Wordsworth, Mr. Scott, by one of the ballads which we reviewed in our fourth number, has already commemorated this subject, and commemorated it in pathetic lines.

The fourth poem is rather abrupt, but contains the best lines in the two volumes; lines which extol a woman, not by amplifying her into an angel, but by representing her as she is. Angels may be very well for dreams; but in real life we prefer woman, simple woman; lovely because she is but human, and interesting even in her weaknesses! Our author defines the phantom of his soul to be

A creature not too bright or good
For human nature's daily food;
For transient sorrows, simple wiles,
Praise, blame, love, kisses, tears, and smiles!
 ['She was a Phantom of delight', *Poems 1807*,
 p. 23, ll. 17–20.]

All of our readers who have ever been fortunate or unfortunate enough to think seriously upon this subject, will acknowledge the force and feeling of this idea, will recall to their minds the delight with which they have gazed on some April countenances, and conclude with us, that one smile or one tear which we ourselves can summon to the features of beauty, is worth all the calm regularity, all the still divinity, that ever was estimated from canvass, or adjusted from a block of marble.

The poem of the Redbreast and Butterfly is puerile beyond the power of imitation. It has been said that a leading fault of the present age, is the eager haste with which children are pressing to imitate men! In our opinion it is at least as disgusting to see men the copyists of children.

The Sailor's Mother is not remarkable, though the sentiment is natural.

The beginning of the first sonnet to the small Celandine, or common Pilewort, is in the stile of the before extracted address to the Daisy; but the latter part is good, because, which is rather unusual throughout these volumes, it actually contains a thought.

> Comfort have thou of thy merit,
> Kindly, unassuming spirit!
> Careless of thy neighbourhood
> Thou dost shew thy pleasant face,
> On the moor, and in the wood,
> In the lane – there's not a place,
> Howsoever mean it be,
> But 'tis good enough for thee.
>
> Ill befall the yellow flowers,
> Children of the flaring hours,
> Buttercups, that will be seen,
> Whether we will see or no;
> Others too, of lofty mien;
> They have done as wordlings do,
> Taken praise that should be thine,
> Like humble celandine!

Then comes another address to the same flower, which is very childish. And it is succeeded by a poem called, *A Character of the Happy Warrior*, very bald and ungrammatical, as *per sample*:

> Who is the happy warrior? Who is he,
> *Whom* every man in arms should wish to be?

The Horn of Egremont Castle is unmeaning, and the Affliction of Margaret common-place. The Kitten with the falling leaves is pretty, and the Seven Sisters a bad imitation of Ovid. Then comes some lines to H. C. a child of six years old, which if the child understood, it must be a very extraordinary child – nay, we have no notion that the author himself would be capable of giving the remotest clue to their interpretation. But all this is only by way of preparation for an Address to the Glow-worm, which is, in our opinion, the very climax and *ne plus ultra* of absurdity. Our readers shall judge for themselves –

[Quotes 'Among all lovely things my love had been', *PW*, II, p. 466; *Poems 1807*, p. 74.]

Pretty innocents!

Another string of flat lines about Lucy is succeeded by an ode to Duty, affecting much feeling, and affording a bad, very bad imitation of the style of Cowley. Then there are more things composed, shewing a tour, chiefly on foot. *Musa pedestris* indeed! All these, except one called Resolution and Independence, which is tolerable, are very silly – one about Beggars,! one about a certain Alice Fell, one to a Sky-lark, and one to the Moon, which thus concludes:

> —Had I
> The power of Merlin, Goddess, this should be:
> And all the stars, now shrouded up in heav'n,
> Should sally forth to keep thee company.
> What strife would then be yours, fair creature, driven
> Now up, now down, and sparkling in your glee!
> But Cynthia, should to thee the palm be given,
> Queen both for beauty and for majesty.
> ['With how sad steps . . .', *PW*, III, pp. 31–2, ll. 8–14.
> *Poems 1807*, p. 91.]

The astronomer in Rasselas was nothing to our hypothetical star-gazer: but we cannot help remembering the reply that was made to the man who said, 'If all churches were one church, what a great church that would be – and if all men were one man, what a great man that would be.'

Then follow twenty sonnets, of which the first is far-fetched, and the second leads to nothing; the third is unintelligible; and the fourth, sixth, and seventh dull; the fifth, eighth, and ninth unmeaning; the eleventh, though not his own, common-place; the twelfth, though a good psalm, yet ill-selected for the subject of a sonnet; the thirteenth, fourteenth, and fifteenth to no purpose; the sixteenth incomprehensible; the eighteenth and nineteenth nonsense. The tenth, as well as the eleventh and twelfth, is a translation from Michael Angelo, but is the only one of the three that possesses much merit. The seventeenth is not without some desert; but the twentieth amused us most. It is a sort of paraphrase of Horace's *Exegi monumentum aere perennius*:[4] but Mr. Wordsworth and Horace do not quite rank together, and Peter Pindar has wittily said,

> Fleas are not lobsters, damn their souls!

This volume concludes with twenty-six sonnets to liberty, of which twenty-one are not worth the labour of perusal. The sixth and tenth are tolerable, the seventeenth and twentieth good, and the twenty-sixth finishes with the following forcible and complimentary lines, applied to the late administration:

> We shall exult, if they who rule the land
> Be men who hold its many blessings dear,
> Wise, upright, valiant; not a venal band,
> Who are to judge of danger which they fear,
> And honour which they do not understand!
>
> ['Another year . . .', *PW*, III, p. 122, ll. 10–14;
> *Poems 1807*, p. 160.]

The second volume begins with some lines eulogistic of Rob Roy, a Scotch outlaw – the strain of this poem might be dangerous if it were not so foolish. The Solitary Reaper and Stepping Westward are poems both innocent of all meaning; the Grave of Ossian excites no poetical idea in our author's mind; and the Matron of Jedburgh is more moral than entertaining – so is the Address to the Sons of Burns. A sonnet, composed at some castle, informs us that though some trees have been cut down, yet, strange to relate, the ground on which they grew is still where it was: and the poem on Yarrow Mr. Wordsworth has long protracted, for the pleasure of concluding it with a nothing. All the first stanzas of this production are evidently borrowed from Horace's *Laudabunt alii claram Rhodon, aut Mitylenen*.[5] The lines to a Highland Girl, with a few errors, are very pretty; we think it but fair to extract them.

[Quotes 'To a Highland Girl', *PW*, III, p. 73; *Poems 1807*, p. 197.]

There is a story about a highland boy going to sea in a wash-tub, which may amuse children in the nursery; and there is a song about a linnet, which will never amuse any body any where. The lines to a young lady, who was in the habit of taking long walks, are forcible and feeling. There are a great many other little pieces, some of which are written upon subjects that give scope for the display of genius; but Mr. Wordsworth has, in very few instances, taken advantage of his opportunity, and these poems, as well as those which we have more minutely criticised, bear the general characteristics of an author easily satisfied with his own productions, however little those productions be likely to satisfy any body else.

Upon the whole we have a most unfavourable opinion of the volumes before us; a few beauties indeed are scattered abroad through their pages; but, like violets, they lie very low, and are difficult of discovery. Mr. Wordsworth has ruined himself by his affectation of simplicity. Most good authors have been content to form themselves on the models of polished writers: Mr. Scott, in the present day, has chosen to copy the language of barbarous ages; but it was reserved for Mr. Wordsworth to imitate the lisp of children.

EDITOR'S NOTES

1. 'by way of pre-eminence (*par excellence*)'.
2. The reviewer refers to the epigraph to Wordsworth's Poems, *1807*, the Latin being from the pseudo-Virgilian text, *Culex* 8–9. Wordsworth clearly alludes to his ambitious philosophical poem, *The Recluse*. *The Excursion* had yet to be brought together, and *The Prelude* was to remain unpublished until his death.
3. Dr Abraham Rees (1743–1825), dissenting minister, editor of Chambers' *Cyclopaedia* and *The New Cyclopaedia* (1802–1820).
4. 'I have constructed a memorial more lasting than bronze' (Horace, *Odes*, III, 30).
5. *Odes*, I, 7, 1: 'Others will praise famous (or "sunny") Rhodes or Mytilene'.

98. Francis Jeffrey

Unsigned review, *Edinburgh Review*, October 1807, XI, 214–31

This author is known to belong to a certain brotherhood of poets, who have haunted for some years about the Lakes of Cumberland; and is generally looked upon, we believe, as the purest model of the excellences and peculiarities of the school which they have been labouring to establish. Of the general merits of that school, we have had occasion to express our opinion pretty fully, in more places than one, and even to make some allusion to the former publications of the writer now before us. We are glad, however, to have found an opportunity of attending somewhat more particularly to his pretensions.

The Lyrical Ballads were unquestionably popular; and, we have no hesitation in saying, deservedly popular; for in spite of their occasional vulgarity, affectation, and silliness, they were undoubtedly characterised by a strong spirit of originality, of pathos, and natural feeling; and recommended to all good minds by the clear impression which they bore of the amiable dispositions and virtuous principles of the author. By the help of these qualities, they were enabled, not only to recommend themselves to the indulgence of many judicious readers, but even to beget among a pretty numerous class of persons, a sort of admiration of the very defects by which they were attended. It was upon this account chiefly, that we thought it necessary to set ourselves against this alarming innovation. Childishness, conceit, and affectation, are not of themselves very popular or attractive; and though mere novelty has sometimes been found sufficient to give them a temporary currency, we should have had no fear of their prevailing to any dangerous extent, if they had been graced with no more seductive accompaniments. It was precisely because the perverseness and bad taste of this new school was combined with a great deal of genius and of laudable feeling, that we were afraid of their spreading and gaining ground among us, and that we entered into the discussion with a degree of zeal and animosity which some might think unreasonable towards authors, to whom so much merit had been conceded. There were times and moods indeed, in which we were led to suspect ourselves of unjustifiable severity, and to doubt, whether a sense of public duty had not carried us rather too far in reprobation of errors, that seemed to be atoned for, by excellences of no vulgar description. At other times, the magnitude of these errors – the disgusting absurdities into which they led their feebler admirers, and the derision and contempt which they drew from the more fastidious, even upon the merits with which they were associated, made us wonder more than ever at the perversity by which they were retained, and regret that we had not declared ourselves against them with still more formidable and decided hostility.

In this temper of mind, we read the *annonce* of Mr Wordsworth's publication with a good deal of interest and expectation, and opened his volumes with greater anxiety, than he or his admirers will probably give us credit for. We have been greatly disappointed certainly as to the quality of the poetry; but we doubt whether the publication has afforded so much satisfaction to any other of his readers: – it has freed us from all doubt or hesitation as to the justice of our former censures, and has brought the matter to a test, which we cannot help hoping may be convincing to the author himself.

Mr Wordsworth, we think, has now brought the question, as to the merit of his new school of poetry, to a very fair and decisive issue. The volumes before us are much more strongly marked by all its peculiarities than any former publication of the fraternity. In our apprehension, they are, on this very account, infinitely less interesting or meritorious; but it belongs to the public, and not to us, to decide upon their merit, and we will confess, that so strong is our conviction of their obvious inferiority, and the grounds of it, that we are willing for once to wave our right of appealing to posterity, and to take the judgment of the present generation of readers, and even of Mr Wordsworth's former admirers, as conclusive on this occasion. If these volumes, which have all the benefit of the author's former popularity, turn out to be nearly as popular as the lyrical ballads – if they sell nearly to the same extent – or are quoted and imitated among half as many individuals, we shall admit that Mr Wordsworth has come much nearer the truth in his judgment of what constitutes the charm of poetry, than we had previously imagined – and shall institute a more serious and respectful inquiry into his principles of composition than we have yet thought necessary. On the other hand, – if this little work, selected from the compositions of five maturer years, and written avowedly for the purpose of exalting a system, which has already excited a good deal of attention, should be generally rejected by those whose prepossessions were in its favour, there is room to hope, not only that the system itself will meet with no more encouragement, but even that the author will be persuaded to abandon a plan of writing, which defrauds his industry and talents of their natural reward.

Putting ourselves thus upon our country, we certainly look for a verdict against this publication; and have little doubt indeed of the result, upon a fair consideration of the evidence contained in these volumes. – To accelerate that result, and to give a general view of the evidence, to those into whose hands the record may not have already fallen, we must now make a few observations and extracts.

We shall not resume any of the particular discussions by which we formerly attempted to ascertain the value of the improvements which this new school has effected in poetry; but shall lay the grounds of our opposition, for this time, a little more broadly. – The end of poetry, we take it, is to please – and the name, we think, is strictly applicable to every metrical composition from which we receive pleasure, without any laborious exercise of the understanding. This pleasure, may, in general, be analyzed into three parts – that which we receive from the excitement of Passion or emotion – that which is derived from the play of Imagination, or the easy exercise of Reason – and that which depends on the character and qualities of the Diction. The two first are the vital and primary springs of poetical delight, and can scarcely require explanation to any one. The last has been alternately overrated and undervalued by the professors of the poetical art, and is in such low estimation with the author now before us and his associates, that it is necessary to say a few words in explanation of it.

One great beauty of diction exists only for those who have some degree of scholarship or critical skill. This is what depends on the exquisite *propriety* of the words employed, and the delicacy with which they are adapted to the meaning which is to be expressed. Many of the finest passages in Virgil and Pope derive their principal charm from the fine propriety of their diction. Another source of beauty, which extends only to the more instructed class of readers, is that which consists in the judicious or happy application of expressions which have been sanctified by the use of famous writers, or which bear the stamp of a simple or venerable antiquity. There are other beauties of diction, however, which are perceptible by all – the beauties of sweet sound and pleasant associations. The melody of words and verses is indifferent to no reader of poetry; but the chief recommendation of poetical language is certainly derived from those general associations, which give it a character of dignity or elegance, sublimity or tenderness. Every one knows that there are low and mean expressions, as well as lofty and grave ones; and that some words bear the impression of coarseness and vulgarity, as clearly as others do of refinement and affection. We do not mean, of course, to say any thing in defence of the hackneyed common-places of ordinary versemen. Whatever might have been the original character of these unlucky phrases, they are now associated with nothing but ideas of schoolboy imbecility and vulgar affectation. But what we do maintain is, that much of the most popular poetry in the world owes its celebrity chiefly to the beauty of its diction; and that no poetry can be long or generally acceptable, the language of which is coarse, inelegant, or infantine.

From this great source of pleasure, we think the readers of Mr Wordsworth are in a great measure cut off. His diction has no where any pretensions to elegance or dignity; and he has scarcely ever condescended to give the grace of correctness or melody to his versification. If it were merely slovenly and neglected, however, all this might be endured. Strong sense and powerful feeling will ennoble any expressions; or, at least, no one who is capable of estimating those higher merits, will be disposed to mark these little defects. But, in good truth, no man, now-a-days, composes verses for publication with a slovenly neglect of their language. It is a fine and laborious manufacture, which can scarcely ever be made in a hurry; and the faults which it has, may, for the most part, be set down to bad taste or incapacity, rather than to carelessness or over-sight. With Mr Wordsworth and his friends, it is plain that their peculiarities of diction are things of choice, and not of accident. They write as they do, upon principle and system; and it evidently costs them much pains to keep *down* to the standard which they have proposed to themselves. They are, to the full, as much mannerists, too, as the poetasters who ring changes on the common-places of magazine versification; and all the difference between them is, that they borrow their phrases from a different and a scantier *gradus ad Parnassum*. If they were, indeed, to discard all imitation and set phraseology, and to bring in no words merely for show or for metre, – as much, perhaps, might be gained in freedom and originality, as would infallibly be lost in allusion and authority; but, in point of fact, the new poets are just as great borrowers as the old; only that, instead of borrowing from the more popular passages of their illustrious predecessors, they have preferred furnishing themselves from vulgar ballads and plebeian nurseries.

Their peculiarities of diction alone, are enough, perhaps, to render them ridiculous; but the author before us really seems anxious to court this literary martyrdom by a device still more infallible, – we mean, that of connecting his most lofty, tender, or impassioned conceptions, with objects and incidents, which the greater part of his readers will probably persist in thinking low, silly, or uninteresting. Whether this is done from affectation and conceit alone, or whether it may not arise, in some measure, from the self-illusion of a mind of extraordinary sensibility, habituated to solitary meditation, we cannot undertake to determine. It is possible enough, we allow, that the sight of a friend's garden spade, or a sparrow's nest, or a man gathering leeches, might really have suggested to such a mind a train of powerful impressions and interesting reflections; but it is certain, that, to most minds, such associations will always appear forced, strained, and unnatural; and that the composition in which it is attempted to exhibit them, will always have the air of parody, or ludicrous and affected singularity. All the world laughs at Elegiac stanzas to a sucking-pig – a Hymn on Washing-day – Sonnets to one's grandmother – or Pindarics on gooseberry-pye; and yet, we are afraid, it will not be quite easy to convince Mr Wordsworth, that the same ridicule must infallibly attach to most of the pathetic pieces in these volumes. To satisfy our readers, however, as to the justice of this and our other anticipations, we shall proceed, without further preface, to lay before them a short view of their contents.

The first is a kind of ode 'to the Daisy,' – very flat, feeble, and affected; and in a diction as artificial, and as much encumbered with heavy expletives, as the theme of an unpractised schoolboy. The two following stanzas will serve as a specimen.

[Quotes 'To the Daisy', ('In youth from rock to rock I went . . .') *PW*, II, pp. 135–6 and footnotes, ll. 9–24; *Poems 1807*, p. 10, ll. 9–24:

> When soothed a while by milder airs . . .
> When such are wanted.]

The scope of the piece is to say, that the flower is found every where; and that it has suggested many pleasant thoughts to the author – some chime of fancy '*wrong or right*' – some feeling of devotion '*more or less*' – and other elegancies of the same stamp. It ends with this unmeaning prophecy.

> Thou long the poet's praise shalt gain;
> Thou wilt be more beloved by men
> In times to come; thou not in vain
> Art Nature's favourite.
> [To the Daisy', *PW*, II, p. 138, ll. 77–80; *Poems 1807*,
> p. 14, ll. 77–80]

The next is called 'Louisa,' and begins in this dashing and affected manner.

> I met Louisa in the shade;
> And, having seen that lovely maid,
> *Why should I fear to say*
> That she is ruddy, fleet, and *strong*;
> *And down the rocks can leap along,*
> Like rivulets in May?
>   I. 7.

Does Mr Wordsworth really imagine that this is at all more natural or engaging than the ditties of our common song writers?

A little farther on we have another original piece, entitled, 'The Redbreast and the Butterfly,' of which our readers will probably be contented with the first stanza. [Quotes stanza.] This, it must be confessed, is 'Silly Sooth' in good earnest. The three last lines seem to be downright raving.

By and by, we have a piece of namby-pamby 'to the Small Celandine,' which we should almost have taken for a professed imitation of one of Mr Philips's prettyisms. Here is a page of it.

> Comfort have thou of thy merit,
> Kindly, unassuming spirit!
> Careless of thy neighbourhood,
> Thou dost show thy pleasant face
> On the moor, and in the wood,
> In the lane; – there's not a place,
> Howsoever mean it be,
> But 'tis good enough for thee.
> Ill befal the yellow flowers,
> Children of the flaring hours!
> Buttercups, that will be seen,
> Whether we will see or no;
> Others, too, of lofty mien;
> They have done as worldings do,
> Taken praise that should be thine,
> Little, humble Celandine!
>> [To the Small Celandine', *PW*, II, pp. 143–4,
>> ll. 41–56; *Poems 1807*, p. 33, ll. 41–56]

After talking of its 'bright coronet',

> And its arch and wily ways,
> And its store of other praise,
>> [To the Same Flower', *PW*, II, p. 145, ll. 31–2;
>> *Poems 1807*, p. 37, ll. 31–2][1]

the ditty is wound up with this piece of babyish absurdity,

> Thou art not beyond the moon,
> But a thing 'beneath our shoon;'
> Let, as old Magellan did,
> Others roam about the sea;
> Build who will a pyramid;
> Praise it is enough for me,

If there be but three or four
Who will love my little flower.
[*Ibid.*, *PW*, II, p. 146, ll. 49–56;
Poems 1807, p. 38, ll. 41–8]

After this come some more manly lines on 'The Character of the Happy Warrior,' and a chivalrous legend on 'The Horn of Egremont Castle,' which, without being very good, is very tolerable, and free from most of the author's habitual defects. Then follow some pretty, but professedly childish verses, on a kitten playing with the falling leaves. There is rather too much of Mr Ambrose Philips here and there in this piece also; but it is amiable and lively.

Further on, we find an 'Ode to Duty,' in which the lofty vein is very unsuccessfully attempted. This is the concluding stanza.

Stern lawgiver! yet thou dost wear
The Godhead's most benignant grace;
Nor know we any thing so fair
As is the smile upon thy face;
Flowers laugh before thee on their beds;
And fragrance in thy footing treads;
Thou dost preserve the stars from wrong;
And the most ancient heavens through thee are fresh and strong.
['Ode to Duty', *PW*, IV, p. 86. ll. 49–56; *Poems 1807*, p. 81, ll. 49–56]

The two last lines seem to be utterly without meaning; at least we have no sort of conception in what sense *Duty* can be said to keep the old skies *fresh*, and the stars from wrong.

The next piece, entitled 'The Beggars,' may be taken, we fancy, as a touchstone of Mr Wordsworth's merit. There is something about it that convinces us it is a favourite of the author's; though to us, we will confess, it appears to be a very paragon of silliness and affectation. Our readers shall have the greater part of it. It begins thus.

She had a tall man's height, or more;
No bonnet screen'd her from the heat;
A long drab-coloured cloak she wore,
A mantle reaching to her feet:
What other dress she had I could not know;
Only she wore a cap that was as white as snow.
['The Beggars', *PW*, II, p. 222, ll. 1–6; *Poems 1807*,
p. 85, ll. 1–6]

Before me begging did she stand,
Pouring out sorrows like a sea;
Grief after grief: – on English land
Such woes I knew could never be;
And yet a boon I gave her; for the creature
Was beautiful to see; a weed of glorious feature!
[*Ibid.*, *PW*, II, p. 223, ll. 13–18; *Poems 1807*, p. 86, ll. 13–8]

The poet, leaving this interesting person, falls in with two ragged boys at play, and 'like that woman's face as gold is like to gold.' Here is the conclusion of this memorable adventure.

They bolted on me thus, and lo!
Each ready with a plaintive whine;
Said I, 'Not half an hour ago
Your mother has had alms of mine.'
'That cannot be,' one answered, 'She is dead.'
'Nay but I gave her pence, and she will buy you bread.'

'She has been dead, Sir, many a day.'
'Sweet boys, you're telling me a lie;
It was your mother, as I say – '
And in the twinkling of an eye,
'Come, come!' cried one; and, without more ado,
Off to some other play they both together flew.
[*Ibid.*, *PW*, II, p. 224, see footnotes, ll. 37–48;
Poems 1807, p. 87, ll. 31–42]

'Alice Fell' is a performance of the same order. The poet, driving into Durham in a postchaise, hears a sort of scream; and, calling to the post-boy to stop, finds a little girl crying on the back of the vehicle.

'My cloak!' the word was last and first,
And loud and bitterly she wept,
As if her very heart would burst;
And down from off the chaise she leapt.

'What ails you, child?' she sobb'd, 'Look here!'
I saw it in the wheel entangled,
A weather beaten rag as e'er
From any garden scarecrow dangled.
['Alice Fell', *PW*, I, p. 233, ll. 21–8; *Poems 1807*,
pp. 93–4, ll. 21–8]

They then extricate the torn garment, and the good-natured bard takes the child into the carriage along with him. The narrative proceeds –
[Quotes *ibid.*, *PW*, I, p. 234, ll. 41–60; *Poems 1807*, pp. 95–6, ll. 41–60:

> 'My child, in Durham do you dwell?' . . .
> The little orphan, Alice Fell!]

If the printing of such trash as this be not felt as an insult on the public taste, we are afraid it cannot be insulted.

After this follows the longest and most elaborate poem in the volume, under the title of 'Resolution and Independence.' The poet, roving about on a common one fine morning, falls into pensive musings on the fate of the sons of song, which he sums up in this fine distich.

> We poets in our youth begin in gladness;
> But thereof comes in the end despondency and madness.
> ['Resolution and Independence', *PW*, II, p. 236, ll. 48–9;
> *Poems 1807*, p. 100, ll. 48–9]

In the midst of his meditations –

> I saw a man before me unawares:
> The oldest man he seemed that ever wore grey hairs.
> [*Ibid.*, *PW*, II, p. 237, ll. 55–6; *Poems 1807*, p. 100, ll. 55–6]

> Motionless as a cloud the old man stood;
> That heareth not the loud winds when they call;
> And moveth altogether, if it move at all.
> At length, himself unsettling, he the pond
> Stirred with his staff, and fixedly did look
> Upon the muddy water, which he conn'd,
> As if he had been reading in a book:
> And now such fredom as I could I took;
> And, drawing to his side, to him did say,
> 'This morning gives us promise of a glorious day.'
> [*Ibid.*, *PW*, II, pp. 237–8, ll. 75–84; *Poems 1807*, p. 102, ll. 82–91]

> 'What kind of work is that which you pursue?
> This is a lonesome place for one like you.'
> He answer'd me *with pleasure and surprise*;
> And there was, while he spake, a fire about his eyes.
> [*Ibid.*, *PW*, II, p. 238, ll. 88–91; *Poems 1807*, p. 103, ll. 95–8]

> He told me *that he to this pond had come
> To gather leeches*, being old and poor:

Employment hazardous and wearisome!
And he had many hardships to endure:
From pond to pond he roam'd, from moor to moor,
Housing, with God's good help, by choice or chance:
And in this way he gain'd an honest maintenance.
[*Ibid.*, *PW*, II, p. 239, ll. 99–105; *Poems 1807*, p. 103, ll. 106–12]

Notwithstanding the distinctness of this answer, the poet, it seems, was so wrapped up in his own moody fancies, that he could not attend to it.

And now, not knowing what the old man had said,
My question eagerly did I renew,
'How is it that you live, and what is it you do?'
He with a smile did then his words repeat;
And said, that, *gathering leeches*, far and wide
He travelled; stirring thus *about his feet*
The waters of the ponds where they abide.
'*Once I could meet with them on every side*;
But they have dwindled long by slow decay;
Yet still I persevere, and find them where I may.'
[*Ibid.*, *PW*, II, p. 239, ll. 118–26; *Poems 1807*, pp. 104–5,
ll. 124–33]

This very interesting account, which he is lucky enough at last to comprehend, fills the poet with comfort and admiration; and, quite glad to find the old man so cheerful, he resolves to take a lesson of contentedness from him; and the poem ends with this pious ejaculation –

'God,' said I, 'be my help and stay secure;
I'll think of the leech-gatherer on the lonely moor.'
[*Ibid.*, *PW*, II, p. 240, ll. 139–40; *Poems 1807*, p. 105, ll. 146–7]

We defy the bitterest enemy of Mr Wordsworth to produce any thing at all parallel to this from any collection of English poetry, or even from the specimens of his friend Mr Southey. The volume ends with some sonnets, in a very different measure, of which we shall say something by and by.

The first poems in the second volume were written during a tour in Scotland. The first is a very dull one about Rob Roy; but the title that attracted us most was 'an Address to the Sons of *Burns*, after visiting their Father's Grave.' Never was any thing, however, more miserable. This is one of the four stanzas.

Strong bodied if ye be to bear
Intemperance with less harm, beware!
But if your father's wit ye share,
 Then, then indeed,
Ye sons of Burns! for watchful care
 There will be need,
 ['To the Sons of Burns', *PW*, III, p. 70 and footnotes,
 ll. 13–18; *Poems 1807*, p. 203, ll. 7–12]

The next is a very tedious, affected performance, called 'the Yarrow Unvisited.' The drift of it is, that the poet refused to visit this celebrated stream, because he had 'a vision of his own' about it, which the reality might perhaps undo; and, for this no less fantastical reason –

Should life be dull, and spirits low,
'Twill soothe us in our sorrow,
That earth has something yet to show,
The bonny holms of Yarrow!
 ['Yarrow Unvisited', *PW*, III, p. 85, ll. 61–4; *Poems 1807*,
 p. 209, ll. 61–4]

After this we come to some ineffable compositions, which the poet has simply entitled, 'Moods of my own Mind.' One begins –

O Nightingale! thou surely art
A creature of a fiery heart –
 ['O Nightingale! Thou surely art', *PW*, II, p. 214,
 ll. 1–2; *Poems 1807*, p. 216, ll. 1–2]

It is afterwards 'a hope;' and 'a love;' and, finally,

O blessed *bird*! the earth we pace
Again appears to be
An unsubstantial, faery place,
That is fit home for thee!
 ['To the Cuckoo', *PW*, II, p. 208, ll. 29–32;
 Poems 1807, p. 233, ll. 29–32]

After this there is an address to a butterfly, whom he invited to visit him, in these simple strains –

This plot of orchard-ground is ours;
My trees they are, my sister's flowers;
Stop here whenever you are weary.
 ['To a Butterfly', *PW*, II, p. 23, ll. 10–2; *Poems 1807*,
 p. 235, ll. 10–12]

We come next to a long story of a 'Blind Highland Boy,' who lived near an arm of the sea, and had taken a most unnatural desire to venture on that perilous element. His mother did all she could to prevent him; but one morning, when the good woman was out of the way, he got into a vessel of his own, and pushed out from the shore.

> In such a vessel ne'er before
> Did human creature leave the shore.
> ['The Blind Highland Boy', *PW*, III, p. 91, ll. 101–2;
> *Poems 1807*, p. 246, ll. 101–2]

And then we are told, that if the sea should get rough, 'a beehive would be ship as safe.' 'But say, what was it?' a poetical interlocutor is made to exclaim most naturally; and here followeth the answer, upon which all the pathos and interest of the story depend.

> A Household Tub, like one of those
> Which women use to wash their clothes!!
> [*Ibid.*, *PW*, III, p. 91, in footnotes, ll. 113–4; *Poems 1807*,
> p. 246, ll. 113–4]

This, it will be admitted, is carrying the matter as far as it will well go; nor is there any thing, – down to the wiping of shoes, or the evisceration of chickens, – which may not be introduced in poetry, if this is tolerated. A boat is sent out and brings the boy ashore, who being tolerably frightened we suppose, promises to go to sea no more; and so the story ends.

Then we have a poem; called 'the Green Linnet,' which opens with the poet's telling us,

> A whispering leaf is now my joy,
> And then a bird will be the *toy*
> That both my fancy *tether*.
> ['The Green Linnet', *PW*, II, p. 140 in footnotes,
> ll. 6–8; *Poems 1807*, p. 253, ll. 6–8]

and closes thus –

> While thus before my eyes he gleams,
> A brother of the leaves he seems;
> When in a moment forth *he teems*
> His little song in gushes:

197

As if it pleas'd him to disdain
And mock the form which he did feign,
While he was dancing with the train
Of leaves among the bushes.
[*Ibid.*, *PW*, II, pp. 140–1 in footnotes, ll. 33–40;
Poems 1807, p. 255, ll. 33–40]

The next is called 'Star Gazers.' A set of people peeping through a telescope, all seem to come away disappointed with the sight; whereupon thus sweetly moralizeth our poet.

Yet, showman, where can lie the cause? Shall thy implement
have blame,
A boaster, that when he is tried, fails, and is put to shame?
Or is it good as others are, and be their eyes in fault?
Their eyes, or minds? or, finally, is this resplendent vault?
['Star Gazers', *PW*, II, p. 219, ll. 9–12; *Poems 1807*, p. 262, ll. 9–12]

Or, is it rather, that conceit rapacious is and strong,
And bounty never yields so much but it seems to do her wrong?
Or is it, that when human souls a journey long have had,
And are returned into themselves, they cannot but be sad?
[*Ibid.*, *PW*, II, p. 219, ll. 17–20; *Poems 1807*, p. 262, ll. 17–20]

There are then some really sweet and amiable verses on a French lady, separated from her own children, fondling the baby of a neighbouring cottager; – after which we have this quintessence of unmeaningness, entitled, 'Foresight.'[Quotes stanzas 1 and 3.]
Afterwards come some stanzas about an echo repeating a cuckoo's voice; here is one for a sample –

Whence the voice? from air or earth?
This the cuckoo cannot tell;
But a startling sound had birth,
As the bird must know full well.
['Yes, it was the mountain Echo', *PW*, II, pp. 265–6 in
footnotes, ll. 4–7; *Poems 1807*, p. 297, ll. 5–9]

Then we have Elegiac stanzas 'to the Spade of a friend,' beginning –

Spade! with which Wilkinson hath till'd his lands,

– but too dull to be quoted any further.

After this there is a Minstrel's Song, on the Restoration of Lord Clifford the Shepherd, which is in a very different strain of poetry; and then the volume is wound up with an 'Ode,' with no other title but the motto, *Paulo majora canamus.*[2] This is, beyond all doubt, the most illegible and unintelligible part of the publication. We can pretend to give no analysis or explanation of it; – our readers must make what they can of the following extracts.

[Quotes 'Ode: Intimations of Immortality', *PW*, IV, p. 280, ll. 51–7; *Poems 1807*, p. 324, ll. 51–7; and *PW*, IV, pp. 283–4, ll. 130–68; *Poems 1807*, pp. 328–30, ll. 132–70:

> – But there's a tree, of many one . . .
> Where is it now, the glory and the dream?
> . . .
> O joy! that in our embers . . .
> And hear the mighty waters rolling evermore.]

We have thus gone through this publication, with a view to enable our readers to determine, whether the author of the verses which have now been exhibited, is entitled to claim the honours of an improver or restorer of our poetry, and to found a new school to supersede or new-model all our maxims on the subject. If we were to stop here, we do not think that Mr Wordsworth, or his admirers, would have any reason to complain; for what we have now quoted is undeniably the most peculiar and characteristic part of his publication, and must be defended and applauded if the merit or originality of his system is to be seriously maintained. In our own opinion, however, the demerit of that system cannot be fairly appreciated, until it be shown, that the author of the bad verses which we have already extracted, can write good verses when he pleases; and that, in point of fact, he does always write good verses, when, by any accident, he is led to abandon his system, and to transgress the laws of that school which he would fain establish on the ruin of all existing authority.

The length to which our extracts and observations have already extended, necessarily restrains us within more narrow limits in this part of our citations; but it will not require much labour to find a pretty decided contrast to some of the passages we have already detailed. The song on the restoration of Lord Clifford is put into the mouth of an ancient minstrel of the family; and in composing it, the author was led, therefore, almost irresistibly to adopt the manner and phraseology that is understood to be connected with that sort of composition, and to throw aside his own babyish incidents and fantastical sensibilities. How he has succeeded, the reader will be able to judge from the few following extracts. The poem opens in this spirited manner –

> High in the breathless hall the Minstrel sate,
> And Emont's murmur mingled with the song. –
> The words of ancient time I thus translate,
> A festal strain that hath been silent long,
>
> 'From town to town, from tower to tower,
> The red rose is a gladsome flower.
> Her thirty years of winter past,
> The red rose is revived at last;
> She lifts her head for endless Spring,
> For everlasting blossoming!'
> ['Brougham Castle', *PW*, II, p. 254, ll. 1–10; *Poems 1807*,
> p. 302, ll. 1–10]

After alluding, in a very animated manner, to the troubles and perils which drove the youth of the hero into concealment, the minstrel proceeds –

[Quotes extensively: *ibid.*, PW ii. p. 256–9, ll. 87–101, ll. 138–60 and ll. 165–72; *Poems 1807*, pp. 307–12, ll. 89–104, ll. 142–64 and ll. 169–76.]

All English writers of sonnets have imitated Milton; and, in this way, Mr Wordsworth, when he writes sonnets, escapes again from the trammels of his own unfortunate system; and the consequence is, that his sonnets are as much superior to the greater part of his other poems, as Milton's sonnets are superior to his. We give the following 'On the Extinction of the Venetian Republic.'

[Quotes 'Once did She hold the gorgeous East in fee', *PW*, III, p. 111; *Poems 1807*, p. 140; and 'Milton! thou should'st be living at this hour', *PW*, III, p. 116; *Poems 1807*, p. 148.]

We make room for this other; though the four first lines are bad, and 'week-day man' is by no means a Miltonic epithet.

[Quotes 'I griev'd for Buonaparte', *PW*, III, p. 110; *Poems 1807* p. 138.]

When we look at these, and many still finer passages, in the writings of this author, it is impossible not to feel a mixture of indignation and compassion, at that strange infatuation which has bound him up from the fair exercise of his talents, and withheld from the public the many excellent productions that would otherwise have taken the place of the trash now before us. Even in the worst of these productions, there are, no doubt, occasional little traits of delicate feeling and original fancy; but these are quite lost and obscured in the mass of childishness and insipidity with which they are incorporated; nor can any thing give us a more melancholy view of the debasing effects of this miserable theory, than that it has given ordinary men a right to wonder at the folly and presumption of a man gifted like Mr Wordsworth, and made him appear, in his second avowed publication, like a bad imitator of the worst of his former productions.

We venture to hope, that there is now an end of this folly; and that, like other follies, it will be found to have cured itself by the extravagances resulting from its unbridled indulgence. In this point of view, the publication of the volumes before us may ultimately be of service to the good cause of literature. Many a generous rebel, it is said, has been reclaimed to his allegiance by the spectacle of lawless outrage and excess presented in the conduct of the insurgents; and we think there is every reason to hope, that the lamentable consequences which have resulted from Mr Wordsworth's open violation of the established laws of poetry, will operate as a wholesome warning to those who might otherwise have been seduced by his example, and be the means of restoring to that antient and venerable code its due honour and authority.

EDITOR'S NOTES

1. Jeffrey seems to read the two poems addressed to the Celandine as one.
2. Virgil, Eclogue IV, I: 'let us sing of somewhat greater things'.

99.

Unsigned review, *The Satirist or Monthly Meteor*, November 1807, I, 188–91

Instead of occupying two duodecimo volumes of wire-wove and hot-pressed paper, with a beautiful type and a large margin, these poems would have been more appropriately invested with a fine gilt wrapping, adorned with wooden cuts, and printed and bound uniformly in all respects with Mother Bunch's tales and Mother Goose's melodies. The author must indeed have been strongly impressed with the truth of the poetical aphorism,

> Men are but *children* of a larger growth,

when he thought his odes to '*Small* Celandines,' 'Daisies,' and 'Butter-flies;' and his silly stories of 'Alice Fell and her Cloak,' 'the Sailor's Mother and the Linnet,' &c. &c. could for a moment gratify the taste of an *adult* public, or stand the inquiry of *mature* criticism.

This gentleman published two volumes of Lyric Ballads some years ago, which were composed on a system of his own: as if poetry was a mechanical art, and performed its operations by certain regulated processes, and not an appeal to the hearts and feelings of mankind. Of this grand system of poetry, which was thus first discovered by Mr. William Wordsworth, about the year of our Lord 1800 and was of course altogether unknown to Homer, Virgil, Shakspeare, Milton, and Dryden, the grand principle was, that nature could only be represented with fidelity by a close imitation of the language, and a constant adoption of the phrases, made use of by persons in the lowest stages of life: as if language were not entirely factitious and arbitrary; as if men of all ranks and situations were not the creatures of habit; as if the expressions of the meanest individuals were not the result of the education which they receive, while those of the higher orders are rendered natural by long usage to the well-informed and accomplished part of mankind.

With its usual sense and good temper the world laughed at the system, without denying justice to Mr. Wordsworth's merit as a poet. The gossipping style of those productions, in which his practice corresponded with his theory, was the object of universal ridicule; but whenever he forgot his system, and consulted his feelings, he displayed genuine talent, and excited more than common interest. We are sorry to say that, in the present publication, he has given a convincing proof of the pertinacious sincerity of his opinions as a critic, by suffering the most humiliating martyrdom in his reputation as a poet.

Fond as he is of the words *nature, modesty, simplicity*, &c. this author perpetually betrays the most magnificent opinion of his own powers. No image can present itself to his eye, no observation, no whim, no fancy, however idle or transitory, can pass through his mind without deriving importance from its accidental contact with so *great a genius*. If a certain *ex-chancellor* were to write a book of the same size, it could not contain a greater number of *I*'s and *me*'s. Almost a ludicrous contrast is produced between the swelling self-sufficiency of the writer, and the extreme insignificance of the object described. He thinks it worth while to give a tame matter-of-fact account of some daffodils blown about with the wind, because he thought of them afterwards; and we may observe generally, that the uninteresting nature of all the appearances he dwells upon, proves the interest which he attaches to himself and his own character. Then he promises us a great effort, a mighty poem, a production that he and his country are to be proud of. We do not perhaps estimate this gentleman's intellect quite so highly as he does himself; yet we certainly think him capable of more than he has yet achieved; and confess, at the same time, that in some instances he has achieved much. But we entertain serious doubts whether a long-indulged habit of such drivelling nonsense as fills with emptiness the far larger part of the volumes now before us, may not incapacitate him from producing any work that shall deserve to be ranked among the higher order of poems. We shall be happy if Mr. W. attends to this friendly caution.

We rarely peruse a modern poem without forming an earnest wish that we had the power of supplying the English *Gradus* with a commodity of new rhymes; and few versifiers would profit more by such an acquisition than Mr. Wordsworth. With all his high pretensions to a pure and unsophisticated phraseology, his sacrifices of sense to sound are numerous and inhuman. The *Small* Celandine is said to be as lively as a *leveret!* that the corresponding line may end with 'nature's *favourite.*' *Twitter* and *glitter* are well enough as mere rhymes; but what words to be placed in the most emphatical part of a line! The Sky-lark, which is honoured by a very wild address, has much too good a taste and too musical an ear to be pleased with the following congratulatory compliment:

> Happy, happy *liver*,
> *With a soul as strong as a mountain river,*
> Pouring forth thanks to the Almighty giver!
> ['To a Sky-Lark', *PW*, II, p. 142, ll. 22–4; *Poems 1807*,
> p. 89, ll. 22–4]

Query. Does the word *liver* here mean a living animal, or a part of the physical body? The use of it in the latter sense is new in our language, but not less elegant on that account. In the former sense the word is not English. Whichever is the true interpretation (which must be left for the consideration of future commentators) the reviewer may truly say with Horace,

203

— Meum
Fervens difficili bile tumet jecur.'

My heated liver swells with bile,
To witness so absurd a style.

What does the reader say to the following lines?

There's a nightingale[1] and two or three *thrushes*,
And a noise of wind that *rushes*,
And a noise of water that *gushes*.
['The sun has long been set', *PW*, IV, p. 9, ll. 5–7; *Poems 1807*,
p. 215, ll. 5–7]

For our own part, we prefer the versification of Master Stephen's posy.

Though fancy sleep,
My love is deep.

Answer. – The deeper the sweeter,
I'll be judged by St. Peter.

Young Knowell. – What has St. Peter to do with this affair?
Master Stephen. – Oh, I put in St. Petre for the sake of the metre.

We have expressed a favourable opinion of Mr. Wordsworth's powers, if
they were vigorously exerted and properly directed; and we admit that a
very small part of the contents of this volume do him honour. The *Happy
Warrior*, though bald, clumsy, and affectedly abstract in the terms
employed, is in a noble strain of thought and feeling. Some of the sonnets also deserve high praise as poetical compositions. But we are sorry
to feel it our duty to remark, that these occasional exhibitions of talent
render him the more inexcusable for having obtruded so much miserable
trash upon the public.

EDITOR'S NOTE

1. The reviewer misquotes; the line should read, 'There's a cuckoo and two or
three thrushes'.

100. James Montgomery (1771–1854)

Letter, unsigned review, memoir and reminiscence, 1807–1812

Montgomery was a dissenter, religious poet, and editor of the Sheffield newspaper, the *Iris*.

a. Letter to Daniel Parken, October or November 1807

In this letter Montgomery explained to Daniel Parken, the editor of the *Eclectic*, his reluctance to undertake the review, partly through the pressure of his own writing, and partly because public opinion was already hostile to Wordsworth:

I am almost sure that you and I differ very widely in our opinions concerning Wordsworth's talents, and perhaps more concerning his performances. My free, sincere, and utterly unbiassed sentiments I send you, not at all dreading your displeasure, because I hold a poet's merits in higher estimation than you do. I know that when you engage me to review any work, it is my own judgment that you require me to exercise, and you do not expect that it shall always be in consonance with yours. I feel exceeding great reluctance to censure the works of a man of high and noble genius, however unworthy of him, because I am aware that the vivid imagination of poets, which I doubt not is always accompanied with equal self-complacency, often seduces them into errors which they know not to be such, but mistake them for excellencies of the purest order, when they are nothing but delirious wanderings from truth and nature. Yet it is hard to punish them for such follies, as if they had been guilty of crimes: lenity is not the character of any existing Review, nor are any of our periodical critics too lavish of praise. I hope that your readers will find as much rigour of censure in this article as will reconcile them to the warmth of commendation which I have most honestly and heartily bestowed on Wordsworth's undeniable merits. The cry is up; and it is the fashion to yelp him down. I belong not to the pack, nor will I wag my tongue or my tail, on any occasion, to please the multitude. I am conscious of no personal partiality to prejudice me in favour of Wordsworth. I am sure the poetry of two men cannot differ much more widely than his does from mine. I hate his baldness and vulgarity of phrase, and I doubt not he equally detests the splendour and foppery of mine; but I feel the pulse of poetry beating through every vein of thought in all his compositions, even in his most pitiful, puerile, and affected pieces. To *you* I need not add that his frigid mention of my name in his first note has not influenced me to speak more favourably of him than I otherwise should have done. It is a proud and almost contemptuous notice which he has taken of me and my 'Daisy' (I won't change *mine* for his *three daisies*), and was more calculated to mortify and provoke a jealous temper than to soothe and disarm one who had the power and the opportunity to humble a rival in the eye of the public. No! I am persuaded, in my own mind, that I have done him justice to the best of my knowledge. I only regret that you will probably derive less satisfaction from the perusal of this essay than you might have done had our opinions been in perfect harmony. You must not be alarmed at the apparent length; for though the first four pages are closely written, the following ones are loose, and the whole will make no more, I believe, than eight of yours at the most. I confess that I tore myself from poetry to criticism, on this occasion, with excessive reluctance. My mind was so alive with images and sentiments connected with my West Indian Poem, that I did violence to my most favourite feelings to undertake this review. I hope nobody but you, and my own binding promise, could have moved me to do it. You will probably find that this article is written with more than usual stiffness; but indeed I could not help it. Only half of my heart was engaged in it, and the other half has been repining all the while at the interruption and loss of time. This is not often the case; but the poem on which I am at present engaged has so deeply and divinely interested me, that it has been great self-denial to suspend my meditations on it just at this time, when I am in the very heart of it. I intended to complete it, if possible, within this year, and I do not yet despair. I can, however, very conscientiously say, that, under these circumstances, I have done my utmost to serve you in the composition of this critique, and I have endeavoured to make the extracts as interesting as possible. I have plucked the most exquisite flowers in Wordsworth's parterre to present to your readers. You yourself will not deny that some of these are very beautiful.

[John Holland and James Everett, *Memoirs of the Life and Writings of James Montgomery, Including Selections from His Correspondence, Remains in Prose and Verse, and Conversations on Various Subjects*, London, 1854–6, II, 183–5]

b. Montgomery's unsigned review in the *Eclectic*, January 1808, IV, 35–43

In this age of poetical experiment, Mr. Wordsworth has distinguished himself, by his 'Lyrical Ballads,' as one of the boldest and most fortunate adventurers in the field of innovation. Casting away, at once and entirely, all the splendid artifices of style, invented in the earliest ages by the fathers of poetry, and perpetuated among all classes and generations of their successors, he avowed, in his Preface to that work, that 'his principal object was to chuse incidents and situations from common life, and to relate and describe them throughout, as far as was possible, in a selection of language really used by men; and at the same time to throw upon them a certain colouring of imagination, whereby ordinary things should be presented to the mind in an unusual way; and further, and above all, to make these incidents and situations interesting by tracing in them, truly, though not ostentatiously, the primary laws of our nature; chiefly as far as regards the manner in which we associate ideas in a state of excitement.' Pref. p. vii. Were these volumes (the *Lyrical Ballads*, &c.) now before us for criticism, however we might admire and commend Mr. Wordsworth's ingenuity in the advancement and vindication of his theory of poetical phraseology; and however we might agree with him, so far as his system would restrict the multitude of epithets that frequently render verse too heavy for endurance, – we would certainly protest against the unqualified rejection of those embellishments of diction, suited to the elevation of enthusiastic thoughts equally above ordinary discourse and ordinary capacities, which essentially distinguish Poetry from Prose, and have been sanctioned by the successful usage of Bards in every age and nation, civilized or barbarous, on which the light of Song has shed its quickening, ennobling, and ameliorating beams. In dramatic verse, assuredly, the writer, through all his characters, should speak the truth of living nature: the language of violent passions should be simple, abrupt, impetuous, and sublime; that of the gentler affections, ardent, flowing, figurative, and beautifully redundant; while, in both instances, every colour of expression, every form of thought, which appeals only to the imagination, and touches not the heart, should be rigorously proscribed. But in narrative, descriptive, and ethic poetry, we know no law of nature, and we will acknowledge none of art, that forbids Genius to speak his mother-tongue, – a language which, in sound and structure, as well as in character and sentiment, exalts itself far above the models of common speech.

A Poet – we speak of him who is really such – is no ordinary man; (Mr. Wordsworth allows him '*more than usual organic sensibility*';) – nor are his compositions the prompt and spontaneous expressions of his own every-day feelings; (Mr. W. declares, that 'he must have thought

long and deeply, to produce poems to which any value can be attached':)
– No! they are the most hidden ideas of his soul, discovered in his
happiest moments, and appareled in his selectest language. Will such a
man array the most pure, sublime, and perfect conceptions of his
superior mind in its highest fervour, only with 'the real language of men
in a state of vivid excitement'. Compare the heroic narratives of Milton,
the magnificent descriptions of Thomson, the solemn musings of
Young, nay even the soliloquies, and frequently the speeches of Shakspeare, in which characters and passions are pourtrayed with unparalleled force and feeling; compare these with 'the real language of men' on
the very same subjects, or in the same situations, however animated,
interested, or excited they may be. The fact is, that poetical sensibility
will, on all occasions, except perhaps in the simple expression of the
highest degree of agony or rapture, suggest language more lively, affecting, and fervent, than passion itself can inspire in minds less tremblingly
alive to every touch of pain or pleasure. Hence the delight communicated by true poetry is generally more deeply transporting, than any that
could be derived from the unassisted contemplation of the objects themselves, which are presented to us by the magic of the author's art: of this
art his *language* is the master-secret; for by that charm he transfuses
into frigid imaginations his warmer feelings, and his brighter views, on
subjects and of things that would only indifferently affect them in nature
and reality.

Mr. Wordsworth is himself a living example of the power which a man
of genius possesses, of awakening unknown and ineffable sensations in
the hearts of his fellow-creatures. His *Cumberland Beggar, Tintern Abbey*,
his *Verses on the naming of Places*, and some other pieces in his former
volumes, have taught us new sympathies, the existence of which in our
nature had scarcely been intimated to us by any preceding poet. But Mr.
Wordsworth must be reminded, that in these, his most successful pieces,
he has attired his thoughts in diction of transcendent beauty. We will
quote two brief passages from *Tintern Abbey*.

[Quotes 'Tintern Abbey', *PW*, II, pp. 261–2, ll. 88–102, and p. 263, ll.
134–45; *LB (1798)*, p. 114, ll. 89–103, and pp. 115–6, ll. 135–46:

> —I have learn'd
> To look on Nature . . .
> And rolls thro' all things!
>
> . . .
>
> Therefore let the moon . . .
> Of tender joy wilt thou remember me!]

This is no more the language, than these are the thoughts, of men in general in a state of excitement: language more exquisitely elaborate, and thoughts more patiently worked out of the very marble of the mind, we rarely meet with in any writer either of verse or prose. For such tales as *Andrew Jones, The last of the Flock, Goody Blake and Harry Gill*, &c. 'the real language of men' may be employed with pleasing effect; but when Mr. Wordsworth would 'present *ordinary* things in an *unusual* way, by casting over them a certain colouring of imagination,' he is compelled very frequently to resort to splendid, figurative, and amplifying language. The following, among innumerable examples from the volumes before us, to which we are compelled reluctantly to turn, will prove that he sometimes succeeds admirably, and sometimes indifferently, in using this poetical language.

> This tiresome night, O Sleep! thou art to me
> *A fly*, that up and down himself doth shove
> *Upon a fretful rivulet*, now *above*,
> Now *on the water* vex'd with mockery.
> ['To Sleep' ('O gentle Sleep! do they belong to thee'), *PW*, III,
> p. 8, ll. 115–8; *Poems 1807*, p. 117, ll. 5–8]

> The winds that will be howling at all hours,
> And are *up gather'd* now, *like sleeping flowers*.
> ['The world is too much with us', *PW*, III, p. 19, ll. 6–7;
> *Poems 1807*, p. 130, ll. 6–7]

> It is a beauteous evening, calm and free;
> The holy time is *quiet as a nun*
> *Breathless with adoration*.
> ['It is a beauteous evening', *PW*, III, p. 17, ll. 1–3;
> *Poems 1807*, p. 131, ll. 1–3]

> Dear Child! dear Girl! that walkest with me here,
> If thou appear'st untouch'd by solemn thought,
> Thy nature is not therefore less divine:
> *Thou liest in Abraham's bosom all the year,*
> *And worshipp'st at the Temple's inner shrine,*
> God being with thee when we know it not.
> [*Ibid.*, *PW*, III, p. 17, ll. 9–14; *Poems 1807*, p. 131, ll. 9–14]

> *Flowers laugh before thee in their beds,*
> *And Fragrance in thy footing treads.*
> ['Ode to Duty', *PW*, IV, p. 86, ll. 9–14; *Poems 1807*,
> p. 81, ll. 53–4]

209

The *cataracts blow their trumpets* from the steep;
The *winds* come to me *from the fields of sleep.*
['Ode: Intimations of Immortality', *PW*, IV, p. 280, ll. 25, 28;
Poems 1807, p. 322, ll. 25, 28]

We need insist no more on the necessity of using, in poetry, a language different from and superior to 'the real language of men,' since Mr. Wordsworth himself is so frequently compelled to employ it, for the expression of thoughts which without it would be incommunicable.

These volumes are distinguished by the same blemishes and beauties as were found in their predecessors, but in an inverse proportion: the defects of the poet, in this performance, being as much greater than his merits, as they were less in his former publication. It is remarkable that we have not, among all the piebald miscellanies before us, a single example of that species of poetry, for which the author's theory of diction and his habits of thinking peculiarly qualify him. The *blank verse* was the glory of his former volumes; in these there is not a trace of it. But songs instead we have, and sonnets, and stories, of every length and form of versification, and of every style and character from sublimity to silliness. Most of these are mere reveries in rhyme, in which the Poet's mind seems to be delightfully dreaming, while his thoughts are romping at random, and playing all manner of mischievous pranks about him; assuming at pleasure the most antic shapes, tricking themselves with the gaudiest colours, sporting at large in every field of fancy, and spurning with gallant independence every rule of art and every sanction of precedent for the government of licentious genius. It would be in vain to attempt to characterize all the contents of these incomparable, and almost incomprehensible volumes. A more rash and injudicious speculation on the weakness or the depravity of the public taste has seldom been made; and we trust that its inevitable failure will bring back Mr. Wordsworth himself to a sense of his own dignity, as well as of the respect due to his readers. The public may often be wrong in its first judgements, but it is always right at last; and Mr. W. can have no hope in its final decision concerning the greater part of the pieces before us.

To do little things gracefully, is sometimes more difficult than to do great things well; but when done, what *are* they? Trifles, that only please by surprize, and only surprize for a moment. Mr. Wordsworth has attempted many little things in these volumes, and few indeed have rewarded him for his trouble. The following is perhaps the best of these.

[Quotes 'A Complaint' ('There is a change'), *PW*, IV, p. 34; *Poems 1807*,
p. 291.]

It would not be easy to quote the *worst*, as a contrast to the *best* of these trifles; the following is probably as bad as any, and almost as bad as can be written by a man of superior talents.

[Quotes 'The sun has long been set', *PW*, IV, p. 9; *Poems 1807*, p. 215.]

The stories in these volumes are generally inferior, both in subject and in handling, to those which Mr. Wordsworth formerly gave the public. *Alice Fell* only shews that it is possible to tell in verse what is scarcely worth relating in prose. *The Blind Boy* is younger brother to Mr. W.'s own inimitable *Ideot Boy*, but very far behind him in merits and accomplishments. The tale, intitled *Fidelity*, is on the same subject as Walter Scott's *Helvellyn*, (on the fate of a traveller who perished on that wild mountain, and whose body was found three months afterwards, with his Dog alive and watching beside his dead master;) and it proves that Mr. Wordsworth, when he pleases, can be as much inferior to another as to himself.

The Sonnets in point of imagery and sentiment, are perhaps the most poetical of all these motley productions; but they are exceedingly unequal, often obscure, and generally heavy in the motion of the verse: the lines too are frequently so intertwisted, that if they were not printed in lengths of ten syllables, it would be difficult to break them into metre at all. The following contains a noble thought, which is carried through to the last word, and is a rare example of excellence either in Mr. Wordsworth or any other English Sonnetteer.

[Quotes 'On the Extinction of the Venetian Republic', *PW*, III, p. 111; *Poems 1807*, p. 140.]

In Mr. Wordsworth's poetry, more perhaps than in that of any other man, we frequently find images and sentiments, which we have seen and felt a thousand times, without particularly *reflecting* on them, and which, when presented by him, flash upon us with all the delight and surprize of novelty.

> The Cattle are grazing,
> *Their heads never raising,*
> There are *forty feeding like one.*
> ['The cock is crowing', *PW*, II, p. 220, ll. 8–10;
> *Poems 1807*, p. 219, ll. 8–10]

> The Swan on still St. Mary's lake
> *Floats double*, Swan and Shadow!
> ['Yarrow Unvisited', *PW*, II, p. 84, ll. 43–4; *Poems 1807*,
> p. 208, ll. 43–4]

O Cuckoo! shall I call thee bird,
Or but a *wandering voice!*
['To the Cuckoo', *PW*, II, p. 207, ll. 3–4; *Poems 1807*,
p. 231, ll. 3–4]

Thrice welcome, darling of the Spring!
Even yet thou art to me
No Bird; but *an invisible thing,*
A voice, a mystery.

The same whom in my school-boy days
I listen'd to; *that Cry*
Which made me look a thousand ways:
In bush and tree and sky.
[*Ibid.*, *PW*, II, p. 207, ll. 13–20; *Poems 1807*,
p. 232, ll. 13–20]

The grass is bright with rain-drops; on the moors
The Hare is running races in her mirth:
And *with her feet* she from the plashy earth
Raises a mist; which, glittering in the sun,
Runs with her all the way, wherever she doth run.
['Resolution and Independence', *PW*, II, p. 235, ll. 10–14;
Poems 1807, p. 98, ll. 10–14]

Who, that after long absence has visited the scenes where he spent the days of childhood, and from which he was separated in youth, has not experienced both the expectation and the disappointment described in the following slovenly lines?

'Beloved Vale!' I said, 'when I shall con
Those many records of my childish years,
Remembrance of myself and of my peers
Will press me down: to think of what is gone
Will be an awful thought, if life have one.'
But when into the vale I came, no fears
Distress'd me; I look'd round, I shed no tears;
Deep thought, or awful vision, had I none.
By thousand petty fancies I was cross'd,
To see the trees, which I had thought so tall,
Mere dwarfs; the brooks so narrow, fields so small.
['"Beloved Vale!" I said', *PW*, III, pp. 2–3, ll. 1–11;
Poems 1807, p. 127, ll. 1–11]

A specimen of Mr Wordsworth's finest talent – that of *personal description* – may be found in a Poem, which we have not room to quote, though we consider it the best in the volume, intitled '*Resolution and Independence*.'

The last piece in this Collection is simply styled '*An Ode*,' and the reader is turned loose into a wilderness of sublimity, tenderness, bombast, and absurdity, to find out the subject as well as he can. The Poet assumes the doctrine of pre-existence, *(a doctrine which religion knows not, and the philosophy of the mind abjures)* and intimates that the happiness of childhood is the reminiscence of blessedness in a former state.

[Quotes 'Ode: Intimations of Immortality', *PW*, IV, p. 281, ll. 58–65; *Poems 1807*, pp. 324–5, ll. 58–65:

> Our birth is but a sleep and a forgetting . . .
> From God, who is our home.]

In allusion to these romantic and unwarranted speculations, he says, in the same Ode, that there are

[Quotes *ibid.*, *PW*, IV, p. 284, ll. 156–68; *Poems 1807*, p. 330, ll. 158–70:

> —Truths that wake
> To perish never . . .
> And hear the mighty waters rolling evermore.]

After our preliminary remarks on Mr. Wordsworth's theory of poetical language, and the quotations which we have given from these and his earlier compositions, it will be unnecessary to offer any further estimate or character of his genius. We shall only add one remark, which truth compels us to make, in spite of a partiality which we feel almost for the faults of such a writer as Mr. W. He says, in the preface to his former volumes, that 'each of the poems' contained therein 'has *a worthy purpose*.' Of the pieces now published he has said nothing: most of them seem to have been written *for* no purpose at all, and certainly *to* no good one.

c. Crabb Robinson's account of a meeting with Montgomery, 20 May 1812

The party was agreeable. Some conversation about Wordsworth. I was warm in his praise. Montgomery seemed not displeased with my eulogy, and in a *tête à tête* expressed his high admiration of him. 'The study of the human heart,' said Montgomery, 'is what I most delight in, and I know no writer so profound in all that respects the affections and feel-ings.' The Leech Gatherer i.e. *Resolution and Independence* he is a great admirer of, but dares hardly praise in company. *The Old Cumberland Beggar* he also referred to. I spoke severely of the *Eclectic* review of Wordsworth. He pleaded on behalf of it, and once again referred to it when I, addressing Montgomery, said he who so praised the better parts of Wordsworth has a right to censure what he does not love. 'And why not extend that to the *Eclectic?* said he. So that a suspicion occured to me of his being the author . . .

[*Henry Crabb Robinson on Books and their Writers*, ed. Edith J. Morley, 1938, I, 84]

d. Montgomery's account of the same meeting

'I entered,' said Montgomery to Mr. Everett, 'into a long argument on the principles of poetry laid down in the celebrated 'Preface,' showing that the poet was often most happy when he departed from his own rules. There was,' continued he, 'an amusing incident connected with *that* review. Not very long after its appearance, I was in London, where I met with Mr. Henry Crabb Robinson, a gentleman of taste, well known as a zealous admirer of Wordsworth, and who, among other topics of discourse, made some observations on Mr. Wordsworth's poetry; he expressed himself as being indignant at the treatment which his friend had received from the reviewers, descanting particularly on the critique in the 'Eclectic!' The writer of that article, he remarked, was the only person among the authors of all the reviews he had read who understood the character of Mr. Wordsworth's poetry, and yet it was evident, on the very face of the matter, that he was afraid, – that he had not *spirit* enough to speak out his full praise.' *Everett*: 'Did you make any reply?' *Montgomery*: 'Not I; – though that very silence would with some persons have been construed into at least a confession of complicity; but I suf-fered the remark to pass, as a matter of course.' *Everett*: 'Were you able to maintain your gravity during his observations?' *Montgomery*: 'O yes; though amused, I listened with perfect composure, conscious as I was of the justice of my critical remarks, and of the kindly spirit in which I had written them.' *Everett*: 'Wordsworth was certainly treated with unjust and indiscriminating severity by some of the reviewers.' *Montgomery*: 'There is no doubt of that. The truth is, Wordsworth's mental scope in his higher moods is too great for the generality of poetic readers. There is always one merit in him, – he follows nature. He is often extremely prosaic; but for this he is almost sure to reward you with deep thought. I was informed that when he saw my critique, and long before he knew by whom it was written, he acknowledged the justice of the general argument.'

[John Holland and James Everett, *Memoirs of the Life and Writings of James Montgomery, Including Selections from His Correspondence, Remains in Prose and Verse, and Conversations on Various Subjects*, London, 1854–6, II, 185–6]

101. Lucy Aikin (1781–1864)

Unsigned review, *Annual Review*, 1807 (published spring 1808), vi, 521–9

The review was generally attributed to Lucy Aikin's aunt, Mrs Barbauld, and clearly Wordsworth himself subscribed to this belief (Christopher Wordsworth, *Memoir of William Wordsworth*, 1851, I, 163). The Aikin family ceased to edit the *Annual Register* in 1808: Southey noted on 20 March 1809, 'the loss of the Aikins is a great gain to the work [*Annual Register*]. Miss Lucy's critiques upon poetry were absolutely nauseating' (*New Letters of Robert Southey*, ed. Kenneth Curry, 1965, I, 506). Crabb Robinson knew of the identity of the reviewer of Wordsworth's volume by 22 May 1814:

> We talked of Wordsworth. Miss Aikin wrote the review of the *Poems* in the *Annual Review*. She is an admirer, she says, of Wordsworth, at the same time that she censures his want of taste . . .
>
> (*Henry Crabb Robinson on Books and their Writers*,
> ed. Edith J. Morley, 1938, I, 143)

Wordsworth and his friends were especially irritated with Arthur Aikin, 'for having had the impudence to omit the reviewal of Wordsworth's poem which he received from me [Southey], and inserting an Aikinist one in its stead' (Letter from Southey to Tom Southey, 9 September 1808, Ms. British Library).

Mr. Wordsworth is a writer whose system and practice of poetry are both so entirely his own, that in order to appreciate as fairly as we wish to do, the value of these volumes, it will be necessary for us to enter somewhat at length into a discussion of the theory of the art. His own theory of it

215

the author has given in the preface to a former work, published before this review existed; and as we do not perceive that his style of writing has since undergone any material alteration, we shall refer to it without scruple, as containing the principles upon which the poems immediately before us have been composed.

On glancing the eye over Mr. Wordsworth's poems, the first thing that strikes the reader is, the extreme simplicity of their language: he may peruse page after page without meeting with any of those figures of speech which distinguish we do not say verse from prose, but a plain style from one that may be called cultured, or ornate. Should he however attribute this peculiarity to indolence or deficiency of skill, Mr. W. would complain of injustice, for he has anticipated the charge, and in the preface to 'Lyrical Ballads' has endeavoured to repel it. The highly metaphysical language employed in this preface, and the spirit of mysticism by which it is pervaded, render it somewhat difficult of comprehension, but this, as well as we can collect, is the substance of that portion of it which is to our present purpose.

It was his intention, he says, in his poems to take incidents and situations from humble life, and describe them in the real language of men in that class, only freed from its grosser vulgarisms. He has preferred such incidents and situations, because the feelings of persons in low life are stronger, less complex, and therefore more easy to be developed, than those of persons who move in a wider circle – their language he has preferred for similar reasons, and also because he thought that any departure from nature in this respect must weaken the interest of his poems, both as being a departure from nature, and because the language which the imagination of even the greatest poet suggests to him, must, in liveliness and truth, fall far short of that which is uttered by men in real life, and under the pressure of actual passions. All that is called poetic diction, he therefore despises, and has shunned with the same care that others seek it, convinced that a poet may give all the pleasure he wishes to do without its assistance. At the same time he has 'endeavoured to throw over his draughts a certain colouring of the imagination, whereby ordinary things should be presented to the mind in an unusual way, and further, and above all, to make these incidents and situations interesting by tracing in them, truly thought not ostentatiously, the primary laws of our nature chiefly as far, as regards the manner in which we associate ideas in a state of excitement.' This last expression savours to us of a jargon with which the public has long been surfeited, and it is evident that not a position is here advanced, which might not easily be combated; but as the practical success of a poet is the true test of the justness of his principles, we shall reserve our remarks on this head till we come to extracts. Anticipating an obvious question, why with his sentiments did he write in rhyme and measure? Mr. W. now proceeds sensibly enough to defend his practice in this respect on the ground of the pleasure which the experience of ages has proved these devices to be capable of affording – he adds, that 'from the tendency of metre to divest language in a certain degree of its reality, and throw a kind of half consciousness of unsubstantial existence over the whole composition, there is little doubt that more painfully pathetic incidents and situations may be endured in verse, especially in rhymed verse, than in prose' – He brings in proof, 'the reluctance with which we recur to the more distressing parts of the Gamester and Clarissa Harlowe, while Shakespeare's writings in the most pathetic scenes never act upon us as pathetic beyond the bounds of pleasure.' Is not Mr. W. aware that these very arguments might equally be urged in favour of that poetic diction which he is so anxious to banish from his pages, and that the same instances might be adduced in its support that he here brings in favour of metre? It is not poetical diction, much more than mere verse, which produces the difference here pointed out between the writings of Shakespeare, and those of More and Richardson? But Mr. W. is persuaded that he has absolutely established it as a principle that in the dramatic parts of his compositions a poet should employ no other language than such as nature would suggest to his characters, (which after all is a very vague direction, since nature is by no means uniform in her promptings of this kind, and education and local circumstances produce endless diversities of style and expression,) and he endeavours to show that even where the poet speaks in his own character, he should employ no other diction than that of good and select prose. He begins by defining a poet as a man 'enbued with more lively sensibilities, more enthusiasm and tenderness, who has a greater knowledge of human nature, and a more comprehensive soul, than are supposed to be common among mankind,' and in fine, as one chiefly distinguished from others, 'by a greater promptness to think and feel without immediate external excitement, and a greater power in expressing such thoughts and feelings as are thus excited in him.' These 'passions and thoughts, and feelings,' he affirms to be the same as those of other men; but even if they were not, he proceeds to insist, that as a poet does not write for poets, but for men in general, in order to excite rational sympathy, he must still express himself as other men do. Now it appears to us in the first place, that this definition of a poet is both imperfect and incorrect. It is only that of a person of strong sympathies, who possesses in an unusual degree the power of imagining and describing the feelings of other human beings. A good novel writer must be all this – a descriptive or lyric poet, though perfect in his kind, need not. But one who really deserves the name of a poet, must certainly add another faculty which is not even hinted at in this definition – we scarcely know how to name it, but it is that kind of fancy, akin to wit, which 'glancing from heaven to earth, from earth to heaven,' pervading, as it were, the whole world of nature and of art, snatches from each its beauteous images combines, adapts, arranges them by a magic of its own, peoples with them its new creations, and at length pours forth in one striking, brilliant, yet harmonious whole.

This faculty, which Mr. W. overlooks, is doubtless the true parent of that diction which he despises; nor will either the frigid reasonings of metaphysicians, or the still more frigid caricaturas and miserable apings of mere versifiers, ever deter the genuine poet from employing it; it is his native tongue, and he must speak it, or be dumb. It is idle and sophistical to contend that because he does not write to poets he must not write like a poet. Many there are who are capable of being moved to rapture by a picture of Raphael or Titian, though they themselves could never guide a pencil – many there are who can follow with their eye the boldest soarings of the Theban eagle, though nature has not lent to them even the rudiments of a wing. If men in general are to be supposed incapable of understanding any expressions but what they would themselves have used in similar circumstances, rich and figurative diction must indeed, on most occasions be proscribed, but let it be remembered that such an interdiction would curtail the eloquence of Burke no less than the poetry of Shakespeare; so sweeping a clause is this, so fatal to the scintillations of wit, and the sports of fancy. Our author afterwards speaks of poetry as a thing too high and sacred to be profaned by the addition of trifling ornaments of style: we cannot well understand what his notion of poetry is, after all, for he here plunges into the very depths of mysticism, but we suppose Virgil and Milton must have had some idea of its power and dignity, and it does appear to us somewhat ridiculous, not to say arrogant, in Mr. Wordsworth, to imagine that he has discovered any thing, either in the trivial incidents which he usually makes the subjects of his narrations, or in the moral feelings and deductions which he endeavours to associate with them, too sublime for the admission of such decorations as these masters have not deemed derogatory from the highest themes they ever touched. But we believe one great source of what we consider as the errors of this writer to be his failing to observe the distinction between rhetorical and poetical diction; the former it is that offends; but in his blind zeal he confounds both under the same note of reprobation. He quotes Dr. Johnson's paraphrase of, 'Go to the ant thou sluggard,' and justly stigmatizes it as 'a hubbub of words;' but is this a specimen of poetical diction? Surely not. It contains not one of those figures of speech, – similes, metaphors, allusions, and the like – which take their birth from that inventive, or combining, faculty which we mentioned above, but is tediously lengthened out by that accumulation of idle epithets, frivolous circumstances, and pompous and abstract terms, with which the rhetorician never fails, in prose or verse, to load his feeble and high sounding pages. It is this, this spirit of paraphrase and periphrasis, this idle parade of fine words, that is the bane of modern verse writing; let it be once thoroughly weeded of this, and it will be easy for the pruning hand of taste to lop away any redundancy of metaphor, personification, &c. which may still remain. Thus much for the system of Mr. Wordsworth, which appears to us a frigid and at the same time an extravagant one; we now proceed to examine what its practical application has produced; and whether our author has succeeded according to his intention, by giving us in plain rhymed and measured prose, matter so valuable and interesting as to be capable of affording pleasure equal, or superior, to that usually produced by poems of a similar class composed in a more ornate and polished style. We shall also examine how far the principle of association, on which many of the pieces are composed, appears to have been productive of beauties or defects.

The contents of these volumes may mostly be reduced under the following heads. Ballads, and narratives of incidents apparently from real life. Addresses to various natural objects – the sky-lark, daisy, &c. Sonnets. An ode or two. Certain little pieces entitled, 'Moods of my own mind,' and a few others of the sentimental and descriptive kind. From the narrative pieces we may select the following.

[Quotes 'Fidelity', *PW*, IV, p. 80; *Poems 1807*, p. 17.]

Here Mr. W. has certainly been fortunate in his subject; the incident is affecting, the scenery picturesque, but has he made a good poem of it, even on his own principles? Surely not. The language is not only prosaic, but generally flat, and in some parts absolutely mean; as in the two last lines of the first verse. The elipsis, 'For sake of which' is a vulgarism which cannot but offend the cultivated reader; and to call the noise of a fish leaping 'a lonely chear,' is certainly an absurdity which could never pass in prose – but, what is worse still, is the coldness and tameness of the sentiments; on the unfortunate man, scarcely one expression of commiseration is bestowed; and even the dog, the hero of the tale, is presented to the mind in so unimpassioned a manner that he excites little or no interest. On the whole, in verse or prose, we know not how the tale could have been more flatly related. But let us take another.

[Quotes 'Alice Fell', *PW*, I, p. 232; *Poems 1807*, p. 92.]

Mr. W. piques himself upon having had in view an end, a purpose, in all his narratives; but we confess if he has had one here, it is more than we can discover. The same remark applies to the 'Beggars,' and though the 'Sailor's mother,' and the piece termed 'Resolution and Independance,' have a more obvious drift, they still appear to us feeble, unimpressive, and intolerably prolix. The Blind Boy is a pretty tale for children; but little more. We cannot consider Mr. W. as much more fortunate in those addresses to natural objects where he attempts something more fanciful; though still in the same plain language.

[Quotes 'To a Sky-Lark', *PW* II, p. 141; *Poems 1807*, p. 88.]

We may here take occasion to remark that these pieces in general are extremely ill rhymed. Forced, imperfect, and double rhymes abounding to an offensive and sometimes ludicrous degree. We may also observe, that one who trusts so much to mere metre, should take a little more pains with it, and not shock our ears with such lines as,

> And though little troubled with sloth,
> Drunken Lark thou would'st be loth.

'Louisa,' exhibits some beautiful ideas disguised in quaint and ridiculous language.

[Quotes 'Louisa', *PW*, II, p. 28; *Poems 1807*, p. 15.]

The Sonnets, a portion of which are dedicated to liberty, are formed on the model of Milton's and have a certain stiffness – but they hold a severe and manly tone which cannot be in times like these too much listened to – they bear strong traces of feeling and of thought, and convince us that on worthy subjects this man can write worthily.

[Quotes sonnets: 'It is not to be thought of that the Flood', *PW*, III, p. 117; *Poems 1807*, p. 150; 'There is a bondage that is worse to bear', *PW*, III, p. 118; *Poems 1807*, p. 153; 'England! the time is come when thou should'st wean', *PW*, III, p. 119; *Poems 1807*, p. 155.]

One of the Odes to Duty, is a meanly written piece, with some good thoughts, the other is a highly mystical effusion, in which the doctrine of pre-existence is maintained. The pieces entitled Moods of my own Mind, are some of them very happy, some quite the reverse. When a man endeavours to make his reader enter into an association that exists in his own mind between daffodils waving in the wind, and laughter – or to teach him to see something very fine in the fancy of crowning a little rock with snow-drops; he fails, and is sure to fail; for it would be strange indeed if any one besides himself ever formed associations so capricious and entirely arbitrary. But when he takes for his theme the youthful feelings connected with the sight of a butterfly, and the song of the cuckoo, he has struck a right key, and will wake an answering note in the bosoms of all who have mimicked the bird or chaced the insect. There is an exquisiteness of feeling in some of these little poems that disarms criticism.

[Quotes 'To a Butterfly' ('Stay near me – do not take thy flight'), *PW*, I, p. 226; *Poems 1807*, p. 213; And 'To the Cuckoo', *PW*, II, p. 207; *Poems 1807*, p. 231.]

There are likewise some 'Elegiac Stanzas' of great pathos, and a perfectly original turn, which increase our regret at the quantity of mere gossip that this author has allowed to escape him.

We have now bestowed upon these volumes a survey more detailed and laborious than our usual practice, or, in some respects, their importance, might seem to require; but we were anxious to combat a system which appears to us so injurious to its author, and so dangerous to public taste.

Mr. W. doubtless possesses a reflecting mind, and a feeling heart; but nature seems to have bestowed on him little of the fancy of a poet, and a foolish theory deters him from displaying even that little. In addition to this, he appears to us to starve his mind in solitude. – Hence the undue importance he attaches to trivial incidents – hence the mysterious kind of view that he takes of human nature and human life – and hence, finally, the unfortunate habit he has acquired of attaching exquisite emotions to objects which excite none in any other human breast. He says himself in the concluding verse of his volumes,

> Thanks to the human heart by which we live,
> Thanks to its tenderness, its joys, its fears,
> To me the meanest flower that blows doth give,
> Thoughts that do often lie too deep for tears.

This is all very well; these are pleasures that we cannot estimate, and of which we should be sorry to deprive a humble recluse; we only wish to hint, that a lasting poetical reputation is not to be built on foundations so shadowy.

102.

Unsigned review, *The Cabinet*, or, *Monthly Report of Polite Literature*,
April 1808, III, 249–52

To those who interest themselves in the transactions of the literary
world, the publication of the present volumes will prove a source of uneas-
iness. They will feel hurt that a man of genius should disgrace himself
by such contemptible effusions, and the conduct of the publishers who
introduce such trash into the world, merely because a name of some
celebrity appears in the title page, whilst works of real merit by an
unknown author would be neglected by them, must also excite the
highest disgust.

Mr. Wordsworth possesses several of the most essential qualities of
the poet. He has a lively fancy, strong feelings, an imagination bold, and
sometimes even sublime, an originallity of expression, and has contemplated the scenery of nature for himself: but in taste he is deficient, and
has still to learn 'the last and greatest art, the art to blot.'[1]

Wanting this, his fancy frequently degenerates into conceit, his feeling
into puerile affectation, his sublimity into bombast, and his originallity
of expression into hardness and obscurity.

The present volumes probably contain a collection of the greatest
absurdities that, under the name of poetry, were ever offered to the
public; and when we have informed our readers that there are many,
many more such ridiculous puerilities as the following, we imagine they
will not be inclined to dispute our assertion.

[Quotes 'The sun has long been set', *PW*, IV, p. 9; *Poems 1807*, p. 215; and
'The cock is crowing', *PW*, II, p. 220; *Poems 1807*, p. 219.]

The above description is evidently from nature, but is rendered incapable
of giving pleasure, from the childish manner in which it is expressed: lest
these extracts should not be deemed sufficient, we have transcribed the
following pretty little story.

> Among all lovely things my love had been;
> Had noted well the stars, all flowers that grew
> About her home; but she had never seen
> A glow-worm, never one, *and this I knew*.
> Cunning fellow![2]
>
> While riding near her home one stormy night,
> A single glow-worm did I chance to espy;

I gave a fervent welcome to the sight,
And from my horse I leapt; *great joy had I.*
                                    Happy dog!

Upon a leaf the glow-worm did I lay,
To bear it with me through the stormy night:
And, as before, it shone without dismay
Albeit putting forth a fainter light.
                          Astonishing circumstance!

When to the dwelling of my love I came,
I went into the orchard quietly;
And left the glow-worm, *blessing it by name,*
Laid safely by itself, beneath a tree.
                              Admirable precaution!

The whole next day, I hoped, and hoped with fear;
At night the glow-worm shone beneath a tree:
I led my Lucy to the spot, *'look here!'*
Oh! joy it was for her, and joy for me!
                            Sympathetic innocence!

After giving the above, it cannot be supposed that we shall disgrace criticism by pointing out minute defects; when the body is past recovery, advice is useless.

Yet even amidst this mass of absurdities, 'these vomittings of a sickly brain,' may sometimes be perceived the traces of strong genius. – Amongst the sonnets are many beautiful compositions: the following, 'To sleep,' is natural, original, and poetical.

[Quotes 'Fond words have oft been spoken to thee, Sleep!', *PW*, III, p. 8; *Poems 1807*, p. 119.]

Those who have gazed on the beauties of the opening morn, will also read the following extract from the poem of 'Resolution and independence' with delight.

All things that love the sun are out of doors;
The sky rejoices in the morning's birth;
The grass is bright with rain drops; on the moors
The hare is running races in her mirth;
And with her feet she from the plashy earth
Raises a mist; which, glittering in the sun,
Runs with her all the way, wherever she doth run.

223

It is impossible to recall the verse which is given to the public: 'Non erit emisso reditus tibi.' yet we hope Mr. Wordsworth, in making a *future* collection of his poems, will reject the greater part of the present volumes. By the merit of his first publication, he had nearly established a theory of poetical simplicity; but we are fearful that by the *de*merit of this he has overthrown it. He has undoubtedly a poetical mind, but 'till it is refined by taste, his productions will be useless to the world, and disgraceful to himself.

EDITOR'S NOTES

1. Pope, *Satires*, v, 281.
2. The sarcastic comments at the close of each stanza were added by the reviewer.

103. Francis Jeffrey

Unsigned review of Crabb's *Poems* (1807), *Edinburgh Review*, April 1808, XII, 132–7

It is not quite fair, perhaps, thus to draw a detailed parallel between a living poet, and one whose reputation has been sealed by death, and by the immutable sentence of a surviving generation. Yet there are so few of his contemporaries to whom Mr Crabbe [*sic*] bears any resemblance, that we can scarcely explain our opinion of his merit, without comparing him to some of his predecessors. There is one set of writers, indeed, from whose works those of Mr Crabbe might receive all that elucidation which results from contrast, and from an entire opposition in all points of taste and opinion. We allude now to the Wordsworth's, and the Southeys, and Coleridges, and all that misguided fraternity, that, with good intentions and extraordinary talents, are labouring to bring back our poetry to the fantastical oddity and puling childishness of Withers, Quarles, or Marvel. These gentlemen write a great deal about rustic life, as well as Mr Crabbe; and they even agree with him in dwelling much on its discomforts; but nothing can be more opposite than the views they take of the subject, or the manner in which they execute their representation of them.

Mr Crabbe exhibits the common people of England pretty much as they are, and as they must appear to every one who will take the trouble of examining into their condition; at the same time that he renders his sketches in a very high degree interesting and beautiful, – by selecting what is most fit for description, – by grouping them into such forms as must catch the attention or awake the memory, – and by scattering over the whole, such traits of moral sensibility, of sarcasm, and of useful reflection, as every one must feel to be natural, and own to be powerful. The gentlemen of the new school, on the other hand, scarcely ever condescend to take their subjects from any description of persons that are at all known to the common inhabitants of the world; but invent for themselves certain whimsical and unheard of beings, to whom they impute some fantastical combination of feelings, and labour to excite our sympathy for them, either by placing them in incredible situations, or by some strained and exaggerated moralization of a vague and tragical description. Mr Crabbe, in short, shows us something which we have all seen, or may see, in real life; and draws from it such feelings and such reflections as every human being must acknowledge that it is calculated to excite. He delights us by the truth, and vivid and picturesque beauty of his representations, and by the force and pathos of the sensations with which we feel that they ought to be connected. Mr Wordsworth and his associates show us something that mere observation never yet suggested to any one. They introduce us to beings whose existence was not previously suspected by the acutest observers of nature, and excite an interest for them, more by an eloquent and refined analysis of their own capricious feelings, than by any obvious or very intelligible ground of sympathy in their situation. The common sympathies of our nature, and our general knowledge of human character, do not enable us either to understand, or to enter into the feelings of their characters. They are unique specimens and varieties of our kind, and must be studied under a separate classification. They have an idiosyncrasy, upon which all common occurrences operate in a peculiar manner; and those who are best acquainted with human nature, and with other poetry, are at a loss to comprehend the new system of feeling and of writing which is here introduced to their notice. Instead of the men and women of ordinary humanity, we have certain moody and capricious personages, made after the poet's own heart and fancy, – acting upon principles, and speaking in a language of their own. Thus, instead of employing the plain vulgar character, which may be read by all the world, these writers make use of a sort of cypher, which can only be learned with pains and study; and, dressing up all their persons in a kind of grotesque masquerade habit, they have given birth to a species of composition more fantastic and unnatural than a pastoral or an opera. Into this unnatural composition, however, they have introduced a great deal of eloquence and beauty, and have put many natural thoughts and touching expressions into the mouths of their imaginary persons. By this means, and by the novelty of their manner, they have seduced many into a great admiration of their genius, and even made some willing to believe, that their conception of character is in itself just and natural, and that all preceding writers have been in an error with regard to that great element of poetry. Many, to be sure, found it impossible to understand either their precepts or their example; and, unable to recognize the traits of our common nature in the strange habiliments with which these ingenious persons had adorned it, gave up the attempt in despair; and, recurring to easier authors, looked on with mixed wonder and contempt, while they were collecting the suffrages of their admirers. Many, however, did understand a part; and, in their raised imaginations, fancied that they admired the whole: while others, who only guessed at a passage here and there, laboured, by their encomiums, to have it thought that there was nothing which passed their comprehension.

Those who are acquainted with the Lyrical Ballads, or the more recent publication of Mr Wordsworth, will scarcely deny the justice of this representation; but in order to vindicate it to such as do not enjoy that inestimable advantage, we must beg leave to make a few hasty references to the former, and by far the least exceptionable of these productions.

A village schoolmaster, for instance, is a pretty common poetical character. Goldsmith has drawn him inimitably; so has Shenstone, with the slight change of sex; and Mr Crabbe, in two passages, has followed their footsteps. Now, Mr Wordsworth has a village schoolmaster also – a personage who makes no small figure in three or four of his poems. But by what traits is this worthy old gentleman delineated by the new poet? No pedantry – no innocent vanity of learning – no mixture of indulgence with the pride of power, and of poverty with the consciousness of rare acquirements. Every feature which belongs to the situation, or marks the character in common apprehension, is scornfully discarded by Mr Wordsworth, who represents this grey-haired rustic pedagogue as a sort of half crazy, sentimental person, overrun with fine feelings, constitutional merriment, and a most humorous melancholy. Here are the two stanzas in which this consistent and intelligible character is pourtrayed. The diction is at least as new as the conception.

226

The sighs which Mathew heard were sighs
   Of one tired out with *fear* and *madness*;
The tears which came to Mathew's eyes
   Were tears of light – *the oil of gladness.*

Yet sometimes, when the secret cup
   Of still and serious thought went round,
He seemed as if he *drank it up*,
   He felt with spirit so profound.

Thou *soul*, of God's best *earthly mould*, &c.
       ['Mathew', *PW*, IV, pp. 68–9, ll. 21–9; *LB (1800)*,
                    pp. 185–6, ll. 25–33]

A frail damsel is a character common enough in all poems; and one upon which many fine and pathetic lines have been expended. Mr Wordsworth has written more than three hundred lines on that subject: but, instead of new images of tenderness, or delicate representation of intelligible feelings, he has contrived to tell us nothing whatever of the unfortunate fair one, but that her name is Martha Ray; and that she goes up to the top of a hill, in a red cloak, and cries 'Oh misery!' All the rest of the poem is filled with a description of an old thorn and a pond, and of the silly stories which the neighbouring old women told about them.

The sports of childhood, and the untimely death of promising youth, is also a common topic of poetry. Mr Wordsworth has made some blank verse about it; but, instead of the delightful and picturesque sketches with which so many authors of moderate talents have presented us on this inviting subject, all that he is pleased to communicate of the rustic child, is, that he used to amuse himself with shouting to the owls, and hearing them answer. To make amends for this brevity, the process of his mimicry is most accurately described.

     —With fingers interwoven, both hands
     Press'd closely, palm to palm, and to his mouth
     Uplifted, he, as through an instrument,
     Blew mimic hootings to the silent owls,
     That they might answer him.—
        ['There was a Boy', *PW*, II, p. 206, ll. 7–11; *LB (1800)*,
                    pp. 131–2, ll. 7–11]

This is all we hear of him; and for the sake of this one accomplishment, we are told, that the author has frequently stood mute, and gazed on his grave for half an hour together!

Love, and the fantasies of lovers, have afforded an ample theme to poets of all ages. Mr Wordsworth, however, has thought fit to compose a piece, illustrating this copious subject, by one single thought. A lover trots away to see his mistress one fine evening, staring all the way at the moon: when he comes to her door,

> O mercy ! to myself I cried,
> If Lucy should be dead!
> ['Strange fits of passion', *PW*, II, p. 29, ll. 27–8]

And there the poem ends!

Now, we leave it to any reader of common candour and discernment to say, whether these representations of character and sentiment are drawn from that eternal and universal standard of truth and nature, which every one is knowing enough to recognize, and no one great enough to depart from with impunity; or whether they are not formed, as we have described them, upon certain fantastic and affected peculiarities in the mind or fancy of the author, into which it is most improbable that many of his readers will enter, and which cannot, in some cases, be comprehended without much effort and explanation. Instead of multiplying instances of these wide and wilful aberrations from ordinary nature, it may be more satisfactory to produce the author's own admission of the narrowness of the plan upon which he writes, and of the very extraordinary circumstances which he himself sometimes thinks it necessary for his readers to keep in view, in order to understand the beauty or propriety of his delineations.

A pathetic tale of guilt or superstition may be told, we are apt to fancy, by the poet himself, in his general character of poet, with full as much effect as by any other person. An old nurse, at any rate, or a monk or parish clerk, is always at hand to give grace to such a narration. None of these, however, would satisfy Mr Wordsworth. He has written a long poem of this sort, in which he thinks it indispensably necessary to apprise the reader, that he has endeavoured to represent the language and sentiments of a particular character – of which character, he adds, 'the reader will have a general notion, if he has ever known a man, *a captain of a small trading vessel*, for example, who, being *past the middle age of life*, has retired upon *an annuity, or small independent income*, to some *village*, or country town, of which he was *not a native*, or in which he had not been accustomed to live.'

Now, we must be permitted to doubt, whether, among all the readers of Mr Wordsworth, there is a single individual who has had the happiness of knowing a person of this very peculiar description; or who is capable of forming any sort of conjecture of the particular disposition and turn of thinking which such a combination of attributes would be apt to produce. To us, we will confess, the *annonce* appears as ludicrous and absurd, as it would be in the author of an ode or an epic to say, 'Of this piece the reader will necessarily form a very erroneous judgement, unless he is apprised, that it was written by a pale man in a green coat, – sitting cross-legged on an oaken stool, – with a scratch on his nose, and a spelling dictionary on the table.'*

From these childish and absurd affectations, we turn with pleasure to the manly sense and correct picturing of Mr Crabbe.

---

* Some of our readers may have a curiosity to know in what manner this old annuitant captain expresses himself in the village of his adoption. For their gratification, we annex the two first stanzas of his story, in which, with all the attention we have been able to bestow, we have been utterly unable to detect any characteristic traits, either of a seaman, an annuitant, or a stranger in a country town. It is a style, on the contrary, which we should ascribe, without hesitation, to a certain poetical fraternity in the West of England, and which, we verily believe, never was, and never will be, used by any one out of that fraternity.

> There is a thorn – it looks so old,
>   In truth you'd find it hard to say,
> How it could ever have been young,
>   It looks so old and gray.
> Not higher than a two-years child,
>   It stands erect, this aged thorn;
> No leaves it has, no thorny points;
> It is a mass of knotted joints,
>   A wretched thing forlorn.
> It stands, erect, and like a stone,
> With lichens it is overgrown.
>
> Like rock or stone, it is o'ergrown
>   With lichens to the very top,
> And hung with heavy tufts of moss,
>   A melancholy crop.
> Up from the earth these mosses creep,
>   And this poor thorn they clasp it round
> So close, you'd say that they were bent,
> With plain and manifest intent,
>   To drag it to the ground;
> And all had join'd in one endeavour,
> To bury this poor thorn for ever,
>
> ['The Thorn', *PW*, II, pp. 240–1, ll. 1–22;
> *LB (1798)*, pp. 69–70, ll. 1–22]

And this, it seems, is Nature, and Pathos, and Poetry.[1]

EDITOR'S NOTE

1. Jeffrey added this last sentence when he reprinted the essay in 1843.

104.

Unsigned notice, *British Critic*, March 1809, XXXIII, 298–9

These are the very poems which are ridiculed in the *Simpliciad*, noticed by us last month; and in good truth well worthy are they, in general, of ridicule; for such flimsy, puerile thoughts, expressed in such feeble and halting verse, we have seldom seen; never in a volume published by a person of the smallest reputation. Mr. Wordsworth seems, in his motto, to promise better things hereafter, and we heartily hope he will keep his word. He says,

> Posterius graviore sono tibi Musa loquetur
> Nostra; dabunt cum securos mihi tempora fructus.[1]

His lines on 'the Character of a happy Warrior,' appear to be a specimen of that *gravior sonus*, and have indeed some fine passages in them. They are conceived throughout with a strength and vigour very unlike their *namby-pamby* brethren. To do the best we can for the author, we will insert the conclusion of this character.
[Quotes 'Character of the Happy Warrior', *PW*, IV, p. 88, ll. 65–85; *Poems 1807*, pp. 43–4, ll. 65–85:

> Tis finally the man, who lifted high . . .
> Whom every man in arms should wish to be.]

It is scarcely to be believed, that the man who could read these lines with pleasure, much less he who was able to write them, could be author of the fooleries of which these scanty volumes are principally composed. What Mr. W. may do if he can cast out the dæmon of bad taste, we know not; but while it continues to possess him, he must afford displeasure to critics, and fit subject for satirists.

EDITOR'S NOTE

1. 'Afterwards my muse will speak to you in a more serious tone, when the seasons give me their fruits in tranquillity.' (Virgil, *Culex*, 8–9). For a discussion of Wordsworth's 'motto', see entry 97.

105.

Unsigned notice, *Poetical Register and Repository for Fugitive Poetry, 1807*
(published 1811), VI, 540–1

Than the volumes now before us we never saw any thing better calculated to excite disgust and anger in a lover of poetry. The drivelling nonsense of some of Mr. Wordworth's poems is insufferable, and it is equally insufferable that such nonsense should have been written by a man capable, as he is, of writing well. But Mr. Wordsworth is a System maker. He has formed an out of the way, incomprehensible system of poetry; and on the altar of that system he sacrifices melody, elegance, spirit, and even common sense. Whenever he deviates from his monstrous system he writes like a man of genius. His volumes contain abundant proofs that he possesses no mean poetical powers. It is to be hoped that he will see his error, and not persist in making murderous attacks upon his own literary reputation.

VII

Poems, 1807: opinions, 1806–1814

106. Walter Scott (1771–1832)

From letters, 1806–1808

a. To Anna Seward, 10 April 1806

I spent some time in their society [that of Wordsworth and Southey] very pleasantly and Southey repaid me by visiting my farm. They are certainly men of very extraordinary powers, Wordsworth in particular is such a character as only exists in romance virtuous, simple, and unaffectedly restricting every want & wish to the bounds of a very narrow income in order to enjoy the literary and poetical leisure which his happiness consists in – Were it not for the unfortunate idea of forming a New School of Poetry these men are calculated to give it a new impulse, but I think they sometimes lose their energy in trying to find not a better but a different path from what has been travelld by their predecessors –

(*Letters of Sir Walter Scott, 1787–1807*, ed. Herbert Grierson, Constable, 1932, I, 287)

b. To Southey, November 1807

Wordsworth is harshly treated in the Edinburgh Review, but Jeffrey gives the sonnets as much praise as he usually does to anybody. I made him admire the song of Lord Clifford's minstrel, which I like exceedingly myself. But many of Wordsworth's lesser poems are *caviare*, not only to the multitude, but to all who judge of poetry by the established rules of criticism. Some of them, I can safely say, I like the better for these aberrations; in others they get beyond me – at any rate they ought to have been more cautiously hazarded.

(*Ibid.*, 390)

c. To Anna Seward, 23 April 1808

I am quite glad you have seen Southey. Delighted with him you must be, yet in conversation (great as he is) he is inferior to Wordsworth, perhaps because he is a deeper and more elaborate scholar. Southey rarely allows you any of those reposes of conversation when you are at liberty to speak, as the phrase is, 'whatever comes uppermost.' But in return, if an idle fellow like me is sometimes a little *gêné*, he is at least informed, and may be the wiser or better for all he hears. What I admire in both is an upright undeviating morality connecting itself with all they think and say and write.

(*Ibid.*, II, 51)

107. Robert Southey

From letters, 1807

a. To John Rickman, mid-April 1807

[Coleridge's] present scheme is to live with Wordsworth[1] – it is from his idolatry of that family that this has begun – they have always humoured him in all his follies, listened to his complaints of his wife, and when he has complained of his itch, helped him to scratch, instead of covering him with brimstone ointment, and shutting him up by himself. Wordsworth and his sister who pride themselves upon having no selfishness, are of all human beings whom I have ever known the most intensely selfish. The one thing to which W. would sacrifice all others is his own reputation, concerning which his anxiety is perfectly childish – like a woman of her beauty: and so he can get Coleridge to talk his own writings over with him, and critise [*sic*] them, and (without amending them) teach him how to do it – to be in fact the very rain and air and sunshine of his intellect, he thinks C. is very well employed and this arrangement a very good one.

(*New Letters of Robert Southey*, ed. Kenneth Curry, 1965, I, 449)

b. To Walter Scott, 4 October 1807

Wordsworth is at Grasmere, and has been there for some months. The defects of his last volumes seem to be more felt than their beauties. I hear many persons speak of the few foolish pieces there with dislike, and scarcely any body with admiration of the sonnets, which are in the very highest strain of poetry.

(*Private Letter-Books of Sir Walter Scott*, ed. W. Partington, 1930, 75)

c. To Walter Scott, 8 December 1807

The reviewal of Wordsworth I am not likely to see, the Edinburgh very rarely lying in my way. My own notions respecting the book agree in the main with yours, though I may probably go a step farther than you in admiration. There are certainly some pieces there which are good for nothing (none, however, which a bad poet could have written), and very many which it was highly injudicious to publish. That song to Lord Clifford, which you particularise, is truly a noble poem. The Ode upon Pre-existence is a dark subject darkly handled. Coleridge is the only man who could make such a subject luminous. The Leech-gatherer is one of my favourites; there he has caught Spenser's manner, and, in many of the better poemets, has equally caught the best manner of old Wither, who, with all his long fits of dulness and prosing, had the heart and soul of a poet in him. The sonnets are in a grand style. I only wish Dundee had not been mentioned.[2] James Grahame and I always call that man Claverhouse, the name by which the devils know him below.

(*Life and Correspondence of Robert Southey*, ed. C. C. Southey, 1849, III, 126)

EDITOR'S NOTES

1. Coleridge was about to separate from his wife.
2. See sonnet, 'In the Pass of Killiekranky'.

108. John Taylor Coleridge (1790–1876)
Letters, a review and reminiscences, 1806–1846

John Taylor Coleridge was Coleridge's able nephew, a lawyer, editor of the *Quarterly* for 1825, a judge from 1835; an intelligent propagandist for Wordsworth.

a. From a letter to S. T. Coleridge, 27 June 1807

In this letter J. T. Coleridge thanks his uncle for a gift (presumably *Lyrical Ballads* and Wordsworth's *Poems*, 1807).

237

Before I meet you, I shall now have read your books with attention, & I dare say with pleasure.

(Ms. Victoria College, Toronto)

b. From a letter to his Uncle George Coleridge, early July 1808

Here we see J. T. Coleridge defending himself against the charge that he had made his Uncle Samuel his mentor.

I have scarcely ever spoken to him in my life, & never had any correspondence with him but a single letter to thank him for the Poems, which he sent me.

(Ms. Bodleian Library)

Despite Uncle George's warnings, Coleridge's influence on his nephew was real. From a letter to his brother James, 1811:

> Every subject he was master of, and discussed in the most splendid eloquence . . . altogether [he] made the most powerful impression on my mind of any man I ever saw.

(*The Story of a Devonshire House*, Lord Coleridge, 1905, 190–2)

c. From a Reminiscence of Thomas Arnold

Undoubtedly Coleridge's influence is apparent in J. T. Coleridge's advocacy of Wordsworth's poetry. This text is from J. T. Coleridge's reminiscence of Thomas Arnold. Arnold became an undergraduate at Corpus Christi, Oxford, in 1811, and was a life-long admirer of Wordsworth.

But, though not a poet himself, he [Arnold] was not insensible of the beauties of poetry – far from it. I reflect with some pleasure, that I first introduced him to what has been somewhat unreasonably called the Lake Poetry; my near relation to one, and connexion with another of the poets, whose works were so called, were the occasion of this; and my uncle having sent me the Lyrical Ballads, and the first edition of Mr. Wordsworth's poems, they became familiar among us. We were proof, I am glad to think, against the criticism, if so it might be called, of the 'Edinburgh Review;' we felt their truth and beauty, and became zealous disciples of Wordsworth's philosophy. This was of peculiar advantage to Arnold, whose leaning was too direct for the practical and evidently useful – it brought out in him that feeling for the lofty and imaginative which appeared in all his intimate conversation, and may be seen spiritualizing those even of his writings, in which, from their subject, it might seem to have less place. You know in later life how much he thought his beloved Fox How enhanced in value by its neighbourhood to Rydal Mount, and what store he set on the privilege of frequent and friendly converse with the venerable genius of that sweet spot.

(*Life of Thomas Arnold*, A. P. Stanley, 1846, 12)

d. From a letter to Rev. G. Cornish, 6 July 1839

This letter, written by Arnold himself, recalls J. T. Coleridge's enthusiasm for Wordsworth. (The Oxford Commemoration was on 12 June 1839.)

I went up to Oxford to the Commemoration, for the first time for twenty-one years, to see Wordsworth and Bunsen receive their degrees; and to me, remembering how old Coleridge inoculated a little knot of us with the love of Wordsworth, when his name was in general a bye-word, it was striking to witness the thunders of applause, repeated over and over again, with which he was greeted in the theatre by Under-graduates and Masters of Arts alike.

(*Ibid.*, 478)

e. From an unsigned review of Coleridge's *Remorse*, *Quarterly Review*, April 1814, xi, 177–81

This review offers a commentary on the Lake poets in general.

. . . our Poets; minute in their analyses and analysing the minutest emotions; preferring, indeed, from the greater skill required in the task, to trace to their causes the slight and transient, rather than the strong and permanent feelings of the mind, they have too often become not so much the painters of nature as the commentators upon her.

By this method they have sacrificed the chance of general popularity for the devoted admiration of a few; and it may be said that the alternative was entirely at their option. But still we think the choice a faulty one; the majority of mankind are little conversant in metaphysical pursuits; whereas it should be at least a principal object of poetry to please generally, and it is one of the highest boasts of genius that its strains, like the liturgy of our church, are not too high for the low and simple, nor yet too low for the wise and learned.

But this is not all; for it may be reasonably doubted, whether, from the continual habit of studying these slighter emotions, certain results, having a tendency to erroneous conclusions in philosophy, do not of necessity follow. For first it seems likely that the heart itself would become more susceptible of emotion from slight causes than those of the generality of men; as it is certain that the mind of the artist, or the connoisseur, will receive the most exquisite delight from parts of a production, which leave the common observer in a state of indifference. Now though it may be desirable that a picture should contain some of these latent beauties, yet it is evident that the artist who built his fame entirely upon them, must resign his claims to genius for the reputation of mere science, and can never aspire to the praise of being a perfect painter.

Again, such a study long continued can scarcely fail of attaching a greater degree of importance to the emotions so raised, than they merit. Whatever we dwell upon with intenseness and ardour invariably swells in our conception to a false magnitude; indeed this is implied by the very eagerness of our pursuit; and if this be true with the weed, the shell, or the butterfly, it is evident how much more strongly it will apply, where the study (as must be the case with all studies conversant about the operations of the soul) unites much of real dignity and importance as the basis on which to build the exaggerations of partial fondness. The native of a flat country gradually swells his mole-hills to mountains; no wonder then, if by constantly beholding, and deeply feeling the grandeur and beauty of their own lakes, Mr. Coleridge and his friends have learned to invest every part with a false appearance of greatness; if, in their eyes, every stream swells to a river, every lake to an ocean, and every headland, that breaks or ornaments their prospect, assumes the awful form of a giant promontory. But what is still worse, the habitual examination of their own feelings tends to produce in them a variation from nature almost amounting to distortion. The slight and subtle workings of the heart must be left to play unobserved, and without fear of observation, if they are intended to play freely and naturally; to be overlooked is to be absolutely restrained. The man who is for ever examining his feet, as he walks, will probably soon move in a stiff and constrained pace; and if we are constantly on the watch to discover the nature, order, and cause of our slightest emotions, it can scarcely be expected that they will operate in their free course or natural direction.

Now if we are justified in any of these suppositions, we cannot wonder that to a large portion of mankind the views of nature exhibited by the Lake Poets, and their own feelings with the excitement of them, should often appear strained, and even fictitious. The majority of their readers have passed glow-worms and bird's-nests, celandines and daisies, without any emotion lively enough to be remembered; and they are surprised, unfairly perhaps, but not unnaturally, that so much sensation should be attributed to so trifling a cause. They lose their fellowship of feeling with the poet, and are therefore at the best but uninterested by the poem.

Another source of peculiarities in the poets under consideration is the particular warmth and energy of their feeling in the contemplation of rural scenery. They are not the tasteful admirers of nature, nor the philosophic calculators on the extent of her riches, and the wisdom of her plans; they are her humble worshippers. In her silent solitudes, on the bosom of her lakes, in the dim twilight of her forests, they are surrendered up passively to the scenery around them, they seem to feel a power, an influence invisible and indescribable, which at once burthens and delights, exalts and purifies the soul. All the features and appearances of nature in their poetical creed possess a sentient and intellectual being, and exert an influence for good upon the hearts of her worshippers. Nothing can be more poetical than this feeling, but it is the misfortune of this school that their very excellences are carried to an excess. Hence they constantly attribute not merely physical, but moral animation to nature. Ocean has an heart, and as might be expected in consequence, all the passions of love, pride, joy, &c.; the moon is at one time merciful, at another cruel, at one time loves, at another hates; and the waves, the stars, the clouds, the music of the sky are all friends to the mariner. These are to be carefully distinguished from the commonplaces of poetry; to say that a river kisses its banks, or that the sea embraces an island are but metaphors borrowed from physical appearances, and bear a broad difference from passages in which an inanimate being performs an external action in obedience to some internal feeling.

To an extension or rather a modification of this last mentioned principle may perhaps be attributed the beautiful tenet so strongly inculcated by them of the celestial purity of infancy. 'Heaven lies about us in our infancy', says Mr. Wordsworth, in a passage which strikingly exemplifies the power of imaginative poetry; and Mr. Wilson, on seeing an infant asleep, exclaims:

> Thou smil'st as if thy thoughts were soaring
> To heaven, and heaven's God adoring.
> And who can tell what visions high
> May bless an infant's sleeping eye!
> ['To a Sleeping Child', *The Isle of Palms*, 1812, 283]

The tenet itself is strictly imaginative; its truth, as matter of philosophy, may well be doubted; certainly in the extent in which they take it, it does not rest on Scripture foundation, and may seem to be contradicted by the experience of every mother, who, in the wayward fretfulness of her infant, finds constant exercise for that unweariable love which, seemingly on this very account, the Eternal Wisdom has so wonderfully implanted in her breast. Still, however, we hold that in poetry that may be allowed to be true which accords with general feeling.[1]

There are yet a few points of no common importance to be noticed, in which we scruple not to rank the Lake Poets above all that have gone before them. In their writings the gentle and domestic virtues of an affectionate heart are uniformly exalted above the splendid and danger-ous heroism which has been too generally the theme of other poets. In their writings women are drawn, as they deserve to be, lofty yet meek; patient and cheerful; dutiful, affectionate, brave, faithful, and pious; the pillars that adorn and support the temple of this life's happiness . . .

Lastly, love is purified from the grossness of passion: it is idle to say, that this is an unattainable exaltation; all models should be perfect, though man remains imperfect, that in striving to reach what is impos-sible we may attain to what is uncommon. Love, with the Lake Poets, becomes what he should be, a devout spirit, purifying the soul, and worshipping God most in his most beauteous or his most noble work.

It would not impair the authority of the preceding remarks were we to admit that they do not apply with precisely the same force to the writings of all the Lake Poets. It appears to us that chance or a congenial mode of thinking has brought into intimate connection minds of very distinct powers and peculiarities. Thus a school of poetry has arisen of which all the members agree in some points, but differ in others; and even where they agree in kind they sometimes differ in degree. In examining their writings, therefore, we are to expect a general resemblance in all, which yet shall be neither so strong nor universal as to obliterate a peculiar character in each.

f. From a letter to J. T. Coleridge from his uncle George Coleridge, 19 July 1818

For John Taylor Coleridge's continuing and considered appreciation of Words-worth, see his reviews in the *British Critic*: of *The Excursion* (entry 153), *Peter Bell* (entry 215), *The Waggoner* (enrty 231), *The River Duddon* (entry 244), and, not included in this volume, *Ecclesiastical Sketches* and *Memorials of a Tour, November 1822*. These articles, and others, were written for the *British Critic* despite the advice of John Taylor Coleridge's uncle, George Coleridge, brother of Coleridge, in his letter of 1818.

Articles in the Quarterly written in that Spirit [of noble purpose] and borne out by Wisdom and sound principle will be more effectually useful than the same Articles in the British Critic from this circumstance – that the latter is more generally known to be a Party-publication. Few open a book now without some prejudice of that kind.

(Ms. Bodleian Library)

But it is doubtful that the *Quarterly*, under the editorship of Gifford, would have been sympathetic to articles on Wordsworth.

g. From J. T. Coleridge's Personal Reminiscence of Wordsworth, dated 1836

. . . He said there was some foundation in fact, however slight, for every poem he had written of a narrative kind; so slight indeed, sometimes, as hardly to deserve the name; for example, 'The Somnambulist' was wholly built on the fact of a girl at Lyulph's Tower being a sleep-walker; and 'The Water Lily,' on a ship bearing that name. 'Michael' was founded on the son of an old couple having become dissolute and run away from his parents; and on an old shepherd having been seven years in building up a sheepfold in a solitary valley: 'The Brothers,' on a young shepherd, in his sleep, having fallen down a crag, his staff remaining suspended midway. Many incidents he seemed to have drawn from the narration of Mrs. Wordsworth, or his sister, 'Ellen' for example, in 'The Excursion;' and they must have told their stories well, for he said his principle had been to give the oral part as nearly as he could in the very words of the speakers, where he narrated a real story, dropping, of course, all vulgarisms or provincialisms, and borrowing sometimes a Bible turn of expression: these former were mere accidents, not essential to the truth in representing how the human heart and passions worked; and to give these last faithfully was his object. If he was to have any name hereafter, his hope was on this, and he did think he had in some instances succeeded;* that the sale of his poems increased among the

---

* You could not walk with him a mile without seeing what a loving interest he took in the play and working of simple natures. As you ascend Kirkstone from Paterdale, you have a bright stream leaping down from rock to rock, on your right, with here and there silent pools. One of Wordsworth's poor neighbours worked all the week over Kirkstone, I think in some mines; and returning on Saturday evenings, used to fish up this little stream. We met him with a string of small trout. W. offered to buy them, and bid him take them to the Mount. 'Nay,' said the man, 'I cannot sell them, Sir; the little children at home look for them for supper, and I can't disappoint them.' It was quite pleasant to see how the man's answer delighted the Poet. J. T. C.

243

classes below the middle; and he had had, constantly, statements made to him of the effect produced in reading 'Michael' and other such of his poems. I added my testimony of being unable to read it aloud without interruption from my own feelings. 'She was a phantom of delight' he said was written on 'his dear wife,' of whom he spoke in the sweetest manner; a manner full of the warmest love and admiration, yet with delicacy and reserve . . .

October 10th. – I have passed a great many hours to-day with Wordsworth, in his house. I stumbled on him with proof sheets before him. He read me nearly all the sweet stanzas written in his copy of the 'Castle of Indolence', describing himself and my uncle; and he and Mrs. W. both assured me the description of the latter at that time was perfectly accurate; that he was almost as a great boy in feelings, and had all the tricks and fancies there described. Mrs. W. seemed to look back on him, and those times, with the fondest affection. Then he read me some lines, which formed part of a suppressed portion of 'The Waggoner;' but which he is now printing 'on the Rock of Names,' so called because on it they had carved out their initials:

W. W. Wm. Wordsworth.
M. H. Mary W.
D. W. Dorothy Wordsworth.
S. T. C. Samuel Taylor Coleridge.
J. W. John Wordsworth.
S. H. Sarah Hutchinson.

This rock was about a mile beyond Wythburn Chapel, to which they used to accompany my uncle, in going to Keswick from Grasmere, and where they would meet him when he returned. This led him to read much of 'The Waggoner' to me. It seems a very favourite poem of his, and he read me splendid descriptions from it. He said his object in it had not been understood. It was a play of the fancy on a domestic incident and lowly character: he wished by the opening descriptive lines to put his reader into the state of mind in which he wished it to be read. If he failed in doing that, he wished him to lay it down. He pointed out, with the same view, the glowing lines on the state of exultation in which Ben and his companions are under the influence of liquor. Then he read the sickening languor of the morning walk, contrasted with the glorious uprising of Nature, and the songs of the birds. Here he has added about six most exquisite lines.

We walked out on the turf terrace, on the Loughrigg side of Rydal

Water. Most exquisitely did the lake and opposite bank look. Thence he led me home under Loughrigg, through lovely spots I had never seen before. His conversation was on critical subjects, arising out of his attempts to alter his poems. He said he considered 'The White Doe' as, in conception, the highest work he had ever produced. The mere physical action was all unsuccessful; but the true action of the poem was spiritual – the subduing of the will, and all inferior passions, to the perfect purifying and spiritualising of the intellectual nature; while the Doe, by connection with Emily, is raised as it were from its mere animal nature into something mysterious and saint-like. He said he should devote much labour to perfecting the execution of it in the mere business parts, in which, from anxiety 'to get on' with the more important parts, he was sensible that imperfections had crept in, which gave the style a feebleness of character.

(*Memoirs of William Wordsworth*, ed. Christopher Wordsworth, 1851, II, 305–11)

EDITOR'S NOTE

1. J. T. C. repeats this paragraph's notions in his review of *The Excursion*: see entry 153.

109.

Wordsworth answers his critics, letters, 1807–1808

a. To Lady Beaumont, 21 May 1807

Trouble not yourself upon their [*Poems*, 1807] present reception; of what moment is that compared with what I trust is their destiny, to console the afflicted, to add sunshine to daylight by making the happy happier, to teach the young and the gracious of every age, to see, to think and feel, and therefore to become more actively and securely virtuous; this is their office, which I trust they will faithfully perform long after we (that is, all that is mortal of us) are mouldered in our graves. I am well aware how far it would seem to many I overrate my own exertions when I speak in this way, in direct connection with the Volumes I have just made public.

I am not, however, afraid of such censure, insignificant as probably the majority of those poems would appear to very respectable persons; I do not mean London wits and witlings, for these have too many bad passions about them to be respectable even if they had more intellect than the benign laws of providence will allow to such a heartless existence as theirs is; but grave, kindly-natured, worthy persons, who would be pleased if they could. I hope that these Volumes are not without some recommendations, even for Readers of this class, but their imagination has slept; and the voice which is the voice of my Poetry without Imagination cannot be heard.

Leaving these, I was going to say a word to such Readers as Mr. Rogers.[1] Such! – how would he be offended if he knew I considered him only as a representative of a class, and not as unique! 'Pity,' says Mr. R., 'that so many trifling things should be admitted to obstruct the view of those that have merit;' now, let this candid judge take, by way of example, the sonnets, which, probably, with the exception of two or three other Poems for which I will not contend appear to him the most trifling, as they are the shortest, I would say to him, omitting things of higher consideration, there is one thing which must strike you at once if you will only read these poems, – that those to Liberty, at least, have a connection with, or a bearing upon, each other, and therefore, if individually they want weight, perhaps, as a Body, they may not be so deficient, at least this ought to induce you to suspend your judgement, and qualify it so far as to allow that the writer aims at least at comprehensiveness. But dropping this, I would boldly say at once, that these Sonnets, while they each fix the attention upon some important sentiment separately considered, do at the same time collectively make a Poem on the subject of civil Liberty and national independence, which, either for simplicity of style or grandeur of moral sentiment, is, alas! likely to have few parallels in the Poetry of the present day. Again, turn to the 'Moods of my own Mind'. There is scarcely a Poem here of above thirty Lines, and very trifling these poems will appear to many; but, omitting to speak of them individually, do they not, taken collectively, fix the attention upon a subject eminently poetical, viz., the interest which objects in nature derive from the predominance of certain affections more or less permanent, more or less capable of salutary renewal in the mind of the being contemplating these objects? This is poetic, and essentially poetic, and why? because it is creative . . . saving that I have expressed my calm confidence that these

Poems will live, I have said nothing which has a particular application to the object of this letter which was to remove all disquiet from your mind on account of the condemnation they may at present incur from that portion of my contemporaries who are called the Public. I am sure, my dear Lady Beaumont, if you attach any importance [to it] it can only be from an apprehension that it may affect me, upon which I have already set you at ease, or from a fear that this present blame is ominous of their future or final destiny. If this be the case, your tenderness for me betrays you; be assured that the decision of these persons has nothing to do with the Question; they are altogether incompetent judges. These people in the senseless hurry of their idle lives do not *read* books, they merely snatch a glance at them that they may talk about them. And even if this were not so, never forget what I believe was observed to you by Coleridge, that every great and original writer, in proportion as he is great or original, must himself create the taste by which he is to be relished; he must teach the art by which he is to be seen; this, in a certain degree, even to all persons, however wise and pure may be their lives, and however unvitiated their taste; but for those who dip into books in order to give an opinion of them, or talk about them to take up an opinion – for this multitude of unhappy, and misguided, and misguiding beings, an entire regeneration must be produced; and if this be possible, it must be a work of *time*. To conclude, my ears are stone-dead to this idle buzz, and my flesh as insensible as iron to these petty stings; and after what I have said I am sure yours will be the same. I doubt not that you will share with me an invincible confidence that my writings (and among them these little Poems) will co-operate with the benign tendencies in human nature and society, wherever found; and that they will, in their degree, be efficacious in making men wiser, better, and happier.

(*MY*, I, 146–50)

b. To Southey, January 1808

As to Jeffrey's Review[2] there is nothing to say, for there is nothing in it that bears the least upon the question, except one sentence where he says, that, whether from affectation or other causes, I have connected my lofty or tender feelings with objects such as a Sparrow's Nest, a Spade, a Leech gatherer, etc. which to the generality of mankind appear, and will continue to appear, ridiculous. Now Mr Jeffrey takes this for granted, which was the thing to be proved; and then proceeds to revile the poems accordingly. That, to a great number of persons, many objects such as I have written upon will be either unknown, indifferent, or uninteresting, or even contemptible there can be no doubt, but I suppose, generally speaking, that these people are, so far, in a state of degradation, at least that it would be better for them if they were otherwise. Mr Jeffrey takes for granted the contrary. Here we are at issue. [*The copyist adds the following*: Mr Wordsworth then proceeds to examine Mr J's theory of diction which he pronounces to be very fallacious.]

(*MY*, I, 162, only a copy of this letter exists)

c. To Sir George Beaumont, *c.* 20 February 1808

Thanks for dear Lady B.'s transcript from your Friend's Letter, – it is written with candour, but I must say a word or two not in praise of it. 'Instances of what I mean,' says your Friend, 'are to be found in a poem on a Daisy' (by the bye, it is on *the* Daisy, a mighty difference). 'and on Daffodils *reflected in the Water*' Is this accurately transcribed by Lady Beaumont? If it be, what shall we think of criticism or judgement founded upon and exemplified by a Poem which must have been so inattentively perused? My Language is precise, and, therefore, it would be false modesty to charge myself with blame.

> – Beneath the trees,
> Ten thousand dancing in the *breeze*.
> The *waves beside* them danced, but they
> Outdid the *sparkling waves* in glee.

Can expression be more distinct? And let me ask your Friend how it is possible for flowers to be *reflected* in water where there are *waves*. They may indeed in still water – but the very object of my poem is the trouble or agitation both of the flowers and the Water. I must needs respect the understanding of every one honoured by your friendship; but sincerity compels me to say that my Poems must be more nearly looked at before they can give rise to any remarks of much value, even from the strongest minds. – With respect to this individual poem, Lady B. will recollect how Mrs. Fermor[3] expressed herself upon it. – A Letter also was sent to me addressed to a friend of mine and by him communicated to me in which this identical poem was singled out for fervent approbation. What then shall we say? Why let the Poet first consult his own heart as I have done and leave the rest to posterity; to, I hope, an improving posterity. The fact is, the English *Public* are at this moment in the same state of mind with respect to my Poems, if small things may be compared with great, as the French are in respect to Shakespear; and not the French alone, but almost the whole Continent. In short, in your Friend's Letter, I am condemned for the very thing for which I ought to have been praised; viz., that I have not written down to the level of superficial observers and unthinking minds. – – Every great Poet is a Teacher: I wish either to be considered as a Teacher, or as nothing.

(*Ibid.*, I, 194–5)

d. To Sir George Beaumont, 8 April 1808

At Lancaster I happened to mention Grasmere in hearing of one of the Passengers, who asked me immediately if one Wordsworth did not live there. I answered, 'Yes.' – 'He has written,' said he, 'some very beautiful Poems; The Critics do indeed cry out against them, and condemn them as *over simple*, but for my part I read them with great pleasure, they are natural and true.' – This man was also a Grocer.

(*Ibid.*, I, 210)

EDITOR'S NOTES

1. Samuel Rogers, (1763–1855), poet and banker.
2. See entry 98.
3. Mrs Fermor (1754–1824), widowed sister of Lady Beaumont.

110. Mrs A. B. Skepper (*c.* 1773–1856)

Extract from a letter to James Montgomery, 18 August 1807

In 1808 Mrs Skepper became the third Mrs Basil Montagu.

I think I told you that Wordsworth and his family spent a month with me, and that Coleridge was with us every day.[1] They both thought highly of your poetry; Mr Coleridge begged that I would present his acknowledgements to you for the pleasure he had derived from your works. I assure you if you knew how very lightly Wordsworth holds the very best of the Modern Poets, you would think his praise a very high compliment.

Mr. Wordsworth is one of the most amiable men I ever knew, he has great power in conversation; he has thought while other men have talked, and now when he chuses [*sic*] to talk, I assure you he makes other men think – he has mild, and modest, yet very firm manners, a perfect consciousness of his own talents, without any arrogance or affectation. – Coleridge talks eloquently, and incessantly, with the air of a man who has been in the habit of haranguing – I understand the Reviewers have made very free with Mr. Wordsworth's new publication, I should suppose that 'learned Body' have at length fallen into the contempt they deserve; I was in company with an attorney's Clerk who is not *twenty years of age*, and he very gravely told me he was sorry to be obliged to 'cut up a friend of mine, but that he should review Wordsworth and he should give him a glorious trimming.'

(Ms. Sheffield City Library)

EDITOR'S NOTE

1. Certainly Wordsworth, Mrs Wordsworth and Sara Hutchinson were in London, staying at 36 Lower Thornhaugh Street, the home of Basil Montagu in late April/early May 1807.

111. Anna Seward

From letters, 1807–1808

a. To Walter Scott, 24 August 1807

Surely Wordsworth must be mad as was ever the poet Lee.[1] Those volumes of his, which you were so good to give me, have excited, by turns, my tenderness and warm admiration, my contemptuous astonishment and disgust. The two latter rose to their utmost height while I read about his dancing daffodils, ten thousand, as he says, in high dance in the breeze beside the river, whose waves dance with them, and the poet's heart, we are told, danced too. Then he proceeds to say, that in the hours of pensive or of pained contemplation, these same capering flowers flash on his memory, and his heart, losing its cares, dances with them again.

Surely if his worst foe had chosen to caricature this egotistic manufacturer of metaphysic importance upon trivial themes, he could not have done it more effectually! Whenever Mr Wordsworth writes naturally he charms me, as in the Kitten and the Falling Leaves; Verses to the Spade of a Friend; Written on Brother's Water Bridge; The Sailor's Mother; three or four of the sonnets, and above all the Leech-Gatherer, which is a perfectly original and striking poem. If he had written nothing else, that composition might stamp him a poet of no common powers. The sonnet written on Westminster Bridge, is beautiful, unaffected, and grandly picturesque.

The ode, is a mixture of his successful and unsuccessful attempts at sublimity. I delight in the five first stanzas; – then it goes rumbling down the dark profound of mysticism, whither my comprehension strives to follow him in vain. The lovely stanzas are a manifest imitation of an ode of Coleridge's, of very superior beauty, beginning, 'Well, if the bard was weather-wise,' &c.[2]

(*Letters of Anna Seward*, ed. Walter Scott, 1811, VI, 366–7)

b. To Walter Scott, 28 April 1808

Is it possible that Wordsworth can be Southey's superior in conversation? so widely as it is the *reverse* in their writings. In yours, and in Southey's all is perspicuity. In Wordsworth and still more in the Author of *Gebir*[3] (a poem most unaccountably admired by the Bards of the Cumberland lakes) we find meaning frequently lost in a maze of dark words.

(*Private Letter-Books of Sir Walter Scott*, ed. Partington, 1930, 260)

EDITOR'S NOTES

1. Nathaniel Lee (1649–1692), tragedian who went mad.
2. 'Dejection' was published in the *Morning Post*, 4 October 1802.
3. W. S. Landor: *Gebir* was published 1798, and much admired by Southey.

112. Some painters' opinions
Diaries, letters and writings, 1807–1814

Farington and John Constable (1776–1837), the landscape painter, observe what they deem a vanity in Wordsworth. Constable had been staying with John Harden at Brathay Hall, Ambleside, in September, and again in October, 1806. Coleridge himself was not in the Lake District at the time of Constable's visit; thus it must have been Wordsworth who repeated Coleridge's remark about 'intense thinking' in the conversation with Mrs Charles Lloyd (of Old Brathay, an old friend of the Wordsworths, married 24 April 1799, died 1830).

In the 1840s Wordsworth recalled again the schoolboy experience described below to explain to Isabella Fenwick what he had meant by 'Obstinate questionings / Of sense. . . . Fallings from us, vanishings' of the *Immortality Ode*. (*Poetical Works*, iv, 463–4).

a. From the Diary of Joseph Farington

13 May 1807:

Lawrence[1] was at Sotheby's[2] last night where Richd. Sharpe[3] expressed disapprobation of Wordsworths poems just published, saying He had carried His system of simplicity too far, and had proceeded to puerility. Sir George Beaumont after Sharpe was gone sd. to Lawrence that 'He supposed the Blood Hounds would now be upon Wordsworth'.

(*The Farington Diary*, ed. Kathryn Cave, 1982, VII, 3044)

12 December 1807:

[Constable reports that the painter David Wilkie (1785–1841)] was offended with Wordsworth who offered to propose subjects to Him to paint, & gave Him to understand that when He could not think of subjects as well as paint them He. wd. come to Him.

Constable remarked upon the high opinion Wordsworth entertains of Himself. He told Constable that while He was a Boy going to Hawkshead school, His mind was often so posessed with images, so lost in extraordinary conceptions, that He has held by a wall not knowing but He was part of it. – He also desired a Lady, Mrs. Loyd, near Windermere when Constable was present to notice the singular formation of His Skull, Coleridge remarked that this was the effect of intense thinking.

I observed to Constable if so, He must have thought in His Mother's womb. At Carlisles,[4] Sotheby sd. that Wordsworths poetry not only surpassed any that had ever been written but wd. probably never be equalled. Thus do these persons bepraise each other.

(*Ibid.*, VIII, 3164–5)

12 January 1808:
Reported to Farington by William Alexander (1767–1816) artist, shortly afterwards Keeper of Prints at the British Museum) who had been visiting the Beaumonts at Dunmow, Essex.

Wordsworth was cried up by Lady Beaumont in the most violent manner, calling Him angelic &c. – Sir George seemed to be cooled.

(*Ibid.*, IX, 3196)

b. From a letter of Lady Beaumont to Dorothy Wordsworth, 1 May 1808

Mr Price[5] is just arrived, and speaks with great pleasure of meeting your brother [Wordsworth] at Coleorton – we agree very much in our opinion of his genius, tho' his [Price's] heart may be less deeply affected than mine, the last volumes he had never seen I believe. I read him the brothers he thought *faultless* and a few others that delighted him, his taste is good in all things, and were his morals pure he would have a true relish for sublime poetry.

(Ms. The Wordsworth Library)

c. More extracts from Farington's Diary

28 March 1809:
I breakfasted with Sir G. & Lady Beaumont, Wordsworth & Coleridge were a subject of our conversation. – Lady B. was enthusiastic in admiration of Wordsworth. She desired me to read His preface to His poems. Sir George was more moderate. He told me & warned me of the danger of not approving it, adding 'That Lady B. was as intolerant in Her opinion as Bishop Bonnor on religious matters.'
    She afterwards sd. to me, that Coleridge & Wordsworth thought the bad taste in writing which now prevails, is owing to works of two celebrated authors, '*Popes translation of Homer, & the Odyssy*' and '*Johnson's*

lives of the Poets.' These models of art and an inflated style have been imitated to the destroying of all simplicity. *The Old Testament* they say, is the true model of simplicity of style. They also highly approve the writings of *Dr. Jeremiah Taylor*, who had also the feelings of a Poet, and of *Cowley.* – Sir George sd. to me 'That Wordsworth & Coleridge by living in a state of seclusion, might engender notions respecting matters of taste that would not be approved by the world.'

(*The Farington Diary*, ed. Kathryn Cave, 1982, IX, 3425–6)

17 June 1809:
At Lady Crews, Lady Beaumont told Lawrence that she Had talked with Rogers of Wordsworth's poems, & that Rogers concurred with Her in admiring the simplicity which is in them, & dwelt particularly on the beautiful idea of the 'Dancing Daffodils' – thus playing off Her want of judgment.

(*Ibid.*, IX, 3490)

d. From Benjamin Robert Haydon's *Autobiography*, August 1809

In August 1809, Sir George Beaumont warned his guests at Coleorton, the two young painters Benjamin Robert Haydon (1786–1846) and David Wilkie (1785–1841):

Wordsworth may walk in; if he do, I caution you against his terrific democractic notions.

(Benjamin Robert Haydon, *Autobiography*, Oxford, 1927, 126)

e. More extracts from Farington's Diary

20 December 1810:
Lysons[6] called . . . He told [me] that while He was at Lord Chesterfield's[7] abt. 9 miles from Sir G. Beaumont's at Cole-orton, the last Autumn, His Lordship spoke of the admiration in which Wordsworth was held at Cole-orton on acct. of His poetry. This induced Him to purchase the last Volume of these poems, which, when He asked for it, Paine, the Bookseller, was surprised, said He had it not, but if His Lordship was in earnest to purchase it He wd. get it for him. Lord Chesterfield said, I

gave seven shillings & sixpence for it, & anybody shall have it for the odd
Sixpence. He then expressed His surprise at the puerile nonsense in it, &
Lysons, on looking into the volume was equally astonished at such stuff
being published.

(*Ibid.*, X, 3828)

17 October 1812:
In the evening Lady Beaumont read some of Wordsworth's poems. Sir
George particularly requested that His 'Tintern Abbey' might be read,
as being an admirable specimen of Wordsworth's poetical powers. 'He
is,' said Sir George, 'as much superior to *Walter Scott* as *Claude* to me in
painting'.

(*Ibid.*, 1983, XII, 4220)

20 October 1812:
After tea Lady Beaumont read some of Wordsworth's poetry of which
she is a great admirer. Sir George, however, admitted that Wordworth's
reputation as a poet wd. have stood higher had the two volumes of His
poems contained only those which would be generally approved. Many
of them are thought to be puerile in their simplicity and these have been
dwelt upon by the Critics & published in reviews to the disadvantage of
His better works.

(*Ibid.*, XII, 4220)

f. From a letter of a Mr Preston of Manchester to William Pearson 1812 (June or July)

In this year, George Dawe (1781–1829) painted Coleridge's portrait.

Just returned from a visit to an eminent artist, Mr. Dawe, I sit down to
discourse a while with you. I wished for your company, you would have
enjoyed the conversation so much. We talked of the Arts – of Coleridge
and of Wordsworth, with whom he is intimate. He repeated a poem of
Coleridge's, from which he has painted a large picture – also one of
Wordsworth's, 'Lines written under a Yew-tree.' – ['Lines left on a Seat
in a Yew-tree?'] 'The Mad Mother' [in later editions, 'Her Eyes are
Wild'], he admires so much, as to speak of it only with enthusiasm.

(*Memoir of William Pearson*, 1863, 27)

g. Sir George Beaumont. From a letter to Wordsworth, 2 June 1814

I wish it had so happened that you could conveniently have visited London this year – Your conversation would certainly have been a cordial to me – As it is I have the consolation to perceive that the film which has so long blinded the public & prevented their being sensible of your excellence is gradually dissolving – & I have no doubt you will soon have 'created the taste by which you are to be relished['] – this consideration makes it doubly grateful to me to hear you are so far advanced in the publication of your great work. Leigh Hunt no great favourite of mine – after some severe sarcasms in verse has thought proper to do you some justice in a note which follows[8] – & taking up a paper of which I had never before heard called the Champion I had the satisfaction to see the author is aware of some of your high qualities.[9]

(Ms. The Wordsworth Library)

h. Lady Beaumont. From a letter to Wordsworth, 2 June 1814

. . . when we called to wish him [Haydon] joy, he spoke with enthusiasm of the happy Warrior, and those 2 lines, 'whose high endeavours [are an inward light / That make the path before him always bright]' he repeated, as if they had cheered him thro all his gloomy path. The privilege of thus sustaining the Soul is given to few.

(*Ibid.*)

EDITOR'S NOTES

1. Sir Thomas Lawrence (1769–1830), portrait painter.
2. William Sotheby (1757–1833), poet and translator.
3. Richard Sharpe (1759–1835), merchant, in hats and West India business; Whig MP.
4. Sir Anthony Carlisle (1768–1840), the London surgeon, a fellow guest at a dinner given by David Pike Watts, Constable's uncle. James Northcote and Benjamin West were also present.
5. Uvedale Price (1747–1829), writer on landscape and the picturesque.
6. Samuel Lysons, the elder (1763–1819), antiquary.
7. Lord Chesterfield (1755–1815).

8. Leigh Hunt's unexpectedly favourable notes to his revised satire, *Feast of Poets*, of 1814 (see entry 134c).

9. The author was Thomas Barnes; for his article in the *Champion* of 28 May 1814 (see entry 135).

113. Elizabeth Vassal Fox, Lady Holland (1770–1845)

Journal entry and Lady Bessborough's report of the Hollands' visit to Dove Cottage, 1807

Journal entry, *c.* 27 August 1807

Lady Holland was staying at the Lowood Hotel, Windermere, when she wrote this opinion of Wordsworth.

– Sent an invitation to Wordsworth, one of the Lake poets, to come and dine, or visit us in the evening. He came. He is much superior to his writings, and his conversation is even beyond his abilities. I should almost fear he is disposed to apply his talents more towards making himself a *vigorous conversationist* in the style of our friend Sharp,[1] than to improve his style of composition. He is preparing a manual to guide travellers in their tour amongst the Lakes. He holds some opinions on picturesque subjects with which I completely differ, especially as to the effects produced by *white* houses on the sides of the hills; to my taste they produce a cheerful effect. He, on the contrary, would brown, or even black-work them; he maintained his opinion with a considerable degree of ingenuity. His objection was chiefly grounded upon the distances being confounded by the glare of white. He seems well read in his provincial history.

(*Lady Holland's Journal*, ed. Earl of Ilchester, 1908, II, 231)

Letter from Lady Bessborough to Lord Granville Leveson-Gower, 5 September 1807

The Hollands apparently called on Wordsworth at Dove Cottage and thought their visit worthy of recounting to Lady Bessborough who in turn sent the news to Lord Granville Leveson-Gower (1773–1846).

257

They went to visit Wordsworth and Southey. The former, with his wife and Sisters, liv'd for some years on £80 p^r ann^m in a Cottage such as the peasants inhabit on the side of Grasmere. His poverty was occasion'd by the late Ld. Lonsdale's purchasing (without the necessary ceremony of paying) his Paternal estate. On the present Ld. L.'s succeeding to it, he *justly* (or, as it is thought for *a Lowther, generously*) paid him, and he has now 300 a year, of which he sees no end; but will perhaps soon find one, as on the strength of it he has taken a larger house. His Sister, who is full of Romance, is quite in despair, Ld. Holland says, at leaving her cottage. Their notions of the picturesque, by Ld. H.'s account, are rather extravagant; the comforts of life, such as a warm house with doors and windows, &c., are monstrous and unpoetical – and a dry walk, monotonous and disgusting in the extreme.

(*Private Correspondence of Lord Granville Leveson-Gower, 1781–1821*, 1917, II, 280)

EDITOR'S NOTE

1. Richard Sharp, friendly aquaintance of both Wordsworth and Coleridge.

114. R. P. Gillies (1788–1858)

Reminiscence, probably of the year 1807

R. P. Gillies was a writer and editor who first met Wordsworth in 1813.

In 1806, the only works of Wordsworth, as yet published, were the 'Lyrical Ballads' in two volumes, and 'Poems,' also in two volumes, bearing date, I think, either that year or 1804. Of these, the second only had fallen in my way, and among our wisest men at Edinburgh (Scott no doubt excepted), the contents were pronounced decidedly, irredeemably bad. The 'Lyrical Ballads' were simple and childish, and the long preface thereto was incomprehensible, but the 'Poems' were really beneath criticism, and merely ridiculous! I remember the said productions were on my table one evening when Chalmers[1] called. He pounced on them as something new, and began to read, but grew very much perplexed, and said: 'Is the man crazy?' Especially, he stumbled and puzzled over the beautiful stanzas on the 'Dog of Helvellyn.' My lamented friend, Dr. Black[2] (afterwards of Coylton), came in, and both of them laughed vehemently at the line: 'What is the creature doing here?' In those days, within the enlightened circles of Edinburgh, to admire the greatest of living poets would have been thought either madness or affectation. Dr. Chalmers, however, took rather a different view of the matter. He pored over the poem, and said at last, 'There is merit here; there is good feeling and good sense, if only the author had known how to express himself properly!'

(*Memoirs of a Literary Veteran*, 1851, I, 229–30)

EDITOR'S NOTES

1. Thomas Chalmers (1780–1847), in later life to become a well-known Scottish theologian.
2. John Black (1777?–1825), Italian scholar and Scottish clergyman.

115. Thomas Wilkinson (1751–1836)

From a letter to Mary Leadbeater, 27 July 1808

Quaker, poet and friend of the Clarksons, through whom he knew Wordsworth, Coleridge, Southey and Charles Lloyd, Thomas Wilkinson wrote this when he had been staying with Mrs Juliet Smith at Coniston and hearing gossip of Francis Jeffrey from Mrs Elizabeth Fletcher of Edinburgh (later of Lancrigg and Wordsworth's close friend).

After all he is rather a clever Fellow and is not far wrong in his criticisms on my friend Wordsworth who is so capable of doing well and sometimes does so indifferently.

(Transcript, Friends House Library)

116. Joanna Baillie (1762–1851)

From letters, 1808–1820

Joanna Baillie (1762–1851), Scottish dramatist and poet: published *Fugitive Verse*, 1790, and three volumes entitled *Plays on the Passions*, 1798, 1802 and 1812, and *Miscellaneous Plays*, 1804. She possibly heard of *Lyrical Ballads*, 1798, from her brother's family (see entry 34). Wordsworth, in turn, may have read her 1798 volume and, in particular, *De Monfort: A Tragedy* where, at the beginning of Act Four, the hero, Rezenvelt remembers when as a boy, hearing an owl hoot, he had 'loudly mimick'd him, till my call / He answer would return, and thro' the gloom / We friendly converse held' (see Jonathan Wordsworth's reprint, *Joanna Baillie: a Series of Plays 1798*, Woodstock Books, 1990, Introduction and 378). In 1812 Crabb Robinson notes, 3 June, that Wordsworth agreed with what Crabb Robinson had reported of what Jeffrey had said in the *Edinburgh Review*: 'Miss Baillie is allowed to have much talent for observation and good sense, but she is denied to have poetic sense'. Wordsworth, Crabb Robinson notes, 'concurs in this judgement, and says he could not read the later volumes' which implies that he had read one or two of her early ones (*Henry Crabb Robinson on Books and Their Writers*, ed. Edith J. Morley, 1935, I, 92).

a. To Walter Scott, 28 October 1808

Joanna and her sister Agnes visited the Lakes, 1808, and, encouraged by Walter Scott, saw both Wordsworth and Southey:

Wordsworth came over to Ambleside which was our headquarters for a little time, and spent a compleat day with us there at our Inn, and took us to see many of his favourate [*sic*] spots in the neighbourhood. He is a man with good strong abilities and a great power of words, but I fear there is that soreness in regard to the world & severity in his notions of mankind growing upon him that will prevent him from being so happy as he deserves to be, for he is I understand a very worthy man.

(*Collected Letters of Joanna Baillie*, ed. Judith Bailey Slagle, 1999, I, 240)

b. To Walter Scott, 21 February 1817

Wordsworth's *Lyrical Ballads*, 2 vols., are certainly known to her by 12 February 1810 for she cites a line from 'Michael' – 'something between a hindrance & a help' (l. 189) – to describe what her own presence would be like if she had come to Edinburgh (*ibid.*, I, 254). And she wryly notes to Scott on 2 January 1812 that she has been condemned by Jeffrey 'with Wordsworth' for a 'childish style of writing' (*ibid.*, I, 295 and below entry 132a). That she was hesitant rather than enthusiastic about Wordsworth's poetry is implicit in her comment to Scott 21 February 1817 where she condemns Byron's description of a thunderstorm in Canto III of *Childe Harold* (stanzas 42 and 43):

What I should consider as bad in Wordsworth I can never believe is good in Lord Byron – I have many things which I wish to ask your advice, notwithstanding your bad taste in poets . . .

(*Ibid.*, I, 364)

c. To Walter Scott, 27 November 1820

On 27 November 1820 she reports meeting Wordsworth in London on his return from a tour of Switzerland:

He is going home with a mind full stored with Lake, clouds, & Mountains for the benefit of the next poem he writes, which from what I learned afterwards from Mrs Hoare, will probably be the continuation of the Wanderer [that is, *The Excursion*, the continuation of which was to be *The Recluse*, largely unwritten except for *Home at Grasmere*]

(*Ibid.*, I, 399)

117. Robert Morehead (1777–1842)

From *Poetical Epistle*, 1813 (written 1808)

The visit to the Lakes took place in the summer of 1798 when Morehead was a student at Balliol, Oxford. He was Francis Jeffrey's cousin.

Can I forget the hallow'd hour I pass'd
In Grasmere chapel, in the lonely waste,
Driven by the rains that patter'd on the lake,
(Perhaps no holier cause) repose to take?
The simple people to each separate hand
Divided, youths and maids in different band;
Of the great power of God, their pastor spoke;

Responsive from the hills loud thunders broke,
From the black smoking hills whose wavering line
Through lead-bound panes was dimly seen to shine.
I felt the voice of Man and Nature roll
The deep conviction on my bending soul!
What if, amid the rural tribe, unknown,
From Wordsworth's eye some moral glory shone,
Some beam of poesy and good combined,
That found the secret foldings of my mind?
(ll. 229–44)

118.

The Simpliciad, extracts, 1808

The author was probably Richard Mant (1776–1848). Mant was an admiring pupil of Joseph Warton at Winchester; he published a volume of poems, 1806; was still a curate in Hampshire when *The Simpliciad: a Satirico – Didactic Poem containing Hints for the Scholars of the New School* appeared anonymously in 1808. Mant's strategy, like that of Francis Jeffrey, is to attack Wordsworth's poems alongside those of Southey and (early) Coleridge. Wordsworth's poems provide more than half the quotations in the footnotes and, yet, arguably seem to contradict the satirist's attack. For an analysis of Mant's methods, see Priscilla Gilman, '"To Kill and Bury the Poor Thorn Forever": "The Thorn" and Mant's *Simpliciad*', *The Wordsworth Circle*, Winter 1996, XXVII, 37–41. Later, when he was Bishop of Down, Connor, and Dromore, he and Wordsworth were guests for dinner at John Bolton's of Storrs, Windermere, and Wordsworth reported of him, 'he was said to be the Author of a forgotten Poem called the Simpliciad – the principal butt of which was to ridicule me, so that I was somewhat drolly placed in such company' (another guest was John Wilson) (letter to Edward Quillinan, 10 September 1830, *LY* II, 324).

TO

Messrs. W–ll––m W–rdsw–rth,
R–b–rt S––th–y, and S. T. C–l–r–dg–.

GENTLEMEN,

ALLOW me to dedicate to you the following Anthology; for it is in fact little more than a collection of flowers, unless I adopt the language of one of your triumvirate, and call them weeds, gathered from certain volumes of miscellaneous poetry.

Rules for the scholars of the old and classical School of Poetry, which was founded by Homer and Sophocles, and of which Virgil and Horace, Milton, Dryden, and Pope, did not disdain to be disciples, were formerly drawn from a contemplation of the works of the first masters: and it occurred to me that a similar practice might be successfully adopted with respect to the NEW, and (what I presume to denominate) the ANTI-CLASSICAL SCHOOL. Without entering nicely into the minutiæ of criticism, it has been my endeavour to execute this task, under the general heads of subject, ideas, diction, and metre. I cannot flatter myself that this Art of Poetry, if I may so term it, will be honoured with your approbation, but if it fail of receiving that of the Public, I am persuaded that its failure will be attributable to no other cause than the weakness of the execution.

I should be guilty of an insolent and a self-evident falsehood, were I to affect to say that the aim of this little piece is not to hold up your new school to ridicule: but I do truly affirm my belief, that in attempting to excite ridicule, I have employed no unfair exaggeration; that the school is incapable of caricature; and that, if a smile be raised by my illustrations, it will be heightened by a perusal of the originals whence they are drawn. 'The force of Nature can no further go;' nor of Art either.

At the same time that I amuse myself, I trust without malignity, at the expence of your Poems, I wish to assure you, that as far as I have any knowledge of your personal characters, I feel for them a high respect. With the friends of humanity and virtue, I venerate your humane feelings and your virtuous principles: with the generality of our countrymen, I acknowledge and admire your talents: but at the same time, with most men of discernment and cultivated minds, I lament the degradation of your genius, and deprecate the propagation of your perverted taste.

I am,

GENTLEMEN,

Your obedient humble servant,

THE AUTHOR.

And will you then the smile, the sigh refuse,
Daughter of heav'n to see the high-soul'd Muse
Condemn'd in leading strings to pipe, and cry,

263

And lisp the accents of the nursery;
Or clad in gipsey rags, with rustic air
To whine with beggars, and with felons swear?

[ll. 9–14]

   F. Then why assault Simplicity? Her lays
Modest and lovely –
   P. Modest! 'tis her praise;
Nor barely modest; Gifford must approve
The friend of mercy, peace, and virtuous love
(Gifford, the dread of every snivelling fool,
That loves and rhimes by Della Cruscan rule.)
And therefore 'tis, Simplicity may claim,
She, or the mongrel that affects her name,
A lighter rod. But for the Muse disgrac'd,
For genius outrag'd, and perverted taste,
The scholar's pity, and the critic's sneer,
And smirking ignorance with stare and leer
Attend her triumph: while to greet the song
Enthusiast Folly draws her mimic throng;
And, as the vapid chorus louder swells,
Her whistle blows, and chimes her coral bells.
   O, that thou ever should'st forego thy claim,
Sweet child of Genius, to thy father's fame,
Renounce the glory of thine elder song,
And ape the whimper of a beldame's tongue!
When smiling mild the glorious chief of Troy
Unlac'd his helmet, and caress'd his boy;
Amid the roaring of th' Ægean deep
When Danae cried, 'O sleep, my infant, sleep;'
When her fond spouse o'er Heliodora shed
The tender tear and gave her to the dead,
Thine was the song: – thine is the song that wakes
Echo, who sleeps by Albion's northern lakes,
[1]Echo, whose birth the cuckoo cannot tell,
Tho' that 'tis sound the bird must know full well;
[2]Where Poets, dozing in lethargic dream,
Such as may Fancy's wayward sons beseem,
Entwine each random weed, that charms their eye,
To hang on wildly-staring Poesy:

264

[3]Poets, who fix their visionary sight
On Sparrow's eggs in prospect of delight,
[4]With fervent welcome greet the glow-worm's flame,
Put it to bed and bless it by its name;
[5]Hunt waterfalls, that gallop down the hills:
[6]And dance with dancing laughing daffodills;
[7]Or measure muddy ponds from side to side,
And find them three feet long and two feet wide:
Poets[8] with brother donkey in the dell
Of mild equality who fain would dwell
With[9] brother lark or brother robin fly,
And flutter with half-brother butterfly;
[10]To woodland shades with liberty repair,
And scorn with pious sneer the House of Pray'r:
[11]Of apostolic daisies learn to think,
Draughts from their urns of true devotion drink:
[12]Woo with fond languishment their chymic maids,
Pray for their [13]Spaniels; [14]consecrate their spades;
[15]Whine over tatter'd cloaks and ragged breeches,
And moralize with gatherers of leeches.

Boast of New Bond-street, and St. Paul's Churchyard,
With 'Lyric Ballads' many a gentle Bard,
Proud of gilt cover, with engravings grac'd,
Courts of mammas and aunts the curious taste.
'Tis their's with greater than the Doctor's skill,
To make by night the screaming infant still;
Or, welcoming day with some melodious air,
Wash his nice hands, and comb his shining hair,
To story told of Gaffer Grumble's wig,
Dame Hubbard's dog, and Betty Pringle's pig.
A simple tale these artless bards rehearse;
The ditty simple, simple is the verse;
But ah! in vain – for know a simpler lay
Wrests from their grasp the nursery prize away!

Bards of the lakes! in sickly thoughts sublime,
The vulgar image, and the doggrel rhime,
Less worthy far of go-cart, pap, and bib,
Your brethren of the cradle and the crib.
What tho' they dare, when Autumn winds are sobbing,
To chaunt a funeral stave o'er poor Cock Robin,

They[16] cannot sing how by some name or other,
All men who know him call Cock Robin brother,
Then bid old Father Adam ope his eyes,
And shudd'ring see this sight beneath the skies,
How Redbreasts hunt and feed on Butterflies.
What though in simple rhimes to nature true,
They sing of roses red and violets blue,
Tis not for them to hymn the spring-day praises
Of [17]patient primroses and [18]dauntless daisies;
Indignant show'r in fiddle-faddle verses.
Blessings on celandines, on king-cups curses;
To scold tall flow'rs, which do as worldlings do,
And will be seen, whether we'll see or no;
While others blithe of heart from week to week
More arch and wily play at hide-and-seek;
To bless [19]mysterious cuckoos; and to sing,
With [20]fancy tether'd to a Linnet's wing,
In numbers shilly-shally, shally-shilly,
So very feeling and so very silly,
That wondering Nonsense proud to see a son
Of Science prate in phrase so like her own,
Dwells on the meagre verse with sparkling eyes,
While o'er degraded Genius Reason sighs.
    Sad is the triumph of the simple Bard!
Her limbs all fetter'd and her cheeks all marr'd,
Nature her violated kingdom feels,
And sense and judgment blur his chariot wheels.
But would ye wish, ye nursery bards, to know
The sources, whence your rivals' glories flow,
Hear, while no brother-mason I impart
The precious mysteries of the sinking art,
And not disposed to dive beneath the flood,
Strip off the buoyant cork from those who wou'd.
I. First choose your theme: not one, whose view supplies
Visions of beauty to poetic eyes,
Charms the rapt soul with scenes of other years,
Or 'opes the source of sympathetic tears.'
Such was the theme, when Southey's feeling song
Invok'd revenge for bleeding Afric's wrong;

And such when Wordsworth bade the Minstrel raise
His festal strain to 'Good Lord Clifford's' praise.
For why to distant lands and ages roam?
Less hackney'd themes invite you nearer home;
Congenial themes, which yield more tasteful food
[21]To poets musing in their fitful mood.
See! with impassion'd flow'rs each bank is teeming;
See! with blue sparrow's eggs each hedge is gleaming;
[22]Ecstatic birds, whose thoughts no bard can measure;
Blossoms that breathe, and twigs that pant with pleasure.
Heaths bloom with cups,[23] the darlings of the eye;
[24]Green fields with grass, that drinks a sense of joy;
[25]Hills have their thorns with clasping mosses hung;
Thorns now so old, you'd say they ne'er were young,
Mosses, so close, you'd say that they were bent
With wicked plain and manifest intent,
As if they all had joined in one endeavour,
To kill and bury the poor thorn for ever.
The village boasts its busy,[26] busy bees;
[27]Old road-menders who dine on bread and cheese;
[28]Poachers, who go, when trade in England fails,
To drink their grog and curse in New South Wales;
[29]Goodies who boil their pottage one and one
By the same fire; and some, who dwell alone;
Beggars, on lies and impudence who thrive,
And cottage girls, who don't know seven from five.
If from such arduous tasks you shrink dismay'd,
Play with your cat, apostrophize your spade:
Or [30]should some donkey cross you on the way,
(Not such as wends with crimson housing gay,
The conscious palfrey of a high-born lass,
But a poor, half-starv'd, plodding, vulgar ass)
'Tis but with gentle hand to give him bread,
And clap his ragged coat, and pat his head,
Lament his sad prophetic fears, approve
His patient merit, and his filial love,
Converse a little with his asking feet,
And praise his hoarse bray, musically sweet;
Then in despite of scornful folly's pother,
Ask him to live with you, and hail him Brother!

267

Such subjects are original, 'tis true;
But then they're very poor and paltry too.
And thro' the frame so swiftly venom speeds,
So hard it is to purge a field from weeds,
'Tis chance but themes like these infect your style,
Debase your thoughts, and make your language vile.
   Not but the bard can wave his wizard wand,
And turn a desert into fairy land,
Of village spoils a manly trophy raise,[31]
And crown a Sofa with a Georgic's praise . . .

                        [ll. 60–222]
               [ll. 223–38, section II, cut]

III. For be your thoughts attir'd like Falstaff's pack,
Poor hungry knaves with lean and shirtless back.
[32]What that attire is, dost thou ask of me?
Come walk abroad, and I will answer thee.
Yon children, 'mid the strawberries at play;
Yon old man breaking stones on the highway;
Yon lieing gipsey with her sea of tears;
Yon convict wretch that laughs and prays and swears;
Only ask them, as thou hast ask'd of me,
What words to use and they will answer thee!
   But tho' you deem the style of art[33] too good
And bright for simple Nature's constant food,
Yet spurn not what belike may help along
[34]Your lagging skeletons of meagre song,
As [35]budding groves wak'd by the vernal tune,
Bestir themselves to spur the steps of June.
For [36]visitings of thought beyond the reach,
The scope, the eye-mark of our English speech,
Behold your mighty master [37]FURIUS brings
New words to temper your sweet jargonings;
Or bids the old in awkward union close,
[38]A hailstone swarm; his godlike task foregoes
Of spitting snow on hoary Alpine rocks,
To [39]steep in silence British weathercocks.
He wills; the [40]rivers trample to the deep,
The [41]cataracts blow their trumpets from the steep,
Awaken'd echoes through the mountains throng,

And [42]kettles whisper their faint undersong.

IV. With loftiest numbers, uncontrol'd by rhime,
In epic glory Milton stands sublime;
Such Thomson chose, and Cowper, to array
In moral beauty the descriptive lay.
The finished couplet Pope's smooth rhimes approve,
For precept terse, or tender tale of love.
While Nature owns the elegiac strains,
In solemn quatrain pensive Gray complains,
Or strikes to loftier verse the varying lyre,
Divides the crown, and rivals Dryden's fire.
But [43]ye for metre rummage Percy's Reliques;
In sapphics limp, or amble in dactylics;
Trip it in Ambrose Philips's trochaics;
In dithyrambics vault; or hobble in prosaics.
Yours [44]be the linnet's note, teem'd forth in gushes;
And yours the drunken lark's, as up he rushes;
[45]And yours the fiery nightingale's, that sings
With skirmish and capricious passagings.
Why fetter Genius? But as e'er you hope
To shun the praise of Dryden and of Pope,
The graceful ease, the stately march decline,
And manly vigour of a classic line.
    Thus subject, image, language, metre cull,
Spite of resisting genius, you'll be dull:
But to th' abyss of bathos would you creep,
Unfailing source of ridicule or sleep,
For themes of sorrow marshal all your art,
And plant your whole artillery at the heart.
    Now the gruff farmer's dozing conscience wake,
With tale of Harry Gill and Goody Blake.
Poor Goody Blake, and cruel Harry Gill!
She stole his hedges, and he used her ill,
And now his teeth they chatter, chatter, still.
Now rouse maternal fears for Betty Foy,
Her lamblike pony, and her idiot boy; . . .

[ll. 239–301]

269

AUTHORITIES.

1   Yes! full surely 'twas the Echo,
           Solitary, clear, profound,
        Answering to Thee, shouting Cuckoo!
           Giving to thee sound for sound.

        Whence the voice? from air or earth?
           This the Cuckoo cannot tell;
        But a startling sound had birth,
           As the Bird must know full well.
           ['Yes, it was the mountain Echo', *PW*, II, p. 265 and
              footnotes, stanzas 1 and 2; *Poems 1807*, p. 297,
                                stanzas 1 and 2]

2   Then ask not wherefore, here, alone,
           Conversing as I may,
        I sit upon this old gray stone,
           And *dream* my time away.
           ['Expostulation and Reply', *PW*, IV, p. 56,
              ll. 29–32; *LB (1798)*, p. 104, ll. 29–32]

     And as *beseem'd the wayward Fancy's child*
     Entwin'd each random weed that pleas'd mine eye.
           [Southey: from dedicatory sonnet to *Poems*]

     Dear native brook! where first young Poesy
     Star'd wildly-eager in her noontide dream.
              [Coleridge: *Poems*, 39]

3   Look, five blue *eggs* are gleaming there!
        Few *visions* have I seen more fair,
        Nor many *prospects of delight*,
        More pleasing than that simple sight!
        ['The Sparrow's Nest', *PW*, I, p. 227, stanza 1; *Poems
        1807*, p. 227, stanza 1. 1807 only; much altered by
                          Wordsworth]

4 He then laid the Glow-worm on a leaf, and carried it away with
him: thereupon what followed, Musa rogata refer:

     When to the dwelling of my Love I came,
     I went into the orchard quietly;

And left the Glow-worm, *blessing it by name,*
    Laid safely by itself, beneath a tree.
        ['Among all lovely things my Love had been', *PW*, II,
            p. 466, stanza 4; *Poems 1807*, stanza 4, p. 74. This
            poem 1807 only; never reprinted by Wordsworth]

These lines require some explanation. The Poet tells us that, 'Among all lovely things his Love had been,' but had never had the good fortune to see a Glow-worm. Judge of his emotions

When riding near her home one stormy night
A single Glow-worm did I chance to espy;
I gave *a fervent welcome* to the sight,
And from my horse I leapt; great joy had I.

The whole next day I hoped, and hoped with fear,
At night the Glow-worm shone beneath the tree:
I led my Lucy to the spot, 'Look here!'
Oh! joy it was for her, and joy for me!
        [*Ibid., PW*, II, p. 466, stanzas 2 and 5; *Poems 1807*, p. 74,
            stanzas 2 and 5]

5   When up she winds along the brook,
                To *hunt the waterfalls.*
                    ['Louisa', *PW*, II, p. 28, ll. 23–4; *Poems 1807*, p. 16,
                        ll. 23–4]

What more he said I cannot tell.
The stream came thund'ring down the dell,
    And *galloped* loud and fast.
        ['The Waterfall and the Eglantine', *PW*, II, p. 130,
            ll. 51–3; *LB (1800)*, p. 154, ll. 51–3; 'galloped'
            removed after 1807]

6   I wander'd lonely as a cloud
            That floats on high o'er vales and hills,
            When all at once I saw a crowd,
            A host of *dancing daffodills.*
                *   *   *   *   *   *
            A poet could not be but gay
            In such a *laughing* company.
                *   *   *   *   *   *
            And then my heart with pleasure fills,
            And *dances with the daffodills.*

The whole poem, consisting of eighteen lines, is exquisite.
[Quotes from 'I wandered lonely as a cloud', *PW*, II, p. 216; *Poems 1807*, p. 223; 'laughing' revised later to 'jocund', 'dancing' revised later to 'golden' and 'laughing' to 'golden'.]

7   This Thorn you on your left espy,
And to the left, three yards beyond
You see a little *muddy pond*
Of water never dry;
I've measur'd it from side to side:
'Tis three feet long, and two feet wide.
['The Thorn', *PW*, II, p. 241 and footnotes, ll. 28–33;
LB (1798), p. 69, ll. 28–33]

8 The following lines are taken from an address to a Young Ass, by S.T.C.[oleridge]

Innocent foal! thou poor despis'd forlorn!
I hail thee BROTHER, spite of the fool's scorn!
And fain would take thee with me, *in the Dell*,
Of peace and *mild equality to dwell.*

9   Up with me! up with me into the clouds!
For thy song, *Lark*, is strong;
Up with me, up with me into the clouds!
Singing, singing,
With all the heavens about thee ringing,
Lift me, guide me, till I find
The spot which seems so to thy mind!

And so forth, through another page: after which,

Hearing thee, or else some other,
As merry a *brother*, &c.
['To a Sky-Lark', *PW*, II, pp. 141–2 in footnotes,
stanza 1 and ll. 26–7; *Poems 1807*, pp. 88–90,
stanza 1 and ll. 26–7]

Of the Robin Redbreast, the same Poet singeth sweetly, that he is

The bird, who by some name or other,
All men who know him, call him *brother*.
['The Redbreast chasing the Butterfly', *PW*, II, p. 149,
ll. 9–10; *Poems 1807*, p. 24, ll. 9–10]

The relationship of the Butterfly is not so clearly settled; but in virtue of his being brother to the Robin Redbreast,

> A *brother* he seems of thine own,
>> [*Ibid.*, *PW*, II, p. 150, l. 36, in notes; *Poems 1807*,
>>> p. 26, l. 39]

I have ventured to give his genealogy as above.

10   *Go thou and seek the House of Prayer!*
      I to the *woodlands* bend my way,
      And meet Religion there!
      She needs not haunt the high-arch'd dome to pray, &c.
      With Liberty she loves to rove.
>> Poems by R.S. I. 59.

I transcribe the passage as I find it. It was written, as appears by the date subjoined, in 1795. It is to be hoped that thirteen years have wrought a change in the author's sentiments.

11 The daisy is a favourite with one of our poets; and with reason: for it is fitting that the flower which is 'Nature's favourite,' should be also 'the Poet's darling.' I select one or two passages from 'the overflowings of his mind,' in praise of that 'sweet silent creature.'

> Thou breath'st with me in sun and air,
> Do thou, as thou art wont, repair
> My heart with gladness, and a share
> Of thy meek nature!
>> ['To the Daisy' ("With little here to do . . ."), *PW*,
>>> II, p. 139, ll. 45–8; *Poems 1807*, p. 270, ll. 45–8]

Again:

> If stately passions in me burn,
> And one chance look to thee should turn,
> I *drink* out of an humbler *urn*
> A lovelier pleasure.
>> ['In youth from rock to rock', *PW*, II, p. 137, ll. 49–52;
>>> *Poems 1807*, p. 12, ll. 49–52]

Again:

> At dusk I've seldom mark'd thee press
> The ground, as if in thankfulness,
> Without some feeling more or less,
>   *Of true devotion.*
> [*Ibid.*, *PW*, II, p. 137, ll. 49–52 in footnotes;
>   *Poems 1807*, p. 12, ll. 61–4]

But I know not whether a more perfect instance of silliness is to be detected in the whole farrago of the school, than the following stanza; mark ye! addressed as well as the foregoing, to the daisy:

> Thou wander'st the wide world about,
> Uncheck'd by pride or scrupulous doubt,
> With friends to greet thee, or without,
>   Yet pleased and willing;
> Meek, yielding to occasion's call,
> And all things suffering from all,
> THY FUNCTION APOSTOLICAL
>   IN PEACE FULFILLING.
> ['Bright Flower! whose home . . .', *PW*, IV, p. 68,
>   ll. 17–24; *Poems 1807*, p. 272, ll. 17–24]

I may be pardoned for exclaiming with Cowper,

> From such apostles O ye mitred heads
> Preserve the church!

12   Spirits of Love –
> Or *with fond languishment* around my fair
> Sigh in the loose luxuriance of her hair –
> Spirits! to you the infant maid was given,
> Form'd by the wond'rous *alchemy* of Heaven.
>   Poems by S.T.C. 37.

13 Such a practice is not very common, I apprehend, but we have the Poet's own words for it, that it even was so:

> I PRAY'D FOR THEE, and that thy end were past,
> And willingly have laid thee here at last.
> ['Tribute', *PW*, IV, p. 79, ll. 11–2; *Poems 1807*, p. 277, ll. 13–4;
>   'pray'd' altered to 'grieved' 1820]

But then 'little Music' was not a common dog: it was not for the usual canine qualities that

> Both man and woman wept when she was dead.
> But for some precious boons vouchsafed to thee
> Found scarcely any where in like degree!
> For love, that comes to all, the holy sense,
> Best gift of God, in thee was most intense;
> A chain of heart, a feeling of the mind,
> A tender sympathy which did thee bind
> Not only to us men, but to thy kind;
> Yea for thy fellow-brutes in thee we saw
> The soul of Love, Love's intellectual law.
>
> > [*Ibid.*, *PW*, IV, pp. 79–80, ll. 22–33; *Poems 1807*, pp. 277–8,
> > ll. 24–35]

Now if the Poet's partiality for his friend's dog did not obscure his understanding, she certainly was a wonderful creature; and were all such, we might be disposed to adopt the practice of one of our bards and pray for our dogs in this world, and the creed of his friend, with respect to their existence in another.

> – Fare thee well! mine is no narrow creed;

Is his valedictory address to a favourite old Spaniel:

> – There is another world
> For all that live and move – a better one!
> > Poems by P. S. I. 142.

Surely this is being wise above what is written.

14 And when thou art past service, worn away,
Thee a surviving soul shall *consecrate*.
> ['To the Spade of a Friend', *PW*, II, p. 76, ll. 27–8; *Poems
> 1807*, p. 301, ll. 27–8]

15 Of the pitiable tales of the tatter'd cloak and the leech-gatherer, I shall have more to say anon. For the circumstance of *the ragged breeches*, I refer to a poem communicated to the Anti-Jacobin Newspaper by a Mr. Higgins: and take this opportunity of recommending to Mr. W. the next time he shall have occasion to request the assistance of a friend, to apply to this gentleman; as I am convinced that the poems of Mr. H. 'will in a great measure

have the same tendency as his own, and that, though there may be found a difference, there will be found no discordance in the colours of their style; as their opinions on the subject of poetry do almost entirely coincide.'

See Preface to Lyrical Ballads.

16 – It was some time before I could discover the cause of the appeal made to Father Adam, and referred to above. But after two or three diligent perusals of the poem, the opening of which follows, I perceived it was the indignation of the bard at seeing (eloquar an sileam? [shall I speak or be silent?]) a robin redbreast chasing a butterfly. Fill'd with horror at the spectacle, the poet bursts forth in this animated and pertinent remonstrance:

> Art thou the bird whom man loves best,
> The pious bird with the scarlet breast,
>   Our little English Robin;
> The bird that comes about our doors
> When autumn winds are sobbing?
> Art thou the Peter of Norway Boors!
>   Their Thomas in Finland,
>   And Russia far inland?
> *The bird, whom by some name or other*
> *All men who know thee call their brother,*
> The darling of children and men?
> *Could Father Adam open his eyes,*
> *And see this sight beneath the skies,*
>   *He'd wish to close them again.*
>
> ['The Redbreast chasing the Butterfly', *PW*, II, p. 149,
> ll. 1–14; *Poems 1807*, p. 24, ll. 1–14]

17 – To the small Celandine:

> Comfort have thou of thy merit
> Kindly, unassuming spirit!
> Careless of thy neighbourhood
> Thou dost show thy pleasant face
> On the moor, and in the wood,
> In the lane – there's not a place,
> Howsoever mean it be,
> But 'tis good enough for thee.

Ill befal the yellow flowers,
Children of the flaring hours!
Butter-cups, that will be seen,
Whether we will see or no;
Others too of lofty mien;
They have done as worldlings do,
Taken praise that should be thine,
Little, humble Celandine.

> ['Pansies, lilies, kingcups, daisies', *PW*, II, pp. 143–4,
> ll. 41–56; *Poems 1807*, p. 33, ll. 41–56]

The poet having expressed his admiration of this little flower
through seven stanzas of this spirit, and having set it on a footing
with the apostolical daisy, by finally saluting it,

> Prophet of delight and mirth,
> Scorned and slighted upon earth,

concludes with declaring his resolution of being more just to its
merits,

> I will sing as doth behove,
> *Hymns in praise* of what I love!

The reader perhaps would exclaim, Ohe, jam satis est! Not so the
poet, who is not contented without supplying another address of
six stanzas in the same gentle strain to the same little flower:
Having regretted that he so long could overlook

> Her *arch and wily* ways
> And her store of other praise,

he continues,

> *Blithe of heart from week to week*
> *Thou dost play at hide-and-seek,*
> While *the patient Primrose* sits
> Like a Beggar in the cold,
> Thou, a Flower of wiser wits,
> Slip'st into thy shelter'd hold, &c.

> ['Pleasures newly found . . .', *PW*, II, p. 145, ll. 31 ff.;
> *Poems 1807*, p. 37, ll. 31 ff.]

18 The reader is already acquainted with some of the daisy's amiable
and Christian virtues; its meekness and humility; its long-suffer-
ing and thankfulness; but its resolution and courage are not less
worthy of admiration as the following lines may testify:

> In shoals and bands, a morrice train,
> Thou greet'st the Traveller in the lane;
> If welcome once thou count'st it gain;
> *Thou art not daunted*,
> Nor car'st if thou be set at naught –
> ['In youth from rock to rock', *PW*, II, p. 136, ll. 17–21;
> *Poems 1807*, p. 10, ll. 17–21]

19

> O blithe new-comer! I have heard,
> I hear thee and rejoice:
> O cuckoo shall I call thee bird
> Or but a wandering voice?
>   * * * *
> Thrice welcome, darling of the spring!
> Even yet thou art to me
> No bird; but an invisible thing,
> A voice, a *mystery*.
>   * * * *
> O *blessed* bird, &c. &c.
> ['To the Cuckoo', *PW*, II, pp. 207–8, ll. 1–4, 13–6 and 29;
> *Poems 1807*, pp. 231–3, ll. 1–4, 13–6 and 29]

20

> A whispering leaf is now my joy,
> And then a bird will be the toy,
>   *That doth my fancy tether*.
> Hail to thee, far above the rest,
>   In joy of voice and *pinion*
> Thou, *Linnet*, in thy green array.
> ['The Green Linnet', *PW*, II, p. 140 in footnotes, ll. 6–13;
> *Poems 1807*, pp. 253–4, ll. 6–13; much revised after 1807]

21 – 'Musings,' and 'Moods of my own mind' are the titles prefixed
by our poets to some of their effusions.

'And madness laughing in his ireful mood', is a noble line from
Dryden.

22   Upon yon tuft of hazel trees
   That twinkle to the gusty breeze,
   Behold him perch'd in *ecstasies.*
   [*Ibid.*, *PW*, II, p. 140, ll. 25–7; *Poems 1807*, p. 255,
                ll. 25–7]

   And 'tis my faith that *every flower*
   Enjoys the air it breathes.
   The *birds* around me hopp'd and play'd;
    Their thoughts I cannot measure:
   But the least motion which they made,
    It was a thrill of pleasure.
   The budding twigs spread out their fan,
    To catch the breezy air,
   And I must think, do all I can,
    That there was pleasure there.
     ['Lines Written in Early Spring', *PW*, IV, p. 58,
       ll. 11–20; *LB (1798)*, p. 69, ll. 11–20]

23   And cups, *the darlings of the eye*,
   So deep is their vermilion die.
    ['The Thorn', *PW*, II, p. 242, ll. 43–4; *LB (1798)*,
             p. 71, ll. 43–4]

24   There is a blessing in the air,
   Which seems a *sense of joy* to yield
   To the bare trees and mountains bare
   And *grass in the green field.*
    ['To My Sister', *PW*, IV, p. 59, ll. 5–8; *LB (1798)*, p. 59,
               ll. 5–8]

25   There is a *thorn, – it looks so old,*
   In truth you'd find it hard to say,
   How it could ever have been young
   It looks so old and grey.
   Up from the earth these mosses creep,
   And this poor thorn they *clasp* it round
   So close, you'd say that they were bent
   With plain and manifest intent
   To drag it to the ground;

And all had joined in one endeavour
To bury this poor thorn for ever.
['The Thorn', *PW*, II, pp. 240–1, ll. 1–4 and 16–22;
LB (1798), pp. 69–70, ll. 1–4 and 16–22, omitting
eleven lines where Wordsworth hints at the thorn's
heroic power by noting, twice, that it 'stands erect',
despite the mosses attempting to drag it down.]

26   Thou wert out betimes, thou *busy, busy bee.*
See Poems by R.S.II. 74.

The appellation is a favourite with the author; it occurs twice four
times in four six-line stanzas.

27   There was an *old man* breaking stones
To *mend the turnpike way*;
He sate him down beside a brook,
And out *his bread and cheese* he took,
For now it was mid-day.
Poems by R.S. II. 91.

The old turnpike-mender is presently joined by a soldier, with his
knapsack on, who enquires 'how far to Bristol town;' and having
received a full and particular answer, about the road and the
foot-path,

The soldier took his knapsack off
For he was hot and dry,
And out *his bread and cheese* he took,
And he sat down beside the brook
To *dine* in company.

After such an introduction as this, with what follows about the
soldier begging his companion to let him lean his back against the
post, for that

In such a sweltering day as this,
A knapsack is the devil;

few readers, it is to be presumed, would have much desire to know
more.

28 See Botany Bay Eclogues; by R. S. Poems, Vol. I. p. 93 and
101.

29   *By the same fire to boil their pottage*
       Two poor old dames, as I have known,
       Will often live in one small cottage;
       But she, poor woman! *dwelt alone.*
       ['Goody Blake and Harry Gill', *PW*, IV, p. 174, ll. 33–6;
           LB (1798), p. 55, ll. 33–6; 'dwelt' revised to 'housed']

30 – For the four subjects alluded to in the two foregoing couplets, I
     refer to the Lyrical Ballads and Poems of W. W. This gentleman,
     who is (I believe) the founder of the simple school, supplies us
     with the most copious catalogue of illustrations of its merit. But I
     know not that he has any one composition, so prolific of beauty, as
     the poem to which allusion is here made: so much so indeed, and
     written withal in a style so different from the other poems by the
     same author, of which simplicity is by no means the characteristic,
     that could I believe him capable of such treachery, I should very
     strongly suspect that his object was to quiz his brethren. The
     allusions above keep so close to the original, that my readers may
     be spared the trouble of perusing the annexed extract, which
     however I transcribe for my own justification.
       [Quotes 'To a Young Ass', by Coleridge, ll. 1–5, 9–14, 23–7, 33–5, with
     copious italics and capitals.]

31 See the Poems of the Rev. George Crabbe, especially The Village
     and The Parish Register.

32 – For the striking form in which this precept is conveyed,
     I am indebted to a poem by R. S. intituled, The Complaints
     of the Poor. It opens in the following beautifully abrupt
     manner.

              And wherefore do the poor complain?
                The rich man ask'd of me; –
              Come walk abroad with me, I said,
                And I will answer thee.

     Having met and conversed with several poor objects, miserable
     enough, Heaven knows, but over whose miseries the poet has
     contrived to throw a strong shade of the ludicrous, they settle the
     question thus:

> I turn'd me to the rich man then,
>   For silently stood he, —
> *You ask'd me why the poor complain,*
> *And these have answer'd thee!*

33   – The two following lines are from a poem, to which there is no
title, and which I have read again and again, but am unable to say
what is the subject of it. It begins, She was a phantom of delight,
and after going on to say that she was an apparition, a shape, an
image, a spirit, and a woman, it calls her

> A creature not *too bright or good*
> *For human nature's daily food;*
>   ['She was a phantom of delight', *PW*, II, p. 213,
>   ll. 17–8; *Poems 1807*, p. 23, ll. 17–8]

whatever it was, it appears to have been too much for the Poet's
senses.

34   I never saw aught like to them,
>   Unless perchance it were
>   *The skeletons of* leaves that *lag*
>   My forest brook along.

35   — the voice
>   Of waters which the winter had supplied,
>   Was soften'd down into a *vernal tone.*
>   *The budding groves* appear'd as if in haste,
>   *To spur the steps of June.*
>   ['It was an April morning', *PW*, II, p. 110, ll. 3 ff.; *LB*
>   *(1800)*, p. 212, ll. 3 ff.]

36   With no restraint but such as springs
>   From quick and eager *visitings*
>   *Of thoughts, that lie beyond the reach*,
>   Of thy few words of *English speech.*
>   ['To a Highland Girl', *PW*, III, p. 74, ll. 38–41; *Poems*
>   *1807*, p. 199, ll. 36–9]

37   Sometimes all little birds that are,
>   How they seemed to fill the sea and air
>   With their *sweet jargoning!*

My reader needs hardly to be reminded that Furius was a Roman poet of genius, but known to us not very favourably by a specimen of his style preserved by Horace and Quinctilian, and imitated above in the 261st verse. Furius hybernas canâ nive conspuit alpes (Furius spattered the winter alps with white snow).

38   When *hailstones* have been falling *swarm on swarm.*
['There is a Flower', *PW*, IV, p. 244, l. 5; *Poems 1807*, p. 221, l. 5]

39   The moonlight *steeped in silentness*
              The steady *weathercock.*

40   The lightning, the fierce wind, and *trampling* waves.

41   *The cataracts blow their trumpets from the steep*,
           No more shall grief of mine the season wrong,
           I hear *the echoes through the mountains throng*,
           The winds come to me from the fields of sleep.
['Ode: Intimations of Immortality', *PW*, IV, p. 280, ll. 25–8;
Poems 1807, p. 322, ll. 25–8]

42   To sit without emotion, hope, or aim,
           By my half-kitchen my half-parlour fire,
           And listen to the flapping of the flame,
           Or kettle whispering its faint undersong.
['Personal Talk', *PW*, IV, p. 73, ll. 11–4; *Poems 1807*,
p. 293, ll. 11–4]

43 – See Lyrical Ballads, and Poems by W. W. and Poems by R. S. passim. 'Dithyrambic, a song in honour of Bacchus, in which anciently, and now among the Italians, the distraction of ebriety is imitated.' (*See Johnson's Dictionary.*) I know no term equally fit to describe that undefinable measure which spurns all rules and betrays a total alienation of mind, as in Vol. I. p. 80, and Vol. II. p. 147, of Poems by W.W. In the former place the reader will find '*The drunken lark.*'
[Quotes 'Up with me! up with me into the clouds', *PW*, II, p. 141; *Poems
1807*, p. 88 . . . and 'Ode: Intimations of Immortality', p. 279]

44   While thus before my eyes he gleams,
           A brother of the leaves he seems,
           When in a moment forth he *teems*,
           His little song in gushes.
['The Green Linnet', *PW*, II, p. 140 in footnotes,
ll. 33–6; *Poems 1807*, p. 255, ll. 33–6]

45   O *nightingale*, thou surely art,
A creature of a *fiery* heart.
['O Nightingale! thou surely art', *PW*, II, p. 214,
ll. 1–2; *Poems 1807*, p. 216, ll. 1–2]

They answer and provoke each other's songs,
With skirmish and capricious passagings.

119. Samuel Taylor Coleridge

Extracts from *The Friend*, 1809–1810: see *The Friend*, II,
ed. Barbara E. Rooke, Routledge, 1969

a. 8 June 1809, p. 25

Coleridge speaks overmodestly of his contribution to *Lyrical Ballads*.

And anonymously I have only contributed the foil of three or four small poems to the volume of a superior mind . . .

b. 10 August 1809, p. 41

Men are ungrateful to others only when they have ceased to look back on their former selves with joy and tenderness. They exist in fragments. Annihilated as to the Past, they are dead to the Future, or seek for the proofs of it every where, only not (where alone they can be found) in themselves. A contemporary poet has exprest and illustrated this sentiment with equal fineness of thought and tenderness of feeling:

> My heart leaps up when I behold
>   A rain-bow in the sky!
> So was it, when my life began;
> So is it now I am a man;
> So let it be, when I grow old,
>   Or let me die.
> *The Child is Father of the Man,*
> *And I would wish my days to be*
> *Bound each to each by natural piety.*
>   WORDSWORTH

I am informed, that these very lines have been cited, as a specimen of despicable puerility. So much the worse for the citer. Not willingly in *his* presence would I behold the Sun setting behind our mountains, or listen to a tale of Distress, or Virtue; I should be ashamed of the quiet tear on my own cheek. But let the Dead bury the Dead! The poet sang for the Living.

c. 28 September, 1809, p. 108

But if my Readers wish to see the Questions of the efficacy of the Principles and popular Opinions for evil and for good proved and illustrated with an eloquence worthy of the Subject, I can refer him with the hardiest anticipation of his thanks to the late Work 'concerning the Relations of Great Britain, Spain, and Portugal' by my honoured Friend, William Wordsworth* quem quoties lego, non verba mihi videor audire, sed tonitrua! [whenever I read him, I seem to hear not words but thunders!]

[Coleridge's footnote reads:]

*I consider this reference to, and strong recommendation of the Work above-mentioned, not as a voluntary tribute of admiration, but as an act of mere justice both to myself and to the Readers of THE FRIEND. My own heart bears me witness, that I am actuated by the deepest sense of the truth of the Principles, which it has been and still more will be my endeavour to enforce, and of their paramount importance to the Well-being of Society at the present juncture: and that the duty of making the attempt, and the hope of not wholly failing in it, are, far more than the wish for the doubtful good of literary reputation or any yet meaner object, are my great and ruling Motives. Mr. Wordsworth I deem a fellow-labourer in the same vineyard, actuated by the same motives and teaching the same principles, but with far greater powers of mind, and an eloquence more adequate to the importance and majesty of the Cause. I am strengthened too by the knowledge, that I am not unauthorized by the sympathy of many wise and good men, and men acknowledged as such by the Public, in my admiration of his Pamphlet.

d. 21 December 1809, p. 233

. . . I have prefixed his Sonnet on Switzerland ['Two voices are there'] from his 'Poems' [1807; *PW*, III, 115], having always thought that it is one of the noblest sonnets in our language, and the happiest comment on the line of Milton – 'The *mountain* Nymph, sweet Liberty', which would be no inapt motto for the whole collection.

e. 28 December 1809, p. 258

Coleridge introduces the passage from the opening book of *The Prelude* beginning: 'Wisdom and Spirit of the Universe!' He gives the title as: 'Growth of Genius from the Influences of Natural Objects on the Imagination in Boyhood and early Youth': it is the first printed reference to the existence of Wordsworth's verse autobiography and to Coleridge's response on hearing what was later *The Prelude* read aloud.

Coleridge introduces Wordsworth's description of skating in the English Lake District with his own account of skating at Ratzeburg in Germany in January 1799, a passage, incidentally, influenced by Wordsworth's poem sent to him the previous month.

Here I stop, having in truth transcribed the Preceding in great measure, in order to present the lovers of Poetry with a descriptive Passage, extracted, with the Author's permission from an unpublished Poem, 'The Growth and Revolutions of an Individual Mind', by WORDSWORTH.

> . . . an orphic Tale indeed,
> a Tale divine of high and passionate thoughts
> To their own music chaunted!
>
> S.T.C.

f. 25 January 1810, p. 290

Coleridge recollects the response of Sir Alexander Ball to hearing *Peter Bell* read aloud from the manuscript when he was in Malta in 1804–5.

Works of Amusement, as Novels, Plays &c. did not appear even to amuse him: and the only poetical Composition, of which I ever heard him speak, was a Manuscript Poem written by one of my Friends, which I read to his Lady in his presence. To my surprize, he afterwards spoke of this with warm interest; but it was evident to me, that it was not so much the poetic merit of the Composition that had interested him, as the Truth and psychological interest with which it represented the practicability of reforming the most hardened minds, and the various accidents which may awaken the most brutalised Person to a recognition of his nobler being.

g. 25 January 1810, p. 292

Coleridge, in describing his feelings about the death of Sir Alexander Ball, uses Wordsworth's unpublished lines of 'The Ruined Cottage', later to be included in the first book of *The Excursion*.

At the thought of such events the language of a tender superstition is the voice of Nature itself, and those facts alone presenting themselves to our memory which had left an impression on our hearts, we assent to, and adopt the Poet's pathetic complaint:

> O Sir! The good die first,
> And those whose hearts are dry as summer dust,
> Burn to the socket.

h. 15 February 1810, p. 327

Coleridge is attacking the language of the economist, Sir James Stuart, who had contrasted the labour a man does for his own subsistence and that which is of benefit to Society. Coleridge attacks the words State and Society: 'And think you it possible, that ten thousand happy human beings can exist together without encreasing each other's happiness? or that it will not overflow into countless channels, and *diffuse itself through the rest of the Society.'
[Coleridge's footnote cites the lines from 'Michael', 411–12, where the old man addresses his son, Luke, on the goodness of their forebears.]

*Well, and in the spirit of genuine philosophy, does the Poet describe such beings as Men

> Who being innocent do for that cause
> Bestir them in good deeds'.
>
> WORDSWORTH

Providence, by the ceaseless activity which it has implanted in our nature, has sufficiently guarded against an innocence without virtue.

120. John Wilson and Alexander Blair (*fl.* 1790–1836)

From *The Friend*, 14 December 1809

The authors (see entry 70), writing under the pseudonym 'Mathetes', pick out Wordsworth as the age's Truth-giver; in this reference to him speaking 'in thunder' they are citing Coleridge's own compliment to Wordsworth's essay on the Convention of Cintra in *The Friend*, 20 September, 1809 (see entry 132c).

From much of its own weakness, and from all the errors of its misleading activities, may generous youth be rescued by the interposition of an enlightened mind: and in some degree it may be guarded by instruction against the injuries to which it is exposed in the world. *His* lot is happy who owes this protection to friendship: who has found in a friend the watchful guardian of his mind. He will not be deluded, having that light to guide: he will not slumber, with that voice to inspire; he will not be desponding or dejected, with that bosom to lean on. – But how many must there be whom Heaven has left unprovided, except in their own strength; who must maintain themselves, unassisted and solitary, against their own infirmities and the opposition of the world! For such there may be yet a protector. If a Teacher should stand up in their generation conspicuous above the multitude in superior power, and yet more in the assertion and proclamation of disregarded Truth – to Him – to his cheering or summoning voice all hearts would turn, whose deep sensibility has been oppressed by the indifference, or misled by the seduction of the times. Of one such Teacher who has been given to our own age, you have described the power when you said, that in his annunciation of truths he seemed to speak in thunders. I believe that mighty voice has not been poured out in vain: that there are hearts that have received into their inmost depths all its varying tones: and that even now, there are many to whom the name of Wordsworth calls up the recollection of their weakness, and the consciousness of their strength.

(pp. 228–9)

121. Byron

Reviews, comments and correspondence, 1807–1814

Byron's view of Wordsworth fluctuates from his vague and favourable review of *Poems 1807* to the negative comments derived from Jeffrey in the *Edinburgh Review* in *English Bards and Scotch Reviewers* (see entries 98 and 103). Thereafter, Rogers, Leigh Hunt and Shelley attempt to overcome Byron's absolute prejudice: the two actual meetings of 11 May 1812 and 18 June 1815 seem to have pleased both men, but the gossip between Rogers, Moore, James Hogg and others (which passed on the private scepticism of both men about each other) led from covert to open hostility and to Byron's brilliant attack in *Don Juan* (see entries 252 and 257).

a. Unsigned review of *Poems 1807*, *Monthly Literary Recreations*, July 1807

See entry 94.

b. From *English Bards and Scotch Reviewers*, published anonymously in March 1809

Wordsworth told his nephew Christopher in early August 1827, 'I never read the "English Bards" through' (*Prose Works of Wordsworth*, ed. Grosart, iii, 462). In 1813 and after, Byron always resists attempts to have the satire republished.

> Next comes the dull disciple of thy school,
> That mild apostate from poetic rule,
> The simple WORDSWORTH, framer of a lay
> As soft as evening in his favourite May,
> Who warns his friend 'to shake off toil and trouble,
> And quit his books for fear of growing double';[1]
> Who, both by precept and example, shows
> That prose is verse, and verse is merely prose,
> Convincing all by demonstration plain,
> Poetic souls delight in prose insane;
> And Christmas stories tortured into rhyme,
> Contain the essence of the true sublime:
> Thus when he tells the tale of Betty Foy,
> The idiot mother of 'an idiot Boy;'
> A moon-struck silly lad who lost his way,
> And, like his bard, confounded night with day,*
> So close on each pathetic part he dwells,
> And each adventure so sublimely tells,
> That all who view the 'idiot in his glory,'
> Conceive the Bard the hero of the story.
>
> (ll. 229–48)

---

* Mr. W. in his preface labours hard to prove, that prose and verse are much the same, and certainly his precepts and practice are strictly conformable.

> And thus to Betty's question he
> Made answer, like a traveller bold,
> The cock did crow to-whoo, to-whoo,
> And the sun did shine so cold, &c. &c.
>
> Lyrical Ballads, page 129.

c. Letter from Wordsworth to his wife, franked by Byron 'London May thirteenth 1812'

Rogers, in 1834, told Crabb Robinson that Byron and Wordsworth chanced to meet at his house 'when Lord Byron called to give an account of the assassin-ation of Perceval' [11 May 1812] (*Henry Crabb Robinson on Books and their Writers*, ed. Edith J. Morely, 1938 I, 436). This letter from Wordsworth to his wife confirms Rogers.

. . . This Letter will be franked by Lord Byron, a Man who is now the rage in London, in consequence of his Late Poem Childe Haroldes pilgrimage. He wrote a satire some time since in which Coleridge and I were abused, but these are little thought of; and the other day I met him here and indeed it was from his mouth that Rogers first heard, and in his presence told us, the murder of Perceval.

(*The Letters of William and Dorothy Wordsworth. A Supplement of New Letters*, ed. Alan G. Hill, 1993, 65).

d. Comments, 1813–1814

The greater force of hostile feeling displayed by Byron from late 1815 stemmed, Wordsworth later believed, from a remark of his own being repeated to Byron: apparently, between 20 June and 7 October 1815, Byron had learnt from Tom Moore, who knew it from Rogers (Crabb Robinson, *op. cit.*, I, 428–9, and *Table Talk of Samuel Rogers*, ed. A. Dyce, 1887, 238), that Wordsworth had told a poetess, possibly Mary Bryan of Bristol, that Byron's 'poetic feeling was per-verted'. Mrs. Bryan dedicated her poems to Wordsworth in 1815 (see entry 252). 'Perverted' does seem to be a word bandied by Wordsworth and Byron about each other. R. P. Gillies, recollecting a walk with Wordsworth in August 1814, writes, 'With Lord Byron he seemed to have least patience; for though cordially admitting his lordship's extraordinary power, and his claims as a man of genius, he yet firmly believed that his application of that power was reprehensible, perverted, and vicious' (*Memoirs of a Literary Veteran*, 1851, ii, 144); and see Byron's letter to Moore, 1 June 1818 (entry 257).

Meanwhile, in Switzerland, in June 1816, Shelley encouraged Byron to like Wordsworth's poetry: the subsequent Canto III of *Childe Harold* is the most Wordsworthian of Byron's works. Macaulay's comment[2] that Byron's borrowing of Wordsworthian material mediated, though unconsciously, between Words-worth and the public has a subtle truth. Wordsworth resented what he con-sidered to be Byron's thefts; Byron's flirtation with Wordsworthian notions was over by 1817–18, when *Don Juan*, including unpublished sections, reflects his vigorous rejection.

From Byron's Journal, 24 November 1813
He [Walter Scott] is undoubtedly the Monarch of Parnassus, and the most *English* of bards. I should place Rogers next in the living list – (I value him more as the last of the *best* school) – Moore and Campbell both *third* – Southey and Wordsworth and Coleridge – the rest οἱ πολλοί[3] – thus: –

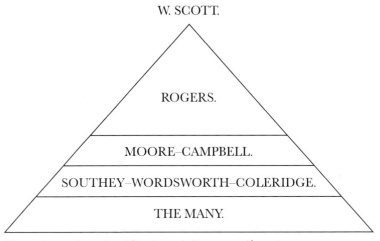

W. SCOTT.

ROGERS.

MOORE–CAMPBELL.

SOUTHEY–WORDSWORTH–COLERIDGE.

THE MANY.

There is a triangular 'Gradus ad Parnassum'[4] – the names are too numerous for the base of the triangle.

(*Byron's Letters and Journals*, 1814–1815, ed. Leslie A. Marchand, 1973–, III, 219–20)

Extract from a letter to James Hogg, probably July or August 1814
Byron's letter no longer exists; Hogg records in his *Memoir* that six letters written to him by Byron, between June 1814 and October 1815, had been stolen (*James Hogg, Memoir*, ed. Douglas S. Mack, Scottish Academic Press, 1972, 37). Crabb Robinson reports Byron's comment on Wordsworth.

1 December 1816. Cargill was telling me the other day that in a letter written by Lord Byron to Hogg the Ettrick Shepherd, in his rattling way he wrote: 'Wordsworth – stupendous genius! damned fool! These poets run about their ponds though they cannot fish. I am told there is not one who can angle – damned fools!'

(*Henry Crabb Robinson on Books and their Writers*, ed. Edith J. Morley, 1988, I, 199)

Clearly, Wordsworth got to know of the letter, for Byron told Medwin that Hogg had told him that he had been unable to resist showing it to the Lake 'fraternity', 'I remember saying, among other things, that the Lake poets were such fools as not to fish in their own waters; but this was the least offensive part of the epistle' (*Conversations of Lord Byron*, ed. Thomas Medwin, 1824, 240). Certainly, by December 1814, Wordsworth was helping Mary Barker with her satire, *Lines Addressed to a Noble Lord* (see entry 251).

Extract from a letter to Thomas Moore, 12 August 1814
Well – and why don't you 'launch?'[5] – Now is your time. The people are tolerably tired with me, and not very much enamoured of ** [Wordsworth], who has just spawned a quarto of metaphysical blank verse, which is nevertheless only a part of a poem.[6]

(Marchand, *op. cit.*, IV, 157)

Extract from a letter to John Murray, 7 September 1814
– There must be many 'fine things' in Wordsworth – but I should think it difficult to make 6 quartos (the amount of the whole) all fine – particularly the Pedlar's portion of the poem – but there can be no doubt of his powers to do about any thing –

(*Ibid.*, IV, 167)

EDITOR'S NOTES

1. Byron's footnote quotes the first stanza of 'The Tables turned'.
2. In his review of Moore's *Life of Byron*, *Edinburgh Review*, June 1830, liii.
3. The masses, i.e. 'the many'.
4. 'Step to Parnassus' – a dictionary designed to assist verse composition.
5. The poem to be launched was *Lalla Rookh*, published 1817.
6. *The Excursion, being a Portion of the Recluse, a Poem*, 1814.

122.

From an unsigned lampoon, 'The Bards of the Lake', the *Satirist or Monthly Meteor*, December, 1809, V, 548–50

The editor and one of the proprietors of the *Satirist* was George Manners (1778–1853), here the probable author, who, travelling south from the western isles of Scotland, had delighted first in Ossian and then in 'the remnants of border minstrelsy.'

By the time I had reached the lakes, which I had proposed to visit in my way, I could think of nothing but the minstrels and the minstrelsy of chivalry and romance. All modern poetry appeared to me to be a composition of affectation, learning, and sentimental refinement, and a hundred other things, with which in fact poetry had nothing to do. – I was not a little delighted, therefore, arriving at the beautiful village of Ambleside, to learn that a brotherhood of modern bards had established themselves there, whose opinions of poetry exactly coincided with mine, and who regulated their practice accordingly. I did not enquire very particularly into the tenets of this sect, being certain that as simplicity and nature were their object, they must be right, by whatever means they attained them. I had very fortunately, on the evening of my arrival the means of judging of their success; and the impression which their impassioned enunciation of their unrivalled strains made upon me is indelible.

I was walking by the side of the neighbouring lake, in company with a friend who had lived some time in the vicinity. As I could think of nothing but the bards, I asked him a thousand questions about them. He was very eloquent in praise of the blameless virtue and pastoral simplicity of their lives, and the admirable harmony that subsisted between them. I was not displeased to hear so fair an account of their private virtues, but it was of their poetry that I wished to speak.

We had just reached the summit of a gentle eminence, and were descending the other side, when in the little vale beneath us, which commanded a beautiful view of the lake, we perceived seated in the grass a groupe of men women, and children; and in the midst of the groupe stood one, who by the energy of his action appeared to be reciting; but he had concluded, and sat down, before we were near enough to hear what he said,

'Behold the bards and their wives and their children?' exclaimed my friend; 'they are rehearsing some of their new poems: this is a frequent custom with them: we will sit down at the foot of yonder beach; where we shall be near enough to hear them: they will not heed us.'

While he spoke, another of the bards arose, and took his station in the midst of the groupe. My friend whispered me, that he had composed some famous *lyrical ballads* and was proceeding to descant on his genius, when the bard began, first announcing his subject to be,

THE HERMIT AND THE SNAIL.

A hermit walk'd forth from his cell one day,
And he met a snail across his way,
And thus to the snail did the hermit say,
    'Silly snail!'

'Is it thy love thou goest to meet;
To woo her in her green retreat?
No—thou hast horns upon thy head,
Thou art already married,
    Silly snail!

I was charmed with the original simplicity of this elegant little composition, to which I did not know what appellation to apply, or in what class of poetry to place it. I perceived that it gave much satisfaction to the brotherhood of bards, though the ladies seemed not altogether to approve the indirect satire contained in it. I had scarcely finished copying it into my book of memoranda, when another bard started from his seat. . . .

123. Walter Scott

From an unsigned essay, 'The Living Poets of Great Britain', *Edinburgh Annual Register for 1808*, 1810, i, part 2, 426–30

Without revealing himself as the author, Scott comments that the author of the article is a 'dashing fellow' (*Letters of Sir Walter Scott, 1787–1807*, ed. Herbert Grierson, Constable, 1932, II, 283), while, on 29 October 1810, William Taylor enquired of Southey, 'Who writes the absurd criticism?' (*Memoir of William Taylor*, 1843, ii, 297). Interestingly, in *A Selection of Fugitive Poetry*, Scott, still anonymous, selects 'Lines written a few miles above Tintern Abbey . . .' (which he mistitles 'On visiting Tintern Abbey'), which is one poem of Wordsworth he does not mention in his review below: he places it, perhaps with some significance, as the last in the two volumes (see *English Minstrelsy, being A Selection of Fugitive Poetry from the Best English Authors with some Original Pieces hitherto unpublished, 1810*, Edinburgh 1810, 256–64).

With the name of Southey those of Coleridge and of Wordsworth are naturally and habitually associated. We do not hold, with the vulgar, that these ingenious and accomplished men are combined to overthrow the ancient land marks of our poetry, and bring back the days of Withers and of Quarles; on the contrary: to those who give themselves the trouble of considering their works attentively, there will appear such points of distinction as argue a radical difference in their taste, and the rules they have adopted in composition. Still, however, connected as they are by habits of friendship, vicinity of residence, and community of studies, some general principles may be pointed out common to all three, and entitling them, more than any other living authors, to the appellation of a school of productions. We regret to say, that the peculiarities which they have in common do not by any means seem to us the most valuable properties of their productions. They are all, more or less, favourers of that doctrine which considers poetry as the mere imitation of natural feeling, and holds that its language ought in consequence to be simplified as much as possible to the expressions of passion in ordinary life. To this proposition Mr Wordsworth adds another yet more doubtful, – that the language of low and rustic life ought to be preferred, because, in his opinion, the essential passions of the heart find a better soil in which they can attain their maturity, and because in that condition of life our elementary feelings co-exist in a state of greater simplicity. Now this appears to us a radical error. Those who have studied the lower orders of society, especially in a mercantile country, must be sensible how much the feelings and talents of that class are degraded, imbruted, and debased by the limited exercise to which they are confined, and the gross temptations to which they hourly give way. Even among the more fortunate inhabitants of a pastoral country, the necessity of toiling for daily bread burthens the mind and quells the powers of imagination: The few passions by which they are strongly actuated are those which are the most simple, the most coarse, and the worst regulated; nor can the expressions which they dictate be considered as proper for poetry, any more than the company of the swains themselves for the society of persons of cultivated taste, manners, and talents. The opposite opinion has led to that affectation of a simple nakedness of style, which has, in some instances, debased even the gold of Southey, and forms a far larger alloy to the coinage of his two friends, which we are about to consider . . . [He suggests that Coleridge has abandoned poetry for 'the mists of political metaphysics', and that he no longer regards himself as a serious poet.]

The feelings of Mr WORDSWORTH appear to be very different. Although hitherto an unsuccessful competitor for poetical fame, as far as it depends upon the general voice of the public, no man has ever considered the character of the poet as more honourable, or his pursuits as more important. We are afraid he will be found rather to err on the opposite side, and, with an amiable Quixotry, to ascribe to those pursuits, and to that character, a power of stemming the tide of luxury, egotism, and corruption of manners, and thus of reforming an age, which we devoutly believe can be reformed by nothing short of a miracle. But in this, as in other particulars, the poetry of Mr Wordsworth accords strikingly with his character and habits. We have made it a rule not to draw the character of the man while we reviewed the works of the author, and our sketch has suffered by this forbearance, for we could have shown, in many instances, how curiously they differed or coincided. But if we durst now raise the veil of private life, it would be to exhibit a picture of manly worth and unaffected modesty; of one who retired early from all that sullies or hardens the heart, from the pursuit of wealth and honours, from the bustle of the world, and from the parade of philosophical pursuits; and who, sitting down contented in a cottage, realized whatever the poets have feigned of content and happiness in retirement. It might have been supposed, that, surrounded by romantic scenery, and giving his attention only to poetical imagery, and to the objects by which they were best suggested, the situation he had chosen was the most favourable for his studies; and that such a happy coincidence of leisure, talents, and situation, ought to have produced poetry more generally captivating than that of Mr Wordsworth has hitherto proved. But we have constant reason to admire the caprices of human intellect. This very state of secluded study seems to have produced effects upon Mr Wordsworth's genius unfavourable to its popularity. In the first place, he who is constantly surrounded by the most magnificent natural subjects of description, becomes so intimately acquainted with them, that he is apt to dwell less upon the broad general and leading traits of character which strike the occasional visitor, and which are really their most poetical attributes, than upon the more detailed and specific particulars in which one mountain or valley differs from another, and which, being less obvious to the general eye, are less interesting to the common ear. But the solitude in which Mr Wordsworth resides has led to a second and more important consequence in his writings, and has affected his mode of expressing moral truth and feeling, as well as his turn of natural description. He has himself beautifully described the truths which he teaches us, as being

> — The harvest of a quiet eye
> That broods and rests on his own heart.
> ['A Poet's Epitaph', *PW*, IV, p. 67, ll. 51–2; *LB (1800)*,
> p. 208, ll. 51–2]

A better heart, a purer and more manly source of honourable and virtuous sentiment beats not, we will say it boldly, within Britain. But the observation of a single subject will not make a skilful anatomist, nor will the copying one model, however beautiful, render a painter acquainted with his art. To attain that knowledge of the human bosom necessary to moral poetry, the poet must compare his own feelings with those of others; he must reduce his hypothesis to theory by actual experiment, stoop to sober and regulated truth from the poetic height of his own imagination, and observe what impulse the mass of humanity receive from those motives and subjects to which he is himself acutely alive. It is the want of this observation and knowledge of the world which leads Wordsworth into the perpetual and leading error of supposing, that trivial and petty incidents can supply to mankind in general that train of reflection which, in his speculative solitude, he himself naturally attaches to them. A reflecting mind and a quick fancy find food for meditation in the most trifling occurrences, and can found a connected and delightful train of deductions upon an original cause as flimsy as the web of a gossamer. The cleaving of a block of wood, the dancing of a bush of wild flowers, the question or answer of a child, naturally suggest matter of reflection to an amiable and reflecting mind, retired from the influence of incidents of a nature more generally interesting. And such are Wordsworth's studies, or, as he himself expresses it,

> The outward shews of sky and earth,
> Of hill and valley he has viewed;

> And impulses of deeper birth
> Have come to him in solitude.
> > [*Ibid.*, *PW*, IV, p. 67, ll. 45–8; *LB (1800)*, p. 208,
> > ll. 45–8]

In this situation, the poet's feelings somewhat resemble those of a person accustomed to navigate a small boat upon a narrow lake, to whom, if he possess an active imagination, the indentures of the shore, which hardly strike the passing stranger, acquire the importance of creeks, bays, and promontories. Even so the impressions made upon the susceptible mind of the solitary poet by common and unimportant incidents; and the train of 'sweet and bitter fancies' to which they give rise are, in the eye of the public, altogether extravagant and disproportioned to their cause. We mark this with sincere regret; for though Mr Wordsworth, to the affectation of rude and bald simplicity, which we have censured in Southey and Coleridge, adds that of harsh and rugged versification, often reduced in harmony several steps below well-written prose, yet his power of interesting the feelings is exquisite, and we do not envy the self possession of those who can read his beautiful pastorals, 'The Brothers' and 'Michael,' without shedding tears; for it may be said of such, that they have no interest in humanity, 'no part in Jacob, and no inheritance in Israel.' It is therefore to be lamented, that Wordsworth should be, upon system, rude in diction and trivial in narrative; and that he should continue to exhibit traits of feeling bordering upon extravagance, and so metaphysically subtile that they are a stumbling block to the ignorant, and foolishness to the learned. But his muse is, we fear, irreclaimable, and pleads the freedom of a Cumbrian mountaineer: –

> > O er rough and smooth she trips along,
> >   And never looks behind;
> > And sings a solitary song
> >   That whistles in the wind.
> > > ['Lucy Gray', *PW*, I, p. 236, ll. 61–4; *LB (1800)*,
> > > p. 160, ll. 61–4]

Somewhat akin to Wordsworth in the train of his poetry, but beneath him in originality of genius, is JAMES GRAHAME, author of the 'Sabbath' and the 'Birds of Scotland.'

124. John Rickman (1771–1840)

From a letter to Southey, 17 January 1810

Here Rickman comments on Coleridge's inclusion in the *Friend* (14 December 1809 and 4 January 1810) of Wordsworth's essay, 'Reply to a letter by Mathetes'.

He should have reserved Mr. Wordsworth's crude didactics for another time if he must needs insert such mountain lore. It seems to me that Wordsworth has neither fun nor common sense in him. He soars far above both, and in my notion makes himself disagreeable and ridiculous accordingly.

(*Life and Letters of John Rickman*, ed. Orlo Williams, 1912, 151)

125. Henry Crabb Robinson

From his diary, 24 July 1811

Southey spoke of Wordsworth in a way that convinced me there is no great attachment between them, Wordsworth, he says, has the fault of overrating his works. He has by him poems that would be universally admired, but he has a miserly feeling concerning them as if by being published they would cease to be his own. He thinks the very worst of his works good enough to be published. Southey would not write a review of his pamphlet, because he knew Wordsworth would not be satisfied with the praise he should give it. I should add that Southey spoke enthusiastically of the pamphlet and of Wordsworth's genius, and said the fault of attaching too great importance to his own writings is his only one.

(*Henry Crabb Robinson on Books and their Writers*, ed. Edith J. Morley, 1938, I, 41)

126. Charles Lamb

From a letter to Wordsworth, 19 October 1810

Here Lamb comments on Wordsworth's second and unpublished Essay on Epitaphs (W. J. B. Owen and Jane Worthington Smyser, eds, *The Prose Works of William Wordsworth*, Oxford, 1974, II, 63–79: for the 'Turgid Epitaph' see p. 73.)

I was much pleased with your continuation of the Essay on Epitaphs. It is the only sensible thing which has been written on that subject & it goes to the Bottom. In particular I was pleased with your Translation of that Turgid Epitaph into the plain feeling under it. It is perfectly a Test. But what is the reason we have so few good Epitaphs after all?

(*The Letters of Charles and Mary Lamb*, ed. E. V. Lucas, I, 104)

127. James Losh

From his diary, 1810–1821

James Losh (1763–1833), having known Wordsworth in a familiar way since at least 1797, is disappointed that Wordsworth's politics have turned away from reform; however, Losh's earlier view that Southey was the greater of the two poets has been revised.

a. 21 October 1810–1821

Wordsworth – with perhaps greater talents and more acquired knowledge than Southey and equal industry and good moral character – shows that gentleness of mind & orderly arrangement of time are essential to the happiness of the individual and those who depend upon him.

(Paul Kaufman, *Notes and Queries*, November 1962, 407)

b. February 1815 [*monthly summary*]

I have read Wordsworth's *Excursion* once through, but must read it a 2nd time before I form any decisive opinion as to its merits. I can already say that it is far too long, in many parts of it tedious and obscure, but full of much beauty and pure and elevated sentiments.

(*Diaries of James Losh*, ed. Edward Hughes (*Surtees Society*, vol. 171), I, 46)

c. 13 September 1821

. . . I called upon my old friend W. Wordsworth, the poet. He looks thin and old but is, I believe, in good health and seems to be contented with his situation. We both (from the wish I have no doubt to avoid unpleasant discussion) avoided the subjects either of general or local politics. Of Wordsworth's talents and character I have spoken elsewhere, and need only say that I think his manners are improved and that he displays less than he used to do, of a desire to give a kind of mysterious importance to common sentiments and common strains of reasoning merely because he considered them to be his own. This fault has infected and overlaid his poetry which notwithstanding, very often shows great vigour of imagination and sweetness of expression.[1]

(*Ibid.*, I, 138)

d. 7 December 1821[2]

I received a long letter from my old Friend William Wordsworth (the Poet) containing a laboured but (in my opinion) very unsuccessful apology for his political *apostasy*. Towards me, however, he expresses himself in the most friendly terms and I mean to reply to him in a mild but decided manner.

(*Ibid.*, I, 144)

EDITOR'S NOTES

1. In his diary, 6 November 1824, Losh makes it clear that for years he had been trying to cure Wordsworth of 'an attempt to make of importance and even to throw a kind of mystery about common and everyday observations; and a dictatorial mode of asserting things which no person ever doubted. Hence, as it seems to me, arises much of the tediousness and obscurity which I believe everyone finds in the works of this able and ingenious man. Wordsworth has

a vigorous mind, considerable learning and (in my opinion) true poetical genius, but he has taken it into his head that he is a great metaphysician, and delivers with an air of dignity, and clothed in oracular language truths or errors (sometimes one and sometimes the other) which when understood, prove not to have been worth enquiring about and quite on the surface. In my long intimacy and correspondence with Wordsworth, I often endeavoured to cure him of this, and until he was spoiled by *over praise* and irritated by *over censure* and ridicule, I flattered myself that my endeavours were not in vain.' (*Ibid.*, II, 16–17; punctuation corrected from the ms at Carlisle City Library.)

2. Wordsworth's letter to Losh is dated 7 December.

128. Henry Crabb Robinson

Extracts from his diary, 1811–1814

a. 8 January 1811

We spoke of Wordsworth and Coleridge. Lamb, to my surprise, asserted Coleridge to be the greater man. He preferred the *Mariner* to anything Wordsworth had written. Wordsworth, he thought, is narrow and confined in his views compared with Coleridge. He does not, like Shakespeare, become everything he pleases, but forces the reader to submit to his individual feelings. This, I observed, lies very much in the lyrical character, and Lamb concluded by expressing high admiration of Wordsworth. He had read many of his things with great pleasure indeed, especially the sonnets, which I had before spoken of as my favourites. Lamb also spoke in high praise of *Hart-Leap Well* as one of Wordsworth's most exquisite pieces, but did not think highly of the *Leech-gatherer* . . .

(*Henry Crabb Robinson on Books and their Writers*, ed. Edith J. Morley, 1938, I, 17)

b. 27 January 1811

With Turner.[1] Turner had read without any pleasure Wordsworth's pamphlet;[2] he thought the feeling throughout affected; he even disliked the period 'Woe to England', etc., and objected to the woe pronounced upon the 'grass on her fields'. I explained this to refer to that unity of the physical and moral world which the Spinozisic poet always beholds.

Turner foolishly said he liked the commentary better than the text; I replied that this must be either flattery or absurdity. On my defending also Wordsworth's lines:

> These forms of beauty have not been to me
> As is a landscape to a blind man's eye,

which I thought contained no image, and, I affirmed, raised a sentiment, he said I was ready to preach from stones and find good in everything. I was half angry when I left him . . .

(*Ibid.*, I, 20)

c. 7 October 1811

. . . At four o'clock read at Mrs. Clarkson's Wordsworth's very fine introduction to Wilkinson's *Drawings of the Lakes*. Wordsworth alone of all writers is inspired by the true spirit of contemplation. Woods, rocks, and lakes, valleys, and mountains are the fields over which his mind most delightfully rambles. With incomparable beauty he has shown how the great elements of natural scenery are combined with the noblest and best feelings of the heart . . .

(*Ibid.*, I, 47)

d. 9 May 1812

The Aikins, though not sensible of the exclusive worth of Wordsworth's poetry, still speak with respect of him. Neither he, however, nor his friends, can or ought to receive a praise that is given him in common with all sorts of pretended poets. Mrs. Barbauld prefers to all others the idyll – the return of a brother who finds his brother and friends all dead.

(*Ibid.*, I, 79)

e. 13 May 1812

[Wordsworth says] 'Wilson's poems are an attenuation of mine. Everything he had he owes to me. This he acknowledges to me, but he ought to have said it to the public also. I have to attack him on that head' (or to that effect). This attenuation is, I have no doubt, the reason why the *Edinburgh* reviewers are disposed to place him above Wordsworth. The most pregnant and significant are the least admired of Wordsworth's poems for the very qualities that make them most admirable. Of course a very inferior poet, he [i.e. Wilson] gives only the weaker and milder features of Wordsworth's poetry with an accommodating spirit, etc., and will have a fair chance of gaining applause with the aid of the malignant pleasure in *so* depreciating a great man.

(*Ibid.*, I, 82–3)

f. 3 June 1812

This entry illustrates how Wordsworth, in conversation, could teach the taste by which he was to be understood.

At four went to Rough's. The poet and Dean Wordsworth and Cargill dined with us. A very pleasant and interesting afternoon. Wordsworth talked much about poetry. He was made to explain *fancy* as opposed to *imagination*, from which it results that fancy forms casual and fleeting combinations in which objects are united, *not* on a permanent relation which subsists and has its principle in the capacity of the *sensible* produced to represent and stand in the place of the abstract intellectual conception, but in a voluntary power of combination which only expresses the fact of the combination with little or no import beyond itself. This is the best explanation I can give. Wordsworth quoted as instances a fine description of cold from Cotton's *Winter* (his own *Kitten and the Falling Leaves* I have mentioned before.) After tea he read us *Benjamin the Waggoner*, a tale of more naïveté than Wordsworth often displays, and with a fine description of a sailor travelling with his ship in model: but I shall refer to it again. Walked with the Doctor to Lambeth Palace and then with Wordsworth to the end of Oxford Road. He talked much of poetry and with great and, to me, laudable freedom of his own poems. He said that perhaps there is as *intense* poetical feeling in *his* as Shakespeare's works, but in Shakespeare the poetical elements are mixed up with other things and wrought into greater works. In him the poetry is *reiner* [more pure]. He contrasted some fine lines from his verses on the Wye, with a popular passage from Lord Byron on solitude. Lord Byron's is a coarse but palpable assertion of the nature of solitude, with an epigrammatic conclusion. In Wordsworth the feeling is involved and the thought clothed in poetic shapes. It is, therefore, no wonder that Wordsworth's description should be forgotten, and Lord Byron's in general circulation.

Wordsworth asserted that Southey was no judge of *his* poems, writing too many of his own to enter into his mind. And on my saying that Southey had praised his unpublished poems as superior to those published, Wordsworth seemed to resent this rather as a depreciation of the latter than a praise of the former. He could not surpass what he had already written. They are the utmost energies of his mind. Before his ballads were published Tobin implored Wordsworth to leave out *We are Seven* as a piece that would damn the book. It became one of the most popular. He related this in answer to a remark that by only leaving out certain poems at the suggestion of someone who knows the public taste he might avoid giving offence. Rogers has said the same, but Wordsworth gives no credit to the assertion. His sonnet in which the wild rose is compared to a village girl* he says is almost the only one of pure fancy. I also mentioned the one on the ship.† He said it expressed the delight he had felt on thinking of the first feelings of men before navigation had so completely made the world known, and while a ship exploring unknown regions was an object of high interest and sympathy.

(*Ibid.*, I, 93–4)

g. 4 June 1812

Read this morning early the prologue to *Peter Bell the Potter*. It is so exquisite a play of imagination, and contains so much of Wordsworth's theory, a vindication of his practice, that I will give an abstract of it.[3]

It opens:

> There's something in a flying horse,
> There's something in a huge balloon;
> But through the clouds I'll never float
> Until I have a little boat
> Whose shape is like the crescent Moon.
> [ll. 1–5]

This little boat is poetic fancy, at least it *may* be considered as such. The poet at once finds himself seated in his canoe, and rapidly takes flight:

> Away we go, and what care we
> For treasons, tumults, and for wars?
> We are as calm in our delight
> As is the crescent Moon so bright
> Among the scattered stars.
> [ll. 26–30]

* 'How sweet it is, when mother Fancy rocks'.
† 'Where lies the Land to which yon Ship must go?'

And in a few words he lightly touches on the wonders of his voyage and this in a tone of levity.

> The towns in Saturn are ill built,
> But Jove is full of stately bowers,
> The Evening Star is not amiss,
> But what are all of them to this,
> This little Earth of ours!
>
> [ll. 41–50]

In other words, what are the fanciful sports of the mind which lead man far from home compared with those exercises of *feeling* which are connected with the ordinary business and connections of life? The boat descends:

> And there it is, the dear green Earth,
> And that's the famed Pacific Ocean!
> Old Andes thrusts yon craggy spear
> Through the grey clouds; the Alps are there,
> Like Waters in commotion.
>
> Yon tawny Strip is Libya's sands,
> That silver thread the River Dnieper;
> And on the skirts of Ocean green
> Is a sweet Isle, of Isles the Queen.
> Ye Faeries from all evil keep her!
>
> [ll. 56–65]

The poet sees his native town. His affections are kindled. This excites the jealousy of his little boat, who makes a speech telling of the fine things she can convey him to, and reproaches him with his faint-heartedness and unworthiness:

> In such a lovely boat to sit,
> And make no better use of it!
>
> [ll. 78–9]

It is necessary, perhaps, to sit in the very boat itself in order to enjoy *its* colloquy. The poet's reply, however, is intelligible, and expresses all that needs be said in his apology:

> My pretty little form of light,
> My sweet and beautiful canoe,
> Now though it grieves me to the heart,
> I feel, I feel that we must part;
> I must take leave of you.

You are a most delightful barge,
But while your pleasure you're pursuing,
Without impediment or let,
My little barge, you quite forget
What on the Earth is doing.
[ll. 111–20]

. . . . . .

Long have I loved what I behold –
The night that calms, the day that cheers,
The common growth of Mother Earth
Suffices me – her tears, her mirth,
Her humblest mirth and tears.

⁴The dragon's wing – the magic ring
I shall not covet for my dower,
If I along that lonely way
With sympathetic heart may stray
And *with a Soul of power.*

These given, what more need I desire
To stir, to soothe, or elevate?
What nobler marvels than the mind
May in life's daily prospect find –
May find, *or there create:*

A potent wand doth Sorrow wield.
What spell so strong as guilty Fear?
Repentance is a tender Sprite:
She dawns, and, smitten by her light,
All troubles disappear.

My shining Pinnace, let us now
Descend from this aerial height;
Then take thy wing, adventurous skiff,
More daring far than hyppogrif,
And be thy own delight.

For me are homelier tasks prepared:
To the stone table in my garden
The Squire is come, and, as I guess,
His little ruddy daughter Bess
With Harry the Churchwarden.
[ll. 131–60]

307

In this transition we have the example, as well [as] the precept. What a spring from the 'long blue field of ether,' and the 'ten thousand stars' beneath the 'wonderful canoe' – to 'Harry the Churchwarden'! And yet the poet will have pleaded his cause in vain, and I expect to hear this same churchwarden brought up in judgment against the author. What stupid attachment to, or rather, what silly antipathy against, certain words of relation on the part of a miseducated public. The church-warden, the vicar, and his dame were all, continues the poet, assembled to hear the tale of Peter Bell the Potter. At the sound of this name 'off flew my pretty little boat,' as if she had been an *Edinburgh* reviewer, for she too was 'all in a trance of indignation.' He finds 'little Bess' and 'Full nine of them or more' assembled to hear the tale – which he instantly began to 'cover his confusion' at the unworthy treatment he had received. I have heard Wordsworth speak of his poems of fancy as if he deemed them not inferior to his poems of imagination, yet Coleridge denies him the former quality, which he at the same time gives to Southey. And this poem might be construed into a confession of a want of that power, a confession, however, I believe he did not intend to make.

Peter Bell the Potter is one of the most delightful of Wordsworth's tales: with infinite imagination, and a great deal of profound psychology interspersed with exquisite description, psychological and natural. Peter himself is portrayed as a wild rover who had braved thirty years in his calling.

> He roved among the vales and streams,
> In the green wood and hollow dell;
> They were his dwellings night and day,
> But Nature ne'er could find the way
> Into the heart of Peter Bell.
>
> In vain, through every changeful year,
> Did Nature lead him as before:
> A primrose by a river's brim
> A yellow Primrose was to him,
> And it was nothing more.
>   [ll. 241–50]

(Lady Mackintosh was once stating to Coleridge her disregard to the beauties of nature which men commonly affected to admire. He said his friend Wordsworth had described her feeling, and quoted the last three lines: 'Yes,' said Lady Mackintosh, 'that is precisely my feeling.') The tale shows how the heart of Peter was wrought on by superstitious terrors, and he was led to feel his human nature and become good and honest. His insensibility is thus further noticed:

> At noon, when by the forest's edge
> He lay beneath the branches high,
> The soft blue sky did never melt
> Into his heart, he never felt
> The Witchery of the soft blue sky.
>
> On a fair prospect some have look'd
> And felt, as I have heard them say,
> As if the moving time had been
> A thing as steadfast as the scene
> On which they gaz'd themselves away.
>
> With Peter Bell I need not tell
> That this had never been the case.
> [ll. 261–72]

Having drawn the character, the poet tells the tale. Peter loses himself in a wood. He is led into a quarry and becomes enraged at the incident. He at length wanders away to a retired spot, where he finds an ass feeding. He resolves to steal the ass, but cannot force him from the river's brink, where he is standing, notwithstanding he beats him unmercifully:

> All, all is silent, rocks and woods,
> All, all is silent far and near,
> Only the Ass with motion dull
> Upon the pivot of his skull
> Turns round his long left ear.
> [ll. 411–15]

A great deal of minute painting follows, and the ass has properties given him, hitherto granted only to the dog and elephant:

> And then upon his side he fell,
> And by the river's brink did lie;
> And as he lay like one that mourn'd
> The patient beast on Peter turned
> His shining hazel eye.

309

'Twas but one mild reproachful look;
And straightway, silent, without fear,
In very sorrow, not in dread,
He turned the eye-ball in his head
Towards the stream so deep and clear.

[ll. 431–40]

The ass's master lay drowned in the river. And when Peter, enraged, attempted to throw the ass in he saw the corse; this excites strong horror. But before this the strange braying of the ass had produced a strange effect upon him:

What is there now in Peter's heart?
Or what the power of that strange sound?
The moon uneasy look'd and dimmer,
The broad blue heavens appeared to glimmer,
And the rocks stagger'd all around.

[ll. 481–5]

The horror described by its effects on Peter occasions the poet to ask what he saw: 'Is it a fiend tied to a stake?' etc.:

Is it some party in a parlour,
Crammed just as they on earth were crammed,
Some sipping punch, some sipping tea,
But as you by their faces see,
All silent and all damned?

[ll. 515–6]

This is the only stanza I wish to have taken out before publication. The image is striking, but its grotesqueness does not suit the accompanying earnest feeling. Wordsworth says, Lady Beaumont also objects to this stanza, and he will therefore think whether he ought not to leave it out.

The ass now manifests joy, and Peter after recovering from a swound has courage to raise the body from the water and mounts the ass, to be led by him to the owner's home. He hears a mournful cry; it is the child of the dead man, seeking him and bewailing him. Peter believes the cry to import his own death, and his conscience is quickened:

The rocks that tower on either side
Build up a wild fantastic scene,
Temples like these among the Hindoos,
And Mosques and Spires among the windows,
And Castles all with Ivy green.

And while the Ass pursues his way
Along this solitary dell,
As step by step he doth advance
The Mosques and Spires change countenance
And look at Peter Bell.

[ll. 681–90]

Other incidents are enunciated: Peter sees blood in a stone. It terrifies him till he finds it proceeds from a wound he had before given the ass.

The poet then digresses, and tells an anecdote of a good man who saw a 'ghostly word' formed of light and shining on his black paper.

This leads the poet to remonstrate with the spirits, which he does in a daring and original style:

And ever where along the turf
They go with smooth and steady pace,
You see driven onward by the wind
A dancing leaf that's close behind
Along that solitary place.

At last he spies the withered leaf,
And Peter is in sore distress,
Where there is not a bush or tree
The very leaves they follow me
So huge hath been my wickedness.

[in var. for ll. 701–10]

Dread spirits! thus to vex the good
How can ye with your functions jar,
Disordering colour, form, and stature!
Let good men feel the *soul of nature*
And see things as they are.

I know you, Potent Spirits! well;
Now with the feeling and the sense
Ye play both with your foes and friends
Most fearful ends,
And this I speak in reverence.

311

But might I give advice to you,
Whom in my fear I love so well;
From men of pensive virtue go,
Dread beings! and your empire show
On hearts like that of Peter Bell.

Your presence I have often felt
In darkness and the stormy night,
And well I know if need there be
Ye can put forth your agency
Beneath the sweet moonlight.

Then coming from the wayward world,
That powerful world in which ye dwell,
Come, Spirits of the Mind! and try
To-night beneath the moonlight sky
What may be done with Peter Bell.
[ll. 761–85]

Peter is not yet free from his evil dispositions, he endeavours, being a 'deep logician,' to reason away his feelings, when the ass turns round and grins on him. Peter is about to retort on the grin with a joke when he hears a noise underground produced by miners. All his fears return redoubled:

Upon the Ass's back he sits
Like one that's riding in a swoon,
Blank as a ghost that can not see,
Whose face, if any such there be,
Is like the eyeless moon.
[in var. for ll. 846–53]

He passes a chapel charmingly described; he is reminded of the place where he married one of his twelve wives and believes a judgment will fall on him that night. The story of the wife is briefly and pathetically related. Peter sees his own figure. At the moment of his utmost dread he passes a tabernacle and hears a pious methodist preaching repentance and forgiveness:

Each nerve, each fibre of his frame,
And all the animal within,
Was weak perhaps; but it was mild
And gentle as an infant child,
An infant that has known no sin.
[ll. 966–70]

The ass leads Peter to the widow. The meeting is described. The wailing boy comes also. The body is fetched by Peter and Farmer Simpson:

> And now does Peter deeply feel
> That man's heart is a holy thing;
> And Nature, through a world of death,
> Breathes into him a second breath,
> E'en like the breath of spring.
>
> [ll. 1071–5]

The operations of these scenes on his mind are described, and the poet concludes with a simple stanza:

> And Peter Bell, who till that night
> Had been the wildest of his clan,
> Forsook his crimes, forsook his folly,
> And after ten months' melancholy
> Became a good and honest man.
>
> [ll. 1131–5]

Benjamin the Waggoner has far less meaning. It is, says Wordsworth, purely fanciful. The good waggoner is addicted to liquor, but on the night of the adventure resists temptation. He gives shelter to a sailor's wife during a storm, and the sailor will treat him at the alehouse. The model of a ship the sailor has with him is shown to the frolicking peasants; but the hours are lost, and the waggoner's master is so enraged at seeing his waggon return with the sailor and his wife, and his own dog wounded by a kick from the sailor's ass, that he turns off poor Benjamin – the horses will obey no one else, so the poet [?] loses both waggon and waggoner. But this tale is told with grace and has delightful passages of description and elegant playfulness. The poem opens with an exquisite [description] of an evening after a hot day:

> Now that the children are abed
> The little glow-worms nothing dread;
> Rich prize as their bright lamps would be,
> Forth they come in company
> And shine in quietness secure
> On the mossy bank by the cottage door,
> As safe as on the loneliest moor.
> In the sky and on the hill
> Everything is hush'd and still;

313

The clouds show here and there a spot
Of a star that twinkles not.
The air as in a lion's den
Is close and hot, and now and then
Comes a tired and sultry breeze
With a haunting and a panting,
Like the stifling of disease.
The mountains seem of wondrous height,
And in the heavens there is a weight;
But the dews allay the heat,
And the silence makes it sweet.*
[in variant forms, Canto I, ll. 7–21]

When the travellers approach the public Benjamin is thus affected:

Although before in no dejection,
He gladdens at the recollection;
His heart with sudden joy is filled,
His ears are by the music thrilled,
His eyes take pleasure in the road,
Glittering before him bright and broad;
And Benjamin is wet and cold,
And there are reasons manifold
That make the food towards which he's yearning
Look fairly like an honest earning.
[Canto ii, ll. 31–40]

This is in the spirit of kindness and indulgence Wordsworth praises in Burns's *Tam o' Shanter*. In describing the dancing and joy in the ale-house the poet concludes:

As if it heard the fiddlers call
The pewter clatters on the wall;
The very bacon shows its feeling,
Swinging from the smoky ceiling.
[*Ibid.*, ll. 66–9]

I must put a limit to copying, or I shall have taken more than Wordsworth might wish to have in writing out of his possession.

(*Ibid.*, I, 94–102)

---

* *N.B.* – Much improved as printed. [Crabb Robinson.] 1849.

h. 6 June 1812

With Charles Lamb. Lent him *Peter Bell*. To my surprise he finds nothing in it good. He complains of the slowness of the narrative, as if that were not the *art* of the poet. Wordsworth says he, has great thoughts, but *here* are none of them. He has no interest in the ass. These are to me inconceivable judgments from Charles Lamb, whose taste in general I acquiesce in, and who is certainly an enthusiast for Wordsworth. But I know no resource against the perplexity arising from the diversities of opinion in those I look up to, but in determination to disregard all opinions and trust to my own unstudied suggestions and natural feelings.

(*Ibid.*, I, 103)

i. 10 August 1812

[?Charles] Aders enjoyed heartily *Tam o'Shanter* and *Holy Willie's Prayer*, etc. I also read to Aders some of Wordsworth, which he did not seem to relish so heartily . . .

(*Ibid.*, I, 106)

j. 12 August 1812

At Blackheath, [at John Flaxman's lodgings] a very agreeable [overnight] visit. At tea read to the ladies Wordsworth's *Brothers*. This pathetic idyll (to which I could have wished a somewhat more polished versification) was more acceptable than the homely tales in a ballad shape . . .

(*Ibid.*, I, 106)

k. 13 August 1812

Coleridge praised *Wallenstein* but censured Schiller for a sort of ventriloquism in poetry, – by the bye, a happy term to express that common fault of throwing the feelings of the writer into the body, as it were, of other personages, the characters of the poem. In *Ruth*, as it stands at present, there is the same fault; Wordsworth had not originally put into the mouth of the lover many of the sentiments he now entertains, and which would better have become the poet himself.

(*Ibid.*, I, 107)

l. 17 October 1812

An agreeable day. Read in the forenoon to Mrs. William Pattisson[5] the extracts from *Peter Bell*. They were only half enjoyed, and I resolved not to endeavour any longer to force a taste for the beauties of my favourite poet where the impressions, if raised, cannot take root . . .

(*Ibid.*, I, 111)

m. 19 October 1812

Forenoon reading to Mrs. William Pattisson and Miranda, Wordsworth's text to Wilkinson's Sketches of the Lakes. We were all greatly delighted with the book. Mrs. William Pattisson seemed deeply to feel its excellence, notwithstanding her readiness to find puerile the peculiarities of Wordsworth's ballad poetry . . .

(*Ibid.*, I, 111)

n. 29 December 1813

After dinner . . . I was allowed to ride my hobby gently, and to praise Wordsworth warmly, and I gave no offence when I abused the other party. I likened the intimacy of Rogers and Lord Byron to a mixture of water-rice gruel and curry, and this was acceded to. But no one, not even Burrell,[6] acceded to my sentiments concerning Wordsworth. Though Burrell has the general feelings which a genuine admirer of Wordsworth must have. Beyond all he has just sentiments concerning the war, and in general on all points that bear upon the moral relations of life, of the highest kind.

(*Ibid.*, I, 133–4)

o. 12 January 1814

Went to W. Taylor's [of Norwich], who had a small party to dine with him, Pitchford and Madge.[7] We had spent a long and pleasant conversation on German literature, Wordsworth, etc. W. Taylor has just notions of Wordsworth as far as notions can suffice to give a just impression of Wordsworth, but he does not feel his peculiar excellence. He complains, and with reason, that Wordsworth wants proportion. He says that he looks at a spider's line with a microscopic eye, and fancies it a cable.

Madge and I admitted that Wordsworth had sensibilities which the great body of mankind could not sympathise with . . .

(*Ibid.*, I, 135)

p. 22 January 1814

I repeated to Madame de Stael Wordsworth's sonnet on the King ['Now that all hearts are glad'], and spoke warmly in his praise. She says Sir James Mackintosh also speaks of him as a man of great talents. But she asked if Wordsworth's style were good, without which, she said, no writer can have immortality.

(*Ibid.*, I, 135)

Some twenty years later, in a letter of 31 July 1835, Crabb Robinson told Wordsworth of this encounter. He may also have spoken to him about it (see below). Wordsworth related the anecdote to his nephew who mis-recorded it in *Wordsworth Memoirs* (1851, ii, 474), attributing to Mackintosh the phrase, 'Wordsworth is not a great poet'. Crabb Robinson, in his own inter-leaved copy of *Memoirs*, commented in a note dated 5 April 1851 on how the reminiscence was 'damaged in the passing through two minds [i.e. Wordsworth's and his nephew's]', and he recalled his earlier words to Wordsworth on the subject of Mme. de Stael and Mackintosh:

> I have no doubt that Sir James Mac[k]intosh told Mad^c. de Stael that y^r. style is bad – for she said to me one day, 'Does Wth. write a good style? It is style that gives duration to works' – and then almost in a breath, and without waiting for my answer went on, 'Mac[k]intosh says that Wth. is not the greatest of the living poets, but the greatest man among the poets'.
>
> (Ms. The Wordsworth Library)

q. 7 February 1814

. . . Dined at the Hall, after which De Quincey, Cargill and others came home with me. We drank tea together, and stayed till late, our conversation chiefly on Lord Byron, to whom we were not favourable, and on Wordsworth, whose admirers were more zealous than his adversaries. De Quincey has a fine and very superior mind. He talks about Wordsworth with the zeal and intelligence of a well-instructed pupil, and his style, with a mixture of pedantry and high-flown sentimentality, evinces a man who thinks while he talks and who has a discriminating judgment and delicate taste . . .

(*Henry Crabb Robinson on Books and Their Writers*, ed. Edith J. Morley, 1938, I, 137)

r. 3 July 1814

Lamb's peculiarities are very interesting. We had not much conversation. He hummed tunes, I repeated Wordsworth's *Daffodils*, of which I am become very fond. Lamb can relish the thieves in the last stage of avarice, ... which is beyond me. At the same time he censures Wordsworth's narrative.

(*Ibid.*, I, 145)

EDITOR'S NOTES

1. Probably Sharon Turner (1768–1847), attorney, historian and friend of Southey.
2. *The Convention of Cintra.*
3. Crabb Robinson's version of *Peter Bell* seems to be similar to that produced by Wordsworth's revisions to Ms. 5 (see note 4)
4. The four stanzas, 'The dragon's wing ...' ff., are added in Wordsworth's hand to Ms. 5 of *Peter Bell*, a fair copy in Sara Hutchinson's hand, dated 1805–6. De Selincourt (*Poetical Works of William Wordsworth*, II, 529) thinks 'they may have been added any time between the writing of this manuscript and the poem's publication' [1819]. Clearly, from Crabb Robinson's evidence, they must have been written well before June 1812 – perhaps Wordsworth's response to criticism of *Poems* (1807).
5. William and Hannah Pattisson of Witham, Sussex; Crabb Robinson was related to William Pattisson.
6. John Palfrey Burrell (dates not known).
7. Rev. Thomas Madge (1786–1870), a prominent Unitarian Minister: at the Octagon Chapel, Norwich, 1811–25, and at Essex Street Chapel, London, 1825–59. A *Memoir ... of ... Madge* by William James, 1871, states: 'Whilst at Norwich Mr. Madge had the pleasure of an introduction to WORDSWORTH, with whom, in his visits to the Lake District, he was for many years privileged to enjoy frequent and friendly intercourse'.

129. Percy Bysshe Shellcy (1792–1822)

From a letter to Elizabeth Hitchener, 15 December 1811

I feel a sickening distrust when I see all I had considered good great & imitable fall around me into the gulph of error . . . Wordsworth (a quondam associate of Southey) yet retains the integrity of his independance, but his poverty is such that he is frequently obliged to beg for a shirt to his back.

(*Letters of Shelley*, ed. F. L. Jones, 1964, I, 208)

130.

From *Modern Poets. A Dialogue, in Verse*, London, 1813, 4

Yet another example of an anonymous satirist abusing Wordsworth without reading him; the comments are based upon Jeffrey's review of John Wilson's *The Isle of Palms* (see entry 132b).

See sing-song ditties bribe the full-grown child,
*In foolscap octaves 'Poems' gravely styl'd;
See now simplicity disjoin'd from sense
To Nature's accent urge the mad pretence;
Pale Learning, stedfast to her classic page,
Unheeded toiling brands a trifling age;
†Moderns in Chronicles for wisdom seek,
Odes yield to ballads, to black-letter Greek.

* Ex. gr. Wilson's 'Isle of Palms' (reputed one of the happiest productions of the Wordsworth school) or any other of those *sweet* compositions.
† Certain recent book sales prove that Chronicles, &c. enjoy no small degree of favour with modern Literati.

No ancient discipline, no youthful toil,
No early vigils, and no midnight oil
Tame the free mind, or chain the ranging soul,
Which roams on earthly limbs from pole to pole.
*The travell'd bard may many a beauty spy,
And thousand miles a thousand lines supply,

131. William Godwin (1756–1836)

From a letter to Wordsworth, 5 March 1811

Godwin met Wordsworth early – at least nine times in February–April and July–August 1795, and four times in July 1796 – but there are no records from this period other than Godwin's terse diary entries. One of these meetings must be the one that Godwin was to recollect in 1826: 'I had the honour, in the talk of one evening to convert Wordsworth, from the doctrine of self-love to that of benevolence – ask him . . . that is perhaps my powerful topic' (microfilm, Bodleian). The relationship was based on the discussion of moral ideas but by late 1798, at least, Godwin's thinking, to Wordsworth, had become too abstract (see W. J. B. Owen and Jane Worthington Smyser, *The Prose Works of William Wordsworth*, Oxford, 1974, I, 103).

On 28 November 1798, Godwin recommended both Coleridge and Wordsworth to his young Scottish friend John Arnott then travelling in Europe: 'you may perhaps meet them on your rambles. They are both extraordinary men, and both reputed men of genius. Coleridge I think fully justifies the reputation' (Kegan Paul, *Life and Letters of Godwin*, 1876, i, 318).

Godwin's diary shows he read *Lyrical Ballads* on 11 April 1799; he praised Coleridge's 'Ancient Mariner' on 9 January 1800; on 1 March 1801, he read the new second Volume and on 8 March the first Volume (with the new Preface). On 9 May he records: 'Northcote sups (Lyrical Ballads)'. Hazlitt in 1830 notes that Godwin had pressed Northcote to admire Wordsworth's poetry, but the date for this is unknown. Some flattery to Wordsworth might be detected in the opening chapter of

---

* A trip to Portugal or Greece seems to be as powerful a stimulant to patrician genius, as a cottage upon the banks of a lake in Westmoreland to plebeian brains. What may we not expect if the excursions of the former should become annual, or the residence of the latter permanent?

Fleetwood (1805): the hero's happy youth is in a pastoral setting where an analysis of his ardent response to the sound of cataracts is attempted.

Fortunately Wordsworth is not among the list of Godwin's former friends who deserted him (Southey is); and an unpublished Wordsworth letter, 21 April 1807, shows that Godwin invited the poet, his wife and Sara Hutchinson to dine: Wordsworth refused, clearly not wanting the families to be intimate, but he arranged to go alone; and their acquaintance respectfully continued. Indeed in the letter of 5 March 1811, signed 'your entire friend', Godwin tries (in vain) to persuade Wordsworth to versify for children the tale of Beauty and the Beast. This request betrays admiration for 'beauty & simplicity' and fear of something 'abstruse'.

. . . I need not tell you that the success would entirely depend upon its suiting a certain class of readers, that is, upon exhibiting as much delicate simplicity as you please, but nothing abstruse, nothing that would repel the young or wrinkle with the frown of investigation the forehead of the fair . . . I ought to have said before, that no one I know of could give the tale in the desired form that beauty & simplicity that you could do & therefore no one, in my apprehension, could do half so much to secure the success of our venture. But though I say this from the bottom of my heart, I would scarcely prevail upon myself to say it at all, because these are trite & threadbare words

(Ms. The Wordsworth Library)

132. Francis Jeffrey

Unsigned reviews, *Edinburgh Review*, 1811–1812

a. From an unsigned review of John Ford's *Dramatic Works*, *Edinburgh Review*, **August 1811**, xviii, 283

. . . Cowper is, and is likely to continue, the most popular of all who have written for the present or the last generation.

Of the poets who have come after him, we cannot, indeed, say that they have attached themselves to the school of Pope and Addison; or that they have even failed to show a much stronger predilection for the native beauties of their great predecessors. Southey, and Wordsworth, and Coleridge, and Miss Baillie, have all of them copied the manner of our older poets; and, along with this indication of good taste, have given great proofs of original genius. The misfortune is, that their copies of those great originals, are all liable to the charge of extreme affectation. They do not write as those great poets would have written: they merely mimic their manner, and ape their peculiarities; – and consequently, though they profess to imitate the freeest and most care-less of all versifiers, their style is more remarkably and offensively artificial than that of any other class of writers. They have mixed in, too, so much of the maukish tone of pastoral innocence and babyish simplicity, with a sort of pedantic emphasis and ostentatious glitter, that it is difficult not to be disgusted with their perversity, and with the solemn self-complacency, and keen and vindictive jealousy, with which they have put in their claim for public admiration. But we have said enough elsewhere of the faults of these authors; and shall only add, at present, that, notwithstanding all these faults, there is a fertility and a force, a warmth of feeling and an exaltation of imagin-ation, about them, which classes them, in our estimation, with a much higher order of poets than the followers of Dryden and Addison; and justifies an anxiety for their fame, in all the admirers of Milton and Shakespeare . . .

b. From an unsigned review of *The Isle of Palms* (1812) by John Wilson, February 1812, xix, 374–5

Crabb Robinson must have had this review in mind when he commented on 13 April 1814:

> Looked into Bowles's sonnets. Mawkish and unreadable. Also Wilson's *Isle of Palms*. 'A *female* Wordsworth' is the designation of this author. A plentiful lack of thought, with great delicacy and even elegance of taste, but without riches or strength of imagination. I could not get on with it, though the poetry is pretty. It is a libel on the great philosophical poet of the Lakes to consider Wilson as his superior. This is one of the most scandalous insults upon Wordsworth by the *Edinburgh* reviewers . . .
> (*Henry Crabb Robinson on Books and their Writers*, ed. Edith J. Morley, 1938, I, 140)

By 25 October 1814 Crabb Robinson had learnt that Wilson had been able to approve this review before publication:

> [Rev. Samuel] Tillbrook is an admirer of Wordsworth. He says that Wilson the poet assured him that Jeffrey, the *Edinburgh* reviewer, declared to him that

he is a great admirer of Wordsworth, and that he had attacked him in the way he has done, not because he himself thinks lowly of him, but because the public think lowly of him. I had heard a similar tale before, but never on such good authority. Jeffrey further asked Wilson to introduce him to Wordsworth, which Wilson refused doing. Wilson and Jeffrey are friends, and the *Edinburgh* review of *The Isle of Palms* was sent to him in manuscript with an offer to omit anything that might be offensive. It seems strange to me that any sincere admirer and disciple of Wordsworth should suffer such an elevation of himself at his master's expense . . .

(*Ibid.*, I, 151)

[Wilson] makes more, to be sure, of a sleeping child, or a lonely cataract – and flies into greater raptures about female purity and moonlight landscapes, and fine dreams, and flowers, and singing-birds – than most other poets permit themselves to do, – though it is of the very essence of poetry to be enraptured with such things: – But he does not break out into any ecstacies about spades or sparrows' eggs – or men gathering leeches – or women in duffle cloaks – or plates and porringers – or washing tubs – or any of those baser themes which poetry was always permitted to disdain, without any impeachment of her affability, till Mr Wordsworth thought fit to force her into an acquaintance with them.

Though Mr Wilson may be extravagant, therefore, he is not perverse; and though the more sober part of his readers may not be able to follow him to the summit of his sublimer sympathies, they cannot be offended at the invitation, or even refuse to grant him their company to a certain distance on the journey. The objects for which he seeks to interest them, are all objects of natural interest; and the emotions which he connects with them, are, in some degree, associated with them in all reflecting minds. It is the great misfortune of Mr Wordsworth, on the contrary, that he is exceedingly apt to make choice of subjects which are not only unfit in themselves to excite any serious emotion, but naturally present themselves to ordinary minds as altogether ridiculous; and, consequently, to revolt and disgust his readers by an appearance of paltry affectation, or incomprehensible conceit. We have the greatest respect for the genius of Mr Wordsworth, and the most sincere veneration for all we have heard of his character; but it is impossible to contemplate the injury he has done to his reputation by this poor ambition of originality, without a mixed sensation of provocation and regret. We are willing to take it for granted, that the spades and the eggs, and the tubs which he commemorates, actually suggested to him all the emotions and reflexions of which he has chosen to make them the vehicles; but they surely are not the only objects which have suggested similar emotions; and we really cannot understand why the circumstance of their being quite unfit to suggest them to any other person, should have recommended them as their best accompaniments in an address to the public. We do not want Mr Wordsworth to write like Pope or Prior, nor to dedicate his muse to subjects which he does not himself think interesting. We are prepared, on the contrary, to listen with a far deeper delight to the songs of his mountain solitude, and to gaze on his mellow pictures of simple happiness and affection, and his lofty sketches of human worth and energy; and we only beg, that we may have these nobler elements of his poetry, without the debasement of childish language, mean incidents, and incongruous images. We will not run the risk of offending him, by hinting at the prosperity of Scott, or Campbell, or Crabbe; but he cannot be scandalized, we think, if we refer him to the example of the dutiful disciple and fervent admirer who is now before us; and entreat him to consider whether he may not conscientiously abstain from those peculiarities which even Mr Wilson has not thought it safe to imitate.

c. 'Rejected Addresses', 10 October 1812

Published on the day of the opening of the rebuilt Drury Lane Theatre, this was an anonymous volume of twenty-one modern parodies purporting to be entries submitted in the competition to provide a suitable address for the opening of the theatre. By James (1775–1839) and Horace (1779–1849) Smith. An unsigned review of this appeared in the *Edinburgh Review*, November 1812, XX, 438–9; the relevant extract begins:

The next, in the name of Mr W. Wordsworth, is entitled 'The Baby's Debut,' and is characteristically announced as intended to have been 'spoken in the character of Nancy Lake, a girl eight years of age, who is drawn upon the stage in a child's chaise, by Samuel Hughes, her uncle's porter.' The author does not, in this instance, attempt to copy any of the higher attributes of Mr Wordsworth's poetry; but has succeeded perfectly in the imitation of his maukish affectations of childish simplicity and nursery stammering. We hope it will make him ashamed of his Alice Fell, and the greater part of his last volumes – of which it is by no means a parody, but a very fair, and indeed we think a flattering imitation. We give a stanza or two as a specimen.

My brother Jack was nine in May,
And I was eight on New Year's Day;
  So in Kate Wilson's shop
Papa, (he's my papa and Jack's)
Bought me last week a doll of wax,
  And brother Jack a top.

Jack's in the pouts, and this it is,
He thinks mine came to more than his,
  So to my drawer he goes,
Takes out the doll, and, Oh, my stars!
He pokes her head between the bars,
  And melts off half her nose!

We pass over this family feud, and the history of her conveyance to the theatre; and proceed to this interesting young lady's observations upon its appearance.

My father's walls are made of brick,
But not so tall, and not so thick,
  As these; and, goodness me!
My father's beams are made of wood,
But never, never half so good,
  As these that now I see.

What a large floor! 'tis like a town!
The carpet, when they lay it down,
  Won't hide it, I'll be bound!
And there's a row of lamps, my eye!
How they do blaze! I wonder why
  They keep them on the ground.

At first I caught hold of the wing,
And kept away; but Mr Thing-
  umbob, the prompter man,
Gave with his hand my chaise a shove,
And said, Go on, my pretty love,
  Speak to 'em, little Nan.

The exit is equally characteristic.

But while I'm speaking, where's papa?
And where's my aunt? and where's mama
  Where's Jack? Oh, there they sit!
They smile, they nod, I'll go my ways,
And order round poor Billy's chaise,
  To join them in the pit.

And now, good gentlefolks, I go
To join mama, and see the show;
  So, bidding you adieu,
I curtsey, like a pretty miss,
And if you'll blow to me a kiss,
  I'll blow a kiss to you.
      [Blows a kiss, and exit.]'

Both Smith brothers were to become admirers of Wordsworth. Horace Smith wrote to his friend, Barron Field:

I hope you told M^r. Wordsworth that I was quite ashamed of the ridicule in the Rejected Addresses (not mine, by the bye) – that I had read his Excursion under my own walnut-trees with infinite delight, and had now the honour of being enrolled among his warm admirers. It must have been a high treat to you to go about with him.'
(Quoted by Barron Field in a letter to Wordsworth, 10 April 1828; Ms. The Wordsworth Library)

Field later noted in his 'Critical Memoir', 1839 (Ms. British Museum), that the author of 'The Baby's Debut' (James Smith),

like hundreds of others, knew nothing of Mr. Wordsworth's poetry then, but what he had read in the Edinburgh Review itself; but he has since done noble justice to one who is now his favorite poet. In the preface to the last edition of the Rejected Addresses, we read:–
'To raise a harmless laugh was our main object, in the attainment of which we were sometimes hurried into extravagance. In no instance were we thus betrayed into a greater injustice than in the case of Mr. Wordsworth – the touching sentiment, profound wisdom, and copious harmony of whose loftier writings we left unnoticed, in the despair of burlesquing them, while we pounced upon his popular ballads, and excited ourselves to push their simplicity into puerility and silliness. With pride and pleasure do we now claim to be ranked among the most ardent admirers of this true poet. And if he himself could see the state of his works, which are ever at our right hand, he would perhaps receive the manifest evidences they exhibit of constant reference and delighted re-perusal, as some sort of *amende honorable*[1] for the unfairness

of which we were guilty, when we were less conversant with the higher inspiration of his Muse.'

Field then records Wordsworth's rather irritated reaction to Jeffrey's comment (see above) on the parody in *Rejected Addresses*:

Mr. Wordsworth was never offended with this professed caricature, as he justly was with Mr. Jeffrey's critical injustice; but he once observed to me that the Mr. Smiths, if their intention was, as Mr. Jeffrey asserted, 'a very fair and even flattering one of Alice Fell, and the greater part of his last volumes', should have printed Alice Fell itself in their book, just as the authors of the celebrated Probationary Odes for the Laureateship, as if in despair of making Tom Warton more ridiculous than he made himself, when they came, to his turn, gave, instead of a parody or burlesque, a real laureate Ode by Warton himself . . .

· EDITOR'S NOTE

1. 'honourable amends', i.e. satisfaction, public apology.

133. Rev. Francis Hodgson (1781–1852)

From *Leaves of Laurel*, 1813

Hodgson was a friend of Byron, as well as of Thomas Denman and J. H. Merivale, both contributors, like him, to the *Critical* and *Monthly* Reviews. This work, edited by 'W. W.' and 'Q. Q.', was written after the death of the Poet Laureate, H. J. Pye, on 11 August 1813.

A child so small, I cannot tell
    How small she was indeed,
Met me, while walking in the dell,
    That's nigh to Pinner mead.
She pull'd me by the coat; and oh!
She look'd, as if she wish'd I'd go,
Where stood a cottage in the lane
That borders upon Pinner plain.

I went with her – and then she said,
'The Poet Laureat, P—e, is dead.'
Ah me! I answer'd sad; and so
We reach'd the little house of woe.

The wicker gate was open'd wide,
The flowers were trodden down beside;
It look'd, as if some friend had past
Eager on P—e to look his last.
I know not – but I heav'd a sigh –
The little child stood weeping by.

We enter'd at the cottage door,
And saw the man who was no more.
That child – I never will forsake her –
Though sneer'd at by the undertaker

With a pitiful sob here the story broke off,
And hard-hearted they felt who were tempted to scoff;
There was something so good in the bard, yet so silly,
That you lov'd him and laugh'd at him too, willy nilly.

(*Leaves of Laurel*, pp. 15–16)

134. Leigh Hunt (1784–1859)

From his writings, 1811–1815

Hunt was a well-known editor, essayist and poet. His attitude to Wordsworth moved from contempt, to praise, to irritated respect; as with Hazlitt, dislike of Wordsworth's politics influenced his critical comments.

a. From *The Feast of Poets*, an unsigned satire, *Reflector*, December 1811, ii. 319

This was apparently based simply on a reading of reviews of Wordsworth.

He [Apollo] turn'd from the rest without even a look;
For Coleridge had vex'd him long since, I suppose,
By his idling, and gabbling, and muddling in prose;

And as to that Wordsworth! he'd been so benurst,
Second childhood with him had come close on the first.   5
These worthies, however, long us'd to attack,
Were not by contempt to be so driven back,
But follow'd the God up, and shifting their place,
Stood full in his presence, and look'd in his face,
When one began spouting the cream of orations,   10
In praise of bombarding one's friends and relations,
And t'other some lines he had made on a straw,
Shewing how he had found it, and what it was for,
And how when 'twas balanc'd, it stood like a spell, –
And how when 'twas balanc'd no longer, it fell!   15
A wild thing of scorn, he describ'd it to be –
But said it was patient to heaven's decree:
Then he gaz'd upon nothing, and looking forlorn,
Dropt a *natural* tear for *that wild thing of scorn!*
Apollo half laugh'd betwixt anger and mirth,   20
And cried, 'Were there ever such asses on earth?'
It is not enough that this nonsense, I fear,
Has half turn'd the fine head of my friend Robert here,
But another bright promise must fairly be lost,
And the gifts of a God by this madman be crost.   25
What! think ye a bard's a mere gossip who tells
Of the ev'ry-day feelings of ev'ry one else;
And that poetry lies, not in something select,
But in gath'ring the refuse that others reject?
Depart and be modest, ye driv'llers of pen,   30
My feasts are for masculine tastes, and for men.'
Then turning to Bob, he said, 'Sit down, I beg;'
But Billy grew sulky and stirr'd not a peg;
While Sam, looking soft and politely dejected,
Confess'd with a tear, that ''twas what he expected,   35
Since Phœbus had fatally learnt to confide in
Such prosers as Johnson and rhymers as Dryden.'

b. From the much-revised *Feast of Poets*, 1814 and 1815

Hunt by now has read Wordsworth for himself (though he avoids making any
comment on *The Excursion*) and the contempt is transformed into a kind of
eulogy.

[Lines 4 and 5 (my numbering) above are altered to:]

And Wordsworth, one day, made his very hairs bristle,
By going and changing his harp for a whistle.

[and lines 30ff. are replaced by:]

Must a ballad doled out by a spectacled nurse
About Two-Shoes or Thumb, be your model of verse;
And your writings, instead of sound fancy and style,
Look more like the morbid abstractions of bile?
There is one of you here, who, instead of these fits,
And becoming a joke to half-thinkers and wits,
Should have brought back our fine old pre-eminent way,
And been the first man at my table to-day:
But resolved as I am to maintain the partitions
'Twixt wit and mere wildness, he knows the conditions;
And if he retains but a spark of my fire,
Will show it this instant, – and blush, – and retire.'
He spoke; and poor Wordsworth, his cheeks in a glow,
(For he felt the God in him) made symptoms to go,
When Apollo, in pity, to screen him from sight,
Threw round him a cloud that was purple and white,
The same that of old used to wrap his own shoulders,
When coming from heaven, he'd spare the beholders:
'Twas culled from the east, at the dawning of day,
In a bright show'ry season 'twixt April and May.
Yet the bard was no sooner obeying his king,
And gliding away like a shadow of spring,
Than the latter, who felt himself touched more and more
Tow'rds a writer whose faults were as one to five score,
And who found that he shouldn't well know what to say,
If he sent, after all, his best poet away,
Said, 'Come, my dear Will, – imperfections apart, –
Let us have a true taste of our exquisite art;
You know very well you've the key to my heart.'

    At this the glad cloud, with a soft heaving motion,
Stopped short, like a sail in a nook of the ocean;
And out of its bosom there trembled and came
A voice, that grew upwards, and gathered like flame:

Of nature it told, and of simple delights
On days of green sunshine, and eye-lifting nights;
Of summer-sweet isles and their noon-shaded bowers,
Of mountains, and valleys, trees, waters, and flowers,
Of hearts, young and happy, and all that they show
For the home that we came from and whither we go;
Of wisdom in age by this feeling renewed,
Of hopes that stand smiling o'er passions subdued,
Of the springs of sweet waters in evil that lie; –
Of all, which, in short, meets the soul's better eye
When we go to meek nature our hearts to restore,
And bring down the Gods to walk with us once more.
   You may think what effect was produced by this strain:
Apollo, put on all his graces again,
With face just inclining, and smiles that agreed;
And Scott looked as who should say 'Lofty indeed!'
And Campbell, as if 'twould be stupid to doubt it;
And Bob, as if he, forsooth, knew all about it;
And Byron, as though he were wrapt in his place;
And Moore, as if pleasure had burst on his face;
And all cried at last, with a passion sublime,
'This, this is the Prince of the Bards of his Time!'
   So the cloud rolled apart, and the poet came forth,
And took his proud seat as was due to his worth;
And Apollo, who felt all his spirits restored,
And wouldn't, for trifles, make gaps at his board,
Twitched Coleridge's ear, who stood yawning askew;
And said, 'There, you lazy dog, sit you down too.'
         (*Feast of Poets*, ll. 309–69 in *Poetical Works of Leigh Hunt*, ed.
         H. S. Milford, 1923, 153–4)

c. From notes to the *Feast of Poets* added to the poem in 1814

[Additions made in 1815 are indicated by pointed brackets.] The notes were seen by Sir George Beaumont who said of them in a letter to Wordsworth of 2 June 1814, they 'do you some justice' (see entry 112g). Hunt, late in life, recorded that 'Byron accused me of making him [Wordsworth] popular upon town' (*Autobiography*, ed. J. E. Morpurgo, 1949, 223). Immediately on reading the new edition of the *Feast of Poets* Byron had written without rancour to Hunt on 9 February 1814, 'I have been at your text, which has much *good* humour in every sense of the word. Your notes are of a very high order indeed, particularly on Wordsworth' (*Works of Lord Byron: Letters and Journals*, ed. R. E. Prothero, 1898–1904, iii, 31).

[The notes are preceded by the verses from the *Feast of Poets* to which they refer.]

> *And Wordsworth, one day, made his very hairs bristle,*
> *By going and changing his harp for a whistle.*

The allusion here scarcely needs a remark; but in revising my verses, and endeavouring to do justice to Mr. Wordsworth, I was anxious, whenever I mentioned him, to show myself sensible of the great powers he possesses, and with what sort of gift he has consented to trifle.

> *And t'other some lines he had made on a straw,*
> *Showing how he had found it, and what it was for,*
> *&c. &c.*

I am told, on very good authority, that this parody upon Mr. Wordsworth's worst style of writing has been taken for a serious extract from him, and panegyrized accordingly, with much grave wonderment how I could find it ridiculous. –

> *And all cried at last with a passion sublime,*
> *'This, this is the Prince of the Bards of his Time!'*

Whatever may be the faults of Mr. Wordsworth, it certainly appears to me, that we have had no poet since the days of Spenser and Milton, – so allied in the better part of his genius to those favoured men, not excepting even Collins, who saw farther into the sacred places of poetry than any man of the last age. Mr. Wordsworth speaks less of the vulgar tongue of the profession than any writer since that period; he always thinks when he speaks, has always words at command, feels deeply, fancies richly, and never descends from that pure and elevated morality, which is the native region of the first order of poetical spirits.

To those who doubt the justice of this character, and who have hitherto seen in Mr. Wordsworth nothing but trifling and childishness, and who at the same time speak with rapture of Spenser and Milton, I would only recommend the perusal of such poems as the Female Vagrant, a little piece on the Nightingale,* the three little exquisite pieces ['Strange

⟨ * Another poem on this bird mentioned in the former edition was, I afterwards found, Mr. Coleridge's; and I had to congratulate myself accordingly on having said what I had, in a previous note, respecting his congeniality with Mr. Wordsworth in point of real powers. It is a pity that all the poems written by Mr. Coleridge are not collected in one publication.⟩

fits of passion', 'She dwelt among the untrodden ways', 'I travell'd among unknown Men' (in 1814 'A slumber did my spirit seal')], another ['Three years she grew'], – the Old Cumberland Beggar (a piece of perfect description philosophized), – Louisa, the Happy Warrior, to H.C., the Sonnet entitled London, another on Westminster Bridge, another beginning 'The World is too much with us,' the majestic simplicity of the Ode to Duty, a noble subject most nobly treated, ⟨and the simple, deep-felt, and calm yet passionate grandeur of the poem entitled Laodamia.⟩ If after this, they can still see nothing beautiful or great in Mr. Wordsworth's writings, we must conclude that their insight into the beauties of Spenser and Milton is imaginary – and that they speak in praise of those writers as they do in dispraise of Mr. Wordsworth, merely by rote.

It may be asked me then, why, with such opinions as I entertain of the greatness of Mr. Wordsworth's genius, he is treated as he is in ⟨some of⟩ the verses before us; I answer, because he abuses that genius so as Milton or Spenser never abused it, and so as to endanger [destroy *1814*] those great ends of poetry, by which it should assist the uses and refresh the spirits of life. From him, to whom much is given, much shall be required. Mr. Wordsworth is capable of being at the head of a new and great age of poetry; and in point of fact, I do not deny that he is so already, as the greatest poet of the present; – but in point of effect, in point of delight and utility, he appears to me to have made a mistake unworthy of him, and to have sought by eccentricity and by a turning away from society, what he might have obtained by keeping to his proper and more neighbourly sphere. Had he written always in the spirit of the pieces abovementioned, his readers would have felt nothing but delight and gratitude; but another spirit interferes, calculated to do good neither to their taste nor reflections; and after having been elevated and depressed, refreshed and sickened, pained, pleased, and tortured, we ⟨sometimes⟩ close his volumes, as we finish a melancholy day, with feelings that would go to sleep in forgetfulness, and full waking faculties too busy to suffer it.

The theory of Mr. Wordsworth, – if I may venture to give in a few words my construction of the curious and, in many respects, very masterly preface to the Lyrical Ballads, is this; – that owing to a variety of existing causes, among which are the accumulation of men in cities and the necessary uniformity of their occupations, – and the consequent craving for extraordinary incident, which the present state of the world is quick to gratify, the taste of society has become so vitiated and so accustomed to gross stimulants, such as 'frantic novels, *sickly* and stupid German tragedies, and deluges of *idle* and *extravagant* stories in verse,' as to require the counteraction of some simpler and more primitive food, which should restore to readers their true tone of enjoyment, and enable them to relish once more the beauties of simplicity and nature; – that, to this purpose, a poet in the present age, who looked upon men with his proper eye, as an entertainer and instructor, should chuse subjects as far removed as possible from artificial excitements, and appeal to the great and primary affections of our nature; – thirdly and lastly, that these subjects, to be worthily and effectively treated, should be clothed in language equally artless. I pass over the contingent parts of the Preface, though touching out, as they go, some beautiful ideas respecting poets and poetry in general, both because I have neither time nor room to consider them, and because they are not so immediate to my purpose. I shall merely observe, by the way, that Mr. Wordsworth ⟨though he has a fine Miltonic ear,⟩ does not seem to have exercised his reflections much on the subject of versification, and must protest against that attempt of his to consider perfect poetry as not essentially connected with metre, – an innovation, which would detract from the poet's properties, and shut up one of the finest inlets of his enjoyment and nourishers of his power, – the sense of the harmonious.*

Now the object of the theory here mentioned has clearly nothing in the abstract, that can offend the soundest good sense or the best poetical ambition. In fact, it is only saying, in other words, that it is high time for poetry in general to return to nature and to a natural style, and that he will perform a great and useful work to society, who shall assist it to do so. I am not falling, by this interpretation, into the error which Mr. Wordsworth very justly deprecates, when he warns his readers against affecting to agree with him in terms, when they really differ with him in taste. The truth which he tells, however obvious, is necessary to be told, and to be told loudly; and he should enjoy the praise which he deserves, of having been the first, in these times, to proclaim it. But the question is, (and he himself puts it at the end of his Preface,) has Mr. Wordsworth 'attained his object?' Has he acted up to his theory? Has he brought back that natural style, and restored to us those healthy and natural perceptions, which he justly describes as the proper state of our poetical constitution? I think not. He has shown that he could do it, and in many [some 1814] instances he has set the example;[1] but the effect of at least many other passages in his poetry, and those, I believe, which he views with

---

⟨ * In the preface to the late edition of his poems, Mr. Wordsworth seems to have tacitly retracted on this head.⟩

most partiality, appears to me to be otherwise: it tends, in my mind, to go to the other extreme of what he deprecates, and to substitute one set of diseased perceptions for another.

Delight or utility is the aim of the poet. Mr. Wordsworth, like one who has a true sense of the dignity of his profession, would unite both; and indeed, for their perfect ends, they cannot be separated. He finds then our taste for the one vitiated, and our profit of the other destroyed, and he says to us, 'Your complexion is diseased; – your blood fevered; you endeavour to keep up your pleasurable sensations by stimulants too violent to last, and which must be succeeded by others of still greater violence: – this will not do: your mind wants air and exercise, – fresh thoughts and natural excitements: – up, my friend; come out with me among the beauties of nature and the simplicities of life, and feel the breath of heaven about you.' – No advice can be better: we feel the call instinctively; we get up, accompany the poet into his walks, and acknowledge them to be the best and most beautiful; but what do we meet there? Idiot Boys, Mad Mothers, Wandering Jews, Visitations of Ague, ⟨Indian Women left to die on the road,⟩ and Frenzied Mariners, who are fated to accost us with tales that almost make one's faculties topple over.* – These are his refreshing thoughts, his natural excitements; and when you have finished with these, you shall have the smallest of your fugitive reflections arrested and embodied in a long lecture upon a thorn, or a story of a duffel-cloak, till thorns and duffel-cloaks absolutely confound you with their importance in life; – and these are his elementary feelings, his calm and counteracting simplicities.

Let the reader observe that I am not objecting to these subjects in behalf of that cowardly self-love falsely called sensibility, or merely because they are of what is termed a distressing description, but because they are carried to an *excess* that defeats the poet's intention, and distresses to no purpose. Nor should I select them as exhibiting a part of the character of Mr. Wordsworth's writings, rather than pass them over as what they really are, the defects of a great poet, – if the author himself had not especially invited our attention towards them as part of his system of counteraction, and if these and his occasional puerilities of style, in their disadvantageous effect upon his readers, did not involve the whole character and influence of his poetry.

⟨ * The last of these 'idle and extravagant stories' was written, it seems, by Mr. Coleridge. The pieces, by the way, supplied by this gentleman, have been left out of the late collection of Mr. Wordsworth's poems.⟩

But how is our passion for stimulants to be allayed by the substitution of stories like Mr. Wordsworth's? He wishes to turn aside our thirst for extraordinary intelligence to more genial sources of interest, and he gives us accounts of mothers who have gone mad at the loss of their children, of others who have killed their's [sic] in the most horrible manner, and of hard-hearted masters whose imaginations have revenged upon them the curses of the poor. In like manner, he would clear up and simplicize our thoughts; and he tells us tales of children that have no notion of death, of boys who would halloo to a landscape nobody knew why, and of an hundred inexpressible sensations, intended by nature no doubt to affect us, and even pleasurably so in the general feeling, but only calculated to perplex or sadden us in our attempts at analysis. Now it appears to me, that all the craving after intelligence, which Mr. Wordsworth imagines to be the bane of the present state of society, is a healthy appetite in comparison to these morbid abstractions: the former tends, at any rate, to fix the eyes of mankind in a lively manner upon the persons that preside over their interests, and to keep up a certain demand for know-ledge and public improvement; – the latter, under the guise of interesting us in the individuals of our species, turns our thoughts away from society and men altogether, and nourishes that eremitical vagueness of sensa-tion, – that making a business of reverie, – that despair of getting to any conclusion to any purpose, which is the next step to melancholy or indifference.

It is with this persuasion, – a persuasion, which has not come to me through the want of acquaintance either with solitude or society, or with the cares of either, – that I have ventured upon the piece of ridicule in the text. Mr. Wordsworth has beautifully told us, that to him

> —the meanest flow'r that blows can give
> Thoughts that do often lie too deep for tears.

I have no doubt of it; and far be it from me to cast stones into the well in which they lie, – to disturb those reposing waters, – that freshness at the bottom of warm hearts, – those thoughts, which if they are too deep for tears, are also, in their best mood, too tranquil even for smiles. Far be it also from me to hinder the communication of such thoughts to man-kind, when they are not sunk beyond their proper depth, so as to make one dizzy in looking down to them. The work of Shakspeare is full of them; but he has managed to apply them to their proper refreshing purposes; and has given us but one fond recluse in his whole works, – the melancholy Jaques. Shall we forget the attractions which this melancholy philosopher felt towards another kind of philosopher, whom he met in the forest, and who made a jest of every thing? Let us be sure, that this is one of the results of pushing our abstractions too far, and of that dangerous art which Mr. Wordsworth has claimed for his simpler pieces, – the giving importance to actions and situations by our feelings, instead of adapting our feelings to the importance they possess. The consequence of this, if carried into a system, would be, that we could make any thing or nothing important, just as diseased or healthy impulses told us; – a straw might awaken in us as many profound, but certainly not as useful reflections, as the fellow-creature that lay upon it; till at last, perplexed between the importance which every thing had obtained in our imaginations, and the little use of this new system of equality to the action and government of life, we might turn from elevating to depreciating, – from thinking trifling things important, to thinking important things trifling; and conclude our tale of extremes by closing in with expedience and becoming men of the world. – I would not willingly disturb the spirit, in which these remarks are written, by unpleasant allusions: but among the numerous acquaintances of Mr. Wordsworth, who have fallen in with his theories, perhaps he may be reminded of some, who have exemplified what I mean. He himself, though marked as government property, may walk about his fields uninjured, from the usual simplicity of his life and from very ignorance of what he has undergone; but those who never possessed the real wisdom of his simplicity, will hardly retain the virtue; and as in less healthy men, a turn for the worst taste of his reverie would infallibly be symptomatic of a weak state of stomach rather than of a fine strength of fancy, so in men of less intellect, the imitation of his smaller simplicities is little else but an announcement of that vanity and weakness of mind, which is open to the first skilful corrupter that wishes to make use of it.

With regard to the language in which Mr. Wordsworth says that poetry should be written, his mistake seems to be this, – that instead of allowing degrees and differences in what is poetical, he would have all poetry to be one and the same in point of style, and no distinction allowed between natural and artificial associations. Nobody will contend with him that the language of nature is the best of all languages, and that the poet is at his height when he can be most fanciful and most feeling in expressions the most neighbourly and intelligible; but the poet may sometimes chuse to show his art in a manner more artful, and appealing to more particular associations than what are shared by the world at large, as those of classical readers for instance. It is true, by so doing, he narrows his dominion, and gives up the glory of a greater and more difficult sway; but he still rules us by a legitimate title, and is still a poet. In the one instance, he must have all the properties of the greatest of his profession, – fancy, feeling, knowledge; – in the other, he requires less feeling, and for knowledge may substitute learning; – a great inferiority no doubt, but still only differing in degree, for learning is but the knowledge of books, as knowledge is the learning of things. Mr. Wordsworth, to illustrate what he means, quotes the following sonnet of Gray, and says that 'the only part of it, which is of any value, is the lines printed in Italics:'

> [Quotes 'In vain to me the smiling mornings shine' as presented in the Preface to the *Lyrical Ballads* and goes on to discuss the kinds of language appropriate for different species of poetry.]

... [Wordsworth] talks of selection in the very midst of what appears to others an absolute contempt of it. Now selection has an eye to effect, and is an acknowledgment that what is always at hand, though it may be equally natural, is not equally pleasing. Who are to be the judges then between him and his faults? Those, I think, who, delighted with his nature, and happy to see and to allow that he has merits of his own superior to his felicitous imitations of Milton, (for the latter, after all, though admired by some as his real excellence, are only the occasional and perhaps unconscious tributes of his admiration,) are yet dissatisfied and mortified with such encounterings of the bellman, as 'Harry Gill and We are Seven;' – who think that in some of the effusions called 'Moods of My Own Mind,'* he mistakes the commonest process of reflection for its result, and the ordinary, every-day musings of any lover of the fields for original thinking; – who are of opinion, in short, that there is an extreme in nature as well as in art, and that this extreme, though not equally removed from the point of perfection, is as different from what it ought to be and what nature herself intended it to be, as the ragged horse in the desert is to the beautiful creature under the Arab, or the dreamer in a hermitage to the waking philosopher in society.

To conclude this inordinate note: Mr. Wordsworth, in objecting to one extreme, has gone to another, – the natural commencement perhaps of all revolutions. He thinks us over-active, and would make us over-

⟨ * This title is omitted in the last edition. – Yet, in objecting to these pieces, it is impossible, I think, for any *poetical* mind not to [be] carried away with the enthusiasm of the song to a Skylark, or not to value the pure and exquisite sentiment wrapped up in the little piece on a Rainbow.⟩

contemplative, – a fault not likely to extend very widely, but which ought still to be deprecated for the sake of those to whom it would. We are, he thinks, too much crowded together, and too subject, in consequence, to high-fevered tastes and worldly infections. Granted: – he, on the other hand, lives too much apart, and is subject, we think, to low-fevered tastes and solitary morbidities; – but as there is health in both of us, suppose both parties strike a bargain, – he to come among us a little more and get a true sense of our action, – we to go out of ourselves a little oftener and acquire a taste for his contemplation. We will make more holidays into nature with him; but he, in fairness, must earn them, as well as ourselves, by sharing our working-days: – we will emerge oftener into his fields; sit dangling our legs over his styles, and cultivate a due respect for his daffodils; but he, on the other hand, must grow a little better acquainted with our streets, must put up with our lawyers, and even find out a heart or so among our politicians: – in short, we will recollect that we have hearts and brains, and will feel and ponder a little more to purify us as spirits; but he will be good enough, in return, to cast an eye on his hands and muscles, and consider that the putting these to their purposes is necessary to complete our part in this world as organized bodies.

Here is the good to be done on both sides; and as society, I believe, would be much bettered in consequence, so there is no man, I am persuaded, more capable than Mr. Wordsworth, upon a better acquaintance with society, to have done it the service. Without that acquaintance, his reputation in poetry, ⟨though very great,⟩ may be little more *salutary* than that of an Empedocles in philosophy or a Saint Francis in religion: – with it, he might have revived the spirit, the glory, and the utility of a Shakspeare.*

⟨ * Since this note, with little variation, was written, Mr. Wordsworth has collected his minor pieces into the two volumes so often referred to, and has published also two new and large poems, the 'Excursion,' and the 'White Doe of Rylstone.' It does not strike me, however, that I should alter it any further in consequence; though I confess I have risen, if possible, in my admiration of this great genius. The White Doe, it is true, which seems to have been written some time back, does not appear to be among his happiest performances, though containing, as almost all his performances do, touches of exquisite beauty. It is a narrative poem; and there is something in this kind of writing too much *out in the world* for the author's habitual powers. Reverie has been his delight; and the Excursion, with some objectionable parts on the old score, is a succession of noble reveries.⟩

EDITOR'S NOTE

1. 'but . . . tends' in *1814* reads: 'but the popular effect of his poetry appears to me to be far otherwise; it gives us puerility for simplicity, affectation for nature; and only tends . . .'

135. Thomas Barnes (1785–1841)

Essay signed 'STRADA', *Champion*, 28 May 1814, 174–5

Editor of *The Times*, 1817–41, Barnes did not meet Wordsworth until precisely one year after the *Champion* article; he wrote to Leigh Hunt:

I met Wordsworth last Sunday,[1] & was a good deal pleased with his unaffected sense. I took an opportunity of introducing Lord Byron's poetry in order to sound him on that subject, & certainly from the opinion which he appears to entertain of Lord B's mind as displayed in his poems, I do not think that he would feel a very high gratification in his company. At any rate, I think it would be a risk to bring together in a small party two persons who I fear would have no points of sympathy about them. If Lord B is half as amiable as Wordsworth appears to be, this is a great pity, for the good & the intelligent ought to amalgamate to be a match for the conspiracy of fools & knaves.

(Quoted by D. Hudson, *Thomas Barnes of The Times*, 1943, 23)

> Hic tamen, et ampera quos diximus, infinores
> Partibus egregiè multis, multoque minores,
> Quanquam multa bene, ac divinitus invenientis
> Ex adylo tanquam cordis responsu dedere
> Sanctius, et multo certa ratione magis, quàm
> Pythin, quo tripode ex Phœbi, lanroque profatur;—
> Principiis tamen in rerum fecere minas.
>
> *LUCRET, Lib.* 1.[2]

Such is the glowing language with which the most eloquent of the Roman poets describes some of his predecessors in natural philosophy. He is devoting his whole faculties to display the absurdities of their system, yet at the same time is eager to lavish upon them all those honours which their high qualities demanded. His eloquence it would not be easy to imitate: but it would be at once possible and decorous for those who attempt to point out the errors of an eminently gifted man to adopt this tone of candid respect. The lines above quoted, with all their praise and all their censure, could scarcely be applied to Empedocles, and his followers, with more accurate propriety, then to Mr. Wordsworth and his school. Like the Sicilian philosopher, he has uttered, from this 'heart's oracular seat,' sounds more true and holy than all the priestesses of Apollo: like him he has shewn a disposition for destruction, by an endeavour to subvert and exterminate some of the old established principles of poetical taste. In naming the school of Mr. Wordsworth, I comply rather with an usual term than express my own opinion: for I am at a loss where I should look for his disciples. 'Tis true that some persons have copied one or two of his worst defects; that babyism of language and thought, which for some inscrutable purpose, he now and then condescends to adopt: but is it thus a man becomes a scholar of Wordsworth? Where is he who has exhibited a kindred elevation of mind, the same intensity of feeling, the same profoundness of view, the same sublimity of moral sense? Surely it is not Mr. Coleridge: there is not a more striking difference between the strut of a grenadier-corporal, and the soul-breathing dignity of the Belvidere Apollo, than exists between the turgid efforts of the pretended scholar, and the easy grandeur of the supposed master. Still less can it be Mr. Southey: he, poor fellow, is forced to ransack every quarter of the globe, say, to tear open the mysteries of every element, for some tale of wonder to rouse his intellect to exertion: whereas, Mr. Wordsworth need but look at the first stick or stone in his way, and he can open to himself visions, rich with all the treasures of poetry and philosophy. He has, indeed, permitted the productions of these gentlemen to appear amidst his own collections: but they are weeds 'which have no business there.' I do not wish to undervalue either of these two poets, but they must not take rank, nor stand side by side, with the first man of the age. Mr Wordsworth belongs to the same class as our Shakespeare, our Spenser, and our Milton; his mind is of the same high, unvulgar cast: purged from the common dimness which obstructs man's vision: his eye, like theirs, looks abroad upon nature, seizing her most retiring beauties, and comprehending her abstrusest harmonies: like theirs, his intellect, with a proud, commanding sagacity, can reach at once the remotest conclusions without the slow process of reasoning, and unravel the most mysteriously-combined motives without those technical auxiliaries which have been invented for the use of ordinary mankind. It would indeed be ridiculous to place him on a footing of perfect equality with the great triumvirate: has he hitherto written nothing of sufficient pretensions to be put in competition with their master-pieces: but his ambition and his qualities are of the same exalted kind, and give us hope that his genius will yet produce fruits corresponding to the magnificence of its promise. Nobody, I think, will deny, that where he is great, none could be greater: that majesty of thought seems natural to him: that whenever he soars into the higher and purer air of intellectual contemplation, he moves about with a facility and conscious dignity which shows that he belongs to that unearthly element. His language too (for in his finest passages he forgets the peculiarities of his own system) has all that abounding vigour and splendour which befit his thoughts, and his blank versification has, to my ear, all the variety, art, and grandeur of the finest music. Milton, though he is said to have been an accomplished musician, has not managed his pauses with half the effect of Mr. Wordsworth, who is reported to be ignorant of the science. In reading the best poems of the latter, you are impressed in the same manner as if you were accompanied by an organ, so that it would be no slight sensual enjoyment to repeat the verses with reference to the cadences alone, without any regard to the meaning.

In glancing at my motto, I find that I have nearly forgot to mention, what most persons have been led to think are the chief parts in this poets character: his defects. As far as regards Mr. Wordsworth himself, I should not think it worth while to descant upon his faults, because he has redeemed them by inimitable beauties: but as there are some simple souls who have confounded his eccentricities with his excellences, have mistaken that for sublime which is in fact only odd, a few words may not be thrown away on an attempt to point out where this poet has erred. He seems to think that the commonest thoughts and feelings are as fit subjects for poetry as the most dignified, and that the most obvious diction is the most poetical. It is heedless to say that all his best pieces are in direct variance with this proposition, abounding as they do with sentiments and phraseology which are exalted utterly beyond the reach of common apprehension: yet he has condescended to write a few poems in conformity with those principles, and a less seductive illustration of their truth could not well be imagined. The failure would have been still greater if he had perfectly accorded in his own rule: but such is not the case: he details indeed some common incidents, but they by no means suggest to him common sentiments or common language. For instance, he takes a morning walk and sees a leech-gatherer, and on this occasion pours out some of the noblest thoughts clothed in the finest and most elaborate diction. But does he mean to say, that, to ten thousand other persons who might have seen the same leech-gatherer, any thought would have occured except that he was a sturdy person with a stupid employment: and could such a thought embodied in such common language excite the slightest interest in any bosom. Mr. Wordsworth has ventured to go further: he has published what he calls the moods of his own mind, and has disclosed the silliest as well as the wisest of his feelings. This experiment is rather to be considered as a hazardous vanity than real magnanimity. It is true that nothing can be more interesting than to view a great mind under all circumstances, in its undress as well as in 'all its bravery:' it is true that simplicity and greatness are so akin, that the most exalted intellects have occasionally been delighted to relapse into the feelings of childhood. – The disclosure however of this tendency should never be made but to the most intimate hearts: the world at large will misunderstand it, and it is not for the interest of virtue that the dignity of the wise and good should be lowered even in the estimation of the most contemptible. Socrates would knuckle down at law with his own children, nor was he ashamed to be caught, for he knew how to abash and overwhelm impertinent folly: but had Socrates carried his bag of marbles to the market-place, and played with the ragged boys of Athens, the profoundest sentence that he could have uttered would not have saved him from scorn and contempt.

Another fault, ascribed to Mr. Wordsworth, belongs rather to his habits of life than to his system of opinions: he has a morbid sensibility which extracts melancholy out of every object, and impresses itself so deeply on the minds of his careful readers, as might unhinge them for the common business of life. Such, at least, is the opinion even of some who admire him. I think the matter is over-rated. There are not ten minds, in an age so nicely organized, so acutely sensitive, as to be in any danger of disorder from the influence of the saddest strains of poetry: and, on account of a possible evil, one cannot consent that Mr. Wordsworth should alter that frame and disposition of mind which is one of his great charms. He had been brought up in the school of nature's beauties and sublimities, and by deep meditation on himself, compared with those wonders of creation, he has acquired an elevation and purity of thinking which has less of earth in it than any poetry in the world, except, perhaps, some of the mournful odes of Petrarch. If he came out more into the world, he might, perhaps, be a merrier personage; but who would not rather have him write sublimely than ludicrously, unless, indeed (which would be too much to expect) he could amuse mankind and himself with such humourous delineations of life as Shakespeare could draw. At any rate, who could endure, what must be one inevitable consequence of much intermixture with society, – that he should waste his time in penning sonnets on Lady Jane's fan, or Lady Bab's slipper?

Mr. Wordsworth is not, indeed, adapted to be a popular poet; he is of too high an order: he writes for men who reflect as deeply as himself. Our greatest poets have not been popular: Shakespeare, notwithstanding his infinite variety, is rather liked, as affording scope to favourite actors, than read in the closet: those who read him do it through the medium of Cibber or Tate, or some other blundering fellow who presumes to alter and fit him for representation. As to Milton and Spenser, they are wholly unknown except to a few poetical readers: every library, indeed, holds their works, and most gentlemen are acquainted with their names; but you might travel from Cornwall to Berwick, and not find twenty persons who have fairly perused Spenser's *Fairy Queen*, or even the *Paradise Lost*. Mr. Wordsworth, therefore, must be content to be less read than the writer of amorous odes and wondrous romances: he may, however, be assured of an eternal memory in the minds of the wise; and that future ages will be eager to point out his name, as one of the proudest specimens of the best English character, distinguished, as it will be, for purity of feeling, for comprehensiveness of intellect, and for a strain of poetry which at once enchants the senses, exalts the understanding, and improves the heart.

STRADA

EDITOR'S NOTES

1. Crabb Robinson noted for 28 May 1815, 'I dined at Collier's with a party assembled to see the poet Wordsworth.' (*Henry Crabb Robinson on Books and their Writers*, ed. Edith J. Morley, I, 167).
2. Barnes draws on lines 734–40 from Lucretius' *De Rerum Natura*, Book I. Lucretius is praising the foremost of the pluralists, Empedocles ('He') but criticises his understanding of the substratum, or the basic substance ('the beginning of things').

> He, however, and those I mentioned earlier, his inferiors by a significantly wide margin and much lesser figures, despite making many fine, inspired

discoveries, and giving their responses, so to speak, from the inner sanctums of their heart with greater holiness and much more assured reasoning than the Pythia [the priestess who delivered the oracles of Pythian Apollo at Delphi] who gives her pronouncements from the tripod and laurel of Apollo, yet in the case of the beginnings of things, they have come to grief . . .

136. J. H. Reynolds (1794–1852)

From a letter to Wordsworth and extract from *The Eden of Imagination*, both 1814

John Hamilton Reynolds was a friend of Keats and a would-be poet. An admirer of Wordsworth, though his prose tended towards the sentimental, even whimsical, rather than the strictly critical. Certainly his reputation as a critic of Wordsworth loses force if John Scott's essay, (wrongly) attributed to Reynolds by L. M. Jones (*Selected Prose of John Hamilton Reynolds*, Harvard, 1966, 13), is removed (see John Scott, *Thanksgiving Ode*, entry 203). Wordsworth himself justly characterised Reynold's literary temper when he commented on his *Naiad*: 'Your Fancy is too luxuriant, and riots too much upon its own creations' (28 November 1816. *MY*, II, 346). But when that temper was touched by irritation, Reynolds became Wordsworth's most entertaining parodist.

a. From a letter to Wordsworth, 12 November 1814

Will you accept of the accompanying little Sketch of rural Scenery? [*The Eden of Imagination* (see entry 136b)] – Written not from immediate observation but from Remembrance – not from the objects themselves before my eye, but from the images of them on my mind. It may appear presumptuous in me to send the offspring of but an ill-stored memory to One who lives in a very friendship with Nature and thinks daily over the wandering streams & in the silent fields: – But I have long wished to thank you for the deep pleasure your Poems have given me – and Time has strengthened my wish – Inclination would fain persuade me that an opportunity now occurs, and I would fain believe her.

To say that I fully enter into your feelings in reading your Poems, would be wrong – For I should imagine no One can Feel so intensely as you do. But I believe I am right in saying that I enter pretty largely into them, and your thoughts always lead me to contemplation and leave me calm. The little blank verse Pieces in the Lyrical Ballads are my favourites – They are full of exquisite feeling & natural description & are clothed in the sweetest & simplest dress: – you show in them how nearly Simplicity & Feeling are related, & prove the importance of flowers & Rocks & Brooks to the mind. For these most particularly and for all I thank you, and from the heart.

It is perhaps very much to be regretted that the World in general, is so ill-calculated to prize the Treasures of Thought which you have discovered to them, or to comprehend even their value. Your poetry is too full of kind-heartedness and philosophical reflection for the present age. If it was placed more out of the reach of simplicity and had less Thought and feeling, it would be more popular.

Living as I do now, in the bustle of London – opportunities occur but seldom of feeding my mind in the fresh clear, & calm Country: – When they do, I lose no time in improving my stock of reflections and preparing for retirement – I look at beautiful scenery in the boldness of Sunshine and in the delicacy of Moonlight with great mental pleasure. – Though where you would find a harvest, I can but glean. The little poem I now send you was composed from the remembrance of scenes in various Counties – And the piece at the end of the pamphlet ['A Recollection'] was written from 'The recollection' of a view I had from a Mountain on the border of North-Wales.

[You] will perhaps pardon the freedom I have treated [your poetry in the] Notes, which ought never to have been inserted. They have too decisive a tone for one of my age – I really now regret their appearance, and intend (if ever the poem should pass to a 2$^\text{d.}$ Edit$^\text{n.}$) totally to strike them out.

In the hope that you will excuse the liberty I have taken in thus writing to you, I beg leave to subscribe myself – Your grateful Admirer

(Ms. The Wordsworth Library)

b. From *The Eden of Imagination*, 1814

The Preface is dated 'August 1814', i.e. before the publication of *The Excursion*.

Let Campbell lead his Hope within my bowers, –
And Wordsworth's* genius illustrate my flowers;
Though he may yet, in some great hour, resign
The simple violet and celandine, –
He may with bolder finger sweep the lyre,
And give to after-times a song of fire.

---

* I know of no one so fit to inhabit this Eden of Imagination as Mr. Wordsworth; he is possessed of ideas and feelings very much above those of common men, and appears (to judge of him by his works) to look deeply and thoughtfully into things. The smallest flowers yield him a pleasure of no ordinary description, and his own words inform us that he can, in the bustle of towns and cities, and in the loneliness of solitude, revive from them recollections of the most refreshing nature –

> 'But oft, in lonely rooms, and 'mid the din
> Of towns and cities, I have owed to them
> In hours of weariness, sensations sweet,
> Felt in the blood, and felt along the heart,
> And passing even into my purer mind,
> With tranquil restoration.'
> LYRICAL BALLADS, VOL. 1.

This passage is from one of those Poems in which Mr. Wordsworth has turned his powers (which are of the highest order) to a proper use, and in which he has awakened his best reflections. For a fine estimate of his genius, see the Notes in Hunt's 'Feast of the Poets.' [See entry 134c for Hunt's 'Fine estimate'.]

VIII

Convention of Cintra: reviews and opinions,
1809–1833

137. Joseph Farington

From his diary, 1809

a. 6 June 1809

Lord Lonsdale[1] asked me if I had seen Wordsworth's new publication on the Cintra Convention. He sd. Wordsworth sent [it] to Him & last night He read a dozen pages of it, & thought it written in a very bad taste, not with plainness & simplicity such [as] is proper to a political subject, but in a style inflated & ill suited to it. – I sd. it was remarkable that in His Poetry He affects a simplicity approaching to puerility, while in Politics in which plain statement & deduction is alone required He assumes the reverse of it.

(*The Farington Diary*, ed. Kathryn Cave, 1982, IX, 3478)

b. 7 June 1809

Mr. Phipps's I dined at. – Lady Beaumont spoke of Wordsworth's pamphlet on the 'Cintra Convention', in very high terms, as above the political writings of Burke & others. – Miss Bowles sd. Stourges Bourne[2] had read it & spoke of the latter part of it particularly, & that the pamphlet was manifestly written by a man of superior abilities. – Sir George said, drily, that Lady Beaumont spoke of the Book as if she was *employed to sell it*. – She sd. she Had caused the sale of some of them.

(*Ibid.*, IX, 3482)

c. 12 July 1809

James Northcote at dinner had spoken of Coleridge's *Friend* as 'strange', even 'contemptible', and Taylor continued in similarly critical vein.

[John] Taylor spoke of Wordsworth's pamphlet on the *Cintra Convention* as being a very poor performance; too heavy to be read through. –

(*Ibid.*, X, 3511)

351

d. 7 April 1810

Lady Beaumont, today, spoke much of Wordsworth, of His great mental powers, of the eloquence in His convention of Cintra, and of His manly contentment in limited circumstances, He having when He first married only £70 a year, & now has not more than £200 a yr. with a wife & 5 children, with an addition of one every year. She sd. that the acquaintance of Coleridge with Wordsworth commenced at a Political Debating Society, where on one occasion Wordsworth spoke with so much force & eloquence that Coleridge was captivated by it & sought to know Him. Wordsworth for all He has published has recd. very little pecuniary profit, not in the whole more than a few hundred pounds.[3]

(*Ibid.*, X, 3628)

EDITOR'S NOTES

1. William Lowther, Earl of Lonsdale (1757–1844). Lord Lonsdale, a close friend of the government, was a supporter of the Convention of Cintra and actively worked against those who wanted a 'County meeting' (at which Wordsworth himself as a freeholder, was expected to speak) to send an Address, protesting to the King. Farington had called on Wordsworth at Allan Bank on 30 September 1808, and had found 'him warm abt. Convention' (*Ibid.*, IX, 3355).
2. William Sturges Bourne (1769–1845), life-long friend of Canning, in Government.
3. Wordsworth's financial return from writing was poor. Farington, 17 May 1808, reports that Sir George Beaumont 'remarked on the hard lot of Poets . . . He sd. Wordsworth has not got £200 by all He has written, & has lived upon £70 a year at Grassmer' (*ibid.*, IX, 3279). On 1 June Sir George 'dwelt much upon the unfortunate situation of Poets compared with that of Painters. He sd. that two of our principal Portrait Painters had got more money within the last seven years than all the poets in this country had obtained. He sd. Wordsworth had got £160 for all He had written & published' (*ibid.*, IX, 3288). Over twenty-five years later, Thomas Moore recorded 'Wordsworth telling me – what certainly is no small disgrace to the taste of the English public – of the very limited sale of his works, and the very scanty sum, on the whole, which he had received for them, – not more I think than about a thousand pounds, in all. I daresay I must have made by *my* writings at least twenty times that sum . . .' (20 February 1835, *Journal of Thomas Moore*, ed. Wilfred S. Dowden, 1987, IV, 1660).

138. James Montgomery

Unsigned review, *Eclectic Review*, July 1809, V, part ii, 744–50

The first thing that will strike the mind, on taking up this pamphlet, will be the *Latinity* of its title; and the second will be the *English* of its contents. Of the former we shall only say, that it is the title of something without a name; – whether an address, speech, letter, or any thing else, to the people of Great Britain, the people of Great Britain must themselves determine. Of the latter, – the *English* of its contents, – we must observe, that it is so exquisitely compounded of words, idioms, and phrases, obsolete and authorized, unprecedented and vernacular, as to form altogether a style of very peculiar gait and character, resembling nothing so nearly as the blank verse of the Westmorland triumvirate of Bards; who, if they have sometimes condescended to degrade poetry into prose, have occasionally deigned to exalt prose into poetry. Of this, the tract before us is an illustrious example. In these Sibylline leaves, (full of portentous and awful denunciations,) snatched from the winds, and stitched loosely together to make a pamphlet of only one day's longer life than a newspaper, there is more of the spirit and fire of genuine poetry, than we have found in many a cream-coloured volume of verse, designed to delight and astonish posterity. The language is at once splendid and obscure, vigorous yet prolix, beautiful, bewildering, and uncouth. The sentiments, ardent, and free, and original, are frequently so clouded with mysticism, subtilized by metaphysical refinement, or emblazoned with imagination, that they appear either too dark, too thin, or too bright, to be steadily viewed, or clearly comprehended. But there is a pulse of philanthropy, that beats through every page (though not through every line), and a soul of patriotism that breathes through the whole body of this work, which raise it, as an offspring of intellect, far above the political ephemera, quickened from the carcases of transient events which Time leaves behind him in his devastating march to Eternity, – ephemera, which flutter for a day, then vanish for ever. Among this imbecile and fugitive race the present gorgeous emanation of Genius is born; and with them it must perish. We therefore seize the earliest opportunity to say something '*concerning*' it, before its freshness and interest are irreparably faded, though we have neither time nor room to do justice to its extraordinary claims, as a great effort of an uncommon mind. It is, self-evidently, the work of a retired man, of deep, enlarged, and patient thought, connected with no political party, warped by no vulgar prejudices, carried away by no sudden or momentary gust of passion; but who, chiefly in solitude and meditation, yet occasionally stimulated by the society of congenial and equally powerful and eccentric minds, may be said to live in the world of war and business only *in the spirit*, and who consequently views men and things in a light peculiar to himself, or participated by none, but the small circle in which he moves. Hence his merits and his faults are so far exclusively his own, that they have all been originally conceived, or deliberately and resolutely adopted, by himself. The sentiments of such a man, cherishing independence of mind as the dearest inheritance of his nature, and reverencing liberty as the supreme good of his country, must be worthy of attention; though we have little hope that they will excite much curiosity, or make any very profitable impression upon the people or governors of this island, to whom they particularly and emphatically appeal. Despising all the common place details of every day business, and overleaping all the petty, thwarting, embarrassing, and disheartening circumstances which must be taken into account by practical politicians, and which generally furnish employment enough for their dwarf faculties, Mr. Wordsworth seems to have discovered the spot which Archimedes desired, from whence he might move the world: here taking his stand, and with a glance embracing the whole surface and horizon of his subject, he decides authoritatively on whatever he reviews, and lays down plans of unparallelled magnitude and complexity, with the confidence of a being of almost infallible intelligence. Whether by this strong effort of superior, but only speculative, talents, he will be able to raise the earth one degree nearer to heaven, or even lift these little portions of the earth on which he peculiarly operates – Spain, Portugal, and Great Britain, – a point above their present degraded level, we shall not attempt to determine. Meanwhile, though we cannot subscribe to all the principles maintained in this pamphlet, particularly the vindictive and sanguinary ones which occasionally are manifested, we have perused its eloquent pages with much pleasure and admiration . . . [A summary of Wordsworth's argument follows.]

139.

Unsigned review, *British Critic*, September 1809, xxxiv, 305–6

In an advertisement to this work we are told, that it 'originated in the opposition which was made by his Majesty's Ministers to the expression, in public meetings and otherwise, of the opinions and feelings of the people concerning the Convention of Cintra.' Our opinion respecting that Convention has already been expressed. It is nearly the same, on the *political* part, with that which has been declared by the highest authority, and, on the *military* part, with that given by the Earl of Moira on the Court of Inquiry. Yet, whatever we might feel, or, as private individuals, express, we can never approve the proceedings of those who, before all the circumstances could be known, prejudged their fellow-subjects, on the eve of a judicial inquiry. The Author before us does not indeed appear to come within that censure, (having, as it appears, first published his sentiments after the inquiry had taken place) yet he argues in support of such prejudication on grounds which we deem fallacious. This subject, however, has been already so fully discussed, and has since been superseded by so many events of equal, if not superior, importance, that we must be excused from enlarging upon this part of his work. Its principal feature must, by every generous mind, be recognised with the warmest approbation. It is a noble and highminded enthusiasm in the cause of the oppressed Spanish and Portuguese nations, with its natural attendant, an indignant disdain of the tyrant who endeavours to enslave them. These general sentiments entitle the Author to our sincere praise, although, in some particulars, his sentiments and our's very widely differ.

After a variety of remarks on the erroneous principles on which (in the Author's opinion) our support to the Spaniards has hitherto been afforded, he proposes two alternatives for our adoption; namely, that we should either put forth our whole strength as a military power, and make ourselves, for a time, upon Spanish ground, principals in the contest, or that we should direct our attention to giving support rather in *things* than in men. The former plan (for the execution of which he requires at least two hundred thousand men to be poured into the Peninsula) he considers, as practicable, though requiring great sacrifices, and argues at some length, to show that the power of our adversary, if once successfully resisted, would soon be broken. 'If this attempt,' he adds, 'be above the strain and temper of the country, there remains only a plan laid down upon the other principles; namely, service (as far as is required) in *things* rather than in men; that is, men being secondary to things.' From a middle course, he thinks, no good is to be expected. Military stores and arms should be furnished with unsailing liberality. Troops also should be supplied, but they should act separately, taking strong positions upon the coast; and, above all, he recommends a floating army, keeping the enemy in constant uncertainty where he is to be attacked. Having stated these plans, the Author censures strongly the want of general and enlarged principles in the statesmen of the present age. We are willing to hope this opinion is carried too far. The rapid fluctuations of public events, and the uncommon difficulties in which the ministers of this country have been frequently placed, since the beginning of the French revolution, may account for many of those apparent inconsistencies which have been observed in the conduct of perhaps every administration. We, however, cordially join in the Author's hope and persuasion, that the tyrant of France will never succeed in completely subjugating the Spanish nation. Some of the principles upon which he founds this opinion are perhaps pushed to the extreme; but, without going so far in this respect, or reasoning wholly upon metaphysical grounds, we cannot but perceive, notwithstanding the errors, the weakness, and (in too many instances) the treachery of their leaders, a determined spirit in the people of Spain which probably will never be subdued.

Upon the whole, the generous spirit which this pamphlet breathes, and the knowledge of human nature, which, in many passages, it evinces, claim attention and applause; although the Author's enthusiasm is not, we think, void of extravagance; although his reasonings partake too much of refinement, and although his style, though it often interests by eloquence, as frequently fatigues by prolixity.

It is hardly possible for a man of ingenuous mind to act under the fear that it shall be suspected by honest men of the vileness of praising a work to the public, merely because he happens to be personally acquainted with the Author. That this is so commonly done in Reviews, furnishes only an additional proof of the morbid hardness produced in the moral sense by the habit of writing anonymous criticisms, especially under the further disguise of a pretended board or association of Critics, each man expressing himself, to use the words of Andrew Marvel, as a *synodical individuum*.[1] With regard however, to the probability of the judgement being warped by partiality, I can only say that I judge of all Works indifferently by certain fixed rules previously formed in my mind with all the power and vigilance of my judgement; and that I should certainly of the two apply them with greater rigour to the production of a friend than that of a person indifferent to me. But wherever I find in any Work all the conditions of excellence in its kind, it is not the accident of the Authors being my contemporary or even my friend, or the sneers of bad-hearted men, that shall prevent me from speaking of it, as in my inmost convictions I deem it deserves.

> no, friend!
> Though it be now the fashion to commend,
> As men of strong minds, those alone who can
> *Censure* with judgement, no such piece of man
> Makes up my spirit: where desert does live,
> There will I plant my wonder, and there give
> My best endeavours to build up his glory,
> That truly merits!
>
> *Recommendatory Verses to one of the old Plays*

EDITOR'S NOTE

1. 'Individual in a synod or association'.

140. Samuel Taylor Coleridge

From *The Friend*, 28 September 1809, ed. Barbara E. Rooke, Routledge, 1969, II, 108

But if my Readers wish to see the question of the efficacy of principles and popular opinions for evil and for good proved and illustrated with an eloquence worthy of the subject, I can refer them with the hardiest anticipation of their thanks, to the late work 'concerning the relations of Great Britain, Spain, and Portugal,' by my honoured friend, William Wordsworth* *quem quoties lego, non verba mihi videor audire, sed tonitrua!* [Whenever I read him, I seem to hear not the words but thunderings!]

---

* I consider this reference to, and strong recommendation of the Work above mentioned, not as a voluntary tribute of admiration, but as an act of mere justice both to myself and to the readers of THE FRIEND. My own heart bears me witness, that I am actuated by the deepest sense of the truth of the principles, which it has been and still more will be my endeavour to enforce, and of their paramount importance to the well-being of Society at the

141. Henry Crabb Robinson

From an unsigned essay reviewing four books, *London Review*,
November 1809, iv, 232–75

... The reader who delights in moral disquisition, is with confidence
referred to Mr. Wordsworth's pamphlet, in which there is a combination
of the philosophic and poetic spirit, unlike any thing which has appeared
before the public since the death of the great orator and statesman so
often mentioned. This encomium and comparison require however to be
qualified and explained, if not for the sake of the Author, at least of his
Reviewer. Three qualities have contributed to raise *Burke* beyond all
popular political writers. 1. A depth of psychological penetration, and a
simplicity of moral remark, delivered sometimes with the familiarity of
the tea-table, and sometimes with axiomatic energy and brevity, by
which many recondite truths have been added to the stock of popular
and national wisdom. 2. A strong and poetic imagination, by which he
could throw a glory round any object which it was his purpose to exalt
and adorn. And, 3. A power of playfully and gracefully combining the
high and the low in nature and in life; by which he could call forth the
inferior sensibilities of men, the sense of ridicule, for instance, to co-
operate with the higher, the sense of moral truth and beauty: hence his
bitter sarcasms, his fine and delicate irony, and that humour which he

---

present juncture: and that the duty of making the attempt, and the hope of not wholly
failing in it, are, far more than the wish for the doubtful good of literary reputation, or any
yet meaner object, my great and ruling motives. Mr. Wordsworth I deem a fellow-labourer
in the same vineyard, actuated by the same motives and teaching the same principles, but
with far greater powers of mind, and an eloquence more adequate to the importance and
majesty of the cause. I am strengthened too by the knowledge, that I am not unauthorized
by the sympathy of many wise and good men, and men acknowledged as such by the
Public, in my admiration of his pamphlet. – *Neque enim debet operibus ejus obesse, quod vivit.
An si inter eos, quos nunquam vidimus, floruisset, non solum libros ejus, verum etiam imagines
conquireremus, ejusdem nunc honor præsentis, et gratia quasi satietate languescet? At hoc pra-
vum, malignumque est, non admirari hominem admiratione dignissimum, quia videre, com-
plecti, nec laudare tantum, verum etiam amare contingit.* PLIN. Epist. Lib. I. [Nor be it any
prejudice to his merit that he is a contemporary writer. Had he flourished in some distant
age, not only his works, but the very pictures and statues of him would have been passionately inquired after; and shall we then, from a sort of satiety, and merely because he is
present among us, suffer his talents to languish and fade away unhonoured and unadmired?
It is surely a very perverse and serious disposition, to look with indifference upon a man
worthy of the highest approbation, for no other reason but because we have it in our power
to see him ... and not only to give him our applause, but to receive him into our
friendship.]

mixed with grave discussions, from which his sincerity and earnestness might be doubted by those who do not know that a man is never more hearty in a cause, than when he calls forth all his faculties to promote it. Of the latter of these three powers, as a writer, Mr. W. possesses comparatively little; he seldom relieves his subject by familiar and colloquial illustrations; he is never ironical without being indignant, and he never relaxes into a playful humour.

In what may be considered as the tragic or serious poetry of their several works, Wordsworth may bear a comparison with Burke, but their eloquence is of different character: the imagery of Burke is more varied and dramatic, that of Wordsworth more intense and lyric: the one receives a coloured glare from his objects; the other reflects the pure light of his own mind. Only one short illustration can be given here. It is thus that W. deplores the convention of Cintra, and the reproach cast upon the country by it.

O sorrow! O misery for England, the land of liberty and courage and peace; the land trustworthy and long approved; the home of lofty example and benign precept; the central orb to which, as to a fountain, the nations of the earth 'ought to repair, and in their golden urns draw light!' – O sorrow and shame for our country; – for the grass which is upon her fields, and the dust which is in her graves; – for her good men who now look upon the day; – and her long train of deliverers and defenders, her Alfred, her Sidneys, and her Milton; whose voice yet speaketh for our reproach; and whose actions survive in memory to confound us, or to redeem!

It is however in reference to the spirit of philosophy which pervades this book, that the comparison may be most safely hazarded. A few sentences only are extracted from the very eloquent remarks on the influence of religion on the Spaniards, and as purified by suffering, which . . . are singularly striking and beautiful

[Quotes 'Whatever mixture of superstition . . . the supreme Disposer of things' (*The Prose Works of William Wordsworth*, ed. W. J. B. Owen and Jane Worthington Smyser, Oxford, 1974, 293–4, ll. 2910–62).]

Yet W. will not possess, or merit to possess, the popularity of Burke, who, being schooled in the House of Commons, always laboured to make himself intelligible to the lowest capacity. W. writes from the woods and lakes, and seems content to be understood and relished by a few like himself: his thoughts are great, but sometimes obscure; his genius is original, and therefore unaccommodating; his style is involved and uncouth, when not impassioned; and he resembles a man who limps till he has walked himself warm: hence the latter half of the pamphlet is better than the former, and he repeats, at the close, the thoughts of the beginning, with great improvement. The reader who grudges his time, may first begin at page 106; but when he has read the latter half, he will hardly choose to leave the former unread . . .

(pp. 264–6)

142. Robert Southey

From a letter to John Rickman, 29 September 1810

You past I think an ill-founded censure on Wordsworth's pamphlett when you said it was not a practical work. I can conceive of nothing of equal practical importance to the philosophy which pervades it, that reliance may be placed on the moral nature of man, and that where there is no principle to rely upon, there can be nothing else, but that is as treacherous as a foundation of sand.

(*New Letters of Robert Southey*, ed. Kenneth Curry, 1965, I, 539)

143. George Canning (1770–1827)

Reported remark to Wordsworth, August 1825

George Canning, when Foreign Secretary, stayed at Storrs Hall, Windermere, August 1825, and met Wordsworth. This was probably the occasion of his remark to the poet, reported by Charles Robinson (1788–1864) (Wordsworth's second cousin) to Christopher Wordsworth, 3 May 1851.

Did you know Mr. Canning assured your Uncle that his Tract on the Convention of Cintra was one of the very few productions of that eventful period that would live, and that it had a most powerful effect in a most righteous cause.

(Ms. The Wordsworth Library)

144. Samuel Taylor Coleridge

From *Table Talk*, 8 April 1833

In H. N. Coleridge's printed text, 1835, II, 146, the passage is dated 8 April 1833; this comment on Wordsworth is suppressed (see *Table Talk*, ed. Carl Woodring, Princeton, 1990, I, 357–8, with the date 5 April).

I wrote the 1st 20 pages or so of W's Cintra pamphlet. But I own my sympathy was W. himself – not much about the Convention – tho' it was a disgraceful proceeding. W. was always subject to violent political humours – or accesses of feeling – I never was.

IX

The Excursion: reviews, 1814–1820

145.

Unsigned notice, *Variety*, 10 September 1814, 5–6

Mr. Wordsworth

Beneath is a short extract from the 'Excursion,' a new poem just published by Mr. Wordsworth, and will be sufficient to satisfy the reader, that this writer perseveres in his long celebrated, and most extraordinary style of composition. With such verses as the following, Mr. W. has now filled the pages of a thick quarto volume; and this, alas, is only the third part of his design. Mr. W. is guilty, it must be confessed, of few or none of the faults which are justly imputed to Moore, to Scott, to Coleridge, and to Byron. If they are all glitter, his coat is of plain frieze. Whether either of them will at once stand the test of criticism, and (what the poet is bound to do,) give delight to his readers, the public taste, knowledge and feeling, must ultimately determine. The 'Excursion' is only the third book of a poem, to be called the 'Recluse,' and of which the first and second books are still to write. The preface to the present volume is a curious *morceau*. Mr. W. has been at work, it seems, to make a poem 'that may live.'

The passage here selected belongs to the description of a Cottage Woman, whose husband has suddenly left her for the army:–

[Quotes *The Excursion*, PW, V, pp. 34–5, Book I, ll. 784–803:

> A momentary trance comes over me . . .
> We sate together, sighs came on my ear,
> I knew not how, and hardly whence, they came.]

146.

Unsigned notice, *New Monthly Magazine*, September 1814, II, 157

Mercy upon the reader, and still more upon the reviewer! for it seems this ponderous volume is only the prelude to two others of an equal size, and similar materials. The race of metaphysical poets was supposed to have been long since extinct; but a wight, more formidable than Cowley, has risen in the person of Mr. Wordsworth; who now ascends into the airy region of metaphysical mysticism, and next plunges into the depths of cabalistic darkness, without relieving the reader either by amusement or information. In a hobbling kind of measure, which the author, we suppose, calls blank verse, a Scotch pedlar delivers tedious prælections on moral principles, the fitness of things, and the harmony of the universe; which are miserably opposed to the sombrous disquisitions of a solitary misanthrope, who having abused his talents in the world, leaves it in disgust – to brood over mortification of his own seeking, and doubts of his own raising. This preparatory course is enough of all conscience, and here ends, we hope, our excursion and entertainment.

147. William Hazlitt

Unsigned review, 'Character of Mr. Wordsworth's New Poem', in three parts: *Examiner*, 21 August 1814, 541–2; 28 August 1814, 555–8; 2 October 1814, 636–8 (*The Complete Works of William Hazlitt*, ed. P. P. Howe, 1930, XIX, 9–25)

Hazlitt published his shortened version in *The Round Table*, 1817, II, pp. 95–112, removing all positive references to Wordsworth himself – including the whole of the first paragraph.

Crabb Robinson noted on 15 October 1814:

I read almost the whole day with interest the *Examiners* for the last three months. They contain an excellent review of Wordsworth's poem by Hazlitt, excepting from this praise some very coarse and cynical remarks on a country life, in which the poor inhabitants of the Lakes are designated as more ignorant, selfish, and worthless than the lower classes elsewhere. Hazlitt delights in bidding defiance to common opinion, and there is a twist about either his head or heart which gives a perverse turn to even his ablest writings.

(*Henry Crabb Robinson on Books and their Writers*, ed. Edith J. Morley, 1938, I, 151)

Mary Wordsworth's comment is similar. She wrote to Dorothy on 29 October:

The conclusion of Hazlitt's Critique is come to us – a curious piece, but it must benefit the sale of the book. You will be amused greatly at the abuse he levies at the Mountaineers . . . he declaims against the Poverty of the Country. – That *nothing good* is to be got – speaks of the want of every thing that is intellectual and elegant, enumerates these wants, and amongst the items courtezans are found – a pretty comment . . .

[continues with a veiled reference to Hazlitt's protection by Wordsworth and flight from the Lakes at the close of 1803 after an escapade involving a country girl].

(*Letters of Mary Wordsworth*, ed. Mary E. Burton, 1958, 24)

Thus, Mary Wordsworth indicates something of a moral judgement against Hazlitt. Wordsworth himself appears to have been ungrateful for the *Examiner* review, and Hazlitt, making comic and exaggerated use of an anecdote, explains this as personal prejudice:

Some time in the latter end of the year 1814 Mr. Wordsworth received an *Examiner* by the post, which annoyed him exceedingly both on account of the expence and the paper. 'Why did they send that rascally paper to him, and make him pay for it?' Mr. Wordsworth is tenacious of his principles and not less so of his purse. 'Oh,' said Wilson, 'let us see what there is in it. I dare say they have not sent it you for nothing. Why here, there's a criticism upon the Excursion in it.' This made the poet (*par excellence*) rage and fret the more. 'What did they know about his poetry? What could they know about it? It was presumption in the highest degree for these cockney writers to pretend to criticise a Lake poet.' 'Well,' says the other, 'at any rate let us read it.' So he began. The article was much in favour of the poet and the poem. As the reading proceeded, 'Ha,' said Mr. Wordsworth, somewhat appeased, 'there's some sense in this fellow too: the Dog writes strong.' Upon which Mr. Wilson was encouraged to proceed still farther with the encomium, and Mr. Wordsworth continued his approbation; 'Upon my word very judicious, very well indeed.' At length, growing vain with his own and the *Examiner's* applause, he suddenly seized the paper into his own hands, and saying 'Let me read it, Mr. Wilson,' did so with an audible voice and appropriate gesture to the end, when he exclaimed, 'Very well written indeed, Sir, I did not expect a thing of this kind,' and strutting up and down the room in high good humour kept every now and then wondering who could be the author, 'he had no idea, and should like very much to know to whom he was indebted for such pointed and judicious praise' – when Mr. Wilson interrupting him with saying, 'Oh don't you know; it's Hazlitt, to be sure, there are his initials to it,' threw our poor philosopher into a greater rage than ever, and a fit of outrageous incredulity to think that he should be indebted for the first favourable account that had ever appeared of any work he had ever

written to a person on whom he had conferred such great and unmerited obligations. I think this statement will shew that there is very little love lost between me and my benefactor.
(Written by September 1818, but unpublished: 'A Reply to "Z"', *The Complete Works of William Hazlitt*, ed. P. P. Howe, 1930, IX, 6)

Certainly, after the *Examiner* review, Hazlitt, while remaining generally fair to the poetry, makes attacks upon the poet personally in his many published comments upon Wordsworth's work. Haydon noted this in his Diary and put it down to Wordsworth's lack of acknowledgement of the *Examiner* review,

> a fine puffing criticism on the Excursion . . . Wordsworth's utter contempt for his [Hazlitt's] character induced him to take no notice whatever of this piece of petty finesse. Hazlitt now became amazed & stung at Wordsworth's neglect, thundered forth those attacks on the whole Lake School, which, on the commonest appearance of any attention on their part, he would have defended their apostasy, & lauded by some paradox their talents.
>
> (Haydon, *Diary*, September 1824, II, 494–5, ed. W.B. Pope, Cambridge, Mass., 1960, 536–48)

Yet Wordsworth, beyond any such petty motive, would in fact feel embarrassed at the praise of a 'heretical' thinker. His brother Christopher had adversely reviewed Hazlitt's *On the Principles of Human Action* in the *British Critic* for November 1806, finding that the work 'was meant to undermine the Christian Religion, and was flat Spinozism', that its author 'seems to hold the ancient and impious doctrine of pantheism'. This book, a 'metaphysical choakpear' in Hazlitt's own later admission, was apparently the subject of conversation between Wordsworth and his 'brother Kit' (see 'A Reply to "Z"', cited above). Hazlitt angrily denounced them both in the *Yellow Dwarf* for 31 January 1818 (*The Complete Works of William Hazlitt*, ed. P. P. Howe, 1930, VII, 251).

---

a. 21 August 1814

In power of intellect, in lofty conception, in the depth of feeling, at once simple and sublime, which pervades every part of it and which gives to every object an almost preternatural and preterhuman interest, this work has seldom been surpassed. If the subject of the Poem had been equal to the genius of the Poet, if the skill with which he has chosen his materials had accorded with the power exerted over them, if the objects (whether persons or things) which he makes use of as the vehicle of his feelings had been such as immediately and irresistibly to convey them in all their force and depth to others, then the production before us would indeed 'have proved a monument,' as he himself wishes it, worthy of the author, and of his country. Whether, as it is, this most original and powerful performance may not rather remain like one of those stupendous but half-finished structures, which have been suffered to moulder into decay, because the cost and labour attending them exceeded their use or beauty, we feel that it would be rather presumptuous in us to determine.

The Poem of the *Excursion* resembles the country in which the scene is laid. It has the same vastness and magnificence, with the same nakedness and confusion. It has the same overwhelming, oppressive power. It excites or recalls the same sensations which those who have traversed that wonderful scenery must have felt. We are surrounded with the constant sense and superstitious awe of the collective power of matter, of the gigantic and eternal forms of Nature, on which, from the beginning of time, the hand of man has made no impression. Here are no dotted lines, no hedge-row beauties, no box-tree borders, no gravel walks, no square mechanic enclosures. All is left loose and irregular in the rude chaos of aboriginal nature. The boundaries of hill and valley are the Poet's only geography, where we wander with him incessantly over deep beds of moss and waving fern amidst the troops of red-deer and wild animals. Such is the severe simplicity of Mr. Wordsworth's taste, that we doubt whether he would not reject a druidical temple, or time-hallowed ruin, as too modern and artificial for his purpose. He only familiarises himself or his readers with a stone, covered with lichens, which has slept in the same spot of ground from the creation of the world, or with the rocky fissure between two mountains caused by thunder, or with a cavern scooped out by the sea. His mind is, as it were, coeval with the primary forms of things, holds immediately from nature; and his imagination 'owes no allegiance' but 'to the elements.'*

The *Excursion* may be considered as a philosophical pastoral poem – as a scholastic romance. It is less a poem on the country, than on the love of the country. It is not so much a description of natural objects, as of the feelings associated with them, not an account of the manners of rural life,

---

* Every one wishes to get rid of the booths and bridges in the Park, in order to have a view of the ground and water again. Our Poet looks at the more lasting and serious works of men as baby-houses and toys, and from the greater elevation of his mind, regards them much in the same light as we do the Regent's Fair, and Mr. Vansittart's permanent erections.' [Hazlitt's reference is to the exhibition opened in August 1814 as part of the nation's celebration of the victory against Napoleon.]

but the result of the Poet's reflections on it. He does not present the reader with a lively succession of images or incidents, but paints the outgoings of his own heart, the shapings of his own fancy. He may be said to create his own materials; his thoughts are his real subject. His imagination broods over that which is 'without form and void,' and 'makes it pregnant.' He sees all things in his own mind; he contemplates effects in their causes, and passions in their principles. He hardly ever avails himself of striking subjects or remarkable combinations of events, but in general rejects them as interfering with the workings of his own mind, as disturbing the smooth, deep, majestic current of his own feelings. Thus his descriptions of natural scenery are not brought home distinctly to the naked eye by forms and circumstances, but every object is seen through the medium of innumerable recollections, is clothed with the haze of imagination like a glittering vapour, is obscured with the excess of glory, has the shadowy brightness of a waking dream. The object is lost in the sentiment, as sound in the multiplication of echoes –

> And visions, as prophetic eyes avow,
> Hang on each leaf, and cling to every bough.

In describing human nature, Mr. Wordsworth equally shuns the common 'vantage-grounds of popular story, of striking incident, or fatal catastrophe, as illegitimate or vulgar modes of producing an effect. He scans the human race as the naturalist measures the earth's zone, without attending to the picturesque points of view, the inequalities of surface. He contemplates the passions and habits of men, not in their extremes, but in their first elements, their follies and vices, not at their height, with all their embossed evils and putrid sores, but as lurking in embryo, the seeds of the disorder inwoven with our very constitution.* He only sympathises with those simple forms of feeling, which mingle at once with his own identity, or with the stream of general humanity. To him the great and the small are the same; the near and the remote; what appears, and what only is. The common and the permanent, like the Platonic ideas, are his only realities. All accidental varieties and individual contrasts are lost in an endless continuity of feeling; like drops of water in the ocean-stream! An intense intellectual egotism swallows up every thing. Even the dialogues introduced in the present volume are soliloquies of the same character, taking different views of the subject. The

---

* 'God knew Adam in the elements of his chaos, and saw him in the great obscurity of nothing.' – *Sir Thomas Browne*. [misremembered from *Pseudodoxia Epidemica*, Bk I, ch. ii]

recluse, the pastor, and the pedlar, are three persons in one poet. We ourselves disapprove of these interlocutions between Lucius and Caius as impertinent babbling, where there is no dramatic distinction of character. But the evident scope and tendency of Mr. Wordsworth's mind is the reverse of dramatic. It resists all change of character, all variety of scenery, all the bustle, machinery, and pantomime of the stage, or of real life, – whatever might relieve or relax or change the direction of its own activity, jealous of all competition. The power of his mind preys upon itself. It is as if there were nothing but himself and the universe. He lives in the busy solitude of his own heart; in the deep silence of thought. His imagination lends life and feeling only to 'the bare trees and mountains bare'; peoples the viewless tracts of air, and converses with the silent clouds!

(*The Complete Works of William Hazlitt*, ed. P. P. Howe, 1930, XIX, 9–11)

b. 28 August 1814

We could have wished that Mr. Wordsworth had given to his work the form of a philosophic poem altogether, with only occasional digressions or allusions to particular instances. There is in his general sentiments and reflections on human life a depth, an originality, a truth, a beauty, and grandeur, both of conception and expression, which place him decidedly at the head of the poets of the present day, or rather which place him in a totally distinct class of excellence. But he has chosen to encumber himself with a load of narrative and description, which, instead of assisting, hinders the progress and effect of the general reasoning. Almost all this part of the work, which Mr. Wordsworth has inwoven with the text, would have come in better in plain prose as notes at the end. Indeed, there is something evidently inconsistent, upon his own principles, in the construction of the poem. For he professes, in these ambiguous illustrations, to avoid all that is striking or extraordinary – all that can raise the imagination or affect the passions – all that is not every way common, and necessarily included in the natural workings of the passions in all minds and in all circumstances. Then why introduce particular illustrations at all, which add nothing to the force of the general truth, which hang as a dead weight upon the imagination, which degrade the thought and weaken the sentiment, and the connection of which with the general principle it is more difficult to find out than to understand the general principle itself? It is only by an extreme process of abstraction that it is often possible to trace the operation of the general law in the particular illustration, yet it is to supply the defect of abstraction that the illustration is given. Mr. Wordsworth, indeed, says finely, and perhaps as truly as finely:

[Quotes *The Excursion*, *PW*, V, pp. 203–4, Book VI, ll. 548–57:

> 'Exchange the Shepherd's frock of native grey
> For robes with regal purple tinged; convert
> The crook into a sceptre; give the pomp
> Of circumstance; and here the tragic Muse
> Shall find apt subjects for her highest art.
> Amid the groves, beneath the shadowy hills,
> The generations are prepared; the pangs,
> The internal pangs, are ready; the dread strife
> Of poor humanity's afflicted will
> Struggling in vain with ruthless destiny.]

But he immediately after declines to avail himself of these resources of the rustic moralist: for the Priest, who officiates as 'the sad historian of the pensive plain' says in reply –

> Our system is not fashioned to preclude
> That sympathy which you for others ask:
> And I could tell, not travelling for my theme
> Beyond the limits of these humble graves,
> Of strange disasters; but I pass them by,
> Loth to disturb what Heaven hath hushed to peace.
> [*Ibid.*, *PW*, V, p. 204, Book VI, ll. 567–72]

There is, in fact, in Mr. Wordsworth's mind (if we may hazard the conjecture) a repugnance to admit any thing that tells for itself, without the interpretation of the poet, – a fastidious antipathy to immediate effect, – a systematic unwillingness to share the palm with his subject. Where, however, he has a subject presented to him, 'such as the meeting soul may pierce,' and to which he does not grudge to lend the aid of his fine genius, his powers of description and fancy seem to be little inferior to those of thought and sentiment. Among several others which we might select, we give the following passage, describing the religion of ancient Greece:

[Quotes *ibid.*, *PW*, V, pp. 136–7, Book IV, ll. 851–87:

> In that fair clime, the lonely Herdsman, stretch'd . . .
> or Pan himself,
> The simple Shepherd's awe-inspiring God.]

The foregoing is one of a succession of splendid passages equally enriched with philosophy and poetry, tracing the fictions of Eastern mythology to the immediate intercourse of the imagination with Nature, and to the habitual propensity in the human mind to endow the outward forms of being with life and conscious motion. With this expansive and animating principle, Mr. W. has forcibly, but somewhat severely, contrasted the cold, narrow, lifeless spirit of modern philosophy:

[Quotes *ibid.*, *PW*, V, pp. 138–40, Book IV, ll. 941–2:

> Now, shall our great discoverers obtain . . .
> To proud self-love her own intelligence?]

From the chemists and metaphysicians our author turns to the laughing sage of France, Voltaire. 'Poor gentleman, it fares no better with him, for he's a wit.'* We cannot, however, agree with Mr. Wordsworth that *Candide* is *dull*. It is, if our author pleases, 'the production of a scoffer's pen,' or it is any thing, but dull. *Rasselas* indeed is dull; but then it is privileged dulness. It may not be proper in a grave, discreet, orthodox, promising young divine, who studies his opinions in the contraction or distension of his patron's brow, to allow any merit to a work like *Candide*; but we conceive that it would have been more in character, that is more manly in Mr. Wordsworth, nor do we think it would have hurt the cause he espouses, if he had blotted out the epithet, after it had peevishly escaped him. Whatsoever savours of a little, narrow, inquisitorial spirit, does not sit well on a poet and a man of genius. The prejudices of a philosopher are not natural. There is a frankness and sincerity of opinion, which is a paramount obligation in all questions of intellect, though it may not govern the decisions of the Spiritual Courts, who may be safely left to take care of their own interests. There is a plain directness and simplicity of understanding, which is the only security against the evils of levity on the one hand, or of hypocrisy on the other. A speculative bigot is a solecism in the intellectual world. We can assure Mr. W. that we should not have bestowed so much serious consideration on a single voluntary perversion of language, but that our respect for his character makes us jealous of his smallest faults.

With regard to his general philippic against the contractedness and egotism of philosophical pursuits, we only object to its not being carried further. We shall not affirm with Rousseau (his authority would perhaps

---

* Love in a Wood [by William Wycherley, 1671].

have little weight with Mr. Wordsworth) – *Tout homme reflechi est mechant*;[1] but we conceive that the same reasoning which Mr. Wordsworth applies so eloquently and justly to the natural philosopher and metaphysician may be extended to the moralist, the divine, the politician, the orator, the artist, and even the poet. And why so? Because wherever an intense activity is given to any one faculty, it necessarily prevents the due and natural exercise of others. The intellectual and the moral faculties of man are different; the ideas of things and the feelings of pleasure and pain connected with them. Hence all those professions or pursuits, where the mind is exclusively occupied with the ideas of things, as they exist in the imagination or understanding, as they call for the exercise of intellectual activity, and not as they are connected with pleasure or pain, must check the genial expansion of the moral sentiments and social affections, must lead to a cold and dry abstraction, as they are found to suspend the animal functions, and relax the bodily frame. Hence the complaint of the want of natural sensibility and constitutional warmth of attachment in those persons who have been devoted to the pursuit of any art or science, – of their restless dissatisfied activity, and indifference to every thing that does not furnish an occasion for the display of their intellectual superiority and the gratification of their vanity. The philosophical poet himself, perhaps, owes some of his love of nature to the opportunity it affords him of analysing his own feelings and contemplating his own powers, – of making every object about him a whole length mirror to reflect his favourite thoughts, and of looking down on the frailties of others in undisturbed leisure, and from a more dignified height.

One of the most interesting parts of this work is that in which the author treats of the French Revolution, and of the feelings connected with it in ingenuous minds, in its commencement and its progress. The Solitary, who by domestic calamities and disappointments had been cut off from society and almost from himself, gives the following account of the manner in which he was roused from his melancholy: –

[Quotes *ibid.*, *PW*, V, pp. 100–2, Book III, ll. 706–39, 749–58 and 768–79:

> From that abstraction I was roused . . .
> Such recantation had for me no charm,
> Nor would I bend to it.]

The subject is afterwards resumed, with the same magnanimity and philosophical firmness:

[Quotes *ibid.*, *PW*, V, pp. 117–8, Book IV, ll. 260–73 and 296–309:

—For that other loss,
The loss of confidence in social man . . .
The vacillating, inconsistent Good.]

In the application of these memorable lines, we should perhaps differ a
little from Mr. Wordsworth; nor can we indulge with him in the fond
conclusion afterwards hinted at, that one day *our* triumph, the triumph
of virtue and liberty, may be complete. For this purpose, we think several
things necessary which are impossible. It is a consummation which cannot happen till the nature of things is changed, till the many become as
the *one*, till romantic generosity shall be as common as gross selfishness,
till reason shall have acquired the obstinate blindness of prejudice, till the
love of power and of change shall no longer goad man on to restless
action, till passion and will, hope and fear, love and hatred, and the
objects proper to excite them, that is, alternate good and evil, shall no
longer sway the bosoms and businesses of men. All things move not in
progress, but in a ceaseless round; our strength lies in our weakness; our
virtues are built on our vices; our faculties are as limited as our being; nor
can we lift man above his nature more than above the earth he treads.
But though we cannot weave over again the airy, unsubstantial dream,
which reason and experience have dispelled –

What though the radiance, which was once so bright,
Be now for ever taken from our sight,
Though nothing can bring back the hour
Of glory in the grass, of splendour in the flower: –

yet we will never cease, nor be prevented from returning on the wings of
imagination to that bright dream of our youth; that glad dawn of the
day-star of liberty; that spring-time of the world, in which the hopes and
expectations of the human race seemed opening in the same gay career
with our own; when France called her children to partake her equal
blessings under her laughing skies; when the stranger was met in all her
villages with dance and festive songs, in celebration of a new and golden
era; and when, to the retired and contemplative student, the prospects of
human happiness and glory were seen ascending, like the steps of Jacob's
ladder, in bright and never-ending succession. The dawn of that day was
suddenly overcast; that season of hope is past; it is fled with the other
dreams of our youth, which we cannot recal, but has left behind it traces,
which are not to be effaced by birth-day odes, or the chaunting of *Te
Deums* in all the churches of Christendom. To those hopes eternal

regrets are due; to those who maliciously and wilfully blasted them, in the fear that they might be accomplished, we feel no less what we owe – hatred and scorn as lasting.

(*Ibid.*, 11–18)

c. 2 October 1814

Poetry may be properly divided into two classes; the poetry of imagination and the poetry of sentiment. The one consists in the power of calling up images of the most pleasing or striking kind; the other depends on the strength of the interest which it excites in given objects. The one may be said to arise out of the faculties of memory and invention, conversant with the world of external nature; the other from the fund of our moral sensibility. In the combination of these different excellences, the perfection of poetry consists; the greatest poets of our own and other countries have been equally distinguished for richness of invention and depth of feeling. By the greatest poets of our own country, we mean Chaucer, Spenser, Shakespeare, and Milton, who evidently possessed both kinds of imagination, the intellectual and moral, in the highest degree. Young and Cowley might be cited as the most brilliant instances of the separation of feeling from fancy, of men who were dazzled by the exuberance of their own thoughts and whose genius was sacrificed to their want of taste. Mr. Wordsworth, on the other hand, whose powers of feeling are of the highest order, is certainly deficient in fanciful invention: his writings exhibit all the internal power, without the external form of poetry. He has none of the pomp and decoration and scenic effect of poetry: no gorgeous palaces nor solemn temples awe the imagination: no cities rise with glistering spires and pinnacles adorned: we meet with no knights pricked forth on airy steeds: no hair-breadth scapes and perilous accidents by flood or field. Either from the predominant habit of his mind, not requiring the stimulus of outward impressions, or from the want of an imagination teeming with various forms, he takes the common everyday events and objects of Nature, or rather seeks those that are the most simple and barren of effect; but he adds to them a weight of interest from the resources of his own mind, which makes the most insignificant things serious and even formidable. All other interests are absorbed in the deeper interest of his own thoughts, and find the same level. His mind magnifies the littleness of his subject, and raises its meanness; lends it his strength, and clothes it with borrowed grandeur. With him, a mole-hill, covered with wild thyme, assumes the importance of 'the great vision of the guarded mount': a puddle is filled with preternatural faces, and agitated with the fiercest storms of passion; and to his mind, as he himself informs us, and as we can easily believe,

—The meanest flow'r that blows can give
Thoughts that do often lie too deep for tears.

The extreme simplicity which some persons have objected to in Mr. Wordsworth's poetry is to be found only in the subject and the style: the sentiments are subtle and profound. In the latter respect, his poetry is as much above the common standard or capacity, as in the other it is below it. His poems bear a distant resemblance to some of Rembrandt's landscapes, who, more than any other painter, created the medium through which he saw Nature, and out of the stump of an old tree, a break in the sky, and a bit of water, could produce an effect almost miraculous.

Mr. Wordsworth's poems in general are the history of a refined and contemplative mind, conversant only with itself and nature. An intense feeling of the associations of this kind is the peculiar and characteristic feature of all his productions. He has described the love of nature better than any other poet. This sentiment, inly felt in all its force, and sometimes carried to an excess, is the source both of his strength and of his weakness. – However we may sympathise with Mr. Wordsworth in his attachment to groves and fields, we cannot extend the same admiration to their inhabitants, or to the manners of country life in general. We go along with him, while he is the subject of his own narrative, but we take leave of him when he makes pedlars and ploughmen his heroes and the interpreters of his sentiments. It is, we think, getting into low company, and company, besides, that we do not like. We take Mr. Wordsworth himself for a great poet, a fine moralist, and a deep philosopher; but if he insists on introducing us to a friend of his, a parish clerk, or the barber of the village, who is as wise as himself, we must be excused if we draw back with some little want of cordial faith. We are satisfied with the friendship which subsisted between *Parson Adams* and *Joseph Andrews*. – The author himself lets out occasional hints that all is not as it should be amongst these northern Arcadians:
[Quotes *The Excursion*, *PW*, V, pp. 166–7, Book V, ll. 411–39:

How gay the habitations that adorn
This fertile valley! . . .
Evince the want and weakness whence they spring.]

377

Though Mr. Wordsworth professes to soften the harsher features of rustic vice, he has given us one picture of depraved and inveterate self-ishness, which we apprehend could only be found among the inhabitants of these boasted mountain districts. The account of one of his heroines concludes as follows: –

[Quotes *ibid.*, *PW*, V, pp. 210–11, Book VI, ll. 741–77:

> A sudden illness seiz'd her in the strength
> Of life's autumnal season . . .
> Though, in this vale, remembered with deep awe!]

We think it is pushing our love or admiration of natural objects a good deal too far, to make it a set-off against a story like the preceding, which carries that concentration of self-interest and callousness to the feelings of others to its utmost pitch, which is the general character of those who are cut off by their mountains and valleys from an intercourse with mankind, even more than of the country-people.

All country people hate each other. They have so little comfort that they envy their neighbours the smallest pleasure or advantage, and nearly grudge themselves the necessaries of life. From not being accustomed to enjoyment, they become hardened and averse to it – stupid for want of thought – selfish for want of society. There is nothing good to be had in the country, or, if there is, they will not let you have it. They had rather injure themselves than oblige any one else. The common mode of life is a system of wretchedness and self-denial, like what you read of among barbarous tribes. You live out of the world. You cannot get your tea and sugar without sending to the next town for it: you pay double, and have it of the worst quality. The small-beer is sure to be sour – the milk skimmed – the meat bad, or spoiled in the cooking. You cannot do a single thing you like; you cannot walk out or sit at home, or write or read, or think or look as if you did, without being subject to impertinent curiosity. The apothecary annoys you with his complaisance; the parson with his superciliousness. If you are poor, you are despised; if you are rich, you are feared and hated. If you do any one a favour, the whole neigh-bourhood is up in arms; the clamour is like that of a rookery; and the person himself, it is ten to one, laughs at you for your pains, and takes the first opportunity of shewing you that he labours under no uneasy sense of obligation. There is a perpetual round of mischief-making and backbit-ing for want of any better amusement. There are no shops, no taverns, no theatres, no opera, no concerts, no pictures, no public-buildings, no crowded streets, no noise of coaches, or of courts of law, – neither courtiers nor courtesans, no literary parties, no fashionable routs, no society, no books, or knowledge of books. Vanity and luxury are the civilisers of the world, and sweeteners of human life. Without objects either of pleasure or action, it grows harsh and crabbed: the mind becomes stagnant, the affections callous, and the eye dull. Man left to himself soon degenerates into a very disagreeable person. Ignorance is always bad enough; but rustic ignorance is intolerable. Aristotle has observed, that tragedy purifies the affections by terror and pity. If so, a company of tragedians should be established at the public expence, in every village or hundred, as a better mode of education than either Bell's or Lancaster's. The benefits of knowledge are never so well understood as from seeing the effects of ignorance, in their naked, undisguised state, upon the common country people. Their selfishness and insensibility are perhaps less owing to the hardships and privations, which make them, like people out at sea in a boat, ready to devour one another, than to their having no idea of anything beyond themselves and their immediate sphere of action. They have no knowledge of, and consequently can take no interest in, any thing which is not an object of their senses, and of their daily pursuits. They hate all strangers, and have generally a nick-name for the inhabitants of the next village. The two young noblemen in Guzman d'Alfarache, who went to visit their mistresses only a league out of Madrid, were set upon by the peasants, who came round them calling out, '*A wolf.*' Those who have no enlarged or liberal ideas, can have no disinterested or generous sentiments. Persons who are in the habit of reading novels and romances, are compelled to take a deep interest in, and to have their affections strongly excited by, fictitious characters and imaginary situations; their thoughts and feelings are constantly carried out of themselves, to persons they never saw, and things that never existed: history enlarges the mind, by familiarising us with the great vicissitudes of human affairs, and the catastrophes of states and king-doms; the study of morals accustoms us to refer our actions to a general standard of right and wrong; and abstract reasoning, in general, strengthens the love of truth, and produces an inflexibility of principle which cannot stoop to low trick and cunning. Books, in Lord Bacon's phrase, are 'a discipline of humanity.' Country people have none of these advantages, nor any others to supply the place of them. Having no circulating libraries to exhaust their love of the marvellous, they amuse themselves with fancying the disasters and disgraces of their particular acquaintance. Having no hump-backed *Richard* to excite their wonder and abhorrence, they make themselves a bug-bear of their own, out of the first obnoxious person they can lay their hands on. Not having the fictitious distresses and gigantic crimes of poetry to stimulate their imagination and their passions, they vent their whole stock of spleen, malice, and invention, on their friends and next-door neighbours. They get up a little pastoral drama at home, with fancied events, but real characters. All their spare time is spent in manufacturing and propagating the lie for the day, which does its office, and expires. The next day is spent in the same manner. It is thus that they embellish the simplicity of rural life! The common people in civilised countries are a kind of domesticated savages. They have not the wild imagination, the passions, the fierce energies, or dreadful vicissitudes of the savage tribes, nor have they the leisure, the indolent enjoyments and romantic superstitions, which belonged to the pastoral life in milder climates, and more remote periods of society. They are taken out of a state of nature, without being put in possession of the refinements of art. The customs and institutions of society cramp their imaginations without giving them knowledge. If the inhabitants of the mountainous districts described by Mr. Wordsworth are less gross and sensual than others, they are more selfish. Their egotism becomes more concentrated, as they are more insulated, and their purposes more inveterate, as they have less competition to struggle with. The weight of matter which surrounds them, crushes the finer sympathies. Their minds become hard and cold, like the rocks which they cultivate. The immensity of their mountains makes the human form appear little and insignificant. Men are seen crawling between Heaven and earth, like insects to their graves. Nor do they regard one another more than flies on a wall. Their physiognomy expresses the materialism of their character, which has only one principle – rigid self-will. They move on with their eyes and foreheads fixed, looking neither to the right nor to the left, with a heavy slouch in their gait, and seeming as if nothing would divert them from their path. We do not admire this plodding pertinacity, always directed to the main chance. There is nothing which excites so little sympathy in our minds, as exclusive selfishness. – If our theory is wrong, at least it is taken from pretty close observation, and is, we think, confirmed by Mr. Wordsworth's own account.

Of the stories contained in the latter part of the volume, we like that of the Whig and Jacobite friends, and of the good knight, Sir Alfred Irthing, the best. The last reminded us of a fine sketch of a similar character in the beautiful poem of *Hart Leap Well*. We conceive that about as many fine things have passed through Mr. Wordsworth's mind as, with five or six exceptions, through any human mind whatever. The conclusion of the passage we refer to is admirable, and comes in like some dying close in music: –

[Quotes *ibid.*, *PW*, V, pp. 262–3, Book VII, ll. 976–1007:

> So fails, so languishes, grows dim, and dies . . .
> And expectations of self-flattering minds!]

If Mr. Wordsworth does not always write in this manner, it is his own fault. He can as often as he pleases. It is not in our power to add to, or take away from, the pretensions of a poem like the present, but if our opinion or wishes could have the least weight, we would take our leave of it by saying – *Esto perpetua!*[2]

(*Ibid.*, 18–25)

EDITOR'S NOTES

1. 'Every reflective man is wicked'.
2. 'Let it be for ever'.

148. Francis Jeffrey

Unsigned review, *Edinburgh Review*, November 1814, XXIV, 1–30

A most damaging attack, all the more influential as its tone was that of a man of assured common sense trying hard to be fair to an obstinately perverse poet. Coleridge, writing to Lady Beaumont on 3 April 1815, called it 'infamous' and continued: 'If ever Guilt lay on a Writer's head, and if malignity, slander, hypocrisy and self-contradicting Baseness can constitute Guilt, I dare openly, and openly (please God!) I will, impeach the Writer of that Article of it' (*Collected Letters of Samuel Taylor Coleridge*, ed. E. L. Griggs, Oxford, 1959–71, IV. 564). Two years later he published precise charges, referring particularly to Jeffrey's

> substitution of assertion for argument; to the frequency of arbitrary and sometimes petulant verdicts, not seldom unsupported even by a single quotation from the work condemned, which might at least have explained the critic's meaning, if it did not prove the justice of his sentence. Even where this is not the case, the extracts are too often made without reference to any general grounds or rules from which the

faultiness or inadmissibility of the qualities attributed may be deduced; and without any attempt to show, that the qualities *are* attributable to the passage extracted. I have met with such extracts from Mr. Wordsworth's poems, annexed to such assertions, as led me to imagine, that the reviewer, having written his critique before he had read the work, had then *pricked with a pin* for passages, wherewith to illustrate the various branches of his preconceived opinions.

(*Biographia Literaria*, 1817, from Chapter XXI)

Even Sydney Smith, a man entirely indifferent to Wordsworth, felt that Jeffrey's review smacked of injustice:

I am much obliged to you for the Review, and shall exercise the privilege of an old friend in making some observations upon it. I have not read the review of Wordsworth, because the subject is to me very uninteresting; but may I ask was it worth while to take any more notice of a man respecting whom the public opinion is completely made up? and do not such repeated attacks upon the man wear in some little degree the shape of persecution?

(*Letters of Sydney Smith*, ed. Nowell C. Smith, Oxford 1953, I, 250)

This will never do. It bears no doubt the stamp of the author's heart and fancy; but unfortunately not half so visibly as that of his peculiar system. His former poems were intended to recommend that system, and to bespeak favour for it by their individual merit; – but this, we suspect, must be recommended by the system – and can only expect to succeed where it has been previously established. It is longer, weaker, and tamer, than any of Mr Wordsworth's other productions; with less boldness of originality, and less even of that extreme simplicity and lowliness of tone which wavered so prettily, in the Lyrical Ballads, between silliness and pathos. We have imitations of Cowper, and even of Milton here, engrafted on the natural drawl of the Lakers – and all diluted into harmony by that profuse and irrepressible wordiness which deluges all the blank verse of this school of poetry, and lubricates and weakens the whole structure of their style.

Though it fairly fills four hundred and twenty good quarto pages, without note, vignette, or any sort of extraneous assistance, it is stated in the title – with something of an imprudent candour – to be but 'a portion' of a larger work; and in the preface, where an attempt is rather unsuccessfully made to explain the whole design, it is still more rashly disclosed, that it is but 'a part of the second part of a *long* and laborious work' – which is to consist of three parts.

What Mr Wordsworth's ideas of length are, we have no means of accurately judging; but we cannot help suspecting that they are liberal, to a degree that will alarm the weakness of most modern readers. As far as we can gather from the preface, the entire poem – or one of them, for we really are not sure whether there is to be one or two – is of a biographical nature; and is to contain the history of the author's mind, and of the origin and progress of his poetical powers, up to the period when they were sufficiently matured to qualify him for the great work on which he has been so long employed. Now, the quarto before us contains an account of one of his youthful rambles in the vales of Cumberland, and occupies precisely the period of three days; so that, by the use of a very powerful *calculus*, some estimate may be formed of the probable extent of the entire biography.

This small specimen, however, and the statements with which it is prefaced, have been sufficient to set our minds at rest in one particular. The case of Mr Wordsworth, we perceive, is now manifestly hopeless; and we give him up as altogether incurable, and beyond the power of criticism. We cannot indeed altogether omit taking precautions now and then against the spreading of the malady; – but for himself, though we shall watch the progress of his symptoms as a matter of professional curiosity and instruction, we really think it right not to harass him any longer with nauseous remedies, – but rather to throw in cordials and lenitives, and wait in patience for the natural termination of the disorder. In order to justify this desertion of our patient, however, it is proper to state why we despair of the success of a more active practice.

A man who has been for twenty years at work on such matter as is now before us, and who comes complacently forward with a whole quarto of it after all the admonitions he has received, cannot reasonably be expected to 'change his hand, or check his pride,' upon the suggestion of far weightier monitors than we can pretend to be. Inveterate habit must now have given a kind of sanctity to the errors of early taste; and the very powers of which we lament the perversion, have probably become incapable of any other application. The very quantity, too, that he has written, and is at this moment working up for publication upon the old pattern, makes it almost hopeless to look for any change of it. All this is so much capital already sunk in the concern; which must be sacrificed if it be abandoned: and no man likes to give up for lost the time and talent and labour which he has embodied in any permanent production. We were not previously aware of these obstacles to Mr Wordsworth's conversion; and, considering the peculiarities of his former writings merely as the result of certain wanton and capricious experiments on public taste and indulgence, conceived it to be our duty to discourage their repetition by all the means in our power. We now see clearly, however, how the case stands; – and, making up our minds, though with the most sincere pain and reluctance, to consider him as finally lost to the good cause of poetry, shall endeavour to be thankful for the occasional gleams of tenderness and beauty which the natural force of his imagination and affections must still shed over all his productions, – and to which we shall ever turn with delight, in spite of the affectation and mysticism and prolixity, with which they are so abundantly contrasted.

Long habits of seclusion, and an excessive ambition of originality, can alone account for the disproportion which seems to exist between this author's taste and his genius; or for the devotion with which he has sacrificed so many precious gifts at the shrine of those paltry idols which he has set up for himself among his lakes and his mountains. Solitary musings, amidst such scenes, might no doubt be expected to nurse up the mind to the majesty of poetical conception, – (though it is remarkable, that all the greater poets lived, or had lived, in the full current of society): – But the collision of equal minds, – the admonition of prevailing impressions – seems necessary to reduce its redundancies, and repress that tendency to extravagance or puerility, into which the self-indulgence and self-admiration of genius is so apt to be betrayed, when it is allowed to wanton, without awe or restraint, in the triumph and delight of its own intoxication. That its flights should be graceful and glorious in the eyes of men, it seems almost to be necessary that they should be made in the consciousness that mens' eyes are to behold them, – and that the inward transport and vigour by which they are inspired, should be tempered by an occassional [sic] reference to what will be thought of them by those ultimate dispensers of glory. An habitual and general knowledge of the few settled and permanent maxims, which form the canon of general taste in all large and polished societies – a certain tact, which informs us at once that many things, which we still love and are moved by in secret, must necessarily be despised as childish, or derided as absurd, in all such societies – though it will not stand in the place of genius, seems necessary to the success of its exertions; and though it will never enable any one to produce the higher beauties of art, can alone secure the talent which does produce them, from errors that must render it useless. Those who have most of the talent, however, commonly acquire this knowledge with the greatest facility; – and if Mr Wordsworth, instead of confining himself almost entirely to the society of the dalesmen and cottagers, and little children, who form the subjects of his book, had condescended to mingle a little more with the people that were to read and judge of it, we cannot help thinking, that its texture would have been considerably improved: At least it appears to us to be absolutely impossible, that any one who had lived or mixed familiarly with men of literature and ordinary judgment in poetry, (of course we exclude the coadjutors and disciples of his own school), could ever have fallen into such gross faults, or so long mistaken them for beauties. His first essays we looked upon in a good degree as poetical paradoxes, – maintained experimentally, in order to display talent, and court notoriety; – and so maintained, with no more serious belief in their truth, than is usually generated by an ingenious and animated defence of other paradoxes. But when we find, that he has been for twenty years exclusively employed upon articles of this very fabric, and that he has still enough of raw material on hand to keep him so employed for twenty years to come, we cannot refuse him the justice of believing that he is a sincere convert to his own system, and must ascribe the peculiarities of his composition, not to any transient affectation, or accidental caprice of imagination, but to a settled perversity of taste or understanding, which has been fostered, if not altogether created, by the circumstances to which we have already alluded.

The volume before us, if we were to describe it very shortly, we should characterize as a tissue of moral and devotional ravings, in which innumerable changes are rung upon a few very simple and familiar ideas: – but with such an accompaniment of long words, long sentences, and unwieldy phrases – and such a hubbub of strained raptures and fantastical sublimities, that it is often extremely difficult for the most skilful and attentive student to obtain a glimpse of the author's meaning – and altogether impossible for an ordinary reader to conjecture what he is about. Moral and religious enthusiasm, though undoubtedly poetical emotions, are at the same time but dangerous inspirers of poetry; nothing being so apt to run into interminable dulness or mellifluous extravagance, without giving the unfortunate author the slightest intimation of his danger. His laudable zeal for the efficacy of his preachments, he very naturally mistakes for the ardour of poetical inspiration; – and, while dealing out the high words and glowing phrases which are so readily supplied by themes of this description, can scarcely avoid believing that he is eminently original and impressive: – All sorts of commonplace notions and expressions are sanctified in his eyes, by the sublime ends for which they are employed; and the mystical verbiage of the methodist pulpit is repeated, till the speaker entertains no doubt that he is the elected organ of divine truth and persuasion. But if such be the common hazards of seeking inspiration from those potent fountains, it may easily be conceived what chance Mr Wordsworth had of escaping their enchantment, – with his natural propensities to wordiness, and his unlucky habit of debasing pathos with vulgarity. The fact accordingly is, that in this production he is more obscure than a Pindaric poet of the seventeenth century; and more verbose 'than even himself of yore;' while the wilfulness with which he persists in choosing his examples of intellectual dignity and tenderness exclusively from the lowest ranks of society, will be sufficiently apparent, from the circumstance of his having thought fit to make his chief prolocutor in this poetical dialogue, and chief advocate of Providence and Virtue, *an old Scotch Pedlar* – retired indeed from business – but still rambling about in his former haunts, and gossiping among his old customers, without his pack on his shoulders. The other persons of the drama are, a retired military chaplain, who has grown half an atheist and half a misanthrope – the wife of an unprosperous weaver – a servant girl with her infant – a parish pauper, and one or two other personages of equal rank and dignity.

The character of the work is decidedly didactic; and more than nine tenths of it are occupied with a species of dialogue, or rather a series of long sermons or harangues which pass between the pedlar, the author, the old chaplain, and a worthy vicar, who entertains the whole party at dinner on the last day of their excursion. The incidents which occur in the course of it are as few and trifling as can be imagined; – and those which the different speakers narrate in the course of their discourses, are introduced rather to illustrate their arguments or opinions, than for any interest they are supposed to possess of their own. – The doctrine which the work is intended to enforce, we are by no means certain that we have discovered. In so far as we can collect, however, it seems to be neither more nor less than the old familiar one, that a firm belief in the providence of a wise and beneficent Being must be our great stay and support under all afflictions and perplexities upon earth – and that there are indications of his power and goodness in all the aspects of the visible universe, whether living or inanimate – every part of which should therefore be regarded with love and reverence, as exponents of those great attributes. We can testify, at least, that these salutary and important truths are inculcated at far greater length, and with more repetitions, than in any ten volumes of sermons that we ever perused. It is also maintained, with equal conciseness and originality, that there is frequently much good sense, as well as much enjoyment, in the humbler conditions of life; and that, in spite of great vices and abuses, there is a reasonable allowance both of happiness and goodness in society at large. If there be any deeper or more recondite doctrines in Mr Wordsworth's book, we must confess that they have escaped us; – and, convinced as we are of the truth and soundness of those to which we have alluded, we cannot help thinking that they might have been better enforced with less parade and prolixity. His effusions on what may be called the physiognomy of external nature, or its moral and theological expression, are eminently fantastic, obscure, and affected. – It is quite time, however, that we should give the reader a more particular account of this singular performance.

It opens with a picture of the author toiling across a bare common in a hot summer day, and reaching at last a ruined hut surrounded with tall trees, where he meets by appointment with a hale old man, with an iron-pointed staff lying beside him. Then follows a retrospective account of their first acquaintance – formed, it seems, when the author was at a village school; and his aged friend occupied 'one room, – the fifth part of a house' in the neighbourhood. After this, we have the history of this reverend person at no small length. He was born, we are happy to find, in Scotland – among the hills of Athol; and his mother, after his father's death, married the parish schoolmaster – so that he was taught his letters betimes: But then, as it is here set forth with much solemnity,

> From his sixth year, the boy, of whom I speak,
> In summer, tended cattle on the hills.
> [*The Excursion, PW*, V, p. 12, Book I, ll. 118–19:]

And again, a few pages after, that there may be no risk of mistake as to a point of such essential importance –

> From early childhood, even, as hath been said,
> From his *sixth year*, he had been sent abroad,
> *In summer*, to tend herds: Such was his task!
> [Omitted 1827 and later]

In the course of this occupation, it is next recorded, that he acquired such a taste for rural scenery and open air, that when he was sent to teach a school in a neighbouring village, he found it 'a misery to him;' and determined to embrace the more romantic occupation of a Pedlar – or, as Mr Wordsworth more musically expresses it,

A vagrant merchant bent beneath his load;
[*Ibid., PW*, V, p. 19, Book I, l. 324]

– and in the course of his pereginations [*sic*] had acquired a very large acquaintance, which, after he had given up dealing, he frequently took a summer ramble to visit.

The author, on coming up to this interesting personage, finds him sitting with his eyes half shut; – and, not being quite sure whether he is asleep or awake, stands 'some minutes space' in silence beside him. 'At length,' says he, with his own delightful simplicity –

> At length I hailed him – *seeing that his hat*
> *Was moist* with water-drops, as if the brim
> Had newly scooped a running stream! –
> —''Tis,' said I, 'a burning day;
> My lips are parched with thirst; – but you, I guess,
> Have somewhere found relief.'
> [*Ibid., PW*, V, p. 23, Book I, ll. 444–6 and 448–50]

Upon this, the benevolent old man points him out a well in a corner, to which the author repairs; and, after minutely describing its situation, beyond a broken wall, and between two alders that 'grew in a cold damp nook,' he thus faithfully chronicles the process of his return.

> My thirst I slaked – and from the cheerless spot
> Withdrawing, straightway to the shade returned,
> Where sate the old man on the cottage bench.
> [*Ibid., PW*, V, p. 24, Book I, ll. 463–5]

The Pedlar then gives an account of the last inhabitants of the deserted cottage beside them. These were, a good industrious weaver and his wife and children. They were very happy for a while; till sickness and want of work came upon them; and then the father enlisted as a soldier, and the wife pined in the lonely cottage – growing every year more careless and desponding, as her anxiety and fears for her absent husband, of whom no tidings ever reached her, accumulated. Her children died, and left her cheerless and alone; and at last she died also; and the cottage fell to decay. We must say, that there is very considerable pathos in the telling of this simple story; and that they who can get over the repugnance excited by the triteness of its incidents, and the lowness of its objects, will not fail to be struck with the author's knowledge of the human heart, and the power he possesses of stirring up its deepest and gentlest sympathies. His prolixity, indeed, it is not so easy to get over. This little story fills about twenty-five quarto pages; and abounds, of course, with mawkish sentiment, and details of preposterous minuteness. When the tale is told, the travellers take their staffs, and end their first day's journey, without further adventure, at a little inn.

The Second book sets them forward betimes in the morning. They pass by a Village Wake; and as they approach a more solitary part of the mountains, the old man tells the author that he is taking him to see an old friend of his, who had formerly been chaplain to a Highland regiment – had lost a beloved wife – been roused from his dejection by the first enthusiasm of the French Revolution – had emigrated on its miscarriage to America – and returned disgusted to hide himself in the retreat to which they were now ascending. That retreat is then most tediously described – a smooth green valley in the heart of the mountain, without trees, and with only one dwelling. Just as they get sight of it from the ridge above, they see a funeral train proceeding from the solitary abode, and hurry on with some apprehension for the fate of the misanthrope – whom they find, however, in very tolerable condition at the door, and learn that the funeral was that of an aged pauper who had been boarded out by the parish in that cheap farm-house, and had died in consequence of long exposure to heavy rain. The old chaplain, or, as Mr Wordsworth is pleased to call him, the Solitary, tells this dull story at prodigious length; and after giving an inflated description of an effect of mountain-mists in the evening sun, treats his visitors with a rustic dinner – and they walk out to the fields at the close of the second book.

The Third makes no progress in the excursion. It is entirely filled with moral and religious conversation and debate, and with a more ample detail of the Solitary's past life, than had been given in the sketch of his friend. The conversation is exceedingly dull and mystical; and the Solitary's confessions insufferably diffuse. Yet there is very considerable force of writing and tenderness of sentiment in this part of the work.

The Fourth book is also filled with dialogues ethical and theologial; and, with the exception of some brilliant and forcible expressions here and there, consists of an exposition of truisms, more cloudy, wordy, and inconceivably prolix, than any thing we ever met with.

In the beginning of the Fifth book, they leave the solitary valley, taking its pensive inhabitant along with them, and stray on to where the landscape sinks down into milder features, till they arrive at a church, which stands on a moderate elevation in the centre of a wide and fertile vale. Here they meditate for a while among the monuments, till the vicar comes out and joins them; – and recognizing the pedlar for an old acquaintance, mixes graciously in the conversation, which proceeds in a very edifying manner till the close of the book.

The Sixth contains a choice obituary, or characteristic account of several of the persons who lie buried before this groupe of moralizers; – an unsuccessful lover, who finds consolation in natural history – a miner, who worked on for twenty years, in despite of universal ridicule, and at last found the vein he had expected – two political enemies reconciled in old age to each other – an old female miser – a seduced damsel – and two widowers, one who devoted himself to the education of his daughters, and one who married a prudent middle-aged woman to take care of them.

In the beginning of the Eighth Book, the worthy vicar expresses, in the words of Mr Wordsworth's own epitome, 'his apprehensions that he had detained his auditors too long – invites them to his house – Solitary, disinclined to comply, rallies the Wanderer, and somewhat playfully draws a comparison between his itinerant profession and that of a knight-errant – which leads to the Wanderer giving an account of changes in the country, from the manufacturing spirit – Its favourable effects – The other side of the picture,' &c. &c. After these very poetical themes are exhausted, they all go into the house, where they are introduced to the Vicar's wife and daughter; and while they sit chatting in the parlour over a family dinner, his son and one of his companions come in with a fine dish of trouts piled on a blue slate; and, after being caressed by the company, are sent to dinner in the nursery. – This ends the eighth book.

The Ninth and last is chiefly occupied with the mystical discourses of the Pedlar; who maintains, that the whole universe is animated by an active principle, the noblest seat of which is in the human soul; and moreover, that the final end of old age is to train and enable us

> To hear the mighty stream of *Tendency*
> Uttering, for elevation of our thought,
> A clear sonorous voice, inaudible
> To the vast multitude whose doom it is
> To run the giddy round of vain delight –
> [*Ibid.*, *PW*, V, p. 289, Book IX, ll. 87–91]

with other matters as luminous and emphatic. The hostess at length breaks off the harangue, by proposing that they should all make a little excursion on the lake, – and they embark accordingly; and, after navigating for some time along its shores, and drinking tea on a little island,

land at last on a remote promontory, from which they see the sun go down, – and listen to a solemn and pious, but rather long prayer from the Vicar. They then walk back to the parsonage door, where the author and his friend propose to spend the evening; – but the Solitary prefers walking back in the moonshine to his own valley, after promising to take another ramble with them –

> If time, with free consent, be yours to give,
> And season favours.
>
> [*Ibid.*, *PW*, V, p. 312, Book IX, ll. 782–3]

– And here the publication somewhat abruptly closes.

Our abstract of the story has been so extremely concise, that it is more than usually necessary for us to lay some specimens of the work itself before our readers. Its grand staple, as we have already said, consists of a kind of mystical morality: and the chief characteristics of the style are, that it is prolix and very frequently unintelligible: and though we are very sensible that no great gratification is to be expected from the exhibition of those qualities, yet it is necessary to give our readers a taste of them, both to justify the sentence we have passed, and to satisfy them that it was really beyond our power to present them with any abstract or intelligible account of those long conversations which we have had so much occasion to notice in our brief sketch of its contents. We need give ourselves no trouble however to select passages for this purpose. Here is the first that presents itself to us on opening the volume; and if our readers can form the slightest guess at its meaning, we must give them credit for a sagacity to which we have no pretension.

> But, by the storms *of circumstance* unshaken,
> And subject neither to eclipse or wane,
> Duty exists; – immutably survive,
> For our support, the measures and the forms,
> Which an abstract Intelligence supplies;
> Whose kingdom is, where Time and Space are not:
> Of other converse, which mind, soul, and heart,
> Do, with united urgency, require,
> What more, that may not perish? Thou, dread Source,
> Prime, self-existing Cause and End of all,
> That, in the scale of Being, fill their place,
> Above our human region, or below,
> Set and sustained; – Thou – who didst wrap the cloud

Of Infancy around us, that Thyself,
Therein, with our simplicity awhile
Might'st hold, on earth, communion undisturbed –
        [*Ibid.*, *PW*, V, pp. 111–12, Book IV, ll. 71–86]

For adoration thou endurest; endure
For consciousness the motions of thy will;
For apprehension those transcendent truths
Of the pure Intellect, that stand as laws,
(Submission constituting strength and power)
Even to thy Being's infinite majesty!
        [*Ibid.*, *PW*, V, p. 112, Book IV, ll. 94–9]

'Tis, by comparison, an easy task
Earth to despise; but to converse with Heaven,
This is not easy: – to relinquish all
We have, or hope, of happiness and joy, –
And stand in freedom loosened from this world;
I deem not arduous: – but must needs confess
That 'tis a thing impossible to frame
Conceptions equal to the Soul's desires.
        [*Ibid.*, *PW*, V, p. 113, Book IV, ll. 130–7]

This is a fair sample of that rapturous mysticism which eludes all comprehension, and fills the despairing reader with painful giddiness and
terror. The following, which we meet with on the very next page, is in the
same general strain: – though the first part of it affords a good specimen
of the author's talent for enveloping a plain and trite observation in all
the mock majesty of solemn verbosity. A reader of plain understanding,
we suspect, could hardly recognize the familiar remark, that excessive
grief for our departed friends is not very consistent with a firm belief in
their immortal felicity, in the first twenty lines of the following passage: –
In the sequel we do not ourselves pretend to recognize any thing.
    [Quotes *ibid.*, *PW*, V, pp. 113–15, Book IV, ll. 146–89:

> From this infirmity of mortal kind . . .
> I cannot doubt that They whom you deplore
> Are glorified.]

If any farther specimen be wanted of the learned author's propensity to
deal out the most familiar truths as the oracles of his own inspired
understanding, the following wordy paraphrase of the ordinary remark,
that the best consolation in distress is to be found in the exercises of

piety, and the testimony of a good conscience, may be found on turning the leaf.

[Quotes *ibid.*, *PW*, V, p. 116, Book IV, ll. 214–27:

> What then remains? . . .
> And his most perfect Image in the world.]

We have kept the book too long open, however, at one place, and shall now take a dip in it nearer the beginning. The following account of the pedlar's early training, and lonely meditations among the mountains, is a good example of the forced and affected ecstasies in which this author abounds.

[Quotes *ibid.*, *PW*, V, p. 13, Book I, ll. 148–61:

> Nor did he fail . . .
> He traced an ebbing and a flowing mind.]

We should like extremely to know what is meant by tracing an ebbing and flowing mind in the fixed lineaments of naked crags? – but this is but the beginning of the raving fit. The young pedlar's sensations at sunrise are thus naturally recorded.

[Quotes *ibid.*, *PW*, V, p. 15, Book I, ll. 203–18:

> —The clouds were touch'd . . .
> That made him; it was blessedness and love!]

In this majestic solitude he used also to read his Bible; – and
[Quotes *ibid.*, *PW*, V, pp. 15–16, Book I, ll. 227–36 in notes:

> There did he see the writing . . .
> for he was meek in gratitude.]

What follows about nature, triangles, stars, and the laws of light, is still more incomprehensible.

[Quotes as a continuous passage *ibid.*, *PW*, V, p. 18, Book I, ll. 263–77 and 293–300.]

The whole book, indeed, is full of such stuff. The following is the author's own sublime aspiration after the delight of becoming *a Motion*, or *a Presence*, or *an Energy* among multitudinous streams.

[Quotes *ibid.*, *PW*, V, p. 125 and footnotes, Book IV, ll. 508–39:

> Oh! what a joy it were, in vigorous health . . .
> Nor let it have an end from month to month!]

We suppose the reader is now satisfied with Mr Wordsworth's sub-limities – which occupy rather more than half the volume: – Of his tamer and more creeping prolixity, we have not the heart to load him with many specimens. The following amplification of the vulgar comparison of human life to a stream, has the merit of adding much obscurity to wordiness; at least, *we* have not ingenuity enough to refer the conglobated bubbles and murmurs, and floating islands to their vital prototypes.

[Quotes *ibid.*, *PW*, V, p. 108, Book III, ll. 967–87:

—The tenor
Which my life holds . . .
Is human Life.]

The following, however, is a better example of the useless and most tedious minuteness with which the author so frequently details circumstances of no interest in themselves, – of no importance to the story, – and possessing no graphical merit whatsoever as pieces of description. On their approach to the old chaplain's cottage, the author gets before his companion,

[Quotes *ibid.*, *PW*, V, pp. 56–7, Book II, ll. 410–33:

—when behold
An object that enticed my steps aside! . . .
. . . and, stooping down, drew forth
A Book,]

And this book, which he

—found to be a work
In the French Tongue, a Novel of Voltaire,'
[*Ibid.*, *PW*, V, pp. 57–8, Book II, ll. 442–3]

leads to no incident or remark of any value or importance, to apologize for this long story of its finding. There is no beauty, we think, it must be admitted, in such passages; and so little either of interest or curiosity in the incidents they disclose, that we can scarcely conceive that any man to whom they had actually occurred, should take the trouble to recount them to his wife and children by his idle fireside: – but, that man or child should think them worth writing down in blank verse and printing in magnificent quarto, we should certainly have supposed altogether impossible, had it not been for the ample proofs which Mr Wordsworth has afforded to the contrary.

Sometimes their silliness is enhanced by a paltry attempt at effect and emphasis: – as in the following account of that very touching and extraordinary occurrence of a lamb bleating among the mountains. The poet would actually persuade us that he thought the mountains themselves were bleating; – and that no thing could be so grand or impressive. 'List!' cries the old Pedlar, suddenly breaking off in the middle of one of his daintiest ravings –

> — 'List! – I heard,
> From yon huge breast of rock, a solemn bleat;
> Sent forth as if it were the Mountain's voice!
> As if the visible Mountain made the cry!
> Again!' – The effect upon the soul was such
> As he expressed; for, from the Mountain's heart
> The solemn bleat appeared to come; there was
> No other – and the region all around
> Stood silent, empty of all shape of life.
> – It was a Lamb – left somewhere to itself!
> [*Ibid., PW*, V, p. 121, Book IV, ll. 402–11]

What we have now quoted will give the reader a notion of the taste and spirit in which this volume is composed; and yet, if it had not contained something a good deal better, we do not know how we should have been justified in troubling him with any account of it. But the truth is, that Mr Wordsworth, with all his perversities, is a person of great powers; and has frequently a force in his moral declamations, and a tenderness in his pathetic narratives, which neither his prolixity nor his affectation can altogether deprive of their effect. We shall venture to give same extracts from the simple tale of the weaver's solitary cottage. Its heroine is the deserted wife; and its chief interest consists in the picture of her despairing despondence and anxiety after his disappearance. The Pedlar, recurring to the well to which he had directed his companion, observes,

[Quotes *ibid., PW*, V, p. 25, Book I, ll. 491–502 and *PW*, V, p. 26, Book II, ll. 516–9:

> —As I stooped to drink . . .
> And they whose hearts are dry as summer dust
> Burn to the socket.
>
> —By some especial care . . .
> Might live on earth a life of happiness.]

The bliss and tranquillity of these prosperous years, is well and copiously described; – but at last came sickness, and want of employment; – and the effect on the kind-hearted and industrious mechanic is strikingly delineated.

[Quotes *ibid.*, *PW*, V, p. 27, Book I, ll. 568–74 and p. 28, Book I, ll. 585–9:

—At his door he stood . . .
Of use or ornament.—

One while he would speak lightly of his Babes . . .
Of the poor innocent children.]

At last, he steals from his cottage, and enlists as a soldier; and when the benevolent Pedlar comes, in his rounds, in hope of a cheerful welcome, he meets with a scene of despair.

[Quotes *ibid.*, *PW*, V, p. 30 and footnotes, Book I, ll. 644–56:

—Having reached the door
I knock'd . . .
Unutterably helpless.]

Hope, however, and native cheerfulness, were not yet subdued; and her spirit still bore up against the pressure of this desertion.

[Quotes *ibid.*, *PW*, V, p. 31, Book I, ll. 686–96:

— Long we had not talked . . .
That seem'd the very sound of happy thoughts.]

The gradual sinking of the spirit under the load of continued anxiety, and the destruction of all the finer springs of the soul, by a course of unvarying sadness, are very feelingly represented in the sequel of this simple narrative.

[Quotes *ibid.*, *PW*, V, p. 32, Book I, ll. 706–22 and p. 33, Book I, ll. 734–8:

—I journey'd back this way . . .
Its pride of neatness. –

The sun was sinking in the west . . .
The voice was silent.]

The desolate woman had now an air of still and listless, though patient sorrow.

[Quotes *ibid.*, *PW*, V, pp. 34–5, Book I, ll. 791–803; p. 35, Book I, ll. 813–22, and p. 36, Book I, ll. 829–31:

—Evermore
Her eyelids drooped . . .

. . . sighs came on my ear,
I knew not how, and hardly whence they came.

—I returned . . .

. . . her House
Bespake a sleepy hand of negligence.'

—Her Infant Babe
Had from its Mother caught the trick of grief,
And sighed among its playthings.]

Returning seasons only deepened this gloom, and confirmed this neglect. Her child died; and she spent her weary days in roaming over the country, and repeating her fond and vain inquiries to every passer by.
[Quotes *ibid.*, *PW*, V, p. 38, Book I, ll. 906–16; omitting ll. 912–13 and substituting 'Meantime' for 'Until':

Meantime her House by frost, and thaw, and rain . . .
Last human Tenant of these ruined Walls.]

The story of the old chaplain, though a little less lowly, is of the same mournful cast, and almost equally destitute of incidents; – for Mr Wordsworth delineates only feelings – and all his adventures are of the heart. The narrative which is given by the sufferer himself, is, in our opinion, the most spirited and interesting part of the poem. He begins thus, and addressing himself, after a long pause, to his ancient country-man and friend the Pedlar –
[Quotes *ibid.*, *PW*, V, p. 89, Book III, ll. 480–7:

You never saw, your eyes did never look . . .
That I remember, and can weep no more.]

The following account of his marriage and early felicity is written with great sweetness – a sweetness like that of Massinger, in his softer and more mellifluous passages.
[Quotes *ibid.*, *PW*, V, p. 91, Book III, ll. 504–23 and p. 92, Book III, ll. 532–49:

—This fair Bride –
In the devotedness of youthful Love . . .
The unendangered Myrtle, decked with flowers

– Wild were our walks upon those lonely Downs . . .
That all the grove and all the day was ours.]

There, seven years of unmolested happiness were blessed with two lovely children.

And on these pillars rested, as on air,
Our solitude.

[*Ibid.*, *PW*, V, p. 95, Book III, ll. 597–8]

Suddenly a contagious malady swept off both the infants.
[Quotes *ibid.*, *PW*, V, p. 98, Book III, ll. 650–2 and p. 99, Book III, ll. 669–79:

> Calm as a frozen Lake when ruthless Winds
> Blow fiercely, agitating earth and sky,
> The Mother now remained.
>
> —Yet stealing slow . . .
> And left me, on this earth, disconsolate.]

The agony of mind into which the survivor was thrown, is described with a powerful eloquence; as well as the doubts and distracting fears which the sceptical speculations of his careless days had raised in his spirit. There is something peculiarly grand and terrible to our feelings in the imagery of these three lines –

> By pain of heart, now checked, and now impelled,
> The Intellectual Power, through words and things,
> Went sounding on, a dim and perilous way!

[*Ibid.*, *PW*, V, p. 100, Book III, ll. 699–701]

At last he is roused from this dejected mood, by the glorious promises which seemed held out to human nature at the first dawn of the French Revolution; – and it indicates a fine perception of the secret springs of character and emotion, to choose a being so circumstanced as the most ardent votary of that far-spread enthusiasm.
[Quotes *ibid.*, *PW*, V, p. 101, Book III, ll. 734–6 and pp. 101–2, Book III, ll. 745–58 as though these were a continuation of the former:

> Thus was I reconverted to the world;
> Society became my glittering Bride,
> And airy hopes my Children.
>
> —If busy Men . . .
> Permitted to descend, and bless mankind.]

On the disappearance of that bright vision, he was inclined to take part with the desperate party who still aimed at establishing universal regeneration, though by more questionable instruments than they had originally assumed. But the military despotism which ensued, soon closed the scence against all such exertions: and, disgusted with men and Europe, he sought for shelter in the wilds of America. In the calm of the voyage, Memory and Conscience awoke him to a sense of his misery.

[Quotes *ibid.*, *PW*, V, pp. 104–5, Book III, ll. 850–5:

> —Feebly must They have felt . . .
> Tender reproaches, insupportable!]

His disappointment, and ultimate seclusion in England, have been already sufficiently detailed.

We must trespass upon our readers with the fragments of yet another story. It is that of a simple, seduced and deserted girl, told with great sweetness, pathos and indulgence by the Vicar of the parish, by the side of her untimely grave. Looking down on the turf, he says –

[Quotes *ibid.*, *PW*, V, pp. 211–12, Book VI, ll. 787–92 and pp. 212–13, Book VI, ll. 811–23 as though these were a continuation of the former:

> As, on a sunny bank, a tender Lamb . . .
> The sheltering Hillock is the Mother's grave.
> There, by her innocent Baby's precious grave . . .
> In the prime hour of sweetest scents and airs.]

Her virgin graces and tenderness are then very beautifully described, and her seduction and lonely anguish passed over very lightly.

[Quotes *ibid.*, *PW*, V, pp. 214–17, Book VI, ll. 869–78, 906–10, 916–27 and 939–48.]

Here the parents of her new nursling, soon forbade her all intercourse with her own most precious child; – and a sudden malady carried it off in this period of forced desertion.

[Quotes *ibid.*, *PW*, V, p. 218, Book VI, ll. 969–87:

> —Once, only once,
> She saw it in that mortal malady . . .
> In the broad day – a rueful Magdalene!]

Overwhelmed with this calamity, she was at last obliged to leave her service.

[Quotes *ibid.*, *PW*, V, pp. 219–20, Book VI, ll. 1000–52:

> But the green stalk of Ellen's life was snapped . . .
> and here is laid
> The mortal Body by her Infant's side.]

These passages, we think, are among the most touching with which the volume presents us; though there are many in a more lofty and impassioned style. The following commemoration of a beautiful and glorious youth, the love and the pride of the valley, is full of warmth and poetry.
[Quotes *ibid.*, *PW*, V, pp. 254–5, Book VII, ll. 714–40:

—The mountain Ash . . .
Our unpretending valley.]

This is lofty and energetic; – but Mr Wordsworth descends, we cannot think very gracefully, when he proceeds to describe how the quoit *whizzed* when his arm launched it – and how the football mounted as high as a lark, at the touch of his toe; – neither is it a suitable catastrophe, for one so nobly endowed, to catch cold by standing too long in the river washing sheep, and die of spasms in consequence. The general reflections on the indiscriminating rapacity of death, though by no means original in themselves, and expressed with too bold a rivalry of the seven ages of Shakespeare, have yet a character of vigour and truth about them that entitles them to notice.
[Quotes *ibid.*, *PW*, V, p. 184, Book V, l. 946 and goes on at once with p. 184, Book V ll. 954–75 as though these were a continuation of the former:

This file of Infants; some that never breathed,
And the besprinkled Nursling, unrequired . . .
And gentle 'Nature grieved that One should die.']

There is a lively and impressive appeal on the injury done to the health, happiness, and morality of the lower orders, by the unceasing and premature labours of our crowded manufactories. The description of night-working is picturesque. In lonely and romantic regions, he says, when silence and darkness incline all to repose –
[Quotes *ibid.*, *PW*, V, pp. 270–1, Book VIII, ll. 167–85:

—An unnatural light,
Prepared for never-resting Labour's eyes . . .
To Gain – the Master Idol of the Realm,
Perpetual sacrifice.]

The effects on the ordinary life of the poor are delineated in graver colours.
[Quotes *ibid.*, *PW*, V, pp. 273–4, Book VIII, ll. 262–82:

—Domestic bliss . . .
That birth-right now is lost.]

The dissertation is closed with an ardent hope, that the farther improvement and the universal diffusion of these arts may take away the temptation for us to embark so largely in their cultivation; and that we may once more hold out inducements for the return of old manners and domestic charities,

[Quotes *ibid.*, *PW*, V, p. 272, Book VIII, ll. 214–27:

> Learning, though late, that all true glory rests . . .
> How weak
> Those Arts, and high Inventions, if unpropped
> By Virtue.]

There is also a very animated exhortation to the more general diffusion of education among the lower orders; and a glowing and eloquent assertion of their capacity for all virtues and all enjoyments.

[Quotes *ibid.*, *PW*, V, pp. 293–4, Book IX, ll. 237–47:

> —Believe it not:
> The primal duties shine aloft – like stars . . .
> The smoke ascends
> To heaven as lightly from the Cottage hearth
> As from the haughty palace.]

The blessings and the necessities that now render this a peculiar duty in the rulers of this empire, are urged in a still loftier tone.

[Quotes *ibid.*, *PW*, V, p. 297, Book IX, ll. 336–54:

> Look! and behold, from Calpe's sunburnt cliffs . . .
> order else
> Cannot subsist, nor confidence, nor peace.]

There is a good deal of fine description in the course of this work; but we have left ourselves no room for any specimen. The following few lines, however, are a fine epitome of a lake voyage.

[Quotes *ibid.*, *PW*, V, p. 305, Book IX, ll. 560–5:

> —Right across the Lake . . .
> Browzed by the side of dashing waterfalls.]

We add also the following more elaborate and fantastic picture – which, however, is not without its beauty.

[Quotes *ibid.*, *PW*, V, p. 300, Book IX, ll. 437–51:

> Then having reached a bridge, that overarched . . .
> Blended in perfect stillness, to our sight!]

Besides those more extended passages of interest or beauty, which we have quoted, and omitted to quote, there are scattered up and down the book, and in the midst of its most repulsive portions, a very great number of single lines and images, that sparkle like gems in the desert, and startle us with an intimation of the great poetic powers that lie buried in the rubbish that has been heaped around them. It is difficult to pick up these, after we have once passed them by; but we shall endeavour to light upon one or two. The beneficial effect of intervals of relaxation and pastime on youthful minds, is finely expressed, we think, in a single line, when it is said to be –

> Like vernal ground to Sabbath sunshine left.
>
> [*Ibid.*, *PW*, V, p. 256, Book VII, l. 781]

The following image of the bursting forth of a mountain-spring, seems to us also to be conceived with great elegance and beauty.

> And a few steps may bring us to the spot,
> Where haply crown'd with flowrets and green herbs;
> The Mountain Infant to the Sun comes forth
> Like human life from darkness. –
>
> [*Ibid.*, *PW*, V, p. 76, Book III, ll. 32–5]

The ameliorating effects of song and music on the minds which most delight in them, are likewise very poetically expressed.
[Quotes *ibid.*, *PW*, V, p. 231, Book VII, ll. 25–30:

> —And when the stream . . .
> That shall not die, and cannot be destroyed.]

Nor is any thing more elegant than the representation of the graceful tranquillity occasionally put on by one of the author's favourites; who, though gay and airy, in general –
[Quotes *ibid.*, *PW*, V, p. 195, Book VI, ll. 292–8:

> Was graceful, when it pleased him, smooth and still . . .
> More winningly reserved.—]

Nor are there wanting morsels of a sterner and more majestic beauty; as when, assuming the weightier diction of Cowper, he says, in language which the hearts of all readers of modern history must have responded –

> —Earth is sick,
> And Heaven is weary of the hollow words
> Which States and Kingdoms utter when they speak
> Of Truth and Justice.
>
> [*Ibid.*, *PW*, V, p. 165, Book V, ll. 378–81]

These examples, we perceive, are not very well chosen – but we have not leisure to improve the selection; and, such as they are, they may serve to give the reader a notion of the sort of merit which we meant to illustrate by their citation. – When we look back to them, indeed, and to the other passages which we have now extracted, we feel half inclined to rescind the severe sentence which we passed on the work at the beginning: – But when we look into the work itself, we perceive that it cannot be rescinded. Nobody can be more disposed to do justice to the great powers of Mr Wordsworth than we are; and, from the first time that he came before us, down to the present moment, we have uniformly testified in their favour, and assigned indeed our high sense of their value as the chief ground of the bitterness with which we resented their perversion. That perversion, however, is now far more visible than their original dignity; and while we collect the fragments, it is impossible not to lament the ruins from which we are condemned to pick them. If any one should doubt of the existence of such a perversion, or be disposed to dispute about the instances we have hastily brought forward, we would just beg leave to refer him to the general plan and the characters of the poem now before us. – Why should Mr Wordsworth have made his hero a superannuated Pedlar? What but the most wretched and provoking perversity of taste and judgment, could induce any one to place his chosen advocate of wisdom and virtue in so absurd and fantastic a condition? Did Mr Wordsworth really imagine, that his favourite doctrines were likely to gain any thing in point of effect or authority by being put into the mouth of a person accustomed to higgle about tape, or brass sleeve-buttons? Or is it not plain that, independent of the ridicule and disgust which such a personification must give to many of his readers, its adoption exposes his work throughout to the charge of revolting incongruity, and utter disregard of probability or nature? For, after he has thus wilfully debased his moral teacher by a low occupation, is there one word that he puts into his mouth, or one sentiment of which he makes him the organ, that has the most remote reference to that occupation? Is there any thing in his learned, abstracted, and logical harangues, that savours of the calling that is ascribed to him? Are any of their materials such as a pedlar could possibly have dealt in? Are the manners, the diction, the sentiments, in any, the very smallest degree, accommodated to a person in that condition? or are they not eminently and conspicuously such as could not by possibility belong to it? A man who went about selling flannel and pocket-handkerchiefs in this lofty

diction, would soon frighten away all his customers; and would infallibly pass either for a madman, or for some learned and affected
gentleman, who, in a frolic, had taken up a character which he was
peculiarly ill qualified for supporting.

The absurdity in this case, we think, is palpable and glaring but it is
exactly of the same nature with that which infects the whole substance
of the work – a puerile ambition of singularity engrafted on an unlucky
predilection for truisms; and an affected passion for simplicity and
humble life, most awkwardly combined with a taste for mystical refinements, and all the gorgeousness of obscure phraseology. His taste for
simplicity is evinced by sprinkling up and down his interminable declamations, a few descriptions of baby-houses, and of old hats with wet
brims, and his amiable partiality for humble life, by assuring us, that a
wordy rhetorician, who talks about Thebes, and allegorizes all the heathen mythology, was once a pedlar – and making him break in upon his
magnificent orations with two or three awkward notices of something
that he had seen when selling winter raiment about the country – or of
the changes in the state of society, which had almost annihilated his
former calling.

149. Charles Lamb

Unsigned review, *Quarterly Review*, October 1814, XII, 100–11

This issue of the *Quarterly* did not appear until December 1814. Lamb, as
Crabb Robinson records on 10 November 1814, was already in some
disquiet about it:

> At half-past nine went to Lamb's. Burney was there. We played a
> rubber and chatted till half-past eleven. Lamb has written a review
> of Wordsworth's poem for the *Quarterly Review* which he says would
> have been fit for the first review but will not do after others. It is
> too slight for a late publication, and it did not appear in the last
> number . . .
> (*Henry Crabb Robinson on Books and their Writers*, ed. Edith J. Morley,
> 1938, I, 153)

By 28 December 1814 Lamb had still not seen the review in print; he
wrote to Wordsworth:

That Review you speak of, I am only sorry it did not appear last month. The circumstances of haste and peculiar bad spirits under which it was written, would have excused its slightness and inadequacy, the full load of which I shall suffer from its lying by so long as it will seem to have done from its postponement. I write with great difficulty and can scarce command my own resolution to sit at writing an hour together. I am a poor creature, but I am leaving off Gin. I hope you will see good will in the thing. I had a difficulty to perform not to make it all Panegyrick; I have attempted to personate a mere stranger to you; perhaps with too much strangeness. But you must bear that in mind when you read it, and not think that I am in mind distant from you or your Poem, but that both are close to me among the nearest of persons and things. I do but act the stranger in the Review. Then, I was puzzled about extracts and determined upon not giving one that had been in the Examiner, for Extracts repeated give an idea that there is a meagre allowance of good things. By this way, I deprived myself of Sr. W. Irthing and the reflections that conclude his story, which are the flower of the Poem. H. had given the reflections before me.[1] *Then* it is the first Review I ever did, and I did not know how long I might make it. But it must speak for itself, if Giffard and his crew do not put words in its mouth, which I expect.

(*The Letters of Charles and Mary Lamb*, ed. E. V. Lucas, 1935, II, 146–7)

Lamb's fears were justified; he wrote to Wordsworth early in January 1815:

DEAR WORDSWORTH,

I told you my Review was a very imperfect one. But what you will see in the Quarterly is a spurious one which Mr. Baviad Gifford has palm'd upon it for mine. I never felt more vexd in my life than when I read it. I cannot give you an idea of what he has done to it out of spite at me because he once sufferd me to be called a lunatic in his Thing. The *language* he has alterd throughout. Whatever inadequateness it had to its subject, it was in point of composition the prettiest piece of prose I ever writ, and so my sister (to whom alone I read the MS.) said. That charm if it had any is all gone: more than a third of the substance is cut away, and that not all from one place, but *passim*, so as to make utter nonsense. Every warm expression is changed for a nasty cold one. I have not the cursed alteration by me, I shall never look at it again, but for a specimen I remember I had said the Poet of the Excurs[n]. 'walks thro' common forests as thro' some Dodona or enchanted wood, and every casual bird that flits upon the boughs, like that miraculous one in Tasso, but in language more piercing than any articulate sounds, reveals to him far higher lovelays.' It is now (besides half a dozen alterations in the same half dozen lines) 'but in language more *intelligent* reveals to him' – that is one I remember. But that would have been little, putting his damnd Shoemaker phraseology (for he was a shoemaker) in stead of mine, which has been tinctured with better authors than his ignorance can comprehend – for I reckon myself a dab at *Prose* – verse I leave to my betters – God help them, if they are to be so reviewed by friend and foe as you have been this quarter. I have read 'It won't do.' But worse than altering words, he has kept a few members only of the part I had done best, which was to explain all I could of your 'scheme of harmonies,' as I had ventured to call it, between the external universe and what within us answers to it. To do this I had accumulated a good many short passages, rising in length to the end, weaving in the Extracts as if they came in as a part of the text, naturally, not obtruding them as specimens. Of this part a little is left, but so as without conjuration no man could tell what I was driving it [?at]. A proof of it you may see (tho' not judge of the whole of the injustice) by these words: I had spoken something about 'natural methodism – ' and after follows 'and therefore the tale of Margaret sh^d. have been postponed' (I forget my words, or his words): now the reasons for postponing it are as deducible from what goes before, as they are from the 104th psalm. The passage whence I deduced it has vanished, but clapping a colon before a *therefore* is always reason enough for Mr. Baviad Gifford to allow to a reviewer that is not himself. I assure you my complaints are founded. I know how sore a word alterd makes one, but indeed of this Review the whole complexion is gone. I regret only that I did not keep a copy. I am sure you would have been pleased with it, because I have been feeding my fancy for some months with the notion of pleasing you. Its imperfection or inadequateness in size and method I knew, but for the *writing part* of it, I was fully satisfied. I hoped it would make more than atonement. Ten or twelve distinct passages come to my mind, which are gone, and what is left is of course the worse for their having been there, the eyes are pulld out and the bleeding sockets are left. I read it at Arch's shop with my face burning with vexation secretly, with just such a feeling as if it had been a review written against myself, making false quotations from me. But I am ashamed to say so much about a short piece. How are *you* served! and the labors of years turn'd into contempt by scoundrels.

But I could not but protest against your taking that thing as mine. Every *pretty* expression, (I know there were many) every warm expression, there was nothing else, is vulgarised and frozen – but if they catch me in their camps again let them spitchcock me. They had a right to do it, as no name appears to it, and Mr. Shoemaker Gifford I

suppose never wa[i]ved a right he had since he commenced author.
God confound him and all caitiffs.
C. L.

(Ibid., II. 148–9)

The volume before us, as we learn from the Preface, is 'a detached portion of an unfinished poem, containing views of man, nature, and society;' to be called the Recluse, as having for its principal subject the 'sensations and opinions of a poet living in retirement;' and to be preceded by a 'record in verse of the origin and progress of the author's own powers, with reference to the fitness which they may be supposed to have conferred for the task.' To the completion of this plan we look forward with a confidence which the execution of the finished part is well calculated to inspire. – Meanwhile, in what is before us there is ample matter for entertainment: for the 'Excursion' is not a branch (as might have been suspected) prematurely plucked from the parent tree to gratify an over-hasty appetite for applause; but is, in itself, a complete and legitimate production.

It opens with the meeting of the poet with an aged man whom he had known from his school days; in plain words, a Scottish pedlar; a man who, though of low origin, had received good learning and impressions of the strictest piety from his stepfather, a minister and village school-master. Among the hills of Athol, the child is described to have become familiar with the appearances of nature in his occupation as a feeder of sheep; and from her silent influences to have derived a character, meditative, tender, and poetical. With an imagination and feelings thus nourished – his intellect not unaided by books, but those, few, and chiefly of a religious cast – the necessity of seeking a maintenance in riper years, had induced him to make choice of a profession, the *appellation* for which has been gradually declining into contempt, but which formerly designated a class of men, who, journeying in country places, when roads presented less facilities for travelling, and the intercourse between towns and villages was unfrequent and hazardous, became a sort of link of neighbourhood to distant habitations; resembling, in some small measure, in the effects of their periodical returns, the caravan which Thomson so feelingly describes as blessing the cheerless Siberian in its annual visitation, with 'news of human kind.'

In the solitude incident to this rambling life, power had been given him to keep alive that devotedness to nature which he had imbibed in his childhood, together with the opportunity of gaining such notices of persons and things from his intercourse with society, as qualified him to become a 'teacher of moral wisdom.' With this man, then, in a hale old age, released from the burthen of his occupation, yet retaining much of its active habits, the poet meets, and is by him introduced to a second character – a sceptic – one who had been partially roused from an overwhelming desolation, brought upon him by the loss of wife and children, by the powerful incitement of hope which the French Revolution in its commencement put forth, but who, disgusted with the failure of all its promises, had fallen back into a laxity of faith and conduct which induced at length a total despondence as to the dignity and final destination of his species. In the language of the poet, he

—broke faith with those whom he had laid
In earth's dark chambers.
[*The Excursion, PW*, V, p. 51, Book II, ll. 247–8]

Yet he describes himself as subject to compunctious visitations from that silent quarter.

—Feebly must they have felt,
Who, in old time, attired with snakes and whips
The vengeful Furies. Beautiful regards
Were turned on me – the face of her I loved;
The wife and mother; pitifully fixing
Tender reproaches, insupportable! –
[*Ibid., PW*, V, pp. 104–5, Book III, ll. 850–5]

The conversations with this person, in which the Wanderer asserts the consolatory side of the question against the darker views of human life maintained by his friend, and finally calls to his assistance the experience of a village priest, the third, or rather fourth interlocutor, (for the poet himself is one,) form the groundwork of the 'Excursion.'

It will be seen by this sketch that the poem is of a didactic nature, and not a fable or story; yet it is not wanting in stories of the most interesting kind, – such as the lovers of Cowper and Goldsmith will recognise as something familiar and congenial to them. We might instance the Ruined Cottage, and the Solitary's own story, in the first half of the work; and the second half, as being almost a continued cluster of narration. But the prevailing charm of the poem is, perhaps, that, conversational as it is in its plan, the dialogue throughout is carried on in the very heart of the most romantic scenery which the poet's native hills could supply; and which, by the perpetual references made to it either in the way of illustration or for variety and pleasurable description's sake, is brought before us as we read. We breathe in the fresh air, as we do while reading Walton's Complete Angler; only the country about us is as much bolder than Walton's, as the thoughts and speculations, which form the matter of the poem, exceed the trifling pastime and low-pitched conversation of his humble fishermen. We give the description of the 'two huge peaks,' which from some other vale peered into that in which the Solitary is entertaining the poet and companion. 'Those,' says their host,

[Quotes *ibid.*, *PW*, V, p. 67, Book II, ll. 695–725:

> —if here you dwelt, would be
> Your prized companions . . .
>
> > alone
> Here do I sit and watch.–]

To a mind constituted like that of Mr. Wordsworth, the stream, the torrent, and the stirring leaf – seem not merely to suggest associations of deity, but to be a kind of speaking communication with it. He walks through every forest, as through some Dodona; and every bird that flits among the leaves, like that miraculous one* in Tasso, but in language more intelligent, reveals to him far higher love-lays. In his poetry nothing in Nature is dead. Motion is synonymous with life. 'Beside yon spring,' says the Wanderer, speaking of a deserted well, from which, in former times, a poor woman, who died heart-broken, had been used to dispense refreshment to the thirsty traveller,

> —beside yon spring I stood,
> And eyed its waters, till we seem'd to feel
> One sadness, they and I. For them a bond
> Of brotherhood is broken: time has been
> When every day the touch of human hand
> Dislodged the natural sleep that binds them up
> In mortal stillness. –
>
> > [*Ibid.*, *PW*, V, p. 24, Book I, ll. 484–90]

---

*   With party-coloured plumes, and purple bill,
A wondrous bird among the rest there flew,
That in plain speech sung love-lays loud and shrill;
Her leden was like human language true;
So much she talkd, and with such wit and skill,
That strange it seemed how much good she knew.
Fairfax's Translation.

To such a mind, we say – call it strength or weakness – if weakness, assuredly a fortunate one – the visible and audible things of creation present, not dim symbols, or curious emblems, which they have done at all times to those who have been gifted with the poetical faculty; but revelations and quick insights into the life within us, the pledge of immortality: –

> —the whispering air
> Sends inspiration from her shadowy heights,
> And blind recesses of the cavern'd rocks:
> The little rills, and waters numberless,
> Inaudible by day-light.
> ['*Ibid.*', *PW*, V, p. 146, Book IV, ll. 1170–14]

'I have seen,' the poet says, and the illustration is an happy one:

> —I have seen
> A curious child, applying to his ear
> The convolutions of a smooth-lipp'd shell
> To which, in silence hush'd, his very soul
> Listen'd intensely, and his countenance soon
> Brighten'd with joy; for murmurings from within
> Were heard – sonorous cadences! whereby,
> To his belief, the monitor express'd
> Mysterious union with its native sea.
> Even such a shell the universe itself
> Is to the ear of faith; and doth impart
> Authentic tidings of invisible things:
> Of ebb and flow, and ever during power;
> And central peace subsisting at the heart
> Of endless agitation. –
> [*Ibid.*, *PW*, V, p. 145, Book IV, ll. 1132–47]

Sometimes this harmony is imaged to us by an echo; and in one instance, it is with such transcendant beauty set forth by a shadow and its corresponding substance, that it would be a sin to cheat our readers at once of so happy an illustration of the poet's system, and so fair a proof of his descriptive powers.

[Quotes *ibid.*, *PW*, V, p. 300, Book IX, ll. 437–51:

> Thus having reached a bridge . . .
> Blended in perfect stillness, to our sight!]

410

Combinations, it is confessed, 'like those reflected in that quiet pool,' cannot be lasting: it is enough for the purpose of the poet, if they are felt. – They are at least his system; and his readers, if they reject them for their creed, may receive them merely as poetry. In him, *faith*, in friendly alliance and conjunction with the religion of his country, appears to have grown up, fostered by meditation and lonely communions with Nature – an internal principle of lofty consciousness, which stamps upon his opinions and sentiments (we were almost going to say) the character of an expanded and generous Quakerism.

From such a creed we should expect unusual results; and, when applied to the purposes of consolation, more touching considerations than from the mouth of common teachers. The finest speculation of this sort perhaps in the poem before us, is the notion of the thoughts which may sustain the spirit, while they crush the frame of the sufferer, who from loss of objects of love by death, is commonly supposed to pine away under a broken heart.

[Quotes *ibid.*, *PW*, V, pp. 114–15, Book IV, ll. 165–85:

—If there be, whose tender frames have drooped . . .
Along the line of limitless desires.]

With the same modifying and incorporating power, he tells us, –
[Quotes *ibid.*, *PW*, V, pp. 142–3, Book IV, ll. 1058–77:

Within the soul a faculty abides . . .
From palpable oppressions of despair.]

This is high poetry; though (as we have ventured to lay the basis of the author's sentiments in a sort of liberal Quakerism) from some parts of it, others may, with more plausibility, object to the appearance of a kind of Natural Methodism: we could have wished therefore that the tale of Margaret had been postponed, till the reader had been strengthened by some previous acquaintance with the author's theory, and not placed in the front of the poem, with a kind of ominous aspect, beautifully tender as it is. It is a tale of a cottage, and its female tenant, gradually decaying together, while she expected the return of one whom poverty and not unkindness had driven from her arms. We trust ourselves only with the conclusion –

[Quotes *ibid.*, *PW*, V, pp. 37–8, Book I, ll. 871–916:

—nine tedious years
From their first separation, nine long years . . .
Last human tenant of these ruined walls!]

411

The fourth book, entitled 'Despondency Corrected,' we consider as the most valuable portion of the poem. For moral grandeur; for wide scope of thought and a long train of lofty imagery; for tender personal appeals; and a *versification* which we feel we ought to notice, but feel it also so involved in the poetry, that we can hardly mention it as a distinct excellence; it stands without competition among our didactic and descriptive verse. The general tendency of the argument (which we might almost affirm to be the leading moral of the poem) is to abate the pride of the calculating *understanding*, and to reinstate the *imagination* and the *affections* in those seats from which modern philosophy has laboured but too successfully to expel them.

'Life's autumn past,' says the grey-haired Wanderer,

> —I stand on winter's verge,
> And daily lose what I desire to keep;
> Yet rather would I instantly decline
> To the traditionary sympathies
> Of a most rustic ignorance, and take
> A fearful apprehension from the owl
> Or death-watch – and as readily rejoice
> If two auspicious magpies crossed my way –
> This rather would I do than see and hear
> The repetitions wearisome of sense,
> Where soul is dead and feeling hath no place. –
>
> [*Ibid.*, *PW*, V, p. 128, Book IV, ll. 611–21]

In the same spirit, those illusions of the imaginative faculty to which the peasantry in solitary districts are peculiarly subject, are represented as the kindly ministers of *conscience*:

> —with whose service charged
> They come and go, appear and disappear;
> Diverting evil purposes, remorse
> Awakening, chastening an intemperate grief,
> Or pride of heart abating.
>
> [*Ibid.*, *PW*, V, p. 135, Book IV, ll. 837–41]

Reverting to more distant ages of the world, the operation of that same faculty in producing the several fictions of Chaldean, Persian, and Grecian idolatry, is described with such seductive power, that the Solitary, in good earnest, seems alarmed at the tendency of his own argument. – Notwithstanding his fears, however, there is one thought so uncommonly fine, relative to the spirituality which lay hid beneath the gross material forms of Greek worship, in metal or stone, that we cannot resist the allurement of transcribing it –

[Quotes *ibid.*, *PW*, V, pp. 132–3, Book IV, ll. 729–62:

—Triumphant o'er his pompous show . . .
Depart, and leave no vestige where they trod.]

In discourse like this the first day passes away. – The second (for this almost dramatic poem takes up the action of two summer days) is varied by the introduction of the village priest; to whom the Wanderer resigns the office of chief speaker, which had been yielded to his age and experience on the first. The conference is begun at the gate of the church-yard; and after some natural speculations concerning death and immortality – and the custom of funereal and sepulchral observances, as deduced from a feeling of immortality – certain doubts are proposed respecting the quantity of moral worth existing in the world, and in that mountainous district in particular. In the resolution of these doubts, the priest enters upon a most affecting and singular strain of narration, derived from the graves around him. Pointing to hillock after hillock, he gives short histories of their tenants, disclosing their humble virtues, and touching with tender hand upon their frailties.

Nothing can be conceived finer than the manner of introducing these tales. With heaven above his head, and the mouldering turf at his feet – standing betwixt life and death – he seems to maintain that spiritual relation which he bore to his living flock, in its undiminished strength, even with their ashes; and to be in his proper cure, or diocese, among the dead.

We might extract powerful instances of pathos from these tales – the story of Ellen in particular – but their force is in combination, and in the circumstances under which they are introduced. The traditionary anecdote of the Jacobite and Hanoverian, as less liable to suffer by transplanting, and as affording an instance of that finer species of humour, that thoughtful playfulness in which the author more nearly perhaps than in any other quality resembles Cowper, we shall lay (at least a part of it) before our readers. It is the story of a whig who, having wasted a large estate in election contests, retired 'beneath a borrowed name' to a small town among these northern mountains, where a Caledonian laird, a follower of the house of Stuart, who had fled his country after the overthrow at Culloden, returning with the return of lenient times, had also fixed his residence.

413

[Quotes *ibid.*, *PW*, V, pp. 201–3, Book VI, ll. 457–83 and ll. 491–521:

—Here, then, they met,
Two doughty champions . . .
                    and that peace,
Which the world wants, shall be for thee confirmed.]

The causes which have prevented the poetry of Mr. Wordsworth from attaining its full share of popularity are to be found in the boldness and originality of his genius. The times are past when a poet could securely follow the direction of his own mind into whatever tracts it might lead. A writer, who would be popular, must timidly coast the shore of prescribed sentiment and sympathy. He must have just as much more of the imaginative faculty than his readers, as will serve to keep their apprehensions from stagnating, but not so much as to alarm their jealousy. He must not think or feel too deeply.

If he has had the fortune to be bred in the midst of the most magnificent objects of creation, he must not have given away his heart to them; or if he have, he must conceal his love, or not carry his expressions of it beyond that point of rapture, which the occasional tourist thinks it not overstepping decorum to betray, or the limit which that gentlemanly spy upon Nature, the picturesque traveller, has vouchsafed to countenance. He must do this, or be content to be thought an enthusiast.

If from living among simple mountaineers, from a daily intercourse with them, not upon the footing of a patron, but in the character of an equal, he has detected, or imagines that he has detected, through the cloudy medium of their unlettered discourse, thoughts and apprehensions not vulgar; traits of patience and constancy, love unwearied, and heroic endurance, not unfit (as he may judge) to be made the subject of verse, he will be deemed a man of perverted genius by the philanthropist who, conceiving of the peasantry of his country only as objects of a pecuniary sympathy, starts at finding them elevated to a level of humanity with himself, having their own loves, enmities, cravings, aspirations, &c., as much beyond his faculty to believe, as his beneficence to supply.

If from a familiar observation of the ways of children, and much more from a retrospect of his own mind when a child, he has gathered more reverential notions of that state than fall to the lot of ordinary observers, and, escaping from the dissonant wranglings of men, has tuned his lyre, though but for occasional harmonies, to the milder utterance of that soft age, – his verses shall be censured as infantile by critics who confound poetry 'having children for its subject' with poetry that is 'childish,' and who, having themselves perhaps never been *children*, never having possessed the tenderness and docility of that age, know not what the soul of a child is – how apprehensive! how imaginative! how religious!

We have touched upon some of the causes which we conceive to have been unfriendly to the author's former poems. We think they do not apply in the same force to the one before us. There is in it more of uniform elevation, a wider scope of subject, less of manner, and it contains none of those starts and imperfect shapings which in some of this author's smaller pieces offended the weak, and gave scandal to the perverse. It must indeed be approached with seriousness. It has in it much of that quality which 'draws the devout, deterring the profane.' Those who hate the Paradise Lost will not love this poem. The steps of the great master are discernible in it; not in direct imitation or injurious parody, but in the following of the spirit, in free homage and generous subjection.

One objection it is impossible not to foresee. It will be asked, why put such eloquent discourse in the mouth of a pedlar? It might be answered that Mr. Wordsworth's plan required a character in humble life to be the organ of his philosophy. It was in harmony with the system and scenery of his poem. We read Pier's Plowman's Creed, and the lowness of the teacher seems to add a simple dignity to the doctrine. Besides, the poet has bestowed an unusual share of education upon him. Is it too much to suppose that the author, at some early period of his life, may himself have known such a person, a man endowed with sentiments above his situation, another Burns; and that the dignified strains which he has attributed to the Wanderer may be no more than recollections of his conversation, heightened only by the amplification natural to poetry, or the lustre which imagination flings back upon the objects and companions of our youth? After all, if there should be found readers willing to admire the poem, who yet feel scandalized at a *name*, we would advise them, wherever it occurs, to substitute silently the word *Palmer*, or *Pilgrim*, or any less offensive designation, which shall connect the notion of sobriety in heart and manners with the experience and privileges which a wayfaring life confers.

EDITOR'S NOTE

1. See Hazlitt, entry 147. Wordsworth sent Lamb's letter to Southey asking him to try to retrieve the manuscript: *Wordsworth Letters*, III, 186; Southey,

in turn, asked his friend Grosvenor Bedford to find Lamb's manuscript 'which has been made the thing it is by Gifford's merciless mutilations . . . If there be a logical arrangement, he is sure to dislocate it by pulling out the middle joint of every articulated paragraph. If there be a felicitous phrase, he is sure to gouge the sentence.' (*Selections from the Letters of Robert Southey*, ed. J. W. Warter, 1856, II, 393)

150. James Montgomery

Unsigned review, *Eclectic Magazine*, January 1815, III (second series), 13–39

Montgomery, no longer a regular reviewer for the *Eclectic*, was sent *The Excursion* by the *Eclectic*'s new owner-editor, Josiah Conder, who wrote to Montgomery on 31 August 1814:

> As to Wordsworth's poem, you shall at least have the reading of it, and high gratification it will afford you. It is noble and elevated, like the mountains of his favourite scenery, and severely beautiful as their embosomed lake, when, tranquil as a mirror, it reflects every cloud and every star of the summer heavens . . .
>
> (*Memoirs of the Life and Writings of James Montgomery*, ed. John Holland and James Everett, 1856, III, 56)

Montgomery had *The Excursion* sent on to his holiday address at Scarborough where, according to his biographers, he 'covered the ample margins of many of its pages with short-hand notes, and thus, almost involuntarily on his part, originated another "Eclectic" article.' (*ibid.*, III, 64). It seems possible that Conder designed to entice Montgomery into doing the review, though his declared intention was to write it himself. Something of his own attitude to Wordsworth is preserved in a letter to Montgomery of 13 October 1814:

> I have great satisfaction in your undertaking Wordsworth. You shall of course do it in your own way, without fettering yourself with any suggestions of my own, the particular bearing of which I have nearly forgotten. The fact is that my opinion of the poem and the poet is very coincident with your own, and I wish him to be done such justice to, as you are sure to do, when you feel your subject. If you can do so as to let me have it by the end of the next month, or even sooner, I shall be particularly obliged, as I hope to put the *Jany N°* *to press by that time*, I hope I shall be able to reserve it for that N°. But on no account would

I tempt you to hurry the article which will require a degree of *elaboration*, I shd suppose, greater than ordinary poems, even those of superior merit, usually demand. I shd like to have the *doctrines* of the work, moral and poetical, fully brought out, and the public made to understand if *possible*, why & in what respects we think him the first poet of the day. Perhaps so absolute an expression is dangerous, where it is difficult to institute a comparison. Surely the author of The Corsair [Byron] is, in the depiction of the workings of the human passions, & in energy of expression, unrivalled by ancient or modern bard. Perhaps Wordsworth is the sublimest poet of the age. He seems to be a compound of Shakespeare & Cowper, tho' in many respects different from both. But I am dictating again – I beg your pardon. But this was not indeed the first book you asked for; I hope it will not be, by a great many the last. I had thought of doing it before I thought of your wishing it. You asked for Southey & I have refused both his poem[1] & Wordsworth's to another reviewer, to send them to you; I may add, I was glad to have *such* an excuse for refusing them, tho' that Reviewer[2] wd have praised the former con amore: the latter he does not appreciate. If you think Wordsworth worth a *double* article, do not scruple to extend it.

(Ms. Sheffield City Library)

By the end of the year the review was printed, and Conder commented to Montgomery on 31 December 1814:

I have but a few minutes which I can take from this busy day, to acknowledge your favour of the 29th of Nov, accompanying the Review of Wordsworth. You will perceive that the article is given entire, being neither divided, nor materially retrenched. All your extracts are retained. That you will cordially approve of all the slight alterations (principally retrenchments) which the Editor has made, is more perhaps than could be under any circumstances expected from a writer; but I beg you to believe that not one has been inconsiderately or capriciously made. The Editor bestowed the utmost care & attention on the article: Indeed we went over it together. It sometimes happens, however, that the very sentences which an Editor is tempted to expunge are those which a writer is the most reluctant to give up. I think that you will own that the spirit & design of your review are preserved inviolate. Let me know what you think of the whole No.

. . . I was particularly gratified with the way in which you take up Wordsworth's moral sentiments. . . . He cannot be offended, he ought to be *impressed*, with what you have advanced. The opening of the article struck me as very beautiful, & the whole, I think, will be highly interesting.

(*Ibid.*)

Montgomery's biographers note Wordsworth's reaction:

'Southey,' says Conder, in a note to Montgomery, 'showed your review
of the "Excursion" to Wordsworth, who was much pleased with it, and
desired him to convey to the author his sense of the very able and very
handsome manner in which the work was treated, and especially of the
spirit in which the criticism is written.'

(*Memoirs of the Life and Writings of James Montgomery*,
ed. John Holland and James Everett, 1856, III, 65)

But Dorothy Wordsworth, though sensible of Montgomery's 'profound
respect and admiration', was surprised that he said 'nothing of the versification', and thought that he spoke with more feeling in a private letter to
John Edwards (see *MY*, II, 214).

Who can behold this beautiful world, and imagine, for a moment,
that it was designed to be the abode of miserable beings? The
earth arrayed in verdure, adorned with flowers, diversified with hill
and dale, engirdled with the ocean, over-canopied with heaven; this
earth so smiling and fruitful, so commodious and magnificent, is
altogether worthy of its Maker, and not only a fit habitation for
Man, created in the image of God, but a place which Angels might
delight to visit on embassies of love. All nature, through all her forms
of existence, calls on man to rejoice with her in the goodness of
the universal Parent. The stars in their courses, the sun and moon in
their changes, by day and by night, display his glory; the seasons in
succession, the land and the waters, reciprocally, distribute his bounty;
every plant in its growth is pleasing to the eye, or wholesome for
food; every animal in health is happy in the exercise of its ordinary
functions; life itself is enjoyment. Yet in the heart of man there is
something which incapacitates *him* from the full fruition of the blessings
thus abundantly dealt around him: something which has introduced
disorder into his mind, and disease into the frame; darkening and
bewildering his intellect; corrupting and inflaming his passions; and
hurrying him by a fatality of impulse to that excess in every indulgence,
which turns aliment into poison, and from the perversion of the social
feelings produces strife, misery, and confusion to families, to nations,
to the world. What is it? It is sin! – This cannot have been in man
from the beginning, otherwise his Creator could not be a God of
holiness, order, and beneficence; nor would He have formed the universe

so excellently fair, and so admirably conducive to the felicity of its inhabitants.

It is true, that we are encompassed with perils from the elements, from accidents, and from the constitution of things; but waiving the inquiry how far these may be the consequences of sin, all the sorrows inflicted by 'the act of God,' in earthquakes, famine, pestilence and storms, are but a drop in the cup of bitterness which man has mingled for himself. Fallen then, as he is, from his primitive state, and shorn of her beauty, though far less in proportion, as nature may be, on account of his transgression, there are still in the human breast those high capacities of enjoyment, connected with improvement, which were his original inheritance; and still throughout the universe there are those forms of sublimity and grace which are calculated to awaken and gratify those capacities: yet, without a new birth, if we may borrow the figure, the noblest powers of the understanding and the imagination remain latent, or, at most, are only passive to receive impressions, not to solicit them, and still less to reproduce them in solitude by reflection. We know that the grossest of rational beings are unconsciously affected by the gaiety and grandeur that surround them in the scenery of morning or midnight, the elevation of mountains, the immensity of forests, the luxuriance of vegetable, and the variety of animal life; yet how much happier would they be if they *knew* their happiness, and *sought* it where they could never fail to find it, in every sight and every sound, melancholy or cheerful, terrible or soothing. Minds opened, refined, and ennobled by education, and led to communion with nature in quest of knowledge and pleasure, which stray hand in hand through all her walks, are prepared to meet the objects of their desire at 'all times and every where:' but hearts, regenerated by the Spirit of God, allied to minds thus expanded, are alone capable of exercising all the energies, and of enjoying all the privileges of the human soul in its intercourse with the visible creation, as the mirror of the power and perfections of Deity; or, rather, as '*the hiding of his power*,' the veil of glory which he has cast round the thick darkness wherein he dwells withdrawn from mortal sight, yet makes his presence felt, wherever there is motion, breath, or being.

It was one of the most captivating dreams of ancient philosophy, one of its infant dreams, for the earliest idolatry sprang from this source, – that there was a living Spirit in every orb of the universe; the sun, the moon, the stars, the earth itself, were conscious beings, acting and re-acting one on another by their respective influences. Superstition afterwards multiplied intelligences through the minor forms of nature,

419

and turned them all into divinities. Hence the sympathetic intercourse, which exalted understandings may hold with animate and inanimate things, as the effects of one great cause, was debased into a false religion, in which the devotees, by a direct inversion of what reason would teach on such a subject, worshipped objects inferior to themselves, creatures of God, or creatures of the imagination. Language itself in its origin was composed of pictures in words; things that *were* representing things that *were not*, and men spoke, as well as wrote, in hieroglyphics, before abstract terms and letters were invented. Poetry in all ages has retained the figures of primitive speech as its most graceful and venerable ornaments: hence its professors have invariably realized the dream of philosophy, and given souls, not only to the host of heaven, but to all the shapes and substances on earth. Mountains, trees, rivers, elements, &c. are personified, apostrophized, and made both the subjects and the objects of hope, fear, love, anger, revenge, and every human affection. With the multitude of poets these are only technical modes of expression employed to charm or astonish their readers; but with Mr. Wordsworth, the Author of the extraordinary volume before us, they are far otherwise. Common place prosopopœias he disdains to use; he has a poetical mythology of his own. He loves nature with a passion amounting almost to devotion; and he discovers throughout her works an omnipresent spirit, which so nearly resembles God in power and goodness, that it is sometimes difficult to distinguish the reverence which he pays to it, from the homage due to the Supreme alone. In proportion, all subordinate identities and phenomena, whether on the earth or in the sky, excite in him joy or wonder, corresponding to the character of simplicity or complexity, beauty or sublimity, inherent in them, and holding mysterious affinity with congenial qualities in the Poet's own soul. Hence, in the poems formerly published, he frequently divulged sensations of rapture, surprise, or admiration, unintelligible to vulgar minds; and avowed sympathies too profound for utterance, in the contemplation of every-day objects, which ordinary eyes pass over as mere matters of fact, no more demanding attention than a truism requires demonstration. Consequently, such passages provoked the scorn of superficial readers, and even incurred the heaviest censure of self-constituted critics in the highest place, solely because the poet, when most solemnly touched, either awakened ludicrous associations, or failed to present his peculiar ideas in such colours as to excite answering emotions in bosoms unaccustomed to feel and reflect after his manner. Few people would be sentimentally struck by the unexpected appearance 'of a host of dancing daffodils' on the margin of a lake, 'whose sparkling waves danced beside them;' and still fewer would carry away the image and treasure it up in memory for the occasional exhilaration of their private thoughts; yet Mr. Wordsworth, after fancifully describing such a merry dance of flowers and sunbeams on the waters, says,

[Quotes the last stanza of 'I wandered lonely as a cloud', *PW*, II, p. 217; *Poems 1807*, p. 224:

Oft when on my couch I lie . . .]

Perhaps every one who has been brought up in the country, the first time he hears the cuckoo in spring, is vividly reminded of the sports of his boyhood, by a sound so familiarly old, that he never remembers *not* to have heard it at that season of the year. None, however, except a poet of the most curious sensibility, who at once lives along the line of past existence, and can dwell on any part of it at pleasure, would be thrown into such a trance, at the call of the cuckoo, as to realize the scenes of infancy with raptures like the following: –

[Quotes the last two stanzas of 'To the Cuckoo', *PW*, II, p. 208; *Poems 1807*, p. 233:

I can listen to thee yet . . .
That is fit home for thee.]

All men, at least in imagination, love the light, the air, the freedom and the quiet of the hills, the woods, and the streams of retirement, incomparably more than the crowded streets, the murky atmosphere, and the prison-like walls of a populous city; but *he* must have an eye purified to behold invisible realities, that surround him like the horses and chariots of fire guarding the prophet and his servant, – and an ear opened to receive ineffable sounds, like the voice of the heavens when they are telling the glory of God, – who, with Mr. Wordsworth, in looking abroad on creation, can listen to 'the still sad music of humanity,' and perceive

A presence that disturbs him with the joy
Of elevated thoughts . . .

And rolls through all things.
['Tintern Abbey', *PW*, II, pp. 261–2, ll. 94–102;
LB (1798), p. 114, ll. 95–103]

Mr. Wordsworth often speaks in ecstatic strains of the pleasures of infancy. If we rightly understand him, he conjectures that the soul comes immediately from a world of pure felicity, when it is born into this troublous scene of care and vicissitude. He tells us, that 'our birth is but a sleep and a forgetting' of our antecedent state; that

> Trailing clouds of glory we do come
> From God who is our home.
>
> Heaven lies around us in our *infancy:* –

but 'the shades of the prison-house' begin to close on the *boy*; the *youth* travels further from this 'east,' yet still accompanied by the vision of diminishing splendour, till at length the *man* perceives it

> —die away
> Into the light of common day!

This brilliant allegory, (for such we must regard it,) is employed to illustrate the mournful truth, that looking back from middle age to the earliest period of remembrance, we find

> That there hath pass'd away a glory from the earth,

since the time, when every fresh object created wonder or delight, and every day's experience was an acquisition of knowledge, a discovery of power, a new kind of enjoyment: but this golden age is gone for ever, and

> —nothing can bring back the hour
> Of splendour in the grass, of glory in the flower.

Such is *Life*, – a gradual receding from beatitude to apathy, which nothing can re-quicken or illumine but the genial influences of nature, cheering, strengthening, and elevating the mind of her votaries. And what is *Death*? Hear it from a meditation on the demise of Mr. Fox.

> A power is passing from the earth
> To breathless nature's dread abyss;
> But when the Mighty pass away,
> What is it *more* than this,
> *That man, who is from God sent forth,*
> *Doth yet again to God return?*
> Such ebb and flow must ever be,
> Then wherefore should we mourn?
> ['Loud is the vale', *PW*, IV, p. 267, ll. 17–24;
> *Poems 1807*, p. 314, ll. 17–24]

The question in the last two lines needs no answer: to that in the four preceding ones we must reply distinctly: – 'It is appointed to men once to die, but *after this the* JUDGMENT.' Heb. ix. v. 27.

Intimations of sensibilities and opinions thus refined and recondite, abound in Mr. Wordsworth's former volumes, from which these extracts are taken; but in the work before us, the fruit of long labour, experience, and meditation, directed by sovereign genius, and executed with consummate skill, the principles and evidence of the Author's system of ethics, are splendidly, if not clearly and fully unfolded. Here we are taught, that communion with those forms of nature which excite no morbid passion, but which possess ineffable[3] affinities to the mind of man, so softens, controls, and exalts his feelings, that, – every asperity of temper being softened down into tranquillity, and every perverseness of reason subdued into willing obedience to truth; – he, whose soul is thus harmonized within itself, cannot choose but seek for objects of kindred love in natures resembling his own. Meanwhile, as the imagination is purified, and the affections are enlarged, the understanding is progressively enlightened, and the subject of this happy change, desiring that which is good, looks for it every where, and discovers it in every thing; till aversion, hatred, contempt, envy, and every malignant or disquieting passion cease to be known, except by name; or if the signs of them are discovered in others, they awaken only compassion, while nothing can abate or destroy the love of God, of Nature, and of Man. By this blissful converse of the human soul with 'the soul of things,' the former grows wiser and better of necessity, while it spontaneously surrenders itself to the moralizing influence of all external circumstances 'working together for good,' till

—whate'er we see,
Whate'er we feel, by agency direct
Or indirect shall tend to feed and nurse
Our faculties, shall fix in calmer seats
Of moral strength, and raise to loftier heights
Of love divine, our intellectual Soul!
[*The Excursion*, *PW*, V, pp. 149–50, Book IV, ll. 1270–5]

Moreover, the soul possesses the power of self-regeneration, and at her own will, by her own activity, in the process of this mystic intercourse with nature, can raise herself from profligacy and wretchedness to virtue and repose. This the Author has endeavoured to exemplify at great length, and with prodigious effect, in the history of one of his characters, *the Wanderer*, as well as to establish it by argumentation in the eloquent advice of that character to another, *the Solitary*, in the fourth book of this poem.

Two questions immediately arise out of the contemplation of this dazzling theory: – Is it *true*? Is it *all*? – True it undoubtedly *is* to a certain extent; but as undoubtedly it is *not all*, – *all* that is necessary to bring in, and constitute, and secure, happiness to man, at once a mortal and an immortal being. The love of Nature is the purest, the most sublime, and the sweetest emotion of the mind, of which the senses are the ministers; yet the love of Nature *alone* cannot ascend from earth to heaven, conducting us, as by the steps of Jacob's ladder, to the love of God; nor can it descend from heaven to earth, leading us by similar gradations to the universal love of Man; – otherwise it had not been necessary for Him, 'who thought it not robbery to be equal with God,' to take upon Himself 'the form of a servant,' and die 'the just for the unjust, that he might bring us to God by HIMSELF.' Every system of ethics which insists not on the extinction of sin in the human soul, by the only means through which sin can be extinguished, and everlasting righteousness substituted, is radically defective; and by whatever subtlety of reasoning, or force of language it may be sustained or recommended, it is a snare to him who receives it as sufficient, because excellent and unexceptionable as it may be, so far as it goes, it falls short of the extremity of a *sinner's* case, and '*all have sinned.*' We do not mean to infer, that Mr. Wordsworth excludes from his system the salvation of man, as revealed in the Scriptures, but it is evident that he has not made 'Jesus Christ the chief corner-stone' of it: otherwise, throughout this admirable poem, he would not so seldom, or, rather, so slightly have alluded to 'redemption in His blood.' The pastor of 'the church among the mountains' indeed, touches delightfully on the Christian's hopes on each side of the grave; but this is only in character, and *his* sentiments are *not* vitally connected with the system of *natural religion*, if we may call it so, which is developed in this poem. The sentiments of the Author, when he speaks in his own person, and of the Wanderer, who is his oracle, *are* connected with it; yet in the fourth book, where a misanthrope and sceptic is to be reclaimed, when there was not only an opportunity, but a necessity for believers in the Gospel to glorify its truths, by sending them home with conviction to the conscience of a sinner, they are rather tacitly admitted, than either avowed or urged; while the soul's own energy to restore itself to moral sanity, by meliorating intercourse with the visible creation, is set forth in strains of the most fervid eloquence, and the theme adorned with the most enchanting illustrations. Now *the Wanderer*

—had early learned
To reverence the Volume which displays
The mystery, the life which cannot die;
[*Ibid., PW*, V, p. 15, Book I, ll. 223–5]

and *the Author*, in the exordium of the sixth book, sufficiently proclaims his orthodoxy by a votive panegyric on the Church of England. If then salvation can be obtained only through faith in the sacrifice of Christ, according to that 'Volume' which the Wanderer reverenced, and according to the doctrines of that 'Church' which the Author acknowledges, how came the terrors of the Lord, and the consolations of His Spirit to make no part even of that discourse which these two zealous preachers of righteousness held with the unbeliever, at the time when his heart might be supposed most accessible to their influence, – when the arrow of Death had just passed *him* by, and slain at his feet one of the four beings, who were the whole human race to him in his little world of solitude? This is not a captious inquiry: we are sure that Mr. Wordsworth must have thought much on the subject; we would hope he thinks rightly. If he does not, we are sorry for his own sake, and not for his only, but for the sake of the thousands, in future generations, who may be his readers; for had the Gospel occasion to be recommended by 'the words which man's wisdom teacheth,' no one living is more eminently gifted for the purpose than Mr. Wordsworth. It is true, that the Gospel has *not* occasion to be thus recommended, yet on what theme can the greatest talents be better employed? It is the cant of ignorance to say, that the truths of religion are unsuitable themes for poetry of the highest order, for then were they unsuitable themes for the harp of David, and for the songs of Angels. It is the cant of scepticism, to say that genius is debased by evangelical notions, and that all sacred poetry must needs be akin to the strains of Sternhold and Hopkins: – Milton and Cowper have rescued these subjects from so ill-founded, so inane a charge. The discussion of this topic would however carry us too far. Mr. Wordsworth *could* so sing of Christ's kingdom, if it has indeed come into his heart, as would for ever set the question at rest; and we hope that in the promised prelude or sequel to this volume, he *will*. 'A Philosophical Poem, containing Views of *Man, Nature*, and *Society*,' would be miserably imperfect if it involved no contemplations on the *eternal* destiny of man. Nature may indeed teach her worshipper, by reason and analogy, that in a future state the good must be happy; but neither reason nor analogy will justify the presumption that the wicked *can* be so. What becomes then of man, when, to use the poet's own phrase, borrowed from Scripture, he who came from God

> doth yet again to God return?
> ['Loud is the vale', *PW*, IV, p. 267, l. 22; *Poems 1807*,
> p. 314, l. 22]

Mr Wordsworth must have been haunted in his retirement by this inquiry, and it is not conceivable that he can have contented himself with a doubtful answer to it. A poet, who seems all eye when he sees, all ear when he listens, all intellect when he reasons, all sensibility when he is touched, cannot have been indifferently affected by the awful burthen of that revelation from God, the authenticity of which he allows, and in the meaning of which *he* must feel himself as deeply interested, as if all the threatenings of the law, and all the promises of the Gospel, were addressed personally to him, and to him alone. We long, therefore, to learn his 'sensations and opinions' on this subject, for we are not satisfied with the scanty intimations of them scattered through this volume. On other subjects we are willing to pay to Mr. Wordsworth, the homage due to his exalted genius, and on this we are anxious to have an opportunity of listening to him with equal deference. But once for all, we must avow our conviction, that 'the moral system' of any man professing Christianity, which does not include, as its immortal principle, 'redemption through the blood of Christ,' is inconsistent with the Author's own creed; and however glorious or beautiful in appearance, it will prove a pageant as unsubstantial as Prospero's vision, which, even while it is contemplated, will vanish, and

> Leave not a rack behind.

After these long preliminaries, which we have introduced to avoid much obscurity and digression hereafter, we shall briefly – we lament that we can only briefly – advert to the contents of this volume.

'*The Excursion*,' it appears, is only 'a portion of a Poem,' and belongs to the second part of a long and laborious work, which is to consist of three parts. This section is published first, because it refers 'more to passing events, and to an existing state of things, than the others were meant to do;' nor does it 'depend on the preceding' so much as to injure its particular interest. The whole work is to be entitled 'THE RECLUSE,' being 'a philosophical Poem, containing views of Man, Nature, and Society;

and having for its principal Subject the sensations and opinions of a Poet living in retirement.' We are further informed, that the Author has written a preparatory piece, which is 'biographical, and conducts the history of his mind to the point, when he was emboldened to hope that his faculties were sufficiently matured for entering upon the arduous labour' of constructing '*a literary work that might live.*' We love to pry curiously into the secrets of a human heart; and since no living Author affords such familiar and complete access to his heart as Mr. Wordsworth does, we rejoice in every opportunity of visiting and exploring its inexhaustible riches of thought, imagery, and sentiment. How these were originally discovered, and how they have been gradually accumulated, we are desirous of knowing; and it is earnestly to be wished, by all his admirers, that he will not withhold from them so reasonable a gratification, as this introductory poem has been long finished.

The preface to '*The Excursion*' concludes with an extract from the preceding portion of the Poem, in which the Author commences his plan, and invokes celestial aid.

[Quotes 'The Excursion', *PW*, V, pp. 3–4, Prospectus, ll. 25–41:

> —Urania, I shall need
> Thy guidance, or a greater Muse . . .
> . . . when we look
> Into our Minds, into the Mind of Man,
> My haunt, and the main region of my Song.]

We have said, that Mr. Wordsworth discerns throughout Nature an omnipresent Spirit, and that it is sometimes difficult to distinguish the reverence which he pays to it, from the homage due to God alone. In the following lines we do not clearly comprehend who is 'the prophetic spirit,' and who 'the dread power;' whether they are two or one; – a creature of the imagination, or the Creator himself; or whether the first be not the creature of imagination, and the second the Creator. If 'the dread power' means *not* God, it is difficult to imagine how the Author can justify the language which immediately follows that phrase, as addressed to any other being.

[Quotes *ibid.*, *PW*, V, pp. 5–6, Prospectus, ll. 83–107:

> – Come thou prophetic Spirit, that inspir'st
> The human Soul of universal earth,
> Dreaming on things to come . . .
> so shall thy unfailing love
> Guide, and support, and cheer me to the end?]

427

Nothing can be more artless than the narrative, or externally more unpretending than the characters of '*The Excursion*;' nor would any thing be more easy (according to the fashionable practice of reviewers) than, with that insidious candour, which tells the truth so as to insinuate a lie, and secure a false impression, to detail the story, and exhibit the persons in such a manner as to cast unmerited ridicule both on the Author and on his subject. With us, however, it is no self-denial to forego the occasion of attempting to shine at the expense of genius such as Mr. Wordsworth's. Selecting men of low estate, and incidents of every-day occurrence, he throws around both such a colouring of imagination as to exalt them far above the stalking heroes, and monstrous adventures of romance. His powers are peculiar; his descriptions, his figures, his similes, and his reflections, are all homogeneous and *unique*. He writes almost as if he had never read, and while he unperceivedly avails himself of the experience and wisdom of others, he seems to utter only his own observations from his own knowledge. Corresponding with this originality of mind, he has invented a style more intellectual than that of any of his contemporaries, and in contradiction to his own theory, (See the Preface to Lyrical Ballads, &c.) as different from the most energetic language of ordinary minds in excitement, as the strain of his argument is elevated above vulgar reasoning. Hence this poem is not more distinguished by depth, compass, and variety of speculation, than by exquisite choice of ornament, and inimitably appropriate diction. The poet possesses the rare felicity of seizing the evanescent forms of thought, at any moment of their change, and fixing them in any point of view, in phraseology so perfect, that the words seem rather the thoughts themselves made palpable, than the symbols of thoughts. No difficulty of mastering his conceptions ever discourages him from attempting the full expression of them; he resolutely faces his subject, fastens on it, wrestles with it, and never quits it till he has won his whole purpose. This may be the true secret of his superiority; others, his equals perhaps in genius, are sooner weary of labour, or impatient of delay, and content themselves with less than the highest attainable reward; Mr. Wordsworth seems always to do his best; he is not satisfied with conquering, he must also triumph. We will offer one example of his success in subduing a most untractable thought, and enriching himself with its spoils.

> —I have seen
> A curious Child, who dwelt upon a tract
> Of inland ground, applying to his ear

    The convolutions of a smooth-lipped Shell;
    To which, in silence hushed, his very soul
Listened intensely; and his countenance soon
Brightened with joy; for murmurings from within
Were heard, – sonorous cadences! whereby,
To his belief, the Monitor expressed
Mysterious union with its native Sea.
Even such a Shell the Universe itself
Is to the ear of Faith; and there are times,
I doubt not, when to You it doth impart
Authentic tidings of invisible things:
Of ebb and flow, and ever-during power;
And central peace, subsisting at the heart
Of endless agitation. Here you stand,
Adore, and worship, when you know it not;
Pious beyond the intention of your thought;
Devout above the meaning of your will.
          [*Ibid.*, *PW*, V, p. 145, Book IV, ll. 1132–50]

We doubt whether any other living writer could have so gracefully presented the image, or so sublimely applied it to elucidate a mysterious subject.

In love there is a certain charm, which renders all things lovely to the eye or the fancy of the lover: the beauty, which he follows with fondness, leaves its light on every object where it has shone. Some such ineffable spell Mr. Wordsworth possesses; the meanest circumstances he raises into dignity; to the homeliest features he communicates grace; whatever, in 'Nature, Man, or Society,' was indifferent to us before, becomes interesting and romantic, when it comes under his notice. He says, in his introduction,

    Beauty, – a living Presence of the earth,
    Surpassing the most fair ideal Forms,
    Which craft of delicate Spirits hath composed
    From earth's materials – waits upon my steps . . .
    . . .

    For the discerning intellect of Man,
    When wedded to this goodly universe
    In love and holy passion shall find these
    A simple produce of the common day.
          [*Ibid.*, *PW*, V, p. 4, Prospectus, ll. 42–55]

Neither is our praise extravagant, nor is this boasting of the Poet self del-usion. The reader who is not affected in the manner we have intimated, will be but very slightly affected by the tenderness, the tranquillity, and the grandeur united, which give inexpressible repose amidst animation, to the scenes and the sentiments of this poem.

On a summer forenoon, the Author walks across a common to a ruined cottage, in a grove, where he meets an ancient friend, of whom he gives some account. This personage, who is distinguished by the appellation of '*The Wanderer*,' was born in Scotland, of poor parents; but having received the rudiments of a plain education, and feeling within himself the motions of a mighty Spirit, that would not let him take root in his native mountain, he becomes one of those travelling merchants – a race now almost extinct – who were wont to carry their shops on their backs, and who were familiarly known in the north of England, by the name of 'Scotchmen.' These itinerants performed their stated rounds as regularly as the seasons, passing from village to village, and calling on families, whom they furnished with drapery and other small wares for use or finery. It was one of the most daring experiments in modern poetry, to make a *quondam* Pedlar the hero of 'a literary work, that might live;' and we will venture to say it has been one of the most successful. Our readers will observe with what ease the Poet lifts him above his mean estate, and invests him with that moral and intellectual dignity, which is not hereditary in the palaces of Princes, but which Nature, or rather the God of Nature, in his sovereign bounty, bestows on select individuals, few in number, remote in locality, distant in time, and scattered through every rank of life.

[Quotes *ibid.*, *PW*, V, ll. 118–62, Book I, pp. 12–13 and pp. 14–15, Book I, ll. 198–218:

> From his sixth year, the Boy of whom I speak,
> In summer, tended cattle on the Hills . . .
> He traced an ebbing and a flowing mind,
> Expression ever varying!
>
> O then what soul was his, when, on the tops
> Of the high mountains . . .
>   it was blessedness and love!]

The manner in which a being, so spiritualized by communion with Nature, profited by his connexion with the world of society, is thus shewn.
[Quotes *ibid.*, *PW*, V, pp. 20–1, Book I, ll. 340–81:

From his native hills
He wandered far . . .
As makes the nations groan.]

Having obtained a small competence, he withdrew from the drudgery of
business; yet still in the summer months, he loved to haunt the paths
which he formerly trod, and journeyed far, – revisiting the scenes to
memory endeared.

His person is thus picturesquely delineated.

Plain his garb
Such as might suit a rustic sire, prepared
For sabbath duties; yet he was a Man
Whom no one could have passed without remark.
Active and nervous was his gait; his limbs
And his whole figure breathed intelligence.
Time had compressed the freshness of his cheek
Into a narrower circle of deep red
But had not tamed his eye; that under brows
Shaggy and grey had meanings which it brought
From years of youth; which, like a Being made
Of many Beings, he had wondrous skill
To blend with knowledge of the years to come,
Human, or such as lie beyond the grave.

[*Ibid.*, *PW*, V, pp. 22–3, Book I, ll. 420–33]

Contemplating this portraiture, we would ask, – Was there ever such a
man formed under such circumstances? and we have no hesitation in
answering – There was not. Mr. Wordsworth's Wanderer is a character
as ideal as Homer's Achilles. The Poet indeed speaks of him as as 'a
being made of many beings;' and assuredly he is *one* made of *two*: – a
man of toil, endowed with the sensibilities, and made wise by the experience, ascribed to the Wanderer, with the learning and refinement of the
Author, a man of leisure, superadded: for Mr. Wordsworth himself, had
he been born in the same sphere, and passed through the same proba-
tion, could never have been more than half the magnificent and venerable being, which his fine imagination has here conceived and bodied
forth. But if this paragon have no prototype in individual man, it has
perfect ideal existence, and therefore poetical reality. It resembles Nature
as the Belvidere Apollo, and the Venus de Medici resemble her, being
defective only in *wanting the defects* of every model of living excellence.

431

With this companion the Author proceeds on 'The Excursion;' and, by the way, the Wanderer relates the history of the former tenant of the ruined cottage; – one instance of that slow and heart-consuming misery which thousands have suffered, during the last twenty years of war, and, in many cases, with aggravated horrors; for though a more pathetic tale than this before us was never told, the effect is produced by innumerable little touches, which imperceptibly work up the picture to the consummation of wretchedness.

The pleasure and independence of *walking*, were perhaps never more worthily celebrated than in the subjoined clause.

> The Wealthy, the Luxurious, by the stress
> Of business roused, or pleasure, ere their time,
> May roll in chariots, or provoke the hoofs
> Of the fleet coursers they bestride, to raise,
> From earth the dust of morning, slow to rise;
> And They, if blessed with health and hearts at ease,
> Shall lack not their enjoyment: – but how faint,
> Compared with our's! who, pacing side by side,
> Could with an eye of leisure look on all
> That we beheld; and lend the listening sense
> To every grateful sound of earth and air,
> Pausing at will; our spirits braced, our thoughts
> Pleasant as roses in the thickets blown,
> And pure as dew bathing their crimson leaves.
> [*Ibid., PW*, V, p. 45, Book II, ll. 97–110]

On the last two of these lines we may remark, that some similes have only an abstract affinity to the things with which they may be combined. These are rarely used by secondary poets, and little understood by careless readers, for they include the most refined and spiritual resemblances. They may be classed with the ideas of the blind concerning objects of vision: – thus one compared the colour of scarlet to the sound of a trumpet; and another supposed the splendour of the sun to be like the intense smoothness of a convex mirror. To *feel* the propriety of these curious conceptions, *we* must imagine, – what indeed we can very imperfectly imagine, – the exquisite sense of hearing and delicacy of touch, which almost compensate the loss of sight to persons born blind. He must have a dull spirit, who, on these things being pointed out, cannot perceive their correspondence; but to discover them is one of the transcendent prerogatives of genius.

In the adjacent glen the Wanderer introduces the Poet to another personage, who is designated '*The Solitary*.' He also is a North Briton, and had been engaged in the Christian ministry; but having lost an amiable wife, and both his children, he became a prey to melancholy, from which he was roused into a temporary frenzy of political zeal for the rights of man, by the shock of the French Revolution. Discovering his error in the disappointment of his hopes, he renounced his sacred function, and with it his faith: and after seeking rest but finding none, either at home or abroad, he has abandoned himself to misanthropy and scepticism, and lives in sullen retirement from the world, with a single family, consisting of four persons, the sole inhabitants of a secluded valley. This unhappy mortal tells his own distressing tale, and gives bitter vent to his despondency: the Wanderer reproves that despondency, and holds out to him motives and means of felicity. Here the Author has put forth all his strength, and it was to this conversation especially, that we alluded in the preamble to this article. The Sceptic twice asks questions concerning the way of salvation revealed in the Scriptures, and in neither case does he receive a direct answer. Describing his unappeasable anguish of spirit during a voyage to America

[Quotes *ibid.*, *PW*, V, p. 105, Book III, ll. 861–9:

> within the cabin stood,
> That Volume . . .
> And by his Nature's ignorance, dismayed.]

Another time, 'in rueful tone, with some impatience in his mien,' he demands,

> —shall the groaning Spirit cast her load,
> At the Redeemer's feet?
> [*Ibid.*, *PW*, V, p. 144, Book IV, ll. 1099–100]

The sum of all the prodigality of eloquent arguments, poured forth by the Wanderer, in reply to the Solitary, comprehending reproof, instruction, and exhortation, amounts to little more than a prescription of air and exercise, and the contemplation of nature, whereby health of body and peace of mind may be restored! If the patient were a mere hypochondriac, devoured by spleen, or overwhelmed with temporal calamity, this advice might perhaps be sufficient; but a 'wounded spirit,' a guilty conscience, 'an evil heart of unbelief,' cannot be healed by the breezes, purified by the streams, or regenerated by the light of the morning. Our limits absolutely preclude us from entering upon any analysis of this most animated division of the poem, which wants nothing but an honest exposition of the *Christian faith*, in addition to accounts of 'the *Jewish, Persian, Babylonian, Chaldean, and Grecian modes of belief*,' to constitute it the most perfect strain of moral poetry in the English, or perhaps in any language. But wanting this 'one thing,' – this 'one thing needful,' – all the glories of philosophy, though displayed with unparalleled splendour, vanish like a florid sunset, leaving the forlorn and disconsolate sinner wandering in darkness, and *still* crying, – 'What shall I do to be saved?'

The following delineation of the contrasted griefs of the Solitary and his Wife, on the sudden loss of their children, may disdain eulogy, and defy censure.

[Quotes *ibid.*, *PW*, V, pp. 99–100, Book III, ll. 650–705:

>   Calm as a frozen Lake when ruthless Winds . . .
>   Only by records in myself not found.]

The origin of Grecian fables is thus elegantly imagined.

[Quotes *ibid.*, *PW*, V, pp. 136–7, Book IV, ll. 851–87:

>   – In that fair Clime, the lonely Herdsman . . .
>   or Pan himself,
>   The simple Shepherd's awe-inspiring God.]

The Poet and his two companions afterwards visit a 'Church Yard among the mountains,' where meeting with 'the Pastor,' he, at their request, records the names and worth of several persons, who lie buried there. These 'short and simple annals of the poor,' – short in detail, and simple in occurrence, – are rendered exceedingly attractive, as well as dignified, by the rich and harmonious style in which they are told; and by many readers they will undoubtedly be deemed the most delightful portions of the work. We must be sparing of quotation. The subsequent remarks on contemplating the epitaphs in a Church yard, though sufficiently obvious, may claim the merit of novelty.

[Quotes *ibid.*, *PW*, V, p. 206, Book VI, ll. 630–45:

>   I, for my part,
>   Though with the silence pleased . . .
>   Of amity and gratitude.]

We will not give utterance to a very harsh suspicion, which almost inevitably obtrudes itself, while we are considering the uniform language of panegyric, which tomb-stones are taught to speak; but we may observe, that if the world of the living resembled the world of the dead, in piety and virtue, this earth would only be a nursery for heaven.

A termagant Woman, of masculine intellect, but sordid views, is thus represented in her last hours.

[Quotes *ibid.*, *PW*, V, pp. 210–11, Book VI, ll. 741–77:

A sudden illness seized her . . .
Though, in this Vale, remembered with deep awe?]

The tale of poor '*Ellen*,' will not yield in tender or tragic interest to any one of the innumerable stories of seduction and desertion, which abound in prose and rhyme. We can only select one beautiful incident, which reads as if it were a real one.

[Quotes *ibid.*, *PW*, V, pp. 214–15, Book VI, ll. 862–93:

—Beside the Cottage in which Ellen dwelt . . .
Bedropped with tears.]

The history of the Priest, who emigrated with his family, like a band of gipsies, from Northumberland, and dwelt in a neighbouring hamlet, is very lively and striking. After a residence of forty years at the rustic parsonage, they all went down to the grave in half of that number of months.

[Quotes *ibid.*, *PW*, V, pp. 238–41, Book VII, ll. 242–91:

Our very first in eminence of years . . .
Were gathered to each other.']

We never met with a more gentle image of Death than the passing cloud: – nor with a more peaceful image of life than in the 'Deaf Man.'

[Quotes *ibid.*, *PW*, V, p. 244, Book VII, ll. 399–427:

There, beneath
A plain blue Stone . . .
Nor husband's love, nor father's hope or care.]

We are reluctantly compelled to refrain from further quotations here. It would be a curious, and not an uninstructive amusement to compare Mr. Wordsworth's Villagers with Mr. Crabbe's, (particularly in the Parish Register,) and with the few which Cowper has sketched in the Task. Crabbe gives low life with all its meanness and misery; Cowper paints it with sprightly freedom as the familiar friend of the Poor; Wordsworth casts over it a pensive hue of thought, that softens its asperities, and heightens its charms, without diminishing its verisimilitude.

From the Church Yard the Pedestrians accompany the Pastor to his home. Much conversation is held by the way on the consequences of manufactures being spread over the face of the country, instead of being confined to a few districts or towns. This subject of course elicits many melancholy, and some noble truths from the golden lips of the Wanderer. The Pastor's family are depicted in such captivating colours, that, as we cannot give the groupe at full length, we shall leave them to the reader's imagination, till he can see them in the book itself. After being hospitably entertained during the heat of the day, the Poet's party in the evening, accompany the Pastor's family, in an excursion on the lake. On their return after sunset, standing on an elevated spot, a vision of glory opens around them, which is thus described.

[Quotes *ibid.*, *PW*, V, p. 306, Book IX, ll. 590–608:

> Already had the sun . . .
> Repeated; but with unity sublime!]

Amid this solemn and magnificent scene, which seems to open the heavens above and around them, the pious Pastor breaks forth into spontaneous prayer. We must conclude our extracts with the opening.

[Quotes *ibid.*, *PW*, V, pp. 307–8, Book IX, ll. 614–46:

> Eternal Spirit! universal God! . . .
> To have a nearer view of Thee, in heaven.]

The company afterwards proceed to the parsonage; the Solitary takes leave at the door; the Poet and the Wanderer remain for the night. Thus '*the Excursion*' is *not* finished; and the Author gives us ground to hope for a sequel; but whether that sequel is to be the third part of the whole Poem, or a second part of this second part, is not quite obvious. At any rate we have to expect two further portions of '*The Recluse*;' and that they will equal this specimen is as much as we dare hope, while we cannot doubt it. Life, however, is short, and the Author may not live to accomplish his task. – Life is short, and many who read this volume may never see another. Mr. Wordsworth did not miscalculate his powers, when he began to compose this 'literary work;' – it *will* live. – It has increased the interest which we always felt in the life and well being of the Author, and the hope of seeing the consummation of the plan is among our most pleasing anticipations.

EDITOR'S NOTES

1. *Roderick* (1814).
2. Probably Cornelius Neale, author of the poem, *Mustapha*.

3. Montgomery had 'inexpressive', and protested at the alteration. See MS. Letter, Conder to Montgomery, 16 January 1815, the Central Library, Sheffield.

151.

Unsigned notice introducing a series of long extracts, *Monthly Magazine*, 30 January 1815, supplement to vol. XXXVIII, 638–49

We here introduce our readers to one of the best poems of this age. The extracts will, we presume, justify this opinion. If any of our readers differ from us, it can only be in regard to the sombre cast of the author's muse, which does not accord alike with every taste; to the mysticism of his theology in which he vainly endeavours to combine certain points of faith with human reason; and to his political sentiments, wherein, in subserviency to popular prejudice, he mistakes cause and effect, and confounds agent and patient. But in the general construction and tone of his poem it is scarcely possible that one reader of sensibility can lay it aside ere he has finished it, or arise from the perusal without feeling the warmest admiration of the amiable character, profound views, and sterling genius of the Author.

152. John Herman Merivale (1779–1844)

Unsigned review, *Monthly Review*, February 1815, LXXVI, 123–36

Merivale, like Denman, his friend from college days (see entry 34), was a considerable contributor to the *Monthly*. This review, revealing dependence upon that in the *Quarterly*, seems to have been written under pressure; Merivale wrote to his father on 18 December 1814:

Here is Charlemagne lying on my bookcase, and, with the greatest avidity to read it, I have snatched at short intervals two or three cantos only out of twenty. There is *Don Roderick* [Southey's *Roderick*, 1814] similarly situated. There is Wordsworth's interminable Poem only just entered upon – here is a review of Salt [*Voyage to Abyssinia*, 1814]

positively promised by a day appointed and yet unfinished. There is an equally positive promise to Gifford [the editor of the *Quarterly*] . . . '
(*Family Memorials*, Anna W. Merivale, Exeter, 1884, 179–80)

Our opinion of the poetical character of Mr. Wordsworth has been freely expressed on more than one occasion; and, although we are aware that we shall be exposed to the charge of *perverseness*, (which is shared with us by a tolerably large majority of poetical readers,) we cannot persuade ourselves to retract that opinion, after a painful and laborious investigation of the volume now before us. Most of our readers, probably, are apprized of the objection made by the admirers of Mr. Wordsworth to every unfavourable judgment passed on his former productions; viz. that such judgment must necessarily be founded on a partial and imperfect view of the case, because the materials from which it was formed were only the disjointed members of a complete but hitherto undeveloped system; and that it was therefore the duty of candid criticism to keep its sentence in suspence until the final disclosure of that system. We will not now stay to contend that this plea is in itself frivolous and untenable, or that, from the moment at which an author chuses to lay himself before the public, he must submit to be judged by that public according to the nature of the case which he has himself made out for their inspection; – and we will confess that the argument, however false, had been so repeatedly pressed on us as to have rendered us perhaps more than duly anxious in our expectations of the promised development: – but, from this time forwards, the argument, such as it is, can never be repeated. A series of verses amounting to nearly 10,000, even though it may form but a portion of a portion of an intended whole, is by much too weighty a matter to be considered in the light of a mere branch, or stray twig, or unimportant excrescence; and, even from the manner in which Mr. Wordsworth announces it, we imagine that neither he himself nor any of his friends can intend that it should be taken otherwise than as that entire and conclusive exposition of his poetical creed, for which we have been so often and authoritatively required to wait in humble expectation.

[Summarises the poem, and notes that Book V is the 'most diversified, and (if the term be not altogether inapplicable) the most amusing part of the poem.]

We do not object to the subjects themselves; which, if not wholly original, afford ample scope both to the descriptive and the didactic genius of the writer. Neither do we quarrel with the characters, or interlocutors of the drama, since they are very suitable to the topics introduced, with the exception of 'The Wanderer.' Nor is our objection to this last-named personage founded on the unpoetical, or undignified, station of life from which he is selected; nor should we (as some ingenious friends of Mr. Wordsworth suggest) be better satisfied with him were he called a *pilgrim*, or a *palmer*, instead of a *pedlar*. If any reader, even with 'Heron's Tour in Scotland'* by his side, can make up his mind to believe that a pedlar would, in his ordinary conversation, use such language as Mr. Wordsworth puts into the mouth of this honest brother of the scrip and wallet, *Pedlar* let him remain, in good sooth: but, till it has been our fortune to meet such another, we cannot place implicit faith in his existence. We allege no fault against the remaining companions of our excursion. 'The Solitary,' on the contrary, is a character well imagined as the vehicle of introducing the moral and philosophical creed of the author; and 'The Pastor' may surely, if any one can, be considered as fitted to the discussion of such high and mystic flights of natural theology as those in which the poet chuses to indulge his imagination.

Proceed we now to the execution of this fearful 'Portion' of a poem. It is in large what the former productions of the same author were in little; only that (speaking *generally* of its comparative merits) it has much less of infantine simplicity, without gaining in nerve that which it has lost in prettiness of feature. Yet the stamp of a poetical mind is throughout apparent; and nobody can refuse to Mr. Wordsworth the possession of those innate qualities of genius which it is even out of his own power wholly to conceal. Still less can he be denied, what all who have ever heard his name pronounced are taught to associate with it, those high moral and intellectual faculties which he constantly enlists in the service of his muse. In this last respect, he does indeed resemble the great pattern of his imitation, Milton; although, in some other points, he may fall far short of such a prototype: – but, having said so much, we have said all; and, brilliant as are the occasional flashes of a genius which no weight of pedantry or of affectation can entirely suppress or extinguish, they serve only to throw light enough on the dark, heavy, confused heaps of nothingness through which they burst, to make us feel more painfully the comparison between the powers given and the purposes to which they have been applied.

The prevailing doctrine of Mr. Wordsworth's poetical system is that of a soul animating and informing all nature; and, not contented with this

---

* Mr. Wordsworth refers to this book, in a note, for his justification of the learned and philosophical pedlar in question.

generalized exposition of the creed in question, he extends it to every individual object, with such constant and unvarying minuteness that not a stream sparkles to the sun, not a leaf trembles to the breeze, not a torrent descends from the hills, not a cloud settles on the brow of a mountain, but stream, sun, leaf, breeze, torrent, hill, cloud, and mountain's brow are sure to be animated at once, as with the touch of Harlequin's wand, and endued with powers of sensation and reflection equal to those that are enjoyed by the poet, or by the most refined and intellectual of his readers. It is true that the poetical world talked much some years ago about *the Loves of the Plants*; – true that we have heard of Dodona's grove, and Tasso's enchanted forest; – and that, in the bold language of eastern metaphor, the little hills are represented as dancing with joy: – but Mr. Wordsworth disdains metaphor and fable. That which he describes is set forth in the colours of reality, not of fiction; – in the language of a devout and sincere believer; – like the honest Swedenborgian, who would stop short in the middle of the street in order to make a bow to St. Paul, and to shake hands with the Prophet Elijah. We will not dispute whether this be strength or weakness of mind; nor whether, if weakness, it be or be not a fortunate weakness for the poet: but we must say that, whether strength or weakness, it is most unfortunate to the reader who is not prepared by a similar process of conversion for a similar reach of mysticism; and we shall not hesitate to declare that, to our duller comprehensions, many fine passages of descriptive poetry are utterly spoiled, and rendered unintelligible, useless, and even disgusting, by the suspicion of affectation which is engendered by this mania. We give the following lines, (which occur almost at the beginning of the poem) by way of example: [Quotes *The Excursion*, *PW*, V, pp. 12–13, Book I, ll. 118–62, and pp. 14–16, Book I, ll. 185–243:

> From his sixth year, the boy of whom I speak,
> Expression ever varying! –
>
> In his heart
> Where fear sate thus, a cherished visitant . . .
> And with a superstitious eye of love.]

In another part of the poem, this doctrine is illustrated by a singular comparison; which we do not mean to censure for lowness, a comparison not being necessarily low because it is familiar: but, on the contrary, if it presents to any reader a more distinct image of that which it is designed to make manifest than it has furnished to us, we shall deem it intitled to great applause on account of its apparent closeness and felicity.

[Quotes *ibid.*, *PW*, V, pp. 144–5, Book IV, ll. 1126–50:

—Access for you . . .
Devout above the meaning of your will.]

So intimately is this mystic principle connected with, and so closely does it pervade, the whole structure of the poem, that it is scarcely possible to turn to any one of the subjects to which it refers without finding it introduced in some form, and, generally speaking, with as little variety as can be well imagined. No doubt, Mr. Wordsworth has higher and nobler aims in his poetry than the mere gratification of his reader's senses; – and indeed the lofty interest and importance of his objects are sufficiently apparent from the summary, with extracts from which we commenced our present remarks. The very passage, also, which we last selected, forms a portion of the correctives of despondency which are announced as the purpose of the fourth book, and presents an illustration of the general scope of argument adduced to combat 'want of faith in the great truths of religion.' Mr. Wordsworth, however, might have borrowed more suitable weapons from the armouries of Hooker or Barrow; and, without deciding whether his effusions be such as to stamp on the opinions and sentiments which they unfold more of 'the character of an expanded and generous quakerism,' or 'of a kind of natural methodism,' we will venture to suggest that neither mysticism nor enthusiasm is the best conductor of misguided mortals back to the precincts of a calm and rational religion.

The originality of Mr. Wordsworth is assumed by a certain class of critics as a matter out of all question; and, as far as the attribute is confined to a certain peculiarity of diction and manner, we believe that it may be correctly ascribed: but, in point of sentiment, (we know that we are broaching an unpardonable heresy, yet we say that, in point of sentiment,) almost all that is not too mystical to be comprehended is too common-place to be tolerated, were it not hidden under a multiplicity of words and phrases, and disguised by those outward peculiarities at which we have just hinted as, in fact, constituting the whole essence of the poet's claim to the great quality now in question. We will not fatigue ourselves and our readers by multiplying quotations in support of so general an assertion, the truth or falsehood of which must necessarily depend not on any detached passages, however numerous or impartially chosen, but on the entire poem.

Nevertheless, we have admitted that, in common (we believe) with all who are capable of feeling true poetry, we are strongly impressed with the conviction that Mr. Wordsworth is himself a true poet; and, saying this after a condemnation apparently sweeping in its effect, it may perhaps be asked in what we hold the evidence of his native powers to consist? We answer, then, that we discover them in the occasional touches of a master's pencil, in the bright but transient gleams of a powerful imagination, in the workings of a fine and high-wrought sensibility, and in that ardent and devoted attachment, that indescribable yearning of the heart, to the grand and beautiful works of the creation, which can exist in full force only in the breast of a poet. It is in the very excess of these feelings, and in the unbounded indulgence of them to the utter exclusion of that intercourse with society, – that habitual collision with the sentiments and opinions of the age, – which is absolutely requisite to keep an enthusiastic mind within the confines of sound and temperate judgment, that a very large proportion of the author's errors and excentricities may perhaps be found. – To return; we are almost as much at a loss to select particular instances of Mr. Wordsworth's beauties as of his defects. They are so infused into each other, that any single page, taken at random, would in some degree answer the purpose; while much more copious and extensive quotations, than we are at liberty to make, would fail to produce the complete effect which we should wish to place before our readers. Perhaps the mode in which this object could be most nearly accomplished, through the medium of a review, would be by selecting the whole of one of his most interesting narratives from the poetical parish-register to which we have before alluded: but, while many of them abound in pathos, and are marked with strong touches both of natural and moral painting, all are unreasonably diffuse and wearisomely pedantic; and none will easily admit of being contracted within the limits that we are obliged to prescribe to ourselves. The extracts which we have already given, however, furnish abundant traces of those powers which we wish to display; and, as a farther proof that even the encumbrance of a false and extravagant system is insufficient to repress the native energies of the mind which gave birth to it, we have only to add other passages of a similar design and tendency.

[Quotes *ibid.*, *PW*, V, pp. 66–7, Book II, ll. 688–725

> In genial mood . . .
> Here do I sit and watch.]

The following are samples of more unexceptionable poetry:
[Quotes *ibid.*, *PW*, V, p. 84, Book III, ll. 299–324, and pp. 293–4, Book IX, ll. 206–54:

—Deities that float . . .
Night hush'd as night, and day serene as day! –

Alas! what differs more than man from man! . . .
So wide a difference betwixt man and man.]

It will not be easily imagined that the peculiar quality, to which our countrymen have agreed in affixing the appellation of 'Humour,' can, under any form or modification, be attributed to Mr. Wordsworth; and, accordingly, in the only instance in which we are aware of his having attempted any thing like it, his failure is pre-eminent. In this respect, he is not to be compared with Cowper, whom in many other points he may be thought to resemble; for Cowper was, undoubtedly, gifted by nature with a very considerable portion of the talent to which we are now referring.

One word must be said, before we conclude, on the subject of versification; – and we have left ourselves no room for more than a word, though, perhaps, a long discussion may be expected from us. Notwithstanding much disfigurement, arising from his inveterate affectation, we are on the whole disposed to consider the blank verse of Mr. Wordsworth as one of the nearest approaches that has yet been made to the majesty of Milton. The preceding extracts will afford our readers ample opportunity of determining whether our judgment be correct. We wish that Mr. W. would condescend to the imitation of his mighty master in points of yet higher importance!

153. John Taylor Coleridge

Unsigned review, *British Critic*, May 1815, III (2nd series), 449–67[1]

The review echoes phrases from J. T. Coleridge's first published comments in the *Quarterly*, April 1814 (see entry 108). Dorothy Wordsworth noted coolly on 28 June 1815, 'I have seen the British Critic which contains a Review by a Friend of the Coleridges' which between ourselves I think a very feeble composition. It was highly praised to me' (*MY* II, 243). Wordsworth invited J.T. Coleridge to meet him for dinner at Sir George Beaumont's London house, on 9 May 1815 (*MY* II, 235–6); it is not clear whether or not he knew that John was his admiring critic.

The name of metaphysical, by which Johnson has distinguished the poetry of Donne, Cowley, and their imitators, might perhaps as justly, though somewhat in a different sense, be applied, in our own days, to that class of writers, in which Mr. Wordsworth holds so distinguished a place. It is not meant that there exists any striking resemblance in their modes of thinking and writing, any farther than as they are both careless how far they wander from common associations of thought and language. Not content, as most imitators of nature have been, with embodying the brighter hues which play on the surfaces of things, both these schools have searched deeply into their hidden workings and mutual attractions; but as their objects were very different, so they did not collect the same materials, nor make the same use of them. The metaphysical poets of the seventeenth century, seem to have sought out for nothing but remote resemblances in things apparently the most unlike: they assemble at will brilliant images from all quarters, and their delight is to shew what rapid, dexterous, and manifold permutations and combinations may be made of them: we are thus perpetually amused by the spirit and luxuriance of the author, but are ready enough to lay down the book for any other gaudy or glittering amusement. For what reason, except that in all this there is nothing to melt or ennoble or calm the spirit? nothing which can be brought to our minds by our daily and hourly occupations and feelings, which comes home 'to our business' and 'bosom,' mixing itself with our goings out and our comings in, our fireside talk and our nightly reveries? The defect will be more distinctly felt, if we look to the result of a different sort of metaphysical observation, as exemplified in the writings of our author and of others his partners in friendship and in fame. These also are metaphysicians, but they have analysed mind and matter, not with a purpose of cold and barren speculation, nor of glittering and useless comparison, like their predecessors just mentioned: but considering that the end of poetry is to instruct through the imagination and the passions, they have regarded every thing naturally felt or imagined by man as being, so far, a proper subject for them; and they have used their abstract knowledge, not to provide playthings for the fancy, but to furnish a clue to the windings of the heart. The consequence is, that their poetry is every where deeply and highly tinctured with feeling: it may be often obscure, sometimes trivial, but it can never be unimpassioned. Peculiar as it seems in its principles, and refined in its operations, we must not expect that it should ever be universally popular, but it will meet with few moderate partizans: where it is admired, it will be beloved and idolized.

Of Mr. Wordsworth this is more especially true, because he has deviated farthest and most avowedly from the ordinary track, and is constantly professing and enforcing his peculiar notions; which, if they be not truely poetical, and such as to furnish not thought only, but materials for thinking, impressions deep and lasting as well as strong impulses, they cannot but afford more disgust than the common frailties of authors, inasmuch as they are more obvious and obtrusive. He owes it therefore to his own fair fame distinctly to set forth the principles, on which rests a practice so repugnant in many instances to his readers' habits of judging. Since his poetry is the shadow of his philosophy, the result of intense reflection and a peculiar way of combining and abstracting, its interest depends in a great measure on a right understanding of the process which formed it. But there are few who have music enough in their souls to unravel for themselves his abstruser harmonies: only let him sound the key-note, and the apparent confusion will vanish: let him make his tones well understood, and they will be to every ear delightful, to every soul elevating: till then they can delight and improve those only, who have fancy enough to transport themselves into the poet's circumstances and mood of mind, and leisure enough to work out with him the speculations and feelings consequent thereupon. In default, however, of time or inclination on his own part, may it be allowed to us, who admire him on principle, to state, more fully than under common circumstances, that conception of his writings, whether rightly or wrongly formed, on which we ground our admiration: discharging thereby, as far as in us lies, our debt of gratitude to the poet, and shewing, perhaps, to some who have paid less attention to the subject, how they may improve themselves by the poem, and unlock all its treasures of noble and benevolent emotions.

The principles, then, which seem to us to shine like a glory round every page of true poetry, and which the present work seems principally intended to enforce, are these; that whatsoever material or temporary exists before our senses, is capable of being associated, in our minds, with something spiritual and eternal; that such associations tend to ennoble and purify the heart; lastly, that the end of descriptive verse is to make them habitual to our minds, and its business, to unfold and exemplify them; to teach men to

> Find tongues in trees, books in the running brooks,
> Sermons in stones, and good in every thing.

Or, as one hath sung yet more divinely,

> Man is the world's high-priest, and doth present
> The sacrifice for all, while they below
> Unto the service mutter an assent,
> Such as springs use that fall, and winds that blow.

Whosoever shall act up to these words in their full import, as Mr. Wordsworth has done, must of course expect to be laughed down by those whose imaginations are too dull to perceive, and whose hearts are too hard to feel aught beyond the hurry and the bustle of the world around them; by those, who can perceive no joy in communing with themselves, or with the works of nature; who like Fleet-street as well as Valcluse, and the Canal in St. James's Park better than Windermere; whose minds are set upon intrigues and fees, business and bustle, places and preferments, and all the toilsome varieties of digging and delving, which 'the least erected spirit that fell' exacts of his votaries. To such as these the retired poet cannot speak: they have not learned the alphabet of his language; but there are many of better and more honest feelings, delighted according to rule by scenery and verse, who are yet so startled by the new and abtruse combinations which this principle has produced, that they throw the book aside in disgust, pronouncing the author puerile or unintelligible; whom, if they had met with earlier in life, before their habits of criticism were formed, they would readily have excused and admired him. These are the men to whom we would fain speak a good word for Mr. Wordsworth and his theory; and, as among them one argument from authority is worth two from speculation, we will refer them in the first place to the direct testimony and example of some of the brightest luminaries of the land. Bishop Hall shall be the first, who, in his Proeme to Occassionall Meditations, thus in few words delivers the rule in question:

Our active soul can no more forbear to think, than the eye can chuse but see when it is open. To doe well, no object should pass us without use; every thing that we see reads us new lectures of wisdom and piety. It is a shame for a man to be ignorant or godless under so many teachers. For me, I would not wish to live longer than I shall be the better for my eyes: and have thought it thankworthy thus to teach weak minds to improve their thoughts upon all like occasions.

But the great teacher as well as exemplar of this branch of Christian discipline was Robert Boyle, whose preface to his Occasional Reflections is as sound in philosophy, as the work itself is rich in poetry and devotion. He has there shewn at large the good effects of the habit on the mind and heart, comprehending all in one word, 'heavenly mindedness.'

There he has taught us to make the whole world a school of wisdom, to transmute every pebble that lies in our way into a precious jewel, every chance breath of air into a whisper from heaven. The exclusion of proud and impure thoughts from the imagination is the least advantage which we might thus ensure to ourselves. The heart also would be partaker of the benefit; for the influence of these two is always reciprocal, and with whatsoever we engage our fancy long, that is sure to become, if within our reach, an object of our hopes or fears. Moreover, by considering all things sensible with respect to some higher power, we are more likely to get an insight into final causes, and all the wonderful ways of Providence; and, above all, it tends to give an habitual sense of the presence of God.

In a word, when the devout soul is come to make that true use of the creatures, as to look upon them as men do upon water, that the sun gilds with his beams; that is, not so much for itself as for the reflective virtue it has to represent a more glorious object: and when she has, by long practice, accustomed herself to spiritualize all the objects and accidents that occur to her, I see not why that practice may not be one of the most effectual means for making good that magnificent assertion of the apostle, 'That all things work together for good to them that love God:' a devout occasional meditation, from how low a theme soever it takes its rise, being like Jacob's ladder, whereof though the foot leaned on the earth, the top reached up to heaven*

The poetical use of this habit is no less obvious than its religious and moral application. Such as may be willing with us to believe, that poetry has for its object the teaching man truth through the fancy and the affections, or, as the same hath been far better expressed, that its essence is 'impassioned imaginative reason:' these will be at no loss to discern how needful it is that the poet should form such associations, before the description of natural objects can form any part of his work. It is bringing fire from heaven to mix up with the clay, ere the Promethean rod can give it life and motion. In proportion as it is successfully practised, all things material become invested with the splendours of mind: till in the end not a form, not a colour, not a motion in the boundless landscape of nature, animate and inanimate, but is waited on by some feeling of the heart, or some shadow bodied forth by the imagination. And whereas the external or historical delineation of each object can be but one, the treasures of poetical description, thus conducted, are as various and inexhaustible as the workings of the mind of man. But even waving what may be paradoxical in this doctrine, and avoiding any discussion which

---

* Boyle's Works, vol. ii. p. 161. folio.

may call up that question with a thousand answers, What is poetry? it may be enough to consider, that in painting with words, no less than with colours, those artists are always considered as the best, who make us feel as well as see their work, and excite sympathy as well as admiration.

It would be a very engaging task to trace the progress of descriptive poetry with a view to this principle, to mark how the great hierophants of nature have instinctively used it as the true key to her high mysteries, and how among her inferior ministers it has had more or less influence according to circumstances of age, nation, and character. Ancient Greece, the land of fair forms, delicious airs, and leisurely contemplative habits, availed herself of it both in her poetry and her mythology to the utter most that her corrupt religion would allow.

[Quotes *The Excursion, PW*, V, p. 136, Book IV, ll. 851–76:

> In that fair clime the lonely herdsman, stretch'd . . .
> Into fleet Oreads sporting visibly.]

The Romans were too busy in governing the world; their skies were less serene, and their religion more civil and less imaginative than the Greek. Accordingly, we find the descriptions of their minor poets in general less touching.

> The woods and shores are forsaken of their nymphs;
> From haunted spring, and dale
> Edg'd with poplar pale,
> The parting genius is with sighing sent.

The influence of the sister art is too apparent: the work is beautiful in its kind, but it lies lifeless before us. This is too often the case in all the Latin poets that we know, except the two mighty enchanters, Virgil and Lucretius, whose descriptions each in their kind possess absolute sway over us, the one by his sweetness captivating the heart; the other by his awfulness thrilling and overpowering the imagination.

When poetry revived in modern Europe, superstition had again been at work, peopling the landscape with a new set of shadows, and, in copying the visible and external forms of things, it was not possible to leave out the airy drapery of sympathies and fancies, wherewith she had invested them. One principal reason, why the descriptions of the Italians and of our own best and oldest bards do so thoroughly enthrall the mind, may be this; that when they wrote, the impressions of chivalrous and monastic enthusiasm were not quite worn out of the surface of nature, and every tree and every spring was haunted by remembrances of love and piety. At the same time, the spirit of the age exercising them in free enquiry, they were ever striking out new combinations, and searching all the depths of analogy; whence it came to pass that they were at once the most imaginative and the most philosophical of all observers; and if ever the archetype of perfect descriptive poetry was present in man's mind, it was extracted from the pages of the poets in the days of Elizabeth, and he who framed it for himself was Milton.

But the blaze of that day was too bright to last: in the next generation, aided by artificial manners and a satirical, heartless spirit of criticism, the form of poetry begun to encroach on its substance, and scenes were described for the mere sake of describing them, on the same principle that versification was turned into a game of battledore and shuttlecock; the reader's desire of amusement at the least possible expence of thought, producing, in the writer, an effort to make the pleasure derivable from his work as near to that of mere animal sensation as might be. Yet many men of sense and spirit were reconciled to the couplet style, by the strong lines which it occasionally produced, forgetting (the exclusive admirers of Dryden especially) that mere condensation of thought is not poetry, and that the true Pierian spring flows bright and pure, as well as deep.

The shackles however were burst by Thomson and Collins and Akenside, and, since their day, the works of nature have not wanted observers able and willing to deduce from them lessons, which Providence, if we may speak it without presumption, intended them to convey. But none have ever entered so profoundly into this theory of their art as those commonly known by the name of the Lake Poets, particularly Mr. Wordsworth, who being by nature endowed with feelings of exquisite delicacy, by fortune placed in the very palace of solitude and contemplation, by education and habit taught to love what is lovely, and revere what is sacred, has made it his daily and hourly business to spiritualize all sensible objects; and hath not been afraid or ashamed of reflecting seriously and deeply (for there is surely room for deep and serious reflection) on the humblest and most trivial accidents of scenery and character.

What he has thus felt, he has made known with too little respect for 'the age of sophists, œconomists, and calculators;' and often, we must in earnest allow, with too manifest a disregard of the common notions of men on poetical subjects. Still, that he is not so thoroughly heretical as many suppose; that where he is wrong, he is wrong by the misapplication of right principles, not by the wilful adoption of erroneous ones, and that where he excels, he excels in the highest kind, even in the walks of

Milton and Spenser, and all those who have immortalized the perishable things which they described, by joining them with the eternal things which all hope or imagine; these are positions which we find forcing themselves more and more on our minds, the more diligently we study his works, and compare them with the remains of those mighty masters.

We have thought proper to preface our remarks on the Excursion with a statement of this principle, which seems to us the key to most of its intricacies and many of its highest beauties. But let us take the author's own exposition of it.

> Trust me, that for th' instructed time will come . . .
> The burthen of existence.
>
> [*Ibid.*, *PW*, V, pp. 148–9, Book IV, ll. 1235–51]

Mr. Wordsworth has embodied this among other favourite speculations in a long Poem, to be called the Recluse, 'as having for its principal subject the sensations and opinions of a poet living in retirement.' And he has selected this, the second of three parts whereof the whole work is to consist, because 'having more reference to passing events and an existing state of things than the others, greater progress was naturally made in it;' nor is it so connected with them as to be hurt by separate publication: for it is in itself nothing like a fragment, but a complete body of thought and imagery, having for its general scope to teach by description, and by simple narrative in form of description, that lesson paramount to all others, which, as we have seen, Boyle drew from the same source, 'That all things work together for good to them who love God and man.'

[Quotes *ibid.*, *PW*, V, p. 110, Book IV, ll. 10–31:

> —One adequate support . . .
> Their lost affections unto Thee, and Thine!]

This is the lesson and the prayer to the teaching of which Mr. Wordsworth has turned the conversation and incidents of a two days' ramble among the mountains of Cumberland. The first book, which is entitled 'The Wanderer,' represents the meeting of the poet with an old friend, one of the chief speakers in the moral dialogues which follow; and gives an account of his education, and habits of life and thought. This man is a sort of philosophical Burns, born in a shepherd's hut, trained among mountains and torrents at a Scottish village school, and by his solitary occupation exercised in reflection and poetry.

[Quotes *ibid.*, *PW*, V, pp. 14–15, Book I, ll. 198–218:

> O then what soul was his, when on the tops . . .
> That made him: it was blessedness and love.]

We could almost wish, not for our own pleasure, but to avoid scandalizing such as feel by rule, that our author had given a being thus educated some higher employment than that of

> A vagrant merchant bent beneath his load.
> [*Ibid.*, *PW*, V, p. 19, Book I, l. 324]

Instinctively, as it may seem, he apologizes for it himself.
[Quotes *ibid.*, *PW*, V, p. 19, Book I, ll. 326–32:

> Yet do such travellers find their own delight . . .
> Or pleas'd their fancies, with the wares he brought.]

And certainly, they who feel no delight in the sublimities of this man's song, and the devout and affecting feelings which he utters, merely because he is called a pedlar, must needs be the slaves of names to an extraordinary degree, and that is a kind of service not very manly nor very philosophical.

With this 'grey-haired wanderer,' the poet surveys a ruined cottage with its garden, and hears from him the tale of its last inhabitant. It is 'an ordinary sorrow of man's life,' yet he has made it singularly affecting. A wedded pair, earning their bread in comfort and industry, are smitten first by famine, then by sickness, then by want of employment.
[Quotes *ibid.*, *PW*, V, pp. 28–9, Book I, ll. 566–91:

> A sad reverse it was for him who long . . .
> Made my heart bleed.]

Finally he is driven to become a soldier: he quits his home without a farewell, and no more is heard of him. The gradual decay of his wife is traced through the different visits of the pedlar, as by one who knows and pities human miseries. The story, besides its inherent beauty, gives great interest to the progress of the poem, by the developement which it affords of the pedlar's character, and his way of drawing comfort from the observation of things natural.
[Quotes *ibid.*, *PW*, V, p. 39, Book I, ll. 939–56:

> Be wise and chearful, and no longer read . . .
> And walk'd along my road in happiness.]

The second book introduces us to a new character, and the third makes us thoroughly acquainted with him. This is a retired man, once a

school-mate of the Wanderer, who having no sound principles, had been first dissipated, then happy in domestic life; but having lost the stay of that happiness, had sunk in despair. Whether his bliss or his despondency be more feelingly described is hard to say.
[Quotes *ibid.*, *PW*, V, pp. 91–2, Book III, ll. 502–49:

> My demerits did not sue in vain . . .
> That all the grove and all the day was ours.]

After her death,

> What followed cannot be review'd in thought . . .
> Went sounding on, a dim and perilous way.
[*Ibid.*, *PW*, V, p. 100, Book III, ll. 680–701]

He was awakened from his trance of sorrows by the French Revolution, and for a time felt all the zeal of a reformer; till being gradually undeceived and disappointed, he retires to that utter solitude in which he is here found, little satisfied with himself, and mistrusting both God and man. Into this man's mouth the Poet has put with great force and probability the usual arguments of sceptics and despondents against a superintending Providence, and the final prevalence of good over evil. And he has answered them by the mouth of the Wanderer in the fourth Book, which is inscribed, 'Despondency Corrected.' Our extracts are becoming too large, but we cannot grudge our readers the delight and improvement to be found in the following passage.
[Quotes *ibid.*, *PW*, V, p. 111, Book IV, ll. 32–65:

> Then, as we issued from that covert nook . . .
> And will possess my portion in content.]

He then points out resources against Despondency, in the contemplation of truth and nature, in a right estimate of our own insufficiency, in the study of natural history, in rural amusements, in rural legends; this affords scope for a noble digression on the origin of mythology, and for an animated assertion of the right which the will and affections, as well as the reasoning faculty, have to be considered in the training of man's mind. In conclusion, the rule of associating things material with things spiritual is enforced, and its effects thus energetically summed up.
[Quotes *ibid.*, *PW*, V, pp. 149–50, Book IV, ll. 1264–75:

> So build we up the being that we are . . .
> Of love divine, our intellectual soul.]

In the Fifth Book, 'the Pastor,' the doctrines begin to be exemplified.

The Solitary has left his cottage to accompany his friends on a part of their ramble, and coming to a church-yard, they are led to consider how far the simple mountaineers, who tenant most of those graves, were concerned with the evils and consolations which they have been speaking of. In good time the Village Pastor appears, and is requested to give an account of his dead flock. This he agrees to, repeating first the arguments of the Wanderer, only with more distinctness in his profession of Christianity. 'Life,' he says,
[Quotes *ibid.*, *PW*, V, p. 185, Book V, ll. 1012–16]

> —is energy of love,
> Divine or human, exercis'd in pain,
> In strife and tribulation, and ordained
> If so approved and sanctified, to pass
> Through shades and silent rest, to endless joy.

This theme is followed up in the sixth and seventh books, called, 'The Church-yard among the mountains;' in which a great number of characters, such as might be supposed gathered together within the precincts of a Cumberland burying ground, are sketched with all the truth of Crabbe's descriptive pencil, and with all the delicacy of Goldsmith's, interspersed with many touches such as none but Wordsworth could throw in. Every one of these has its beauty, some sterner and some lighter: but the longest and most interesting is that of Ellen, the forsaken penitent. Perhaps all poetry might be fairly challenged to produce a passage of sweeter and simpler beauty than the following:
[Quotes *ibid.*, *PW*, V, pp. 214–5, Book VI, ll. 855–87:

> It was the season sweet, of budding leaves . . .
> His darkness doth transcend our fickle light.]

In the eighth book we are conducted to the parsonage, and in the ninth make an afternoon's voyage over a neighbouring lake, with the return from which the poem closes, the effect upon the solitary being good, but not complete enough to be called conversion. These two books furnish scenes well calculated to come in aid of these arguments of hope and comfort which fill those before them. A happy family, and a fine summer's evening, are sights of themselves well-nigh sufficient to cure despondence. In this part of the work we find some political digression; the eighth book contains a dissertation on manufactures, and their baneful result on the souls and bodies of their slaves: And in the ninth, the sight of two free-hearted and joyous children draws from

453

the wanderer a discourse on the natural activity, and consequent freedom of mind: whence he gathers it to be the duty of a nation in no wise to consider her children as mere instruments for making money, but to give them as far as may be an equality of that moral and religious instruction, whereon the true liberty depends, and for the sake of which alone outward freedom is to be valued.

We close our extracts with the pastor's thanksgiving, regretting only that we cannot insert the whole of that high-minded prayer of which it forms the conclusion.

[Quotes *ibid.*, *PW*, V, pp. 310–11, Book IX, ll. 724–54:

—O ye who come . . .
From whom all gifts descend, all blessings flow.]

It will naturally be asked, by those who are strangers to the work, how it is that we despair of the popularity of a poem so noble in design, and so rich in the best ingredients of beauty as these passages, and countless more, prove the Excursion to be. One word may account for our fears: the author is too intent on his system. Looking exclusively to the sacred lesson which he had to teach, he has been too careless on the one hand as to his manner of teaching it, too refined on the other in forcing it on all occasions into notice. To the former cause may be ascribed many prosaic lines, and some whole paragraphs, chiefly of description, which, though they succeed in placing the scenes described full in the attentive reader's eye, and in preparing him, if he be at all used to such reflections, for the moral or religious discussion which is to follow, must needs be wearisome to the mass of those, whose judgment makes the fashion of the day in these matters. For example:

[Quotes *ibid.*, *PW*, V, p. 76, Book III, ll. 50–60:

Upon a semicirque of turf-clad ground . . .
A fragment, like an altar, flat and smooth, &c.]

But the crying sin of Mr. Wordsworth is too much refinement in the application of spiritual associations to natural objects. Agreeing with him to the full in considering this as the essence of Descriptive Poetry, we yet feel and lament that he has not sufficiently distinguished between the common feelings of mankind and the wanderings of his own solitary spirit. He is too familiar with his art to see where the beginner finds difficulty. He listens to a lamb bleating, or gazes on the flight of a bird; and the visionary associations which spring up within him he takes for the ordinary stirrings of the heart, which all men who have leisure to feel at all, must feel as well as himself at the like objects. He passes abruptly from the picture to the result of the reverie it produced, and makes his writings obscure and fantastical for want of a little care in unravelling a thread of ideas so familiar to himself that he deems it easy to all mankind. This was to be expected from a man of strong imagination, living in the shadow of mountains, amidst the roar of winds and waters, and talking daily with Nature about the secret things of Providence. If Mr. Wordsworth had reflected enough on this tendency of a life like his, he would probably have smoothed off many allusions which now come so abrupt and unexpected as to startle even his more experienced readers; and by so doing he would have come nearer the end of poetry; which is not perfected, until to every man according to his measure the cup of delight and instruction be full.

His occasional lapses into childish and trivial allusion may be accounted for, from the same tendency. He is obscure, when he leaves out links in the chain of association, which the reader cannot easily supply: he is puerile, when he sets before us some object commonly accounted low or uninteresting, and leaves us to use it for ourselves to the same purpose of fancy or feeling, unto which it hath become in his own mind habitually instrumental. In his descriptions of children this is particularly the case, because of his firm belief in a doctrine, more poetical, perhaps, than either philosophical or christian, that

Heaven lies about us in our infancy.

Though the tenderness and beauty resulting from this opinion be to us a rich overpayment for the occasional strainings and refinements of sentiment to which it has given birth, it has yet often served to make the author ridiculous in common eyes, in that it has led him to state his own fairy dreams as the true interpretation and import of the looks and movements of children, as being even really in their minds.[2]

Such are the faults of composition, into which the habit of associating what we see and hear with what we believe and hope will be most apt to betray a mind, that can think and feel intensely. But there is an error in conduct to which it often leads, which it may be pardonable to mention here, because it is closely connected with the course and object of this work. That root of bitterness which lies so deeply imbedded in our nature, putting forth its shoots to lay hold of every wholesome plant, and poison it in return for its support – our original corruption – hath not failed to mingle itself even with our habits of pure and devout meditation, enticing us to rest satisfied with ourselves, if we have formed holy imaginations, and longed after heavenly things, though we have not embodied our feelings in active zeal and charity. This is the sin which most easily besets the fervid and melancholy mind, smitten with the love of scenery and poetical meditation: and if not duly checked by a strong practical sense of duty, its effects are but the more lamentable for the nobleness of the heart in which it abides. At once restless and indolent, ever turning giddily round in a maze of his own making, without advancing a single step in the race of glory and benevolence; if ever human mind became pitiable in the eyes of men and angels, it is that man's, who spends his life in beating the air with the strength of right principles habitually separate from his practice. The Excursion, however, though its subject be so dangerous, is so far from deserving any censure in this kind, that all its tendencies are strong in encouragement of real, industrious, social virtue. The two men of sentiment, the Pastor and the Wanderer, are both represented as doing good to all within their sphere. And in the following passage the exercise of duty is recommended to the solitary as the chief and only comfort of the sick soul.

[Quotes *ibid.*, *PW*, V, p. 116, Book IV, ll. 214–38:

> —What then remains? – To seek . . .
> In the sublime attractions of the grave.]

Who can estimate the advantage which would result to mankind, if all men endowed with Mr. Wordsworth's talents would devote them to the expression, by their life and writings, of sentiments pure and ennobling like these? Is it indeed for purposes of vanity or applause, or to be the plaything of an idle hour, that Poetry was sent into the world? that a few are gifted above their fellows with eyes that can see deep into their own minds, and wide around them on the operations of Nature and Providence: with a tongue that can wield all the powers of language for gracefulness or terror: with the port and march almost of superior beings, bowing all hearts to receive their words as it were an oracle? Are all these things for our amusement, or are they talents, for the use of which we shall be called to a severer account, in proportion as they are more rare and precious than those even of the monarch or conqueror. These are awful questions, and it nearly concerns every man of poetical genius to ask them of his own heart, and to act conscientiously up to the answer he receives: that the noblest faculties of our nature may be employed to the noblest ends, and the reason, the fancy, and the affections concur in doing good to mankind, and giving glory to God.

EDITOR'S NOTES

1. This review was reprinted in *Analectic Magazine*, October 1815, VI, 273–91.
2. J. T. C. echoes his own earlier notion here; see entry 108e.

154.

Unsigned notice, *La Belle Assemblée; or, Bell's Court and Fashionable Magazine*, May 1815, XI, 224–5

The 'Bell' alluded to in the sub-title is John Bell (1745–1831), the magazine's successful publisher.

This poem, which, as the title-page specifies, is but a portion of the *Recluse*, abounds with much interest, and with many striking passages. The author, in the commencement, meets with a valued and respected friend, whom, in the work, he styles a Wanderer, and who leads him first to the retreat of a Solitary, and next to the dwelling of the Pastor. The different sentiments expressed by each character in the piece are skillfully and admirably displayed, and the description of the churchyard and the burial places among the mountains, is given in a manner to interest deeply the feelings of the heart, and excite the reflections of the thinking mind. The address of the Priest to the Supreme Being, and his parting with the Solitary, conclude this portion of Mr. Wordsworth's celebrated poem, from which we lay before our readers the following extracts.

[Quotes passages mainly from *The Excursion*, Book I, and from the story of Ellen, Book V, and concludes:]

The address of the Priest to the Supreme Being, as it is too exquisite to bear mutilation, and too long for our limits, we must refer our readers to the perusal of the poem, which will, we venture to assert, amply repay them for their time and attention.

155. Charles Abraham Elton (1778–1853)

Unsigned review, *The British Review and London Critical Journal*,
August 1815, VI, 50–64

Although Josiah Conder in a letter of 26 August 1815 attributed the
article to Rev. J. W. Cunningham, an evangelical clergyman of the Church
of England, Jared Curtis has discovered it was the work of Elton, a minor
poet, translator and reviewer, whose *Poems* (1804) reveal an admiration of
Wordsworth. Although the magazine was evangelical in tone, reviewing
'secular works in a Christian spirit', according to Hannah More, a friend
of the editor, William Roberts (*Life, Letters, and Opinions of William
Roberts*, Arthur Roberts, London, 1850, 65n), Elton's article is characterised by being a defence of *Lyrical Ballads* and an answer to critics such
as Jeffrey who had already attacked the *Excursion*. Three years later, and
for a nine-year period, Elton was to leave the Church of England and
sympathise with the Unitarians, and hence the reviews (see also *The White
Doe*, entry 184) are less pietistical than might be expected. However, in
1836, after he returned to the Church of England, his son, A. H. Elton,
noted in his diary a comment on Wordsworth's atheism, 'My father
alluded to atheistical sentiment in Wordsworth. In one of his Odes to
Lucy he says –

> No motion has she now, no force
> She neither hears nor sees
> Roll'd round in earth's diurnal course
> With rocks and stones and trees!'
> (See Jared Curtis, 'Charles A. Elton and Wordsworth's
> "New Poem": A Study in Taste', *The Wordsworth
> Circle*, Winter 1980, XI, 36–42)

It must be avowed, that this poem is as a 'sealed book' to no inconsiderable number of readers. To those whose imaginations have been kept
continually on the stretch, and whose curiosity has been perpetually
stimulated, by wonders of romance; by tales of Gothic chivalry; by don-
jon, and keep, and battlement, and banner; or by wild mythologies and
exotic manners, American, or Indian, or Turkish; the quiet simplicity, the
mere mental elevation of 'the Recluse,' offer little attraction: to those,
also, who have habituated themselves to consider an uniformly raised
and artificial diction, sparkling sentiment, and traditionary popular verse,
as the essentials of poetry, and who have been familiar in poetical

458

description with such scenes and persons as daily life presents in the crowded town, or the civilized and busy village, the deep reasonings and moral disquisitions of this poem will appear only like metaphysical homilies; the simple dignity of style, and Miltonic rhythm, like the nakedness of prose; the characters unnatural and visionary. For those who are hackneyed in the ways of men, who have engaged in the bustling agitation of political interests, with all their heart-burnings and virulent jealousies, and sleepless tossings of feverish ambition, this poem is composed in far too unworldly a spirit. For those who see nothing in the nature of men and things but a blind mechanism of matter, dabblers in a cold sceptical philosophy, doubters of all truth which they cannot touch and dissect, and bring close under their own mole-sighted optics; whose conception of an immaterial universe resembles that which the blind possess of colours, and the deaf of musical sounds; whose sense of ridicule is their test of truth; who see nothing in the preternatural creations of a Shakspeare, but the walking ghosts of an old woman's fire-side tale; and amidst the daring grandeur of character and imagery which blazes in the Paradise Lost, can dwell only on the substance of devils cut in twain and re-united, or the burlesque of cannon in heaven; the spots of human frailty; the sinkings of towering genius, to which faultless mediocrity never falls; for those, lastly, who can see nothing venerable, or interesting, or awful, or touching; nothing of moral wisdom, nothing of pathos, nothing of poetry, in the page of sacred writ, the oracle of revolving ages, the comfort of affliction; the sole anchor and resting-place for the hope of after-existence, blissful and incorruptible: for all such the poem of 'The Recluse' is a sealed volume. To this poem it is necessary that the reader should bring a portion of the same meditative disposition, innocent tastes, calm affections, reverential feelings, philosophic habits, which characterize the poet himself; for readers of another kind we greatly fear, (and we deeply sympathize in the author's shame and mortification,) that this poem 'will never do.'*

We have usually observed, that they who were most pleased with the 'Lyrical Ballads,' were men with strong minds, and with a propensity to metaphysical studies; a presumption this, that the simplicity of these ballads was not quite so infantile as has been often asserted; and we have remarked, that such men have been more particularly pleased with those very pieces, which have been quoted in companies as subjects of merriment, and have been shouted down with arrogant scorn by supercilious

* See Edinb. Rev. No. 47.

pretenders to criticism. Touches of nature and philosophy stole, however, into the public mind, in spite of the scoffs, the warnings, and anathemas of these guardians of taste; and as, perhaps, no publication ever produced so great a stirring of the general feeling, such a bristling up of alarmed prejudices, and such a perplexed consciousness of inexplicable delight, none, perhaps, ever made in so short a period so deep and affecting an impression. But the alleged infantilities of style and subject were insisted upon with such perserving acrimony, as to frighten effectually away the timid and self-wondering approbation of a portion of the public. They who had been secretly affected with pleasure grew ashamed of their feelings, and were eager to recant their applause, and to join the safe side of the laughers.

In the course of life most persons must have experienced the mortification of finding their frankness misplaced: have exposed their hearts with a facility of which they have instantly repented: have abandoned themselves in easy unsuspiciousness to a child-like freedom of confidence, and have suddenly perceived that they have had the misfortune, neither to be appreciated nor understood by those, on whom, in their unreserved and unguarded openness, they had playfully leaned. In this predicament we think that Mr. Wordsworth has not unfrequently placed himself; he has given his readers credit for too great quickness of apprehension and too liberal a good-nature: he has supposed that they would humour his disposition; fall in with his frame of mind, and understand his intention, when, in fact, they have wanted the first stimulus of curiosity, which would be necessary to induce a persuasion that to endeavour to understand it was worth the trouble. It has never occurred to many of them, that a man, who had shown himself, at least on some occasions, capable of high feelings, rich conceptions, and intelligible harmonies, was not very likely to lisp and drivel with the no-meaning of a moping or tittering idiot; that something might possibly lie deeper than the surface; some touches of original sentiment suggested by the close observation of nature and of man; that, in short, the fault imputed to the poet might probably be the fault of his readers, whose tastes had been pampered with a different aliment, and who were too opinionative or too indifferent even to prepare themselves to listen.

The cause of this indifference, or of this more than indifference, a pre-disposition to dislike; a pre-determination, like that of Sterne towards the mendicant friar, not to bestow a single sous; a resolution not by any means to confess themselves pleased, or, still less, convinced of the possibility of being pleased by such methods; the *cause* of this state of feeling, so little favourable to a candid hearing of the poet, must be sought in the vanity of self-love; in the sensitive alarm, lest a willingness to be touched or delighted in a new way might imply, that they had been heretofore in the wrong; that by allowing the poet to have succeeded in opening sources of poetic pleasure, of which they were not before aware, they must, at the same time, allow his superiority to themselves. The general herd of readers, who know little of poetry further than that it is verse, and the cultivated critical few, seem, in this instance, to have reasoned alike: in both the feeling of antipathy has been equally alive, and for reasons equally vulgar and unphilosophical.

In drawing up the body of reasons why the poetry of Mr. Wordsworth could not possibly be received as poetry, the censors of the Lyrical Ballads seem to lay a mighty stress on the daringness of the innovation; an innovation as old as the dog of Ulysses, and the deer of Jacques; which consists in awakening sympathy by a few slight strokes of artless incident, and in appealing to the primitive simple feelings of the human heart.

[There follows a paragraph on the absurd though prevailing habit of judging a writer by the standard of an earlier writer, and another paragraph on
the kinds of poetry written by Pope and Dryden.]

. . . It is not necessary to tread in the steps of Pope and Dryden, in order to deserve the name of poet. The attempt to prescribe a straitened and beaten path to the diversified faculties of men will everlastingly be foiled by the calm and lofty self-confidence of irrepressible genius.

The question respecting Mr. Wordsworth properly is not 'Does he resemble this or that poet?' but, 'Does he attain the purpose which he has proposed to himself; does he affect the passions; does he awaken the moral sentiment; does he bring us acquainted with appearances of nature which we have hitherto heedlessly overlooked, or with experiences and powers in our own minds, of which he had been heretofore unconscious?'

Connected with the same prejudice in favour of a particular master, we discover another cause of the dislike, or disappointment, which some have felt, or affected, with regard to the Lyrical Ballads, in the notion that certain subjects are absolutely interdicted as themes of poetry, and that certain incidents do not furnish enough of *story*. Several of the minor poems that have a narrative air, describe occurrences perfectly simple; awakening some recollection of our common nature; marking some retired features of character, or some delicate and fleeting impression of thought, which the imagination, or reflection of the reader is to open out and improve. They may often be characterized as solitary impulses, or *fragments* of feeling, which are likely to elude cursory

461

observation, to excite the stare of unreflecting readers, and to offend, beyond all hope of pardon, those who regard such small incidents, and familiar moods, and simple elements of thought and emotion, as beneath the dignity of what they call poetry, and as worthy only of being celebrated in nursery-rhymes. One of these pieces records a lover's fancy while riding slowly, just before the setting of the moon, towards the cottage of his mistress:

> When down behind the cottage roof
>   At once the planet dropp'd,
> What fond and wayward thoughts will slide
>   Into a lover's head! –
> 'Oh mercy! to myself I cried,
>   If Lucy should be dead!'
>   ['Strange fits of passion', *PW*, II, p. 29, ll. 23–8; *LB*
>   (1800), p. 151, ll. 23–8]

Perhaps every mind has, at one time or other, and probably more than once, felt this undefinable and unaccountable suggestion, both sudden and transitory, of a superstitious presentiment of calamity from some such trivial occurrence; yet this it required one nicely conversant with the minutest parts of our mental constitution to observe and to register; and this is the passage on which the most doughty of Mr. Wordsworth's critics has betrayed so sheer an ignorance of the nature of poetry, as to exclaim, 'and here *the story* ends!'

But if the finer essence of poetry be wanted, and that deep and thrilling sentiment, which at once wraps the heart in a contagious softness, where shall we find them, if not in the Lyrical Ballads?

[Quotes 'Three years she grew', *PW*, II, p. 215–16, stanzas 5 and 7; *LB* (1800), p. 194, stanzas 5 and 7.]

We shall notice only one more charge against Mr. Wordsworth: He has not drawn his *characters* like those of other poets; a presumptuous originality, in which he is, however, supported by the example of Shakspeare; who, we fear, sinned not seldom in forming individuals for himself. Mr. Wordsworth has chosen to represent a village schoolmaster; not, truly, with the obvious every-day manners of the rustic pedagogue's profession, as Goldsmith has drawn him, and drawn him excellently for his purpose, but with the peculiarity of a particular likeness, with a reputation from his younger days of quaint humour, blithe sociality, and a love of harmless merriment; now occasionally saddened, in the sobering latter autumn of his life, by recollections of domestic bereavement, and a growing inclination to indulge fits of melancholy and musing. He has drawn him, in short, with precisely those contradictions to general experience which are for ever occurring in nature; those freaks of disposition, and eccentricities of thinking and acting, which break through the mechanical boundaries and accidental limitations of station and profession, and perpetually mock the previous calculations of ordinary observers. Yet at the bar of these latter superficial inquirers; these spruce, factitious beings, who read human character in the streets of cities, in drawing-rooms, and colleges, will the poet of nature, the profound philosopher of the heart, stand eternally arraigned. But his page will live, when the breath of criticism shall have perished, and the laugh of insult shall have passed away: it will live, because it has a vital principle within it, like that which makes Shakspeare the darling of children and the companion of men; because he that fills this high and genuine function of the poet, 'meek Nature's priest,' has looked abroad on the immutable forms of beauty and goodness, moulding and influencing the moral man, and spreading through the grandeur of creation the visibility of God; because he has descended into the most private recesses of the mind, and shown to man that depth of intellectual knowledge, the mystery of himself.

We have dwelt thus long on Mr. Wordsworth's former poems, because, as being illustrative of the author's habits of feeling and reflection, they are naturally linked with his meditative work; of which the introductory part is designed to trace the growth of the writer's mind from boyhood up to the state of man. 'The Excursion' embraces only the middle portion of the work, which is to be entitled The Recluse, and which will form, when completed, a philosophical poem on Man, Nature, and Society. The third part, like the first, will have for its subject the sensations and opinions of the poet himself, as experienced and formed in the meditation of rural retirement. The intermediate poem, which is now before us, assumes a dramatic form. It has a sufficiency of narrative to interest all those who suppose that story-telling is its primary object; and what we regard as still more valuable, it abounds with solemn, pious, and elevated views of human nature and of providence, and is infused and illuminated with 'the thoughts that breathe,' and 'the words that burn.'

The idea of a ramble among the mountains, in which different characters meet and exchange their ideas, is exceedingly well imagined, for the purpose of giving a form, a connexion, and an interest, to the subjects discussed; which appear to arise unaffectedly from the circumstances, and are enlivened by reciprocations of argument, of appeal, and reply.

We shall endeavour to exhibit the poetical power of Mr. Wordsworth in that quality which is essentially poetical: that faculty of creative imitation which gives a shape and real existence to the conceptions of the fancy; which brings us intimately acquainted with unknown characters; places us actually in the midst of distant scenes: amidst the wild and beautiful phenomena of Nature in the loneliness and loveliness of her native majesty; and enables us to see and feel as he himself felt and saw.

> Pectus inaniter angit,
> Irritat, mulcet, falsis terroribus impiet
> Ut magus, et modo me Thebis, modo ponit Athenis.[1]

Our notice is attracted in the opening of the poem to an old man: of whom the poet is in search during a hot summer's noon, and whom he finds stretched on a bench, beside a cottage, now in ruins:

> Supine 'the wanderer' lay:
> His eyes, as if in drowsiness, half-shut,
> The shadows of the breezy elms above
> Dappling his face.
>
> [*The Excursion*, *PW*, V, p. 23, Book I, ll. 438–41]

When it is discovered that this 'wanderer' is a travelling pedlar, nothing can be more easy than to turn such a character into ridicule: to talk of Welsh flannels and brass buttons; and to inquire how such a man could possibly have cherished romantic feelings or meditative habits. They, however, who know any thing of the mountainous districts of our island, know that it is not uncommon to meet with men in a humble station of life, superior in mental attainments to what the inhabitants of the cultivated champaign countries of the South would be at all likely to apprehend, or easily to believe. Were this, however, otherwise, the poet, as we have instanced in the case of Mathew, 'the grey-hair'd man of glee,' would have a perfect right to suppose such a character: for the every-day experience of human life will have shown him that the faculties of men, so far from being cramped by circumstances, perpetually escape from them, and follow the irresistible bent of some strong, and probably inborn, propensity. If the cheapening of duffel and sheeting be supposed necessarily to confine and degrade the intellect, so might the cutting out of soles and upper-leathers for ladies' shoes: yet the author of 'The Baviad,' and of the matchless version of Juvenal, worked mathematical problems with an awl, in default of pen and paper: and Bloomfield, while occupied with the hammer and the lap-stone, meditated a genuine English Georgic, agreeably descriptive of local scenery, and of rural manners and incidents.

It is an arrogant ignorance of the nature of the human mind that ventures thus to prescribe to the poet his probabilities of character. They, indeed, who sneer at the fine sentiments of a pedlar have conveniently overlooked the whole of his existence, prior to his taking up this wandering occupation: which among the solitary villages of Cumberland or Scotland must be acknowledged to be precisely that which affords a man *no* opportunities of conversing with the scenes of nature. All the innumerable items that contribute to fill up the sum of human character: all the imperceptible, yet indelible, impressions of early childhood; all the obscure vestiges of thought; the expanded inclinations; the stimulated tastes; the created fondnesses or aversions; which are brought about by a thousand causes: by circumstance or chance that has eluded remembrance, or that would baffle analysis: all, in short, that prepares the foundations and builds up the future structure of the man, is left completely out of the account. It is, indeed, far more easy to ask with 'the mob of Gentlemen who *think* with ease,' 'How should a shoe-maker write poetry? How can a pedlar philosophize?'

The whole process of mind in this intelligent mountaineer is, in fact, traced by Mr. Wordsworth with beautiful consistency and truth. We extract the description of those first hints which a child collects from external nature, and of which the impression never forsakes him. The school-house, which the boy-herdsman frequented during the winter,

[Quotes *ibid.*, *PW*, V, p. 12, Book I, ll. 122–31:

>Stood alone,
>Sole building on a mountain's dreary edge . . .
>To whom he might confess the things he saw.]

This boy is now an old man: the pensive historian of many who have died before him. He tells the painfully interesting story of a kind-hearted woman who dwelt in the ruined cottage; and who, after her husband had left her in the hope of bettering his condition by a soldier's life, pined away in his protracted absence, and died. The reflections on the desolate well are original, and affecting in the highest degree:

[Quotes *ibid.*, *PW*, V, pp. 24–5, Book I, ll. 484–94:

>Beside yon spring I stood . . .
>Green with the moss of years.]

465

The most interesting personage of the poem is distinguished by the name of 'the Solitary.' The conception of this character indicates a deep knowledge of the motives of human action. It is the instance of an amiable and cultivated mind, shattered and thrown from the balance of its principles by the heavy stroke of affliction, in the sudden and complex loss of a wife and two children. Such a tumultuous interest as that produced by the French revolution would naturally seize on such a mind; left naked of all that constituted its resources and enjoyments; and eagerly grasping at an occasion to fill the dreadful and insupportable vacuum by scenes of political agitation; and by a transfer of individual affections to the whole human race. A sceptical distrust of Providence from the imagined insufficiency of religious consolations; a tendency to bitter questionings of the reality of virtue, and the certainty of revealed truth, might also be natural food for a despair thus disdainful of comfort. But in deducing this taint of infidelity by necessary consequence from the spirit which operated the revolution in France, the reasoning is unphilosophical. Mr. Wordsworth, as we conceive, has mistaken the signs of the times; and has seen nothing but the agency of evil in the subversion of an ancient government and hierarchy. We venture to regard the French revolution as not only a *scourge*, but a *mean*: we see in it, through all its progresses and relapses, the hand of that Being, who by his mysterious agency educes good of evil, preparing by the shock of principles and passions, the collision of opinions, and the conflict of experiments; a recognition of justice and virtue in rulers and people; and probably the universal downfall of anti-christian superstition and of lawless power.

Our introduction to the Recluse is prepared with much of well-contrived interest. The old man and his companion, while on their way to his retired cottage, are startled by the characteristic local circumstance of a dirge chaunted in the hollow of the mountains:

> From out the heart
> Of that profound abyss a solemn voice,
> Or several voices in one solemn sound,
> Was heard ascending: mournful, deep, and slow,
> The cadence as of psalms.
>
> [*Ibid.*, *PW*, V, p. 55, Book II, ll. 372–6]

> 'God rest his soul!'
> The wanderer cried, abruptly breaking silence;
> 'He is departed, and finds peace at last!'
>
> [*Ibid.*, *PW*, V, p. 55, ll. 382–4]

Passing on, they find between the angle, formed by a rock and a ruinous wall, a rustic seat screened by a pent-house of sods. The plan betrays the hand of children; who have cut the turf into walks, as a miniature garden, and reared babyish houses of stones and moss; an incident very much beneath the dignity of great wits, but interesting, perhaps, to those fond and silly beings who love the ways of children. One of the props of these artificial fairy palaces is a book: and this book is the 'Candide' of Voltaire.

> 'Gracious Heaven!'
> The wanderer cried: 'It cannot but be his:
> And he is gone!'
> [*Ibid.*, *PW*, V, p. 57 and footnotes, ll. 436–8]

> Here, then, has been to him
> Retreat within retreat: a sheltering place
> Within how deep a shelter! He had fits
> E'en to the last of genuine tenderness,
> And loved the haunts of children.
> [*Ibid.*, *PW*, V, p. 58, ll. 445–9]

The burial had, however, belonged to another: and they encounter the Recluse:

> I knew from the appearance and the dress
> That it could be no other: a pale face,
> A tall and meagre person, in a garb
> Not rustic, dull and faded, like himself.
> [*Ibid.*, *PW*, V, pp. 59–60, ll. 498–501]

After a repast, described with an appropriation of poetry to the purposes of common life, by some poets perhaps carried a little too far, and by others squeamishly rejected, they walk abroad amidst this calm and beautiful assemblage of rural images:
[Quotes *ibid.*, *PW*, V, p. 75, Book III, ll. 1–10:

> A humming bee, a little tinkling rill . . .
> And cloudless sky.]

The Solitary relates his history: and while describing the dreariness of his state of mind during a voyage across the Atlantic, breaks out into an apostrophe, which is full of the bitter wisdom of melancholy experience:
[Quotes *ibid.*, *PW*, V, p. 104, Book III, ll. 842–50:

> Ye Powers,
> Of soul and sense . . .
> Will conscience prey.]

To promote the cheerfulness of those who consider pure poetry as a most risible absurdity, a most wild and unintelligible sort of raving, we extract the following passage:
[Quotes *ibid.*, *PW*, V, pp. 145–6, Book IV, ll. 1147–82:

> Here you stand:
> Adore and worship, when you know it not . . .
> Faint, and still fainter.]

The company of the ramblers is increased by a rural vicar; who points out the graves in a mountain church-yard, and gives the stories and the characters of those who are buried beneath its turf. The description which we shall select seems new to poetry; and leaves in our opinion no room for doubt whether Mr. Wordsworth be, or be not, a poet:
[Quotes *ibid.*, *PW*, V, p. 244, Book VII, ll. 395–416:

> Almost at the root
> Were all things silent, wheresoe'er he moved.]

The description of the joys of blooming youth and sportive innocence, and the sad reverse of blighted youth and poisoned innocence in a beautiful cottage girl, is so enchantingly poetical and tender, that we cannot part with Mr. Wordsworth without again holding him forth to the taste of his countrymen in the following specimen:
[Quotes *ibid.*, *PW*, V, pp. 211–14, Book VI, ll. 791–849:

> —An infant there doth rest . . .
> Such fate was hers.]

We end with the opinion with which we set out: this poem 'will never do' for persons without poetical enthusiasm, nor for persons without devotional warmth. 'The great, vulgar, and the small,' will not understand it; and by consequence it will not please them. But the writer may watch with calmness and confidence the fluctuations of taste; and despise, without any emotion of anger, the sarcasms of petulant conceit, sitting in judgment on superior intellect. If the present age be not fitted to receive his poem with reverence and gratitude, that age assuredly will come.

EDITOR'S NOTE

1. 'By illusions he tortures [my] heart, provokes, soothes, fills it with fabricated fears like a magician, and puts me now in Thebes, now in Athens.' (Horace, *Epistles*, II, 1, 211–13)

156.

Unsigned review, *The Philanthropist or Repository for Hints and Suggestions Calculated to Promote the Happiness of Man*, late 1815,[1] V, 342–63

> On 11 April 1815 Dorothy Wordsworth suggested (see *MY*, II, 230) to the Clarksons that they might undertake this review after they had sent her a recipe of what it might contain; probably the same hints were passed on to the editor, William Allen (1770–1863), a Quaker, a pharmacist, and a reformer. The review concludes 'To be continued', but there is no sequel.

It is the duty of THE PHILANTHROPIST to sanction whatever tends to the moral and intellectual improvement of mankind; and it is immaterial to us, whether or no such improvement result from the labours of the agriculturist, the manufacturer, or philosopher, that great triumvirate, on whom (politically speaking) depend the prosperity and happiness of every civilized country.

Of these three classes of society, the last, though least in number, is not so in importance; and it were well for the moral interests of the world, if every man of letters would, like a prudent father, duly train up the children of his imagination in such a manner, that when introduced to the world they might become the moral agents of virtue and philanthropy; and so carry home to the author of their existence the love and admiration of his fellow-creatures, and the invaluable blessings of an approving conscience.

We do not mean by this observation to insinuate that a respectable author does not take such precautions, nor are we ungenerous enough to suppose that philosophy and religion do not of themselves suggest them to the votaries of literary fame.

But there is one department of literature, which, from the peculiar licenses it allows, is apt to mislead the judgement of its followers, and inculcate a notion that it is not amenable at all times to the strict laws of morality and virtue.

To this fatal delusion the Muse of every country owes her disgrace; and it is to be lamented that the evil charms of wit and genius have too often polluted the pure streams of Castaly, and disorganized that natural harmony which ought to exist between the Muses and the Graces.

Without dwelling on this painful subject, we may observe that fashion and popular taste, nowadays, have sanctioned a species of poetry which ill accords with our national character, and may in many respects be likened to poetical novels and tales, or to musical and romantic dramas, the highest aim of whose author is to please the eye and the ear, to play round the senses, but never touch the soul. There are, it is true, occasional beauties interpersed, and sketches of nature so drawn as to keep up a sufficient interest till the tale be told, which then passes away like a dream, needing neither after thought nor interpretation. Compositions of this kind require only to be perused to be understood. Philosophical reflections are quite excluded. The œconomy of the universe; the scale and the sword of divine justice and mercy; the connexion between the material and immaterial world; moral agency, cause and effect, and all that ought to interest the rational and thinking part of mankind, are never considered. The amiable virtues sometimes appear, but seldom the severer ones; the pictures have colouring, but need solidity and keeping. The Muse does not act in the twofold character of painter and sculptor, and the forms she pourtrays want the solemn majesty and the animating inspirations of philosophy and truth.

There is however another Muse, who disdains to creep along her earthy path with reptile pace, and, boldly soaring towards that sacred temple which stands on high, looks down upon the scene below, and catches all that is sublime and beautiful. She strikes the rock with her lyre, and the living waters of Poesy gush forth; she treads the mountain and holds communion with the cloudy spirit of the storm, and the sunny shades that dance in the sunbeams; if she descend into the valley, Rural Happiness and Simplicity are her handmaidens; in the populous city she walks hand in hand with Industry and Benevolence; and when conducted by the inward and invisible monitor, amid the visible associations of life and death, the urn and the cypress, Faith allied to Hope and Fear support her through the vale of tears, and open to her view the distant dawn of the promised Land. In short, wherever she treads, her ways are ways of pleasantness and peace. Our readers must not look beyond this imperfect outline (of what we consider as the highest and most edifying species of Poetry) for metaphysical proprieties of unity in time and place, or for obsolete definitions and models of ancient and modern excellence; nor shall we enlarge upon the present state of British poetry, a topic which would carry us beyond our prescribed limits. Criticism we wish to avoid, and would not draw further comparisons (if comparison can be drawn) between the Muse educated in the confined schools of fashion and popular taste, and the same being trained up in the free and boundless expanse of nature. As philanthropists, we would abstain from all bitter and personal allusion, pleased rather with the title of panegyrists than of critics, and happy whenever the press furnishes us with new subjects of praise and commendation – happier still when persuaded that the labours of the poet will be ultimately blessed by the pensive gratitude and moral improvement of his enlightened readers.

In this belief we have now taken up the poem of The Excursion; and in order that a fair estimate may be formed of the nature and design, (of the whole poem of The Recluse, of which this forms the second part,) we cannot do better than quote a portion of the author's own preface:

[Quotes from the *Preface* to the *Excursion*: 'It may be proper to state . . .'
to the end with small omissions, and then quotes immediately the whole
of the verse *Prospectus*.]

The interest of our readers will already be excited by the perusal of this specimen, given as a prospectus of the whole poem of The Recluse, and they will perceive that the powers of its author are nearly allied to those which have immortalized the muse of Milton.

It might not be deemed improper, previous to the introduction of our friends amid the scenes of The Excursion, to make them acquainted with the characters and dispositions of their fellow travellers. But minute details of all these conversational agents would delay our outset too long; and they are better able when called on to speak for themselves. – Nevertheless, in exception to this remark, we feel inclined to say a little on the character of the Wanderer.

Some critics have objected to the introduction of this personage, as being deficient in dignity and interest, because holding no higher station in life than that of an itinerant pedlar –

> A vagrant merchant bent beneath his load.
> [*The Excursion, PW*, V, p. 19, Book I, l. 324]

Is such a character, say they, fit companion for the high and lofty muse? Can such noble sentiments and doctrines proceed from the mouth of vagrant Industry? Can such a being descant upon the order and beauty of Nature, and describe in glowing colours the relations between the upper and the lower world? or, to sum up the whole, Can a low-born pedlar think like a philosopher, and speak like an orator?

Such objections at first sight seem just and reasonable, but vanish on a nearer view of the picture, when Truth has corrected the false colouring in which association had confounded the portraits of the ancient and modern, the northern and southern pedlars. Now the unfitness of companionship, which has been urged against the character of the Wanderer, may be easily obviated, by observing that all travellers, whether poets or not, should, if necessary, take such guides as are best qualified by occupation and pursuit to point out the intended route, and to describe the objects of interest (be they material or intellectual) which pervade it. Innumerable examples in support of this opinion may be quoted both from the ancient and modern poets; and we must still insist upon the propriety of our author's selecting this peripatetic philosopher for the companion of his excursion, which leads him among secluded vales and mountain fastnesses, whose inhabitants and annals were best known to that person who had made the former the constant agents of his traffic, and the latter the common-place-book of his memory.

With respect to the other alleged characteristic incongruities of mental endowment and low-born origin, these too may be as easily reconciled, unless any should be found hardy enough to assert that genius and talents are the exclusive rights of education and rank; that the gems of wisdom are only to be found united with the baubles of art and circumstance; that physical and mental capacities are not one and the same qualities in the prince and the pedlar; that moral excellence and worth are to be neglected and undervalued because blind fortune wants the instinct, and poverty the power, to cherish them: but let us listen awhile to the Muse, and hear with what beauty and truth she sings of talents uncultured, and of genius unrevealed:

[Quotes *ibid.*, *PW*, V, pp. 10–11, Book I, ll. 77–97:

> Oh many are the poets that are sown
> By nature . . .
> Belov'd and honor'd – far as he was known –]

The occupations of our Wanderer's infancy and boyhood were divided between the school, over which his stepfather presided, and the summer tendance of cattle on the hills of Athol:

[Quotes *ibid.*, *PW*, V, pp. 14–15, Book I, ll. 198–218:

Oh then what soul was his, when on the tops . . .
His mind was a thanksgiving to the Power
That made him – it was blessedness and love.]

The scanty libraries of this schoolmaster and of the village priest served to people the infant regions of thought with legendary tales – giants, ancient ballads, and the common-place stock of a nursery education. When further advanced in knowledge and years, elementary works of science and the sacred page of song became his constant companions. Pensive habits and pursuits of this kind could not fail to engender in a mind naturally prone to arrange and calculate, that succeeding admiration of the order and harmony in nature, which is so remarkable in all the moral and philosophical reflections of the Wanderer.

In the strict discipline of the Scotch kirk, and under the guidance of a pious mother, were imbibed those principles of veneration for the divine influence which correct the common propensities to vice, and teach the duties and sympathies due to God and man.

No sooner had youthful manhood fortified the body, and education qualified the mind, than this child of promise was summoned by his parents

—to select the course
Of humble Industry which promised best
To yield him no unworthy maintenance.
[*Ibid.*, *PW*, V, p. 18, Book I, ll. 309–11]

Not in vain did his mother recommend him to take a school in the adjoining village: – he complied for a short time with her wishes; but the wandering spirit, which he had no power to exorcise, still haunted him, and at last led him forth, amid parental blessings, in the humble calling of a pedlar.

From this time, like the celebrated hero of the Odyssey, he saw 'cities, men and manners;' and at length, by thrift and honesty, in life's autumn was enabled to reap the golden harvest of competence and content; to look up with grateful ecstasy to that Power which had been pleased to realize the visionary schemes of his youth, and reconduct him to his native hills, where now
[Quotes *ibid.*, *PW*, V, p. 21, Book I, ll. 386–96:

His calling laid aside he lived at ease . . .
Thus had he lived a long and innocent life.]

Such is the personage whom our author had known from his childhood,

473

and whom he has chosen for the companion and guide of his excursion. We have already carried our readers into the middle of the first book, where the poet meets with this ancient friend by appointment, and whence their pilgrimage of observation commences. After a short walk they arrive at the ruins of a deserted cottage and garden. The Wanderer relates the history of its last inhabitants, and depicts with beauty and truth the miserable consequences of war, as operating upon the industrious habits of the labouring classes. The story is too long to be quoted, and too much of a whole to be separated. It abounds with simplicity and pathos naturally arising from the subjects it embraces; – an industrious and loving husband obliged, by want of employment, to tear himself from his family, enlist for a soldier, and, secretly leaving the price of his liberty and his happiness, to abandon his wife and his children without a farewell look or embrace; and, in the silence of night, steal away like a thief from all he held dearest on earth. His forlorn wife and widow never more hear tidings of him; and, after years of sorrow, her industrious habits are turned by grief to melancholy wanderings; her cottage and her garden and her children become neglected, and all the duties of life are forgotten in the restless expectation of her husband's return. Her youngest child dies; and she herself at last fell a victim to heart-wasting despondency and lingering hope, and dreams that ended in the grave.

We augur that, on the perusal of this tale, our readers will feel a sensation similar to that of the author himself, who says,

> I turn'd aside in weakness, nor had power
> To thank him for the tale which he had told.
> [*Ibid.*, *PW*, V, p. 38, Book I, ll. 919–202]

A village inn receives the travellers, and affords them a resting-place for the evening.

The opening of the second book draws a cheerful comparison between the characters of the ancient harper and the pedlar; and the poet then breaks out into admiration of his guide's lore and sensibility, which were continually called forth by the natural objects which surrounded them; the animal world, the mountains and their streams, the villages and their huts and houses, the hospitality of the cotters, and their gratitude for kind counsel and advice in the hour of mental distress.

[Quotes *ibid.*, *PW*, V, pp. 43–4 and footnotes, Book II, ll. 57–80:

> Greetings and smiles we met with all day long . . .
> With softened spirit even when it condemned!]

474

After three days of such pleasant travel, the Wanderer reminds his companion that he has a solitary friend to visit at a distance, and that they must straightway proceed.

The independence of the pedestrian is then contrasted with the noise of pomp and equipage, and the journey again commenced, their spirits braced, and their thoughts

> Pleasant as roses in the thickets blown
> And pure as dew bathing their crimson leaves!
> [(*Ibid.*, *PW*, V, p. 45, Book II, ll. 109–10]

This distant friend, to whom the Wanderer promises to introduce the poet, is distinguished in The Excursion by the name of the Solitary, and is, like the pedlar, a person of Scotch descent and lowly parentage, yet one who, by the advantages of a quick apprehension, and of studious habits in youth, had qualified himself so as to become a minister of the kirk; and after a while he entered the army as a chaplain. Prompted

> Partly thro' lack of better hopes, and part
> Perhaps incited by a curious mind,
> In early life he undertook the charge
> Of chaplain to a military troop
> Cheer'd by the highland bag-pipe as they marched
> In plaided vest, his fellow-countrymen.
> [*Ibid.*, *PW*, V, p. 48, Book II, ll. 172–7]

In a few lines which immediately succeed these, the poet has drawn to the life a portrait, of which we fear there are at this day too many resemblances both in the British army and navy. How they came there is another question; and why they do but little good there may perhaps be easily conjectured: – but to the passage and characters in question –

[Quotes *ibid.*, *PW*, V, p. 48, Book II, ll. 178–90:

> This office filling, and by native pow'r . . .
> Ambition to attempt, and skill to win!]

The fruits of this marriage were two lovely children; and the gay chaplain having left the army is represented as living in happy retirement, till

[Quotes *ibid.*, *PW*, V, p. 49, Book II, ll. 198–210:

> In the course of one undreaded year . . .
> So lived he – so he might have died.]

From this state of apathy the Solitary is suddenly roused by the bursting

475

out of the French revolution; and hastening to the scene of madness and fury, he

> – from the pulpit zealously maintained
> The cause of Christ and civil liberty
> As one –
> [*Ibid.*, *PW*, V, pp. 49–50, Book II, ll. 220–2]

This 'intoxicating service' was however of short duration; for, mingling with those who from repeated excesses and victories had sold themselves to pride and infidelity, he also became an infidel, and by means of specious argument and smooth tongued eloquence easily seduced others,

> – who most boldly drew
> Hopeful prognostications from a creed
> Which in the light of false Philosophy
> Spread like a halo round a misty moon,
> Widening its circles as the storms advance!!
> [*Ibid.*, *PW*, V, p. 51, Book II, ll. 258–62]

We would advise our readers at this particular part of the Sceptic's (for so the Solitary is sometimes called) history to pause awhile and reflect – on the probable chances of such an one's falling off from his ancient faith – on the sudden manner in which infidelity may be engrafted on personal pride and vanity – These will not prove unprofitable considerations. And then the poet's description – of inward remorse, and of the fallacy and weakness of a creed built on the sandy foundations of arrogance and self-sufficiency, will receive its due tribute of praise and sympathy –

[Quotes *ibid. PW*, V, p. 52, Book II, ll. 278–92:

> – His moods
> Of pain were keen as those of better men . . .
> Are as vain billows in a tossing sea.]

Disappointed in his visionary hopes and dreams of liberty, and despised by men who appeared to thrive in fame and win what he desired – yet in themselves

> – weak men,
> Too weak even for his envy or his hate –
> [*Ibid.*, *PW*, V, p. 52, Book II, ll. 302–3]

the Solitary quits France, and, losing all pleasure and tranquillity, wanders about in foreign lands, till weary of his restless pilgrimage of discontent, he at last sets himself down in one of the most retired and smallest of the vales of his native country. Hither our travellers are hastening; and arriving within sight of their destined place of rest, the poet gives the following description of its loneliness and beauty.

[Quotes *ibid.*, *PW*, V, pp. 54–5, Book II, ll. 358–69:

> In rugged arms how soft it seems to lie . . .
> Sickness, or accident, or grief, or pain.]

This little valley, or mountain Urn as the poet calls it, contained but one abode inhabited by the Sceptic, a young child, an elderly woman, and an old man. As the visitants are descending the side of one of the impending hills, their ears are suddenly struck by these awful sounds:

> – Shall in the grave thy love be known,
> In death thy faithfulness?
> [*Ibid.*, *PW*, V, p. 55, Book II, ll. 381–2]

The Wanderer at first apprehends the death of the Sceptic; but the sounds are afterwards discovered to proceed from an unseen band of rustics conducting the funeral ceremonies of the old man, one of the late inmates of the lonely dwelling, whose life had fallen a sacrifice to the effects of a mountain storm to which the feebleness of age had been all night exposed.

Ere the cottage is gained, the poet's attention is arrested by a small pent or baby-house formed by cottage children in a chasm of the mountain. In this recess is found a single volume of the works of Voltaire, that wildering pilot of the Sceptic's fearful voyage!

After a few moral reflections from the Wanderer on the incident alluded to, the poet thus introduces an interesting picture, contrasting the forlorn appearance of despondency, with that of infant innocence and sorrow needing consolation and support.

[Quotes *ibid.*, *PW*, V, pp. 59–60, Book II, ll. 497–511:

> Behold the man whom he had fancied dead! . . .
> His body is at rest, his soul in heav'n.]

The meeting of the Solitary and the Wanderer is painted in glowing colours; we would fain present the picture to our reader's view, but necessity obliges us to curtail our intended extracts. We have yet a long track to pursue, and many beautiful flowers to select, as well as majestic forms to notice, by the way side.

We therefore hasten to the end of this second portion of The Excursion, and must unwillingly pass over in silence the Wanderer's description of the ancient funeral ceremonies of Scotland; the inner chamber of the Solitary's abode; his narrative of the old man's death; and of his own vision of a heavenly city fancifully depicted in the cloudy architecture of the golden skies which succeeded the storm, and the powerful effect this spectacle produced upon him while beholding it. Our readers will readily form some idea of the brilliant and grand assemblage of objects which an imaginary scene of this kind is fitted to give birth to in the creative mind of Mr. Wordsworth, and we again regret that the passage is too long for insertion. We must, however, in justice to our poet's descriptive powers, (and ere we close this second book,) treat our readers with the following passage, which describes a part of the view opposite to the Solitary's cottage window, and the companionship which the distant prospect of two mighty mountain peaks often afford him during the changeful appearances of nature:

[Quotes *ibid.*, *PW*, V, p. 67, see footnotes, Book II, ll. 694–725:

> Those lusty twins on which your eyes are cast, . . .
> Here do I sit and watch!]

Where, in the whole fields of ancient and modern poetry, shall we find a spot more fertile in sublime and beautiful imagery than this? a composition containing the results of many a morning, noon, and midnight study, sketched amid the fitful changes of elements and seasons, and finished by the masterly touches of science and reflection.

The Solitary having entertained his guests with a short and simple repast, the trio quit the house, and commence a ramble on the hills. This introduces us to the opening of the third book of the poem, which is entitled 'Despondency,' and develops still more of the character of the Sceptic, and of his belief (or inclination to believe) in the doctrines of Chance and Materialism; and the confession of these principles is drawn from him by the contemplation of some huge masses of rock fantastically placed, and bearing the resemblance of a Druidical Cromlek. This object, which the poet has made the productive cause of a difference of sensations in the feelings of the Solitary and of the Wanderer, had at first been overlooked while the party were in doubt which path they should pursue; whether or no they should ascend the hill, and seat themselves, like Cicero's academicians, beneath the shade of a yew-tree, or trace the mountain stream to its source: – but let us hear how eloquently, and with what peculiar truth and simplicity, the scene is described:

[Quotes *ibid.*, *PW*, V, pp. 75–6, Book III, ll. 22–35:

> – Shall we take this pathway for our guide? . . .
> Like human Life from Darkness.]

But to return to the subject of discussion. The Wanderer's mind is suddenly affected by the sight of the rocky masses before alluded to, and vents itself in the following remark:

> Among the rocks and stones methinks I see
> More than the heedless impress that belongs
> To lovely Nature's casual work. They bear
> A semblance strange of Power intelligent
> And of design not wholly worn away.
> [*Ibid.*, *PW*, V, p. 77, Book III, ll. 80–4]

The accompaniments of the supposed Cromlek are then made the touchstones of pleasant thoughts and moral reflections, which end for a time in the following apostrophe to Contemplation:

[Quotes *ibid.*, *PW*, V, p. 78, Book III, ll. 101–12:

> Hail, Contemplation! from the stately tow'rs . . .
> Lost in unsearchable Eternity.]

Some idea of the desponding nature of the Solitary's mind, and of the fatal bias which unbelief would give to the equal scale of divine Justice, may be drawn from the following quotation, which forms one of the links in the chain of argument adopted by the Sceptic while reverting to the rocks assembled on Salisbury Plains, the pyramids of Egypt, and the marble ruins in the sandy deserts of Syria, all of which, in his opinion,

> —if the spirit be oppressed by sense
> Of instability, revolt, decay,
> And change and emptiness, these freaks of Nature
> And her blind helper Chance do *then* suffice
> To quicken and to aggravate, to feed
> Pity and scorn and melancholy pride.
> [*Ibid.*, *PW*, V, p. 79, Book III, ll. 137–42]

The Sceptic next proceeds in eloquent language to support the notion that thought and intellect, and all the wide fields of nature abounding in scenes that allure the sense and lift the soul through time and space, are all vain and useless, as affording no assurance of a future state; no

—better sanctuary
From doubt than the senseless grave!
[*Ibid.*, *PW*, V, p. 81, Book III, ll. 223–4]

At this point of the argument he is reproved by the Wanderer, who reminds him of the words

His body is at rest, his soul in heaven;
[*Ibid.*, *PW*, V, p. 82, Book III, l. 229]

addressed to the child lamenting, in the second book, the death of the old man.

The Solitary, without being offended at the rebuke, goes on to enumerate such opinions of ancient and modern philosophers as agreed in the doctrines of Chance and Materialism, and looked no further than the present scene for happiness and enjoyment. He nevertheless confesses that, while under the influence of his former creed, and amid the tender cares of an amiable wife and family, he experienced days of happiness and visions of ecstasy, when, as he says, he was free

To explore the destiny of human kind
Not as an intellectual game pursued
With curious subtilty, thereby to cheat
Irksome sensations; but by love of Truth
Urged on –
[*Ibid.*, *PW*, V, p. 83, Book III, ll. 284–8]

and again speaking of his visionary bliss, wanting however the assurance of Faith,
[Quotes *ibid.*, *PW*, V, p. 84, Book III, ll. 299–306:

—Deities that float . . .
By flowers embellished, and by springs refreshed!]

Retired amid the beautiful scenes of Devonshire, and enjoying a paradise of uninterrupted conjugal and parental felicity, the mental state of the Solitary seems to have greatly improved; and this progressive amendment he describes to have taken place while his
[Quotes *ibid.*, *PW*, V, p. 94, Book III, ll. 554–83:

—tender mate became
The thankful captive of maternal bonds . . .
And infants' smile, awaited my return!]

This extract, with others which we might select from the Sceptic's own narrative of the death of his children and wife, seem intended by the poet to create in his readers a redeeming interest for this victim of unbelief and despondency: the descriptions we allude to abound in pathos, and the calm and unruffled resignation of the wife is beautifully contrasted with the vehement grief of the desponding husband. These melancholy scenes we shall pass over, as well as the manner in which the Sceptic is disappointed in the termination of the French revolution, and in his voyage to America; and shall end our extracts from the 3d book, with the pensive and desponding comparison which the Sceptic, ever seeking rest yet finding none, draws between the course of his own life and that of a mountain stream descending into the valley. We have seen similar pictures before, but never one so highly finished, and so richly fraught with the ornaments of nature and philosophy: – but we hasten to lay it before our readers –

[Quotes *ibid.*, *PW*, V, pp. 107–8, Book III, ll. 956–91:

> Enough is told! Here am I – ye have heard . . .
> The unfathomable gulph – where all is still!!]

'Despondency corrected' forms the title of the fourth book of The Excursion, and it will easily be conjectured for whom this correction is intended. Whether or no our author has succeeded in the subject, the future judgement of his readers must decide. We do not wish to bias the opinion of the public, but particular experience admonishes us that it is our duty to recommend a frequent and reflective study of this portion of The Excursion.

The very best of us, from the natural frailty of our condition and the instability of human affairs, are at times too apt to suffer the clouds of despondency to arise and darken those beautiful visions which bless our day dreams, and, in the trance of bodily and mental distress, create for the disembodied soul a short-lived paradise of spiritual ecstasy.

There is, we should hope, no rational being (the register of whose life is not too much blotted by guilt) but must sometimes feel this sort of spiritual transport; and the enjoyment is so pure, that it seems the only foretaste of those joys (that the eye hath not seen or the ear heard) which favoured mortality can experience.

To qualify the mind for frequent impressions of this kind, is a study well worth the attention of every intelligent being; and some of the readiest modes of attaining that qualification will be to fortify the heart against the encroachments of discontent and despondency, to contemplate with care and reflection the works of the Creation, and thus be led from things below to look on things above – By analogy and the inherent impulses of imitation to compare the order of the universe, and to feel the necessity of organizing our own works so as faintly to resemble those which bear the impress of perfect Intelligence.

The vacant hours of idle thoughtlessness will then be turned to good account. Things will begin to have something more than a nominal value and association; substances and relations, primary and secondary causes, cease to be mere metaphysical distinctions; and the mind become a kingdom peopled by natural and elementary subjects, under the government and discipline of its individual sovereign. It is thus that the estate of the retired and unwealthy philosopher, though unblessed by the smiles of fortune and patronage, is nevertheless supported by the benevolence of Nature and Religion, whose endless supplies are made the active agents of gratitude and consolation.

We will not however forestall the arguments, nor vainly attempt to aim at the eloquence, of our Poet; but recommend again and again a frequent study of the 'Despondency corrected,' which, in our judgement, contains the best test of the mighty powers of its author's intelligence, and will enable our readers to draw from it some inference of the sublimity and beauty of the poet's moral and religious system supported on the basis of Virtue and Faith; – of his philanthropy, from the almost apostolic earnestness with which he sets about the conversion of misguided and desponding humanity; – of his imagination and poetical genius, from the originality and depth of his thoughts; – the elegance of expression, the truth and propriety of his metaphors and similes; – the fitness of his epithets; – and lastly, from the majestic simplicity and harmonious cadence of his numbers, &c. – To these poetic excellencies we think the Muse of Mr. Wordsworth fairly entitled; and are aware that, for this poor though grateful acknowledgement of the mental improvement and pleasure which we have received from the study of the work before us, we stand exposed to the censure of some who affect to despise what we have commended. We however feel persuaded that from Philanthropists the Poet will meet with that consideration and esteem, which those who have a deeper insight into the human heart will be ready to bestow. By these the pages of a poem like The Excursion, embracing all the best interests of humanity, will not be devoured with that disgusting rapacity which disgraces the poetic feasts of our Fashionables, who like locusts overrun the territories of every circulating library; and after all their travels cannot even boast with the map-devouring mouse,

A river or a sea
Was to me a dish of tea,
And a kingdom bread and butter.

No; rivers and seas and kingdoms are to these triflers mere objects of transient eye-service, and nothing better. But to return to our subject: –
The Sceptic, in the course of his painful narrative, having evinced symptoms of native feeling, which called forth the partial sympathy and pity of his hearers, the Wanderer, commencing his remonstrances,

—with firm voice
That did not falter tho' his heart was mov'd,
[*Ibid.*, *PW*, V, p. 110, Book IV, ll. 8–9]

strikes at once at the root of the Sceptic's mental disease; and boldly telling him the main causes of its origin and continuance, makes the folly and injustice of adhering to a particular creed deduced from individual experience, and not from the general distributions of Providence, the next argument of reproof:

[Quotes *ibid.*, *PW*, V, p. 110, Book IV, ll. 10–27:

—one adequate support
For the calamities of mortal life . . .
To the dishonor of his holy Name!]

This remark, so truly and feelingly expressed, is tempered by the following short and supplicatory prayer in favour of desponding mortality:

Soul of our souls, and safeguard of the world,
Sustain Thou only canst the sick of heart,
Restore their languid spirits, and recall
Their lost affections unto Thee and thine!
[(*Ibid.*, *PW*, V, p. 110, Book IV, ll. 28–31]

EDITOR'S NOTE

1. The preceding article is dated 22 September.

157.

Unsigned notice, *Literary Gazette*, 23 December 1820, IV, 837

The Octavo Edition of Wordsworth's Excursion.
We do not usually conceive ourselves called upon to notice second editions of works; especially such as evince no variation from their predecessors, except in size and price. We must however claim the privilege of deviating from our accustomed mode in the case of Wordsworth's Excursion. Indeed a quarto, of the price of two guineas, is likely only to be known by report to the majority of readers of poetry; and the consequence is, that though this beautiful poem has been published, we believe, more than six years, it has, from its size and cost, been as inaccessible to numbers, whom its contents would have delighted, as if it had continued in manuscript.

Nothing can be more remote from our purpose, than any idea of entering into an elaborate critique on the poem now before us; for although from its hitherto limited circulation, we might fill column after column with extracts that would probably be new to many of our readers, and must elicit admiration from all; we are not sure that we should be authorized to do this by a work, which, in point of fact, has been already long known to the public by name; and which is now, we hope, likely to be universally read and duly appreciated. But we cannot consent to let the second edition of such a poem only have its appearance announced in the common advertisements of the trade. This would indeed be a lasting disgrace to us as conductors of a Journal, claiming the proud appellation of a Literary Record. Our department in criticism is, we are sensible, comparatively an humble one: promptitude, and fairness, are the qualities by which we consider our notifications most likely to be rendered really valuable to our readers. *We* do not pretend either to dictate to the taste of the present age, or to anticipate the judgment of posterity. Exceptions, however, do occur, if they only prove the existence of the general rule; and believing this to be one of them, we are induced to congratulate it's author and the public on the appearance of The Excursion, in a form which may enable the lovers of poetry to judge for themselves of it's merits. The result of that judgment we are quite willing to commit to pure taste, and genuine feeling; but we should be equally unjust to the author, and ourselves, did we not express our belief, that if a faith at once meek and sublime; a genius, at the same time pure, lofty, and ennobling; a philosophy, equally comprehensive, and profound; be qualities likely to render the public decision favorable, the Excursion has nothing to fear. It is a volume to which the lover of nature may turn with delight, for its enchanting pictures of scenery, and its patriarchal views of character; the admirer of poetry, for almost every better charm which his favorite science can exemplify; the philosopher, for the profoundness and majestic simplicity of many of its speculations; and the christian, for the unaffected piety and devotional sublimity it so abundantly displays.

X

The Excursion: some opinions, 1812–1818

158. Henry Crabb Robinson

Undated reminiscences added to his diary entry for 27 February 1812

Richard Cargill (*fl.* 1790–1822), a native of Jamaica, was taught 'oratory' by John Thelwall and studied law with William Rough (1772–1838); he became first a barrister and then took holy orders. Rough was a friend of Christopher Wordsworth at Cambridge (see entry 7) and later became judge (1830) and Chief Justice of Ceylon. Wordsworth, 31 December 1814, reports to Catherine Clarkson that Rough was one of those who had declared of *The Excursion*: 'there has been nothing equal to it since Milton's day.' Cargill, met Crabb Robinson in 1812.

(MY, II, 182)

a.

One day ... I met him [Cargill] by chance and asked him by chance what he thought of Wordsworth's *Ecclesiastical Sketches*. He had not read them. I expressed my surprise. 'Do you no longer love Wordsworth?' 'It is as impossible', he answered, 'for one who has ever really loved Wordsworth to cease loving him, as it is for a Christian to cease being a Christian. But the religious poems of Wordsworth are those precisely which I do not love. In fact, I doubt whether Wordsworth is a Christian, if I am to judge of him from *The Excursion*. I think that no better than atheism. This he afterwards defined to consist in a faith in redemption by Christ and the means of redemption ...

(*Henry Crabb Robinson on Books and their Writers*, ed. Edith J. Morley, 1938, I, 65)

b.

At the time I became acquainted with him [in 1812] ... I was an enthusiast for Wordsworth and probably I had considerable influence in making him also an enthusiast for Wordsworth. The same taste had cemented my friendship for Rough.

(*Ibid.*)

159. Robert Southey

From letters, 1814–1816

a. To Henry Southey, 11 March 1814

Wordsworth is going to the press with eight books of his Recluse, – the great work of his life – about 8000 verses. The Old Cumberland Beggar in the Lyrical Ballads is one of the loppings of this poem, & will show you its pitch.

(Ms. Bodleian Library)

b. To J. Neville White (brother of Henry Kirke White), 7 September 1814

Have you seen Wordsworth's poem? If not, read it, if you can, before you see the author. You will see him with the more pleasure, and look with more interest at the scenery which he describes.

(*A Selection from the Letters of Robert Southey*, ed. J. W. Warter, London, 1856 II, 376)

c. To Bernard Barton, 19 December 1814

Wordsworth's residence and mine are fifteen miles asunder, a sufficient distance to preclude any frequent interchange of visits. I have known him nearly twenty years, and, for about half that time, intimately. The strength and the character of his mind you see in the Excursion, and his life does not belie his writings, for, in every relation of life, and every point of view, he is a truly exemplary and admirable man. In conversation he is powerful beyond any of his contemporaries; and, as a poet, – I speak not from the partiality of friendship, nor because we have been so absurdly held up as both writing upon one concerted system of poetry, but with the most deliberate exercise of impartial judgment whereof I am capable, when I declare my full conviction that posterity will rank him with Milton . . .

(*Life and Correspondence of Robert Southey*, ed. C.C. Southey, 1849, IV, 91)

d. To Walter Scott, 24 December 1814

Southey repeated this on 27 December in a letter to William Taylor.

Jeffrey I hear has written what his admirers call a *crushing* review of the Excursion. He might as well seat himself upon Skiddaw and fancy that he crushed the mountain. I heartily wish Wordsworth may one day meet with him, and lay him alongside, yard-arm and yard-arm in argument.

(*Ibid.*, IV, 97)

e. To Henry Southey, 16 January 1815[1]

I have heard from many quarters of Lord Byron's praise, and regard it just as much as I did his censure. Nothing can be more absurd than thinking of comparing any of my poems with the Paradise Lost. With Tasso, with Virgil, with Homer, there may be fair grounds of comparison; but my mind is wholly unlike Milton's, and my poetry has nothing of his imagination and distinguishing character; nor is there any poet who has, except Wordsworth: he possesses it in an equal degree. And it is entirely impossible that any man can understand Milton, and fail to perceive that Wordsworth is a poet of the same class and of equal powers. Whatever my powers may be, they are not of that class.

(*Ibid.*, IV, 105)

f. To Chauncey Hare Townshend, 17 August 1816

Have you read The Excursion? and have you read the collection of Wordsworth's other poems, in two octavo volumes? If you have not, there is a great pleasure in store for you. I am no blind admirer of Wordsworth, and can see where he has chosen subjects which are unworthy in themselves, and where the strength of his imagination and of his feeling is directed upon inadequate objects. Notwithstanding these faults, and their frequent occurrence, it is by the side of Milton that Wordsworth will have his station awarded him by posterity.

(*Ibid.*, IV, 194–5)

EDITOR'S NOTE

1. Date corrected from Ms. Bodleian Library.

160. Thomas Poole (1765–1837)

From a letter to Wordsworth, 9 July 1814

I am truly glad that you'r about to publish at last, at least part of one of your great Poems. I trust it will make you known as you are; and it seems to me the only difference between you and the World has been – as to the manner of executing the *minor* parts. All allow you the greatest essentials of a Poet in a *super eminent degree*. Can you alter your opinions as to those minor Parts?

(Ms. The Wordsworth Library)

161. Charles Lamb

From a letter to Wordsworth, 9 August 1814

It is the noblest conversational poem I ever read. A day in heaven. The part (or rather main body) which has left the sweetest odour on my memory (a bad term for the remains of an impression so recent) is the Tales of the Church yard. The only girl among seven brethren, born out of due time and not duly taken away again – the deaf man and the blind man – the Jacobite and the Hanoverian whom antipathies reconcile – the Scarron-entry of the rusticating parson upon his solitude – these were all new to me too. My having known the story of Margaret (at the beginning), a very old acquaintance, even as long back as I saw you first at Stowey, did not make her reappearance less fresh. I don't know what to pick out of this Best of Books upon the best subjects for partial naming.

That gorgeous Sunset is famous, I think it must have been the identical one we saw on Salisbury plain five years ago, that drew Phillips from the card table where he had sat from rise of that luminary to its unequall'd set, but neither he nor I had gifted eyes to see those symbols of common things glorified such as the prophets saw them, in that sunset – the wheel – the potter's clay – the wash pot – the wine press – the almond tree rod – the baskets of figs – the fourfold visaged head, the throne and him that sat thereon.

One feeling I was particularly struck with as what I recognised so very

492

lately at Harrow Church on entering in it after a hot and secular day's pleasure, – the instantaneous coolness and calming, almost transforming, properties of a country church just entered – a certain fragrance which it has – either from its holiness, or being kept shut all the week, or the air that is let in being pure country – exactly what you have reduced into words but I am feeling I cannot. The reading your lines about it fixed me for a time, a monument, in Harrow Church, (do you know it?) with its fine long Spire white as washd marble, to be seen by vantage of its high scite as far as Salisbury spire itself almost –

I shall select a day or two very shortly when I am coolest in brain to have a steady second reading, which I feel will lead to many more, for it will be a stock book with me while eyes or spectacles shall be lent me.

There is a deal of noble matter about mountain scenery, yet not so much as to overpower and discountenance a poor Londoner or South country man entirely, though Mary seems to have felt it occasionally a little too powerfully, for it was her remark during reading it that by your system it was doubtful whether a Liver in Towns had a Soul to be Saved. She almost trembled for that invisible part of us in her.

(*The Letters of Charles and Mary Lamb*, ed. E. V. Lucas, 1935, II, 126–7)

162. Henry Crabb Robinson

Extracts from his diary, 1814–1815

a. 13 August 1814

I stole out of the theatre to call on Madge, at whose apartments I found the new great poem of Wordsworth, *The Excursion*. I could only look into the preface, and read a few extracts with Madge. It is a poem of formidable size, and I fear too mystical to be popular. But it will, however, put an end to the sneers of those who consider him or affect to consider him as a puerile writer who attempts only little things. But it will draw on him the imputation of dullness possibly. Still it will, I trust, strengthen the zeal of his few friends. My anxiety is great to read it.

(*Henry Crabb Robinson on Books and Their Writers*, ed. Edith J. Morley, 1938, I, 147)

b. 4 October 1814

Schlegel conversed in English with me, and he was curious to inquire about our English poets. He had received a favourable impression of Lord Byron from Madame de Stael, who considers him as the best of our poets. I objected to him the want of a repose and an intellect calmly contemplating the passions it regulates, at least in the poetic representation of them. This Schlegel assented to. I repeated to him three of Wordsworth's sonnets, *Westminster Bridge*, *Switzerland*, and *The King*. He seemed to be pleased with them all, and took a list of his and Southey's works with evident interest. But he said he was more curious to know the general character of English literature than to be acquainted with any one work.

(*Ibid.*, I. 149)

c. 30 October–11 November 1814

Oct. 30th . . . I read some extracts from Wordsworth's poem out of the *Examiner*, but it did not seem to please greatly . . .

Nov. 2nd . . . Sat at home this evening from six to half-past eight reading Wordsworth's *Excursion*. I have yet read but little of this exquisite work. I have, however, already no doubt that it will be for other reasons as unpopular as his other works, and that it will be highly admired by his former admirers . . .

And afterwards I called at the Godwins' and saw the young people, and then returned and read Wordsworth again till past midnight with high delight.

Nov. 4th. I spent part of the morning at home and continued Wordsworth's poem. The fourth book I found by no means dull or uninteresting, though purely reasoning, and the book has hitherto had in my mind greater beauties and fewer faults that I anticipated . . .

Nov. 6th . . . The evening was spent partly in chat and partly in attending to Wordsworth. Mrs. Clarkson read the first two books with great effect . . .

Nov. 8th . . . I chatted, however, with Burrell, a man who *ought* to love Wordsworth, but who almost scorns and derides the poem. He has no tolerance for the mystical passages of the work . . .

Robley came to my chambers to read Wordsworth while I went to Islington . . . I returned and took tea at my chambers with Robley. I read passages of the poem to him. He left me about eight . . .

Nov. 10th. . . . At breakfast . . . I read the conclusion of the fourth book of Wordsworth's poem – transcendently beautiful . . .

Nov. 11th . . . . I also read part of the fifth book of *The Excursion*, but it is far inferior to the fourth, perhaps to any preceding book. It is the first part of the work that I found heavy.

(*Ibid.*, I. 151–3)

d. 2–3 January 1815

Jan. 2nd . . . I took tea and played chess with T. Isaac, and after supper began to read Wordsworth. But we broke off soon, Pattison not liking it. I was offended and shut up my book.

Jan. 3rd . . . *The Excursion* on the second perusal gratified me still more than the first, and my own impressions were not removed by the various criticisms I about this time became acquainted with. I also read to Mrs. William Pattisson the *Eclectic Review*. It is a highly encomiastic article, rendering ample justice to the poetical talents of the author, but very reasonably raising a doubt as to the religious character of the poem. It is pointedly insinuated that Nature is a sort of God throughout, and consistently with the Calvinistic orthodoxy of the reviewer the lamentable error of representing a love of nature as a sort of purifying state of mind, and the study of nature as a sanctifying process, is emphatically pointed out. It must be owned that the *written word* is but sparingly and even feebly adverted to even where the occasion called for an elaborate statement of religious principles. The *Eclectic* reviewers charitably hope this will still come; I do not expect it. ⟨I recollect Wordsworth saying to me: 'I have no need of a Redeemer'; but I believe his religion to be like [that] of the German metaphysicians, a sentimental and metaphysical mysticism in which the language of Christianity is used, which is a sort of analogy to this poetical and philosophical⟩ religion. Wordsworth is too upright a man to be guilty of any wilful deception; but perhaps he is himself not perfectly clear on the subjects on which his mode of thinking and feeling is anxiously inquired after by his religious admirers. Mrs. William Pattisson perceived the want of this doctrinal merit in his poem, and was at the same time offended with some hyper-orthodox assertions as to the influence of baptism, which Wordsworth seems to represent as actually washing away the stains of original sin.

Mrs. William Pattisson further objected to Wordsworth a want of sensibility, or rather passion, and she even maintained that one of the reasons why I admired him so much is that I never was in love. We disputed on this head, and it was at last agreed between us that Wordsworth has no power because he has no inclination to describe the *passion* of an unsuccessful lover, but that he is eminently happy in his description of connubial felicity. Mrs. Pattisson allowed him to possess sensibility, but a sensibility extended over a great number of objects even inanimate, and not concentrated on the nearest and best objects of affection.

We also read the *Edinburgh* review of the poem. It is a very severe and contemptuous article. Wordsworth is treated as incurable, and the changes are rung with great vivacity on the old keys – affectation, bad taste, mysticism. He is reproached with having written more feebly than before. Some of the blows will have effect, I fear, but not all. A ludicrous statement of the story is given, which will not impose on many, for Homer or the Bible might be so represented. There is little novelty in the attack on Wordsworth, and [it] will do little mischief among those who are already acquainted with the *Edinburgh Review* articles; but it will close up the eyes of many who might have otherwise recovered their sight.

Perhaps, after all, *The Excursion* will leave Mr. Wordsworth's admirers and contemners where they were. Each will be furnished with instances of excellence and deformity to strengthen his own persuasions. Certainly I could wish for a somewhat clearer development of the author's opinions, for the retrenchment of some of the uninteresting interlocutory matter, and for the exclusion of one tale, the angry and avaricious and unkind woman, and curtailments in most of the other narratives. But with these deductions from the worth of the poem, I do not hesitate to place the poem among the noblest works of the human intellect, and to me it is one of the most delightful. What is good, is of the best kind of goodness, and the passages are not few which place the author on a level with Milton. It is true, Wordsworth is not an epic poet . . . Wordsworth is purely and exclusively a lyric poet, in the extended use of that term.

I conversed with Mrs. Clarkson at Bury on the Sunday about the poem. She read me an exceedingly sensible letter from Miss Smith[1] in which the radical objection made by the *Eclectic Review* was also urged by her though a Unitarian, and with great force; so that Mrs. Clarkson was troubled by the letter. She had also received a letter from Wordsworth himself in which he mentioned the favourable as well as unfavourable opinions he had already heard of. He said that Dr. Parr, who had signalized his judgment in the opinion he avowed that Ireland's forgeries were the work of Shakespeare, had said his work was hardly inferior to Milton. Other great men were named as admirers. Mrs. Clarkson and I agreed that it might be useful to copy Miss Smith's letter. ⟨I found Mrs. Clarkson quite able to parry objections against Wordsworth, and very anxious for assistance in the good work of defending him.⟩ I afterwards found at Norwich that Wordsworth's book had few admirers there. Madge was almost the single apostle of the poet of the Lakes . . .

(*Ibid.*, I, 158–60)

e. 1 February 1815

. . . Alsager is become a warm partizan of Wordsworth. *The Excursion* has converted him. He declares that Wordsworth gives him more delight than any other poet. He is more enthusiastic on this than on any subject. Burrell is but a cold and imperfect admirer of Wordsworth.

(*Ibid.*, I, 160)

EDITOR'S NOTE

1. Martha Frances ('Patty') Smith, eldest daughter of William Smith, MP for Norwich.

163. William Cookson (1754–1820)

From a letter to Wordsworth, 20 August 1814

Cookson was Wordsworth's maternal uncle; a tutor to George III's sons; Canon of Windsor; early friend of Joseph Farington and William Wilberforce. This letter was written from his vicarage at Binfield, near Windsor.

Accept my best thanks for the Present of your Volume, which has afforded the greatest Pleasure to all the Members of this Family who have had the opportunity of perusing it. For my own Part I am particularly grateful with it on account of the amiable and cheering Light in which you have represented revealed Religion and of the Respect which you have every where shown for the religious, and, especially, the clerical character. Notwithstanding I cannot help entertaining a Fear that the Poem will not be in the common Sense of the Word, *popular*, although if deservedly appreciated it cannot fail I think of being cherished & approved by *gentle* Hearts and lofty Minds. After all, should my apprehensions prove true, your Friends will have some consolation in reflecting that Popularity has lost much of its ancient value, when it is perceived to set with so strong a Gale towards Moore and Byron and such like writers of the present Day.

(Ms. The Wordsworth Library)

164. William Taylor (1765–1836)
Extracts from letters to Robert Southey, 1814–1815

Taylor, of Norwich, was a writer, translator and prolific reviewer, and a Unitarian.

a. 5 September 1814

Your friend Wordsworth has a most zealous admirer in our Octagon minister, Mr. Madge. He read, at our Philosophical Society, a dissertation on the poems of Wordsworth, in which he placed them above everything past, present, or to come. I approve the simplicity, love the feeling, and admire the painting they display, yet my enthusiasm has not attained so high a pitch. I have however not hitherto read 'The Excursion'.

(*Memoir of the Life and Writings of William Taylor*, ed. J. W. Robberds, 1843, II, 424)

b. 1 March 1815

Poets should live in cities; the leisure of the country spoils them. That bucolic contemplation of nature, which spends its ennui in watching for hours the eyelet-holes of a rill's eddies, is very well for a goat-herd, and may grace an eclogue; but where fates of empires are at stake, the attention should not be invited to settle on any phenomena, not stimulant enough to arrest the attention of a busy man. The engineer, who is sent to reconnoitre, is not to lose his time in zoologizing, entomologizing, botanizing and picturesquixing, as Pelayo does on his way to Covadonga. I can at most concede to Homer that he may get his dinner. Your heroes never Travel in seven-league boots, but rather a la Humboldt. Wordsworth carries further than you the narratory manner, and the magnification of trifles, but you Wordsworthize too often.

(*Ibid.*, II, 455)

165. Mary Shelley (1797–1851) and Percy Bysshe Shelley

Journal entries, sonnet and reminiscence by Haydon, 1814–1816

a. From Mary Shelley's Journal, 14–16 September 1814

Shelley and Mary Godwin, after the six weeks abroad in which they became avowed lovers, arrived back in England on 13 September 1814. On the next day, to their hotel in Oxford Street, Shelley

brings home Wordsworth's 'Excursion', of which we read a part, much disappointed. He is a slave.

Thursday, 15 September:
Mary reads the 'Excursion' all day, and reads the 'History of Margaret'[1] to P. B. S.

16 September:
Read the 'Excursion' and [Southey's] 'Madoc'.

(*Mary Shelley's Journal*, ed. F. L. Jones, 1947, 15)

Shelley and Mary at the end of 1814 have *The Excursion* in the list of books read (*ibid.*, 32); they list it again in 1815 (*ibid.*, 48). On 22 April 1815, they 'look over WW's poems' – almost certainly *Poems* 1815 published the week before (*ibid.*, 45). Shelley never met Wordsworth but probably Mary did in 1842 when she was invited by Rogers to meet him at breakfast. (*Letters of Mary Shelley*, ed. F. L. Jones, 1944, II, 157).

b. Sonnet, 'To Wordsworth', published 1816

POET of Nature, thou hast wept to know
That things depart which never may return:
Childhood and youth, friendship and love's first glow,
Have fled like sweet dreams, leaving thee to mourn.
These common woes I feel. One loss is mine
Which thou too feel'st, yet I alone deplore.
Thou wert as a lone star, whose light did shine
On some frail bark in winter's midnight roar:
Thou hast like to a rock-built refuge stood
Above the blind and battling multitude:
In honoured poverty thy voice did weave
Songs consecrate to truth and liberty, –
Deserting these, thou leavest me to grieve,
Thus having been, that thou shouldst cease to be.

c. From Haydon's Diary, 23 January 1817

Shelley said he could not bear the inhumanity of Wordsworth in talking of the beauty of the shining trout as they lay after being caught [see *The Excursion*, VIII, ll. 558–69], that he had such a horror of torturing animals it was impossible to express it.

(*Diary of B. R. Haydon*, ed. W. B. Pope, Cambridge, Mass., 1960, II, 89)

EDITOR'S NOTE

1. F. L. Jones identifies this as a novel by Adam Fergusson, but undoubtedly what Mary read to Shelley was the story of Margaret from the First Book of the *Excursion*, two lines from which Shelley later used in the Preface to *Alastor*.

166. Catherine Clarkson (1772–1856)

From a letter to Dorothy Wordsworth, 25 December 1814

Wife of Thomas Clarkson, the slave-trade abolitionist; she was intimate with the Wordsworths from 1801 when the Clarksons were living at Eusemere Hill, Ullswater.

I told you of the pleasure which my first greedy devouring of the Excursion had given me – the second increased my admiration but deadened my hopes with respect to the impression likely to be made by it on others. I read the first Book aloud to Mr. Clarkson who listened with earnest attention & deep feeling. He said there were parts which he must read to himself & think about. He means to give the whole work a very attentive perusal & doubt not he will give William a strict account of his feelings respecting it. It is melancholy to think that the scale of it will depend much upon the character given of it in Reviews & on this account I very much wish that Coleridge would review it for the Edinburgh – I hear of two of their body (neither of them Jeffray) who carried the book to Malthus's home – one of them read many of the finest passages with great feeling & expressed the highest admiration – the other followed reading in a dry sarcastic tone passages which he thought to be & attempted to make appear ridiculous. I have been spending a fortnight at Parridon & Mr. Smith came down from London & said he had heard a discussion of the Poem but I could not learn by whom – the opinion given was that it was very fine but *un peu pesant*.[1] I give you the very words. Something was said about reading it aloud in the family but it went off – I was asked to leave it and I did. Mr. Smith [William Smith (1756–1835), MP for Norwich] said that he wished to see it but I know Mr. Smith's ideas about Poetry so well that I do not expect much admiration from him. Yet he has a tast for the tender & pathetic & will I am sure admire the story of Margaret – The interest excited by L^d. Birons Poems shews that the thirst for 'outrageous stimulation' is by no means allayed & though there is matter enough in the single story of the Solitary to form the subject of an epic poem it is told so simply that as the Man was not actually one of the poor Louis' executioners & did not actually preach Atheism & occasion a few dozen suicides or become so inveterate a misanthrope as to detirmine upon doing all the evil he could I am afraid it will make but little impression. I am afraid also that the class of men likely to enter into the Spirit of the Poem those who have a sacred respect for human nature & are by nature & principle religious have not delight enough in Poetry to seek after the work or entirely to relish its merits if brought before them. I fear too that the religious will think that too much is attributed to the power of nature independent of its author, & that this tends to lessen the value of revelation. These are my fears & I am therefore prepared for the worst. I have heard nothing of the sale except that Tillbrooke disposed of five Copies. The very few whom I have heard speak of it say that it will give the greatest delight to Williams former admirers but that it will not make many converts – We shall see. I am not without hope in the midst of my fears. At Parridon I saw the Examiner – Hazlitts observations are much below what I should have expected from him & the libel upon human nature contained in his remarks upon the northern peasantry is an abomination of abominations.

(British Library, Additional Ms. 41, 186, F27ᵛ–28)

EDITOR'S NOTE

1. 'A bit weighty/heavy'.

167. Francis Horner (1778–1817)

From a letter to his sister, Anne, 19 January 1815

I am much struck with the beauty of some passages, which are extracted in the Review from Wordsworth's new poem, they ought to have softened the barbarity of the critic. The plan of the poem is radically against all propriety and good taste, and his obscure inelegant Platonism must be wearisome; but the last few pages of the Review contain about half a dozen passages, that ought to shelter a multitude of faults. – It is odd enough, however, that a much more favourable impression of this work is to be had, from the Edinburgh sentence of execution with all its savage texture, than from the Quarterly studied panegyric of the Excursion.

(Ms. London School of Economics)

168. Thomas Babington Macaulay (1800–1859)

From a letter to Hannah Moore, 16 January 1815

The historian Macaulay recalled late in life, 14 September 1852, that it was at Hannah Moore's house at Barley Wood that he, aged 10, had first taken down *Lyrical Ballads*: 'With what delight and horror I read the Ancient Mariner!' (*Life of Macaulay*, ed. G. O. Trevelyan, 1876, II, 573).

Every eminent writer of poetry, good or bad, has been publishing within the last month, or is to publish shortly. Lord Byron's pen is at work over a poem as yet nameless. Lucien Buonaparte has given the world his 'Charlemagne.' Scott has published his 'Lord of the Isles,' in six cantos, a beautiful and elegant poem; and Southey his 'Roderick the last of the Goths.' Wordsworth has printed 'The Excursion,' (a ponderous quarto of five hundred pages,) *'being a portion of the intended poem entitled "The Recluse."'* What the length of this intended poem is to be, as the Grand Vizier said of the Turkish poet, 'n'est connu qu'à Dieu et à M. Wordsworth.'[1] This forerunner, however, is, to say no more, almost as long as it is dull; not but that there are many striking and beautiful passages interspersed; but who would wade through a poem

> —where, perhaps, one beauty shines
> In the dry desert of a thousand lines?

(*Letters of Hannah Moore to Zachary Macaulay*, ed. Arthur Roberts 1860, 69–70)

EDITOR'S NOTE

1. 'Known only to God and Mr. Wordsworth'.

169. William Johnson Fox (1786–1864)

From a letter to Crabb Robinson, received 6 February 1815

Fox was a Unitarian, and an editor of the *Monthly Repository*, later a politician.

I confess I was rather surprised by your remarks on the Excursion, but not disheartened – If by Wordsworth's peculiar excellencies you mean a moral feeling at once correct, refined, and profound – Imagery beautiful, simple, & original – and above all a life-giving spirit which infuses soul into every object & makes the material face of Nature beam with intellect & sensibility, these I can discover and admire – for the elevated delight which they inspire I have been often indebted to Wordsworth, & have always felt that they placed him at an immeasurable height above Scott & the other Rhyming Romancers of the day – Still in reading him I am often vexed at what gives you no offence, or perhaps excites your admiration – I am not, as [Thomas] Madge says, *initiated* or *fraternized* – I am accustomed to be alternately scorned for admiring too little, & ridiculed for admiring too much – His *prose* is my delight – He ranks, in my opinion, with the best writers of the best age of English literature – His prose is a rich combination of the swelling majesty of Milton with the luxuriant imagery of Jeremy Taylor – If you read the Essay on Epitaphs to Mrs P[attisson], I think her pleasure could not be inferior even to yours[1] – But you are probably wondering, all this time, what occasioned my *surprise* – It was, your almost identifying Wordsworth with the German poets – My ignorance must be my excuse for having supposed that there were so few points of resemblance that it was very possible to be an Infidel as to the one, and an Enthusiast as to the other – If their prose writers resemble him I wish nothing better – What I have seen of their translated poetry bears a nearer affinity to that of our elder Dramatists – with his it appeared almost in contrast – He is generally gentleness itself – his beings of this world are *men* – but they are men of simple, honest hearts & unaspiring minds – & even these he gladly leaves to commune with the benignant spirits of mildest influence who brood over his solitary haunts. – They delight in the strongest, darkest, wildest emotions which distract the soul – and their supernatural beings are called from hell's deepest caverns to lower over the battle or guide the lightning – I shall be surprised to see the fevered Genius of their poetry hushed into his mood of pure and pensive thought and 'breathless with adoration'.

(*Henry Crabb Robinson and the Wordsworth Circle*, ed. E. J. Morley, 1927, I, 82–4)

EDITOR'S NOTE

1.   Crabb Robinson had mentioned to Fox his failure of 3rd. January 1815 (see entry 162d) to persuade Mrs. William Pattisson to be enthusiastic about *The Excursion* ('my late reading of the Poem to Hannah', *Books and their Writers*, iii, 849).

170. Sir George and Lady Beaumont
From their letters to the Wordsworths, 1814–1818

The Beaumonts were stalwart in support of Wordsworth, especially the *Excursion*, but Dorothy Wordsworth came to recognise an over-zealousness in Lady Beaumont: 'I am afraid her zeal will outrun her discretion, and prevent her from aiding the sale of the work as were she more moderate in her expressions she might do' (*MY*, II, 202).

a. Lady Beaumont to Wordsworth, 4 July 1814

I cannot help wanting to know why the excursion is substituted for the Recluse if it be a part of that work, I remember the beautiful opening at the beginning of deliberating long before settling upon what subject to chuse.[1]

(Ms. The Wordsworth Library)

b. Beaumont to Wordsworth, 20 November 1814

I had a letter from the Bishop of London[2] a few days since, he is enchanted by the Excursion – indeed I have heard but one opinion on the subject – Your friends the reviewers will be at a loss how to chuse their extracts –

(*Ibid.*)

c. Beaumont to Wordsworth, 30 November 1814

As to the Excursion I shall not attempt to express the delight the instruction & the enthusiasm with which it inspires me – the feeling is universal or will shortly be so – I verily think the vision near the end of the 2[d] book[3] is the fairest flower of British Poesy – it perfectly fascinates me – Pray tell me if it was not suggested by that marvellous effect we saw in returning thro Patterdale amongst the mountains of Ulswater [*sic*] – Into every crevice & hollow of the hills the clouds poured in profusion, & no shape regular or fantastic, no colour brilliant or solemn, no light splendid or awful, was omitted by the setting sun in that glorious display – I remember you were struck dumb for an hour at least, & then you told me words might do little but not much in describing it – you have proved yourself mistaken –

(*Ibid.*)

d. Lady Beaumont to Wordsworth, 17 January 1815

With fingers half-frozen, and a head benumbed with cold, I cannot help writing to you, if only to rectify a mistake I made in my last letter – in speaking of the price of the Excursion as a reason for the tardiness of the Sale, when upon looking over the numerous works now teeming from the press, whether Novel, or Epic, 2 guineas is the established price.

(*Ibid.*)

e. Beaumont to Wordsworth, 17 January 1815

Dr. Wordsworth [the poet's brother] tells me Ld. Calthor[p]e[4] & Ly. Olivia Sparrow[5] who visited you, belong to the powerful evangelical Sect, and her ardour will not rest in silence. I have obtained you a new admirer in Mr. S. Bourne[6] a great friend of Mr Cannings & now in office – he, and Mrs Bourne are now reading the Excursion at their own fireside with great delight – the calm and philosophical Mr Hayley[7] is touched, and Mrs Opie[8] raves: but independent of those lower gratifications an author must naturally feel as a reward for his labours, I am sure this work must be spiritualising the mind, prepare it for the shocks of mortal life, and to consider death as the friend, not the enemy of Man.

(*Ibid.*)

f. Beaumont to Wordsworth, early 1815

The Excursion rises upon my imagination every day – & I am glad to find everybody sensible of its excellence – Still however they fail to do it full justice – indeed that is scarce possible.

(*Ibid.*)

g. Lady Beaumont to Wordsworth, 29 April 1815

The Excursion will go off very slowly as being only the portion of a larger work, persons of moderate incomes consider its present price and future accompanyments as out of their reach; and those persons living in retirement a[re] those most fitted to be benefitted by it, this Difficulty I do not see how it could have been removed.

(*Ibid.*)

h. From the Diary of Joseph Farington, 21 May 1815

Sir G. Beaumont's I dined at – In the course of Conversation *Poetry* was a Topick. Sir George mentioned the high encomiums for Wordsworth's '*Excursion*' in the *Ecclectic Review*. Wordsworth had seen it, and could not but be pleased with the statements expressed in it. The *Edinburgh Review* He never reads. He does not wish to have the opinions and *ribaldry* of *Jeffries*, the author of it, floating in His memory, for however much He may despise such matter He would not have it buz in His thoughts, when occupied on any subject when Poetry engages His mind. He added that he does not read the [blank] Review.

(*The Farington Diary*, ed. Kathryn Cave, XIII, 4625–6)

i. Lady Beaumont to Wordsworth, [? 2, franked 5] October 1815

I was surprised to hear Mr J. Smith[9] has read the Excursion of which he speaks with a[s] much approbation as he can feel for so high a cast of thought, he has not a meditative turn. In returning from the eating room with dear Lady Mulgrave we read together some of your smaller poems and feel when thus employed that 'other pleasures be, sweeter even than gaiety.'

(Ms. The Wordsworth Library)

j. Beaumont to Wordsworth, 8 January 1817

Westal[10] is here, & last night we read the opening of the Excursion to him, he was astonished, & it brought you before me in such a magnificent character, that I cannot refrain from expressing the admiration I feel of your powers – This will be the fifth time of my reading the work, & every time with redoubled delight – Westal has never either heard or read it before!

(*Ibid.*)

k. Lady Beaumont to Dorothy Wordsworth, 17 December 1818

Mr [George] Dance has just left us, at 78 his feelings are so vivid that on hearing Sir George read the deaf & blind Man [*The Excursion*, VII, 395–536], and the story of poor Ellen [*The Excursion*, VI. 787–1052] he was so overpowered for a quarter of hour after, as not to be able to speak – such is the power of a real poet on the human heart.

(*Ibid.*)

EDITOR'S NOTES

1. Coleridge had lent Lady Beaumont a Ms. copy of the first two books of the *Prelude* in March 1804 (*Collected Letters of Samuel Taylor Coleridge*, ed. E. L. Griggs, 1956–1971, II, 1104).
2. Dr William Howley (1766–1848), Bishop of London, 1813–1828, afterwards Archbishop of Canterbury. He dined with Wordsworth's family while holidaying at Rydal in the summer of 1819. His daughter married Beaumont's cousin (and heir).
3. *The Excursion*, II, ll. 829–60. Sir George repeats much of this in a letter of 20 February 1820 where it becomes clear that Lady Beaumont was also present on that excursion through Patterdale.
4. Lord George Calthorpe (1787–1851), a cousin of the wife of Wilberforce.
5. Lady Olivia Sparrow (died 1863), friend and correspondent of Hannah More.
6. Not quite a new admirer: see entry 137b (*Convention of Cintra*, 7 June 1809).
7. William Hayley (1745–1820), Cowper's biographer, sometime patron of Blake.
8. Amelia Opie (1769–1853), writer.
9. James Smith, author of the parody of Wordsworth in *Rejected Addresses*; through Lord Mulgrave's patronage he held a government post with the Board of Ordnance.
10. William Westall (1781–1850), topographical artist.

171. R. P. Gillies (1778–1858)

From letters to Wordsworth, 1815–1816

Wordsworth to his Scottish friend Gillies, on 14 February 1815

I hope that you continue to like the Excursion. I hear good news of it from many quarters. But its progress to general notice *must* be slow. Your opinion of Jeffrey is just – he is a depraved Coxcomb; the greatest Dunce, I believe, in this Island, and assuredly the Man who takes most pains to prove himself so.

(*MY*, II, 197–8)

a. Gillies' reply, 28 February

Never was there any book in the world which gained so much by repeated perusals as that most inestimable of all works 'The Excursion'. I have not read anything since I returned to town, but the Excursion is the first book I shall have recourse to. Scott's Lord of the Isles I tried before I left Edin: but could make nothing of it. I expect more from his Guy Mannering which is on our table at present, but wch I have not yet looked into. – Jeffrey's friends occasionally insist that his taste is not really depraved & that he *knows* perfectly well that every thing he has said of your poetry only proves its superiority. I am however perfectly convinced that his real character is exactly what you have described.

(Ms. The Wordsworth Library)

b. Gillies to Wordsworth, 10 April 1816

After discussing his own work and ideas about poetry, he notes:

I regret very much that for a long time past I have not read any of 'The Excursion'; which is in truth a direct confession of the unsettled state of my own mind, which was not capable of understanding what to understand & appreciate *fully* requires considerable and indeed very great exertion, & also a sufficient [amount] of freedom from preconceived errors –

(*Ibid.*)

c. On 15 October 1816, Gillies indicates that he has been ill

Every day I think a thousand times (or rather constantly) of passages in your admirable writings – yet I put off the study of 'The Excursion' untill more tranquil in my own mind, and more likely to understand & appreciate its contents – But I have no right to enter on a subject to which I am inadequate. I know that you must hear enough in respect to your publications, & there *increasing influence on the world* from those who from their own mental powers are better entitled to attention than I can possibly be. – . . . [In a postscript, he adds] When I say that I *put off* the *study* of 'The Excursion' I mean the more complete and careful study of *the whole*; for it is that Work that I so constantly refer by recollection.

(*Ibid.*)

172. Dorothy Wordsworth

From a letter to Sara Hutchinson, 18 February 1815

From all hands we hear the same story that Jeffrey has played the fool, has suffered his malignity to cheat him into producing passages as fit matter for ridicule, which are so beautiful that even the eyes of his worshippers must be opened. Old Mrs Lloyd[1] is enraptured with the Book – It expresses what she habitually feels; in a manner that she had never either the power to express or conceive – and that passage where he says the 'raving begins'[2] is one that she should have selected as among the finest that ever were composed. Mr. de Quincey writes – but I will give you his own brief words. 'Miss J[oanna] Hutchinson must have been amongst people who read nothing but novels, because I find far more persons acquainted with the Excursion than I thought likely: among others I could not help smiling to find two fervent admirers, Unitarians, from whom you anticipated nothing but hostility!'

(*MY*, II, 202)

EDITOR'S NOTES

1. Mary Lloyd (née Farmer), 1751–1821, Charles Lloyd's mother and a Quaker.
2. See Jeffrey's *Edinburgh* review, entry 148.

173. Samuel Taylor Coleridge

From letters, 1815

a. To Lady Beaumont, 3 April 1815

Of the Excursion, excluding the tale of the ruined Cottage, which I have ever thought the finest Poem in our Language, comparing it with any of the same or similar Length, I can truly say, that one half the number of it's Beauties would make all the beauties of all his Contemporary Poets collectively mount to the balance; but yet – the fault may be in my own mind – I do not think, I did not feel, it equal to the Work on the Growth of his own spirit. As proofs meet me in every part of the Excursion, that the Poet's genius has not flagged, I have sometimes fancied, that having by the conjoint operation of his own experiences, feelings, and reason *himself* convinced *himself* of Truths, which the generality of persons have either taken for granted from their Infancy, or at least adopted in early life, he has attached all their own depth and weight to doctrines and words, which come almost as Truisms or Common-place to others.

From this state of mind, in which I was comparing Wordsworth with himself, I was roused by the infamous Edinburgh Review of the Poem. If ever Guilt lay on a Writer's head, and if malignity, slander, hypocrisy and self-contradicting Baseness can constitute Guilt, I dare openly, and openly (please God!) I will, impeach the Writer of that Article of it.

(*Collected Letters of Samuel Taylor Coleridge*, ed. E. L. Griggs, Oxford, 1956–1971, IV, 564)

b. To Wordsworth, 30 May 1815

I feared that had I been silent concerning the Excursion, Lady B. would have drawn some strange inference – & yet I had scarcely sent off the Letter before I repented that I had not run that risk rather than have approach to Dispraise communicated to you by a third person –. But what did my criticism amount to, reduced to it's full and naked Sense? – This: that *comparatively* with the *former* Poem the excursion, as far as it was new to me, had disappointed my expectations – that the Excellences were so many and of so high a class, that it was impossible to attribute the inferiority, if any such really existed, to any flagging of the Writer's own genius – and that I conjectured that it might have been occasioned by the influence of self-established Convictions having given to certain Thoughts and Expressions a depth & force which they had not for readers in general. – In order therefore to explain the *disappointment* I must recall to your mind what my *expectations* were: and as these again were founded on the supposition, that (in whatever order it might be published) the Poem on the growth of your own mind was as the ground-plat and the Roots, out of which the Recluse was to have sprung up as the Tree – as far as the same Sap in both, I expected them doubtless to have formed one compleat Whole, but in matter, form, and product to be different, each not only a distinct but a different Work. – In the first I had found 'themes by thee first sung aright' –

[Quotes ll. 12–47 of his own 'To William Wordsworth Composed on the Night after his Recitation of a Poem on the Growth of an Individual Mind!']

Indeed thro' the whole of that Poem 'με Αὔρα τις εἰσέπνευσε μυστικωτάτη.' *This* I considered as 'the EXCURSION'; and the second as 'THE RECLUSE' I had (from what I had at different times gathered from your conversation on the Plan) anticipated as commencing with you set down and settled in an abiding Home, and that with the Description of that Home you were to begin a *Philosophical Poem*, the result and fruits of a Spirit so fram'd & so disciplin'd, as had been told in the former. Whatever in Lucretius is Poetry is not philosophical, whatever is philosophical is not Poetry: and in the very Pride of confident Hope I looked forward to the Recluse, as the *first* and *only* true Phil. Poem in existence. Of course, I expected the Colors, Music, imaginative Life, and Passion of *Poetry*; but the matter and arrangement of *Philosophy* – not doubting from the advantages of the Subject that the Totality of a System was not only capable of being harmonized with, but even calculated to aid, the unity (Beginning, Middle, and End) of a *Poem*. Thus, whatever the Length of the Work might be, still it was a *determinate* Length: of the subjects announced each would have it's own appointed place, and excluding repetitions each would relieve & rise in interest above the other –. I supposed you first to have meditated the faculties of Man in the abstract, in their correspondence with his Sphere of action, and first, in the Feeling, Touch, and Taste, then in the Eye, & last in the Ear, to have laid a solid and immoveable foundation for the Edifice by removing the sandy Sophisms of Locke, and the Mechanic Dogmatists, and demonstrating that the Senses were living growths and developements of the Mind & Spirit in a much juster as well as higher sense, than the mind can be said to be formed by the Senses –. Next, I understood that you would take the Human Race in the concrete, have exploded the absurd notion of Pope's Essay on Man, Darwin, and all the countless Believers – even (strange to say) among Xtians of Man's having pro-gressed from an Ouran Outang state – so contrary to all History, to all Religion, nay, to all Possibility – to have affirmed a Fall in some sense, as a fact, the possibility of which cannot be understood from the nature of the Will, but the reality of which is attested by Experience & Conscience – Fallen men contemplated in the different ages of the World, and in the different states – Savage – Barbarous – Civilized – the lonely Cot, or Borderer's Wigwam – the Village – the Manufacturing Town – Sea-port – City – Universities – and not disguising the sore evils, under which the whole Creation groans, to point out however a manifest Scheme of Redemption from this Slavery, of Reconciliation from this Enmity with Nature – what are the Obstacles, the *Antichrist* that must be & already is – and to conclude by a grand didactic swell on the necessary identity of a true Philosophy with true Religion, agreeing in the results and differing only as the analytic and synthetic process, as discursive from intuitive, the former chiefly useful as perfecting the latter – in short, the necessity of a general revolution in the modes of developing & disciplining the human mind by the substitution of Life, and Intelligence (considered in it's different powers from the Plant up to that state in which the differ-ence of Degree becomes a new kind (man, self-consciousness) but yet not by essential opposition) for the philosophy of mechanism which in every thing that is most worthy of the human Intellect strikes *Death*, and cheats itself by mistaking clear Images for distinct conceptions, and which idly demands Conceptions where Intuitions alone are possible or adequate to the majesty of the Truth. – In short, Facts elevated into Theory – Theory into Laws – & Laws into living & intelligent Powers – true Idealism necessarily perfecting itself in Realism, & Realism refining itself into Idealism. –

Such or something like this was the Plan, I had supposed that you were engaged on –. Your own words will therefore explain my feelings – viz – that your object 'was not to convey recondite or refined truths but to place commonplace Truths in an interesting point of View.' Now this I supposed to have been in your two Volumes of Poems [1815] as far as was desirable, or p[ossible,] without an insight into the whole Truth – . How can common [trut]hs be made permanently interesting but by being *bottomed* in our common nature – it is only by the profoundest Insight into Numbers and Quantity that a sublimity & even religious Wonder become attached to the simplest operations of Arithmetic, the most evident properties of the Circle or Triangle –.

(*Ibid.*, 572–6)

EDITOR'S NOTE

1. 'a most mystical breeze breathed upon me' (Aristophanes, *Frogs*, 313–14).

174. John Edwards (1772–1845)
From letters, 1814–1817

Wordsworth called Edwards, a poet and a liquor merchant from Derby, the 'ingenuous Poet' in *Essay on Epitaphs*, reprinted from the *Friend* as a note to *Excursion* V, and Edwards gratefully told him in a letter of 22 November 1814, 'My name will now be transmitted to posterity most honorably associated' (Ms. The Wordsworth Library); yet at the same time Edwards felt that he must wait for the *Excursion* until it appeared in a cheaper octavo edition. However, in the spring he had a copy, and pleased Rydal Mount by sending them an enthusiastic response to the poem which he had received from James Montgomery.

a. To Wordsworth, 11 March 1815

I need not lengthen this letter by detailing my own opinion of the poem, since I can with more pleasure give you an extract from a letter written to me by my friend Mr. Montgomery the poet, of Sheffield, a most amiable man, wherein, I was surprised and much encouraged to see my own previous thoughts embodied in his beautiful and energetic language. I had before been gratified with his Critique on your Poem in the Eclectic

Review, which I hope you have seen; but he gives a bolder and more faithful exposition of its merits in his private correspondence. He writes as follows:

'The Poem in my opinion, an opinion confirmed by repeated perusal of it, is incomparably the greatest and the most beautiful work of the present age of poetry, and sets Mr. Wordsworth beyond controversy above all the living and almost all the dead of his fraternity. I assure you that the spirit of that book, which I read first at Scarborough in September last, so possessed me, that I have scarcely yet recovered my relish for any other modern verse. The peculiar harmony of rhythm, felicity of language, and splendour of thought, for awhile made all beside poor or feeble in comparison, I am gradually returning to sober feelings, and though the transcendent powers of Wordsworth are not at all diminished in my estimation, those of others his contemporaries are recovered their natural size and shape and coloring, which they had before almost lost to my eye'. It adds afterward: 'You have got a passport to posterity signed by Wordsworth'.

Encouraged by this corroboration of my own sentiments & failings, I took the liberty of making a slight correction in the Edinburgh Reviewer's critique, when it passed thro' my hands. He says 'nobody is more disposed to do justice to your great powers than himself'. My note begins. 'Erratum, for justice, read injustice', defending this correction by a few arguments signed with my initials. I should not have mentioned this trivial note, if it had not led to something better. A person whom I respect challenged me on account of my expressed opinion, the validity of which he questioned. I told him I would rather he judged for himself, and lent him the book, which he has perused with great pleasure, and now declared it an exquisite and most admirable poem. The parts of the Excursion which have afforded me the highest pleasure, are the sublime discourses, speeches and descriptions of the 3rd and 4th books & in part of the 5th, but I shall oftener refer for a milder gratification to your annals of the poor.

(Ms. The Wordsworth Library)

On 10 May 1817 Edwards sent a letter defending Wordsworth to the editor of the newly founded *Literary Gazette* (i, 257–8). It was published on 17 May 1817 and signed 'J. E.'. Edwards objected to the 'contemptuous treatment' of Coleridge and Wordsworth in a previous issue when a correspondent assigned it 'as their portion of the national epic which he proposes should be undertaken by the poetical brotherhood, to describe the unsophisticated death of an aid-de-camp's horse'. Edwards parries this species of abuse chiefly by quotation of Coleridge's judgment, and of Wordsworth's works. He cites passages from the *Convention of Cintra*, *Excursion*, *White Doe* and *Thanksgiving Ode* volume, and ends,

> Not Ossian, with his thousand ghosts shrieking on the hollow wind, is more awfully sublime.

175. Priscilla Wordsworth (1781–1815)

From a letter to her sister-in-law, Hannah, 'a few days before Waterloo' (fought 18 June 1815)

What an eventful period this is! I never felt so depressed by the outward state of things as at this moment. The external face of the world seems to me full of discouragement. Have you read W.'s 'Excursion'? I hope you have. It is a noble work – and cannot, I think, be read without profit.

(*Charles Lamb and the Lloyds*, ed. E. V. Lucas, 1898, 250)

XI

Poems, 1815 and *The White Doe of Rylstone*:
reviews and opinions, 1808–1820

176. Samuel Taylor Coleridge

From a letter to Wordsworth, 21 May 1808

This is a reply to Wordsworth's passionate defence to him of the *White Doe* (19 April 1808; *MY*, I. 221–3). The criticism is of a text no longer extant, for the poem was revised before its publication in 1815 (see *The White Doe of Rylstone*, ed. Kristine Dugas, Cornell, 1988, 31–56). The revision and the delayed publication show that Wordsworth, though magisterial in his letters, was attentive to his friends' views, which here include those of Charles and Mary Lamb. Beyond this, Coleridge's remarks indicate how the attacks upon *Poems* (1807) had made him nervous for Wordsworth's success. Clearly the pressure of reader's tastes is acutely felt. When the poem was published, Wordsworth was prickly in its defence; once at a dinner in London with Humphry Davy and his wife (according to the latter's conversation with Tom Moore), Wordsworth too forcibly showed his 'exceeding high opinion of himself'.

> & she mentioned that one day, in a large party, Wordsworth, without anything having been previously said that could lead to the subject, called out suddenly from the top of the table to the bottom, in his most epic tone 'Davy!' and (on Davy's putting forth his head in awful expectation of what was coming) said 'Do you know the reason why I published [my] The White Doe in quarto?' – 'No, what was it?' 'To show the world my own opinion of it.'
>
> (*The Journal of Thomas Moore*, ed. W.S. Dowden *et al.*, 1983, I, 356)

In my re-perusals of the Poem it seemed always to strike on my feeling as well as judgement, that if there were any serious defect, it consisted in a disproportion of the Accidents to the spiritual Incidents, and closely connected with this, if it be not indeed the same, – that Emily is indeed talked of, and once appears; but neither speaks nor acts in all the first ¾ths of the Poem: and as the outward Interest of the Poem is in favor of the old man's religious feelings, and the filial Heroism of his band of Sons, it seemed to require something in order to place the two Protestant Malcontents of the Family in a light, that made them *beautiful*, as well as virtuous – In short, to express it *far* more strongly than I *mean* or *think* in order, in the present anguish of my spirits, to be able to express it [at] all, that ¾ths of the Work is every thing rather *than* Emily; *then*, the last almost a separate (& doubtless most exquisite Poem) wholly *of* Emily. – The whole of the Rout and the delivering up of the Family by Francis I never ceased to find not only *comparatively* very heavy, but to me quite obscure, as to Francis's motives. And on the few, to whom within my acquaintance the Poem has been read either by yourself or me (I have, I believe, read it only at the Beaumonts') it produced the same effect. – Now I had conceived two little Incidents, the introduction of which joined to a little abridgement, and lyrical precipitation of the last Half of the third, I had thought, would have removed this defect – so seeming to me – and bring to a finer Balance the *Business* with the *Action* of the Tale. But after my receipt of your Letter concerning Lamb's censures I felt my courage fail – and that what I deemed a harmonizing would disgust you, as a *materialization* of the Plan, & appear to you like insensibility to the power of the history in the mind . . .

. . . I should most deeply regret the withdrawal of a Poem so pecu-liarly your's, and beyond any other *in rhyme* illustrative of your charac-teristic excellences – tho' I may now add, that it being not only sense, but sense that demands thought in the Reader, & will not leave him to a lax free-will, that the metre being – as you observed of your poem in general, rather dramatic than lyric, i.e. not such an arrangement of syllables, not such a metre, as acts a priori and with complete self-subsistence (as the simple anapestic in its smoothest form, or the praise of Bacchus in Dryden's Ode) but depending for it's beauty always, and often even for it's metrical existence, on the *sense* and *passion* – I have something like the same suspicion that you entertained concerning Xtabel, how far this would or would not be an obstacle to it's popular-ity – Lamb & Miss Lamb, who evidently read it – he twice thro', he said – with no genial effort, no exertion from sympathy, are for the very reason that disqualifies them as Judges concerning it's *true merit*, no unfair Specimens of perhaps the majority of readers of Poetry, espe-cially in the perusal of a new Poem, which does not employ the com-mon excitements of lively interest, namely, curiosity, and the terror or pity from unusual external Events & Scenes – convent dungeons &c &c –

I beg to be understood solely as referring to *the Public*, not *the People*, according to your own distinction – and this only for a while – and chiefly influenced by the wish, that two publications should not succeed each other, both failing in their *first general* Impression – & perhaps in some measure, by comparing it's *chances* of immediate Sale with the almost *certainty* of the great popularity of either Peter Bell, or Margaret, or even the Salisbury Plain –

God forbid, your Sister should ever cease to use her own Eyes and heart, and only her own, in order to know how a Poem *ought* to affect mankind; but we must learn to see with the Eyes of others in order to guess luckily how it *will* affect them – Neither do I *wish* her to learn this; but then I would have her learn to entertain neither warm Hopes or confident Expectations concerning Events dependent on minds & hearts BELOW the distinct Ken of her Sympathies. Let her only reflect that (even *excluding* the effect of, Routs & continued personal gossip, &c &c, yet) the great majority of the modern Buyers of new Poems read at least 20 whole *Novels* of 2, 3, 4, 5 Volumes each, for ONE poem – You have slightly mentioned this in the Preface to the L. B. – but it deserves to be dwelt on at length –.

(*Collected Letters of Samuel Taylor Coleridge* , ed. E. L. Griggs, Oxford, 1956–71, III, 107–13)

177.

Unsigned review, *Theatrical Inquisitor*, June 1815, VI, 445–50

If the present race of authors was to be judged of from the quantity, and not the quality of their productions, the voice of censure would be wholly silenced; quarto succeeds to quarto, and poem to poem, in such rapid succession, that the public has no time for pause or doubt. At the very instant they are adjusting their critical scales to weigh the merit of one production, their attention is called off to the perusal of another. There is, indeed, scarcely one of our modern poets, who could not, out of his own works, furnish a very decent library, although it might not be so extensive as the Bodleian.

Mr. Wordsworth is a man of undoubted talent, there is enough scattered throughout his works to prove it; and yet, as the matter now stands, out of all his productions, there is not one which any writer of common taste and understanding would wish to own. There is almost a perverseness of taste, a sickliness of sentiment, an affectation of excessive feeling, on all occasions, which are utterly in opposition to real merit. It is scarcely possible to read his works for the first time, without being dizzy;

there is a wonderful appearance of meaning and mysterious sublimity, which on being considered more minutely, proves to be nothing but a meteor – yet with these defects, and while they last, they are insuperable obstacles to real fame. Mr Wordsworth is a man of first-rate talent, who might do honour to himself and his country; in many respects his genius towers above that idol of prejudice, Walter Scott; with equal powers of versification, he has a higher tone of feeling, a more intimate knowledge of the human heart. With such qualifications, it is his own fault that he wants success. Without entering into any minute description, we shall merely subjoin a few specimens of his virtues and errors, which will be more satisfactory than pages of criticism.

[Quotes, without a break between the first two passages, *The White Doe of Rylstone*, *PW*, III, pp. 281–6, ll. 15–99]

There is a glowing melody in these lines that is truly exquisite; at the same time it is impossible not to feel an unfitness of the language to the subject; it is like supporting the roof of a cottage on the massy columns of a temple.

178. John Scott (1784–1821)

Review signed 'S*', *Champion*, 25 June 1815, 205–6

Wordsworth had written to Sir George Beaumont, 23 June 1814, explaining that De Quincey had told him that Scott, editor-owner of the *Champion*, 1814–16, 'though once a desperate Enemy of mine, may become in time what the Quakers call, a convinced friend.' Scott's first meeting with Wordsworth on 13 June a year later (see entry 258) is enthusiastically described by Haydon: 'He shook us both in explaining the principles of his system, his views of man, & his objects in writing.' Wordsworth's explanations seem to inform Scott's review.

Mr Wordsworth has lately published a second edition of his smaller poems, and with them he has given a dissertation, which, as it is an explanation of his principles, is of course a defence of his practice. His large work, the *Excursion*, a noble poem in blank verse, has been some time out; and the other day he presented us with the *White Doe of Rylstone*, a poem founded on a legendary historical tale. We do not think the last his best. The narrative part will be most attentively perused by readers, and it does not seem to be most successfully accomplished: the *White Doe* is the inspiration of the poem, and the most beautiful passages are connected with this fair and gentle mysterious creature.

The story may be shortly told. [Summarises poem.]

The Poem opens with a lively picture of 'sprinklings of blythe company', – 'of lasses, and of shepherd grooms', trooping down the hills on a fine Sabbath morning to attend public worship in the ruined chapel, which, 'In covert like a little nest', 'remaineth one protective part' of 'Bolton's mouldering Priory'. They fill the church-yard; – but the clustered standers and sitters suddenly disappear:

> And scarcely have they disappear'd
> Ere the prelusive hymn is heard,
> With one consent the people rejoice,
> Filling the church with a lofty voice!
> [*The White Doe of Rylstone.*, *PW*
> III, p. 284, ll. 35–8]

The sound of psalm-singing becomes hushed: the Priest is known to be reciting the liturgy: but

> The only voice which you can hear,
> Is the river murmuring near.
> [*Ibid.*, *PW*, III, p. 285, ll. 47–8]

These preliminary circumstances are sketched with much feeling, for their natural beauty; and by their gentle and pure influence, throw the reader into a happy mood for the introduction of the most interesting living agent in the poem. From under the arch bound with ivy, that gives entrance to the church-yard,

> And right across the verdant sod,
> Towards the very house of God,
> Comes gliding in, with lovely gleam –
> Comes gliding in, serene and slow,
> Soft and silent as a dream,
> A solitary Doe!
> [*Ibid.*, *PW*, III, p. 285, ll. 54–8]

[And continues to quote ll. 59–147 with omissions, *ibid.*, *PW*, III, pp. 285–7]

The rest of the poem we leave unnoticed, as a reward to the curiosity of the reader.

It has been boldly said of Mr. Wordsworth, – 'his diction has no where any pretensions to elegance or dignity; and he scarcely ever condescended to give the grace of correctness or melody to his versification.'* The reader, if he have never perused any of Mr. W.'s poetry before,† will judge whether the writer of the above pieces of touching harmony, which his ear will tell him are admirably tuned in soft beauty of expression to the delicious moral music of the strain of feeling, is likely to have sent out to the world four volumes of poetry, the diction of which should *no where* have *any pretensions* to elegance or dignity! We must maintain, on the contrary, that the great attracting body of these four volumes of Mr. Wordsworth's early poetry, – that which alone rivets the attention of candid and discriminating judges, and fixes the writer's place among the lights of fame, is of this unimpugnable kind, – legitimate in its kindred to the works of the long-standing and revered 'dynasties of genius', – sanctioned by established precept, by the general sense of excellence, and even by the very prejudices which are wedded to the 'old oracles of poetical wisdom'; – therefore not to be decried without incurring the guilt and shame of treason against the acknowledged and rightful heirs of immortality. We may affirm this without disputing about the quality of those peculiar passages, which have been seized upon and dragged forward to a prominency which their number does not entitle them to receive, for the purpose of depreciating the sterling value of Mr. Words-worth's talent, by including the bulk of persons to estimate him in the whole according to a few suspicious specimens. Of these we shall say, that some of them have been objected to, as in former times certain sublime doctrines were to the Jews stumbling blocks, and to the Greeks foolish-ness; and that others of them, as they gallantly encounter the arbitrary associations, the despotic dogmas, the standard etiquettes and fashions, of a highly artificial social state, – which is surely liable to at least the sus-picion of being in some measure diseased, – may very possibly be less in the wrong than their critics. It is a sound maxim in politics, that, at certain intervals, the established institutions of government should be returned to their elements, in order that the wanderings of practice from original principles, and (what are more insidious) those violations of spirit which

---

* This sweeping stigma was uttered as part of a review [by Jeffrey: see entry 98] of two volumes, that contained among many, many other specimens of exquisite language, clothing an exquisite fancy in 'fit sound', – the following sonnet, which for mellifluous flow of words, and deep solemn tenderness of sentiment, is not to be put in the second rank by any production, of a similar kind, of any place or of any times –

[Quotes 'Earth hath not anything to show more fair'.]
† This is but too probable a supposition.

creep in under the guise of observances of the letter, may be corrected, and the forms and style of measures be brought back to the significancy of real purpose. In the same way Literature, in a country that has long been pursuing, amidst the pamperings and profusions of high civilization, a course of increasing refinement of artifice, extending to every exertion of the hand, the temper, and the intellect, is apt to lose its native qualities in those adornments which were at first intended only to set them off, and to get away from all its true objects through pursuing them too far, or to miss them entirely in consequence of the first care being that the steps by which it is sought to arrive at them may be nice, delicate, clever, and showy. To prevent this evil, or hinder it from arriving at its last stage, it is highly useful that men of vigorous talent, whose feelings are quickly excited, and when excited are powerful in their effects, should refer poetry back to its elements, which consist of what Wordsworth calls '*the plain humanities of nature*'. It is quite clear, however, that in doing this they must come in contact with the artificial frame of public taste, formed as has been described, and that they must lay themselves open to the critics of a day, when ladies' routes are quite as literary as their favourite quarto poems, when reviews are more substantial than books, – when poets dine with princes, and have leisure besides to do jobs for the booksellers, bringing themselves five or six thousand pounds a year. It is quite clear that this is a day for '*smooth rubbed*' souls to flourish and have fame; – the art will then be held in more esteem than the essence: the shew of sharpened wit will bear away the palm from earnest feeling; and a lucky parodist, or a ballad-monger whose publisher fleeces the 'clean-shirted rabble', his customers, – the studious readers on rose-wood tables, – under pretence of procuring for their impatience '*A Mail Coach Copy*', will be carried triumphantly through six or eight editions, – when the true poet, as described in the following fine verses, will scarcely drag through one: –

> The outward shews of sky and earth,
> Of hill and valley he has viewed;
> And impulses of deeper birth
> Have come to him in solitude.

> In common things that round us lie,
> Some random truths he can impart,
> – The harvest of a quiet eye,
> That broods and sleeps on his own heart.
> ['A Poet's Epitaph', *PW*, IV, p. 67, ll. 45–52; *LB (1800)*,
> p. 208, ll. 45–52]

These are Wordsworth's verses, – and have they 'no pretension to elegance or dignity of diction'? We doubt not that many of our readers will be startled to find that eight lines so simply beautiful, so chastely sublime, can be taken from the works of an author whose writings they have never read, but have seen quoted in broken lines to be ridiculed for their quaintness and vulgarity. But the truth is, that the sneer of professional criticism, got up for drawing-rooms, to supply the comments for fashionable coteries, will ever find most of its natural prey in the finest works of those

> Who give us nobler loves, and nobler cares, –
> The Poets who on earth have made us heirs
> Of truth and pure delight by Heavenly Lays.
> ['Personal Talk', *PW*, IV, p. 75, ll. 52–4; *Poems 1807*, p. 296,
> ll. 52–4]

In one of Shakespeare's best Sonnets we find the following lines,

> And art made *tongue-ty'd* by authority?

Modern criticism would pounce ferociously on the phrase 'tongue-ty'd', which it would represent as consigning the author to eternal ridicule, – there being no redemption for him in the exquisite conclusion –

> Tir'd with all these, from these I would be gone,
> *Save that to die, I leave my love alone*
> [Shakespeare's Sonnet, 66]

The next Sonnet but one, seems to be levelled against the sin of wig-making: – it begins with these lines –

> Thus is his cheek the map of days outworn,
> When beauty liv'd and died as flowers do now.

But what of these, or their companions. The subject is enough to render it execrable in the estimation of persons who scoff at one of the deepest pieces of poetical pathos in the English Language, because the sufferer is described to be the wife of a weaver! We allude to a story in Wordsworth's *Excursion*, of which he says –

> —Tis a common tale,
> An ordinary sorrow of man's life,
> A tale of silent suffering.'
> [*The Excursion*, *PW*, V, p. 24, Book I, ll. 636–8]

We do not, however, mean to conceal our opinion, that Mr. Wordsworth often most unguardedly and unnecessarily exposes himself to the enemy. A stricter principle of selection than this author chooses to exercise, seems to us essential to Poetry. We would suggest that a Poet should discriminate between all that he feels, and what he can successfully convey: and, with deference, we would say, that Mr. Wordsworth often neglects to do this. He has told us that to him

> the meanest flower that blows can give
> Thoughts, that do often lie too deep for tears: –

but if there are narrower limits to language than to his thoughts, he should, in his publications stop within the former, – for otherwise what takes place? That which is rich and dignified in its original existence, is rendered mean and poor in the process by which it is brought forward to challenge admiration. There are, no doubt, intense faculties, to which the seeming degrees and varieties of the earth are much lessened by the penetration of their possessor into the general system of things. There is one

> Who sees with equal eye, as God of all,
> A Hero perish, or a Sparrow fall,

but it is neither pleasing nor useful to have all objects and events placed on an equality before mankind, – for the level must, with the generality, be brought about by reducing what is high, – and not by raising what is low.

But Mr. Wordsworth is a Poet of the first class: his mind is, what he has described, – 'a mansion for all lovely forms'; – his memory is

> —a dwelling place
> For all sweet sounds and harmonies.

He is now before the public in a variety of works, – of unequal merit certainly, – but in their collective testimony proclaiming him the greatest poetical genius of the age. It may be a question how far he is right and how far he is wrong: critics may employ themselves and amuse their readers in picking out what they think objectionable passages, – but his heavenly faculty raises him above the application of their rules, and even (which is the privilege only of the few first rates) places him out of the reach of being substantially injured by his own defects. It is said that the Booksellers do not find by the sale that his poetry is popular: the fact is no otherwise of importance than as illustrative of what we have been long ago told – that *the children of the world are wiser,* (that is to say more lucky) *than the generation of light.*

As for the effect of this on Mr. Wordsworth himself, it is sufficient to say that he is Nature's votary, and

[Quotes 'Tintern Abbey', *PW*, II, pp. 262–3, ll. 122–34; LB (*1798*), p. 115, ll. 123–35:

> —Nature never did betray
> The heart that loved her . . .
> Our cheerful faith that all which we behold
> Is full of blessings.]

179.

Unsigned review, *British Lady's Magazine,* July 1815, II, 33–7

At the close of 1814 Mary Lamb had written about needlework for this periodical. Then she was ill between December and February. The review is a vigorous apologia for Wordsworth's poetry and Donald Reiman plausibly suggests (*The Romantics Reviewed: Contemporary Reviewers of British Romantic Writers. Part A. The Lake Poets,* ed. Donald H. Reiman, Garland, New York and London, 1972, i, 208) that the writer could be Mary Lamb or someone like her who was personally acquainted with Wordsworth.

At a time when a just and general taste, which prevails for the best productions of our ancient masters of poetry, has led to a fervour of pursuit that has ransacked all the hidden literary stores, it seems strange that the works of the author now before us should have met with such unmerited obliquy. The name of no living poet is perhaps better known than that of Mr. Wordsworth, but there is no man whose works, if read, are less understood, or as to whose merits or defects so many persons, capable of forming a judgment of their own, have taken their opinions upon trust. The censure which has been applied to his productions, as undeserved as it has been indiscriminate, would almost lead us to doubt the existence of that admiration of the works of our older bards, and to fear, at least, that it was established on a foundation as superficial and unstable as the vagaries of fashion, with no hold upon the heart and understanding.

For the system of Mr. Wordsworth, called peculiar, is only so as compared with the writers claiming the same title of the present day. He does
not set up in this latter age, while before him are all the glorious
examples of his forefathers (those more than kindred ancestors of poetry,
even to remotest times), to establish new rules and new laws of his divine
pursuit; and there is no notion so mistaken as to suppose that his principles are other than those by which great poets in all ages have been
governed. He treads in a path once familiarly beaten, though long forsaken; and, if he have not the merit of discovering it, he does claim the
praise of being the first to retrace it by the almost obliterated prints of
the hallowed footsteps of his predecessors. This additional applause may
also be his, that, walking in their spirit, he has carried it even further than
many of the greatest names that hitherto guided him, and has struck the
shell of poetry in scenes that had seldom, if ever, been wakened by its
melody.

To a certain extent this proceeding has been a novelty, but assuredly
not an innovation: it may be new to modern readers, but the foundations
of the system of his poetry are as ancient and as venerable as the foundation of the system of the world.

With regard to the result of the perseverance in that system – the
productions which Mr. Wordsworth has laid before the world, – if we are
not prepared at all times to enter fully into the enjoyment of them, we
have only ourselves to blame, and our own insensibility to regret. If,
through the eye of a poet, this author receives faint and delicate impressions upon his mind, afterwards transferred upon his paper, in the pleasure of which we are not prepared to participate, it ought to be a subject of
lamentation as regards ourselves, and of admiration with regard to him.
But, if we are not able to follow all the wanderings of his fancy, if he
draws honey from flowers in which we can perceive, with our duller
sense, neither fragrance nor flavour, if he, among the inferior and more
trifling objects of the creation, discovers subjects that impress some
important truth, some moral lesson, or afford some pleasing contemplation, some excitement to soothe sorrow or augment joy, so far we are
losers, and so far Nature has endowed him with superior means of
enjoyment and happiness. Of this kind are many of his smaller poems;
but those who are not capable of entering into their spirit, even those
who have most decidedly expressed their aversion to them, have not
denied the merits of many of his longer performances, and some have
candidly acknowledged the delight they received.

It is not, however, necessary, in speaking of the work now under review, 'the White Doe of Rylstone,' to enter further into this subject, or to dwell upon the justification of what may be deemed the peculiarities of Mr. Wordsworth, because this poem is almost entirely free from them, and we think will be perused by all classes, by all poetical sects, with a pleasure that experiences no drawback by the insertion of passages for which the reader's mind is not prepared. It was written, as the author informs us, in the year 1807, soon after he had made an excursion to the principal scene of action, and is founded upon an event that took place in the twelfth year of the reign of Queen Elizabeth, called the rising in the North. . . .

[The events of the Rising are retold here and the part in it played by the Norton family as added by Percy in his ballad.]

This addition is a great improvement to the story; and Mr. Wordsworth has included others that much heighten its interest and augment its beauty, particularly that which gives the first title to the poem 'the White Doe of Rylstone.' The foundation for this insertion is contained in Dr. Whitaker's 'History of Craven;' which, after referring to the desolate state of Rylstone and Bolton Priory, not far distant, states that it was a tradition among the aged people of the neighbourhood, that, not long after the dissolution of the monasteries, a white doe continued to make a weekly pilgrimage from Rylstone over the fells of Bolton, and was constantly found in the abbey church-yard during divine service; after the close of which she returned home as regularly as the rest of the congregation. Mr. Wordsworth is a strong and able advocate in favour of the more than half-reasoning affection and sympathy of dumb animals, particularly those of this graceful and poetical species, as may be seen by the poem of 'Hart-leap-well' among his lyrical ballads; and the mode in which he connects this tradition, related by Dr. Whitaker, with the story of the fate of the family of the Nortons, is as follows: –

[The review continues with summary and extensive quotation.]

Thus concludes 'the White Doe of Rylstone,' of which we can scarcely pretend to have given even an imperfect sketch, partly from want of room, and partly (with unfeigned diffidence we say it) from incapacity to estimate worthily a man of Mr. Wordsworth's mind. This feeling is, we are happy to say, becoming more general; and although perhaps the poem now before us will not contribute to raise him in the admiration of his friends, we doubt whether it will not render him more popular. Some persons may be apt to draw comparisons, but they will be no less injurious to the work than to the man.

530

180.

Unsigned notice, *New Monthly Magazine*, July 1815, III, 564

Although this notice may seem of derisory brevity, five out of the six other newly published poems mentioned are accorded their titles and authors only.

In a note appended to this costly volume we read that 'the poem of the White Doe of Rylstone is founded on a local tradition, and on the ballad in Percy's Collection entituled, "The Rising of the North." The tradition is as follows. – 'About this time,' not long after the dissolution of the monasteries, 'a white doe, say the aged people of the neighbourhood, long continued to make a weekly pilgrimage from Rylstone over the falls of Bolton, and was constantly found in the Abbey church-yard during divine service, after the close of which, she returned home as regularly as the rest of the congregation.' – Such is the foundation of the present piece, upon which Mr. Wordsworth has framed a story drawn from the narrative of the Nortons, who were engaged in the northern insurrection that took place in the 12th year of Queen Elizabeth. Of the poem itself we shall give a short specimen, and if that does not satisfy the reader, he will do well to purchase the book, and judge for himself: –

> Fast the church-yard fills: – anon
> Look again, and they all are gone;
> The cluster round the porch, and the folk
> Who sate in the shade of the Prior's oak.
> [*The White Doe of Rylstone, PW*, III, p. 284, ll. 31–4]

181.

Unsigned review of *Poems* (1815), *The Excursion, The White Doe of Rylstone, Augustan Review*, August 1815, I, 343–56

In these works the author employs the simple and the heroic styles; but his merit consists in the former. A portion of the first article was published some years ago under the title of 'Lyrical Ballads;' and many of the other miscellaneous pieces have appeared at subsequent periods. The present edition is 'enlarged and diversified,' and contains,

1st. *Poems referring to the period of Childhood:* an embellishment to one of which ('Lucy Gray') is the frontispiece to the first volume. – The author's simplicity of manner and style renders him happy in some of these little pieces. We are pleased with the lines addressed 'to a Butterfly' – 'Alice Fell' – 'The Idle Shepherd Boys,' and 'The Blind Highland Boy.' We meet, however, with some lines, which, by the introduction of unmeaning particles, are rendered very heavy and insipid,

> His mother, too, no doubt, above
> Her other children, him *did* love.
> ['The Blind Highland Boy', *PW*, I, p. 89, ll.26–7;
> *Poems 1807*, p. 241, ll. 26–7]

Among these pieces we find an 'Address to a Child,' and the 'Mother's Return,' – written by a female friend of the author's, the latter of which only is entitled to any praise.

2nd. *Juvenile Pieces.* These chiefly consist of extracts from works published in 1793 and 1798. 'The Female Vagrant' is interesting, but by placing a dash after the word *wept*, instead of the word *end*, in the following stanza, the effect which the author intended to produce is destroyed.

> —She ceased and weeping turned away,
> As if because her tale was at an end
> She wept; – because she had no more to say
> Of that perpetual weight which on her spirit lay.
> ['Guilt and Sorrow', *PW*, I, p. 118, ll. 447–50]

3rd. *Poems founded on the Affections.* These commence with a dialogue, in familiar blank verse, between a priest and a youth, in which the latter is informed that his brother is dead. We term it *familiar* verse, as it is destitute of every thing dignified: indeed we can see no difference between the following lines and *common* prose – nay, the very commonest of prose.

> Of this they took no heed, but one of them
> Going by chance, at night, into the house
> Which at that time was James's home, there learned
> That nobody had seen him all that day:
> The morning came and still he was unheard of.
> ['The Brothers', *PW*, II, p. 12, ll. 373–7; *LB (1800)*, p. 146,
> ll. 386–90]

Except the 'Complaint of a Forsaken Indian Woman,' the rest of these poems might very well have been classed with the author's childish and juvenile pieces.

4th. *Poems of the Fancy.* These trifles (for trifles we must call them) serve, in the words of the author, for 'a pretty baby-treat,' and nothing else.

5th. *Poems of the Imagination.* Fancy and imagination are, by lexicographers, improperly considered as synonimous terms. Mr. Wordsworth tells us that the former is of a light, and the latter of a serious nature. One of these poems (which has no title, but might have been called *Lucy* or *the Darling,*) has more of the character of Shenstone's productions than any of the rest.

[Quotes the first and last verses of 'Three years she grew in sun and shower', *PW*, II, pp. 214–16; *LB (1800)*, pp. 193–4]

6th. *Poems proceeding from Sentiment and Reflection.* These are commendable chiefly for their morality; but they might with equal propriety have been placed with those of the Imagination.

7th. *Miscellaneous Sonnets.* 8th. *Sonnets dedicated to Liberty.* 9th. *A Second Part of Sonnets dedicated to Liberty.* A sonnet should be harmonious, as a compensation for its brevity. In some of these we meet with discordant sounds, and lines composed entirely of monosyllables:

> Wisdom *doth* live with children round her knees:
> Books, leisure, perfect freedom and the talk
> Man holds with week-day man in the hourly walk,
> *By which true Sway* DOTH *mount; this is the stalk*
> *True Power* DOTH *grow on, and her rights are these.*
> ['I grieved for Buonaparte', omitting l. 12, *PW*, III, p. 111,
> ll. 9–14; *Poems 1807*, p. 138, ll. 9–14]

The succeeding poems are – 10. *On the Names of Places.* – 11. *Inscriptions* – 12. *Referring to the period of Old Age.* – 13. *Epitaphs and Elegiac Poems* – And 14. *An Ode.* These trifles are in general moral and inoffensive. The Elegiac Stanzas were 'suggested by a picture of Peele castle in a storm, painted by Sir George Beaumont;' to which the frontispiece of the second volume refers, but of which no mention is made, either in the engraving or in the contents of the work. The ode contains 'Intimations of Immortality from recollections of early childhood.'

The author, in his *New preface*, tells us the powers requisite for the production of poetry, are, '1. Those of Observation and Description.' '2. Sensibility.' '3. Reflection.' '4. Imagination and Fancy.' '5. Invention,'

– which most people understand by *Imagination*. – 'And lastly, Judgment.' Many are endowed in a greater or less degree with all these qualifications, and yet are no poets. Taste – especially a taste for what is beautiful and sublime, and truly dignified in nature and art, is requisite to a good poet.

In the essay supplementary to the preface, the author takes a retrospect of the poetical literature of this country during the greater part of the last two centuries, for the purpose of proving the small number of real judges of poetry. Shakspeare and Milton, we are told, had a paucity of readers. Pope 'bewitched the nation by his melody, and dazzled it by his polished style, and was himself blinded by his own success.' Thomson's 'Seasons,' the author acknowledges, were universally and justly admired. The number of judges consequently encreased; and where is the wonder if we compare the population and mental improvement of the different periods? After mentioning the names of Dryden, Warton, Collins, Dr. Percy, &c., but omitting those of Prior, Young, Churchill, Goldsmith, &c., Mr. Wordsworth infers – 'That every author, as far as he is great, and at the same time original, has had the task of *creating* the taste by which he is to be enjoyed.' This is hyperbolical reasoning. Civilization creates taste and discernment of worth; and literary merit will always find admirers in an enlightened nation.

In the *old* preface, which is given at the end of the second volume, Mr. Wordsworth contends that the language of a *large portion* of *every* good poem should be strictly the language of prose, when prose is well written. 'The truth of this assertion,' he adds, 'might be demonstrated by innumerable passages from almost all the poetical writings, even of Milton himself.' He then quotes one of Gray's sonnets as an example, and tells us, that except in the rhyme, the language is the same as that of prose. Why not have quoted himself – since every page of his writings abounds with apt examples of prosaic verse? But besides rhyme and metre, other qualities are necessary to good poetry – such as artificial arrangement, appropriate epithets, striking metaphors, harmonious cadence, &c.

The *Excursion* now demands consideration. It is written in blank verse, a species of English composition which is in imitation of the hexameter verse of the Romans, and which like it admits of much transposition, elision, &c. Though it is not, like the hexameter, composed of *spondees* and *dactyls*, it is, in many instances, equally majestic. Milton's grandeur is remarkable, and he frequently makes the sound an echo to the sense. This is doubtless the proper English metre for an epic or heroic poem. It may be said that Thomson's poem of the 'Seasons' is disjointed; but it embraces one year, and the vicissitudes of that year are so painted, that no want of connection appears. The 'Night Thoughts' of Young demanded the dignity of blank verse: and Mr. Wordsworth has judged it necessary to his Excursion. But notwithstanding the melancholy subjects which the Excursion contains, readers in general would probably have been better pleased had he contented himself with rhyme, and an humbler species of compostion. The *Excursion*, though a bulky quarto, is announced in the title page as only a *portion* of a poem, and the preface states that it belongs to a *second* part of a laborious work. The *first* not having been completed to the author's satisfaction, the second division has been published (as usual), at the *earnest entreaties* of some valued friends – 'its interest not depending, in any great degree, on the preceding part.' The want of connection is therefore candidly acknowledged; and as a kind of *prospectus* of the *whole* poem, a passage is given in the preface, from the conclusion of the first book of the 'Recluse,' *not yet published.*

The 'Excursion,' which is dedicated in a neat sonnet to the Earl of Lonsdale, is divided into nine books; and the first person introduced to the reader's notice is the author himself! He reaches a ruined cottage on a common, during a summer forenoon, and there meets the wanderer, whom he had known from his childhood, and after whom the first book is called. While resting under the shade of the trees that surrounded the ruined cottage, the wanderer gives an account of its last inhabitants. Margaret, deserted by her husband who had joined a troop of soldiers, had told her 'piteous tale' to the wanderer, 'with many tears.' Having left her for awhile he returns, and is informed by a stranger, 'that she was used to ramble far.' She is described as 'tender and deep in her excess of love,' yet during her absence

> —From within
> Her solitary infant cried aloud,
> Then, like a blast that dies away self-stilled,
> The voice was silent –
> [*The Excursion PW*, V, p. 33, Book I, ll. 735–8]

She returns when the cottage clock strikes eight, and tells the wanderer

> That she had parted with her elder child
> To a kind master on a distant farm,
> Now happily apprenticed.
> [*Ibid., PW*, V, p. 34, Book I, ll. 760–2]

535

She confesses that by her occasional rambles she has done herself and helpless infant much wrong. The *neglected* babe at length dies, and the mother is left alone. A final parting takes place between her and the wanderer. – We meet with no striking beauties in this book, no energetic thoughts: on the contrary, it abounds with egotism, and unnecessary tautologies. For instance:

> From his sixth year, the boy *of whom I speak,*
> In Summer, tended cattle on the hills
> [*Ibid.*, *PW*, V, p. 12, Book I, ll. 118–19]

> From early childhood, even, as hath been said,
> *From his sixth year,* he had been sent abroad
> *In summer,* to *tend herds.*
> [*Ibid.*, (1814–20 only) *PW*, V, p. 14, Book I, cf. ll. 197–9]

Harsh words are introduced for no reason:

> —The countenance of the man
> Was hidden from my view.
> [*Ibid.*, *PW*, V, p. 9, Book I, ll. 43–4]

Countenance makes a very inharmonious dissyllable, and is properly used afterwards as a trisyllable. *Visage* would have been better. Many of the lines have a very flat, prosaic, puerile tendency. They really are not poetry.

> —These favored beings,
> All but a scattered few, live out their time
> Husbanding that which they possess within,
> And go to the grave unthought of. Strongest minds
> Are often those of whom the noisy world
> Hears least.
> [*Ibid.*, *PW*, V, p. 11, Book I, ll. 88–93]

> And 'twas a rueful thing to see the looks
> Of the poor innocent children. 'Every smile,'
> Said Margaret to me, here, beneath these trees,
> 'Made my heart bleed.'
> [*Ibid.*, *PW*, V, p. 28, Book I, ll. 588–91]

Some parts of this book may, however, be justly admired. We select the following:

[Quotes *The Excursion*, *PW*, V, p. 20, Book I, ll. 361–71;

> Unoccupied by sorrow of its own . . .
> With those whom he saw suffer.

and, *PW*, V, p. 36, Book I, ll. 829–31

> —Her Infant Babe
> Had from its mother caught the trick of grief,
> And sighed among its playthings.]

[A summary of *The Excursion*, Book II, follows.]

The language of this book is variable – descending from grandeur, which it sometimes reaches, to absolute poverty and meanness.

[Summary of Book III.]

The incidents in this book are few, and not calculated either to charm or surprise the reader. The language however is more regular, and the metre more correct.

[Summarises with quotation of Books IV, V, VI.]

This book [Book VI] is uncommonly interesting; but contains a great many very unmetrical lines.

The seventh Book, which is a continuation of the subject, might have been dispensed with, by blending some parts of it with the preceding. The interest of a poem should gradually rise. The sixth Book is certainly better than the fifth; but the subject becomes tedious in the seventh, and this poet is seldom very lively.

[Summaries of Books VIII and IX follow.]

The defects of this publication are numerous; and may be ascribed to Mr. Wordsworth's want of classic taste, and his ignorance, real or affected, of what constitutes the true dignity and charm of poetry. We frequently, however, meet with passages which are reputable to his head; and the moral and religious tendency of the whole work does infinite credit to his heart.

The subject of this poem, [*The White Doe*] which is in seven Cantos, is admirably adapted to Mr. Wordsworth's simplicity of style; for *Calliope* is not that gentleman's happiest muse. In the first Canto we are introduced to the church-yard:

[Quotes *The White Doe of Rylstone*, *PW*, II, p. 283, ll. 1–8]

> From Bolton's old monastic tower . . .
> Trooping to that summons holy.]

He varies his measure, we think, too suddenly:

> Fast the church-yard fills – anon,
> Look again – they all are gone;
> The cluster round the porch, and the folk,
> Who sate in the shade of the Prior's oak.
>
> > [*Ibid.*, *PW*, III, p. 284, ll. 31–4]

We like the introduction of the Doe:
[Quotes *ibid.*, *PW*, III, p. 285, ll. 49–58

> > —When soft, the dusky trees between . . .
> > A solitary Doe.]

The harmony of these lines is greatly assisted by the well introduced alliteration. The author pursues his theme in a happy manner, adding to the vivacity of his subject by an occasional increase of rhyme. We meet, however, as usual, with discordant lines, sufficient to counterbalance almost any degree of harmony:

> > Now doth a delicate shadow fall –
> > Falls upon her like a breath,
> > From some lofty arch or wall,
> > As she passes underneath.
> >
> > > [*Ibid.*, *PW*, III, p. 286, ll. 87–90]

[Summary and quotation follows:]
The anxiety of Emily, when told that her father and brothers, save one, were doomed to die, renders the fifth Canto exceedingly interesting. In the sixth we read of the escape of Francis, and his sudden death:
[Quotes *ibid.*, (1815–43), *PW*, III, pp. 328–9 in footnotes, ll. 1483–519

> > His weaker hand the banner held . . .
> > And the body was left on the ground where it lay.]

We object to this needless Alexandrine; and would rather have said,

> While on the ground the mangled body lay.

[The rest of the poem is briefly summarised.]
This poem will be read not without pleasure; and we trust that the author will never choose a loftier subject for the exercise of his muse. If he would but consent to abandon slovenly metre, and addict himself to good plain prose, his unceasing benevolence, and his turn of thought always so moral and religious, might render him a highly respectable Essayist.

182. Francis Jeffrey

Unsigned review, *Edinburgh Review*, October 1815, XXV, 355–63

This, we think, has the merit of being the very worst poem we ever saw imprinted in a quarto volume; and though it was scarcely to be expected, we confess, that Mr Wordsworth, with all his ambition, should so soon have attained to that distinction, the wonder may perhaps be diminished, when we state, that it seems to us to consist of a happy union of all the faults, without any of the beauties, which belong to his school of poetry. It is just such a work, in short, as some wicked enemy of that school might be supposed to have devised, on purpose to make it ridiculous; and when we first took it up, we could not help fancying that some ill-natured critic had taken this harsh method of instructing Mr Wordsworth, by example, in the nature of those errors, against which our precepts had been so often directed in vain. We had not gone far, however, till we felt intimately, that nothing in the nature of a joke could be so insupportably dull; – and that this must be the work of one who honestly believed it to be a pattern of pathetic simplicity, and gave it out as such to the admiration of all intelligent readers. In this point of view, the work may be regarded as curious at least, if not in some degree interesting; and, at all events, it must be instructive to be made aware of the excesses into which superior understandings may be betrayed, by long self-indulgence, and the strange extravagances into which they may run, when under the influence of that intoxication which is produced by unrestrained admiration of themselves. This poetical intoxication, indeed, to pursue the figure a little farther, seems capable of assuming as many forms as the vulgar one which arises from wine; and it appears to require as delicate a management to make a man a good poet by the help of the one, as to make him a good companion by means of the other. In both cases, a little mistake as to the dose or the quality of the inspiring fluid may make him absolutely outrageous, or lull him over into the most profound stupidity, instead of brightening up the hidden stores of his genius: And truly we are concerned to say, that Mr Wordsworth seems hitherto to have been unlucky in the choice of his liquor – or of his bottle holder. In some of his odes and ethic exhortations, he was exposed to the public in a state of incoherent rapture and glorious delirium, to which we think we have seen a parallel among the humbler lovers of jollity. In the Lyrical Ballads, he was exhibited, on the whole, in a vein of very pretty deliration; but in the poem before us, he appears in a state of low and maudlin imbecility, which would not have misbecome Master Silence himself, in the close of a social day. Whether this unhappy result is to be ascribed to any adulteration of his Castalian cups, or to the unlucky choice of his company over them, we cannot presume to say. It may be, that he has dashed his Hippocrene with too large an infusion of lake water, or assisted its operation too exclusively by the study of the ancient historical ballads of 'the north countrie.' That there are palpable imitations of the style and manner of those venerable compositions in the work before us, is indeed undeniable; but it unfortunately happens, that while the hobbling versification, the mean diction, and flat stupidity of these models are very exactly copied, and even improved upon, in this imitation, their rude energy, manly simplicity, and occasional felicity of expression, have totally disappeared; and, instead of them, a large allowance of the author's own metaphysical sensibility, and mystical wordiness, is forced into an unnatural combination with the borrowed beauties which have just been mentioned.

The story of the poem, though not capable of furnishing out matter for a quarto volume, might yet have made an interesting ballad; and, in the hands of Mr Scott, or Lord Byron, would probably have supplied many images to be loved, and descriptions to be remembered. The incidents arise out of the short-lived Catholic insurrection of the Northern counties, in the reign of Elizabeth, which was supposed to be connected with the project of marrying the Queen of Scots to the Duke of Norfolk, and terminated in the ruin of the Earls of Northumberland and Westmoreland, by whom it was chiefly abetted. Among the victims of this rash enterprize was Richard Norton of Rylstone, who comes to the array with a splendid banner, at the head of eight tall sons, but against the will and advice of a ninth, who, though he refused to join the host, yet follows unarmed in its rear, out of anxiety for the fate of his family; and, when the father and his gallant progeny are made prisoners, and led to execution, at York, recovers the fatal banner, and is slain by a party of the Queen's horse near Bolton priory, in which place he had been ordered to deposit it by the dying voice of his father. The stately halls and pleasant bowers of Rylstone are wasted and fall into desolation; while the heroic daughter, and only survivor of the house, is sheltered among its faithful retainers, and wanders about for many years in its neighbourhood, accompanied by a beautiful white doe, which had formerly been a pet in the family; and continues, long after the death of this sad survivor, to repair every Sunday to the church-yard of Bolton priory, and there to feed and wander among their graves, to the wonder and delight of the rustic congregation that came there to worship.

This, we think, is a pretty subject for a ballad; and, in the author's better day, might have made a lyrical one of considerable interest: Let us see, however, how he deals with it since he has bethought him of publishing in quarto.

The First Canto merely contains the description of the doe coming into the church-yard on Sunday, and of the congregation wondering at her. She is described as being as white as a lily, – or the moon, – or a ship in the sunshine; – and this is the style in which Mr Wordsworth marvels and moralizes about her through ten quarto pages.

> What harmonious pensive changes
> Wait upon her as she ranges
> Round and through this Pile of state,
> Overthrown and desolate!
> [*The White Doe of Rylstone*, *PW*, III, p. 285–6, ll. 79–82]

> The presence of this wandering Doe
> Fills many a damp obscure recess
> With lustre of a saintly show;
> And, re-appearing, she no less
> To the open day gives blessedness.
> [*Ibid.*, *PW*, III, p. 285 in footnotes, ll. 100–4]

The mothers point out this pretty creature to their children; and tell them in sweet nursery phrases –

> Now you have seen the famous Doe!
> From Rylstone she hath found her way
> Over the hills this sabbath-day;
> Her work, whate'er it be, is done,
> And she will depart when we are gone.
> [*Ibid.*, *PW*, III, p. 289, ll. 185–9]

The poet knows why she comes there, and thinks the people may know it too: But some of them think she is a new incarnation of some of the illustrious dead that lie buried around them; and one, who it seems is an Oxford scholar, conjectures that she may be the fairy who instructed Lord Clifford in astrology; an ingenious fancy which the poet thus gently reproveth –

Ah, pensive scholar! think not so!
But look again at the radiant doe!
[*Ibid.*, *PW*, III, p. 292, ll. 308–9]

And then closes the Canto with this natural and luminous apostrophe to
his harp.

But, harp! thy murmurs may not cease, –
Thou hast breeze-like visitings;
For a Spirit with angel wings
Hath touched thee, and a Spirit's hand:
A voice is with us – a command
To chaunt, in strains of heavenly glory,
A tale of tears, a mortal story!
[*Ibid.*, *PW*, III, p. 293, ll. 330–6]

The Second Canto is more full of business, and affords us more insight
into the author's manner of conducting a story. The opening, however,
which goes back to the bright and original conception of the harp, is not
quite so intelligible as might have been desired.

The Harp in lowliness obeyed:
And first we sang of the green-wood shade,
And a solitary Maid;
Beginning, where the song must end,
With her, and with her sylvan Friend;
The friend who stood before her sight,
Her only unextinguished light, –
Her last companion in a dearth
Of love, upon a hopeless earth.
[*Ibid.*, *PW*, III, pp. 293–4, ll. 337–45]

This solitary maid, we are then told, had wrought, at the request of her
father, 'an unblessed work.'

A Banner – one that did fulfil
Too perfectly his headstrong will:
For on this Banner had her hand
Embroidered (such was the command)
The Sacred Cross; and figured there
The five dear wounds our Lord did bear.
[*Ibid.*, *PW*, III, p. 294, ll. 352–7]

The song then proceeds to describe the rising of Northumberland and Westmoreland, in the following lofty and spirited strains.

> Two earls fast leagued in discontent,
> Who gave their wishes open vent;
> And boldly urged a general plea,
> The rites of ancient piety
> To be by force of arms renewed;
> Glad prospect for the multitude!
> And that same Banner, on whose breast
> The blameless Lady had exprest,
> Memorials chosen to give life,
> And sunshine to a dangerous strife;
> This Banner, &c.
> [*Ibid.*, *PW*, III, pp. 294–5, ll. 368–78]

The poet, however, puts out all his strength in the dehortation which he makes Francis Norton address to his father, when the preparations are completed, and the household is ready to take the field.
[Quotes *ibid.*, *PW*, III, p. 295, ll. 380–95

> —Francis Norton said,
> 'O Father! rise not in this fray – . . .
> And live at home in blissful ease.']

The warlike father makes no answer to this exquisite address, but turns in silent scorn to the banner,

> And his wet eyes are glorified,
> [*Ibid.*, *PW*, III, p. 295, l. 404]

and marches out at the head of his sons and retainers.

Francis is very sad when left thus alone in the mansion – and still worse when he sees his sister sitting under a tree near the door. However, though 'he cannot chuse but shrink and sigh,' he goes up to her and says,
[Quotes *ibid.*, *PW*, III, pp. 297–8, ll. 454–75

> Gone are they, – they have their desire . . .
> For faithful we must call them, bearing
> That soul of conscientious daring.]

After a great deal more as touching and sensible, he applies himself more directly to the unhappy case of his hearer, – whom he thus judiciously comforts and flatters.

[Quotes *ibid.*, *PW*, III, p. 299, ll. 530–45

> Hope nothing, if I thus may speak . . .
> Espouse thy doom at once, and cleave
> To fortitude without reprieve.]

It is impossible, however, to go regularly on with this goodly matter. – The Third Canto brings the Nortons and their banner to the head quarters of the insurgent Earls; and describes the first exploits of those conscientious warriors, who took possession of the Cathedral of Durham,

> Sang Mass, – and tore the book of Prayer, –
> And trod the Bible beneath their feet.
>   [*Ibid.*, *PW*, III, p. 304, ll. 713–14]

Elated by this triumph, they turn to the south.

> To London were the Chieftains bent;
> But what avails the bold intent?
> A Royal army is gone forth
> To quell the Rising of the North;
> They march with Dudley at their head,
> And in seven days' space, will to York be led! –
> And Neville was opprest with fear;
> For, though he bore a valiant name,
> His heart was of a timid frame.
>   [*Ibid.*, *PW*, III, pp. 306–7, ll. 783–94]

So they agree to march back again; at which old Norton is sorely afflicted – and Francis takes the opportunity to renew his dehortations – but is again repulsed with scorn, and falls back to his station in the rear.

The Fourth Canto shows Emily walking by the fish ponds and arbours of Rylstone, in a fine moonshiny night, with her favourite white Doe not far off.

> Yet the meek Creature was not free,
> Erewhile, from some perplexity:
> For thrice hath she approached, this day,
> The thought-bewildered Emily.
>   [*Ibid.*, *PW*, III, p. 314 and footnotes, ll. 1012–15]

However, they are tolerably reconciled that evening; and by and by, just a few minutes after nine, an old retainer of the house comes to comfort

her, and is sent to follow the host and bring back tidings of their success.
– The worthy yeoman sets out with great alacrity; but not having much
hope, it would appear, of the cause, says to himself as he goes,

> 'Grant that the moon which shines this night
> May guide them in a prudent flight!'
> [*Ibid.*, *PW*, III, p. 317, ll. 1117–18]

Things however had already come to a still worse issue – as the poet very
briefly and ingeniously intimates in the following fine lines.

> Their flight the fair moon may not see;
> For, from mid-heaven, already she
> Hath witnessed their captivity.
> [*Ibid.*, *PW*, III, p. 317 and footnotes, ll. 1123–5]

They had made a rash assault, it seems, on Barnard Castle, and had been
all made prisoners, and forwarded to York for trial.

The Fifth canto shows us Emily watching on a commanding height
for the return of her faithful messenger; who accordingly arrives forthwith, and tells, 'as gently as could be,' the unhappy catastrophe which he
had come soon enough to witness. The only comfort he can offer is, that
Francis is still alive.

> To take his life they have not dared.
> On him and on his high endeavour
> The light of praise shall shine for ever!
> Nor did he (such Heaven's will) in vain
> His solitary course maintain;
> Not vainly struggled in the might
> Of duty seeing with clear sight.
> [*Ibid.*, *PW*, III, p. 320, ll. 1213–19]

He then tells how the father and his eight sons were led out to execution;
and how Francis, at his father's request, took their banner, and promised
to bring it back to Bolton priory.

The Sixth canto opens with the homeward pilgrimage of this unhappy
youth; and there is something so truly forlorn and tragical in his situation, that we should really have thought it difficult to have given an
account of it without exciting some degree of interest or emotion. Mr
Wordsworth, however, reserves all his pathos for describing the whiteness of the pet doe, and disserting about her perplexities, and her high

545

communion, and participation of heaven's grace; and deals in this sort with the orphan son turning from the bloody scaffold of all his line with their luckless banner in his hand.

[Quotes *ibid.*, *PW*, III, pp. 325–6 and footnotes, ll. 1393–418

> He looked about like one betrayed . . .
> Without a thought to such intent?']

His death is not much less pathetic. A troop of the Queen's horse surround him, and reproach him, we must confess with some plausibility, with having kept his hands unarmed, only from dread of death and forfeiture, while he was all the while a traitor in his heart. The sage Francis answers the insolent troopers as follows.

> 'I am no traitor,' Francis said,
> 'Though this unhappy freight I bear;
> It weakens me, my heart hath bled
> Till it is weak – but you beware,
> Nor do a suffering Spirit wrong,
> Whose self-reproaches are too strong!'
> [*Ibid.*, *PW*, III, p. 328, ll. 1470–5]

This virtuous and reasonable person, however, has ill luck in all his dissuasions; for one of the horsemen puts a pike into him without more ado – and

> There did he lie of breath forsaken!
> [*Ibid.*, *PW*, III, p. 328 and footnotes, l. 1496]

And after some time the neighbouring peasants take him up, and bury him in the churchyard of Bolton priory.

The Seventh and last canto contains the history of the desolated Emily and her faithful doe; but so very discreetly and cautiously written, that the most tender-hearted reader may peruse it without the least risk of any excessive emotion. The poor lady runs about indeed for some years in a very disconsolate way in a worsted gown and flannel nightcap; but at last the old white doe finds her out, and takes again to following her – whereupon Mr Wordsworth breaks out into this fine and natural rapture.

Oh, moment ever blest! O Pair!
Beloved of Heaven, Heaven's choicest care!
This was for you a precious greeting, –
For both a bounteous, fruitful meeting.
Joined are they, and the sylvan Doe
Can she depart? can she forego
The Lady, once her playful Peer?
[*Ibid.*, *PW*, III, p. 334, ll. 1665–71]

That day, the first of a reunion
Which was to teem with high communion,
That day of balmy April weather,
They tarried in the wood together.
[*Ibid.*, *PW*, III, p. 334, ll. 1680–3]

What follows is not quite so intelligible.

When Emily by morning light
Went forth, the Doe was there in sight.
She shrunk: – with one frail shock of pain,
Received and followed by a prayer,
Did she behold – saw once again;
Shun will she not, she feels, will bear; –
But wheresoever she looked round
All now was trouble-haunted ground.
[*Ibid.*, *PW*, III, p. 335, ll. 1694–1701]

But we make out that the lady's loneliness was cheered by this mute associate; and that the doe, in return, found a certain comfort in the lady's company –

Communication, like the ray
Of a new morning, to the nature
And prospects of the inferior Creature!
[*Ibid.*, *PW*, III, p. 338, ll. 1829–31]

In due time the poor lady dies, and is buried beside her mother; and the doe continues to haunt the places which they had frequented together, and especially to come and pasture every Sunday upon the fine grass in Bolton churchyard, the gate of which is never opened but on occasion of the weekly service. – In consequence of all which, we are assured by Mr Wordsworth, that she 'is approved by Earth and Sky, in their benignity;' and moreover, that the old Priory itself takes her for a daughter of the

Eternal Prime – which we have no doubt is a very great compliment,
though we have not the good luck to understand what it means.

> And aye, methinks, this hoary Pile,
> Subdued by outrage and decay,
> Looks down upon her with a smile,
> A gracious smile, that seems to say,
> 'Thou, thou art not a Child of Time,
> But Daughter of the Eternal Prime!'
> [*Ibid., PW*, III, p. 340, ll. 1905–10]

183. Bernard Barton (1784–1849)

From a letter to Wordsworth, and the accompanying poem, 22 December 1815

Although the Quaker poet Barton made a habit of writing to leading
authors, the validity of the experience he records here need not be questioned. Among his favourite authors, according to his daughter, was
'Wordsworth in his lowlier moods' (*Poems and Letters of Bernard Barton*,
ed. Lucy Barton [his daughter], 1853, xxxvi–vii). (For Wordsworth's
pleased reply to Barton's letter, see 12 January 1816, *MY*, II, 269–7.)

Esteemed Friend

In turning over the last Edin. Rev. I met with the Critique on the
White Doe of Rylstone, and the preceding Stanzas were composed
pretty directly after the perusal of it. They bear indeed evident marks of
haste, but I hope they likewise express, though feebly, the gradual progress which thy Poetry has made in my estimation. When a Boy I
perused it with a pleasure few Books before or since have ever [given to]
me but when a few years since I came to mix more in the [world] I was I
own in some degree shamed out of my early favo[urites] and distrusted
my own early judgement. I have since however, partly in the school of
disappointment, and partly I hope in that of improving experience,
reverted with renew'd pleasure to my former impressions and the favourite of my childish fancy is the charm and endear'd companion of my
hours of retirement. Judging of others by myself, I hope that many such

instances are to be met with: and I believe I may say not in flattery but in sober simple truth that few Poets will in the Hour of affliction be oftener recurred to than Thyself.

To Wm. Wordsworth, on reading the Critique on his White Doe in the Edinburgh Review –

> There was a time, with spirits light and gay,
>   When simple marvels pleas'd my young desire;
> Then Wordsworth, in thy Page from day to day,
>   I found that rapture youthful minds require;
> And, with my elder Sister, o'er thy Lay,
>   Ponder'd beside our quiet Parlour Fire
> Still finding, in thy legendary Store
> Some tale, which oftener read, still pleas'd the more.
>
> Then unto virtue, pleasing was the smart,
>   And the tear precious in compassion shed
> For Her, who pierc'd by poverty's keen dart,
>   Did meekly bear the taunts unmerited
> Utter'd by Harry Gill; until her heart
>   Found vent in supplication, short and dread: –
> Awfully mighty in her impotence
> Trusting to one above for her defence.
>
> Visions I saw, call'd forth by magic
>   With fairy prospects was thy page then fraught;
> Till in the Landscape chilling darkness fell
>   And I was by cold, rigid Critics taught
> That all my favourite Lays were, truth to tell,
>   By Reason scorn'd, by manhood reckon'd naught:
> And I was told to think, with fancied Pride,
> Thy once lov'd Page to childish Love allied.
>
> To me thy soothing fiction ceas'd to flow,
>   To me thy matchless melody was mute;
> Awhile seduc'd by Bards of loftier show
>   I sought mid flaunting flowers for richer fruit:
> But 'twas not theirs such banquet to bestow;
>   So I desisted from the vain pursuit,
> And turn'd once more to share with thee content,
> The blameless feast of fancies innocent –

549

It sooth'd me, it beguil'd me then to hear
   Thy pensive *wanderer's* pure and lofty strain,
Address'd to Him, who, losing all held dear,
   Retir'd from busy life as full of pain,
As pain unmingl'd – with attentive ear,
   I heard thy simple Sage to him explain
The Christian's comfort in affliction's hour
With all the Poets and the Prophet's power.

Then too thy Village Pastor's tales could please,
   Tales told of those now lull'd in dreamless sleep:
Their trials past, their humble destinies –
   Gathering fresh interest from each grassy heap:
Wakening with gentle touch those sympathies
   Which in the inmost heart their dwelling keep.
And link the loftiest to the lowliest doom
Alike the trembling tenants of the tomb.

Then could the tragic Tale of Norton's fate
   Please and instruct; and o'er the mournful Page
Which pictur'd that fair Lady and her Mate
   Roving the Earth in helpless pilgrimage.
Fond Fancy ponder'd: pleas'd to contemplate
   Scenes which have rous'd a Critic's harmless rage
But sweet to gentler Readers, who would bless
A happy hour with holier happiness.

He serves the Muses erringly and ill
   Whose aim is pleasure light and fugitive:
Wordsworth! 'tis thine the Mandate to fulfill
   Which God and Nature to the Poet give!
To raise our thoughts, to elevate our Will
   And bid our better feelings wake and live
And for this cause thy Muse may proudly claim
The Amaranthine wreath of pure and hallow'd Fame!
(Ms. Wordsworth Library)

550

184.

Unsigned review, *British Review*, November 1815, vi, 370–7

The author was possibly Charles Abraham Elton (1778–1853).

It is usually thought a recommendation of any poem to say, that it is popular. But are the most popular poems always those which essentially deserve the distinction? We are bold enough to doubt of this, and to suspect that a genuine poet who has high aspirings, and who looks to that mental elevation, that inward sense of moral dignity, and that enthusiasm of sentiment and taste, which accompanies his labours, as their great reward, – who looks to the soothing of his common-life anxieties and the visions of his pillow, as among the privileges of his sublime vocation, will be apt to distrust a popularity too rapidly and easily acquired.

Pure poetry is in fact a mystery to the million, and may without any impeachment of its excellence be unintelligible to the sciolist in belles lettres and the drawing-room critic, or fail to amuse or strike the super-ficial multitude. I banish *you*, said Coriolanus to the Roman rabble: and so the poet may exclaim when driven into temporary exile by the light-minded, and those who float, as it were, upon the surface of society. Among men who have drunk of the well of knowledge, how few are there to whom the muse has opened those recesses of her precious repository which contain the furniture of a poet's mind.

The popular feeling is now, however, more just than at the period which has been styled the English Augustan Age: and although it can scarcely be considered in its highest possible state of improvement, as likely to become favourable to poetry, purely imaginative or philo-sophical; yet it is encouraging to perceive that the French rules of criti-cism, which resembled the figure-gardening in the Spectator, and which threatened to reduce all English poetry to a polished and featureless mannerism, has gradually been superseded by one more vigorous and more national. Goldsmith set an example of original sentiment; of ease, and nature, and tenderness. Glover exhibited in his Leonidas the simple outline of an ancient statue. Cowper has, as it were, crept into the bosom confidence of half his countrymen. The cold brilliancy of Darwin's mere material poetry dazzled for a while; but its gleam was that of an ignis fatuus. General taste has, upon the whole, within this last half century, been simplified, purified, and invigorated. Men have begun to be weaned from the persuasion that poetry is something necessarily striking and dazzling, and epigrammatic, and antithetical, squared and balanced by rule and measure, and made up of established periphrases, conventional phrases, and traditional metaphors; forming altogether a sort of poetic cypher; a symbolical diction as unlike as possible to the language immemorially spoken by men and women and children. They have begun to give up the expectation that every word and line in poetry must be essentially different from prose; to perceive that to call a line flat or lagging is sometimes the dictate of an inflexible and prejudiced ear, not knowing or not considering that poetry has its reliefs as well as painting. They have begun to admit that poetry, like prose, must have her moods of relaxation; her easy moments; her bye-passages and resting-places: to discover, in short, that poetry is not a being of mere artifice, moving in buckram and sparkling with embroidery; but that, like the mountain shepherdess, she searches the woods and the meadows for her fairest and freshest ornaments, assumes all the changing colours, and follows all the vagrant varieties of primitive nature: 'MILLE habet ornatus; mille decenter habet'[1].

The turbulent era of the French revolution, bringing with it a succession of gigantic and astounding events, roused the spirits of men to a pitch of unnatural excitement. Literature, for ever operated upon by external causes, and poetry more especially, caught the contagion. Goblin novels, infidel and obscene, ballads of witchcraft, and tales of wonder and of terror, came like a cloud upon us, and 'darkened all the land' of genius.

At length a poet, truly deserving that name, conceived the project of gratifying this appetite for stimulating novelties by resorting to the times of border heroism, and exhibiting the rude characters and picturesque manners of that gallant age in the new and striking form of lyrical epopœia: recommended also by a singular strength and distinctness in the representation of sensible objects, by an animating impetuosity in the description of busy action, and a boldness and relief in the display of individual character, scarcely exceeded since the time of Homer. A similar experiment has been tried with respect to eastern manners: and that, too, with a peculiarity of powers which may claim the honour of invention; with much of wildness and of melancholy, much of thought and of sentiment. These productions, though open to many exceptions, have done good, independently of the example afforded of a daring poetic spirit, by diffusing a taste for poetical reading among all classes; by recalling conversation from insipid trifling, and disposing it to critical discussion. But the result has, perhaps, been injurious to the moral value of poetry, and perhaps to its interests in general. The sublimations of a spiritual philosophy; the pure ideal of the imagination; the fine and ethereal essence of feeling, are disregarded with a coarse and vulgar contempt as visionary obscurities: admiration is reserved for the dazzle and the bustle of adventure; for incidents so arranged as to embrace the complicated interest of a novel; and for characters in which a capricious and incongruous mixture of virtues and vices, which never did and never could meet and mingle in the self-same human being, are conceived in a spirit of forced and overstrained enthusiasm, and applied to pamper the outrageous craving of a diseased and insatiable appetite for distortion and eccentricity.

In attempting to interest mankind in a species of poetry composed of mere simple elements, Mr. Wordsworth has had to contend with the prejudices of two descriptions of readers. Those who, accustomed to the refined language of Pope or the smooth couplets of Hayley and Rogers, cry out on a common or trivial expression or a loose line, as if they had made a notable detection of poetic insufficiency; and those who, aware of the natural variety and relief of these occasional softenings of tone, yet expect a certain supernatural vehemence of passion; a rapidity of detail; a stirring and hurrying excitement; a constant 'darkening of the gloomy and illuminating of the splendid.' Neither the ballad character of the poem before us, nor the quiet and passive fortitude and meek sympathy which are its object, will stand the touchstone of artificial criticism, or float on the breath of popular applause. It is a song fitted to a calmer and better age, and a less sophisticated audience: such as might have reck-oned among its hearers a Spenser and a Sydney. It might be said of it, in the language of the Arcadian, 'Behold! he cometh to you with a tale which holdeth children from play, and old men from the chimney cor-ner.' Yet, after all, we cannot let Mr. Wordsworth escape from our hands without correction. His extreme love of simplicity has sometimes betrayed him into affectation, and by affectation he has been carried into excess. Sometimes we discern in his compositions an inverted labour – a studious departure from grace, and a fastidious disdain of cultivation; as if ease implied the absence of ornament, and nature delighted in discord. It is to be regretted that Mr. Wordsworth, with his powers of harmony and delicate apprehension of metrical beauty, should ever forget that, however grave or sublime, affecting or noble the sentiment, if it pretend to array itself in verse, it must adopt its characteristic embellishments, or sink below the level of prose.

The historical part of the poem is grounded on the great northern insurrection in the twelfth year of Elizabeth, 1509; which forms the subject of one of the ballads in Dr. Percy's collection, entitled 'The Rising in the North.' The Duke of Norfolk had been committed to the Tower by Elizabeth, on the discovery of a negotiation for marrying him with Mary, Queen of Scots, in which several of the English nobility were implicated: and the Earl of Northumberland, on being commanded to repair to the English court, took up arms, on the plea of settling the succession of the crown, and restoring the ancient religion. His standard-bearer was Richard Norton, whose sons, with the exception of the eldest, marched at his side; and on the banner were embroidered the cross and the five wounds of Christ. They entered Durham, and with a zeal of catholicity which would have refreshed the heart of Dr. Drumgoolee, *trampled on the Bible*, and heard mass. They then proceeded towards London, but were obliged to follow the example of a certain nameless king of France, and having marched up the hill, to march down again. On a retrograde movement occasioned by the difficulty of supplies, Westmoreland's men slunk away, and Northumberland, hearing of the advance of the Earl of Sussex, disbanded his levies, and with the other leaders escaped into Scotland. Norton, however, according to the old ballad, laying siege to Barnard Castle, entered it with his eight sons by escalade; but not being followed, they were overpowered by the garrison within, taken, and executed. With this event Mr. Wordsworth has connected a local tradition recorded in Dr. Whitaker's history of the Deanery of Craven; that about the time of this insurrection being quashed, 'a white doe long continued to make a weekly pilgrimage from Rylstone over the falls of Bolton, and was constantly found in the abbey church-yard during divine service, after the close of which she returned home as regularly as the rest of the congregation.'

The old gentleman with his thumb-screw zeal and his paganized Christianity is obviously not much entitled to our condolence. The characters in which the interest of the poem is absorbed are those of his daughter and his eldest son, who had been educated by their mother in the purer faith of the reformed religion; the one a beautiful emblem of Christian meekness and resignation, the other a no less affecting instance of Christian courage in the difficult task of braving even a father's scorn, and submitting to the unworthiest imputations from a clear and intrepid sense of duty.

Francis, though he has the fortitude to dissuade his father from this ill-digested and hot-brained enterprise, and to refuse to lift a sword in the cause, attends him to the field unarmed. When all has failed, he still clings to him. The heart of old Norton is softened at the magnanimity of his son; and feeling his ruling superstition 'strong in death,' he confides to Francis, as the condition of his blessing and forgiveness, the charge of placing the consecrated banner on the shrine of St. Mary in Bolton Priory. This charge Francis accepts; wrests the standard from a soldier who was bearing it in mockery before the prisoners as they went to the scaffold, and, protected by the sympathy of the crowd, bears it off in safety; but is pursued by horsemen and cut down. The desolate state of his sister; her estrangement from home after falling on her brother's grave; her melancholy, her recognition by the doe, which had become wild since the dispersion of the family in which it was reared; and the gradually soothing effects which this renewed companionship produces, are naturally and pathetically told. The young lady, however, pines away: and it is to her grave that the doe repairs in its sabbath pilgrimage.

[Quotes *The White Doe of Rylstone*, *PW*, III, pp. 284–5, ll. 43–62, and pp. 285–6, ll. 79–99:

> A moment ends the fervent din . . .
> And she is left alone in heaven. –
>
> What harmonious pensive changes . . .
> And where no flower hath leave to dwell.]

The different conjectures of those who pass the church-yard respecting the visit and the nature of this creature, as put into the mouth of the old soldier, the great lady, and the Oxford scholar, are characteristic and poetically imagined: but we must limit our extracts. The following passage from the interview between Francis and Emily, will exemplify Mr. Wordsworth's peculiar power of conveying to the mind a still and deep impression of sadness.

[Quotes *ibid.*, *PW*, III, p. 299, ll. 521–9, and pp. 299–300, ll. 546–65

> For thee, for thee, is left the sense.
> Of all we lov'd and lov'd so well: –
>
> For we must fall, both we and ours: –
> Herself belov'd in Rylstone Hall.]

We think the poem should have ended with the following lines:

> But chiefly by that single grave,
> That one sequester'd hillock green,
> The pensive visitant is seen.
> [*Ibid.*, *PW*, III, p. 340, ll. 1898–900]

The additional stanza is stiff and affected:

> And aye, methinks, this hoary pile,
> Subdued by outrage and decay,
> Looks down upon her with a smile:
> A gracious smile, that seems to say,
> 'Then, thou art not a child of Time,
> But daughter of th' eternal prime.'
> [*Ibid.*, *PW*, III, p. 340, ll. 1905–10]

At the end of the volume is a ballad, entitled 'The Force of Prayer,' or the Founding of Bolton Priory.' There is little to warrant the former title. A lady built the Priory on her son being drowned in the river wharf, while leaping with his grey-hound in a leash across 'the strid,' – a chasm between rocks. Time brought with it resignation: 'slowly did her succour come:' but the 'force of prayer' would lead us to expect something out of the common routine of things; and the disappointment gives a flatness to the close of the ballad. It had better have been called simply 'the Founding of Bolton Priory.'

'The White Doe' is prefaced by a beautiful proëm in the octave measure, addressed to the author's wife. We select a few lines illustrative of the high order of moral faculties which this writer possesses, and prophetic, as we think, of the durability of this his legendary tale:

> He serves the muses erringly and ill
> Whose aim is pleasure light and fugitive:
> Oh that my mind were equal to fulfill
> The comprehensive mandate which they give!
> Vain aspiration of an earnest will!
> Yet in this moral strain a power may live.
> ['Dedication' to *The White Doe of Rylstone*, *PW*, III,
> pp. 282–3, ll. 57–62]

EDITOR'S NOTE

1. 'She has a thousand costumes, she wears a thousand gracefully' (Tibullus III, 8. 14).

185.

Unsigned review (possibly a last contribution to the magazine by Francis Hodgson). *The Monthly Review*, November 1815, LXXVIII, 225–34

Despite the irritated tone, Wordsworth is called 'a man of acknowledged genius'; the essay is an attack on Wordsworth's theories and what the writer considers the silliness of some poems.

After all that the public has known of the productions of Mr. Wordsworth, and all that we have said concerning them, it is scarcely necessary for us now to observe that the sum and substance of his poetical character may be comprehensively described under one quality; viz. a strong admiration of the beauties of external nature. Accustomed to visit rocks and mountains rather than cities or market-towns, and cherishing a strict intimacy with the plants and flowers of his neighbourhood while he has maintained, comparatively, but little converse with men and women, he has contracted such habits of composition as were the natural consequence of so recluse and peculiar a mode of life. This simple explanation of a series of phænomena intitled Poems, and scientifically distributed by the author into classes of 'Imagination,' 'Fancy,' 'Affections,' 'Sentiment and Reflection,' &c., &c. will probably give little satisfaction to that author himself, or to his few though ardent votaries: but the '*raison suffisante*' for *all* Mr. Wordsworth's writings is nevertheless to be found in his 'local habitation;' where he has long been giving 'a name to airy nothings,' and, with much, very much indeed, of the real genius of a poet, has been wasting that genius on unworthy though innocent subjects, and displaying every variety of a whimsical and inveterately perverted taste which it is possible to conceive.

In a preface to the 'Poems' before us, which is not remarkable for clearness of idea nor for humility of tone, a fresh attempt is made to give that air of invention and novelty to Mr. W.'s writings which it seems to be his main object to claim. He wishes to be the founder of a school or system in poetry; and he endeavours to refer all his chance-effusions, all his walking thoughts, suggested by the stocks and stones or the old men and children that he encounters, to some particular class of composition, in which this or that faculty of the human mind has been appropriately exercised. Thus in the present volumes we have a poem belonging to the class of 'Fancy,' with no possible distinguishing characteristic from another in the class of 'Imagination;' 'the Affections' lay claim to a third, which might as well have been ranked under the head of 'Sentiment and Reflection,' and, in short, we have here such a pompous classification of trifles, for the most part obvious and extremely childish, that we do not remember to have ever met with so 'Much Ado about Nothing' in any other author. That we may not incur the faintest imputation of over-stating the confusion or the assumption of this celebrated preface, (which our readers will observe is 'entirely new,' and to be distinguished from that which was formerly prefixed to the Lyrical Ballads and is now printed again at the end of this work,) we shall make some extracts from it; – extracts, we confess, which give us pain to read, but which it is our duty to accompany with a proper degree of reprehension.

After some warm and therefore most pleasing commendation of Spenser, Shakspeare, and Milton, as distinguished by their power of imagination, Mr. W. thus proceeds:

If, bearing in mind the many poets distinguished by this prime quality, whose names I omit to mention; yet justified by a recollection of the insults which the ignorant, the incapable, and the presumptuous have heaped upon these and my other writings, I may be permitted to anticipate the judgment of posterity upon myself; I shall declare (censurable, I grant, if the notoriety of the fact above stated does not justify me) that I have given, in these unfavourable times, evidence of exertions of this faculty upon its worthiest objects, the external universe, the moral and religious sentiments of man, his natural affections, and his acquired passions; which have the same ennobling tendency as the productions of men, in this kind, worthy to be holden in undying remembrance.

We beg permission to subjoin to this extraordinary passage, as we cannot help considering it, the following still more extraordinary quotation and note. Viewed in conjunction with what we have just cited, we think that they give no unamusing insight into the opinions of poet, on subjects as important as his own present reveries and his own future reputation:

> I gazed – and gazed* – but little thought
> What wealth the shew to me had brought:
> For oft when on my couch I lie
> In vacant or in pensive mood,

* All those readers who are acquainted with Mr. Wordsworth's productions must remember his field of Daffodils. *Rev.*

They† flash upon that inward eye
Which is the bliss of solitude,
And then my heart with pleasure fills,
And dances with the Daffodils.

That note we also subjoin: it alludes to 'The Horn of Egremont Castle,' and the well known 'Goody Blake and Harry Gill;' as far as such personages can be honoured with that description: viz. 'This POEM, and the ballad which follows it, as they rather *refer to the imagination than are produced by it*, would not have been placed here, but to avoid a needless multiplication of the *classes*.' Needless, indeed! It is really almost incredible that a man of acknowledged genius, and of very considerable cultivation of mind, should attach such unmeaning consequence to trifles lighter than air; and more ludicrous, in many instances, than those who have not seen them can imagine. 'Goody Blake and Harry Gill' *referring to the imagination*!!! We shall shortly present our readers with some specimens of these wondrously distinct poems: but first we must introduce them to the author's *metaphysical* and *egotistical* lucubrations, which occupy so large a portion of his Preface and Supplementary Essay.

In the series of poems placed under the head of Imagination, I have begun with one of the earliest processes of nature in the development of this faculty. Guided by one of my own primary consciousnesses, I have represented a commutation and transfer of internal feelings, co-operating with external accidents to plant, for immortality, images of sound and sight, in the celestial soil of the imagination. The boy, there introduced, is listening, with something of a feverish and restless anxiety, for the recurrence of the riotous sounds which he had previously excited; and, at the moment when the intenseness of his mind is beginning to remit, he is surprised into a perception of the solemn and tranquillizing images which the poem describes. – The poems next in succession exhibit the faculty exerting itself upon various objects of the external universe; then follow others, where it is employed upon feelings, characters, and actions; and the class is concluded with imaginative pictures of moral, political, and religious sentiments.

To the mode in which fancy has already been characterized as the power of evoking and combining, or, as my friend Mr. Coleridge has styled it, "the aggregative and associative power," my objection is only that the definition is too

---

† The subject of these stanzas is rather an elementary feeling and simple impression (approaching to the nature of an ocular spectrum) upon the imaginative faculty, than an *exertion* of it. The one which follows is strictly a Reverie; and neither that, nor the next after it in succession, 'The Power of Music,' would have been placed here except for the reason given in the foregoing note.

general. To aggregate and to associate, to evoke and to combine, belong as well to the imagination as to the fancy; but either the materials evoked and combined are different; or they are brought together under a different law, and for a different purpose. Fancy does not require that the materials which she makes use of should be susceptible of change in their constitution, from her touch; and, where they admit of modification, it is enough for her purpose if it be slight, limited, and evanescent. Directly the reverse of these, are the desires and demands of the Imagination. She recoils from every thing but the plastic, the pliant, and the indefinite. She leaves it to Fancy to describe Queen Mab as coming,

> In shape no bigger than an agate stone
> On the fore-finger of an alderman.

Having to speak of stature, she does not tell you that her gigantic angel was as tall as Pompey's pillar; much less that he was twelve cubits, or twelve hundred cubits high; or that his dimensions equalled those of Teneriffe or Atlas; – because these, and if they were a million times as high, it would be the same, are bounded: the expression is, 'His stature reached the sky!' the illimitable firmament! – When the Imagination frames a comparison, if it does not strike on the first presentation, a sense of the truth of the likeness, from the moment that it is perceived, grows – and continues to grow – upon the mind; the resemblance depending less upon outline of form and feature than upon expression and effect, less upon casual and outstanding, than upon inherent and internal, properties: – moreover, the images invariably modify each other. – The law under which the processes of Fancy are carried on is as capricious as the accidents of things, and the effects are surprizing, playful, ludicrous, amusing, tender, or pathetic, as the objects happen to be appositely produced or fortunately combined. Fancy depends upon the rapidity and profusion with which she scatters her thoughts and images, trusting that their number, and the felicity with which they are linked together, will make amends for the want of individual value: or she prides herself upon the curious subtilty and the successful elaboration with which she can detect their lurking affinities. If she can win you over to her purpose, and impart to you her feelings, she cares not how unstable or transitory may be her influence, knowing that it will not be out of her power to resume it upon an apt occasion. But the Imagination is conscious of an indestructible dominion; – the soul may fall away from it, not being able to sustain its grandeur, but if once felt and acknowledged, by no act of any other faculty of the mind can it be relaxed, impaired, or diminished. – Fancy is given to quicken and to beguile the temporal part of our nature, Imagination to incite and to support the eternal. – Yet is it not the less true that Fancy, as she is an active, is also, under her own laws and in her own spirit, a creative faculty. In what manner Fancy ambitiously aims at a rivalship with the Imagination, and Imagination stoops to work with the materials of Fancy, might be illustrated from the compositions of all eloquent writers, whether in prose or verse; and chiefly from those of our own country.

To this ingenious but far from sound passage, we think, most readers will find something to object; although it contains much to amuse and even a certain portion of instruction. The truth appears to be that, amid all his seemingly accurate distinctions, Mr. Wordsworth has often capriciously attributed to one power that which belongs by equal right to another, and has missed the broad and plain distinction of Professor Stewart, (see his 'Elements,' pp. 284, 285.) that the office of Fancy is to collect materials for the Imagination. Such, however, are Mr. Wordsworth's metaphysics:* but, on referring to his Supplementary Essay, we find still more ample reason to admire the clearness and cogency of argument by which he establishes his own claim to originality, (for, likes Achilles in the Iliad, he is seldom out of the author's sight,) and proves the principal point which he has in view; namely, that all great poets except Thompson have been neglected at their first appearance; *ergo*, that the time is yet to come at which Mr. Wordsworth's own fame will attain its maturity. This prophecy is not merely implied, it is directly and plainly delivered by the prophet himself, of himself, and for his own benefit. '*Vanitas vanitatum, omnia vanitas!*' Well, indeed, might the wise man, or the most ordinary of mortal sages, thus exclaim, when perusing some of Mr. W.'s presages of his own immortality. Let our readers digest that which we are about to quote, and with which we shall be contented as an example of the author's prose-performances, criticisms, or good auspices relating to his own future support from the *people*: – the *people*, whom he emphatically separates from the *public*: meaning, we presume, those who are hereafter to be taught to read, the *mox erudiendum vulgus*,[1] the unborn children of Joseph Lancaster, as contradistinguished from the progeny of the universities or the literary swarm of the metropolis now in existence.

Mr. W. takes a brief and rapid notice of some of the leading English poets, the temporary neglect of whose writings evidently consoles him in the comparative unpopularity† of his own, and then thus proceeds, alluding to Johnson's Lives of the Poets:

As I do not mean to bring down this retrospect to our own times, it may with propriety be closed at the era of this distinguished event. From the literature of other ages and countries, proofs equally cogent might have been adduced that the opinions announced in the former part of this essay are founded upon

---

* He is pleased, among other curious judgments, to disapprove the title of 'Metaphysical Poets,' which Johnson has bestowed on Cowley and some others.
† The word *popular* is evidently unpleasing to the author's ear, notwithstanding his fondness for 'the *people*.' This is capricious.

truth. It was not an agreeable office, nor a prudent undertaking, to declare them, but their importance seemed to render it a duty. It may still be asked, where lies the particular relation of what has been said to these volumes? – The question will be easily answered by the discerning reader who is old enough to remember the taste that was prevalent when some of these poems were first published, seventeen years ago; who has also observed to what degree the poetry of this island has since that period been coloured by them; and who is further aware of the unremitting hostility with which, upon some principle or other, they have each and all been opposed. A sketch of my own notion of the constitution of fame has been given; and, as far as concerns myself, I have cause to be satisfied. The love, the admiration, the indifference, the slight, the aversion, and even the contempt, with which these poems have been received, knowing, as I do, the source within my own mind, from which they have proceeded, and the labour and pains, which, when labour and pains appeared needful, have been bestowed upon them, – must all, if I think consistently, be received as pledges and tokens, bearing the same general impression though widely different in value; – they are all proofs that for the present time I have not laboured in vain; and afford assurances, more or less authentic, that the products of my industry will endure.

To complete the modesty of this picture of '*Myself*' by an author, we subjoin the concluding paragraph of the Essay:

Towards the public the writer hopes that he feels as much deference as it is intitled to: but to the people, philosophically characterized, and to the embodied spirit of their knowledge, so far as it exists and moves, at the present, faithfully supported by its two wings, the past and the future, his devout respect, his reverence, is due. He offers it willingly and readily; and, this done, takes leave of his readers, by assuring them – that, if he were not persuaded that the contents of these volumes, and the work to which they are subsidiary, evinced something of the "Vision and the Faculty divine;" and that, both in words and things, they will operate in their degree, to extend the domain of sensibility for the delight, the honour, and the benefit of human nature, notwithstanding the many happy hours which he has employed in their composition, and the manifold comforts and enjoyments they have procured to him, he would not, if a wish could do it, save them from immediate destruction; – from becoming at this moment, to the world, as a thing that had never been,

Emendaturis ignibus ipse darem.[2]

Credat Judæus Apella.[3]

We[4] are so thoroughly overwhelmed by the high and mighty tone of this author's prose, that we really must have immediate recourse to his verse, in order to get rid of the painful humiliation and sense of inferiority which he inflicts on his readers. There, (*Dieu merci!*) we are comforted by silliness instead of system; by want of harmony instead of abundance of pride; by downright vacancy instead of grandeur and presumption. Will any one believe that the critic who speaks so contemptuously of other severe critics, and yet is very gall and vinegar himself, – and the poet, – are the same person? We will not pain him farther than by contrasting the titles, or a few lines only, of his pitiable, seriously pitiable frolics of versification, with the pompous language just quoted

Pull the primrose, sister Anne!
Pull as many as you can!

Oft I had heard of Lucy Gray.

Spade! with which Wilkinson half tilled his lands.

The little orphan, Alice Fell.

Clarkson! it was an obstinate hill to climb.

There's George Fisher, Charles Fleming, and Reginald Shore.

Fair Ellen Irwin, when she sate.

Nay, Betty, go! good Betty, go!

What is't that ails young Harry Gill?

'Twas little Barbara Lewthwaite, a child of beauty rare.

Jones! when from Calais southward you and I
Travelled on foot together, &c.

This '*class*' we could increase and diversify largely: but, craving leave to call it the '*Class of Names,*' we shall proceed to the '*Class of Nonsense,*' which is still more fruitful, and on which we should dwell at more length, if it were not in vain to attempt to do justice to this part of our subject. We shall therefore deem it sufficient to give one entire specimen, although perhaps rather hackneyed, of the '*class*' in question; and then let our readers judge of the value of that author's criticisms, who, after having himself thus written, dares to treat Dryden and

Pope with the arrogant disrespect which is manifest in the essay above mentioned.*

[Quotes 'The Star-Gazers'. *PW*, II, p. 219; *Poems 1807*, p. 261]

So much for the detached and the connected childishness of this author. We are aware that we may be told by the admirers of Mr. Wordsworth that this is one of his *early* absurdities, and must not be brought forwards as the test of his present improvement. Why, then, does he republish it? But, besides the fact that the year 1807 has not very long elapsed, we are not sure whether we have not selected a poem which is a favourite with its author; and which, notwithstanding the unpoetical and unmeaning character of it, will be *gazed* at by '*the people*' with more delight than the stars in Leicester-square: although we cannot ourselves well imagine the mind of the critic

That does not *slackly* go away, as if dissatisfied,

not only from this poem, but from nine-tenths of the collection before us.

Having executed an unpleasant task in endeavouring, as our duty enjoined, to moderate the unusual arrogance of this writer, by condensing some specimens of it into one mass, and by illustrating his favourable sentiments of himself with a few examples of his practical skill in the ridiculous, we shall now turn with real pleasure to the remaining tenth part of these volumes, in which we find much that will give rational pleasure to the reader.

We begin with 'an Extract from the Conclusion of a Poem, composed upon leaving School,' so far back as the year 1786.

> Dear native regions, I foretell
> From what I feel at this farewell,
> That, wheresoe'er my steps shall tend,
> And whenso'er my course shall end,
> If in that hour a single tie
> Survive of local sympathy,
> My soul will cast the backward view,
> The longing look alone on you.
> 'Thus, when the sun, prepared for rest,
> Hath gained the precincts of the west,

---

* The passage cited from Dryden is far from deserving the censure with which this critic loads it, (pages 358, 359, vol. i) and his attack on Pope is exactly the same as that of Mr. Elton, which we noticed in a late Number.

> Though his departing radiance fail
> To illuminate the hollow vale,
> A lingering light he fondly throws
> On the dear hills where first he rose.

This youthful production certainly gave a promise of purer taste than a love for singularity, and a spirit of imaginary system,* have subsequently permitted to ripen into maturity. The poem of 'Yarrow visited,' composed in 1814, is of peculiar softness and beauty; and we only omit to quote it, as well as the charming lines 'written while sailing in a Boat at Evening,' and those in 'Remembrance of Collins,' which are perhaps still more delightful, in order to make room for a longer and equally pleasing proof of Mr. Wordsworth's poetical abilities, and (with the painful exception above noticed) of his most amiable tone of mind. We quote it indeed in preference to any of the later compositions, of whatever description. We shall not, however, transcribe the first and the last stanzas of this poem, although strongly characteristic of the author's peculiarities; since we cannot persuade ourselves that they do not injure the effect of the natural sorrows of a lover, the object of whose affections has been snatched from him by death.

> Oh, move, thou cottage, from behind that oak!
> Or let the aged tree uprooted lie,
> That in some other way yon smoke
> May mount into the sky!
> The clouds pass on! they from the heavens depart:
> I look – the sky is empty space;
> I know not what I trace;
> But, when I cease to look, my hand is on my heart.
>
> O! what a weight is in these shades! Ye leaves,
> When will that dying murmur be supprest?
> Your sound my heart of peace bereaves,
> It robs my heart of rest.
> Thou thrush, that singest loud – and loud and free,
> Into yon row of willows flit,
> Upon that alder sit;
> Or sing another song, or choose another tree.

---

* Mr. Wordsworth should remember that the *notice* which he has gained from the public has principally arisen from these faults.

Roll back, sweet rill! back to thy mountain-bounds,
And there for ever be thy waters chained!
For thou dost haunt the air with sounds
That cannot be sustained;
If still beneath that pine-tree's ragged bough
Headlong yon waterfall most come,
Oh let it then be dumb! –
Be any thing, sweet rill, but that which thou art now.

Thou Eglantine, whose arch so proudly towers,
(Even like a rainbow spanning half the vale)
Thou one fair shrub, oh! shed thy flowers,
And stir not in the gale.
For thus to see thee nodding in the air,
To see thy arch thus stretch and bend,
Thus rise and thus descend, –
Disturbs me, till the sight is more than I can bear.

Mr. W.'s sonnets in honour of liberty may boast, in many instances, of distinguished merit; and they seem to have been called forth by the genuine feelings of joy or indignation, as patriotism successfully opposed tyranny, or was cruelly oppressed by it, in the late eventful struggles. Why will Mr. Wordsworth ever be so untrue to himself, as to desert the manly and vigorous style of this burst of poetry?

A PROPHECY. – *February* 1807.
High deeds, O Germans, are to come from you!
Thus in your books the record shall be found,
'A watchword was pronounced, a potent sound,
Arminius! – all the people quaked like dew
Stirred by the breeze – they rose, a nation, true,
True to itself – the mighty Germany,
She of the Danube and the northern sea,
She rose, – and off at once the yoke she threw.
All power was given her in the dreadful trance –
Those new-born kings she withered like a flame.'
– Woe to them all! but heaviest woe and shame
To that Bavarian who did first advance
His banner in accursed league with France,
First open traitor to her sacred name!

EDITOR'S NOTES

1. 'the soon to be educated public'.
2. 'I would give (them) myself to the flames to improve'.
3. 'Appella the Jew might believe it' (Horace, *Satires*, I, 5). Jews were regarded as superstitious. 'It' in Horace means that incense might melt without fire.
4. The first two sentences in this paragraph were quoted by Barron Field in his Ms. Life, 1839; Wordsworth in 1840 annotated them: 'All this extract is now read by me for the first time'.

186.

Unsigned review, *Monthly Review*, November 1815, LXXVIII, 235–8

We had scarcely completed the preceding notice of Mr. Wordsworth's new poems and re-publications, when we were called to listen again to his lyre, or harp, or hurdy-gurdy, (as it too often may be denominated,) and to sympathize with his 'White Doe of Rylstone.' We hoped to be able to meet him now with a less interrupted pleasure than before: but indeed this is not yet the case. So tired, however, are we with pointing out errors which we fear must be now regarded as incurable, that, after having remarked that all the author's usual excentricities of thought and defects in composition are to be found in the thin quarto before us, we shall resign the wearisome office of censure for the present, and amuse ourselves and our readers with a few extracts which display elegance and tenderness of manner.

It must previously be observed that this poem is founded on a local tradition, and on the ballad in Percy's Collection, (a book to which Mr. Wordsworth very gratefully acknowledges his manifold obligations,) intitled 'The Rising of the North.' [Summarises the tradition.]

As the part of this poem which is concerned with human affairs is, in our apprehension, very inferior to that in which the supernatural Doe is depicted, we shall confine our selections to the latter; and, as the introduction of this extraordinary animal and the final dismissal of her are among the most successful passages, they are those which we shall now transcribe, submitting them without farther criticism to the qualified approbation of the discerning reader.

The people being all gone into church at Bolton Abbey,

[Quotes *The White Doe of Rylstone*, *PW*, III, pp. 284–6, ll. 35–99

    —scarcely have they disappeared . . .

    And where no flower hath leave to dwell.]

We have no room for an ampler description of this visionary and soothing creature: but we must not withhold the pleasure which we have
promised, and shall therefore extract the account of her last appearance.

Emily, the sole remaining branch of the Nortons, is introduced as
wandering about her paternal scenes, accompanied by this gentle animal,
who has been wondrously restored to her mistress:

[Quotes *ibid.*, *PW*, III, pp. 338–9, ll. 1811–70

    But most to Bolton's sacred pile . . .

    Was buried by her mother's side.]

A very pleasing engraving, from a landscape painted by Sir George
Beaumont, is prefixed to the volume.

187.

Unsigned review, *Gentleman's Magazine*, December 1815, LXXXV,
524–5

In this Poem Mr. Wordsworth has displayed a richness of fancy and a
tenderness of feeling which place him in a high rank among the living
Poets of his Country. It is not merely by proving himself to be endowed
with those qualities that he merits this distinction; it is by the power
which he exercises, apparently without effort, over the minds of his
readers; by the artless and natural touches with which he excites and
kindles emotions congenial with his own; and by his skill in awakening
those simple tones of real pathos, to which every heart, alive to the
charms of Poetry, must vibrate in unison. Heretofore he has been censured, and even ridiculed, for debasing these powers, for the homeliness
of his diction, and the want of dignity in his characters; but in the present
case such censure would be misplaced, and the ingenious severity of
criticism will not easily find matter for ridicule.

The Poem is founded partly on the ballad in Dr. Percy's collection,
entitled 'The Rising of the North,' and partly on a local tradition.
[The plot of the ballad is expounded and the tradition of the doe's visits.]

From these materials the Poet has constructed a singularly pathetic and interesting tale, in which the mysterious Doe is introduced as having been the favourite of Emily in childhood and early youth; as recognizing her in the desolation of her grief among the wilds of Craven; as being her constant companion in her seclusion; and, finally, as the meek pilgrim of Nature, that returned on every Sabbath, to lie down, in simple homage by her grave.

[Extensive quotation ends the review.]

188. Josiah Conder (1789–1855)

Unsigned review, *Eclectic Review*, January 1816, V (second series), 33–45

Conder had again hoped that Montgomery would undertake the review (see entry 150). He wrote to Montgomery on 26 August 1815:

> What do you say to Wordsworth's White Doe? Will it be fair to pass it over in silence? will it be possible, after our review of the Excursion, to notice it at all? I can hear but one opinion of this White Doe, – that it is an unaccountable piece of wanton silliness. Lest you shd not have seen it, I enclose a copy for your *opinion* at least if you will not review it.
>
> (Ms. Sheffield City Library)

This time Montgomery was not persuaded and Conder wrote the article himself. He wrote to Montgomery on 13 December 1815:

> Wordsworth's White Doe for credit sake must not be passed over. I wished you to take it in hand, as you did Wordsworth's Excursion so much *con amore*. I remember, too, being much pleased with an article (I believe of yours) on Wordsworth's minor poems in the former series [see entry 100b]. But you have declined it, probably from feeling that you could not maintain in reviewing it, the high tone of your former article. I have endeavoured, as much as possible, to steer clear of lowering your estimate, as well as of losing our own credit by praising Wordsworth through thick and thin. It will give me great satisfaction to find that you approve of my article. The Monthly and British Reviews have already noticed it.
>
> (*Ibid.*)

Southey apparently did not entirely approve of the article. He wrote to Conder on 18 March 1816:

Another reading, and you and I shall not differ about the 'White Doe'. The faults are glaring and on the surface; admit them, and then read for the beauties. There is neither impiety nor nonsense there – there is much mysticism. This evening I came upon a text in the Wisdom implying pre-existence in the belief of its writer: 'For I was a witty child, and had a good spirit. *Yea rather, being good, I came into a body undefiled.*' This notion will explain a good deal in Wordsworth.

(Josiah Conder: A Memoir, E. R. Conder, 1857, 179)

It is one of the worst effects resulting from the malignant abuse or the incompetent discharge of the office of the critic, that it has a tendency to render a man of superior genius unduly and proudly inattentive to the suggestions of his contemporaries. He is led to repay himself for the injustice with which he may have been assailed, by investing himself with the sullen, independent feeling of conscious merit.

Mr. Wordsworth must feel that his character as a poet, has not been justly appreciated by his contemporaries; and this feeling, though operating in an amiable and ingenuous mind, has betrayed him into the language of arrogant egotism. He is conscious that he has been estimated by his faults rather than by his excellencies, the former only being on a level with the minds of his critics: for, in respect of the latter, he soars far above them. His poems have been tried by the eye and by the ear, for these, his critics could exercise with nicety; while with the plastic spirit that breathed in his numbers, they could hold no converse, for the only converse to be held with a poet's mind, is that of sympathy. The feelings of the reader must be strung to a pitch in unison with those of the poet himself, or they will not vibrate in reply.

That all persons who have a capacity for the pleasures and emotions of poetry, should derive equal gratification from the same class of compositions, must, we think, be regarded as neither desirable nor possible. Even among persons of real sensibility, the natural strength of imagination, the relative degree in which the faculties of the mind have received cultivation, as well as the moral habits of the individual, will very considerably modify the power of intellectual enjoyment. There are few minds in which the love of poetry does not form a sort of intellectual instinct; an instinct often blind and indiscriminating, yet having reference to something nobler than the wants of the physical being, and valuable as connected with a peculiar degree of moral sensibility, incident to the first development of the imagination and of the passions. The poetry which aims at popularity, must be adapted to that numerous class of readers, in whom this instinctive feeling exists, but who have stopped short at a very low degree of mental cultivation, or whose imagination has been neglected, amid the pursuits of after life. The rude idea which their infantile fancy first pictured, the broad features of romance, and the common objects of passion, will be the most likely to interest persons of this description; for poetry will engage them chiefly by carrying them back to the age of poetry, when ideal objects were more nearly balanced with the realities of life. In their amusements, both individuals and nations long retain the feelings and characteristics of their childhood. They are the last traces of the correspondent periods of intellectual progress that disappear. In maturer life poetry is considered as an amusement, because it originated and expired, as a passion, in the season of amusement, and its higher purpose was never regarded.

We shall perhaps make ourselves more clearly understood, by adverting to the success of Walter Scott's first production, as an illustration of these remarks. Throughout his poems, there is, perhaps, scarcely a sentiment expressed, or a feeling described, which the humblest intellect would find it difficult to understand, or the most common character fail to realize. He has not scrupled to employ all the common-place of poetry which first captivated our imagination, and so far as amusement is concerned, he has completely succeeded. In the vividness which his descriptions seem to impart to the faded colours of romance, in the feeling of novelty which he awakens by the most familiar images, and in the sprightliness and grace with which he tells the oft-told tale, we recognise the hand of no ordinary poet; although the materials of his composition are all ordinary. His 'Lay of the Last Minstrel' is the happiest of his productions, and bears most evidently the glow of those feelings which the author brought warm from the study of the *reliques* of ancient minstresly. In imitating these, he seemed to have unconsciously transferred to himself the feelings of the ideal harper, while he transformed us into the children who listened to him. His subsequent poems have pleased as imitations of his first, but the same strain frequently repeated, palls at length upon the ear. Those who have but little taste for poetry, begin to be tired even of Mr. Scott's, and those who have taste, begin to ask for something better.

Poetry, to be extensively popular, must, we have ventured to affirm, possess a universality of character. It is certain, however, that this sort of poetry cannot be of a very high order; and if there be no higher kind, the art must be considered as affording little that is adapted to minds of superior intelligence. Accordingly, this is the light in which it has been regarded by many persons, who have paid but little attention to the objects for which it is chiefly to be valued. As we ascend higher in the scale of intellectual cultivation, not only the class on which the poet's popularity depends, is diminished in point of numbers, but the varieties of character and habit which then become increasingly prominent, render it more difficult for an author to make himself intelligible to the feelings of each individual. Even if the pre-eminent character of his genius, together with the nature of his subject, in some rare instance, succeed in conciliating the sympathy or the homage of all intelligent minds, it will be found that the pleasure derived by various individuals from the same production, relates to different qualities, proceeds from different causes, and is obtained by a different effort of the mind. In some, it will be a spontaneous act of sympathy giving birth to pleasurable emotion; in others, the pleasure will be consequent upon the operation of the judgement, and of a more artificial nature. To whom will the perusal of Paradise Lost be a study and a task, which the reader forgets to repeat? Not to the man of cultivated fancy and poetical feeling; who, in his amusements, preserves the dignity of a thoughtful being. On the other hand, by what proportion of his readers can Milton be really understood? Not, surely, by the thousands in successive generations, who lay out their first pocket-money on a half-crown edition of Paradise Lost, awed and captivated by the religious nature of the subject; and receiving as almost authentic, the history the poet gives of our first parents. Yet, there is a high degree of pleasure, perhaps a degree more powerful than that of which the critic partakes, and it is a salutary pleasure too, which may be derived from the perusal of our great poet's greatest work, even by those who very imperfectly understand it. This pleasure, since it springs from the imagination, must be called a poetical pleasure, although poetry is rather the exciting occasion of it, than its proper source. Words imperfectly understood, are often found to convey an indefinite meaning, quite as impressive as their simple import; and, in this way, a subject above the conceptions of the reader, will often furnish hints which the mind follows out into an episode framed of its own associations. But, it is not by minds of this description, nor by hundreds of his readers, nor by thousands of his admirers, still less by the bulk of the admirers of Mr. Scott, or by the ridiculers of Mr. Wordsworth, that Milton can be understood or appreciated.

Poetry consists of the external forms which the noblest thoughts and feelings of our nature have adopted as their appropriate expression. The materials upon which the imagination works, are composed of earthly elements, but its model is the ideal prototype of a fairer creation existing within the mind of the poet; a day dream of perfection cherished in the hope of realizing the vision. The cultivation of the imagination, provided it does not interfere with the development of the other faculties, must be deemed beneficial, inasmuch as it is productive of a correspondent increase of sensibility, and is conducive to the exercise of the purest affections. By causing the past and the future to preponderate over the present, it exalts man, according to Dr. Johnson's fine observation, in the scale of intellectual being. Its natural effect, however, will be to produce a degree of abstractedness from objects of customary interest, to introduce a fondness for speculation, and, in certain situations, to give a peculiarity to the mental character. Now, poetry, more than any other production of the intellect, is the expression of character, having been invented for the purpose of communicating and transmitting those sentiments and feelings which constitute character; sentiments and feelings common indeed to all, but the consciousness of which is confined to those who have made the phenomena of their own minds the subject of habitual attention. The objects with which these feelings become in some respects arbitrarily associated, will be determined by the peculiar habits of the individual; and if these have abstracted him from the ordinary pursuits of life, the objects of his sensibility or taste, will be probably peculiar; and his character, which can be understood only by sympathy, – influencing the character of his productions, will render them unintelligible, and consequently uninteresting to the feelings of common readers.

The class of poets generally termed the metaphysical, were doubtless men of strong imagination and of real poetical feeling; but their habits led them to associate the indefinite ideas which are connected with the deepest emotions, with mere intellectual abstractions, thus substituting a sort of hieroglyphic language, instead of the vocal and living expression of the passions. The forms in which they imbodied their fancies, were artificial; but there is no question that, in many instances at least, a peculiar sensibility, tenderness, and refinement, were the sources of productions the most foreign to the sympathy of common readers. We can easily believe that an astronomical problem, though far enough from being itself a poetical production, may, by suggesting a train of sublime associations, become invested with a mysterious power of affecting the feelings in a way strictly analogous to poetry. In like manner, pure metaphysical abstractions may take the place of the common objects of human sympathy, in the minds of individuals who are more strongly under the influence of their own speculations, than of the impressions received through their external senses.

Mr. Wordsworth exhibits the singular combination of the metaphysical poet, and the enthusiastic lover and minute observer of external nature. He has a mind which grasps the whole compass of poetry; and where he comes in contact with the ordinary sympathies of human nature, no living poet leaves so strongly the impression of a master genius: at times, however, he retires into a region distant from all intellectual intercourse, and becomes shrouded in impervious mysticism. Recondite and obscure as his meanings often are, and perverse as his choice of objects and expressions may appear, he is never justly chargeable with want of meaning. What subject or what style soever he selects, he seems always more than equal to his task, while those of his faults which most nearly resemble failure, are evidently the result of design. His descent is as deliberate as his highest flight is easy: in both he discovers eccentricity, but eccentricity without weakness.

Faults, however, such as Mr. Wordsworth chooses to commit, are not easily overlooked by the intolerance of taste. His bold and determined non-conformity to the creeds and rules of established usages, marks him out as a poetical schismatic. For our own parts, we contend, even in the world of taste, for an enlarged toleration. If a poet like Mr. Wordsworth, chooses to narrow out for himself a path on the confines of mysticism, inaccessible to common minds, there let him play the Solitary: transformed into an insect, let him fondle flowers, and, like Ariel, lie sheltered in a cowslip's bell, or 'under the blossom that hangs on the bough': – then, half resuming humanity, let him delight to indue the nobler life of animal consciousness with reflex intelligence, and realize the fables of the Pythagorean; the same propensity which led the grosser imaginations of the old heathens to carry their uninformed sympathy with inferior and even inanimate nature, into idolatry. Through all these changes we may recognise the poet's power, but we cannot accompany him; and we would gladly, when the Proteus again becomes man, fix him in that shape for ever.

Strictly speaking, it will generally, perhaps always, be found, that a writer's peculiarities are his faults: in their excellencies men resemble each other. The latter are uniform though various, like all the productions of nature; for they spring from natural endowment; the former result from the eccentricity of growth, and originate in the character. From a character with which ordinary persons cannot sympathize, of the inner springs of which they can know little – and such a character, judging from his productions, we must conceive Mr. Wordsworth's to be – we may naturally expect a degree of singularity in its productions, which ill deserves to be submitted to the flippancy of opinion, but which must, nevertheless, interfere with the impression that their excellencies are adapted to produce.

We shall now very briefly acquaint our readers with the nature of the poem which has excited these rather lengthened remarks.

[Quotes the first paragraph of Wordsworth's note to the *White Doe*.]

The feeling in which we conceive the poem to have originated, and to which it is adapted to minister, is a contemplative melancholy, such as beautiful and romantic scenery, aided by associations of ancient grandeur, and by some wild tradition, is exquisitely calculated to inspire. In this frame of mind, the poem will not fail to please; it is the light by which the painting was coloured, and it seems flat in the glare of other feelings. Nothing can be less calculated to gratify the expectations raised by the title, of some busy narrative of lofty adventure, such as Walter Scott's Tales had led us to associate with the metre, than our Author's first canto, in which the reader is forced to stand in Rylstone Church-yard, and look all the while at a White Doe, and listen all the while to a rhapsody, the import of which he is not led to perceive, upon its whiteness, and brightness, and famousness, and holiness. We must pronounce it to be a great error, that the Author should not have attended more to the circumstances necessary to engage a reader's sympathy: it is requisite that he be prepared for the feeling the Author designs to convey. The mysterious tie of instinctive fondness which attaches some animals to mankind, is a subject highly susceptible of poetical treatment; and the particular tradition referred to in the poem, when known to be a tradition, becomes highly pleasing. The circumstance itself, unconnected with the interest it receives from having been the subject of belief and credulous wonder in former days, strikes us as puerile, and as unworthy of the labour bestowed in drawing the reader's attention to it. Instead, therefore, of the mysterious interest which the mute heroine might have been made to awaken, we follow her without curiosity, and resent her after-intrusion, as that of an impertinent spectre. We are persuaded that this first canto will in many cases effectually prejudice persons against the whole poem: it nevertheless contains some exquisite painting. We transcribe the opening.

[Quotes *The White Doe of Rylstone, PW*, III, pp. 283–5, ll. 1–48:

> From Bolton's old monastic tower . . .
> Is the river murmuring near.]

The entrance of the Doe is described rather too much in the style of *'The Isle of Palms*,' and the apology which the Author gives for tracking the steps of the 'bright creature' as a work meet 'for sabbath hours,' is in that peculiar dialect of feeling, to us unintelligible, to which we have before adverted, as endangering at least the popularity of the writer who employs it. The following lines describe the still and graceful pace of the animal.

[Quotes *ibid.*, *PW*, III, pp. 285–7, ll. 79–120:

What harmonious pensive changes . . .
Is that lordly chamber's hearth?]

The succeeding five cantos are devoted to 'A tale of tears, a mortal story,' and narrate the fate of the Nortons. We think it is simply and beautifully told, and we shall not *do* it into prose. The story is, however, so much more like history, than romance, so destitute of plot, and so purely tragical, that it forms a much better subject for a ballad, than for a poem of seven cantos, in which the reader is led to expect more of incident and detail.

Francis Norton, the elder brother, who vainly endeavours to dissuade his father from joining the discontented earls in the ill-advised rebellion, is made to predict to his sister, in the following pathetic lines, the fatal issue of the adventure to his family.

[Quotes *ibid.*, *PW*, III, pp. 299–300, ll. 546–55:

For we must fall, both we and ours . . .
One desolation, one decay!']

The fourth canto opens with a passage of exquisite description.
[Quotes *ibid.*, *PW*, III, pp. 311–13, ll. 938–76:

From cloudless other looking down . . .
His last words in the yew-tree shade.]

The sixth canto narrates the death of Francis, and with this the interest of the Poem, as a tale, terminates. The seventh is wholly occupied in depicting the gradual process by which the mind of Emily attained a state of holy fortitude and peaceful resignation, and the pleasure which she received in her solitude, from the mute sympathy of the only friend left her, – the sharer of her youthful measures, and the remembrancer of all the painful past, – the sylvan doe of other years. The natural workings of the heart are in this canto, minutely and faithfully portrayed, and the feelings of the Solitary are evidently the transcript of character. The whole is calculated to leave the impression of a quiet landscape at sunset; but comparatively few persons will receive this impression, or partake in the mystical fondness of the poet for Emily's faithful follower, which leads him to dilate upon the subject to extravagance. We cannot in justice to our Author, refuse admission to the following extracts.

[Quotes *ibid.*, *PW*, III, pp. 331–9, ll.1568–870, with omissions:

> 'Tis done; – despoil and desolation . . .
> Was buried by her Mother's side.]

With these lines we wish the Poem had terminated: but Mr. Wordsworth chose to return to *The White Doe*, and chose to conclude his Poem with a mystical couplet, which, with such phrases as 'heavenly glory', applied to his own strains, and 'beloved of heaven, heaven's choicest care,' in reference to the 'White Doe,' and other similar expressions, we consign to the happy unintelligibility which envelops them from common intellects. In a poem of Mr. Wordsworth's, they must have a meaning, and we would hope a good meaning: had we met with them elsewhere, we confess we should have deemed them to be significant only of absurdity.

Prefixed to the poem are some beautiful stanzas addressed to Mrs. Wordsworth, which come home to the fancy and to the heart. They afforded us, after all, more pleasure than any thing in the volume.

189. Rev. William Rowe Lyall (1788–1857)[1]

Unsigned review, *Quarterly Review*, October 1815, XIV, 201–25

Of the two publications selected for this article, the latter only can be said to come regularly under our cognizance; the contents of the former having been, for the most part, many years before the public: our attention, therefore, must be principally devoted to the prefatory and post-prefatory essays. The topics which these embrace are in themselves of some importance, and such as our author, from the nature of his pursuits, would seem to be professionally qualified to illustrate. We must, therefore, bespeak the patience of our readers for a few remarks upon some of his opinions; premising that we offer them, not so much in the hope of being able to throw any new light upon the subject, as from a wish to obviate an idea which we suspect has gone abroad, that because we admire the poetical talents of Mr. Wordsworth, we are therefore to be numbered as implicitly entertaining all the tenets of his poetical system.

Among those who are really qualified to judge for themselves in matters of taste, we think that one opinion only is entertained respecting the productions of Mr. Wordsworth, – that they exhibit a mind richly stored with all the materials from which poetry is formed; – elevation of sentiment – tenderness of heart – the truest sensibility for the beauties of nature – combined with extraordinary fervour of imagination, and a most praiseworthy love of simplicity both in thought and language. It would appear, however, upon a first view of the fact, that he has by no means turned these valuable endowments to their greatest advantage. If the business of the poet be to please, Mr. Wordsworth's endeavours have hitherto not met with the most flattering success. He professes, indeed, to be well content; – *neque te ut miretur turba, labores,*[2] is his motto; but even among those with whose applause he declares himself so satisfied, we doubt whether he can number the whole of that class whom Horace was so proud to reckon among his admirers.

It is indeed true, that the productions of our author furnish no very striking proofs of that large and vigorous understanding with which all the writings of the poet just mentioned, as of every other *great* poet, are so strongly impregnated: but neither are the productions of his competitors particularly imposing in this respect: and since they have managed to gain, notwithstanding, such a high place in the public estimation, compared with his own, it seems natural enough that he should be desirous of explaining the reasons for what would appear to be, at first sight, a very mortifying distinction.

Accordingly, in the essay subjoined to the volumes before us, Mr. Wordsworth professes to shew, that a fate similar to his, has in all ages been that of poets greatly endowed with originality of genius; and that the want of contemporary popularity affords a just criterion of a poet's demerits, only in the case of writers whose compositions have evidently been designed to meet the popular taste prevailing at the time. This essay may be considered as forming a supplement to the preface (now re-published) with which a former edition of his poems was accompanied, and in which the general principles upon which he professes to compose, are explained and enforced at considerable length.

With regard to the style in which Mr. Wordsworth writes, we doubt whether it can be greatly praised. There is indeed a raciness about his language, and an occasional eloquence in his manner, which serve to keep the reader's attention alive. But these advantages are more than counteracted by that same ineffectual straining after something beyond plain good sense, which is so unpleasant in much of his poetry. In other respects the comparison is in favour of the latter. Instead of that graceful softness of murmur which forms so principal a charm in his poetic effusions, his prose is distinguished by a tone which, in any other person, we should feel ourselves called upon to treat with some little severity. For a writer to protest that he *prides* himself upon the disapprobation of his contemporaries, and considers it as an evidence of the originality of his genius, and an earnest of the esteem in which he will be held by succeeding generations, is whimsical enough, to say the least of it; but Mr. Wordsworth ought, at all events, to be consistent with himself; and since he derives so many auspicious assurances from the opposition which his opinions have met with, he should speak with a little more moderation of those by whom they happen to be opposed. He should remember, moreover, that the public, and those who profess to be the organs of the public voice in these matters, have at least as much right to dislike *his* poetical taste, as he has to dislike *theirs*. If he voluntarily steps forward to make an attack upon the latter, the burthen of proof rests clearly upon him: to be in an ill temper merely because his opponents will not at once surrender at discretion, is surely most unreasonable.

It appears to us, that whatever difference of opinion may be entertained respecting the peculiarities of Mr. Wordsworth's poetical compositions, we might admit, in nearly all their extent, the poetical doctrines which he wishes to introduce, without materially touching upon the questions about which the public are really at issue with him. For example, it is a prominent tenet with him that the *language and incidents of low and rustic life* are better fitted for the purposes of his art, than the language and incidents which we have hitherto been accustomed to meet with in poetry; his reasons are: –

Because in that condition of life the essential passions of the heart . . . with the beautiful and permanent forms of nature.

['Preface to the Lyrical Ballads']

Now all this may be true, for aught that we know to the contrary; it may be very wrong, in a metaphysical point of view, for a person to have a predilection for other subjects; but the fact obviously is, that people do not resort to poetry for metaphysical instruction; and the question about which Mr. Wordsworth's readers are interested is, whether other subjects do not afford equal or superior pleasure, not whether they throw greater or less light upon the 'elementary feelings,' and 'essential passions,' and 'primary laws of our nature.' Let us suppose a person were to express a distaste for the subject of the poem, at vol. i. p. 328, upon a bed of daffodils; it would probably not at all alter his opinion to say that 'the subject is an elementary feeling and simple impression (approaching to the nature of an ocular spectrum) upon the imaginative faculty;' nor will the pleasure which most readers will probably receive from the lines at vol. i. p. 297, with which the 'Poems of the Imagination' are introduced, be at all augmented, by being told – what few would otherwise have guessed – that the poet was describing 'a commutation, or transfer of internal feelings, cooperating with internal accidents, to plant for immortality images of sound and sight in the celestial soil of the imagination.'[3] How far poetry, upon the principles of Mr. Wordsworth, is capable of being made subservient to a metaphysical analysis of the human mind, is an inquiry which we apprehend to be quite foreign to our present purpose; the question about which the public are at issue with him is, whether the doctrines which he wishes to establish are likely to open purer or more copious sources of poetical delight than those at which his readers hitherto have drunk.

With respect, then, to the 'primary laws of our nature,' 'elementary feelings,' 'essential passions,' and so forth: – if we are to understand by these words the passions of anger and jealousy, and love and ambition, and all the modifications of moral pleasure and pain which it is the appropriate business of poetry to delineate, we are not aware of any good reason which would lead us to suppose that these feelings are not just as frequently and as powerfully excited in such scenes as Homer, Virgil and Milton have chosen, as in those to which Mr. Wordsworth professes to devote his muse. But we are told that in the scenes of 'low and rustic life,' they *co-exist in a state of more simplicity*, may be *more easily comprehended, more accurately contemplated*, and so on. No doubt, in proportion as we advance in years, or in station, or in knowledge, our feelings and passions embrace a greater variety of objects, and become more and more complicated and mixed. But although this may be a very sufficient reason why Mr. Wordsworth should prefer subjects taken from low life, it is plainly no reason whatever why his readers should. As in every other production of human intellect, so in poetry; the superior pleasure which one subject affords rather than another, is mainly ascribable to the comparative degree of mental power which they may require; and this, it is plain, must be proportioned to the difficulties that are to be overcome, and not, as in the case of our author's favourite subjects, to the facilities which they afford.

These last, unquestionably, are susceptible, in a high degree, of poetical embellishment; and though Mr. Wordsworth is, we think, occasionally somewhat unlucky in the topics which he selects, yet we know not any writer who, upon the whole, has painted them with more pathos and fidelity. In themselves, however, they would not appear to be of the most difficult nature; it requires no extraordinary degree of judgment and penetration to discriminate the broad rough lines by which the characters of people in low life are commonly chalked out; nor can it require, considering the few and simple objects about which their thoughts must necessarily be conversant, any extraordinary force of imagination to enter into their feelings; natural sensibility, acquaintance with their manners, and a love of the scenes in which they pass their lives, are of course indispensable; other auxiliary qualities may be called in to advantage; but for those higher and rarer qualifications, which have their foundations in the understanding, and not in the mere liveliness of a susceptible imagination, we imagine the poet would seldom find occasion.

But Mr. Wordsworth is an advocate, not only for the 'incidents' of 'low and rustic life,' as better suited than any other for poetry, but also for its 'language,' which, on several accounts, he considers as being 'a far more philosophical language than that which is frequently substituted for it by poets.' Now, to talk of one language as being more *philosophical* than another, is, perhaps, not a very philosophical way of speaking; but be it as he supposes; still, we think, he will not deny, that the most convenient language, either for a poet or any other man to make use of, is that by which he can with most precision make himself understood by those to whom he addresses himself. Does our author then write for people in low and rustic life, or for people in high and educated life? If for the former, good; but if for the latter, surely to select a language in which, as he himself partly confesses, vol. ii. p. 390, he necessarily exposes himself to the danger of raising opposite ideas to those which he intended to convey, is paying to mere sounds (be they ever so philosophical) an homage which we can never be brought to believe that they deserve.

It is possible, no doubt, while describing such subjects as Mr. Wordsworth chiefly delights in, to pitch the language in too high a key; and this, perhaps, is a fault which pastoral writers have been too much in the habit of committing. But although we admit that there are some phrases and a sort of diction which a poet cannot, without in some sense violating costume, put into the mouths of characters belonging to a *low and rustic condition of life*, yet to avoid this fault is very different from putting into their mouths, phrases which persons of education have actually banished from their vocabulary. We are told indeed, that the language of 'low and rustic life' should be adopted 'purified from its real defects,' and 'from all lasting and rational causes of dislike and disgust.' But the truth is, if the language of low life be purified from what *we* should call its *real defects*, it will differ only in copiousness from the language of high life; as to *rational and lasting causes of dislike and disgust*, it is plain that on the subject of language no such causes can, in any instance, be assigned. We suspect that in criticism Mr. Wordsworth feels no great reverence for constituted authorities, or he would, perhaps, have called to mind the lines, beginning

> Multa renascentur quæ jam cecidêre, cadentque
> Quæ nunc sunt in honore vocabula, si volet *Usus*;
> Quem penes arbitrium est, et jus, et norma loquendi.[4]

Language, as every body knows, consists merely of arbitrary signs which stand for whatever it may have pleased custom to enact; and whatever changes may happen among them, are occasioned not by 'rational causes' but by accidental associations of one sort and another, of which, in general, we defy the most profound metaphysician to give any philosophical account. If a poet has the humour of despising them, he has clearly a right to consult his own pleasure upon the subject; but the chances are that he will draw down such a flight of small critics upon his head – and perhaps deservedly – as will, in all probability, soon teach him the greatness of his mistake.

But although we cannot bring ourselves to approve of Mr. Wordsworth's project for substituting the language of 'low and rustic life' in place of that which we are accustomed to meet with in poetry; yet, in many respects, we feel pretty much disposed to coincide with him in disapproving of the latter. We think, with him, that the language of poetry ought to be language really used by men, and constructed upon the same principles as the language of prose. That this cannot be affirmed of that peculiar sort of diction technically called *poetical*, a slight inspection of the poetry which has prevailed in this country since the Restoration will, we think, sufficiently prove. How far Mr. Wordsworth's account of the origin and distinctive character of this artificial phrase-ology is just and satisfactory, we are, perhaps, not competent to decide; as far, however, as we were able to enter into his meaning, his observations upon the subject seemed in general well-grounded. To us it appears, that this diction does not essentially consist in any particular choice or arrangement of the words; for, to take the instance quoted by our author, Gray's sonnet to West, with the exception of the 6th, 7th, 8th, 13th and 14th lines, consists, as he justly observes, 'almost entirely of this diction, though not of the worst kind.' If, however, Mr. Wordsworth will refer to the remaining lines, he will immediately perceive that they do not consist 'of the language of passion wrested from its proper use;' perhaps the contrary is the fault which may be found with them; neither are the words inverted from their natural order, or such as, taken separately, would seem to belong to any particular condition of life; but the sun is 'the golden fire of reddening Phœbus;' the song of the birds is their 'amorous descant;' the grass of the fields is their 'green attire;' the produce of the earth is its 'wonted tribute;' and so forth. – Now, as addressed to our *reason*, all these expressions are perfectly intelligible; and supposing poetry to be nothing more than the art of paraphrasing our ideas, this sort of diction may furnish room for the display of much fancy and ingenuity. It is, however, manifest, that this indirect way of signifying things, is not the language of present feeling; and that the effect of it is to fix the imagination rather upon the real or fanciful analogies which objects may seem to possess among one another than upon the particular relations in which they actually stand to us. In those subjects in which Pope and Dryden chiefly excelled, where the poet addresses himself to the fancy and understanding rather than to the heart, we know not but that the method of versification to which we are alluding, may produce a good effect; indeed, in one point of view, it would seem to be that which nature points out. But when the business of the poet is to present us with an image of the scenes and objects among which we are placed, not in abstract description, but as they relate immediately to our feelings, his expressions cannot, as we conceive, be too free from rhetorical ornament. That the exclusion, or at least a more moderate use of this, need not interfere with the utmost degree of strength, nor the most refined harmony and elegance of language, is fully proved by many passages in the writings of our old and excellent dramatists; and indeed it is doing Mr. Wordsworth himself nothing more than justice to say, that in his happier hours of inspiration, when his theories and eccentricities happen to be laid aside, no writer of the day seems to understand better the exact key in which the language of this last kind of poetry should be pitched. Unfortunately these hours are not so frequent with Mr. Wordsworth, as the lovers of poetry could wish; and upon the causes of this we shall now trouble our readers with a few remarks, which will, perhaps, assist us to explain the reasons why his popularity is less – we will not say than he deserves, for this would be to prejudge the question – but less than such talents as he possesses have commonly conferred.

It is impossible to take up the works of Mr. Wordsworth without remarking that, instead of employing his pen upon subjects of durable and general interest, he devotes himself almost exclusively to the delineation of himself and his own peculiar feelings, as called forth by objects incidental to the particular kind of life he leads. Now, although this be a plan apparently contrived to gratify the pleasure which poets, as our author tells us, take in their 'own passions and volitions,' rather than any curiosity which the reader, generally speaking, can be supposed to feel upon the subject, yet, in common cases, it is productive of no very *positive* inconvenience. Poets, as well as other people, feel, for the most part, pretty much alike; so that what is true with respect to any individual, will commonly be true with respect to mankind at large, under the same circumstances. As long as the feelings of the poet are founded on such occasions as ordinarily give rise to them, although the subjects of his effusions may be particular, yet the interest and the application of them will be, to a great degree, general. But the fact is, that the habits of Mr. Wordsworth's life are not more different from those of people in general, than are the habits of his mind; so that not only the incidents which form the subjects of his poetry, are such as the greater part of his readers take much less interest in, than he imagines, but the feelings, moreover, with which he usually contemplates them are often such as hardly any person whatever can participate.

For example: a sensibility for the beauties of nature is, no doubt, a highly commendable quality, and to illustrate it is, we admit, the great business of descriptive poetry; nevertheless, however warmly we may sympathize with Mr. Wordsworth in his rapturous admiration of the great and striking features of nature; – though we cannot but think that even on this subject, his feelings are tuned much too high for the sobriety of truth; – yet when we are called upon to feel *emotions which lie too deep for tears even with respect to the meanest flower that blows*, to *cry for nothing, like Diana in the fountain*, over every ordinary object and every common-place occurrence that may happen to cross our way, all communion of feeling between the poet and those who know no more of poetry than their own experience and an acquaintance with the best models will bestow, is necessarily broken off. But it would be difficult to convey a just idea of the extent to which the peculiar habits of Mr. Wordsworth's mind have affected the character of his writings by citing particular examples. Our readers, however, will probably be able to judge for themselves, when they learn that, instead of looking upon this sort of exuberant sensibility to which we allude as a disadvantage, he regards it as a qualification of singular value; and formally places it, under the technical name of *poetic*, which he always distinguishes from merely *human* sensibility, among what he considers as being the characteristical attributes of the poetical character.

Our author justly observes, that 'poets do not write for poets alone, but for men. Unless, therefore, we are advocates for that admiration which depends upon ignorance, and that pleasure which arises from hearing what we do not understand, the poet must descend from his supposed height, and in order to excite rational sympathy, he must express himself as other men express themselves.' vol. i. p. 384. Nothing can be more true; but surely Mr. Wordsworth cannot but perceive, that if a poet, in order to excite rational sympathy, must *express* himself as other men express themselves; by a still stronger reason it would seem to follow that *he must descend from his supposed height*, and *feel* as other men feel.

Nothing is more easy to conceive than a sense of vision infinitely, more acute than that with which it has been thought necessary to endow the human race. Nevertheless, however advantageous the gift of such a superiority might be considered, in a general point of view, yet it would really be inconvenient to a person desirous of turning painter; because, admitting that his pictures might be ever so admirable upon a supposition that other people's organs of sight were constructed upon the same principles as his own, yet they would clearly be of no value whatever except to himself, if we suppose the contrary to be the fact. It is precisely the same in the case of poetry; the merit of a poet does not essentially consist, as is sometimes supposed, in the possession of sensibilities different from or more intense than those of other people, but in the talent of awakening in their minds the particular feelings and emotions with which the various objects of his art are naturally associated. For this purpose he must, of course, consult his own feelings; it is, however, only so far as he knows them to be in unison with those of mankind at large, that he can safely trust himself to their direction; because, if they preserve not the same relative subordination and the same proportions among each other that they possess in the minds of people in general, it is plain that his compositions must appear to the greater part of his readers like pictures constructed upon false principles of perspective, and whatever resemblance they may bear to objects as they appeared to his own mind, may bear no more resemblance to objects as they appear in nature than the fantastical devices of an Indian screen.

We are far from meaning to assert, by way of a general proposition, that the merit of a poem is to be measured by the number of its admirers; different classes of composition, no doubt, are adapted to different classes of readers: whatever it requires extraordinary powers of mind to produce, it must require some corresponding superiority of mind to understand; and we think Mr. Wordsworth intimates somewhere that this is partly the predicament in which his poetry stands. We shall not dispute upon this point; nevertheless we may remark that, although the above consideration will afford a satisfactory explanation of Quintilian's observation, that the Iliad is projected upon so vast a scale, as to require considerable greatness of mind even to comprehend its merits; yet this way of evading the dilemma to which Mr. Wordsworth's indifferent success has reduced him, will hardly apply to his case, upon a supposition at least, that his poetry really is what it professes to be: because, when a poet's avowed object is merely to trace in the plain and intelligible language of every-day life, those 'great and simple affections,' those 'elementary feelings' and 'essential passions' which are assumed, by definition, to be common to all men alike, – it would seem but reasonable to expect that it would find readers in every class of society. But then the poet must be supposed truly to perform what he promises; his poetry must not contain a mere portraiture of his own mind in those points in which he differs from other people, and with respect to which none but his particular friends can be supposed to feel an interest; but an image of human nature in general.

Our familiar matter-of-fact way of talking about an art which Mr. Wordsworth seems to think belongs rather to the divine than to human nature, will not, we fear, tend to impress him with a very favourable opinion of our profoundness; – mais la vérité est comme il peut; truth is as it happens, and not always exactly as men of fine imaginations wish it to be. – Accordingly, although we would not choose to be classed among those to whom our author alludes, 'who converse as gravely about a *taste* for poetry, as they express it, as if it were a thing as indifferent as a taste for rope-dancing,' yet we candidly confess, that we see nothing at all wonderful or mysterious about the art; nor, if we may judge from experience, any reason to suppose that it requires greater or more uncommon talents than any other among the higher productions of human intellect. In reply to this, Mr. Wordsworth will probably place us in that unhappy sub-division of critics, in which, he says, 'are found those who are too petulant to be passive to a genuine poet, and too feeble to grapple with him: men, who take upon them to report of the course *he* holds, whom they are utterly unable to accompany – confounded if he turn quickly upon the wing, dismayed if he soar steadily into "the region;" men of palsied imaginations and indurated hearts.' All we can say is, that whenever Mr. Wordsworth's own flights are through 'the region' of truth and nature, and sober sense, we accompany him with pleasure; but when he penetrates into the *terra Australis* beyond, then, indeed, our inclination to continue of the party, as well as our ability, leaves us.

Having thus stated our opinions at length, upon the critical dissertations, we shall proceed to give our readers some idea of the poem.

The 'White Doe of Rylstone' is so out-of-the-way a production, in many respects, that we are not sure but it would be wiser in us gravely to 'shake the head' at such a ballad sort of poem, than to risk our authority with the public by recommending it to them as a beautiful performance. It is not, indeed, free from the singularities which arise from the particular point of view in which Mr. Wordsworth likes to look at things; but in the present instance, they fall in not unhappily with the whimsical nature of the subject, and give a tone of colouring to the poem, which, however peculiar, is far from being unpleasing. As a mere narrative, it does not possess much interest; the story is told, as it were, in scraps; a few prominent scenes are selected, and the circumstances which connect them left pretty much to the reader's imagination; and after all, instead of a denouement, we have merely the explanation of a certain strange phenomenon which had puzzled rather than interested our curiosity.

That the poem contains many beauties – exquisite tenderness of feeling, and often great happiness combined with the utmost simplicity of expression, will abundantly appear from the extracts which we shall make; but then, in other parts, it is just as much distinguished for obscurity and flatness; and throughout there is a something, not only about the rhythm and the language, but also about the turn of the thoughts and sentiments, which often left us at a loss to determine whether the hesitation which we felt, even as to being pleased, proceeded from mere fastidiousness on our part, or from a mistaken taste in Mr. Wordsworth. The poem, we admit, is written with simplicity; and so far as this is the indigenous growth of his own mind, it has our warmest praises. But Mr. Wordsworth's love of this first quality of all good poetry has made him resort to artificial means for producing it; so that instead of the polished simplicity which belongs to an age of so much refinement as the present, he affects that rude kind which the writings of our forefathers exhibit, and which expressed the genuine character of the times. Now, be the merits of this last what it may when met with in our old ballads, it is plain, that in the present advanced stage of society, it can never be *natural* to a man like Mr. Wordsworth; in *his* writings, the manner which he studies is necessarily an affectation; and be the imitation ever so successful, a discriminating taste still perceives a something which is different from the native flavour of original simplicity . . .

At Bolton Priory, in Yorkshire, it seems, there is a tradition about a White Doe, who on every Sabbath-day, during the time of divine service, used to pay a visit to the church-yard; the problem which the poem proposes to solve, is, why the White Doe should do this? Mr. Wordsworth satisfactorily explains it, by means of an old ballad, in Percy's Reliques, called the 'Rising of the North;' and containing a succinct account of the total destruction which fell upon the Nortons, an ancient family of Yorkshire, in consequence of their share in that fatal act of rebellion.

The first Canto opens with the introduction of the 'White Doe;' and she is ushered in with some very pleasing lines . . .

[Straightforward summary and extensive quotation follows with some few sentences of a critical nature.]

These lines (with which the second Canto closes) in spite of some expressions which made our critical nerves *wince* a little, afford no unfavourable specimen of that peculiar tenderness of manner for which we think the poem is chiefly remarkable.

The third Canto opens with spirit . . .

The fourth Canto brings the reader back to Rylstone Hall. The description, with which it opens, of the old mansion by moonlight, is among the most successful passages of the poem. The sober tone of the language is well suited to the repose which belongs to the subject . . .

The above description is not without poetry.

[Quotes *The White Doe of Rylstone*, *PW*, III, p. 329, ll. 1501–23.]

We have, however, quoted it, chiefly because it relates an important circumstance in the story; in other respects, we fear, the language is too quaint to be generally pleasing.

Our readers now know why the 'White Doe' came from Rylstone to Bolton Priory every Sabbath day during the time of divine service. Whether the explanation will not, upon the whole, disappoint the curiosity which its mysterious appearance excited, we shall not attempt to determine: more particularly as the decision of the question will not very greatly affect the merits of the work, considered as a poem, however it may affect its popularity, considered merely as a story. In the former point of view, we think that our extracts will fully justify the praises which we have bestowed upon it; but we have also said, that it possesses great blemishes, and it now becomes the unpleasant part of our duty to instance a few particular examples.

Mr. Wordsworth, as our readers must have perceived, aims at great simplicity of language; but even supposing no objections to exist against the particular sort of which he is ambitious, still we must be permitted to observe, that mere simplicity of language is no merit at all, if it be purchased at the expense of perspicuity; and this is a price which our author is continually paying for it. We dislike minute criticism, not only for Horace's reason, of *non ego paucis*, &c.[5] but because we know that in the hands of unfair critics it is an engine by which a writer may be made to appear any thing they please; nevertheless as an example of what we mean, take the following passage: Mr. Wordsworth means to say, that Emily sate upon a primrose bank, neglecting outward ornaments, and having in her countenance a melancholy which seemed not to belong to the sweetness and gentleness of its natural expression; which is thus laboriously signified: –

> Upon a primrose bank—
> – – – – – – – –
> Behold her like a Virgin Queen
> Neglecting in imperial state
> These outward images of fate,
> And carrying inward a serene
> And perfect sway, through many a thought
> Of chance and change, that hath been brought
> To the subjection of a holy
> But stern and rigorous melancholy!
> The like authority, with grace
> Of awfulness, is in her face –
> There hath she fixed it; yet it seems
> To o'er-shadow by no native right
> That face which cannot lose the gleams,
> Lose utterly the tender gleams,

Of gentleness and meek delight
And loving-kindness ever bright. –
[*Ibid., PW*, III, p. 332, ll. 1590–605]

Surely Mr. Wordsworth cannot need to be told, that such an unaccountable way of expressing himself as this, notwithstanding the humbleness
of the style, is directly the reverse of simple. This, perhaps, is an extreme
instance; but the fault is of perpetual recurrence. Again, with respect to
his words themselves; we will not say that they are often too familiar,
because we suspect Mr. Wordsworth does not regard that as a fault: but
the truth is, that in the senses to which he applies them, they are often
absolutely devoid of meaning – The following lines really would seem to
have been written by a 'Lady of Quality.'

> The day is placid in its going
> To a lingering motion bound;
> Like a river in its flowing;
> Can there be a softer sound –
> [*Ibid., PW*, III, pp. 287–8 and footnotes, ll. 148–51]

Speaking of the Doe, wandering through sun and shade,

> What *harmonious pensive changes*
> Wait upon her as she ranges
> Round and through the hall of state!
> [*Ibid., PW*, III, pp. 285–6, ll. 79–81]

In this last quotation, we perceive the kind of impression which Mr.
Wordsworth meant to convey; but in the following, we are equally at a
loss to understand either the sense in which he uses his words, or the
propriety of the sentiment which he intends them to express.

> For *deepest sorrows* that *aspire*
> Go *high*, no *transport* ever higher.
> [*Ibid., PW*, III, p. 324, ll. 1352–3]

But it is unnecessary to accumulate instances of the extraordinary want
of precision with which Mr. Wordsworth is in the habit of expressing
himself; he seems to think that if words only have a good character, and
mean something pleasant when by themselves, whether they have any
relation to one another in a sentence is a matter of no great importance.
Hence it is, for we can no otherwise account for it, that Emily is always
called the 'consecrated Emily,' and that every pleasant thought is a

'dream' a 'vision,' or a 'phantom,' just as it happens. But it is irksome to expatiate upon particular faults; a task which we the more willingly abridge, because they are more than redeemed by that true feeling of poetry with which the poem is pervaded. In this, as in any other line of poetry to which he may dedicate himself, Mr. Wordsworth has some-thing to learn and a good deal to unlearn; whether he will endeavour to do either at our suggestion, is, perhaps, more than doubtful; he seems to be *monitoribus asper* ['harsh to advisors', Horace, *Ars Poetica*, l. 163], in a degree which is really unreasonable; however, this is his business; all we can say is, that if he is not now or should not be hereafter, a favourite with the public, he can have nobody to blame but himself.

EDITOR'S NOTES

1. Lyall was to conduct the *British Critic*, 1816–17, but contributed articles on Douglas Stewart's philosophy in the *Quarterly Review*, 1812 and 1815 (VI. 1–36 and XII. 281–317).
2. 'You should not work hard for the crowd to admire you' (Horace, *Satires*, I, 10, 73).
3. Wordsworth's comment on 'There was a boy' in the Preface to *Poems* (1815); but it should begin: 'a commutation and transfer of internal feelings, cooper-ating with external accidents to plant, for immortality . . .'
4. 'Many words which have now fallen out of use will be revived, and many which are now in vogue will fall if that is the will of Usage, in whose hands is the power to decide the law and rule of speech' (Horace, *Ars Poetica*, 70–2).
5. Horace, *Ars Poetica*, 351–2: 'I shall not be offended by a few blemishes'.

190. Henry Crabb Robinson

Extract from his diary, 30 March 1816

I read the last number of the Quarterly Review.[1] An article on Words-worth's *White Doe* I thought judicious. One remark sufficiently accounts for the unpopularity of Wordsworth. He himself says in vindication of his style that a poet to touch the reader must speak as he speaks, and the reviewer remarks, much more then must he feel as his reader feels. While therefore Wordsworth is excited by objects which excite no other

591

man – and in his poems he develops the object so interesting to him and so uninteresting to others, he cannot succeed in awaking sympathy however great his excellencies . . .

(*Henry Crabb Robinson on Books and their Writers*, ed. Edith J. Morley, 1938, I, 181)

EDITOR'S NOTE

1. See entry 189.

191.

Unsigned review, *European Magazine*, March 1816, LXIX, 237–9

In the general cast and character of this poem, there is something very analogous to those chivalrous legends so popular in ancient times, and for which the taste of the present age has been successfully excited by the fertile and romantic genius of Walter Scott. The Rising of the North, under the Earls of Northumberland and Westmoreland, in the reign of Elizabeth; the tragic fate of the Nortons, of Rylstone, who distinguished themselves in that rash insurrection; and the mysterious tradition of a white doe, which, for years after, performed a weekly pilgrimage to the grave of the last of their race, are themes which would spontaneously call forth the enthusiasm of the later minstrels, and particularly of him who sung the restoration of the good Lord Clifford. The severest of Mr. Wordsworth's critics were startled into admiration by the lofty and animated strain of that fine ballad; and must, we think, be equally constrained to applaud this nobly pathetic tale. It certainly merits that epithet, by the picture which it presents of a meek and lovely lady, whose solitary grief for the extinction of her parent, and her brothers, is refined and exalted into triumphant resignation, and by the interesting light in which the poet has exhibited this transition.

It would be doing our readers an ill grace to obtrude upon them an abstract of the story of this poem, and by that means impair the enjoyment which they must reap from the perusal of the work itself; an enjoyment not indeed allied to gaiety, but the more lasting, because it consists in a kindlier, though deeper emotion. We shall therefore merely state so much as may be necessary to explain the passages which our limits will allow us to cite, in illustration of its merits.

The tradition, on which the poem is founded, has been mentioned by Dr. Whitaker, in his History of the Deanery of Craven. 'About this time,' not long after the dissolution, 'a white doe, say the aged people in the neighbourhood, long continued to make a weekly pilgrimage from Rylstone, over the fells of Bolton, and was constantly found in the Abbey Church-yard during divine service; after which she returned home as regularly as the rest of the congregation.' – *Notes on the Poem.*

[Summary and ample quotation follow.]

The meeting of Norton and his sons, with the Earls at Brancepeth, is described with great animation and energy; it is characterized by that union of warlike gallantry with religious zeal, which marked the later ages of English chivalry. The sudden and total failure of this 'rash levy,' the fate of the brave Norton, with his eight sons, and the high-souled devotedness of Francis, are narrated and portrayed in a free and vigorous flow of poetry, which carries the reader along, without allowing him to pause, until he contemplates the fulfilment of the elder brother's prediction, in the saintly suffering of his orphan sister.

[More summary and quotation.]

These, and a multitude of other passages shew, that in this poem Mr. Wordsworth has given another proof of his ability to achieve the high purposes of poetry; which are, not to give delight alone, but to awaken and refine those feelings that belong to the imperishable part of our nature.

192. Mrs Basil Montagu (1773–1856)

From letters to James Montgomery, 1819–1820

a. 23 March 1819

A poet's admirers are the worst nurses for his offspring – they persuade him the weakest are likely to live, and they overlay him as well as his bantlings, by their ill-judged caresses. Happily in your case, your severity more than counteracts this officious fondness – Posterity will regret that Wordsworth did not shake off these little flowery fetters which imprisoned his judgement, I say *posterity* will regret it, because I feel that his contemporaries have rather rejoiced in the self approbation which has lowered this giant mind occasionally to their own pigmy level.

(Ms. Sheffield City Library)

b. 14 September 1820

When this letter was written the Montagus were staying at Bolton Abbey, the setting for *The White Doe*.

I wish the White Doe of Rilston had fallen into your hands instead of Wordsworth's – She grew tame and meagre in his company – He should have confined himself to some Monkish Legend, and left that tender and delicate pair to you.

(*Ibid.*)

XII

Letter to a Friend of Robert Burns: reviews and opinions, 1816–1817

193. James Gray (1770–1830)

From a letter to Wordsworth, 28 November 1815

James Gray was a schoolmaster, first at Dumfries and then at the High School, Edinburgh, 1801–1822. He was a poet, linguist and a friend of Robert Burns. Here he writes directly to Wordsworth, expressing his admiration. The letter is remarkable in being further evidence of Wordsworth's conversational powers – obviously Wordsworth had spoken eloquently of his concept of *The Recluse*, even as he was to discuss it with Haydon and George Ticknor (see entries 258 and 275). Arguably, Wordsworth's talking about the poem did not help him to write it. Gray had contributed to Alexander Peterkin's *A Review of the Life of Robert Burns*, 1815, and it was on receiving this publication that Wordsworth wrote to James Gray *A Letter to a Friend of Robert Burns*, 1816.

Dear Sir

In a number of years, your lakes and mountains 'unvisited' was one of those untouched treasures, one of those things in hope, to which the mind looks forward with so much delight. Yet it was not your sunny Lakes, nor your green glens nor your romantic mountains, beautiful as I understood them to be, which alone brightened the prospect, I was well aware that your glens contained other objects of higher interest. To confess the truth, I was too much delighted by every thing I saw and heard at Rydale Mount, to suffer the day I passed there to live like a fair vision in the memory only, your kindness made me hope more important results. I am one of those beings who are ever making a surrender of their hearts to goodness, talent and genius, not reflecting how little it is worthy of acceptance, and it would have been very wonderful, if I had escaped from your house without being made captive. Before I saw the Author of the Excursion, I did not think it possible that he could rise in my esteem, but a few hours of his conversation convinced me I was wrong, for I soon discovered a justness of feeling and taste, an extent of information and a glow and rapidity of spoken eloquence which would have alone exulted their possessor to the very pinnacle of intellectual eminence. I am quite aware that the fashions of the world proscribe this mode of address, so Mr Jeffrey has told us in his review of Burns's letters, but I detest the cold and heartless correctness of the 'many headed monster' and tho I should not think it necessary to tell a man that I thought him a villain or a fool, nothing shall deprive me of the delight I feel in speaking my opinion of great genius even in the presence of its possessor. Poetry has been to me all my life I may say, a kind of mental opium, it not only deadens the painful feeling of those cares and sorrows with which my path has been thick enough strewn, but excites in my mind visions of delight and joy to which it were otherwise a total stranger and I am not sure, if even you can judge of the avidity with which I have devoured your pages and the debt of gratitude I owe to the man who could furnish me such a feast. In a conversation that passed at your house respecting Burns I was delighted, tho not surprised to discover that you were one of the few individuals I had met who had taken a true view of the character of that extraordinary man. I am happy to be able now to inform you that his brother Gilbert, a man of a sound head and some skill in composition is about to undertake a vindication of the poets named from the calumnies of reviewers and pamphleteers. He is engaged by Caddel and Davies to superintend a new edition, and to add what new matter he can furnish in elucidation of his Brother's life, character and genius. I repeated to him some of the remarks you had made, which struck him so much that he is exceedingly desirous of obtaining your opinion as to the best mode of conducting the defence. I send you a review of the Life of Burns, by a friend of mine, in it among others, you will find a beautiful little letter from Gilbert, and one from me. This review was lately published in an Edin^h Edition. Gilbert has asked me to write another letter for his edition. I knew the poet intimately for several years before his death and I think it only a duty to correct the errors and misrepresentation of these men who have err'd thro ignorance and lied thro malevolence. Your friend Mr De Quincy, has charmed every one who has seen him. His heart and understanding are without a flaw. I have seldom seen a man of as much of that native simplicity of character which is the concomitant of true genius, and of so much learning with so perfect a freedom from that affectation and pedantry which so often disgrace it. I trust the Recluse is in progress. It is a work which will exalt it's [*sic*] Author to the rank of our Shakespeare and Spenser. There is certainly not any poem of the present age which has so fair a claim to a long career of glory and which is so certain of obtaining it, unless the principles of our nature are to be changed. I question if ever there was a creation of genius that contained so many profound views of the intellectual nature of man and so many simple, pathetic and enchanting pictures of life. The pathos of the story of Margaret and the Solitary is really quite intolerable. If any evidence were wanting, I have enough, in the tears of my wife and in my own which have been mingled again and again over the page. Remember me in the language of gratitude and admiration to Mrs Wordsworth and Miss Wordsworth, gratitude for their kindness to a stranger and admiration of their genius. It is really unfair that any one family should have made such a monopoly of this rarest of all qualities. After the corner of a little glen somewhere in the vicinity of Rydale and Elery! I should without a sigh bid farewell to great cities. I am sorry that I have not been able to procure a more respectable copy of the pamphlet I send.

I have the honour to be

Dear Sir

With admiration and esteem

James Gray

(Ms. Wordsworth Library)

194. Charles Lamb

From a letter to Wordsworth, 26 April 1816

Lamb had corrected the proofs of Wordsworth's *Thanksgiving Ode* and *Letter to a Friend of Robert Burns*. He carefully avoids giving any critical comment on the poems.

With regard to the works, the Letter I read with unabated satisfaction. Such a thing was wanted, called for. The parallel of Cotton with Burns I heartily approve; Iz. Walton hallows any page in which his reverend name appears. 'Duty archly bending to purposes of general benevolence' is exquisite.[1] The Poems I endeavored not to understand, but to read them with my eye alone, and I think I succeeded. (Some people will do that when they come out, you'll say.)

(*The Letters of Charles and Mary Lamb*, ed. E. V Lucas, 1935, II, 190)

EDITOR'S NOTE

1. Wordsworth's phrasing in his summary of Burn's 'Tam o'Shanter' was 'conjugal fidelity archly bends to the service of general benevolence'.

195. R. P. Gillies

From a letter to Wordsworth, 9 May 1816

I have now not only to assure you of my gratitude for your highly-valued letter, but also to return thanks for your inestimable publications of *Poems*[1] & the Letter respecting Burns which have been sent to me from Longmans & co – though I read them over more than once (& indeed frequently) yet I have never since their arrival been in a situation to read with that degree of individual attention which I should have wished. – Above all I was struck on the first perusal with the sonnet addressed to 'R. B. Haydon Esqre' which has continued to impress my remembrance as the most interesting Sonnet I ever met with & which I think cannot be sufficiently praised – my attention has been so much engaged by the Letter on the character of Burns that I have been led to compose three stanzas in Tasso's manner about him, which if I thought them tolerable I should communicate in this letter.

(Ms. The Wordsworth Library)

EDITOR'S NOTE

1.   This must be *Thanksgiving Ode*, 1816, since it contained the sonnet to Haydon.

196.

Unsigned review, *Critical Review*, July 1816, IV, 51–8

This review has been attributed to John Payne Collier (1789–1883), literary editor of the *Critical Review*, close friend of Henry Crabb Robinson and personally known to both Wordsworth and Coleridge (see Oskar Wellens, 'John Payne Collier: the Man Behind the Unsigned *Times* Review of "Christabel", 1816,' *The Wordsworth Circle*, Spring 1982 XIII, 68–72). Wellens notes Collier's 'vigorous campaign for Wordsworth's public recognition' and adds that Collier, even gratuitously, introduces Wordsworth, or quotations from him, in reviews, among which are: Walter Scott's *The Antiquary*, 1816 (*Critical Review*, May 1816, III, 500); John Wilson's *The City of the Plague*, 1816 (*ibid.*, August 1816, IV, 190); John Scott's *The House of Mourning*, 1817 (*ibid.*, April 1817, V, 352); and James Hogg's

The Poetic Mirror, All the living Bards of Britain, 1816 (*ibid.*, November 1816, IV, 466–7); this last serves to characterise the campaign:

> There is nothing in the history of literature that gives us greater pleasure than the growing estimation of which the productions of [Wordsworth] is held. The principles upon which he started as an author were so repungant to what had until then almost appropriated to itself the name of poetry, that he had many difficulties and repugnancies to overcome: – those who had habitually considered poetry to depend more upon the language, that upon the thought that language conveyed – who had been accustomed to admire full-sounding bombastic lines as the very quintessence of excellence – would not at first relish productions composed of *the real language of men in a state of vivid sensation*, which is the very foundation of the system of Mr. Wordsworth: they who have been used to hear the most familiar expressions tricked in the ponderous trappings of phraseology, for a time could endure nothing else, but within the last few years a rapid improvement in this respect has taken place, and the public begin to perceive that they had been misled by those who had little else but words to give them: a vocabulary which supply all the materials for their effusions; and if a thought now and then did creep in almost without the knowledge of the author, 'he thank'd his stars, for he was in good luck.'

Dr. Currie, the editor of the poems, and the compiler of the Life of Burns, which was published in 1800 for the benefit of the family of the poet, then lately deceased, has been repeatedly blamed for the manner in which he executed his task, and the object of the pamphlet which forms the subject of the present article, is through a Mr. Gray of Edinburgh, to give some advice to Mr. Gilbert Burns relative to the best mode of vindicating the memory of his brother, by the correction of the errors of his biographer, and by the omission of certain parts of Dr. Currie's publication, which Mr. Wordsworth and others contend ought never to have been printed. The chief ground of complaint against Dr. Currie is, that he has either done too much, or not done enough; if he thought it right to lay before his readers so many of the private letters of Burns, he ought to have placed them in such a series as would have shewn the connecting links of impulse, and to have accompanied them with those observations that would have placed the offences of the poet, therein with bitter remorse confessed, in a fair point of view; if the crime be detailed, at least it ought to be related with some of the incitements and allurements without which crime is never committed. Upon this point Mr. Wordsworth well remarks:

601

'Would a bosom friend of the author . . . it would have been absurd to attempt it.'
[Quotes 'Letter to a Friend of Robert Burns'; see *The Prose Works of William Wordsworth*, ed. W.J.B. Owen and Jane Worthington Smyser, 1974, 120, ll. 122–40]

The conclusion therefore is, that such letters of the poet as communicate no useful information, and only gratify those who sooth their own vices by the discovery that others like them have offended, ought to have been completely excluded. The soul-sick confessions of a sensitive mind can never be taken as literally true; but although Dr. Currie has certainly been censurable in this respect, we think he is not quite as much to blame as Mr. Wordsworth contends. At the time Dr. Currie's edition appeared, Burns had but recently died, and his biographer had a very difficult course to steer between personal delicacy on the one hand, and public expectation on the other . . .

That Dr. Currie has however gone too far we are very ready to admit; he seems to have forgotten, that when a man like Burns, of an open and generous disposition, reprobates his own vices, he is much less to be believed than if he applauded his own virtues; it does not follow, because he says it, that it must be true, or that if it be true, it is necessary to publish it. Upon the duties of a biographer in the abstract Mr. Wordsworth well and truly observes, that 'biography, though differing in some essentials from works of fiction, is nevertheless like them an *art* – an art, the laws of which are determined by the imperfections of our nature, and the constitution of society. Truth is not here as in the sciences and in natural philosophy, to be sought without scruple, and promulgated for its own sake, upon the mere chance of its being serviceable; but only for obviously justifying purposes, moral or intellectual.' He follows it by some other remarks equally just.

'Silence is a privilege of the grave . . . guardians of rational public freedom.'
[Quotes *ibid.*, 121–2, ll. 199–230]

It is not to be wondered that Mr. Wordsworth on this occasion should stand forward in vindication of a man of so many estimable and admirable qualities as Burns, not merely from a natural love of justice, but from a peculiar resemblance between the minds and the stiles of the two poets – we speak of the mind and state of Burns before they became infected by the society and habits into which he fell in the later years of his life. As all true poetry has the same foundation, so all true poets must have some principles in common; and the chief difference between Burns and

Wordsworth is, that the former was energetic, simple, and unaffected, in all his earlier and better pieces using the common language of men in a state of excitement because he knew no other; and the latter because he holds it to be the very essence of his art. It is this quality that constitutes the principal charm of the productions of the Scottish bard; and as at the period to which we allude he knew of no other school, he never deviated from the rules which it prescribes. Our readers may not at first be sensible of this similarity, but if they will carefully examine the productions of Mr. Wordsworth, they will find that our opinion is borne out, not only in principle but in practice. We need only quote from the letter before us the subsequent eloquent passages to shew how well its author understands and how deeply he enjoys the better part of the works of Burns.

'But you will perhaps accuse me of refining too much . . . though there was no moral purpose, there is a moral effect.' . . .

[Quotes *ibid.*, 123–4, ll. 261–323]

197.

Unsigned review, *Scots Magazine and Edinburgh Literary Miscellany*, August 1816, LXXVIII, 605–12

. . . Among these champions for justice to the memory of departed genius appears now the celebrated Wordsworth, known as a politician, a philosopher, and a poet; and if this production of his be considered as containing the sentiments of one man of genius and feeling communicated, as it at first was, in private to another, it appears to us calculated to excite no common degree of interest, On the other hand, whoever turns to it in hopes of finding any thing decisive with regard to the real character of our national bard, either as a private individual, a poet, or an epistolary writer, will be disappointed. Neither is there any distinct view or statement adduced, that enables us to judge what portion of Burns's posthumous works ought in future to be published, though the title page certainly led us to expect it.

Nevertheless, considering the production in the first-mentioned light, or considering it in any light which we please, it is impossible to read it without feeling deep sensations of grief for the depressed and perilous lot of genius in this life, and of regret that a principle so baneful should exist in our nature, as to induce many to delight in injuring the memory of the illustrious dead.

Mr Wordsworth, whether in prose or verse, has not only a peculiar mode of expressing his ideas, but the ideas themselves seem to be framed on a peculiar structure, and to branch out in an irregular ramification, which an ordinary mind could in no degree encompass. His associations are singular. He never proceeds in a regular gradation of ascent to the top of any eminence, from whence he can give a distinct view of the object of his research, but goes on with a kind of ambling majesty, dwelling with equal concern on things of no moment, and on scenes of the utmost grandeur. – His mind grasps the trivial and the great with equal avidity – elucidates them as chance or caprice may direct, and abandons them again with equal unconcern.

If Mr Wordsworth would condescend to take human nature as it is, and neither embarrass himself with establishing literary principles, that are at best equivocal, nor affect to despise the judgement and feelings of the greater part of his species, we know of no man more calculated to delight or influence the human heart. But desirable as this may be, we fear it is in vain to hope for its accomplishment; for with all the heart and feeling of a poet, he is dictatorial, abstruse, and often affected in the highest degree. That such adverse ingredients should exist in the same great mind is a matter of regret – that they do preside in the formation of it, is a fact – but how they do, or why they should, Dr Spurzheim alone can inform us.

Our extracts from the pamphlet, as we go along, will bear evidence to such incongruity: in the mean time, we must premise that there is one leading principle laid down in Mr Wordsworth's letter with which we most cordially agree – it is, that the public have nothing to do with a man's private life and character in its estimation of him as a poet. It is his writings alone that the man of genius lives: these mankind have a right to discuss – to compare one sentiment of these with others, and to censure or applaud as their various creeds, feelings, and general principles may prompt. That there should be a diversity of feelings on such subjects is natural; and we blame no-one, whether critic or divine, for uttering and publishing his sentiments on them with perfect freedom: truth, by being searched into, is never injured: but we think it should always be kept in view, that an author can never be accountable to posterity for any thing farther than he himself sanctions – than is published with his own consent, and under his own name; far less for the imperfections of his nature, and the blemishes in his life, unless he had blazoned and defended them to the world. [Attacks a 'zealous Christian writer of the present day' who censures Burns for his injurious and ribald verses of which he is not in truth the author.] But because some venal publisher has been sordid enough to collect all these, all the lewd and fulsome rhymes, ancient and modern, that exist in a whole realm, and tho', in order to give publicity to such a miscellany, he gives out that it is the production of Burns, – is the bard of nature, who has so often delighted our hearts, to be blamed for this, and his name branded with infamy? It is really more than human patience can bear. Well may we apply the sentiments of Mr Wordsworth –

The poet was laid where these injuries could not reach him . . . this is indeed to be 'crushed beneath the furrow's weight!'
    [Quotes *ibid.*, 121, ll. 175–85]

. . . We must then contend for the privilege of authors, that with what they never meant the world should see, the world has nothing to do. Mr W. expresses himself with great energy, truth, and beauty on this subject.

The general obligation upon which I have insisted . . . whether they lived happily or miserably.
    [Quotes *ibid.*, 122, ll. 231–65]

No one will, we conceive, read the following passage without being struck with the genuine propriety and truth of the remarks.
    [Quotes three further long passages from the *Letter* with similar approving remarks.]
. . . What remains to be noticed in Mr W.'s work, is a most awful and tremendous attack on the Editor of the Edinburgh Review, whom, we believe, Mr W. supposes he has quite overthrown, and rendered impotent and despicable for ever. The bard, quitting the playful and happy humour of his supposed opponent, when rallying Mr W. and his associates on their whimsical peculiarities, breaks forth into the degrading rhapsody which follows, and which we are truly sorry to see from the pen of a man, whom, we believe, the whole nation are disposed to admire, provided he would suffer them.

The only excuse for the writer is, that he has done it under the influence of anger, and that which is done thus, is never well done. After all, we think the Reviewer has done the poetical character of Burns ample justice; and the only error with which he can be impeached is, the too common one of contrasting his poetical powers with his private character, or making any use of the one, to throw odium upon the other, whereas the two things are existences perfectly different. Indeed, this whole system of scraping up private ancedotes, and posthumous scraps, and thence pretending to form an estimate of a departed *literary char-*

605

acter, is unjust, beyond all sufferance. A poet must draw to himself the bad features of the human character, before he is enabled to define the more perfect ones which he means to lay before the public; he must sketch before he draws; but, are these rude sketches to be afterwards produced as tokens of the artist's incapacity? To know mankind, he must also mix with them; and who can reasonably blame him for conforming to the manners of those with whom he is obliged to associate?

But it is too apparent, that it was not the Reviewer's sentiments of Burns that kindled the fierceness of Mr W's wrath. There is a soreness felt nearer home than any thing that relates to Burns: but Mr W. has exposed himself, not the journalist. There is nothing that amuses or delights a critic so much as this rebellion of chiefs and principalities against his laws and regulations, especially if he is endowed with the same 'portion of malignity' which it seems the critic in question is possessed of, as it gives him an opportunity of imposing his laws upon them in future with still greater severity. We can, however, assure Mr W. and we do it in perfect sincerity, that is the opinion of many who have considered the circumstances with deep and interested attention, that if it had not been for the sentiments avowed by this detested Reviewer, this 'intoxicated despot,' Mr W. would not have stood so high, by many degrees, in the public estimation as he does at present. There are a few who read poetry for the sake of enjoying its beauties, who might, and would have discovered the poetic powers of his mind; but these are a very limited number compared with the multitude that read a work merely because it is the fashion to do so, and who, of course, read it very partially. Among these Mr W. never could have been popular. There is so much wire-drawn minuteness in his pictures of life, mixed with so much affectation of Miltonic pomp and fustian, that he never fails to leave impressions on the mind which make the true gold too generally overlooked. This might ever have been the case, if it had not been for the sentiments boldly avowed by this 'infatuated slanderer,' by whom the gigantic powers of Mr W.'s mind are highly appreciated and minutely pointed out.

We took up this small work principally for the purpose of giving a little more publicity to Mr W.'s sentiments with regard to the life and character of Burns, which we deemed conformable to reason, and likewise that we might hint to the friends of the poet who are now engaged in supplying materials for an additional account of his life, by his own brother, Gilbert Burns, that they have no cause to be enraged at all those who mention any imperfection or blemish in the character or life of the bard. The public have, we believe, already formed a very just and not at all unfavourable estimate; but if these friends go on as they have begun, combating trifles that are obvious to every one, they will, by allowing nothing, confirm all that the most prejudiced have dared to insinuate – by open candour and truth we do not think the character of our loved and regretted bard can ever be truly injured.

198. John Wilson (1785–1854)

Three letters to *Blackwood's Edinburgh Magazine*: June 1817, signed 'By a Friend of Robert Burns'; October 1817, signed 'D'; November 1817, signed 'N'

These letters, an attack on Wordsworth, a defence, and a further attack provoked two anonymous pamphlets, *A Review of Blackwood's Edinburgh Magazine for October 1817* (1817), and *Hypocrisy Unveiled* (1818); these criticised *Blackwood's* for inconsistency towards Wordsworth and declared that the three letters were the work of one author.

John Wilson's behaviour seems to need explanation. It appears that it was Blackwood's (or the editors') intention that James Irving, a correspondent of Wordsworth, should write a defence to palliate the anonymous attack (Wilson's) of June 1817. Straight away, on 21 June 1817, William Blackwood wrote to Wordsworth,

> I hope you will pardon the liberty I take in sending you a copy of the third number of the Edin^h Magazine of which I am the publisher. The Observations therein contained on your "Letter to a Friend of Burns" have excited great indignation in the minds of many of your friends here; and M^r. Wilson M^r. Gray and M^r. Irving have expressed themselves very strongly on the subject. The last mentioned Gentleman communicated to me this day his determination to answer the obnoxious Paper in our next number. I therefore have thought it my duty to send you the Magazine as I feel anxious to know if [you] would consider the paper in question worthy of any notice. Should I not have the honour of hearing from you, I shall conclude from your silence that you do not think it should be noticed, and therefore without the sanction of your authority I shall not venture to publish Mr. Irving's reply . . .
>
> (Ms. National Library of Scotland)

Wordsworth, it appears, replied at once, consenting to Mr. Irving's defence providing that 'especial care be taken . . . not to implicate Gilbert

Burns [brother of the poet].' He goes on to give the publisher a general warning:

> I have lost no time in answering your Letter; and as the best return which I can make for your attention, I venture to observe that your infant publication must unavoidably fall into discredit if it be made the vehicle of the malignant passions by which this anonymous article is disfigured. There are certain indecencies in writing which *no* merit can atone for. The Philosophy of Plato could not have been endured if it had been accompanied with the manner of Thersites. If this be true, what becomes of your correspondence?
>
> (Draft letter. *MY* II, 389, and probably addressed to Blackwood and not to James Irving (to whom merely a copy was sent) as the editors have it.)

The defence by Irving did not appear however: Blackwood quarrelled apparently with those first editors, Cleghorn and Thomas Pringle (a friend of Irving). Wordsworth must have written about its non-appearance to Blackwood, for the latter wrote to Wordsworth on 20 October 1817:

> I was duly honoured with yours of the 8th and have to thank you for your polite Attention. I have never heard a syllable from Mr Irving, and I cannot help being vexed at his Silence, as I depended so completely upon him. I waited till the last moment and then applied to my friend M^r. Wilson who was so good as to furnish me with the Article which you will see in the Number which I now send you. I also beg leave to inclose you a note I rec$^{d.}$ from M^r. Wilson when he sent me his communication, as I think this will explain the way he has written it, better than anything I could say.
>
> (Ms. National Library of Scotland)

Wilson's note, surviving on a half sheet of paper as though specifically written in order to be torn off and sent to Wordsworth, contains of course no indication that the June attack was also Wilson's work:
14 October,

> I send you [Blackwood] the Article you requested me to write concerning Mr Wordsworth's celebrated Letter to Mr Gray – having had but a single day to write it, and even that day much broken in upon, it is a very imperfect composition; tho, I hope completely Justificatory of the Poet's character, which should never have been attacked had you not told me that Mr Irvine had volunteered him a defence, or rather an attack [on the June article, presumably]. I could have made mine much better than it is, by the allowance of a little more time, he had the advantage of seeing Mr Wordsworth, & of learning had he chosen, what his sentiments or wishes were.
>
> (Ms. Wordsworth Library)

Wilson followed this October defence, signed 'D', with the second attack in November, signed 'N'; even if his aim was merely to enliven the controversy, there is a curious basic ambivalence towards Wordsworth.

a. June 1817

. . . First, his [Wordsworth's] advice to Gilbert Burns [the brother of the poet]. The utter dullness, triteness, and absurdity, of this part of the Letter are almost beyond credibility. – 'I strenuously recommend, that a concise life of the poet be prefixed from the pen of Gilbert Barns, who has already given public proof how well qualified he is for the undertaking.' This is really humorous. What was Mr Wordsworth dreaming about? All this was fixed long ago; – there was no need of any recommendation from him. What would he think of the understanding of a correspondent who should recommend him *to go on with his Poem, the Recluse*, and who at the same time gave him advice *how* to write it. – 'If it be deemed adviseable to reprint Dr Currie's narrative, without striking out such passages as the author, *if he were now alive*, would probably be happy to efface, let there be notes attached to the most obnoxious of them, in which the misrepresentations may be corrected, and the exaggerations exposed.' – What novelty, ingenuity, and profundity of thought! We entreat Mr Gilbert Burns to pay particular attention to this advice; for it may probably not have occurred to him, that he must not aid and abet the calumniators of his brother's memory. – 'I know no better model as to proportion, and the degree of detail required, nor, indeed, as to the general execution, than the *life of Milton by Fenton*.' These three passages are the most important that we could discover; and we hope that Mr Gilbert Burns' gratitude will be in proportion to the value of the advice. The pompous inanity of all this is unaccountable, – and affords a melancholy proof how vanity, self-conceit, arrogance, and presumption, finally undermine the intellect, and can reduce a tolerably strong understanding to the very lowest level. The other advices which he gives form a complete system of mystification. He tells Mr Gilbert Burns to speak the truth, – and that boldly – but he is not to speak all the truth – yet he is not told what to conceal; – then he is to consult his conscience; – then he is to beware of undue partiality; – and, finally, 'to fix the point to which Burns' moral character had been degraded!' – And here we may remark, that Mr Gilbert Burns had better inform the public what degree of truth there is in the following stanza of Mr Wordsworth, while that gentleman himself will be pleased to shew its consistency with

609

the abuse he throws on Dr Currie, for un-undisguisedly admitting that Burns was too much addicted to the use of spirits. In an address to the Sons of Burns, Mr Wordsworth thus speaks of their deceased father:

> Strong-bodied, if ye be *to bear*
> *Intemperance with less harm*, beware!
> But if your father's wit ye share,
> *Then, then, indeed!*
> Ye sons of Burns, of watchful care
> There will be need.

Mr Wordsworth himself has here said, in miserable doggrel, what Dr Currie has said in elegant prose.

The second part of the letter contains Mr Wordsworth's notions on biography, and these, we think, if modified and qualified, tolerably rational and judicious, though delivered with a most laughable solemnity and true Wordsworthian self-importance . . .

But when Mr Wordsworth brings his specific charge against Dr Currie, what is it? – He accuses him of narrating Burns' errors and misfortunes, without affording the reader any information concerning their source or cause. This error of the biographer, he says, gave him 'acute sorrow,' excited 'strong indignation,' 'moved him beyond what it would become him to express.' Now Mr Wordsworth might have spared himself all this unnecessary emotion; for the truth is, that no man can, with his eyes open, read Dr Currie's Life of Burns, and the multitude of letters from and to the poet which his edition contains, without a clear, distinct, and perfect knowledge of all the causes from which the misfortunes and errors of that mighty genius sprung . . .

We had hoped, after all, to part with Mr Wordsworth in tolerably good humour, and with a smile on our faces; but what follows is too deplorable to be laughed at; and if he will make a fool of himself, he cannot well blame us for recording his folly. The secret cause of all his intemperate zeal in the needless vindication of Burns now betrays itself; and, as if maddened by a sudden sense of intolerable wrong, he falls foul of the Editor of the Edinburgh Review with a violence that must discompose the nervous system of that learned and ingenious person. It seems that Mr Peterkin, in his very heavy and dry Essay [of observations on the criticisms of Burns' life and genius in the *Edinburgh* and *Quarterly* reviews], had made several quotations from the Edinburgh and Quarterly Reviews. The last of these articles is far more severe on Burns' failings than the first. But Mr Wordsworth passes the Quarterly Review quietly over; and, with the voice and countenance of a maniac, fixes his teeth in the blue cover of the Edinburgh. He growls over it – shakes it violently to and fro – and at last, wearied out with vain efforts at mastication, leaves it covered over with the drivelling slaver of his impotent rage.

But what will be thought of Mr Wordsworth, when he tells us that he has never *read* the offensive criticism in the Edinburgh Review! He has only seen the garbled extract of Mr Peterkin. What right, then, has he to talk big of injustice done to the dead, when he is himself so deplorably deficient in justice to the living? But Mr Wordsworth must not be allowed to escape that castigation which his unparalleled insolence deserves. The world is not to be gulled by his hypocritical zeal in the defence of injured merit. It is not Robert Burns for whom he feels, – it is William Wordsworth. All the while that he is exclaiming against the Reviewer's injustice to Burns, he writes under the lash which that consummate satirist has inflicted upon himself, and exhibits a back yet sore with the wounds which have been in vain kept open, and which his restless and irritable vanity will never allow to close.

We shall not disgrace our pages with any portion of the low and vulgar abuse which the enraged poet heaps upon the Editor of the Edinburgh Review. It is Mr Wordsworth's serious opinion, that that gentleman is a person of the very weakest intellects – that his malignity is neutralized by his vanity – that he does not possess one liberal accomplishment – and that he is nearly *as imbecile as Buonaparte!* Mr Wordsworth's friends should not allow him to expose himself in this way. He has unquestionably written some fine verses in his day; but, with the exception of some poetical genius, he is, in all respects, immeasurably inferior, as an intellectual being, to the distinguished person whom he so foolishly libels.

We wish to have done with this lyrical ballad-monger . . .

(*Blackwood's Edinburgh Magazine*, I, 261–6)

b. October 1817

I BEG leave to make a few remarks on a Paper which appeared in the Third Number of the Edinburgh Monthly Magazine, respecting Mr Wordsworth's Letter to Mr Gray, on the best mode of composing a memoir of the life of Robert Burns. Had the writer of that Paper confined himself to the question under discussion, I should not have thought it necessary to oppose his opinions, however erroneous they may be; but as he has endeavoured to represent Mr Wordsworth's feelings and motives in an odious and contemptible light, and has shewn greater anxiety to vituperate that truly great Man than to vindicate the character of Burns, I shall, in a few words, expose the weakness and the malignity of this anonymous Calumniator . . .

[Quotes passages from the article in the previous issue and replies fulsomely in Wordsworth's favour, yet asserts that 'Mr. Jeffrey is the best Professional Critic we now have.']

It should, however, be held in mind by Mr Wordsworth's admirers, among whom are to be found every living Poet of any eminence, that, with all the fearlessness of original genius, he has burst and cast away the bonds which were worn very contentedly by many great writers. Mr Wordsworth is a man of too much original power not to have very often written ill; and it is incredible that, mid all his gigantic efforts to establish a system (even allowing that system to be a right one), he has never violated the principles of taste or reason. He has brought about a *revolution* in Poetry; and a revolution can no more be brought about in Poetry than in the Constitution, without the destruction or injury of many excellent and time-hallowed establishments. I have no doubt that, when all the rubbish is removed, and free and open space given to behold the structures which Mr Wordsworth has reared, in all the grandeur of their proportions, that Posterity will hail him as a regenerator and a creator. But meanwhile some allowance must be made for them who, however ignorantly, adhere to their ancient idols; and for my own part, I can bear all manner of silly nonsense to be spoken about Wordsworth with the most unmoved tranquillity. I know that if he has often written ill, Milton and Shakespeare have done so before him. Johnson has said, that we cannot read many pages of Shakespeare, 'without contempt and indignation;' and Hume says, that the same divine Poet cannot, for two pages together, 'preserve a reasonable propriety.' The same critic says, that at least a third of Paradise Lost is 'almost wholly devoid of harmony and elegance – nay, of all vigour of imagination.' Now, neither Samuel Johnson nor David Hume were dunces. Let us therefore believe that neither is Mr Francis Jeffrey a dunce,—and let Mr Wordsworth be contented with sharing the fate of Milton and Shakespeare.

But in a subject of this nature, why should we dwell on any disagreeable or painful altercations between men of Power. Here there is a noble prospect, without any drawback or alloy, to delight our souls and our imagination. A Poet distinguished for the originality of his genius, – for his profound knowledge of the human heart, – for his spiritual insight into all the grandeur and magnificence of the external world, – for a strain of the most serene, undisturbed, and lofty morality, within whose control no mind can come without being elevated, purified, and enlightened, – for a Religion partaking at once of all the solemnity of faith, and all the enthusiasm of poetry, – and, to crown all with a perfect consummation, a Poet who has realized, in a life of sublime solitude, the visions that have blessed the dreams of his inspiration, – He comes forward with a countenance and a voice worthy of himself and the Being of whom he speaks, – and vindicates, from the confused admiration, or the vulgar reproaches of ordinary minds, a Bard who is the pride of his native land, and a glory to human nature, – while he speaks of his failings with such reverential pity – of his virtues with such noble praise, that we see Burns standing before us in all his weakness and all his strength, – the same warmhearted, affectionate, headstrong, fervid, impassioned, imprudent, erring, independent, noble, high-minded, and inspired Man, that won or commanded every soul, and whose voice, omnipotent in life, speaks with a yet more overpowering sound from the silence of the grave.

(*Ibid.*, II, 65–73)

c. November 1817

. . . I hope I may be permitted to say without offence, in the pages of your Magazine, that, so far as Mr Wordsworth is concerned, all the kindness of feeling, and all the very masterly rhetoric of N. have, on the present occasion, been most egregiously misapplied. On looking back to the Third Number of Blackwood's Magazine, I own I was astonished to find, that although N. has written seven pages, under the name of 'A Vindication of Mr Wordsworth,' he has nevertheless, by some strange oversight (whether intentional or otherwise it is not for me to determine), left the character of that gentleman exactly as it stood before he took his pen in his hand, and offered not a single word which can have the effect of sheltering him from those accusations of egotism, spleen, and scurrility, which had originally been brought against him, with apparently so much reason, by your English correspondent the 'Observer.' . . .

Indeed, were I to fix upon what sort of person I should fancy the least likely to give good counsel to a biographer of Burns, I have little hesitation in saying, that I should select just such a one as Mr Wordsworth, – a man who, if it be true that he possesses poetical genius, most certainly possesses no other quality in common with Robert Burns; – a retired, pensive, egotistical *collector of stamps*; one who has no notion of that merry, hearty life, that Burns delighted in; and one that seems to be completely overflowing with envy, malignity, and a thousand bad passions, of which Burns' nobler nature, whatever defects it might otherwise have, was at all times entirely incapable. How can a melancholy, sighing, half-parson sort of gentleman, who lives in a small circle of old maids and sonnetteers, and drinks tea now and then with the solemn Laureate, have any sympathy with the free and jolly dispositions of one who spent his evenings in drinking whisky punch at mason lodges with Matthew Henderson and David Lapraik? To my view it would be scarcely less absurd in Gilbert Burns to send Mr Wordsworth a long letter concerning the proper method of drawing *the Recluse* to a conclusion, than it was in Mr Wordsworth to prescribe rules to Gilbert with regard to that Memoir of his illustrious brother, which he is so well qualified in every way to make exactly what it should be, without the officious hints of any Laker in existence . . .

. . . Who . . . does not at once perceive that the true objects of the author's concern were not Robert Burns and Dr Currie, but himself and Mr Jeffray, and those reviews of the *Lyrical Ballads*, the *Excursion*, and the *White Doe*, which he so credibly informs us he has never read? That Mr Wordsworth should have been extremely nettled by the sarcasms of the Edinburgh Review, seems to be abundantly natural; but that he, if he be a man of genius, should at all times and on every occasion stand howling on the highway, and entreating all mankind to look at his blisters, – appears, to say the least of it, extremely injudicious. Cannot Mr Wordsworth content himself with sitting at home and carping at Mr Jeffray, in the midst of his own little knot of kindred worshippers at Keswick . . .

(*Ibid.*, II, 201–4)

198a. William Hazlitt

From the seventh of his *Lectures on the English Poets*, 'On Burns and the old English Ballads': given at the Surrey Institution, Great Surrey Street, near Blackfriars Bridge, 24 February 1818

See entry 256j, pp. 887–90.

XIII

'Thanksgiving Ode': reviews and opinions, 1816–1817

199. Henry Crabb Robinson

From his diary, 15 May 1816

I forwarded to Miss H. M. Williams,[1] Wordsworth's Thanksgiving Ode recently published.

I supped with Mrs. Thornthwaite and read Wordsworth's ode. It has heavy passages, but the commencement and conclusion are both fine indeed. His assertion that the great calamities of life are the instruments of Providence, though very trite, was never expressed with more force and beauty.

> He puts the Earthquake on its still design
> ['Ode. 1815', l. 94, *PW*, III, p. 154]

deserves to pass into a proverb. The verses on the Russian Winter are, perhaps, the most delightful in the volume. There are beautiful sonnets on the Battle of Waterloo. The volume is worthy of Wordsworth, but it will have the fate of his other works. It was not relished by the party I had to read to this night . . .

(*Henry Crabb Robinson on Books and Their Writers*, ed. Edith J. Morley, 1938 I, 182)

EDITOR'S NOTE

1. Helen Maria Williams (1762–1827), to whom Wordsworth addressed a youthful sonnet, had lived mainly in France for more than twenty years.

200. John Scott (1783–1821)

From a letter to Wordsworth, 29 May 1816

I have read your [*Thanksgiving*] Ode with delight, – and acknowledge its gift from the Author, with a truly proud pleasure. Professedly contemplative and abstracted, it conveys all the active interests & picturesque exhibitions of the great events which it celebrates, before the mind of the reader, by the energy, majesty, brightness, and rapidity of its imagery, language, & strain of feeling. Living as we do in the very time of these deeds, it seems as if their sublimity sets at nought particular description, and invites to that general exaltation of spirit, that indulgence of moral joy, philosophical triumph, & devout thankfulness, which meet, and breathe intensely purely in your Ode, and stamp it one of the few primordial productions, all the elements of which are genuine and great. It is the hymn of a high & well-tuned Soul, the poetic harmonies of which have been called into play by the ardour of patriotic affection. Excuse me, I beg, my Dear Sir, for being thus unreserved, although addressing Yourself; my expressions are the dictates of my understanding & the overflowings of my heart. I owe you gratitude for your kindness, – and I have for many years paid to your genius the tribute of deep & earnest admiration. I cannot but be of opinion that the other Poets who have taken Waterloo for their theme have totally failed: a Gentleman wrote rather favourably of Mr Southey's [*Poet's Pilgrimage to Waterloo*] in the Champion but I confess it appears to me poor. I have not felt myself strong enough to enter thoroughly as yet into the business of my Journal: – one or two of the first articles I have put together, but in general I have been obliged to friends. I would not willingly have seen any one but myself take your ode for a subject in the Champion, & this has been the cause of delaying the honor it must have in paying homage to so fine a Poem. I confess I should have been jealous of any one's stepping in before me here, and I hope you will accept with indulgence the feeble attempt you will soon see. Your Letter on Burns seems perfectly called for & just: it is eloquent, & convincing. But I have not been able to gather from it, your exact opinion on a point of great importance, as it strikes me, viz – how the strength of faculty which forms what is called talent should be permitted to affect the judgment which, for the sake of society, ought to be passed on the moral conduct of individuals so distinguished. I am particularly led to the consideration of this question, as well by your Printed Letter, as by some doctrines recently broached by my antagonists in the Exam^r. one of whom is Mr Hazlitt – a powerful writer, – but an inconclusive & dangerous one. My doubts do not apply to the case of Burns at all – on it you are quite clear & irrefutable: but how far are we to extend that allowance which is claimed for the strong impulses, & irritable feelings that usually form part of the constitution of powerful intellects? If it be recognized as an established position, that genius is naturally allied to irregularity, the decorous dullness of common minds will not unfairly treat with apprehension and disdain the pretensions of men of talent to regulate the affairs of society, and adjust disputed obligations & duties. Yet what seems to be the highest, most natural, & most useful province of talent? Excuse me for thus propounding my hesitations; I have no doubt that ten words of explanation as to your sentiments on this matter would settle me in complete coincidence with them.

(Ms. The Wordsworth Library)

201. Josiah Conder

From an unsigned review, *Eclectic Review*, July 1816, VI, second series, 4–8[1]

Conder's preference lies obviously with the work of his friend, Southey, whose *Poet's Pilgrimage to Waterloo* (1816), is the other poem upon which this article centres.

It is not with any view of bringing our two greatest living poets into direct comparison with each other, that we have coupled a publication of Mr. Wordsworth's with that of his friend. It is interesting, however, to observe the characteristic difference between the two authors. Mr. Wordsworth, always metaphysical, loses himself perpetually in the depths of abstraction on the simplest subject; and frequently employing words as the arbitrary signs of recondite and mystical meanings, exhibits a singular inequality of style, varying from Miltonic majesty of thought and diction, to apparent poverty and meanness. It is only at intervals that he comes within reach of the sympathy of ordinary readers. We never think of claiming kindred with Mr. Wordsworth as a man of the same nerve and texture and heart's blood with ourselves. He looks on nature with other than human senses. He appears to regard God and man through the medium of a philosophy taught in no secular and in no sacred schools. Mr. Southey, on the contrary, is never to be mistaken for any other than a husband, a father, a friend; – a man whose sympathies all link him to his country and his fellow-men; whose errors whether poetical or political, proceed from the warmth of feeling or the force of prejudice, and are never the deliberate sins of a perverse intellect, or the indications of dubious principles. Moral objects seem in his mind to hold the place of metaphysical ones, and he takes too much interest in the passing scenes of the real world, to cultivate the habit of severe abstraction. Whatever he writes, is at least interesting. It bears the stamp of character, – of the man and of the poet. Wordsworth *can* interest. He has written some whole poems, and there are passages in all his poems, that are fitted with exquisite skill to find their way to the heart. But in much of his loftiest poetry he is any thing but interesting. When he aims to teach, he fails to please. He aspires to sit in Milton's chair; but the spirit whose nightly visitation Milton enjoyed, was not the spirit of mere poetry. The spirit of Milton has not rested upon Mr. Wordsworth, unless it be in some of his noble sonnets, in which he more than rivals the great puritan champion of liberty. Southey and Wordsworth have some obvious peculiarities of diction in common, but the resemblance is very superficial. Wordsworth's affectation lies more in the thoughts than in the manner. If Southey be at any time chargeable with a fault of this kind, it will be found confined to the expression; his thoughts are always natural. The poems of the one are altogether so different from those of the other, that it is not conceivable that Wordsworth could have written Madoc or Roderick, or Southey, the Excursion. Wordsworth displays at times an intellectual grandeur and a depth of pathos, peculiarly his own. Southey excels in force of dramatic conception, in the development of character, and in the expression of the tender affections. Wordsworth's poetry, if we may be allowed so trite a comparison, reminds us of a mountain torrent issuing from some unknown solitude, and rolling its rarely navigable waters through barren and uninhabited regions, over rocks and shallows, now lingering round some green and sunny islet, now thundering in precipitous grandeur, now tamely diffusing its waters over a wide spread channel. Southey's is the mighty stream, eccentric, but clear, rapid, and beautiful, that loves the imaged heavens on its surface, and the racy verdure of the earth, and flows and murmurs for man.

We have described the productions of both these original poets freely, as though they were not living authors, whom it is our bounden duty, as critics, to treat with sparing praise and salutary censure. We have spoken of them as we feel, and as we believe, in a few years, their readers will generally feel, when they shall live only in their works, and their critics shall be forgotten. But it is time that we proceed to the business of reviewing.

We cannot approve of the avowed object of Mr. Wordsworth's publication, whatever credit be due to him for the patriotism to which it owes its existence. When he speaks of Great Britain having 'distinguished herself above all other countries for some 'time past,' by a course of action so worthy of commemoration, we wish to know more definitely to what course of action he refers; and as we are always fearful of being imposed upon by abstractions, what portion of the nation is intended by Great Britain, – the cabinet, the army, or the people. To whom are we to ascribe that great moral triumph, the splendour of which, not all the present distresses are able to obscure? It is too much for Mr. W. to expect that the 'national wisdom' which he so highly eulogizes, will sanction that unmingled admiration of the measures of the present Government, which, in the height of his exultation, he seems desirous of producing; as if the stamp of moral greatness and of disinterested patriotism, were impressed on all their councils for the last ten years, and one steady purpose had been the simple spring of all their policy!! But this is not all. Mr. Wordsworth adds,

'Nor is it at the expense of rational patriotism, or in disregard of sound philosophy, that the author hath given vent to feelings tending to encourage a martial spirit in the bosoms of his countrymen, at a time when there is a general outcry against the prevalence of these dispositions! – The nation would err grievously, if she suffered the abuse which other states have made of military power, to prevent her from perceiving that no people ever was, or can be independent, free or secure, much less great, in any sane application of the word, without martial propensities, and an assiduous cultivation of military virtues.'

We shall not stop to dispute with Mr. Wordsworth: we should just as soon encounter Dr. Johnson in argument. Were we obliged to admit that the assertion receives too melancholy countenance from historic fact, it is execrable in principle. It sets at defiance all attempts to introduce the meliorating tendencies of the Gospel into the policy of governments, and takes for granted that the maxims of Christian morality are wholly nugatory and inapplicable to national transactions. It is not worth while to point out the bearing of the military virtues on the civil character of a people. Mr. Wordsworth considers apprehensions in reference to that point, as arising from the 'delusive influence of an honourable jealousy.' Upon this subject he has the satisfaction of being of coincident sentiments with the right honourable Lord Castlereagh. But now for the poetry.

The ode composed on the morning of the day appointed for general thanksgiving, is marked with all the peculiarities of Mr. Wordsworth's genius. Few readers will be able to follow in the track of thought, or to enter into the sentiments of the Author, nor shall we attempt to give a commentary upon so desultory and irregular a production. No poetry could be further removed from a popular style, than that in which this ode is cast; except in an occasional stanza of the following kind.

> Preserve, O Lord, within our hearts
> The memory of thy favour,
> That else insensibly departs,
> And loses its sweet savour!
> ['Thanksgiving Ode', *PW*, III, p. 160, ll. 161–4]

And again,

> For these, and for our errors,
> And sins that point their terrors,
> We bow our heads before thee, and we laud
> And magnify thy name, Almighty God!
> But thy most dreaded instrument
> *In working out a pure intent*,
> Is man, arrayed for mutual slaughter, –
> Yea, Carnage is thy daughter!
> ['Ode, 1815', *PW*, III, pp. 154–5 and footnotes,
> ll. 102–7: text revised 1832]

What strange and revolting phraseology, to use the mildest term, is this! How utterly at variance with the language of truly Christian devotion. How unmeet an offering.

> On the high day of thanks before the *Throne of Grace!*

The second ode, bearing the same date, is less elaborate, and more pleasing. It consists of an allegorical description of the various methods of festive and honorary commemoration of the deeds of the victors of Waterloo. Among the 'Miscellaneous 'Pieces,' there is a very fine ode, beginning –

> Who rises on the banks of Seine.

We are tempted however to select, as the most pleasing specimen of what Mr. Wordsworth can achieve, an exquisite composition 'in recollection of the expedition of the French into Russia.'

[Quotes 'The French Army in Russia, 1812–13', *PW*, III, p. 140 and the sonnet on the same occasion, 'Ye Storms, resound the praises of your King!' *PW*, III, p. 141.]

EDITOR'S NOTE

1. Marked 'J. C.' in the London Library copy of the *Eclectic*.

202.

Unsigned review, *British Critic*, September 1816, VI, second series, 313–15

The first [poem] is an Ode for the Morning of the Day appointed as a General Thanksgiving, January, 1816. The opening invocation to the sun is finely conceived and well expressed . . .

There is fire, we would almost say an awful strain of piety which pervades the whole, which is interrupted by fewer of those peculiarities of expression, which have afforded, and with some justice, the deriders of Mr. Wordsworth so much amusement . . .

Among the smaller poems we have some good lines occasioned by the Battle of Waterloo. Of the inscription for a national monument we approve; but we are more pleased with the following:

[Quotes 'The bard, whose soul is meek as dawning day'.]

The following strain, on the same subject, is indeed of a higher mood; we shall willingly extract it, as it does Mr. Wordsworth the highest credit.

[Quotes 'Oh, for a kindling touch of that pure flame'.]

From the specimens of this collection which we have been enabled to exhibit, our readers will be decidedly of opinion, that Mr. Wordsworth has gained character by the poems now before us.

203. John Scott

Unsigned review, *Champion*, 20 October 1816, 334–5

This article was rightly attributed to Scott by T. R. Hughes, *London Mercury*, April 1930. 24: Leonidas M. Jones, knowing that Scott had sold the *Champion*, was led to assign it to J. H. Reynolds.

Scott introduced has review of the 'Thanksgiving Ode' by his essay:

'Popular poetry – Periodical Criticism', published on 13 October 1816, 326–7. Leonidas M. Jones argues that the reference there to 'personal circumstances of interruption' points to Reynolds as author since Reynolds had been taking a long vacation at Exeter (see *Selected Prose of John Hamilton Reynolds* (1966), p.448); but Scott's letter to Wordsworth cited above (entry 200) adequately explains Scott's delay. Scott attacks the concept of 'popular poetry' (a theme touched upon in his review of *The White Doe*, see entry 178 above) and takes his keynote from Wordsworth's 'Essay Supplementary to the Preface' (1815) which argues against 'the senseless iteration of the word, *popular*, applied to new works in poetry, as if there were no test of excellence in this first of the Fine Arts, but that all men should run after its productions . . .'. Scott declares: ' We think it is clear that Genius has essentially nothing to do with what is called popularity . . .'. Scott delightedly quotes Wordsworth's dismissive view: 'But a small quantity of brain is necessary to produce a considerable quantity of admiration, provided the aspirant will accommodate himself to the likings and fashions of his day.' He points to Wordsworth's key arguments: 'Every author, as far as he is great, and at the same time *original*, has had the task of creating the taste by which he is to be enjoyed'; again: 'Genius is the introduction of a new element into the intellectual universe: – or, if that be not allowed, it is the application of powers to objects on which they had not been before exercised, – or the employment of them in such a manner as to produce effects hitherto unknown.' Scott himself concludes: 'But at present we resist what is strange to us, as something that is inferior to us: we question it, – not ourselves.' Scott's argument implies that Wordsworth is the victim of such critics as the editor of the *Edinburgh Review* [Francis Jeffrey] who undervalues Wordsworth because he is not, in Scott's own words, 'capable of exerting, within his own mind, a corresponding energy' to that of the poet.

Considering the subject of Mr. Wordsworth's Poem, this tardy notice of it might be deemed out of time, were not its author one who writes more for 'all time,' than for any particular time present. There is no one so little dependent as he is on occasion, – and on what are commonly called means. Indeed, both his attributed faults, and superlative excellence, chiefly proceed from this circumstance, that, whatever his subject may be, the soul and imagination of the poet make the all in all of the performance. Every thing that proceeds from him is an emanation of himself: – he creates it in his own image, – and, without meaning to suggest any improper analogy, we would say, that he it is who sees that it is good. This is the proper exercise and sole province of genius, – which exists, in quality of its divinity, in itself and for itself. It makes no advances or concessions: – it is the privilege of all that all may come to worship it; – those who will not, may enjoy the perversity for their pains, – those who cannot, may keep themselves in countenance by their numbers.

Mr. Wordsworth, we have heard, and on good authority, is not a popular poet: – we are very sure he is an admired one; and as to popularity, though it is a desirable thing for any weekly newspaper, yet we do not know that it is absolutely necessary for the Cartoons, or the Sampson Agonistes. However, on this delicate subject we, perhaps, too frankly expressed ourselves last week: – at all events we need not now add to these remarks.

Asking, therefore, no further questions about popularity, let us simply inquire whether there is one of our readers who will confess himself dead to the charm of any of the following passages, and yet profess to be alive to the beauties of those works which the canons of criticism have established in the rank of master models and examples of poetical skill, grace, and power? The Ode in question, is a devout and patriotic hymn for the morning of the day appointed for a general thanksgiving, with reference chiefly to the splendid victory of Waterloo, – the successful termination of the war being the immediate and inevitable consequence of that great exploit. Mr. Wordsworth, in a prose dissertation, has said of poetry that it is 'the spontaneous overflow of powerful feelings: – it takes its origin from emotion remembered in tranquillity.' Where can be found a more sublime illustration of this assertion, than in the opening of the poem now under notice; – and in reading it, we will do well to recollect another of his fine explanations of the poetic mind, – in which he terms it 'the mirror of the fairest and most interesting qualities of nature.'

[Quotes 'Thankgiving Ode' *PW*, III, pp. 155–6 and footnotes, ll. 1–35:

> Hail universal Source of pure delight! . . .
> Once more, heart-cheering Sun, I bid thee hail!
> Bright be thy course to day, – let not this promise fail!]

Whatever may be thought and felt of such poetry as this, we are quite sure that all will agree it is not likely to be ever deemed or called *popular* poetry. Mr. Wordsworth's warmest admirers will be the most earnest to affirm this. We shall give an example, from the works of another, and an earlier author – an author too of some note – of poetry which we presume to think very admirable, – but which it would also be ridiculous to dignify with the epithet *popular*. Mr. Murray, who has disposed of so many editions of Lord Byron's works, would not have cause to envy the copy right of such verses as follow.

[Quotes Milton's 'Samson Agonistes', ll. 652–80:

> Many are the sayings of the wise
> In antient and in modern books enroll'd . . .
> To some great work, thy glory,
> And people's safety, – which in part they effect.]

We apologise to our readers for being so tedious: – we know that we make the above long quotation at considerable risk, – particularly during the present dull time for newspapers: and we are sure our publisher will see it with grief of soul. But when one is a good deal piqued in behalf of favourite opinions, hazard is not much thought of. We have been vexed and mortified, even nigh unto death, by sensible ladies and reading gentlemen on the subject of Mr. Wordsworth poetry. One fair correspondent writes, from the neighbourhood of that seat of taste, Edinburgh, to know whether we really do, in our hearts, think, that Mr. Wordsworth has ever composed any thing so pretty as the *Pleasures of Hope?* A judicious friend is puzzled to know the meaning of one of Mr. Wordsworth's lines; – and a witty one asks if '*Harry Gill's* teeth are yet done chattering. – Now, to cut short all this, we have given them the last extract, – no matter whence taken, or from whom: – and we warrant it to them as excellent, standard poetry, of the first genius, and of immortal fame. Neither their sentiments or ours have any thing at all to do with this decision: – it *is* so – the thing is settled, – and we warn them that it can only now be denied to the shame of the dunce who denies it. If any one, lady or gentleman, will step forward and declare conscientiously, that they *doat* [*sic*] upon the lines beginning 'many are the sayings of the wise:' – that they could read them from morning to night; that they could do nothing but read them; that Lord Byron's *Farewell* was not half so touching: that his verses to the *Star of the Legion of Honour* were not so sublime: – if they will declare that they feel quite struck by these lines, – and add, after making this declaration *sincerely*, that they cannot see any high degree of power and beauty in the great body of Mr. Wordsworth's poetry, – we pledge ourselves never to write another line, or say another word in admiration of it.

If we have already said enough to excite some suspicions of the truth in a certain class of breasts – such as are full of quick sensibilities, but which have not been sufficiently scrupulous in questioning the nature of their excitement – we would recommend to these persons, – as nothing is

more difficult of cure than a taste debauched from simplicity and truth, –
to read the opening passage of Mr. Wordsworth's Ode *twice or three times
over*. If they will read it aloud, and with an intonation characterized by
feeling, the process will be assisted. They will then, if we are not much
mistaken, speedily feel the growing charm spreading and warming
within them; the charm which proceeds from 'the unostentatious beauties of a pure style.' But at this stage of the recovery, it is most essential for
them to avoid all relapses of tea-table criticisms; to repress all inward
movements of self-sufficiency; and, we think, it would be no more than
prudent, to keep, at this time, any thick pamphlet-looking work, with
blue covers [*Edinburgh Review*] out of sight for a day or two. We only
advise this latter precaution, however, till the patient has acquired a little
strength. 'In the higher poetry,' says our author, 'an enlightened critic
chiefly looks for a reflection of the wisdom of the heart and the grandeur
of the imagination.' But one can only recognize the fidelity of the images
by sympathising with the qualities: – and this leads us to state of Mr.
Wordsworth's poetry that it must actually bring the mind of the reader
up to a full and thorough participation and communion with itself,
in all its views, enjoyments, and discoveries, – or it has no effect upon
him at all. In this it essentially differs from the greatest number of
examples of modern poetry. These, – instead of encouraging, inviting,
and strengthening the minds of those who engage in them, to make an
advance of themselves, – seize their readers off their legs as it were, carry
them away hastily for a temporary excursion, independently entirely of
their own powers – whirl them about with violence amidst a hubbub of
words, false sentiments, and misplaced ornaments, – and end by setting
them down precisely where they found them, – not having made an inch
of mental progression or acquired one new insight into the properties or
combinations of nature. It requires no explanations to point out the
superior difficulties of Mr. Wordsworth's task; – he gives the intellectual
part of those who apply to him, something serious and severe to do: –
how should he be popular with the million? He turns the soul inward, to
muse upon and enjoy its own realities: – if nature has made it in any case
empty, what can the poet do? If the arbitrary and artificial fashions of
society, and the common occupations, of sordid life, have made it the
victim of low or false impression, – have entangled it in false analogies,
and given it, at the same time, an unshakeable self-confidence, – what
can the poet do? This last consideration may serve to convince, how ill-
adapted a very late period of society is, for the immediate appreciation of
the original efforts of any great contemplative genius. People are all then

proud of their own knowledge, and their own attainments: it follows that they are then most likely to withstand any attempt to extend that dominion over their spirits, 'by which they are to be humbled and humanized, in order that they may be purified and exalted.' At an earlier period of human affairs, men's hearts are more full of generous confidence, and of that elevated disposition from which proceeds a frank submission; – then, too, the voices of the naturally incapable have no means of assuming a disgusting and fatal ascendency.

We do not feel that we have any thing to do as critics in this instance, but to explain the general principles of our favourable opinion, and to leave examples of the poetry to speak for themselves. We have quoted the opening of the Ode, which we consider distinguished by a majesty of thought and expression, not less elevated and imposing for being also benign and harmonious. 'The *depth*, and not the tumult of the soul' – (to quote one of our author's own fine lines) – is apparent in the next passage, – which follows the other, encreasing the swell of the music.

> Mid the deep quiet of this morning hour,
> All nature seems to hear me while I speak, –
> By feelings urged, that do not vainly seek
> Apt language, ready as the tuneful notes
> That stream in blithe succession from the throats
>   Of birds in leafy bower,
> Warbling a farewell to a vernal shower.
> ['Thanksgiving Ode', *PW*, III, p. 156–7, ll. 36–42]

Milton, in his fragment of the History of England, says, 'I have determined, in speaking of the antient and rejected British fables, to bestow the telling over even of these reputed tales, be it for nothing else but in favour of our English Poets and rhetoricians, who by their art well know how to use them judiciously.' Some of our present enlighteners of public opinion, will feel great contempt for this regard paid to the imaginative honours and decorations of our country; as they will sneer at the following burst of tender feeling towards her.

> Land of our fathers! precious unto me
> Since the first joys of thinking infancy!
> When of thy gallant chivalry I read,
> And hugged the volume on my sleepless bed!
> O England! – dearer far than life is dear,
> If I forget thy prowess, never more

Be thy ungrateful son allowed to hear
Thy green leaves rustle, or thy torrents roar.
[*Ibid.*, *PW*, III, pp. 159–60, ll. 138–9 in footnotes, and
ll. 139–44]

If all this be childishness, as some will say it is, it only proves that 'the child is father to the man.'

The following passage, descriptive of the spreading of the good news, affords a remarkable example of what we mentioned in the beginning of this article; – viz. Mr. Wordsworth's power independently of subject, – his originality in the handling of all subjects, – and his habit of embellishing purely from the stores of his own imagination.

[Quotes 'Ode, 1815', *PW*, III, pp. 152–3, ll. 8–36 and footnotes. Three lines omitted, originally part of the 'Thanksgiving Ode'.

Fly ministers of Fame . . .
How virtue triumphs, from her bondage freed!]

The regular reader of the *Champion* knows how cordially we join in feeling with the admirers and celebrators of the victory to which this fine poem is devoted. Yet there is a beatific abandonment, and a spiritual fullness of faith about Mr. Wordsworth, which we can only contemplate with envying wonder, being ourselves far behind him in this respect, encompassed with fears, doubts, and misgivings. We do not mean, however, to enter here on any political considerations: – suffice it for us to say, that the twenty first of his Sonnets dedicated to Liberty, in the 2d volume of the last edition of his Lyrical Ballads, &c. speaks the language of our present poor frame exactly. He has now, however, outgrown all his weaknesses, and supplied all his barrenness. He has been caught up into the third heaven – whether in the body or out of the body we cannot tell – but unassisted earthly vision, when he takes this course, cannot follow him further than the clouds. It is in the excess of this saintly rapture that he describes the 'blest angels,' welcoming the hideous defeat of the French 'with a choral shout!' We wish we could be admitted with him into these regions of perfect confidence and perfect joy. But alas! we still remain where he was when he wrote the following beautiful and touching lines: –

[Quotes 'England! The time is come when thou shouldst wean!', *PW*, III, p. 119.]

204.

Unsigned review, *Dublin Examiner*, November 1816, II, 18–25

Despite the irreverence, a style common to all their reviews, a furtive respect for the *Excursion* is detectable.

There are in the North of England half a dozen lakes, and as many lake-poets. (This we mention for the information of our continental readers.) These gentlemen have long since contracted a habit of conferring upon the world, from among their body, a babe and a book, at the expiration of, at most, every nine months. We have, for obvious reasons, in choosing a subject for animadversion, preferred to select a specimen from among their productions of the latter kind, and the work which now lies before us, will be consequently found, to all intents and purposes, a *book*, being indeed 'a sequel to the Author's Sonnets, dedicated to Liberty;' and 'therefore printed uniformly with the two volumes of his Poems, in which those Sonnets are collected, to admit of their being conveniently bound up together.'

The particular tenets, to which the extravagancies, or (to dulcify the epithet,) peculiarities characteristic of the style of this North-Anglian horde may be referred, are sufficiently known, to warrant our declining to enter upon the discussion of them. Suffice it to observe, that one of the gentlemen, a very good laureate, and classical scholar, has, by the assumption of a well-known passage in Lucian, as a motto to one of his most celebrated, but, at the same time, lawless works, abundantly manifested his disposition to wrest the τὸ δόξχν τῷ ποιητῇ[1] of the above author, into a sanction for poetical licentiousness; while the hymner of the 'Thanksgiving Ode' at present before us, emulates the impartiality of that luminary, whom the opening lines of the aforesaid Ode are intended to celebrate, who, while his

orient visitations smite
The haughty towers where monarchs dwell;
['Ode. 1816', *PW*, III, pp. 155–6, ll. 4–5]

sheers

the low threshold of the Peasant's cell!
[*Ibid.*, l. 7]

who, while he gilds the dome, does not disdain the dunghill. It is thus with his encomiast. We fancy we behold him going forth of a morning a bog-trotting, in search of ideas or subjects for composition, with all the humility which Peter Pindar recommends to young limners: if, per-adventure, he lifts up his head, and lights upon a sun, he is ready enough, no doubt, to write a 'Thanksgiving Ode' to it, but equally content to pick

> rich lumps of *Album Græcum.*[2]

and, by due castigation, performed with the aid of his poetical pistil and mortar, to knead them into good, plausible lake poems. There is, in fact, no object whatsoever beneath his attention, from the well-defined

> Houshold-Tub, like one of those
> Which women use to wash their clothes.
> ['The Blind Highland Boy', *PW*, III, p. 88; *Poems 1807*,
> p. 239, ll. 113–14]

to the

> Spade! with which Wilkinson hath till'd his lands,
> ['To the Spade of a Friend', *PW*, IV, p.75, l. 1; *Poems 1807*,
> p. 299, l. 1]

from

> The leech-gatherer on the lonely moor.
> ['Resolution and Independence', *PW*, III, p. 240, l. 140;
> *Poems 1807*, p. 105, l. 147]

to the battle of Waterloo, which revives such a multitude of letter-press recollections. No poet, or poetess, or poetaster from St. Paul of Abbotsford, Esq. to the prophet on whom we are at present holding inquest, has refrained from poor Waterloo.

Yes – a prophet: for whoever will take the trouble of glancing over Page iv of the advertisement prefixed to the Thanksgiving Ode and Co, will find therein sundry notable predictions, respecting the accomplish-ment of which we are equally desirous and incredulous. However averse we may be to a state of war, we are still too little enthusiastic and pur-blind, to trumpet forth a panegyric *en avance* upon a doubtful millennium, and in truth, were it not for the very express terms in which Mr. W. states, that this little work has been published for the purpose of 'being conveniently bound up together' 'with two volumes of Sonnets' &c. we do not know – but – having one of Joanna Southcote's pamphlets in our hands – we – might be wicked enough – to – but we wash our hands of the prophet, and hasten to the poet, and the Thanksgiving Ode, being the bell-wether, first claims our attention.

After an opening invocation to the Sun, the author proceeds to state how the fells, and the fields, and all the lakes seem to listen to him while he sings; and no wonder they should, 'for,' says he, (and says it well,)

> I speak, –
> By feelings urged, that do not vainly seek
> Apt language, ready as the tuneful notes
> That stream in blithe succession from the throats
> Of birds in leafy bower,
> Warbling a farewell to a vernal shower.
> ['Ode. 1816', *PW*, III, pp. 156–7, ll. 37–42]

Now, since these old lakes have been so long habituated to hearken to poetic recitation, and have, moreover, produced many fine passages themselves, (particularly in 'The Excursion,') it is very natural that they should have come forth upon this occasion, to listen to Mr. Wordsworth chaunting matins, as it was besides a remarkably fine morning.

After creating a new peer (Lord Honour) – introducing a passage in prose, about Britain – talking of diving for glory – and

> Assaulting without ruth
> The citadels of truth;
> While the *old forest of civility*
> Is doomed to perish, to the last fair tree.
> [*Ibid.*, *PW*, III, p.158 and footnotes, ll. 107–12,
> with omissions]

('it was the mor pitté.') he gratifies his readers with the following very pregnant and emphatic line, which we would recommend to the attention of all partitioned and subjugated countries: –

> — O PROSTRATE LANDS, CONSULT YOUR AGONIES!
> [*Ibid.*, *PW*, III, p. 159, l. 126]

To pursue, in this detailed manner, the analysis of the entire poem, would extend this critique to a compass exceeding that of the work criticized. We also feel it an ungracious task, to animadvert upon the eccentricities of an author, who has produced – if not entire works – at least considerable portions of poems, (particularly of the descriptive kind,) which are too overwhelming for admiration, and of an altogether oppressive sublimity. From these kindly dispositions towards Mr. Wordsworth, we were gratified to find that the latter half of this poem presents more matter for approbation than for censure, and therefore hasten with pleasure to the duty of recording some of the leading beauties, applying, however, as in conscience bound, such occasional discipline as his magnificent but capricious Muse is almost continually incurring. But we shall be first permitted to make one short observation, suggested by the passage in page 12, (although not exactly a case in point,) where Mr. Wordsworth dwells upon the transmission '*De Paris au Perou, du Japon jusqu'à Rome*,'[3] of the following *Italian* distich of his: –

> — *The shock is given – the Adversaries bleed –*
> *Lo, Justice triumphs! Earth is freed!*
> ['Ode. 1815', *PW*, III, p. 152, ll. 17–18]

One of the most striking characteristics of Walter Scott's poetic style is the rapidity with which he occasionally hurries the reader along, even across all the stubble of a long 'muster-roll' of Celtic names of places, wondering at the ease of the motion, and unfatigued by the flight. We should, indeed, in such cases, be inclined to consider this celebrated author endowed with that faculty of 'ubiquity,' which he ascribes to Bonaparte, and of which he represents his own Malise possessed. Now we think it is just the reverse with Mr. Wordsworth. Whenever, in perusing his works, we have been obliged to catch hold of his poetic mantle, for the purpose of being assisted from trisyllable to trisyllable, far from mistaking it for 'the winged robe' of Loke, we have rather found the wearer possessed of an unwieldy, Vulcanic locomotion.

The following passage contains so much sterling ore, that we have been induced to quote it at length, notwithstanding the alloy of 'sweet savour,' (*alias*, the odour of sanctity,) – of the anti-rhyme of 'omen,' and 'coming,' – and of the 'medicable wounds:' –

[Quotes 'Ode. 1816', *PW*, III, pp. 160–1, ll. 161–75, and 'Ode. 1815', *PW*, III, pp. 153–4 and footnotes, ll. 16–86:

> Preserve, O Lord! within our hearts . . .
> Her hope of lasting glory for the whole.

> — Yet might it well become that City now . . .
> Unheard by them, their deeds shall celebrate!]

To the succeeding passage we have strong objections, as depicting the Deity in too prominent a light, as the author of evil. We select however the following powerful image: –

> — The fierce Tornado sleeps within thy courts –
> He hears the word – he flies –
> And navies perish in their ports;
> For Thou art angry with thine enemies!
> ['Ode. 1815', *PW*, III, p. 154, ll. 98–101]

The concluding passage is very pleasing; but we could have dispensed with the sing-song, or namby-pamby (Mr. Wordsworth has our full permission to choose which epithet he pleases) of the following lines: –

> Of mysteries revealed,
> And judgments unrepealed, –
> Of earthly revolution,
> And final retribution, –
> ['Ode. 1816', *PW*, III, p. 163, ll. 238–41]

We shall close our remarks on the Thanksgiving Ode, by transcribing the opening lines of the passage just mentioned: –
[Quotes *ibid.*, *PW*, III, p.162, ll. 205–19:

> But hark – the summons! – down the placid Lake . . .
> As if the fretted roof were riven.]

The ode which immediately succeeds that we have just dispatched commences thus: –

> WHEN the soft hand of sleep had *closed the latch*
> On the tired household of corporeal sense . . .
> ['Ode. 1814', *PW*, III, p.143]

A celestial, or, at least, aerial 'Visitant' is then introduced, who 'may be' 'Saint George,' and who delivers forthwith some twenty lines of poetry, in a neat and appropriate manner, very much in the style of Mr. Wordsworth himself, in which he enjoins both 'Virgins,' and 'Matrons grave,' to present the warriors of Waterloo with silver medals, to be duly appended to their button-holes by 'green chaplets,' that is, ribbons of threepenny breadth. After this, in compliance with the manducating propensities of our English brethren, we find

> The feast dealt forth with bounty unconfined;
> [*Ibid.*, *PW*, III, p.146, l. 70]

where we shall leave the Homeric heroes at their roast-beef and plum-pudding, and pass on to a brief consideration of the 'Miscellaneous Poems.'

The first of these is a monster in literature – a poem in fourteen lines, not a sonnet!! In the second, we are, we presume, presented with a delineation of Mr. Wordsworth's proper character, his skill in making prophecies (both of past as well as of future events,) not forgotten: –

> He whose experienced eye can pierce the array
> Of past events,—to whom, in vision clear,
> The aspiring heads of future things appear,
> Like mountain-tops whence mists have roll'd away:
>> ('Occasioned by the Battle of Waterloo. February, 1816)
>> ['The Bard . . .', *PW*, III, p. 150, ll. 5–8]

It had been well however, if Mr. Wordsworth had published this very pleasing little poem a short time after the battle of Waterloo, as it is intended to furnish a canon, according to which candidate Pæan-hymnsters should examine themselves, before they presume to point the pen, or skewer, for Waterloo purposes. As this wholesome measure might have startled the consciences of some of them, by convincing them of their inability adequately to chaunt the praises of Prince Arthur, we should probably have been saved from much English, Scotch, Irish-English, and English-Latin absurdity.

It is now high time to think of bidding farewell to Mr. Wordsworth, both prophet and poet. There is one notable piece of information, how-ever, contained in his poem, 'composed &c.' ['Humanity, delighting to behold'] which we conceive he would be little obliged to us for passing over in silence, and it is our apprehension of incurring his disapproba-tion, that alone induces us to extend this long article a little further. In Homer's Iliad, mention is made of certain horses who had the North-wind for their sire . . . now as such queer horses would be of incalculable advantage for conveying expresses, drawing flying artillery, and lovers to Gretna Green &c. &c., we have often wondered that antiquaries never turned their thoughts towards tracing the stock, and discovering whether any of the breed still remained, or whether, the race was completely extinct. What then was our surprise and satisfaction at finding – pursuant to the following lines: –

> Fleet the Tartar's reinless steed, –
> But fleeter far the pinions of the Wind,
> Which from Siberian caves the monarch freed,
> And sent him forth, with squadrons of his kind,

And bade the Snow their ample backs bestride,
And to the battle ride; –
['Humanity, delighting to behold', *PW*, III, p. 141,
ll. 26–31]

at finding – we repeat – that the descendants of those very same windy
animals were instrumental in chasing the French out of Russia, and that
their 'monarch' wisely kept them pent up in 'Siberian caves' (that is – in
Ulysses-bags, or, balloons, from *cavus*, 'hollow,') until a fit opportunity
should arrive of sending them forth, bestrode by flakes of 'Snow,' well
booted and spurred. What has become of those Æolians— whether it is
to Mr. Sadler, father or son, or to the æronauts or æronautesses of Ham-
burgh, or Paris, that they have been presented – or whether they now
form a very handsome stud for Mr. M. G. Lewis, being bestowed upon
him, as a compliment well merited by his fine Poem, 'The Cloud King' –
we leave it to more skilful antiquaries to determine. This interesting
discovery we are the more pleased at promulgating, as it serves for a
parallel to that of the black Jews in India, descendants of the ten tribes
and a half, who were lost, or mislaid, after the captivity.

EDITOR'S NOTES

1. 'What seemed good to the poet'/'what the poet decides', Lucian, *How to
   Write History*, 8.4: in poetry (in contrast to history) freedom is absolute and
   there is one law/rule—the will/decision of the poet.
2. Greek quotation book.
3. 'From Paris to Peru, from Japan as far as Rome'.

205.

Unsigned review, *Monthly Review*, January 1817, LXXXII, 98–100

A sacredness belongs to poetry, as we have always thought, which ill
adapts it to the bustle and business of contemporary transactions.
Whether the feeling of dislike which we own that we entertain for
'Odes written on the Occasion of Recent Public Events,' and for all such
every-day effusions, arises from their number and from their general

mediocrity; or whether some suspicion of adulation always attaches to the poetry which celebrates living merit; or, lastly, and perhaps most efficiently, whether the perusal of the high-flown descriptions in prose which the newspapers of the new æra contain, on every opportunity of rejoicing for a victory, pre-occupies our minds, and indisposes us to the repetition of the same images and ideas in the pages of their poetical brethren; whether, we say, either or all of these causes may be said to influence our taste, we cannot with cordial pleasure enjoy the very best of these gazettes in verse. Mr. Wordsworth, indeed, has written a little Thanksgiving of his own; and so peculiarly his own, that we do not see to what human being, place, circumstance, or time, saving Mr. W. W. in good spirits on a fine Sunday morning, among the Lakes, it has more than a general reference. It is composed in all that *composing* placidity of style which is so characteristic of this rural and romantic personage; and it is very pious, and so far so good: but it is also very quaint, and very prosaic. The thoughts are sometimes poetical: but the expressions, according to the author's happy theory of familiarity in the language of verse, are often of the most conversational cast; and the whole effect of the poem is very much that of a moderate dose of magnesia, inspirited with a small quantity of lemon-juice. We shall offer our readers a tea-spoon full or two of this harmless mixture . . .

We select . . . [a] little example of the tranquil and the resigned. The fondness of Mr. W. W. for 'green leaves' and 'roaring torrents' is curiously exemplified in this passage.

> Land of our fathers! *precious unto me*
> Since the first joys of thinking infancy;
> When of thy gallant chivalry I read,
> And hugged the volume on my sleepless bed!
> O England! – dearer far than life is dear,
> If I forget thy prowess, never more
> Be thy ungrateful son allowed to hear
> Thy green leaves rustle, or thy torrents roar!
> But how can *He* be faithless to the past,
> Whose soul, intolerant of base decline,
> Saw in thy virtue a celestial sign,
> That bade him hope, and to his hope cleave fast!
> ['Ode. 1816', *PW*, III, pp. 159–60 in footnotes, ll. 138–9]

Surely this is very tame and uninteresting; very unlike what we were accustomed to read as poetry in our youth. We must say, too, that the conclusion is in the same insipid manner; – a manner which, if we had not been prepared for it by various degrees of *prosaic verse*, slowly mounting from the worst parts of Thomson up through Cowper and Southey into Wordsworth, would have been instantly rejected by the public as a gross imposition, in pretending to assume the remotest shape of poetry.

It is astonishing what we can be brought to bear by due gradations. The Indian Jugglers did not *swallow* their swords at once, and with facility: – but alas! we, the descendants of those who were enraptured by Dryden and Pope, (to look no farther back into the long succession of English genius,) we have been brought so low by the repeated exercise of unworthy patience and degrading toleration, that *we* can *swallow* any thing; and even the incredible hardihood of dividing prose into fantastic sections, and calling it verse, is now committed not only with impunity but with honour! – We are weary with expostulation, and we are sure that our readers would be equally tired with ampler quotation. We shall therefore merely add, for their information, that the pamphlet now before us contains a few dull and aukward sonnets and other minor poems at the end of the Thanksgiving Ode; and transcribing for their amusement four happy little lines from that ode, which rival any of the flowers of methodism that we have lately encountered in the shape of *hymns* or *whims*, or whatever they may be intitled:

> Preserve, O Lord! within our hearts
> The memory of thy favour,
> That else insensibly departs,
> *And loses its sweet savour!*
> [*Ibid.*, *PW*, III, p. 160, ll. 161–4]

XIV

'Peter Bell' and 'The Waggoner': reviews and opinions, 1819

206. Charles Lamb

From a letter to Wordsworth, 26 April 1819

Peter Bell (not the mock one) is excellent. For its matter, I mean. I cannot say that the style of it quite satisfies me. It is too lyrical. The auditors to whom it is feigned to be told, do not *arride me*. I had rather it had been told me, the reader, at once. Hartleap Well is the tale for me, in matter as good as this, in manner infinitely before it, in my poor judgment. Why did you not add the Waggoner? Have I thanked you though, yet, for Peter Bell? I would not *not have it* for a good deal of money . . .

. . . The mock P. B. had only this effect on me, that after twice reading it over in hopes to find *some*thing diverting in it, I reach'd your two books off the shelf and set into a steady reading of them till I had nearly finished both before I went to bed. The two of your last edition, of course, I mean. And in the morning I awoke determining to take down the Excursion. I wish the scoundrel imitator could know this.

(*The Letters of Charles and Mary Lamb*, ed. E. V. Lucas, 1935 II, 241–2)

207.

Unsigned review, *Literary Gazette*, 1 May 1819, III, 273–6

Possibly by the editor, William Jerdan (1782–1869). Jerdan, up to 1813, had been editor of the *Satirist* and had published then a parody of Wordsworth; from 1813 to 1817 he had been partner/editor with John Taylor on the Tory *Sun*. The mocking tone here might suggest Jerdan as the author. For Jerdan's later more sympathetic interest in Wordsworth, see *Autobiography of William Jerdan* (1853), IV, 237–40.

There are, it is said, a considerable number of persons who not only admire the style of those who have been called the *Lake School* of poets, but who uphold their productions as the only true and genuine poetry extant. It seems impossible that any thing backed by such a number of opinions should be utterly worthless; but, with every disposition to defer to the judgment of others, we are sorry to say that we can by no means become converts to this way of thinking. Unfortunately, PETER BELL seems to us to possess more of the deformities and fewer of the beauties which are occasionally scattered over the author's productions than many of his former publications; insomuch that all our unfavourable impressions are strengthened and confirmed, and all our wishes to be *pleased* most *unpleasantly* baffled. This may arise, perhaps, from the poem being an early effort; for the dedication (to Mr. Southey) informs us that it 'first saw the light' in 1798, though pains have since been bestowed to 'fit it for filling *permanently* a station, however, humble, in the literature of the country.' Mr. Wordsworth adds that such has been the aim of all his endeavours in poetry, which have been sufficiently laborious to prove that he deems the art not lightly to be approached. In the present instance, as in former instances, this labour appears to be ill bestowed. One man polishes diamonds, and produces gems fit for a monarch's crown; another polishes muscle shells, and the utmost attainment of his art is a toy for children.

Peter Bell is a strange story, written to shew that supernatural agency may be dispensed with, and yet the imaginative faculty 'be called forth as imperiously, and for kindred results of pleasure, by incidents, within the compass of poetic probability, in the humblest departments of daily life.' The framework for this demonstration is not unworthy of the proposition. The Hero, a low and abandoned vagrant (whose character our extracts will develop more particularly) roaming at night for pleasure or for plunder, finds a lean ass on the bank of a river, which he determines to steal. 'Your dull ass,' however, 'never mends his pace with beating,' and this ass will not stir at all, but bends ruefully over the water. In the water is the drowned body of its master, which it has watched, without tasting food, for four days and nights. The apparition of this corse terrifies the marauder; he drags it out, and mounts the ass in search of the friends of the deceased, whom the animal now willingly trudges along to find. On their road Peter is appalled by loud shrieks in a wood, proceeding from the dead man's son; by some drops of blood upon the road proceeding from the ass's head, which he had broken; by some subterranean noises proceeding from a corps of miners; and by some earthly noises proceeding from a public house, which the conscience-stricken rider now avoids with horror. The ass finally turns up a lane where the widow of its drowned owner resides; the catastrophe is unfolded; the body buried; and Peter Bell

> Forsook his crimes, repressed his folly,
> And, after ten months melancholy,
> Became a good and honest man.
>> [*Peter Bell*, *PW*, II, p. 382, ll. 1133–5]

How he manages this with '*twelve wives*,' for such is the number assigned to him by the author, we are not informed: as they had all equal claims upon him, it may be supposed that he lived in a goodly and honest manner with them all, voluntarily inflicting upon himself the Hungarian punishment for polygamy.

To this story, far too mean, as we think, for dignity, and far too insignificant for an interest and pathos to be sustained through three long parts, is prefixed a rhapsody under the title of Prologue, beginning thus:

> There's something in a flying horse,
> There's something in a huge balloon;
> But through the clouds I'll never float
> Until I have a little Boat,
> Whose shape is like the crescent-moon.
>
> And now I *have* a little Boat,
> In shape a very crescent moon:
> Fast through the clouds my Boat can sail;
> But if perchance your faith should fail,
> Look up – and you shall see me soon!
>> [*Ibid.*, *PW*, II, pp. 331–2, ll. 1–10]

This seems to be a plagiarism from the equally well-painted piece of imagination –

> There was an old woman went up in a blanket
> Twenty times as high as the moon,
> Where she was going ne'er a one asked her,
> But in her hand she carried a broom.

Only *this old woman* had an object; while Mr. Wordsworth has none, and if he were addressed in the same style he could not give so satisfactory an answer:

> *Old woman, old woman, old woman*, quoth I,
> Where are you going, you're flying so *high*:
> I'm going to sweep the cobwebs from the sky,
> And you may follow *me* – if you can fly?

We must follow the author, whose prologue thus proceeds, after noticing his friends' affright at his skiff and him:

> Meanwhile I from the helm admire
> The pointed horns of my canoe:
> [*Ibid., PW*, II, p. 332, ll. 16–17]

Quære – how can a helmsman sit *in* a boat so as to see both stem and stern at once? Perhaps just in the same way as he *dives upward* in the ensuing verse;

> Away we go, my Boat and I –
> Frail man ne'er sat in such another;
> Whether among the winds we strive,
> Or *deep* into the *heavens* we *dive*,
> Each is contented with the other.
>
> Away we go – and what care we
> For treasons, tumults, and for wars?
> We are as *calm* in our delight
> As is the crescent-moon so bright
> Among the scattered stars.
> [*Ibid., PW*, II, p. 332, ll. 21–30]

This *calm* was 'striving among the winds' only four lines before:

> Up goes my Boat between the [two] stars
> Through many a *breathless* field of light:
> [*Ibid., PW*, II, p. 332, ll. 31–2]

Though we never saw a *breathing* field, this is evidently no place for us to take breath in, so we run on through all the signs of the Zodiack, and over all the planets, still casting a glance however to the earth, where, in metre truly doggerel,

> Yon tawny slip is Libya's sands –
> That silver thread the river Dnieper –
> And look, where clothed in brightest green
> Is a sweet isle, of isles the queen;
> Ye fairies from all evil keep her!
> [*Ibid., PW*, II, p. 334, ll. 61–5]

We are glad to descend from the clouds to the poet's abode, even though he there introduces us to the company who are to hear his tale in such sad sportive simplicity as he imagines this to be.

> To the stone table in my garden,
> Loved haunt of many a summer hour,
> The Squire is come; – his daughter Bess
> Beside him in the cool recess
> Sits blooming like a flower.
>
> With these are many more convened;
> They know not I have been so far –
> I see them there in number nine
> Beneath the spreading Weymouth pine –
> I see them – there they are!
> [*Ibid.*, *PW*, II, p. 337, ll. 156–65]

How like an old nurse bo-peeping with a baby?

> There sits the Vicar and his Dame;
> And there my good friend, Stephen Otter;
> And, ere the light of evening fail,
> To them I must relate the tale
> Of Peter Bell the Potter.
> [*Ibid.*, *PW*, II, p. 337, ll. 166–70]

Miss Betsy is quite delighted with the Bard's arrival from his aerial excursion, where it was likely enough that Peter Bell the potter would go to pot, and thus *naturally* exclaimed –

> 'Oh, here he is!' cried little Bess –
> She saw me at the garden door,
> 'We've waited anxiously and long,'
> They cried, and all around me throng,
> Full nine of them, *or more!*
> [*Ibid.*, *PW*, II, p. 338, ll. 176–80]

However sickly and absurd this last line may be considered, it is no unfit prelude to the story itself, of which having given the outline, we shall now quote some passages. Among the Hero's other rambles

645

> —he had been at Inverness;
> And Peter, by the mountain rills,
> Had danced his rounds with Highland lasses;
> And he had lain beside his asses
> On lofty Cheviot Hills –
> [Ibid., PW, II, p. 340, ll. 221–5]

Two of these lines might be mended with this Potter-Don-Juan. But we leave the suggestion to Mr. W. and journey on.

> And he had trudged through Yorkshire dales,
> Among the rocks and winding *scars*;
> Where deep and low the hamlets lie
> Beneath their little patch of sky.
> And little lot of stars:
> [Ibid., PW, II, p. 340, ll. 226–30]

With any thing less *winding* than *scars* (abrupt angular and precipitous ravines or faces of rock) we are unacquainted; the phrase is as much nature as the namby-pamby about little lots of stars is poetry. But of Peter? Peter, we have mentioned, is a worthless rascal –

> Of all that lead a lawless life,
> Of all that love their lawless lives,
> In city or in village small,
> He was the wildest far of all; –
> He had a dozen wedded wives.

> Nay, start not! – wedded wives – and twelve!
> But how one wife could e'er come near him,
> In simple truth I cannot tell;
> For be it said of Peter Bell,
> To see him was to fear him.
> [Ibid., PW, II, pp. 341–2, ll. 276–85]

> He had a dark and sidelong walk, –
> [Ibid., PW, II, p. 342, l. 306]

That is, like a crab; but how a walk can be dark, unless figuratively spoken of blindness, we do not comprehend. His particular nocturnal perambulation, and meeting with the ass, the subject of this poem, being fully and faithfully delineated, the tale advances, though slowly, through pleonasms.

> All, all is silent, rocks and woods,
> All still and silent – far and near;
> Only the ass, with motion dull
> Upon the pivot of his skull
> Turns round his long left ear.
>
> Thought Peter, What can mean all this?
> [*Ibid.*, *PW*, II, p. 348, ll. 411–16]

And we think what can all this mean? The pillory being put down by Act of Parliament, not only asses, but rogues, may now turn their long left ears on the pivots of their skulls, only, perhaps Mr. Curtis the aurist will object to the anatomy of the figure. If that celebrated practitioner would think it a *foolish*, Peter Bell declares it to be a *desperate* trick.

> 'Ill cure you of these desperate tricks' –
> And with deliberate action slow,
> His staff high-raising, in the pride
> Of skill, upon the ass's hide
> He dealt a sturdy blow.
> [*Ibid.*, *PW*, II, p. 349, ll. 421–5]

He continues to belabour the ass, as the author continues to be-labour his poetry; but nevertheless neither of them makes way. Indeed the parallel effect on ass and poem (if we may personify it) seems to run, as the saying is, on all fours.

> Upon the beast the sapling rings, –
> Heav'd his lank sides, his limbs they stirred;
> He gave a groan – and then another,
> Of that which went before the brother,
> And then he gave a third.
>
> All by the moonlight river side
> He gave three miserable groans;
> ' 'Tis come then to a pretty pass,'
> Said Peter to the groaning ass,
> 'But I will bang your bones!'
> [*Ibid.*, *PW*, II, p. 349, ll. 441–50]

Having disposed of this birth of male twin groans, we have a sort of parody upon them in

> A loud and piteous bray,

647

which the *banging* elicited. The effect of this bray is quite *supernatural,* though the author pretends to have dispensed with its agency.

> This *out-cry* (of the ass) on the heart of Peter
> Seems like a *note of joy* to strike, –
> Joy on the heart of Peter knocks; –
> But in the echo of the rocks
> Was something Peter did not like.
> [*Ibid., PW*, II, p. 351, ll. 466–70]

If this be not maudlin trash, we cannot tell what is: but it is the same throughout.

> Among the rocks and winding crags –
> Among the mountains far away –
> Once more the ass did lengthen out
> More ruefully an endless shout
> The long dry see-saw of his horrible bray.
>
> What is there now in Peter's heart?
> Or whence the might of this strange sound?
> The moon uneasy looked and dimmer,
> The broad blue heavens appeared to glimmer,
> And the rocks staggered all about [should read 'around'].
> [*Ibid., PW*, II, pp. 351–2, ll. 476–85]

At the braying of an ass – truly, the *moon* has too much to do in this business. Peter, in revenge, resolves to throw the donkey into the water, but meets 'a startling sight' in the pool. After many equally pertinent inquiries, touching this sight, it is asked,

> Is it a party in a parlour?
> Crammed just as they on earth were crammed—
> Some sipping punch, some sipping tea,
> But as you by their faces see,
> All silent and all damned!
> [*Ibid., PW*, II, p. 354, in footnotes, ll. 515/6]

We suspect the conclusion is a pun on a water dam, but for the rest of the verse we again profess our ignorance of meaning, never having seen such a damned, silent, face-betrayed, punch-sipping, tea-drinking party in a parlour on earth, as is here alluded to. But after all, reader, what do you think the spectacle at the bottom of the river really is? It is, in short, the drowned body of the ass's master.

> Ah well-a-day for Peter Bell! –
> He will be turned to *iron* soon,
> Meet statue for the court of Fear.
>> [*Ibid.*, *PW*, II, p. 355, ll. 521–3]

Would not *Bell-metal* be more appropriate?

He falls into a trance, but wakes again, and '*feels* the glimmering of the moon,' (still harping on the *moon*). He then mounts the ass, and trusts to the wiser brute to find out the dead man's relatives. The cry of a wood-boy, 'distrest,' by looking at a dark cave, and shrieking fearfully in consequence of discovering this appalling and wonderful phenomenon assails them on their route, and here our ass, which, like the Devil in Milton, may fairly challenge the post of hero in competition with Peter Bell the potter, proves himself an *uncommon scholar*, for

> Of that intense and piercing cry
> The listening ass doth *rightly spell*:
> Wild as it is *he* there can *read*
> Some intermingled notes that plead
> With touches irresistible;
>> [*Ibid.*, *PW*, II, p. 362, ll. 651–5]

This miraculous power in the ass works conviction in his rider, who from observing such knowledge in a beast, begins to think vengeance and visitation for his past crimes will overtake him. They trudge on, and one of their pieces of landscape is thus poetically described:

> The rocks that [t]ower on either side
> Built up a wild fantastic scene;
> Temples like those among the *Hindoos*,
> And mosques, and spires, and abbey *windows*,
> And castles all with ivy green.
>> [*Ibid.*, *PW*, II, p. 364, ll. 681–5]

But the *enchantment* of this scene is to come:

> And while the ass pursues his way,
> Along this solitary dell,
> As pensively his steps advance,
> The mosques and spires *change countenance*
> And *look at* Peter Bell.
>> [*Ibid.*, *PW*, II, p. 364, ll. 686–90]

Would it not have been more natural if Peter Bell had changed countenance and looked at them? Peter's *next* alarm is at 'a *dancing* leaf,' where there is no tree nor bush, and his *next* at a drop of the ass's blood, as stated in our outset. The *next* fact in this poem, whence the *supernatural* is excluded, is in an episode about a word self-written in flame upon a pious book which a 'gentle soul' was reading; and the *next* again, introduced with due solemnity, for

> The ass turned round his head – and *grinned* –
> [*Ibid.*, *PW*, II, p. 370, l. 825]

is the 'appalling process' of a 'murmur pent within the earth,' and occasioned by a troop of miners blasting with gunpowder 'some twenty fathoms under ground.' The *next* conscience striker is a ruined chapel, which reminds Peter of that 'in the shire of Fife,' where he married his '*sixth* wife.' The last of all is an apparition of himself, and of a Highland girl whom he had seduced to death. What is most remarkable in this place is, that the ass does not heed these imaginary terrors:

> Calm is the well-deserving brute,
> *His* peace, hath no offence betray'd; –
> [*Ibid.*, *PW*, II, p. 376, ll. 936–7]

What however crowns Peter's compunction and remorse is a voice from the tabernacle: –

> Within, a fervent methodist
> Is preaching to no heedless flock.
> [*Ibid.*, *PW*, II, p. 376, ll. 944–5]

The poem now becomes, we doubt not with the best of meaning, but in truth very profanely sacred: the recognition of the ass by the drowned man's distracted family is however feelingly told, and, with fewer puerilities than any other part, the sincere repentance of Peter Bell concludes the tale.

We gladly take our leave of it. There are perhaps half a dozen fine passages, but nothing can in our mind redeem the besetting absurdity of the whole. It convinces us more and more that the system on which Mr. Wordsworth builds his rhyme is radically wrong; that no talent can render that pathetic which is essentially ludicrous, nor great which is decidedly vulgar, nor delightful which is glaringly disgusting. That any thing like genius should be employed on such a mass of folly as Peter Bell presents, is indeed both astonishing and vexatious. Having no view of it but as a gross perversion of intellect, we have freely delivered our sentiments: we should be sorry to hurt the author's self-love by applying the argumentum ad ridiculum, but considering his example as most injurious to the poetic character of our country, we cannot compromise our public sense of the error so far as to spare our personal feelings.

There is, as a frontispiece, a pretty design by Sir George Beaumont, of a picturesque and romantic scene, not unworthy the pencil of Salvator. It is, however, very ill engraved, and looks like rotten ice. Four sonnets upon wild views by Westall are added to the principal poem.

208. Leigh Hunt

Unsigned review, *Examiner*, 2 May 1819, 282–3

This is another didactic little horror of Mr. Wordsworth's, founded on the bewitching principles of fear, bigotry, and diseased impulse. *Peter Bell* is a potter, who has rambled about the country, and been as wilful, after his fashion, as any Lake poet. His tastes indeed are different. He sees no beauty in mere solitariness, and is not alive to the abstract sentiment of a ditch; neither does he dance with daffodils. He is, in fact, a little over social, chusing rather to dance with gypsies, and having had no less than a dozen wives. He is like the Friar in Chaucer; he

> *Will* drinke the liquor of the vine,
> And have a joly wenche in everie towne.

One day, however, losing himself in a wood, he meets with a stray jack-ass, who lies upon the ground by a river's side, and looks mysterious. *Peter* has a royal contempt for inferior animals (not that the Poet so words it, but such is the fact), and belabours the poor jack-ass in a dreadful manner, till it groans and then looks into the water, and then at *Peter*. He looks in his turn, and in the water what does he see? This is a question which the Poet himself asks his Readers, putting a number of samples of horrid sights, by way of help to their memories. Of course they cannot answer him; but it turns out that one thing at least which *Peter* did see was the corpse of a man newly drowned, the owner of the jack-ass. The animal's attachment makes the first impression on

651

Peter's imagination; he sees him inclined to show him the way to the deceased's house, and accordingly rides him thither, where he finds the widow and children bitterly lamenting. For the final impression resulting from this scene he is also prepared, as he rode along, by the sound of a Damnation Sermon, which a Methodist is vociferating from a chapel. The consequence is that after a melancholy of eleven months, he is thoroughly reformed, and has a proper united sense of hare-bells and hell-fire.

Now all this, we conceive, is as weak and vulgar in philosophy as can be. It is the philosophy of violence and hopelessness. It is not teaching ignorance, but scourging it. If Mr. Wordsworth means to say that fear may occasionally do good, we grant it; but we say that nine times out of ten, it does harm, and is likely to make a man's after-thoughts desperate and resentful, and still oftener selfish and servile. The very hope of such things as Methodism is founded in hopelessness, and that too of the very worst sort – namely, hopelessness of others, and salvation for itself. *Peter Bell* is an ill-taught blackguard. There is his whole history. The growth of such persons must be prevented by good and kind teaching. If they are suffered to grow up without it, and are then to be dosed with horrors proportioned to the strength of the disease inflicted on them, they have as much right to complain as any that suffer from them. It is no more incumbent on them to think themselves objects of God's anger (thus giving them a bad idea of God, as well as man) than it is on the most didactic of the Lake Poets to think himself wise and virtuous. The good old fable of the son who bit off his mother's ear at the gallows is, and will ever remain, worth a thousand such stories.

We are really and most unaffectedly sorry to see an excellent poet like Mr. Wordsworth returning, in vulgar despair, to such half-witted prejudices; especially when we meet with such masterly descriptions as the following. It is a portrait as true in the colouring as any of Mr. Crabbe's, and deeper thoughted.

[Quotes *Peter Bell*, *PW*, II, pp. 342–3, ll. 291–320:

> A savage wildness round him hung
> As of a dweller out of doors . . .
> Against the wind and open sky.]

But what is to be said to the following Methodistical nightmare? It is part of the questions of which we spoke, when *Peter* sees the spectacle in the water.

Is it a fiend that to a stake
Of fire his desperate self is tethering?
Or stubborn spirit doom'd to yell
In solitary ward or cell,
Ten thousand miles from all his brethren?
[*Ibid.*, *PW*, II, p. 354, ll. 511–15]

Is it a party in a parlour?
Cramm'd just as they on earth were cramm'd—
Some sipping punch, some sipping tea,
But, as you by their faces see,
All silent and all damn'd!
[*Ibid.*, *PW*, II, p. 354, ll. 515–16]

What pretty little hopeful imaginations for a reforming philosopher! Is Mr. Wordsworth in earnest or is he not, in thinking that his fellow-creatures are to be damned? If he is, who is to be made really better or more comfortable in this world, by having such notions of another? If not, how wretched is this hypocrisy?

Mr. Wordsworth, in the course of his mystic musings on *Peter* has the following passage on a jackass's grin:

Let them whose voice can stop the clouds –
Whose cunning eye can see the wind –
Tell to a curious world the cause
Why, making here a sudden pause,
The Ass turn'd his head – and *grinn'd*.

Appalling process! – I have mark'd
The like on heath – in lonely wood,
And, verily, have seldom met
A spectacle more hideous – yet
It suited Peter's present mood.
[*Ibid.*, *PW*, II, p. 370, ll. 821–30]

Pray admire the way in which the poet first begs the question about a meaning in the ass's grin, and then calls upon those who 'can see the wind' to disprove it. Surely the burden of the proof lies upon the ass's worthy spectator. We refer him however, if he still makes his call, to the Learned Pig.

Yet it is in this morbid spirit that Mr. Wordsworth writes, for the benefit of the world!

The poem is dedicated in an odd shy way, that has anything but the look of sincerity, to 'Robert Southey, Esq. P. L.,' that is to say (for Mr. Wordsworth has left it unexplained), not *Precious Looby*, but *Poet Laureat*. It has a Proem also, which the author thinks it necessary to inform us was written some years back, about an aerial living Boat which he can ride if he chuses about the upper regions, but declines so doing for the benefit of the lower. There are fine passages in it, but Mr. Wordsworth should never affect vivacity. It leads him to expose himself in such unwieldy levities as these –

> There's something in a flying horse,
> And something in a huge balloon;
> But through the clouds I'll never float
> Until I have a little boat,
> Whose shape is like the crescent-moon.
>
> And now I *have* a little boat,
> In shape a very crescent-moon, &c.
> [*Ibid.*, *PW*, II, pp. 331–2, ll. 1–7]

The pamphlet concludes with three sonnets on some of Mr. Westall's landscapes. The first is a fine one, though running off into the old vein. The conclusion of one of the others is very melancholy, and would let us into the secret of Mr. Wordsworth's philosophy, if nothing else did. He forsakes the real cause of the world, and then abuses what he has injured. And yet this is he who would make us in love with the visible creation!

> Vain earth! – false world! Foundations must be laid
> In Heav'n; for, mid the wreck of *is* and *was*,
> Things incomplete and *purposes betrayed*
> Make sadder transits o'er truth's mystic glass
> Than noblest objects utterly decayed.
> ['Was the aim frustrated', *PW*, III p. 37, ll. 10–14]

Alas! Alas for the *ci-devant* patriots, and *soi-disant* philosophers! We happen to write this article on the First of May; and thanks to greater poets than Mr. Wordsworth, and to the nature whom he so strangely recommends, can enjoy the beautiful season on earth, without thinking the less hopefully of heaven.

209. Henry Crabb Robinson

Extracts from his diary, May 1819

a. 3 May 1819

Calling on Walter (I dined also with Walter, Fraser and Barnes there), Fraser I attacked on a trimming article in yesterday's *Times* about Catholic Emancipation, and Barnes attacked me about *Peter Bell*. But this is a storm I must yield to. Wordsworth has set himself back ten years by the publication of this unfortunate work . . .

(*Henry Crabb Robinson on Books and their Writers*, ed. Edith J. Morley, 1938, I, 230)

b. 11 May 1819

Lamb spoke of *Peter Bell*, which he considers as one of the worst of Wordsworth's works. The lyric narrative Lamb has no taste for, he is disgusted by the introduction, which he deems puerile, and the story he thinks ill told, though he allows the idea to be good . . .

(*Ibid.*)

210.

Unsigned notice, *Gentleman's Magazine*, May 1819, LXXXIX, 441–2

THIS delectable Tale cannot but excite the admiration of the present times; and will undoubtedly be considered by *Prince Posterity* as one of the brightest gems in the Author's collected volumes. It is not the ephemeral production of the day; but 'has, in its manuscript state, nearly survived its minority; for it first saw the light in the summer of 1798.'

In a Prefatory address to his worthy friend Mr. Southey, the Poet says, [Quotes the greater part of the address.]

The opening of the Poem is elegantly simple; perhaps sublime: [Quotes the 'Prologue' to *Peter Bell*, *PW*, II, pp. 331–2, ll. 1–10:

> There's something in a flying horse . . .
> Look up – and you shall *see me* soon!]

Seen him we have – and *wept* (as many other tender readers will) at the singular adventures of *Peter Bell the Potter* – at the untimely death of the *sixth* of his *twelve wives* – and at the instinct of the braying friend, who, after having lost his original master in the river, and remained for four days too sorrowful to eat, though in the middle of a fine pasture, conducted Peter Bell, first to the place where lay the drowned cottager; and then led him safely to the dwelling of the afflicted widow.

The Tale is so pleasingly melancholy, that we leave it to the good taste of those who will eagerly devour it, and haste to the conclusion:

[Quotes the last three stanzas, *ibid.*, *PW*, II, p. 346 and footnotes:

> Here ends my Tale . . .
> Became a good and honest man.]

Four Sonnets are affixed to the Volume; and it has a most beautiful Frontispiece, of romantic scenery, engraved by Bromley, from a Picture by Sir George Beaumont, Bart.

211.

Review signed 'J. B.' *European Magazine*, May 1819, LXXV, 445–8

The present period is rich in the master-spirits of poetry – perhaps at no time have more brilliant names adorned the poetical annals of our country than in our day – Even the age of Elizabeth, the Augustan æra of our poetry in point of number and excellence, cannot be said to have surpassed our latter times.

In the first rank of the bards of our own day, Mr. Wordsworth may justly be classed. With that boldness which is the characteristic of genius, he has chosen a path rarely trodden by poets, and has shed over his uninviting and apparently sterile subjects an elegance and brilliancy which nothing but the energetic influence of such talents as he possesses could have communicated.

In his choice of these subjects, he seems rather to have been actuated by the discriminating influence of his own judgment, than the desire of gaining popularity; for with his high poetical feelings, it cannot be doubted, that had he chosen the more common subjects on which verse is employed, he would have succeeded better in obtaining the applause of the less reflecting part of his readers: – but an enthusiastic admirer of

Nature in all her forms, he appears to be so completely devoted to his passion, that he despises the common machinery of poetry, and trusting to the inspiration of 'the Goddess of his idolatry,' floats gently down the current of his imaginations, and supplies by the naked beauty of his Muse the absence of all ornament, '*Nuda si, ma contenta.*'[1]

His is the poetry of solitude, the very eloquence of the inanimate objects of Nature, and revives in our minds the impressions made by her beauties in those days of happy youth, when every breath of heaven, every flower which bloomed beneath our feet, spoke to the soul in a tone which awoke a vibrating chord of feeling. It penetrates the callousness which an intercourse with the world, and all its intricacies and disappointments, have collected round the heart. It is like the breathing silence of a summer's evening, where all is distinct and invigorating, but solemn, still, and gentle.

He sees with microscopic eyes the numerous beautiful productions which present themselves too frequently unheeded to the cursory observer, and exhibits with minute discrimination the harmonies which have lost their influence from their frequent occurrence; like a stranger in the land, he points out excellencies and discovers combinations which the denizens had never beheld, or to which their frequent familiarity had deadened their admiration.

The tale is preceded by a prologue, in which the poet takes occasion, in a playful and ingenious manner, to point out the inclination of his genius, which is under the form of a flying boat. After a long excursive range into regions of air and fancy, the poet wishes to return to his dear earth

[Quotes *Peter Bell*, *PW*, II, pp. 336–7, ll. 131–50:

Long have I loved what I behold . . .
'Tis lodg'd within her silent tear.]

The substance of the tale is the most simple in its organization that can he imagined; its intent is to paint the effect produced on the mind of a reprobate vagabond by the mute force of solitude and of natural objects. The gradual progress from the first softening impulse to reflection on his guilty courses, thence to remorse, and finally to repentance, is developed in the most pathetic and masterly manner.

He two and thirty years, or more,
Had been a wild and woodland rover.
[*Ibid.*, *PW*, II, p. 339, ll. 206–7]

*   *   *   *   *   *

[Then quotes *ibid.*, *PW*, II, pp. 340–2, ll. 241–95 and p. 343, ll. 311–15:

> He rov'd among the vales and streams . . .
> Of mountains and of dreary moors.
>
> His forehead wrinkled was and furr'd . . .
> Beneath the glaring sun.]

'One beautiful November night,' Peter Bell is bewildered in a thick wood on the banks of the River Swale – after journeying some time, he arrives at

> — of earth a small green spot,
> With rocks encompass'd round. –
> [*Ibid.*, *PW*, II, p. 345, ll. 369–70]
>
>   *   *   *   *   *   *
> When turning round his head he sees
> A solitary Ass.
> [*Ibid.*, *PW*, II, p. 346, ll. 384–5]

With the laxity of principle which he possesses, Peter does not hesitate to appropriate the ass to himself, at least for the purpose of carrying him out of the wood – but to his astonishment the ass is unmoved by his beating – his rage is excessive, and he falls on the poor animal with redoubled brutality, but still in vain; the ass falls down, and turns towards him 'his shining hazel eye.'

> 'Twas but one mild reproachful look,
> A look more tender than severe;
> And straight in sorrow, not in dread,
> He turn'd the eyeball in his head
> Toward the river deep and clear.
> [*Ibid.*, *PW*, II, p. 349, ll. 436–40]

The ass braying in the still silence of the scene has an appalling effect on the mind of Peter – he recovers, however, from this, and

> —in resolute mood, once more
> He stoops the ass's neck to seize –
> Foul purpose quickly put to flight!
> For in the pool a startling sight
> Meets him, beneath the shadowy trees.
> [*Ibid.*, *PW*, II, p. 353 and footnotes, ll. 496–500]

The effect of the object he sees in the river is admirably described.

> He looks – he ponders – looks again;
> He sees a motion – hears a groan; –
> His eyes will burst – his heart will break –
> He gives a loud and frightful shriek,
> And drops, a senseless wight, as if his life were flown.
> [Ibid., PW, II, p. 355, ll. 526–30]

Upon his recovery from the swoon into which his terror had thrown him, he discovers what had frightened him to be the body of a dead man at the bottom of the river, the master of the ass, which he draws to the bank, when 'full suddenly the ass doth rise!

> His staring bones all shake with joy –
> And close by Peter's side he stands:
> While Peter o'er the river bends,
> The little ass his neck extends,
> And fondly licks his hands.
> [Ibid., PW, II, p. 357, ll. 561–5]

Peter Bell mounts the ass, who is now not unwilling, in hopes of being led by him to the cottage of the drowned man. Our limits will not allow us to trace the progress of the change in his feelings during the journey. Among the subjects which wring his heart 'to strong compunction and remorse,' is the following –

> But more than all his heart is stung
> To think of one, almost a child:
> A sweet and playful Highland girl,
> As light and beauteous as a squirrel,
> As beauteous and as wild!
> [Ibid., PW, II, p. 374, ll. 886–90]

[And quotes *ibid.*, *PW*, II, p. 375, ll. 901–30:

> But when she follow'd Peter Bell . . .
> My mother! Oh my mother!]

In his route, Peter passes by a chapel where 'a fervent Methodist is preaching,' and hears him hold forth the promises of the gospel dispensation to repentant sinners –

[Quotes *ibid.*, *PW*, II, p. 376, ll. 954–60:

And though your sins be red as scarlet . . .
He melted into tears.]

Peter arrives at length at the dwelling of the poor man, where the distress of his widow is painted in touching and powerful colours.

> Beside the woman Peter stands;
> His heart is opening more and more;
> A holy sense pervades his mind;
> He feels what he for human kind
> Had never felt before.
>   [*Ibid.*, *PW*, II, p. 380, ll. 1051–5]

The most eloquent and pathetic description is reserved to the last part of the poem, and forms a climax to the whole no less admirable in the idea than felicitous in the execution – it is the return of the son of the dead man, who has been seeking him in vain.

[Quotes *ibid.*, *PW*, II, pp. 381–2, ll. 1101–20:

> But he who deviously hath sought . . .
> 'Oh! God, I can endure no more!']

Let the frivolous scoff at and the hard-hearted despise such poems as this; but we do not envy that man his strength of mind who reads Peter Bell without being beguiled of tears, or who rises from the perusal without the finer and more amiable feelings of his nature being strongly excited.

EDITOR'S NOTE

1. 'Naked, yes, but happy.'

212.

Unsigned reviews, *Theatrical Inquisitor and Monthly Mirror*, XIV,
May–June 1819

a. May 1819, 369–76

Mr. Wordsworth is a Gentleman, who stands high in the literature of
our country; and though his poems do not possess that commanding
superiority over all contemporaneous productions, nor that peculiar
conformity to any fashionable style, which might occasion them to be
read with general and eager enthusiasm, on their first appearance; they
possess that genuine merit, which secures for them a large body of
admirers, amongst people of undoubted taste, and a permanent station
amongst our standard Poets. Mr. Wordsworth, we believe, is one of that
number of gentlemen, who from their residence, their intimacy, or some
coincidences in style of writing, are termed the Lake Poets; each of these
is marked by some peculiarity, which pervades his works and stamps
on them a character. Such are Messrs. Coleridge, Campbell, Crabbe,
Southey, and Montgomery. There are two characteristics, which may be
observed in Mr. Wordsworth's poems, which at a glance, may seem
inconsistent with each other, but which are nevertheless remarkable in all
his writings; the first is a mixture of refined and intricate metaphysic
with his poetry, which, though he differs widely from him in other
respects, reminds us forcibly of Cowley; in his most important productions, he philosophizes continually. We are not, for our own parts, much
inclined to admire philosophy in verse; and think that to expound science, or convey new theories, is not the province of poetry; though our
language does boast some didactic poetry, which will be coeval with its
duration. Imagination is the grand faculty for poetry. The other peculiarity of Mr. Wordsworth is an affectation of simplicity in the diction,
which is carried, sometimes, to such an excess, as to expose him to
well founded ridicule; this is more observable in his later productions.
The effect of this manner varies perpetually with the use of it; sometimes
it produces a most touching pathos, and at others degenerates into
laughable puerilty.

The Poem before us is preceded, by what is termed a prologue, in
which by an odd mixture of allegorical and plain expression, the author
disclaims all the higher regions of imagination; all supernatural machinery, and all heroic actions, and declares his resolution of relating, a simple

tale, to a little party, assembled in his garden. And simple enough the tale is indeed.

We remember in some one of Mr. Wordsworth's productions, we think it was in the Excursion, he expresses great disgust at the rustic character, declaring all the ideas of honest simplicity and guilelessness to be mere fancies, and representing the peasantry to abound as much in vices and evil passions, as the inhabitants of cities, which became additionally disgusting from the rude and untamed shape in which they appeared. [Not Wordsworth's view, but Hazlitt's: see entry 147.]

Peter Bell, the hero of the tale before us, is produced as a case in point, or an illustration of the above remark.

> A Potter, Sir, he was by trade,
> *   *   *   *   *   *   *
> And, wheresoever he appeared,
> Full twenty times was Peter feared,
> For once that Peter was respected.
>
> He two and thirty years or more,
> Had been a wild and woodland rover;
> [*Peter Bell, PW,* II, p. 339, ll. 201–7]

Cornwall, Dover, Caernarvon, Sarum, Lincoln, Doncaster, York, Leeds, Carlisle, the Lowlands of Scotland, Ayr, Aberdeen, Inverness, and the Cheviot Hills had fallen within the compass of his rambles. We must here stop to remark one pretty idea in the versification.

> Where deep and low the hamlets lie
> Beneath their little patch of sky,
> And little lot of stars.
> [*Ibid., PW,* II, p. 340, ll. 228–30]

But all this peregrination was lost upon the untoward soul of Peter.

> As well might Peter, in the Fleet,
> Have been fast bound a begging debtor; –
> He travelled here, he travelled there; –
> But not the value of a hair
> Was heart or head the better.
> [*Ibid., PW,* II, p. 340, ll. 236–40]

The adamantine nature of Peter's heart and his insensibility to nature are deduced from two circumstances; first, because

> A primrose by the river's brim
> A yellow primrose was to him,
> And it was nothing more.
> [*Ibid.*, *PW*, II, p. 341, ll. 248–50]

And secondly, because

> Small change it made in Peter's heart
> To see his gentle pannier'd train,
> *With more than vernal pleasure feeding*,
> Where e'er the tender grass was leading,
> It's earliest green along the lane.
> [*Ibid.*, *PW*, II, p. 341, ll. 251–5]

Had these been the only reasons for judging Peter insensible, we fear that we are ourselves in danger of the same imputation; for we have never been able to discover, any more than Peter, any thing more, in '*a yellow primrose*,' than a yellow primrose itself. Neither are we quite alive to the sensations to be produced by seeing a company of asses with '*more than vernal pleasure feeding.*'

A more serious accusation than these however follows,

> He had a dozen wedded wives!
> [*Ibid.*, *PW*, II, p. 341, l. 280]

This is rendered still more remarkable by the lines which immediately follow, nor is the difficulty thus started ever done away.

> But how one wife could e'er come near him,
> In simple truth I cannot tell;
> For be it said of Peter Bell,
> To see him was to fear him.
> [*Ibid.*, *PW*, II, p. 342, ll. 282–5]

This same Peter, such as he is however, in the course of a nocturnal ramble, pursued, with what intent we are not informed, passes through a quarry, in which is found a small patch of verdure by which flows a river. Near this river stands an ass, and Peter, with an aptitude of disposition very natural, immediately inclines to make this ass his own property. In this determination the ass is by no means disposed to acquiesce, being an ass of extraordinary sagacity, as appears. –

> 'What's this' cried Peter, brandishing
> A new-peel'd sapling white as cream;
> *The ass knew well what Peter said.*
> [*Ibid.*, *PW*, II, p. 346 in footnotes, ll. 395–6]

Peter, by no means delighted with a sagacity which opposed his pleasure, from 'brandishing' proceeds to exercise the 'new-peel'd sapling,' upon the poor quadruped. The first blow brings him upon his knees; the next rolls him over on his side; and a rapid succession which followed produced only 'three miserable groans.' But this, so far from exciting the compassion of Peter, draws from him this exclamation.

> But I will bang your bones!
> [*Ibid.*, *PW*, II, p. 349 in footnotes, l. 450]

That he may execute this threat more vigorously,

> Peter halts to gather breath,
> And now full clearly it was shown,
> (What he before in part had seen,)
> How gaunt was the poor ass and lean,
> Yea wasted to a skeleton.
> [*Ibid.*, *PW*, II, p. 350 in footnotes, ll. 451–5]

Peter soon perceived the inefficacy of 'banging,' upon such an ass, and adopts another plan.

> *   *   'You little mulish dog,
> I'll fling your carcase like a log,
> Head foremost down the river.'
> [*Ibid.*, *PW*, II, p. 350, ll. 458–60]

On proceeding to execute this design however, he is deterred by a 'loud and piteous bray' from the poor beast, which is once or twice repeated; his spirits are daunted and his courage shaken, for

> In the echo of the rocks
> Was something Peter did not like.
> [*Ibid.*, *PW*, II, p. 351, ll. 469–70]

Recovered however from his terrors, he once more attempts to consign this skeleton of an ass to the river –

[Quotes *ibid.*, *PW*, II, p. 353 in footnotes, ll. 496–530:

> Whereat, in resolute mood, once more . . .
> And drops, a senseless weight, as if his life were flown!]

664

The sight which had this terrible effect on Peter was the corpse of a drowned man, whom, when he returns to his senses from the swoon, he proceeds to drag from the river. Upon this the ass revives, and touching the man, Peter comes to the conclusion that

> * * * * he is the master
> Of this poor miserable ass –
> [*Ibid.*, *PW*, II, p. 358, ll. 584–5]

By some symptoms, he judges that the man had been four days in the river, which accounts in some measure, for the wretched appearance of the ass. This beast –

> That Peter on his back should mount
> He shows a wish well as be can.
> [*Ibid.*, *PW*, II, p. 358, ll. 591–2]

With which Peter complies, for this reason –

> I'll go, I'll go, whate'er betide,
> He to his home my way will guide,
> The cottage of the drowned man.
> [*Ibid.*, *PW*, II, p. 358 in footnotes, ll. 593–5]

Peter accordingly mounts and away trudges the ass. On their journey, Peter is alarmed: a loud and piercing cry, which proceeds from a lad whom he finds wandering about the country, of whom however he takes no notice but proceeds. The transactions of the night taken together seem to have had a surprising effect on the heart of Peter; his wonted hardihood of conscience has left him; he is filled with indefinable dreads and apprehensions; the cry of the boy; the appearance of the rocks, as they pass, even the rolling of a leaf on the pathway; all strike his heart as omens of evil. Proceeding along a lane, he perceives stains of blood on the road and on the stones as they pass; these strike fresh terrors to his soul, till he finds that the blood has issued from a wound which he himself had given the ass.

The third part of the poem opens with a curious anecdote, of the authenticity of which we beg leave to doubt, and which seems to border a little upon those regions of the imagination which the poet has expressed an anxiety to avoid.

[Quotes *ibid.*, *PW*, II, pp. 367–8, ll. 736–60:

> I've heard of one, a gentle soul . . .
> Out of the bottom of his heart.]

665

The author proceeds however to affirm, that he is acquainted by experience with the nature of such agency, and invokes it in behalf of Peter Bell.

[Quotes *ibid.*, *PW*, II, pp. 368–9 in footnotes, ll. 761–85:

> Dread Spirits! to torment the good . . .
> What may be done with Peter Bell!]

(*To be Continued.*)

b. June 1819, 441–46

We will, as Mr. Wordsworth does, after a digression, remind our readers where we left off, by the following couplet.

> Our travellers, ye remember well,
> Are thridding a sequestered lane;
> And Peter many tricks is trying,
> And many anodynes applying,
> To ease his conscience of its pain.
> [*Ibid.*, *PW*, II, p. 369, ll. 796–800]

It appears, that in this, he is tolerably successful for –

> * * * Peter is a deep logician
> Who hath no lack of wit mercurial;
> 'Blood drops – leaves rustle – yet,' quoth he,
> 'This poor man never, but for me,
> 'Could have had Christian burial.'
> [*Ibid.*, *PW*, II, p. 370, ll. 806–10]

The thumps upon Peter's conscience, however, are not yet at an end, the next is one of the most curious that a mortal imagination ever conceived.

> Let them whose voice can stop the clouds –
> Whose cunning eye can see the wind –
> Tell to a curious world the cause
> Why, making here a sudden pause,
> The Ass turn'd round his head – and *grinn'd*.
> [*Ibid.*, *PW*, II, p. 370, ll. 821–5]

Upon this occasion, which we should have thought highly whimsical, he proceeds to remark

Appalling process! – I have mark'd
The like on heath – in lonely wood,
And, verily, hath seldom met
A spectacle more hideous – yet
It suited Peter's present mood.

And, grinning in his turn, his teeth
He in jocose defiance show'd –
[*Ibid., PW*, II, pp. 370–1, ll. 826–32]

This circumstance of the Ass, by a preternatural flexibility of the neck, turning round his face completely to Peter, and grinning; and Peter grinning in return, must have formed a tableau, which would have made a worthy frontispiece to this work.

The noise of some miners underground, next alarms Peter, and induces him to imagine, that the ground is about to open and swallow him up. The noise of the carousers in a public house, which they pass, brings home to Peter's conscience, in its awakened state, the memory of his former dissoluteness. The principal crime which weighs on his heart, and aggravates his terrors is this.

[Quotes the account of the fate of the Highland girl who married Peter
Bell, *ibid., PW*, II, pp. 374–5, ll. 886–930:

But more than all, his heart is stung . . .
'My mother! oh my mother!'

and summarises the rest of the poem with extensive quotation.]

Our extracts from this Poem have been so copious, that our readers are in a situation to come to a correct opinion of its merits. We have been thus lavish in quotation, because the poetry is so very uneven, and has parts of such different degrees of merit, that it is not easy to stamp on it a general character. The action of the Poem seems to be repentance – to show the powerful operation of circumstances, in themselves indifferent, to awaken the conscience and generate the work of repentance, in the heart of a desperately wicked man – that Mr. Wordsworth's experience may have acquainted him with cases similar to this, and his observations, on rustic life; have encountered some Peter Bell, is very possible; but there is nothing in the circumstances of this story calculated very forcibly to arrest the attention, or convey any particular lesson. It undoubtedly possesses some very fine passages, and these will be found amongst our quotations; but they are where he deviates from that extreme simplicity which he appears to have prescribed to himself, and rises into those regions of imagination, which he in his prologue disclaims. In taking up

667

this line of simple narrative, we think Mr. Wordsworth has certainly mistaken his *forté*; it is evident from the poem before us, that his powers are evinced only when he deviates from it, and his affectation of it frequently sinks into downright puerility, and is sometimes truly ludicrous. What can be more outrageous than the idea of the Ass turning round and grinning? The Poem altogether wants interest and dignity; the hero is a person, for whom, of all others, we are least likely to feel any degree of sympathy, and this, we think, a vital defect; the action of the tale is too trifling to arrest the attention; hardly sufficient to induce the reader to proceed through the intervening narrative, from one beautiful passage to another. Mr. Wordsworth has certainly not added to his reputation by the production of 'Peter Bell;' and we think it a great pity, that powers like his, should not be concentrated on some work worthy of them.

c. Unsigned review of *Peter Bell, a Lyrical Ballad* (Reynolds), June 1819, 449–50

The reviewer is impatient with the imitation, and concludes:

Much as we regret that his merit should suffer that deterioration which it does from his excessive vanity, we are not pleased to see him handled quite so roughly as he is in the work before us: much of affectation as there may be in his lines, there is doubtless much also of real feeling; and the sensibility of a man of talent should always be shielded by his admirers, from the rude attack of those who are so greatly inferior to him. This parody possesses none of that acuteness and delicacy which gives the keen and irresistible edge to satire; it is coarse and ungentle; and, we think, will excite more of indignation amongst Mr. Wordsworth's admirers, than it will exultation in his enemies.

213.

Unsigned review, *Literary Chronicle and Weekly Review*, 29 May 1819, I, 20–1

A brief and mocking summary precedes the following conclusion.

Of all Mr. Wordsworth's poems, this is decidedly the worst; it possesses all the faults of the Lake school, without any of its beauties; and although there is an entire exclusion of every thing ornamental, we had almost said poetical, yet its simplicity is truly ridiculous, and calculated only for the nursery; nor will any defence of it which Mr. Wordsworth or his admirers can set up, ever make Peter Bell fill a permanent situation in the literature of the country, as its author has the vanity to anticipate, unless indeed the public taste should become so far perverted, as not to distinguish between the puerilities of some modern poets and the lofty and impassioned diction of those whose works have stood the test of ages, and who will be read with delight when Mr. Wordsworth and the Lake school will be entirely forgotten.

214.

Unsigned notice, *Monthly Magazine*, XLVII, 1 June 1819, 442

Mr. WORDSWORTH, the father of the baby school of the Lakes, has published some rhimes for the nursery, under the title of *Peter Bell the Potter*, so superlatively silly, as to be beneath grave criticism, or any expression of contempt contained in the idiom of the English language. We thought *The Excursion*, of the writer, had beauties which counterbalanced certain puerilities of the same kind: but *Peter Bell* is all puerility, and has, perhaps, no counterpart even in the juvenile repositories of Tabart or Marshall.

215. John Taylor Coleridge[1]

Unsigned review, *British Critic*, June 1819, XI (second series), 384–603

> The opening critical remarks do not promise the praise of *Peter Bell* with which the essay concludes; the advocacy is skilful, throwing out allusions against Leigh Hunt, Byron, Shelley, and Keats (several of whom, if not all, were adversely reviewed by J. T. Coleridge).

The sentiments with which we regard Mr. Wordsworth as a poet, have been long before the public, in one of our earliest numbers; and a fuller consideration of his writings leaves us still satisfied with the opinions we there expressed. We think that there is no one of the present day, and none but the few giants of preceding ages, who have excelled him in some of his productions; in these and in parts of others he has displayed a splendour and purity of diction, a force, and skilful harmony of measure, with a depth, a truth, a tenderness, and a solemn sublimity of sentiment, which in their union remind us forcibly of the happiest, and most golden moments of the immortal Petrarch. Competent judges will not complain of this praise as exaggerated; and they only, who are miserably ignorant of the capabilities of a simple style, or (to speak more correctly) of the meaning of the terms implicity in style, will be surprized to hear us make mention of a diction which they have been accustomed to hear characterised as fit only for the mouths of nurses and infants. But without entering into that argument, which is foreign to our present purpose, we will satisfy ourselves with opening a single volume as it lies before us, and recommending those who doubt *the fact*, to the perusal of Ruth, or an exquisite little poem, beginning. 'Three years she grew in sun and shower.' If they have formed their notions of simplicity in style from the pages of modern criticism, we can promise them at least the pleasure of a surprise from the perusal of these poems.

Still in our consideration of what Mr. Wordsworth might have been from what he sometimes is, we confess, regretfully, that he seems to us to have failed; not merely failed in the acquisition of present popularity, which he justly values at a very low rate, (for to the poet, beyond all other writers, the favourable judgment of an artificial and fashion-mongering age, offers but a doubtful assurance of real and abiding fame,) but also in our opinion he has not laid grounds for his permanent and unambiguous rank as an English Classic so high, as his peculiar powers, and the meritorious study which he has bestowed in the cultivation of them would have led us to anticipate for him. In every age, so long as our language be intelligible, whether living or dead, Wordsworth will have enthusiastic admirers, and to go a step farther, there will always be among them such admirers as a poet may with reason be most proud of; but we are much in error if in any age the ablest of those admirers will be able satisfactorily to answer the objections urged against him by candid and feeling readers of a different persuasion. We say this, reasoning partly from our own feelings, but still more from those of the ablest and fairest judges whom we have been able to consult; we scarcely ever met with a single person, whose opinion on the subject we valued, and who was open to express it, that could say he had read any whole poem of Wordsworth's composition, longer than a mere sonnet, without being obliged to get over, and subdue, in some part of it, offensive and disturbing feelings; to forget something that shocked his taste, and checked that full current of admiration, which the remainder excited; the latter feeling perhaps after all predominated, yet the mind was left in a state of incomplete satisfaction.

We are ourselves warm, very warm admirers of Wordsworth; yet if our opinion be worth asking, we must give it nearly in the words which we have written above. This is a fact, of which those who 'care for such things,' will consider it worthy of inquiry to ascertain the causes; and as we have never, we believe, attempted to develope them, though perhaps they may be deduced from our former reasoning, we will take the opportunity which Peter Bell affords us, to say a few words upon it. We see no cause for departing from the account which we have before given of the principles, on which Mr. Wordsworth's poetical system is built; they seem to us to be two in number, with an important corollary deducible from them; we perfectly agree in the truth and importance of the two first, and we are precluded from denying the abstract truth, though we doubt of the practical expediency of the last. The principles are, first, that 'whatsoever material or temporary exists before our senses, is capable of being associated in our minds with something spiritual and eternal;' and, secondly, that it is the business of the poet to see all things with a view to this capability of association, and to familiarize the process to his own, and to his reader's mind; the corollary is, that if all things are equally capable of the process, and in the availing itself of that capability, the true and essential excellence of poetry consists, then the commonest external thing, the most every day occurrence of life, or the meanest appearance of nature is equally capable of being made the ground-work or subject of poetry with the noblest and most uncommon.

We have said that these principles are true; on such subjects there is always danger of writing in a way which may seem mystical to many readers; we would earnestly desire to avoid this except at the expence of truth. As surely then as every human body contains within it an intellectual soul, so surely, we hold, does every thing external, animate and inanimate, *bear reference* to things internal and immaterial, which reference becomes apparent, and is brought as it were into action by the powers of analogy and association, in feeling acute and imaginative, that is to say, in poetical minds. The simplest truth sometimes assumes a solemn air, when formally announced, and such we fear may be the case

671

with the present; but our proposition less regularly put is merely this, that every external object is capable of exciting in a poetical mind some analogous internal idea, and as a beautiful and irresistible proof of the truth of this we would refer our readers to Boyle's Occasional Reflections, where they will find the noblest, and most poetical train of thoughts often deduced from what might otherwise have seemed the most unpromising and unproductive ground-work. Admitting the truth of this proposition, it is clear, beyond dispute, that the internal idea to which the external object gives rise, is by far the more important of the two, considered either as the subject of communication or reflection; to take up our former comparison it is as the soul to the body of that from which it springs, and the poet or the painter, whose representation of externals fails to excite in minds sufficiently sensible the proper internal association, fails precisely in the noblest, and most essential part of his duty, and neglects to draw from things without the more important meaning and lesson which they are capable of conveying from within.

These principles then are not only true, but so far as poetry itself may be considered as one among many engines bestowed upon man by God for the improvement of his moral nature, no less than the mere adornment of his earthly existence, they must undoubtedly be ranked among moral, and highly important truths. Nor if we look at poetry merely as a source of intellectual pleasure, can we doubt that these principles are in that point of view equally considerable. We will not affirm that no pleasure is derivable from a merely exact delineation of any scene of nature or art, but we are sure that it is lame and poor to that vivid, and, as it were, electric delight, which the mind receives from a description, acting, not so much by itself, and in finished details, as by rousing the creative power within, and enabling it to see in more perfect beauty that which is only sketched, and faintly traced by the describer. It is not indeed easy to ascertain comparative quantities of pleasure; we may safely, however, appeal to the lovers of poetry for the truth of our last assertion: they will find it illustrated and proved in every page of our greatest poets; it is hardly possible to read a single description of Milton's, which does not contain some one or more words, the key notes, as it were, of the association, giving life to the whole passage, and limiting, not indeed the precise train, but the general direction of the correspondent thoughts and images which arise in the reader's mind.

Simple and self-evident as these propositions now are to ourselves, they were certainly lost sight of by the majority of our intermediate poets from the restoration down to a late period; laborious and unimpassioned

description clothed in a conventional set of terms, and a language artificial, and often grossly misapplied, were substituted for the natural and
individual, though highly cultivated, and highly raised poetry, which had
gone before. So far then as our author revived, enforced, and exemplified
these principles, so far as he manfully protested against, and very ingeniously demonstrated, the abuses of modern poetic diction by the indiscriminate and conventional use of those terms, metaphors, and figures,
which had their merit in ancient poetry, from the propriety and dramatic
truth of their application, so far as he evinced that it was as absurd to
make passion and imagination speak the language of poetical *convention*
as it would be to confine them to the terms of the schools or the courts;
thus far he is entitled to our highest praises, and our warmest thanks; he
by so doing unfettered the tongue of the Muse, and replaced in her hand
the sceptre of power.

But when we come to the practical consequences which he has always
maintained, and too often exemplified, we must in honesty hold a more
measured language, and admit, that we see in them the excesses, from
which no manliness or strength of mind seems able to guard the reviver
of an old, or the inventor of a new system. We have said that we cannot
deny the abstract truth of his corollary; if it be true that all things are
capable of the process, and that in pursuing the process lies the true
business of the poet, then any thing, that which is low as well as that
which is high, is capable of being the subject of poetry. We grant it, and
we grant no more; Wordsworth, as it appears to us, has advanced one
step farther, and in that step the fallacy lies; he has substituted the words
'more fit for' in the place of 'capable of,' and has therein committed the
same error which a statuary would, who, because all stone was capable of
the process, in the performance of which his art lay, should therefore
choose to execute his groupes in granite, rather than in Parian marble.
Wordsworth might have been well content simply to have established
the truth of his proposition; he must have well known that merely as
abstract truth, it was not so unimportant, as ignorant men would have
imagined. To know that all nature, low as well as high, was equally
submitted to his jurisdiction and within his province, was sure, on many
occasions, to give a poet's hand that freedom and spirit which are inconsistent with the fear of overstepping certain limits, and straying into a
forbidden country. To know this also was, in another view, important,
because it implied and flowed from the still more important knowledge
of the true principle of all poetical capability; when he announced that
all things were subjects of poetry, he did so from correctly reasoning how

it was that any single thing might be. Thus learned in the principles of his art, and gifted by nature as he is with the main ingredients of poetic genius, there seem to us to have been no bounds to the excellence which he might have maintained, but those which he has unfortunately set to himself, and these may be described in a single sentence; he has not suffered his poetry to be the expression merely of his natural and unperverted feelings; but *he has devoted it to the developement and maintenance of a system*. Because he has discovered and maintained successfully, that good poetry may be written on a celandine or a daisy, he seems to have acted as if better poetry could be written on them than on subjects of a higher degree; he has neglected to take into the account that poetry is a communicative art, that the state of the recipient is to be considered, as well as that of the communicant; that it is little to have mixed up all the essential ingredients of poetic pleasure if they are to be neutralized or overpowered by certain accompanying feelings of disgust or ridicule.

We are aware that the poet himself will deny the grounds of our conclusion; he will declare, perhaps, that though his writings are in faithful adherence to a certain system, yet he writes with unshackled freedom, that it is an unconscious adherence, and undeviating, only because the system itself is built upon the laws of our nature. Such an answer, it is evident, will apply with equal force to a false and a true system; it is making the inveteracy of the habit its justification; but, indeed, with all our old, our unfeigned, our respectful, and even affectionate deference for Wordsworth, we are bold to say that he is no competent judge in this matter. That he writes under the impulse of a glowing and real enthusiasm we do not intend to deny; on the contrary, we are very sure that he feels whatever he describes himself as feeling in the contemplation of a bird's nest, or the sudden gleaming of a bunch of daffodils; but we cannot therefore conclude either that the thoughts which they excite are so important, as that they should form the principal subject of a wise man's contemplations; or that it is proper for a poet to make such feelings the principal topic of his communications to the world.

After all, what is poetry, or when do a certain train of thoughts, images, and words become poetry? certainly they are so when they first rise in the poet's mind; and a man may be a poet, in the full and common sense of the word, who has never committed a poem to paper or even recited a line to his friend. A man may satisfy himself with the solitary pleasure of such creations, content with his own vivid perceptions, and exulting within himself in the consciousness of his uncommunicated strength; he may feel no desire to communicate what has delighted himself, he may seek for no applause beyond that of his own breast. When this is the case, the world has no right to question him upon the subject or the manner of his meditations; but the moment the poet communicates to others, it is evident that as he has now a new object, so there is also a new party to be consulted in the attainment of that object. The poet who recites, or writes, or publishes, has clearly, in so doing, an object beyond the pleasure of poetic composition; he seeks for praise, for immortal fame, or to suit a poet's delicacy, he seeks to communicate pleasure to others. The process by which he arrives at that object is the exciting feelings correspondent to those which he has himself experienced; and he attains his object more completely, the greater number of persons he succeeds in thrilling with these similar emotions. Poets may coquette it if they please, and disclaim a desire of applause or fame; but he who publishes, must, by all fair rules of interpretation, be held to desire something external, either glory to himself, or the communication of pleasure to others; in either case the number of those who applaud, or who are pleased, is an essential part of the complete attainment of the object. We are aware of the distinction between popularity and fame, we give Wordsworth full credit for despising the former and desiring only the latter; but in this he is only a better arithmetician than many of his contemporaries; it is only because he knows that the popularity of to-day is no assurance for the fame of to-morrow, and that he whose admirers are the most judicious, and whose fame lasts the longest, will in the end have the greater number of readers.

The question then with a poet must always be, how can I excite in the greatest number of my fellow-creatures emotions similar to those which I feel myself? and when this is the question, it is obvious that he must take into the account something more than merely his own sensibilities, and the causes of excitement *to them*; he is bound to examine into the same things as they belong, or refer to others. His own constitution may be one of peculiar delicacy; circumstances may have rendered it morbid, or at least cherished its sensibilities to excess; his habits of life may have directed them into an uncommon channel, or may have attached importance to that which the mass of the world has been accustomed to consider trifling. In all these cases, the medium of communication between the poet and his readers, is disturbed; to say the least, he comes among them and proffers his thoughts for their acceptance, just as one buried for many years in the interior of Africa, might appear in the market here, with a string of cowries for his medium of commerce; they may have been valuable where they were procured, and may have cost him many a day's labour under a burning sun; they may indeed be intrinsically as fit for the purpose as gold and silver, or more perishable paper; but he must not expect to purchase with them here the article of which he stands in need. When this too happens, the poet must not too hastily conclude, any more than the African, that all the world is wrong, and he alone right; if, indeed, he is conscious of powers which may constrain the age and fashion, hearts and habits to his own bent, it is all well, at least for him, and his object will be attained in his own way. But since the poet has no controul over circumstances; since there will be always in the world bustle, and contention, and wars, and commerce, and litigation, it is perhaps greater wisdom to despair of altering that which flows from them, to renounce an attempt which the most vigorous son of the Muse has never made with success, and so far as may be done, without cramping the free step of genius, to accommodate oneself to the feelings and reasonings of others. In saying this, we are not the advocates of an unworthy compliance; the 'diversity,' as a lawyer would say, is to be noted between that which is the sickly and short-lived fashion of the day, and that which, proceeding from permanent causes, may be fairly expected to be itself permanent; the slave of the former deliberately renounces the very object, which we have supposed to be honestly and properly in the poet's view.

It will scarcely be asked how we apply this to Wordsworth, or how it accounts for that want of success, which we lament in his poetry. All objects or appearances in nature are intrinsically capable of that speculation and association which are the basis of poetical pleasure; a large class of them, however, from other circumstances, apparently permanent in their nature, and from inveterate counter-associations, whether reasonable or not, are either esteemed by the mass of men as trifling, or felt to be disgusting; when these, therefore, are made the subjects of grave or delicate speculation, the poet's associations and the reader's are at direct variance; and even if the powers of the former, with the intrinsic justice of his thoughts, should prevail over the mere habits and feelings of the latter, it is evident that a victory obtained by a struggle does not and cannot impart that full and perfect pleasure which it is the business of poetry to bestow. This we take to be a just account of the dispute between Wordsworth and the mass of his readers; there was something more than playful and good-humoured satire in the critic, that talked of the 'consecration of chicken,' and such other disgusting subjects in a review of his poetry; but saving the malice of the remark, it is undoubtedly true, that according to Wordsworth's principles carried to their full

extent, (carried, let it be remembered, much farther than even his Quix-
otism has ever ventured in practice,) there is nothing too trifling for
grave, too disgusting for pleasant speculation; the greatness, the goodness, the wisdom of the Creator are as fairly deducible from the fly that
feeds upon corruption, nay from the corruption itself on which it feeds,
as from the purest lily, the brightest sun-rise, the most glorious canopy
of stars, or the fairest woman, that were ever celebrated by poet.

Two remarks remain to be made, one addressed to readers, the other
with great respect to the poet himself. To the former, we would say, that
if they have formed their opinions of Wordsworth from public reputation, from illiberal and unjust criticism, from any thing but an attentive
and impartial study of his writings, they impeach their own justice; have
done the poet great wrong, and themselves yet greater. We have stated
our objections to certain of his opinions, and we repeat that we think he
has shewn a perverse preference for the maintenance and exemplification
of a system to the yielding to the nobler and more genial current of his
natural feelings. Still, if we reject from the list of his poems whatever are
most open to these objections, those in which the inventor or the reviver
of a system predominates over the natural poet, enough and more than
enough will yet remain in the volumes of Wordsworth, to reward with
the richest fruits that poetry can bestow, a candid and attentive reader. It
is pitiable and maudlin folly to consider poetry as the mere recreation of
idleness, in which it is a fault if the mind is called upon for a moment's
exertion; it is prejudice to take up our opinions for granted, and without
examination, upon the word of a single critic; it is injustice for a single
fault of taste to reject all the writings of any poet; let our readers only
stand clear of this folly, and avoid this prejudice and this injustice, and we
promise them that they will find in Wordsworth, poems, which it is a
misfortune at least, we will not venture to say a disgrace, to be incapable
of feeling and admiring.

We have also to address a few words to the poet himself. His writings
are devoted to the cause of religion and morality, and in that holy cause
we scarcely know a more zealous, a more fearless, or more eloquent
advocate; it is quite refreshing to turn from the tawdry voluptuousness
of one contemporary poet, or the gloomy misanthropy of another; the
vague aspirations of this man, the cold scepticism of that, or the shocking blasphemy of a third, to the pure, manly, single-minded morality of
Wordsworth. We give him credit too for feeling as he writes, and we are
sure, that to promote virtue and purity, is, with him, beyond all profit, all
praise, all pleasure. Upon this ground we take our stand, and we beseech

him to consider, that whatever prevents his general acceptation, diminishes his power of doing good; we think he must be satisfied by a trial of so many years, that while he writes as he writes now, projecting his system at every angle, and presenting so many sides obvious to the perversions of ridicule and malice, he may indeed have a few passionate admirers, whoze zeal and weight may suffice to console wounded vanity, but he never can have that general influence, nor produce that powerful effect, which of all living poets he is by nature most capable of producing. We do not prescribe the manner or the measure of alteration to the poet, we appeal to the man and the moralist, whether some alteration, some yielding to prejudices, if they be permanent, some departure from the very *summum jus*[2] of abstract truth, be not both possible and expedient.

It is high time for us to come to the poem itself, which has furnished us with an excuse for so long a preface. It is introduced by a prologue, in which the poet explains his preference of the earth, and subjects connected with the daily feelings, and occurrences of man over all that is supernatural and marvellous. This is attempted to be done in a playful fiction of a

Little boat,
In shape a very crescent moon.
[*Peter Bell, PW*, II, p. 332, ll. 6–7]

In which the poet describes himself as taking a voyage in the air, but soon becoming tired of stars and planets, and begging to be reconveyed to earth. The boat cries shame upon him for a poet of faint heart, but offers to convey him, since heaven is too high for him, and the music of the spheres troubles him, to see all the wonders of the earth, and of fairy land; the poet rejects even this offer, and persists in being set down in his own garden, where round the stone table, 'beneath the spreading Weymouth pine,' a party of friends are assembled to hear him tell the tale of 'Peter Bell the Potter.' Playfulness is not Wordsworth's forte, and we think that in all the lighter parts of this *jeu d'esprit* he has failed; in these parts too he has indulged himself in the use of those familiar forms of speech, to which nothing can reconcile us in poetry that is in other passages so serious and philosophical as this. But there is something very glowing and tender in the expression of his feelings when he hangs over 'the town where he was born,' and the following stanzas are no less beautiful and well expressed, than true in the positions which they lay down.

[Quotes *ibid.*, *PW*, II, pp. 336–7, ll. 121–50:

> There was a time when all mankind . . .
> 'Tis lodg'd within her silent tear.]

The poem itself opens with a stanza, which Wordsworth seems to have placed boldly *in limine*, as a note of defiance to his critics, and a test of the passive obedience of his disciples.

> All by the moonlight river side
> It gave three miserable groans,
>   ' 'Tis come then to a pretty pass,'
>   Said Peter to the groaning Ass,
>   'But I will bang your bones.'
>   [*Ibid.*, *PW*, II, p. 349 and footnotes, ll. 446–50]

We are as far as the poet himself can be from thinking that Peter the potter ought to storm at a poor ass in downright heroics; but we beg to observe, that the tale might, in this part at least, have been as well conducted without making him speak at all; the speech is merely inserted *ornamenti gratiâ*; and if it was incorrect to make him speak in any other than forms and phrases inseparably connected with low and ridiculous associations, we think there can be no doubt, that the poet should have sacrificed the dramatic effect for the sake of excluding such associations, and merely told us in his own person and *in his own language*, that Peter beat the ass very unmercifully. Not, however, to renew an argument on which we have already said so much, we will only say one word with reference to the few lines which we addressed in the last page to Wordsworth himself, and upon a point on which we are sure that we must be better judges than he himself can be. Of all the persons who take up Peter Bell, we will venture to say, that a very large proportion, (and among them persons who might have been delighted and instructed with the tale if they could have been got fairly into it without prejudice on their minds) will take the colouring of their opinion, and receive a fatal disgust from this very unfortunate stanza. The poet may smile at this, the critic may hold for nothing judgments so formed, but the zealous moralist cannot consider such a fact as unimportant.

The audience who are assembled to hear the tale, very naturally expostulate upon this abrupt beginning, and in the manner of their doing so, Wordsworth has fallen into an inconsistency with his own position, which as an *argumentum ad hominem*, we cannot pass over without noticing to him.

'Good sir,' the vicar's voice exclaimed,
'You rush at once into the middle;'
And little Bess, with accents sweeter,
Cried 'O dear sir, but who is Peter?'
Said Stephen ''tis a downright riddle.'
[*Ibid., PW*, II, p. 339 in footnotes, ll. 195–6]

We have no fault to find with this, but

The Squire said, 'sure as Paradise
Was lost to man by Adam's sinning
This leap is for us all too bold, &c.'
[*Ibid., PW*, II, p. 339 and footnotes, ll. 196–8]

Now there may be some propriety in the squire's talking of a bold leap, but upon the same principle that Peter was found to talk of 'pretty passes,' and 'banging bones,' we contend that the squire's simile should have been, 'sure as a gun,' or 'sure as Carlisle race was lost to me by Adam's bolting,' or any other such form of speech. The fall of man, and the loss of Paradise are evidently dramatically improper in the mouth of the village squire.

This interruption, however, recalls the poet, and he begins his tale regularly, by an account of the occupation, habits, and character, of Peter Bell. This is admirably done in the best style of narration, with the truest pencil of moral delineation. Peter was by trade an 'itinerant potter,' and in his vocation had travelled through all parts of Ireland; he had been in the large towns, and cities, and through the most retired hamlets in inland vallies, or 'along the indented coast.' Nature, however, in all her varied forms of loveliness and majesty, had produced no effect upon his stubborn heart, he had learned from her, indeed, whatever she could teach of wildness and cunning, which in his mind had been compounded with all the low vices of the city, but to use the beautiful words of the Poet,

[Quotes *ibid., PW*, II, p. 341, ll. 246–75:

In vain through every changeful year . . .
As ever ran a felon's race.]

The character of the hero being fully drawn, the little incident which forms the ground-work, rather than the subject of the poem, commences. In one of his rambles, Peter was wandering alone by moonlight, near the river Swale, and seeing a path that promised him a shorter road than the one in which he was travelling, he strikes into it and loses his way. Following, however, the path, he comes to an old quarry, where it ends; nothing daunted, however, by the gloominess of the quarry, and in that kind of vexation which a man feels who has wantonly thrown himself out of his right road, he pushes on through the aperture of the quarry, and at length emerges –

> And behold
> A scene of soft and lovely hue!
> Where blue and grey, and tender green,
> Together made as sweet a scene
> As ever human eye did view.
>
> Beneath the clear blue sky he saw
> A little field of meadow ground,
> But field, or meadow, name it not;
> Call it of earth a small green plot
> With rocks encompass'd round.
>
> The Swale flow'd under the grey rocks, &c.
> [*Ibid.*, *PW*, II, p. 345, ll. 361–71]

There is something very exquisite to our feelings in these few lines of description; the drawing, it will be observed, is very general, a blue sky, a little meadow, rocks around, and a stream flowing under them; it is, we believe, in the very generality of the drawing, and the fewness of the features, that the charm consists; scarcely any one can wander much in countries but of common beauty, and be a real lover of nature, who will not be able to associate this description with some secluded glade, some little island in the woods, which arrested his steps in passing, and which it is delightful to have brought again to his memory. We could name several favourite spots upon both shores of Devonshire, that instantly rose to our recollection upon reading the lines.

In this lonely spot Peter finds nothing but a solitary ass, which he instantly determines upon stealing, and the poet as usual makes him announce this determination, and address the ass in language, the only recommendation of which in his eyes can be that he supposes it dramatically correct. But a moment's observation suffices to shew that it has not even that merit; it is not humorous enough to excite a smile, and the poet has no intention of making us laugh; but it is low enough, and ridiculous enough to disturb our feelings. Peter Bell himself would never have so spoken, and we cannot conceive the merit of a false and artificial lowness.

> 'With better speed I'll back again,
> And, lest the journey should prove vain,
> Will take yon Ass my lawful prize.'
> [*Ibid.*, *PW*, II, p. 346 in footnotes, ll. 385–6]

To so much of the speech we have no objection; it is the language in which our best poets would have clothed the same ideas, remembering that they were not bound to give the potter's own words, not to speak precisely as he would have spoken, but with all their own cultivation of mind, and addressing themselves to cultivated minds to speak *for* him; just as a person narrates a dialogue in low life, without *mimicking* the accents, provincialisms, or vulgarities of the speakers. But to pursue.

> Off Peter hied – 'A comely beast,
> Though not so plump as he might be;
> My honest friend, with such a platter
> You should have been a little fatter,
> But come, sir, come with me.'
> [*Ibid.*, *PW*, II, p. 346 in footnotes, ll. 385–6]

This is no more the language of Peter Bell, than of Peter the Great; it is indeed, exactly the manner in which full grown school-boys, smart, and frolicksome, would have expressed themselves upon such an occasion; and if the speech has not the merit of *propriety*, we really do not see in such a poem as this, what merit it has of any kind.

Peter leaps on the ass to ride him away, but finds that he cannot move him from the spot, in vain he spurs, and pulls, and 'bangs,' – the ass is resolutely obstinate, and with his head hanging over the stream, and his eyes bent on it remains precisely in the place in which Peter found him. He groans, indeed, under the cruel treatment which he receives, and the savage observes his lank sides wasted almost to a skeleton, but without any commiseration; on the contrary, in a fit of brutal passion he determines to throw the poor creature into the river. At the moment when he is about to execute the determination, the ass brays most loudly and piteously, Peter is startled by the echo from the rocks in the stillness of the night; the bray is repeated, and with still greater effect upon Peter; at length, summoning up his resolution, he returns to his savage purpose, but on stooping to execute it, a ghastly sight meets his eyes under the water, the appearance of a dead man's face, he shrieks, and falls senseless in a swoon by the side of the river.

The whole of this, to which it is impossible to do justice in a mere analysis, is admirably done; its merit, indeed, lies principally in that of which it is impossible to convey any idea in an analysis, namely, in the gradual impression of circumstances upon the hard and insensible heart of the savage; time, place, solitude, his own wanton and unlawful purpose, the strangeness of the resistance, the sudden noise redoubled by the echo in the still night, all these conspiring to produce that feeling of something supernatural, to which the most brutal nature is, perhaps, the most susceptible, and which, in Peter's mind, is consummated by the shocking close of the adventure.

He awakes from his swoon, the first, perhaps, into which he had ever fallen; the gradual return of recollection, and sense, is very well described. With his staff he immediately begins to sound the river, and at the sight of this the faithful animal, who had been watching, as our readers will have before now anticipated, the body of his drowned master, is roused to the liveliest joy and animation; he licks his hands with his tongue, and expresses in the most sensible manner his gratitude for Peter's endeavours to draw the body to land. These endeavours are at length successful, and moved by the dumb show of the animal, who seems to implore him to mount his back, Peter leaps on him, and without a moment's delay the earnest creature sets off, as may be supposed, for his poor master's home.

We have seldom read a journey so beautifully conceived, so well described as this, it is little to say that it is full of the exquisite painting of nature, and that the scenes selected for the pencil are admirably in harmony with the incidents, and with the changing feelings of Peter.

This part of the poem, by far the longest, is entitled to higher praise; Wordsworth has here put forth all his powers, both in the 'moving incident,' and in tracing the various changes in the mind of his principal personage, from wonder to a sort of desperate and unresisting conviction of guilt, with an anticipation of speedy and inevitable punishment; a wild remorse for his past evil courses, a natural relapse to thoughtless hardheartedness, a renewed remorse softening down to the deepest, and most painful repentance, and then the awakening of all those kindly and human feelings, which the circumstances before his eyes might breathe into the gentlest heart. Our readers must not, however, suppose that it is *merely* a scientific analysis of the workings of the human heart under given circumstances; it is that certainly, but it is much more; we should be as little disposed to commend a mere lecture on moral anatomy, as they could be to enjoy it. But to the commonest readers we can give our assurance, that they will find this a most pathetic tale; for ourselves we will confess that we have seldom met with one, over which, when we read it aloud, we find it so difficult to restrain our feelings.

The issue of the tale may well be supposed, and we decline the task of analysing the incidents, for we would neither rob them of their beauty and interest, nor anticipate the pleasure of our readers. Peter Bell becomes a 'good and honest man,' after months of sober melancholy, and rational repentance, and the ass is for many years the laborious, and useful servant of the unfortunate widow and her family. Our extracts have been very numerous already, indeed we may seem to have devoted an unreasonable portion of our number to remarks on so short a poem; but we cannot refrain still from adding to both. We have two extracts to make for which we must still find room, as they serve to put beyond a doubt Wordsworth's power in two of the essentials of poetry, picturesque drawing, and pathetic narration. In the course of the journey homewards to the cottage of the dead man, both Peter and the ass are startled by a shrill and doleful cry; the ass knows it well, for it proceeds from his master's son, who had been now for four days seeking his unfortunate father. The boy is not yet introduced actually into the poem, but the poet turning to 'little Bess,' who was much affected by this part of the story, tells her that the cry 'comes from the entrance of a cave;' and then exclaims.

> *I see a blooming wood boy there,*
> And if I had the power to say
> How sorrowful the wanderer is,
> Your heart would be as sad as his
> Till you had kiss'd his tears away.
>
> *Holding a hawthorn branch in hand,*
> *All bright with berries ripe and red,*
> *Into the cavern's mouth he peeps,*
> *Thence back into the moonlight creeps;*
> What seeks the boy?—the silent dead –
>
> 'His father.'
>   [*Ibid., PW*, II, pp. 361–2, ll. 631–41]

Confining ourselves to the five lines which we have printed in Italics, the only descriptive lines of the passage (unless indeed the epithet 'sorrow-ful,' in the third line may more correctly be so considered) we do not know that in all the compass of English poetry we can turn to a more *complete* picture. No pencil can set the scene more perfectly before the eye, and yet our readers will not fail to remark that two or three general features are all the materials with which this *completeness* of effect is produced. The hawthorn branch 'with berries ripe and red,' might to an inattentive observer of the reality have seemed an unimportant feature, not worthy of introduction, nor properly to be introduced in so general a sketch; yet no one can study the picture, without remarking what a life and individuality, what a determinate character it gives to the more considerable features. We may seem to attach too much importance to such a trifle, and to discourse on it with disproportionate earnestness, but it is in fact intimately connected with, and a strong illustration of the truth of those principles in poetry, which we have uniformly laboured to enforce, and to which we are convinced both readers and writers must return, if the former would either really delight in, or the latter successfully imitate, Shakspeare, Spenser, or Milton, the great triad of English poetry.

The other, and the last extract which we shall make, is of a kind in which Wordsworth has, on several occasions, shewn himself eminently successful, and the present, perhaps, may fearlessly stand in competition with the best of his preceding efforts. Taken by itself, and apart from the context, we think it must strike the reader as a beautiful specimen of pure and simple pathos, but it loses somewhat by being read as an extract, for it occurs in the original very naturally, and conduces much to the reformation produced in Peter's mind. He passes a little ivied chapel (a scene by the way most exquisitely described) and in the ruminating self-accusing mood into which he has been thrown, he remembers that in such a ruin, 'in the shire of Fife,' he had deceived a poor girl, and married her his sixth wife. He passes on by an alehouse, whence issues the noise of a carousing, and drunken party, but this sound, once so pleasing to him, now affects him with other sensations, and turns him more wildly and gloomily to the consideration of all his past irregular and wicked life.

[Quotes *ibid.*, *PW*, II, pp. 374–5, ll. 886–930:

> But more than all his heart is stung
> To think of one almost a child,
> A sweet and playful highland girl,
> As light and beauteous as a *squirrel**,
> As beauteous and as wild . . .
>
> 'My mother, Oh! my mother.']

---

* Does Mr. Wordsworth pronounce squirrel '*squirl*;' this is not his only offence against rhyme; the more remarkable, because haste and inattention are none of his faults. *Rev.*

We must not allow ourselves to extend these remarks any further, as there are some subjects, and some books, upon which it takes some 'beating of the brain' to produce an article of the adequate size, so there are others, and among them the present, upon which we find it hard to check our pen, but upon consideration of the patience of our readers. Our last extract speaks for itself, and we would decline talking upon poetry with any one who was incapable of feeling its beauty; to such a man poetry must be as colour to the blind, or music to the deaf. Neither can it be necessary to sum up our formal opinion of the poet, or the poem; we have treated both with freedom, but it is manifest, that profound admiration predominates in our minds over all other feelings of an opposite nature. But we do fear, lest our expressions may seem exaggerated to many among our readers, whose bosoms glow with poetic pleasure as warmly as our own, and whose judgments may be more matured, and better disciplined. To such persons we feel anxious to justify ourselves for our own sakes and we will venture to add, for their own. When we first read Peter Bell, it was in the midst of business, and with that impatient haste, which one feels with regard to the 'last new poem' of a favourite author; we laid it down, we confess, much disappointed, and should have been ready to condemn, as injudicious and exaggerated, such a critique as we are now closing. As, however, we were to render an account of the poem to the public, it was natural to recollect, that it was more fair to distrust ourselves, than to condemn another on so hasty a perusal. We accordingly again read it, with a good deal of attention, and with a total change of opinion; we found that Peter Bell was worthy of its author's fame, and that its unobtrusive beauties, fairly weighed, and properly brought to light, were more than a counterbalance to the staring defects, which had influenced our first judgment. What has happened to ourselves, we shall venture to think may happen to other, and even wiser men; and we hope we may without presumption, urge upon them the propriety also of doing as we did, the giving the poet a second and a more attentive consideration. The man who reads a poem, as a lady does a newspaper, for the births, deaths, murders, and marriages it contains, who takes it up without a thought in his head, and puts it down again with no accession, but what scantily suffices for his table talk the same day at dinner, will waste his time on Peter Bell, or indeed any production of its author. Wordsworth demands from his readers, not only the sacrifice of many prejudices, and the conquest of some reasonable dispositions to laughter, or mortification, but also an open heart, and a patient exercise of his intellect.

People may doubt, whether a poet has a right to demand all these, but of this we are certain, that he who can, and will grant them, will derive from Wordsworth nearly as high gratification as any poet is capable of bestowing.

EDITOR'S NOTES

1. Identified as the work of J. T. Coleridge by the extract from his Diary published in *Life and Correspondence of John Duke Lord Coleridge*, ed. E. H. Coleridge, 1904, i, 13.
2. 'highest law'.

216.

Unsigned review, *Monthly Review*, August 1819, LXXXIX, 419–22

> The sour note of this review is continued in the review that immediately follows it, a review of Reynolds's *Peter Bell*, in which it is claimed that it is 'a most superfluous extravagance' to write in imitation of Wordsworth since his own writing is itself a caricature.

This infantine pamphlet is dedicated to Robert Southey, Esq. *P. L.* or Poet Laureate, by William Wordsworth, Esq. *L. P.* or Lake Poet. It is, in truth, 'a right merry and conceited' small production; worthy of the bard to whom it is offered, and worthy of him also by whom it is produced. All past, present, and (probably) future performances, by the same author, must sink into nothing before Peter Bell. No lisping was ever more distinctly lisped than the versification of this poem; and no folly was ever more foolishly boasted than that of the writer, whether in style or subject-matter. The former is the style of Mr. Newbery's best gilded little volumes for nurseries; the latter is a subject for any of the Cheap Repository Tracts, intended for the reformation of the lowest of the lower orders.

With this brief but sufficient preface, we introduce Peter Bell and his poet to our readers:

[Quotes *Peter Bell*, *PW*, II, pp. 339–40, ll. 201–35:

—A potter, Sir, he was by trade . . .
Sure never man like him did roam!]

Can Englishmen write, and Englishmen read, such drivel, – such daud-
ling, impotent drivel, – as this!

Oh were not all Rome's ancient vigour fled,
Could such lines *gender* in a Roman head?
(*Persius, by Brewster*)

as we must for ever ask our degenerate, our unblushing countrymen.
Weak indeed must be the mind that, by any process of sophistry, or long
practice of patience, can be reconciled to the aforesaid drivel. We feel the
force of custom to be *almost* omnipotent: but, however *dulled* and *deadened* our sense of propriety, our sense of poetry, or sense of every kind
may have been by the eternal repetition of similar imbecilities, we *should*
have thought that, until the very brains were extracted, no head could
hold such unmeaning prittle-prattle as the above; – no tongue, we *are*
persuaded, tied by the thinnest silk of shame, would ever have poured it
forth. – We really waste *words*, however, on what is scarcely *Word's-
worth*; and, suffering this infatuated poetaster to condemn himself out of
his own mouth, we shall intersperse very few farther remarks with his
modicums of matchless vanity.

Some well-meaning, and, in one case, witty individuals have published
parodies of Peter Bell, the potter, and of his brother, the Waggoner. We
shall be required briefly to notice these parodies, as well as their originals:
but in fact the originals themselves are the parodies, or rather the gross
burlesques of all that is good in poetry. It is like travestying Cotton's
Travesties of Homer and Virgil, to parody Wordsworth's own parodies
of other illustrious poets. Nay, he is the buffoon of Nature herself; and,
by lowering her grand and general associations of physical and moral
beauty into petty pastry-cook details of fruit and flowers, he presents to
some a *ludicrous*, and to all an *unfaithful* portrait of his pretended original.
We say pretended; for in fact it is not Nature, but his own narrow, whimsical, unpoetical idea of Nature, which this strange writer worships. It is,
however, true that rays of reason escape through these hallucinations; as
for instance:
[Quotes *Peter Bell*, *PW*, II, pp. 368–9, ll. 761–85:

Dread Spirits! to torment the good . . .
What may be done with Peter Bell!]

Yet what is all this about? About a man who was reading in his room at midnight, when all grew suddenly dark, and on the paper, in letters of light, was formed a *word* – *too* something or other to be mentioned!!! Oh dear! Oh dear! and this is written for full-grown men and women! We can only say that, if a nurse were to talk to any of their children in this manner, a sensible father and mother would be strongly disposed to dismiss her without a character.

Peter sees a number of strange things in the water, the product of his own guilty fancy; like the faces on the trees in the wooden tail-pieces in Bewick's Quadrupeds. Among other scenes is the following:

> Is it a party in a parlour?
> Cramm'd just as they on earth were cramm'd –
> Some sipping punch, some sipping tea,
> But, as you by their faces see,
> All silent and all damn'd!
> [*Ibid.*, *PW*, II, p. 354 in footnotes, ll. 515–16]

Fie, fie, Mr. Wordsworth!*

217. H. St. John

Review signed 'H. St. John', *Kaleidoscope, or Literary and Scientific Mirror* (a Liverpool weekly), 6 March 1821

Henry St. John, the pseudonym used here, was the name of that sage man of politics, the First Viscount Bolingbroke (1678–1751). The review is a mixture of facetiousness, cheap wit and cautious praise.

This work has been considered by the admirers of Mr. Wordsworth, as his *chef-d'œuvre*; and I have therefore selected it as the subject of my remarks. It is not without pain that I am necessitated, from the best of my judgment, to condemn it altogether; and to say, that although in some of the passages an ardent admirer of poetry may descern some slight germs of genius and traces of originality, yet, as a whole, I certainly consider it the most ridiculous attempt at poetry ever aspired to, were it even by one of mediocre talents.

---

* We are compelled, with regret, to announce that Mr. W.'s 'Waggon' having broken down on the road, the *Waggoner* is remanded for examination till the next month.

In the first place, I must, in common justice to the author, confess, that his preface, in some respects, is well adapted, and consistent with the rest of the work; he there expresses a hope that it will not be totally unworthy of 'filling, permanently, a station, however humble, in the literature of his country.' In this, he will not be disappointed; as I think the book will everlastingly be cited as a specimen of the dearth of genius among the poets of the 19th century. Mr. W. afterwards observes, that such 'has always been the aim of all his endeavours in poetry.' I cannot doubt the success of his laudable aims, from the reason above stated, through [*sic*] probably the author intended it in a different way.

At the conclusion of his preface, which is dedicated to Mr. Southey, he alludes to the frequent occasions in which their names have been coupled together, 'for evil and for good.' Heaven knows, our reviewers have often enough conjoined the names of these worthies in the former; but, as to the latter, I must apologise for my ignorance, in confessing that I never heard a syllable in praise of their united efforts in any way.

But to commence with the poem. The first verse of what the writer terms the prologue runs thus:

> There's something in a flying-horse,
>   And something in a huge balloon:
> But through the clouds I'll never float,
> Until I have a little boat,
>   Whose shape is like the crescent moon.
> [*Peter Bell*, *PW*, II, p. 331, ll. 1–5]

This may, no doubt, be very fine; but I must venture to say, that, though the poet has discovered something in these wonders, it grieves me that I can find nothing like sense or connexion throughout the whole prologue. The author may, perhaps, laugh: and say, 'Am I first to write poetry, and then give people sense to understand it?' Certainly not: but let him write sense at once, and then the difficulty is obviated. There is no great hardship in composing incomprehensible nonsense, and then calling it metaphysical. Whether Mr. W.'s poetry is the more incomprehensible from being stupid, or the more stupid from being incomprehensible, I will not take it upon me to say; but it often amuses me to hear those who pretend great admiration for his genius, affirm very coolly, that he is too deep for the generality of his readers. I wonder what Gray would have thought of it.

At length, after wading through the prologue, we arrive at the poem: the ostensible hero is a wild rover, named Peter Bell; and we have a few pages descriptive of his travels. In this place, I must observe, that, though my animadvertions have been thus pointed and severe, I must not so far lose sight of candour and justice (like most of our Reviewers) as to select from the poem those passages only, from the abundant specimens it affords, which may tend to accredit my assertions, and leave, unregarded, those parts which, like thinly-scattered gems in the mine, sparkle the more brilliantly, contrasted with the rubbish that surrounds them. Such parts indeed there are, and they plainly show Mr. Wordsworth to be a man of genius, and a deep observer of human nature. What can be more beautiful than the two following? In these few lines he has described what others could scarcely attempt in as many pages.

> He rov'd among the vales and streams,
>   In the green wood and hollow dell;
> They were his dwellings night and day, –
> But *nature* ne'er could find the way
>   Into the heart of Peter Bell.
>
> In vain, through every changeful year,
>   Did Nature lead him as before;
> A *primrose* by a *river's brim*,
> A *yellow primrose* was to him,
>   And it *was nothing* more.
>   [*Ibid.*, *PW*, II, pp. 340–1, ll. 241–50]

Pursuing the description of this wild and savage outlaw, he breaks into a beautiful strain. Who that ever gazed on the calm blue sky, and melted away into the kindly but lofty emotions a lovely prospect gives rise to, but must feel deeply and intensely on reading the following lines?

> At noon, when by the forest's edge
>   He lay beneath the branches high,
> The soft blue sky did never melt
> Into his heart, he never felt
>   The witchery of the soft blue sky!
>
> On a fair prospect some have look'd
>   And felt, as I have heard them say,
> As if the morning time had been
> A thing as steadfast as the scene
>   On which they gaz'd themselves away.
>   [*Ibid.*, *PW*, II, p. 341, ll. 261–70]

This Peter, it seems, has very little idea of enjoying fine prospects, and not much leisure, one would think, even if he had the taste; for he had 'a dozen wedded wives.'

To proceed with the tale: – [Summary begins . . .]

Mr. Wordsworth seems to take singular pleasure in observing each motion of the Ass's ears. I am sorry no other poetical idea could be produced to break the dreadful pause. What Lord Byron said to Coleridge will apply inimitably well to this wonderful bard:

'Yet none in lofty numbers can surpass
The bard who SOARS to eulogise an ass;
How well the subject suits his noble mind,
A *fellow-feeling* makes us *wondrous kind!*'

After divers resolute attacks on the Ass (which, by the bye, from the respect paid to it by the poet, one would be apt to mistake for the hero of the piece) Peter Bell stoops to seize and drag him away by violence, but is suddenly struck by some startling sight in the pool. After many sagacious conjectures as to what this frightful spectacle can be, the author proceeds gravely to ask

Is it a party in a parlour?
Cramm'd just as they on earth are cramm d –
Some sipping punch, some sipping tea,
But, as you by their faces see,
All silent and all damn'd!
[*Ibid., PW*, II, p. 354 in footnotes, ll. 515–16]

Independent of the *striking beauty* of this passage, and its absolute freedom from vulgarity, I may add, that, though I do not pretend to know in what kind of a circle Mr. W. moves, yet, from his poetical ideas, (which are of course, taken from the feelings which a man's society gives rise to) I may be permitted to imagine that his cannot be the most select; at any rate, situated as I am, among the third or fourth class, it has never been my fortune to visit any of these tea-and-punch cramming parties; and, I feel rather sorry to find, that a gentleman of such refined taste as Mr. Wordsworth should descend so low.

The reader will hardly guess that this sight, so appalling to the rover, turns out to be a *dead man's* face, which he sees in the stream!

Master Bell forthwith falls into a trance, and so concludes *part first.*

Languidly rousing from his death-like slumber, the potter looks around him,

And feels the glimmering of the moon,
And to stretch forth his hand is trying, &c.
        [*Ibid.*, *PW*, II, p. 355 in footnotes, ll. 537–8]

The last line reminds me strongly of what an old and dear friend used
to say, 'that he never considered a man intoxicated who could lie on the
ground without laying hold of it; but if in *lying down*, he clung fast to
the earth to *keep him up*, he certainly then was completely *done*.' But to
return:

The ass is a wondrous creature. The animation in his countenance
when he endeavours to induce Peter to raise the body out of the stream;
his subsequent wailings and grief; his bending on his knees (not very like
an elephant) in order to prevail on Peter to mount; and his returning
homewards with him, all bespeak a very superior intellect. The poet
seems, for the moment, to have forgotten that the Christian, and NOT
the Mahometan religion, is prevalent in England. This mistake, we may
conjecture, originates in his ardent desire of displaying the marvelous
talents of the ass; 'the mosques change contenance' at sight of this
wonder-working animal.

> While the ass pursues his way
>   Along the solitary dell,
> As pensively his steps advance,
> The *mosques* and *spires* change *countenance*,
>   And look at Peter Bell!
>   [*Ibid.*, *PW*, II, p. 364, ll. 686–90]

The pair pursue their way through devious paths. I never heard before,
that withered leaves were sent on earth for the punishment of the
wicked, but *here* they are made the chief instrument of Peter's chastise-
ment: one of them gives him a very long chase, and it is with difficulty
that the potter escapes its clutches. The passage is so sublime that
I can't refrain from quoting it in full. Mark the awful pause at the
beginning:

> How blank! but whence this rustling sound
>   Which, all too long, the pair hath chased!
> A dancing leaf is close behind;
> Light plaything for the sportive wind
>   Upon the solitary waste.

> When Peter spies the withered leaf,
> It yields no cure to his distress,
> 'Where there is not a bush or tree,
> The very leaves they follow me,
> So huge hath been my wickedness!'
> [*Ibid.*, *PW*, II, p. 365, ll. 701–10]

Why the leaves should follow him *because* of his wickedness, I am really at a loss to say. How very admirably reasoned and connected!

Some other agonies which an awakening conscience torments this man of sin with, are then depicted, and so closes *part the second*.

At the opening of *part third*, the spirits of the Mind are invoked, and invited to try their influence on the mind of Peter Bell. There is something noble and lofty in this invocation; and indeed the poet seems to have caught an inspiration from their power, far transcending his ordinary attempts.

One more touch at the ass, and the author soars to what should be his proper region.

> Let them whose voice can stop the clouds –
> Whose cunning eye can see the wind –
> Tell to a curious world the cause
> Why making here a sudden pause,
> The ass turned round his head – and grinned.
>
> Appalling process! I have marked
> The like on heath – in lonely wood,
> And, verily, have seldom met
> A spectacle more hideous – yet
> It suited Peter's present mood;
>
> And, grinning in his turn, his teeth
> He in jocose defiance show'd.
> [*Ibid.*, *PW*, II, pp. 370–1, ll. 821–32]

Who can imagine anything more sublime than the spectacle of the ass and Peter hideously grinning at each other. The latter, however, is suddenly alarmed at a tremendous rumbling sound, seeming to proceed from the centre of the earth, and his compunction is again awakened. The deep and tender feeling breathed through the following passage, would recompense one for more than *even all* the poet's nonsense. It is astonishing that a man possessed of such powers should so constantly misapply them. My remarks would tend only to weaken the effect of this episode, which is written in the very soul and spirit of poetry. Nothing I have ever read has so completely excited the tender luxury of the mind, with all its loftier enthusiasm, as these lines:

[Quotes the 'Highland Girl' episode, *ibid.*, *PW*, II, pp. 374–6, ll. 886–935:

> But more than all, his heart is stung . . .
> This miserable vision!]

The arrival of Peter at the house of the deceased, and the grief of the widow are described with much pathos; and, to conclude,

> Peter Bell, who, till that night,
> Had been the wildest of his clan,
> Forsook his crimes, repressed his folly,
> And, after ten month's melancholy,
> Became a good and honest man.
> [*Ibid.*, *PW*, II, p. 382, ll. 1131–5]

'PETER BELL' AND 'THE WAGGONER'

218. Josiah Conder

Josiah Conder (?), Unsigned review, *Eclectic Review*, July 1819, xii (second series), 62–76

Marked 'X' in the London Library copy of the *Eclectic*. 'X' seems to be Conder's way of identifying his own work in this volume, as 'J. C.' was, in an earlier volume; one essay, continued from one volume to the next, is marked first, 'J. C.', then 'X'. On 8 July 1819 Crabb Robinson wrote of this review:

Read . . . an able criticism on *Peter Bell* in the *Eclectic Review*, which, though severe, I felt to be for the greater part just. It is written by one who understands, as well as feels, the excellence of Wordsworth as well as his great faults. I could not but feel the force of the remark that to dwell as Wordsworth does on the meanest of objects, exerting on them all the force of his intellect, evinces a sort of insanity. The author has too sarcastically reproached Wordsworth with conceit, and seems to impute as vice what is, I believe, mere peculiarity of taste; nor do I think he can be justly reproached with having lost the faculty of distinguishing great and small, noble and mean . . .

(*Henry Crabb Robinson on Books and their Writers*, ed. Edith J. Morley, 1938, I, 233–4)

Mr. Wordsworth has facetiously affixed the following motto on the title page of 'The Waggoner:'

> What's in a NAME?
> Brutus will start a spirit as soon as Cæsar.

And truly, a better answer to the demand could not have been given, than that which is tacitly supplied by the incongruous names of Brutus and Peter Bell, Cæsar and Benjamin the Waggoner. If the gifted biographer of the two modern heroes, was insensible to this incongruity, it would suffice to shew, what upon other grounds we have had reason to suspect, that as he is himself devoid of any talent for humour, so he is, through a singular simplicity of mind, insusceptible of the ludicrous. We imagine that this in *sooth* furnishes the key to that part of Mr. W.'s poetical character, which is written in cipher. The ludicrous always arises from contrast, from the juxta-position of incongruities, such as dignity and meanness, solemnity and insignificance. But an object is dignified or insignificant to us, according to the associations with which our imagination invests it; and it is possible that the imagination shall have been so accustomed to exert itself with intense interest upon things comparatively mean and trifling, and to appropriate these as the source of intellectual pleasure, that no adequate feelings shall be left for all that is in itself grand, or important, or captivating; and the relative magnitude of this latter class of objects shall be lost in the estimate of the mind, for want of a standard of measurement. Now it is obvious, that, to this individual, no such incongruity will be apparent between objects of vastly different dimensions and opposite character, as is to others the foundation of the ludicrous. No object in nature, taken simply by itself, partakes of this character. Take, for instance, one of Mr. Wordsworth's favourite heroes, a donkey; an animal upon whom has rested an unmerciful load of unmerited obloquy and ridicule. It must be familiar to the lovers of the picturesque, that not the noble horse itself forms so congruous and pleasing an object in a landscape. It is not its form, but the vulgarizing circumstances of degradation to which the poor drudge is subjected, that render it liable to become ridiculous. Array the poor beast in the caparison of a war horse, or, what comes to much the same thing, deck him out in the sentimental honours of heroic or elegiac verse, and the incongruity between the native character of the object, and the qualities of the style, will make itself irresistibly felt as in the highest degree amusing. But Mr. Wordsworth, we think we have a right to say, does not feel this. In the extensive horizon of his capacious intellect, all distant interests it should seem are dwarfed, while, as he lies recumbent, a shrub, or a blade of grass, acquires from nearness a microscopic magnitude occupying the whole field of vision. Or perhaps, in the profound abstraction of his contemplative solitude, princes and potters, heroes and donkeys, would pass before him in the landscape as things of scarcely perceptible difference of configuration, and as possessing equal claims upon his sovereign attention. Under such circumstances, a *simplicity* would soon come to pervade all the associations of ideas excited by external objects, which would forbid the impertinent intrusion of the ludicrous. And when the philosopher came back to the busy world of human action and interests, no doubt it must appear both unaccountable and provoking, to find that the subjects of his elevated lucubrations and rhapsodies, were deemed fit sport only for the critic's sneer and the public's laugh.

It is not the titles of these poems, the mere names of Peter Bell and the Waggoner, which are ridiculous. That effect, so far as it preceded the publication of the poems themselves, arose from the pompous *annoncé* of these tales, which seemed like the ushering of a washer-woman into a drawing-room. It was this which gave fair scope for the good humoured *hoax* which was played off by the author of the spurious Peter Bell. But how nobly, we thought, might Mr Wordsworth, if he has really in his possession and at his command, the talents which we have always given him credit for, how nobly might he revenge himself! We had only to suppose that when Peter Bell appeared, it should prove to be a tale of that highly picturesque and imaginative character which has given immortality to the name of Tam a Shanter, combining with the homeliness of style which the title bespoke, the deep tragic feeling of some of our old English ballads, or at least some portion of high moral interest; or, not to exact so high a task, we had only to imagine that it should prove such a tale as Cowper, or as Crabbe would have framed of similar materials, possessing either the pensive playfulness and high moral excellence which distinguish the writings of the one, or the strong graphic fidelity of representation peculiar to the coarse pencil of the other. It was surely no impertinent or idle supposition, that Mr. Wordsworth might be found to have produced under the titles he has chosen, two poems of merit and interest sufficient, fully to overpower whatever ludicrous associations any *travestie* of his style should have previously awaked.

But Mr. Wordsworth, we regret to say, has not done this. We must add that the public, though it has just reason to be dissatisfied, will be, and on that very account will be, indisposed to do justice to what he has done. The bad taste which is the condemning sin of his poetry, will revolt the reader at the outset.

Peter Bell was meant to be a tragi-comic tale, but Mr. Wordsworth cannot be comic, and it is well known to what ungraceful expedients persons devoid of native humour are seduced to resort by a misdirected ambition. To see a man trying to be playful and sportive, to whose rigidity of form, and unelastic tread, and solemnity of voice, the tones and attitudes of humour or of grace are incapable of being communicated, is a spectacle which only the malicious can take delight in. Persons under the influence of this desire of imitating entertaining qualities foreign from their own character, will descend to a coarseness and flippancy of style, into which they would on no other occasion have deviated, and to which a person of *true* humour or *true* wit, would have felt himself under no such necessity of having recourse. We cannot in any other way account for the vulgarisims which occur in the tale of Peter Bell. But we must proceed to our specimens. The poem opens with the following stanza:

> All by the moonlight river side
> It gave three miserable groans;
> ''Tis come then to a pretty pass,'
> Said Peter to the groaning Ass,
> 'But I will *bang* your bones!'
> [*Peter Bell, PW*, II, p. 339, ll. 191–5]

This our readers will readily think, is vulgar and unpromising enough; but there are worse passages still. Before they come to the tale itself, however, we must inform them that this tale has a prologue, in which the poet holds parley with a celestial boat of light, that transports him, much in the same way as the wooden horse did Don Quixote, through the regions of air. This radiant boat, instinct with life and intelligence, turns out to be an allegorical representation of the poet's fancy, which tempts him to venture into the higher region of romantic invention.

> I know secrets of a land
> Where human foot did never stray;
> Fair is the land as evening skies
> And cool, – though in the depth it lies
> Of burning Africa.
>
> Or we'll into the realm of Faery,
> Among the lovely shades of things;
> The shadowy forms of mountains bare,
> And streams, and bowers, and ladies fair;
> The shades of palaces and kings!
> [*Ibid.*, *PW*, II, p. 335, ll. 96–105]

The allegory is not well-managed: the reader does not for some time catch a glimpse of its purpose, but there are some very pleasing stanzas. The Poet thus replies to the adventurous sprite imbodied in the airy vehicle:

[Quotes *ibid.*, *PW*, II, p. 337, ll. 121–55:

> There was a time when all mankind . . .
> And be thy own delight!]

The next page accordingly introduces us to his good friend

> Stephen Otter,
> and Peter Bell the Potter.

Peter Bell is a wicked man, a fearful man. He had a dozen wedded wives, and does not love primroses. He attempted, one November night, to steal a stray ass, but the ass would not leave the spot where it was stationed. He '*banged* and *banged*' the poor creature till his arm ached, but still it would not stir. At length, leaning down upon the beast, he discovers in the pool 'a startling sight,' the corse of the poor brute's master. Peter swoons with fright, but on recovering himself resolves to take up the body, and then to let the ass carry him, if it will, to the cottage of the drowned man. The poor beast, now docile and thankful, acquits himself with all the fidelity of instinct, and Peter's hard heart, which had been previously subdued by terror, now relents to humanity and repentance at the sight of the fatherless family.

He

> —who till that night
> Had been the wildest of his clan,
> Forsook his crimes, repressed his folly,
> And, after ten months' melancholy,
> Became a good and honest man.
>
> [*Ibid.*, *PW*, II, p. 382, ll. 1131–5]

Such is the Tale. A more extraordinary conversion never excited the scorn of the sceptic, in the annals of what is termed Methodism. Strange to say, however, a 'Methodist' preacher is introduced by our Poet, as contributing, though in a very subsidiary degree, to work this strange metamorphosis. It is, perhaps, the first time such an incident was pressed into the service of poetry, and we give Mr. W. credit for venturing upon something like an honest reference to the fact of the efficacy of such preaching, although we cannot commend the manner in which he has made Scripture to jingle in his verse. The chief part in the effecting of this transformation of a hardened ruffian into 'a good man,' is, however, of course assigned to other *machinery*; and the Poet must be allowed to have shewn no small skill in describing the natural workings of the conscience and feelings, under the strong excitement, first of terror, and then of tenderness. When Mr. Wordsworth refrains from all attempt at humour, and forgets to be vulgar upon system, he seldom fails to interest by that natural pathos of manner, in which he is excelled by few of his contemporaries. The poor animal, with his freight, is pursuing his way homeward, and after passing through a gloomy grove of beech, reaches a narrow dell in the open moonlight. Peter's mind has not recovered from the horror and self-reproach produced by the sight of the drowned man, and as he rides along,

> The rocks that tower on either side
> Build up a wild fantastic scene;
> Temples like those among the Hindoos,
> And mosques, and spires, and abbey windows,
> And castles all with ivy green:
>
> And, while the Ass pursues his way,
> Along this solitary dell,
> As pensively his steps advance,
> The mosques and spires change countenance,
> And look at Peter Bell!
>
> [*Ibid.*, *PW*, II, p. 364, ll. 681–90]

Other circumstances occur to work up his terrified fancy to the highest pitch of excitement. The ass suddenly turns round its head and grins at him, at which Peter gives a grin responsive, when, at the moment, an explosion produced by a troop of miners some twenty fathoms under ground, confounds his forced mirth, and confirms all the suggestions of conscience as to his impending doom.

[Quotes *ibid.*, *PW*, II, pp. 371–6, ll. 846–940:

> But, as an oak in breathless air . . .
> A voice to Peter's ears ascends,
> Resounding from the woody glade.]

That voice is the voice of the 'fervent methodist,' preaching to no heedless flock, and exhorting them to repent, while yet they may find mercy, and to save their souls alive.

[Quotes *ibid.*, *PW*, II, pp. 376–7, ll. 956–70:

> Even as he pass'd the door . . .
> An infant that has known no sin.]

Arrived at the poor man's cottage, Peter has to encounter a scene which calls forth emotions to which he has long been a stranger. A little girl who had been sent to the meeting-house in hope of gaining some tidings, at the sight of the well known steed and his rider, shrieks out. 'My father! here's my father!' The sound reaches the poor widow's ears.

> Her joy was like a deep affright;
> And forth she rushed into the light,
> And saw it was another!

> And instantly, upon the earth
> Beneath the full-moon shining bright,
> Close at the Ass's feet she fell.
> [*Ibid.*, *PW*, II, p. 378, ll. 1008–13]

Peter, when she recovers, with difficulty gets out his tale, and while the woman is venting her passionate grief, he stands beside her trembling with perturbation.

[Quotes *ibid.*, *PW*, II, pp. 380–2, ll. 1052–120:

> His heart is opening more and more . . .
> 'Oh! God, I can endure no more!']

We know not how these extracts may affect our readers; but we will confess, that, in spite of the imbecilities of style which run through the narrative, and in spite of our determination not to allow Peter Bell, the potter, to gain upon our feelings, the Poet got the better of us, and we closed the Tale, resolved, even at the imminent risk of being set down for *Lakers* ourselves, to do its Author justice.

With the best intentions in the world, we sat down to the perusal of 'The Waggoner', for 'What's in a name?' Benjamin doubtless may start a spirit as well as Peter. This poem, it seems, existed in manuscript thirteen years ago, and therefore, though it does not pretend to 'the high tone of imagination and the deep touches of passion aimed at in the former poem,' yet, it must be supposed to come forth as the approved production of the Author's matured judgement. *Voyons.*

Benjamin 'the good, the patient, and the tender-hearted,' is the driver of 'a lordly wain,' who makes his horses do their work better up the hills of Cumberland by patience and fair words, than others can by all the eloquence of the whip. Howbeit, the said Benjamin was a frail mortal, and on a wet, blowing night, a light in a public house, and the squeak of a fiddle, had charms for him which he could not always withstand. One fatal night, he fell into company with a sailor and his wife. 'The Sailor, sailor now no more, but such he had been heretofore,' in return for the Waggoner's good offices in giving his wife a snug birth in the machine, treats him with a jolly bowl at the Cherry-tree. There they are seduced to tarry, till the owner of the waggon, alarmed at the lateness of its arrival, sallies forth, and on discovering this fresh instance of good Benjamin's infirmity, moreover, spying on the guardian mastiff's head, a wound received from the Sailor's steed,

> A wound, where plainly might be read
> What feats an Ass's hoof can do,
> [*The Waggoner, PW*, II, p. 203, Canto IV, ll. 175–6]

gives the said Benjamin his discharge. He, the hero of this most interesting piece of *Lake* history,

> When duty of that day was o'er,
> Laid down his whip – and served no more.
> Nor could the waggon long survive
> Which Benjamin had ceased to drive;
> [*Ibid.*, *PW*, II, p. 203, Canto IV, ll. 185–8]

and so, the good people of that country had

—two losses to sustain;
We lost both waggoner and wain!!!
[*Ibid.*, *PW*, II, p. 203, Canto IV, ll. 195–6]

Such is actually the sum and substance of this poem in four cantos! This
is the whole catastrophe to which the reader's attention is summoned by
all the pomp of verse. But it is fair to let the Poet assign in his own words,
his reason for composing this 'adventurous song.'
[Quotes *ibid.*, *PW*, II, pp. 203–5, Canto IV, ll. 197–269:

Accept, O Friend, for praise or blame . . .
Could keep alive when He was gone!]

Now, who would wish to disturb the innocent 'bliss' of this poet with the
shy spirit? Let Mr. Wordsworth write on, if it so please him, and let him
dream that inanity like this, the very garrulousness of dotage, is to
occupy 'a permanent place in the literature of his country. The lord of
Rydal Mount may safely disdain the pity which one might be led to
express for a man under less independent circumstances, labouring under
a similar delusion. He neither seeks a precarious living from his pen, nor
hangs upon the sentence of the critic for his praise. But there are many
who have never been of the number of his guests or of his flatterers, who
yet have ranked among his most genuine admirers, and whose mortification will not be small at being constrained to recognise in these productions the unequivocal marks of that tincture of imbecility which is the
latent cause of the eccentric action of true genius. That imbecility, they
have been hitherto backward to admit as at all compatible with so much
undoubted talent; they have attributed the peculiarities of style on which
with so much malignant pleasure the party-critic has fastened, to originality, to the seduction of system, to retired habits, or at worst to bad taste.
Yet, what is bad taste, but in other words an imbecility of judgement,
more or less, in reference to the objects and the qualities of things with
which the imagination is conversant? Wherever bad taste is characteristically predominant, it argues in some part of the mental constitution a
defect, a defect of genius, for we know of no sound definition of genius
which excludes the idea of taste. Shakspeare had exquisite taste. Milton's
taste was still more refined. All our best poets exhibit this quality in a
greater or less degree of perfection, and they are read in proportion as
they exhibit it. But Mr. Wordsworth's system pours contempt on all
those finer rules which his predecessors have worked by: he is for bringing in a Gothic horde of potters and pedlars and waggoners upon the

classic regions of poetry: he has attempted to set up a new reign of taste, and he has sacrificed his genius in the adventure.

Mr. Wordsworth has one chance of being read by posterity. It rests upon his finding some judicious friend to do for him the kind office which Pope did for Parnell, and which has probably saved his fame. If Wordsworth's best pieces could be collected into one volume, some of his early lyrics, a few of his odes, his noble sonnets, all his landscape sketches, and the best parts of the Excursion, while his ideots and his waggoners were collected into a bonfire on the top of Skiddaw, the 'Sybilline leaves' would form a most precious addition to our literature, and his name and his poetry would live, when his system, and his absurdities, and his critics should be forgotten.

As for ourselves, Mr. Wordsworth will probably set lightly enough by our praises or our censure; but we feel we owe him our best thanks. We have derived from some of his poetry the highest pleasure, and even from his worst productions we have gained something of moral value, in which we should be glad that our readers should participate. If amid the anxious bustle and collision of scenes to which the calm beauty of nature, and the intense solitude of her mountain recesses, seem to disown all relation, the imagination being scarcely able to realize them as different aspects of the same world, – if jaded with the fatigues and impertinences of an artificialized state of society, we have suffered ourselves to dwell at times with envy on the blissful occupants of green mounts and shady burns, and to envy more especially the man whose gifted fancy could people the solitudes of nature with the sociable sprites of the ideal world, – it has served more than perhaps any thing to reconcile us to our humbler lot, and less aspiring labours, to perceive at what a price this life of intellectual luxury is often purchased; how certainly a man suffers in the entireness of his moral being for withdrawing himself from the active service and warfare of common life, when his affections have not laid hold of the nobler realities with which the faith and hope of the Christian are then most conversant.

It is true that, to a benevolent mind, the meanest participant of humanity, be he a potter, a pedlar, or what he may, is, in reference to the essential qualities and circumstances of his being, most interesting, but this interest arises from regarding him under an aspect widely different from that in which the poet or the artist views the hero of his narrative, or the subject for which he prepares the canvas. His imagination is governed by impulses of a quite different kind, by habits and trains of thought wholly foreign from moral considerations. When, therefore, as *objects of the imagination*, things mean, trifling, and even of a degraded nature, are chosen and dwelt upon, and when the energies of thought are lavished upon subjects like these, we are warranted in saying, that the mind of the individual, whatever be its native power, and its power may remain undiminished, has lost some portion of its sanity.

We have spoken of Mr. Wordsworth's noble sonnets. The following two amply justify the application of that epithet.

[Quotes 'I watch, and long have watch'd, with calm regret', *PW*, III, p. 22; and 'Composed by the Side of Grasmere Lake', *PW*, III, p. 127]

219.

Unsigned review, *Literary and Statistical Magazine for Scotland*, August 1819, III, 314–19

The character of Wordsworth's poetry is too well known to require any description; and yet it would not be very easy to describe it were we called to execute the task. It may be conceived to bear nearly the same relation to the metaphysical school of the seventeenth century, whose founders were Cowley and Donne, which the speculations of the later Platonists bore to those of the older academies. Philosophy, in both cases, extended its bounds, and became more familiar in its applications. It left its high places and lofty pursuits, and came down to dwell with ordinary men, decorating their every-day callings, and shedding a lustre over their simplest thoughts and affections, by associating them with poetical ideas, or with such trains of deep and beautiful reflection, as a view of their condition might be supposed to suggest to a cultivated mind. The metaphysics of Wordsworth are those of the feelings, not of the intellect. He traces the links of that chain which connects the emotions of the heart with sights and sounds, and other objects of the external senses; giving himself no trouble about the generation of ideas properly so called, or about the subsequent processes of reasoning and judging. Wordsworth is only metaphysical, therefore, in as much as he habitually embodies in verse his own reveries, and sentiments, and reflec-tions, and dreams on human things as they lie before him, allowing himself to be wrapped up so closely in spiritual visions, and surrounded so thickly by the creatures of his own thought, that he entirely leaves behind him the material world, which had served to suggest these seraphic imaginations. Perhaps the epithet *mystical* would describe the nature of this poet's writings more truly than metaphysical; and it is only in compliance with the general fashion of speaking on this subject, that we have permitted ourselves to use the latter term.

With much delicacy and feeling, there is also much absurdity in the productions of Wordsworth. He touches the heart one moment, and the next he excites our ridicule. He delights by a soft, plaintive, and musical language, expressing ideas of the truest poetic beauty; and all at once you have something so excessively grotesque both in thought and words, that it is impossible not to laugh outright, whilst you are compelled to wonder at the marvellous incongruity of the author's manner. Nay, he seems to study, and to pique himself upon eccentricity; to set at defiance every rule of writing and of criticism, and to chuckle in secret over the amazement and disgust which he prepares for his reader. Take for instance the first and second stanzas in Peter Bell.

These verses are the commencement of a prologue which contains many beauties of a superior order, and yet we have seen several persons throw down the 'Tale' with indignation, upon the mere reading of the first stanza. The object of the said prologue, too, is neither more nor less than a defence of his singular choice of subjects to write upon, and was meant to show, that the 'Imagination not only does not require for its exercise the intervention of supernatural agency, but that though such agency be excluded, the faculty may be called forth as imperiously, and for kindred results of pleasure, by incidents within the compass of poetic probability, in the humblest departments of daily life.' The 'little boat,' then, is the faculty of Imagination, in which the poet is supposed to be carried through the most exalted regions of nature and of fancy, that he might be supplied with materials for more stately writing. The result will appear.

[Quotes *Peter Bell*, *PW*, II, pp. 332–4 and footnotes, Prologue, ll. 21–80–1:

> Away we go, my boat and I – . . .
> Just three good miles an hour.]

The tale of Peter Bell may be told in three sentences.

[The reviewer tells the tale in some ten sentences and long extracts.]

. . . the interview with the poor widow is the most pathetic part of the poem; and it is no doubt rendered more pathetic by the simplicity of style peculiar to Wordsworth. But he is too fond of the ass. This quadruped is a great favourite with painters, both from the picturesque effect which its presence produces, and also from the associations with which its name is connected in scripture history, and in the simple and more innocent periods of remote antiquity. It does not, however, suit the poet so well; and in the present case, the incessant bursts of passion and regard directed towards the half-starved brute, and mixed with those of sorrow for the woman and her fatherless babes, only serve to break in upon our feelings, and to excite our disgust . . .

The story of the Waggoner is still more barren of incident than that of Peter Bell . . . [Relates story.]

It must strike every reader, that the fine talents of Wordsworth are completely thrown away on such subjects as these. It is in fact impossible to give interest or dignity to such a tale as the Waggoner; and all the beauty which this poem contains, is drawn from the description of the scenery through which the waggon was wont to pass, and with which honest Ben and his team had in reality no more connection than the raven which flew over it, or the wind which swept along its surface. Every subject is indeed to a certain extent capable of poetical decoration, and the more unpromising the materials, the greater, perhaps, the merit of the author; but what would we think of a poet who should task his muse to celebrate the uses and motions of a dust cart, or the morning operations of a street scavenger! There are limits below which poetry can never descend with success; and if the *res lecta potenter*[1] means any thing as a critical maxim, it must imply that every species of writing is best exercised on a certain order of topics, as well as that different men excel in different things: And notwithstanding the great powers of Wordsworth in description and narrative, we can assure him that any small degree of success which may have attended his exertions, will never bring men to think that poetry may profitably scatter its beauties on washing-tubs, baby-clothes, bull-dogs, and donkies.

EDITOR'S NOTE

1.   'Subject chosen in accordance with one's ability' (Horace, *Ars Poetica*, 40).

220. Juliet Smith (*fl.* 1760–1840)

From a letter to Thomas Wilkinson of Yanwath, 22 October 1819

Mrs Juliet Smith of Tent Lodge, Coniston, was mother of the precocious authoress Elizabeth Smith (1776–1806). With another daughter, Kitty, she had visited Dove Cottage on 5 June 1802.

. . . were you charm'd with 'Peter Bell the Potter'? I was assured one of the Author's strenuous Admirers declared, that the line respecting the Ass who 'on the pivot of his skull turn'd his long left Ear,' was the finest in the Poem!! I replied, I am satisfied, if that's the *best* what must be the rest – Have you seen 'Benjamin the Waggoner'? that Out Herods Herod! The Horses *think*, *reflect* & even *pray*, but their Driver does none of these – I verily believe such a production never went to the Press before –

(Ms. Friends' House Library)

221.

Unsigned review, *Edinburgh Monthly Review*, December 1819, II, 654–61

M^R. WORDSWORTH is undoubtedly a man of genius. To be convinced of this, we have only to turn to any of his numerous publications; in all of which, a reader of ordinary discernment will perceive the gleams of a brilliant fancy occasionally bursting upon the sombre pictures of humble life, which it is his high pleasure to delineate. But while we admit his inspiration, and that it is, therefore, in his power to furnish a delicious banquet to the lovers of genuine poetry, we feel painfully convinced, that he does not often choose to afford the expected gratification. Of what avail are his talents, we ask, if he do not exert them in the manner that is likely to gratify public taste? Why has he not listened to the advice of those periodical writers, who, notwithstanding all their defects and their prejudices, must be allowed to possess the best opportunities of ascertaining what that taste is? It is, or at least ought to be, for the public that every poet writes; and we conceive it to be his bounden duty, while in fact he is a candidate for popular favour, to sacrifice some of his own trivial predilections to the general opinion of his readers. To the didactic and the satirical poet, indeed, it is admitted as a licence to contravene preva- lent habits and sentiments; but these can rarely be neglected with impun- ity where mere taste is concerned. Mr. Wordsworth, however, having acquired renown as the head of a far-famed poetical school, may be desirous of preserving his title and dignities unimpaired. If this be his object, we think him peculiarly fortunate in the publication of the pres- ent poems, which are composed according to the most rigid rules of the sect, and display a lowliness and simplicity of conception, equalled indeed by the homeliness of the language in which they are clothed, that we should think not likely to be excelled by the effusions of any sub- sequent disciple. We forbear at present from all general criticism, and confine ourselves to a short analysis, which, we believe, will justify the sentence now pronounced. Let us begin with Peter Bell.

This poem consists of a prologue and three parts. In the prologue, the author steps into his 'little boat, twin sister of the crescent moon;' and, in order, no doubt, to be fitted for the arduous undertaking in which he is about to engage, takes a trip through the etherial regions. We extract the following description of the appearance of our earth and island, which we are glad to find make so good a show at a distance.

[Quotes *Peter Bell*, *PW*, II, pp. 333–4 and footnotes, ll. 56–65:

> And there it is, the matchless Earth! . . .
> Ye fairies from all evil keep her!]

The object of the prologue, as we are told in the dedication, somewhat fortunately, for it may be questioned if we could have made the discovery ourselves, is to shew, that 'the imagination not only does not require for its exercise the intervention of supernatural agency, but that, though such agency be excluded, the faculty may be called forth as imperiously, and for kindred results of pleasure, by incidents, within the compass of poetic probability, in the humblest departments of daily life.' After this, our readers will probably be not a little astonished to be told, that there are no less than two instances of the intervention of supernatural agency in the poem before us. The author's view of this subject will be found, it is believed, in the following extract:

[Quotes *ibid.*, *PW*, II, pp. 336–7, ll. 131–50:

> Long have I lov'd what I behold . . .
> 'Tis lodg'd within her silent tear.]

709

The poet then civilly asks permission to descend from his airy carriage, alleging, in his excuse, that he must relate to some of his friends, the tale of Peter Bell the potter. At this the boat flies off in scorn, and leaves the bard to make the best of his way to the place where his audience is convened.

As for the tale itself, let the following brief outline suffice. [Summary.]

The most important living personages in this pathetic tale, for we put the corpse entirely out of the question, are Peter Bell and the ass; and so great are the respective claims to notoriety of these worthy characters, that we are, for a time, at some loss to determine to which of them the name of hero ought to be given. The reason of our concluding in favour of the the latter may be shortly stated. Peter Bell, we conceive, is but a common every-day sort of animal, – saving that he has more wives than ordinary in our clime; and his prototype may be seen, frequently enough, trudging along the public roads. The ass, on the other hand, being rather a rare creature of its kind, and exciting as deep an interest as his two-legged fellow-adventurer, is *a fortiori* entitled to pre-eminence. Perhaps we are warranted in this conclusion by the indications which we think we can perceive of the author's own attachment, notwithstanding his selection of a title which promises nothing but human qualities. It is indeed impossible sufficiently to appreciate the great pains which he has taken to render our favourite worthy of all the commiseration and admiration we can bestow; and, undoubtedly, nothing withholds us from applauding the success of his very generous labour, but a conviction, that, with all its excellencies, and notwithstanding all our own defects, an ass is too far beneath us in the scale of nature, to permit our sympathizing in its history.

We do not intend to follow Peter regularly through the whole of his various peregrinations, because we think we shall perform a more grateful task, and better study our readers' gratification, by presenting them with a few of the many beautiful passages which are scattered through this motley composition. Even the finest of them, we must premise, however, are not free from the faults to which we have slightly adverted. Take the following extract as an instance:

[Quotes *ibid.*, *PW*, II, pp. 360–2, ll. 611–50:

> When hark, a burst of doleful sound! . . .
> Hovering around with dolorous moan!]

The following passage is a fit comparison for the foregoing. It describes Peter's state of mind, when his conscience, awakened from the lethargy in which it had been so long sunk, begins to take a survey of the past. Pathos and vulgarity – thrilling thought and disgusting quaintness of expression, have rarely so combined to neutralize verse.

[Quotes *ibid.*, *PW*, II, pp. 374–5, ll. 886–930:

> But more than all, his heart is stung . . .
> My mother! Oh my mother!]

Another passage, which, though rather long, we extract entire, will afford our readers a fair opportunity of forming a correct judgment of the author's comico-lugubrious peculiarities of matter and manner. Peter, arriving at the cottage door of the drowned man, is met by a little girl –

[Quotes *ibid.*, *PW*, II, pp. 378–80, ll. 1001–70:

> She to the meeting-house was bound . . .
> Seven are they, and all fatherless!]

What a pity it is that so exquisite a picture as is presented to us in this poem, should be wilfully marred by a puerile affectation of simplicity! We say, unhesitatingly, affectation – because we are perfectly convinced that no one, of the rank and education of a gentleman, could or would employ the ideas and expressions to which we allude, without a conscious effort to do so; and we add the epithet puerile, because the object for which they are employed, is unworthy the ambition of any individual of our sex that has been a dozen years out of the nursery.

We must now shortly advert to the other poem, which is very appropriately called the Waggoner. It celebrates a nocturnal adventure of an honest warm-hearted Waggoner, whose chief failing happens to be an over-fondness for a social glass. We are introduced to him walking slowly along by the side of his team, on a fine evening in the delightful month of June, and accompany him past two public houses, which, notwithstanding his propensity, he has sufficient self-denial to avoid. Whilst indulging in self-gratulations on this mighty victory over his master passion, he is overtaken by a thunder storm, the description of which we willingly extract. Perhaps it is owing in a great measure to the situation in which it stands, that it is relished by us; as, in truth, like a flower in the midst of a desert—it seems the more beautiful from the objects with which it is contrasted. But be this as it may, we conceive it worthy of commendation.

[Quotes *The Waggoner*, *PW*, II, p. 183, Canto I, ll. 152–79:

> The thunder had begun to growl— . . .
> Still sit upon Helm-crag together!]

711

This storm, so finely described, is, as might be expected, the prelude to a very important adventure. Our hero is accosted by a female, who proves to be the wife of an old sailor, and who carries an infant in her arms. Having placed her with her little charge in the waggon, the sailor next comes forward, and shortly entices Benjamin into a public house, where they both get drunk. The consequence is, that our waggoner does not arrive at his destination by the time appointed; and that his master, who comes in a rage to ascertain the cause of the delay, dismisses him from his place.

These two poems, the author tells us, were published separately, because, 'from the higher tone of imagination, and the deeper touches of passion aimed at' in Peter Bell, the Waggoner could not accompany it without disadvantage. On the same principle, we think he ought not to have allowed the many beautiful passages to be found in both poems to lose their effect by being associated with objects so contemptible and ludicrous as those with which they are surrounded.

Of the Sonnets appended to both poems, we shall merely say, that they are free of one glaring defect, so abundant in all the author's larger works – vulgarity of expression.

We could not close our first year's lucubrations, without noticing, however briefly and imperfectly, the productions of an author, for whose talents and genius and moral purity, we entertain unfeigned respect, though we may feel somewhat grieved at the manner in which they are generally displayed. Notwithstanding the extraordinary pains which he assures us have been bestowed upon these poems, to render them worthy of a favourable reception from the public, and of filling a *permanent* station in the literature of his country, we deem it utterly impossible that they ever can be popular. They have passages, it is true, which require only to be read in order to be admired, and which may probably shine in some future specimens of English poetry; but, considered as a whole, neither of these pieces, we apprehend, is possessed of sufficient buoyancy to enable it to float down the stream of immortality; and the only permanence that we think can be promised them is in the gulf of oblivion.

'THE WAGGONER'

222. Charles Lamb

From a letter to Wordsworth, 7 June 1819

This letter was written in response to Wordsworth's dedicating *The Waggoner* to Lamb.

You cannot imagine how proud we are here of the dedication. We read it twice for once that we do the poem – I mean all through – yet Benjamin is no common favorite – there is a spirit of beautiful tolerance in it – it is as good as it was in 1806 – and will be as good in 1829 if our dim eyes shall be awake to peruse it . . .

I re-read the White Doe of Rylston – the title should be always written at length – –

Manning had just sent it home and it came as fresh to me as the immortal creature it speaks of. M. sent it home with a note, having this passage in it, 'I cannot help writing to you while I am reading Wordsworths poem. I am got into the 3rd Canto, and say that it raises my opinion of him very much indeed.* 'Tis broad; noble; poetical; with a masterly scanning of human actions, absolutely above common readers. What a manly (implied) interpretation of (bad) party-actions, as trampling the bible, &c.' – and so he goes on.
*N.B. M – from his peregrinations is 12 or 14 years *behind* in his knowledge of who has and who has not written good verse of late.

I do not know which I like best, the prologue (the latter part specially) to P. Bell, or the Epilogue to Benjamin. Yes, I tell stories, I do know. I like the last best, and the Waggoner altogether as a pleasanter remembrance to me than the Itinerant. If it were not, the page before the first page would and ought to make it so.

The sonnets are not all new to me. Of what are, the 9th I like the best. Thank you for that to Walton. I take it as a favor done to me, that, being so old a darling of mine, you should bear testimony to his worth in a book containing a dedi—

I cannot write the vain word at full length any longer.

If as you say, the Waggoner in some sort came at my call, O for a potent voice to call forth the Recluse from his profound Dormitory, where he sleeps forgetful of his foolish charge The World.

(*The Letters of Charles and Mary Lamb*, ed. E. V. Lucas, 1935, II, 249–51)

223.

Unsigned review,[1] *Blackwood's Edinburgh Magazine*, June 1819, V, 332–4

The Waggoner is a poem of a kind whereof Mr Wordsworth's muse had not hitherto afforded any example. It is lightly and playful, written in a dancing, merry, irregular measure, sometimes almost Hudibrastic in its cadences and rhymes. It abounds in passages which Mr Crabbe might have written; but nobody, we are sure, who might have seen it published anonymously would have suspected it to be a production of the Great Poet of the Lakes.

Over the whole of this playfully written narrative, however, there is diffused a certain delicacy of touch and feeling, which we (who pretend to be pretty well skilled in all the poetry of the day) do not think any living poet, except Wordsworth, could have scattered so easily over so unpromising a theme. The story is nothing more than a fragment of the history of a certain poor man, who was long employed in driving a huge waggon, with eight horses, in the neighbourhood of the poet's residence, and whose good temper and skill in this his calling had been more than sufficient to counterbalance, in the eyes of the people among whom he travelled, some little besetting infirmities of drunkenness and dissipation and delay. His master, however, was less merciful in his judgment of these failings, and the present little poem narrates how he turned off poor Benjamin, one fine summer morning, for having deferred the arrival of the waggon beyond its appointed time, by sitting for several merry hours in a hedge ale-house – tempted to this excess chiefly by the charming conversation of a wayfaring showman, who had once been a sailor under Lord Nelson, and who now carried about with him a mimic three-decker, with all her tackle complete, for the temptation and gratification of the curiosity of the Dalesmen of Cumberland.

The Poem has come into our hands just as our last sheet is going to press, so that we have no time for any thing like criticism – nor indeed does the case require it. Those who do not perceive the beauty of the passages we shall quote, deserve to be pitied; but they do not deserve to be argued with.

[Quotes *The Waggoner*, *PW*, II, p. 189, Canto II, ll. 52–69:

> Blithe souls and lightsome hearts have we . . .
> The very bacon shows its feeling,
> Swinging from the smoky ceiling!

and *ibid*., pp. 202–5, Canto IV, 11. 171–269:

> With eager eyes the Master pries . . .
> And of his stately Charge, which none
> Could keep alive when He was gone!]

Mr Wordsworth has added twelve Sonnets; we have made room for five of them . . .

EDITOR'S NOTE

1. Attributed to John Wilson by A. L. Strout (*A Bibliography of Articles in Blackwood's Magazine*, Lubbock, Texas, 1859).

224.

Unsigned review, *Literary Gazette*, 12 June 1819, III, 369–71

The review is possibly by Jerdan, see entry 207.

What's in a name?

– – – – – –

Brutus will start a spirit as soon as Caesar.

Or, in other words, one sort of subject is as fitting for poetry as another, – the mean is equal to the dignified, the affected to the affecting, the childish to the pathetic. Mr. Wordsworth produces his character in rags; he is a Guy Faux, like Peter Bell, or a low-lived fellow like this Benjamin the Waggoner. There is indeed more of nature about the latter; his beggar's garb has some spangles upon it, nay, some tags of bullion; but still the original sin of his nature disfigures the whole; and while we observe with pleasure his few and scattered poetical beauties, we are compelled to think them accidental, seeing that his deformities are pervading and systematic.

This Poem is addressed to Mr. Charles Lamb, and the writer, as usual, attaching importance to what is of no consequence, informs us that it was read to his dedicatee in the year 1806; but was not added to Peter Bell, lest it should appear to disadvantage by the side of 'the higher tone of imagination, and the deeper touches of passion aimed at in the former.'!! Our readers, who agreed with us in the opinion we expressed of that silly farrago, will appreciate the modesty of the author's sentiment; and be prepared to expect an indescribably ridiculous performance in any thing which could be so bad as to dread injury from being

> . . . Worse than worst
> Of those, that lawless and uncertain thoughts
> Imagine.

But in this case, as in many others, the author seems to us to have formed a wrong estimate. Master Benjamin, though absurd enough, is not quite so absurd as Master Peter; the spectacle is not so ludicrous in this mezzo-tint, as in the attempt upon the 'higher tones and deeper touches;' there is a little more common sense about Mr. Wordsworth's Waggoner than about his Tinker, a little more nature and a little less pretension, so that upon the whole, were it not set up as a standard of all excellence, we could be content to let it pass as an endurable composition, in which a few good ideas and some accurate descriptions of scenery served to contrast a mass of imbecile trifling and low peculiarities.

We confess without hesitation our general contempt for the Lake school, and for the powers that minister to it withal. What credit can be given for verses which any boy of ten years old could write? We shall quote some of the best, or rather the least absurd, passages in this silly poem; and by way of illustration we give some doggrels written in our presence, on the model of the leader of the *Aqueous*, and in scorn of him.

> DRURY LANE
> The play is over, – like a tide
> The rabble fill the portals wide,
> Some squeezing out, some rushing in,
> With stamp and squall, and growl and grin.

[Some 30 lines of this.]

But there is nothing to prevent this jingle of rhyme from going on to any extent: this poetry is as good (or as bad) as Mr. Wordsworth's, and it was written by a friend in the few minutes that we were writing these observations. If any collection of rugged names and raggamuffin allusions is poetry, we see no reason why the Fleet prison and Avemaria Lane should not take a classical place beside Gimmer-crag, and Nathdale Fell; but, if Mr. Wordsworth is only to be tried by the picturesque, let us see what *we* can do by the system of merely providing rhyme for rhyme, and letting the sense take its chance;

> Tis lovely to stand on the Autumn hill,
> When the Sun is down and the air is still,
> And rushing thro' the forest trees
> Comes the sigh of the evening breeze –

[8 more lines.]

This is doggrel, and written with no reference beyond that of letting one line correspond in harmony with the other; and of such material is the mass of the nonsense called Wordsworth's poetry.

Before quoting those parts of the Waggoner which strike us as most fairly illustrating its merits and demerits, we shall briefly relate the story . . . [Summary]

The poem begins abruptly, as if one of the springs were broken:

> 'Tis spent – this burning day of June!
> Soft darkness o'er its latest gleams is stealing;
>
> – – – – – –
>
> Confiding glow-worms, 'tis a night
> Propitious to your earth-born light!
>
> – – – – – –
>
> The air, as in a Lion's den,
> Is close and hot; –
>
> (*Lo, a second Daniel!*)
>
>   . . . And now there
> Comes a tired and sultry breeze
> With a haunting and a panting,
> Like the stifling of disease; –
>
> [*The Waggoner*, *PW*, II, pp. 177–8, Canto I, ll. 1–2, ll. 7–8
>   and ll. 15–19]

Here in eighteen lines at the beginning of the Waggoner, we have specimens in plenty of what the Lakeists admire, but which we hold to be extravagant foolery usurping the semblance of poetic imagery, 'Soft darkness' is hard to understand; 'confiding glow-worms' with their 'earth-born light,' still more unintelligible; and 'a tired breeze with a haunting,' quite a lusus naturæ. Nevertheless they serve to introduce the subject in a way entirely a la Wordsworth. We have just been told that except the buzzing of the Dor-hawk, that solitary *bird*, there was nothing but

> Silence deeper far than that of deepest noon –
> [*Ibid.*, *PW*, II, p. 177, Canto I, l. 6]

Yet the author bursts out with

> *Hush*, there is some one on the stir!
> Tis Benjamin the Waggoner –
> [*Ibid.*, *PW*, II, p. 178, Canto I, lll. 22–3]

As if the Dor-hawk, the only noisy creature in creation at the time, cared one jot for Benjamin, or would cease its own wheelings to listen to his wheels! We do not insist upon the trite vulgarity of being 'on the stir,' as the poem abounds with similar expressions, under the utterly mistaken idea that whatever low terms the Lake Bards and their followers please to employ, become immediately exalted into poetical fitness by the mere honour of their selection. Thus, for example, we hear of the driver that

> Many a breathing fit he takes.
> [*Ibid.*, *PW*, II, p. 178, Canto I, l. 37]

At a shower of rain

> He starts – and, at the admonition
> Takes a survey of his condition.
> [*Ibid.*, *PW*, II, p. 183, Canto I, ll. 158–9]

When he meets the Sailor, this doggrel ensues:

> Then Benjamin entreats the man
> Would mount, too, quickly as he can.
> [*Ibid.*, *PW*, II, p. 186, Canto I, ll. 253–4]

And he replies—

'Go you your way, and mind not me;
For I must have, whate'er betide,
My Ass and fifty things beside, –
Go, and I'll follow speedily!'
[*Ibid.*, *PW*, II, p. 186, Canto I, ll. 258–61]

Now truly if this be poetry, why, – the following is also poetry.

To a little tent hard by
Turns the Sailor instantly;
For when at closing-in of day
The Family had come that way; –
[*Ibid.*, *PW*, II, pp. 186–7, see footnotes, Canto I,
ll. 264–7]

But it is vain to follow out these glaring defects with the hope of bring-ing this School to a sense of what is due to the Muse – she is to them a dirty pot-girl, and, as with depraved tastes of another kind, the more homely the better. Nay, even black stockings and uncleanliness come, from this species of indulgence, to be preferred to well-dressed beauty and refinement. Our Waggoner and his friend are described,

. . . After their high-minded riot,
Sickening into thoughtful quiet.
[*Ibid.*, *PW*, II, p. 199, Canto IV, ll. 71–2]

And as if one nasty image were not enough, the horses straining their utmost efforts are painted with the accuracy of a beastly Dutchman, and all that is filthy enlarged upon, as other writers might dwell on a charming picture:

And the smoke and respiration
Rising like an exhalation,
Bends with the mist, – a moving shroud,
To form – an undissolving cloud;
Which with slant ray the merry sun
Takes delight to play upon.
[*Ibid.*, *PW*, II, p. 200, Canto IV, ll. 102–7]

'Then did the Sun on dunghill shine,' as our friend Pistol says, for we are sure the God of Day is vilified by being accused of delighting to play upon any such unsavoury ('undissolving!') cloud.

If Swift's definition of a good style be correct, this composition of Mr. Wordsworth is not only indifferent poetry, but bad language. No one can allow that the annexed passages are examples of 'proper words in proper places;' on the contrary, they are improper words adopted for rhymes' sake, expletives to eke out the measure, or expressions which do not convey the meaning of the writer. Of a sign it is said, that it

> Offered a greeting of good ale
> To all who entered Grasmere Vale;
> And *called on him* [i.e. bid him] who must depart
> To leave it with a joyful heart.
>> [*Ibid.*, *PW*, II, p. 179, Canto I, ll. 54–7]

Of the waggon-team, when Benjamin exhorts them to proceed,

> The ranks were taken with *one mind*.
>> [*Ibid.*, *PW*, II, p. 182 and footnotes, Canto I, l. 133]

(i.e. one mind of eight horses!)

A storm.

> The road is *black* before his eyes,
> *Glimmering faintly* where it *lies*;
> Black is the sky – and every hill,
> Up to the sky, is blacker *still*:
>> [*Ibid.*, *PW*, II, p. 183, Canto I, ll. 160–3]

The angry master discharging the waggoner on account of the ass having kicked the dog:

> . . . This aggravation,
> This complicated provocation,
> A hoard of grievances unsealed;
> All past forgiveness *it repealed*; –
>> [*Ibid.*, *PW*, II, p. 203, Canto IV, ll. 177–80]

> A nobler ship *did* never swim.
>> [*Ibid.*, *PW*, II, p. 191, Canto II, l. 119]

> The Waggoner with prompt *command*,
> *Summons* his horses to a stand.
>> [*Ibid.*, *PW*, II, p. 185, Canto I, ll. 223–4]

Other blemishes of other sorts might be multiplied, but this is no pleasing task, nor would we perform it but for the arrogant claims put forward by this class of writers, and we shall only cite two of bad grammar. The Sailor

Intent to use his utmost haste,
Gained ground upon the waggon fast –
And *gives* (gave) another lusty cheer;
– – – – – –

        [*Ibid., PW,* II, pp. 187–8, Canto II, ll. 16–18]

The Cherry Tree:

Thence the sound – the light is there
As Benjamin is now aware,
Who neither heard nor saw – *no more*
Than if he had been deaf and blind –
    [*Ibid., PW,* II, p. 188 and footnotes, Canto II, ll. 23–6]

Than which four lines of more faulty construction are not to be found in any author, from Taylor the water poet to the lowest scribbler of the Lakes.

We now arrive at the more agreeable office of endeavouring to extract specimens of Mr. Wordsworth's better parts. Benjamin's victory over the first ale-house (which reminds us of that of a great drinker, who swore he would pass the door of the tap where his morning dram was wont to be swallowed; kept his oath, but immediately returned to reward his constancy with a double allowance) and the approach of the storm, are neatly given:

[Quotes *ibid., PW,* II, pp. 182–3, Canto I, ll. 146–57:

While Benjamin in earnest mood . . .
Fell with the weight of drops of lead; –

and ll. 194–204:

He is astounded, wonder not . . .
A rending o'er his head begins the 'fray again.]

The description of the assemblage at a village tavern is a spirited drawing:
[Quotes *ibid., PW,* II, pp. 189–90, Canto II, ll. 52–100:

Blithe souls and lightsome hearts have we . . .
But enjoy their own the more!]

This shews that if the choice of subject were mended, the author might paint more passably: his local scenery is also, in some places, accurate and natural. These are, we presume, the 'gleams of fancy' which he tells us have been shed on his tale,

Like pleasant sunbeams shifting still
Upon the side of a distant hill,
[*Ibid.*, *PW*, II, p. 204, Canto IV, ll. 204–5]

insomuch, that 'Nature might not be gainsaid,' and he accordingly published the 'adventurous song.' These reasons, and a four-and-sixpenny
book added to the five-and-sixpenny Peter Bell, will, it is trusted, satisfy
the reading public. For ourselves, we will part on good terms with the
author, and therefore subjoin two of the best sonnets our taste enables us
to select from the twelve which conclude these pages.

[Quotes 'The Wild Duck's Nest', *PW*, III, p. 9; and 'I watch, and long
have watched, with calm regret', *PW*, III, p. 22.]

225.

Unsigned review, *European Magazine*, June 1819, LXXV, 531–3

Probably the work of J. B. (see J. B.'s review of Peter Bell, entry 211).

We are so great admirers of Mr. Wordsworth's genius, that we had hailed
with pleasure the unusual fertility of his Muse; but 'what a falling off is
here!' our disappointment is proportioned to our anticipated gratification. As soon as *Peter Bell* was published, *The Waggoner* was announced;
and before the relish of the excellence of the former had subsided, the
insipidity of the latter came full upon our critical palate. It is, perhaps,
this immediate contrast which is as injurious to *the Waggoner* as its
intrinsic defects.

The dedication to Mr. Charles Lamb seems shyly to insinuate that it
has been published with his approbation, if not at his request; if this be
so, his friendship must have blinded the judgment of the most clear-
sighted critic of the present day; and we may venture to assert, that had
the poem been written by any one, other than his friend, none *could* have
discovered its blemishes, more readily than Mr. Lamb.

The subject is not so well adapted for Mr. Wordsworth's talents as
those which he generally selects, nor is the execution more happy than
the subject; – they are both fitter for a nursery song, than to assist
in establishing the author in that station among the first poets of the

country, to which, with all his faults, he is undoubtedly entitled. There is none of the elegant painting of the silent objects of Nature, no pathetic delineations of deep feeling, which adorn his other poems, and for which Peter Bell is so eminently remarkable.

The story, if story it may be called, is of a good tempered silly sort of a Waggoner, for whom good liquor has irresistible charms, driving his team along the road through the mountains, in the neighbourhood of the Lakes, in the close of a very hot day in June. The description at the commencement is in the author's usually excellent style.

[Quotes *The Waggoner*, *PW*, II, pp. 177–8, Canto I, ll. 1–21:

> 'Tis spent—this burning day of June! . . .
> And the silence makes it sweet.]

Our friend Benjamin, 'that frail child of thirsty clay,' after making violent resolutions of sobriety, and passing two public-houses without yielding to his inclinations, is overtaken by a violent thunder tempest, during which he falls in with a sailor, and his wife, and child, who are also exposed to *the pelting of the pitiless storm*. The sailor has in his suite 'a solitary ass,' dragging a model of a ship. The ass is to Mr. Wordsworth's poetry what the *White horse* is to Wouvermann's paintings, always in the fore-ground[1] – or like the jack at bowls – no play without him.

Benjamin, whose head and heart seem of a congenial softness, gives the woman the shelter of his waggon, and himself, the sailor, *and the ass*, follow on foot.

The second canto begins with a most novel and ingenious method of telling the hour, by informing you what it *would* have been by the clock of a certain church, if that church had, *par hasard*, happened to have had a clock.

[Quotes *ibid.*, *PW*, II, p. 187, Canto II, ll. 1–9:

> If Wytheburn's modest House of Prayer . . .
> Its bead-roll of midnight.]

And this is the awful period at which all Benjamin's good resolves are to fail before the attraction of a fiddle and a full tankard. – (Beer, rascally beer, was the first parent of the sophisters and the fallacies.)
[Summary and quotation.]
The description of the rustic fête at the Cherry Tree is given with a vigorous jollity, more like the effusions of poor Burns, than those of the 'musing melancholy' author – the subject seems to have inspired him.

[Quotes *ibid.*, *PW*, II, p. 189, Canto II, ll. 52–81:

723

> Blithe souls and lightsome hearts have we . . .
> All care with Benjamin is gone . . .
> A Cæsar past the Rubicon!]

After the exhibition of the sailor's ship to the guests of the Cherry Tree, and two hours' toping, '*Again behold them on their way.*'

The poet then pictures the feelings of the drunken men in very rapturous terms, but a water-drinker like Mr. Wordsworth paints the delights of drunkenness rather too warmly for the reality – at least we (who are *not* water-drinkers) think so. And the only excuse for the application of such lines as the following to the two drunken fools, will be, to believe that the author was himself a little *dans less histoires* when he wrote them.

[Quotes *ibid.*, *PW*, II, pp. 193–4, Canto III, ll. 31–44:

> —While they coast the silent lake,
> Their *inspiration* I partake;
> *Share their empyreal spirits* – yea . . .
> What *tears of rapture,*'—]

Maudlin drunk too! From this fellowship arises an offer on the part of Benjamin to tether the ass (*two* are good company where *three* are none) to the waggon, by way of getting rid of him; but there is unfortunately a mastiff also tied under the waggon, whose convenience had not been consulted in the arrangement, and who was

> —not well pleased to be
> So very near such company.
> [*Ibid.*, *PW*, II, p. 194 in footnotes, Canto III,
> ll. 60–3]

These new allies under the waggon are by no means such good friends as their biped masters; and the ass, who by the way, is not so well bred as Mr. Wordsworth's asses, in general, are, kicks the poor dog on the head, as a means of teaching him better manners.

> The ass uplifting a hind hoof,
> *Salutes* the mastiff on the head,
> And so were better manners bred,
> And all was calm and quieted.
> [*Ibid.*, *PW*, II, p. 196, Canto III, ll. 106–9]

The *impression* which this made on the dog was not easily effaced, as the sequel shews.

724

They proceed: – the following is an elegant description of a circumstance which in any other hands would either be offensive or nothing – the horses pulling up hill:

[Quotes *ibid.*, *PW*, II, pp. 200–1, Canto IV, ll. 99–115:

> Tugging all with might and main – . . .
> Him and his enemies between!]

But, alas! all 'this outward glory' cannot shield poor Benjamin from the ire of his master, who, in consequence of his delay, has come to look for him. He is angry at finding the vagabond inside and outside passengers of his waggon – angry at Benjamin's loitering – but most angry when he discovers the trifling remembrance which the ass had bestowed on his noble mastiff, on whose head

> —there plainly might be read
> What *feats* an ass's *hoof* can do.
> [*Ibid.*, *PW*, II, p. 203, Canto IV, ll. 175–6]

We suspect that the author meant something like a pun in this last line – but as this is an infirmity to which all frail mankind are obnoxious, in Christian charity we pass it. The consequence of the master's anger is Benjamin's discharge.

> And thus, and through distemper'd blood
> On both sides, Benjamin the good,
> The patient, and the tender-hearted,
> Was from his team and waggon parted;
> When duty of that day was o'er,
> Laid down his whip, and served no more.
> [*Ibid.*, *PW*, II, p. 203, Canto IV, ll. 181–6]

And the waggon and team were after that reduced to eight sorry carts, 'unworthy successors of thee!' as Mr. W. has it, apostrophising the waggon.

When such a man as Mr. W. will condescend to write in the silly style in which he has here indulged, it can hardly be wondered at, that some persons shall be found to parody, and others to vilify his works; for it is his own fault that he is placed within reach of the puerile ridicule of the one, or the unprincipled abuse of the other.

725

EDITOR'S NOTE

1. Philip Wouvermann (1619–1668), Dutch painter of battle and hunting scenes.

226.

Unsigned review, *General Review or Weekly Literary Epitome*, June 1819, I, 36–46

That a mind capable of noble things, like that of Mr. WORDSWORTH, should pervert and debase its powers, by descending to compose such childish doggrel as this, is one more instance of the melancholy infirmity of human nature. So strongly does this reflection operate upon our own minds, that notwithstanding the insipidity and ridiculousness of the present poem, the respect we entertain for the author, with all his faults, restrains us from speaking of him in the language of derision. If indeed there were even a hope that ridicule would have the effect of reforming him, it would be desirable to use it: but he is absolutely incurable; he is equally proof against the bitter satire of enemies, and the sincere admonition of friends. The power of man cannot reach his malady: to attempt to apply to it a remedy therefore would be useless, and to mock what is irremediable in an object that has still claims to reverence, would be censurable. If Mr. WORDSWORTH will look back upon what he once was, or, to speak with more propriety, on what he might have been, and contrast it with what he now is, he will then perceive with how much reason he may adopt the words of the celebrated Duke of Marlborough, when in the decline of life and afflicted with palsy, he said to a person who was observing the Duke's portrait, 'Yes, that WAS a great man.' As, however, it is next to impossible to read the production we are noticing without a propensity to laughter, we must be excused if we inadvertently yield to an emotion of risibility in going through its pages.

The *Waggoner* appears to have lain very quietly in the author's drawer ever since the year 1806, as a companion to *Peter Bell*. The first canto opens by informing the reader that it is the close of 'a burning day of June,' – in brief, it is night. The second stanza deserves notice.

[Quotes, *The Waggoner*, PW, II, pp. 177–8, Canto I, ll. 7–21:

> Confiding glow-worms, 'tis a night . . .
> *And the silence makes it sweet.*]

What is to be understood by this? That '*a haunting and a panting like the stifling of disease*' is *sweet*? Surely, Mr. WORDSWORTH cannot think this description happy. – But let us proceed: –

> Hush, there is some one on the stir!
> 'Tis Benjamin the Waggoner; –
> [*Ibid.*, *PW*, II, p. 178, Canto I, ll. 22–3]

This important personage is thus introduced. The poem then goes on to acquaint us that he is driving his team along the road: his progress is minutely traced over the 'lower ground, and the craggy hill;' and we are gratified with the knowledge that 'his whip is dumb all the while;' moreover it is not omitted to be stated, that the horses were strong, that BENJAMIN, their driver, was patient, and that the former were pleased to win the praises of the latter. Having gained this interesting intelligence, we find that BENJAMIN experiences some alarm; but there does not appear any other cause for his apprehensions than that he happens to be passing the poet's house at the time, where every thing is very quiet. Pray was the 'simple water-drinking bard' mentioned in this place, in the habit of frightening poor BENJAMIN by reciting to him any of his verses? – Be this as it may.

[The reviewer summarises the poem in similar mocking vein and quotes extensively.]

We have extended this article to a length much greater than the intrinsic merit of the production deserves. But the name of WORDS-WORTH still excites curiosity and interest: had '*The Waggoner*' been the work of an inferior writer, we should probably have let it sink unnoticed into obscurity; but coming from the pen of a man whose name stands so high as this gentleman's, we could not pass it over in silence, nor dismiss it in a brief paragraph.

227.

Unsigned review, *Theatrical Inquisitor and Monthly Mirror*, June 1819,
XIV, 447–9

The above production has quickly trod on the heels of Peter Bell, and we may imagine that the honor of the press were decreed to them by their author at one and the same moment. The preface assigns the following reason for the separate publication of the Waggoner: – 'From the higher tone of imagination, and the deeper touches of passion aimed at in the former, I apprehended this little piece could not accompany it without disadvantage.' Excessive egotism is a weakness incidental to poets, and one from which Mr. Wordsworth can lay no claims to exemption; this feeling occasions him to attach a degree of importance to the merest trifle which comes from his hands, that exposes him to a good deal of ridicule. We have above given our opinion of Peter Bell; the poem does possess some touches of feeling; but we are inclined to apprehend, that no one but its author will ascribe to it a high tone of imagination, or any thing worthy of the name of passion. It is beyond a doubt, that a tone of deep feeling is a characteristic of Mr. Wordsworth's writings; but it is lamentably impaired by an insufferable affectation, from which it is never free. This defect not unfrequently betrays him absolutely into the bathos; and a passage of high pretensions is sometimes marred by an unlucky quaintness of expression, at once *recherché* and ridiculous. The study of simplicity often produces downright puerility; and his elaborate endeavors to raise into political importance persons, things, situations, and feelings, with which a cultivated imagination cannot sympathize, and with which the dignity of an epic can claim no affinity, must ever prove futile: he may degrade his name down to these topics, but he can never invest them with sublimity or beauty, or chain down the imaginations and sympathies of his readers to that level on which his own expand. What was there, either in the character of Peter Bell, or the incidents which occurred to him, at all calculated to excite any of the tender or agreeable emotions? contempt and disgust, which in an ardent imagination might be fomented into horror, were the first and most powerful sensations it produced; his repentance was effected by such trivial incidents, and so impressed on us the weak and uncultivated mind of the man, that it was destitute of interest. The distress of the poor cottage widow, which was the subject of the last twenty or thirty lines, was the only passage in the piece which partook of pathos, nor was it even there very forcible. Mr. Wordsworth may think that sentiments of this kind betray a great want of sensibility; but we again assure him, that whatever importance the affairs and feelings of rustics may have acquired in his estimation, he will find it more than even his talents can accomplish, to raise them into the higher walk of poetry. Pastoral poets have attempted to invest the *affaires champêtres* with a degree of the *beau idéal*, which have rendered their productions pleasing to the imagination; but if we are to come to the sober reality of rusticity, the *Ballad* is the very highest region of poetry it can hope to attain. No one has ever depicted these things more faithfully, imparted to them a higher tone of feeling, or rendered them more interesting, than *Robert Bloomfield*: he treated them with a simplicity which became them, totally divested of affectation; nor do we ever hope to see rustic personages and rustic feelings elevated to a higher importance in the scale of the imagination. Peter Bell might have furnished a very pretty Ballad, and so might the Waggoner. We do not know to what particular order of poetry Mr. Wordsworth would refer these productions. Peter Bell was divided into *three parts*, the Waggoner appears in *four cantos*. This sounds a little like epic; but when we consider that the journey of a waggoner from Rydalmere to Keswick, who is overtaken by a storm, turns into a public-house, gets drunk with a lame sailor, and is discharged in the morning by his master for loitering on the road, – forms the action of the poem, we can hardly bring ourselves to believe that Mr. Wordsworth himself can refer the Waggoner to the class of epics.

In attributing to it an importance inferior to that of Peter Bell, Mr. Wordsworth is right: it is entirely destitute of those touches of feeling, which marked the former; and, indeed, of all interest whatever. It possesses little of poetic beauty of any kind; and, indeed, had it been more adorned than it is, we should have deplored the waste of poetry on a subject so insignificant.

228.

Unsigned notice, *Monthly Magazine*, 1 July 1819, XLVII, 540

We have seen, read, pitied, and laughed at, Mr. WORDSWORTH's second folly of *The Waggoner*; and we have seen other opinions than our own on the subject of 'Peter Bell:' but we know too much of the *secret* history of periodical criticism, to be shaken in the opinion we have expressed. Some SONNETS, printed at the end of *the Waggoner*, prove that Mr. W. can command respect when he is serious; and that he plays the fool only when he attempts to be merry. But that Mr. W. is capable of something better than 'Peter Bell.' and 'The Waggoner,' will be evident on perusing the last of these sonnets:

[Quotes 'Eve's lingering clouds extend in solid bars', *PW*, III, p. 127]

229.

Unsigned notice, *Gentleman's Magazine*, August 1819, LXXXIX, 143–4

MR. WORDWORTH's productions cannot possibly be charged with precipitancy; the present Poem having been written so far back as the year 1806; and, notwithstanding 'the higher tone of imagination, and the deeper touches of passion, aimed at in *Peter Bell*,' we cannot but think 'The Waggoner' is, to say no more of it, not less meritorious than the former Poem. The style is simply elegant, and unaffected; and we have accompanied honest *Benjamin and his Team*, with much satisfaction, through their long and weary journey over the rough and romantic roads of

> Rydal heights and Dunmail-raise,
> And all their fellow banks and braes.
> [*The Waggoner*, *PW*, II, p. 182, Canto I, ll. 140–1]

. . .

The Sailor's narrative of the Battle of the Nile is excellent; and the conviviality of the little party at the Inn is well described.

[Brief summary and quotation end the review.]

230.

Unsigned review, *Monthly Review*, September 1819, XC, 36–40

'THE WAGGONER,' and 'SONNETS,' in the same little drab-coloured pamphlet! Well! Our ancestors would have stared at these things: but we receive them with a good-humoured smile, and our taste is proportionably improved.

Mr. Wordsworth appears determined to try how far he can trample on the degraded poetry of his country. 'Keep it down,' seems to be his prevailing principle; and well may he add, 'now it is down.' He asks us, in his motto,

> 'What's in a name?
> Brutus will start a spirit as soon as Cæsar!'

and, *therefore*, 'the Waggoner' will do as well as Brutus. Beautiful reasoning! and beautifully illustrated in the poem itself.

This tale is dedicated to Charles Lamb, Esq., to whose own poetical performances we hope soon to call the attention of the favoured few, who rejoice in the productions of the modern antique school: but Mr. Wordsworth apologizes for not adding *the Waggoner* to 'Peter Bell,'* (as Mr. Lamb, it seems, had wished; and the whole communication is *very* interesting to the public!) on account of 'the higher tone of imagination, and the deeper touches of passion,' attempted in 'Peter Bell! – *Risum teneatis, amici!*[1]

For ourselves, we confess honestly that we consider 'the Waggoner' to be one of the best and most ingenious of *all* Mr. Wordsworth's poems. It manifests, occasionally, a classical style of language and versification which is wholly superior to his native manner; and, were it not for the internal evidence of several instances of extreme folly, we should really be disposed to suspect that some lighter and more joyous hand had here been at work. Throughout the piece, or at all events very frequently, we perceive a sly covert sort of irony, an *under-tone* of playfulness, smiling at the mock heroics of the author; and preserving that difficult but exact spirit of bombast, which betrays a consciousness of misapplied sublimity, without rendering it quite gross and ridiculous. Let our readers judge. Mr. Wordsworth's 'Waggoner,' who was wont, for many years, to carry the heavy goods (Mr. W.'s own works included) from the lakes to

---

* See our last Review.

London, after most exemplary habits of sobriety, was tempted to stay too long at an ale-house with a drunken sailor, carrying a ship about as an exhibition, and is obliged to make unusual exertions up a northern hill to recover lost time. At this juncture, the *Pickwood* of those parts 'pricks forth from Keswick' to look after his waggon; when the exultation of inebriety (a state which Mr. Wordsworth has described with a degree of feeling that we should scarcely have expected) has passed away from the waggoner and his marine companion.

[Quotes *The Waggoner*, *PW*, II, pp. 199–201 and footnotes, Canto IV, ll. 83–116:

> They are drooping, weak, and dull . . .
> Alas, what boots it?]

This concluding question intimates the catastrophe of the story. Benjamin, with all his itinerary and vehicular virtues, is dismissed by his inexorable master; and the waggon droops, decays, and ceases to travel, in consequence. 'Eight sorry carts' supply its place; and, passing by Mr. Wordsworth's interesting windows, they will probably produce no more than 'eight sorry poems,' in the course of the next season. We subjoin the passage in which the cheerful effects of intoxication are so livingly depictured.

[Quotes *ibid.*, *PW*, II, pp. 193–4, Canto III, ll. 22–55:

> Now, heroes, for the true commotion . . .
> Might trudge it alongside each other!]

When our readers have paused a moment to digest this last and very elegant line, we beg to ask them whether these results of conviviality are not most naturally represented?

'He best can paint them who shall feel them most.'

We call on Mr. Southey, on Mr. Coleridge, on Mr. Lamb, and on the *arbiter elegantiarum ac bibendi*[2] himself, to join in our sincere admiration of that truly picturesque couplet,

> What *solemn, vacant,* interlacing,
> As if they'd fall asleep embracing!
> [*Ibid., PW*, II, p. 194, Canto III, ll. 46–7]

Seriously, we can no longer endure to hear the poets of so festive a school called the '*Water* Poets of the Lakes;' and from the strong spirit of humour evidently displayed in this memorable passage, we more than suspect where Mr. Wordsworth's real *forte* lies: we exhort him to cultivate his talent for the ridiculous; and we earnestly request him no longer to *laugh in his sleeve* at his 'solemn, vacant' admirers, but to come forth in that character for which nature has plainly designed him, 'the Prince of Poetical Burlesque.'

We must not dismiss this little work without a word of compliment to the versatility of genius that is exhibited, on all occasions, by its author. 'The Waggoner' has driven a small load of 'Sonnets' with him to town, and some of them breathe the true *simplicity* of the writer; as, for instance, when he calls building an imaginary castle on a rock an *'innocent scheme!'* or tells us that good old Isaac Walton, in his plain love of nature, was guilty of the metaphysical quaintness of *'exhorting'* us

> To reverent watching of each *still report*
> That nature utters from her *rural shrine.*
> [Written upon a blank leaf in 'The Complete Angler',
> *PW*, III, pp. 9–10, ll. 5–6]

This *'still report,'* or φωνη ἀφωνος[3] of nature, is a very remarkable thing; and we call the attention of every patient listener to watch and wait for it; or, peradventure, it may escape a common hearkening.

Most prominently and peculiarly does Mr. Wordsworth stand forth, *all himself,* in that unrivalled Sonnet, ycleped 'The *Wild-duck's Nest*;' for, at the end of this *idiosyncratical* production, the poet exclaims

> I gaze—*and almost wish to lay aside
> Humanity,* weak slave of cumbrous pride.
> ['The Wild Duck's Nest', *PW*, III, p. 9, and footnotes, ll. 13–14]

Gaze at what? At a wild-duck's nest! Oh, 'Goosy-goosy-Gander!' friend of our infancy, resign thine honours! and thou, 'Happy, happy, happy Fly,' acquaintance of our manhood, sink into deep forgetfulness, before an author who wishes (almost) to lay aside *humanity,* at the sight of a wild-duck's nest!

Is it, in sober seriousness, possible that these things should be uttered by a person capable of composing the following sonnet?

[Quotes 'Captivity – Mary Queen of Scots', *PW*, III, p. 33.]

EDITOR'S NOTES

1. 'Could you restrain your laughter, friends?' (Horace, *Ars Poetica*, 5).
2. 'master of refinements and drinking'.
3. 'voiceless voice'.

231. John Taylor Coleridge

Unsigned review, *British Critic*, November 1819, XII (second series), 464–79

Identified as the work of John Taylor Coleridge from the extract from his diary published in *Life of Lord Coleridge*, ed. E. H. Coleridge, 1904, i, 13.

We owe Mr. Wordsworth some apology for having interposed so great a space between our notices of the present and his last preceding poem; the delay has been occasioned by circumstances over which we had no controul, and did not proceed from any reluctance to our present task; or from any difficulty which we felt in forming our own opinion upon the place to be assigned to the present poem; neither has it been so long, we trust, as to make it at all necessary to repeat the general notions respecting Mr. Wordsworth's poetical creed, with which we troubled our readers in remarking on Peter Bell. Under this impression we shall be able to compress in shorter compass all that we wish to say respecting this later, and in its way, scarcely less beautiful production of his muse.

Some few general remarks are, however, necessary; even here, before we proceed to analyze the poem itself; for the path pursued in it is very different from that of the former one; it is, indeed, in some respects, a very peculiar one; and as in judging of every effort of human wit it must always be essential to understand rightly the object of the author, and to estimate duly the reasonableness of that object, we shall not mis-spend our readers time, or our own, if we devote a short portion of it to explain what we conceive to have been Mr. Wordsworth's peculiar object in the present poem, and to make a few observations on its merit in that respect.

His object seems to us to have been to select a story of which the characters are not high, nor the events strange or pathetic, but of which neither the one nor the other are essentially low or vulgar, nor wholly devoid of interest; to treat this story without exaggeration of any kind; neither throwing more of morality or passion into it than a story of such a class may fairly possess, nor yet giving it a ludicrous effect by ironical exaltation, or trivial reduction of it below its natural level; but designing to draw from it all the fair and reasonable interest which it is capable of producing; giving it, too, all the poetical ornament which the incidents admit, and yet showing from time to time, by a subdued under-tone of humour, by a playful hint, conveyed in an epithet or comparison, that he is master of himself, aware of the real rank of his subject, and not pursuing it with disproportionate zeal. Whatever may be thought of such an object in poetry, it is certain that the interest of a poem, written in pursuance of it, cannot be very universally, nor very speedily communicated; all those causes of poetic emotion, which operate on every mind, and in a moment; sublimity or loveliness of character, strange and moving incidents, glowing or lofty comparisons, thoughts, or language, are all, by the terms of statement, almost necessarily absent. When we admit this, we think ourselves bound to admit also, as a consequence too clear to be disputed, that such a poem can never be ranked among the highest classes of poetry, however, excellent in its execution, and however it may demonstrate high powers in the poet. It is also evident that such a poem cannot stand much chance of pleasing those whose taste has been exclusively formed by food of a more stimulating kind; there are too many readers in whom, if we could analyse the pleasure which they derive from poetry, we should find that it was precisely the same as that which a novel affords them; they read as a boy reads Tom Jones, skipping the introductory chapters, for the story only: if there are plenty of adventures, a chivalrous hero, a beautiful heroine, and a good tragic villain, they are vehemently delighted; and they would be equally so if the poem were stripped of every thing which is characteristic of it as a poem, and were ushered into the world as the last new novel from the Minerva Press. To these readers the Waggoner must be very dull indeed; a character, to be sure, which the author has the consolation of knowing that many of the noblest poems in the language share with it, and that they still survive in spite of the deadly imputation. That, however, which is not the highest nor of universal acceptation, is not, therefore, without its value; and we will state in a few words what we conceive the value to be of that which is now under consideration.

We speak with hesitation, but so far as our recollection serves us, this is a new class of poetry; we do not remember any poet who has considered that large range of subjects which lye among the ordinary occurrences of life, and which are calculated neither to raise a glow of enthusiasm, to excite a tear of sympathy, or provoke strong emotions of ridicule, as being among the legitimate materials of poetry, or capable of imparting true poetic pleasure, when treated in the way we have described above. It is necessary to make our remark on the novelty of this class of poems, with the qualifications which we have annexed to it, because every one, as well as ourselves, is aware that poetry abounds with the most successful instances of the treatment of such subjects in other ways, and with different objects. To mention a familiar example: nothing can be more trivial than the subject of Pope's most happy effort, the Rape of the Lock; nothing in itself can be less poetically interesting than many of the features and parts on which the most attention was evidently bestowed by the author; but it is clear that the interest is created by treating and describing them not as they really are; 'familiar things (to use the words of Johnson on the same subject) are made new' by not treating them as familiar things, and attaching to them a mock dignity and importance. We are pleased by the well proportioned and well sustained incongruity between the things themselves as they really exist, and the masquerade dress in which the gorgeous and laboured, and slily serious language of the poet exhibits them. It must not be supposed that we mention this circumstance of novelty as attaching any great importance to it; novelty, indeed, in the kind or style of poetry, is always a suspicious circumstance on the first presumption; at the same time it is not conclusive, and it must be admitted that it is something to have opened a new path to the region of purest and highest intellectual pleasure, even though it may not lead us to the most delightful tract in it; we have no desire, indeed, to follow him who would lead us in bye and crooked paths from the mere desire of novelty, or from perverted taste; but if the new road be in itself pleasant, and direct, we certainly are indebted to the guide who opens it for us.

It is a less ambiguous and more important advantage, that these subjects oblige the poet to greater care and industry in disposing and finishing the detail of the poem, than it is the fashion of the present race of poets to bestow on that part of their works. It is very convenient for the indolence both of those who write, and those who read poetry, to make genius all in all, and to reduce the necessary qualifications of a good poem simply to the display of poetic power. While this notion, however, prevails, we will confidently assert that no good poem will ever be produced, and that those who abide by this maxim will never be permanently and generally admired as great poets, nor enlightened or effective reformers of the public taste as critics. Let us give to nature 'the honour due,' and give it in full measure; let us admit in some sense the truth of the adage *poeta nascitur non fit*,[1] or rather let us admit, without reserve, that he must be *born* such, but let us add, that he must be *made* such also. He must be born a poet in the same degree and sense as the sculptor, the painter, the musician, must receive their first impress and destiny, as it were, from nature; but a good poem was never written any more than an exquisite groupe, or a perfect strain, composed, without the combination of study, labour, learning, and all those numerous adjuncts besides, which in their aggregate form the education of the man. This is a simple truth, so simple that an apology might seem necessary for enforcing it, if it were not completely lost sight of by too many in the present day; we have urged it before now, perhaps, but we feel that it can scarcely be too much insisted on; poets must not be too proud to admit that poetry is in the strictest sense of the word *an art*; and they must neither be too indolent nor too impatient to make themselves masters of its rules; while critics cannot with consistence refuse to admit as true a maxim, upon which, in great measure, rests the necessity for, and use of their calling; unless poetry be an art, it may well be asked what are the principles of criticism, and what certainty can there be in her decrees.

To call poetry an art may seem, but it cannot justly be said, to derogate from its high dignity; human pride, indeed, by a strange apparent inconsistency, delights rather in that which is given us, than in that which we work out for ourselves; we are always more pleased to display our natural gifts than our acquired accomplishments; and we desire to attain to excellence so quickly, as to seem to have been born to it, not so much from a love of ease, or impatience for the object, as because it seems to imply a superiority over those who arrive at the same point by the slower progress of diligence and labour; though there can be no doubt that these latter have really the most ground to be proud of the eminence to which they have reached. Thus we find very few poets who have the sound sense to remember with delight, or relate with satisfaction, the difficulties they have overcome, the pains they have taken, or the improvement they have made; they are pleased rather to tell the world in how short a time, and in spite of what distractions, the perfect poem 'sprung armed' from the brain. From this feeling it is, perhaps, in a great degree, that they are so jealous of any thing like the interference of rules; but even if we allow them the reasonableness of the feeling, which we are very far from doing, the jealousy would still remain wholly groundless. We by no means intend to set nature and discipline on a level; the former may do much without the latter, but the latter is wholly nugatory without the former to work on; as in music, natural taste may produce a sweet melodist, though not a good musician without the aid of education; while the greatest diligence and ablest instruction would produce nothing really delightful, where nature had denied a sweet or flexible organ, a precise ear, or delicate touch. Our position, therefore, does not tend to open the monopoly of poetry, to lower its value, or increase the number of poets, but to add grace and perfection to those whom nature has already admitted; we are

737

not introducing weeds or common flowers into the allies of Paradise, but pruning, or correcting the luxuriance and wasteful growth of the beautiful treasures that grow there already.

We have wandered too far from our purpose, but our readers will have no difficulty in seeing how we mean to apply the digression which we have made. It is essential to a poet to interest his reader; wherever, therefore, the charm derivable from the characters and incidents of a story is less strong, and wherever the manner in which it is told is intended not to exaggerate it beyond its natural power, it becomes absolutely necessary for the poet to look for an interest of some other kind; to carry his reader on by the happy arrangement of his narrative, by the justness and apposite introduction of his images, by the verity and liveliness of his pictures, by the correctness of his language and its fitness to the matter, by the modulation and variety of his measures. He who excels in these points will not, indeed, excite in us the highest kind, or the greatest degree of poetic pleasure; we shall not hang over his page with the turbulent and breathless delight, with which we listen to the lays of the great masters of his art; the blasts of the trumpet will not stir up our spirits and hurry us away to the 'press of war;' the pealing strains of the organ will not elevate us to heaven; but we are quite sure that he will not he an unsuccessful poet; there is 'a charm in the Flemish scene' even in poetry; the beauties of detail steal on us, we know not how, they twine round us, and lay fast hold, we know not why. If the poetry on which we are remarking leads necessarily to attention to them, as we think it does, it will certainly be beneficial both to the art itself, and eventually to public taste; not by rendering it minute and captivated by trifles, but more simple, and less standing in need of strong stimulants to action.

Another advantage of this species of poetry, and that by which, perhaps, it will maintain the strongest hold on its readers, is the force which it is capable, and peculiarly capable, of giving to the 'ethic' part of a poem. We are compelled to borrow a term from Aristotle, for which we do not know any exactly corresponding in English; a poem, or narration, is said by him to be 'ethic' when in general, and especially in slight particulars, and by incidental touches it discloses the habitual moral preferences either of the author himself, or his personages, in points of conduct or matters of feeling. And the 'ethic' effect of a poem may, in accordance with this, be said, when we use it in a good sense, to be that moral sympathy and human fellow-feeling, that emotion of benevolent regard which a writer excites in the minds of his readers, either towards himself or his characters, by the amiable and good-natured thoughts, or actions, or remarks, which he indicates as habitual to himself, or makes to seem so in them. This was a matter, on which it is evident, from many passages in his critical works, that great student of nature laid considerable stress both in oratory and poetry: that he was right in so doing there can be no question; whoever has attended public debates of any kind, in our senate, or in our courts of justice, will doubtless have observed the favourable impression often made merely by certain slight touches of manner, by good-natured turns, simple expressions, unforced declarations of opinions on moral questions, which create in the audience a notion of the candour, and honesty, and good temper of the speaker; we could name advocates at the bar, and even lecturers in our hospitals, who owe some part, at least, of their success, to this circumstance. In poetry the effect is the same; nothing more disposes the mind to take pleasure in a poem, and to form a favourable judgment of it, than to be made to take part with the personages of it, to enter into their trains of thought, and to wish, if we may so express ourselves, to have to do with such characters. It is matter of nice judgment so to dispose events, and so to express thoughts, that the former may seem naturally to give occasion for the latter, and the latter not to be ostentatiously, or formally obtruded. But the class of poetry now under consideration, presents the greatest facilities for this, for it is rather in the ordinary and daily events of life, under petty crosses, or slight gratifications in the bosoms of our families, and in the middle walks of society, that occasions are afforded for the exercise of those habits of forbearance, kind judging, friendliness, simplicity, equanimity, which as they evidence themselves by kind words, kind thoughts, and kind acts, procure for us the character of amiable men. The Waggoner himself is a strong exemplification of these remarks; a great part of the charm of the poem, and the friendly regret which we feel at the close, is to be found in the amiableness of his character, his patience with, and care of his horses, his feelings for the poor woman and her child in the storm, the unsuspicious, and unthinking good fellowship which he contracts with the sailor, and even in the very weakness by which he is betrayed to his ruin. For our own parts we are not aware of any affected or false sentiment, nor are we ashamed to say, that there is something very pleasing to us in the affection of his horses for him. Virgil speaks of a different, but not a more natural nor so amiable a feeling in the

Plausæ sonitum cervicis amare.[2]

It would, however, be an authority, if any were wanting, for lines such as these.

[Quotes *The Waggoner*, *PW*, II, p. 180–1, Canto I, ll. 99–109:

> And now the conqueror essays . . .
> He thus pursues his thoughts at leisure.]

These remarks very naturally lead us to the poem itself, which has furnished the excuse for them, and from which they have detained us too long. Indeed, when we consider how much we have written by way of preamble, and how slight a performance the poem itself will appear to many, we fear that we shall be thought to have preserved no proportion between the two; and many, perhaps, will be of opinion that we might better have spared ourselves any remarks on the poem, than devoted so much of our number to it.

The subject of the poem is slight indeed; – the hero is the conductor of a common road waggon, whose dismissal from his place in consequence of an unfortunate indulgence in his propensity to good fellowship forms the catastrophe. It should seem hard to frame a serious and interesting poem from such materials; let us by an examination a little more detailed see how Mr. Wordsworth has succeeded. The first Canto opens with a very accurate description of evening closing in upon a sultry, and burning day of June; in the midst of the deep and heavy silence, the waggoner (somewhat unfortunately we think called Benjamin) is introduced; the lines do not contain any thing very striking, except the exactness and particularity with which the sound of his approaching waggon is described, and which sufficiently mark that the poet is telling truly, what he has often really remarked.

[Quotes *ibid.*, *PW*, II, p. 178, Canto I, ll. 22–39:

> Hush there is some one on the stir . . .
> Yet all the while his whip is dumb.]

Poor Benjamin, it seems, had been warned by his master against his besetting sin of loitering at the ale-houses on the road, and was now returning with his charge, safe so far, and full of the best resolutions for the remainder of his stage to Keswick. The Dove and Olive Bough had been a place of danger to him, the first house on the ascent from the lower ground, but here 'beyond his wish he is secure;' for a poet; we presume Mr. Wordsworth himself, harbours there now. He passes the house, and a mile farther on the road reaches the Swan; – here we would notice one of those playful hints (they are in general so slight, that we can call them by no other name) which we alluded to in the beginning of this article, and which the poet has scattered here and there to preserve the due keeping of the poem –

that frail child of *thirsty clay*.
Of whom I frame this rustic lay,
Could tell with self-dissatisfaction
Quaint stories of the bird's attraction.
[*Ibid.*, *PW*, II, p. 180, Canto I, ll. 93–6]

The Swan however for this time is past in safety; – and the conqueror (for so he is now called) begins to ascend Dunmail-Raice; as the horses toil up the long and steep hill, their gentle guide partly in soliloquy and partly in address to them, informs us of all that we want to know of his failings and his merits; the former had led him into many quarrels with an unkind master, the latter were such that no one but himself was adequate to the conduct of the waggon over this mountainous tract of country, and he retained his place in spite of all provocation for want of a fit successor. Benjamin however was little disposed to repeat his fault, and he congratulates himself that having passed the Swan, he is now safe from temptation for the night. It is perhaps no instance of uncommon ingenuity thus to lay before us the information necessary for entering into the story that follows; – yet in such a poem as this, many writers would have used the less lively, and elegant method of introducing it by previous narration.

While Benjamin is thus busily meditating, the darkness becomes more compleat, the sky more gloomy, and at last a thunder storm bursts on his head, of that violent kind which might be expected to follow such a day. This is one of the incidents, which may naturally occur in the humblest story, and in the description of which such ornament is allowable as, without departing from the general colouring, may yet elevate, and add interest to the story. Mr. Wordsworth has made full use of it; – a thunder storm in the mountains at night is a thing well suited to his powers, and familiar probably to his experience. He has described it with peculiar reference to the spot in which the waggon had then reached in the ascent. We will cite a few lines, which have not this relation, but which strike us as peculiarly true, and characteristic of such a scene.

He is astounded—wonder not –
With such a charge in such a spot –
Astounded in the mountain gap
By peals of thunder clap on clap!
And many a terror – striking flash,
And somewhere, as it seems, a crash

741

> Among the rocks; with weight of rain,
> And rattling motions long and slow,
> That to a dreary distance go –
> Till breaking in upon the dying strain,
> A rending o'er his head begins the 'fray again.
>
> [*Ibid.*, *PW*, II, p. 184, Canto I, ll. 194–204]

Few descriptions can be finer than this in its general effect; and if we examine its different members we shall find them for the most part of equal merit – the 'crash among the rocks,' undefined by the 'somewhere,' and 'as it seems;' the 'weight' of rain, the 'rattling motions' that pass on to a 'dreary distance,' and most of all perhaps the 'rending o'er his head' (than which no more apt expression for the commencement of a near and violent thunder peal can be imagined) are all incidents which we recognise indeed, as familiar in such scenes, but which are very forcibly and happily brought together here, with all the effect of novelty. A severe critic however might make his objections even here; we doubt whether it is correct to speak of 'rattling motions' being 'slow;' celerity seems to us to be implied in the very idea of any motion that rattles; and they who love the preservation of metaphors will find fault with the strange confusion of them in the two last lines; a rending may indeed break in upon a dying strain; both the metaphors are borrowed from physical sounds though of different kinds; but how a rending is to begin again an affray it is hard to conceive; with an inaccuracy, not very common to him, Mr. Wordsworth has mixed a metaphor borrowed from the physical, with one derived from a merely imaginary world; – the first burst of near thunder is really like an actual rending of the heavens, and may well be so expressed; – continual and repeated peals of thunder give to the imagination the idea of war in heaven, and therefore an affray is no bad term for them; – but there is a manifest incongruity between the two ways of considering the subject, and they cannot properly be made use of together.

Two other lines we must cite, in which we have no fault to find –

> There came a flash – a startling glare,
> And all Seat-Sandal was laid bare.
>
> [*Ibid.*, *PW*, II, p. 185, Canto I, ll. 229–30]

This is a common incident in lightning in a dark night, but it is one always extremely solemn, and never we believe witnessed without emotion, – the glare of livid light flashing suddenly on the eye (suddenly, for when does lightning, however often repeated, and however we may wait and watch for it, not come at last suddenly, and unexpected) appals us; and then the momentary glance on a distant prospect seems like a vision of another world, Mr. Wordsworth has noticed the incident in a truly picturesque manner; he sketches, it at a stroke simply and shortly, and leaves us to the reflections which he knows cannot but arise in our minds.

In the midst of this dreadful storm Benjamin and his charge proceed cautiously and safely to the summit, where is supposed to lie buried King Dunmail, the last king of Cumberland; this little tradition Mr. Wordsworth introduces in six lines with the same good effect of duly sustaining his subject which we have before noticed in his treatment of the storm. In this spot Benjamin is startled by a female voice piteously imploring shelter, and too kind-hearted to make any question about admitting her, 'in the pelting of such a pitiless storm,' he bids her get in under the cover of the waggon. The person imploring is a woman with her infant, the wife of a wounded and discharged sailor, which last addresses him also, and is invited to the same shelter; but he has the charge of an ass, a cart with all the family store, and utensils, and something beside of which more will appear in the sequel. Gipsy like, he had pitched his tent for the night on the turf by the road side; the storm was too violent for such a tenement, and having packed up his whole property he pursues the waggon, which is now descending the hill towards another house of temptation, the Cherry Tree. Two things are noticeable here; one the address of the sailor in that style of *imperfect copy* instead of *general imitation*, which we had occasion to censure so much in Peter Bell; we will not again enter on that subject, but simply stating that Mr. Wordsworth should speak for the sailor, and not the sailor for himself, observe that in the following lines neither Mr. Wordsworth, nor the sailor are speaking, but a character between both –

> 'Good brother why so fast'
> I've had a glimpse of you – *avast* –
> Or since it suits you to be civil
> Take her at once – for good or evil.'
> [*Ibid.*, *PW*, II, p. 188, Canto I, ll. 237–40]

It is clear that Mr. Wordsworth would never have ended the first couplet with the word 'avast,' and that if the sailor had ended the second, he would have pressed the word 'devil' into the service instead of 'evil,' by some contrivance or other.

The other thing which we notice as a fault here, is the manner of relating the incident, which is such that it is impossible not to suppose that something really tragic is to arise from it; we never heard any one that had read the poem who did not suppose the rough sailor to have been guilty of or meditating some crime which was to be developed in the issue of the poem; and the real conclusion has therefore always struck them as lame and impotent.

It was midnight when the storm ceased, and if Benjamin had thought himself safe from temptation when he passed the Swan in triumph, he might certainly now feel more secure that all danger was over; we should have supposed that in the vales and mountains of Cumberland no house of entertainment was open at such an hour; but alas, there is nothing more true than that our sins often beset us, when we the least expect them. The sailor having packed up his property had now reached the waggon, and by his cheer roused the waggoner's attention to the lights streaming and the fiddle squeaking from the Cherry Tree before them; Benjamin immediately remembers that it is the merry night of the village of Wytheburn, by which appropriate name it seems that the 'assemblies' of the northern villages are denominated.

[Quotes *ibid.*, *PW*, II, p. 188, Canto II, ll. 31–40:

> Although before in no dejection . . .
> Look fairly like a lawful earning.]

Benjamin's failings and conduct, remind us of the reforming dram-drinker, who having by a great effort and as it should seem to his own astonishment, forced himself to pass unentered one of his favorite haunts, exclaimed in rapture, 'well done resolution, I must give thee a glass for that;' our hero yields, and no great wonder that he did; but what shall we say of Mr. Wordsworth himself, who has described himself before in the poem as a 'water-drinking bard,' and who now sings with enthusiasm.

> A steaming bowl – a blazing fire
> What greater good can heart desire?
> 'Twere worth a wise man's while to try
> The utmost anger of the sky –
> To *seek* for thoughts of painful cast
> If such be the amends at last.
>
> [*Ibid.*, *PW*, II, p. 189, Canto II, ll. 70–5]

We know not in poetry so down-right, and desperate a declaration as

this; if there be any justice in the argument, by which Horace convicts Homer of vinous propensities, certainly Mr. Wordsworth in spite of his watery professions must at least be a sincere and hearty lover of 'good cheer.' Will it be thought too great a departure from the grave dignity of our office, if we observe that the lines strong, simple, and flowing are admirably adapted for convivial music; in the hands of the unfortunate Callcot how much might have been made of them.

Benjamin and the sailor are soon the happiest of the happy there, when the latter, his professional enthusiasm growing warmer as he did himself, limps out and returns with his most valuable possession – 'a ship of lusty size,' which he was in the habit of drawing about behind his little cart, and exhibiting for gain. This part of the story is told in a very pleasing and lively manner –

[Quotes *ibid.*, *PW*, II, p. 191, Canto II, ll. 113–34:

> This, cries the sailor, a third-rate is . . .
> Here lay the French – and *thus* came we.]

This last and dexterous introduction of the name of Nelson compleats poor Benjamin's ruin; his patriotic feelings are inspired, and he calls for another and a double bowl; the mastiff from beneath the waggon rattled his chain, and gave a monitory growl in vain, he heard it, but he drank in spite, and it was not till after two hours 'hearty stay that the horses moved again towards Keswick.'

The waggoner and his new friend travel on together in all the fondness, and excess of convivial intimacy; indeed the hearty rustic soon finds the care which the sailor is obliged to bestow on his ass, cart, and the vanguard, too great an interruption of their social converse, and he therefore purposes to tether them to the waggon, that they, as

> brother should with brother
> [*Ibid.*, *PW*, II, p. 194, Canto III, l. 54]

might walk on side by side, enjoying unrestrained the talk and society of each other. This arrangement is made to the great annoyance of the aristocratic mastiff, who whatever might be the rule of precedence between the two masters, certainly thought himself degraded by his fellowship with the ass, and ceased not to annoy him by growling and showing his teeth, till he was silenced by an ugly blow on the head, which taught him better manners, but which was sorely revenged on the unfortunate Benjamin in the sequel.

We have remarked on the spirit of good fellowship with which Mr.

Wordsworth introduces his travellers to their 'steaming bowl and blazing fire;' he commemorates with no less the first results of their compotation. We should be sorry even in a page so light as this, to say any thing that might seem to encourage excess of any kind; but who is there among us settling down in the soberer years of manhood, who does not sometimes remember with something of unpainful regret, or even of playful delight, the first glow of a convivial evening, when as the spirits warmed we sensibly felt ourselves more generous, more open, more affectionate, when suspicions gave way, and intimacy too long restrained by scruples, doubts, or bashfulness, was cemented in a moment.

There might be something with all this a little ludicrous to a cold stander by, but considering its effect on the heart we should hardly consider it very censurable, if *it were possible*, which we do not think it is, to restrain it within the precise bounds described, and to limit the frequency of the excitement. In the following lines Mr. Wordsworth seems to us to have felt the enthusiasm, and seen the ridicule, and to have preserved the effect of both, however seemingly incongruous with great skill.

[Quotes *ibid.*, *PW*, II, pp. 193–4, Canto III, ll. 22–47:

> Now heroes for the true commotion . . .
> As if they'd fall asleep embracing.]

The poem now hastens to a conclusion, morning comes, when after all the turbulent glee, and riotous exaltation of the night, the waggoner and his friend are becoming weak and dull, in the emphatic language of the poet –

> *Sickening* into thoughtful quiet;
> [*Ibid.*, *PW*, II, p. 199, Canto IV, l. 72]

not so the poet himself; the morning has no such effect on him, but he launches out into a very noble and spirited description of the mountainous scenery in the neighbourhood of Keswick; these are among the most pleasing lines in the poem, but our limits forbid us the indulgence of extracting them, they are full of truth we doubt not in the drawing, and we are sure they are full of the richest imagination in the colouring.

Benjamin's master has sallied forth from Keswick, rendered anxious for the fate of the waggon by the delay in its arrival, and the known frailty of its guide; he meets it ascending the hill, and Benjamin, who has luckily espied him at some distance, by the side of his horses, self-collected, steady, and assuming 'a careless air and open mien;' alas, how little can all this avail him, the sailor limping on the turf by the road side near him, the ass, the ship, the woman and child, and last and worst of all, the wound on the favourite mastiff's head, speak too plainly the events of the night, and the cause of the delay. Benjamin is dismissed the service, and with the waggoner the country lost the wain also, for no one was found capable of conducting it, and the surly master was reduced to substitute 'eight sorry carts' for the stately charge of the kind and good, and patient but frail Benjamin.

Our readers cannot but perceive that the waggoner is a favourite with us; we have been indeed much pleased with an examination of its details, in which we imagine we see much poetical skill, and we feel that there is much poetical spirit in the conception of the characters, and the general management of the story. We part with him with regret, but we will candidly confess, that we do not expect the generality of our readers to participate in these feelings, at least in any thing like an equal degree; the nature of the subject will be a stumbling block to many; it is easy to call it 'a poem on the discharge of a drunken waggoner,' and to ask whether that is fit matter for poetry, to be gravely written by a philosophical poet, or seriously read by full-grown men. We will not repeat what we have said on this head; if that has failed to convince or persuade, let the poet speak for himself, and try if he cannot justify or excuse himself more successfully than his critics; he attempts to do so by way of epilogue; we have no doubt of the actual truth of the statement, and we believe it is what passes commonly in the breast of true poets.

[Quotes *ibid.*, *PW*, II, pp. 203–4, Canto IV, ll. 197–215:

Accept, O Friend, for praise or blame . . .
Until the debt, I owe, be paid.]

EDITOR'S NOTES

1. 'A poet is born, not made.'
2. 'To love the sound of patting its neck' (Virgil, *Georgics*, III, 186).

XV

'The River Duddon': reviews and opinions,
1820–1821

232. Charles Lamb

From a letter to Dorothy Wordsworth, 25 May 1820

I have volunteer'd to reply to your Note, because of a mistake I am desirous of rectifying on the spot – There can be none, to whom the last Vol. of W. W. has come more welcome than to me. – I have traced the Duddon in thought, & with repetition, along the banks (alas!) of the Lea – unpoetical name – it is always flowing & murm[uri]ng, & dashing in my ears – The story of Dion is divine – the genius of Plato falling on him like moonlight the finest thing ever express'd. Then there is Elidure – & Kirkstone Pass – this last not new to me – & let me add one of the sweetest of all to me, The Longest Day. – Loving all these as much as I can love Poetry, new to me, what could I wish or desire or extravagantly desiderate in a new Vol. That I did not write to W. W. was simply that he was to come so soon, & that flattens Letters. –

(Ms. Jonathan Wordsworth)

233.

Unsigned review, *Literary Gazette*, 25 March 1820, IV, 200–3

This volume will be published next week; and we are called upon to give our opinion upon it, as far and as correctly as one perusal admits. Under such circumstances, it is a very gratifying relief to our minds to have a report almost unmixedly favourable to make. We consider these poems to be by much the least mannered and most beautiful of any that this distinguished individual has ever written. There is a tenderness which runs through them of the truest nature; their pathos is genuine and affecting; many of their images bear the impress of genius, and touches of soul are thickly sown over them; . . . and, to those who are familiar with our sentiments respecting the mis-called simplicities of Peter Bells, Waggoners, Daffodils, &c., it will not seem a slight recommendation of the forthcoming work, that it is almost entirely unstained with similar

751

puerilities. We might perhaps instance two or three pretty conceits; but they are in a very minor degree objectionable, when compared with what of the same kind have preceded them; while the noble thoughts clothed in fine language are infinitely more abundant. Some of the adjectives and epithets may be questioned, as quaint or inapplicable; but others are happily chosen and eminently appropriate. In short, the blemishes are trifling in themselves and thinly scattered; the excellencies great and numerous.

'The River Duddon,' is a composition consisting of thirty-three Sonnets, suggested by various views of that stream, and reflections arising out of them. The second, an address to the river which flows from Wrynose Fell, at first through a mountain district, and thence through a more cultivated tract, for twenty-five miles, and enters the Irish sea, is highly poetical,

[Quotes 'Child of the Clouds . . .', Sonnet II, *PW*, III, p. 246]

The third is rather formal in its rhymes; and the fourth does not meet our ideas so strikingly as that which follows it.

> Sole listener, Duddon! to the breeze that play'd
> With thy clear voice, I caught the fitful sound
> Wafted o'or sullen moss and craggy mound,
> Unfruitful solitudes, that seem'd to upbraid
> The sun in heaven! . . .
> . . . light as endless May
> On infant bosoms lonely Nature lies.
> ['Sole listener, Duddon! to the breeze that play'd', Sonnet V,
> *ibid.*, p. 248]

The 'Sullen Moss' is exquisite, coupled as it is with the transmission of sound; nor will the lovers of poetry fail to notice either the original thought of the 'Unfruitful solitudes,' that seem to upbraid the sun in heaven, or the concluding image, which is as sweet as lovely. It is not our intention to canvas each separate sonnet, but we shall briefly mention and quote what occurs to us as most remarkable. The seventh is simple, but we are not aware why the wren is styled 'darkling.' The eleventh, entitled 'The Fairy Chasm,' claims a place for its fancy.

[Quotes 'No fiction was it . . .', Sonnet XI, *ibid.*, p. 250]

The fifteenth is grandly descriptive –

[Quotes 'From this deep chasm . . .', Sonnet XV, *ibid.*, p. 252]

The following, the 21st, possesses a most interesting tenderness and flush of imagination, and is, if at all, very little inferior to the best of the series.

[Quotes 'Whence that low voice . . .', Sonnet XXI, *ibid.*, p. 255 and then 'I thought of thee . . .', Sonnet XXXIV, *ibid.*, p. 261]

To this poem of strung Sonnets, is appended a few notes and a biographical memoir of a Mr. Walker, a lowly but eminently virtuous clergyman. Then follows Vaudracour and Julia, a tale of lawless and hapless love. Its opening is charming –

[Quotes 'Vaudracour and Julia', *PW*, II, pp. 59–61, ll. 1–53:

> O happy time of youthful lovers . . .
> A man too happy for mortality!]

We confess that we know no parallel to this in the whole range of English amatory poetry. The picture is full of living grace, and every heart must feel its magical power. The sequent misfortunes of the lovers gives augmented force and beauty to the delightful simile of the sea fowl sporting unconscious amid blast or billow. Julia becomes a mother ere a wife. Violence separates her from Vaudracour; and a convent encloses her griefs, while imbecile apathy deadens the fiercer sorrows of her beloved. We refrain from dwelling more at length upon the story, in order to find space for examples of the shorter productions, which we can transplant whole into our page. The 'Lament of Mary Queen of Scots on the eve of a New Year,' is apt for this purpose.

[Quotes 'The Lament of Mary Queen of Scots', *PW*, II, pp. 37–40]

The pathetic tone and elegant versification of this lament need no comment. From an ode to Lycoris we select a passage worthy of being its companion.

[Quotes 'Ode to Lycoris', *PW*, IV, pp. 95–6, ll. 19–54:

> In youth we love the darksome lawn . . .
> Be hopeful Spring the favourite of the soul!]

The model of L'Allegro is not far forgotten here; nor in the following felicitous allusions to Ambition, notwithstanding a somewhat of ruggedness in the verse, are we disposed to find a less flattering comparison for the poet.

[Quotes 'Enough of climbing toil . . .', *PW*, IV, pp. 96–8]

The 'Brownie's Cell' is of a mingled character, of much that is good and a little that is indifferent. For example, we cannot appreciate

> —Him whose *smile*
> *Shot lightning* through this lonely isle.
> ['The Brownie Cell', *PW*, III, p. 98, ll. 41–2]

But neither can we be blind to the surpassing sweetness of a scene where

> —flowers delight,
> And all is lovely to the sight . . .
> . . . when the viewless wren
> Is warbling near the BROWNIE's Den.
> [*Ibid.*, pp. 99–100, ll. 79–90]

The poem written in sight of Wallace's Tower, at Cora Linn, cannot be passed in silence. It speaks in the grandest voice of inspiration.

[Quotes 'Composed at Cora Linn in sight of Wallace's Tower', *ibid.*, iii. pp. 100–2]

Largely as we have riffled Mr. Wordsworth of his 'honied sweets,' and pleased as we are to dwell on the praises of a bard who has sometimes offended our taste, and never delighted us so highly before; we must yet, ere we take our leave, request attention to the verses addressed by him to his brother, as a dedication of this volume. They display so amiable a mind, that in them we learn to admire the man, as well as the poet, who has drawn so much music from a rustic custom.

[Quotes 'To the Rev. Dr. Wordsworth', *ibid.*, III, pp. 244–5]

We have little to add, but that besides what we have selected or noticed, the lovers of the muse will find much to admire in this truly charming volume.

In addition to what we have noticed, a prose description of the country of the lakes will be found a very agreeable performance; and other poems, entitled Dion, The Pilgrim's Dream, Artegal and Elidure – a fact and imagination, The Prioress's Tale from Chaucer, September, Odes, Inscriptions, Sonnets, &c. which we can only name, would of themselves form a volume conferring immortality, and ranking their author, even with those hitherto most sceptical of his powers, among the foremost bards of the age.

234.

Unsigned review,[1] *Blackwood's Edinburgh Magazine*, May 1820,
VII, 206–13

THERE is something exquisitely discouraging in the conclusions to
which a calm review of the effects of contemporary criticism in England
must lead every man of tolerably sound judgment; and in regard to no
department of literary exertions are these necessary conclusions so discouraging as in that of the criticism of Poetry. This age has unquestionably produced a noble band of British Poets – . . . Scott, and Byron, and
Wordsworth, and Southey, and Coleridge – . . . Yet, when a man asks of
himself, for a moment, what has really been said – what *remarks* worthy
of the name have really been uttered concerning any one of these Poets –
how lamentably must we feel the worthlessness of all the criticism of the
most critical age ever the world produced. . . . Who can suppose for a
moment that the applauses of our Reviewers have contributed a single
iota to the splendour of the reputation of the highest? The utmost
vanity of the vainest critic alive, can scarcely lead him to flatter himself
that the fame of Byron, for example, would have been one whit less, had
he never acknowledged, by one expression of admiration, that his spirit
was capable of understanding the mastery of Byron.

It is an easier matter, however, to prevent Reputation from beginning
to rise, than to lend her effectual aid after her ascent has once been
triumphantly begun: and therefore it is, that we consider the total
failure of all the attempts which have been made to check the fame
of Wordsworth, as a still more convincing proof of the imbecility
concerning which we speak, than any one circumstance besides in
the literary history of our time. If the shafts of dishonest malice have
at any moment wounded the high spirit of the Poet himself – and if
the pertinacity of the wicked zeal with which he has been persecuted,
has prevented his genius from going abroad so speedily and so widely
in its workings as nature meant it to do – the fault of the critics has not
been small . . .

Nothing is more common than to talk about the unpopularity of
Wordsworth; – but, after all, we are inclined, to doubt very much,
whether at any moment for many years past, he can, with any propriety,
be said to have lain under the reproach of unpopularity. The true Acceptation of a Poet does not surely consist in the wideness to which his name

is blown on the four winds of heaven. Ever since Wordsworth began to write, he has fixed the attention of every genuine lover and student of English Poetry; and all along he has received from these the tribute of honour due to the felt and received power of his genius. And – much as is our admiration of some of his contemporaries, whose excellencies have been more universally applauded – we rather think that they may have more reason to envy Wordsworth for the depth of meditation which his productions have called forth, than he can have to envy them for any of their more buoyant and resplendent symbols of successful art. Besides, if we be not greatly mistaken, Wordsworth has been read by just as many on account of his *Poetry*, as ever read the most popular of his contemporaries for the sake of *Poetry*. Nay, more, we doubt, whether the writings of Spencer, or of Dryden, or even of Milton himself, be at this instant truly familiar to a larger portion of the Reading Public of England than those of Wordsworth.

The way in which the fame of this poet had been attacked by the Edinburgh Reviewers, has already frequently induced us to speak of the philosophical spirit in which the more peculiar productions of his genius are conceived: but in the present volume, while the native strength and originality of his genius are most perfectly preserved, not a few of his customary singularities of style and manner are unquestionably less prominent than any of his former publications. . . . If the passages which we quote do not suffice to make our readers loath for ever all the cant about 'Lakish Ditties,' 'Pond Poets,' &c. and acknowledge at once that this author is a genuine English classic, in the purest and highest sense of the term, we shall despair for ever of the effects of poetry – . . .

The first part of this volume is occupied with a series of Sonnets, which may be considered as forming something not unlike one poem – The subject, the river Duddon; a stream which, flowing down one of the most beautiful valleys in the country of the Lakes, has, throughout the whole of his life, been familiar and dear to the eye and the imagination of the poet. The idea of forming a poem on such a subject, belongs originally, as Mr Wordsworth mentions, to his illustrious friend, Mr Coleridge; who, many years ago, used to talk of writing 'The Brook.' It has been the fortune of Coleridge to see not a few of his plans executed by other hands than his own; but we are much mistaken if the present near approach to 'The Brook,' will give him any thing but pleasure. It is impossible for us to enter upon any analysis; but we give the following six as specimens of the whole thirty-three Sonnets.

[Quotes 'What aspect bore the Man . . .', Sonnet VIII, *PW*, III, pp. 251–2; 'O Mountain Stream . . .', Sonnet XIV, *ibid.*, pp. 251–2; 'From this deep chasm . . .', Sonnet XV, *ibid.*, p. 252; 'Whence that low voice . . .', Sonnet XXI, *ibid.*, p. 255; 'A love-lorn Maid . . .', Sonnet XXII, *ibid.*, p. 255; 'No record tells . . .', Sonnet XXIX, *ibid.*, pp. 258–9.]

Our next extract shall be *Dion*, a magnificent strain of most classical and energetic poetry, imbued intensely with the spirit of ancient grandeur, and enriched with all the depth and gracefulness of Mr Wordsworth's own most poetical philosophy. It will remind those acquainted with his earlier works, of the *Laodamia*; and satisfy them that have never seen that production, how absurdly the charge of 'silly simplicity' has been brought against the general tenour either of the thought or the language of Mr Wordsworth. The truth is, that among all the English poets who have written since Milton, there is none, except Gray, who has ever caught the true inspiration of the Grecian Lyre with the same perfect dignity as the great poet of the Lakes. Talking of language merely – we remember nothing in the whole poetry of his contemporaries, to be compared with the uniform and unlaboured stateliness of his march in the Laodamia, the Sonnets to Liberty, and the following piece:

[Quotes 'Dion', *PW*, II, pp. 272–8.]

The deep breath of simple unconscious grace diffused over the whole of this poem will, if we may judge from ourselves, to the mind of every reader

> Call up him that left half told
> The story of Cambuscan bold.

Indeed the effect of the whole of the extracts we have made, will, we nothing doubt, be quite sufficient to convince every one who has made the character of English poetry his study, that so far from deserving to be held up to derision as a fanciful and conceited innovator, Mr Wordsworth (judged by the genuine spirit of his writings) is entitled to be classed with the very highest names among his predecessors, as a pure and reverent worshipper of the true majesty of the English Muse. Had he never written some few pieces, which are indeed most dear and precious to us, but the conception as well as execution of which we can easily conceive to be of far more questionable excellence in the eyes of the greater part of those who read them for the first time, we are satisfied that the most malignant critics would never have dared to say one word in derogation from the sublimity or the elegance of his compositions.

But we can imagine nothing less enviable than the feelings with which, at this time of day – after he has lived to throw into shade the errors (granting them to have been errors) of a few of his earlier pieces, by the solid and reposing grandeur of the main structure of his poetry – than the reflections which his pertinacious detractors must make in spite of themselves on the conduct which they for so long a period adopted in regard to him. The senseless and boyish clamours with which they pursued a few trivial singularities of one of the proudest of men, probably served no purpose whatever, except that of confirming him in the belief, that what such people took upon them to consider as wrong, must of necessity be right. – Had they been silent in regard to the Betty Foys and the Alice Fells, we should in all likelihood have had fewer of that class – while, had they given the praise that was due to such poems as Ruth, Michael, and Laodamia, it is not impossible that these might, long ere now, have been followed up by many more productions equally free, as they must be allowed to be, from any of the real or supposed faults of the others.

Of the genius of Mr Wordsworth, in short, it is now in the hands of every man to judge freely and fully, and for himself. Our own opinion, ever since this Journal commenced, has been clearly and entirely before them; and if there be any one person, on whose mind what we have quoted now, is not enough to make an impression similar to that which our own judgment had long before received – we have nothing more to say to that person in regard to the subject of poetry. We conclude with a few specimens of the more miscellaneous part of this volume – which will be sufficient to shew, that that is nothing inferior to the other parts. To those who have long been familiar with Wordsworth, and sensible to his merits, the 'Pass of Kirkstone' will be additionally acceptable, on account of its connexion with the train of thought in one of the grandest of his early pieces, the Ode, 'Intimations of Immortality.'

[Quotes 'The Pass of Kirkstone', *PW*, II, pp. 278–80; 'On the Death of his Majesty (George III)', *PW*, III, pp. 40–1; 'Hint from the Mountains', *PW*, II, pp. 151–2]

The volume is concluded with a very singular and striking prose description of the County of the Lakes; but of this we must defer our notice till some future opportunity – contenting ourselves, in the meantime, with assuring our readers, that it is by far the best specimen of the prose style of Wordsworth which has ever been given to the world.

EDITOR'S NOTE

1. Attributed to Lockhart and Wilson (A. L. Strout, *A Bibliography of Articles in Blackwood's Magazine*, Lubbock, Texas, 1959) and Lockhart alone (G. Macbeth, *John Gibson Lockhart*, Illinois, 1935, 212).

235.

Unsigned review, *London Magazine* (Gold's), June 1820, I, 618–27

... Almost every century has produced some great literary sovereign. ... Cowley ... first offers himself to our notice as the great literary monarch of his day. ... In process of time, however, ... the meteor of metaphysical fancy faded and the divine Shakespeare ... announced the speedy arrival of a clear and cloudless sky. ... The third school of poetry ... has Pope for its principal founder, and has been justly defined as the artificial.

... It is not our intention to enter into any regular discussion on the merits of the different systems, we leave them to the decision of abler hands, while we wend our way onwards to the fourth and last school, which has the object of our present review for its great founder and its boast. The reaction of any thing, whether in politics, religion, morality, or literature, is generally proportioned to the necessity that caused it. It was perhaps on this account that the new system, which has been termed the Lake-school of poetry, distinguished itself in its earliest dawn by its extreme peculiarities. Professing to take nature and sensibility, for its 'guide, philosopher, and friend,' it judiciously discarded all meretricious ornaments, and resolved to be conspicuous for its strict adherence to the dictates of genuine sensibility. Aware of the necessity of a radical reform in the house of commons of literature, it set out by its extreme and lasting opposition to any thing that savoured of a mechanical process; disgusted with the complete ossification that the soul of poetry had sustained during the earlier part of the eighteenth century, it prescribed its nostrums to be administered by the hands of nature, unassisted by art. With the modesty usually attendant on superior ability, it appears in preference to any originality of its own, to have combined the beauties of the metaphysical and the natural schools. It possesses all the homely simplicity, the deep feeling, and the intense love of external nature that characterizes the one, with the metaphysical subtlety, and meditative spirit, that forms the principal attractions of the other. In the writings of Wordsworth in particular, to which, as the founder of this embryo system, our subject naturally inclines us, there is a quiet peaceable spirit of philosophy, uninfluenced by the gaudy decorations of art, and looking out, 'from the loop-holes of retreat,' on the glittering pomp and pageantry of the world and its enjoyments, that forms the highest boast of his school. He is evidently an enthusiastic worshipper of nature, but he does not worship her in glittering epithets, and tame classical allusions; he pays reverence to her works in the devotional purity of his heart; and records her attractions rather under the impulse of sensibility than of imagination. In every flower that blooms, in every breeze that blows, in every stream that ripples, in every star that shines in the gay vaulted ceiling of the air, he sees fit subjects for the deepest contemplation and reflection. A code of morality, far superior to the pride of worldly theology, or the garbled system of popular religion, is read in the endless volume of external nature. Every object teems with intelligence, with intelligence that may humble the pride of man, and inspire proper thoughts of devotion and morality. It was this feeling of enthusiasm for the works of nature, and for life in its more rude, modest, and lowly stages, that first startled the aristocrats of literature, and subjected the sensitive poet to the caustic lash of illiberality and ridicule. They could not conceive the possibility of divesting poetry of the cumbrous drapery of art. They could not admit the existence of any beauty in nature, if unrecorded in the usual routine of description. If the moon-beam was to be mentioned, it was either to be eulogized as *the chaste sister of Phœbus*, or *the goddess of the silver bow*, or not to be mentioned at all: the critics would as soon have thought of describing it as the poet of feeling would describe it, as of calling it green cheese.

It is not to be wondered at then, if a system which professed to have nature for its guide, and humility for its handmaid, and which was in every respect so diametrically opposed to the reigning schools of the day, should have been considered as a daring and an idle innovation on established principles. Those critics, who were unable to discover flaws where they most essayed to detect them, and who read in the transcripts of their own hearts, the poet's faithful adherence to nature, still joined in the hue and cry that was universally excited against the professors of the new system, and imagined that they had destroyed the hydra, when in fact they had only bruised one of his fifty heads. The light fanciful song of that lyre, which could at times respond to the deep fitful strains of

inspiration, were attacked with all the bigotry of criticism; and the graceful badinage with which the poet, in his livelier hours, occasionally condescended to sport, were taken as criterions of his general powers, when
his more lofty and impassioned flights were purposely disregarded and
despised. The 'Excursion,' which abounds every where in beauties of the
highest description, and which, taken as a meditative philosophy, is
grand, or, as a poem, unequalled by any production of the present day,
and which may also be considered as the touchstone of its author's talent,
has met with little or no encouragement. Its modest and retiring beauties, lovely as the summer violet, sweet as the balmy breath of evening; its
somewhat fastidious rejection of the ruling systems of the day; its
delineation of the humbler characters of life, and its metaphysical dif-
fuseness, have rendered it but idly adapted to the effects of general
circulation. But with all these popular disadvantages, it is a work that
must immortalize the genius of its author; it is the work to which future
ages will turn as the grand luminary of its era; and long after the poet
that traced the sentiments is mouldering in the dust, his spirit shall
survive in his productions, pure, fresh, and indestructible. Before we
conclude our disquisition, we shall offer a few cursory observations on
the style and writings of Wordsworth, as an accompaniment to his
review that follows. He is evidently, as we have previously mentioned, a
deep searcher into the works of nature; like the Abyssinian traveller that
discovered the sources of the Nile, he has worshipped her at her foun-
tainhead, and inhaled draughts of inspiration; but in his anxious wish to
delineate her inmost thoughts, and her most trifling peculiarities, he has
led himself into numerous errors, both of sentiment and versification,
that notwithstanding the general tone of passion and fidelity that pervades his works, have subjected him to the charge of affectation and
puerility. Well aware of the stronger feeling of sincerity that is met with
among the lower classes than the higher orders of society; acquainted
with the dramatic effects that might be produced, if properly elicited;
and the novelty of the attempt at representing them; he has drawn forth
what from its intrinsic modesty, and its timid sensitiveness, was unable to
encounter the rude blast of popular opinion, and has consequently failed
in his attempt. The different poems on these lowly and familiar subjects
in the associated work of the Lyrical ballads, were both interesting and
delightful, if considered with regard to individuals to whom a knowledge
of the author, or an intimate acquaintance with the spirit of his works,
might impart additional pleasure in the perusal. But when estimated
with reference to the greater number of the reading public, to whose

refined ears, fastidious taste, and over excited sensibility, such writings were wholly unentertaining, were certainly merited failures. Had they possessed less peculiarities of idiom and feeling; had the occasional ruggedness of their versification been softened down, and their inter-jectional phrases been diminished, they would then perhaps have been less remarkable, but would have sustained less animadversion than at present. As they are now constituted, they form a remarkable, instance of the diversity of taste carried to the utmost latitude of opinion. The literary world is divided into opposite parties. Of those who enthusiastically admire, and those who as cordially despise them. But with respect to the following stanzas there can be but one undivided opinion; and never did Collins, in his more exquisite moments of scusibility [an unrecorded word: possibly 'sensibility'?], pen so tender, so delicate a poem.

[Quotes 'She dwelt among the untrodden ways', *PW*, II, p. 30, apparently from memory.]

Artifice, in the composition of poetry, as has been amply testified in the numerous swarm of drones that revelled in the sweets of the Augustan age, may certainly do a great deal – it may please by its correctness, and instruct by its occasional sprinkling of the good things of devotion and morality; but it will never attain that depth of feeling, that intuitive perception of beauty, which induces the genuine poet, as in the instance above, to 'snatch a grace beyond the reach of art,' and bear away the palm of honor and triumph.

Another distinguishing feature that characterizes the writings of Wordsworth, is the accurate and minute manner in which he places his description before the mind's-eye of his readers. This is a quality attain-able only by those in whom a deep knowledge of the objects described produces a corresponding fidelity of delineation; and this talismanic power our author inherits in common with some of the first writers of our country – a word, a sentiment, acts with magical influence on our souls; draws forth the hidden sensibilities of the heart; lets in a long stream of sunshine on our darkened imagination, and makes us purer and greater than before. In this peculiar power of placing the objects described in immediate review before us; in handing us the intellectual telescope, and in bidding us behold the far-off glories of the country that were before seen darkly through the vista of the fancy, he stands alone, unapproachable and unrivalled. Other poets, in their highest moments of inspiration, may possess more glittering imagery and more fanciful analysis, but there is none who reveals the naked truth beaming in its natural simplicity, so gracefully, so exquisitely, as Wordsworth.

But while we do justice to the general accuracy of his description we must object to the individual instances of almost ludicrous fidelity, that prompted the maudlin tale of Goody Blake and Harry Gill, and the Star-gazer, in which neither the fancy is elevated, the heart bettered, nor the reason strengthened. But such trifling peculiarities, though they may for a time sully, can never diminish the native genius of Wordsworth. His palace is the edifice that was built on the rock; the winds came, and the floods descended, but it stirred not, for its foundation was of adamant. He has raised to himself a deathless monument of glory; he has fixed it as the landmark of future ages, to show where the spirit of poesy remains enshrined, and the sensibilities of nature are consecrated; and while in his voyage down the stream of life towards the regions of immortality, his genius gathers glory as it proceeds, the bards of other times, who have so often been the themes of his praise and the subjects of his adoration, shall welcome him home to the everlasting temple of fame, as the brightest and the purest offering of Time to Eternity.

In the poems before us, there is less of the idiomatic peculiarities, and more of the modest philosophical beauties, than in any preceding works of the author. The principal poem in the collection, which consists of a connected series of sonnets in praise of the river Duddon, is distinguished for its intense love of nature, and its beautiful adaptation of morality with description. The sonnets entitled Hints for the Fancy, and the Conclusion, will exemplify our opinions:

[Quotes 'On, loitering Muse . . .', Sonnet XII, *PW*, III, p. 251; 'I thought of Thee . . .', Sonnet XXXIV, *ibid.*, p. 261; summary and extract from 'Vaudracour and Julia', *PW*, II, pp. 59–61.]

The verses addressed to a Lady on the Longest Day are so exquisitely and naturally beautiful, that we shall make no apology for the extract:

[Quotes 'The Longest Day, addressed to my Daughter, Dora', *PW*, I, pp. 249–51, and 'Inmate of a mountain-dwelling', *PW*, II, pp. 286–7.]

It is surprising that such beautiful specimens of poetry as those we have extracted, should ever have been permitted to slumber in oblivion. Such, however, is the fact; and it is equally certain that those aristocrats of literature, the Edinburgh Reviewers, have ever been among the foremost to vituperate and vilify the existing school of poetry. More occupied in the dignified and the striking, than the gentle and unassuming, they are unable to appreciate properly the beauty of the latter. Accordingly, we find them turning from the tender, quiet, lowly subjects of poetry with a look of the most ineffable contempt. What is the consequence? The dogmas of their Review, which has for some time been considered as the model of approbation, are regarded with infinite respect; and illiberal ignorance, shielding itself under the banners of literary bigotry, joins in the hue and cry, and can always contrive to sneer, when generally unable to convince. Another object that retards the success of the Lake school is, that their system is too pure and too metaphysical to entrap the applauses of the social community. Let us suppose, for an instant, that one-half of England are able to judge with correctness, and that the remainder take their opinions from the critical sagacity of their acknow-ledged superiors; the chances of the success of the new school of poetry, among the reading public, will then both *pro* and *con* be equally bal-anced. But then let us suppose, in continuation, that one-third of the reading half, particularly among the elders, attached to the productions of former days, and reluctant to admit innovation, which tends to over-throw the prejudices of their youth, are either unwilling or unable to enter into the poetical spirit of the reformers. This circumstance alone will greatly retard the popularity of the new system. Again; to pursue the estimate, let it be imagined that another third (as is generally the case) are struck more with the artificial than the simple – the dazzling than the humbler graces of versification; there will then only be left one more third who are able to drink in the freshness of the school of poetry and disseminate their opinions. It is seldom that a new system (whatever direction it may take) is successful; – mankind must be convinced of its utility before they will subscribe to its opinion, and even then reluctantly admit the innovation. On this principle these poets cannot yet expect unqualified applause – the system which originates with themselves is yet in embryo – the conception is great, but the machines are not yet sufficiently softened by practice. The harrow of cultivation must pass frequently over the rich, but still untilled-ground; and the buds of genius, that will then spring from the fecundity of the soil, shall attest the value and beauty of the ground from whence they sprung, and diffuse their fragrance around.

236.

Unsigned review, *European Magazine*, June 1820, LXXVII, 523–25

It has been peculiarly unfortunate for Wordsworth, that poetry is not always read in the disposition of mind which ought to accompany such on occupation. Fashionable readers open the last new Poem of any popular author, in much the same frivolous temper as they would take up a newspaper; they read only to be on a par with their neighbours, and, if capable of feeling, reserve the exercise of that capacity for such authors as the taste or fashion of the day may point out as most fitting to awaken it. Professed critics read, for the most part, for the mere purpose of displaying their own critical acumen: and decided partizans, whether political or theological, have no spare sympathies to throw away on pure poetry. Even among the real lovers of poetry, there is often a lamentable deficiency of taste; and that which, by its splendour, powerful delineation of passion, graceful narrative, or gorgeous description, will most easily stimulate a pampered taste, is generally preferred to such as may possess infinitely higher merit; simply because that merit is of an unobtrusive, chaste, and dignified nature. For these reasons, we believe, Wordsworth's poetry is really enjoyed by comparatively few: but in the estimation of those who do enjoy it, he is surpassed by none, and equalled by few of his contemporaries: to us, we confess, he appears beyond all comparison the most truly sublime, the most touchingly pathetic, the most delightfully simple, the most profoundly philosophical, of the poetical spirits of the age.

The present volume is a very welcome addition to his former productions. It consists of a series of Sonnets, bearing the name of the river which has given rise to them; and various other minor poems; together with a prose description of the country of the Lakes, and a Memoir of a humble but truly reverend Divine, once a resident in this romantic district: almost as interesting as the poetry itself.

The Sonnets, bearing collectively the title of 'The River Duddon,' ought to be read '*seriatim*:' we shall, therefore, venture on none of them. – 'Julia and Vaudracour,' a tale of hapless love, or rather a brief sketch of one, has in it passages of poetical beauty, which might, we think, almost defy competition; and would even suffer little by comparison with the pages of the mighty Master to whom Wordsworth alludes in the following exquisite tribute: –

[Quotes 'Vaudracour and Julia', *PW*, II, pp. 62–63, ll. 87–94:

> such theme
> Is, by innumerable poets . . .
> In the unrelenting east.]

Yet even Shakspeare himself, we think, could scarcely have given a more magnificent picture of the intoxicating happiness of Love in early life, than the following: –

[Quotes *ibid*, pp. 60–61, ll. 36–53:

> his present mind
> Was under fascination . . .
> A man too happy for mortality.]

Our next extract, and we are afraid it cannot be a very short one, exhibits this delightful poet, neither in his simplest nor his sublimest strain, but in the engaging character of an instructor of youth in the precepts of moral wisdom; and to us there is something irresistibly touching, and powerfully persuasive, in his mode of inculcating the truth he wishes to impress. The following are stanzas 'addressed to—, on the longest Day.'

[Quotes 'The Longest Day, addressed to my Daughter, Dora', *PW*, I, pp. 250–1, omitting the first stanza.]

Passing over several short pieces, we come to one 'Composed at Corra Linn, in Sight of Wallace's Tower;' the conclusion of it is, we think, in a style of genuine sublimity.

[Quotes 'Composed at Cora Linn, in Sight of Wallace's Tower', *PW*, III, pp. 101–2 and footnote, ll. 19–48:

> Along thy banks, at dead of night . . .
> –prepar'd to slake
> Their thirst in tyrants' blood!]

The next, inscribed to the Author's Brother, is equally honourable to the genius and feeling of the poet; but we cannot give the whole, and do not like to give part: – we must let it go.

'Dion' is a classical gem: we can only afford to give the superb image with which it opens.

[Quotes 'Dion', *PW*, II, pp. 272–3 and footnote, ll. 1–19:

> Fair is the Swan, whose majesty, prevailing . . .
> From heaven, upon her chosen favourite!]

We conclude our extracts from this fascinating volume, with the two following sonnets; each admirable in its way: the one elegantly beautiful, the other solemnly impressive.

[Quotes 'Lady! I rifled a Parnassian Cave', *PW*, III, pp. 28–9 and 'On the Death of his Majesty (George III)', *ibid*., pp. 40–1.]

We must now take our leave of Mr. Wordsworth; and we do so with renewed feelings of love and admiration for his genius. His poetry may not be the most popular in the present day: it may be less frequently quoted, than that of some among his contemporaries, in crowded drawing-rooms, and less admitted in fashionable circles: but we believe he is again regaining his ground in the public estimation. Critics of indubitable taste and talent have of late manfully avowed their partiality, and honourably bestowed their praises: but let critics say what they please, his poetry must, and will live; for it has an enduring principle of vitality within itself, which proclaims its origin, and will ultimately perfect its praise.

237.

Unsigned review, *Literary Chronicle and Weekly Review*, July 1820, II, 420–2

Nothing is more natural than that the Lake poet should select a river for the subject of his muse; but what a name and what a river for inspiring a poet's imagination, Duddon! – And yet the sonnets Mr. Wordsworth has written on it will make the name, obscure and uncouth as it is, pretty widely known. His success in this instance, reminds us of an anecdote rather apt to the purpose. Two footpads, after a most desperate struggle, succeeded in robbing a poor Scotchman of sixpence. In retiring with their booty, one of them exclaimed to the other, 'what a resistance the fellow made, and that too only for a sixpence. I suppose if the fellow had had eighteen pence, he would have beaten us both!' And when we see the beautiful verses Mr. Wordsworth has written on this insignificant river, with its barbarous name, we may exclaim, – what would he not have written had the majestic Thames employed his muse. We will not quarrel with a poem on account of the name; but there is really something in it. Walter Scott, (we love to call him by the familiar name he has ennobled beyond the honours a sovereign can confer,) has been particularly happy, not only in the titles of his works, but also in the quaint and significant names he has given to his personages, 'Marmion,' 'The Lady of the Lake,' 'the Lay of the Last Minstrel.' How harmonious! why they are in themselves almost poetical. Mr. Wordsworth, on the contrary, has scarcely even chosen a good title for any of his works; witness his 'Peter Bell,' and 'Benjamin the Waggoner.' But he will probably say, What's in a name?

It has been often remarked, that authors are seldom good judges of their own works. Milton is said to have preferred his 'Paradise Regained' to 'Paradise Lost;' and Mr. Wordsworth is a striking instance of an author not appreciating the relative merits of his productions; or he would never have disgraced his name by the puerilities of Peter Bell and Benjamin the Waggoner, when he was able to write such pieces as are contained in the work before us.

There are very few poets of the present day respecting whom so much diversity of opinion exists as Mr. Wordsworth. One party laud him to the skies as the poet of nature, while others think he carries his affectation of simplicity to a ridiculous extent. We are of opinion, that *in medio tutissimus ibis*[1]: and having, on a former occasion remarked on the style of Mr. Wordsworth, and on the Lake School generally, we shall only observe that the present volume possesses all the beauties and very few of the defects of this writer. We think it by far his best production. The subjects are more appropriate, – the images more natural, – the landscape richer in variety, and the pathos deeper and more genuine and affecting.

. . . [The sonnets] are of various degrees of merit, but most of them are very pretty; some are distinguished by their natural simplicity, and others by their grandeur and sublimity. We select as specimens the two following: –

[Quotes 'Whence that low voice . . .', Sonnet XXI, *PW*, III, p. 255 and 'But here no cannon . . .', Sonnet XXXIII, *ibid.*, p. 260.]

The poem of 'Vaudracour and Julia,' which by the author is said to be founded on an event that occurred in France, is a tale of illicit love . . .

. . . Nothing can be finer than the poet's description of the power of love on a youthful heart: –

[Quotes 'Vaudracour and Julia', *PW*, II, pp. 60–1, ll. 10–53:

A town of small repute . . .
A man too happy for mortality!]

This is true poetry, – it speaks to every heart, – the most prejudiced person must acknowledge its force and beauty, while the admirers of the poet will admit, that in this effort, he has surpassed the brightest of his former productions.

[Quotes 'The Longest Day, addressed to my Daughter, Dora', *PW*, I, pp. 250–1.]

Who that reads this volume of Mr. Wordsworth's poems, or the extracts we have made from it, will not involuntarily exclaim, *O si sic omnia!*[2]

EDITOR'S NOTES

1. 'In the middle you will go safest' (Ovid, *Metamorphoses*, II, 137).
2. 'O that he had done/said everything thus!'

238.

Unsigned notice, *Ladies' Monthly Museum*, August 1820, XII
(third series), 95

Peter Bell, and Benjamin, the Waggoner, had given us almost a disgust to Mr. Wordsworth's Muse; for to such a ridiculous height has he carried his affectation of simplicity in these two last productions, that he left us little hope of seeing his genius break the fetters of his school. It has done so, however, and it now bursts upon us with a brilliancy and pathos, a grandeur and a true simplicity, which, if he always wrote thus, would, indeed, entitle him to be called the poet of Nature.

The River Dudden is the principal poem; the author describes, in a series of sonnets, thirty-three in number, the various beauties of scenery which adorn its course, and which he has painted in general in the most felicitous manner: the mind must have, indeed, little relish for the beauties of nature, that is not fired with enthusiasm in perusing his description of them. In Vaudracour and Julia, he paints the power of love in a manner at once so natural, and so exquisitely poetical, that we regret we cannot extract some passages. The remaining poems, though not entitled to such high praise as those we have noticed, are nevertheless extremely pretty. If our pleasure is now and then damped by the author's relapsing into the peculiarities, or defects, whichever our readers chuse to call them, of his school, it must be owned that these instances are rare, and we must not quarrel with what is excellent, merely because it is not quite perfect.

239.

Unsigned review, probably by Josiah Conder. *Eclectic Review*, August 1820, XIV (second series), 170–84

This publication is designed to form, together with 'The Thanksgiving Ode,' 'The Tale of Peter Bell,' and 'The Waggoner,' the third and last volume of the Author's Miscellaneous Poems. Mr. Wordsworth appears to be satisfied that he has written enough; quite enough, at least, for the illustration of his theory, which if the Public do not by this time understand or appreciate, it is not his fault: with this volume therefore, the indignant Author closes his metrical labours. But a poet has lived too long, who has written quite enough. Measured by this rule, Mr. Wordsworth's literary existence has long touched upon superannuation: the Author of the Excursion is almost forgotten in the Author of Peter Bell, and the Poet's warmest admirers are beginning to be ashamed of standing out for the genius of a man who, whether in the wantonness of self-conceit, or from infirmity of judgement, could, in an age of brilliant competition like the present, deem such productions as those worthy of the Press. It is evident that Mr. Wordsworth has felt the universal ridicule which they brought upon him, from the manner in which he calls upon his friend Peter, in the following sonnet, not to mind the naughty critics. It is entitled, a 'Sonnet on the detraction which followed the publication of a certain poem.' '*See Milton's Sonnet*,' it is added, 'beginning "A Book was writ of late called Tetrachordon."' We shall see into that matter presently.

> A Book came forth of late called, 'Peter Bell;'
> Not negligent the style; – the matter? good
> As aught that song records of Robin Hood,
> Or Roy, renowned through many a Scottish dell;
> But some (who brook these hacknied themes full well,
> Nor heat, at Tam o' Shanter's name, their blood)
> Wax'd wroth, and with foul claws, a harpy brood –
> On Bard and Hero clamorously fell.
> Heed not, wild Rover once through heath and glen
> Who mad'st at length the better life thy choice,
> Heed not such onset! nay, if praise of men
> To thee appear not an unmeaning voice,

Lift up that grey-haired forehead, and rejoice
In the just tribute of thy Poet's pen!
['On the Detraction which followed the Publication of a
certain Poem', *PW*, III, p. 11]

Mr. Wordsworth has very frequently puzzled us before now by the equivocal character of his lighter productions: his gravity is often so facetious, and his humour is often so grave, that we have been at a loss to know whether to take him as in jest or in earnest. This is the case with the above lines. We should certainly have supposed from the reference to Milton's burlesque sonnet, that Mr. Wordsworth meant on this occasion to be jocose. But on looking the Poet steadfastly in the face while addressing his friend Peter in the latter half of the sonnet, we could not discern the least relaxation of feature that betrayed a latent smile, and were compelled to conclude that he was in very sober earnest. Now, if we are right, it seems unaccountable why the reader should be referred to Milton's sonnet at all, unless Mr. Wordsworth, in whom we have frequently observed a sort of half-concealed fidgetty ambition to be taken for a cousin-german of the great patriot-bard, has really, in the simplicity of his mind, mistaken the character of that *jeu d' esprit*. Some persons had, it seems, laughed at the Greek title of Milton's treatise, just as the public were diverted at the title of Peter Bell. Thus far the parallel holds. But we do not learn that the public laughed at Milton's book, and he could not, therefore, have been seriously hurt at the jokes passed upon 'a word on the titlepage.' It afforded him however, as he thought, a good occasion for turning the joke upon his polemical assailants, on the ground of the far more uncouth and cacophonous combination of vocables of which their names were composed. 'Gordon' is evidently brought in to supply the rhyme; but 'Colkitto, Macdonnel, or Galasp,' those rugged names 'that would have made Quintilian stare and gasp,' were at that period not yet familiarized to Southern ears; and Milton, who hated every thing Scotch, and had an exquisite ear, was no doubt unaffectedly diverted at these barbarous appellatives. And then in the close of the sonnet he has a good fling at his opponents for their dislike of Greek, which was the only sin of his title.

Thy age, like ours, O Soul of Sir John Cheek,
Hated not learning worse than toad or asp,
When thou taught'st Cambridge, and King Edward, Greek.

But to descend to Mr. Wordsworth. In our notice of his Peter Bell, we had occasion to remark, that his title confirmed us in the suspicion that, as he is himself devoid of any talent for humour, so he is, through a singular simplicity of mind, insusceptible of the ludicrous. Were not this the case, he would scarcely have trusted his name and that of his friend Peter, so near that of Milton, in the present instance; nor would he have blundered in his serious imitation of a burlesque poem; nor would he have called upon Peter Bell, at least in the hearing of the public, to lift up his grey-haired forehead, and rejoice in having such a poet as our Author's eccentric self, to write about him; nor, lastly, would he have been now at any loss to know why the formal annunciation of a poem with such a title, and coming from Mr. Wordsworth, should have excited more merriment than the title of the thrilling and matchless 'Tam a Shanter' of a poet who *could not* be ridiculous.

We take it, however, as a good sign, that Mr. Wordsworth has been made sensible of the fact, that the public do not wish for any more Peter Bells. How depraved soever their taste, how unjust soever their ridicule, the thing will not do again. And he seems determined to please the lovers of euphony this time by at least half of his titlepage, by the melodious names of Vaudracour and Julia. 'The River Duddon' stands boldly forward, indeed, in defiance of all ludicrous associations; but it has had this name given it, and cannot help itself. We question whether Mr. W. does not think it the most sweetly sounding title of the two.

The contents of the volume are very miscellaneous. A third part is occupied with the topographical description of the Lake country; and it forms by no means the least valuable portion. The Notes to the Sonnets contain a prose memoir of the Rev. Robert Walker, curate of Seathwaite, the abstract of whose character is given in 'The Excursion.' He appears to have been a man of very singularly primitive character, and incomparably more deserving of poetical honours, than most of our Author's Lakers. The reader must excuse us, if we suffer Mr. Wordsworth's prose for once to detain us from his poetry . . .

[By summary and extensive quotation gives a fair indication of Wordsworth's prose 'Memoir of the Rev. Robert Walker', *PW*, III, pp. 510–22.]

We really feel indebted to Mr. Wordsworth for having presented us with the full-length portrait of a man of such sterling and almost obsolete excellence. It shall cancel us half the defects of his poetry. And poetry after all, be it of the best quality, is exceedingly less affecting than such a simple record of unvarnished realities. The Sonnet on Seathwaite Chapel, we thought passably good, till we had read the Note which is given in illustration of it; and then we found it miserably inadequate to the theme. And this tempts us to suspect that Mr. Wordsworth is not so much to blame, after all, for the choice of many of his subjects, as for writing ballads and lyrical pieces about them, instead of throwing them into the form of honest prose. In some of his narrative poems, however, where he has adopted a free blank verse, which is the species of poetry by far the best suited to his habits of thinking and style of composition, he has risen to a very unusual height of excellence. The Excursion, with all its faults, assuredly contains some of the most exquisite blank verse in the language. It is remarkable, that both his prose and his blank verse are in general quite free from the puerilities and vulgarities which disfigure many of his lyrical pieces. The diction of the former, as well as that of his sonnets, is frequently, in direct opposition to his theory, extremely elevated and richly figurative; sometimes to an excess bordering upon affectation. The River Duddon flows through a series of thirty-three sonnets which are for the most part of no ordinary beauty. Here and there, a little metaphysical mud, or a *Lakish* tincture, mingles with the stream, and it occasionally runs somewhat shallow; but the general character of the series is that of very noble descriptive poetry. They are the growth of many years: the following, which stands the fourteenth, was the first produced; others being added upon occasional visits to the Stream, or as recollections of the scenes upon its banks awakened a wish to describe them.

[Quotes 'O Mountain Stream! the shepherd and his cot', Sonnet XIV, *PW*, III, pp. 251–2.]

In thus breathing a lonely sentiment into the material elements of picturesque beauty, no living poet has shewn greater skill and fancy than Mr. Wordsworth. The next we shall select, is, it is true, no more than a sonnet; but pages of description are compressed within the compass of fourteen lines, and hours of feeling are concentered in the spirit which animates them.

[Quotes 'Child of the clouds! remote from every taint', Sonnet II, *ibid.*, pp. 246–7.]

The following is in a different strain: it is entitled 'The Faery Chasm,' and is singularly elegant.

[Quotes 'The Faery Chasm', 'No fiction was it of the antique age', Sonnet XI, *ibid.*, p. 250.]

In the twenty first sonnet of the series, there occurs a strange catachresis, if we may not rather term it metaphor run mad. Memory is described as breaking forth 'from her unworthy seat, the cloudy stall of Time;' the precise import of which expressions we do not quite enter into. And then to the Poet's eye, this metaphysical abstraction is embodied in a palpable form – 'Her glistening tresses bound:' this would seem bold enough; yet the Author might think himself justified in venturing thus far by the exquisite line of Collins;

> And Hope enchanted smiled, and waved her golden hair.

But Mr. Wordsworth wants just that one thing which Collins possessed in perfection – taste. The Author of the Ode on the Passions knew by instinct the precise boundary line between the sublime and the extravagant, between figure and nonsense. He never for a moment loses himself amid his own imagery, or confounds the figurative with the physical. But Mr. Wordsworth goes on to define the appearance of the glistening tresses of Memory, and to compare them to 'golden locks of birch;' and then forgetting altogether, as it should seem, the imaginary being he has conjured up, his mind fastens upon the new idea, one that relates to a simple object of perception: –

> – golden locks of birch that rise and fall
> On gales that breathe too gently to recal
> Aught of the fading year's inclemency.

['Whence that low voice? . . .', Sonnet XXI, *ibid.*, p. 255, ll. 12–14.]

If these last lines have any intelligible connexion with the idea of Memory as introduced in the foregoing part of the stanza, we confess that it eludes our dull apprehensions.

Vaudracour and Julia is a tale in blank verse, which was originally intended, we presume, to form an episode in some future portion of 'The Excursion.' The incidents are stated to be facts, no invention having as to them been exercised. It is a touching and melancholy tale of unfortunate love, and told in Mr. Wordsworth's happiest manner. From the lyrical pieces which follow it in order, we cannot do otherwise than select the very beautiful stanzas entitled

LAMENT OF MARY QUEEN OF SCOTS,

[Quotes 'Lament of Mary Queen of Scots', *PW*, II, pp. 37–40.]

The odes are the least pleasing compositions in the volume, being for the most part very affected and very enigmatical. There are, however, some exceptions. The one bearing date September, 1816 [*sic*], merits transcription as a varied specimen of the contents of the volume.

[Quotes 'September 1819', *PW*, IV, pp. 98–9.]

There is among the Inscriptions also, a short piece written in a style with which we have not been accustomed to meet in our Author's productions.

[Quotes 'Not seldom, clad in radiant vest . . .', *ibid.*, p. 206.]

We can make room for only two more specimens: they are in themselves sufficient to justify all the praise that has been bestowed on Mr. Wordsworth's sonnets.

[Quotes 'The stars are mansions built by Nature's hand', *PW*, III, pp. 32–3.]

The other sonnet is on the death of his late Majesty.

[Quotes 'On the Death of his Majesty (George III), *ibid.*, pp. 40–1.]

'The Prioress's Tale' from Chaucer, is a very ill-chosen subject for the experiment of exhibiting the Father of English Poetry in a modern form. The legend is so exquisitely absurd, that it must have been designed as a burlesque on the lying martyrological wonders of the Romish priesthood. It is that of a poor innocent child who had his throat cut by some wicked Jews, because he was too fond of singing Ave Maria, but who continued, by aid of the blessed Virgin, to reiterate the same articulate sounds which he had been wont to utter while living, till his corpse was found, and then, was able to give information against his murderers; but the spirit could not obtain its discharge till a grain was taken off of his tongue which the Virgin had placed there. When Chaucer wrote, such fables were not too gross for the vulgar credulity; but we know not for what purpose they are transplanted into modern poetry. To Mr. Wordsworth, indeed, we can conceive that such tales would recommend themselves by their very puerility; that he would be even melted into tears by the affected solemnity of a sly old humorist like Chaucer; and that what was meant by him for satire, might be mistaken by our Author for pathos.[1]

We deem it quite unnecessary to repeat that our respect for Mr. Wordsworth's talents remains unaltered. The copious extracts we have given from the present volume, sufficiently evince that those talents are of a very high order. But we have so fully expressed our opinion on this point, in our reviews[2] of the Excursion, and of 'The White Doe of Rylstone,' as well as subsequently in noticing the unfortunate pair, Peter Bell and Benjamin the Waggoner, that we will not run the hazard of wearying our readers by saying more upon the subject. It is certain, that while he has been as a poet ridiculously, because indiscriminately and immeasurably lauded on the one hand, he has been very ignorantly and flippantly depreciated on the other. For the latter circumstance, however, he may thank chiefly himself, and, next to himself, his friends, who have taught him to despise the warning voice of public opinion, which, however wayward and arbitrary in its first decisions, is sure to be mainly just at last. Had his judgement but been as correct as his imagination is powerful, had the purity of his taste been equal to the simplicity of his feelings, had his understanding been as sound as his heart, we hope, is warm – though we have a deeply rooted distrust of all sentimentalists and *sensationists* in this respect, – the critic's task would have been far more easy, and, to our feelings, far more pleasant. We should not then have been disposed to acquiesce in thinking that he had written enough; too much, indeed, for his permanent reputation, unless he adopts our suggestion, namely, to entrust to some competent friend the reducing of his writings, by a rigid selection, to the due compass of 'Sybilline leaves,' and to make a bonfire of the refuse – his potters, waggoners, and ideots, on the top of Skiddaw. The present volume ought, however, to do him at least this service with the public; it should be accepted as an ample atonement for his last offence, for there is a weight of sterling good poetry in it far more than adequate to turn the scale in his favour. From this time forth, therefore, it ought to be held a breach of courtesy and kindness, to say one word more of Benjamin the Waggoner or of Peter Bell.

EDITOR'S NOTE

1. There is no evidence to support the reviewer's strange idea that the 'Prioress's Tale' was meant to be satirical.
2. See entries 150, 188, 218.

240.

Unsigned review, *Literary and Statistical Magazine for Scotland*, August 1820, I, 323–8

This is a very miscellaneous volume, consisting of poetry and prose, biographical sketches, critical remarks, and lastly, of a topographical description of the country of the Lakes. The poem from which the work is named, is neither long nor very interesting. It amounts to between thirty and forty stanzas, some of which are extremely beautiful; but as a whole, it has nothing striking, either in design or effect. The imagination of the author appears to have had no other guide than the localities with which the Duddon is connected; on which account a foot-path, or a turn-pike road, would have answered his purpose just as suitably as the stream, which 'rises upon Wrynose Fell, on the confines of Westmorland, and enters the Irish sea between the isle of Walney, and the lordship of Millum.'

The following sketch of a country parson moved us not a little. The example, presented in it, is unquestionably more wonderful than instructive: but let the reader judge for himself.

[Quotes a substantial part of the 'Memoir of the Rev. Robert Walker', *PW*, III, pp. 510–22, in notes.]

As specimens of the poetry contained in this volume we have selected the following.

[Quotes 'Lament of Mary Queen of Scots', *PW*, II, pp. 37–40; 'The stars are mansions built by Nature's hand', *PW*, III, pp. 32–3; 'On the Death of his Majesty (George III), *ibid.*, pp. 40–1.]

241.

Unsigned review, *British Review*, September 1820, XVI, 37–53

Of Sir John Denham, Johnson says, in commenting on his Cooper's Hill, 'he seems to have been, at least among us, the author of a species of composition that may be denominated *local poetry*, of which the fundamental subject is some particular landscape, to be poetically described, with the addition of such embellishments as may be supplied by historical retrospection or incidental meditation.' By *author*, we presume Dr. Johnson to have intended the introducer or inventor, and in this character we cannot but consider the mind of his country as under great obligations to his genius. The mere natural imagery of landscape, the display of colour and magnificence, 'the pomp of groves and garniture of fields,' have been consecrated in poetry from its earliest essays, and its earliest essays are almost coeval with nature itself; but those local interests and affections by which history, or memory, or moral similitudes, endear and animate particular scenes, imparting to them a sort of mute intelligence and tacit discourse, have given a decided superiority to the descriptive poetry of very recent days. Many unnoticed, many accidental, and many untraceable circumstances, have concurred to generate this intermixture of living pathos with the description of inanimate existences; but it seems obvious to ascribe it in part to the multiplied associations, attenuated feelings, and cherished illusions, into which life has spread itself with a sort of luxuriance in the progress of refinement, and partly to the higher principles and more mental enjoyment with which of late years the theory of landscape and ornamental scenery has been cultivated and ennobled. In the place of the fairies and divinities, and the cold mythology of the Naiads and the Dryads, our fountains and our groves are rendered interesting or sacred by affinities, recollections, and resemblances, which make them a part of the moral of life, and connect them with the finest properties and feelings of the mind.

If we are to date the introduction of what Dr. Johnson has called 'local poetry' from the time of Sir John Denham, we can consent to allow little more to the poet and his age than the general merit of a first conception. When we compare his Cooper's Hill, or indeed any of the specifically descriptive poetry, either of the period to which Johnson has assigned its introduction, or of the period which followed, we mean that of Pope and Thomson, with the poetry of our own time in the same department, it seems, to our judgments, that the present æra may fairly claim the credit of having originated that sentimental manner of describing particular landscapes which carries the picturesque into the heart, and annexes an interior feeling to what was formerly in its most luxuriant dress the source only of a superficial ecstacy and transient delight. Among the writers who have purchased this distinction for the times in which we live, the author of the little book of poems now before us deserves, in our opinion, a very honourable place. He has entitled himself to this place by an intensity of natural expression, and a thoughtful original delineation of local scenery, which have exalted him to a dignified independence upon traditional imagery, hereditary similes, and the stores of superficial common-place. From these obvious resources he has turned himself to those treasures of contemplative wealth, which, by adding their value to rural objects, and all the possible combinations of scenery, general, local, and domestic have philosophized, and spiritualized, and raised into commerce with the soul, those beauties and sublimities of nature which, in the dress of our old poetry, produced admiration without emotion; stimulating the fancy indeed, but leaving the ideas that slumber in the heart unawakened or unengaged. To Mr. Wordsworth we do really think the praise of this new style of local poetry eminently belongs. We hardly know where to look for a greater abundance of those vivid displays which exhibit the points of contact between our own interior constitution and the objects of external nature which surround us, developing, in the habitudes and associations of the mind, the springs of a superadded delight in each prospect that presents itself.

As a cultivator of this local poetry, Mr. Wordsworth has with good judgment adopted a distinguishing simplicity of style. It is to the simple elemental passions, as they singly display themselves, that his descriptions and allusions are necessarily restricted: the scenes of unsophisticated nature with which his muse is occupied know nothing of the complications of sentiment or emotion to which the tumults and agitations of crowded life furnish constant occasion. The theme is simple, and calls for simplicity of dress and decoration. Where this simplicity is lost sight of, descriptive poetry may be brilliant and beautiful, but it can no longer communicate with the heart; its alliance with moral feeling is cut off: it has no longer any common medium of expression with the impulses of genuine affection.

But while, in order to maintain this consonance and responsiveness of character between the scenes of external nature, and the operations of mind, Mr. Wordsworth, and others who have adopted his taste, have properly estimated the importance of a simple, and apparently artless manner, the excess and extravagance to which they have frequently carried the principle have been the means of bringing it under reproach and contempt, or of recommending a practice detrimental and degrading to our national muse. Poetry is, after all, an ornamental art, and pledged by its very undertaking to become the medium of embellishment: it must achieve something beyond prose, or, it might as well be prose. Simplicity may, without the sacrifice of its proper character, assume both grace and elevation; and we speak it in discommendation of Mr. Wordsworth, and of a certain school to which he may be regarded as belonging, that in many instances they seem to have forgotten the distinction between a natural and unlaboured expression of feeling, and a language at the farthest remove from poetical elevation. To mistake a mean and prostrate diction for the dialect of the poet, is among the follies generated by the affectation of treating things in a new way. It is an inverted ambition; and as there is no dignity in its endeavour, there is the greater disgrace in its fall; by a disappointment well deserved, its very eagerness for distinction precipitates it into common-place. We shall by and by illustrate these observations by a passage or two from some of the pieces now under review. We will first address ourselves to the more pleasurable task of doing justice to the many excellencies which are scattered through these poems, and which may be said almost uniformly to characterize the principal piece, called 'The River Duddon,' consisting of a series of sonnets accompanying the flow of that pleasing river with a succession of incidental reflections beautifully appropriate. For the purpose of interweaving the moral with the picturesque, a more ingenious thought could not have entered the mind of a poet than that of following the variegated course of a river, sometimes calm or slightly agitated, sometimes urged into torrents by its straitened banks, rocky barriers, and precipitous falls; passing at one time through verdant meads, at another through dark defiles, till, widening into a broad and glittering expanse, it bares its bosom to the heavens, and finally sinks into its oblivious repose in the ultimate receptacle of waters, – majestic emblem of eternity! It seems to us, that by following up these diversities of appearance with a series of sonnets, in which he has borrowed, from the changeful aspects of the river in its course, a succession of tender and pathetic allusions to human life, and its affecting vicissitudes, Mr. Wordsworth has with great art and effect contrived to harmonize into one general impression of accumulated interest an assemblage of little pieces distinct in their subjects, and which, without some point of union, might be apt to fatigue attention by a recurrence of the same structure without continuity of interest, or progression of sentiment.

Such, we think, is the character, and such are the advantages of the subject which this poet has chosen for a series of connected sonnets; and though it seems that 'this series of sonnets was the growth of many years,' and the product of 'occasional visits to the stream, as recollections of the scenes upon its banks awakened a wish to describe them;' yet the effect produced by the order in which they are arranged, is that of a continuous effort of expanding thought produced by a single object pleasingly diversified by accident and combination.

It was with great delight that we read many years ago the loco-descriptive poem of Lewesdon Hill, by the present public orator of Oxford; nor can we recollect any production of a similar kind which has since afforded us equal gratification, unless it be the 'River Duddon' of the writer on whom we are now commenting. They proceed in the same tenor of illustrative description, drawing from nature without any strain after similitudes, or analogies, an allusive morality that gives life to the landscape, and makes it converse with the heart. Of the meditative character of Mr. Wordsworth's muse, these sonnets on the River Duddon are a lively specimen, and we cannot but think that the more this style of poetry engages him, the more his reputation will be advanced. We may observe, too, that the demand which descriptive poetry makes upon the imagination for dress and colouring of language, has seemed to divert him from that unaccountable addiction to a frigid and creeping idiom, halting between prose and verse, in which the class of writers to which he belongs is so prone to indulge. Where his language maintains the level of his thoughts, the whole composition stands before us as a structure of suitable elevation and chaste magnificence.

All our readers may not know that the river Duddon rises upon Wrynese Tell [*sic for* Fell], on the confines of Westmoreland, Cumberland, and Lancashire; and after dividing Lancashire from Cumberland for about twenty-five miles, discharges itself into the Irish Sea. But for the sake of enabling them to read the extracts, which we shall present to them, with the intelligence which is necessary to their due impression, we will further inform them, from 'Mr. Green's Guide to the Lakes,' that in the scenery through which the Duddon winds its course to the sea, 'the face of nature is displayed in a wonderful variety of hill and dale; wooded grounds and buildings; amongst the latter, Broughton Tower, seated on the crown of a hill, rising elegantly from the valley, is an object of extraordinary interest. Fertility on each side is gradually diminished, and lost in the superior heights of Blackcomb, in Cumberland, and the high lands between Kirkby and Ulverstone. The road from Broughton to Seathwaite is on the banks of the Duddon, and on its Lancashire side it is of various elevations. The river is an amusing companion, one while brawling and tumbling over rocky precipices, until the agitated water becomes calm again by arriving at a smoother and less precipitous bed; but its course is soon again ruffled, and the current thrown into every variety of form which the rocky channel of a river can give to water.' For a specimen of Mr. Wordsworth, take the fourteenth stanza.

[Quotes 'O Mountain Stream! the shepherd and his cot', Sonnet XIV, *PW*, III, pp. 251–2.]

The tributary stream making its way to the Duddon with precipitate haste, sprinkling refreshment and invigorating the verdure of the thirsty fields through which it hurries, is celebrated with a charming simplicity in the nineteenth sonnet.

[(Quotes 'My frame hath often trembled with delight', Sonnet XIX, *ibid.*, p. 254.]

From among the seven or eight concluding sonnets, it is difficult to make a choice, each of them is so well worthy of being presented to our readers. Every character of the river is impressive, and not the least so in the softest and serenest part of its course. But the poet has, without dissipating the idea which belongs to the integrity of the single sonnet, beautifully pourtrayed the variations of the river's temper, within the compass of fourteen exquisite lines.

[Quotes 'The old inventive Poets, had they seen', Sonnet XX, *ibid.*, p. 254.]

The sheepwashing is very poetically described. It has all that picturesque exactness into which the writer of taste and feeling knows so well how to descend without degrading his muse. There is a transmutation in the poet's touch by which a value is given to the little and the low, while the strictest fidelity in the representation is preserved. Such, we think, is the character of the following sonnet.

[Quotes 'Sad thoughts, avaunt! – the fervour of the year', Sonnet XXIII, *ibid.*, pp. 255–6.]

Take again the view here presented of the church of Ulpha, and the churchyard, with all the pensive features and moral quietude of the scene, as an example of what we hesitate not to say of Mr. Wordsworth, that, apart from his unfortunate propensity to mistake meanness for simplicity, and to discredit his own funds and resources, by affecting poverty in the midst of abundance, he possesses a compass of poetical expression, a sentimental chastity of imagination, and an elevation of moral feeling, which entitle him to rank with that small number to whom his country is indebted for the gifts of genius without the corruption of principle.

[Quotes 'The Kirk of Ulpha to the pilgrim's eye', Sonnet XXXI, *ibid.*, pp. 259–60]

The two following sonnets conduct the river to its home, with a peaceful pomp of expression and placid composure of accompanying allusion, terminating very naturally and gracefully together the process of thought and the course of the stream.

[Quotes 'Not hurled precipitous from steep to steep', Sonnet XXXII, *ibid.*, pp. 260.]

And then follows the verses which, though not the last of the series, would, we think, have closed it with more impressiveness of effect than those by which it is in the next sonnet concluded

[Quotes 'But here no cannon thunders to the gale', Sonnet XXXIII, *ibid.*, pp. 260.]

Of 'Vaudracour and Julia,' the poem which follows, we cannot speak in the same terms of praise as of the sonnets, of which we have just taken our leave. It is one of those examples of failure from ambitious sinking to which Mr. Wordsworth is occasionally abandoned. The tale has nothing in it very new; but the breaking of lovers' hearts, and the bursting of nature's ties by the artificial arrangements and usages of society, can never cease to command our sympathies. Vaudracour, a youth of high birth, living with his parents in a small town among the mountains of Auvergne, woos a maid of the same place, of great charms, but unhappily sprung from a plebeian stock. Their union is implacably opposed by the stern parents of the young man; and the interdict only serves, as might be expected in a case of virtuous love, to confirm the affections of the youthful pair. We shall not follow the story to its catastrophe, which we do not think would be estimated at the value of the room it would demand; enough has been told to introduce the extract, which we think will afford a fair specimen of the style; of which the merit, it would seem, in the opinion of Mr. Wordsworth, and the rest of this humble school, consists in telling a story in verse, as one gossip would tell it to another over their tea, or in a stage-coach. The angry father is made to threaten; and the effect of the menace is related in the following explicit and matter-of-fact language.

[Quotes 'Vaudracour and Julia', *PW*, II, pp. 62–3, ll. 120–35:

> 'You shall be baffled in your mad intent . . .
> And wore the fetters of a criminal.']

Now the meaning of the terms and phrases in the above passage are certainly not subject to mistake; and as far as perspicuity is desirable, and it is without doubt an indispensable requisite in all composition, there is merit in this style of poetry; but it is a merit which is shared in equal degree by every well-drawn contract for the hire of a house, or the minutes of the proceedings of a turnpike meeting; and if the extracted passage be poetry, the documents alluded to are only not poetry, because they are not metrical. We venture, however, to think, that a flat and frigid diction cannot be exalted into poetry by rhyme or rhythm; and that something more than plain good-sense, and clear statement, is of the essence of that species of composition, which from the first ages of the world men have agreed to call poetry. Of the diction of poetry we should say emphatically it should be that 'in qua non eminent venæ nec ossa numerantur: sed temperatus ac bonus sanguis implet membra, et exsurget toris, ipsos quoque nervos rubor tegit et decor commendat.'[1]

We are not ignorant or unwilling to allow that there is a great beauty in the use of familiar words, skilfully applied and combined, and that some of the most affecting and sublime passages in our great poets are constituted of materials of the cheapest quality: but they are no longer cheap or ordinary in the place into which we find them transplanted; and in giving to them this new value lies the profound secret of the poetical artist. It is by arrangement, and disposition, and combination, that he draws out the latent powers of language, and by the contact of new affinities, mysteriously varies its nature, and endows it with new properties. But if words or phrases of vuglar origin still retain in their new situation the savour of their plebeian stock, they retain also their full disqualification for the post and preferment to which they are advanced. Poets, such as Shakspeare and Milton, have each been the fountain of honour, from which sometimes a language of the lowest birth has derived a nobility of rank. Something doubtless is to be ascribed to the prerogative of transcendent excellence, and something to prescription, and the reconciling effect of time and usage; but the magic really resides in that fine and discriminative tact, which at once detects the capabilities of homely expressions, and snatches them warm and breathing from the intercourse of common life, to impart their freshness and stamina, and to take on themselves another nature.

But the phraseology and idiom of vulgar life is not irrespectively and absolutely poetical; nor is carelessness of phrase, the franchise of the muse's votary. We live, indeed, in times unfavourable to discipline in all its departments; men claim to write at their ease, as well as to live at their ease; but either habit is equally grounded in mistake and ends in equal disappointment. To be really at ease, can only consist with being secure of doing well, and this security is only to be arrived at by much preparatory labour, save in some few instances of felicitous endowment. It may be a proper object of a writer's ambition to avoid the appearance of study, but this semblance of facility is in general the fruit only of perseverance, and the consummation of skill. Nothing so deceives and betrays as this appearance of ease in the great models of imitation. The character of labour is lost in the maturity of attainment, and what seems to move with the smallest effort is frequently the least gratuitous in its origin, or facile in contrivance. Thus unfortunately the ease of impertience is mistaken for the ease of accomplishment, as well in composition as in manners; and to this error we owe the quantity of flippant colloquial trash, which at the present period claims to be poetry, and has its claim extensively allowed. With these men of low standard and presumptuous claims, we are far from intending to class Mr. Wordsworth; but we cannot help regretting that his example should afford countenance to an affectation, so destructive of sound taste, and so encouraging to unqualified pretenders. If all that the poet has to do is to come intelligibly to the point, and deliver himself like a man of business, the inference is strong on the side of the aphorism, that a poet is born such, and not made; for who can not be a poet, on such easy terms, if he will relinquish his last or his spade, and take up the pen. If it is but to lessen the danger which threatens us, in this age of scribes and scholars, of the daily multiplication of rhyming plough-boys, and inspired shoe-makers, we conjure Mr. Wordsworth not to give the sanction of his broad example to a mode, of versifying within the competency of 'most men, many women, and some children,' to attain.

That Mr. Wordsworth touches the bottom from choice and not necessity, and that his will and not his poverty consents, we think is plainly proved by a great part of his productions, and especially by the specimens contained in the book before us, in which he shows himself not merely acquainted with the deepest operations of feeling, and conversant with all the springs of natural tenderness, but a master of poetical expression. To justify this remark, we will lay before our readers, what we do not fear to call a most exquisite ode, which the poet tells us was composed upon an evening of extraordinary splendor and beauty:

[Quotes the ode, 'Had this effulgence disappeared', *PW*, IV, pp. 10–13.]

The little song on the September month is full of a sort of cheerful pathos exquisitely borrowed from the scenery of this mellow season. Our readers will, we are sure, sympathise with our admiration of it.

[Quotes 'September 1819', *PW*, IV, pp. 98–9.]

The Ode to 'the Pass of Kirkstone' is singularly beautiful, and forces us to transgress the bounds to which those who delight in this sort of poetry less than ourselves will think we should confine our extracts: we must make our appeal to those who feel the like infirmities with ourselves in these matters.

[Quotes 'The Pass of Kirkstone', *PW*, II, pp. 278–80.]

These charming specimens are with us a decisive proof of the power of Mr. Wordsworth's mind to sustain itself, if, by a strange perverseness of bias, it were not frequently otherwise disposed, at a very lofty level of poetic composition. But we lament to say there is a frequent recurrence of his bad habits and downward ambition throughout this little collection. His genius has a lofty bearing, looking heaven-ward towards the eagle's path; art and imitation combine to keep it down, and compel it to breathe a grosser atmosphere in a lower scale of thought and sentiment. His inequalities are as great as those supposed in his 'Pilgrim's Dream,' between the star and the glow-worm; which little poem we should select as one of those instances of that depression of taste which interrupts the triumphs of his genius. Not even a dream can cover the extravagance of a dialogue between a glow-worm and one of those celestial luminaries which rational conjecture contemplates as a world of souls; but Mr. Wordsworth has exhibited them in controversy together concerning their respective pretensions, in which, for the sake of the instruction, the weight of sentiment and morality inclines to the side of the reptile. When a worm reasons, perhaps we ought to think it enough, and not expect it to rhyme also; but wherever the attempt is made, it is our duty to mark the failure; and Mr. Wordsworth must allow us to say, that even in lines the most creeping we cannot allow the words, 'no' and 'know,' to stand for rhyme.

The Poem 'addressed to — on the longest day;' The 'Hint from the Mountains, for certain political aspirants;' 'Dion;' the poem, beginning with 'Lady, I rifled a Parnassian cave;' would leave the collection improved by their absence in case of another edition; and we are compelled to say of 'the Prioress's Tale,' that it has failed, to our imagination at least, to

> Call up him who left half told
> The story of Cambuscan bold.

We should be glad that this tale should not be thrice told, but that this collection should, by leaving it out of a future edition, be further improved in negative merit. It is horrible in its facts, disgusting in its narration, and odiously profane in its language.

We ought not to close the book without giving due praise to the prose dissertation on the peculiar scenery of the lakes, at the end of the book. The Essay was published some years ago, as we are told in the advertisement, as an introduction to some views of the lakes by the Rev. Joseph Wilkinson, and is now, with emendations and additions, attached to this volume. It certainly is of value as an illustration of the poems now under our review, but we rate its absolute merit very high. Among many topics of rural beauty, it contains an ingenious illustration of the advantages which winter has over summer in the display of mountainous prospect; a very interestingly picturesque description of the disposition and effect of the cottages in the vales; and more particularly of the gradual formation of woody scenery, by nature and time. We think we shall be excused if we lay before our readers what occurs on the last-mentioned subject.

[Quotes 'A Guide through the District of the Lakes', *The Prose Works of William Wordsworth*, ed. W. J. B. Owen and J. W. Smyser, 1974, II. pp. 219–20, ll. 2106–52.]

We always leave Mr. Wordsworth with regret, but on no occasion have we left him with so much regret as on the present. He has touched in these poems some of the finest springs of natural pathos; and we do really think that there is enough in the collection before us to fix the wreath upon his brows too firmly to be torn off by his own hands in any of his fits of prosaic depression, or temporary rage for simplicity.

EDITOR'S NOTE

1. Tacitus, *Dialogus*, 21. Tacitus compares literary style to the human body, finding beautiful that eloquence 'in which the veins are not prominent and the bones cannot be counted; but moderate, healthy blood fills out the limbs and swells up on the muscles and a ruddy complexion covers the very sinews and a gracefulness makes it attractive.'

242.

Unsigned notice, *Gentleman's Magazine*, October 1820, XC, II, 344–6

The Poems in this Volume are marked by the same apparent ease and elegant simplicity which characterize the productions of Mr. Wordsworth. The first of them, affectionately inscribed to his brother (the Rev. Dr. Christopher Wordsworth) consists of XXXIII. Sonnets, 'called forth by one of the most beautiful streams of his native County;' and is illustrated by some entertaining Notes; particularly an excellent Biographical Memoir of the Rev. Robert Walker, who lived to the age of 93, and was Curate of Seathwaite 67 years.

[The remainder of the notice consists of extracts.]

243.

Unsigned review, *Monthly Review*, October 1820, XCIII, 132–43

It would indeed be a satisfaction to the professional critic, and a reward for his long labours, if he could entertain the remotest idea of any *direct* effect being produced by them, on the extravagant mistakes of genius, and on the corruptions of cotemporary taste. It might be Utopian to form an expectation of this nature; but it perhaps may not be wholly chimerical to entertain the pleasing hope that an *indirect* effect is, in some distinguished cases, so produced; and that the re-action of literary opinion produces an amendment in style which no individual censor, or body of censors, can accomplish. In this comparatively slow result of criticism, in this good produced by the circuitous diffusion of truth, the critic only shares the common lot of all who work for the improvement of their fellow-men. Especially may he console himself with the reflection, that his superiors in the great council of the nation, who *criticize* on so much ampler a scale, are forced, like himself, to wait for this same *round-about* result of their patriotic orations: ministers being quite as incorrigible as authors by any *direct* appeal; and the well-informed of the community, – whose judgment needs only to be awakened and recalled to sound principles, whether of government or of literary composition, in order to demand and to secure the necessary changes in practice, – being at last the *rational reformers* by whom the prevailing evils are corrected. It certainly gives us sincere satisfaction to observe an improvement in Mr. Wordsworth, from whatever cause it arises. He has been *put on his mettle*, and starts for the present prize with a spirit and a beauty that have rarely characterized him in any passages of his long poetical course. We meet with poems in this volume which, in our judgment, would reflect honour on any of Mr. W.'s cotemporaries, and (which we consider as much higher praise) would stand a comparison with their neighbours if inserted among the minor efforts of the muse of old. The happiest of these productions, we think, are to be found among the miscellanies here printed; and not in the Sonnets on the river Duddon, although several of these are *very* happy; nor in 'Vaudracour and Julia,' which we regard as but a moderate composition. It is impossible to restrain a passing smile at the *fineness* of this title of 'Vaudracour and Julia,' when contrasted with 'Peter Bell,' and 'The Waggoner.' Mr. W. is determined to shew that he is at least as various as the singer in Horace; and that, if he can sound 'the very base string of humility,' he can also strike the chords to the most 'holiday and lady' measures of which the harp is capable.

In serious truth, we view the major portion of the present volume as a practical recantation, as a distinct palinodia, sung in his best style, of all Mr. Wordsworth's poetical theories, or rather heresies, concerning the identity of the language of prose and verse, &c. &c. He has here proved himself to be endowed with very considerable powers (which, indeed, we never doubted,) as a poet of the genuine classical stamp; and condescending to return to the established models of taste, he has frequently written in a dignified, elegant, and pathetic manner. We shall enable our readers to partake in our own gratification, at witnessing the dawn of a purer and nobler exertion of intellect in a writer of acknowledged ability, and of great amiableness of disposition; as far, we mean, as that can be indicated by the tone of sentiment which pervades his works.

The first little poem which we shall quote has appeared in the newspapers, and may (for aught that we are here informed, or remember at this moment,) have been published elsewhere before: but, attended as it now is by a selection of more adorned and laboured efforts than we usually witness in Mr. W., we consider it as here first introduced to the world in fitting company; and we hope we may add, as the harbinger of many similar strangers whom we are to know hereafter.

[Quotes 'Composed at Cora Linn, in Sight of Wallace's Tower', *PW*, III, pp. 100–2.]

Is it possible to believe that the same pen which produced 'Alice Fell' and 'Peter Bell,' and the whole family of *paupers* in condition and versification, should also have struck forth these noble lines; and that they should proceed from an author perverted enough to maintain such degrading dogmas of poetical belief, as those which characterize that celebrated specimen of absurdity, the '*lyrical*' preface of Mr. Wordsworth? We trust that we shall have no future occasion to address this distinguished heretic again, as we have done of yore;

> Oh! fling away the *worser* part of thee,
> And live the purer with the nobler half.

Let us listen again:
[Quotes 'Dion', *PW*, II, pp. 273–6, ll. 18–76:

> Five thousand warriors – O the rapturous day! . . .
> His flight, mid eddying pine-tree tops!]

Our readers need hardly be reminded of the story in Plutarch.

In the same animated strain of feeling, and the same ornamented cast of expression, this altered and amended poet* sings on another occasion: [Quotes 'Departing summer hath assumed', *PW*, IV, p. 100, ll. 25–48:

> For deathless powers to verse belong . . .
> Her own Æolian lute.]

We are not *quite* assured of the *hallow'd* nature of the Lesbian page; nor do we *entirely* approve the expression of 'Passion's *finest* finger;' which, of course, must be her *little* finger. This poem is dated September, 1819.

From the lines 'On the Pass of Kirkstone,' we select the ensuing *general* and glowing picture†: [Quotes 'The Pass of Kirkstone', *PW*, II, pp. 278–80, ll. 21–86:

> Ye plowshares sparkling on the slopes! . . .
> 'Whate'er the weak may dread, the wicked dare,
> Thy lot, O man, is good, thy portion fair!']

With the sincere and benevolent piety of Mr. Wordsworth, it is impossible not to sympathize.

It becomes now our unwilling duty to point out some remaining *Wordsworthianisms* in this volume. The foregoing extracts betray some slighter indications of those quaintnesses, and pedantries, and 'affectations', as our good old friend Sir Hugh Evans would have called them; – such, for example, as

> Imprison'd mid the formal props
> Of *restless ownership!*
>> [*Ibid.*, ll. 23–4]

but we shall leave the reader to discover and in due degree to condemn the rest, while we proceed to some more striking peculiarities of this description.

'Vaudracour and Julia' is an attempt, we presume, to record a love-story, in all the less impassioned part of it, so very soberly and so very prosaically, that the most fanciful reader shall not be able to imagine it to be in verse, except from the shape and appearance of the lines in the page. Certainly, if it be prose in these passages, it wastes a great deal of

---

* If indeed Mr. W. be not here returning to his own early and most natural character, ere false theories corrupted his imagination.

† The epithet *general* will furnish the clue to much of our praise of Mr. W.'s present effusions, and to much of our censure on his past vagaries. He has usually forgotten the admirable advice to the poet in Rasselas.

the margin by its mode of publication. Yet, in this said Vaudracour, &c. we sometimes are delighted by a most touching, beautiful, and natural bursting forth of poetry. These, however, are not the parts which constitute that kind of merit which we are now solicitous to honour in Mr. Wordsworth. It is not a feverish and occasional energy; it is rather his raised and improved style (whether he has really written many of these poems anew, or only collected some of his best and older compositions into one *gentlemanly* volume,) that pleases us throughout the work; – and, in furtherance of our *visionary* design of contributing to the establishment of his poetical repentance, we shall here request him to forgive our notice of those peculiarities, yet adhering to his muse, to which we alluded above.

[Quotes 'Vaudracour and Julia', *PW*, II, pp. 62–3, ll. 120–49:

> You shall be baffled in your mad intent . . .
> Is man, subjected to despotic sway.]

To say nothing of the pervading *prosiness* of this extract, in one part of it we discover the true spirit of 'Wordsworth's edition of *animated* nature.' The secret is to confound the properties of *vegetable* and *animal* life; and, on many occasions, to ascribe to herbs, plants, and flowers, nay even to stocks and stones, the reasoning powers and passionate attributes of mankind. This is the whole receipt; and Mr. Wordsworth has no patent for it: since the poets of the antient world, and their successors, the classical moderns, have (although more sparingly and judiciously) used the same wand of transmutation, and metamorphosed the inhabitants of one region of nature into the likeness of very different classes in another. It certainly is competent, therefore, to any versifier to tread in the same track; and, if he chuses, to become as absurd by the extravagant abuse of this *old liberty*, and still more by pretending that it is a *new invention* of his own, as even the author of the 'Lyrical Ballads' himself.

The 'seed of the dandelion,'

> —suffered not to use
> Its natural gifts for purposes of *rest*,
> [*Ibid.*, p. 63, ll. 138–9]

and the

> —leaf-clad bough,
> Within the vortex of a foaming flood,
> *Tormented*,
> [*Ibid.*, p. 63, ll. 142–4]

have several parallels in this volume: but, thanks to *common sense* and *common censure!* they are not so eternally repeated as in the other works of Mr. Wordsworth.

We are by much too plain men to relish (or perhaps fully to comprehend) the poetical morality of the subjoined passage:
[Quotes *ibid.*, p. 61, ll. 54–68:

So passed the time, till, whether through effect . . .
The promise of a mother.

To our old English understandings, it seems less heinous for the lovers to be overcome by an unguarded moment, than for either of them to be '*inwardly prepared* to turn aside from law and custom,' &c. We can fancy the indignant zeal of injured virtue, with which a poet, or perhaps a critic, of the *Lake school* (for such prodigies even as the last do actually exist!) would have censured the above sentiment in any of our classical effusions; in the Eloisa, for instance, where indeed it *is*, unfortunately, to be found. It is rare that we have to reprove Mr. Wordsworth for any such mistake as this.

Let us now attend to some of the Sonnets on the 'River Duddon.' They are in number thirty-three; and certainly, whatever variety they may display in their uniformity, that number is sufficient for *one* river. The chain of connection, indeed, with this stream is often rather undiscoverable, consisting solely in the name of 'Duddon;' in which, if there be nothing mystical, (and of this we cannot be certain in any poem by Mr. W.) if there really *is* no more than meets the ear, we own that we are not greatly struck with its poetical effect: but,

—'What's in a name?'
'*Duddon*' will stir a spirit as well as '*Tiber!*'*

Let us try, then.
[Quotes 'Change me, some god, . . .' Sonnet VII, *PW*, III, pp. 248–9]
The 'unculled flow'ret of the glen,' and 'darkling wren,' and the persons who would *prefer* to be either of these to Laura's bird or nosegay, are truly Wordsworthian. The bird and nosegay themselves are in a *finer* manner: but really we descry some symptoms of *finery* in this volume (so surely do extremes meet!) in the author's own style. For example:

---

* See the motto to 'Peter Bell.'

> Or survey the bright dominions
> In the gorgeous colours drest,
> Flung from off the *purple pinions*,
> Evening spreads throughout the west.
> ['Inmate of a mountain-dwelling', *PW*, II, p. 207, ll. 21–4]

Do not our readers recollect a certain 'Song by a Person of Quality?' Who would have expected to see Mr. Wordsworth justly incur a comparison with it?

In that peculiar *seeming-wise* manner which so many of our cotemporaries have attained, Mr. Wordsworth stands pre-eminent. So, in the following passage, where the birth of the Duddon is commemorated, what can be more solemn, mystical, and pregnant with *apparent* meaning than these lines?

> But *as* of all those tripping lambs not one
> Outruns his fellows, *so* hath nature lent
> To thy beginning nought that doth present
> Peculiar grounds for hope to build upon.
> ['How shall I paint thee?', Sonnet III, *PW*, III. p. 247,
> ll. 5–8]

In the subjoined verses, we see a specimen of that extravagant taste which, not contented with so far *animalizing* a river as to make it *undaunted*, (an allowable and antient liberty,) must proceed to describe it as running a race with the traveller, and laughing at his inferiority in speed!

> Starts from a dizzy steep the undaunted rill
> Rob'd instantly in garb of snow-white foam;
> And laughing dares the adventurer, who hath clomb
> So high, a rival purpose to fulfil;
> Else let the dastard backward wend, and roam,
> Seeking less bold achievement, where he will!
> ['Take, cradled Nursling . . .', Sonnet IV, *ibid.*, p. 247, ll. 9–14.]

We could point out many instances of this school-boy fault; this early imitation of Ovid, in his worst propensity of extending a liberty into a licentious usage, and dwelling on his ideas till they are good for nothing; but the clue which we have afforded in the last passage will enable any attentive reader to discover the peculiar error of Mr. Wordsworth, – the love of chattering with, and listening to the gabble of, the inanimate things which he has endeavoured to animate.

It appears to us that the great difference between Mr. Wordsworth's *plain* and his *ornamented* manner is this: in the former, all is told as distinctly, and with as laboured a minuteness of explanation, as we should attempt in addressing a child on any subject that he could not otherwise understand; while, in the latter, the author, like all other poets, and with no originality but that of his thoughts, (the greatest and the best originality), addresses the cultivated imagination, and endeavours to awaken appropriate feelings and fancies by figurative words, which really mean much 'more than meets the ear.'

We cannot afford room for additional extracts, and must therefore be contented with referring the reader to sonnets 5th, 8th, 10th*, and 11th, 17th, (perhaps) 20th, 26th, 29th, 31st, and 32d. The remainder are more or less marked and disfigured by decided *Wordsworthianisms*.

Of the miscellanies, we have yet to refer to those which occur at page 87. and 92.; and we think very well of several passages in the others. We have also to mention a most interesting account of the Reverend Robert Walker, in the notes; and to say, in conclusion, that the Tour to the Lakes seems to us to be as topographically useful as it is *poetically picturesque*.

244. John Taylor Coleridge

Unsigned review, *British Critic*, February 1821, XV, 113–35

John Taylor Coleridge wrote to Keble 16 December 1820:

> . . . I am now at work in a general examination of Wordsworth's powers as a poet without reference to his system . . .
>
> (Ms. Keble College Library)

The account is general and defensive; however, the attack on Wordsworth's heretical view concerning pre-existence in the 'Immortality Ode' is one of the first to appear in print; it is prompted by the last stanza of 'On an

---

* The conclusion of the 10th sonnet is a complete *return* into the regions of antiquity, from the borders of the lakes. Mr. W. is certainly *improving*.

> 'The frolic loves, who, from yon high rock, see
> The struggle, clap their wings for victory.'
>
> ['Not so that Pair whose youthful spirits dance', Sonnet X, *ibid.*,
> p. 250, ll. 13–14]

extraordinary evening of splendour and beauty' where the same heresy is detected.

In our previous notices of Mr. Wordsworth's productions, we have for the most part confined our attention either to the particular work which might happen to be before us, or to the peculiarities of his system of poetry; our limits have naturally precluded us, from entering upon a consideration rather distinct from either of the two just mentioned, yet essential to the forming a correct judgment of him as a poet, we mean the individual qualifications which he has brought either natural or acquired, to the development and support of that system, in other words, what are his pretensions generally to the high character of a poet. We have the gratification of thinking that our remarks were not wholly without the effect, which we aimed at producing, either on the poet himself, or the public, and having so good an opportunity as the present volume affords us, we are the more emboldened to solicit our reader's attention, not indeed to an elaborate, or very regular essay upon the genius and information of Wordsworth, but to a few desultory, and, we hope, brief remarks upon them.

Humorous, and we regret to add, malevolent criticism has been busy with Mr. Wordsworth's poetry, and it has done its work; there are many who read a great many verses, and profess to be enthusiastically fond of poetry; many who pretend to take a great interest in the progress of national taste and literature, and who are respected as judges, who know Wordsworth only by the reports and extracts of periodical criticism. Of these, some in consequence regard him as a childish driveller, as a writer of ballads too stiff for the nursery, and too silly for the drawing-room; others again, and these we believe begin now to form the larger class, consider him a great indeed, but a wild and unequal genius, throwing off now and then, and by accident, poems of exquisite beauty, but these not sufficient in importance, or quantity, to redeem the great mass of careless and absurd writing of which he has been the author. On premises such as these, it is unfair to judge of any writer, but Wordsworth is of all men the most certain to suffer by a judgment so grounded; where a man writes on a system, it is easy to select the faults, and they become perhaps the more salient and repulsive by separating the passages in which they are found from the context, and it requires no knowledge of the system to make the fault very apparent; but the beauties depend so much, and in some cases so entirely on being taken with the context, or as parts of the system, that it is difficult to convey a fair notion of them in extract, or to persons who will not take the trouble of understanding the system. Wordsworth is eminently, and as we think, faultily a systematic writer, and so long as he is known only by the criticisms, or extracts of reviews, he will be imperfectly known: whether the review be favorable or adverse, he will still be imperfectly known, but the effect of the former is to stimulate others to read and judge for themselves, the end of the latter is to prejudice the mind, and stop up the true road of inquiry. It must be well known to the readers of this journal, that our general opinion of Wordsworth is highly favourable, but they also know that our praise is by no means unqualified, and we are inclined to think that what we have said against him in the course of our notices, may weigh as heavily as any thing that has fallen from the more indiscriminate censure of other pens. We have said, and we say again, that he has many things to be blamed in him, and we have tried to account for them; it is not for us to say whether we have done so successfully or not, but we feel confident that what is blameable in him cannot be attributed to imbecility on the one hand, or to irregularity or carelessness on the other; the first is not his misfortune, nor are the latter his faults.

The task which we have now proposed to ourselves, is of a more pleasing nature; and we proceed to it with proportionable interest and spirits. In such an enquiry it is obvious that the primary consideration will be the moral feeling and intellectual power of the poet's mind; these being the faculties by which he is to distinguish what is true and just in all the subject matter of poetry from that which is false and meretricious. To a mind whose moral feelings are pure, and whose perceptive power is clear and unimpeded, many truths, the sublimest truths, those in the declaration and illustration of which poetry exults most and is most magnificently triumphant, are as it were intuitive; the mind does not go through the process of reasoning upon them, but it *enunciates* them as an oracle: it promulgates the truth, it rejects the fallacy, it welcomes that which is good and just with a congenial glow, it adorns it with even more than its own beauty, it dwells upon it with the fondness of love.

[Shakespeare's sublime power of perception is discussed.]

Of this high qualification we think Mr. Wordsworth is gifted with a large endowment; his mind is quick to perceive, and warm to cherish the beauty of moral truth; he holds no parley with what is only specious, or comes enforced by a pretended plea of necessity or expedience; it is the wise and good and beautiful in all things that he never fails to see where they exist, and never fails to celebrate where he sees them. The

Excursion is not our favourite of his works, but no man could have written that poem without this power and feeling of which we have been speaking – it happens to be lying by us, and we will not deny our argument the benefit, nor ourselves the pleasure of illustrating what we have advanced by the following splendid example, which seems to us to be conceived and expressed in what we would call the oracular manner of Shakspeare.

[Quotes *The Excursion*, *PW*, V, pp. 142–3, Book IV, ll. 1058–77:

Within the soul a faculty abides . . .
From palpable oppressions of despair.]

The property, which it is next in order to consider in forming any estimate of a poet, is his reasoning or argumentative power, that power by which he is to draw conclusions from the premises, which may have been assumed only from the faculty just considered. We express ourselves thus, because undoubtedly it is not necessary in poetry that the grounds *from* which we reason, should be always true or philosophical in themselves; it is sufficient if the reasoning *from* those grounds be always logically correct. The poet moves in a world of his own creation, he may announce facts, or doctrines from that world, of which the truth will not be strictly inquired into, if they do not too violently offend against our common sense; but when he reasons upon them, or from them, he must use the common weapons of mankind and use them under the common rules and discipline of mankind . . .

. . . This faculty, so essential to good writing, is however of far less dignity than the one first considered, and we believe any one of common sense may by industry attain to it – every writer therefore is inexcusable who does not possess it, for no man has a right to obtrude his thoughts on the world, unless he has been at the pains so to discipline his mind, as at least to attain all the correctness in his power. It is not then as matter of high praise that we ascribe to Wordsworth the character of a correct arguer, for we could have had no pleasure in his poetry, if he had not been such, and being so, it might yet be possible that we should remain unpleased. But he certainly is both a correct and skilful reasoner; and the Excursion, were we at liberty to refer to it again, would in the course of its long discussions furnish us with many instances, both of his adroitness and regularity in argument.

The poet's knowledge is the next point which we should regularly consider, but this will branch out into so many points of view, that we prefer to say a few words previously on two less comprehensive topics;

his diction, and metrical ear. It has often struck us with surprise that Wordsworth's style should have been considered low, and too simple: undoubtedly phrases of the most colloquial plainness and turn do occasionally, perhaps too often, occur in his poetry, but the general character of his diction has always seemed to us, to be rather raised above, than depressed below his subject. And indeed, if we do not mistake, the objection to the style has arisen from the confused notions of the objectors, who have transferred the fault which they intended to impute to his subjects, to the language in which he has treated of them, and have taken for granted, that the words were low, because the thoughts appeared to them to be low. No unprejudiced critic however can hesitate to place Wordsworth very high in the scale of poets, so far as mere style is concerned − without the appearance of imitation it is more like that of Shakspeare or Milton, than any modern writer's: in the present volume indeed is a very striking and intelligible proof, how much his style is of the *same kind* with that of the latter of our two great poets; the poem of Artegal and Elidure, will appear to any one to be written with Wordsworth's common diction. No one, we are persuaded, will perceive any difference in that respect between it, and the remaining poems of the volume; yet if any one will take the trouble to refer to Milton's History of England, from which the story is taken, he will find not merely words and phrases, but nearly whole sentences embodied into the poem, which harmonize however completely with the colouring of the rest, and do not give the least idea of two distinct masters. The fact is, that however different the direction and occupation of Wordsworth's mind has been from that of Shakspeare, or Milton, however they have taken broader views, and, if we may use the expression, only 'touched and gone' on subjects and trains of thought, to which he has devoted all the intensity of a reflective mind, and elaborately unravelled and examined, still we imagine that he has been a long and deep student of their writings, that he has sounded the principles on which they thought and wrote, and so transfused them into himself, as to make their manner of expression habitual and natural to him. At all events his style is very English, very unaffected, very free from tiresome mannerisms, at the same time that where his subject will admit, and sometimes perhaps almost beyond the fair proportion of his subject, it is lofty, ornate, and even gorgeous. As a specimen of these latter qualifications, we will cite the opening of a noble poem on the story of Dion, taken from Plutarch's Life.

[Quotes 'Dion', *PW*, II, pp. 272–4, first two stanzas:

> Fair is the swan, whose majesty prevailing . . .
> Help under every change of adverse fate.]
>
> [1820]

We have quoted this passage as a specimen of rich and lofty diction, but we might have instanced it for the peculiar and felicitous appropriateness of it in the whole and in every part to the subject matter. The simile of the swan silently gliding on the calm lake in the moonshine, as it is in itself a most beautiful idea, so is it in its detail all most poetically worked out, and most happily expressed. We need not point out to our readers many epithets, descriptive of the swan's form or motions, which it would be impossible to alter without injury to the passage; but this is a merit very generally diffused through Wordsworth's writings; his epithets always have a force, and add a new and valuable idea.

Yet with all these advantages of a strong conceptive, and clear reasoning power, aided by an excellent diction, Wordsworth is not always so intelligible a writer, as from these circumstances might fairly be expected. We are not now speaking of the difficulty which arises from depth or novelty of thought, but of that which appears to us attributable to indistinctness in the poet's own idea, connection of irrelevant thoughts or images, or imperfect description. For example, in a sonnet on the death of the late King, he speaks of him as one

> Whose universe was gloom, immersed in gloom,
> Darkness as thick as life o'er life could fling –
> ['On the Death of his Majesty' (George III), *PW*, III, p. 40,
> ll. 3–4]

The first line *we suppose* may allude to the mental, and visual darkness which clouded the latter years of our excellent King, if so we think it very imperfectly expressed; but the second line we really are unable, after all our pains, to attach any meaning to; neither can we feel confident that we understand the sense intended to be expressed by the last lines of the same sonnet:

> The nation hears
> In this deep knell – silent for threescore years
> *An unexampled voice of awful memory.*
> [*Ibid.*, p. 41, ll. 12–14]

They may have two or three meanings, but we can fix on none. As an instance of the obscurity which arises from too rapid a transition from one train of images to another, we will cite a few lines from the poem to the present Master of Trinity College, which is a great favorite with us, and as a whole is a most exquisite production. The stanzas turn on the village carols, which he describes as having been just sung under his window on Christmas Eve.

> How touching, when at midnight sweep
> Snow muffled winds, and all is dark
> To hear – and sink again to sleep –
> Or, at an earlier call, to mark
> By blazing fire the still suspense
> Of self-complacent innocence
> The mutual nod – the grave disguise
> Of hearts with gladness brimming o'er;
> And some unbidden tears that rise
> For names once heard, and heard no more,
> Tears brightened by the serenade
> For infant in the cradle laid.
>
> ['To the Rev. Dr. Wordsworth', *ibid*., p. 245, ll. 37–48]

The first three lines are clear, and the remainder of the passage, if it *was* clear, would be exquisitely beautiful; but we are not sure that we understand it; and if we do, the transition is too rapid and wide to be followed by merely a catch word here and there, but no direct relation. We will give one instance of obscurity, arising from imperfect description, and then have done with this minute criticism:

> Enough – for one soft vernal day
> If I a bard of ebbing time
> And nurtured in a fickle clime
> May haunt this horned bay;
> Whose amorous water multiplies
> The flitting halcyon's vivid dyes;
> And smoothes its liquid breast – *to show*
> *These swan-like specks of mountain snow*
> White, as the pair that slid along the plains
> Of Heaven, when Venus held the reins.
>
> ['Ode to Lycoris', *PW*, IV, pp. 94–5, ll. 9–18]

The epithet 'ebbing' cannot be well understood in an extract, but the preceding lines make it clear and forcible; our objection is to the words printed in italics; they are evidently meant to describe and paint something to the reader, which the poet saw before him actually, when he wrote; and if the reader could *in fact* be placed by the side of the poet, he might see that the language was striking and expressive enough; but without this advantage, we really cannot tell what the object was which was displayed in the water, and scarcely even whether it was a reflection or the thing itself. We may expose ourselves to the imputation of great dullness, but we rather imagine that a poet may deceive himself; and that those who live with him and know what he knows, and see what he sees, may deceive themselves in judging of his descriptions; no notice can be too slight, no hint too rapid to convey a clear idea when we know the original, and the slighter or more rapid the notice or hint are, the more delight we receive, the more vivid is the impression. But it cannot be the same with strangers; they have no picture of the whole within to connect and explain the sketch given of the past, the hint to *them* awakens no *recollections*, no associations. We remember a fanciful fashion of exchanging miniatures of the eye only, or of a lock of hair, instead of the whole face or figure; it was fanciful, but undoubtedly among intimates, the picture of the eye might suffice to recall the face; as that of the face commonly does to recall the whole figure; but such a fashion, either in painting or poetry, can only recall what is known; it cannot impart what is unknown; it may subsist between the members of a family, or the companions of retirement, but it cannot satisfy the world. We need hardly guard ourselves to Wordsworth himself, nor indeed to our readers in general, from being supposed to be the advocates of minute and unsparing description; that too often degenerates into mere tame copy; the true mean is between both; we must not have *every* feature so laboriously drawn, that there is no room left for the play of our own imagination; but we require so much to be done, that our imagination be at least directed in a certain definite train; every description should be on the face of it, without note from the author, or knowledge of the reader, *intelligible*; the kind and character of the thing described should be put beyond a doubt.

The metrical ear of Wordsworth is next to be considered, and we cannot agree with the great critic of British poetry, in regarding this as a matter of small importance in any poet, or on any subject.

[Discussion of Milton's metrical care, his 'nice and humorous' attention to his versification.]

. . . we can trace in [Wordsworth] great marks of diligence in this respect; he appears to us to be in some respects the most practised and skilful metrist of the age; and if we are not mistaken, he is indebted for his success not so much to a good natural ear, as to the diligence we have been speaking of, and the patient study of the best models. Our reason for thinking this is, that he is incomparably more excellent in his blank verse, than in his lyric measures; now it seems to us that no gift of nature, nothing but care and study will suffice to make a good writer of blank verse; and we think that with but a moderate share of the former, these latter will seldom fail of success. Without entering into the dispute between blank verse and heroic rhyme, we presume that it will be admitted that the beauty of the former consists in its endless variety of pauses, the lengthened flowing sweep of the period when the subject requires it, and also from its adequacy to sustain any train of thoughts or images, however weighty or sublime they may be – blank verse can never, if we may use the term, 'break down' under the dignity of the subject. Now it is manifest that these are the beauties of care and study; an unpractised or careless writer of blank verse, with a good ear, will in general run into the fault of a cloying sweetness and sameness; each line will be good, but the whole strain too short, too unvaried, and the several strains too much like each other. When he mends, and feels the necessity of variety, his change will be too abrupt, and he will fancy his object accomplished merely by breaking the chime of his numbers, by a line here and there harsh in itself, and which has no relation in the general framing of the measure with those which precede and follow it – a discord clumsily thrust into the music, and not leading the ear again by nice gradations into the original key. It is not till after longer practice that the real music of blank verse is attained – we think Wordsworth has mastered this difficulty; many of his shorter poems are models of this kind of versification, and the lines written a few miles above Tintern Abbey, have often been cited by able judges, with the highest praise in this respect. The present volume contains but little blank verse, and a short poem indeed is rather a partial mode of trying such a question; if we would bring an author fairly to the bar, we should examine his longer works, and we think Wordsworth may boldly challenge criticism upon the metre of his Excursion. We will, rather for the sake of delighting our readers, and shewing what Wordsworth can do in this way, than with a view of deciding the question, cite a few lines, to which we have turned almost by hazard – independently of the grandeur of the poetry, the measure seems to us to be constructed with the greatest skill and taste.

[Quotes *The Excursion*, *PW*, V, p. 307, Book IX, ll. 614–35:

            Eternal Spirit! Universal God! . . .
            Time's weary course.]

We have said that we do not think Mr. Wordsworth so fortunate in his lyric measures, as in the construction of his blank verse; neither has he in our opinion attained any high degree of positive excellence in this way. Passages indeed may be found, and especially in his loftier odes of very elaborate and exquisite versification; that most difficult but most sublime ode in the second volume of his Poems, to which he has affixed no title, and which we hardly know how better to designate than by calling it the Platonic Ode, is full of strains, in which the metre is so adapted to the feeling as to prove the most perfect acquaintance with the mystery of versification. But these are exceptions, and their excellence depends on a circumstance which is connected with what we imagine to be the cause of Mr. Wordsworth's general failure in lyric metres; the subject matter did not require the sweetness or rapidity of lyrics, and it is in these qualities, and especially the last, that he is generally deficient; all that can be effected by the artful construction of an intricate strain, Mr. Wordsworth has done, and will do; and this is enough for subjects which might as well have been treated of in such blank verse as the Tintern Abbey Lines: but where the thought is lighter and more properly lyric, where the measure should be less involved the melody more simple and sweet, and the current of words more strong and rapid, we will confess that he generally disappoints us. It may be vulgar taste, but we will plead guilty to receiving pleasure from the tune itself in lyric poetry; our satisfaction even in noble poetry, is rendered incomplete, when our ears are disappointed by the immeasurable postponement of the recurrent rhyme, or when the correspondent line comes halting to us a foot or syllable shorter than its mate. We know that there are occasions in irregular metres where the feeling calls for a shorter line, to be a pause and a basis, as it were, on which the whole strain may rest; no man knows the use of this short line better than Wordsworth; but we are now speaking of alterations in the length of lines, which add nothing to the force of the feeling, and for which we can assign no cause but the mere caprice of a bad ear; take the following instance from the beautiful passage we have already once quoted.

> Fair is the swan whose majesty prevailing
> O'er breezeless water on Locarno's lake
> *Bears him on while proudly sailing*
> He leaves behind a moon illumined wake, &c.
> ['Dion', *PW*, II, p. 272 and footnote, ll. 1–4]

These lines, though part of a long strain, are in themselves a mere quatrain, and the rudest ear must be shocked by the shortness of the third line, and the change from the iambic to a trochaic foot.

We pass on with pleasure to speak of the cultivation of Wordsworth's mind, the knowledge of books, and of nature inanimate and human, which he brings to his poetry. Of the former, the volume now before us presents greater evidence than his earlier productions, it is more classical in its manner, more classical in its allusions. Yet we imagine Mr. Wordsworth to be less book learned than any great poet of our nation who has preceded him; his habits are evidently less studious, and more contemplative; he is rather disposed to Find 'tongues in trees, books in the running brooks,' &c.

And certainly much of the peculiar charm of his poetry, the individuality and truth of his descriptions of external nature, as well as the depth which he has reached in his examinations of the human heart are owing to this part of his character. Indeed, without this he could not have written the more important part of his poems; still we have often missed in him the pleasure, which as zealous though imperfect scholars, we always derive from classic allusion, and we have felt it to be something like an imputation upon a great modern poet not to evince in his writings a more intimate acquaintance with, and a more imitative admiration of the great masters of antiquity. For after all, consistently with every rational theory of poetry, the great poets of Greece and Rome must ever stand objects of the highest interest, and most attentive study to modern poets; they may, and they certainly did, want whole classes of important ideas and sublime subjects which are open to their successors of later ages; but what they had they made such use of, and the Grecian poets were so favoured by the excessive beauty of their language, that with all our advantages, it may well be doubted whether we can produce any thing as a model so safely to be followed, as many of their productions. But independently of this consideration, every English gentleman, who reads poetry, cannot fail to receive additional pleasure, when it reminds him of those studies which are associated in his mind with the most delightful recollections; and the English poet is wanting to himself who neglects to give his poetry an ornament so effective, and to be added with so little comparative difficulty. This is not the case with Wordsworth in the present volume; he recalls to our recollection in several places Sophocles, and even Pindar, but what perhaps is singular, and could not have been expected, we trace our favourite Horace the most frequently. As a lyric poet, Wordsworth has much to learn of Horace; his clearness, his beautiful transitions, his moral conveyed in a hint, and not in an essay, his conclusions seemingly so abrupt and unprepared, yet so complete and so precisely where they should be. Recollecting these qualities in Horace, we are not afraid to call our reader's attention to the second Ode, entitled, 'September'. It is almost too long for an extract, yet we know not how to give what we consider the Horatian parts of it their full effect, unless we transcribe the whole.

[Quotes 'Departing Summer hath assumed . . .', *PW*, IV, pp. 99–101.]

But delightful to us as poems of this kind are, it is not in such that Wordsworth's genius is most powerful, or is best pleased to expatiate; he is not to be characterized, in the common sense of the term, as a scholar-like poet; it is in contemplation of external nature, and in meditation on the mysterious workings of his own heart, and especially in the effects produced by the former on the latter that he is most profound, and most pleased to be employed. As an observer of nature, limiting the term to the inanimate world around us, he seems to us to unite at once a more exquisite taste, a more intimate knowledge and a more ardent zeal than any poet that has ever preceded him. We do not mean to say that he has better described common appearances, but he has seen more, and he draws what he has seen with the fidelity of a portrait painter, and his pictures have, in consequence, all the indescribable and forcible individuality of real portraits. His scenery is sometimes very remarkable, perhaps we have ourselves seen nothing like it in nature, yet we cannot help feeling sure that the poet has, and that it is thence that he derives the power of making us see it so perfectly in his description; so, on the other hand, it is sometimes very common; a few features of ordinary occurrence make it up, a flowing stream, a hanging tree, a cavern, a meadow, or any such common incident; yet even in such a case we shall be sure to find some individualizing trait thrown in, which gives a reality to it, and makes us feel that he is describing some real spot where the event in narration occurred. Again, it is not only in the features themselves, and their disposition, that Wordsworth is so feelingly *true* and forcible, but every incident of light and shade, of time and season is kept in perfect correctness and harmony; we not only see the wood the rock or the river, as they really are, but we see them exactly as they would be at that time of the day, in that season of the year, and from that spot in which we are supposed to be placed. Perhaps Wordsworth has sometimes carried this too far, and given his pictures a too finished, and too artificial appearance from the overflowing of this abundant knowledge of his subject; the omnia nimis is the cleaving frailty to excellence in any particular department of taste; what we do well, we delight to do too often, and we try to do too well. But this occasional excess is a small drawback from the great beauty that results from the practice in general; we cannot press too much upon our younger poets the necessity of striving for this great qualification. Wordsworth has, indeed, an exquisite eye for nature, but he owes his descriptive excellence to his great love of nature, his great acquaintance with nature; they too must describe not what they fancy in their study, not *what they have seen described elsewhere*, but what they have seen themselves. This rule is founded in common sense, and it is universal; principles may be drawn from the study of models, but in practice, if we would be true and forcible, we must not *copy* copies, but *imitate* originals. It is very well in sculpture to extol the antique, and far be it from us to detract from its merit, or deny the utility of its study, but if our artists would rival what they admire, they must look to *nature*; instead of disputing upon the comparative merits of the horses of Lysippus and of Phidias, let them become more familiar with real barbs and racers, in the studs of this country they will find better models than either.

To return, however, to Wordsworth, and to instance a little of what we have been just remarking, it might be supposed that the appearances of the sky would be favourite subjects with him; the magnificence and beauty of evening skies are common topics; it is a remark we must all of us have made a great many times, that such or such a sky would be declared unnatural in a picture or a poem, and a common artist in either way would shrink from attempting to give the detail of them; it is easy, in either art, to give perhaps the general effect, but it is only the free and fearless hand of a master that can venture on the minuter incidents of such a scene that make the picture a portrait. Now let us turn to the following lines, from a poem composed on an evening of extraordinary splendour and beauty.

[Quotes 'Composed on an Evening of extraordinary Splendour and Beauty', *ibid.*, pp. 11–13, ll. 19–80:

> This silent spectacle – the gleam
> The shadow – and the peace supreme . . .
> 'Tis past – the visionary splendour fades
> And night approaches with her shades.]

We have added the last stanza to our quotation, though it is not descriptive, and may lead us for a moment out of our way, when we have little room to allow for a digression; but we have added it because it alludes to a part of Mr. Wordsworth's creed, which we did not hope to see again professed by him at this time of day, we mean the notion of the pre-existence of the soul in heaven, or in some state far superior to the present. In a passage of exquisite poetry he announces this doctrine elsewhere.

[Quotes the stanza from the 'Immortality Ode', beginning

Our birth is but a sleep and a forgetting . . .]

A more poetical theory of human nature cannot well be devised, and if the subject were one, upon which error was safe, we should forbear to examine it closely, and yield to the delight we have often received from it in the ode from which the last extract is made. The heavenliness of infancy is a sweet idea, and no one can have watched, with a parent's attention, the waking eye of a placid infant without fancying that it really had communion with something unearthly; the clear, quiet, untroubled look, together with the voluntary yet unexplained change and motions, seem to hold a language, which though unintelligible to us, may find a correspondent among other beings in a higher sphere. If, therefore, we had met the doctrine in any poet but Mr. Wordsworth, we should have said nothing; but we believe him to be one not willing to promulgate error, even in poetry, indeed it is manifest that he makes his poetry subservient to his philosophy; and this particular notion is so mixed up by him with others, in which it is impossible to suppose him otherwise than serious; that we are constrained to take it for his real and sober belief. But not to say that it is unwarranted by Scripture, and contradicted by common experience, we would ask him, if he has ever considered to what consequences he must be led by the admission of its truth; if the soul of each individual comes, like an emanation from the bosom of the Creator, 'trailing clouds of glory,' pure, heavenly, and unspotted, what becomes of original sin, and the fall of man, and if they are abandoned, where is the atonement – in one word, (and the consequence cannot stop shorter,) where is Christianity? We have held up Mr. Wordsworth as a great moral teacher, and undoubtedly such is the general effect of his poems, and such, we are convinced, is the design of all; but we are bound by a sacred duty to protest against a philosophy which substitutes a visionary notion of human purity, and a mystic appeal to the influences of external nature for the plain, unerring, and heart-controuling doctrines of Scripture. We are sure we need not tell, though we may venture to remind Mr. Wordsworth, that for the last eighteen hundred years there has been no moral philosophy, but Christian philosophy.

The digression into which we have been led has a little anticipated some part of what we should have remarked on Mr. Wordsworth's acquaintance with human nature – we have stated that we consider him erroneous in his fundamental theory, but we do not mean to deny him the praise of very accurate observation of the human heart. Next to external nature the human heart has been his favourite study, and every page of his works is full of proof, that his study has been very successful. He has watched and traced with minute precision its workings in every age and condition, and under an immense variety of circumstances; the Brothers, a poem, which it is almost impossible to read without a tear, the Two April Mornings, the Fountain, Michael, and Ruth, among a number of others, and very many of the tales introduced in the Excursion, are proofs beyond contradiction with how true a hand he can touch the strings of human feeling. In the volume before us is a beautiful ballad, entitled Repentance, which turns on the regret of a dalesman for having sold his little patrimony; we cannot spare room to cite it, but it is another proof, on a subject which we should have thought not likely to have fallen within a poet's range, of this same skill in the human heart. We have before expressed our opinion of Peter Bell in this respect; but indeed it would be endless to cite all the instances which our intimacy with Wordsworth's writings presents to us of this high poetical qualification. We shall rather devote a few words to some exceptions and restrictions which seem to us necessary to be made in our commendation. In the first place, intimate as we believe him to be with the human heart, he is by no means gifted with dramatic skill; he knows the effect which given circumstances will produce on a given character, but he does not distinguish well whether the patient himself will always be conscious of that effect; and if he be, whether he will naturally express that consciousness. For example, Dion beholds the spectre of a giant-woman violently sweeping at the end of a gallery. After bidding her depart in vain,

[Quotes 'Dion', *PW*, II, p. 277, ll. 94–101:

> Ye Gods, thought he, that servile implement
> Obeys a mystical intent!
> Your minister would brush away
> The spots that to my soul adhere;
> But should she labour night and day
> They will not, cannot disappear –
> *Whence angry perturbations, and that look*
> *Which no philosophy can brook.*]

Undoubtedly the remembrance of a sin committed would produce perturbations in the mind of such a man as Dion, and such perturbations
were not proper for the mind of a favourite disciple of Plato; and Dion
might have naturally enough declared this of a third person; but at such a
moment it was by no means natural for him to draw this cool deduction
from his own feelings, and apply it to himself. So again, in the lines
which a little precede those just quoted, in which he is bidding the
spectre avaunt, and declaring that he would rather see the torch, and
snaky whip,

> And the long train of doleful pageantry
> Which they behold whom vengeful Furies haunt;
> [*Ibid.*, p. 276, ll. 85–6]

It is clearly unnatural to make *him* add

> Who while they struggle from the scourge to flee
> Move where the blasted soil is not unworn
> And in their anguish bear what other minds have borne.
> [*ibid.*, p. 276, ll. 87–9]

The mistake is in suffering the agitated individual to speak the reasonings
of the stander-by calmly reflecting on his case.

Another circumstance has led Mr. Wordsworth into errors of a different and more obvious kind; a poet's own mind will naturally enough be
the text-book from which he will draw many of his axioms as to the
workings of other minds; it will be the rule by which he will measure, but
our author has not always sufficiently remembered, that peculiar habits
and studies, peculiar trains of circumstances, and we may reasonably add,
very remarkable powers make *his* own mind by no means a safe index to
the movements of others . . . .

One more qualification of a poet, an indispensable one to the attainment of excellence . . . and his severest critics will not deny that Mr.
Wordsworth possesses it; we mean an exalted and worthy notion of his
art. The value which he assigns to his office is high, but not beyond its
fair claims; poetry is undoubtedly a gift of God to man, for great and
useful purposes, often the precursor of civilization, and always its most
brilliant ornament; the fairest flower of the human intellect, and its most
delightful and elegant recreation; the refiner of our pleasures, and yet a
faithful handmaid of the virtues; the poet who thinks otherwise of her,
or lower than this, not only debases the gift, but is unworthy of it, and
can never attain to the excellence which he does not comprehend. It is

not possible, we believe, to find a great poet in any age or language an exception to this rule; a consciousness of their own dignity, widely different from the assumed importance of the mere versifier, is inseparable from all true poets; and we believe Mr. Wordsworth does not overstep this proper line, but feeling himself to be a poet, he is right to demand the consideration which is payable to every real poet.

. . . enough has been said, we trust, to excite the interest of our readers, and to convince them that at least there must be something more in the man, who has called forth all these remarks, than other critics have been willing to allow him. If they shall be induced to read for themselves we shall be satisfied; faults they will undoubtedly find, but they are not the faults of a weak or careless writer, and if we can judge of others by ourselves, they will derive a pleasure higher in degree, and almost different in kind, from that which is afforded by any other modern poet. We never rise from Wordsworth without feeling ourselves elevated; there is, perhaps, a tendency to mysticism in the enthusiasm which he excites, but it is pure, meditative and satisfactory.

We never like to close an article, however long, without at least some direct notice of the book which forms its title, and though we have quoted largely from the volume before us in the course of our general remarks, yet we have said scarcely any thing of its particular character or merits. We must do both in a few words; it has less of Mr. Wordsworth's peculiarities than any preceding volume, and furnishes less food for the humorous critic; but it is more than commonly soft and sweet; a mild and moral pensiveness runs through the whole of it, and it gives us the idea of a mind not weakened indeed, but mellowed and sobered by time, and willing to concede something, in order that mankind, who cannot be benefited by poetry unless they be pleased by it, may be allured gradually to theories somewhat too repulsive in their original and naked simplicity. The gem of the volume is a set of Sonnets on the River Duddon, in which the poet, following the stream from its mountain source down to its mixing with the sea, seizes on all the incidents by the way that strike his attention. This is a beautiful idea; each incident has the completeness and unity essential to a sonnet, while the stream is the connecting link, or rather the pervading string of the pearl necklace that unites and harmonizes the whole. The Sonnets are in general very beautiful, we are almost at a loss which to select for our readers, but contenting ourselves with referring them to the 9th, 10th, 19th, 21st, 29th, 31st, and 32nd,[1] we will close this long article by extracting the last, which exhibits at once the classical turn of allusion noticed by us before as frequent in this volume, and at the same time elevates the mournful and querulous strain of the heathen poet by moral and religious reflections, which occur so readily and instinctively, as it were, to Wordsworth's mind, and which he knows so well how to express.

[Quotes 'I thought of Thee, my partner and my guide', Sonnet XXXIV, *PW*, III, p. 261.]

EDITOR'S NOTE

1. The last three sonnets are now numbered 30, 32, and 33.

XVI

Later opinions, 1815–1820

245. Charles Lamb

From letters to Wordsworth, April 1815

a. 7 April 1815

You have made me very proud with your successive book presents. I have been carefully through the two volumes to see that nothing was omitted which used to be there. I think I miss nothing but a Character in Antithet. manner which I do not know why you left out; the moral to the boys building the giant, the omission whereof leaves it in my mind less complete; and one admirable line gone (or something come in stead of it) 'the stone-chat and the glancing sand-piper,' which was a line quite alive. I demand these at your hand.[1] I am glad that you have not sacrificed a verse to those scoundrels. I would not have had you offer up the poorest rag that lingered upon the stript shoulders of little Alice Fell, to have atoned all their malice. I would not have given 'em a red cloak to save their souls. I am afraid lest that substitution of a shell (a flat falsification of the history) for the household implement as it stood at first, was a kind of tub thrown out to the beast, or rather thrown out for him. The tub was a good honest tub in its place, and nothing could fairly be said against it. You say you made the alteration for the 'friendly reader,' but the malicious will take it to himself. Damn 'em; if you give 'em an inch &c. The preface is noble and such as you should write: I wish I could set my name to it – Imprimatur – but you have set it there yourself, and I thank you.[2] I had rather be a doorkeeper in your margin, than have their proudest text swelling with my eulogies. The poems in the volumes which are new to me are so much in the old tone that I hardly received them as novelties. Of those, of which I had no previous knowledge, the four yew trees and the mysterious company which you have assembled there, most struck me – 'Death the Skeleton and Time the Shadow –' ['Yew-Trees', *PW*, II, p. 10, 1. 27–8] It is a sight not for every youthful poet to dream of – it is one of the last results he must have gone thinking on for year for. Laodamia is a very original poem; I mean original with reference to your own manner. You have nothing like it. I should have seen it in a strange place, and greatly admired it, but not suspected its derivation . . .

I am almost sorry that you printed Extracts from those first Poems

[*Evening Walk* and *Descriptive Sketches*], or that you did not print them at length. They do not read to me as they do all together. Besides they have diminished the value of the original (which I possess) as a curiosity. I have hitherto kept them distinct in my mind as referring to a particular period of your life. All the rest of your poems are so much of a piece, they might have been written in the same week – these decidedly speak of an earlier period. They tell more of what you had been reading.

(*The Letters of Charles and Mary Lamb*, ed. E. V. Lucas, 1935, II, 153–4)

b. Postmarked 28 April 1815

The more I read of your two last volumes, the more I feel it necessary to make my acknowledgm^{ts}. for them in more than one short letter. The Night Piece^3 to which you refer me I meant fully to have noticed, but the fact is I come so fluttering and languid from business, tired with thoughts of it, frightened with fears of it, that when I get a few minutes to sit down to scribble (an action of the hand now seldom natural to me – I mean voluntary pen-work) I lose all presential memory of what I had intended to say, and say what I can . . .

 – So I had meant to have mentioned Yarrow Visited, with that stanza, 'But thou that didst appear so fair – ' than which I think no lovelier stanza can be found in the wide world of poetry – yet the poem on the whole seems condemned to leave behind it a melancholy of imperfect satisfaction, as if you had wronged the feeling with which in what pre-ceded it you had resolved never to visit it, and as if the Muse had determined in the most delicate manner to make you, and *scarce make you*, feel it. Else, it is far superior to the other ['Yarrow Unvisited'], which has but one exquisite verse in it, the last but one, or the two last – this has all fine, except perhaps that *that* of 'studious ease and generous cares' has a little tinge of the *less romantic* about it. The farmer of Tilsbury vale is a charming counter part to poor Susan, with the addition of that delicacy towards aberrations from the strict path which is so fine in the Old Thief and the boy by his side, which always brings water into my eyes. Perhaps it is the worse for being a repetition. Susan stood for the representative of poor Rus in Urbe.^{4} There was quite enough to stamp the moral of the thing never to be forgotten. 'Fast volumes of vapour'^{5} &c. The last verse of Susan was to be got rid of at all events. It threw a kind of dubiety upon Susan's moral conduct. Susan is a servant maid. I see her trundling her mop and contemplating the whirling phenomenon thro' blurred optics; but to term her a poor outcast seems as much as to say that poor Susan

was no better than she should be, which I trust was not what you meant
to express. Robin Goodfellow supports himself without that *stick* of a
moral which you have thrown away, – but how I can be brought in felo
de omittendo for that Ending to the boy builders is a mystery. I can't say
positively now – I only know that no line oftener or readier occurs than
that 'Light hearted boys, I will build up a giant with you.'[6] It comes
naturally with a warm holyday and the freshness of the blood. It is a
perfect summer Amulet that I tye round my legs to quicken their motion
when I go out a Maying. (N.B.) I don't often go out a maying. – *Must* is
the tense with me now. Do you take the Pun? Young Romilly is divine,
the reasons of his mother's grief being remediless.[7] I never saw parental
love carried up so high, towering above the other Loves. Shakspeare
had done something for the filial in Cordelia, and by implication for the
fatherly too in Lear's resentment – he left it for you to explore the depths
of the maternal heart. I get stupid, and flat and flattering – what's the use
of telling you what good things you have written, or – I hope I may add –
that I know them to be good. Apropos – when I first opened upon the
just mentioned poem, in a careless tone I said to Mary as if putting a
riddle 'What is good for a bootless bean?' to which with infinite presence
of mind (as the jest book has it) she answered, a 'shoeless pea.' It was the
first joke she ever made. Joke the 2d I make – you distinguish well in
your old preface between the verses of Dr. Johnson of the man in the
Strand, and that from the babes of the wood. I was thinking whether
taking your own glorious lines –

> And for the love was in her soul
> For the youthful Romilly –

which, by the love I bear my own soul, I think have no parallel in any of
the best old Balads, and just altering it to –

> And from the great respect she felt
> For Sir Samuel Romilly –[8]

would not have explained the boundaries of prose expression and poetic
feeling nearly as well. Excuse my levity on such an occasion. I never felt
deeply in my life, if that poem did not make me, both lately and when I
read it in MS. No alderman ever longed after a haunch of buck venison
more than I for a Spiritual taste of that White Doe you promise. I am
sure it is superlative, or will be when *drest*, i.e. printed. All things read
raw to me in MS. – to compare magna parvis[9], I cannot endure my own
writings in that state. The only one which I think would not very much

win upon me in print is Peter Bell. But I am not certain. You ask me about your preface. I like both that and the Supplement without an exception. The account of what you mean by Imagination is very valuable to me. It will help me to like some things in poetry better, which is a little humiliating in me to confess. I thought I could not be instructed in that science (I mean the critical), as I once heard old obscene beastly Peter Pindar in a dispute on Milton say he thought that if he had reason to value himself upon one thing more than another it was in knowing what good verse was. Who lookd over your proof sheets, and left *ordebo*[10] in that line of Virgil?

(*Ibid.*, II, 157–9)

EDITOR'S NOTES

1. Lamb seems unaware that 'A Character in the Antithetical Manner' had also been omitted from the editions of *Lyrical Ballads* of 1802 and 1805, and that the last stanza, the 'moral', of 'Rural Architecture' had been cut out of the 1805 edition: this stanza was restored in 1820, as was l. 27 of 'Lines Left upon a Seat in a Yew-tree': 'The stone-chat, or the glancing sand-piper'. The poem, 'A Character', was not reprinted until the edition of 1837.
2. A reference to the Preface to the 1815 volumes, where Wordsworth quotes and acknowledges Lamb's comments on the Imagination: see Lamb's essay, 'On the Genius and Character of Hogarth', *The Reflector* 3, 1811.
3. 'The sky is overcast', first published in 1815, though composed seventeen years before at Alfoxden. Wordsworth also drew Crabb Robinson's attention to this poem: see entry 246d, 9 May 1815.
4. 'The Country in the City' (Martial, XII, 57. 21).
5. Line 7 of 'The Reverie of Poor Susan': it should read 'Bright volumes of vapour'.
6. Wordsworth must have indicated that it was Lamb himself who was responsible for the omission (in 1805) of the last verse of 'Rural Architecture'. Lamb seems to have forgotten this early critical remark and, of course, to have been unaware that the verse had been omitted in 1805. It is interesting that Wordsworth took sufficient notice of Lamb's now positive comments to restore the verse in 1820.
7. See 'The Force of Prayer'.
8. Romilly (1757–1818), the great legal reformer.
9. 'Great to small'.
10. Lamb is pointing out that Wordsworth has allowed a misprint in his quotation from Virgil's *Eclogues*, I, 75–6: the word 'ordebo' should be 'videbo' meaning, in the context, 'shall I see'.

246. Henry Crabb Robinson
From his diary, April–June 1815

a. 16 April 1815

... In the evening in my chambers enjoyed the looking over Wordsworth's new edition of his poems. The supplement to his preface I wish he had left unwritten, for it will afford a triumph to his enemies. He betrays resentment and that he has suffered pain. His reproaches of the bad taste of the times will be ascribed to merely personal feelings, and to disappointment. But his manly avowal of his sense of his own poetic merits, I by no means censure. His preface contains subtle remarks on poetry, but they are not clear or intelligible. And I wish he would incorporate all his critical ideas into a work of taste in either the dialogue or novel form. Otherwise his valuable suggestions are in danger of being lost. His classification of his poems displeases me from an obvious fault, that it is partly subjective and partly objective. The new poems appear to be not numerous and chiefly sonnets ...

(*Henry Crabb Robinson on Books and their Writers*, ed. Edith J. Morley, 1938, I, 165)

b. 23 April 1815

... [With the Roughs.] Read Wordsworth and collated some of the old poems in the former and new edition. We were, in general, satisfied with the alterations ...

(*Ibid.*)

c. 7 May 1815

... I read some of Wordsworth's poems, particularly the extracts from his first published works, which are in so different a style from his subsequent works as not to be recognised as his; and I could not relish them though they appear to be full of those elaborately fine descriptions which have given reputation to other and inferior poets ....

On coming home I found a card from Wordsworth, and running to Lamb I found him and Mrs. Wordsworth there. After sitting half an hour with them I walked with them to their lodgings near Cavendish Square.

Mrs. Wordsworth appears to be a mild and amiable woman, not so lively or animated as Miss Wordsworth, but like her, devoted to the poet. We chatted, of course, about the new edition, etc. of which hereafter.

(*Ibid.*, 165–6)

d. 9 May 1815

. . . I took tea with the Lambs. Mr. and Mrs. Wordsworth were there. We had a long chat. I regret that I can relate but little. Wordsworth ⟨is, as he was before, most acutely sensible to a censure, however slight. I told him I did not like his supplementary preface against the reviewers because it betrayed anger. He denied that there is any expression of anger in the preface, though he has nothing but contempt, etc.

Wordsworth is by no means satisfied with Hunt's judgment of him, yet on the⟩[1] representation by Brougham that Hunt had been pleased with his poems he sent him a copy of them.

Wordsworth, in answer to the common reproach that his sensibility is excited by objects which produce no effect on others, admits the fact and is proud of it. He says that he cannot be accused of being insensible to the real concerns of life. He does not waste his feelings on unworthy objects. For he is alive to the actual interests of society. I think the justification complete. If Wordsworth expected immediate popularity, he would betray an ignorance of public taste reproachful to a man of observation.

Wordsworth spoke of the changes in his new poems. He has substituted 'ebullient' for 'fiery', speaking of the nightingale, and 'jocund' for 'laughing' applied to the daffodils; but he will probably restore the original epithets.[2] We agreed in preferring the original reading. But on my gently alluding to the lines: 'Three feet long and two feet wide', and confessing that I dared not read them out in company, he said 'they ought to be liked.'[3]

Hazlitt said in his ferocious way at Alsager's that 'if Lamb in his criticism had found but one fault with Wordsworth he would never have forgiven him.' And some truth there is in the extravagant statement.

Wordsworth particularly recommended to me among his Poems of Imagination *Yew Trees* and a description of Night.[4] These, he says, are among the best for the imaginative power displayed in them. I have since read them. They are fine, but I believe I do not understand in what their excellence consists. Wordsworth himself, as Hazlitt has well observed, has a pride in deriving no aid from his subject. It is the mere power which he is conscious of exerting in which he delights, not the production of a work in which men rejoice on account of the sympathies and sensibilities it excites in them. Hence he does not much esteem his *Laodamia*, as it belongs to the inferior class of Poems Founded on the Affections. Yet in this, as in other peculiarities of Wordsworth, there is a *German* bent in his mind.

(*Ibid.*, 165–6)

e. 1 June 1815

... Long, Collier, Cargill, and myself disputed a little about Wordsworth's merits, Long being a little unpleasant to the rest of us from an apparent desire to depreciate Wordsworth. I was proud to have Wordsworth in my chambers, but my pride only was gratified, for I was vexed to a degree which exceeded my pleasure at my inability to ask others, especially Alsager, who was, I believe, somewhat offended at my in-attention ...

JUNE 4th ... Came home to read *The White Doe of Rylstone* by Wordsworth. This legendary tale will be less popular than Walter Scott's from the want of that vulgar intelligibility and that freshness and vivacity of description which please even those who are not of the vulgar. Still, the poem will be better liked than better pieces of Wordsworth's writing. There is a delicate sensibility, an exquisite moral running through the whole, but it is not the happiest of his narrative poems ...

(*Ibid.*, 168)

f. 6 June 1815

... W. Taylor enjoys nothing so much as an extravagant speculation – the odder the better. He spoke of Wordsworth: praised his conversation, which he likes better than his poetry. Says he is solid, dignified, simple, and eloquent. But he observed that Wordsworth seemed unwilling to render full justice to Southey. 'I told him,' said W. Taylor, 'I thought Southey the greatest poet and the greatest historian living, and he looked surprised.' 'No great matter of surprise,' I answered, 'that Wordsworth should think himself a greater poet than Southey.' 'I never thought,' replied Taylor, 'that he could presume to make any comparison' ...

(*Ibid.*, 168–9)

EDITOR'S NOTES

1. Passage in angle brackets in shorthand in the original.
2. Wordsworth did restore the original epithet in 'O Nightingale! thou surely art', but not in 'I wandered lonely as a cloud'.
3. 'The Thorn', l. 33. This anticipates Coleridge's more famous criticism of this line.
4. 'A Night-piece'.

247. Robert Southey

From a letter to J. Neville White (1775–1820), 8 May 1815

Wordsworth is in town. Have you seen the new edition of his poems? I do not hesitate to say that in the whole compass of poetry, ancient or modern, there is no collection of miscellaneous poems comparable to them, nor any work whatever which discovers greater strength of mind or higher poetical genius.

(*A Selection from the Letters of Robert Southey*, ed. J. W. Warter, London, 1856, II, 409)

248. William Lisle Bowles (1762–1850)

From his poem, 'The Two Sailors – written at Greenwich June 13th 1815'[1]

Wordsworth is identified as:

> He whose MUSE in Vision *high and holy*,
> Marks all things with a quiet melancholy –

(see Mark L. Reed, *Wordsworth: Chronology of the Middle Years, 1800–1815*, Harvard, 1975, 607.)

EDITOR'S NOTE

1. Revised and published as 'The Greenwich Pensioners'.

249. Thomas Wilkinson

From a letter to Wordsworth, 22 June 1815

Wilkinson thanks Wordsworth for the gift of his *Poems* (1815); interestingly, now aged 64, and with a taste formed in the eighteenth century, he picks out for admiration the extracts from Wordsworth's early (now revised) *Descriptive Sketches . . . in the Alps*. The admirer of *The Excursion* from York was Marianne Fothergill (1786–), who wrote to Wilkinson 12 June 1815 (see Wilkinson MSS, Friends House, Euston Road, London); she had told Wilkinson on 29 March of her reluctance to read the poem after reading Jeffrey's review (see entry 148); she further had reported that the poem had been voted in, then out, then in again by her book subscription library, its members clearly affected by the warring reviewers. The 'lovely Campbells' to whom Wilkinson showed Wordsworth's 'Seven Sisters' were probably the daughters of the Rev. David Campbell, Minister at Southend, Argyllshire.

Poetry has been an object of my affection from my earliest years. I remember with what avidity I copied the first verses I saw, which as far as I can now recollect were those of Bunyan and Quarles. Beginning with and deriving Pleasure from such Authors, thou wilt readily conceive the Increse of such Pleasures when I became acquainted with a Milton and a Cowper, a Collins and a Goldsmith, the two last of which to me possess a *Charm* in their Writings which like other charms is difficult to define, but which unquestionably confirms them to be Poets: that charm I also feel the force of in many parts of the two elegant Volumes thy kindness has transmitted to me, which after perusing and re-perusing I shall set up as a Monument in my little Library of thy Friendship. I never knew any Volumes that one would like so well to take with one into the Fields, and there sit down under a Tree to read: this I have done and shall continue to do, possessing at this Time, for which I am obliged to thee, a portion I trust, of the spirit with which they were written. The subjects are numerous and well adapted to the rural Reading I have hinted at, and when so reading it will heighten the Enjoyment to suppose they were several of them wrote in such circumstances. Thy Journey among the Alps is new to me, the Pictures there are vivid, as the Time of Life in which they were drawn; I hope thou hast not omitted many of them, I wish thou hadst given us them all: still more I wish thou hadst finished the Fragment of the 'Danish Boy', thou hast interested us in no common degree, and it is with one does not know what. I have not yet got hold of the Excursion, therefore it is yet one of those objects to which we look forward with the hope of pleasurable Feelings, nay indeed more, for the Introduction of *Virtuous* Feeling is a predominant Merit in thy Pages. A Friend of mine some time ago wrote me from York that she had got the Excursion ordered for their Library and her name down for the Perusal. She now writes me 'I have finished the Excursion, and have derived more pleasure from the Perusal than I had anticipated. The Author is a *virtuous Poet*, a man of quick Discernment and exquisite feeling, a lover of God, and of Nature, possessing an Imagination of the *first order*. The Excursion will not meet with praise from the Multitude, but will delight the solitary and reflective. Many of his Descriptions of Nature are sublime and beautiful, his knowledge of the human Heart profound, his delineations of it masterly, impressive, and affecting. His Muse seems sometimes to vanish amidst Clouds and Darkness but soon again emerges in brightness – This Work will afford *thee* very great Pleasure.' Since I began writing I have been visited by three lovely Campbells from Argyleshire. I was acquainted with some of them 27 years ago, and have seen none of them; the survival of such old friendships was mutually pleasing – I showed them thy 'own lovely Campbells' and they were interested.

(Ms. The Wordsworth Library)

250. Walter Savage Landor (1775–1864)

From letters, 1815–1822

Landor was first Southey's friend and, then, through Southey from about 1814 to 1834 a friend of Wordsworth's. Thereafter, perhaps believing that Wordsworth had spoken ill of Southey, he became critical and in 1842 published a second imaginary conversation in which he attacked Wordsworth (see *Blackwood's Magazine*, December 1842, LII, 687–715). It was then that Wordsworth described Landor as 'a man so deplorably tormented by ungovernable passion. . . . His character may be given in three words; a mad-man, a bad-man, yet a man of genius, as many a mad-man is' (April 1843, *LY*, IV, 438). Though Landor kept his reservations about Wordsworth's poetry, when his friend and biographer John Forster showed him 'a noble passage from Wordsworth's Prelude', Landor exclaimed: 'O si sic omnia scripsisset! [O that everything were written in this way] Higher it would be difficult to go. Here the wagoner's frock shows the coat of mail under it. Here is heart and soul' (*Landor: A Biography*, John Forster, II, 423).

---

a. To Miss Margaret Holford (d. 1852), the date probably 1815

This letter is in response to a published defence of Wordsworth's poems sent to him by Miss Holford.

I am not surprised that the criticism stands higher in your estimation than in mine. It is evidently the composition of a zealous and indignant friend. The poems, in my opinion, are far above the necessity of any such defence. The attack was not only weak but wicked. *Weak*, because a man of genius must know, and, minds alone can be ignorant, what breadth of philosophy, what energy and intensity of thought, what insight into the heart, and what observation of nature, are requisite for the production of such poetry. *Wicked*, to behold such signal gifts not merely with disrespect, but with irreverence and malice.

(*Walter Savage Landor: A Biography*, John Forster, 1869, I, 319)

b. To Southey, December 1817

The first of your magnificent books that I took out of the box was Wordsworth. I would have given eighty pounds out of a hundred that he had not written that verse,

> Of high respect and gratitude sincere.
> > [l. 8 of the Dedication of the *Excursion* to the
> > Earl of Lonsdale]

It is like the verses of the Italians, Spanish, &c. quite colloquial; and '*high* respect,' an expression borrowed from the French, is without intrinsic sense. Wordsworth has the merit, the rarest of all merits and the most difficult to be certain of, to avoid street-and-house language and to be richly endowed with whatever is most simple, pure and natural. In his Lyrical Ballads he has sometimes disappointed me, just as an Æolian harp has done when I expected a note more. These books have wakened me up. I shall feed upon them till I fall asleep again, but that will not be until I have devoured all.

(*Ibid.*, I, 438)

c. To Southey, late 1818

It is very very long indeed since I heard from you. I forget whether in my last letter or the preceding I mentioned that I had received the books. I am reading over and over again the stupendous poetry of Wordsworth. In thoughts, feeling, and images not one amongst the ancient equals him, and his language (a rare thing) is English. Nations are never proud of living genius. Surely no country under heaven has produced in twenty years so much excellent poetry and such a rich latter-math of what approaches to good as our own in the last twenty.

(*Ibid.*, I, 446)

d. To Southey, 30 January 1820

It appears to me an age since I heard from you, nor have I yet received the new poem of Wordsworth. A poem given by him, as I have just been telling my friend Walter Birch, is like a kingdom given by Alexander of Cyrus.

(*Ibid.*, I, 456)

e. To Wordsworth, 23 September 1820

Sir,

Whether the distinction you have conferred on me in the present of your poems, ought to subject you to the taxation of a letter from Italy, and to the heavier one of time, seized & driven away from your studies, has exercised my casuistry two entire days. To have thanked you however, through Mr Southey would not satisfy my sense of duty. You know, or you could not have sent me this volume [*The River Duddon*, 1820], the impression it has made upon my mind. The only thing I can add, uncertain to you, is that I perceive in some pieces a slight shade of variation in manner from your former works. Nothing in Pindar is more like anything else in Pindar than the Ode composed at Cora Linn. Of all compositions in modern language the higher ode is most difficult. Perhaps our own is the only one in which it can exist, the only one that has enough of sweetness flexibility & force, and above all, that does not remind us of something better in its own family.

(Ms. The Wordsworth Library)

f. To Southey, November 1820

I received the books about six weeks ago, if my recollection is right, and wrote immediately to Wordsworth a letter of thanks, waiting to hear from you whether I might send the heavy folios. They shall be dispatched by the first English ship from Leghorn . . . in whatever Wordsworth writes there is admirable poetry; but I wish he had omitted all that precedes 'There was a time' (p. 9) in Peter Bell. The first poet that ever wrote was not a more original poet than he is, and the best is hardly a greater.

(*Walter Savage Landor: A Biography*, John Foster, I, 468)

g. To Wordsworth, 22 February 1822

I have been employed for about a month in composing some *Imaginary Conversations of Literary Men & Statesmen* and about as long in transcribing them. I am wanting for some opportunity of Sending them to be printed. I have inscribed them to you, in a few lines[1] . . . Say something of the Recluse. I have read the Excursion through, four times, & several parts four times four.

(Ms. The Wordsworth Library)

h. To Wordsworth, 8 September 1822

. . . may I venture to confess that I came to the reading of your poems with strong prejudice against them; acquired from the very men who are now my converts – and that, until I had seen Southey at Bristol [April 1808] . . . I had read nothing more of them than what I casually met with in throwing a glance on some Review. I loved them afterwards the more warmly for my past injustice and the more attentively I examined them, the more convinced was I that my enthusiasm was rightly placed.

(Ms. The Wordsworth Library)

EDITOR'S NOTE

1. *Imaginary Conversations*, published from 1824, but not dedicated to Wordsworth.

251. Mary Barker (1774–1850)

From a satire, *Lines Addressed to a Noble Lord*, by 'one of the Small Fry of the Lakes', 1815

Mary Barker (later Mrs Slade Smith) came to live near her admired Southey at the lodge of Greta Hall, Keswick. Her verses appear to have been revised by Wordsworth himself, perhaps on three occasions (see Mark L. Reed, *Wordsworth: Chronology of the Middle Years, 1800–1815*, Harvard, 1975, 557–601 *passim*.). Wordsworth must have seen Byron's comment on him in a letter to Hogg (see entry 121d) Despite the help Miss Barker received, it is difficult not to agree with Crabb Robinson, who said, when he received a copy of the privately printed poem, 'Not a good satire, and far below the Rejected Addresses.' (*Henry Crabb Robinson on Books and their Writers*, ed. Edith J. Morley, 1938, I, 167). The objects of attack are both Byron and Jeffrey. Wordsworth told Sara Hutchinson: 'Miss B. is a cunning jade as to her verses' but goes on to suggest that he has been considerably involved with the text and then begs Sara to keep this fact secret (*MY*, II, 175–6). Wordsworth's letter makes it clear that Miss Barker's attitude to Byron is ambiguous: 'the fair Authoress would be very happy to see his crackbrained, skull-bearing Lordship at Greta Hall [none] the less.' Indeed, the lines below are scarcely satirical, being a defence of Wordsworth and his fellow poets choosing to live and work in retirement in a sanative and pastoral world. Mary Barker's Ms., in the Wordsworth Library, is discussed by Jonathan Wordsworth in *Mary Barker and William Wordsworth: Lines Addressed to a Noble Lord, 1815*, Woodstock Books, 2001.

VIII.

Come then – discontented creature!
Come, and glory in thy nature!
See the joys of innocence,
See the Wise Man's recompence!
Every echo of our mountains,
Every streamlet of our fountains,
Tribute pays, and witnesses
To our Poets' happiness.
Blest and blessing here live they
For this frail life's transient day,
Fix'd yet soaring, bound yet free,
For Time and for Eternity.

IX.

Sweeter strains were never sung
Greenwood bowers or shades among,
Never heard the listening Earth,
From the moment of her birth,
Nobler-sounding minstrelsy,
Than, in holy extacy
Here enwrapt, our Poets chaunt
Beneath this gorgeous firmament:
Gentle hearts their persons loving,
Lofty minds their works approving.

X.

Not to glitter and decay,
Not to live a Summer's day;
Not for praise, nor in despite
Do our Poets think and write.
Nature formed them, bounteously
Sons of Immortality;
Great, above thy mind's conceiving:
Good, beyond thy heart's believing.
Sacred union! which defies
Envious tongues and evil eyes;
All little critics of the day;
All cares what foes, or friends may say;
Higher aspirations theirs!
Nobler hopes and worthier cares.

252. Mary Bryan (*fl.* 1815)

A Dedication to Wordsworth, 1815

Mary Bryan, brought up in North Curry, near Taunton, Somerset, was, by
1815, the widow of Edward Bryan, a Bristol printer and bookseller. She
published her *Sonnets and Metrical Tales*, Bristol, to help support her six
children (see J. R. de Jackson, *Romantic Poetry by Women: A Bibliography,
1770–1835*, Oxford, 1993, 43 and Jonathan Wordsworth's reprint of
Sonnets and Metrical Tales in Woodstock Books, 1996). Bryan clearly

continued her husband's press as 'Mary Bryan and Co. City Printing-office, 52 Corn Street' (living at 9 Clarence Place) until 1823; and, per-haps, as 'Bryan and Co' until 1825. For a sympathetic account of her poetry, suggesting her appropriate use of Wordsworth's Matthew and Lucy poems, see Stuart Curran, 'Isabella Lickbarrow and Mary Bryan: Wordsworthian Poets', *The Wordsworth Circle*, XXVII, 1996, 113–118.

Bryan presumably sent Wordsworth the volume in 1815 (her Preface is dated 1 August 1815); it was sold from Wordsworth's library in 1859 (see Rydal Mount Sale Catalogue, item 600). Unintentionally, the events sur-rounding her publication had a greater impact. There can be little doubt that Mary Bryan is the unidentified poetess to whom Wordsworth wrote so candidly about Byron's 'perverted' taste. Three separate accounts exist of Wordsworth's anecdote – the first by Crabb Robinson, 17 June 1833; the second by Thomas Moore, 20 February 1835; and the clearest, from Alexander Dyce. Moore's account and Crabb Robinson's hint that Rogers himself was suspected to be the 'good-natured friend' who so poisonously repeated Wordsworth's private opinion. Some such incident between June and October 1815 would account for Byron's dramatic change to hostility and anger towards Wordsworth (see entry 257). Wordsworth's conversation with the Rev. Alexander Dyce (1798–1869) is undated, but Dyce emphasises that Wordsworth's account I noted down at the time'.

Lord Byron's hatred towards me originated thus. There was a woman in distressed circumstances at Bristol, who wrote a volume of poems, which she wished to publish and dedicate to me. She had formed an idea that, if she became a poetess, her fortune would be made. I endeavoured to dissuade her from indulging such vain expectations, and advised her to turn attention to something else. I represented to her how little chance there was that her poems, though really envincing a good deal of talent, would make any impression on the public, and I observed that, in our day, two persons only (whom I did not name) had succeeded in making money by their poetry, adding that in the writings of the one (Sir Walter Scott) there was little poetic feeling, and that in those of the other (Lord Byron) it was perverted. Mr Rogers told me that when he was travelling with Lord Byron in Italy, his lordship confessed that the hatred he bore me arose from a remark about his poetry which I had made to that woman, and which some good-natured friend had repeated to him.

(*Recollections of the Table-Talk of Samuel Rogers*, ed. Alexander Dyce, 1887, 237–8; for Crabb Robinson's account see *Crabb Robinson on Books and Their Writers*, ed. Edith J. Morley, 1938, I, 428–9; and for Thomas Moore's account, see *The Journal of Thomas Moore*, ed. Wilfrid S. Dowden, 1987, IV, 1660–1.)

TO W.W————————H, ESQ.

THOU! who dost well reprove the sordid fear,
    That spoils the springs of bliss – wasting life's powers,
O wilt thou *mourn* th' ungenial influence here,
    One moment pausing o'er these wither'd flowers?

Like thee thro' many a darling haunt I stray'd;
    And if to thee sublimer views were given,
Dear were the scenes my *ling'ring* steps delay'd –
    As dear the silent grove – the starry Heav'n.

Far in the shelter'd vale, I never knew
    To mark great nature in her wonders drest;
Around her child her tend'rest charms she threw,
    And smiling, hid me in her tranquil breast.

No sordid wishes drew me from her bowers –
    Not such the passion that these strains reveal;
No sordid cares consume my wasting powers –
    My infant spoilers wear the bloom they steal.

– O, happiest of Poets, as of men,
    Who dost delight to shew with feelings true,
The maiden, dearest in her native glen,
    Spontaneous graces blending with her view –

Hast thou ne'er watch'd her cheek's decaying bloom?
    Hide – hide it ever from thy cheerful ken –
The faded mourner should not ask a tomb,
    To chill thy breast – O, happiest of men!

Poet of Nature's – Reason's – Beauty's light –
    Who nobly scorn'd the Muse by custom drest:
If too long dazzled, the bewilder'd sight
    Mark not her glories in her simpler vest;

The futile glare at length will cease to charm,
    At length awakening truth delight to find
A Muse with genuine hopes, and passions warm;
    Too wise for form – 'Too pure to be refin'd.'*

---

*   *Too pure to be refin'd.*
See Wordsworth's Address to the Spade of his Friend.

A short time since appeared in a daily Journal a criticism on 'The Excursion,' beginning
thus: – 'Now that Mr. W. no longer the companion of a Leech-gatherer, and the panegyrist

253. John Gibson Lockhart (1794–1854)
Extracts from letters and essays, 1815–1821

Lockhart was the son-in-law of Sir Walter Scott, and his biographer; editor of the *Quarterly Review* from 1825. Lockhart's youthful interest in Wordsworth (see (a) and (b) below) led to friendly declarations about Wordsworth's poetry in his anonymous *Peter's Letters to his Kinsfolk* (1819), a work that seconded the essay in *Blackwood's* on *The White Doe* (this essay is almost certainly by Lockhart. See (f)). Of *Peter's Letters*, late in 1819 Sara Hutchinson, not altogether delighted (or undelighted), wrote: 'it is praise & censure so extravagant that you see in a moment that they have no principle at all – William cuts a great figure in the book' (*Letters of Sara Hutchinson*, ed. K. Coburn, 1954, 166). For the epigraph to his novel, *Matthew Wald* (1824), Lockhart chose the opening quatrain of Wordsworth's 'The Fountain'. Indeed, the theme of that poem – old Matthew's gaiety having an undercurrent of secret melancholy – is crudely and explicitly exploited at the close of the novel: the Wordsworthian notion is gothicised. Yet, Lockhart was irritated when, at a meeting between Wordsworth and Walter Scott in August 1825, he realised that Wordsworth did not recognise in his father-in-law a poet of equal stature; and his later scepticism about Wordsworth's writing seems to be part of a deeper scepticism about poetry itself.

---

of a Spade, directs his talents to their proper objects, &c.' Impressed with the highest opinion of the merits of this performance, it surpasses belief that this Poet can now have excelled some of his former writings. I have not yet read the Poem, but supposing a change in his opinions to have taken place, never can he, with all his present powers, impair the strength or beauty of that everlasting monument of argumentative truth – his Preface to his Lyrical Pieces.

Probably this critic had merely heard that the 'Leechgatherer' and the 'Spade,' &c. had been the subjects of this Poet's muse, and content with estimating great and little by that scale, which wealth and pride have long preponderated, had never read these pieces; if he had actually perused them, pitiable are the defects of such a perception. There are, that are 'deaf to the voice of the charmer, charm he never so wisely' – but I have heard that these Poems are generally and duly esteemed. – In the regular reviews of some years past, I am wholly unread, simply, because the numerous productions of uncommon interest of this period, pouring their treasures at once upon my amazed and delighted mind, have almost engrossed it.

a. From a letter to J. H. Christie (died 1876), 3 January 1815

I am grieved that W.[1] takes offence at my tolerance for some of the Wordsworth school: I am not sure that I would say so much as I have said after reading the 'Excursion,' at least the Jeffreys (*sic*) give one a bad scent of it. But from their having omitted to quote any of several divine passages which I have read I doubt not they are unfair.

(*Life of Lockhart*, Andrew Lang, 1897, I, 81)

b. From a letter to Christie, 3 January 1816

Lockhart by 1818 had revised his opinion of the *White Doe*.

By way of qualifying myself for forming a sane judgment on a subject more than once discussed between us, I have lately read over *all* Wordsworth – prose and verse. The 'Doe' is certainly wretched, but not quite so bad as 'The Force of Prayer.' The 'Excursion' I enjoyed deeply – particularly the character of the Solitary, and the description of the Churchyard and its inhabitants. One of these sketches pleased me more than anything of this day's poetry I have ever read, unless it be O'Connor's Child and Michael; it was that of the young man 'all hopes Cherished for him who suffered to depart – Like blighted buds; or clouds that mimicked land – Before the sailor's eye; or Diamond drops – That sparkling decked the morning grass, or aught – That *was* attractive, and had ceased to be.[2] The whole picture is exquisite. The *Examiner* has well characterised Wordsworth as a poet – who, had he written but half of what he has, would have deserved to be immortal. He certainly has more prosing and less variety than I thought it possible for a man of genius and learning, such as his.

(*Ibid.*, I, 102–3)

c. Unsigned essay. 'Essays on the Lake School of Poetry. No. 1 Wordsworth's *White Doe of Rylstone.' Blackwood's Edinburgh Magazine*, July 1818, III, 369–81

Though A. L. Strout (*A Bibliography of Articles in Blackwood's Magazine, 1817–25*, Lubbock, Texas, 1959) assigns this essay to Wilson, Lockhart is the probable author. The opening sentence repeats the notion in Lockhart's essay of the previous month (*Blackwood's*, June 1818, III, 297), that the 'present age of English poetry . . . boasts three great masters . . .'. In that June essay Wordsworth receives unequivocal praise:

Wordsworth is a poet of profounder sentiment; his delight has been in solitude, and he has therefore spoken less to the ordinary passions of active men.
His familiarity has, indeed, been

> Not with the mean and vulgar works of man,
> But with high objects, with enduring things,
> With life and nature.
>
> [*Prelude* (1805), I, ll. 435–7, first published in *The Friend*, 19,
> 28 December 1809]

Yet the majesty of this country, the sacred and secure repose of her freedom,
have not been witnessed without filial awe and admiration by this serene and
solitary bard. The vulgar declamations of demagogues, the hypocritical
dogmas of self-constituted judges, have never deceived the stately intellect
that holds its converse with the

> Wisdom and spirit of the universe,
> The soul that is the eternity of thought.
> [*Ibid.*, 428–9]

His patriotism has been like his poetry, affectionate, tender, and beautiful, but
at the same time strong, rational, and sublime.

Again, the reference to Raphael in the July essay reminds us that Lockhart was to
write fervently 'On the Great MADONNA of Dresden' in *Blackwood's*, for the
following month, August 1818.

THE three great master-spirits of our day, in the poetical world, are Scott,
Wordsworth, and Byron. But there never were minds more unlike to
each other than theirs are, either in original conformation or in the
course of life. It is great and enduring glory to this age, to have produced
three Poets, – of perfectly original genius, – unallied to each other, –
drinking inspiration from fountains far apart, – who have built up superb
structures of the imagination, of distinct orders of architecture, – and
who may indeed be said to rule, each by a legitimate sovereignty, over
separate and powerful provinces in the kingdom of Mind. If we except
the Elizabethan age, in which the poetical genius of the country was
turned passionately to the drama, and which produced an unequalled
constellation of great spirits, we believe that no other period of English
literature could exhibit three such Poets as these, standing in conspicuous
elevation among a crowd of less potent, but enlightened and congenial
Worthies.

If Byron be altogether unlike Scott, Wordsworth is yet more unlike
Byron. With all the great and essential faculties of the Poet, he possesses
the calm and self-commanding powers of the Philosopher. He looks over

human life with a steady and serene eye; he listens with a fine ear 'to the still sad music of humanity.' His faith is unshaken in the prevalence of virtue over vice, and of happiness over misery; and in the existence of a heavenly law operating on earth, and, in spite of transitory defeats, always visibly triumphant in the grand field of human warfare. Hence he looks over the world of life, and man, with a sublime benignity; and hence, delighting in all the gracious dispensations of God, his great mind can wholly deliver itself up to the love of a flower budding in the field, or of a child asleep in its cradle; nor, in doing so, feels that Poetry can be said to stoop or to descend, much less to be degraded, when she embodies, in words of music, the purest and most delightful fancies and affections of the human heart. This love of the nature to which he belongs, and which is in him the fruit of wisdom and experience, gives to all his Poetry a very peculiar, a very endearing, and, at the same time, a very lofty character. His Poetry is little coloured by the artificial distinctions of society. In his delineations of passion or character, he is not so much guided by the varieties produced by customs, institutions, professions, or modes of life, as by those great elementary laws of our nature which are unchangeable and the same; and therefore the pathos and the truth of his most felicitous Poetry are more profound than of any other, not unlike the most touching and beautiful passages in the Sacred Page. The same spirit of love, and benignity, and etherial purity, which breathes over all his pictures of the virtues and the happiness of man, pervades those too of external nature.

We shall now direct the attention of our readers to the 'White Doe of Rylstone,' a poem which exhibits in perfection many of Wordsworth's peculiar beauties, and, it may be, some of his peculiar defects. It is in itself a whole; and on that account we prefer beginning with it, in place of the 'Lyrical Ballads,' or the subsequent 'Poems' of the author, which contain specimens of so many different styles; and still more, in place of the 'Excursion,' which, though a great work in itself, is but a portion of a still greater one, and will afford subject matter for more than one long article.

This Poem is prefaced by some stanzas addressed to the wife of the Poet, in which a touching allusion is made to severe domestic afflictions, (the death, we believe, of two children 'whom all that looked on loved,') that direfully interrupted, for a while, the flow of imagination in his soul, but the softened memory of which blended at last, not undelightfully, with the mournful and tragic character of this 'tale of tears.' No verses in the language are more simply yet profoundly affecting; and we are sure that they will dispose every feeling mind to come to the perusal of the Poem itself with the most kindly and sympathetic emotions.

[Quotes the whole of the dedication to the *White Doe*, 64 lines, *PW*, III, pp. 281–3.]

The Poem is founded on a wild and beautiful tradition, that in former times a White Doe, coming over the hills from what once were the demesnes of Rylstone Hall, in Yorkshire, visited, every Sabbath morning, during the time of divine service, the burial-ground and the ruined part of Bolton Abbey. The Poet undertakes to give a poetical character to this solitary and mysterious creature, and to connect with its Sabbath visit to the holy place a tale of human passions.

The first canto begins with an animated and picturesque description of the assemblage of people to divine service in a rural chapel built within the heart of the solemn ruins,

> When faith and hope were in their prime,
> In great Eliza's golden time.

[There follows a summary of the poem using copious and lengthy extracts.]

It will be soon seen, by those who have not read this Poem, that in it Mr. Wordsworth has aimed at awakening the feelings and affections through the medium of the imagination. There are many readers of Poetry who imperiously demand strong passion and violent excitement, and who can perceive little merit in any composition which does not administer to that kind of enjoyment. Such persons will probably consider this Poem feeble and uninteresting, as they will do numerous productions that have, nevertheless, established themselves in the literature of our country. But it is owing to a defect of imagination that the beauty, apparent and delightful to others, shines not upon them. All those magical touches, by which a true Poet awakens endless trains of thought in an imaginative mind, are not felt at all by persons of such character. It is wonderful what influence a delicate tune, or shade, or tone, may have over the poetical visions of a poetical reader. In poetry, as in painting, gentle lineaments, and sober colouring, and chastened composition, often affect and delight the mind of capable judges more than even the most empassioned efforts of the art. But, to the vulgar, – and even to minds of more power than delicacy or refinement, such delineations carry with them no charm – no authority. Many persons, in some things not only able but enlightened, would look with untouched souls on the pictures of Raphael, – and turn, undelighted, from the countenance and the eyes of beings more lovely than human life, – to the rapturous con-templation of mere earthly beauty. If we do not greatly err, the Poem we have now been analyzing possesses much of the former character, and will afford great delight on every perusal, – new and gentle beauties stealing and breathing from it like fragrance from perennial flowers.

Indeed, the tradition on which the Poem is founded must, to an unimaginative mind, appear childish and insignificant; but to purer spir-its, beautifully adapted to the purposes of Poetry. The creature, with whose image so many mournful and sublime associations are connected, is by nature one of the loveliest – wildest – of the lower orders of cre-ation. All our ordinary associations with it are poetical. It is not the first time that a great Poet has made this fair animal the friend of human innocence. During the happy days of the Lady Emily, we can figure to ourselves nothing more beautiful than her and her mute favourite gliding together through the woods and groves of Rylstone-hall; and when utter desolation comes over that Paradise, and the orphan is left alone on the hopeless earth, a more awful bond of connexion is then felt to subsist between the forlorn lady and the innocent companion of her days of blessedness. We willingly attribute something like human reason and human love to that fair creature of the woods, – and feel the deep pathos implied in such communion between a human soul in its sorrow with an inferior nature, that seems elevated by its being made the object of tender affection to a being above itself. A ring, a lock of hair, a picture, a written word of love, would be cherished with holy passion, by a solitary heart that mourned over their former possessor. To the Lady Emily nothing remained of all she had loved on earth, – nothing but the play-mate of herself and youthful brothers, – the object which the dead had loved in their happiness, – and which, with a holy instinct, forsook the wild life to which it had returned, when the melancholy face of its protector once more shone among the woods.

Of Emily herself little need be said. From the first moment she is felt to be orphaned, – all her former happiness is to us like a dream, – all that is real with her is sorrow. In one day she becomes utterly desolate. But there is no agony, no convulsion, no despair: profound sadness, settled grief, the everlasting calm of melancholy, and the perfect stillness of resignation. All her looks, words, movements, are gentle, feminine, subdued. Throughout all the Poem an image of an angelical being seems to have lived in the Poet's soul, – and without effort, he gives it to us in angelical beauty.

The character and situation of Francis, the eldest brother, are finely conceived, and coloured in the same calm and serene style of painting. He is felt to be a hero, though throughout branded with the name of coward. It required some courage in a Poet to describe a character so purely passive. There is, we think, a solemnity, and piety, and devotion, in the character that becomes truly awful, linked, as they are, throughout, with the last extremities of human suffering and calamity.

But we must conclude, – and we do so with perfect confidence, that many who never have read this Poem, and not a few who may have read extracts from it with foolish and unbecoming levity, will feel and acknowledge, from the specimens we have now given, that the 'White Doe of Rylstone' is a tale written with singularly beautiful simplicity of language, and with a power and pathos that have not been often excelled in English Poetry.

d. From *Blackwood's Magazine*, April 1819, Vol. V, 97, the opening of the fifth article 'On the Cockney School of Poetry'.

The two greatest egotists of the present day are *absque omni dubio*,[3] Mr Wordsworth, and Mr Leigh Hunt. It is strange that one of the best and wisest of poets and men, should in any respect bear resemblance to such a thing as the Examiner. But there are reasons for everything, and we shall try to account for the phenomenon.

Mr Wordsworth is a man of high original genius, whose reputation in the general ear lags far, very far behind its merits. The world knows little or nothing about Mr Wordsworth. What can fine ladies understand about Ruth? or fine gentlemen about Michael? Who, that wears black silk breeches or a crimson sattin petticoat, cares a farthing about the gray headed pedlar with his substantial coat of Galashiels cloth, or for Lucy Fell with her 'little gray cloak?' One might as well imagine a Geraldine sighing in solitude over a leading article of the sulky Scotsman, or feeding her midnight dreams with dim shadows of the Ettrick Shepherd and his top-boots.

> There are things that may not be,
> There is a rule in destiny.

Mr Wordsworth may perhaps look very long before he finds fit audience; when he does find them, there is no question they must be 'few.' His words are all of the φωναντα σμνετοισι[4] kind; and even Mr. Jeffrey, with all his cleverness, has, for these ten years, been railing at the contents of a book shut – to whose cipher he has no key.

It is no great wonder that a mind such as Mr Wordsworth's, finding that its productious were not tasted as they should be, should have gathered itself all into itself. His genius came down to us like a beautiful unknown bird of heaven, wheeling around us, and courting us in its innocence, with colours we had never seen before, and wild sweet melodies to which our ears were strangers. But we repelled our visitor, and he has taken him to the air above us, where he finds serene joy in the consciousness of his soaring,

> And singeth sweetly to the cloud he cleaves.

It is no wonder that he should have learned almost to forget the existence of those who rejected him; and that egotism is pardonable in him, which would infallibly expose any other man of his genius to the just derision even of his inferiors. The egotism or *nosism* of the other luminaries of the Lake School, is at times extravagant enough, and amusing enough withal, but these also are men of great genius, and though not in the same degree, they are sharers in the excuse which we have already made for Mr Wordsworth.

e. From *Peter's Letters*

i

The critics who ridicule Mr Wordsworth, for choosing the themes of his poetry among a set of objects new and uninteresting to their minds, would have seen, had they been sufficiently acute, or would have confessed, had they been sufficiently candid, that, had he so willed it, he might have been among the best and most powerful masters in other branches of his art, more adapted for the generality of mankind and for themselves. The martial music in the hall of Clifford was neglected by the Shepherd Lord for the same reasons which have rendered the poet that celebrates him such a poet as he is.

> Love had he seen in huts where poor men lie,
>> His daily teachers had been woods and rills;
> The silence that is in the starry sky,
>> The sleep that is among the lonely hills.
>> ['Song at the Feast of Brougham Castle', *PW*, II, p. 25,
>> ll. 161–4; *Poems 1807* p. 312, ll. 165–8.]

Before a man can understand and relish his poems, his mind must, in some measure, pass through the same sober discipline – a discipline that calms, but does not weaken the spirit – that blends together the understanding and the affections, and improves both by the mixture. The busy life of cities, the ordinary collisions of sarcasm and indifference, steel the mind against the emotions that are bred and nourished among those quiet vallies, so dear to the Shepherd Lord and his poet. What we cannot understand, it is a very common, and indeed a very natural thing, for us to undervalue; and it may be suspected, that some of the merriest witticisms which have been uttered against Mr Wordsworth, have had their origin in the pettishness and dissatisfaction of minds, unaccustomed and unwilling to make, either to others or to themselves, any confessions of incapacity.

(*Peter's Letters to his Kinsfolk*, 1819, I, 122–3)

ii.

The true characteristic of science consists in this, – that it is a thing which can be communicated to, and made use of by, all men who are endowed with an adequate share of mere intellect. The philosophy of moral feeling must always, on the other hand, approach nearer to the nature of poetry, whose influence varies according as it is perused by individuals of this or that character, or taste. The finest opening to any book of psycology and ethics in the world, is that of Wordsworth's Excursion. That great poet, who is undoubtedly the greatest master that has for a long time appeared in the walks of the highest philosophy in England, has better notions than any Scotch metaphysician is likely to have, of the true sources, as well as the true effects, of the knowledge of man.

[Quotes Preface to *Excursion*, PW, V, pp. 3–4, ll. 25–41:

. . . Urania, I shall need . . .
My Haunt, and the main region of my song.]

(*Ibid.*, p. 14, Book I, ll. 178–80)

iii.

Even the commanding, majestic intellect of Wordsworth has not been able to overcome the effect of the petty warfare kept up against it by a set of wits, one of whom only might have been expected to enter with some portion of intelligence into the spirit of so great and original a poet. To find fault with particular parts of Mr Wordsworth's poems, or with particular points in the Psycological system upon which the whole structure of his poetry is built, this might have been very well either for the

Reviewers, or the readers of the Review. But the actual truth of the case is something very different, indeed, from this. The reading public of Edinburgh do not criticise Mr Wordsworth; they think him below their criticism; they know nothing about what he has done, or what he is likely to do. They think him a mere old sequestered hermit, eaten up with vanity and affectation, who publishes every now and then some absurd poem about a Washing-Tub, or a Leech-Gatherer, or a Little Grey Cloak. They do not know even the names of some of the finest poems our age has produced. They never heard of Ruth, or Michael, or the Brothers, or Hart-Leap Well, or the Recollections of Infancy, or the Sonnets to Buonaparte. They do not know, that there is such a thing as a description of a Church-yard in the Excursion. Alas! how severely is their ignorance punished in itself. But after all, Mr Wordsworth can have no very great right to complain. The same people who despise, and are ignorant of him, despise also, and are ignorant of all the majestic poets the world has ever produced, with no exceptions beyond two or three great names, acquaintance with which has been forced upon them by circumstances entirely out of their controul. The fate of Homer, of Æschylus, of Dante – nay, of Milton – is his.

(*Ibid.*, II, 143–4)

f. From the anonymous pamphlet of April/May 1821, *John Bull's Letter to Lord Byron* (ed. A. L. Strout, 1947)

In my humble opinion, there is very little that will really stand the test of half a century, except the *Scotch* novels of Sir Walter Scott and *Don Juan*. *They* will do so because they are written with perfect facility and nature – because their materials are all drawn from nature – in other words, because they are neither made up of cant, like Wordsworth and Shelley . . .

Mr Wordsworth may write fifty years about his 'dales men'; if he paints them truly, it is very well; if untruly, it is no matter, but you know what neither Mr Wordsworth nor any Cumberland stamp-master ever can know. You know the society of England . . .

EDITOR'S NOTES

1. John Williams (1761–1818), Welsh, a Balliol friend.
2. *Excursion*, VI, 313–18.

3. 'Without any doubt'.
4. 'That speak to the wise' (Pindar, *Olympian*, 2, 85).

254. Mary Russell Mitford (1787–1855)

From letters, 1815–1819

Her slight and varying opinions are expressed forcibly. In 1817 Talfourd drew her towards Wordsworth's poetry; the authoress Barbara Hofland fed her with gossip, 1818–1819; in 1824 Haydon's distress led her to attack Wordsworth; in 1835 an apparent discourtesy to Talfourd provoked another outburst; in 1836 three meetings at dinner with Wordsworth delighted her; in 1842 Coleridge seemed the greater poet, and in 1845 Lamartine; in 1852 she prefered the earlier to the later Wordsworth.

a. To Sir William Elford (1749–1837), banker, politician and amateur artist

13 February 1815:

Are you, my dear friend, of the Wordsworth school? I think not; so I may venture to say that I do not much like that either. There is such a waste of talent – such imagination buried alive – in that vast wordy wilderness; such powers lavished upon a pedlar; such poetry thrown away on dull metaphysics – that antidote to poetry. Who is it says that 'when one man is talking to another who does not understand him, and when he that is talking does not understand himself, that is metaphysics?'*

(*Life of Mary Russell Mitford*, ed. A. G. L'Estrange, 1870, I, 303)

13 September 1817:

The exercise, which I do dearly love, is to be whirled along fast, fast, fast, by a blood horse in a gig; this, under a bright sun, with a brisk wind full in my face, is my highest notion of physical pleasure; even walking is not so exhilarating. Besides this experiment upon my bodily taste, I have been

---

* Miss Mitford was never able to trace this definition beyond Mrs. Charles Kemble, whose description of metaphysics was, 'When A talks to B and C, and B and C don't understand him, and A does not understand himself, that's metaphysics.'

making one of the same nature on my mind – trying to learn to admire Wordsworth's poetry. I do not mean by 'admire' merely to like and applaud those fine passages which all the world must like, but to admire *en masse* – all, every page, every line, every word, every comma; to admire nothing else, and to admire all day long. This is what Mr. Wordsworth expects of his admirers (I had almost said his worshippers); and, strange to say, a large proportion of the cleverest young men in London (your friend Mr. Haydon among the rest) do pay him this homage.

One of the circle, a Reading gentleman of the name of Talfourd – of whom, by the way, when he has completed his studies for the bar, the world will one day hear a good deal – talked to me about Mr. Wordsworth's genius till I began to be a little ashamed of not admiring him myself. Enthusiasm is very catching, especially when it is very eloquent. So I set about admiring. To be sure, there was the small difficulty of not understanding; but that, as Mr. Talfourd said, did not signify. So I admired. But, alas! my admiration was but a puny, flickering flame, that wanted constant relighting at Mr. Talfourd's enthusiasm, and constant fanning by Mr. Talfourd's eloquence. He went to town, and out it went for good. After all, I should never have done for a disciple of Mr. Wordsworth. I have too much self-will about me – too much spirit of opposition. By-the-by, I wonder how Mr. Haydon manages. Docility is not *his* characteristic. I suppose there is a little commerce of flattery, though Mr. Wordsworth not only exacts an entire relinquishment of all other tastes besides taste for his poetry, but if an unlucky votary chances to say, 'Of all your beautiful passages I most admire so and so,' he knocks him down by saying, 'Sir, I have a thousand passages more beautiful than that. Sir, you know nothing of the matter.' One's conscience may be pretty well absolved for not admiring this man: he admires himself enough for all the world put together.

The best estimate I ever met with of Wordsworth's powers is in Coleridge's very out-of-the-way, but very amusing 'Biographia Literaria.' It is in the highest degree flattering, but it admits that he may have faults; and Mr. Lamb, who knows them both well, says he is sure Mr. Wordsworth will never speak to Mr. Coleridge again.

(*Ibid.*, II, 10–11)

9 November 1818:
An account of the Wordsworths' domestic habits from a report by Mrs Hofland of a conversation with a friend who had visited the poet. Barbara Hofland was

the wife of T. C. Hofland, a landscape painter (he painted near Hallsteads on Ullswater, for the Marshalls, Wordsworth's friends).

'The Wordsworths never dine, you know; they hate such doings; when they are hungry they go to the cupboard and eat. And really,' observes Mrs. Hofland, 'it is much the best way. There is Mr. Wordsworth, who will live for a month on cold beef, and the next on cold bacon; and my husband will insist on a hot dinner every day. He never thinks how much trouble I have in ordering, nor what a plague my cook is!' So you see the Wordsworth regimen is likely to spread.

(*Ibid.*, II, 44)

29 June 1819:
Another account of an opinion of Mrs. Hofland's.

'Sir W. E.'s picture is a very beautiful natural scene, most beautifully and honestly painted – not slipped over like a whitewasher, as Mr. Turner does things, and as your favourite, Mr. Wordsworth, writes poems' (by-the-by, Mrs. Hofland is mistaken there – Wordsworth is the highest finisher of any poet going); 'but done as if the thing was worth doing – as I take it everything should be, if done at all.'

(*Ibid.*, II, 62–3)

255. Thomas Noon Talfourd (1795–1854)
From his writings, 1815–1835

Talfourd was a lawyer, writer of poems, poetic drama and criticism, and Lamb's first biographer.

a. From the Preface to *Ion*, Talfourd's poetic tragedy, first privately printed 1835

Here Talfourd recalls his introduction to Wordsworth's writings (before 1815).

. . . my taste and feeling, as applied to poetry, underwent an entire change,[1] consequent on my becoming acquainted with the poetry of Wordsworth. That power which, slighted and scoffed at as it was then, has since exerted a purifying influence on the literature of this country, such as no other individual power has ever wrought; which has not only given to the material universe 'a speech and a language' before unheard, but has opened new sources of enjoyment even in the works of the greatest poets of past days, and imparted a new sense by which we may relish them; – which, while on the one hand it has dissipated the sickly fascinations of gaudy phraseology, has, on the other, cast around the loveliest conditions a new and exquisite light, and traced out the links of good by which all human things are bound together, and clothed our earthly life in the solemnities which belong to its origin and its destiny – humbled the pride of my swelling conceits, and taught me to look on the mighty works of genius, not with the presumption of an imitator, but with the veneration of a child. For the early enjoyment of this great blessing, which the sneers of popular critics might otherwise have withheld from me for years, I am indebted to my friend Mr. Baron Field, a worthy and beloved associate of the most original poets and thinkers of our time, who overcame my reluctance to peruse what the 'Edinburgh Review' had so triumphantly derided. The love of contemplative poetry, thus inspired, led me, in such leisure as I could attain, rather to ponder over the resources of the profoundest emotions, or to regard them as associated with the majestic forms of the universe, than to follow them into their violent conflicts and mournful catastrophes . . .

b. Essay signed 'T. N. Talfourd, of the Middle Temple', 'An Attempt to Estimate the Poetical Talent of the Present Age, Including a Sketch of the History of Poetry, and Characters of Southey, Crabbe, Scott, Moore, Lord Byron, Campbell, Lamb, Coleridge, and Wordsworth', *The Pamphleteer*, V, 413–71, 1815

The section on Wordsworth (462–7) is a generalised expression of positive feeling for Wordsworth's poetry, rare indeed at that time, and it asserts his supremacy among contemporary writers. This essay of the youthful Talfourd was published by his friend, A. J. Valpy, editor of *The Pamphleteer*, and son of the Headmaster at Reading School where Talfourd had been head scholar.

To the consideration of Mr. WORDSWORTH's sublimities we come with trembling steps, and feel, as we approach, that we are entering upon holy ground. At first, indeed, he seems only to win and to allure us, to resign the most astonishing trophies of the poet, and humbly to indulge, among the beauties of creation, the sweetest and the lowliest of human affections. We soon, however, feel how faint an idea of his capacities we have entertained by classing him with the loveliest of descriptive poets, and how subservient the sweetest of his domestic pictures are to the grandeur of his lofty conceptions. That his writings abound with sketches of rural scenery, arises merely from his peculiar love of nature, and from his constant residence among the magnificent regions where his genius has been gradually unfolding.

Secluded from the anxieties and dissipations of the world, he has experienced all his seasons of elevated abstraction among the solitudes of the country; – there he has often soared into the heaven of heavens – and the very humblest of its charms – its lowliest and most retiring graces – have been linked in his associations to the loftiest sublimities of our nature. Whilst he seems to be walking, in vacancy of thought, through the favorite nooks of his little grove, or dreaming over some narrow rivulet, he is rapt in celestial thoughts, and drinking of that deep bliss which assures and anticipates the joys of a brighter existence. He loves the bushes, and blades of grass, the humble daisies, and small celandines, because they have all given the first spring to a train of holy contemplation reaching far – far beyond 'the visible diurnal sphere.' The kindly influence he ascribes to beautiful scenery, is first imparted to it by the wonder-working magic of his fancy, and then reflected in his poems. Thus all the prospects which he delineates are enchanted with a spell more potent than faery lore, or the marvels of old romance, – they are filled with innumerable loves and graces, which we recognize as contributing to form all that is noble or divine in man – abound with gleams of half-extinguished thought, and recollections of almost-forgotten bliss – and open between some aged thorns or forky eminences of the landscape, glimpses which fill us, even to overflowing, with serenity and rapture and peace. The sweet mellowness of his portraits and the exquisite delicacy of his coloring form only the fore-ground of his pictures – the vestibule of his solemn temples – the flowers that cling round the portals of an unbounded Eden. We linger among them with fond delight, till amidst the stirring leaves or gentle blossoms a vista opens to our view, which displays the finest qualities and the richest destiny of our species, and fills us with a confusion of mysterious joy which it were vain to analyse or describe. He rises from the lowliest vale into the purest and most exalted regions of poetical spirits, with a majesty so easy that he is nearly beyond our gaze, before we perceive whither our aching eyes are pursuing him. He has enlarged the resources of the mind, and discovered new dignities in our species. At a single touch of his genius, a glorious light is thrown on the inmost recesses of the soul – the veil of our nature is withdrawn – and all the sweetest and most amiable of its sympathies – the deep and secret springs of its purest virtues – its fine bloom, uninjured by the corruptions which are floating around it – appear encircled with a bright and celestial medium. The most searching eyes observe in his productions a depth of thought which they are unable to fathom – eminences rising far into an imaginative glory which they cannot penetrate. Above all others, he has discerned and traced out the line by which the high qualities of intellectual greatness are intimately united with the most generous exertions, and the holiest principles of moral goodness. His perceptions of truth, derived as they are from the intuitive feelings of his heart, are clear and unclouded, except by the shadows which are thrown from the vast creations of his fancy. Where no ungifted philosopher in verse would write an Essay on Man to elaborate his principles of virtue, Mr. Wordsworth breathes a few simple images which touch the inmost chords of the bosom, and the sentiments he desires to inculcate are engraven there for ever. Set before him the meanest and most disgusting of all earthly objects, and he immediately traces the great chain by which it is linked to the great harmonies of nature – sweeps through the most beautiful and touching of all human feelings, in order to show the mysterious connection, – and at last enables us to perceive the union of all orders of animated being, and the universal workings of the great Spirit that lives and breathes in them all. Deducing from all objects the most amiable charities, as well as the loftiest hopes, he feels a charm in all things among which he moves – finds the gentleness of heaven in the landscape – delight in every humble flower – joy in the brooks – life in the fountains – voices in the silence – 'Sermons in stones and good in every thing.'

Yet Mr. Wordsworth is regarded, by the great majority of readers, as an affected and childish rhymer, who vents a mawkish sensibility in miserable verses. The same causes which have rendered Mr. Scott the Apollo of milliners and magazines, have excluded the greatest genius of the age from the honors of their applause. He is indeed far beyond the visual powers of ordinary minds; and our self-love naturally inclines us to despise that which we are unable to enjoy. Unquestionably there are beautiful pictures of rustic life, gentle sketches of retiring character, and passages of a majestic elevation and swelling harmony, scattered among his works, which the humblest capacity need only read to admire. But the sneers of critics, whom the multitude have been accustomed to follow, prevents them from obtaining a pleasure which all who can feel would certainly feel. They have learned to despise beauties, because they are intermingled with pauses of interest, or rather to overlook what is manifestly excellent, because it is surrounded with brightness which they are unable to perceive. The Review, whence a thousand petty wits have drawn their ridicule against Mr. Wordsworth, professes to decide his fate by quoting a few of his verses, which appear mere madrigal to the common eye, and on the score of these insulated passages, represents him as unworthy of perusal. It is obvious that by this method of criticism, Milton and Shakspeare might have been long ago stamped as proverbially absurd, or consigned to speedy oblivion. If the essence of poetry be to produce delight, the injustice of such a standard may easily be rendered obvious. In order to set off the faults against the excellence of a poet, we must show that the former torture us with as acute a misery as the latter transport us into elevated rapture. But it is impossible that such a proportion in any degree whatever should exist: for it is one of the many striking reasons which demonstrate how far the blessings outweigh the calamities of life, that the loftier pleasures, which throw a glory round our being, are not balanced by any painful sensations arising from their contraries. We are filled, for instance, with a thousand delightful associations crowding in confusion upon us when we wander amidst the listening stillness of a lovely seclusion, or gaze on wild and mountainous regions; but we experience no corresponding disgust when we travel through dusty roads and unvaried fields, we carry the beauty of the former into the barrenness of the latter, and even array it in new grace by the mingling of imagination with memory. So, while we are awakened into strange bliss, by the magic touches of a superior genius, we feel no agony when the power which has enraptured us is slumbering. A critic, indeed, will find his chief gratification in unveiling the weaknesses of the loftiest minds, but the true lover of the Muses will only pass them over, and regard them as mere negations in his estimate of the author. He would not obliterate all the puns and obscenity with which the scenes of Shakspeare are intermingled, at the expence of one of his more felicitous images. And yet Wordsworth is neglected, because a reviewer, in a fit of spleen, has selected two or three passages from his works, which he has contrived to render ludicrous. But he alone is not the cause which deters the world from admiring. There are deeper causes of the unpopularity of Wordsworth, which we shall endeavour concisely to explain.

In the first place he appears, in a great degree, indifferent to human applause. His hopes, and views, and aspirations, are directed to more substantial objects than the changeable breath of Man, which so fill and expand his mind as to enable him to look, with an undazzled eye, on the darling rewards of genius. Nor does this proceed from any antisocial spirit, any want of love for Man, or of sympathy with the general feeling. It is perhaps the truest and most signal stamp of the loftiest powers, and contributes in the end to soften and mature them. The love of fame, which burns so fiercely in most poetical spirits, while it tends to display their capacities to the world, despoils them of their loveliest bloom. They learn to mark and analyse their deepest and most sacred feelings – not to nourish them for a richer soil hereafter – but to exhibit them to an admiring world. There is a kind of violation in thus laying open the sanctuary, and its sparkling treasures, to the vulgar gaze; in putting it in the power of every pretender to sensibility to imitate the language of the holiest emotions, and of every unfeeling critic to deride them. A poet of delicate and exalted perceptions should no more rejoice in the promiscuous admiration of his muse than of his mistress. He should feel his world, his glory and his fame, in the kindling divinity within him, and yield to all the impulses of heaven in the solitude which has witnessed his earliest rapture. There is nothing so hostile to that sweet abstraction, and to those delicious dreamings, which are broken if we touch them, as the attempt to transfuse them into the rules of metrical compositions, and to fit them for the amusement of the public. Perhaps, therefore, the brightest poetical spirits have florished and disappeared in the retirements amidst which they arose; men who felt their peculiar joys too sensibly to impart them, who were caught up into the 'third heaven' of inspiration, and heard voices which it was not possible for them to convey in mortal language. Such might have been the case with Shakspeare, who appears to have been nearly destitute of the love of fame, had he not been compelled to write for the stage; and thus, in the haste of his unstudied compositions, unavoidably to let fall those brilliant sparks of his heavenly flame, which have lighted us into the darkest caverns of the heart, and diffused a celestial glow on the loveliest regions of the fancy. Mr. Wordsworth's soul is composed of the same divine materials, and he finds in them the fulness of his joy. The whispering groves – the golden clouds – and the old long-remembered seats among the woods, all bear the record of his fame, and awaken in his mind gentle gleams of half-forgotten pleasure. The summer evening's faintest sigh has more charms for him, than the acclamations of towered cities; for its breathing sweets revive in his memory images of devotion and love. And thus he has written, absorbed in sublime contemplations, without adapting his language or his subjects to the tastes of the world, and has failed of acquiring laurels which his better sense would lead him to disdain.

Another cause, derived from the former, of the comparative obscurity of his writings, is the apparently trifling effusions with which they are chequered. Many, even of his admirers, are unable to conceive how a man of his intellectual power could have produced them. The truth is, they have sprung from the depth and richness of his thoughts, and have been given to the world with that carelessness to its applause, which indicates the purity of his genius. They are the feeble expressions of a heart too big for utterance, and filled, even to the overflow, with strong conceptions. They are little portions of a deep train of thought, which would some-times burst forth by reason of its rich copiousness, into a slight and transient display; and the poet, not considering that the reader's mind could not perceive all the previous emotions of his own, has left little sketches of feeling in carelessness to our wonder. He is carried away too much with his own conceptions to reflect how imperfectly he has expressed them. Less gifted writers are able to elaborate their imagin-ations with skill, but his are too mighty to be easily wielded. Their powers of language are greater than their depth of feeling, and their anxiety to be applauded is more potent than their wish for internal pleasure, while his thoughts overmaster his words, and he cares not enough for fame to stoop to polish them. We are unfortunately without a clue to the sensations by which they were excited, and therefore we see nothing in them but the most ordinary objects celebrated in feeble and unmelodious verse. But let some happy coincidence let us into the sensa-tions of the poet, and all the mystery will vanish, and we shall feel with surprise and delight that those small and retired springs, over which we were musing in the midst of breathing solitudes, and which the careless traveller passes unheeded, are of a depth, which we cannot fathom, and exhibit the breakings-forth of a mighty river, which is winding on in silence to the ocean in its dark and subterraneous channel, hewn out by unearthly hands.

We must remember too that all the favorite themes of Mr. Words-worth are personal; that with all his intensity of intellect, he has little expansion beyond himself. Thus his system of metaphysics is drawn rather from the history of his own mind, than from an extended acquaintance with his species. He throws the glory of his own imagin-ation over the whole of nature, and imputes the instincts, the feelings, and the loves to all mankind, which he discovers in his own bosom. He represents the earliest days of childhood, not merely as attractive from the winning gentleness of infantine smiles, and from the loveliness of unspotted innocence, but he surrounds them with a celestial brightness, he discerns amidst their little anxieties and budding hopes a radiance from afar, and from their mysterious impulses and fairy imaginings, extracts a noble proof of the origin and the destiny of man. Sublime as this prospect appears, when it first blazes on the eye, we may venture to assert that at least with the great mass of our species, its objects are chiefly ideal. And even those whom the majestic verse and the exalted enthusiasm of the poet have beguiled into a belief of their truth, must confess that they were wholly unacquainted with these supposed facts in the history of their moral being, which now seem to harmonise with all the delicious remembrances of early affection. Mr. W. has thrown the noon-tide majesty of his soul over the blushing dawn of his fancy, as he has shed the lustre and the bloom of his genius on the universe he surveys. In the holiness of his imagination all appears bright, and solemn, and serene; and his theories may rather be regarded as prophetic of what we may be in a loftier stage of being, than as descriptive of what we are on earth. No man of feeling ever perused his nobler poems for the first time, without finding that he breathed in a purer and more elevated region of poetical delight, than any which he had before explored. To feel, for the first time, a communion with his mind, is to discover loftier faculties in our own. He seems like a being scarcely of this world – like a mind exhibited before its time, to shew to what an eminence our nature is capable of attaining – or like a star dwelling apart, which not only sheds around the most pure and blessed influences, but precedes the dawn of brighter days on the spheres with which it is connected.

c. From an essay signed S. N. D. (the terminal letters of Thomas Noon Talfourd), 'On Poetical Scepticism', *Monthly Repository*, 1816, XI

From a note in section 2
After defending Unitarianism from Wordsworth's charge against it as 'being from the calculating understanding' (*Poems*, 1815), Talfourd writes:

It is almost needless to observe, that these observations leave untouched the merits of Mr. W's. poetry. Here indeed he is far above my feeble praise. In acute sensibility, in the philosophy of nature, in the delineation of all that is gentle in man, and in the power of rendering earthly images ethereal, I believe him to be surpassed by none in ancient or modern times. But I would confine poetry and reason to their respective uses. I would no more allow the former to usurp the place of the latter, than I would suffer a spirit of conceited criticism to deprive me of my purest enjoyments.

(p. 218)

From section 3:
After the epigraph, 'Heaven lies about us in our infancy', Talfourd expands ideas and perceptions taken from the 'Immortality Ode' in order to combat 'the peculiar doctrines' of Calvinism, especially the insistance upon original sin:

[Calvinism] will not spare even those enchanted regions which seem fresh and glorious to us still; – the only spots of life on which we can dwell with an undisturbed sense of joy. It enters them like a withered enchantress, to change their loveliness into a melancholy waste, to extinguish the pure and heavenly light shed over them, and to enshroud them with a gloom relieved by nothing but a fitful gleam from beneath.

Nothing surely need be said to prove the near connexion of the loftiest sublimities of poetry with the sacred feelings of childhood. The first touch of inspiration – the beautiful dawnings of fancy – the bright visions of celestial beauty – the shapes of unearthly loveliness, dimly seen – the reverential awe, and the mounting hopes which nothing on earth could satisfy – are the darling treasures of genius. They are 'the fountain light of all its day.' Perhaps a poet may almost be defined as one who possesses all those feelings of childhood with the expanded intellect of maturer years. He is one who preserves all the images of his early life in the inmost sanctuary of his soul. The emotion of primal innocence lives for ever, as a pure flame on the altar of that holy of holies; and forms the vital principle of all his moral and intellectual being. And this true 'spark of heavenly flame' it is the first object of Calvinism to extinguish! . . .

Surely this cannot be a poetical creed. On the contrary it is the peculiar delight of a true poet to trace out the kindly emotions in the midst of their holiest seclusion, to exhibit pictures of lowly goodness on which the soul can repose, as well as to kindle it into a sympathy and almost participation with the deeds of sublimer virtue. He sees a 'spirit of good even in things evil.' To him the human mind appears majestic, even in ruins. He rejoices to find that there are some feelings, and those the holiest with which heaven has blessed us, to be found in every land where the dwellings of man can be traced – high instincts of conjugal devotion, of parental tenderness, of filial love, of romantic affection, and of veneration, however blind, for a superior intelligence – which prove to him 'that we have all of us ONE HUMAN HEART.'*

(pp. 279–80)

d. 19 March 1819

Talfourd spoke on Wordsworth's poetry in a debate on the comparative merits of Wordsworth and Byron as poets, at a literary club, the Athenaeum, which met at the Crown and Rolls office in Chancery Lane. After a week for members' consideration, Byron was accorded nine votes, and Wordsworth six. This result was an improvement on that of a debate two years earlier (Talfourd was then president) when Byron had received seven votes, and Scott and Wordsworth together two votes.

(See Mary Moorman, *William Wordsworth, A Biography: The Later Years, 1803–1850*, Oxford, 1965, 321–2)

* Mr. Wordsworth arrives at this conclusion, in his 'Old Cumberland Beggar,' after a vein of philosophical poetry, as beautiful as ever the purest heart and the holiest imagination suggested. He takes as mean an object as the country in which his scene is laid could supply. A poor aged mendicant regularly visiting the scattered hamlets to receive alms, and traces out his importance to the general welfare, and the useful purposes for which he lives. He exhibits him as a record which binds together the memory of past charities, as impelling the villagers to goodness by 'the mild necessity of use,' and as giving 'the first kind touch of sympathy and love' to the youth amidst the mountains – In the midst of these reflections he exclaims,

> Man is dear to man; – the poorest poor
> Long for some moments in a weary life
> When they can know and feel that they have been
> Themselves the carvers, and the dealers out
> Of some small blessings; – have been kind to those
> Who needed kindness – for this single cause,
> That we have all of us one human heart.
> ['The Old Cumberland Beggar', *PW*, IV, p. 239, ll. 147–53;
> *LB (1800)*, p. 204, ll. 140–6]

In the same poem, as an example of the blessedness of this humble charity, he gives the picture of one poor woman who, 'though prest herself with her own wants,' as the mendicant makes his weekly call, 'takes one unsparing handful for his scrip,' and

> Returning with invigorated heart
> Sits by her fire and builds her hope in heaven.
> [*Ibid.*, *PW*, IV, p. 239, ll. 160–1; *LB (1800)*, p. 204, ll. 153–4]

This is finer than the finest things in Cowper. It comes over the heart with an absolute conviction of its reality; and fills it at once with a cordial love for its species. No one can read the whole of this exquisite poem, and be *for the time* a Calvinist. If Mr. Wilberforce should write for ages on the total corruption of man – these lines would be more than an answer to the most eloquent exaggerations he could produce.

e. Anonymous essay, 'On the Lake School of Poetry: Mr. Wordsworth', *New Monthly Magazine*, 1 October 1820, XIV, No. 81

This piece, which includes a mocking account of 'The Idiot Boy', probably provoked Talfourd into writing his major statements about Wordsworth (f. and g. below).

. . . But see with what a start of admiration the bard kens Johnny again. Behold the effective power of the passionate interrogatory:

> Who's yon that near the waterfall
> ['The Idiot Boy', *PW*, II, p. 77, l. 347; *LB (1798)*,
> p. 97, l. 357]
>
> Sits upright on a feeding horse.
> [*Ibid.*, *PW*, II, p. 77, l. 351; *LB (1798)*, p. 97, l. 361]

For a guinea, every reader knows as well as Mr. W. But there is a doubt whether every one will equally recognize him with that fervent warmth of the poet, with that mixed feeling of love and wonder so finely described in this line,

> 'Tis *Johnny! Johnny!* as I live.
> [*Ibid.*, *PW*, II, p. 77, l. 356; *LB (1798)*, p. 97, l. 366]

To be sure, Betty knew him; she runs up, and Johnny *burrs* as usual. This shews Mr. Wordsworth's great art in the epopœia; it shews his power in the creation of character – one of the highest prerogatives of the poet. *Johnny* is the only hero, with whom we are acquainted, that preserves consistency of action throughout – he is equally *unique* in the beginning, middle, and end. *He burrs* . . .

I could quote a great many of those fanciful follies, but I abstain. There is one curious thought which struck me very much; it may be admired at first sight, but if looked into it will be discovered to be very incongruous, calling an infant's smiles *'feelers of love.'* ['Address to my infant daughter, Dora', *PW*, II, p. 174, l. 72] What affinity is there between a child's innocent seraph smiles and the disgusting members of some loathed reptile or insect?

There is a great propensity to such thoughts in the Lake poetry. Mr. Wordsworth tells us, it is in the fine arts, as in the affairs of life, and as in the scriptural apothegm, no man can obey two masters. Lord Byron tells us openly, we 'must not set up Coleridge, Wordsworth, Southey.' And I think a little *'Anthropomorphitism,'* or some sort of *morphitism*, is necessary for our heathen imaginations, ere we can worship them. We cannot adore that *unknown* poetical *god*, living in the cloudy imaginations of the Bards of the Lakes. If we must be made intellectual Ixions of – to embrace a cloud – we must at least be tempted by the phantom of Juno. Mr. Wordsworth has gone far to prove that every great and original mind must create that taste by which its productions are to be appreciated and admired. We will allow that Mr. Wordsworth is a master-spirit, and has given a tone to the most of the poetical writings of this age. We should be glad to see his intuitive knowledge of the human heart, his holy communion between the phenomena of the external universe and the internal feelings, when it does not dive into mysticism, imitated; but we must protest against the taste, that would adopt his idiotry, his affectation, his riddling and ridiculous rusticity. We (I mean the literary and poetical world, assured of their sameness of thinking on this subject,) should be sorry to find the sweet chirpings of the grasshoppers, or the divine harmonies of the nightingales of the English poesy, turned into the hoarse and ominous creakings of *Winandermere frogs.*

(pp. 365, 367)

f. Essay signed T. N. T. 'On the Genius and Writings of Wordsworth', *New Monthly Magazine*, 1 November 1820, XIV, 498–506[2]

Our readers will be disappointed if they expect to find in this article any of the usual flippancies of criticism. Were we accustomed to employ them, its subject would utterly confound us. Strange is their infatuation who can fancy that the merits of a great poet are *subjected* to their decision, and that they have any authority to pass judicial censures, or confer beneficent praises, on one of the divinest of intellects! We shall attempt to set forth the peculiar immunities and triumphs of Wordsworth's genius, not as critics, but as disciples. To him our eulogy is nothing. But we would fain induce our readers to follow us 'where we have garnered up our hearts,' and would endeavour to remove those influences by which malignity and prejudice have striven to deter them from seeking some of the holiest of those living springs of delight which poets have opened for their species.

A minute discussion of Wordsworth's *system* will not be necessary to our design. It is manifestly absurd to refer to it as a test of his poetical genius. When an author has given numerous creations to the world, he

855

has furnished positive evidence of the nature and extent of his powers, which must preclude the necessity of deducing an opinion of them from the truth or falsehood of his theories. One noble imagination – one profound and affecting sentiment – or one new gleam cast on the inmost recesses of the soul, is more than a sufficient compensation for a thousand critical errors. False doctrines of taste can endure only for a little season, but the productions of genius are 'for all time.' Its discoveries cannot be lost – its images will not perish – its most delicate influences cannot be dissipated by the changes of times and of seasons. It may be a curious and interesting question, whether a poet laboriously builds up his fame with purpose and judgment, or, as has most falsely been said of Shakspeare, 'grows immortal in his own despite,' but it cannot affect his highest claims to the gratitude and admiration of the world. If Milton preferred Paradise Regained to Paradise Lost, does that strange mistake detract from our revering love? What would be our feeling towards critics, who should venture to allude to it as a proof that his works were unworthy of perusal, and decline an examination of those works themselves on the ground that his perverse taste sufficiently proved his want of genius? Yet this is the mode by which popular Reviewers have attempted to depreciate Wordsworth – they have argued from his theories to his poetry, instead of examining the poetry itself – as if their reasoning was better than the fact in question, or as if one eternal image set up in the stateliest region of poesy, had not value to outweigh all the truths of criticism, or to atone for all its errors!

Not only have Wordsworth's merits been improperly rested on his system, but that system itself has been misrepresented with no common baseness. From some of the attacks directed against it, a reader might infer that it recommended the choice of the meanest subjects; and their treatment in the meanest way; and that it not only represented poetry as fitly employed on things in themselves low and trivial, but that it forbad the clustering any delicate fancies about them, or the shedding on them any reconciling and softening lustre. Multitudes, indeed, have wondered as they read, not only that any persons should be deluded by its perverse insipidities, but that critics should waste their ridicule on an author who resigned at once all pretensions to the poetic art. In reality, this calumniated system has only reference to the diction, and to the subjects of poetry. It has merely taught, that the *diction* of poetry is not different from that of prose, and suggested that themes hitherto little dwelt on, were not unsuited to the bard's divinest uses. Let us briefly examine what ground of offence there is in the assertion or application of these positions.

Some have supposed that by rejecting a diction as peculiar to poetry, Wordsworth denied to it those qualities which are its essence, and those 'harmonious numbers' which its thoughts 'voluntarily move.' Were his language equivocal, which it is not, the slightest glance at his works would shew that he could have no design to exclude from it the stateliest imaginings, the most felicitous allusions, or the choicest and most varied music. He objected only to a peculiar phraseology – a certain hacknied strain of inversion – which had been set up as distinguishing poetry from prose, and which, he contended, was equally false in either. What is there of pernicious heresy in this, unless we make the crafty politician's doctrine, that speech was given to man to conceal his thoughts, the great principle of poetry? If words are fitly combined only to convey ideas to the mind, each word having a fixed meaning in itself, no different mode of collocation can be requisite when the noblest sentiment is to be embodied, from that which is proper when the dryest fact is to be asserted. Each term employed by a poet has as determinate an office – as clearly means one thing as distinguished from all others – as a mathematician's scientific phrases. If a poet wishes lucidly to convey a grand picture to the mind, there can be no reason why he should resort to another mode of speech than that which he would employ in delivering the plainest narrative. He will, of course, use other and probably more beautiful words, because they properly belong to his subject; but he will not use any different order in their arrangement, because in both cases his immediate object is the same – the clear communication of his own idea to the mind of his reader. And this is true not only of the chief object of the passage, but of every hinted allusion, or nice shade of feeling, which may adorn it. If by 'poetic diction' is intended the vivid expression of poetic thoughts, to annihilate it is to annihilate poetry; but if it means certain ornamental phrases and forms of language not necessary to such expression, it is, at best, but a splendid error. Felicity of language can never be other than the distinct expression of felicitous thought. The only art of diction in poetry, as in prose, is the nice bodying forth of each delicate vibration of the feelings, and each soft shade of the images, in words which at once make us conscious of their most transient beauty. At all events, there was surely no offence in an individual's rejecting the aid of a stile regarded as poetic, and relying for his fame on the naked majesty of his conceptions. The triumph is more signal when the Poet uses language as a mirror, clear, and itself invisible, to reflect his creations in their native hues, – than when he employs it as a stained and fallacious medium to exhibit its own varieties of tint, and to shew the objects which it partially reveals in its own prismatic colouring.

But it is said that the subjects of Wordsworth's poetry are not in themselves so lofty as those which his noblest predecessors have chosen. If this be true, and he has yet succeeded in discovering within them poetical affinities, or in shedding on them a new consecration, he does not surely deserve ill of his species. He has left all our old objects of veneration uninjured, and has enabled us to recognize new ones in the peaceful and familiar courses of our being. The question is not whether there are more august themes than those which he has treated, but whether these last have any interest, as seen in the light which he has cast around them. If they have, the benefits which he has conferred on humanity are more signal, and the triumph of his own powers is more undivided and more pure, than if he had treated on subjects which we have been accustomed to revere . . .

His office is, indeed, more arduous than if he selected those subjects about which hallowing associations have long clustered, and which other poets have already rendered sacred. But if he can discover new depths of affection in the soul – or throw new tinges of loveliness on objects hitherto common, he ought not to be despised in proportion to the severity of the work, and the absence of extrinsic aid! Wordsworth's person are not invested with antique robes, nor clad in the symbols of worldly pomp, but they are 'apparelled in celestial light.' By his power 'the bare earth and mountains bare' are covered with an imaginative radiance more holy than that which old Greek poets shed over Olympus. The world, as consecrated by his poetic wisdom, is an enchanted scene – redolent with sweet humanity, and vocal with 'echoes from beyond the grave.'

We shall now attempt to express the reasons for our belief in Wordsworth's genius, by first giving a few illustrations of his chief faculties, and then considering them in their application to the uses of philosophical poetry.

We allude first to the descriptive faculty, because though not the least popular, it is the lowest which Wordsworth possesses. He shares it with many others, though few, we think, enjoy it in so eminent a degree. It is difficult, indeed, to select passages from his works which are merely descriptive; but those which approach nearest to portraiture, and are least imbued with fantasy, are master-pieces in their kind. Take, for example, the following picture of masses of vapour receding among the steeps and summits of the mountains, after a storm, beneath an azure sky; the earlier part of which seems almost like another glimpse of Milton's heaven; and the conclusion of which impresses us solemnly with the most awful visions of Hebrew prophecy:

[Quotes *The Excursion*, *PW*, V, pp. 71–3, Book II, ll. 829–69

> — A step,
> A single step, which freed me from the skirts
> Of the blind vapour . . .
> . . . forms uncouth of mightiest power,
> For admiration and mysterious awe!]

Contrast with this the delicate grace of the following picture, which represents the white doe of Rylstone – that most beautiful of mysteries – on her Sabbath visit to the grave of her sainted lady: –

[Quotes *The White Doe of Rylstone*, *PW*, III, pp. 285–7, ll. 49–147, with omissions:

> Soft – the dusky trees between
> And down the path through the open green . . .
> Even so, without distress, doth she
> Lie down in peace, and lovingly.]

What, as mere description, can be more masterly than the following picture of the mountain solitude, where a dog was found, after three months' watching by his master's body – though the touches which send the feeling of deep loneliness into the soul, and the bold imagination which represents the huge recess as visited by elemental presences, are produced by higher than descriptive powers? –

> It was a cove, a huge recess,
> That keeps till June December's snow;
> A lofty precipice in front,
> A silent tarn below!
> Far in the bosom of Helvellyn,
> Remote from public road or dwelling,
> Pathway, or cultivated land;
> From trace of human foot or hand.
>
> There, sometimes does a leaping fish
> Send through the Tarn a lonely cheer;
> The crags repeat the raven's croak
> In symphony austere;

Thither the rainbow comes, the cloud;
And mists that spread the flying shroud,
And sun-beams; and the sounding blast,
That, if it could, would hurry past,
But that enormous barrier binds it fast.

['Fidelity', *PW*, IV, pp. 80–1, ll. 17–33; *Poems 1807*,
pp. 18–19, ll. 17–33]

We must abstain from farther examples of the descriptive faculty, and allude to that far higher gift which Wordsworth enjoys in his profound acquaintance with the sanctities of the soul. He does not make us feel the strength of the passions, by their violent contests in a transient storm, but the measureless depth of the affections when they are stillest and most holy. We often meet in his works with little passages in which we seem almost to contemplate the well-springs of pure emotion and gentle pathos, and to see the old clefts in the rock of humanity whence they arise. In these we may not rarely perceive the true elements of tales of the purest sentiment and most genuine tragedies. No poet has done such justice to the depth and the fulness of maternal love. What, for instance, can be more tear-moving than these exclamations of a mother, who for seven years has heard no tidings of an only child, abandoning the false stay of a pride which ever does unholy violence to the sufferer? –

Neglect me! no, I suffer'd long
From that ill thought; and, being blind,
Said, 'Pride shall help me in my wrong;
Kind mother have I been, as kind
As ever breathed:' and that is true;
I've wet my path with tears like dew,
Weeping for him when no one knew.
My son, if thou be humbled, poor,
Hopeless of honour, or of gain,
Oh! do not dread thy mother's door;
Think not of me with grief or pain:
I now can see with better eyes;
And worldly grandeur I despise,
And fortune with her gifts and lies.

['The Affliction of Margaret', stanzas 5 and 6, *PW*, II,
pp. 48–9, ll. 29–42; *Poems 1807*, p. 55, ll. 29–42]

How grand and fearful are the following conjectures of her agony! –

> Perhaps some dungeon hears thee groan,
>   Maim'd, mangled by inhuman men;
> Or thou upon a desert thrown
>   Inheritest the lion's den;
> Or hast been summon'd to the deep,
> Thou, thou and all thy mates, to keep
> An incommunicable sleep.
>   [*Ibid.*, stanza 8, *PW*, II, p. 49, ll. 50–6; *Poems 1807*, p. 56,
>   ll. 50–6]

And how triumphant does the great instinct appear in its vanquishing even the dread of mortal chilness – asking and looking for spectres – and concluding that their appearance is not possible, because they come not to its intense cravings: –

> I look for ghosts; but none will force
> Their way to me: 'tis falsely said
> That ever there was intercourse
> Between the living and the dead;
> For surely then I should have sight
> Of him I wait for day and night,
> With love and longings infinite.
>   [*Ibid.*, stanza 9, *PW*, II, p. 49, ll. 57–63; *Poems 1807*,
>   pp. 56–7, ll. 57–63]

Of the same class is the poem on the death of a noble youth, who fell in attempting to bound over a chasm of the Wharf, and left his mother childless. – What a volume of thought is there in the little stanzas which follow: –

> If for a lover the lady wept,
>   A solace she might borrow
> From death, and from the passion of death, –
>   Old Wharf might heal her sorrow!
>
> She weeps not for the wedding-day,
>   Which was to be to-morrow:
> Her hope was a farther-looking hope,
>   And her's is a mother's sorrow!
>   ['The Force of Prayer', *PW*, IV, p. 90, ll. 41–8]

Here we are made to feel not only the vastness of maternal affection, but its difference from that of lovers. The last, being a passion, has a tendency to grasp and cling to objects which may sustain it, and thus fixes even on those things which have swallowed its hopes, and draws them into its likeness. Death itself thus becomes a passion to one whom it has bereaved; or the waters which flowed over the object of once happy love, become a solace to the mourner, who nurses holy visions by their side. But an instinct which has none of that tendency to go beyond itself, when its only object is lost, has no earthly relief, but is left utterly desolate. The hope of a lover looks chiefly to a single point of time as its goal; – that of a mother is spread equally over existence, and when cut down, at once the blossoming expectations of a whole life are withered for ever.

Can any thing be more true or intense than the following description of remorse, rejecting the phantoms of superstitious horror as powerless, and representing lovely and uncomplaining forms of those whose memories the sufferer had dishonoured by his errors, casting their silent looks perpetually upon him:

> — Feebly must they have felt
> Who, in old time, attired with snakes and whips
> The vengeful Furies. *Beautiful* regards
> Were turn'd on me – the face of her I loved;
> The wife and mother pitifully fixing
> Tender reproaches, insupportable!
> [*The Excursion*, PW, V, pp. 104–5, Book III, ll. 850–5]

We will give but one short passage more to shew the depth of Wordsworth's insight into our nature – but it is a passage which we think unequalled in its kind in the compass of poetry. Never surely was such a glimpse of beatific vision opened amidst mortal affliction; such an elevation given to seeming weakness; such consolation ascribed to bereaved love by the very heightening of its own intensities. The poet contends, that those whom we regard as dying broken-hearted for the loss of friends, do not really perish through despair; but have such vivid prospects of heaven, and such a present sense that those who have been taken from them are waiting for them there, that they wear themselves away in longings after the reality, and so hasten to enjoy it: –

> – Full oft the innocent sufferer sees
> Too clearly; feels too vividly; and longs
> To realize the vision with intense
> And overconstant yearning – there – there lies

The excess by which the balance is destroy'd.
Too, too contracted are these walls of flesh,
This vital warmth too cold, these visual orbs,
Though inconceivably endow'd, too dim
For any passion of the soul that leads
To extasy; and, all the crooked paths
Of time and change disdaining, takes its course
Along the line of limitless desires.
      [*Ibid., PW*, V, pp. 114–15, see footnotes, Book IV, ll. 174–85]

But the imaginative faculty is that with which Wordsworth is most eminently gifted. As the term IMAGINATION is often very loosely employed, it will be necessary for us here to state as clearly as possible our idea of its meaning. In our sense, it is *that power by which the spiritualities of our nature and the sensible images derived from the material universe are commingled at the will of the possessor.* It has thus a two-fold operation – the bodying forth of feelings, sentiments, and ideas, in beautiful and majestic forms, and giving to them local habitations; and the informing the colours and the shapes of matter with the properties of the soul. The first of these workings of the faculty supplies the highest excellences of the orator, and of the philosophic bard . . .

In the second mode of its operation, it moves over the universe like the spirit of God on the face of the waters, and peoples it with glorious shapes, as in the Greek mythology, or sheds on it a consecrating radiance, and imparts to it an intense sympathy, as in the poems of these more reflective days. Although a harmonizing faculty, it can by the law of its essence only act on things which have an inherent likeness. It brings out the secret affinities of its objects; but it cannot combine things which nature has not prepared for union, because it does not add, but transfuses. Hence there can be no wild incongruity, no splendid confusion in its works. Those which are commonly regarded as its productions in the metaphorical speeches of 'Irish eloquence,' are their very reverse, and may serve by contrast to explain its realities. The highest and purest of its efforts are when the intensest elements of the human soul are mingled inseparably with the vastest majesties of the universe; as where Lear identifies his age with that of the heavens, and calls on them to avenge his wrongs by their community of lot; and where Timon 'fixes his everlasting mansion upon the beached shore of the salt flood,' that 'once a day with its embossed froth the turbulent surge may cover him,' scorning human tears, but desiring the vast ocean for his eternal mourner!

Of this transfusing and reconciling faculty – whether its office be to 'cloath upon,' or to spiritualize – Mr. Wordsworth is, in the highest degree, master. Of this abundant proofs will be found in the latter portion of this article; at present we will only give a few examples. The first of these is one of the grandest instances of noble daring, completely successful, which poetry exhibits. After a magnificent picture of a single yew-tree, and a fine allusion to its readiness to furnish spears for old battles, the poet proceeds:

> — But worthier still of note
> Are those fraternal four of Borrowdale,
> Join'd in one solemn and capacious grove;
> Huge trunks! – and each particular trunk a growth
> Of intertwisted fibres serpentine,
> Upcoiling, and inveterately convolved, –
> *Not uninformed by fantasy and looks*
> *That threaten the profane; – a pillar'd* shade
> Upon whose grassless floor of red-brown hue,
> By sheddings from the *pining* umbrage tinged
> Perennially – beneath whose sable roof
> Of boughs, as if for *festal purpose* deck'd
> By *unrejoicing berries*, ghostly shapes
> May meet at noon-tide – *Fear* and *trembling Hope*,
> *Silence* and *Foresight* – *Death* the *Skeleton*
> And *Time* the *Shadow* – there to celebrate,
> As in a natural temple scatter'd o'er
> With altars undisturb'd of mossy stone,
> United worship; or in mute repose
> To lie, and listen to the mountain flood
> Murmuring from Glamarara's in most caves.
> ['Yew-Trees', *PW*, II, p. 210, ll. 13–33]

Let the reader, when that first glow of intuitive admiration which this passage cannot fail to inspire is past, look back on the exquisite gradations by which it naturally proceeds from mere description to the sublime personification of the most awful abstractions, and the union of their fearful shapes in strange worship, or in listening to the deepest of nature's voices. The first lines – interspersed indeed with epithets drawn from the operations of mind, and therefore giving them an imaginative tinge – are, for the most part, a mere picture of the august brotherhood of trees, though their very sound is in more august accordance with their

864

theme than most of the examples usually produced of 'echoes to the sense.' Having completely set before us the image of the scene, the poet begins that enchantment by which it is to be converted into a fitting temple for the noontide spectres of Death and Time, by the general intimation that it is 'not uninformed by fantasy and looks that threaten the profane' – then by the mere epithet *pillared* gives us the more particular feeling of a fane – then, by reference to the actual circumstances of the grassless floor of red-brown hue, preserves to us the peculiar features of the scene which thus he is hallowing – and at last gives to the roof and its berries a strange air of unrejoicing festivity – until we are prepared for the introduction of the phantasms, and feel that the scene could be fitted to no less tremendous a conclave. The place, without losing one of its individual features, is decked for the reception of these noon-tide shades, and we are prepared to muse on them with unshrinking eyes. How by a less adventurous but not less delightful process, does the poet impart to an evening scene on the Thames at Richmond, the serenity of his own heart, and tinge it with softest and saddest hues of the fancy and the affections! The verses have all the richness of Collins, to whom they allude, and breathe a more profound and universal sentiment than is found in his sky-tinctured poetry.

[Quotes 'How richly glows the water's breast', *PW*, I, p. 40; and 'Remembrance of Collins', originally written as a single poem, *PW*, I, p. 210, ll. 1–12]

The following delicious sonnet, inspired by the same scene, is one of the latest effusions of its author. We do not here quote it on account of its sweet and intense recollection of one of the divinest of poets – nor of the fine unbroken ligament by which the harmony listened to by the later bard is connected with that which the earlier drank in, by the lineage of the songsters who keep up the old ravishment – but of that imaginative power, by which a sacredness is imparted to the place and to the birds, as though they performed unresting worship in the most glorious of cathedrals.

[Quotes 'Fame tells of groves – from England far away', *PW*, III, p. 41]

The following 'Thought of a Briton on the subjugation of Switzerland,' has an elemental grandeur imbued with the intensest sentiment, which places it among the highest efforts of the imaginative faculty.

[Quotes 'Two voices are there; one is of the sea', *PW*, III, p. 115]

We have thus feebly attempted to give some glimpse into the essence of Wordsworth's powers – of his skill in delineating the forms of creation – of his insight into the spirit of man – and of his imaginative faculty. How he has applied these gifts to philosophical poetry, and what are the results of his contemplation, by their aid, on the external universe – human life – individual character – the vicissitudes of individual fortune – society at large – and the prospects of the species – we shall next proceed more particularly to examine.

g. Essay signed T. N. T., continuation of 'On the Genius and Writings of Wordsworth', *New Monthly Magazine*, 1 December 1820, XIV, 648–55

The spirit of contemplation influences and directs all Wordsworth's poetical faculties. He does not create a variety of individual forms to vivify them with the Promethean fire of dramatic genius, and exhibit the living struggle of their passions and their affections in opposition to each other, or to destiny. 'The moving accident is not his trade.' He looks on humanity as from a more exalted sphere, though he feels his kindred with it while he gazes, and yearns over it with deepest sympathy. No poet of ancient or modern times has dared so entirely to repose on the mere strength of his own powers. Others, indeed, have given hints of the divinest truths, even amidst their wildest and most passionate effusions. The tragedies of Sophocles, for example, abound in moralities expressed with a grace and precision which often ally the sentiment to an image, and almost define it to the senses. In Shakspeare the wisdom is as much deeper as the passion is intenser; the minds of the characters, under the strongest excitements of love, hope, or agony, grow bright as well as warm, and in their fervid career shed abroad sparkles of fire, which light up for an instant the immost sanctuaries of our nature. But few have ventured to send into the world essentially meditative poems, which none but the thoughtful and the gentle-hearted can truly enjoy. Lucretius is the only writer of antiquity who has left a great work of this description; and he has unhappily lavished the boundless riches of his genius on doctrines which are in direct opposition to the spirit of poetry. An apostle of a more congenial faith, Wordsworth, stands pre-eminently – almost alone – a divine philosopher among the poets. It has been his singular lot, in this late age of the world, to draw little from those sources of interest which incident and situation supply – and to rest his claim to the gratitude and admiration of the people on his intense and majestical contemplations of man and the universe.

The philosophical poetry of Wordsworth is not more distinct from the dramatic, or the epic, than from the merely didactic and moral. He has thrown into it as much of profound affection, as much of ravishing loveliness, as much of delicate fantasy, as adorn the most romantic tales, or the most passionate tragedies. If he sees all things 'far as angel's ken,' he regards them with human love. His imagination is never obscured amidst his profoundest reasonings, but is ever active to embody the beautiful and the pure, and to present to us the most august moralities in 'clear dream and solemn vision.' Instead of reaching sublime conclusions by a painful and elaborate process, he discloses them by a single touch, and fixes them on our hearts for ever. So intense are his perceptions of moral beauty, that he feels the spirit of good however deeply hidden, and opens to our view the secret springs of love and of joy, where all has appeared barren to the ungifted observer. He can trace, prolong, and renew within us, those mysterious risings of delight in the soul which 'may make a chysome child to smile,' and which, when half-experienced at long intervals in riper age, are to us the assurances of a better life. He follows with the nice touch of unerring sympathy all the most subtle workings of the spirit of good, as it makes its little sanctuaries in hearts unconscious of its presence, and blends its influences unheeded with ordinary thoughts, hopes, and sorrows. The old prerogatives of human-ity, which long usage has made appear common, put on their own air of grandeur while he teaches us to revere them. When we first read his poetry, we look on all the mysteries of our being with a new reverence, and feel like children who, having been brought up in some deserted palace, learn for the first time the regality of their home – understand a venerableness in the faded escutcheons with which they were accus-tomed to play – and feel the dim figures on the stained windows, or on the decaying tapestry, which were only grotesque before, speaking to their hearts in ancestral voices.

The consecration which Wordsworth has shed over the external world is in a great measure peculiar to his genius. In the Hebrew poetry there was no trace of particular description – but general images, such as of tall cedars, of sweet pastures, or of still waters, were alone permitted to aid the affections of the devout worshipper. The feeling of the vast and indistinct prevailed; for all in religion was symbolical and mysterious, and pointed to 'temples not made with hands, eternal in the heavens.' In the exquisite master-pieces of Grecian inspiration, free nature's grace was almost excluded by the opposite tendency to admire only the def-inite and the palpable. Hence the pictures of nymphs, satyrs, and deities, were perpetually substituted for views of the magnificence of earth and heaven. In the romantic poetry of modern times, the open face of nature

867

has again been permitted to smile on us, and its freshness to glide into our souls. Nor has there been wanting 'craft of delicate spirits' to shed lovelier tinges of the imagination on all its scenes – to scatter among them classical images like Ionic temples among the fair glades and deep woods of some rich domain – to call dainty groups of fairies to hold their revellings upon the velvet turf – or afford glimpses of angel wings floating at even-tide in the golden perspective. But the imagination of Wordsworth has given to the external universe a charm which has never else, extensively at least, been shed over it. He has not personified the glorious objects of creation – nor peopled them with beautiful and majestic shapes – but, without depriving them of their own reality, has imparted to them a life which makes them objects of affection and reverence. He enables us at once to enjoy the contemplation of their colours and forms, and to love them as human friends. He consecrates earth by the mere influences of sentiment and thought, and renders its scenes as enchanted as though he had filled them with Oriental wonders. Touched by him, the hills, the rocks, the little hedgerows, and the humblest flowers – all the grandeurs and the tendernesses of creation – shine in a magic lustre 'which never was by sea or land,' and which yet is strangely familiar to our hearts. These are not hallowed by him with 'angel visits,' nor by the presence of fair and immortal shapes, but by the remembrances of early joy, by lingering gleams of a brightness which has passed away, and dawnings of a glory to be revealed in the fulness of time. The lowliest of nature's graces have power to move and to delight him. 'The clouds are touched, and in their silent faces does he read unutterable love.' He listens to the voice of the cuckoo in early spring, till he 'begets again the golden time of his childhood,' and till the world, which is 'fit home' for that mysterious bird, appears 'an airy unsubstantial place.' At the root of some old thorn, or beneath the branches of some time-honoured tree, he opens the sources of delicious musing, and suggests the first hints which lead through a range of intensest humanities to the glories of our final destiny. When we traverse with him the 'bare earth and mountains bare,' we feel that 'the place whereon we are standing is holy ground;' the melancholy brook can touch our souls as truly as a tragic catastrophe; the splendours of the western sky give intimation of 'a joy past joy;' and the meanest flowers, and scanty blades of grass, awaken within us hopes too rapturous for smiles, and 'thoughts which do often lie too deep for tears.'

To give all the instances of this sublime operation of the imaginative faculty in Wordsworth, would be to quote the far larger portion of his

works. A few lines, however, from the poem composed on the Banks of
the Wye, will give our readers a deep glimpse into the inmost heart of his
poetry, and of his poetical system, on the communion of the soul of man
with the spirit of the universe. In this rapturous effusion – in which, with
a wise prodigality, he hints and intimates the profoundest of those feelings which vivify all he has created – he gives the following view of the
progress of his sympathy with the external world: –
[Quotes 'Tintern Abbey', *PW*, II, pp. 261–2, ll. 72–102, *LB (1798)*, pp.
113–14, ll. 73–103:

> — Nature then
> (The coarser pleasures of my boyish days . . .
> All thinking things, all objects of all thought,
> And rolls through all things.]

There are none of the workings of our poet's imaginative faculty more
wonderful in themselves, or more productive of high thoughts and
intense sympathies, than those which have for their objects the grand
abstractions of humanity – Life and Death, Childhood and Old Age.
Every period of our being is to him not only filled with its own peculiar
endearments and joys, but dignified by its own sanctities. The common
forms of life assume a new venerableness when he touches them – for he
makes us feel them in their connexion with our immortality – even as the
uncouth vessels of the Jewish law appeared sublime to those who felt
that they were dedicated to the immediate service of heaven. He ever
leaves us conscious that the existence on whose beginning he expatiates,
will endure for ever. He traces out those of its fibres which are eternal in
their essence. He discovers in every part of our earthly course manifold
intimations that these our human hearts will never die. Childhood is, to
him, not only the season of novelty, of innocence, of joyous spirits, and of
mounting hope – but of a dream-like glory, which assures to us that this
world is not our final home. Age, to him, is not a descent into a dark
valley, but a 'final eminence,' where the wise may sit 'in awful sovereignty'
as on a high peak among the mountains in placid summer, and commune
with heaven, undisturbed by the lesser noises of the tumultuous world.
One season of life is bound to another by 'the natural piety' which the
unchanging forms of nature preserve, and death comes at last over the
deep and tranquil stream as it is about to emerge into a lovelier sunshine,
as 'a shadow thrown softly and lightly from a passing cloud.'
    The Ode in which Wordsworth particularly developes the intimations
of immortality to be found in the recollections of early childhood, is, to

our feelings, the noblest piece of lyric poetry in the world. It was the first poem of its author which we read, and never shall we forget the sensations which it excited within us. We had heard the cold sneers attached to his name – we had glanced over criticisms, 'lighter than vanity,' which represented him as an object for scorn 'to point its slow unmoving finger at' – and here – in the works of this derided poet – we found a new vein of imaginative sentiment opened to us – sacred recollections brought back on our hearts with all the freshness of novelty, and all the venerableness of far-off time – the most mysterious of old sensations traced to a celestial origin – and the shadows cast over the opening of life from the realities of eternity renewed before us with a sense of their supernal causes! What a gift did we then inherit! To have the best and most imperishable of intellectual treasures – the mighty world of reminiscences of the days of infancy – set before us in a new and holier light; to find objects of deepest veneration where we had only been accustomed to love; to feel in all the touching mysteries of our past being the symbols and assurances of our immortal destiny! The poet has here spanned our mortal life as with a glorious rainbow, terminating on one side in infancy, and on the other in the realms of blessedness beyond the grave, and shedding even upon the middle of that course sweet tints of unearthly colouring. The following is the view he has given of the fading glory of childhood – drawn in part from Oriental fiction, but embodying the profoundest of elemental truths: –

[Quotes 'Ode: Intimations of Immortality', stanza V, 'Our birth is but a sleep, and a forgetting' ff., p. 281, *PW*, IV.]

But the following is the noblest passage of the whole; and such an outpouring of thought and feeling – such a piece of inspired philosophy – we do not believe exists elsewhere in human language: –

[Quotes *ibid.*, 'O joy! that in our embers . . .', stanza IX, *PW*, IV, p. 283.]

After this rapturous flight the author thus leaves to repose on the quiet lap of humanity, and soothes us with a strain of such mingled solemnity and tenderness, as 'might make angels weep:'

[Quotes *ibid.*, 'What though the radiance which was once so bright . . .', stanza X and XI, l. 176, *PW*, IV, pp. 284–5.]

The genius of the poet, which thus dignifies and consecrates the abstractions of our nature, is scarcely less felicitous in its pictures of society at large, and in its philosophical delineations of the characters and fortunes of individual man. Seen through the holy medium of his imagination, all things appear 'bright and solemn and serene' – the asperities of our earthly condition are softened away – and the most gentle and evanescent of its hues gleam and tremble over it. He delights to trace out those ties of sympathy by which the meanest of beings are connected with the general heart. He touches the delicate strings by which the great family of man are bound together, and thence draws forth sounds of choicest music. He makes us partake of those joys which are 'spread through the earth to be caught in stray gifts by whoever will find' them – discloses the hidden wealth of the soul – finds beauty every where, and 'good in every thing.' He draws character with the softest pencil, and shades it with the pensive tints of gentlest thought. The pastoral of The Brothers – the story of Michael – and the sweet histories in the Excursion which the priest gives while standing among the rustic graves of the churchyard, among the mountains, are full of exquisite portraits, touched and softened by a divine imagination which human love inspires. He rejoices also to exhibit that holy process by which the influences of creation are shed abroad in the heart, to excite, to mould, or to soften. We select the following stanzas from many passages of this kind of equal beauty, because in the fantasy of nature's making 'a lady of her own,' the object of the poet is necessarily developed with more singleness than where reference is incidentally made to the effect of scenery on the mind: –

[Quotes 'Three years she grew in sun and shower', *PW*, II, pp. 214–15, ll. 1–30; *LB (1800)*, pp. 93–4, ll. 1–30.]

But we must break off to give a passage in a bolder and most passionate strain, which represents the effect of the tropical grandeur and voluptuousness of nature on a wild and fiery spirit – at once awakening and half-redeeming its irregular desires. It is from the poem of 'Ruth,' – a piece where the most profound of human affections is disclosed amidst the richest imagery, and incidents of wild romance are told with a Grecian purity of expression. The impulses of a beautiful and daring youth are thus represented as inspired by Indian scenery:

[Quotes 'Ruth', *PW*, II, p. 231, ll. 121–44:

The wind, the tempest roaring high,
The tumult of a tropic sky . . .
 . . . needs must have their share
Of noble sentiment.]

We can do little more than enumerate those pieces of narrative and character, which we esteem the best in their kind of our author's works. The old Cumberland Beggar is one of those which linger most tenderly on our memories. The poet here takes almost the lowliest of his species – an aged mendicant, one of the last of that class who made regular circuits amidst the cottages of the north – and after a vivid picture of his frame bent with years, of his slow motion and decayed senses, he asserts him not divorced from good – traces out the gentle links which bind him to his fellows – and shews the benefit which even he can diffuse in his rounds, while he serves as a record to bind together past deeds and offices of charity – compels to acts of love by 'the mild necessity of use' those whose hearts would otherwise harden – gives to the young 'the first mild touch of sympathy and thought, in which they find their kindred with a world where want and sorrow are' – and enables even the poor to taste the joy of bestowing. This last blessing is thus set forth and illustrated by a precious example of self-denying goodness and cheerful hope, which is at once more tear-moving and more sublime than the finest things in Cowper: –

> — Man is dear to man; the poorest poor
> Long for some moments in a weary life
> When they can know and feel that they have been,
> Themselves, the fathers and the dealers out
> Of some small blessings; have been kind to such
> As needed kindness, for this single cause,
> That we have all of us one human heart.
> – Such pleasure is to one kind being known,
> My neighbour, when with punctual care, each week
> Duly as Friday comes, though prest herself
> With her own wants, she from her chest of meal
> Takes one unsparing handful for the scrip
> Of this old mendicant, and, from her door
> Returning with invigorated heart,
> Sits by her fire, and builds her hope in Heaven.
> ['The Old Cumberland Beggar', *PW*, IV, p. 262, ll. 976–82;
> *LB (1800)*, p. 204, ll. 140–54]

Then, in the Excursion, there is the story of the Ruined Cottage, with its admirable gradations, more painful than the pathetic narratives of its author usually are, yet not without redeeming traits of sweetness, and a reconciling spirit which takes away its sting. There, too, is the intense history of the Solitary's sorrows – there the story of the Hanoverian and the Jacobite, who learned to snatch a sympathy from their bitter disputings, grew old in controversy and in friendship, and were buried side by side – there the picture of Oswald, the gifted and generous and graceful hero of the mountain solitude, who was cut off in the blossom of his youth – there the record of that pleasurable sage, whose house death, after forty years of forbearance, visited with thronging summonses, and took off his family one after the other, 'with intervals of peace,' till he too, with cheerful thoughts about him, was 'overcome by unexpected sleep in one blest moment,' and as he lay on the 'warm lap of his mother-earth,' 'gathered to his fathers.' There are those fine vestiges, and yet finer traditions, and conjectures, of the good knight Sir Alfred Irthing, the 'mild-hearted champion' who had retired in Elizabeth's days to a retreat among the hills, and had drawn around him a kindred and a family. Of him nothing remained but a gentle fame in the hearts of the villagers, an uncouth monumental stone grafted on the church-walls, which the sagest antiquarian might muse over in vain, and his name engraven in a wreath or posy around three bells with which he had endowed the spire. 'So,' exclaims the poet, in strains as touching and majestic as ever were breathed over the transitory grandeur of earth –

> So fails, so languishes, grows dim and dies,
> All that this world is proud of. From their spheres
> The stars of human glory are cast down;
> Perish the roses, and the flowers of kings,
> Princes and emperors, and the crowns and palms
> Of all the mighty, withered, and consumed.
> [*The Excursion*, *PW*, V, p. 262, Book VII, ll. 976–82]

In the Excursion, too, is the exquisite tale of Poor Ellen – a seduced and forsaken girl – from which we will give one affecting incident, scarcely to be matched, for truth and beauty, through the many sentimental poems and tales which have been founded on a similar woe:
[*Ibid.*, *PW*, V, pp. 214–15, Book IV, ll. 862–93:

> — Beside the cottage in which Ellen dwelt . . .
> To the blank margin of a Valentine,
> Bedropp'd with tears.]

With these tear-moving expressions of ill-fated love, we may contrast the following rich picture of the affection in its early bloom, from the tale of Vaudracour and Julia, which will shew how delightedly the poet might have lingered in the luxuries of amatory song, had he not chosen rather to brood over the whole world of sentiment and passion: –
[Quotes 'Vaudracour and Julia', *PW*, II, pp. 60–1, ll. 39–53:

> Arabian fiction never fill'd the world . . .
> A man too happy for mortality]

Perhaps the highest instance of Wordsworth's imaginative faculty, exerted in a tale of human fortunes, is to be found in 'The White Doe of Rylstone.' He has here succeeded in two distinct efforts, the results of which are yet in entire harmony. He has shewn the gentle spirit of a high-born maiden gathering strength and purity from sorrow, and finally after the destruction of her family, and amidst the ruin of her paternal domains, consecrated by suffering. He has also here, by the introduction of that lovely wonder, the favourite doe of his heroine, at once linked the period of his narrative to that of its events, and softened down the saddest catastrophe and the most exquisite of mortal agonies. A gallant chieftain, one of the goodliest pillars of the olden time, falls, with eight of his sons, in a hopeless contest for the religion to which they were devoted – the ninth, who followed them unarmed, is slain while he strives to bear away, for their sake, the banner which he had abjured – the sole survivor, a helpless woman, is left to wander desolate about the silent halls and tangled glades, once witnesses of her joyous infancy – and yet all this variety of grief is rendered mild and soothing by the influences of the imagination of the poet. The doe which first with its quiet sympathy excited relieving tears in its forsaken mistress, which followed her a gentle companion through all her mortal wanderings, and which years after made Sabbath visits to her grave, is like the spirit of nature personified to heal, to bless, and to elevate. All who have read the poem aright, will feel prepared for that apotheosis which the poet has reserved for this radiant being, and will recognize the imaginative truth of that bold figure, by which the decaying towers of Bolton are made to smile upon its form, and to attest its unearthly relations: –

> There doth the gentle creature lie
> With these adversities unmoved;
> Calm spectacle, by earth and sky
> In their benignity approved!
> And aye, methinks, this hoary pile,
> Subdued by outrage and decay,
> Looks down upon her with a smile,
> A gracious smile, that seems to say,
> 'Thou art not a Child of Time,
> But daughter of the eternal Prime!'
> [Quotes 'The White Doe of Rylstone', *PW*, III, p. 340,
> ll. 1901–10]

Although Wordsworth chiefly delights in these humanities of poetry, he has shewn that he possesses feelings to appreciate and power to grasp the noblest of classic fictions. No one can read his Dion, his Laodamia, and the most majestic of his sonnets, without perceiving that he has power to endow the stateliest shapes of old mythology with new life, and to diffuse about them a new glory. Hear him, for example, breaking forth, with holy disdain of the worldly spirit of the time, into this sublime apostrophe: –

> Great God! I'd rather be
> A Pagan suckled in a creed outworn:
> So might I, standing on some pleasant lee,
> Have glimpses which might make me less forlorn;
> Have sight of Proteus coming from the sea,
> Or hear old Triton blow his wreathed horn!
>> ['The world is too much with us', *PW*, III, p. 19, ll. 9–14;
>> *Poems 1807*, p. 130, ll. 9–14]

But he has chosen rather to survey the majesties of Greece, with the eye of a philosopher as well as of a poet. He reviews them with emotions equally remote from pedantry and from intolerance – regarding not only the grace and the loveliness of their forms, but their symbolical meaning – tracing them to their elements in the human soul, and bringing before us the eldest wisdom which was embodied in their shapes, and speedily forgotten by their worshippers. Thus, among 'the palpable array of sense,' does he discover hints of immortal life – thus does he transport us back more than twenty centuries – and enable us to enter into the most mysterious and far-reaching hopes of a Grecian votary: –

[Quotes *The Excursion*, *PW*, V, pp. 132–3, Book IV, ll. 735–62

> — A *Spirit* hung,
> Beautiful region! o'er thy Towns and Farms . . .
> And countless generations of mankind
> Depart: and leave no vestige where they trod.]

We must now bring this long article to a close – and yet how small a portion of our author's beauties have we even hinted! We have passed over the clear majesty of the poem of 'Hart leap well' – the lyrical grandeur of the Feast of Brougham Castle – the masculine energy and delicate grace of the Sonnets which with the exception perhaps of one or two of Warton and of Milton far exceed all others in our language – 'The Waggoner,' that fine and hearty concession of a water-drinker to the joys of wine and the light-hearted folly which it inspires – and numbers of smaller poems and ballads, which to the superficial observer may seem only like woodland springs, but in which he who ponders intently will discern the breakings forth of an under-current of thought and feeling which is silently flowing beneath him. We trust, however, we have written or rather quoted enough to induce such of our readers as hitherto have despised the poet on the faith of base or ignorant criticism to read him for themselves, especially as by the recent appearance of the Excursion in octavo, and the arrangement of the minor poems in four small volumes, the whole of his poetical works are placed within their reach. If he has little popularity with the multitude, he is rewarded by the intense veneration and love of the finest spirits of the age. Not only Coleridge, Lloyd, Southey, Wilson, and Lamb – with whom his name has been usually connected – but almost all the living poets have paid eloquent homage to his genius. He is loved by Montgomery, Cornwall, and Rogers – revered by the author of Waverley – ridiculed and pillaged by Lord Byron! Jeffrey, if he begins an article on his greatest work with the pithy sentence *'this will never do,'* glows even while he criticises, and before he closes, though he came like Balaam to curse, like him 'blesses altogether.' Innumerable essays, sermons, speeches, poems – even of those who profess to despise him – are tinged by his fancy and adorned by his expressions. And there are no small number of young hearts, which have not only been enriched but renovated by his poetry – which he has expanded, purified, and exalted – and to which he has given the means of high communion with the good and the pure throughout the universe. These, equal at least in number to the original lovers of Shakspeare or of Milton, will transmit his fame to kindred spirits, and whether it shall receive or be denied the honour of fashion, it will ever be cherished by the purest of earthly minds, and connected with the most majestic and undecaying of nature's scenery.

Too many of our living poets have seemed to take pride in building their fame on the sands. They have chosen for their subjects the diseases of the heart – the sad anomalies of humanity – the turbulent and guilty passions which are but for a season. Their renown, therefore, must necessarily decline as the species advances. Instead of tracing out the lineaments of the image of God indelibly impressed on the soul, they have painted the deformities which may obscure them for a while but can never utterly destroy them. Vice, which is the accident of our nature, has been their theme instead of those affections which are its groundwork and essence. 'Yet a little space, and that which men call evil is no more!' Yet a little space, and those wild emotions – those horrid deeds – those strange aberrations of the soul – on which some gifted bards have delighted to dwell, will fade away like the phantoms of a feverish dream. Then will poetry, like that of Wordsworth, which even now is the harbinger of a serener day, be felt and loved and held in undying honour. The genius of a poet who has chosen this high and pure career, too, will proceed in every stage of being, seeing that 'it is a thing immortal as himself,' and that it was ever inspired by affections which cannot die while the human heart shall endure. The holy bard even in brighter worlds will feel, with inconceivable delight, the connection between his earthly and celestial being – live along the golden lines of sentiment and thought back to the most delicious moments of his contemplations here – and rejoice in the recognition of those joys of which he had tastes and intimations on earth. Then shall he see the inmost soul of his poetry disclosed – grasp as assured realities the gorgeous visions of his infancy – feel 'the burthen of the mystery of all this unimaginable world,' which were lightened to him here dissolved away – see the prophetic workings of his imagination realized – exult while 'pain and anguish and the wormy grave,' which here were to him 'shapes of a dream,' are utterly banished from the view – and listen to the full chorus of that universal harmony whose first notes he here delighted to awaken!

h. A letter from Talfourd to Wordsworth, 1 December 1820

Temple, 1st December 1820

My Dear Sir,

The neglect of the Printers has prevented me from obtaining the Copy of the New Monthly Magazine until this Morning; but I hope it may yet be in time for your acceptance before you leave Cambridge. The Article which is concluded in its pages is, I am sensible, a most imperfect view even of those qualities of your poetry which it professes to develope; for it is very far indeed from expressing my own feelings respecting them; and I believe that there is more in them than I can even *feel*. If it should induce any who have been hitherto strangers to these vast stores of sentiment and imagery of which it would afford a glimpse, to enter on their full contemplation, I shall greatly rejoice; – but I am most anxious that you should receive the imperfect essay as a private expression of deep gratitude, and as though it were breathed in no ear but your own. Instead of making the most of my feelings for the purpose of effect I have studiously restrained them, lest to those who have never read your works, my seeming extravagance should defeat my aim. I might have said with truth, what I most deeply feel, that there is no writer who has ever lived to whom I personally owe the obligation which I owe to you, whose verse has so slid into the very current of my blood, and has so mingled with all my thoughts, hopes, and joys. There is no sympathy of my nature which you do not enoble nor any day of my life which you do not make happier. I am sure, you will feel that these acknowledgements are not mean flattery to you, but fitting homage to the divine spirit which is in you. It was my intention to expose in detail the manifold plagiarisms of Byron and others from your Poems; but I found my time would not permit, and I feared to extend my remarks beyond the Editor's wishes. This is a duty which I hope hereafter to discharge, and also to take a summary review of all the chief attacks which have been made on your fame.

I have received the Excursion and prize it as I ought. And now with most fervent wishes for the long continuance and happiness of the life of him who has so enriched mine, I have the honour to subscribe myself

Yours most gratefully and respectfully,

Thomas Noon Talfourd.

P. S. Present my best respects to Mrs & Miss Wordsworth.

(Ms. The Wordsworth Library)

EDITOR'S NOTES

1. Talfourd in 1847 recollects that his first published remarks in *The Pamphleteer*, 1815, 'found no echo except those which mocked me in the youths of my acquaintance – even among the most studious & gifted of them'. But he explains that he himself had previously been among those who had mocked Wordsworth's poetry. 'I knew indeed how lately I had myself turned from its contemplation with distaste; how when towards the close of my schooldays I had joined with some of my schoolfellows, who had by chance become possessed of a volume of the Lyrical ballads in pronouncing them below contempt; how personally I had contrasted the compact couplets of Pope's Homer and the pomp & glitter of Thomson's Seasons with the homely verse and simple diction of the lake poet. But thus it is in the progress of individual mind as of the species; the advancement after the first stage of intellectual association, is not from the simple to the ornate but from the ornate to the simple . . .

(Ms. Reading Public Library; from the draft of a lecture given on 21 October 1847).

2. Reprinted with the essay of December 1820, *Talfourd's Miscellaneous Writings*, 1842, 125–59.

256. William Hazlitt

From his writings, 1815–1818

a. From an unsigned note on Milton's *Comus*, *Examiner*, 11 June 1815

... Samson Agonistes is almost a canonisation of all the high moral and religious prejudices of his maturer years. *We* have no less respect for the memory of Milton as a patriot than as a poet. Whether he was a *true* patriot, we shall not enquire: he was at least a *consistent* one. He did not retract his defence of the people of England; he did not say that his sonnets to Vane or Cromwell were meant ironically; he was not appointed Poet-Laureat to a Court which he had reviled and insulted; he accepted neither place nor pension; nor did he write paltry sonnets upon the 'Royal fortitude' of the House of Stuart, by which, however, they really lost something.[*]

[Hazlitt's footnote]

[*] In the last edition of the works of a modern Poet, there is a Sonnet to the King, complimenting him on 'his royal fortitude.' The story of the Female Vagrant, which very beautifully and affectingly describes the miseries brought on the lower classes by war, in bearing which the said 'royal fortitude' is so nobly exercised, is very properly struck out of the collection.[1]

(*The Complete Works of William Hazlitt*, ed. P. P. Howe, 1930, V, 233)

b. From a report in Crabb Robinson's Diary, 15 June 1815

Crabb Robinson (ironically, it was Hazlitt who, *c.* 1799, first introduced him to Wordsworth's poetry) discussed Hazlitt's *Examiner* attack with Wordsworth who happened to be in London.

I called on Wordsworth for the first time at his lodgings. He was luckily at home, and I spent the forenoon with him, walking. We talked about Hazlitt in consequence of a malignant attack on Wordsworth by him in Sunday's *Examiner*. Wordsworth that very day called on Hunt, who, in a manly way, asked whether Wordsworth had seen the paper of the morning, saying, if he had, he should consider his call as a higher honour. He disclaimed the article. The attack by Hazlitt was a note in which, after honouring Milton for being a consistent patriot, he sneered at

Wordsworth as the author of 'paltry sonnets upon the royal fortitude,' etc. and insinuated that he had left out the *Female Vagrant*, a poem describing the miseries of war sustained by the poor. This led to Wordsworth's mentioning the cause of his coolness towards Hazlitt. It appears that Hazlitt, when at Keswick, narrowly escaped being ducked by the populace, and probably sent to prison for some gross attacks on women. ⟨He even whipped one woman, *more puerorum*[2] for not yielding to his wishes.⟩ The populace were incensed against him and pursued him, but he escaped to Wordsworth, who took him into his house at midnight, gave him clothes and money (from three to five pounds). Since that time Wordsworth, though he never refused to meet Hazlitt when by accident they came together, did not choose that with his knowledge he should be invited.

(*Henry Crabb Robinson on Books and their Writers*, ed. Edith J. Morley, 1938, I, 169–70)

c. From an essay, 'On Manner', signed 'T. T.', *Examiner*, 27 August 1815[3]

The poem, 'Gipsies', was written and published not recently, as Hazlitt implies, but in 1807. For Keats's comment see entry 263f.

A strolling gipsy will offer to tell your fortune with a grace and an insinuation of address that would be admired in a court.*

[Hazlitt's footnote]

* Mr. Wordsworth, who has written a sonnet to the King on the good that he has done in the last fifty years, has made an attack on a set of gipsies for having done nothing in four and twenty hours. 'The stars had gone their rounds, but they had not stirred from their place.' And why should they, if they were comfortable where they were? We did not expect this turn from Mr. Wordsworth, whom we had considered as the prince of poetical idlers, and patron of the philosophy of indolence, who formerly insisted on our spending our time 'in a wise passiveness.' Mr. W. will excuse us if we are not converts to his recantation of his original doctrine; for he who changes his opinion loses his authority. We did not look for this Sunday-school philosophy from him. What had he himself been doing in these four and twenty hours? Had he been admiring a flower, or writing a sonnet? We hate the doctrine of utility, even in a philosopher, and much more in a poet: for the only real utility is that which leads to enjoyment, and the end is, in all cases, better than the means. A friend of ours from the North of England proposed to make

Stonehenge of some use, by building houses with it. Mr. W.'s quarrel with the gipsies is an improvement on this extravagance, for the gipsies are the only living monuments of the first ages of society. They are an everlasting source of thought and reflection on the advantages and disadvantages of the progress of civilisation: they are a better answer to the cotton manufactories than Mr. W. has given in the *Excursion*. 'They are a grotesque ornament to the civil order.' We should be sorry to part with Mr. Wordsworth's poetry, because it amuses and interests us: we should be still sorrier to part with the tents of our old friends, the Bohemian philosophers, because they amuse and interest us more. If any one goes a journey, the principal event in it is his meeting with a party of gipsies. The pleasantest trait in the character of Sir Roger de Coverley, is his interview with the gipsy fortune-teller. This is enough.

(*The Complete works of William Hazlitt*, ed. P. P. Howe, 1930, IV, 45–6)

d. From 'On the Doctrine of Philosophical Necessity', unsigned, *Examiner*, 10 December 1815

> — For I had learnt a sense sublime
> Of something far more deeply interfused,
> Whose dwelling is the light of setting suns,
> And the round ocean and the living air
> And the blue sky, and in the mind of man,
> A motion and a spirit that impels
> All thinking things, all objects of all thought,
> And rolls through all things.

PERHAPS, the doctrine of what has been called philosophical necessity was never more finely expressed than in these lines of a poet, who, if he had written only half of what he has done, would have deserved to be immortal. There can be no doubt that all that exists, exists by necessity; that the vast fabric of the universe is held together in one mighty chain, reaching to the 'threshold of Jove's throne'; that whatever has a beginning, must have a cause; that there is no object, no feeling, no action, which, other things being the same, could have been otherwise; that thought follows thought, like wave following wave; that chance or accident has no share in any thing that comes to pass in the moral or the physical world; that whatever is, must be; that whatever has been, must have been; that whatever is to be will be necessarily.

(*Ibid.*, XX, 60)

e. From *The Examiner*, 24 December 1815, unsigned

The 'thankless office' Hazlitt once attempted was his review of *The Excursion*, see entry 147.

We have been urged several times to take up the subject of Mr. Wordsworth's Poems, in order to do them justice. In doing this, we should satisfy neither his admirers nor his censurers. We have once already attempted the thankless office, and it did not succeed. Indeed we think all comment on them superseded by those lines of Withers, which are a complete anticipation of Mr. Wordsworth's style, where, speaking of poetry, he says, –

> In my former days of bliss
> Her divine skill taught me this,
> That from every thing I saw
> I could some invention draw;
> And raise pleasure to her height
> Through the meanest object's sight; –
> By the murmur of a spring,
> Or the least bough's rustling,
> By a daisy whose leaves spread
> Shut when Titan goes to bed;
> Or a shady bush or tree,
> She could more infuse in me
> Than all Nature's beauties can
> In some other wiser man.
> [From 'The Shepherd's Hunting', 1615]

(*Ibid.*, XX, 68)

f. From 'Shakespeare's Female Characters', *Examiner*, 28 July 1816, unsigned

One of the finest passages in Mr. Wordsworth's poems is that where he has given us his opinion of Desdemona:

> Books, dreams, are each a world; and books, we know,
> Are a substantial world, both pure and good,
> Round which, with tendrils strong as flesh and blood,
> Our pastime and our happiness may grow;
> . . . . . .

Matter wherein right voluble I am,
Two let me mention dearer than the rest,
The gentle lady wedded to the Moor,
And heavenly Una with her milk-white lamb.
['Personal Talk', *PW*, IV, p. 74, ll. 33–42]

(*Ibid.*, XX, 88)

g. From an unsigned essay, 'Literary Notices', No. 20, *Examiner*, 22 December 1816

Hazlitt throws equal contempt on Wordsworth's 'Jacobin' (i.e. radical) poetry, and his 'anti-Jacobin' (i.e. reactionary) politics: both are seen to be the result of egotism. Hazlitt re-worked this passage, making it perhaps less political; for his Lecture of 1818 (see j(2) below). Crabb Robinson, on both occasions, showed open indignation with Hazlitt. On 22 December 1816, he records:

> . . . After tea went to Basil Montagu's. Hazlitt was there. I could not abstain from adverting to a scandalous article in this morning's *Examiner* in which he attacks Wordsworth. Hazlitt, without confessing himself the author, spoke as if he were but did not vindicate himself boldly. He said: 'You know I am not in the habit of defending what I do. I do not say that all I have done is right.' . . .
> I carefully abstained from shaking hands with Hazlitt.
> (*Henry Crabb Robinson on Books and their Writers*, I, ed. Edith J. Morley, 1938, 200–1)

The spirit of Jacobin poetry is rank egotism. We know an instance. It is of a person who founded a school of poetry on sheer humanity, on ideot boys and mad mothers, and on Simon Lee, the old huntsman. The secret of the Jacobin poetry and the anti-jacobin politics of this writer is the same. His lyrical poetry was a cant of humanity about the commonest people to level the great with the small; and his political poetry is a cant of loyalty to level Bonaparte with kings and hereditary imbecility. As he would put up the commonest of men against kings and nobles, to satisfy his levelling notions, so for the same reason, he would set up the meanest of kings against the greatest of men, reposing once more on the mediocrity of royalty. This person admires nothing that is admirable, feels no interest in any thing interesting, no grandeur in any thing grand, no beauty in any thing beautiful. He tolerates nothing but what he himself creates; he sympathizes only with what can enter into no competition with him, with 'the bare earth and mountains bare, and grass in the green field.' He sees nothing but himself and the universe. He hates all greatness, and all pretensions to it but his own. His egotism is in this respect a madness; for he scorns even the admiration of himself, thinking it a presumption in any one to suppose that he has taste or sense enough to understand him. He hates all science and all art; he hates chemistry, he hates conchology; he hates Sir Isaac Newton; he hates logic, he hates metaphysics, which he says are unintelligible, and yet he would be thought to understand them; he hates prose, he hates all poetry but his own; he hates Shakespeare, or what he calls 'those interlocutions between Lucius and Caius,' because he would have all the talk to himself, and considers the movements of passion in *Lear*, *Othello*, or *Macbeth*, as impertinent, compared with the Moods of his own Mind; he thinks every thing good is contained in the 'Lyrical Ballads,' or, if it is not contained there, it is good for nothing; he hates music, dancing, and painting; he hates Rubens, he hates Rembrandt, he hates Raphael, he hates Titian, he hates Vandyke; he hates the antique; he hates the Apollo Belvidere; he hates the Venus de Medicis. He hates all that others love and admire but himself. He is glad that Bonaparte is sent to St. Helena, and that the Louvre is dispersed for the same reason – to get rid of the idea of any thing greater, or thought greater than himself. The Bourbons, and their processions of the Holy Ghost, give no disturbance to his vanity; and he therefore gives them none.

(*The Complete Works of William Hazlitt*, ed. P. P. Howe, 1830, VII, 144–5)

h. From *Characters of Shakespeare's Plays*, 1817

Hazlitt's attack on Wordsworth's lack of interest in the experience of sexual love is echoed in Shelley's 'Peter Bell the Third'.

The only evil that even in apprehension befalls the two lovers [*Romeo and Juliet*] is the loss of the greatest possible felicity; yet this loss is fatal to both, for they had rather part with life than bear the thought of surviving all that had made life dear to them. In all this, Shakespear has but followed nature, which existed in his time, as well as now. The modern philosophy, which reduces the whole theory of the mind to habitual impressions, and leaves the natural impulses of passion and imagination out of the account, had not then been discovered; or if it had, would have been little calculated for the uses of poetry.

It is the inadequacy of the same false system of philosophy to account for the strength of our earliest attachments, which has led Mr. Wordsworth to indulge in the mystical visions of Platonism in his Ode on the Progress of Life. He has very admirably described the vividness of our impressions in youth and childhood, and how 'they fade by degrees into the light of common day,' and he ascribes the change to the supposition of a pre-existent state, as if our early thoughts were nearer heaven, reflections of former trails of glory, shadows of our past being. This is idle. It is not from the knowledge of the past that the first impressions of things derive their gloss and splendour, but from our ignorance of the future, which fills the void to come with the warmth of our desires, with our gayest hopes, and brightest fancies. It is the obscurity spread before it that colours the prospect of life with hope, as it is the cloud which reflects the rainbow. There is no occasion to resort to any mystical union and transmission of feeling through different states of being to account for the romantic enthusiasm of youth; nor to plant the root of hope in the grave, nor to derive it from the skies. Its root is in the heart of man: it lifts its head above the stars. Desire and imagination are inmates of the human breast. The heaven 'that lies about us in our infancy' is only a new world, of which we know nothing but what we wish it to be, and believe all that we wish. In youth and boyhood, the world we live in is the world of desire, and of fancy: it is experience that brings us down to the world of reality. What is it that in youth sheds a dewy light round the evening star? That makes the daisy look so bright? That perfumes the hyacinth? That embalms the first kiss of love? It is the delight of novelty, and the seeing no end to the pleasure that we fondly believe is still in store for us. The heart revels in the luxury of its own thoughts, and is unable to sustain the weight of hope and love that presses upon it. – The effects of the passion of love alone might have dissipated Mr. Wordsworth's theory, if he means any thing more by it than an ingenious and poetical allegory. *That* at least is not a link in the chain let down from other worlds; 'the purple light of love' is not a dim reflection of the smiles of celestial bliss. It does not appear till the middle of life, and then seems like 'another morn risen on mid-day.' In this respect the soul comes into the world 'in utter nakedness.' Love waits for the ripening of the youthful blood. The sense of pleasure precedes the love of pleasure, but with the sense of pleasure, as soon as it is felt, come thronging infinite desires and hopes of pleasure, and love is mature as soon as born. It withers and it dies almost as soon!

(*Ibid.*, IV, 250–1)

i. From the conclusion to the essay, 'On the Character of Rousseau', from *The Round Table*, 1817

Rousseau, in all his writings, never once lost sight of himself. He was the same individual from first to last. The spring that moved his passions never went down, the pulse that agitated his heart never ceased to beat. It was this strong feeling of interest, accumulating in his mind, which overpowers and absorbs the feelings of his readers. He owed all his power to sentiment. The writer who most nearly resembles him in our own times is the author of the *Lyrical Ballads*. We see no other difference between them, than that the one wrote in prose and the other in poetry; and that prose is perhaps better adapted to express those local and personal feelings, which are inveterate habits in the mind, than poetry, which embodies its imaginary creations. We conceive that Rousseau's exclamation, '*Ah, voila de la pervenche*,'[4] comes more home to the mind than Mr. Wordsworth's discovery of the linnet's nest 'with five blue eggs,' or than his address to the cuckoo, beautiful as we think it is; and we will confidently match the Citizen of Geneva's adventures on the Lake of Bienne against the Cumberland Poet's floating dreams on the Lake of Grasmere. Both create an interest out of nothing, or rather out of their own feelings; both weave numberless recollections into one sentiment; both wind their own being round whatever object occurs to them. But Rousseau, as a prose-writer, gives only the habitual and personal impression. Mr. Wordsworth, as a poet, is forced to lend the colours of imagination to impressions which owe all their force to their identity with themselves, and tries to paint what is only to be felt. Rousseau, in a word, interests you in certain objects by interesting you in himself: Mr. Wordsworth would persuade you that the most insignificant objects are interesting in themselves, because he is interested in them. If he had met with Rousseau's favourite periwinkle, he would have *translated* it into the most beautiful of flowers. This is not imagination, but want of sense. If his jealousy of the sympathy of others makes him avoid what is beautiful and grand in nature, why does he undertake elaborately to describe other objects? *His* nature is a mere Dulcinea del Toboso, and he would make a Vashti of her. Rubens appears to have been as extravagantly attached to his three wives, as Raphael was to his Fornarina; but their faces were not so classical. The three greatest egotists that we know of, that is, the three writers who felt their own being most powerfully and exclusively, are Rousseau, Wordsworth, and Benvenuto Cellini. As Swift somewhere says, we defy the world to furnish out a fourth.

(*Ibid.*, IV, 92–3)

j. From *Lectures on the English Poets*, 1818

These lectures were given in January and February 1818; they were repeated in April and May, and published in the same year. P. G. Patmore, under the signature, 'A. Z.', reported the lectures extensively in *Blackwood's* for April 1818, but omitted passages of personal attack upon Wordsworth, thus gleaning the praise and tempering the abuse.

Hazlitt's attack on Wordsworth had been provoked by Wordsworth's less than moderate tone in his *Letter to a Friend of Robert Burns*, 1816. But Wordsworth's tone had its origins in the hostile reviews of Francis Jeffrey of, first, *The Excursion*, 1814 and, second, *The White Doe*, 1815 (see entry 182). To the first review Wordsworth made a reply in his 'Essay, Supplementary to the Preface', published with his *Poems*, 2 vols, 1815, and his reply to the second review is his *Letter to a Friend of Robert Burns*. There Wordsworth told his new friend, James Gray (see entry 193), that Robespierre was 'one of the vainest men that the most vain country on earth has produced'; and declared that Napoleon had been 'an intoxicated despot.' Napoleon was a hero to Hazlitt, so Wordsworth's comments would not be seductive; nor would his linking Robespierre with his tormentor, Jeffrey: 'It is a descent which I fear you will scarcely pardon, to compare these redoubtable enemies of mankind with the anonymous conductor of a perishable publication'. Wordsworth's restraint, shown in his 'Essay, Supplementary to the Preface', is abandoned: 'It is notorious that this presevering Aristarch [Jeffrey], as often as a work of original genius comes before him, avails himself of that opportunity to re-proclaim to the world the narrow range of his own comprehension.' (*The Prose Works of William Wordsworth*, ed. W.J.B. Owen and J.W. Smyser, 1974, III, 127). Altogether, the level of abuse spiralled down through Jeffrey, Wordsworth, Hazlitt and, finally, to Crabb Robinson listening to Hazlitt's lecture: 'Hazlitt was so contemptuous towards Wordsworth, speaking of his letter about Burns, that I lost my temper and hissed; but I was on the outside of the room. I was led to burst out into declamations against Hazlitt which I afterwards regretted, though I uttered nothing but the truth. Hazlitt abused Wordsworth in a vulgar style, imputing to him the mere desire of representing himself as a superior man.' (*Henry Crabb Robinson on Books and Their Writers*, ed. Edith J. Morley, 1938, I. 220.)

(1) *From Lecture 7, 'On Burns and the Old English Ballads'*

It has been usual to attack Burns's moral character, and the moral tendency of his writings at the same time; and Mr. Wordsworth, in a letter to Mr. Gray, Master of the High School at Edinburgh, in attempting to defend, has only laid him open to a more serious and unheard-of responsibility. Mr. Gray might very well have sent him back, in return for his epistle, the answer of Holofernes in Love's Labour's Lost: – '*Via* goodman Dull, thou hast spoken no word all this while.' The author of this performance, which is as weak in effect as it is pompous in pretension, shews a great dislike of Robespierre, Buonaparte, and of Mr. Jeffrey, whom he, by some unaccountable fatality, classes together as the three most formidable enemies of the human race that have appeared in his (Mr. Wordsworth's) remembrance; but he betrays very little liking to Burns. He is, indeed, anxious to get him out of the unhallowed clutches of the Edinburgh Reviewers (as a mere matter of poetical privilege), only to bring him before a graver and higher tribunal, which is his own; and after repeating and insinuating ponderous charges against him, shakes his head, and declines giving any opinion in so tremendous a case; so that though the judgment of the former critic is set aside, poor Burns remains just where he was, and nobody gains any thing by the cause but Mr. Wordsworth, in an increasing opinion of his own wisdom and purity. 'Out upon this half-faced fellowship!' The author of the Lyrical Ballads has thus missed a fine opportunity of doing Burns justice and himself honour. He might have shewn himself a philosophical prose-writer, as well as a philosophical poet. He might have offered as amiable and as gallant a defence of the Muses, as my uncle Toby, in the honest simplicity of his heart, did of the army. He might have said at once, instead of making a parcel of wry faces over the matter, that Burns had written Tam o' Shanter, and that that alone was enough; that he could hardly have described the excesses of mad, hairbrained, roaring mirth and convivial indulgence, which are the soul of it, if he himself had not 'drunk full ofter of the ton than of the well' – unless 'the act and practique part of life had been the mistress of his theorique.' Mr. Wordsworth might have quoted such lines as –

> The landlady and Tam grew gracious,
> Wi' favours secret, sweet, and precious; –

or,

> Care, mad to see a man so happy,
> E'en drown'd himself among the nappy;

and fairly confessed that he could not have written such lines from a want of proper habits and previous sympathy; and that till some great puritanical genius should arise to do these things equally well without any knowledge of them, the world might forgive Burns the injuries he had done his health and fortune in his poetical apprenticeship to experience, for the pleasure he had afforded them. Instead of this, Mr. Wordsworth hints, that with different personal habits and greater strength of mind, Burns would have written differently, and almost as well as *he* does. He might have taken that line of Gay's,

> The fly that sips treacle is lost in the sweets, –

and applied it in all its force and pathos to the poetical character. He might have argued that poets are men of genius, and that a man of genius is not a machine; that they live in a state of intellectual intoxication, and that it is too much to expect them to be distinguished by peculiar *sang froid*, circumspection, and sobriety. Poets are by nature men of stronger imagination and keener sensibilities than others; and it is a contradiction to suppose them at the same time governed only by the cool, dry, calculating dictates of reason and foresight. Mr. Wordsworth might have ascertained the boundaries that part the provinces of reason and imagination: – that it is the business of the understanding to exhibit things in their relative proportions and ultimate consequences – of the imagination to insist on their immediate impressions, and to indulge their strongest impulses; but it is the poet's office to pamper the imagination of his readers and his own with the extremes of present ecstacy or agony, to snatch the swiftwinged golden minutes, the torturing hour, and to banish the dull, prosaic, monotonous realities of life, both from his thoughts and from his practice. Mr. Wordsworth might have shewn how it is that all men of genius, or of originality and independence of mind, are liable to practical errors, from the very confidence their superiority inspires, which makes them fly in the face of custom and prejudice, always rashly, sometimes unjustly; for, after all, custom and prejudice are not without foundation in truth and reason, and no one individual is a match for the world in power, very few in knowledge. The world may altogether be set down as older and wiser than any single person in it.

Again, our philosophical letter-writer might have enlarged on the temptations to which Burns was exposed from his struggles with fortune and the uncertainty of his fate. He might have shewn how a poet, not born to wealth or title, was kept in a constant state of feverish anxiety with respect to his fame and the means of a precarious livelihood: that 'from being chilled with poverty, steeped in contempt, he had passed into the sunshine of fortune, and was lifted to the very pinnacle of public favour'; yet even there could not count on the continuance of success, but was, 'like the giddy sailor on the mast,' ready with every blast to topple down into the fatal bowels of the deep!'. He might have traced his habit of ale-house tippling to the last long precious draught of his favourite usquebaugh, which he took in the prospect of bidding farewel for ever to his native land; and his conjugal infidelities to his first disappointment in love, which would not have happened to him, if he had been born to a small estate in land, or bred up behind a counter!

Lastly, Mr. Wordsworth might have shewn the incompatibility between the Muses and the Excise, which never agreed well together, or met in one seat, till they were unaccountably reconciled on Rydal Mount. He must know (no man better) the distraction created by the opposite calls of business and of fancy, the torment of extents, the plague of receipts laid in order or mislaid, the disagreeableness of exacting penalties or paying the forfeiture; and how all this (together with the broaching of casks and the splashing of beer-barrels) must have preyed upon a mind like Burns, with more than his natural sensibility and none of his acquired firmness. . . .

. . . It is hardly reasonable to look for a hearty or genuine defence of Burns from the pen of Mr. Wordsworth; for there is no common link of sympathy between them. Nothing can be more different or hostile than the spirit of their poetry. Mr. Wordsworth's poetry is the poetry of mere sentiment and pensive contemplation: Burns's is a very highly sublimated essence of animal existence. With Burns, 'self-love and social are the same' –

> And we'll tak a cup of kindness yet,
> For auld lang syne.

Mr. Wordsworth is 'himself alone,' a recluse philosopher, or a reluctant spectator of the scenes of many-coloured life; moralising on them, not describing, not entering into them. Robert Burns has exerted all the vigour of his mind, all the happiness of his nature, in exalting the pleasures of wine, of love, and good fellowship: but in Mr. Wordsworth there is a total disunion and divorce of the faculties of the mind from those of the body; the banns are forbid, or a separation is austerely pronounced from bed and board – *a mensâ et thoro*. From the Lyrical Ballads, it does not appear that men eat or drink, marry or are given in marriage. If we lived by every sentiment that proceeded out of mouths, and not by bread or wine, or if the species were continued like trees (to borrow an expression from the great Sir Thomas Brown), Mr. Wordsworth's poetry would be just as good as ever. It is not so with Burns: he is 'famous for the keeping of it up,' and in his verse is ever fresh and gay. For this, it seems, he has fallen under the displeasure of the Edinburgh Reviewers, and the still more formidable patronage of Mr. Wordsworth's pen.

This, this was the unkindest cut of all.

(*Ibid.*, V, 128–32)

(2) *From Lecture 8, 'On the Living Poets'*

Mr. Wordsworth is the most original poet now living. He is the reverse of Walter Scott in his defects and excellences. He has nearly all that the other wants, and wants all that the other possesses. His poetry is not external, but internal; it does not depend upon tradition, or story, or old song; he furnishes it from his own mind, and is his own subject. He is the poet of mere sentiment. Of many of the Lyrical Ballads, it is not possible to speak in terms of too high praise, such as Hart-leap Well, the Banks of the Wye, Poor Susan, parts of the Leech-gatherer, the lines to a Cuckoo, to a Daisy, the Complaint, several of the Sonnets, and a hundred others of inconceivable beauty, of perfect originality and pathos. They open a finer and deeper vein of thought and feeling than any poet in modern times has done, or attempted. He has produced a deeper impression, and on a smaller circle, than any other of his contemporaries. His powers have been mistaken by the age, nor does he exactly understand them himself. He cannot form a whole. He has not the constructive faculty. He can give only the fine tones of thought, drawn from his mind by accident or nature, like the sounds drawn from the Æolian harp by the wandering gale. – He is totally deficient in all the machinery of poetry. His *Excursion*, taken as a whole, notwithstanding the noble materials thrown away in it, is a proof of this. The line labours, the sentiment moves slow, but the poem stands stock-still. The reader makes no way from the first line to the last. It is more than any thing in the world like Robinson Crusoe's boat, which would have been an excellent good boat, and would have carried him to the other side of the globe, but that he could not get it out of the sand where it stuck fast. I did what little I could to help to launch it at the time, but it would not do. I am not, however, one of those who laugh at the attempts or failures of men of genius. It is not my way to cry 'Long life to the conqueror.' Success and desert are not with me synonymous terms; and the less Mr. Wordsworth's general merits have been understood, the more necessary is it to insist upon them. This is not the place to repeat what I have already said on the subject. The reader may turn to it in the Round Table. I do not think, however, there is any thing in the larger poem equal to many of the detached pieces in the Lyrical Ballads. As Mr. Wordsworth's poems have been little known to the public, or chiefly through garbled extracts from them, I will here give an entire poem (one that has always been a favourite with me), that the reader may know what it is that the admirers of this author find to be delighted with in his poetry. Those who do not feel the beauty and the force of it, may save themselves the trouble of inquiring farther.

[Quotes 'Hart-leap Well', *PW*, II, pp. 249–54; *LB (1800)*, pp. 125–32]

Mr. Wordsworth is at the head of that which has been denominated the Lake school of poetry; a school which, with all my respect for it, I do not think sacred from criticism or exempt from faults, of some of which faults I shall speak with becoming frankness; for I do not see that the liberty of the press ought to be shackled, or freedom of speech curtailed, to screen either its revolutionary or renegado extravagances. This school of poetry had its origin in the French revolution, or rather in those sentiments and opinions which produced that revolution; and which sentiments and opinions were indirectly imported into this country in translations from the German about that period. Our poetical literature had, towards the close of the last century, degenerated into the most trite, insipid, and mechanical of all things, in the hands of the followers of Pope and the old French school of poetry. It wanted something to stir it up, and it found that something in the principles and events of the French revolution. From the impulse it thus received, it rose at once from the most servile imitation and tamest common-place, to the utmost pitch of singularity and paradox. The change in the belles-lettres was as complete, and to many persons as startling, as the change in politics, with which it went hand in hand. There was a mighty ferment in the heads of statesmen and poets, kings and people. According to the prevailing notions, all was to be natural and new. Nothing that was established was to be tolerated. All the common-place figures of poetry, tropes, allegories, personifications, with the whole heathen mythology, were instantly discarded; a classical allusion was considered as a piece of antiquated foppery; capital letters were no more allowed in print, than letters-patent of nobility were permitted in real life; kings and queens were dethroned from their rank and station in legitimate tragedy or epic poetry, as they were decapitated elsewhere; rhyme was looked upon as a relic of the feudal system, and regular metre was abolished along with regular government. Authority and fashion, elegance or arrangement, were hooted out of countenance, as pedantry and prejudice. Every one did that which was good in his own eyes. The object was to reduce all things to an absolute level; and a singularly affected and outrageous simplicity prevailed in dress and manners, in style and sentiment. A striking effect produced where it was least expected, something new and original, no matter whether good, bad, or indifferent, whether mean or lofty, extravagant or childish, was all that was aimed at, or considered as compatible with sound philosophy and an age of reason. The licentiousness grew extreme: Coryate's Crudities were nothing to it. The world was to be turned topsy-turvy; and poetry, by the good will of our Adam-wits, was to share its fate and begin *de novo*. It was a time of promise, a renewal of the world and of letters; and the Deucalions, who were to perform this feat of regeneration, were the present poet-laureat and the two authors of the Lyrical Ballads. The Germans, who made heroes of robbers, and honest women of cast-off mistresses, had already exhausted the extravagant and marvellous in sentiment and situation: our native writers adopted a wonderful simplicity of style and matter. The paradox they set out with was, that all things are by nature equally fit subjects for poetry; or that if there is any preference to be given, those that are the meanest and most unpromising are the best, as they leave the greatest scope for the unbounded stores of thought and fancy in the writer's own mind. Poetry had with them 'neither buttress nor coigne of vantage to make its pendant bed and procreant cradle.' It was not 'born so high: its aiery buildeth in the cedar's top, and dallies with the wind, and scorns the sun.' It grew like a mushroom out of the ground; or was hidden in it like a truffle, which it required a particular sagacity and industry to find out and dig up. They founded the new school on a principle of sheer humanity, on pure nature void of art. It could not be said of these sweeping reformers and dictators in the republic of letters, that 'in their train walked crowns and crownets; that realms and islands, like plates, dropt from their pockets': but they were surrounded, in company with the Muses, by a mixed rabble of idle apprentices and Botany Bay convicts, female vagrants, gipsies, meek daughters in the family of Christ, of ideot boys and mad mothers, and after them 'owls and night-ravens flew.' They scorned 'degrees, priority, and place, insisture, course, proportion, season, form office, and custom in all line of order': − the distinctions of birth, the vicissitudes of fortune, did not enter into their abstracted, lofty, and levelling calculation of human nature. He who was more than man, with them was none. They claimed kindred only with the commonest of the people: peasants, pedlars, and village-barbers were their oracles and bosom friends. Their poetry, in the extreme to which it professedly tended, and was in effect carried, levels all distinctions of nature and society; has 'no figures nor no fantasies,' which the prejudices of superstition or the customs of the world draw in the brains of men; 'no trivial fond records' of all that has existed in the history of past ages; it has no adventitious pride, pomp, or circumstance, to set it off; 'the marshal's truncheon, nor the judge's robe'; neither tradition, reverence, nor ceremony, 'that to great ones 'longs, it breaks in pieces the golden images for poetry, and defaces its armorial bearings, to melt them down in the mould of common humanity or of its own upstart self-sufficiency. They took the same method in their new-fangled 'metre ballad-mongering' scheme, which Rousseau did in his prose paradoxes – of exciting attention by reversing the established standards of opinion and estimation in the world. They were for bringing poetry back to its primitive simplicity and state of nature, as he was for bringing society back to the savage state: so that the only thing remarkable left in the world by this change, would be the persons who had produced it. A thorough adept in this school of poetry and philanthropy is jealous of all excellence but his own. He does not even like to share his reputation with his subject; for he would have it all proceed from his own power and originality of mind. Such a one is slow to admire any thing that is admirable; feels no interest in what is most interesting to others, no grandeur in any thing grand, no beauty in anything beautiful. He tolerates only what he himself creates; he sympathizes only with what can enter into no competition with him, with 'the bare trees and mountains bare, and grass in the green field.' He sees nothing but himself and the universe. He hates all greatness and all pretensions to it, whether well or ill-founded. His egotism is in some respects a madness; for he scorns even the admiration of himself, thinking it a presumption in any one to suppose that he has taste or sense enough to understand him. He hates all science and all art; he hates chemistry, he hates conchology; he hates Voltaire; he hates Sir Isaac Newton; he hates wisdom; he hates wit; he hates metaphysics, which he says are unintelligible, and yet he would be thought to understand them; he hates prose; he hates all poetry but his own; he hates the dialogues in Shakespeare; he hates music, dancing, and painting; he hates Rubens, he hates Rembrandt; he hates Raphael, he hates Titian; he hates Vandyke; he hates the antique; he hates the Apollo Belvidere; he hates the Venus of Medicis. This is the reason that so few people take an interest in his writings, because he takes an interest in nothing that others do! – The effect has been perceived as something odd; but the cause or principle has never been distinctly traced to its source before, as far as I know.

(*Ibid.*, V, 156–64; this passage builds upon his 1816 essay: see entry 256i.)

k. From a review of Byron's *Childe Harold's Pilgrimage*, canto iv, *The Yellow Dwarf*, 2 May 1818, unsigned

This will never do. It is more intolerable than even Mr. Wordsworth's arbitrary egotism and pampered self-sufficiency. *He* creates a factitious interest out of nothing: Lord Byron would destroy our interest in all that is. Mr. Wordsworth, to salve his own self-love, makes the merest toy of his own mind, – the most insignificant object he can meet with, – of as much importance as the universe: Lord Byron would persuade us that the universe itself is not worth his or our notice; and yet he would expect us to be occupied with him.

> —The man whose eye
> Is ever on himself doth look on one,
> The least of Nature's works, one who might move
> The wise man to that scorn which wisdom holds
> Unlawful ever.
>
> ['Lines left upon a seat in a Yew-tree', *PW*, I, p. 94, ll. 55–9;
> *LB (1798)*, p. 40, ll. 51–5]

These lines, written by one of these two poets, might be addressed to both of them with equal propriety.

(*Ibid.*, XIX, 36)

1. From a review of *Letters of Horace Walpole*, *Edinburgh Review*, December 1818, unsigned

. . . a single letter from the pen of Gray, is worth all the pedlar-reasoning of Mr. Wordsworth's Eternal Recluse, from the hour he first squats himself down in the sun to the end of his preaching. In the first we have the light unstudied pleasantries of a wit, and a man of feeling; – in the last are talked to death by an arrogant old proser, and buried in a heap of the most perilous stuff and the most dusty philosophy.

(*Ibid.*, XVI, 142)

EDITOR'S NOTES

1. Hazlitt's implication that Wordsworth omitted 'The Female Vagrant' from *Poems* (1815) is incorrect: the first 130 lines were excluded and also two stanzas of a radical tendency.
2. 'in the manner of boys'.
3. Republished in *The Round Table*, 1817.
4. 'So here's some periwinkle!'

257. Byron

From his letters and writings, 1815–1821, including reminiscences
from Joseph Farington and Thomas Medwin

To Crabb Robinson, in 1834, Rogers claimed that he brought Lord Byron
and Wordsworth 'together to a tête-à-tête dinner. Wordsworth tried to
talk his best and talked too much – he did not appear to advantage' (*Henry
Crabb Robinson on Books and their Writers*, ed. Edith J. Morley, 1938,
I, 436). The date of this dinner was probably 18 June 1815, the day of
the Battle of Waterloo: Byron hoped 'Buonaparte wd be victorious';
Wordsworth 'maintained He had no chance whatever if the allies kept
together' (see Mark L. Reed, *Wordsworth: Chronology of the Middle Years,
1800–1815*, Harvard, 1975, 498–9).

George Ticknor, the American scholar and traveller, reported a conversation on 20 June 1815 in which Byron explained that he had suppressed
English Bards and Scotch Reviewers at Roger's request and because he 'was
now the friend of Moore, the correspondent of Jeffrey and intimate with
the Wordsworth School, and had a hearty liking for them all, – especially
as they did not refuse to know one who had so much abused them' (*Life,
Letters and Journals of George Ticknor*, ed. E. S. Hillyard, London, 1876, I,
58). June 1815 was a period of relative happiness in Byron's short marriage; Lady Byron was later to remember her husband speaking well of
Wordsworth, 'after meeting at the same table'. Crabb Robinson reported
to Mary Wordsworth, 26 February 1854 (The Wordsworth Library Ms.),
that Lady Byron told him (on 12 February) 'that Lord B. notwithst
[andin]g his invincible recklessness, and in spite of what he had written,
spoke of Mr. W. with great respect, even reverence towards his person
praising his dignified manners after meeting at the same table.' Anyhow,
this sweetness has disappeared by October 1815, probably because of
Rogers reporting to Byron an adverse opinion that Wordsworth had sent to
a lady in Bristol (see entry 251). A conversation with Wordsworth
reported by Thomas Moore, 2 February 1835, records Wordsworth's view
of why Byron turned against him 'in speaking of Byron's attacks upon
himself seemed to think they all originated in something Rogers told
Byron of a letter written by him (Wordsworth) to a lady who applied
to him for contributions to some miscellany – Being in a little fit of
abstraction at the monment I did not well attend to the particulars of this
anecdote, but it seemed to imply some gratuitous mischief-making, on the
part of Rogers, that, imperfectly as I recollected the facts, I pronounced at
once that Wordsworth must have been misinformed on the subject. He

said he would ask Rogers about it & I intended to do the same, but it went out of my mind.'
(*The Journal of Thomas Moore*, ed. Wilfrid S. Dowden, 1987, 1658–59.)

---

a. From a letter to Leigh Hunt, 7 October 1815

– Pray don't make me an exception to the 'Long live King Richard' of your bards in 'the feast' – I do allow him to be 'prince of the bards of his time'[1] upon the judgment of those who must judge more impartially than I probably do. – I acknowledge him as I acknowledge the Houses of Hanover & Bourbon the – not the 'one eye'd Monarch of the blind' but the blind Monarch of the one-eyed. I merely take the liberty of a free subject to vituperate certain of his edicts – & that only in private. –

(*Byron's Letters and Journals, 1814–1815*, ed. Leslie A. Marchand, 1973, IV, 316–17)

b. From the diary of Joseph Farington, 23 October 1815

[John] Taylor told me that He frequently meets Lord Byron in the *Green Room* at Drury Lane Theatre, His Lordship being one of the super-intending Managers. Lord Byron spoke of Wordsworth as being wrapt up in self approbation as a Poet, and holding other Poets as beneath Him. On the contrary His Lordship held Southey & others in higher consideration. –

(*The Diary of Joseph Farington*, ed. Kathryn Cave, 1984, VIII, 4722)

c. From a letter to Hunt, 30 October 1815

Byron attacks Wordsworth for his poetry since *Lyrical Ballads* and for his criticism of Pope's Homer in 'Essay, Supplementary to the Preface' in *Poems* (1815).

– I take leave to differ from you on Wordsworth[2] as freely as I once agreed with you – at that time I gave him credit for promise which is unfulfilled – I still think his capacity warrants all you say of *it* only – but that his performances since 'Lyrical Ballads' – are miserably inadequate to the ability which lurks within him: – there is undoubtedly much natural talent spilt over 'the Excursion' but it is rain upon rocks where it stands & stagnates – or rain upon sands where it falls without fertilizing – who can understand him? – let those who do make him intelligible. – Jacob Behman – Swedenborg – & Joanna

Southcote are mere types of this Arch-Apostle of mystery & mysticism – but I have done: – no I have not done – for I have two petty & perhaps unworthy objections in small matters to make to him – which with his pretension to accurate observation & fury against Pope's false translation of the 'Moonlight scene in Homer'[3] I wonder he should have fallen into – these be they. – He says of Greece in the body of his book – that it is a land of

> *rivers – fertile* plains – & *sounding* shores
> Under a cope of *variegated* sky
> [*The Excursion*, PW, V, p. 131, Book IV, ll. 719–20]

The rivers are dry half the year – the plains are barren – and the shores *still* & *tideless* as the Mediterranean can make them – the Sky is anything but variegated – being for months & months – but 'darkly – deeply – beautifully blue.' – The next is in his notes – where he talks of our 'Monuments crowded together in the busy &c. of a large town' – as compared with the 'still seclusion of a Turkish cemetery in some *remote* place' – this is pure stuff – for *one* monument in our Churchyards – there are *ten* in the Turkish – & so crowded that you cannot walk between them – they are always close to the walks of the towns – that is – merely divided by a path or road – and as to '*remote* places' – men never take the trouble in a barbarous country to carry their dead very far – they must have lived near to where they are buried – there are no cemeteries in 'remote places' – except such as have the cypress & the tombstone still left when the olive & the habitation of the living have perished.[4] – These things I was struck with as coming peculiarly in my own way – and in both of these he is wrong – yet I should have noticed neither but for his attack on Pope for a like blunder – and a peevish affectation about him of despising a popularity which he will never obtain. – I write in great haste – & I doubt – *not* much to the purpose – but you have it hot & hot – just as it comes – & so let it go. – By the way – both he & you go too far against Pope's 'so when the Moon &c.' it is no translation I know – but it is not such *false* description as asserted – I have read it on the spot –

(Marchand, *op. cit.*, IV, 324–6)

d. From a letter to John Murray, 15 July 1817

Have you had no new Babe of Literature sprung up to replace the dead – the distant – the tired & the *re*tired? no prose – no verse – no *nothing*?

No infant Sotheby whose dauntless head
Translates misunderstood a deal of German;[5]
No city Wordsworth more admired than read –
No drunken Coleridge with a new 'Lay Sermon.'[6]

(*Ibid.*, V, 251–3)

e. From a letter to the same, 15 September 1817

With regard to poetry in general: I am convinced the more I think of it – that he [Moore] and *all* of us – Scott – Southey – Wordsworth – Moore – Campbell – I – are all in the wrong – one as much as another – that we are upon a wrong revolutionary poetical system – or systems – not worth a damn in itself – & from which none but Rogers and Crabbe are free – and that the present & next generations will finally be of this opinion. – I am the more confirmed in this – by having lately gone over some of our Classics – particularly *Pope* –

(*Ibid.*, V, 264–6)

f. From a letter to the same, 12 October 1817

– I leave the Irish Clergyman and the new Orator Henley[7] to battle it out between them – satisfied to have done the best I could for *both* – I may say this to *you* – who know it. – Mr. Coleridge may console himself with the 'fervour – the almost religious fervour' of his and Wordsworth's disciples as he calls it – if he means that as any proof of their merits – I will find him as much 'fervour' in behalf of Richard Brothers[8] and Joanna Southcote – as ever gathered over his pages – or round his fireside. He is a shabby fellow – and I wash my hands of, and after him. –

(*Ibid.*, V, 267–9)

g. From a letter to Thomas Moore, 1 June 1818

Byron refers to Leigh Hunt's Preface to *Foliage*, see entry 259h

– Did you read his skimble-skamble about [Wordsworth] being at the head of his own *profession*, in the *eyes* of *those* who followed it? I thought that Poetry was an *art*, or an *attribute*, and not a *profession*; – but be it one, is that * * * * * * at the head of *your* profession in *your* eyes? I'll be curst if he is of *mine*, or ever shall be. He is the only one of us (but of us he is not) whose coronation I would oppose. Let them take Scott,

Campbell, Crabbe, or you, or me, or any of the living, and throne him; –
but not this new Jacob Behmen, this ＊＊＊＊ whose pride might have kept
him true, even had his principles turned as perverted as his *soi-disant*
poetry.

(*Ibid.*, VI, 45–8)

h. From the Preface and Dedication to *Don Juan* (1818), both unpublished in Byron's lifetime

J. C. Hobhouse (1786–1869) spoke for several of Byron's friends when he urged
him not to publish any part of *Don Juan*: 'Neither Southey, Wordsworth, nor
Coleridge have any character except with their own crazy proselytes, some fifty
perhaps in number: so what harm can you do them, and what good can you do
the world by your criticism?' (Leslie A. Marchand, *Byron: A Biography*, 1957, II,
765).

From the Preface:
In a note or preface (I forget which) by Mr. W. Wordsworth to a poem,
the Subject of which, as far as it is intelligible, is the remorse of an
unnatural mother for the destruction of a natural child, the courteous
Reader is desired to extend his usual courtesy so far as to suppose that
the narrative is narrated by 'the Captain of Merchantman or small trading vessel, lately retired upon a small annuity to some inland town, etc.,
etc.' I quote from memory, but conceive the above to be the sense, as far
as there is Sense, of the note or preface to the aforesaid poem – as far as it
is a poem.

The poem, or production, to which I allude, is that which begins with
– 'There is a thorn, it is so old' – and then the Poet informs all who are
willing to be informed, that its age was such as to leave great difficulty in
the conception of its ever having been young at all – which is as much as
to say, either that it was Coeval with the Creator of all things, or that it
had been *born Old*, and was thus appropriately by antithesis devoted to
the Commemoration of a child that died young. The pond near it is
described, according to mensuration,

> I measured it from side to side:
> 'Tis three feet long, and two feet wide.

Let me be excused from being particular in the detail of such things, as
this is the Sort of writing which has superseded and degraded Pope in
the eyes of the discerning British Public; and this Man is the kind

of Poet, who, in the same manner that Joanna Southcote found many thousand people to take her Dropsy for God Almighty re-impregnated, has found some hundreds of persons to misbelieve in his insanities, and hold him out as a kind of poetical Emanuel Swedenborg – a Richard Brothers, a person Tozer – half Enthusiast and half Impostor.

This rustic Gongora and vulgar Marini of his Country's taste has long abandoned a mind capable of better things to the production of such trash as may support the reveries which he would reduce into a System of prosaic raving, that is to supersede all that hitherto by the best and wisest of our fathers has been deemed poetry, and for his success – and what mountebank will not find proselytes? (from Count Cagliostro to Madame Krudener) – he may partly thank his absurdity, and partly his having lent his more downright and unmeasured prose to the aid of a political party, which acknowledges its real weakness, though fenced with the whole armour of artificial Power, and defended by all the ingenuity of purchased Talent, in liberally rewarding with praise and pay even the meanest of its advocates. Amongst these last in self-degradation, this Thraso of poetry has long been a Gnatho in Politics, and may be met in print at some booksellers and several trunk-makers, and in person at dinner at Lord Lonsdale's.

The Reader, who has acquiesced in Mr. W. Wordsworth's supposition that his 'Misery oh Misery' is related by the 'Captain of a small, etc.,' is requested to suppose, by a like exertion of Imagination, that the following epic Narrative is told by a Spanish Gentleman in a village in the Sierra Morena in the road between Monasterio and Seville, sitting at the door of a Posada, with the Curate of the hamlet on his right hand, a Segar in his mouth, a jug of Malaga, or perhaps 'right Sherris,' before him on a small table containing the relics of an Olia Podrida: . . .

(*Byron's Don Juan*, ed. T. G. Steffan and W. W. Pratt, Edinburgh 1957, II, 3–7)

From the Dedication:

> And Wordsworth, in a rather long 'Excursion,'
>   (I think the quarto holds five hundred pages),
> Has given a sample from the vasty version
>   Of this new system to perplex the sages;
> 'Tis poetry – at least by his assertion,
>   And may appear so when the dog-star rages –
> And he who understands it would be able
> To add a story to the Tower of Babel.

You – Gentlemen! by dint of long seclusion
   From better company, have kept your own
At Keswick, and, through still continued fusion
   Of one another's minds, at last have grown
To deem as a most logical conclusion,
   That Poesy has wreaths for you alone:
There is a narrowness in such a notion,
Which makes me wish you'd change your lakes for Ocean.

I would not imitate the petty thought,
   Nor coin my self-love to so base a vice,
For all the glory your conversation brought,
   Since gold alone should not have been its price.
You have your salary; was't for that you wrought?
   And Wordsworth has his place in the Excise.
You're shabby fellows – true – but poets still,
And duly seated on the Immortal Hill.

(*Ibid.*, stanzas IV–VI)

i. From *Don Juan*, 1819

Thou shalt believe in Milton, Dryden, Pope;
   Thou shalt not set up Wordsworth, Coleridge, Southey;
Because the first is crazed beyond all hope,
   The second drunk, the third so quaint and mouthy:
With Crabbe it may be difficult to cope,
   And Campbell's Hippocrene is somewhat drouthy:
Thou shalt not steal from Samuel Rogers, nor
Commit – flirtation with the muse of Moore.

[Canto I, ccv]

'Go, little Book, from this my solitude!
   I cast thee on the waters – go thy ways!
And if – as I believe, thy vein be good,
   The World will find thee after many days.'
When Southey's read, and Wordsworth understood,
   I can't help putting in my claim to praise –
The four first rhymes are Southey's every line:
For God's sake, reader! take them not for mine.

[Canto I, ccxxii]

All are not moralists, like Southey, when
    He prated to the world of 'Pantisocracy';
Or Wordsworth unexcised, unhired, who then
    Seasoned his pedlar poems with Democracy;
Or Coleridge long before his flighty pen
    Let to the Morning Post its aristocracy;
When he and Southey, following the same path,
Espoused two partners (milliners of Bath).

Such names at present cut a convict figure,
    The very Botany Bay in moral geography;
Their loyal treason, renegado rigour,
    Are good manure for their more bare biography;
Wordsworth's last quarto, by the way, is bigger
    Than any since the birthday of typography;
A drowsy, frowzy poem, called the 'Excursion,'
Writ in a manner which is my aversion.

He there builds up a formidable dyke
    Between his own and others' intellect;
But Wordsworth's poem, and his followers, like
    Joanna Southcote's Shiloh and her sect,
Are things which in this century don't strike
    The public mind, – so few are the elect;
And the new births of both their stale Virginities
Have proved but Dropsies, taken for Divinities.
                                    [Canto III, xciii–xcv]

We learn from Horace, 'Homer sometimes sleeps;'
    We feel without him, – Wordsworth sometimes wakes, –
To show with what complacency he creeps,
    With his dear '*Waggoners*,' around his lakes.
He wishes for 'a boat' to sail the deeps –
    Of Ocean? – No, of air; and then he makes
Another outcry for 'a little boat,'
And drivels seas to set it well afloat.

If he must fain sweep o'er the ethereal plain,
    And Pegasus runs restive in his 'Waggon,'
Could he not beg the loan of Charles's Wain?
    Or pray Medea for a single dragon?

Or if, too classic for his vulgar brain,
  He feared his neck to venture such a nag on,
And he must needs mount nearer to the moon,
  Could not the blockhead ask for a balloon?

'Pedlars,' and 'Boats,' and 'Waggons!' Oh, ye shades
  Of Pope and Dryden, are we come to this?
That trash of such sort not alone evades
  Contempt, but from the bathos' vast abyss
Floats scumlike uppermost, and these Jack Cades
  Of sense and song above your graves may hiss –
The 'little boatman' and his *Peter Bell*
Can sneer at him who drew 'Achitophel'!

                                        [Canto III, xcviii–c]

j. From Byron's 'Reply to Blackwood's', Ravenna, 15 March 1820

Of the 'lofty-minded, virtuous' Wordsworth, one anecdote will suffice to speak his sincerity. In a conversation with Mr. – upon poetry, he concluded with, 'After all, I would not give five shillings for all that Southey has ever written.' Perhaps this calculation might rather show his esteem for five shillings than his low estimate of Dr. Southey; but considering that when he was in his need, and Southey had a shilling, Wordsworth is said to have had generally a sixpence out of it, it has an awkward sound in the way of valuation. This anecdote was told me by persons who, if quoted by name, would prove that its genealogy is poetical as well as true. I can give my authority for this; and am ready to adduce it also for Mr. Southey's circulation of the falsehood before mentioned.

Of Coleridge, I shall say nothing – *why*, he may divine.

I have said more of these people than I intended in this place, being somewhat stirred by the remarks which induced me to commence upon the topic. I see nothing in these men as poets, or as individuals – little in their talents, and less in their characters, to prevent honest men from expressing for them considerable contempt, in prose or rhyme, as it may happen. Mr. Southey has the *Quarterly* for his field of rejoinder, and Mr. Wordsworth his postscripts to *Lyrical Ballads*, where the two great instances of the sublime are taken from himself and Milton. 'Over her own sweet voice the stock-dove broods;' that is to say, she has the pleasure of listening to herself, in common with Mr. Wordsworth upon most of his public appearances. 'What divinity doth hedge' these persons, that we should respect them? Is it Apollo? Are they not of those who called

Dryden's *Ode* 'a drunken song?' who have discovered that Gray's *Elegy* is full of faults, (see Coleridge's *Life*, vol. i. *note*, for Wordsworth's kindness in pointing this out to him,) and have published what is allowed to be the very worst prose that ever was written, to prove that Pope was no poet, and that William Wordsworth is?

....

At the same time Mr. Southey was favouring the public with *Wat Tyler* and *Joan of Arc*, to the great glory of the Drama and Epos. I beg pardon, *Wat Tyler*, with *Peter Bell*, was still in MS., and it was not till after Mr. Southey had received his Malmsey butt, and Mr. Wordsworth* became qualified to gauge it, that the great revolutionary tragedy came before the public and the Court of Chancery. Wordsworth was peddling his lyrical ballads, and brooding a preface, to be succeeded in due course by a postscript, both couched in such prose as must give peculiar delight to those who have read the prefaces of Pope and Dryden; scarcely less celebrated for the beauty of their prose, than for the charms of their verse.

Wordsworth is the reverse of Molière's gentleman who had been 'talking prose all his life, without knowing it;' for he thinks that he has been all his life writing both prose and verse, and neither of what he conceives to be such can be properly said to be either one or the other . . .

These three personages, Southey, Wordsworth, and Coleridge, had all of them a very natural antipathy to Pope; and I respect them for it, as the only original feeling or principle which they have contrived to preserve . . .

. . . A paper of the *Connoisseur* says, that 'it is observed by the French, that a cat, a priest, and an old woman, are sufficient to constitute a religious sect in England.' The same number of animals, with some difference in kind, will suffice for a poetical one. If we take Sir George Beaumont instead of the priest, and Mr. Wordsworth for the old woman, we shall nearly complete the quota required; but I fear that Mr. Southey will but indifferently represent the CAT, having shown himself but too distinctly to be of a species to which that noble creature is peculiarly hostile.

---

* Goldsmith has anticipated the definition of the Lake poetry, as far as such things can be defined. 'Gentlemen, the present piece is not of your *common epic poems*, which come from the press like paper kites in summer; there are none of your Turnuses or Didos in it; *it is an historical description of nature.* I only beg you'll endeavour to make your souls in unison with mine, *and hear with the same enthusiasm with which I have written.*' Would not this have made a proper proem to the *Excursion*, and the poet and his pedler? It would have answered perfectly for that purpose, had it not unfortunately been written in good English

Nevertheless, I will not go so far as Wordsworth in his postscript, who pretends that *no* great poet ever had immediate fame; which being interpreted, means that William Wordsworth is not quite so much read by his cotemporaries as might be desirable. This assertion is as false as it is foolish. Homer's glory depended upon his present popularity . . .

. . . Ariosto was permitted to pass free by the public robber who had read the *Orlando Furioso*. I would not recommend Mr. Wordsworth to try the same experiment with his *Smugglers* . . .

There will be found as comfortable metaphysics, and ten times more poetry in the *Essay on Man*, than in the *Excursion* . . .

(*Works of Lord Byron*, ed. R. E. Prothero, 1904, IV, 474–95)

k. 'Epilogue', a parody of the beginning of *Peter Bell* scribbled in the margin of Byron's copy of the poem and dated, Ravenna, 22 March 1820

> THERE's something in a stupid ass;
> And something in a heavy dunce;
>   But never since I went to school
>   I heard or saw so damned a fool
> As William Wordsworth is for once.
>
> And now I've seen so great a fool
> As William Wordsworth is for once;
>   I really wish that Peter Bell
>   And he who wrote it, were in hell,
> For writing nonsense for the nonce.
>
> I saw the 'light in ninety-eight,'
>   Sweet Babe of one-and-twenty years!
> And then he gave it to the nation,
>   And deems himself of Shakspeare's Peers.
> He gives the perfect works to light!
>   William Wordsworth – if I might advise:
> Content you with the praise you get,
> From Sir George Beaumont, Baronet,
>   And with your place in the Excise.

(W. Hamilton, *Some Parodies of the Works of English and American Writers*, 1888, V, 105)

l. From a letter to John Murray, 23 April 1820

– I have erased the six stanzas about those two impostors Southey and Wordsworth – (which I suppose will give you great pleasure) but I can do no more – I can neither recast – nor replace – but I give you leave to put it all in the fire if you like – or *not* to publish – and I think that's sufficient; . . .

– I love Scott and Moore – and all the better brethren – but I hate & abhor that puddle of water-worms – whom you have taken into your troop in the *history*[9] line I see. –

(Marchand, *op. cit.*, VII, 82–3)

m. From a letter to the same, 12 August 1820

. . . – but no *more modern* poesy – I pray – neither Mrs. Hewoman's – nor any female or male Tadpole of Poet Turdsworth's – nor any of his ragamuffins. –

(*Ibid.*, VII, 158)

n. From a letter to Douglas Kinnaird, 31 August 1820

Murray has the play – which is at least as good as Mr. Turdsworth's Peter Bell.

(*Ibid.*, VII, 167)

o. From a letter to Murray, 31 August 1820

. . . I believe that (except Milman perhaps) I am still the youngest of the fifteen hundred first of living poets – as Wm Turdsworth is the oldest –

(*Ibid.*, VII, 168–9)

p. From a letter to Francis Hodgson, 22 December 1820

The Scoundrels of Scribblers are trying to run down *Pope*, but I hope in vain. It is my intention to take up the Cudgels in that controversy, and to do my best to keep the Swan of Thames in his true place. This comes of Southey and Turdsworth and such renegado rascals with their systems. I hope you will not be silent; it is the common concern of all men of common sense, imagination, and a musical ear.

(*Ibid.*, VII, 252–3)

q. **Extracts from Byron's controversy with W. L. Bowles on the merits of Pope, written Ravenna, 25 March 1821**

. . . In the present rank fertility of 'great poets of the age,' and 'schools of poetry' – a word which, like 'schools of eloquence' and of 'philosophy,' is never introduced till the decay of the art has increased with the number of its professors – in the present day, then, there have sprung up two sorts of Naturals; – the Lakers, who whine about Nature because they live in Cumberland; and their *under-sect* (which some one has maliciously called the 'Cockney School'), who are enthusiastical for the country because they live in London. It is to be observed, that the rustical founders are rather anxious to disclaim any connexion with their metropolitan followers, whom they ungraciously review, and call cockneys, atheists, foolish fellows, bad writers, and other hard names not less ungrateful than unjust. I can understand the pretensions of the aquatic gentlemen of Windermere to what Mr. Braham terms '*entusymusy*,' for lakes, and mountains, and daffodils, and buttercups; but I should be glad to be apprized of the foundation of the London propensities of their imitative brethren to the same 'high argument.' Southey, Wordsworth, and Coleridge have rambled over half Europe, and seen Nature in most of her varieties (although I think that they have occasionally not used her very well); but what on earth – of earth, and sea, and Nature – have the others seen? Not a half, nor a tenth part so much as Pope. While they sneer at his Windsor Forest, have they ever seen any thing of Windsor except its *brick*?

. . .

The grand distinction of the under forms of the new school of poets is their *vulgarity*. By this I do not mean that they are *coarse*, but 'shabby-genteel,' as it is termed. A man may be *coarse* and yet not *vulgar*, and the reverse. Burns is often coarse, but never *vulgar*. Chatterton is never vulgar, nor Wordsworth, nor the higher of the Lake school, though they treat of low life in all its branches. It is in their *finery* that the new under school are *most* vulgar, and they may be known by this at once; as what we called at Harrow 'a Sunday blood' might be easily distinguished from a gentleman, although his clothes might be the better cut, and his boots the best blackened, of the two: – probably because he made the one, or cleaned the other, with his own hands.

(Prothero, *op. cit.*, V, 522–92)

r. Thomas Medwin (1788–1869) records a conversation with Byron, which must have taken place in late 1821, or 1822

Byron, not having read *Peter Bell*, is understandably inaccurate about it, and Wordsworth, of course, had never been associated with Pantisocracy.

I said to him, 'You are accused of owing a great deal to Wordsworth. Certainly there are some stanzas in the Third Canto of "Childe Harold" that smell strongly of the Lakes: for instance –

> "I live not in myself, but I become
> Portion of that around me; – and to me
> High mountains are a feeling!"'

'Very possibly,' replied he. 'Shelley, when I was in Switzerland, used to dose me with Wordsworth physic even to nausea; and I do remember then reading some things of his with pleasure. He had once a feeling of Nature, which he carried almost to a deification of it: – that's why Shelley liked his poetry.

'It is satisfactory to reflect, that where a man becomes a hireling and loses his mental independence, he loses also the faculty of writing well. The lyrical ballads, jacobinical and puling with affectation of simplicity as they were, had undoubtedly a certain merit*: and Wordsworth, though occasionally a writer for the nursery masters and misses,

> "Who took their little porringer,
> And ate their porridge there,"

now and then expressed ideas worth imitating; but, like brother Southey, he had his price; and since he is turned tax-gatherer, is only fit to rhyme about asses and waggoners. Shelley repeated to me the other day a stanza from 'Peter Bell' that I thought inimitably good. It is the rumination of Peter's ass, who gets into a brook, and sees reflected there a family circle, or tea-party. But you shall have it in his own words:

---

*   Or Wordsworth unexcised, unhired, who *then*
                Season'd his pedlar poems with democracy.
                      Don Juan, Canto III. Stanza 93.

"Is it a party in a parlour,
Cramm'd just as you on earth are cramm'd?
Some sipping punch, some sipping tea,
And every one, as you may see,
All silent and all d——d!"
[*Peter Bell*, 11. 515/6, misquoted: the stanza used by Shelley
as the motto for his *Peter Bell the Third*.]

There was a time when he would have written better; but perhaps Peter thinks feelingly.

'The republican trio, when they began to publish in common, were to have had a community of all things, like the ancient Britons; to have lived in a state of nature, like savages, and peopled some "island of the blest" with children in common, like ——. A very pretty Arcadian notion! It amuses me much to compare the Botany Bay Eclogues, the Panegyric of Martin the Regicide, and "Wat Tyler," with the Laureate Odes, and Peter's Eulogium on the Field of Waterloo. There is something more than rhyme in that noted stanza containing

"Carnage is God's daughter!"* –

(*Conversations of Lord Byron . . . at Pisa . . . 1821 and 1822.* A new edition, 1824, 236–9)

EDITOR'S NOTES

1. See Leigh Hunt, *The Feast of Poets*, 1815.
2. See Hunt, *ibid.*, particularly the Preface, (see entry 259a).
3. Pope's *Iliad*, VIII, ll. 687–98.
4. In an 'Essay upon Epitaphs' added to the notes in the first edition of *The Excursion*, Wordsworth says: 'Let a man only compare in imagination the unsightly manner in which our Monuments are crowded together in the busy, noisy, unclean, and almost grassless Church-yard of a large Town, with the still seclusion of a Turkish Cemetery, in some remote place . . .'
5. Sotheby's translation of Wieland's *Oberon*, 1798.
6. Coleridge first 'Lay Sermon', *The Statesman's Manual*, was published in 1816: the second, *On the Existing Distresses and Discontents*, appeared in 1817.
7. Byron compared Coleridge to John Henley whom Pope had ridiculed as 'Zany of thy age' (*Dunciad*, Book III, l. 206).
8. Richard Brothers (1757–1824) believed that, in 1795, he was to be revealed

* Wordsworth's *Thanksgiving Ode*.

910

to be Prince of the Hebrews and ruler of the world. He was arrested and confined as a lunatic.

9. Probably Southey's *History of the Peninsular War*, first volume published December 1822, though dated 1823.

258. Benjamin Robert Haydon (1786–1846)

Letters and extracts from his diary, 1815–1817

Haydon was a painter and diarist. His comments are often extreme but, despite the neurotic contradictions, his opinions accumulate into a major statement. Haydon is constantly trying to place, without separating them, both the artist and the man. Until 1820 there is admiration; with Wordsworth's refusal in that year to lend him money, resentment grew and culminated in the passionate outburst of 1824; the relationship was restored in 1831; in 1842 there is an Indian summer of affection; in 1845 there came an ironic note, a Browningesque indictment that perhaps 'for a handful of silver he left us'.

In his Diary Haydon often records the vivid fragmentary opinions of others.

a. Diary entry, 13 June 1815

Haydon, through Sir George Beaumont, had recently met Wordsworth, in May 1815.

I had a cast made yesterday of Wordsworth's face. He bore it like a philosopher. [John] Scott was to meet him at Breakfast. Just as he came in the Plaister was covered over. Wordsworth was sitting in the other room in my dressing gown, with his hands folded, sedate, steady, & solemn. I stepped in to Scott, & told him as a curiosity to take a peep, that he might say the first sight he ever had of so great a poet was such a singular one as this.

I opened the door slowly, & there he sat innocent & unconscious of our plot against his dignity, unable to see or to speak, with all the mysterious silence of a spirit.

When he was relieved he came into breakfast with his usual cheerfulness, and delighted & awed us by his illustrations & bursts of inspiration. At one time he shook us both in explaining the principles of his system, his views of man, & his objects in writing.

911

Wordsworth's faculty is describing all these intense feelings & glimmerings & doubts & fears & hopes of Man, as referring to what he might be before he was born & to what he may be hereafter. He is a great Being, and will hereafter be ranked as one who had *a portion* of the spirit of Homer, Virgil, Dante, Tasso, Shakespeare, Chaucer & Milton, but as one who did not possess the power of wielding these feelings to any other purpose but as referring to himself and as wishing to make others feel by personal sympathy. This is, in my opinion, his great characteristic distinction.

We afterwards called on Hunt, and as Hunt had previously attacked him & has now reformed in his opinions, the meeting was interesting. Hunt paid him the highest compliments, & told him that as he grew wiser & got older he found his respect for his powers & enthusiasm for his genius encrease. Hunt was ill or it would have been his place to call on Wordsworth. Here again he really burst forth with burning feelings & I never saw him so eloquent as today.

I afterwards sauntered along to Hampstead with him with great delight. Never did any Man so beguile the time as Wordsworth. His purity of heart, his kind affections, his soundness of principle, his information, his knowledge, his genius, & the intense & eager feelings with which he pours forth all he knows affect, enchant, interest & delight one. I don't know any man I should be so inclined to worship as a purified being . . .

Wordsworth is original surely on this principle – he has one part (& perhaps the finest) of the genius of the great but he has not all. He has not the lucidus ordo [clearness of order]; he does not curb, direct his inspirations for a positive moral, but leaves them to be felt only by those who have a capacity to feel with equal intensity. The moral is not obvious, only the feeling; but he that can feel the feeling will feel the moral too.

(*The Diary of Benjamin Robert Haydon*, ed. W. B. Pope, Harvard, 1960, I, 450–2)

b. From a letter to Wordsworth, 29 December 1815

Wordsworth, on 21 December, had sent Haydon a letter containing copies of three recently composed sonnets, one of them addressed to the painter, 'High is our calling, Friend'.

Since the Freedom of my native Town was voted me in honor of Solomon I have never been so shaken as I was, on reading your exquisite Sonnetts;

the last is the highest honor that ever was payed or ever can be payed to me; reflect what I must feel, my dear Sir, when the first effusion of Poetry, that was ever addressed to me has been addressed by our greatest Poet – I declare to you I was so affected on recognising the feelings of my own bosom so sublimely put forth, that I felt as if they had been reech-oed by some inspired being to stimulate & encourage me – your writing me such a fine thing is a proof you think I deserve it, and be assured that I will continue by the greatest efforts, and most invincible constancy, to render myself daily more worthy of such a high honor–I have felt melan-choly ever since, as if I was elevated so exceedingly, with such a drunken humming in my brain, that my nature took refuge in acquired humble-ness and gratitude to God. This Year has been to me a Year of glorious retribution – without any effort on my part, my miseries have been redressed, my talents acknowledged, and my great object advanced and just as the winding up comes a Sonnet from you to carry me to the conclusion of it with glory – You are the first English Poet that has done compleat justice to my delightful art – never was so just & true a compliment paid to it in English verse before as

> Whether the instrument of words she use
> Or Pencil, pregnant with etherial hues

This is the truth; Every other Poet has shown a thorough ignorance of its nature before – seeming not to know that the mind was the source the means only different – If for this only, you will have the gratitude of every Painter; – Indeed I cannot say to you – My dear Sir enough about them, I let [John] Scott read them, and he was exceedingly affected, and thought them what they are, some of your finest and worthy of Milton though completely your own – a heart

> Tho sensitive, yet in the weakest part
> Heroically fashioned – to infuse
> *Faith* in the whispers of the lonely muse –

This went to my heart strings – how often have I leaning over a fire nearly out – with my Picture before me untouched for the day, for want of money to pay a model – how often for a short time have misgivings made my heart sink, and then has something made me start, I have felt as if a superior being had reflected a beam of light from a ball into my very marrow, and I have had a sensitive ring through my frame as if something had whispered 'Go on' inside my bosom – Eleven years and a half ago, the very first Sunday after I left my Father and arrived in

913

Town, I went to the new Church in the Strand, with the most awful feeling, and kneeling I prayed God to bless my exersions, to grant I might reform the taste of my Country, to grant that before thirty I might be at the head of my Art, and to grant no obstructions however great, might stop me, but that I might sacrifice myself with delight, if requisite – Constantly has this assisted me, – and judge my dearest Sir, of my intense feeling, to find you so grandly put forth all the secrets of my soul – I had reverence for your inspiration before, I now revere you with sympathy – God bless you forever, and grant that the World may be enlightened to feel the intensity of your Poetry and do you full and ample justice before you leave it – I will keep them as long as the materials will last, and then artificial means shall preserve them like an ancient manuscript – If I could express myself twenty times as strong I would, to convey you my sensations –

(Ms. The Wordsworth Library)

c. From a letter to Sir George Beaumont, 21 January 1816

Could a distrust of my powers have urged me to begin a picture larger than the one that failed, and to have brought the world again in my favour? Perhaps you know the 'Happy Warrior?' In that sublime sonnet my principles are breathed in every line –

> Who is the Happy Warrior? Who is he
> Whom every man in arms should wish to be?
> It is the generous spirit, who, when brought
> Among the tasks of real life, hath wrought
> Upon the plan that pleased his childish thought.
> Whose high endeavours are an inward light
> That make the path before him always bright;
> Who, with a natural instinct to discern
> What knowledge can perform, is diligent to learn.
> ['Character of the Happy Warrior' *PW*, IV, pp. 86–8, ll. 1–9]

>   * * * * *

> Who comprehends his trust, and to the same
> Keeps faithful with a singleness of aim;
> And therefore does not stoop, nor lie in wait
> For wealth, or honours, or for worldly state.
> [Ibid., ll. 39–42]

914

*   *   *   *   *

Who, whether praise of him must walk the earth
For ever, and to noble deeds give birth,
Or he must go to dust without his fame,
And leave a dead unprofitable name,
Finds comfort in himself and in his cause.

[*Ibid.*, ll. 77–81]

Oh Wordsworth, it is impossible for me to express the delight I have experienced, and the gratitude I feel to you for the effusions of your sublime spirit: they have supported and inspired me when even my nature tended to suspect my enemies might be right, and the aspirations of my heart mere delusion! They have indeed never failed to inspire –

Faith in the whispers of the lonely muse
When the whole world seem adverse to desert.

['High is our calling, Friend', ll. 7–8]

(*B. R. Haydon: Correspondence and Table Talk*, ed. F. W. Haydon, 1876, I, 295)

d. From a letter to Wordsworth, 18 November 1816

If you remember my dear Sir, at the time you breakfasted with me you gave [John] Scott and I an account of the scope of your intentions with regard to the Recluse – I yet remember how I was affected at your powerful description, and Scott and I have often talked of it, with great delight – You would do me the greatest favour if you would write me, what you then said – it appeared to me at the time as grand an intention as ever entered the conception of any Poet, and it would be a memento I would keep as long as I breath, if you would so honour me as I have requested – now do not hesitate, but let the next letter you write me be a full exposition of your feelings, of your intentions and a full development of your plan, with respect to that sublime Poem –

(Ms. The Wordsworth Library)

e. 31 December 1816

Haydon sent Wordsworth Keats's admiring sonnet, 'Great spirits now on Earth are sojourning', see entry 263a.

f. From a letter to Wordsworth, 15 April 1817

Haydon attempts to explain the attacks of Hazlitt and Leigh Hunt, particularly in *The Examiner*. Haydon's own position at this stage was close to that of John Scott, editor of *The Champion*.

With respect to Haslitt [*sic*], I think his motives are easily enough disernible had you condescended to visit him, when he praised your excursion just before you came to Town his vanity would have been soothed & his virulence softened – he was conscious from what an emergency you had helped to rescue him – he was conscious of his conduct while in your neighbourhood – and then your taking no notice of his praise, added to his acid feelings – I see him scarcely ever and then not at my own house – But Leigh Hunt's weathercock estimation of you I cannot account for, nor is it worthwhile to attempt it – He first attacks you when he had never read you, then a friend (M^r. Barnes) Brought him your Excursion pointed out your Sonnets and he began to find really that he should have looked through a Poets Works before he came to a conclusion on the genius displayed in them – he then recanted – When you were in town you visited him – you remember what he said with an agitated mouth – 'The longer I live, and the older I grow, I feel my respect for your Genius increase, Sir'. These were *his* words – Before a month was over – I again percieved doubt & hums, and ha's, instead of the momentary enthusiasm for you displayed for about that time – Scott and I and all his Friends accounted for it in the usual way – knowing he never holds one opinion one month he does not sophisticate himself out of before the next is over – You explained your political principles to him, & he said he was satisfied – I think you did a great deal too much – When first I knew Leigh Hunt, he was really, a delightful fellow, ardent in virtue & perceiving the right thing – in everything but Religion – he now finds no 'end in wond'ring mazes lost' perplexes himself, and pains his Friends – his great error is inordinate personal vanity & he who pampers it not is no longer received with affection – I am daily getting more estranged from him – and indeed all his old Friends are dropping off – John H[unt] is truly a noble character – it was for him I got th[e] drawings to have a bust made of you – it was made in clay, and he has a cast – but when you [come] to Town, a young Sculptor will make for us a real bust from the life –

(Ms. The Wordsworth Library)

g. Haydon compares Wordsworth with Shakespeare and Milton, 22 December 1817

Wordsworth sat to me today & I began to put his head into my Picture. He read all the book of 'Despondence Corrected' in his Excursion in the finest manner.

Wordsworth's great power is an intense perception of human feelings regarding the mystery of things by analyzing his own, Shakespeare's an intense power of laying open the heart & mind of man by analyzing the feelings of others acting on themselves. The moral in Shakespeare is inferred from the consequences of conduct, that of Wordsworth is enforced by a previous devellopement of Duty. Shakespeare is the organ of Nature; Wordsworth of Piety, Religion, & Virtue. Wordsworth lays down the duty of man, from which to swerve is to do wrong. Shakespeare has no moral code, and only leaves it at the option of all how to act by shewing the consequences of such & such conduct in acting. Wordsworth tries to render agreable all that hitherto has alarmed the World, by shewing that Death, the Grave, futurity are the penalties only to go to a happier existence. Shakespeare seems reckless of any principles of guidance. He takes futurity, Death, & the Grave as materials to act on his different characters, and tho' one may be horrified one moment in reading what Claudio says of Death,[1] we may be reconciled the next by attending to what the Duke has said of Life,[2] and be uncertain which to believe, and leave off in intense and painful distraction.

In grief & the troubles of life Shakespeare solaces by our finding similar feelings displayed by others in similar situations; that is sympathy. In Grief & in misery the comfort & consolation Wordsworth affords is by consolidating the hopes & glimmerings man has from a higher power into a clear & perceptible reality. What we hope he assures us of. What we fear he exhibits without apprehension; of what we have a horror he reconciles us to, by setting it before us with other associations. Wordsworth is the Apostolic Poet of Piety & Pure thoughts, and Shakespeare, dear Shakespeare, the organ of nature herself, with all her follies & captivations & beauties & vices. Wordsworth's feelings are exclusive, because his intensity of purpose is so strong. His object is to reform the World, by pointing out to it how it *ought to be*; Shakespeare to delight it, by shewing Nature herself how she is. It would be the height of absurdity to say that the Power of dear Shakespeare, in its infinite variety, does not entitle him to the highest place over all Poets, but in moral scope & height of purpose, Milton & Wordsworth have greater intention &

nobler views than Shakespeare has shewn; take any one power separately
& compare it with theirs. They have *but one*, but that one is the highest
on Earth; it is to guide Man to deserving, endless happiness in futurity.

(*Diary of Benjamin Robert Haydon*, op. cit., II, 171–2)

h. From Haydon's Diary, 28 December 1817

This is the most immediate and the fullest account of a famous gathering.
Haydon later, in 1824 and 1842, added to and varied details of the scene; his
footnotes indicate and his letters suggest that he more than once reread this
entry, and the dinner was to become for him the point marking Wordsworth's
fall in his estimation.

The 'Friend' was Thomas Monkhouse (1783–1825). Lamb's allusion to
Wordsworth's calling Voltaire a 'dull fellow' must be to the lines on 'a novel of
Voltaire' in *The Excursion* (II. ll. 484–6), 'this dull product of a scoffer's pen . . .'.
Joseph Ritchie died in Libya in 1819, aged 31. The 'Comptroller of the Stamp
Office' was John Kingstone, deputy comptroller. Landseer (1769–1852) was the
father of three boys who were then Haydon's pupils: Edwin became the best
known.

Wordsworth dined with me; Keats & Lamb with a Friend made up the
dinner party, and a very pleasant party we had. Wordsworth was in fine
and powerful cue. We had a glorious set to on Homer, Shakespeare,
Milton, & Virgil. Lamb got excessively merry and witty, and his fun in
the intervals of Wordsworth's deep & solemn intonations of oratory was
the fun & wit of the fool in the intervals of Lear's passion. Lamb soon
gets tipsey, and tipsey he got very shortly, to our infinite amusement.
'Now, you rascally Lake Poet,' said Lamb, 'you call Voltaire a dull fellow.'
We all agreed there was a state of mind when he would appear so – and
'Well let us drink his health,' said Lamb. 'Here's Voltaire, the Messiah of
the French nation, & a very fit one.'

He then attacked me for putting in Newton, 'a Fellow who believed
nothing unless it was as clear as the three sides of a triangle.' And then he
& Keats agreed he had destroyed all the Poetry of the rainbow, by
reducing it to a prism. It was impossible to resist them, and we drank
'Newton's health, and confusion to mathematics!' It was delightful to see
the good Humour of Wordsworth in giving in to all our frolics without
affectation and laughing as heartily as the best of us.

By this time other visitors began to drop in, & a Mr. Ritchie, who is
going to penetrate into the interior of Africa. I introduced him to
Wordsworth as such, & the conversation got into a new train. After

some time Lamb, who had seemingly paid no attention to any one, suddenly opened his eyes and said, alluding to the dangers of penetrating into the interior of Africa, 'and pray, who is the Gentleman we are going *to lose?*' Here was a roar of laughter, the *victim* Ritchie joining with us.

We now retired to Tea, and among other Friends, a Gentleman who was *comptroller of the Stamp Office* came. He had been peculiarly anxious to know & see Wordsworth. The moment he was introduced he let Wordsworth know *who* he officially was. This was an exquisite touch of human Nature. Tho' Wordsworth of course would not have suffered him to speak indecently or impiously without reproof, yet he had a visible effect on Wordsworth. I felt pain at the slavery of office. In command men are despotic, and those who are dependent on others who have despotic controul must & do feel affected by their presence. The Comptroller was a very mild & nice fellow but rather weak & very fond of talking. He got into conversation with Wordsworth on Poetry, and just after he had been putting forth some of his silly stuff, Lamb, who had been dozing as usual, suddenly opened his mouth and said, 'What did you say, Sir?' 'Why, Sir,' said the Comptroller, in his milk & water insipidity, 'I was saying &c., &c., &c.' 'Do you say so, Sir?' 'Yes, Sir,' was the reply. 'Why then, Sir, I say, hiccup, you are – you are a silly fellow.' This operated like thunder! The Comptroller knew nothing of his previous tipsiness & looked at him like a man bewildered. The venerable anxiety of Wordsworth to prevent the Comptroller being angry, and his expostulations with Lamb, who had sunk back again into his doze, as insensible to the confusion he had produced as a being above it; the astonishment of Landseer the Engraver, who was totally deaf, & with his hand to his ear & his eye was trying to catch the meaning of the gestures he saw; & the agonizing attempts of Keats, Ritchie, & I to suppress our laughter; and the smiling struggle of the Comptroller to take all in good part, without losing his dignity, made up a story of comic expressions totally unrivalled in Nature. I felt pain that such a Poet as Wordsworth should be under the supervisorship of such a being as this Comptroller. The People of England have a horror of Office, an instinct against it. They are right. A man's liberty is gone the moment he becomes official; he is the Slave of Superiors, and makes others slaves to him. The Comptroller went on making his profound remarks, and when any thing very *deep* came forth,* Lamb roared out,

---

* Such as 'Pray, Sir, don't you think Milton a very *great genius?*' This I really recollect. 1823.

> Diddle iddle don
> My son John
> Went to bed with his breeches on
> One stocking off & one stocking on,
> My son John.

The Comptroller laughed as if he marked it, & went on; every remark Lamb chorused with

> Went to bed with his breeches on
> Diddle iddle on.

There is no describing this scene adequately. There was not the restraint of refined company, nor the vulgar freedom of low, but a frank, natural license, such as one sees in an act of Shakespeare, every man expressing his natural emotions without fear. Into this company, a little heated with wine, & Comptroller of the Stamp Office walked, frilled, dressed, & official, with a due awe of the powers above him and a due contempt for those beneath him. His astonishment at finding where he was come cannot be conceived, and in the midst of his mild namby pamby opinions, Lamb's address deadened his views. When they separated, Wordsworth softened his feelings, but Lamb kept saying in the Painting [room], 'Who is that fellow? Let me go & hold the candle once more to his face –

> My son John
> Went to bed with his breeches on –

& these were the last words of C. Lamb. The door was closed upon him. There was something interesting in seeing Wordsworth sitting, & Keats & Lamb, & my Picture of Christ's entry towering up behind them, occasionally brightened by the gleams of flame that sparkled from the fire, & hearing the voice of Wordsworth repeating Milton with an intonation like the funeral bell of St Paul's & the music of Handel mingled, & then Lamb's wit came sparkling in between, & Keats's rich fancy of Satyrs & Fauns & doves & white clouds, wound up the stream of conversation. I never passed a more delightful day, & I am convinced that nothing in Boswell is equal to what came out from these Poets. Indeed there were no such Poets in his time. It was an evening worthy of the Elizabethan age, and will long flash upon 'that inward eye which is the bliss of Solitude.' Hail & farewell!*

---

* Since writing this, poor Ritchie is dead! He died on this route 1819. Lamb's feeling was prophetic.

Keats too is gone! How one ought to treasure such evenings, when life gives us so few of them. 1823, Nov.

Lamb is gone too! Monkhouse, the other Friend, is gone. Wordsworth & I alone remain of the party. If the Comptroller lives I know not. Jany. 24, 1837.

[*Ibid.*, 173–6]

i. From a letter to Wordsworth, 12 September 1818

How do you do, my dear Sir, with the Recluse? I hope these abominable politics will no longer interfere with your Poetry – I am very anxious that this Poem should be all arranged and put out of the way of accident – or Death. – Keates has been in your neighbourhood lately – and called upon you – but you were not at home.

(Ms. The Wordsworth Library)

j. From a letter to Wordsworth, 20 April 1820

I received your last Volume of Duddon river &c last night for which and for all your kind remembrances of me my dear Sir accept my sincere thanks – there are things in it as fine or perhaps finer than in any of your other works.

> We men, who in our morn of youth defied
> The elements, must vanish – be it so!
> Enough, if something from our hands have power
> To live, and act, and serve the future hour.

This is my favourite bit in the whole volume – and what I have been thundering in my painting room and in the fields, ever since I have read it –

(Ms. The Wordsworth Library)

EDITOR'S NOTES

1. See *Measure for Measure*, III, i, 118–31.
2. *Ibid.*, III, i, 5–41.

259. Leigh Hunt

Letters and writings 1814–1818, including reminiscences from
Henry Crabb Robinson, Benjamin Robert Haydon and John Scott

a. From the Preface to the second edition of the *Feast of Poets*, dated 11 July 1815

As to the principal poet alluded to, the Author does not scruple to
confess, that his admiration of him has become greater and greater
between every publication of 'The Feast of the Poets.' He has become a
convert, not indeed to what he still considers as his faults, but, to use a
favourite phrase of these times, to the 'immense majority' of his beauties;
– and here, it seems to him, lies the great mistake, which certain intelligent critics persist in sharing with others of a very different description.
It is to be observed, by the way, that the defects of Mr. Wordsworth are
the result of theory, not incapacity; and it is with their particular effect
on those most calculated to understand him that we quarrel, rather than
with any thing else. But taking him as a mere author to be criticised, the
writers in question seem to regard him as a stringer of puerilities, who
has so many faults that you can only wonder now and then at his beauties; whereas the proper idea of him is that of a noble poet, who has so
many beauties that you are only apt now and then, perhaps with no very
great wisdom, to grow impatient at his faults.

b. Henry Crabb Robinson. From entry in his Diary, 8 December 1814

Despite the new admiration for Wordsworth, Hunt, at least initially, was quite
unable to like the *Excursion*. Thomas Barnes (see entry 135), formerly a schoolfellow and still a close friend of Hunt's, discussed his sensitivity with Crabb
Robinson who recorded the following in his Diary.

Hunt has been so put out of sorts by Wordsworth's *Excursion* that it
makes him uncomfortable to hear it mentioned in company, and his
friends therefore avoid the subject out of tenderness to him. Hunt at first
ridiculed Wordsworth as a contemptible writer; then he mingled warm
praise with reproof, and now he dislikes his great poem so much that,
probably because he is dissatisfied with his own sentiment and dares not
avow it, he is made unwell by hearing it mentioned.

(*Henry Crabb Robinson on Books and their Writers*, ed. Edith J. Morley, 1938, I, 156)

c. Letter to Wordsworth, 28 May 1815

Hunt however had told Henry Brougham (probably before the appearance of the *Excursion*) that he admired Wordsworth's poetry, and Wordsworth, hearing of this, sent him his *Poems* (1815) (see *MY*, II, 195). Hunt acknowledged the gift in a letter of 28 May 1815:

Whatever may be the objections, which I have ventured to make to some parts of your poetical theory, & which perhaps will not exist with persons who felt your poetry less than myself, I am known for one of the most ardent of your general admirers, & even hope that I have not been altogether uninstrumental in procuring you some, who knew as little of you at first as I did. My objections, such as they are, still exist; but my admiration has been increased since the publication of the Excursion, & I have been delaying [fro]m day to day in hopes of sending you the second edition of a little work which [I publishe]d last year, & which contains a suitable increase in its mention of you. [Illness?] however, as well as the habit of delay, has hitherto prevented me; & [I can] no longer, in decency, omit to return you some acknowledgement for your [? two v]olumes of poems. When I send you the book I allude to, you will also receive the first edition of it, together with a publication in which it had p[revi]ously appeared in a lesser shape; for you will thus see how you have g[rown] upon me in proportion to my own knowledge & experience; nor should I chuse in justice to my own feelings, erroneous or otherwise, to disguise from you anything I have said.

(Ms. The Wordsworth Library)

d. Benjamin Robert Haydon. Letter to Wordsworth, 27 November 1815

Leigh Hunt thought he *might* try to bring Byron and Wordsworth together at dinner in early June 1815. Thomas Barnes, knowing that Wordsworth was against Byron's poetry, reluctantly advised against it. Hunt met Wordsworth on 11 June, the day on which Hazlitt's first attack appeared in the *Examiner*. Hunt disclaimed Hazlitt's article. (For an account of their conversation see Haydon letter, 258a). There was no break until 1816.

Leigh Hunt's respect for you seems to increase daily. His Brother it is who has had your bust made.

(Ms. The Wordsworth Library)

e. Unsigned article. *The Examiner*, 18 February 1816, 97–9

Yet a critical note (seconding the barbed asides of Hazlitt in the *Examiner* for June, August and December 1815, see entries 256a, 256c, 256d, 256e) appears to sound again in Hunt's writing, with Wordsworth's publication of the three patriotic sonnets on the victory at Waterloo. These sonnets were printed in John Scott's paper, The *Champion*, on 4 February, 1816. Hunt commented on them sharply in this unsigned article.

HEAVEN MADE A PARTY TO EARTHLY DISPUTES – MR. WORDSWORTH'S SONNETS ON WATERLOO.

The reader will be good enough to consider the following extracts and the comments on them as appendages to what we said in our last respecting the Holy Alliance, and the making Heaven a party to earthly disputes. We make no apology to him for introducing criticism on verses among our political articles. Poetry has often been made the direct vehicle of politics. To go up to very lofty authority, both HOMER and VIRGIL are supposed to have had political designs in their great poems; – TYRTÆUS fairly beat up for recruits with lyre, instead of drum; – DANTE was not content with sending his political adversaries to the devil rhetorically, but fairly disposed them about the dominions of that personage; – MILTON, besides his political sonnets, took an opportunity in his *Paradise Lost* of insinuating some lessons to Kings, which it might not be amiss to recollect now-a-days*; – the poetical wits of their respective ages, the ANDREW MARVELLS, DRYDENS, THOMAS MOORES, have most of them done great as well as lively service to their respective political creeds; – in short, not to heap up precedents, the state of existing European intellect, which we have so often described of late as opposed to the violated promises of the Allies, renders it a matter of curiosity to know what can be said on their side of the question, that has any thing intellectual to boast of.

It would be well indeed for them if the writer, whom we are about to notice, were entirely on their side; for whatever theoretical faults he may have in his productions, and however little he may be appreciated for the beauties they possess, having had the misfortune, in fact, to have the former studiously thrust forward and the latter kept in the back-ground,

---

* It is well known that the *Licenser* under King Charles the 2d hesitated at that noble simile about the eclipse, which

——————with fear of change
Perplexes Monarchs.

he is no mean person, and will, we doubt not, possess the ear of posterity. He is what can be very rarely said, a true poet; and we should think him so, if he had written nothing but his Sonnets on *Milton*, on Westminster Bridge, the one beginning 'The world is too much with us,' – nay, if he had written only that single line, which he quotes in his Preface with so just a confidence,

> Over his own sweet voice the stock-dove broods.

But it would be monstrous, in our opinion, if a Poet like Mr. WORDS-WORTH (the SCOTTS and SOUTHEYS we do not care for) *could* accompany such men as the Allied Sovereigns and their Ministers in all their destitutions of faith and even common intellect; and what we quarrel with him for in the present instance, is, first, that while he is understood not to do so, and indeed to have very great objections to some of their characters and proceedings, he leaves it to be supposed by his readers that the case is otherwise, and that he really thinks the *results* of the Battle of Waterloo will be as fine as the thing itself; – and second, that forgetting the very strong tone, of another sort, which he is known to have held in the earlier part of his life, he undertakes to settle matters with as summary a confidence as he did then, and to pronounce on this and that political view of a subject, that Heaven thinks precisely as he does. For the general propriety of assumptions of this nature we refer him to what we said in our last *Examiner*, always of course excepting, with regard to himself, whatever is attributed there to sheer want of intellect.

As to the Battle itself, in which 'The strong-armed English spirits conquered France' – DRAYTON – there can be but one opinion about it among those who really wish and know how to make the proper compliment to their countrymen, and who do not confound with it a counter-setting up of one general to another. It was won by the *English* literally speaking, – by that national spirit, character, and physical strength, which such politicians would have done away long before this, had the precursors of Mr. WORDSWORTH's *youth*, the MILTONS and MARVELLS, suffered it. – But to the point before us.

We do not mean in general to criticise any thing from other journals; but as we intended to say something on the following Sonnets that have appeared from the pen of Mr. Wordsworth, we thought it as well to do so in the present place. It is true, they are by no means among his best; but they have other calls upon us, which are worth answering in these portentous times. The author is not a man to be overlooked, even when in our opinion he is most descending from his proper height. Like Musæus in a very different sort of company, he is a head and shoulders taller than any of the strange, courtly sets, among whom he sometimes has a fancy for getting, perhaps for that very reason. What we have to say in the present instance we shall subjoin to each sonnet.

I.

INSCRIPTION FOR A NATIONAL MONUMENT, IN COMMEMORATION OF THE BATTLE OF WATERLOO.

Intrepid Sons of Albion! – not by you
Is life despised! – ah no – the spacious earth
Ne'er saw a race who held, by right of birth,
So many objects to which love is due;
Ye slight not life – to God and Nature true;
But death, becoming death, is dearer far,
When duty bids you bleed, in open war:
Hence hath your prowess quelled that impious crew.
Heroes, for instant sacrifice prepared,
Yet filled with ardour and on triumph bent,
Mid direst shocks of mortal accident,
To you who fell, and you whom slaughter spared,
To guard the fallen, and consummate the event,
Your country rears this sacred monument.

With regard to this Sonnet, which has nothing particular in it as to poetry, we have little more to observe than that the Poet has been singularly unfortunate in complimenting his countrymen on their attachment to life, – a passion which was certainly never found out in *Englishmen* before, whatever virtues they may possess to warrant it. The probability is indeed, that the virtues of this nation, which are many and sturdy ones, are not a little owing to the very absence of those native relishes of existence, which help perhaps to render some of their neighbours at once so lively and so irregular. As to the old phrase however, 'that impious crew,' – which has been in use among enemies of all sorts, when they got particularly angry with the other side, and wished to make Heaven a party with their own notions, we refer the reader to what we have already said on this point in the conclusion of our last week's article.

II.

OCCASIONED BY THE SAME BATTLE.

The Bard, whose soul is meek as dawning day,
Yet trained to judgments righteously severe;
Fervid, yet conversant with holy fear,
As recognizing one Almighty away;
He whose experienc'd eye can pierce the array
Of past events, – to whom, in vision clear,
The aspiring heads of future things appear,
Like mountain-tops whence mists have roll'd away;
Assoiled from all encumbrance of our time,
He only, if such breathe, in strains devout
Shall comprehend this victory sublime;
And worthily rehearse the hideous route,
Which the blest angels, from their peaceful clime
Beholding, welcomed with a choral shout*.

This is a very noble strain of versification, to say the least of it, – very varied and sonorous; and the simile in the middle is worthy of the music. But here again we must refer to our protest against the enlistments of Heaven in earthly quarrels. It is something worse [than] begging the question, especially when we know all that the Allied Sovereigns have done in France, in Italy, Poland, Spain, &c. &c. For our parts, we certainly do not pretend to be 'meek as dawning day,' nor 'assoiled from all the time's encumbrance'; and so, it seems, we must not pretend to comprehend '*this* victory sublime.' However, we endeavoured to comprehend a former victory sublime, or rather to make the best of it, and encourage those who won it to do what was right; and we know what we got by our verses, as witness the nations above-mentioned, to say nothing of more private remuneration, though we could tell a very pretty religious story upon that too. But is Mr. Wordsworth sure, after all, that he sees the mountain-tops he speaks of? Did he not think he saw *others* some years ago, of a very different altitude? and may he not still have to find that 'Alps on Alps arise?' We grievously suspect as much.

---

* In the above is a line taken from Spenser:

> And, hanging up his arms and warlike spoil,
> From all this world's encumbrance did himself assoil.
> *Note by the Author.*

III.

O, for a kindling touch of that pure flame
Which taught the offering of song to rise
From thy lone bower, beneath Italian skies,
Great Filicaia! – With celestial aim
It rose, – thy saintly rapture to proclaim,
Then, when the imperial city stood released
From bondage, threatened by the embattled East,
And Christendom respired; from guilt and shame
Redeemed, – from miserable fear set free
By one day's feat – one mighty victory.
Chaunt the Deliverer's praise in every tongue!
The cross shall spread, – the crescent hath wax'd dim,
He conquering, – as in earth and heav'n was sung, –
HE CONQUERING THROUGH GOD, AND GOD BY HIM!*

In this third Sonnet the author really seems to have sunk to the pitch of
Mr. Southey. He certainly has not been kindled with the flame he cries
out for; though much as we admire Filicaia, we think Mr. Wordsworth
nevertheless a greater poet. He has got into an awkward business here
altogether. Filicaia was an Italian poet of no mean order, whose infirmities turned him into a devotee. The Canzoni Mr. Wordsworth speaks of
were addressed to the gallant King he mentions, and to the Emperor
Leopold, on the preservation of Vienna from the Turks, and Filicaia, in
return for the attacks of 'that impious crew,' – quegli empi, – was desirous of carrying Christian vengeance into their own quarters. Probably he
was the last of Christian poets, who would have revived the Crusades.
Mr. Wordsworth therefore, in the first instance, is longing for the flame
that inspired Catholic superstition, and which it must be allowed was a
pretty warning one. In the next place, it is true that John Sobieski, King
of Poland, was a fine sovereign, and remained so; but it is true also, that
he was a popular and elected one, a circumstance upon which Filicaia
compliments him, and the spirit of which sort of sovereignty, even in [its]
remotest degree, the late victories, we find, are to put down. The
Emperor also, who is complimented with him, and of whom a thousand
fine things are prophecied by the poet, – discerned, of course on the

---

* [Wordsworth quotes four lines from Filicaia's Canzone, or Ode to John Sobieski, King
of Poland, upon his raising the siege of Vienna.] This, and his other poems on the same
occasion, are superior, perhaps, to any Lyrical pieces produced in any age or country, with
the exception of those in the Hebrew Scriptures.

Note by the Author.

'mountain-tops' of those times, – turned out such a knave and tyrant, that he was very near losing one of his crowns. In short, Filicaia, though a devotee, and inclined well enough to praise a despotic sovereign where religion was concerned, was also a lover of freedom in the abstract. He did not scruple, even in those times, to be the friend and panegyrist of the Whig Lord Somers: *and he has left some noble sonnets that shew what he would have felt for ITALY, had he lived now.* Mr. Wordsworth should have gone for countenance on the present occasion to another lyric poet, Guidi, who made such a noise about the beheaders of Charles the 1st, including, of course, our Poet's friend *Milton*, whose tone of thinking, by the way, comes out very singularly sometimes among these panegyrics on modern princes, and the restoration of discarded dynasties, Mr. Wordsworth, we should think, must feel some strange qualms on that point, especially as in one of his sonnets he expressly said, that Milton ought to 'be living at that hour,' and that the times 'had need of him.' As to the other Italian poets, it ought not to be forgotten that they were for the most part strenuous advocates of independence, – that Tasso and Ariosto loved it, – that Dante suffered banishment for it, – and that Petrarch did not hesitate, when a struggle arose in his time between freedom in its most popular shape, and the pretensions of the 'legitimate,' to risk his old patrician acquaintances, rather than not join in the cause of 'the many against the few.' See his letters and life, and the fine Canzone addressed to the Tribune *Rienzi*, beginning 'Spir[i]to gentil,'[1] which Filicaia himself had evidently read to some purpose.

We hope to see many more of Mr. Wordsworth's sonnets, but shall be glad to find them, like his best ones, less Miltonic in one respect, and much more so in another.

f. Letter from John Scott to Wordsworth, 29 May 1816

Wordsworth was not to remain ignorant of the authors of the *Examiner* attacks. John Scott, hearing from Wordsworth that he had sent Hunt a copy of *Poems* (1815), felt it his duty to let the poet know that it was Hunt and Hazlitt who were responsible for the unsympathetic *Examiner* comments. Scott was clearly surprised that Wordsworth should have thought of Hunt as a proper recipient of his *Poems*, but the reason for this, he acknowledged, was that Wordsworth was not in the habit of reading the *Examiner*.

. . . with the exception of a momentary freak of respect, you have personally & by name been treated with insolence & ignorant abuse in that Paper. Mr Hunt was instructed for a time by some of his companions (particularly a Mr Barnes) in his value of your poetry, – but it had previously been treated by him with much stupid & unwitting disrespect. Twice then you have wounded his vanity, by throwing a splendour around a political side, opposite to his own – and he & his Coadjutor Mr Hazlett, are in the pretty constant habit of alluding to you in slighting language. Mr Hazlett has written in the Exam^r a very capital notice of the Excursion, – but consistency or good principle of any kind, furnishes no obstacle to the gratification of his malevolence, when it is excited by any personal offence. If you had not mentioned to me Mr Hunt's name, & that you had sent him your Poems, I certainly should never have entered into this disagreeable statement.

(Ms. The Wordsworth Library)

g. From a review of Keats's *Poems* 1817, *The Examiner*, 1 June 1817, 345

It was the Lake Poets in our opinion (however grudgingly we say it, on some accounts) that were the first to revive a true taste for nature; and like most Revolutionists, especially of the cast which they have since turned out to be, they went to an extreme, calculated rather at first to make the readers of poetry disgusted with originality and adhere with contempt and resentment to their magazine common-places. This had a bad effect also in the way of re-action; and none of those writers have ever since been able to free themselves from certain stubborn affectations, which having been ignorantly confounded by others with the better part of them, have been retained by their self-love with a still less pardonable want of wisdom. The greater part indeed of the poetry of Mr. Southey, a weak man in all respects, is really made up of little else. Mr. Coleridge still trifles with his poetical as he has done with his metaphysical talent. Mr. Lamb, in our opinion, has a more real tact of humanity, a modester, Shakspearean wisdom, than any of them; and had he written more, might have delivered the school victoriously from all its defects. But it is Mr. Wordsworth who has advanced it the most, and who in spite of some morbidities as well as mistaken theories in other respects, has opened upon us a fund of thinking and imagination, that ranks him as the successor of the true and abundant poets of the older time. Poetry, like Plenty, should be represented with a cornucopia, but it should be a real one; not swelled out and insidiously *optimized* at the top, like Mr. Southey's stale strawberry baskets, but fine and full to the depth, like a heap from the vintage.

h. From the Preface to *Foliage, or, Poems Original and Translated,* 1818

[Not the least cause for the downfall of the French school of poetry has been] the accession of a new school of poetry itself, of which Wordsworth has justly the reputation of being the most prominent ornament, but whose inner priest of the temple perhaps was Coleridge – a man who has been the real oracle of the time in more than one respect, and who ought to have been the greatest visible person in it, instead of a hopeless and dreary sophist. . . . Wordsworth,[2] whose ground is morals, has not succeeded so well as either [Byron or Moore] in one sense of the word; but taking everything into consideration, the novelty of his poetical system, and the very unattractive and in my opinion mistaken nature of his moral one, he has succeeded still more; and is generally felt among his own profession to be at the head of it.

(*Leigh Hunt's Literary Criticism*, ed. L. and C. Houtchens, 1956, 129–31)

EDITOR'S NOTES

1. 'Gentle spirit'.
2. For Hunt's hostile review of *Peter Bell*, 1819, see entry 208.

260. John Hamilton Reynolds (1796–1852)

From letters and writings, 1815–1816

a. Essay signed 'R', 'Mr. Wordsworth's Poetry', *Champion*, 9 December 1815, 398

– Perhaps you may not be disinclined to permit me to continue a little further, the remarks on Mr. WORDSWORTH's Poetry, which have, from time to time, appeared in the *Champion*. It is an important subject, nearly concerning the character of the present age for taste, for feeling – in fact, for every moral and mental quality that can do it honor in future estimation, or conduce to its present enjoyment of the worthiest means of gratification.

Mr. Wordsworth has the power of calling forth the retired thoughts and fleeting recollections of the mind, more exquisitely than any poet of later times. He breathes the same air of philosophy that Milton and Jeremy Taylor breathed before him: – though, in the latter, there is indeed a singularly rich enthusiasm that defies similarity. Mr. Wordsworth's sublimities are of the same nature with the sublimities of these noble Poets – bold in their rise and steady and beautiful in their elevation.

We have generally remarked, that persons of deep intellect, beautiful fancies, and gentle affections, are readers of Mr. Wordsworth's Poetry. – It is true, these are not in him, that haughty melancholy and troubled spirit which so peculiarly distinguish Lord Byron, – nor the wild and melodious fancy, the wanted pleasantry, or lightsome mirthfullness of Moore; – neither are there the gentlemanly prettinesses, and snatches of antiquity of Scott: – (who, by the way, is nothing better than an artful libeller of chivalrous heroes.) The truth is, Mr. Wordsworth describes natural feelings and natural beauties – his thoughts come from him, purified through the heart. – He indulges in calm reasonings and rich reflections, and invites us to the feast, concluding that we have the same appetites with himself. – Of the Lyrical ballads, – we can imagine him to have composed many in the fields, with all his feelings fresh about him. – We can imagine him to have suffered his memory to wander at times so long in the fairy grounds of Childhood, – that the present seemed to fade, and the past seemed to brighten into life. We can believe that he may often have wept, over his own pure and fine reflections, such tears as were made sacred by the charm of his own mind. We never touch on the Lyrical Ballads without feeling that we are busied with the innocent and the beautiful. There have been no Pastoral Poems so truly sweet since the days of Sydney – none in which the simplicities of poetry and philosophy are so gracefully blended. The pieces by Shenstone, misnamed Pastoral, are totally destitute of feeling. We can get no other idea than that the shepherd walked about very discontented, – very amorous, and very affected. Shenstone deserves all the hard things that have been said of him by Gray and Dr. Johnson, – for it is very clear that he wrote merely from 'vanity and vexation of spirit.' All his descriptions of rural happiness are artificial. He would make us believe that the fields are for ever green, the sheep for ever feeding, and that the shepherds have nothing to do but to make love and play on a pipe.

To those who have been close observers of nature, the poetry of Mr. Wordsworth is indeed a treasure. We have never heard the sound of a closing gate* on a still summer's evening, or the 'tremulous sob of the complaining owl' breaking the silence of night – without recollecting his descriptions with a thrilling delight. They have melody

> — like of a hidden brook
> In the leafy month of June – ,
> That to the sleeping woods all night,
> Singeth a quiet tune.
> COLERIDGE'S *Ancient Mariner.*

The Lyrical Ballads had, on their first appearance, much to contend against. They introduced a new system to the world, and one that, if received, could not fail to overthrow the artificial one so long adopted. They came forward in the dress of nature, not tricked out in a fantastical habit, and sought to revive gentle tastes, quiet feelings, and innocent affections. But 'the million' saw nothing beyond the surface, – they could not reach where the calm philosophy rested: – these Poems, therefore, were violently opposed, and, as it would seem, overpowered. But they remained alive in the hearts and minds of a few, and have been quietly gaining strength up to the present hour.

We are convinced that the name of Wordsworth will

> In Fames' eternal volume shine for aye.

It is associated in our minds with all that is great and beautiful in human intellect. In the following extract from the Supplementary Essay, printed in his two volumes of poems lately re-published – it will be seen that he feels within him that mental elevation which must command posterity.

'The love, the admiration, the indifference, the slight, the aversion, and even the contempt, with which these poems have been received, knowing, as I do, the source within mine own mind, from which they proceded, and the labour and pains, which, when labour and pains appeared needful, have been bestowed upon them, – must all, if I think consistently, be received as pledges and tokens, bearing the same general impression though widely different in value; – they are all proofs that for the present time I have not laboured in vain, and afford assurances, more or less authentic, that the products of my industry will endure.'

---

*   Sound of clos'd gate, across the water borne, –
       Hurrying the feeding hare through rustling corn.

These lines are from Mr. Wordsworth's Poem, entitled, '*An Evening Walk,*' &c. [(1793) ll. 441–2] which was published in his youthful days, and is now become very scarce.

We cannot conclude without protesting against the expensive manner in which the two last of Mr. Wordsworth's Poems have been published. Mr. Wordsworth writes for persons of intellect and feeling, and not for brainless young men, and ladies of fashion. – In the quarto volume Mr. Wordsworth is altogether out of the reach of common readers; – he is as much above their pockets as their understandings.

b. Extract from 'The Pilgrimage of Living Poets to the Stream of Castaly', signed 'J. H. R.', *Champion*, 7 April 1816

Reynolds begins by declaring himself 'one of those who pant for distinction, but have not within them that immortal power which alone can command it.' He then dreams of the stream of Castaly to which poets come in pilgrimage: Byron, Scott, Moore, Southey, Crabbe, Montgomery, Campbell, Hunt, Coleridge, Lamb, Lloyd, and last, Wordsworth, who is treated less mockingly than any other poet.

Last came a calm and majestic figure moving serenely towards the stream: – the Celandines and small flowers sprang up to catch the pressure of his feet, – the sun-light fell with a finer glow around, – spirits rustled most mirthfully and musically in the air, and a wing every now and then twinkled into sight, – (like the autumn leaf that trembles and flashes up to the sun) – and its feathers of wavy gold were almost too sparkling to be looked upon; – the waters of Castaly ran brighter as he approached, and seemed to play and dimple with pleasure at his presence. It was Wordsworth! In his hand he held a vase of pure chrystal, – and, when he had reached the brink of the stream, the wave proudly swelled itself into his cup: – at this moment the sunny air above his brow, became embodied, – and the glowing and lightsome Spirit shone into being, and dropt a garland on his forehead; – sounds etherial swelled, and trembled, and revelled in the air, – and forms of light played in and out of sight, – and all around seemed like a living world of breathing poetry. Wordsworth bent with reverence over the vase, and declared that the waters he had obtained should be the refreshment of his soul; – he then raised his countenance, – which had become illumined from the wave over which he had bowed, – and retired with a calm dignity.

c. **Sonnet, signed 'J. H. R.',** *Champion,* **18 February 1816**

O, Wordsworth! when my heart hath been oppress'd,
With many griefs, – and all the world look'd sad;
To thee I've owed a mild return of rest,
And of young Hope, soft smiling; thou hast clad
My heart with quietness, – and given my breast
A proneness to be gentle, if not glad.
Long in thy mountain solitude mayst thou
Live happy! Peace the guardian of thy hours!
And may the roses, and the jasmine's flowers
Creep kindly o'er thy cot, and fragrance throw
To the free air, that best of earthly dowers.
May sound of green leaves rustling on the bough, –
And song of birds, – and distant waterfall; –
Cheer thee; – and pure affections blend with all.

d. **A letter to Wordsworth, August 1816**

Wordsworth took Reynold's request seriously, and firmly, though kindly, suggested that Reynold's poem, *The Naiad: a Tale,* 1816, would 'be better without the first 57 lines . . . and without the last 146' (*MY,* II, 345–6).

Will you accept the accompanying little Poem as a slight but sincere token of gratitude for many happy hours which your Volumes have given me. You will find that I have inscribed it to our mutual friend, Mr Haydon, – through whose hands it will be conveyed to you. Should you have leisure to point out to me any passages which you may think objectionable; I shall feel happy at being able to benefit the Poem by your suggestions.

I have read your late pamphlet on Burns (which Mr Leigh Hunt was kind enough to lend me) with great pleasure. It is very ably thought & written. The thanks-giving Odes are noble Poems, & well bespeak the heart & mind that gave them birth.

(Ms. The Wordsworth Library)

e. **From a letter to Benjamin Haydon, 28 September 1816**

. . . I am glad you have sent the Copy to Wordsworth for me: – Oh Haydon when I think of the sunlike genius, & fine firm principle of that Noble Poet; – I think higher of human nature, of the age in which I live.

935

He is the Milton of our day. He has twined the pillars of the Temple of Philosophy with the loveliest flowers of Poetry. He has turned by the touch of his genius, the mountain air of his country into words. Liberty breathes through his Poetry, as the wind wanders over his Hills. Thought is the friend of his retirement. I long to see Wordsworth.

(*The Letters of John Hamilton Reynolds*, ed. Leonidas M. Jones, University of Nebraska, Lincoln, 1973, 5.)

f. *Peter Bell. A Lyrical Ballad*

The circumstances of Reynolds' writing of *Peter Bell* is related by 'Fitzhopkins' in *Notes and Queries*, 10 February 1866, 127:

I knew Reynolds, and often talked to him about *Peter Bell*. Wordsworth's poem had been advertised, but its publication was from time to time put off. Some literary men were guessing at the cause of this delay, and one said, 'Wordsworth is keeping it back to elaborate.' 'Elaborate!' said Reynolds, 'I'll see if I can't get one out before him.' He set to work that afternoon, and sent his poem to the printer the next evening. I think it was out about a fortnight before Wordsworth's. Reynolds was a great admirer of Wordsworth, and though rather averse to continuous exertion, had read through *The Excursion*. Up to the publication of *Peter Bell*, they were literary friends, and occasionally exchanged letters. The joke annoyed Wordsworth, who gave up the acquaintance.

Though Keats is to review the poem (see entry 263n), it confirmed a separation of sympathy between himself and Reynolds, to whom he had written the great letters on poetry the previous year. By 18 March 1819, Keats notes: 'Reynolds is completely limed in the law; he is not only reconciled to it but hobby-horses upon it' (*Keats Letters*, II, 78; also, *Shelley and His Circle*, ed. D. H. Reiman, 1973, VI, 806–7).

The poem was published anonymously, 15 April 1819, one week before Wordsworth's *Peter Bell* appeared. The parody had the motto, 'I do affirm that I am the REAL Simon Pure' (from Mrs Centlivre's *Bold Stroke for a Wife*, 1718). The poem has charm as well as irony, probably because, as Keats put it, 'the writer of it has felt the finer parts of Mr. Wordsworth' (see entry 263n). Coleridge wrote to Taylor and Hessey, 22 April 1819, admiring the notes more than the verse: 'But be the verses what they may, they are all *morally* fair – & the Preface & Notes are very droll and clever.' (*Collected Letters of Samuel Coleridge*, ed. E. L. Griggs, Oxford, 1956–71, IV, 939.) The poem was immediately successful. The text given here is that of the third edition, also 1819 (was there a second edition?); it has some additions: stanzas 13, 40, 41, and two foot-notes, that on *The White Doe* and that on stanza 2.

PREFACE.

IT is now a period of one-and-twenty years since I first wrote some of the most perfect compositions (except certain pieces I have written in my later days) that ever dropped from poetical pen. My heart hath been right and powerful all its years. I never thought an evil or a weak thought in my life. It has been my aim and my achievement to deduce moral thunder from buttercups, daisies*, celandines, and (as a poet, scarcely inferior to myself, hath it) 'such small deer.' Out of sparrows' eggs I have hatched great truths, and with sextons' barrows have I wheeled into human hearts, piles of the weightiest philosophy. I have persevered with a perseverance truly astonishing, in persons of not the most pursy purses; – but to a man of my inveterate morality and independent stamp, (of which Stamps I am proud to be a Distributor) the sneers and scoffings of impious Scotchmen, and the neglect of my poor uninspired country-men, fall as the dew upon the thorn, (on which plant I have written an immortal stanza or two) and are as fleeting as the spray of the waterfall, (concerning which waterfall I have composed some great lines which the world will not let die.) – Accustomed to mountain solitudes, I can look with a calm and dispassionate eye upon that fiend-like, vulture-souled, adder-fanged critic, whom I have not patience to name, and of whose Review I loathe the title, and detest the contents. – Philosophy has taught me to forgive the misguided miscreant, and to speak of him only in terms of patience and pity. I love my venerable Monarch and the Prince Regent†. My Ballads are the noblest pieces of verse in the whole range of English poetry: and I take this opportunity of telling the world I am a great man. Mr. Milton was also a great man. Ossian was a blind old fool. Copies of my previous works may be had in any numbers, by application at my publisher.

Of PETER BELL I have only thus much to say: it completes the simple system of natural narrative, which I began so early as 1798. It is written in that pure unlaboured style, which can only be met with among labour-ers; – and I can safely say, that while its imaginations spring beyond the reach of the most imaginative, its occasional meaning occasionally falls

---

* A favourite flower of mine. It was a favourite with Chaucer, but he did not understand its moral mystery as I do.

Little Cyclops, with one eye.

Poems by ME.

† Mr. Vansittart, the great Chancellor of the Exchequer, is a noble character: – and I consecrate this note to that illustrious financier.

far below the meanest capacity. As these are the days of counterfeits*, I am compelled to caution my readers against them, 'for such are abroad.' However, I here declare this to be the true Peter; this to be the old original Bell. I commit my Ballad confidently to posterity. I love to read my own poetry†: it does my heart good.

W.W.

N.B. The novel of Rob Roy is not so good as my Poem on the same subject.

PETER BELL.

1.

Iᴛ is the thirty-first of March,
A gusty evening – half past seven;
The moon is shining o'er the larch,
A simple shape – a cock'd-up arch,
Rising bigger than a star,
Though the stars are thick in Heaven.

2.

Gentle moon! how canst thou shine
Over graves and over trees,
With as innocent a look
As my own grey eye-ball‡ sees,
When I gaze upon a brook?

---

* The White Doe of Rylstone is not of my writing. If it be a serious imitation of my style, I venerate the author; but if it be meant as a joke against me, – I cannot but weep at its remorseless cruelty. I neither know the tragic *Doe*, nor am I acquainted with the tragic *Buck*, – though both these poetical creatures have of late piteously moaned over their buffettings of fortune – 'But let the stricken *deer* go weep,' as Bacon philosophically hath it.

†   Often have I sigh'd to measure
                      By myself a lonely pleasure,
                      Sigh'd to think I read a book
                      Only read perhaps by me.
                           Poems. i. 249 [from Wordsworth's second poem addressed
                                  to the Lesser Celandine: 'Pleasures newly found are
                                        sweet' (written 1802, published 1807)]

‡ My eyes are grey. Venus is said to have had grey eyes. Grey eyes please me well, – being, as a friend of mine finely saith, 'beautiful exceedingly.'

3.

Od's me! how the moon doth shine:
It doth make a pretty glitter,
Playing in the waterfall;
As when Lucy Gray doth litter
Her baby-house with bugles small.

4.

Beneath the ever blessed moon
An old man o'er an old grave stares,
You never look'd upon his fellow;
His brow is covered with grey hairs,
As though they were an umbrella.

5.

He hath a noticeable look*,
This old man hath – this grey old man;
He gazes at the graves, and seems,
With over waiting, over wan,
Like Susan Harvey's† pan of creams.

6.

'Tis Peter Bell – 'tis Peter Bell,
Who never stirreth in the day;
His hand is wither'd – he is old!
On Sundays he is us'd to pray,
In winter he is very cold‡.

7.

I've seen him in the month of August,
At the wheat-field, hour by hour,
Picking ear, – by ear, – by ear, –
Through wind, – and rain, – and sun, – and shower,
From year, – to year, – to year, – to year.

---

*   'A noticeable man with large grey eyes.'
                                        Lyrical Ballads.
† Dairy-maid to Mr. Gill.
‡ Peter Bell resembleth Harry Gill in this particular:

'His teeth they chatter, chatter, chatter.'

I should have introduced this fact in the text, but that Harry Gill would not rhyme. I reserve this for my blank verse.

8.

You never saw a wiser man,
He knows his Numeration Table;
He counts the sheep of Harry Gill*
Every night that he is able,
When the sheep are on the hill.

9.

Betty Foy – *My* Betty Foy,
Is the aunt of Peter Bell;
And credit me, as I would have you,
Simon Lee was once his nephew,
And his niece is Alice Fell.†

10.

He is rurally related;
Peter Bell hath country cousins,
(He had once a worthy mother)
Bells and Peters by the dozens,
But Peter Bell he hath no brother.

11.

Not a brother owneth he,
Peter Bell he hath no brother;
His mother had no other son,
No other son e'er call'd her mother;
Peter Bell hath brother none.

12.

Hark! the church-yard brook is singing
Its evening song amid the leaves;
And the peering moon doth look
Sweetly on that singing brook,
Round‡ and sad as though it grieves.

---

* Harry Gill was the original proprietor of Barbara Lewthwaite's pet-lamb; and he also bred Betty Foy's celebrated poney, got originally out of a Night-mare, by a descendant of the great Trojan horse.

† Mr. Sheridan, in his sweet poem of the Critic, supplies one of his heroes with as singularly clustering a relationship.

‡ I have here changed the shape of the moon, not from any poetical heedlessness, or human perversity, but because man is fond of change, and in this I have studied the metaphysical varieties of our being.

13.

The little leaves on long thin twigs
Tremble with a deep delight,
They do dance a pleasant rout,
Hop and skip and jump about
As though they all were craz'd to night.

14.

Peter Bell doth lift his hand,
That thin hand, which in the light
Looketh like to oiled paper;
Paper oiled, – oily bright, –
And held up to a waxen taper.

15.

The hand of Peter Bell is busy,
Under the pent-house of his hairs;
His eye is like a solemn sermon;
The little flea severely fares,
'Tis a sad day for the vermin.

16.

He is thinking of the Bible –
Peter Bell is old and blest;
He doth pray and scratch away,
He doth scratch, and bitten, pray
To *flee* away, and be at rest.

17.

At home his foster child is cradled –
Four brown bugs are feeding there*;
Catch as many, sister Ann,
Catch as many as you can†
And yet the little insects spare.

---

* I have a similar idea in my Poem on finding a Bird's Nest: –

Look! *five* blue eggs are gleaming there.

But the numbers are different, so I trust no one will differ with the numbers.
† I have also given these lines before; but in thus printing them again, I neither tarnish their value, nor injure their novelty.

18.

Why should blessed insects die?
The flea doth skip o'er Betty Foy,
Like a little living thing:
Though it hath not fin or wing,
Hath it not a moral joy?

19.

I the poet of the mountain,
Of the waterfall and fell,
I the mighty mental medlar,
I the lonely lyric pedlar,
I the Jove of Alice Fell,

20.

I the Recluse – a gentle man*,
A gentle man – a simple creature,
Who would not hurt, God shield the thing,
The merest, meanest May-bug's wing,
Am tender in my tender nature.

21.

I do doat on my dear wife,
On the linnet, on the worm,
I can see sweet written salads
Growing in the Lyric Ballads,
And always find them green and firm.

22.

Peter Bell is laughing now,
Like a dead man making faces;
Never saw I smile so old,
On face so wrinkled and so cold,
Since the Idiot Boy's grimaces.

* See my Sonnet to Sleep: –

I surely not a man ungently made.

B

23.

He is thinking of the moors,
Where I saw him in his breeches;
Ragged though they were, a pair
Fit for a grey old man to wear;
Saw him poking, – gathering leeches.*

24.

And gather'd leeches are to him,
To Peter Bell, like gather'd flowers;
They do yield him such delight,
As roses poach'd from porch at night,
Or pluck'd from oratoric† bowers.

25.

How that busy smile doth hurry
O'er the cheek of Peter Bell;
He is surely in a flurry,
Hurry skurry – hurry skurry,
Such delight I may not tell.

26.

His stick is made of wilding wood,
His hat was formerly of felt,
His duffel cloak of wool is made,
His stockings are from stock in trade,
His belly's belted with a belt.

27.

His father was a bellman once,
His mother was a beldame old;
They kept a shop at Keswick Town,
Close by the Bell, (beyond the Crown),
And pins and peppermint they sold.

---

* See my story of the Leech-gatherer, the finest poem in the world, – except this.
†   'Ah!' said the Briar, 'blame me not.'
                                    Waterfall and Eglantine.
Also, –

The Oak a Giant and a Sage,
His neighbour thus address'd.

28.

He is stooping now about
O'er the grave-stones one and two;
The clock is now a striking eight,
Four more hours and 'twill be late,
And Peter Bell hath much to do.

29.

O'er the grave-stones three and four,
Peter stoopeth old and wise;
He counteth with a wizard glee
The graves of all his family,
While the hooting owlet cries.

30.

Peter Bell, he readeth ably,
All his letters he can tell;
Roman W, – Roman S,
In a minute he can guess,
Without the aid of Dr. Bell.

31.

Peter keeps a gentle poney,
But the poney is not here;
Susan who is very tall*,
And very sick and sad withal,
Rides it slowly far and near.

32.

Hark! the voice of Peter Bell,
And the belfry bell is knelling;
It soundeth drowsily and dead,
As though a corse th' 'Excursion' read;
Or Martha Ray her tale was telling.

---

*   *Long Susan* lay deep lost in thought.
                    The Idiot Boy.

33.

Do listen unto Peter Bell,
While your eyes with tears do glisten:
Silence! his old eyes do read
All, on which the boys do tread
When holidays do come – Do listen!

34.

The ancient Marinere lieth here,
Never to rise, although he pray'd, –
But all men, all, must have their fallings;
And, like the Fear of Mr. Collins*,
He died 'of sounds himself had made.'

35.

Dead mad mother, – Martha Ray,
Old Matthew too, and Betty Foy,
Lack-a-daisy! here's rout full;
Simon Lee whose age was doubtful†,
Simon even the Fates destroy.'

36.

Harry Gill is gone to rest,
Goody Blake is food for maggot;
They lie sweetly side by side,
Beautiful as when they died;
Never more shall she pick faggot.

---

* See what I have said of this man in my excellent supplementary *Preface*.
† I cannot resist quoting the following lines, to shew how I preserve my system from youth to age. As Simon was, so he is. And one and twenty years have scarcely altered (except by death) that cheerful and cherry-cheeked Old Huntsman. This is the truth of Poetry.

> In the sweet shire of Cardigan,
>   Not far from pleasant Ivor-hall;
> An old man dwells – a little man –
>   I've heard he once was tall;
> Of years he has upon his back,
>   No doubt, a burthen weighty;
> He says he is threescore and ten,
>   But others say he's eighty.

These lines were written in the summer of 1798, and I bestowed great labour upon them.

37.

Still he reads, and still the moon
On the church-yard's mounds doth shine;
The brook is still demurely singing,
Again the belfry bell is ringing,
'Tis nine o'clock, six, seven, eight, nine!

38.

Patient Peter pores and proses
On, from simple grave to grave;
Here marks the children snatch'd to heaven,
None left to blunder 'we are seven;' –
Even Andrew Jones* no power could save.

39.

What a Sexton's work† is here,
Lord! the Idiot Boy is gone;
And Barbara Lewthwaite's fate the same,
And cold as mutton is her lamb;
And Alice Fell is bone by bone.

40.

Stephen Hill is dead and buried,
Reginald Shore is crumbling – crumbling,
Giles Fleming – Susan Gale – alas!
Death playeth in the church-yard grass
His human nine-pins – tumbling – tumbling.

41.

But Peter liveth well and wisely,
For still he makes old Death look silly,
Like those sage ducks of Mrs. Bond,
Who, not of killing over fond,
Turn a deaf ear to dilly, dilly.

* Andrew Jones was a very singular old man. – See my Poem,

'I have that Andrew Jones – he'll breed,' &c.
† 'Let thy wheelbarrow alone, &c.' See my poem to a Sexton.

42.

And tears are thick with Peter Bell,
Yet still he sees one blessed tomb;
Tow'rds it he creeps with spectacles,
And bending on his leather knees,
He reads the *Lake*iest Poet's doom.

43.

The letters printed are by fate,
The death they say was suicide;
He reads – 'Here lieth W. W.
Who never more will trouble you, trouble you:'
The old man smokes who 'tis that died.

44.

Go home, go home – old Man, go home;
Peter, lay thee down at night,
Thou art happy, Peter Bell,
Say thy prayers for Alice Fell,
Thou hast seen a blessed sight.

45.

He quits that moon-light yard of skulls,
And still he feels right glad, and smiles
With moral joy at that old tomb;
Peter's cheek recals its bloom,
And as he creepeth by the tiles,
He mutters ever – 'W. W.
Never more will trouble you, trouble you.'

HERE ENDETH THE BALLAD OF PETER BELL.

SUPPLEMENTARY ESSAY.

I BEG leave, once for all, to refer the Reader to my previous Poems, for illustrations of the names of the characters, and the severe simplicity contained in this affecting Ballad. I purpose, in the course of a few years, to write laborious lives of all the old people who enjoy sinecures in the text, or are pensioned off in the notes, of my Poetry. The Cumberland Beggar is dead. He could not crawl out of the way of a fierce and fatal post chaise, and so fell a sacrifice to the Philosophy of Nature. I shall commence the work in heavy quarto, like the Excursion, with that 'old, old Man,' (as the too joyous Spenser saith.) – If ever I should be surprised into a second edition of my whole Poems, I shall write an extra-supplementary Essay on the principles of simple Poetry. I now conclude, with merely extracting (from my own works) the following eloquent and just passage (my Prose is extremely good) contained in the two volumes lately published, and not yet wholly disposed of: –

> A sketch of my own notion of the Constitution of Fame has been given; and as far as concerns myself, I have cause to be satisfied. – The love, the admiration, the indifference, the slight, the aversion, and even the contempt, with which these Poems have been received, knowing, as I do, the source within my own mind, from which they have proceeded; and the labour and pains which, when labour and pains appeared needful, have been bestowed upon them, – must all, if I think consistently, be received as pledges and tokens, bearing the same general impression though widely different in value; – they are all proofs that for the present time I have not laboured in vain; and afford assurances, more or less authentic, that the products of my industry will endure.

Lyrical Ballads, Vol. i, p. 368

261. Samuel Rogers (1763–1855)
From a letter to Walter Scott, July 1816

Samuel Rogers was a banker and author of the popular *Pleasures of Memory* (1792) – over 22,000 copies had been printed by 1816, the year of the nineteenth edition. Byron praised his poetry in *Don Juan* but savaged his backbiting in a satire dated 1820. Rogers was a personal friend of Wordsworth and an admirer, with reservations, of Wordsworth's poetry. For his role in causing Byron to dislike Wordsworth, see entry 252.

Our knowledge of Rogers' opinions of Wordsworth largely come through records of Rogers' conversation: a certain inconsistency perhaps comes from the fact that Rogers always liking to speak for effect rather than absolute truth. Henry Crabb Robinson reports, 29 November 1835, '[Rogers] spoke very highly of Wordsworth, but with qualifications which would not satisfy Wordsworth's admirers. He thinks he is likely, now, to be overlauded as before he was underrated. I was least prepared for his affirming that Wordsworth is a careless versifier – he thinks his blank verse better than his rhymes' (*Henry Crabb Robinson on Books and their Writers*, ed. Edith J. Morley, 1938, I. 434.). Crabb Robinson came to think that Rogers' maverick comments were perhaps motivated by envy and suggests Byron's bitter verse comment on Rogers 'is justly drawn: 'Tis but envy when all's done' (18 February 1838, *ibid.*, II, 547). In 1842 Rogers surprised Crabb Robinson by applying a remark about Burns to Wordsworth: 'He is great in verse, greater in prose, and greatest in conversation. So it is of all great men. Wordsworth is greatest in conversation.' Crabb Robinson then continues: 'This is not the first time of [Rogers] preferring prose to verse . . .' (*ibid.*, II, 614). However, in his undated *Table-Talk*, Rogers praises neither the blank verse nor the prose, but Wordsworth's sonnets: 'I never attempted to write a sonnet, because I do not see why a man, if he has anything worth saying, should be tied down to fourteen lines. Wordsworth perhaps appears to most advantage in a sonnet, because its strict limits prevent him from running into the wordiness to which he is somewhat prone. Don't imagine from what I have just said, that I mean to disparage Wordsworth: he deserves all his fame' (*Recollections of the Table-Talk of Samuel Rogers*, ed. A. Dyce, 1887, 210). Rogers' personal graciousness to Wordsworth, which certainly would boost Wordsworth's self-esteem, is illustrated by Rogers' gift of *Paradise Lost* 1669 on 13 November 1820:

> My dear Wordsworth. Pray accept this little volume, one of the most precious that I can give or you receive. It will acquire a new value by becoming yours.
>
> (Written in the front of the book: The Wordsworth Library)

Coleridge is now at Highgate, and in better health than usual. he is printing some letters to his friend Wordsworth [*Biographia Literaria*, 1817] on his theory of poetry, a theory certainly very assailable . . .

(*The Private Letter-Books of Sir Walter Scott*, ed. W. Partington, 1930, 185)

262. James Hogg (1770–1835)

From the *Poetic Mirror*, 1816

James Hogg, the 'Ettrick Shepherd', published the *Poetic Mirror*, a volume of parodies, anonymously in 1816. The three Wordsworth parodies are in the form of first-person narrations, pointed clearly at the *Excursion*.

Hogg, in his autobiographical *Memoir* of 1832, revised 1833, recounts his first meeting with Wordsworth; James Wilson (1795–1856) was the younger brother of Wordsworth's maverick admirer, John Wilson. Wordsworth visited Hogg (and went with him to the vale of Yarrow) in August 1814; on 11 September Hogg was at Rydal Mount, and with Wordsworth on the terrace along with Wilson, Lloyd, and De Quincey. A brilliant meteor appeared and Hogg told Dorothy Wordsworth not to fear, for it was 'a triumphal airch, raised in honour of the meeting of the poets.' De Quincey reported to Hogg that Wordsworth overheard this and said, 'Poets? Where are they?' (Mary Moorman, *William Worsworth, A Biography: The Later Years, 1803–1850*, II, 276). Hogg was offended; hence the parodies (in later years he thought it possible that De Quincey had lied, and regretted the verses). (*Memoir of the Author's Life*, ed. D. S. Mack, 1972, 68–71)

But the poems, perhaps the most subtle of any parodies of Wordsworth, offer more than irritation; they catch Wordsworth's long sentences, his studied exclamations, his associative argument, his juxtaposition of heightened and domestic language, his liking for the polysyllabic or technical term, his observing and unhurried narrator always at hand to catch a rumour or deliver a meditation. The strength of the poems is that the absurdity can break into seriousness, not least in 'James Rigg', where a man's sudden blindness is described.

---

a. From 'The Stranger', first published in *The Edinburgh Annual Register, 1814* (1816); subtitled, 'A Farther Portion of "The Recluse"'

A stranger asks a boy to hold his horse, and does not return; the butter in the boy's basket melts; the horse is difficult to manage, and finally runs off. The boy's tale is not believed. Months later, the poet, 'Wordsworth', and his friends, supposedly Hogg, Southey and Wilson, discover a skeleton in the lake (the stranger's?). They are filled with a sense of the momentous as a tadpole approaches the skeleton.

The reference to 'sexual intercourse' draws upon the Preface to *Lyrical Ballads* (1800) where Wordsworth says that the pleasure received from metrical language

'. . . derives from the perception of similitude in dissimilitude. This principle is
the great spring of the activity of our minds and their chief feeder. From this
principle the direction of the sexual appetite, and all the passions connected with
it, take their origin.'

> A boy came from the mountains, tripping light
> With basket on his arm – and it appear'd
> That there was butter there, for the white cloth
> That over it was spread, not unobserved,
> In tiny ridges gently rose and fell
> Like graves of children cover'd o'er with snow;
> And by one clumsy fold the traveller spied
> One roll of yellow treasure, all as pure
> As primrose bud reflected in the lake.
> 'Boy,' said the stranger, 'wilt thou hold my steed
> Till I walk round the corner of that mere?
> When I return I will repay thee well.'
> The boy consented – touch'd his slouching hat
> Of broad unequal brim with ready hand,
> And set his basket down upon the sward.
>
> The traveller went away – but ere he went
> He stroak'd his tall brown steed, and look'd at him
> With kind, but yet not unregretful eye.
> The boy stood patient – glad was he to earn
> The little pittance – well the stripling knew
> Of window in the village, where stood ranged
> The brown and tempting cakes – well sprinkled o'er
> With the sham raisin and deceitful plum,
> And, by corporeal functions sway'd, his mind
> Forestall'd the luxury with supreme delight.
>
> Long, long he patient stood – the day was hot . . .
> The stranger came not back . . .
>
>   – The horse went round
> Most unrespective, and, not satisfied
> With whisking his dark tail in furious guise,
> He broke on all propriety, with snort
> Like blustering cannon, or the noise that bursts
> From heaven in thunder through the summer rain.
> The boy was stunn'd – for on similitude,

In dissimilitude man's sole delight,
And all the sexual intercourse of things
Do most supremely hang. – The horse went round,
Jerk'd with his nose, and shook his harness so
The boy wax'd desperate, and – O impious elf!
He cursed that hungry beast – the horse went round,
And round, and round; and pulling in his head
To his fore-pastern, upward made it spring
So forcibly, the poor boy's feeble arm
Was paralyzed – his hold he lost – and off
Like lightning flew the steed, that never more
Was in these regions seen! – Some did report,
Though, I believe, the tale was all untrue,
That a right wayward bard[1], whom I regret
As having left these mountains, where alone
True genius uncontaminate can thrive,
Was seen cantering through Chester on that horse;
And others, that he afterwards became
The horse of a strange youth, not unrenown'd
In early life, who undertook the charge
Of chaplain to a military troop,
Cheer'd by the Highland bagpipe and the drum . . .

    Late did I journey there with bard obscure[2]
From Scotland's barren wastes – barren alike
Of verdure, intellect, and moral sense, –
To view that lonely tarn. – He too was there,
The changeful and right feeble bard now stiled
The Laureate[3] – he too of the Palmy Isle[4],
The man of plagues, horrors, and miseries,
Disgrace of that sweet school, that tuneful choir
Named from these peaceful waters – he who framed
An imitation of that lay divine
Which is inimitable. – Not inept,
Our conversation ran on books and men:
The would-be songster of the Scottish hills[5].
In dialect most uncouth and language rude
Lauded his countrymen, not unrebuked,
Reviewers and review'd, and talk'd amain
Of one unknown, inept, presumptuous bard,

The Border minstrel[6] – he of all the world
Farthest from genius or from common sense.
He too, the royal tool, with erring tongue,
Back'd the poor foolish wight, and utter'd words
For which I blush'd – I could not chuse but smile.
'Yet,' said I, tempted here to interpose,
'You must acknowledge this your favourite
Hath more outraged the purity of speech,
The innate beauties of our English tongue,
For amplitude and nervous structure famed,
Than all the land beside, and therefore he
Deserves the high neglect which he has met
From all the studious and thinking – those
Unsway'd by low caprices of the age,
The scorn of reason, and the world's revile.'
More had I said derisive – yes, by heaven!
Much more I would have said, but that just then
He of the Palms with startled eye look'd round,
And such an eye, as any one may guess
To whom that eye is known – for he beheld
What I yet shudder to define. – 'Great God!'
The youth exclaim'd, 'see what is lying there!'
He of the laurel, who was next to him,
Nay, haply nigher to the shore than he,
Stared in amaze, for he can nothing see;
And in his haste, instead of looking down
Into the water, he look'd up to Heaven:
A most preposterous habit, which the bard
Practises ever and anon – I look'd
Into the peaceful lake, and there beheld
The bones of one who once in mortal life
Had lived and moved – a human skeleton!
I may not say what horrors shook my frame!
The bones seem'd loose, nor film nor ligament
Bound them together, yet each one maintain'd
Its proper place, as loth to break the mould
In which a human soul once householded.
It was a ghastly sight! – where once the heart
Of feeling and of passion play'd, or beat
With ardent throb, lay the dark filmy mud

That gathers in the deep, and on the bones
Appear'd thin soapy spots of greenish hue;
The jaws upon the nape-bone had fallen down,
The scull seem'd looking up – there had he died!
His back upon the sand, his face to heaven!

My mind, borne on the influence of truth,
Turn'd instantly upon the poor boy's tale.
Rightly I judged, for there indeed we saw
All that remain'd of him, the stranger wight,
That lonely wanderer of the mountain reign.

It boots not here to tell all that was said.
The Laureate, sighing, utter'd some few words
Of most sublime and solemn tendency.
The Shepherd spoke most incoherent stuff
About the bones of sheep, that on the hills
Perish unseen, holding their stations so.
And he, the tented Angler of the lakes,
Alias the Man of Palms, said nothing meet.
He was o'ercome with feeling, – it is known
To many, and not quite to me unknown,
That the youth's heart is better than his head.

Glad of this opportunity, I said,
Still pointing to the bones, 'Access for you
Is yet preserved to principles of truth,
Which the imaginative will upholds
In seats of wisdom, not to be approach'd
By the inferior faculty that moulds
With her minute and speculative pains
Opinions ever changing – I have seen
Regenerative Nature prostrate lie
And drink the souls of things – of living things
And things inanimate, and thus hold up
The beings that we are – that change shall clothe
The naked spirit ceasing to deplore
The burden of existence, her dull eye
To other scenes still changing still unchanged.
The thinking thoughtless school-boy, the bold youth
Of soul impetuous, and the bashful maid,

All cogitative yield obedience up.
And whence this tribute? wherefore these regards?
Not from the naked heart alone of man,
Though framed to high distinction upon earth,
As the sole spring and fountain-head of tears,
His own peculiar utterance for distress
Or gladness – it is not the vital part
Of feeling to produce them, without aid
From the pure soul, the soul sublimed and pure
With her two faculties of eye and ear,
Not without such assistance could the eye
Of these benign observances prevail;
Thus are they born, thus foster'd, and maintain'd,
And by the care prospective of our wise
Forefathers, who, to guard against the shocks,
The fluctuation, and decay of things.
There lies the channel and original bed,'
Continued I, still pointing to the lake,
'From the beginning hollow'd out and scoop'd
For man's affections, else betray'd and lost,
And swallow'd up 'mid desarts infinite.
This is the genuine course, the aim and end
Of prescient reason, all conclusions else
Are abject, vain, presumptuous, and perverse.'

The men were thunderstruck; the Angler most.
That man of palms and plagues, vile copyist!
Seem'd compassed in wonder – in my face
Wistful he gazed, and ever and anon
He utter'd a short sound at every pause,
But further ventured not – upon the ear
Of the poor shepherd all these breathings fell
Like sounds of distant waters – like the rain,
The treasures of the sky, on the firm flint,
So moveless his impenetrative soul,
He scratch'd his poll – the Laureate look'd to heaven.

More had I said, resuming the discourse
Of subterraneous magazines of bones,
The faint reflections of infinitude,
The moon and the unvoyageable sky,

And all the high observances of things,
But that, chancing again to turn my eyes
Toward the bosom of that peaceful mere,
I saw a form so ominous approach
My heart was chill'd with horror – through the wave
Slowly it came – by heaven I saw it move
Toward the grizly skeleton! – Its shape
Was like a coffin, and its colour such,
Black as the death-pall or the cloud of night!
At sight of such a hideous messenger,
Thus journeying through the bowels of the deep,
O'er sluggish leaf and unelaborate stone,
All Nature stood in mute astonishment,
As if her pulse lay still – onward it came,
And hovering o'er the bones, it linger'd there
In a most holy and impressive guise.
I saw it shake its hideous form, and move
Towards my feet – the elements were hush'd,
The birds forsook their singing, for the sight
Was fraught with wonder and astonishment.
It was a tadpole – somewhere by itself
The creature had been left, and there had come
Most timeously, by Providence sent forth,
To close this solemn and momentous tale.

b. 'The Flying Tailor – Further Extract from "The Recluse," a Poem'

Hogg seems to have in mind here, particularly at the beginning, Books VI and VII of the *Excursion*, entitled 'The Churchyard among the Mountains'.

IF ever chance or choice thy footsteps lead
Into that green and flowery burial-ground
That compasseth with sweet and mournful smiles
The church of Grassmere, – by the eastern gate
Enter – and underneath a stunted yew,
Some three yards distant from the gravel-walk,
On the left-hand side, thou wilt espy a grave,
With unelaborate head-stone beautified,
Conspicuous 'mid the other stoneless heaps
'Neath which the children of the valley lie.

There pause – and with no common feelings read
This short inscription – 'Here lies buried
The Flying Tailor, aged twenty-nine'!

    Him from his birth unto his death I knew,
And many years before he had attain'd
The fulness of his fame, I prophesied
The triumphs of that youth's agility,
And crown'd him with that name which afterwards
He nobly justified – and dying left
To fame's eternal blazon – read it here –
'The Flying Tailor!'

                        It is somewhat strange
That his mother was a cripple, and his father
Long way declined into the vale of years
When their son Hugh was born. At first the babe
Was sickly, and a smile was seen to pass
Across the midwife's cheek, when, holding up
The sickly wretch, she to the father said,
'A fine man-child!' What else could they expect?
The mother being, as I said before,
A cripple, and the father of the child
Long way declined into the vale of years.

    But mark the wondrous change – ere he was put
By his mother into breeches, Nature strung
The muscular part of his economy
To an unusual strength, and he could leap,
All unimpeded by his petticoats,
Over the stool on which his mother sat
When carding wool, or cleansing vegetables,
Or meek performing other household tasks.
Cunning he watch'd his opportunity,
And oft, as house-affairs did call her thence,
Overleapt Hugh, a perfect whirligig,
More than six inches o'er th' astonish'd stool.
What boots it to narrate, how at leap-frog
Over the breech'd and unbreech'd villagers
He shone conspicuous? Leap-frog do I say?
Vainly so named. What though in attitude

The Flying Tailor aped the croaking race
When issuing from the weed-entangled pool,
Tadpoles no more, they seek the new-mown fields,
A jocund people, bouncing to and fro'
Amid the odorous clover – while amazed
The grasshopper sits idle on the stalk
With folded pinions and forgets to sing.
Frog-like, no doubt, in attitude he was;
But sure his bounds across the village green
Seem'd to my soul – (my soul for ever bright
With purest beams of sacred poesy)
Like bounds of red-deer on the Highland-hill,
When, close-environed by the tinchel's chain,
He lifts his branchy forehead to the sky,
Then o'er the many-headed multitude
Springs belling half in terror, half in rage,
And fleeter than the sunbeam or the wind
Speeds to his cloud-lair on the mountain-top.

No more of this – suffice it to narrate,
In his tenth year he was apprenticed
Under a Master Tailor by a strong
And regular indenture of seven years,
Commencing from the date the parchment bore,
And ending on a certain day, that made
The term complete of seven solar years.
Oft have I heard him say, that at this time
Of life he was most wretched; for, constrain'd
To sit all day cross-legg'd upon a board,
The natural circulation of the blood
Thereby was oft impeded, and he felt
So numb'd at times, that when he strove to rise
Up from his work he could not, but fell back
Among the shreds and patches that bestrew'd
With various colours, brightening gorgeously,
The board all round him – patch of warlike red
With which he patched the regimental-suits
Of a recruiting military troop,
At that time stationed in a market town
At no great distance – eke of solemn black

Shreds of no little magnitude, with which
The parson's Sunday-coat was then repairing,
That in the new-roof'd church he might appear
With fitting dignity – and gravely fill
The sacred seat of pulpit eloquence,
Chearing with doctrinal point and words of faith
The poor man's heart, and from the shallow wit
Of atheist drying up each argument,
Or sharpening his own weapons only to turn
Their point against himself, and overthrow
His idols with the very enginery
Reared 'gainst the structure of our English church.

Oft too, when striving all he could to finish
The stated daily task, the needle's point,
Slanting insidious from th' eluded stitch,
Hath pinch'd his finger, by the thimble's mail
In vain defended, and the crimson blood
Distain'd the lining of some wedding-suit,
A dismal omen! that to mind like his,
Apt to perceive in slightest circumstance
Mysterious meaning, yielded sore distress
And feverish perturbation, so that oft
He scarce could eat his dinner – nay, one night
He swore to run from his apprenticeship,
And go on board a first-rate man-of-war,
From Plymouth lately come to Liverpool,
Where, in the stir and tumult of a crew
Composed of many nations, 'mid the roar
Of wave and tempest, and the deadlier voice
Of battle, he might strive to mitigate
The fever that consumed his mighty heart.

But other doom was his. That very night
A troop of tumblers came into the village,
Tumbler, equestrian, mountebank, – on wire,
On rope, on horse, with cup and balls, intent
To please the gaping multitude, and win
The coin from labour's pocket – small perhaps
Each separate piece of money, but when join'd
Making a good round sum, destined ere long

All to be melted, (so these lawless folk
Name spending coin in loose debauchery)
Melted into ale – or haply stouter cheer,
Gin diuretic, or the liquid flame
Of baneful brandy, by the smuggler brought
From the French coast in shallop many-oar'd,
Skulking by night round headland and through bay,
Afraid of the King's cutter, or the barge
Of cruising frigate, arm'd with chosen men,
And with her sweeps across the foamy waves
Moving most beautiful with measured strokes.

It chanced that as he threw a somerset
Over three horses (each of larger size
Than our small mountain-breed) one of the troop
Put out his shoulder, and was otherwise
Considerably bruised, especially
About the loins and back. So he became
Useless unto that wandering company,
And likely to be felt a sore expense
To men just on the eve of bankruptcy.
So the master of the troop determined
To leave him in the work-house, and proclaim'd
That if there was a man among the crowd
Willing to fill his place and able too,
Now was the time to shew himself. Hugh Thwaites
Heard the proposal, as he stood apart
Striving with his own soul – and with a bound
He leapt into the circle, and agreed
To supply the place of him who had been hurt.
A shout of admiration and surprise
Then tore heaven's concave, and completely filled
The little field, where near a hundred people
Were standing in a circle round and fair.
Oft have I striven by meditative power,
And reason working 'mid the various forms
Of various occupations and professions,
To explain the cause of one phenomenon,
That since the birth of science hath remain'd
A bare enunciation, unexplain'd

By any theory, or mental light
Stream'd on it by the imaginative will,
Or spirit musing in the cloudy shrine
The Penetralia of the immortal soul.
I now allude to that most curious fact,
That 'mid a given number, say threescore,
Of tailors, more men of agility
Will issue out, than from an equal shew
From any other occupation – say
Smiths, barbers, bakers, butchers, or the like.
Let me not seem presumptuous, if I strive
This subject to illustrate; nor, while I give
My meditations to the world, will I
Conceal from it, that much I have to say
I learnt from one who knows the subject well
In theory and practice – need I name him?
The light-heel'd author of the Isle of Palms,
Illustrious more for leaping than for song.

    First, then, I would lay down this principle,
That all excessive action by the law
Of nature tends unto repose. This granted,
All action not excessive must partake
The nature of excessive action – so
That in all human beings who keep moving,
Unconscious cultivation of repose
Is going on in silence. Be it so.
Apply to men of sedentary lives
This leading principle, and we behold
That, active in their inactivity,
And unreposing in their long repose,
They are, in fact, the sole depositaries
Of all the energies by others wasted
And come at last to teem with impulses
Of muscular emotion, not to be withstood,
And either giving vent unto themselves
Innumerous feats of wild agility,
Or terminating in despair and death.

    Now of all sedentary lives, none seems
So much so as the tailor's. – Weavers use

Both arms and legs, and, we may safely add,
Their bodies too, for arms and legs can't move
Without the body – as the waving branch
Of the green oak disturbs his glossy trunk.
Not so the Tailor – for he sits cross-legg'd,
Cross-legg'd for ever! save at time of meals,
In bed, or when he takes his little walk
From shop to alehouse, picking as he goes
Stray patch of fustian, cloth, or cassimere,
Which, as by natural instinct, he discerns,
Though soil'd with mud, and by the passing wheel
Bruised to attenuation 'gainst the stones.

Here then we pause – and need no farther go,
We have reached the sea-mark of our utmost sail.
Now let me trace the effect upon his mind
Of this despised profession. Deem not thou,
O rashly deem not, that his boyish days
Past at the shop-board, when the stripling bore
With bashful feeling of apprenticeship
The name of Tailor, deem not that his soul
Derived no genial influence from a life,
Which, although haply adverse in the main
To the growth of intellect, and the excursive power,
Yet in its ordinary forms possess'd
A constant influence o'er his passing thoughts,
Moulded his appetences and his will,
And wrought not, by the work of sympathy,
Between his bodily and mental form,
Rare correspondence, wond'rous unity!
Perfect – complete – and fading not away.
While on his board cross-legg'd he used to sit,
Shaping of various garments, to his mind
An image rose of every character
For whom each special article was framed,
Coat, waistcoat, breeches. So at last his soul
Was like a storehouse, fill'd with images,
By musing hours of solitude supplied.
Nor did his ready fingers shape the cut
Of villager's uncouth habiliments

With greater readiness, than did his mind
Frame corresponding images of those
Whose corporal measurement the neat-mark'd paper
In many a mystic notch for aye retain'd.
Hence, more than any man I ever knew,
Did he possess the power intuitive
Of diving into character. A pair
Of breeches to his philosophic eye
Were not what unto other folks they seem,
Mere simple breeches, but in them he saw
The symbol of the soul – mysterious, high
Hieroglyphics! such as Egypt's Priest
Adored upon the holy Pyramid,
Vainly imagined tomb of monarchs old,
But raised by wise philosophy, that sought
By darkness to illumine, and to spread
Knowledge by dim concealment – process high
Of man's imaginative, deathless soul.
Nor, haply, in th' abasement of the life
Which stern necessity had made his own,
Did he not recognize a genial power
Of soul-ennobling fortitude. He heard
Unmoved the witling's shallow contumely,
And thus, in spite of nature, by degrees
He saw a beauty and a majesty
In this despised trade, which warrior's brow
Hath rarely circled – so that when he sat
Beneath his sky-light window, he hath cast
A gaze of triumph on the godlike sun,
And felt that orb, in all his annual round,
Beheld no happier nobler character
Than him, Hugh Thwaites, a little tailor-boy.

Thus I, with no unprofitable song,
Have, in the silence of the umbrageous wood,
Chaunted the heroic youthful attributes
Of him the Flying Tailor. Much remains
Of highest argument, to lute or lyre
Fit to be murmur'd with impassion'd voice;
And when, by timely supper and by sleep
Refresh'd, I turn me to the welcome task,

With lofty hopes, – Reader, do thou expect
The final termination of my lay.
For, mark my words, – eternally my name
Shall last on earth, conspicuous like a star
'Mid that bright galaxy of favour'd spirits,
Who, laugh'd at constantly whene'er they publish'd,
Survived the impotent scorn of base Reviews,
Monthly or Quarterly, or that accursed
Journal, the Edinburgh Review, that lives
On tears, and sighs, and groans, and brains, and blood.

c. 'James Rigg – Still Further Extract from "The Recluse," a Poem'

ON Tuesday morn, at half-past six o'clock,
I rose and dress'd myself, and having shut
The door o' the bed-room still and leisurely,
I walk'd down-stairs. When at the outer-door
I firmly grasp'd the key that ere night-fall
Had turn'd the lock into its wonted niche
Within the brazen implement, that shone
With no unseemly splendour, – mellow'd light,
Elicited by touch of careful hand
On the brown lintel; and th' obedient door,
As at a potent necromancer's touch,
Into the air receded suddenly,
And gave wide prospect of the sparkling lake,
Just then emerging from the snow-white mist
Like angel's veil slow-folded up to heaven.
And lo! a vision bright and beautiful
Sheds a refulgent glory o'er the sand,
The sand and gravel of my avenue!
For, standing silent by the kitchen-door,
Tinged by the morning sun, and in its own
Brown natural hide most lovely, two long ears
Upstretching perpendicularly, then
With the horizon levell'd – to my gaze
Superb as horn of fabled Unicorn,
Each in its own proportions grander far
Than the frontal glory of that wandering beast,
Child of the Desart! Lo! a beauteous Ass,
With panniers hanging silent at each side!

964

Silent as cage of bird whose song is mute,
Though silent yet not empty, fill'd with bread
The staff of life, the means by which the soul
By fate obedient to the powers of sense,
Renews its faded vigour, and keeps up
A proud communion with the eternal heavens.
Fasten'd to a ring it stood, while at its head
A boy of six years old, as angel bright,
Patted its neck, and to its mouth applied
The harmless thistle that his hand had pluck'd
From the wild common, melancholy crop.

   Not undelightful was that simple sight,
For I at once did recognize that ass
To be the property of one James Rigg,
Who for the last seven years had managed,
By a firm course of daily industry,
A numerous family to support, and clothe
In plain apparel of our shepherd's grey.
On him a heavy and calamitous lot
Had fallen. For working up among the hills
In a slate-quarry, while he fill'd the stone,
Bored by his cunning, with the nitrous grain,
It suddenly exploded, and the flash
Quench'd the bright lustre of his cheerful eyes
For ever, so that now they roll in vain
To find the searching light that idly plays
O'er the white orbs, and on the silent cheeks
By those orbs unillumined calm and still.

   Quoth I, I never see thee and thy ass,
My worthy friend, but I methinks behold
The might of that unconquerable spirit,
Which, operating in the ancient world
Before the Flood, when fallen man was driven
From paradise, accompanied him to fields
Bare and unlovely, when the sterile earth
Oft mock'd the kindly culture of the hand
Of scientific agriculture – mock'd
The shepherd's sacrifice, and even denied
A scanty pittance to the fisherman,

Who by the rod or net sought to supply
His natural wants from river or from mere.
Blind were these people to the cunning arts
Of smooth civility – men before the Flood,
And therefore in the scriptures rightly call'd
Antediluvians!

         While thus I spake
With wisdom, that industrious blind old man,
Seemingly flatter'd by those words of mine,
Which, judging by myself, I scarcely think
He altogether understood, replied,
While the last thistle slowly disappear'd
Within the jaws of that most patient beast:
'Master!' quoth he, – and while he spake his hat
With something of a natural dignity
Was holden in his hand – 'Master,' quoth he,
'I hear that you and Mrs. Wordsworth think
Of going into Scotland, and I wish
To know if, while the family are from home,
I shall supply the servants with their bread,
For I suppose they will not all be put
Upon board-wages.'

         Something in his voice,
While thus he spake, of simplest articles
Of household use, yet sunk upon my soul,
Like distant thunder from the mountain-gloom
Wakening the sleeping echoes, so sublime
Was that old man, so plainly eloquent
His untaught tongue! though something of a lisp,
(Natural defect,) and a slight stutter too
(Haply occasion'd by some faint attack,
Harmless, if not renew'd, of apoplex)
Render'd his utterance most peculiar,
So that a stranger, had he heard that voice
Once only, and then travell'd into lands
Beyond the ocean, had on his return,
Met where they might, have known that curious voice
Of lisp and stutter, yet I ween withal
Graceful, and breathed from an original mind.

Here let me be permitted to relate,
For sake of those few readers who prefer
A simple picture of the heart to all
Poetic imagery from earth or heaven
Drawn by the skill of bard, – let me, I say,
For sake of such few readers, be permitted
To tell, in plain and ordinary verse,
What James Rigg first experienced in his soul,
Standing amid the silence of the hills,
With both the pupils of his eyes destroyed.

When first the loud explosion through the sky
Sent its far voice, and from the trembling rocks
That with an everlasting canopy
O'ershadow Stickle-Tarn the echoes woke,
So that the mountain-solitude was filled
With sound, as with the air! He stood awhile,
Wondering from whence the tumult might proceed,
And all unconscious that the blast had dimm'd
His eyes for ever, and their smiling blue
Converted to a pale and mournful grey.
Was it, he thought, some blast the quarrymen
Blasted at Conniston, or in that vale,
Called from its huge and venerable yew,
Yewdale? (though other etymologists
Derive that appellation from the sheep,
Of which the female in our English tongue
Still bears the name of ewe.) Or did the gun
Of fowler, wandering o'er the heathery wilds
In search of the shy gor-cock, yield that voice
Close to his ear, so close that through his soul
It rolled like thunder? Or had news arrived
Of Buonaparte's last discomfiture,
By the bold Russ, and that great heir of fame
Blucher, restorer of the thrones of kings?
And upon Lowood bowling-green did Laker
Glad of expedient to beguile the hours,
Slow moving before dinner, did he fire
In honour of that glorious victory,
The old two-pounder by the wind and rain
Rusted, and seemingly to him more old

Than in reality it was, though old,
And on that same green lying since the days
Of the last landlord, Gilbert Ormathwaite,
Name well-remember'd all the country round,
Though twenty summer suns have shed their flowers
On the green turf that hides his mortal dust.
Or was it, thought he, the loud signal gun
Of pleasure-boat, on bright Winander's wave,
Preparing 'gainst some new antagonist
To spread her snowy wings before the wind,
Emulous of glory and the palmy wreath
Of inland navigation? graceful sport!
It next perhaps occurr'd to him to ask,
Himself, or some one near him, if the sound
Was not much louder than those other sounds,
Fondly imagined by him, – and both he,
And that one near him instantly replied
Unto himself, that most assuredly
The noise proceeded from the very stone,
Which they two had so long been occupied
In boring, and that probably some spark,
Struck from the gavelock 'gainst the treacherous flint,
Had fallen amid the powder, and so caused
The stone t' explode, as gunpowder will do,
With most miraculous force, especially
When close ramm'd down into a narrow bore,
And cover'd o'er with a thin layer of sand
To exclude the air, else otherwise the grain,
Escaping from the bore, would waste itself
In the clear sky, and leave the bored stone
Lying unmoved upon the verdant earth,
Like some huge creature stretch'd in lazy sleep
Amid the wilderness, – or lying dead
Beneath the silence of the summer sun.

   This point establish'd, he was gently led
By the natural progress of the human soul,
Aspiring after truth, nor satisfied
Till she hath found it, wheresoever hid,
(Yea even though at the bottom of a well,)
To enquire if any mischief had been done

By that explosion; and while thus he stood
Enquiring anxiously for all around,
A small sharp boy, whose task it was to bring
His father's breakfast to him 'mid the hills,
Somewhat about eleven years of age,
Though less than some lads at the age of eight,
Exclaim'd – 'Why, father, do you turn the white
Of your eyes up so?' At these simple words
Astonishment and horror struck the souls
Of all the quarrymen, for they descried,
Clear as the noon-day, that James Rigg had lost
His eyesight, yea his very eyes were lost,
Quench'd in their sockets, melted into air,
A moisture mournful as the cold dim gleam
Of water sleeping in some shady wood,
Screen'd from the sunbeams and the breath of heaven.

  On that he lifted up his harden'd hands,
Harden'd by sun, and rain, and storm, and toil,
Unto the blasted eye-balls, and awhile
Stood motionless as fragment of that rock
That wrought him all his woe, and seem'd to lie,
Unwitting of the evil it had done,
Calm and serene, even like a flock of sheep,
Scatter'd in sunshine o'er the Cheviot-hills.
I ween that, as he stood in solemn trance,
Tears flow'd for him who wept not for himself,
And that his fellow-quarrymen, though rude
Of soul and manner, not untouchingly
Deplored his cruel doom, and gently led
His footsteps to a green and mossy rock,
By sportive Nature fashion'd like a chair,
With seat, back, elbows, – a most perfect chair
Of unhewn living rock! There, hapless man,
He moved his lips, as if he inly pray'd,
And clasp'd his hands and raised his sightless face
 Unto the smiling sun, who walk'd through heaven,
Regardless of that fatal accident,
By which a man was suddenly reduced
From an unusual clear long-sightedness
To utter blindness – blindness without hope,

So wholly were the visual nerves destroyed.
'I wish I were at home!' he slowly said,
'For though I ne'er must see that home again,
I yet may hear it, and a thousand sounds
Are there to gladden a poor blind man's heart.'

He utter'd truth, – lofty, consoling truth!
Thanks unto gracious Nature, who hath framed
So wondrously the structure of the soul,
That though it live on outward ministry,
Of gross material objects, by them fed
And nourish'd, even as if th' external world
Were the great wet-nurse of the human race,
Yet of such food deprived, she doth not pine
And fret away her mystic energies
In fainting inanition; but, superior
To the food she fed on, in her charge retains
Each power, and sense, and faculty, and lives,
Cameleon-like, upon the air serene
Of her own bright imaginative will,
Desiderating nothing that upholds,
Upholds and magnifies, but without eyes
Sees – and without the vestige of an ear
Listens, and listening, hears – and without sense
Of touch (if haply from the body's surface
Have gone the sense of feeling) keenly feels,
And in despite of nose abbreviate
Smells like a wolf – wolf who for leagues can snuff
The scent of carrion, bird by fowler kill'd,
Kill'd but not found, or little vernal kid
Yean'd in the frost, and soon outstretch'd in death,
White as the snow that serves it for a shroud.

Therefore James Rigg was happy, and his face
Soon brighten'd up with smiles, and in his voice
Contentment spoke most musical; so when
The doctor order'd his most worthy wife
To loose the bandage from her husband's eyes,
He was so reconciled unto his lot,
That there almost appear'd to him a charm
In blindness – so that, had his sight return'd,

I have good reason to believe his happiness
Had been thereby scarcely at all increased.

   While thus confabulating with James Rigg,
Even at that moment when such silence lay
O'er all my cottage, as by mystic power
Belonging to the kingdom of the ear,
O'erthrew at once all old remembrances –
Even at that moment, over earth, and air,
The waving forest, and the sleeping lake,
And the far sea of mountains that uplifted
Its stately billows through the clear blue sky,
Came such a sound, as if from her dumb trance
Awaken'd Nature, starting suddenly,
Were jealous of insulted majesty,
And sent through continent and trembling isle
Her everlasting thunders. Such a crash
Tore the foundations of the earth, and shook
The clouds that slumber'd on the breast of heaven!
It was the parlour-bell that suddenly
An unknown hand had rung. I cast my eyes
Up the long length of bell-rope, and I saw
The visible motion of its iron tongue,
By heaven I *saw* it tinkling. Fast at first,
O most unearthly fast, then somewhat slower,
Next very slow indeed, until some four
Or half-a-dozen minutes at the most,
By Time's hand cut from off the shorten'd hour,
It stopp'd quite of itself – and idly down,
Like the sear leaf upon th' autumnal bough
Dangled!

EDITOR'S NOTES

1. A reference possibly to Coleridge.
2. Hogg.
3. Southey.
4. Wilson.
5. Hogg.
6. Scott.

263. John Keats (1795–1821)

From his letters and writings, 1817–1819, including reminiscences from Benjamin Robert Haydon and Benjamin Bailey

Keats's admiration for Wordsworth, aroused by his meeting both Leigh Hunt and Benjamin Robert Haydon in October, is attested by his sonnet of 19 or 20 November 1816: 'Great Spirits now on Earth are sojourning'; and less clearly in 'Sleep and Poetry' (complete by December 1816) where Keats finds a true music of poetry 'has been upstirred / From out its crystal dwelling in a lake / By a swan's ebon bill' (224–6). *The Excursion*, Book IV, was for Keats a seminal experience. Hunt, reviewing Keats's *Poems* (1817) in the *Examiner*, 6 July 1817, notes that Keats (in 'I stood tiptoe') 'alludes to the origin of the other lovely tales of mythology, on the ground suggested by Mr Wordsworth in a beautiful passage of his *Excursion*.' Haydon in his copy of the *Excursion* (at Cornell University) has written against IV, 858–64: 'Poor Keats used always to prefer this passage to all others.'

By early 1818, Keats's admiration of Wordsworth is put to the test by, first, the political-literary attacks in the *Examiner*, from Hunt and Hazlitt. Second, by his meetings with Wordsworth himself, December 1817 to January 1818; and, third, by his hearing some of Hazlitt's Lectures on the English Poets, late January to early March, 1818, where the notion of Wordsworth's egotism was forcibly presented. Thereafter, Wordsworth is a poet whose power Keats seriously feels, but rather as something alien to his own poetic personality.

a. From a letter of B. R. Haydon to Wordsworth, 31 December 1816

Keats's sonnet, composed 19–20 November 1816, was published in *Poems* (1817).

I copy out a Sonnet by a Young Poet Keats addressed to me, but beginning with you – I should wish very much to know what you think of it – he promises a great deal – and said in a letter to me when I promised to enclose it to you – 'The idea of your sending it to Wordsworth puts me out of breath, you know with what Reverence I should send my well wishes to him' &c –

Great Spirits now on Earth are sojourning
He of the Cloud, the Cataract, the Lake
Who on Helvellyn's summit wide awake
Catches his freshness from archangels wing . . .
[Continues with references to Hunt and Haydon.]
These These will give the World another heart
And other Pulses – hear ye not the hum
Of mighty workings? —
Listen awhile ye Nations and be dumb! –

he is quite a Youth, full of eagerness & enthusiasm, and what greatly recommends him to me, he has a very fine head! – he is now writing a longer sort of poem of Diana & Endymion, to publish with his smaller productions, and will send you a copy as soon as it is out – I need not say his reverence for you my dear Sir is unbounded –

(Ms. The Wordsworth Library)

Wordsworth, pleased and interested, found the sonnet 'of good promise' and 'very agreeably concluded' (*MY*, II, 360–1).

b. Item 1251 of Sotheby's catalogue for June 1896

A copy of Keats's *Poems* (1817) inscribed, 'To W. Wordsworth with the author's sincere reverence'. The book is described as a 'fine uncut copy'.

c. From a letter to Haydon, 11 May 1817

'Tis good too that the Duke of Wellington has a good Word or so in the Examiner A Man ought to have the Fame he deserves – and I begin to think that detracting from him as well as from Wordsworth is the same thing.

(*Letters of John Keats*, ed. H. E. Rollins, 1958, I, 144)

d. From a letter to J. H. Reynolds, September 1817

Keats was staying at Oxford with Benjamin Bailey (1791–1853), a decided admirer of Wordsworth.[1]

Wordsworth sometimes, though in a fine way, gives us sentences in the Style of School exercises – for Instance.

973

The lake doth glitter
Small birds twitter &c.
['Written in March [1802], While Resting at
the Bridge at the foot of Brother's Water,'
ll. 3–4]

Now I think this is an excellent method of giving a very clear description
of an interesting place such as Oxford is –

The Gothic looks solemn, –
The plain Doric column
Supports an old Bishop & crosier;
The mouldering arch,
Shaded o'er by a larch,
Lives next door to Wilson the hosier . . .

(*Ibid.*, I, 151–2)

e. From a letter of Benjamin Bailey to R. M. Milnes, Keats's first biographer, 7 May 1849

Bailey recollects his Oxford conversations with Keats of late September and early
October, 1817.

Our conversation rarely or never flagged, during our walks, or boatings,
or in the Evening. And I have retained a few of his opinions on Literature
& Criticism which I will detail.

The following passage from Wordsworth's ode on Immortality was
deeply felt by Keats, who however at this time seemed to me to value this
great Poet rather in particular passages than in the full length portrait, as
it were, of the great imaginative & philosophic Christian Poet, which he
really is, & which Keats obviously, not long afterwards, felt him to be.

Not for these I raise
The song of thanks & praise;
But for those obstinate questionings
Of sense & outward things,
Fallings from us, vanishings;
Blank misgivings of a creature
Moving about in worlds not realized,
High instincts, before which our mortal nature
Did tremble like a guilty thing surprized.
['Ode: Intimations of Immortality', ll. 140–8]

The last lines he thought were quite awful in their application to a guilty finite creature, like man, in the appalling nature of the feeling which they suggested to a thoughtful mind.

Again, we often talked of that noble passage in the Lines on Tintern Abbey: –

> That blessed mood,
> In which *the burthen of the mystery*,
> In which the heavy & the weary weight
> Of all this unintelligible world
> Is lightened.
>
> ['Tintern Abbey', ll. 37–41]

And his references to this passage are frequent in his letters. – But in those exquisite stanzas: –

> She dwelt among the untrodden ways,
> Beside the springs of Dove –
>
> [1–2]

ending, –

> She lived unknown & few could know
> When Lucy ceased to be;
> But she is in her grave, & oh,
> *The difference to me* –
>
> [9–12]

the simplicity of the last line he declared to be the most perfect pathos.

Among the qualities of high poetic promise in Keats was, even at this time, his correct taste. I remember to have been struck with this by his remarks on that well known & often quoted passage of the Excursion upon the Greek Mythology, – where it is said that

> Fancy fetched
> Even from the blazing Chariot of the Sun
> A beardless youth who touched a golden lute,
> *And filled the illumined groves with ravishment.*

Keats said this description of Apollo should have ended at the 'golden lute,' & have left it to the imagination to complete the picture, – *how* he 'filled the illumined groves.' I think every man of taste will feel the justice of the remark.[2]

(*The Keats Circle*, ed. H. E. Rollins, Harvard, 1948, II, 274–6)

f. From a letter of Keats to Benjamin Bailey, 28–30 October 1817

Keats is discussing Hazlitt's footnote to his essay 'On Manner', (see Hazlitt, entry 256c, 27 August 1815).

Now with respect to Wordsworth's Gipseys I think he is right and yet I think Hazlitt is right and yet I think Wordsworth is rightest. Wordsworth had not been idle he had not been without his task – nor had they Gipseys – they in the visible world had been as picturesque an object as he in the invisible. The Smoke of their fire – their attitudes – their Voices were all in harmony with the Evenings – It is a bold thing to say and I would not say it in print – but it seems to me that if Wordsworth had thought a little deeper at that Moment he would not have written the Poem at all – I should judge it to [has *deleted*] have been written in one of the most comfortable Moods of his Life – it is a kind of sketchy intellectual Landscape – not a search after Truth – nor is it fair to attack him on such a subject – for it is with the Critic as with the poet had Hazlitt thought a little deeper and had been in a good temper he would never had spied an imaginary fault there.

(*Letters of John Keats*, ed. H. E. Rollins, 1958, I, 173–4)

g. From a letter to Haydon, 10 January 1818

Also evey [*sic*] day older I get – the greater is my idea of your atchievements [*sic*] in Art: and I am convinced that there are three things to rejoice at in this Age – The Excursion Your Pictures, and Hazlitt's depth of Taste.

(*Ibid.*, I, 203)

h. Keats to Benjamin Bailey, 23 January 1818

'I have seen a great deal of Wordsworth.'

There were at least five, and possibly six, meetings between Wordsworth and Keats. They met on 28 December 1817 at Haydon's famous dinner party (with Lamb berating John Kingston, the newly appointed Commissioner of Stamps – Wordsworth's superior (see entry 258h)); possibly Keats had been introduced by Haydon some days[3] before this and it was at the *first* meeting at Thomas Monkhouse's, 28 Queen Anne Street West, that Keats recited the 'Hymn to Pan' and Haydon, in 1845, reports that 'Wordsworth drily said "a Very pretty piece of Paganism" –' (*The Keats Circle*, ed. H. E. Rollins, Harvard, 1948, II, 143–4). Haydon's comment of 1845 that Keats 'never forgave' Wordsworth seems untrue. They also met on 31 December upon Hampstead Heath; on 3 January, when Keats called at 48 Mortimer Street where Wordsworth was staying: to Keats's surprise, after he had been kept waiting, Wordsworth (with his wife and, probably, Sara Hutchinson) appeared with a stiff collar, departing to dine with Kingston. Keats himself had declined Kingston's invitation – 'not liking that place' – but he arranged to dine with Wordsworth on Monday, 5 January. On this occasion, perhaps, Mary Wordsworth prevented Keats from disagreeing on a point with Wordsworth by putting her hand upon his arm: 'Mr. Wordsworth is never interrupted' (Cowden Clarke, 'Recollections of Keats', *Atlantic Monthly*, January 1861, Vol. VII, 97). Monkhouse also invited Haydon; the weather was too bad for the painter's eyes and he declined but wrote: 'Keats will be with you punctually – he went into the City' (Ms. Mr. Jonathan Wordsworth). Whether this invitation was for 5 January or another occasion is not clear. Wordsworth left London 20 January; on 21 February Keats wrote to his brothers: 'I am sorry that Wordsworth has left a bad impression wherever he visited in Town – by his egotism, Vanity and bigotry – yet he is a great Poet if not a Philosopher' (*Letters*, I, 235). Wordsworth felt no hostility towards Keats: he wrote to Haydon 16 January 1820: 'How is Keates, he is a youth of promise too great for the sorry company he keeps' (*MY*, II, 578).

i. From a letter to J. H. Reynolds, 3 February 1818

It may be said that we ought to read our Contemporaries. that Wordsworth &c should have their due from us. but for the sake of a few fine imaginative or domestic passages, are we to be bullied into a certain Philosophy engendered in the whims of an Egotist – Every man has his speculations, but every man does not brood and peacock over them till he makes a false coinage and deceives himself – Many a man can travel to the very bourne of Heaven, and yet want confidence to put down his halfseeing. Sancho will invent a Journey heavenward as well as any body. We hate poetry that has a palpable design upon us – and if we do not agree, seems to put its hand in its breeches pocket. Poetry should be great & unobtrusive, a thing which enters into one's soul, and does not startle it or amaze it with itself but with its subject. – How beautiful are the retired flowers! how would they lose their beauty were they to throng into the highway crying out, 'admire me I am a violet! dote upon me I am a primrose! Modern poets differ from the Elizabethans in this. Each of the moderns like an Elector of Hanover governs his petty state, & knows how many straws are swept daily from the Causeways in all his dominions & has a continual itching that all the Housewives should have their coppers well scoured: the antients were Emperors of vast Provinces, they had only heard of the remote ones and scarcely cared to visit them. – I will cut all this – I will have no more of Wordsworth or Hunt in particular – Why should we be of the tribe of Manasseh, when we can wander with Esau? why should we kick against the Pricks, when we can walk on Roses? Why should we be owls, when we can be Eagles? Why be teased with "nice Eyed wagtails,"[4] when we have in sight 'the Cherub Contemplation'? – Why with Wordsworths 'Matthew with a bough of wilding in his hand'[5] when we can have Jacques 'under an oak &c' – The secret of the Bough of Wilding will run through your head faster than I can write it – Old Matthew spoke to him some years ago on some nothing, & because he happens in an Evening Walk to imagine the figure of the old man – he must stamp it down in black & white, and it is henceforth sacred – I don't mean to deny Wordsworth's grandeur & Hunt's merit, but I mean to say we need not be teazed with grandeur & merit – when we can have them uncontaminated & unobtrusive.

(*Ibid.*, I, 223–4)

j. From a letter to Reynolds, 3 May 1818

My Branchings out have been numerous: one of them is the consideration of Wordsworth's genius and as a help, in the manner of gold being the meridian Line of worldly wealth, – how he differs from Milton. – And here I have nothing but surmises, from an uncertainty whether Miltons apparently less anxiety for Humanity proceeds from his seeing further or no than Wordsworth: And whether Wordsworth has in truth epic passion, and martyrs himself to the human heart, the main region of his song – In regard to his genius alone – we find what he says true as far as we have experienced and we can judge no further but by larger experience – for axioms in philosophy are not axioms until they are proved upon our pulses . . .

. . . I will return to Wordsworth – whether or no he has an extended vision or a circumscribed grandeur – whether he is an eagle in his nest, or on the wing – And to be more explicit and to show you how tall I stand by the giant, I will put down a simile of human life as far as I now perceive it; that is, to the point to which I say we both have arrived at – ' Well – I compare human life to a large Mansion of Many Apartments, two of which I can only describe, the doors of the rest being as yet shut upon me – The first we step into we call the infant or thoughtless Chamber, in which we remain as long as we do not think – We remain there a long while, and notwithstanding the doors of the second Chamber remain wide open, showing a bright appearance, we care not to hasten to it; but are at length imperceptibly impelled by the awakening of the thinking principle – within us – we no sooner get into the second Chamber, which I shall call the Chamber of Maiden-Thought, than we become intoxicated with the light and the atmosphere, we see nothing but pleasant wonders, and think of delaying there for ever in delight: However among the effects this breathing is father of is that tremendous one of sharpening one's vision into the heart and nature of Man – of convincing ones nerves that the World is full of Misery and Heartbreak, Pain, Sickness and oppression – whereby This Chamber of Maiden Thought becomes gradually darken'd and at the same time on all sides of it many doors are set open – but all dark – all leading to dark passages – We see not the ballance of good and evil. We are in a Mist – *We* are now in that state – We feel the 'burden of the Mystery,' To this point was Wordsworth come, as far as I can conceive when he wrote 'Tintern Abbey' and it seems to me that his Genius is explorative of those dark Passages. Now if we live, and go on thinking, we too shall explore them. he is a Genius and superior [to] us, in so far as he can, more than we, make discoveries, and shed a light in them – Here I must think Wordsworth is deeper than Milton – though I think it has depended more upon the general and gregarious advance of intellect, than individual greatness of Mind – . . .

[Milton] did not think into the human heart, as Wordsworth has done – Yet Milton as a Philosopher, had sure as great powers as Wordsworth – What is then to be inferr'd? O many things – It proves there is really a grand march of intellect – , It proves that a mighty providence subdues the mightiest Minds to the service of the time being, whether it be in human Knowledge or Religion –

(*Ibid.*, I, 278–81)

k. From a letter to Monkhouse, 21 June 1818

I was very much gratified in hearing from Haydon that you so great a Lover of Wordsworth should be pleased with any part of my Poem [*Endymion*]. In hopes of seeing you soon after my return and speaking of my visit to Rydal –

(*Ibid.*, I, 297)

After Keats called at Rydal Mount on 27 June, he wrote to his brother George: '[Wordsworth] was not at home nor was any Member of his family – I was much disappointed.' (*Ibid.*, I, 302). Keats would be hoping to hear from Wordsworth what his opinion of the newly published *Endymion* was: Keats had already sent a copy to Thomas Monkhouse and it appears he had sent a copy to Wordsworth (now in the possession of Mr Harry Oppenheimer) which is inscribed in Wordsworth's hand, 'W Wordsworth Rydal Mount May 25'.

l. From a letter to R. Woodhouse, 27 October 1818

As to the poetical Character itself, (I mean that sort of which, if I am any thing, I am a Member; that sort distinguished from the wordsworthian or egotistical sublime; which is a thing per se and stands alone) it is not itself – it has no self – it is every thing and nothing – It has no character – it enjoys light and shade; it lives in gusto, be it foul or fair, high or low, rich or poor, mean or elevated – It has as much delight in conceiving an Iago as an Imogen. What shocks the virtuous philosopher, delights the camelion Poet.

(*Ibid.*, I, 386–7)

m. From a letter to George and Georgiana Keats, 15 April 1819

– Wordsworth is going to publish a Poem called Peter Bell – what a perverse fellow it is! Why wilt he talk about Peter Bells – I was told not to tell – but to you it will not be tellings – Reynolds hearing that said Peter Bell was coming out, took it into his head to write a skit upon it call'd Peter Bell. He did it as soon as thought on it is to be published this morning, and comes out before the real Peter Bell, with this admirable motto from the 'Bold stroke for a Wife' '"I am the real Simon Pure"'

(*Ibid.*, II, 83–4)

n. From a letter to George and Georgiana Keats, 21 April 1819

The notice drafted here was printed, with some slight changes, in the *Examiner* for 25 April 1819. He laments Reynolds' spleen and Wordsworth's lapses that allow room for the attack.

When Reynolds was here on Monday – he asked me to give Hunt a hint to take notice of his Peter Bell in the Examiner – the best thing I can do is to write a little notice of it myself which I will do here and copy it out if it should suit my Purpose – *Peter-Bell* There have been lately advertized two Books both Peter Bell by name; what stuff the one was made of might be seen by the motto, 'I am the real Simon Pure'. This false florimel has hurried from the press and obtruded herself into public notice while for ought we know the real one may be still wandering about the woods and mountains. Let us hope she may soon appear and make good her right to the magic girdle – The Pamphleteering Archimage we can perceive has rather a splenetic love than a downright hatred to real florimels – if indeed they had been so christened – or had even a pretention to play at Bob Cherry with Barbara Lewthwaite: but he has a fixed aversion to those three rhyming Graces Alice Fell, Susan Gale and Betty Foy; and now at length especially to Peter Bell – fit Apollo. It may be seen from one or two Passages in this little skit, that the writer of it has felt the finer parts of Mr Wordsworth, and perhaps expatiated with his more remote and sublimer muse; This as far as it relates to Peter Bell is unlucky. The more he may love the sad embroidery of the Excursion; the more he will hate the coarse Samplers of Betty Foy and Alice Fell; and as they come from the same hand, the better will be able to imitate that which can be imitated. to wit Peter Bell – as far as can be imagined from the obstinate Name – We repeat, it is very inlucky – this real Simon Pure is in parts the very Man – there is a pernicious likeness in the scenery a 'pestilent humour' in the rhymes and an inveterate cadence in some of the Stanzas that must be lamented – If we are one part amused at this we are th[r]ee parts sorry that an appreciator of Wordsworth should show so much temper at this really provoking name of Peter Bell – ! This will do well enough – I have coppied it and enclosed it to Hunt – You will call it a little politic – seeing I keep clear of all parties. I say something for and against both parties – and suit it to the tune of the examiner – I mean to say I do not unsuit it – and I believe I think what I say nay I am sure I do – I and my conscience are in luck to day – which is an excellent thing –

(*Ibid.*, II, 93–4; omitting deleted variants)

EDITOR'S NOTES

1. In 1841 Bailey sent Wordsworth a pamphlet of adulatory poems privately printed by the Wesleyan Press, Colombo, Ceylon (where Bailey was then living). The earliest of Bailey's tributes is dated Townfield, North Briton, July 1827. The pamphlet also includes stanzas by 'W.R.' Bailey's hand-written dedication to Wordsworth is, 'To W. Wordsworth Esqr. With the deep and affectionate respect of one, who has been intimately acquainted with his

published Works, for more than a Quarter of a Century. B. Bailey. Colombo, Ceylon. June 29. 1841.' (Ms. The Wordsworth Library).

2. For a full account of the Wordsworth poems, 56 in all, which editors believe Keats quotes or alludes to, see Beth Lau, 'Keats's Reading of Wordsworth: An Essay and Checklist', *Studies in Romanticism*, 1987, 26, 105–50.

3. See T. O. Mabbott, *Notes and Queries*, 10 May 1941, 328, and Sotheby's catalogue for 25 July 1978, p. 295–6, Lot 399.

4. Leigh Hunt, 'The Nymphs', II, 170.

5. 'The Two April Mornings', ll. 59–60.

264. Sarah Wedgwood (1776–1856)

From a letter to Jessie Allen, 26 February 1817

Sarah was the younger sister of Josiah, John and Thomas Wedgwood, all of whom knew Wordsworth: she would further know of him through Basil Montagu who had, perhaps briefly, fallen in love with her in 1797 and also because of Coleridge's close friendship with Thomas (d. 1805). Both Josiah and John had married sisters of Jessie Allen. Sarah's remarks relate to *Poems (1815)*.

We are reading the new edition of Wordsworth's poetry, in which there are several new things. I like some of them very much, yet I don't know if we (meaning by 'we' the Miss Allens and myself) have not admired Wordsworth rather above his merits. My present notion is (how surprised he would be to hear that any human being could have such a notion) that he has not understanding enough to be a very fine poet. [She then attacks Coleridge's *The Statesman's Manual* (1816), noting that Coleridge 'has the vilest way of writing that ever man had; he is as insolent as his brother-Lakers, takes the same high ground, no mortal can tell why, except that it pleases them to think that their proper place is on a throne . . .'.]

(*Emma Darwin: a Century of Family Letters*, ed. Henrietta Litchfield, 1915, I, 109–10)

265 William Whewell (1794–1866)

From his letters, 1817–1822

Whewell was a philosopher and mathematician, Fellow and Master (1841) of Trinity College, Cambridge. It was Julius Hare, Hugh James Rose and Coleridge's *Biographia Literaria* that brought Wordsworth to Whewell's sceptical notice. Whewell later recollected his first acquaintance in 1817, or earlier, with Julius Hare: 'My tastes were the common vulgar tastes of that day, the tastes to which the "Rejected Addresses" so successfully appealed. I began our intercourse by ridiculing some passages, and especially the "solemn bleat" of the "Excursion."' (*Life of Dr. Whewell*, Mrs Stair Douglas, 1881, 34.) Whewell's interest in Wordsworth developed into friendship with the poet, and in 1838 he contributed a sonnet to Dora Wordsworth's album, beginning 'Daughter of that good man whose genuine strain / Patiently uttered oft in evil days / Called English poesy from erring ways / Of laboured trifling, insincere and vain'. On 12 October 1841 he married Cordelia Marshall, the daughter of Dorothy's oldest friend, Jane Marshall, and, within the week, succeeded Wordsworth's brother Christopher as Master of Trinity. In 1845 he dedicated his *Elements of Morality*, 2 vols., 1845, to the poet: 'in your Poems, at the season of life when the mind and the heart are most wrought on by poetry, I, along with many others, found a spirit of pure and comprehensive morality, operating to raise your readers above the moral temper of those times. I shall rejoice if it appear from the following pages, that such influences have not been wasted upon me. (*LY*, IV, 673)

a. To Hugh James Rose (1795–1838), 31 July 1817

Rose was a Cambridge friend who had been corresponding with Coleridge.

I have just got through a new book of your friend Coleridge's, his 'Biographia Literaria,' which I suppose you have seen. It contains an account of himself, which in many places is amusing enough; but it appears to me to be of considerable consequence from the critical parts of it, which will, I think, completely change the state of the question about the 'Lake School.' For to my astonishment I find it full of good sense and fair rational criticism, and containing a condemnation of all those parts of

Wordsworth, both of his theory and his practice, to which I should object – denying his whole theory about poetical diction and the resemblance of poetry to real life, and low life, and blaming almost all those poems which he has written upon his theory, condemning his prosaic style, his puerilities, his mystical and inflated language, and wonderments about the most every-day things, his *matter of factness*, his attachment to pedlars, his deification of children, and in short everything, or almost everything, that other people have made a pretext for laughing at the whole, he takes out and laughs at by itself.

Now it may be very true that all this makes but a very small part of the whole, but nevertheless it always appeared to me so woven and matted in with the rest as to give a tinge to the whole mass; it was in consequence of that, that I never entirely got over the repulsion I felt to Wordsworth, for there were so many passages, obviously favourites of the poet, where I could not feel any sympathy with him, that I could not but doubt whether I had really any sympathy with him when I appeared to have. Even yet I much doubt whether Wordsworth would allow that man to understand his poems who talks of them as Coleridge does. If it be so, the whole imaginary fabric of a new school of poetry, which seemed as if it were to be built up to the skies and to the borders of the universe, for out-topping the Tower of Babel, turns out to be nothing but a little furbishing and beautification (as the churchwardens call it) of the parish church. Just get rid of stale epithets and stale personifications, and one or two other errors that had crept in, and all our poets will turn out to be good poets. I am glad of it, because I had much rather have my objects of admiration increased than diminished.

The negative part of Coleridge's system is (as is the case with most systems) true or verisimillimum. As for the positive part, we are all abroad again. His poetics are, I think, false; and as for his metaphysics, they are as before, muddy with their own turbulence. I can make nothing of them. How the man who wrote the critique on Wordsworth could write 'Christabel,' I cannot conceive. If I were to judge from this book, I should take Coleridge's talent to lie in wit more than in poetry; his similes and metaphors are delightfully lively. Upon the strength of Coleridge's knowledge of Wordsworth's meaning, I have sent for Wordsworth's poems.

(*Ibid.*, 28–9)

b. To Rose, 30 August 1817

I was much astonished to find that Coleridge takes his critical grounds so low. It is not so much the absolute extent of his disapprobation of Wordsworth which made me consider it as indicating a revolution in Lake criticism, as the principles on which he founds it and those are obviously such that they will irresistibly extend themselves much further than he has carried them; his critique on the Daffodils,[1] for instance, might serve as a model for similar strictures on all Wordsworth's Wordsworthian poems. It pleases me to find that it is in consequence of his theory that Wordsworth has got wrong. What has a poet to do with a theory? Let him mind his business, or it will be the worse for him.

. . . if you think it inconsistent to admire both Wordsworth and Pope, you would do me the favour to believe that it may nevertheless be my case: nay, more, that I may admire one or the other, or neither, according to the state of the barometer.

(*Ibid.*, 31)

c. To Rev. Henry Wilkinson, Headmaster of Sedbergh School, 5 September 1821

I was with Wordsworth part of two days, and was very much gratified with his company. The only thing to complain of is that he is not half as Wordsworthian as his admirers, and I am more and more puzzled that a man of his acuteness and good sense should write poems with white rabbits[2] and wagon drivers for their heroes. I have since seen him here on an expedition somewhere or other among the hills, which he has great propensities for climbing whenever he can get a fine day.

(*Ibid.*, 67)

d. To Rev. Henry Wilkinson, 21 May 1822

As to Wordsworth, I do not like any sonnets, and I think most of his faults are aggravated when he takes to that species of writing. His harshness of expression and his determination to dwell upon feelings which are very sincere and vivid in himself, but which he can never be sure of conveying to other people, are all concentrated when he is confined to fourteen lines. Since I saw him, I think I admire his beauties as much as ever, but I have lost that mysterious respect with which I used to look at his faults with a sort of suspicion that there might be something in them.

I have not yet found any Wordsworthian to invent a meaning for that strange stanza in the ode which in other respects I admire as you do.

(*Ibid.*, 77)

EDITOR'S NOTES

1. Coleridge advanced as Wordsworth's 'fifth and last' defect 'thoughts and images too great for the subject' (*Biographia Literaria*, 1817, II, chapter 22).
2. A jocular reference to *The White Doe*.

266. Percy Bysshe Shelley

From letters and writings, 1817–1822, including reminiscences from Henry Crabb Robinson and Thomas Medwin

a. From Crabb Robinson's Diary, 6 November 1817

Shelley spoke of Wordsworth with less bitterness [than he had of Southey], but with an insinuation of his insincerity, etc. The passage about baptism in *The Excursion*, it is not easy to defend. [See *The Excursion*, V, ll. 261 *ff.*]

(*Henry Crabb Robinson on Books and their Writers*, ed. Edith J. Morley, 1938, I, 212)

b. From a letter about Godwin's *Mandeville*, signed E. K. (i.e. 'Elphin Knight'), *The Examiner*, 20 December 1817, 826

About this time Shelley had been disputing with W. T. Baxter claiming that Wordsworth as a poet was superior to Thomas Campbell. (See *Shelley and his Circle*, ed. Donald Reiman, 1973, V, 382)

Godwin has been to the present age in moral philosophy what Wordsworth is in poetry. The personal interest of the latter would probably have suffered from his pursuit of the true principles of taste in poetry, as much as all that is temporary in the fame of Godwin has suffered from his daring to announce the true foundation of morals, if servility and dependance and superstition had not been too easily reconcileable with

Wordsworth's species of dissent from the opinions of the great and the prevailing.

c. From a letter of Shelley to Thomas Peacock, 25 July 1818

What a beastly and pitiful wretch that Wordsworth! That such a man should be such a poet! I can compare him with no one but Simonides, that flatterer of the Sicilian tyrants, and at the same time the most natural and tender of lyric poets.

(*The Letters of Shelley*, ed. F. L. Jones, 1964, II, 26)

d. From a letter to Peacock, 17/18 December 1818

The weather is usually like what Wordsworth calls the 'first fine day of March', sometimes very much warmer, though perhaps it wants that 'each minute sweeter than before' which gives an intoxicating sweetness to the awakening of the earth from its winter's sleep in England.

(*Ibid.*, II, 60–61)

e. From a letter to Charles Ollier, 15 October 1819

The 'article in question', a review of *The Revolt of Islam* printed in the *Quarterly Review* for April 1819 (published in September), was not by Southey, but by John Taylor Coleridge.

Southey wrote the article in question, I am well aware. Observe the impudence of the man in speaking of himself. The only remark worth notice in this piece is the assertion that I imitate Wordsworth. It may as well be said that Lord Byron imitates Wordsworth, or that Wordsworth imitates Lord Byron, both being great poets, and deriving from the new springs of thought and feeling, which the great events of our age have exposed to view, a similar tone of sentiment, imagery, and expression. A certain similarity all the best writers of any particular age inevitably are marked with, from the spirit of that age acting on all.

(*Ibid.*, II, 127)

f. Extracts from *Peter Bell the Third*, 1819

Shelley (like J. H. Reynolds with his *Peter Bell, A Lyrical Ballad*) had not read Wordsworth's *Peter Bell* when at Florence in October 1819 he wrote *Peter Bell the Third*; he had read in the *Examiner*, first, Keats's notice of Reynolds' anticipatory burlesque (see Keats's letter 21 April 1819), and second, Hunt's review of the real Peter Bell [see entry 208]. He delighted to invent a third poem, a rambling fantasy generally concerned with the fable of a poet who failed. The poem was published posthumously in 1839.

Peter's natural gifts are outlined, ll. 273–327:

> All things that Peter saw and felt
>   Had a peculiar aspect to him;
> And when they came within the belt
> Of his own nature, seemed to melt,
>   Like cloud to cloud, into him.
>
> And so the outward world uniting
>   To that within him, he became
> Considerably uninviting
> To those who, meditation slighting,
>   Were moulded in a different frame.
>
> And he scorned them, and they scorned him;
>   And he scorned all they did; and they
> Did all that men of their own trim
> Are wont to do to please their whim,
>   Drinking, lying, swearing, play.
>
> Such were his fellow-servants; thus
>   His virtue, like our own, was built
> Too much on that indignant fuss
> Hypocrite Pride stirs up in us
>   To bully one another's guilt.
>
> He had a mind which was somehow
>   At once circumference and centre
> Of all he might or feel or know;
> Nothing went ever out, although
>   Something did ever enter.
>
> He had as much imagination
>   As a pint-pot; – he never could
> Fancy another situation,
> From which to dart his contemplation,
>   Than that wherein he stood.

Yet his was individual mind,
    And new created all he saw
In a new manner, and refined
Those new creations, and combined
    Them, by a master-spirit's law.

Thus – though unimaginative –
    An apprehension clear, intense,
Of his mind's work, had made alive
The things it wrought on; I believe
    Wakening a sort of thought in sense.

But from the first 'twas Peter's drift
    To be a kind of moral eunuch,
He touched the hem of Nature's shift,
Felt faint – and never dared uplift
    The closest, all-concealing tunic.

She laughed the while, with an arch smile,
    And kissed him with a sister's kiss,
And said – 'My best Diogenes,
I love you well – but, if you please,
    Tempt not again my deepest bliss.

'Tis you are cold – for I, not coy,
    Yield love for love, frank, warm, and true;
And Burns, a Scottish peasant boy –
His errors prove it – knew my joy
    More, learnèd friend, than you.

*Under the influence of one, 'a mighty poet – and/A subtle-souled
psychologist', alas, mad (Coleridge), Peter's best poetry is written*, ll. 403–47:

At night he oft would start and wake
    Like a lover, and began
In a wild measure songs to make
On moor, and glen, and rocky lake,
    And on the heart of man –

And on the universal sky –
    And the wide earth's bosom green, –
And the sweet, strange mystery
Of what beyond these things may lie,
    And yet remain unseen.

For in his thought he visited
  The spots in which, ere dead and damned,
He his wayward life had led;
Yet knew not whence the thoughts were fed
  Which thus his fancy crammed.

And these obscure remembrances
  Stirred such harmony in Peter,
That, whensoever he should please,
He could speak of rocks and trees
  In poetic metre.

For though it was without a sense
  Of memory, yet he remembered well
Many a ditch and quick-set fence;
Of lakes he had intelligence,
  He knew something of heath and fell.

He had also dim recollections
  Of pedlars tramping on their rounds;
Milk-pans and pails; and odd collections
Of saws, and proverbs; and reflections
  Old parsons make in burying-grounds.

But Peter's verse was clear, and came
  Announcing from the frozen hearth
Of a cold age, that none might tame
The soul of that diviner flame
  It augured to the Earth:

Like gentle rains, on the dry plains,
  Making that green which late was gray,
Or like the sudden moon, that stains
Some gloomy chamber's windowpanes
  With a broad light like day.

For language was in Peter's hand
  Like clay while he was yet a potter;
And he made songs for all the land,
Sweet both to feel and understand,
  As pipkins late to mountain Cotter.

PERCY BYSSHE SHELLEY

*The Reviewers' intemperate condemnation of Peter's early and best poetry
disturbs the poet: he writes a perverse poetry* [Shelley's reference is chiefly to
the *Excursion*] *which the devilish critics praise*, ll. 569–640:

> One single point in his belief
>   From his organization sprung,
> The heart-enrooted faith, the chief
> Ear in his doctrines' blighted sheaf,
>   That 'Happiness is wrong';
>
> So thought Calvin and Dominic;
>   So think their fierce successors, who
> Even now would neither stint nor stick
> Our flesh from off our bones to pick,
>   If they might 'do their do.'
>
> His morals thus were undermined: –
>   The old Peter – the hard, old Potter –
> Was born anew within his mind;
> He grew dull, harsh, sly, unrefined,
>   As when he tramped beside the Otter.
>
> In the death hues of agony
>   Lambently flashing from a fish,
> Now Peter felt amused to see
> Shades like a rainbow's rise and flee,
>   Mixed with a certain hungry wish*.

---

* See the description of the beautiful colours produced during the agonizing death of a
number of trout, in the fourth part of a long poem in blank verse, published within a few
years (*The Excursion*, VIII, ll. 568–71). That poem contains curious evidence of the gradual
hardening of a strong but circumscribed sensibility, of the perversion of a penetrating but
panic-stricken understanding. The author might have derived a lesson which he had
probably forgotten from these sweet and sublime verses: –

> This lesson, Shepherd, let us two divide,
> Taught both by what she* shows and what conceals,
> Never to blend our pleasure or our pride
> With sorrow of the meanest thing that feels.
>   * Nature.
>   ['Hartleap Well', *PW*, II, p. 254, ll. 177–80]

991

So in his Country's dying face
   He looked – and, lovely as she lay,
Seeking in vain his last embrace,
Wailing her own abandoned case,
   With hardened sneer he turned away:

And coolly to his own soul said; –
   'Do you not think that we might make
A poem on her when she's dead: –
Or, no – a thought is in my head –
   Her shroud for a new sheet I'll take:

'My wife wants one. – Let who will bury
This mangled corpse! And I and you,
My dearest Soul, will then make merry,
As the Prince Regent did with Sherry, – '
'Ay – and at last desert me too.'

And so his Soul would not be gay,
   But moaned within him; like a fawn
Moaning within a cave, it lay
Wounded and wasting, day by day,
   Till all its life of life was gone.

As troubled skies stain waters clear,
   The storm in Peter's heart and mind
Now made his verses dark and queer:
They were the ghosts of what they were,
Shaking dim grave-clothes in the wind.

For he now raved enormous folly,
   Of Baptisms, Sunday-schools, and Graves,
'Twould make George Colman melancholy
To have heard him, like a male Molly,
   Chanting those stupid staves.

Yet the Reviews, who heaped abuse
   On Peter while he wrote for freedom,
So soon as in his song they spy
The folly which soothes tyranny,
   Praise him, for those who feed 'em.

'He was a man, too great to scan; −
A planet lost in truth's keen rays: −
His virtue, awful and prodigious; −
He was the most sublime, religious,
   Pure-minded Poet of these days.'

As soon as he read that, cried Peter,
   'Eureka! I have found the way
To make a better thing of metre
Than e'er was made by living creature
   Up to this blessèd day.'

Then Peter wrote odes to the Devil; −
   In one of which he meekly said:
'May Carnage and Slaughter,
Thy niece and thy daughter,
May Rapine and Famine,
Thy gorge ever cramming,
   Glut thee with living and dead!'

g. From a letter of Shelley to Maria Gisborne, 8 May 1820

As an excuse for mine and Mary's incurable stupidity I send a little thing about Poets; which is itself a kind of an excuse for Wordsworth & [word heavily deleted]. You may shew it Hunt if you like. [The poem was probably 'Chameleons feed on light and air'.]

(*The Letters of Shelley*, ed. F.L. Jones, 1964, II, 195)

h. From a letter to Charles Ollier, 14 May 1820

Shelley was of course wrong in thinking that Wordsworth's sister was called Emma.

If 'Peter Bell' be printed (you can best judge if it will sell or no, and there would be no other reason for printing such a trifle), attend, I pray you, particularly to completely concealing the author; and for Emma read Betty, as the name of Peter's sister. Emma, I recollect, is the real name of the sister of a great poet who might be mistaken for Peter.

(*Ibid.*, II, 196)

i. From a letter to John Gisborne, 10 April 1822

Shelley is remembering the passage from the *Prelude* (1805, X, 690–728). He almost certainly read this when it was published separately in *Poems* (1815); if he had seen it in *The Friend*, 26 October 1809, he could hardly have failed to remember Coleridge's own powerful commentary entitled, 'Enthusiasm for an Ideal World' (*The Friend*, ed. B. Rooke, I. 227). One element that Shelley might have disliked in the passage is the reservation with which Wordsworth presents his youthful revolutionary zeal; but it is more likely that the contrast between Goethe and himself on the one hand and Wordsworth on the other is accounted for by Shelley's own powerful sense that reality involves more than this life.

I have been reading over & over again Faust, & always with sensations which no other composition excites. It deepens the gloom & augments the rapidity of the ideas, & would therefore seem to be an unfit study for any person who is a prey to the reproaches of memory, & the delusions of an imagination not to be restrained. – And yet the pleasure of sympathizing with emotions known only to few, although they derive their sole charm from despair & a scorn of the narrow good we can attain in our present state, seems more than to cure the pain which belongs to them. – Perhaps all discontent with the *less* (to use a Platonic sophism) supposes the sense of a just claim to the *greater*, & that we admirers of Faust are in the right road to Paradise. – Such a supposition is not more absurd, and is certainly less demoniacal than that of Wordsworth – where he says –

> This earth,
> Which is the world of all of us, & where
> *We find our happiness or not at all.*

As if after sixty years of suffering here, we were to be roasted alive for sixty million more in Hell, or charitably annihilated by a coûp de grace of the bungler, who brought us into existence at first.

(*The Letters of Shelley*, ed. F. L. Jones, 1964, II, 406–7)

j. From a letter of Thomas Medwin to Edward Quillinan, 17 May 1846

Shelley was a great admirer who is not of Wordsworth. – I never saw him but once – at Geneva when there with Mrs W & his Sister. They were at the Couronne – I have his face before me still – the *beau ideal* of that of a Poet & his voice & manner for I once or twice conversed with him at the

Hotel. – I think of him as of 'some particular Star he is so much above me.'

(Ms. The Wordsworth Library)

k. From a letter of Medwin to Quillinan, February [? 1847]

By the way what admirable sonnets Wordsworth has written. – That on Milton for instance – on London – . Shelley admired them much but used to read – I have often heard him – with wonderful delight the Tintern Abbey & Laodamia. – If W. had written nothing but the last he would have been immortalized –.

(Ms. The Wordsworth Library)

267. J. W. Croker (1780–1857)

From a letter to William Blackwood, 2 February 1818

J. W. Croker, Tory politician and essayist, is here commenting on John Wilson's abusive review of *Biographia Literaria*.

I have to thank you for your last number, [of *Blackwood's Edinburgh Magazine*] which I like much better than the former. I own I was distressed at the attacks on Messrs. Wordsworth and Coleridge, who are certainly respectable writers, to say the least of them, and, I understand, worthy men. I never saw either of them but once at dinner, and therefore I am impartial.

(*John Wilson Croker*, M. F. Brightfield, 1940, 229)

268. Peter George Patmore (1786–1855)

From his writings, 1818–1823

Peter George Patmore, father of Coventry Patmore; author, admirer of Hazlitt, a second in John Scott's fatal duel, 1821, and sometime editor of the *New Monthly Magazine*.

a. Two sonnets praising Wordsworth, signed P.G.P., *Blackwood's Edinburgh Magazine*, February 1818, II, 512–3

Behold yon Moon! with what a sober joy
She treads her destined path! her quiet beam
Sinks to the heart, and bids its vital stream
Flow on in peace. She gazes from on high
With looks of love. Her comprehensive eye
Takes in the visible world – which then doth seem
With conscious bliss to flash, and spread, and gleam,
And kindle into brightness far and nigh.
   Such, Wordsworth, is thy song – such is its power,
Its purity, its beauty. Thus it moves
'In naked majesty,' – tho' tempests lower
And threaten and deform the land it loves,
Athwart the gloom its warning splendors fall:
Those splendors borrow'd from the source – the Sun of all.

London, Sept. 1813.

Wordsworth, thy name is precious to mine ear!
It comes not on my spirit like the shout
Of riotous mirth,– scattering its noise about
Till joy becomes half intermix'd with fear,–
But to my heart it sinks in tones of clear,
Deep, pure, perpetual music. Mists of doubt,
That cling around my being, and put out
The lights of life, at that name disappear.
   O, for a poet's voice, that I might frame
A lay of fitting thanks! I would not sing,
Like the proud nightingale's, a song of flame;
But, like the stock-dove's – ever murmuring
Of quiet, inward bliss – ever the same;–
Perpetual as my thanks – pure as their spring.

London, 1817.

b. *Blackwood's Edinburgh Magazine*, April 1818, II, passim

Patmore reported Hazlitt's Lectures on the English Poets, but omitting
Hazlitt's abuse of Wordsworth. For Hazlitt's full comments see entry 256j.

---

c. From a long essay under the pseudonym Count de Soligny

Taking Wordsworth and Byron as the two poets who 'possessed a higher degree of genius than any other of their contemporaries', Patmore considered both were great, even though it is 'not possible to conceive of two human beings more diametrically opposite to each other in almost everything than Wordsworth and Byron'. He suggests:

Wordsworth is all contemplation, and Byron all passion; or in the one, passion seems to be perpetually hushed to sleep in the arms of contemplation, and in the other, contemplation forever strangled in its birth by the throes of passion. Byron's poetical character exhibits the very essence, the concentration of all the powers and attributes of man – a personification of our *human* nature, in all the shadows of its gloom, and in all the light of its glory. – Wordsworth would almost seem to be an incarnation of some loftier and less earthly nature, permitted for a time to sojourn in this lower world, in order to teach man the possible purity and grandeur of his destinies, and beckon him onward to deserve and enjoy them.

(From *Letters on England*, 1823, II, 7–19)

269. John Wilson (1785–1854)

From his writings, 1818–1819

a. Extract from 'Letters from the Lakes', purporting to be 'Written during the Summer of 1818. Translated from the German of Phillip Kempfherhausen', signed P. K. *Blackwood's Edinburgh Magazine*, January 1819, IV. 403 and March 1819, IV, 735–44

Blackwood himself marked these as by Wilson (see A. L. Strout, 'Authorship of Articles in Blackwood's', *The Library*, 1956, II, 192) and the intimacy of the flattering portrait of Wordsworth at home left little doubt of the authorship to the Wordsworth circle. They were not at all pleased when the 'Letters' were reprinted locally. Sara Hutchinson wrote to her cousin John Monkhouse, 7 May 1819:

M[r] Wilson wrote those 'Letters' which appeared in the [Carlisle] *Patriot &c*, pretending to be written by a German – they were copied into the

[Westmoreland] *Gaz:* without M^r De Q[uincey']s [the editor] knowledge. W^m stopt their going on – I believe they came out originally in *Blackwoods Edin: Magazine* which now takes upon it to praise W^m through thick & thin –

(*Letters of Sara Hutchinson,* ed. Kathleen Coburn, 1954, 155)

The second letter, which contains brief but extravagant praise of Wordsworth, attributed to Southey, was reprinted in the *Carlisle Patriot,* in two parts, on 3 and 20 February. The following extract is from the third and final essay.

. . . I soon entered the house, and was shewn into the parlour, where Mr Wordsworth and his family were assembled to breakfast. The name of Southey acted like a talisman in my favour, and I also found that my name was not unknown to the family as that of a foreigner resident in Ambleside. Their kind and affable reception of me soon relieved me from any temporary embarrassment, and when I told the circuit I had made, they seemed pleased that a foreigner should feel so enthusiastically the beauties of their country. I soon found that even the ladies well knew every step I had taken, and that the poet's wife and sister had trodden with him the mountains and cliffs I had just traversed. Our conversation became every moment more kind and animated, and the room was filled with gentle voices and bright smiles. I know not how to describe to you the great Poet himself. They who have formed to themselves, as many have foolishly done, the idea of a simple pastoral poet, who writes sweet and touching verses, would be somewhat astounded to find themselves in the presence of William Wordsworth. There seemed to me, in his first appearance, something grave almost to austerity, and the deep tones of his voice added strength to that impression of him. There was not visible about him the same easy and disengaged air that so immediately charmed me in Southey – his mind seemed to require an effort to awaken itself thoroughly from some brooding train of thought, and his manner, as I felt at least, at first reluctantly relaxed into blandness and urbanity. There was, however, nothing of vulgar pride in all this, although perhaps it might have seemed so, in an ordinary person. It was the dignity of a mind habitually conversant with high and abstracted thoughts – and unable to divest itself wholly, even in common hours, of the stateliness inspired by the loftiest studies of humanity. No wonder if at first I felt somewhat abashed before such a man – especially when the solemnity of his manner was rendered more striking by the mild simplicity of his wife, and the affectionate earnestness of his sister. But I soon saw how finely characteristic all this was of the man. By degrees he became more lively and careless – and he shewed his politeness towards me his guest and a stranger, by a number of familiar and playful remarks addressed to the members of his own family. I could not help feeling that there was something extremely delicate in this. Often have I been oppressed and almost disgusted with the attention heaped and forced upon me because a stranger, to the utter neglect and seeming forgetfulness of the master of the house towards his own family. But here the kind affections continued in full play – I did not act as a dam to stop the current of domestic enjoyment – and when I saw Mr Wordsworth so kind, so attentive, and so affectionate, to his own happy family, I felt assured that the sunshine of his heart would not fail also to visit me, and that he was disposed to think well of a man before whom he thus freely indulged the best feelings of his human nature.

The features of Wordsworth's face are strong and high, almost harsh and severe – and his eyes have, when he is silent, a dim, thoughtful, I had nearly said melancholy expression – so that when a smile takes possession of his countenance, it is indeed the most powerful smile I ever saw – gives a new character to the whole man, and renders him, who before seemed rather a being for us to respect and venerate, an object to win our love and affection. Smiles are, assuredly, not the abiding light on that grand countenance; but at times they pass finely over it, like playful sunbeams chasing each other over the features of some stern and solemn scene of external nature, that seems willingly to yield itself for a while to the illumination. Never saw I a countenance in which CONTEMPLATION so reigns. His brow is very lofty – and his dark brown hair seems worn away, as it were, by thought, so thinly is it spread over his temples. The colour of his face is almost sallow; but it is not the sallowness of confinement or ill health, it speaks rather of the rude and boisterous greeting of the mountain-weather. He does not seem a recluse philosopher, who pores over the midnight oil in his study; but rather a hermit who converses with nature in his silent cell, whose food is roots and herbs, and whose drink is from

> Wherever fountain or fresh current flowed
> Against the eastern ray, translucent pure.
> With touch ethereal of Heaven's fiery rod.

I at once beheld, in his calm and confident voice – his stedfast and untroubled eyes – the serene, expansion of his forehead – and the settled dignity of his demeanour – that original poet, who, in an age of poetry, has walked alone through a world almost exclusively his own, and who has cleared out for himself, by his own labour, a wide and magnificent path through the solitary forests of the human imagination.

After breakfast I accompanied Mr Wordsworth and his family to Grassmere Church, distant about two miles from Rydal Mount; and as we walked along, it was delightful to observe with what mingled respect and familiarity our group was saluted by all the peasants. I have not been able to observe any love of poetry among the lower orders of the people here, as in many parts of our own Germany; but the influence of a great man's character is felt in his neighbourhood, even by those who are either wholly ignorant, or but imperfectly aware of its nature; and besides, Wordsworth, during his long life of study, has been a frequent visitor in all the cottages round; and I remarked in particular, that the old men, as they passed by, addressed him with an air of reverence, inspired no doubt by the power and wisdom of his conversation, and also by the benevolence and charities of his life. As we walked along towards the simple house of God, occasionally talking cheerfully with the shepherds and their families, I almost forgot the poet in the man – the great, if not lost, was absorbed, as it were, in the good; and I less envied William Wordsworth his glory as a prevailing poet, than his happiness as a philanthropist and a Christian.

I was greatly charmed with divine service as it was performed in the church of Grassmere. The congregation were most attentive and devout, and took part in the solemn ordinances of religion with a staid and sober fervour alike remote from enthusiasm and indifference – while the young priest who officiated, son of the rector of the parish, and who had received a classical education at Oxford, read the service with much feeling and simplicity. There seemed around me neither vice, ignorance, poverty, nor unhappiness – at least, the sanctity of the place prevailed for a while over them all; and when the choir of young maidens and boys breathed forth its music, I thought that I had never heard the praises of God sung with one united soul of so much innocence, purity, and devotion. When I looked around upon so many young and beautiful – upon so many old and venerable faces – all happy and tranquil in the holy business of the day – I could not but think of the calm which such a day must carry forwards into all the coming week; and the Sabbath seemed to me, like a sacred fountain from which the regular hand of religion removes the seal, that the fresh-gushing waters of comfort may for ever continue to overflow the land.

After divine service Mr Wordsworth's family returned home, while he proposed to conduct me into a neighbouring valley, named Easdale, that had long been one of his favourite haunts. This valley lies immediately behind the wooded shoulder of a hill that forms the north-west boundary of Grassmere, and I found it indeed worthy of the poet's love. Till we reached a waterfall, about a mile up the valley, it was wooded and cultivated; but it afterwards became wild and sterile, and our journey terminated at a small lake or tarn of deepest solitude, and in great part surrounded with lofty rocks. Here, Wordsworth informed me, that he had meditated, and even composed, much of his poetry; and certainly there could not be a fitter study for a spirit like his, that loves to brood, with an intensity of passion, on those images of nature which his imagination brings from afar and moulds into the forms of life. It was in this naked solitude that many of the richest and loftiest passages of the 'Excursion' were composed. I now walked with the poet himself through the scene of his inspiration; and when I looked at the bare rocks, the dim tarn, and the silent precipices, I thought, what is nature without the poet's soul to illuminate it? and what is our love of nature, unless refined and elevated by the true feeling of its poetry?

Wordsworth spoke to me, for he saw that I desired it, of poetry – and he seemed to me, as he spoke, like an inspired man. Though his language was far beyond the pitch of conversation, yet it was neither pedantic nor high-flown; for it rolled out as from a soul filled with ideas and images, and his voice and manner kindled into an enthusiasm which they soon communicated. His speech was continuous as the flow of a free torrent, that seems to meet with no impediments but those of its own seeking, and such as it delights to overcome. It was evident, that poetry was the element in which he lived, and breathed, and had his being. Other poets, at least all I have ever known, are poets but on occasions – Wordsworth's profession is that of a poet; and therefore when he speaks of poetry, he speaks of the things most familiar, and, at the same time, most holy to his heart. For twenty years has he lived in this grand country, and there devoted his whole soul to his divine art. When he speaks most earnestly, it may almost be said that he soliloquizes; for he seems to obey strong internal impulses of thought, and the presence of the person to whom he speaks serves merely to give his eloquence something of a didactic character; yet rarely, if ever, does he become mystical. Indeed, nothing surprised me so much in this great poet, as his strong sense and strict logic – with which the very highest imagination, and the deepest passion, were united in a way that I have never seen exemplified in the conversation of any other man.

I soon saw that he applied to all kinds of poetry the very highest standard – that he was intolerant of all compositions that had not a lofty aim, and that the poetry of action was in his eyes unworthy of being

1001

thought of in comparison with that of contemplation. He seemed to venerate some of the mighty masters of old with such perfect veneration, that he had but little to spare for his contemporaries. Yet it would be most unjust to say of him, that he was either jealous or envious of their fame. He rated the worth of several of them very high, and with great discrimination; but it was clear that his soul was with them of elder times; and who shall say, but in this he obeyed the voice of truth – the only voice to which in his solitude Wordsworth cares to listen.

I must not venture to repeat to you mere fragments of the conversation of this extraordinary man; for his very simplest illustrations, and his most ordinary remarks, appeared, somehow or another, all connected with – all part of – a system; and though there seemed to me, when I listened to him, and still seems to be perfect truth in all his general views of poetry – yet, in order to give a true impression of them to another person, it would be necessary to narrate the whole course of his argument, and to present it in all its bearings. On this account might Wordsworth's conversation, more easily than that of any other man, be misrepresented, by being given piecemeal; and it would be a dangerous thing indeed, to attempt to imitate the bold and sweeping eloquence of his philosophical conversation. What is it that often makes almost the identical words true from one man's lips, and altogether false from those of another?

From poetry the conversation turned to criticism, and I was gratified to hear Wordsworth speak in terms of the highest praise of our two great philosophers of criticism, William and Frederick Schlegel. He said, that the former, in his book on dramatic literature, almost always saw into the soul of truly great writers, and characterized their genius with a singular felicity; but that he often missed the distinguishing traits of inferior minds, and that it was then, and then only, that we observed him to be a foreigner, imperfectly acquainted with the details of our poetical literature. But of his love of high truths, his capacity to discern, and his eloquence to express them, it was not possible, he said, to speak too warmly, and that his own country could as yet boast of no such philosophical critic. Mr Coleridge, he said, was the only man he knew in Britain entitled to lecture upon Shakespeare; and that such was the richness, and beauty, and wildness, of his aerial and romantic imagination, that he did not doubt Mr Coleridge would, in lecturing on the Midsummer Night's Dream, or the Tempest, cast forth images and rays of fancy, that would render more wonderful even those wonderful creations. He thought that Mr Coleridge might far surpass Schlegel in some departments of philosophical criticism; and that were he to reduce the lectures to a systematic shape, which he has more than once delivered, on the characters of Shakespeare, England would not have to yield to Germany the honour of having produced the best expositor of the genius of her greatest poet. Of the periodical criticism of Britain he spoke with almost unqualified contempt. That it often displayed acuteness, talent, and even sensibility, he well knew; and no doubt, said he, many good hints might be found scattered through its voluminous records; but, for his own part, he had never seen any important principles laid down there, nor did he see how a poet could become wiser in his own art by aid of the instructions, however kindly meant, of such critics. The very spirit in which they were of necessity written, did of necessity prevent such disquisitions from being of a high character, even if the critic were a man of high intellect. But *that*, he said, was impossible; for that the office of a periodical critic was one beneath the dignity of a great mind – that such a critic, in order to please, to startle, or astonish – without doing which he could acquire no character at all – must often sacrifice what he knew to be truth – that he must mingle truth with falsehood, or, at least, with error; and that he who wrote avowedly and professionally to the public, must respect, nay, take advantage, of its prejudices or its ignorance; and if so, surely, whatever might be the advantages or disadvantages of such writings to the public, they were not worthy much notice from a poet who devoted his whole life to the study of his art, – who in his solitude sought truth, and truth alone; and who, unless he knew that it was amply deserved, and wisely bestowed, would be miserable under the world's applause. This is a faint sketch indeed of Wordsworth's opinion on this subject. Suffice it to say, that he delivered these opinions without anger and without arrogance; and that while he spoke, I could not but look on him as the most eloquent of men, and, at the same time, the most unanswerable.

Ere we approached his beautiful residence, our conversation had turned upon general politics; and Wordsworth carried into that science the same lofty principles – the same faith in the high destinies of man, that had just given such surpassing dignity to his opinions on poetry. To me, who had been so frequently distressed, even in the most enlightened societies of England, by the paltry and vexatious wrangling about party creeds, and the fretful and seemingly irrational opposition of Whig and Tory – it was not only delightful in itself, but a fine relief from such wearisome and unprofitable contests, to hear the affairs of Europe spoken of with the same calm wisdom, and the same unprejudiced earnestness, with which a philosopher might be supposed to speak of the mighty events of former ages. He said, that as I had done him the honour to make myself acquainted with his publications, he would refer me to them for what was called his political opinions; and that it was satisfactory to him, a recluse student among the hills, to think, that none of his dearest and most sacred beliefs had been shewn foundationless by the events of the last twenty awful years. Living, as he had done, in solitude, his mind, he said, had not perhaps been subjected, so much as the minds of those living in the world, to the disturbing, and confounding, and weakening power of popular rumours, and popular fears – so that it was left lying at anchor of its own inward strength, and not liable to be blown about by every shifting blast. He thought that he had perceived throughout the history of man certain great principles acting, if not uniformly, at least with a tendency whose progress nothing could entirely arrest or change. To them he had made frequent reference in his poetry, and more especially in his Sonnets to Liberty – as well as in his prose tract on the Affairs of Spain; and all who interested themselves about him, would there see that he had never despaired of Europe, even in her darkest days; and that he had, not obscurely or dimly, but with all the confidence in truth inspired by a knowledge of the past history of oppression – all along emphatically described the power of Bonaparte as a power that could not endure; but that,

> If old judgments held their sacred course,

would soon be shattered into shapeless and irretrievable ruin. Of Bonaparte himself, he spoke as of a man utterly destitute, at all times of his career, of that imperfect and disturbed moral grandeur which preserved from contempt and hatred some of the wicked ones of antiquity. He had longed and desired to find something great, generous, true, in his heart, that the present age might not have had the degradation of bowing the knee before such an ignoble idol; but all was cold and barren there – nor did he exhibit any one feature of character that arrests and commands our admiration in some splendid and magnificent barbarian. But the human mind was apt, often blindly, to attribute that grandeur which existed in great events, to the character of the man by whose agency these events were brought to pass; and thus they looked on him, who had overturned old, and created new dynasties – and before whom the aspect of the world grew pale, as necessarily in his nature a truly great being – though, when looked at, apart from the dazzling splendour of his achievements, he stood in his own native littleness, without one faculty or one accomplishment on which his admirers could pronounce a high and unqualified eulogium. He then, in a strain of irresistible eloquence, contrasted his character with that of the first Cæsar; and though perhaps he leaned rather too much to the side of the 'mighty Julius,' yet I could not but feel how far beneath the image of the imperial Roman shrunk that of the conqueror of our Germany. Ambition, and all its concomitant vices, evils and crimes, he could have almost forgiven – had the object and aim of that ambition been in any way reconcileable with any lofty views of that human nature over which it sought the ascendancy of unlimited power, or with any generous enjoyment in the heart of him who obeyed its impulses; but Bonaparte had evidently no knowledge – no feeling of the diviner qualities of the soul of man – he knew not that his own highest elevation was to be sought in the elevation of human nature; – his sole triumph was in superiority, – not the only real superiority of mental power, but the accidental one of brute force: while he burned with impatience to root out, or to cut down, or to blast for ever, all those faculties, desires, and virtues, which entitle mankind to the name of civility, and thus to turn back, as it were, the human mind many centuries in its career.

But our walk was now at an end; for we were at the gate of Rydal Mount, and were met there by kind and happy eyes, that had been looking out impatiently for our return. Mr Wordsworth was received by his family with as much eager delight as if he had been absent for days, and I came in for my share of the kindness of such kind hearts. During the calm summer evening we sat in a sort of hanging garden, beneath the shadow of some old pine-trees; and if during the day I was instructed by the wisdom of his mind, so now was I charmed by the goodness of his heart; for young and old were alike the objects of his affections, that wandered carelessly among them all, and seemed, in that quiet garden of Eden, at once shadow and sunshine, breeze and calm.

b. Unsigned review. *Blackwood's Edinburgh Magazine*, May 1819, V, 130–6

This piece was first attributed to John Wilson, but without proof, by A. L. Strout (*A Bibliography of Articles in Blackwood's Magazine, 1817–1825*, Lubbock, Texas, 1959). The evidence for Wilson's authorship explains both the hasty composition of the review and its laudatory tone. On 6 May 1819, Wilson, then in Peebles, sent four articles to Blackwood in Edinburgh, indicating in a covering letter (National Library of Scotland) that two of them – an article on Religion in the Highlands and a review of Mrs Brunton's *Emmeline* – required some little further work which he would turn to when he returned to Edinburgh on 12 May. He must also have turned to *Peter Bell* at that time, the middle of the month in which the review was published, for on the outside of Wilson's letter is a memo in Lockhart's hand (Lockhart appears to have been acting as editor as well as writing his *Peter's Letters* for *Blackwood's*, see entry 253e): 'Peter Bell', and then the list – '4/Brunton/Highlands'; i.e., the four articles sent from Peebles, two of them needing attention, and one other on *Peter Bell*. In all Wilson, I suggest, contributed five articles to *Blackwood's* for May 1819, and had little time to spare for a detailed consideration of Wordsworth's poem.

Additional grounds for proposing Wilson's authorship are provided by the mis-spelling of 'Christabelle' (see the last sentence in the review); this form of the word occurs also in Wilson's review of *Yarrow Revisited* (May 1835).

The laudatory tone of the review can be seen to be closely connected with Wilson's mention of 'Christabel' for this must have been part of *Blackwood's* campaign – in which there was no success – to try to persuade Coleridge to write for the magazine. Blackwood tried personally, while his friend and agent in London, William Davies, the publisher, advocated a more oblique approach. He wrote to Blackwood, 27 April 1819 (posted 29 April):

> What is said of your Cockney Poetry of the 25th. Nº about Mr Wordsworth [see 253d] so perfectly accords with Mr Coleridge's conversation on Friday last, that I have no fears of his being dissatisfied on that part – but I discover that Mr W is a very great favourite with Mr C. I am rather inclined to recommend that you occasionally say something kind and conciliatory, about Mr W., in your future Nᵒˢ, though merely to show a kindly feeling towards Mr C.

(Ms. National Library of Scotland)

Davies even got the Rev. Dr Robert Jones (1780–1844, *not* Wordsworth's friend) in London to write on *Peter Bell* (and on Reynold's parody), but this was not published and Blackwood explained to Jones, 22 May 1819:

> You will see by this number that there is an article on Peter Bell, and like the former ones on Wordsworth very very laudatory. The Editor and several of our writers are passionate admirers of the Lake School.

(Ms. *ibid.*)

AFTER allowing a considerable time to elapse without offering any thing to the public, Mr Wordsworth has at last printed a short poem, which, we are told in the preface, has been lying by him for twenty years. Such retentiveness is certainly quite at variance with the practice of the other authors of the present times, whose works are generally more than half printed before their conclusions are written, or even determined upon. Mr Wordsworth has probably long since relinquished the belief that any of his compositions can ever be bought up with the avidity of popular curiosity, and, therefore, it is to be supposed, that when, in the course of the leisure of a rural life, he happens to employ himself about an '*ingrato caseus urbi*,'[1] he is in no haste to push it into the market. He has often been counselled by critics about taking more pains to adapt his mode of composition to the prevalent tastes of mankind; but, if he wishes to have light on that subject, he should at once resort for advice to the booksellers, who are indisputably the best judges, and whose authority should be considered as paramount, in the present age, to that of any critic whatever. – As his genius leads him very strongly to the discussion of moral questions, perhaps, if he would be persuaded to venture forth with a volume of sermons, under a feigned name, he might have a better chance of attaining to that success which, as yet, he has so sparingly enjoyed.

The present poem of Peter Bell is of the narrative kind; and even those readers who are most averse to moralizing and reflection, will find a thread of story extending throughout the composition. It has more of the interest of suspended curiosity than almost any other of the tales of the same author; but this is not saying much for it on that score. The diction, throughout a great part of it, is highly animated and poetical, and more especially in the introduction; which, although it relates to the choice of the subject, is no ways connected with the incidents afterwards introduced. No preternatural, nor even any splendid or extraordinary machinery is made use of; and the poem exemplifies a principle which Mr Wordsworth has often insisted on, namely, that the strength and importance of the emotions which are brought into play, can be made to communicate the highest poetical interest to the circumstances which excite them, although these circumstances may be quite homely and familiar in themselves. Although this principle be true, and was never more remarkably proved than by the present poem; yet we must certainly concur with those who maintain that its truth can never be adduced as a reason for preferring incidents and circumstances that are disagreeably homely, and forcing them to become poetical by means of the skill with which they are rendered the occasions of emotion, when other circumstances of a more dignified and agreeable sort can be equally well made to answer the same end. Nevertheless, it is a great chance whether, if Mr Wordsworth had studied to find more dignified incidents and circumstances, he would not have lost some part of his originality among the hackneyed conceptions of former poets. If he had assumed any of the materials in common use, he must have had to struggle with all that host of factitious associations which attach themselves to ideas that have long been separated from actual modes of life, and employed only in the artificial combinations of literature. He wished once more to visit the field of nature, and take possession of whatever harvest of poetical materials still remained unsullied by frequent handling. All the other living poets, who have described present modes of existence, have been compelled to seek for poetry in scenes of life similar to those depicted by Wordsworth. Situations of pure invention are seldom interesting, and have never been varied or numerous. With the exception of Walter Scott, living poets seem little inclined to seek for new poetical situations in the history of the past.

The story of Peter Bell is that of a harsh, profligate, and brutal character, who by means of a succession of circumstances acting upon his imagination, is gradually mollified into tenderness and repentance. Like the great Pedlar in the Excursion, he is an itinerant merchant, videlicet, a seller of pottery wares. A perpetual change of situation, and an ignorance of what is next to be met with, are ingredients which wherever they are introduced can scarcely fail to bring something of a romantic feeling along with them. One moonlight night, Peter Bell strikes into a bye-path in order to shorten his way, and loses himself in a wood. On emerging from the wood, he comes to a small meadow, where he finds a solitary ass standing near a stream of water. Being out of humour with losing his way, he determines to steal it as a recompence for his trouble; but, upon his attempting to lead it away, it refuses to stir. He drubs and cudgels it without effect; for some unknown power seems to fix it to the spot. At length, Peter Bell perceives, by the moonlight, the face of a dead man lying in the stream; and after recovering from the horror into which he was thrown by such a sight, he finds means to twist his staff among the hair of the corpse, and to drag it upon the bank. The ass shews the utmost satisfaction when this is done, and allows Peter Bell, who is now touched with remorse for his cruelty, to mount it, that it may carry him to the house of its drowned master. In pursuing his journey, he hears among the rocks the cries of the son of the deceased searching for his father; and his stubborn nerves, having been already shaken with what had passed, are visited by a feeling of sympathy and humanity to which he had before been a stranger. He does not meet with the seeker; but, in pursuing his ride, a variety of circumstances combine to operate on his mind. He perceives blood flowing from the wounds which he had inflicted on the faithful ass. He sees objects and hears sounds that recall the past scenes of his past life. In passing a meeting-house he hears a preacher quoting texts from Scripture, which he applies to himself. And, lastly, having arrived at the door of the drowned person, he witnesses the agonies of the widow. When she has gone to procure assistance, and he has dismounted, one of the children comes home, and recognizing the ass, imagines that his father has returned along with it, and embraces the animal with transports of joy and affection. This spectacle entirely over-powers Peter Bell, and such an effect is wrought upon him, that he leaves off his former profligate habits, and becomes an altered character.

This is the whole subject of the poem; but without having read the composition itself, it is impossible to conceive what a fine effect, and what profound pathos are drawn forth from these leading ideas. The chief fault is the dallying prolixity of some parts, which is the more felt, because there is a progressive interest. Upon the whole, it is equal to any of the lyrical ballads, both in the excellence and originality of the general idea conveyed by it, and also in the poetical merits of the execution. As for the fine and picturesque animal, which occupies so important a place in the story, it would be foolish to laugh at it, when, if properly considered, it is capable of exciting emotions so much better than those of derision. Mr Wordsworth is not in the least shy about his subject; but, when it is first discovered standing on the meadow, he makes its name the last word in a stanza, where it is rendered still more emphatic by serving as a rhyme. In order to judge fairly of Mr Wordsworth's poetry, a truth which he hints at in his preface should always be kept in view. There is certainly a radical distinction between that species of poetry whose ultimate object is to strike the imagination and interest the curios-ity, by means of splendid objects and extraordinary events, and that other species which founds its charm upon the exhibition of the relations which sentiments and emotions bear to each other within the human mind. In the first species, there is no comparison of feelings, nor any mere problem determined. Our pleasure consists in the direct impression made by images upon the imagination, or of incidents drawing us blindly along under the influence of personal sympathy; and therefore, the nature of the images and incidents employed, is here the most important of all considerations. In the other species of poetry, that developement, collision, or other relation of internal feelings, which the poet chooses for his subject, generally partakes of the nature of a universal truth, and is capable of being represented by means of a thousand different forms; and therefore, the images or situations employed, should be considered only in the light of symbols or vehicles, and not as materials of poetry. That relation of feelings which, in such a case, constitutes the true subject of the poem, would retain the same fundamental interest, although the means by which it was expressed were to be shifted through all the varieties of splendid and familiar, or of coarse and refined. Its eternal and universal nature would only be rendered more apparent, without being either vulgarised or exalted, by the outward aspect of the circumstances, in which it made its temporary abode.

[Quotes long extracts from *Peter Bell* interspersed with summary.]

A few more stanzas bring the tale to a conclusion. It will probably be considered as one of the best which have been produced by this author, and has every chance of circulating more extensively than some of his other writings. It is as likely to attract popular attention as Coleridge's Christabelle, for instance, which had a considerable success.

EDITOR'S NOTE

1. 'A cheese for the ungrateful city', Virgil, Eclogue I. 34: '[Although . . . and rich] cheese was pressed for the ungrateful city [my hand would never return home laden with money]'.

270. William Howison (died 1850, aged about 57)

From his writings, 1818

Howison was a lawyer, distinguished in records from two other, apparently unrelated, lawyers of the same name by the addition of 'tertius'; son of William Howison 'senior' of Clydegrove, the address associated with William 'tertius' after 1834; and described as 'residing in Alva Street, Edinburgh'. As a youth of 16 he was known to Scott through his writing the successful 'Polydore', an imitation ballad (see Lockhart's *Life of Scott*, 1837, V, 288–9).

a. 'Some Remarks on the Use of the Preternatural in Fiction', *Blackwood's Edinburgh Magazine*, September 1818, III, 649

This was Howison's first published comment on Wordsworth. He observes that there are six novels written to represent modern manners to one that resorts to 'the old machinery of spectres and mysteries.'

The greatest poets of the present time, however, have not disdained to continue the use of it; and indeed some of Scott's works excite the feelings of superstitious fear and traditional awe in a degree that has never been surpassed. Wordsworth's fictions in this line have exquisite beauty, and may be said to represent the spontaneous and creative superstition of the human mind, when acted upon by impressive circumstances. The poems of the Thorn, Lucy Gray, and Hartleap Well, are instances of this. The poem of the Danish Boy is a beautiful superfluity of fancy, but is too entirely poetical to please common readers. Lord Byron's strength lies in a different direction; and the spectres which appear in his poetry are not the product of imagination working upon what is unknown and invisible, but are created by the passions of the heart striving to embody their own objects. The world of spirits is not an object of interest to him for its own sake, and when he resorts to it, he does so only for the images of what he loved or hated on earth. Mr Coleridge has perhaps the finest superstitious vein of any person alive. The poem of Christabel is the best model extant of the language fit to be employed for such subjects. It was the greatest attempt, before Walter Scott's poems, to turn the language of our ancient ballads to account in a modern composition, and is perhaps more successful in that respect than the Lay of the Last Minstrel itself. Indeed Christabel may be considered as a test by which to try men's feeling of superstition, and whoever does not perceive the beauty of it, may rest assured that the world of spectres is shut against him, and that he will never see 'any thing worse than himself.'

b. Unsigned essay. No. 11 of 'Essays on the Lake School of Poetry: On the Habits of Thought inculcated by Wordsworth', *Blackwood's Edinburgh Magazine*, December 1818, IV, 257–63

Although this strange piece was edited by J. F. Ferrier into John Wilson's *Works* (1856, V, 392*ff.*), William Blackwood's attribution of it – based on fees paid – to the eccentric Howison is clearly correct (for Blackwood's list see A. L. Strout, 'Authorship of Articles in *Blackwood's*', *The Library*, 1956, XI, 192; for Strout's contradictory acceptance of Ferrier's candidate, Wilson, as author, see his *Bibliography . . . Blackwood's Magazine, 1817–1825*, 1959).

In 1827 Howison's essay, signed 'B. M.' (for *Blackwood's Magazine*) was chosen by Amédée Pichot for the major part of his introduction to the pirated and extensive selection from Wordsworth's poetry in *The Living Poets of England*, Paris, 1827, I. 289–412.

Howison's eccentricity became more marked. In his *Grammar of Infinite Forms*, 1823, he associated Wordsworth with Michaelangelo and Dante as

having Etruscan characteristics – a certain 'recluseness', the 'rejecting and excluding all that is not within a certain line ... Wordsworth who has the power of
finding out much within any given limits.' Howison developed an elaborate
theory of personality types, each named from the 'Twelve Nations', and in 1826
he noted, 'The Etruscan character must be that which appears in Wordsworth,
whose poetry expresses a taste for the serene and tranquil pleasures of retirement,
which allows the mind gently to balance its feelings, and, by excluding all disproportioned and transitory influences, to enjoy a repose favourable to delicacy of
organization and to impartiality of taste.' (*The Contest of Twelve Nations.*)

As in this country the investigations of metaphysicians have been directed chiefly towards the laws of intellect and association, and as we have
nothing which deserves the name of philosophy founded upon an examination of what human nature internally says of itself, or upon enquiries
into the dependance of one feeling upon another; in short, as we have
neither any Platonism, nor even any philosophy of the passions, we must
turn to the poets, if we wish to hear what our literature says upon these
subjects; for, by our speculative men, they have been left in utter silence,
darkness, and uncertainty. If the practical turn of mind, which has always
been characteristic of our nation, has led to these neglects, there is nothing more to be said; for the works of intellectual men should be moulded
according to the character of those who are to read them: and nothing
can obtain much influence over life, if it finds not a broad foundation in
the popular mind. Nevertheless, if philosophers profess to examine what
human nature is, in the abstract, the peculiarities of their auditors will
not serve as an excuse for slurring over particular branches of the subject,
as if they had no existence.
. . .

Two things may be chiefly observed in Mr Wordsworth's poetry;
namely, first, an attempt to awaken in the minds of his countrymen,
certain *lumieres* which they do not generally possess, and certain convictions of moral laws existing silently in the universe, and actually modifying events, in opposition to more palpable causes, in a manner similar to
what is said to be taught by the philosophy of the Hindoos; and, secondly, a thorough knowledge of all the beauties of the human affections,
and of their mutual harmonies and dependancies. In both of these
things, he has scarcely had any precursors, either among the poets or
philosophers of his country. Some traces of the convictions above alluded
to, may be found in Spenser, and some fainter traces in Milton; whose
turn of genius was decisively ascertained by the circumstance of his
greater success in handling a subject, taken from the historical parts of

the Old Testament, than one from the Christian Gospel. As for those who came after Milton, scarcely any thing above the level of actual existence appears in their writings; and, upon the whole, it would seem that the kind of sublimity with which the English have always been chiefly delighted, consists merely in an exhibition of the strength of the human energies, which, in our most esteemed poems and plays, are frequently not even elevated by self-devotion; witness Coriolanus, Richard the Third, Satan in Paradise Lost, the Giaours and Corsairs, &c. of modern days. In these pieces, elements of human nature, which are by no means of the highest kind, are represented boiling and foaming with great noise, and their turbidity is falsely taken for the highest kind of nobleness and magnificence.

Mr Wordsworth has not followed out the national spirit in this, but has turned off into a totally different sphere of reflection, from whence no kind of strength appears great, because all strength is limited, and cannot appear sublime, if contrasted with strength a single degree above it. His contemplative Platonism searches for some image of perfection to admire, and perceives that the beauty of no limited being can consist in strength, but in its conformity to the moral harmony of the universe. Hence he can see no greatness in the movements of the mind, if they tend to no higher object than self-aggrandisement, which has ever its bounds that make it appear little; and, therefore, those objects, which appear to him endowed with poetical beauty, are often such as appear homely to the eyes of others who measure them by a different standard. The small admiration he entertains for the undisciplined energies of human nature leads him to a somewhat contemptuous estimation of active life, even when conduct is submitted to the restraints of morality. He thinks little has been done for the mind, unless those internal movements, also, which are without result in action, have been tuned into beauty and regularity, and a complete balance and subordination established among the feelings by dint of long continued meditation. On this subject his ideas cannot fail to recal to remembrance those Indian doctrines, which taught that the first step towards the perception of high moral truth, was the establishment of a certain stillness and equability within the mind. But Mr Wordsworth should have proposed these Braminical notions elsewhere; for they are totally at variance with the stirring and tumultuous spirit of England. No philosophy or religion, purely contemplative, has ever taken a strong hold of the English mind; and no set of English devotees, however much they professed to be dead to the world, have been able to keep their hands out of temporal affairs.

They have always found something that called for their interference, and have exchanged the pleasures of abstract contemplation, for the zeal of partisanship. Mr Wordsworth seems averse to active life, chiefly, because he is afraid of losing sight of impressions which are only to be arrived at in the stillness of contemplation; and because he sees a risk, that the lower and coarser feelings being stirred into activity, amidst the bustle, may lose their subordination, and rise up so as to obscure the bright ideal image of human nature, which he would wish to retain always before him. Notions like these, however, must always appear ridiculous to the majority in England, where life is estimated as it produces external good or mischief. But, although Mr Wordsworth's ideas have not met with a very flattering reception, he seems no way blind to the manly integrity and substantial excellences of character that adorn his country, and which have so deep a root there, that, as Madame de Stael observes, they have never ceased to flourish even, under the influence of speculative opinions, which would have withered them up elsewhere. Indeed, the moral speculations of England have been very much a separate pastime of the understanding, which began and ended there, without ever drawing a single reflection from the depths of human nature. A remarkable trait in the history of our philosophy is, that Christianity has been as it were transposed by Paley into a more familiar key, and adapted throughout to the theory of utility; so that David Hume himself might almost play an accompaniment to it. And Paley has obtained a great deal of credit, for the performance of this good office to his countrymen.

One of the causes which have prevented Mr Wordsworth's writings from becoming popular, is, that he does not confine himself, like most other poets, to the task of representing poetical objects, or of moving our sympathies, but, also, proposes and maintains a system of philosophical opinions. In most of his poems, and in the Excursion especially, he scarcely makes poetry for its own sake, but chiefly as a vehicle for his doctrines, and the spirit of these doctrines is, unfortunately for his success, at variance with the philosophy at present most fashionable in this country. Although possessed of the requisite genius, he does not seem to care for composing poems, adapted to the exclusive purpose of taking hold of the feelings of the people; and, among the philosophers, he is rejected because he holds a different language from them. Besides, the habits of thought, in which he chiefly delights, are not calculated to produce that strength and vividness of diction, which must ever constitute one of the chief attractions of poetry. Imagination seems insufficient of itself to produce diction always nervous and poetical, without the aid of human passion and worldly observation. It is from these that the greatest poignancy of words must spring. As for the saltness of sagacity and wit, Mr Wordsworth looks down upon it as a profane thing, and is well entitled to do so. If he were to descend into so low a region as that of jesting, he would probably succeed no better than old David Deans did, when he attempted a joke at his daughter's marriage dinner. But, as Mr Wordsworth never jests, so his writings, perhaps, have some claim to be exempted from the pleasantries of others; which, indeed, can scarcely be directed with much success or effect against a person who faces ridicule so systematically, and who has always counted upon it beforehand.

Mr Wordsworth has been thought to have more affinity to Milton than any other poet. If this is the case, the affinity is rather in manner than in substance. Milton has no idealism, not even in the Paradise Regained, where there was most scope for it. His poetry is, for the most part, quite literal; and the objects he describes have all a certain definiteness and individuality, which separates them from the infinite. He has often endeavoured to present images, where every thing should have been lost in sentiment. It is generally agreed, that among the most successful parts of Paradise Lost, are those which represent the character of the fallen angel; and yet these sublime and tragical soliloquies are founded chiefly on personal feeling; which, although it may be made a source of consummate pathos and dramatic beauty, is certainly not the region of the human mind, from whence the highest possible impressions are to be drawn. Terrible acts of divine power, and, on the other hand, force of will, and obdurate pride in the rebel spirits, are the highest moral elements exhibited; but, if we look to what composes some of the finest passages in Wordsworth, we shall be inclined (theoretically at least) to prefer them to the best of Milton, as conveying more exalted meaning, whether the poetical merit of the vehicle be equal or not. The sublimity drawn from terror, collision, tumult, or discord, of any kind, has always the disadvantage of being transient; and, therefore, cannot be considered as equal to those openings into immutable brightness and harmony, which are sometimes to be met with in Wordsworth. One beauty cannot fail to strike the reader of his poetry; and that is, the perfect homogeneousness of its spirit. A systematic correspondence pervades the whole, so that the perusal of one piece frequently leads the reader's own mind into a tract of thought, which is afterwards found to be developed by the poet himself, in some other performance. The defects of his poetry originate in the same system of thought which produces its beauties. They are not the result of casual whims, or imperfections of taste. Certain great convictions of sentiment have so completely pervaded his mind, as to produce a degree of consistency in all its emanations, that we vainly look for in works founded upon observation. It is remarkable that even the external characteristics of his poetry are similar to what we are told an analogous turn of internal thought anciently produced among the Hindoos. 'From the descriptive poems of the Indians,' says Schlegel, in his lectures on the history of literature, 'we must seek to gather what influence those opinions had on human life and all its relations and feelings; what sort of poetry, and what sort of feeling of the lovely and beautiful, were produced among the Indians by the adoption of ideas to us so foreign and unaccountable. The first things which strike us in the Indian poetry are, that tender feeling of solitude, and the all-animated world of plants, which is so engagingly represented in the dramatic poetry of the Sokuntola; and those charming pictures of female truth and constancy, as well as of the beauty and loveliness of infantine nature, which are still more conspicuous in the older epic version of the same Indian legend. Neither can we observe, without wonder and admiration, that depth of moral feeling with which the poet styles conscience 'the solitary seer in the heart, from whose eye nothing is hid,' and which leads him to represent sin as something so incapable of concealment, that every transgression is not only known to conscience, and all the gods, but felt with a sympathetic shudder by those elements themselves which we call inanimate, by the sun, the moon, the fire, the air, the heaven, the earth, the flood, and the deep, as a crying outrage against nature, and a derangement of the universe.'

Whoever wishes to understand Mr. Wordsworth's philosophical opinions, will find them developed in their most perfect form, in the Excursion; but those who wish to judge merely how far he possesses the powers commonly called poetical, will do best to read his Lyrical Ballads, and smaller Poems, where pathos, imagination, and knowledge of human nature, are often presented by themselves, without any obtrusive or argumentative reference to a system. At the same time, the reverential awe, and the far extended sympathy with which he looks upon the whole system of existing things, and the silent moral connexions which he supposes to exist among them, are visible throughout all his writings. He tunes his mind to nature almost with a feeling of religious obligation; and where others behold only beautiful colours, making their appearance according to optical laws, or feel pleasant physical sensations resulting from a pure atmosphere, or from the odoriferous exhalations of herbage, or enjoy the pleasure of measuring an extended prospect, as an amusement for the eye, this poet (whether justly or not) thinks he traces something more in the spectacle than the mere reflection of his own feelings, painted upon external objects, by means of the association of ideas; or, at least, seems to consider what we then behold as the instantaneous creation of the mind.

[Quotes *The Excursion*, *PW*, V, p. 14, Book I, ll. 198–209, and *ibid.*, pp. 14–16, ll. 227–32

> Oh then what soul was his, when on the tops
> Of the high mountains, he beheld the sun . . . *ff.*]

The relation which the consideration of moral pain or deformity bears to this far-extended sympathy with the universe, is alluded to in another passage of the Excursion.

[Quotes *ibid.*, p. 36. ll. 932–55

> My friend, enough to sorrow you have given . . .
> Appeared an idle dream, that could not live
> Where meditation was.]

Notions like those of Mr Wordsworth are evidently suited only to a life purely contemplative; but that universality of spirit, which becomes true philosophy, should forbid, in persons of different habits, any blind or sudden condemnation of them. No individual can say what are all the internal suggestions of the human faculties, unless he has varied his mode of existence sufficiently to afford fit opportunities for their developement. – The facts of consciousness are admitted to be as much facts as those of the senses; but, at the same time, we cannot get individuals to agree what they are, and, while things remain in this state of uncertainty, the first duty is certainly that of liberality of mind.

Wordsworth's habit of dwelling as much upon the rest of the universe as upon man, has given his poetry an air of greater joyfulness and sunshine, than it could have possessed if human life had been his more constant theme. He turns with ever new delight to objects which exhibit none of the harshness and discrepancy of the human world.

> The blackbird on the summer trees,
>   The lark upon the hill,
> Let loose their carols when they please,
>   Are quiet when they will.
> With nature do they never wage
>   A foolish strife; they see

> A happy youth, and their old age
> Is beautiful and free.
> > ['The Fountain', *PW*, IV, p. 72, ll. 37–44)]

> Down to the vale this water steers,
> > How merrily it goes,
> 'Twill murmur on a thousand years,
> > And flow as now it flows.
> > > [*Ibid.*, in footnote, ll. 21–4]

When he does turn his attention upon life, we find always the most beautiful echoes of Christian tenderness and sorrow. In an elegy, suggested by a picture representing a storm, he alludes to the bitter recollection of a domestic loss which had befallen him, and is pleased to see the image of pain reflected in external nature.

[Quotes 'Peele Castle', *PW*, IV, p. 260, ll. 45–60:

> Oh 'tis a passionate work! – Yet wise and well . . .
> Not without hope we suffer and we mourn.]

Surely nothing can be finer than this. It is impressed with the true character of that kind of social sentiment, which is drawn from a source not liable to fail. In his sonnets, we see what form citizenship is made to assume, when growing up in contiguity with the other habits of mind cultivated by Wordsworth. How these compositions, so pregnant with feeling and reflection, upon the most interesting topics, should not have been more generally known, is a problem difficult to be solved. The following is one of them, containing reflections on the moral effects of slavery.

[Quotes 'There is a bondage . . .', *PW*, III, p. 118]

As Mr Wordsworth's habits of thought, and not his merely poetical powers, were meant to form the subject of this discussion, we have not adverted to some of his detached performances, which are master-pieces in their way. These would offer a separate subject for criticism. But, as they are little known (in Scotland especially), we shall quote the whole of one of his most exquisite minor pieces.

[Quotes 'Ruth', *PW*, II, pp. 227–235]

In some respects Mr Wordsworth may be considered as the Rousseau of the present times. Both of them were educated among the mountains, at a distance from the fermentations of social life, and acquired, from their way of existence, certain peculiar sentimental habits of meditation, which were pitched in a different key from the callous, sarcastic, and practical way of thinking, prevalent among their contemporaries of the cities. Rousseau mingled in the throng; but found himself there like a man dropped out of the clouds. The peculiarity of his habits made him wretched; and his irritation perverted the employment of his genius. Mr Wordsworth has acted more wisely in keeping aloof, and continuing to cultivate his mind according to its pristine bias, and forbearing to grapple too closely with the differently educated men of cities. Rousseau makes a fine encomium upon the mountains, which, as it is connected with the present subject, we shall quote: – 'A general impression (which every body experiences, though all do not observe it) is, that, on high mountains where the air is pure and subtle, we feel greater lightness and agility of body, and more serenity in the mind. The pleasures are there less violent; the passions are more moderate; *meditations receive there a certain great and sublime character proportioned to the objects that strike us*; a certain tranquil pleasure which has nothing sensual. We are there grave without melancholy; quiet without indolence; contented with existing and thinking, all too lively pleasures are blunted, and lose the sharp points which render them painful; they leave in the heart only a slight and agreeable emotion; and thus an happy climate makes the passions of mankind subservient to his felicity, which elsewhere are his torment. I question whether any violent agitation or vapourish disorder could hold out against such an abode if continued for some time; and I am surprised that baths of the salutary and beneficial air of the mountains are not one of the principal remedies of medicine and morality.'

271. Robert Morehead (1777–1842)

From an essay, 'Observations on the Poetical Character of Dante', signed 'D.' *Edinburgh Magazine*, September 1818, N.S. III, 226–8

It may be a singular observation, but we believe it to be a just one, that the modern school of poetry which has arisen in this country within the last thirty years, comes closer to the manner of Dante than any other; and this very remarkable poet actually combines many of the leading traits of the most eminent of our distinguished contemporaries. They do not know it, and probably never thought of it, but he is really at the head of their school, – and, if they would go to him with the same devotion with which poets in general have drank from the fountain of Homer, they would find much light thrown, by his comprehensive genius, on the path which they are seeking to trace, and which they have as yet only imperfectly found. It has been the great object of modern poets to overthrow every poetical idol, and to seek for the sources of their inspiration in nature alone, and in their own genius. All the classical images and *formulæ* which had acquired a sort of prescriptive dominion in the regions of Parnassus, (here is one of them) are now banished as fetters upon the originality of genius, and the natural flow of sentiment; and this, we may say, Dante has done of old as thoroughly as it ought to be done. He has his allusions to these things when any good is to be got by them, and never expresses any thing like contempt for them; but his mind is completely unfettered by them to a degree that is not to be found in any other poet previous, perhaps, to Mr Wordsworth; and the reverence which, with all his freedom, he entertains for his old poetical masters, is a feeling which Mr Wordsworth would not be the worse of imbibing from him.

The modern school, with Mr Wordsworth at its head, has a contempt for the established language of poetry; and he, it is well known, even goes so far as to propose the adoption of a low and familiar diction, approaching to the language of a vulgar prose. Now Dante seems to have apprehended all that was just and sound in this idea, and to have, moreover, perceived, what Mr Wordsworth has not, the precise bounds and limits to which it ought to be carried. No diction can be more familiar, more the language of conversation, more taken out of the unnatural forms of a false poetical elevation, than his, yet none can be less vulgar, less childish, more constantly bearing the impression, and reflecting the images of a powerful, unwavering, and highly cultivated mind.

For a natural diction suited to the force and imagery of a strong poetical genius, Lord Byron is, perhaps, the modern poet whose style most closely resembles Dante's; there is a strength and a compression in both in which Wordsworth and his peculiar school are greatly defective.

One of Wordsworth's finest peculiarities is perfectly possessed by Dante, and much better applied, besides, by the old, than by the modern poet; we mean that close observation of nature by which images that have escaped both the common race of men, and much more, the common race of poets, have been marked, and secretly contemplated, and made the subject of musings, which are connected in the mind of the genuine pupil of nature with much moral and refined wisdom. The error of Wordsworth is, that he makes observations of this kind the great staple of his poetry, and by this means he has become as fantastic, and as much of a humourist, as the melancholy Jacques himself. Dante lived among political intrigues, and the turmoils of factions, yet it is astonishing, that he had as fine an eye for these glimpses of nature in which 'the vision and the mystery' are contained, as the poet who has passed all his days musing on the banks of Grassmere, or Rydal-water. But the Chief Magistrate of Florence, as our poet was in one year, and an exile from his country, as he was in the next, knew very well that the mind of a being like man, which has strong interests to engage it in the present life, and strong hopes and fears to lead it forward into futurity, cannot be permanently occupied with, though it may, with deep feeling, take a sidelong glance at, dancing daffodils, or the reflection of a lamb in a smooth lake. The same sort of images, therefore, which, in Wordsworth, seem so often puerile and ridiculous, by being brought upon his fore-ground, and made the subject matter of long poems or descriptions, Dante glances at with wonderful effect, as similes for illustrating the profound invisible truths of eternity, which he professes to reveal to an awe-struck and astonished world.

[Quotes some five lengthy similes from Henry Cary's version of Dante's *Divine Comedy*.]

These similes, we maintain, are infinitely more in the character of Wordsworth's images than of Homer's, and almost all the similes of Dante are in this strain of minute refinement, derived either from nature or art, as it may happen, as if he purposely avoided those broad outlines of objects which had been traced over and over again by so many preceding poets.

There is another singular resemblance between Dante and Wordsworth, which particularly struck us in Mr Cary's version of the old poet. In the Paradiso, especially, he indulges to an excess in certain long bewildered metaphysical and theological discussions, which are extremely in the wandering unsatisfactory style of our good friend the Pedlar in the Excursion. We have not here compared the translation with the original, and are unable as yet to say how far the resemblance holds in the Italian; but we really believe we should have sometimes thought that we had taken up by mistake the Excursion instead of the Paradiso, were it not that the one volume is a large quarto, and the other one of the smallest possible duodecimos. This mystical style of writing, however, is very excusable, or rather was scarcely to be avoided in the oldest poet of Christian Europe, a contemporary, moreover, of Thomas Aquinas; and the only wonder is, that, in the nineteenth century Mr Wordsworth should have carried it so much farther, and interwoven it so much more closely with the tissue of his poem.

272. C. H. Terrot (1790–1872)

Extract from his anonymous verses, *Common Sense*, 1819, and his
accompanying footnote, both reprinted in the *Monthly Review*, May
1820, XCII, 98–100

Nephew of Wordsworth's college friend, William Terrot; he lived at
Haddington, Scotland, from 1814; Bishop of Edinburgh, 1841–72. If for
no other reason, Charles Terrot would know of Wordsworth through his
evangelical uncle, William, Vicar of Grindon, Co. Durham, whose
reunion with the poet at Rydal Mount in October 1814 is so mischiev-
ously described by Mary Wordsworth (*Letters of Mary Wordsworth*, ed.
Mary Burton, 26).

> What shall I say of Wordsworth? that I praise
> The pure and spotless tenor of his lays:
> But that his rhymes are bad, his sense obscure,
> His diction childish, and his fancy poor:
> That if he be a poet, well I wot
> Milton and Shakespeare, Pope and Gray were not:
> If verse be just the talk of common men,
> Dealt out by line, and measured eight or ten:
> If knights and heroes, kings and gods, be toys,
> Compared with duffle cloaks, and idiot boys –
> Thou shalt be read, when Homer is forgotten,
> And the great Goth in dust and worms is rotting;
> Then shalt thou live the joy of babes and men –
> But, gentle Wordsworth, hope it not till then.

'Few poets have been more reviewed, or less read, than Wordsworth. He
has a few idolaters, to whom he is ὁ ποιητης[1]: while the common run of
readers and critics will scarcely allow him to be a poet at all. I hold with
the million. Mr. Wordsworth has given us his notions of poetry in certain
philosophical prefaces, which have very much the air of translations from
the German. Among other canons, he observes, "the reader cannot be
too often reminded that poetry is passion." As an illustration of this, the
reader may take –

> The Vicar did not hear the words: and now
> Pointing towards the cottage, he entreated

That Leonard would partake his humble fare;
The other thanked him with a fervent voice,
But added, that the evening being fine
He would pursue his journey.
['The Brothers', *PW*, II, p. 13, ll. 412–7]

Is not this passion? Are not these thoughts that breathe, and words that burn?'

Common Sense was reviewed in the *Edinburgh Monthly Review* for December 1819 (II, 674) and another comment was added:

The note on Wordsworth we consider better than the text; which last merely amplifies, in no very remarkable verse, Porson's notorious repartee to an idolater of Southey's Thalaba, who said that his favourite would be admired when Homer and Milton were forgotten. – 'Perhaps he may, – but not till then.' The passage quoted in this note is a specimen of those rags in which Wordsworth often voluntarily clothes himself, thereby forfeiting much otherwise deserved popularity; for, that Wordsworth is a great poet, needs no other proof than the fact, that the question has been mooted and disputed for so many years.

EDITOR'S NOTE

1. 'The poet/maker'.

273. Robert Southey

From later letters, 1819

a. To W. S. Landor, 3 January 1819

I was quite certain that you would appreciate Wordsworth justly. Nations, you say, are not proud of living genius. They are proud of it only as far as they understand it; and the majority, being incapable of understanding it, can never admire it, till they take it upon trust: so that two or three generations must pass before the public affect to admire such poets as Milton and Wordsworth. Of such men the world scarcely produces one in a millenium; – has it, indeed, ever produced more than two? for Shakspeare is of a different class. But of all inferior degrees of poets no age and no country was ever so prolific as our own: every season produces some half dozen poems, not one of which obtains the slightest attention, and any one of which would have the author celebrated above all contemporaries five-and-twenty years ago.

(*A Selection from the Letters of Robert Southey*, ed. J. W. Warter, 1856, III,109–10)

b. To Henry Southey, [? late April] 1819

Have you seen Wordsworth's Peter Bell, to which I have the honour of being dedicatee? It is a truly original poem. There are one or two lines which might easily have been made unexceptionable, – & seem placed as if to invite mockery. And in one part I think the Poet is hardly serious enough for his subject, – where he is asking *what* Peter saw in the water. But the latter part has passages which can hardly be read without tears, – & the Prologue is exquisite in its kind, – & indeed the whole, – take it as a whole, what no man but Wordworth could have written.

(Ms. Bodleian Library)

c. To W. S. Landor, 7 May 1819

Wordsworth has just published a little poem Peter Bell, to the tune of his 'Idiot Boy', and of the same pitch, with fine things in it, and a prologue which you will be much pleased with. I told him what you said of his poem, and he desires to send you this when an opportunity offers.

(*A Selection from the Letters of Robert Southey*, ed. J. W. Warter, 1856, III, 133)

d. To Wade Brown (d. 1821), 15 June 1819

'I think you will be pleased with Wordsworth's "Waggoner," if it were only for the line of road[1] which it describes. The master of the waggon was my poor landlord Jackson; and the cause of his exchanging it for the one-horse-cart was just as is represented in the poem; nobody but Benjamin could manage it upon these hills, and Benjamin could not resist the temptations by the way-side.

(*Life and Correspondence of Robert Southey*, ed. C. C. Southey, 1849, IV, 348)

EDITOR'S NOTE

1. The road from Keswick to Ambleside.

274.

Unsigned biographical account, 'Memoir of William Wordsworth, Esq.
(With a Portrait)', *New Monthly Magazine*, 1 February 1819, XI, 48–50

This is the earliest attempt at a detailed life. It was accompanied by the
first published engraving of Wordsworth (of the Carruthers portrait,
1817). Richard Scambler, the Wordsworths' Ambleside apothecary since
1808, had been approached, and Mary Wordsworth expressed the family's
distaste for the idea:

> We have been applied to by Mr Scambler for communications towards
> the 'Life' that is to appear in the Mag: He has been written to, and I
> believe has supplied something – but we would not give ear to it. It is an
> unbelievable thing for anybody to seek for such information as they
> require during the existence of any one – this at least is my view of the
> subject. A precious morsel of Biography no doubt the production will
> be, appear in public when it may.
>
> (*Letters of Mary Wordsworth*, ed. Mary Burton, 1958, 50)

It was possibly Alaric Watts who approached Scambler and wrote the
account: Watts (1797–1864) was sub-editor of *New Monthly* from 1818 to
April 1819. The Memoir was reprinted in the Galignani collected edition
of Wordsworth's poems, Paris, 1827.

Thomas Monkhouse, Mary Wordsworth's cousin, who owned the portrait of Wordsworth by Carruthers, painted 1817, must have given Henry
Meyer the opportunity to make an engraving of it; this remained the only
published portrait of Wordsworth until 1831. Mary Wordsworth, on 6
December 1818, hoped that Monkhouse would not lend his authority to
the 'Life'

> I wish they may not send the 'Life' that the Mag: people mean to give of
> W. to you for dates or anything else. For you, (as one of the family),
> having aught to do with it, will give a sort of sanction to any absurdities
> which it may contain – for no doubt that your having seen it, will be
> made known.
>
> (*Ibid.*, 43)

MEMOIR OF WILLIAM WORDSWORTH, ESQ.
(*WITH A PORTRAIT*)

The penury of literary biography is a complaint of long standing, and the
justness of it is evident in the scanty memorials that have been left of the

learning and genius of former days. Anxious to redeem our own times from the charge of negligence, our constant efforts are employed in collecting from primary sources accurate information concerning the characters whose portraits give interest to our numbers. It is seldom, indeed, that the materials so obtained are copious or various, because pre-eminent merit is generally of a retiring nature, and the delicacy of friendship is not easily prevailed upon to be communicative.

Such is the apology which we have to offer, whenever our narratives are contracted within narrow limits, and when the memoir is brief, because the dignity of truth prevents us from drawing upon invention to supply the paucity of facts. We trust, however, that in the present instance the biography will be found substantially correct, and prove equally satisfactory to those who esteem the subject of it for his private worth, and those who, knowing him only by his writings, admire him for the use which he has made of his talents.

WILLIAM WORDSWORTH was born at Cockermouth, of a highly respectable family, April 7, 1770. At the age of eight years he was sent to Hawkshead school, in that part of Lancashire which is separated from the county to which it belongs by Westmoreland and the sea. The grammar school of Hawkshead was founded and endowed in the reign of Queen Elizabeth, by the venerable Edwin Sandys, archbishop of York, and it has ever been accounted one of the best seminaries in the north of England. Two of its living ornaments are the subject of this sketch, and his brother Dr. Christopher Wordsworth, the present chaplain to the House of Commons, rector of Lambeth, and dean of Bocking; whose extremely acute and erudite letters on the Greek definitive article in confirmation of the late Granville Sharpe's Rule, procured him the patronage of the Archbishop of Canterbury, and the valuable preferments which he now so deservedly enjoys.

The two boys were educated at the same school, and though they had but little similarity of taste, a strong fraternal attachment subsisted between them, of which a striking instance occurred while they were both very young: when one being furiously assailed by a much more powerful lad than himself, the other, with affectionate gallantry, planting himself by the side of his brother, fought with such spirit, that the aggressor was obliged to desist.

Of William, it is said, by those who were his contemporaries at school, that in his classical attainments he was considerably above par, when compared with boys of his own age; while in English composition, both prose and verse, he frequently obtained the distinguished commendation of Mr. Taylor, the headmaster, who was a man of great critical judgment. The chief delight of the youth, even at a very early age, consisted in reading and reciting passages of the best of our poets. Before the morning hour of repairing to school, he has been often seen and heard in the sequestered lane, either alone, or with a favourite companion, repeating aloud beautiful passages from Thomson's Seasons, and sometimes comparing, as they chanced to occur, the actual phenomena of nature with the descriptions given of them by the poet. At the age of thirteen, his genius was indicated in verses on the vacation, which procured him the praise of the master; but it should seem that this incipient effort did not quite satisfy himself, since we are told that at the next returning season of welcome relaxation from scholastic discipline, he composed another poem on the same subject, which was also applauded by those to whom it was shewn. This stirring of the spirit of poesy within was kept up and invigorated by the romantic scenery which tempted his youthful steps to ramble among the mountains, and along the margin of the lake of Esthwaite, near the school of Hawkshead.[1]

Having laid in a good stock of grammar learning, William Wordsworth removed, in October, 1787, to the university of Cambridge, where he was matriculated a student of St. John's, as his brother, sometime afterwards, was of Trinity College. Here our author continued long enough to complete his degrees in arts, but without aspiring to, or attaining, the academical honours of wrangler or prizeman. During one of the long vacations, he made a pedestrian excursion through part of France, Switzerland, the Savoy, and Italy, accompanied by a college friend. Of this tour he wrote an account, under the title of 'Descriptive Sketches in Verse,' which was printed in 1793; in which year also he published, 'An Evening Walk, an Epistle in Verse, addressed to a Young Lady from the Lakes in the North of England.'

Whether Mr. Wordsworth was intended for any of the learned professions, we have not the means of knowing, but if such was the case, he disappointed the expectation of his friends, by leaving the university altogether soon after his return, and amusing himself in wandering over different parts of the country. At length he took a cottage in the hamlet of Alfoxden, not far from Bridgewater, in Somersetshire, where he either contracted or renewed an intimate friendship with Mr. Coleridge. In this remote part of the kingdom, they lived almost in a state of seclusion, employing their hours either in climbing the Quantock hills, traversing the winding shores of the bay, or in sitting at home, planning literary works. Sometimes, indeed, they visited the only little inn of the village, but here their conversation was above the frequenters of the place, and their character altogether such as to excite surprise and curiosity. At this time the violence of the revolutionary tempest in France occasioned much observation and dispute, not only in the metropolis and large towns, but in every obscure nook and corner of the British isles. Such a subject could not, therefore, fail to be agitated in the public house where our two friends occasionally spent their evenings. Wordsworth had no turn for politics, and was generally silent, but his friend, being at that period a zealous reformist, took such an active part in the questions which arose, as to beget a suspicion, in one person, that these two strangers were spies or incendiaries. This sagacious politician was no other than the lawyer of the village, and having once formed this idea in his fertile brain, it soon acquired the figure and substance of reality. Every action of the sojourners was accordingly watched by a person employed for the purpose; who, true to his trust, traced their footsteps, and without being seen by them, placed himself in a situation where he could hear their discourse when they sat upon a craggy cliff observing the dashing of the waves on the beach. Sometimes he would meet them, as it were by accident, in their walks, and by entering into familiar chat with them, draw the conversation on by degrees to politics, merely to catch some clue to a discovery. All these arts, however, produced nothing, and the man, very much to his honour, gave so faithful a report of all his observations, that no farther inquiry was made, nor were the two friends apprised of the snare that had been laid to entrap them, till a long time afterwards, when all suspicion was completely removed.

It was during this retirement on the coast of Somersetshire, that the 'Lyrical Ballads' were planned and in part written, 'as an experiment,' says Mr. Coleridge, whether subjects, which from their nature rejected the usual ornaments and extra colloquial style of poems, in general, might not be so managed in the language of ordinary life as to produce the pleasurable interest, which it is the peculiar business of poetry to impart.[*]

These Ballads, with some other poems, appeared first in one small volume in 1798, in which year the author and his sister made a tour through part of Germany, where they fell in with Mr. Coleridge, who, through the liberality of the late Mr. Wedgworth [for Wedgwood], had been enabled to prosecute his studies in a foreign university. How long the travellers continued abroad, we are not informed, but in 1800, we find Mr. Wordsworth settled at Grassmere, in Westmoreland, where, or

---

[*] Biographia Literaria, vol, ii. p. 3.

at Rydall, in that neighbourhood, he has continued to dwell ever since. In 1803, he married Miss Mary Hutchinson, of Penrith, a young lady of the most respectable connexions and exemplary character, who has brought him five children, of whom three, two sons and a daughter, are still living. With such inducements to active exertion, and the aid of potent friends, who hold his merits in high estimation, the poet might no doubt have distinguished himself in public life to the lucrative advantage of his family. But alike indifferent to the temptations of ambition and riches, he seems to have imbibed the spirit of Hooker, who besought his patron to remove him from the bustle and intrigues of the world, to a situation 'where he might see God's blessings spring from his mother earth, and eat his bread in peace and privacy.'

The picturesque beauties of Windermere, and the scenery of the neighbourhood, proved more attractive charms than the pleasures of artificial society; and here, in the bosom of a happy circle, our author enjoys the utmost tranquility, on a moderate income, arising from a patrimonial estate, and the situation of distributor of the stamps for the counties of Cumberland and Westmoreland, which office he owes to the personal friendship of the Earl of Lonsdale.

In 1807 Mr. Wordsworth gave to the public a miscellaneous collection of poems, in two small volumes, of which a new and considerably improved edition made its appearance in the year 1815. – Among the many additions which the author thought proper to make to this last impression, were a preface and supplementary essay, both directed to the same object – that of applying his principle of simplicity in composition to every species of poetry.

The next original production of Mr. Wordsworth was of a different cast, and one that from his turn and habits could hardly have been expected. This was a bulky political pamphlet, printed in the year 1809, with a title remarkable for its elliptical abruptness and prolixity. – 'Concerning the Relations of Great Britain, Spain, and Portugal, to each other, and to the common enemy, at this crisis; and specifically as affected by the Convention of Cintra; the whole brought to the test of those principles by which alone the Independence and Freedom of Nations can be preserved or recovered.'

In this performance ministers were censured, not for intermeddling in the affairs of the peninsula, but for neglecting to pour into the heart of Spain all their military resources. The essay is written in an energetic strain, and reflects credit upon the patriotic feelings of the author.

In 1814 Mr. Wordsworth published the first portion of his long-promised performance of 'The Recluse;' in a large and splendid quarto. To this part he gave the title of 'The Excursion;' but of the rest of the work, nothing has yet seen the light, unless the story of 'The White Doe of Rylstone; or, the Fate of the Nortons,' which appeared in the same form in the following year, be considered as an episode of the great poem.

This last piece closes the list of our author's publications, on which we shall observe, that if the character of a man is to be inferred from his literary progeny, that of Mr. Wordsworth is at once stamped with the genuine marks of native excellence; for no liberal reader of his poems can rise from the perusal of them without sentiments of respect for that spirit of virtue which breathes in every line. But we are assured that the poet is one who writes from the heart, and who lives as he writes. They who know him most intimately, speak of him as constantly discharging all the relative duties of the husband, father, and friend, with scrupulous fidelity and the most affectionate tenderness. He is universally esteemed in his neighbourhood for the benevolence of his disposition, the courteousness of his manners, his readiness to relieve the distressed, and to promote every design calculated for the general benefit. To this summary of pre-eminent talent and substantial worth, we may add, that he is a firm friend to the constitution, which is the same as saying that he is a loyal subject of the king, and a sincere member of the Church of England.

EDITOR'S NOTE

1. The earliest known comment on Wordsworth's poetry was recorded by William Knight in his *Life of William Wordsworth*, 1889. 'That he did write verses was known to all his schoolfellows; and I am indebted to a nephew of Southey's, the Rev. Mr Hill of Warwick, for the fact, told him by the poet, that one of his very prosaic schoolfellows at Hawkshead once addresses him thus: "I say, Bill, when you write poems, do you *always* invoke the Muse?"' (1. 38). Hill's own manuscript version is recorded in a copy of Knight's *The English Lake District as Interpreted in the Poems of Wordsworth*, 1878: 'As an illustration of Hawkshead life I will write down an Anecdote which Wordsworth himself told me pronouncing the words in true Westmorland fashion. One day after he gained some credit from his Master for some English verses – a bigger boy took him by the arm and led him off into the fields, & when he had got him quite apart, gravely said to him "I say, Bill, when thoo writes verse dost thoo invoke t'Muse?" (James A. Butler, 'The Muse at Hawkshead: Early Criticism of Wordsworth's Poetry', *The Wordsworth Circle*, XX, Summer 1989, 140). Herbert Hill, 1810–92, married Bertha, Southey's daughter in 1839.

275. George Ticknor (1791–1871)

From his journals, 1819–1837

George Ticknor was Professor of Modern Languages at Harvard. These extracts from his Journals indicate how the power of Wordsworth's personality and conversation could blend with, and supplement a response to, the poetry.

a. 21 March 1819

Ticknor records a visit to Rydal Mount. He was 28 at the time and very shortly to be a Professor at Harvard.

An extremely pleasant drive of sixteen miles . . . brought me to Wordsworth's door, on a little elevation commanding a view of Rydal water . . . It is claimed to be the most beautiful spot and the finest prospect in the lake country, and, even if there be finer, it would be an ungrateful thing to remember them here, where, if anywhere, the eye and the heart ought to be satisfied. Wordsworth knew from Southey that I was coming, and therefore met me at the door and received me heartily. He is about fifty-three or four, with a tall, ample, well-proportioned frame, a grave and tranquil manner, a Roman cast of appearance, and Roman dignity and simplicity. He presented me to his wife, a good, very plain woman, who seems to regard him with reverence and affection, and to his sister, not much younger than himself, with a good deal of spirit and, I should think, more than common talent and knowledge. I was at home with them at once, and we went out like friends together to scramble up the mountains and enjoy the prospects and scenery . . . we returned to dinner, which was very simple, for, though he has an office under the government and a patrimony besides, yet each is inconsiderable . . .

His conversation surprised me by being so different from all I had anticipated. It was exceedingly simple, strictly confined to the subjects he understood familiarly, and more marked by plain good-sense than by anything else. When, however, he came upon poetry and reviews, he was the Kahn of Tartary again, and talked as metaphysically and extravagantly as ever Coleridge wrote; but, excepting this, it was really a

1031

consolation to him. It was best of all, though, to see how he is loved and respected in all his family and neighbourhood. . . . The peasantry treated him with marked respect, the children took off their hats to him, and a poor widow in the neighbourhood sent to him to come and talk to her son, who had been behaving ill. . . .

In the evening he showed me his manuscripts, the longest a kind of poetical history of his life, which, in the course of about two octavo volumes of manuscripts, he has brought to his twenty-eighth year, and of which the 'Excursion' is a fragment. It is in blank verse, and, as far as I read, what has been published is a fair specimen of what remains in manuscript. He read me 'Peter Bell, the Potter,' a long tale, with many beauties but much greater defects; and another similar story, 'The Waggoner' . . . the whole amused me a good deal; it was a specimen of the lake life, doctrines, and manners, more perfect than I had found at Southey's, and, as such, was very curious.

(*Life, Letters, and Journals of George Ticknor*, 1876, I, 287)

b. 1 and 2 September 1835

Ticknor records a kind reception, despite the illness of Wordsworth's sister Dorothy and daughter Dora and the recent death of Sara Hutchinson.

And he talked about Campbell, the reviewers, and their effect on his own reputation, etc., all in the most kindly and frank spirit, describing to us 'The Recluse,' his unpublished poem, and repeating in illustration of his opinions, passages from his own works, in his own peculiarly sonorous recitative.

(*Ibid.*, I, 287)

c. 1837

Ticknor had met Wordsworth several times in 1837 – in Rome, Como, Venice, Munich – during Wordsworth's tour with Crabb Robinson. For the third time, Wordsworth discusses with Ticknor the unfinished *Recluse*, and here most fully expresses his powerlessness to finish the third part of *The Recluse*, unwritten except for *Home at Grasmere*.

RICHARD HENRY DANA, SR. (1787–1879)

We were expected at Wordsworth's, and were most heartily welcomed, with real frank kindness, as old friends . . . and we took the meal with them. It was simple as possible. . . . Afterwards we walked an hour . . . on the terraces and through the little grounds, while Mr. Wordsworth explained the scenery about us, and repeated passages of his poetry relating to it. Mrs. Wordsworth asked me to talk to him about finishing the Excursion, or the Recluse; saying, that she could not bear to have him occupied constantly in writing sonnets and other trifles, while this great work lay by him untouched, but that she had ceased to urge him on the subject, because she had done it so much in vain. I asked him about it, therefore. He said that the Introduction, which is a sort of autobiography, is completed. This I knew, for he read me large portions of it twenty years ago. The rest is divided into three parts, the first of which is partly written in fragments, which Mr. Wordsworth says would be useless and unintelligible in other hands than his own; the second is the Excursion; and the third is untouched. On my asking him why he does not finish it, he turned to me very decidedly, and said, 'Why did not Gray finish the long poem he began on a similar subject? Because he found he had undertaken something beyond his powers to accomplish. And that is my case.' We controverted his position, of course, but I am not certain the event will not prove that he has acted upon his belief. At any rate, I have no hope it will ever be completed, though after his death the world will no doubt have much more than it now possesses.'

(*Ibid.*, II, 167)

276. Richard Henry Dana, Sr. (1787–1879)

From a review of Hazlitt's *Lectures on the English Poets. Delivered at the Surrey Institution*, Philadelphia, 1818 (*North-American Review*, III, March 1819, 318–22)

Richard Henry Dana, Sr., a poet and journalist, makes a strong defence of Wordsworth against Hazlitt's attack, his remarks coming at the end of a long essay in which he surveys, as Hazlitt does, a range of English poets from Chaucer to the present day. Dana finds the personal attacks unacceptable:

These things afford entertainment; but when we reflect upon the manner in which he brings before those who attended his lectures, some of his old acquaintance and their friends, we feel nothing but disgust at him, and doubt of the true refinement of an age in which a polite and well educated audience would allow of such gross personalities. If Mr. Hazlitt is blind to the beauties of the living poets, it is of little consequence to them or to us, but we are offended at the vulgarity of the attack upon the characters of Wordsworth and Coleridge, nor does he rise in our estimation by seeking to make, out of the faults of Burns, a defence for licentiousness, and a rude attack upon a well principled man.

We hope that the English are not losing their reserve, and their reverence of domestic and individual privacy. Strangers who visit them may find it inconvenient, and coarse-minded people rail about it. It is connected with their best feelings, and when they become the mere creatures of society, they will put off that character which has made them respected.

(*North-American Review*, III, March 1819, 322)

Though there were private individuals – such as William Cullen Bryant (1794-1878)[1] – who were reading Wordsworth with rapture ten years before Bryant's poems appeared in America in 1821, the one example of critical enthusiasm for Wordsworth in the United States was this review by Dana: it helped prepare the way for the first major edition of Wordsworth's poetry in America (*The Poetical Works of William Wordsworth*, in four volumes, Boston, 1824) since the publication of *Lyrical Ballads*, Philadelphia, 1802. Importantly, we note that Dana's remarks are bolstered by his reading of Coleridge's *Biographia Literaria*, 1817:

What with the variety of faces we have seen, and such mixed and continued talking, we feel too much exhausted to say more than a passing word to Mr. Wordsworth. Besides, it is getting quite late, and our readers must be growing as weary as we are. We must take another time, when we can begin fresh, and have the day before us. We hope it will not be long before Mr. Wordsworth will give us such an opportunity, when we shall be glad to visit him and his country friends, to take a seat by him in his retired dwelling 'green, to the very door,' and 'in the plain presence of his dignity,' learn to feel a kindred self-respect, and becoming pure through his teaching, have our minds opened to the beauties that make happy thoughts for him.

Mr. Wordsworth, with a mind perfectly original, with an imagination full of forms of beauty and grandeur, and with powers of description unsurpassed by any poet of this age, has such an air of plain truth in telling his stories and giving the characters of those he is speaking of, – puts into the mouths of his personages sentiments so very simple, though elevated, and makes his scenery so like that which we see every where, that we lose the impression while reading him, that we are taken out of the world and reality into the regions of imagination and poetry, – we are wholly absorbed in what we are about in this new state of things, and deluded into all the earnestness with which the concerns of life affect us. When we read other men, we look at the scenery they are describing, with the sense upon us that it is seen by us through the imagination; but in Wordsworth this is lost, and every thing he shows us appears to the eye with the same distinctness and immediate reality, as if the object itself was directly before us.

It may at first seem strange that the poetical interest should be so deep, where there is so slight a departure from plain experience. It is the change wrought in ourselves that gives it. It is we and the pleasures, the business and desires of life that have been a delusion; we are made to feel a serious concern in what we find in him, and reality itself becomes idle and unimportant. He brings right thoughts and pure wishes into our minds and hearts, clears our dim imaginations, and the poetry of our being becomes its truth. He has formed another creation, but it is one within ourselves – the mountains and valleys, the rivers and plains are the same, and so are the trees and the smaller plants, they are no greener, nor are the clouds passing over them any brighter than before. To our eyes they are the same as when we saw them yesterday; but a new sense is in our hearts, new and delightful relations have grown out from them, running over the earth and twisting themselves about every little thing upon it that has life, and connecting its being with our own. A moral sense is given to all things; and the materials of the earth which seemed made only for homely uses, become the teachers of our minds and ministers of good to our hearts. Here the love of beauty is made religion, and what we had falsely esteemed the indulgence of idle imaginations, is found to have higher and more serious purposes, than the staid affairs of life. The world of nature is full of magnificence and beauty; every thing in it is made to more than a single end. The fruit that nourishes us is fair to the eye, that we may find in it a second and better delight. Lasting and purifying pleasures are awakened within us and happy thoughts and images brought into being. In the luxury of this higher existence, we find a moral strength, and from the riot of imagination comes our holiest

1035

calm. It is true that other poets have given this double existence to creation, bestowing a moral and intellectual being upon the material world, but they have done it by hasty suggestions and rapid and short hints, with other purposes in view. Mr. Wordsworth carries us through all its windings,– he touches the strings of our hearts, and the vibration make us feel that they rest upon and connect themselves with every thing in nature.

If poetry of this kind has peculiar beauties, Mr. Wordsworth must remember that it is but a small class of society that can see or feel them. He must not be impatient if the larger portion give the name of mysticism to what they were not born to understand. In truth, what one poet sees to be the choicest parts in another, are not what the world at large ever think of turning to. That which is more obvious, and no doubt very good, is what pleases them, and they are gratified with the thought that they have a sense of the whole. Shakespeare is more read than any work except the bible, yet how many understand a tithe of Shakespeare?

No poet since Milton seems so thoroughly imbued with old English and the truly poetical language, as Mr. Wordsworth. There is no affectation in the use of these, or ill sorting of old and modern phrases, but every word comes from him naturally. His versification, though sometimes tame, is for the most part filled with varied harmony. His main fault in his 'Excursion' is too much rambling and lengthening out, places, of the sentiments and conversation. A little more compactness in such parts would give them life and energy. This appears to be accidental, and by no means a frequent fault. Mr. Coleridge's criticism, in his 'Life and Opinions,' upon Mr. Wordsworth, has more good taste and philosophy in it, than any that has been written upon Mr. Wordsworth, or any other man in modern times. We must except from this, however, his objections to the Pedler. We think that characters enough like him for the purposes of poetry, must have been common in Scotland,– he is in agreement with the scenery, and certainly has an imaginative interest, which it would have been difficult to have given to an accomplished gentleman – a trio of them would have been rather too much.

We regret closing so very abruptly with Mr. Wordsworth, and are no less sorry that we cannot find place for Mr. Coleridge. He is a man of too much originality and genius to be described in half a dozen lines.

(*Ibid.*, 318–20)

EDITOR'S NOTE

1. Bryant had published a Wordsworthian blank verse meditation 'Thanatopsis' in the *North-American Review*, 1817, and in R. H. Dana's essay, 'The Writer of the Idle Man to his Old Friends', *Poems and Prose Writings*, Boston, 1833, Dana tells of conversations with Bryant in which Bryant describes the effect produced upon him by his reading Wordsworth's *Lyrical Ballads* for the first time: 'a thousand springs seemed to gush up at once in his heart, and the face of nature of a sudden to change into a strange freshness and life'.

277. Hans Busk (1772–1862)

From letters to Wordsworth 1819–1820

Busk, scholar, poet and country gentleman, was a neighbour of Wordsworth's brother-in-law, Thomas Hutchinson. Wordsworth possessed three poems by Hans Busk, published in 1819: *The Banquet*, *The Dessert* and *The Vestriad*, all apparently presented to him. Wordsworth reciprocated by presenting, on publication, *Peter Bell*, *The Waggoner*, and *The River Duddon*. Busk appears to have visited, or even lived in, the Lakes for, referring to the *Duddon* volume, he speaks of 'the peculiar gratification of retracing in its pages Scenes & sentiments for which I have had an early & strong attachment'. Whether the contact with Wordsworth was through Busk having an estate in Radnorshire, near the Hutchinsons, or was merely a literary contact is not clear.

a. Letter to Wordsworth, 29 April 1819

I have received the little Bijou which you have done me the honour to send, & think the time you mention to have been employed in polishing it, has been well and most successfully bestowed – It is truly surprising how out of such simple materials you could have worked it to so brilliant an effect as it is indeed pétillant d'Esprit et de graces, and in my opinion is a jewel fit to adorn the front of any poet's wreath –

The skiff excursion is much to my taste; and in an unworthy production which I hope some time or other to have the satisfaction of presenting to you, you will perceive I just launched one by way of experiment, tho' I soon quitted it for a less dangerous vehicle – it is not exactly adapted for the voyage I had to undertake –

In so beautiful a Poem as 'Peter Bell' a preference of any particular passage seems almost an injustice to the rest, but I cannot omit to mention how much I was struck with –

> Where deep & low the hamlets be
> Beneath their little patch of sky
> And little lot of stars:

and this

> A primrose by a river's brim
> A yellow primrose was to him,
> And it was nothing more.

And the stanza that begins

> On a fair prospect some have looked &c

Perhaps the impressive lines of Stanza 29 in the Prologue, would have had a more striking effect upon many readers had they formed the concluding verse of the poem –

I think you have satisfactorily illustrated the proposition which you wished to establish, and that your work will become a permanent ornament to our poetical libraries – Thanking you for the high gratification I have received from the perusal –

(Ms. The Wordsworth Library)

b. From a letter to Wordsworth, 25 May 1819, in which Busk comments on Reynold's parody of *Peter Bell* (see entry 260f)

I see you have a proper indulgence for the Poet who treading on your heels thought no doubt 'Omnia *belle* dicere'[1]: Peter Bell's left-hand wife so far from doing him any harm: increases his consequence & he can afford half a dozen – Great men are only caricatured – A work must be excellent in itself or it cannot be parodied with any effect – If the parody be worth nothing, it drops stillborn – if it be good it is a proof of the merit of the original – these things stamp an Author's importance more decidedly than direct praise –

We wonder at the temerity of the little feather'd chirpers that attend the hawk in his airy excursions, but they feel themselves secure in their insignificance & when he rises to his native heights they are entirely enveloped in the clouds and lost to our sight –

Hoc damnum tibi non videtur esse
Si quod Roma legit poeta carpit[2]

(Ms. The Wordsworth Library)

c. Letter to Wordsworth, 24 June 1819

I have received your kind & esteemed present, & see you have placed a new Waggoner with attendant satellites in the skies.

You have both in this piece & in 'Peter Bell', according to my way of thinking, given most striking & pleasing delineations of the picturesque & beautiful; & embellished Nature in her own true colors.

Whatever half-informed & unreflecting criticks may advance, those who have applied their minds to this species of composition, well know that the difficulty of the task is often in the inverse ratio of the familiarity of the subject; & that simplicity which is one of the highest charms, is one of the hardest accomplishments of the Muse.

Poetry perhaps, in all its range of fascinating powers, affords no treat more engaging than the naïvités of rural scenery & primitive rustic habits sketched by the hand of science, taste & sensibility – while Detraction herself cannot deny your stanzas numberless beauties from this source, the eye of Admiration derives additional pleasure from the contrasting spots which Envy seeks to scatter over the page & which only serve to heighten its lustre, & increase its effect.

I have before said how much I appreciate the talent which can give so fine a polish & brilliance to these crystal ores of our native mountains; & I need only add that whatever *lapidaries* may, I do not esteem this the less tho' it may have somewhat *more color* than the last.

But lest, in an unqualified encomium, the dictates of my feelings should appear to assume the voice of flattery, I must show you that I can find fault & not without reason. – Tho' I allow, generally speaking, it is with books as with animals, that those which are longest in coming to maturity are also the longest lived, yet in your transgression of the rule laid down by Horace, & your extension of his merciless ter ternos *more* unmercifully to ternidenos annos,[3] you will not, I am sure, be countenanced by any of your friends, & most certainly not by me. – It has been said ars longa, vita brevis: but ars brevis, vita brevida,[4] would be more characteristic of the perishable state of things in this life, which whether as to ourselves or our works, is but the infancy & babyhood of immortality. – But whilst I am exhorting you to despatch, I am perhaps actually interrupting your employment, & occasioning that very delay I so much deprecate. – I shall only add therefore that I am, notwithstanding the severity of my criticisms . . .

(Ms. The Wordsworth Library)

d. Letter to Wordsworth, 2 May 1820

Your last publication which reached me on Thursday I assure you I received with great pleasure as the token of remembrance from one for whom I entertain the truest esteem & on whose good Opinion I set the highest value – and in perusing it have felt much interest & delight in the fresh & numerous instances it affords of the amiable disposition, just conceptions, & elevated & extensive capacity of the writer. –

In addition to the admiration which the talents it everywhere displays must create in every reader, I have had the peculiar gratification of retracing in its pages Scenes & sentiments for which I have had an early & strong attachment & which from the captivating dress of bea[u]tiful [*sic*] imagery in which you have decked them, derive new & irresistible charms –

Perhaps not invariably, but generally speaking undoubtedly, those are the best writings that enter the deepest into our minds & none take a firmer hold upon us certainly than they which make us pleased with ourselves. If envy & ill nature interpose not to p[r]event their Operation a state of feeling is produced extremely favourable to the author's intentions & a part of the Complacency excited is, as is but just, set down to his account whilst a portion of the benefit real or imaginery which is produced is & often unfairly assumed to our own. – Now these emotions are never more successfully raised than in cases where the work we meet with revives & embodies & embellishes & reassembles that train of lively familiar & cherished ideas, the first fruit of agreeable associations which early Fancy once tricked out in her richest colouring & which however impoverished & impaired by the withering hand of Time still float in the recollection & solicit the attention with the importunity of old acquaintances who know their value & presume upon their services & to whom we are both unwilling & ashamed to deny the scanty leasings of our vacant hours – 'Tis almost as if [in] a [tedious] absence we received back t[h]e offspring of our youth with powers & faculties developed, improved, matured & perfected from the beneficent hand of some faithful friend & skilful preceptor. Hence it is that simplicity & sublimity are such powerful recommendations & lasting ornaments of all works of art for wherever the task is not vitiated, & sometimes where it is, there resides not seldom unconsciously a native & inherent admiration of these two striking attributes of nature – But it is perhaps idle if not impertinent to insist longer in this to one whose works afford so excellent a commentary on my text. My paper does not permit me to particularize the prominent passages which afforded the most pleasure in the first reading & indeed as the ladies have got the book from me I shall content myself with mentioning the following from M^{rs}. B^{s}. notation – the 2 ['Child of the clouds . . .'], 7 ['"Change me, some God, . . ."'], 15 ['From this deep chasm . . .'], 21 ['Whence that low voice . . .'], & 26 ['Return, content! . . .'], Stanza of Duddon (the only unpoetical thing in which is the name) the Commencement of Dion & conclusion of Lycoris – The Brownies' Cell throughout & the 3^{d} & 5 Inscription in the Hermitage – . . .

(Ms. The Wordsworth Library)

EDITOR'S NOTES

1. 'To say everything well/neatly'.
2. Martial, XI, 24, 5–8:

> You do not think this is a loss
> If what Rome reads the poet criticises.

3. Busk alludes to the thirteen years between the composition and the publication of *The Waggoner*; 'ter ternos' = 9; 'ternidenos annos' = 13 years.
4. Perhaps this should read: 'ars brevis, vita brevior' – 'art is short, life shorter.

278. Sir George Beaumont

From a letter to Washington Allston, 29 May 1819

Allston was an American painter and Coleridge's companion in Italy.

Our friend Wordsworth has just published his 'Peter Bell,' which has brought all the minor wits about his ears, and although he seems insensible to the hum and venom of these gnats, I own I wish he would reserve

these small poems, which afford such scope for ridicule and misrepresentation to injure and traduce him, for future publication, whatever their
merits and beauties may be, and every man of feeling will allow them to
be great, and come forward with his great works. Yet I have no doubt
time will do him ample justice, and although the good his works must
effect sooner or later is indisputable, yet I am unwilling the present
generation should pass away without receiving the full advantages of his
instructions, or he himself pass through life without his due share of
fame, and his family lose the profits of his honorable labors. I send you,
by the kindness of your friend Mr. Leslie, a copy of 'Peter Bell.'

(*Life and Letters of Washington Allston*, ed. J. B. Flagg, 1893, 156)

279. John Scott

Unsigned review, *London Magazine*, March 1820, I, 275–85

Scott had just founded the *London Magazine*, published by Taylor and
Hessey. It was characterised by its support of good writing, not least in
original work – its brilliant contributors including Lamb, de Quincey and
Hazlitt. Scott's essay is an overview of Wordsworth, strongly influenced
by Coleridge's *Biographia Literaria*, 1817. He follows Coleridge in attacking Francis Jeffrey, editor of the *Edinburgh Review*. Within the year Scott
is to die in a duel, the result of his attacks upon Lockhart and *Blackwood's
Magazine*.

THE little island of Ischia is one of those fragments of a land of volcanoes
which have been flung into the sea, and now freckle the light face of the
bay of Naples. The three days we spent there last year, in the house of a
priest, with little of his company, and none of any one's else, will for ever
remain hoarded in the *museum* of our memory, as one of the rarest and
fairest specimens of existence; a thing 'to dream of, not to tell.'

We were seated in the shade, on the priest's balcony, one beautiful
Sunday morning. A woman, with the high and fanciful white head-dress
of the island, was moving below amongst the green leaves of the vines,
and loudly singing a religious ballad of her native place. The sun was
shining, bright and hot, on the main land, where were the Elysian fields,

their tombs, and the promontory of Misena full in front; the lake of Acheron and the Stygian river, grey and steaming, a little on the left; the ruins of Cumea, and the Sybil's cave, were just visible in the distance; and a path of silver lay across from these objects, undulating over the small swellings of the summer water, up to the deep blue of the basin of Lacco, close at our feet. At this moment a stirring breeze suddenly sprung up, and caused all the features of this beautiful sight to quiver like arrows: − it also brought a brigantine in full sail round the headland of the island, and placed the stately vessel in the very midst of the picture, with its canvas hanging like clouds round its lofty masts, and its topmost streamer spreading quietly over them, like the sceptre of an unquestioned monarch.

Very common poetry, we think, would not be apt to intrude itself on so regal a scene; yet we confess that we felt it as but a glorious visible realization of Wordsworth's lines −

> Or, like a ship, some gentle day,
> In sunshine sailing far away,
> A glittering ship, that hath the plain
> Of ocean for her vast domain.*
>
> (*The White Doe of Rylstone PW*, III, p. 285,
> Canto I, ll. 63−66)

Perhaps this may not be exactly the fit introduction to an article of a critical nature; but the circumstance suggested itself so forcibly to our minds in writing the name of Wordsworth at the head of the page, that we could not resist the temptation of going into the description. It leads us, however, naturally enough, to notice one of the distinguishing qualities of this author's writing − distinguishing him, that is to say, amongst most of his contemporaries, and resembling him to the other greatest masters of English song: we mean that perfect harmony with the elements of moral and physical beauty, which causes his poems to form a delightful text-book to nature herself in the most striking of her works.

---

* These are taken from the White Doe of Rylstone; a poem of which the Edinburgh Review says, 'the authors here appear in *a state of love and maudlin imbecility*, which would not have misbecome Master Slender himself, in the close of a social day!' No. 50, p. 356. The reader is requested to support, if he can, another specimen of this maudlin sottish weakness, as the magnanimous Reviewer terms it:
[Quotes *The White Doe of Rylstone*, PW, III, pp. 284−5, Canto I, ll. 43−62:

> A moment ends the fervent din, . . .
> And she is left alone in heaven.]

There hangs about the finest passages of some of the most able poets of our day, an air of force and artifice, which, however high our admiration of them in the closet may go, excludes them from our recollection when we are in the immediate presence of the sacred power from whence proceeds poetical inspiration: their lustre seems then to go out, like that of the most magnificent chandelier that ever was suspended from the roof of a palace, when exposed to the face of a starry sky – Wordsworth, however, never quit us on these solemn occasions: he is with us, as one who has a right to be wherever there is a display of natural sublimity, grandeur, or beauty. He does not disturb the august silence and secret influence of the spot or moment, by officious interference or overstrained invitations and excitements; but, like Moses and Elias in the Transfiguration, he is at once a fellow worshipper and a superior being, whose more intimate communion with the glories before which we are prostrate, only adds to the simplicity of his zeal, and the humility of his devotion.

In all the sterling poets – the immortal masters of the art – a soul of truth and sincerity appears to be the animating spirit of their productions, far above all ambition of composition, yet producing its greatest success. It is this which enables them to penetrate while they please; which causes them to flash on the mind, with the force of lightning, the characteristic and essential qualities of objects, – that which we most feel about them, and are often the least able to express. Wordsworth certainly has more of this power than any other living poet: his lines connect themselves more permanently and easily with the scenery of nature, and the workings of thought and passion, than those of his contemporaries and rivals. They strike on our minds, at the moment of observation, like the light of day, to illustrate and embellish. The passage we have just quoted from him furnishes an instance: – how perfectly, how musically, how gracefully, does it accord with the actual image of the thing represented! and, at the same time, how true and suitable the sentiment which it adapts to the image, to give it a moral life, and an influence over the feelings. The sails of the brigantine in the sun, the stateliness of her port, her gentle yet commanding motion, as if master of herself and all about her, – her superiority over the expanse in which she moves, her singleness in it, her fitness for it, – all conspire to give to her the air and character of sovereignty. This privilege of great poets to touch nature, as it were, with Ithuriel's spear, causing her to start up under it in her true shape and genuine character, is suggested, though not expressly named, by the remark of a living critical writer on Milton's description of the moon, as appearing

Like one that had been led astray,
Through the heaven's wide pathless way.

'In this couplet,' says the writer in question, 'there is more intense observation, and intense feeling of nature (as if he had gazed himself blind in looking at her), than in twenty volumes of descriptive poetry.' – Pindar, when he makes the sun travel in 'the *vast desarts* of the air,' affords another instance of the power of imagination stamping the impression of truth; and there is a striking analogy of thought between the English and the Greek bard in the two passages. Lord Byron's description of the morning,

————smiling as if earth contained no tomb,

though more exclusively sentimental than the two we have just alluded to, is equally real in its spirit, and, like the others, seems to call up in the mind reminiscences of former feelings, to bring back lost ideas and images, 'first affections,' and 'shadowy recollections' – the long passed hour

Of splendour in the grass, of glory in the flower.
['Ode: Intimations of Immortality' *PW*, IV, p. 284, l. 179]

We have heard that, immediately before the first publication of the Lyrical Ballads, Mr. Coleridge waited on an eminent bookselling house, to ask whether, in the opinion of the partners, a series of Poems *in the manner of Tenier's paintings*, was likely to attract popular notice and favour. We do not think it improbable that Mr. Coleridge took such a step, but we cannot compliment it in any way. The Booksellers only know what has succeeded, not what will: – indeed who does? And, while the gentlemen in question were unduly flattered in one respect, they were, we think, almost insulted in another; for Mr. Coleridge is well aware that there is no real resemblance between the character of Wordsworth's works and that of Teniers; but he made use of a bungling illustration, as, in his opinion, most suitable to the parties to whom he was speaking. He was, however, mistaken in this; for to be right is almost always to be intelligible, and *vice versa*. Although the Poems of Wordsworth often relate to familiar characters and incidents, and the Paintings of Teniers always do, no two sets of productions can be imagined more dissimilar the one to the other. The works of the Dutch artist are valuable, beyond measure, for their *literal* truth; the feature which, where it is the most prominent in Mr. Wordsworth's, is very often the least pleasing, or rather the most repulsive. Teniers never leads his spectators further than the mere objects he represents; but he gives these so richly endowed with their proper qualities, and so fully charged with the force of their own peculiar natures, that we are well contented to rest with them. Wordsworth, on the contrary, renders his familiar scenes and characters interesting, only by causing them to suggest and illustrate a certain system of thought and feeling which belongs rather to him than to them; it is rather their latent capabilities, than their apparent properties, which form the value of these in his poetry; and when he is minutely descriptive of their common daily habits, for the sake of elucidating the philosophy of their relative natures, he is evidently too far removed from real companionship with what he represents, for the representation to be pleasant. The familiarity strikes us as assumed for the moment; and the loquacious imbecility, childish trifling, and vulgar bluntness, which he often introduces, contrast disagreeably with the solemnity of the purpose of their introduction, and the betrayed gravity and apostolic fervour of the author. The boors, and boors' wives, and children, of Teniers, appear in his pictures for the purpose of enjoying themselves in good earnest in their own way: there they are, – to act and speak for themselves in and about that which concerns them. If you tickle them, will they not laugh? and if you give them a jug of ale, will they not drink? They will, heartily; and without being conscious that they are furnishing experiments in the philosophy of human nature: but Mr. Wordsworth's peasants are brought in, pretty much as Surgeon Carlisle, the lecturer, brings in Sam, the academy model, to shew the students how a man moves his legs when he walks forwards and how when he walks backwards! In the lecturer this proceeds from quackery; in the poet it is system.

The Waggoner we think one of the finest, if not the very finest, of Mr. Wordsworth's professed sketches from common life; but a waggoner by Teniers would be altogether different, we suspect, – and so would a Highland carrier, depicted by the author of the Scotch Novels. One and the other would give us individuals of their class, of whom we might afterwards think, without any conscious reference to the painter or writer: – but it is *Wordsworth's* Waggoner, *Wordsworth's* Beggar, *Wordsworth's* Sailor, or *Wordsworth's* Schoolmaster, we name in our minds, when recalling the subjects of some of the most celebrated of his compositions. His poetical characters are all marked with the impress of his own personal one; and therefore we think it, on the whole, a pity, that he should attempt any thing but pieces where this impress would be the best of recommendations. In spite of his familiarity of phrase, and long drawn-out minuteness of description, his hedge-menders and ditch-cutters would be shyly looked at by the set at the Swan or the Red Lion, we fear. They would be set down for Methodists, or fellows that could not take their own parts. Even his old women, though they gossip tediously, do not gossip heartily, and would be slightly estimated at the village conclave of a summer evening. The reason of this is, that they are one and all of the Wordsworth fashion, and that is not by any means the true style of pot-houses and gossipping-matches. Mr. Wordsworth's intimacy with these classes is of a speculative not a practical nature: when he imitates their language, it is as the nurse imitates the broken words and ill-put-together phrases of a child – in doing which she generally utters greater nonsense than the child would have done.

This criticism applies to Mr. Wordsworth's compositions only as they may be called, or are intended to be considered, representations of familiar or common life; and it has been particularly suggested by the allusion to Tenier's paintings, so ill-judged and unfounded, as it appears to us to be at least. Mr. Coleridge, in his Biographia Literaria, gives a better account of the object and character of his friend's poems, when he describes the circumstances that attended the original conception of the plan of the Lyrical Ballads: –

> Mr. Wordsworth was to propose to himself as his object, to give the charm of novelty to things of every day, and to excite a feeling analogous to the supernatural, by awakening the mind's attention from the lethargy of custom, and directing it to the loveliness and the wonders of the world before us: an inexhaustible treasure, but for which, in consequence of the film of familiarity and selfish solicitude, we have eyes, yet see not, ears that hear not, and hearts that neither feel nor understand.
>
> Vol. II. p. 2.

In his endeavours to effect this noble object, Mr. Wordsworth particularizes only to generalize.

> From their gross matter he abstracts their forms,
> And draws a kind of quintessence from things.

It is not to the denomination of an object in the common catalogue of life, that he trusts to excite sympathy. 'What's in a name,' he asks? He considers every thing alike as a link in the vast chain that comprehends the universe; and, as great names interfere too much with the moods of his own mind, are not so tractable as little ones, with which he can do as he pleases, he very often gives a preference to the latter. His ambition as a poet he thus describes for himself:

```
                                          ─By words
```
Which speak of nothing more than what we are,
Would I arouse the sensual from their sleep
Of Death, and win the vacant and the vain
To noble raptures.

['Preface' to *The Excursion*, *PW*, V, p. 5, ll. 58–62]

In pursuing this great purpose, Mr. Wordsworth connects the simplest and commonest images with the rarest and often the most complicated thoughts and feelings: – by which we may see what a mistake it is to speak of him as a writer, aiming at simplicity, and failing in the attempt. Mere simplicity does not enter into his plan we believe, and certainly has nothing to do with his system. He is fearless in the familiarity of his expressions, because he is conscious of the depth, grandeur, and importance of his sentiments. A flower gives him thoughts 'too deep for tears:' – in the bright blue eggs of a sparrows nest he sees 'a vision of delight,' and the Colonade of the Louvre would not probably touch him so sensibly. Let those only sneer at him for this, who are prepared to sneer at the power of seeing 'with equal eye,'

A hero perish, or a sparrow fall.

That people in general do not thus see, we admit; but they do not now laugh at Newton for gazing on soap-bubbles in their flight. The very simplicity and apparent triviality of an object, when it falls in the way of a mind full of the order of nature, and of the associated recollections of life, will often cause it to excite the sensibility more quickly and powerfully than qualities of a high and rare cast. When nature hath 'linked to her fair works the human soul,' it will not fail to derive from even the 'daisy,' or the 'small celandine,'

[Adaptation of 'Lines Written in Early Spring' *PW*, IV, p. 58, ll. 5–6:

Some apprehension;
Some steady love; some brief delight;
Some memory that had taken flight;
Some chime of fancy, wrong or right;
Or stray invention.
'To the Daisy' ('In youth from rock to rock . . .')
PW, II, p. 136, ll. 44–8]

But let the poet explain this for himself: he does it eloquently, and touchingly, as it seems to us, in some lines addressed to the former of these flowers, of which the Edinburgh Reviewers pronounce, that they are 'flat, feeble, and affected.' – No. 21, p. 218.

[Quotes *ibid.*, *PW*, II, p. 137, ll. 49–64:

> If stately passions in me burn, . . .
> Hath often eased my pensive breast
> Of careful sadness.]

All this seems very laughable to the Edinburgh Reviewers. So much about a daisy! The poet could not have said more about a crowned head, or one that has been uncrowned! We do not imagine, however, that their tone of feeling in this respect can be fairly considered as indicating the standard of public sensibility. The poet may sometimes push his levelling principles too far, and where he does so he becomes amenable to criticism; but what is to be said of the heart or head of a man who picks out the following exquisite stanza, to support a charge of childishness and affectation, brought against our author in the most caustic language of worldly scorn?

[Quotes 'My heart leaps up when I behold', *PW*, I, p. 226]

The Edinburgh Reviewers actually seize on this passage, deep as it is in sentiment, musical in expression, and inspired in feeling, as ridiculous, – probably because of the three admirable lines with which it closes! The doctrine of him who said that *of little children is the kingdom of heaven*, was foolishness to the Greeks. Mr. Wordsworth, in statelier language than that which we have quoted a little way back, gives at once a winning picture of his own heart, and an eloquent justification of his feelings, and the poetical system founded on them, in the following verses taken from another of his works:

[Quotes *Peter Bell*, *PW*, II, p. 336–7, ll. 131–50:

> Long have I lov'd what I behold, . . .
> 'Tis lodg'd within her silent tear.]

It is only with the very thoughtful; perhaps we should say the very contemplative, that this cast of poetry, stripped of external 'pomp and circumstance,' is likely to be in high favour: – but the coarse, the vain, and the malignant would alone have sneered at it, if the better feelings of the public had not been perverted, on a subject of which it was imperfectly master, by the influence of flippancy and ignorance, accidentally possessing an opportunity of doing much mischief in this way. We do not think that Mr. Wordsworth, considering the general character of his compositions, had a right to calculate on that extensive and immediate popularity which has fallen to the lot of some of his contemporaries, who are certainly inferior to him in poetical power; – but

that he should be insulted in his capacity of poet – he being the author of
the Excursion and the Lyrical Ballads, in which works there is more of
magnificent and touching poetry than in all the other volumes of English verse, which have appeared from the time of Milton up to the present day – is an infamy attaching disgrace to the period. As for those
principally concerned in it, they already feel that they have committed an
irremediable fault, connecting them in reputation for ever with the very
dregs of the taste and judgment of their time. What are we to say of the
critic who gives the following passage, not less distinguished for purity
and distinctness of language and description, than for sublimity of
sentiment, as the continuation of '*a raving fit?*' *Edinburgh Review*, No.
53, p. 12.

> ——The clouds were touched,
> And in their silent faces did he read
> Unutterable love. Sound needed none,
> Nor any voice of joy; his spirit drank
> The spectacle. – *   *   *   *
> In such access of mind, in such high hour
> Of visitation from the living God,
> Thought was not; in enjoyment it expired.
> No thanks he breathed, he proffered no request;
> Rapt into still communion that transcends
> The imperfect offices of prayer and praise,
> His mind was a thanksgiving to the power
> That made him; – it was blessedness and love.

[*The Excursion, PW*, V, Book I, p. 15, ll. 203–7, 211–28]

This is not poetry, we repeat, that ought to be so presently popular as
the Lady of the Lake, or the Pleasures of Hope; – nor ought the
Samson Agonistes of Milton to be so, were it now to appear: – but that
a critic of celebrity, holding a distinguished place in intelligent society,
should quote it as a specimen of raving, is a circumstance not well
calculated to make us exult in the effects of high civilization, and the
diffusion of public information, as it is called. Without such misleaders
of sentiment, Mr. Wordsworth's poetry would have had fair play, and
would have found the estimation to which it is entitled. No one would
have been able to talk of his pieces that had not read them, and this
alone would be a great point gained for him, for, generally speaking,
those who read him admire him. When people are good enough to tell
us that they cannot understand Wordsworth, we willingly take their

words for the fact, and think of Doctor Johnson, who hoped he had not said any thing that could be understood by a chatty individual, then in his company. Lycidas and the Samson Agonistes, are compositions of the highest order of poetry, but if they were lying on one table in a fashionable drawing-room, and the Bride of Abydos on another hard by, we venture to say, that few male, or female hands, would approach to open their covers. Nor does this fact condemn either Milton or the public: – the former has received his due portion of fame from the public voice, – but he has received it only in the fulness of time, which, in his case, has not been retarded by Edinburgh Reviews. Had they existed in his days, how much would their Editor have made of the '*Tetrachordon*' sonnet, and how little of the *Hymn to the Nativity!* He would have picked out the following, probably as a specimen of 'exquisite raving.'

> The stars with deep amaze,
> Stand fix'd in stedfast gaze,
>   Bending one way their precious influence,
> And will not take their flight,
> For all the morning light,
>   Or Lucifer that often warn'd them thence;
> But in their glimmering orbs did glow,
> Until their Lord himself bespake, and bade them go.
>
> And, though the shady gloom
> Had given day her room,
>   The sun himself withheld his wonted speed,
> And hid his head for shame,
> As his interior flame
>   The new-enlightened world no more should need;
> He saw a greater sun appear,
> Than his bright throne, or burning axle-tree could bear.
>
> The shepherds on the lawn,
> Or e'er the point of dawn,
>   Sat simply chatting in a rustic row;
> Full little thought they then,
> That the mighty Pan
>   Was kindly come to live with them below;
> Perhaps their loves, or else their sheep,
> Was all that did their silly thoughts so busy keep.

This is not at all in the style of the most popular modern poetry; and yet we are far from intimating that what is popular at present does not deserve to be so. It possesses many distinguished qualities of its own, and we shall have the pleasure of dwelling on them in the future course of these articles: – but we must protest against considering the present taste as the standard of excellence, or the criticisms on poetry in the Edinburgh Review as the voice even of the present taste. The latter might possibly be better than it is; but, when left to itself, we are sure it is much better than these criticisms. The finest line in Campbell's Gertrude of Wyoming, was cited, in the journal in question, among the objectionable passages; and, while very overstrained praise was bestowed by it on Southey's Don Roderick, the Reviewer took occasion to protest against one of the most poetical ideas in the book. How, he asks, can we commit our sympathies, without distrust, to the hands of a writer who introduces *the shocking tameness of the sea-birds*, which flew round about the fallen monarch in his retreat, as intolerable to his feelings? If he be right, Cowper, as well as Southey, must be pronounced ignorant of the human heart, and the nature of human sympathies, for in the verses 'supposed to be written by Alexander Selkirk,' we find the following lines: –

> The beasts that roam over the plain,
> My form with indifference see;
> They are so unacquainted with man,
> *Their tameness is shocking to me.*

It would not be worth while to follow Mr. Wordsworth's traducers further into particulars: – it is of more consequence to inquire if he have faults that have given to these a very considerable advantage over him, which he might have withheld from them if he had so pleased. If such faults exist, it is important that they should be stated and estimated, in justice even to his genius, for mischief is always done to reputation by concealing any part of a case which is on the whole an excellent one. Some of our remarks in an earlier part of this article will have already convinced the reader that we are no sticklers for the poetic infallibility of Mr. Wordsworth; but we will go further than this, and now state broadly, that he has, in our conceptions at least, misconceived, in some very important respects, the true nature and end of poetry, and that, still more often, he perverts in practice the principles of his theory where they are sound and valuable.

When Mr. Wordsworth thus addresses the flower of the small celandine,

> Thou art not beyond the moon,
> But a thing 'beneath our shoon:'
> Let, as old Magellan did,
> Others roam about the sea;
> Build who will a pyramid;
> Praise it is enough for me
> If there be but three or four
> Who will love my little flower: –
>> ['To the Same Flower' ('Pleasures newly found are
>> sweet') *PW*, II, p. 146, ll. 49–56]

when he thus addresses it, we say, he lets us into the source of the characteristic and besetting faults of his system; for in this passage we see, not only the intensity of his feeling for the quieter and less ostentatious beauties of nature, – which is one of the most distinguishing of the properties of a true poet, – but also a spirit of scorn and dislike towards the more heroic and brilliant manifestations of passion and enterprise. From these he seems to turn with distaste, and rather in an ill-temper than otherwise: but angry contempt is very apt to throw a man off his guard, and we think it has done so to Mr. Wordsworth. He seems sometimes determined, not only to make us admire what is humble, but also what is in itself little: – not only is he disdainful of the accidents and accessaries of grandeur, but he often seems enamoured of the mere circumstances of silliness, vulgarity, and weakness, independently of any thing else. Now, we apprehend, that, if the two be put in the balance, the former will be found the more valuable for the poet's purpose; and that if it be Mr. Wordsworth's intention to discard what is accidental or extraneous, the last ought to be rejected by him as well as the first. To 'trace maternal passion through many of its more subtle windings,' he states to have been his object in the composition of the 'Idiot Boy;' and it is an object worthy of the skill and feeling of the greatest of poets, and to be most happily effected perhaps by placing the scene of the story in humble life: – but how does it assist this object to lengthen out the composition, beyond its natural interest, by the eternal repetition of such names as 'Betty Foy,' and 'Susan Gale,' and by such expletive verses as the following: –

> Beneath the moon that shines so bright,
> Till she is tired, let Betty Foy

With girt and stirrup fiddle-faddle;
But wherefore set upon a saddle
Him whom she loves, her Idiot Boy?
['The Idiot Boy' *PW*, II, p. 68 in footnotes, ll. 11/12]

Such a verse is absolutely disagreeable, first because, having no perceptible connection with the author's object, there is nothing to raise it above the degradation of the common vulgar associations which its language suggests: secondly, because the author's business being with a passion, and a very serious one, this trifling is out of place: and thirdly, because, though it might pass, and even be admired, in a picture where the artist succeeded in giving the exact lineaments of nature in its most homely situations and characters, – where pathos, rudeness, interest, and insignificance should be all mingled up together, exactly as we would be likely to find them in the corresponding conditions of real life, – it is only felt as an incongruity in a composition by an author who does not give, and who cannot give, the real, genuine, hearty, every-day look to his rustic or vulgar characters. We repeat that he goes in amongst these as a philosopher and moralist, not as a companion; and his sketches shew them stiff, awkward, and unnatural, as if they were sensible of his presence, and felt embarrassed by it. The poet, therefore, never being able to conceal himself, or to prevent his own disposition from giving their general hue to all his pieces, ought to preserve consistency in them, by causing his incidents and characters to attend, as satellites, the course of his own mind, following its natural movements, and strictly dependent on its influence. Parodies of 'the unmeaning repetitions, habitual phrases, and other blank counters which an unfurnished or confused understanding interposes at short intervals, in order to keep hold of his subject, which is still slipping from him,'* must appear as mere awkward incongruities in such compositions, and unpleasantly ruffle and disturb the sympathies of their readers.

Let us take as an example the poem of the 'Sailor's Mother.' – How poetically does it open!

[Quotes 'The Sailor's Mother' *PW*, II, p. 54, ll. 1–12:

One morning – (it was cold and wet,
A foggy day in winter time) . . .
I looked at her again, nor did my pride abate.]

---

* Coleridge – See his excellent criticism on Wordsworth's Poetry. – Biographia Literaria, Vol. 2d.

Here is most evident the grand imagination of the poet, 'drawing all things to one, making things animate and inanimate, beings with their attributes, subjects with their accessaries, take one colour and serve to one effect.'* We see in these lines the vision of a dignified female form, approaching through the gloom, with the trappings of poverty hanging about her like darker folds of the wintry mist; and in this way the subject should have been pursued, and all such subjects, by Mr. Wordsworth. – In 'the old Cumberland Beggar,' he has done so consistently: – this piece is altogether in harmony with the following lines, forming its noble conclusion:

[Quotes 'The Old Cumberland Beggar' *PW*, IV, p. 239, ll. 162–97:

> Then let him pass, a blessing on his head! . . .
> So in the eye of Nature let him die.]

What the Edinburgh Reviewers might say to these lines it is scarcely worth while to inquire: the public will feel them properly, and honour the genius and sensibility from whence they proceed: – but, when, from the grand imaginative opening of 'the Sailor's Mother,' which we have quoted above, the poet drops us abruptly into the commonest colloquial language of the poor, clumsily given, and without the vivacity of reality, – we are startled and disappointed at first, and on consideration offended. We ask ourselves, why is this put into the shape of poetry at all, and furnished with rhymes and metre? Poetry includes *ornamental qualities* in its very essence: common scolding is not fit for poetry, however energetic; yet the natural language of anger is well adapted for the poet's use. Something, however, is to be done by him, beyond giving the mere passion, or feeling, or incident: he is to *celebrate*, and celebration supposes array, selection, and adornment. It is not of gold ore that the monarch's crown is made, but of gold drawn forth from surrounding impurities, foreign to its nature and accidental to its condition. The naturalist may find it most interesting in its former state: but Mr. Wordsworth does not represent himself as a mere naturalist; – it has been his endeavour, he says, to give the natural language, of his characters 'purified from what appears to be its real defects, from all lasting or rational causes of dislike or disgust.' This being his principle, we think him often wrong in his practice. 'Dislike and disgust' are, to be sure, strong words; but, Coleridge has told him, with sufficient reason, that 'it is impossible to imitate truly a dull and garrulous discourse, without repeating the effects of dullness and garrulity.'

---

* Charles Lamb upon the genius of Hogarth.

One of three things seems necessary to be done, in order that bare representations of common life may be made pleasant in works of a poetical cast. 1st. The author must be entirely lost in the composition, and the reader's attention be solely attracted to the accuracy of the description, creating a sense of delight by that quality alone, if for no other reason: or, 2dly, the reader must be made to lose himself, in regard to all his usual associations of ideas and feelings with circumstances, by being thrown into another period or place, where such associations would be inapplicable: or, 3rdly, the sense of humour or pleasantry must be excited in his mind, and contrast be thus rendered a source of amusement and satisfaction.

Mr. Wordsworth, in his familiar dramatic pieces, does not observe, or aim to observe, either of the two first conditions: and in regard to the third, whenever he attempts humour or pleasantry, he is positively bad. Nothing can be more uncouth than his attempts at levity of manner. A disagreeable sense of contrast and contradiction, is in every respect, then, excited by his compositions of this stamp, – and to this may be traced that portion of the public distaste which has been fairly experienced towards the author. But these objectionable compositions do not form *one-fourth* of his published works; and the large mass of these is composed of high and pure poetry, majestic in expression, exquisite in sensibility, philosophic in thought, lofty in imagination, and splendid in imagery. That no poetical power, equal to his, exists in the present day, would admit of no debate, if the question were only to be debated by those who are masters of the evidence. Who of our present poets has produced such a passage as the following, which we quote as a specimen of his steady strain, vying in strength, dignity, and simplicity, with the greatest productions of the greatest spirits?

[Quotes *The Excursion, PW*, V, Book VI, pp. 203–4, ll. 542–57:

> ——Say what meant the woes
> By Tantalus entailed upon his race, . . .
> Struggling in vain with ruthless destiny.]

Of his sonnets we say nothing, because their excellence seems to be universally acknowledged. If tender melody, running in unison with pathos of story and sentiment, be demanded, where shall we find any thing to excel these lines: –

[Quotes *ibid., PW*, V, Book VI, pp. 211–2, ll. 787–805:

> As, on a sunny bank, a tender Lamb, . . .
> Till the stars sicken at the day of doom.]

1056

Or poor Ellen's complaint of the faithlessness of her lover: –
[Quotes *ibid.*, *PW*, V, Book VI, pp. 214–5, ll. 867–85:

> 'Ah why,' said Ellen, sighing to herself, . . .
> Of his triumphant constancy and love.]

But the object of this article is not so much to quote or to review, as to offer some observations on Mr. Wordsworth's poetry, considered generally. This we have imperfectly done, with reference both to its merits and its defects. It is more easy to see and describe the latter than to do justice to the former. His errors are, in a great measure, to be traced to his system; and in reading his works we find, in every page almost, reason to join with Coleridge in saying of the author – 'I reflect with delight how little a mere theory, though of his own workmanship, interferes with the processes of genuine imagination in a man of true poetic genius, who possesses, as Mr. Wordsworth, if ever man did, most assuredly does possess, 'THE VISION AND THE FACULTY DIVINE.'

280. Thomas Samuel Mulock (1789–1869)

Report of a meeting between Mulock and Wordsworth in Switzerland, 20 September 1820 (reminiscences from Henry Crabb Robinson, Mary Wordsworth, Dorothy Wordsworth and Edward Kenealy

a. From Henry Crabb Robinson's Diary, 20 September 1820

A stranger hearing my name pronounced on the walk made himself known to us as a Mr. Mulock, a lecturer on English Literature at Geneva and Lausanne. He had letters to Mr. Monkhouse, to whose lady he had rendered services. Before he had been with us five minutes he took Mr. Monkhouse aside, and without any apology intimated to him that the world made comments on his having left Mrs. Monkhouse and Miss Horrocks at Geneva, and very seriously advised him as to his duty as a married man. His conversation began with me by saying that he considered all Mr. Wordsworth's religious poetry as atheism – whose school of poetry he had been 'castigating'. On my remonstrating on this harsh position, he burst out into a furious ultra-Calvinistic rant that all religion was founded on a recognition of the fall of man – that all declamations about God as recognized in the beauties and wonders of nature were

mystical nonsense. In perfect consistency with his contempt for Words
worth he avowed the highest admiration of Lord Byron, a greater poet
than Shakespeare; he saw in his works the profoundest views of the
depravity of human nature – not indeed spiritual views, but though not
spiritually-minded, Lord Byron has developed the human heart, and the
intense truth of all his poetry is its great excellence. I admitted that Lord
Byron's works do exhibit a most depraved and corrupt heart, but
observed that he shares this merit with Voltaire, Lord Rochester, and all
the obscene and profligate writers of Italy and France. Mr. Mulock did
not feel the observation. Of course, these speculative opinions could not
offend Mr. Monkhouse or me, but that seeing us with Mr. Wordsworth,
and knowing us to be his friends, he should express his contempt of his
writings to us in the grossest terms, and at the same time obtrude himself
into his company, appeared to us an instance of indelicacy quite unex-
ampled. I did not conceal my opinion of him. In the evening he forced
Mr. Wordsworth into an argument, and on coming up I heard him utter
such impertinences to Mr. Wordsworth that I could not help interfering,
and assisted in putting an end to the unpleasant conversation. I said:
'Mr. Wordsworth, you are not aware that this gentleman is a lecturer
by profession. He has been lecturing Mr. Monkhouse on the duties of
a husband, you on poetry, and I dare say will soon instruct me in law,
and Mrs. Wordsworth how a lady should conduct herself.' This served
to divert the lecturer's attention from Wordsworth to me, and the
controversy ended . . .

[22 September 1820]

. . . At night I was at the Chisholms'. He is a Scotch physician and a very
respectable man. . . . A literary party, too; the only prominent man
Sismondi . . . he resembles Rogers the poet; has the air of a scholar. We
talked of Wordsworth. I was desirous to counteract the effect of
Mulock's lectures, and I therefore read and expatiated and I believe with
effect.

[24 September 1820]

I then accompanied Trotter to Dr. Chisholm's. I read *Ruth* to the ladies.
Made progress in unperverting them and in generating a love for
Wordsworth, and wished I could have devoted a week to the task. They
enjoyed very much what I did read to them. . . .

(*Henry Crabb Robinson on Books and Their Writers*, ed. Edith J. Morley, 1938, I,
246–7)

b. From the Journal of Mary Wordsworth, kept during a tour of the Continent, 1820

21 September 1820.

We have had merry conversation about our officious acquaintance [Mulock] – but wish we had not met with him, on every other account than that we get our Rydal letters a day sooner – It is a curious coincidence that this letter contains a notice of a Gentleman a stranger to us having called at Rydal who had been on a pilgrimage to the 'River Duddon' & who was such an admirer of William's Poetry that he, to show his respect, had called his son by W^{ms} Name – & that this same letter was brought to us by one who in the course of the day expressed his own opinion to M^r. Robinson, uncalled for, that never was such a heap of trash gathered together as appeared in the four volumes! – Where lies the truth? Posterity will decide! – Glad shall I be to lay hold of those said four Volumes when we reach Geneva tomorrow.

(Ms. The Wordsworth Library)

c. From Dorothy Wordsworth's Journal

19 September 1820.

[Mulock] favoured [Crabb] R. [obinson] and our poet himself with free criticisms of the 'Lyrical Ballads', not concealing that he highly disapproved of that kind of poetry, as childish and silly.

(*Journals of Dorothy Wordsworth*, ed. De Selincourt, II, 299)

d. From the Diary of Edward Kenealy, May 1869

The report of Mulock's reminiscence almost fifty years later at least establishes that Wordsworth's argument with Mulock, from which Crabb Robinson rescued him, was about the merits of Byron's poetry.

May. – Dined with Muloch, who talked as usual without ceasing. He mentioned having met Wordsworth and his sisters at Lausanne. He walked with Wordsworth, who had never been there before, and showed him the Castle of Chillon, 'the subject of Byron's beautiful poem.' 'Do you call that beautiful?' says Wordy. 'Why, it's nonsense. What means "Eternal Spirit of the chainless mind?"' Muloch said there was a very deep and very fine meaning in it. But Wordsworth flew into a rage, and from words they came almost to blows. And Muloch, instead of going back to breakfast with him, rushed off and left him.

(*Memoirs of Edward Vaughan Kenealy*, ed. Arabella Kenealy, 1908, 239)

281. The Etonians: W. M. Praed (1802–1839) and H. N. Coleridge (1798–1843)

From the *Etonian*, 1820

W. M. Praed, while at Eton, edited the ten numbers of *The Etonian*: his pseudonym was 'Mr. Courtenay'. One of the contributors, who are all identified at the end of the tenth issue, was Henry Nelson Coleridge, Coleridge's nephew and brother of John Taylor Coleridge: his pseudonym was 'Gerard Montgomery' (to the confusion of scholars this was a name also used by John Moultrie, another *Etonian* contributor). It seems clear that Wordsworth knew the magazine: on 13 March 1821 he wrote to Crabb Robinson praising a 'Youngster [Moultrie] who writes verses in the Etonian, to some of which our Cumberland Paper has introduced me, & some I saw at Cambridge' (*Correspondence of Henry Crabb Robinson with the Wordsworth Circle*, ed. Edith J. Morley, Oxford, 1927, I, 100).

a. Notice by Praed introducing H. N. Coleridge's essay b., *Etonian*, November 1820

'The Essay on Wordsworth,' said Mr. COURTENAY, 'is a powerful attempt to counteract the effects of a groundless prejudice against one of the first poets of the day. Wordsworth, whose glowing genius and intense feeling his most severe critics cannot but allow, has been too long a stranger to the bookshelves of Etonians. We may be allowed to hope that the efforts of my Honourable Friend will induce our schoolfellows to *read* before they *ridicule*. I feel convinced that "The Etonian" will have strong claims upon the gratitude of his readers, although the only service he renders to them should be the introduction of Wordsworth to their acquaintance.' (*Loud cries of hear.*)

(*The Etonian*, I. 98)

b. Henry Nelson Coleridge, from an essay, 'On Wordsworth's Poetry', *Etonian*, November 1820, I, 99–104, signed 'G. M.'

. . . I have just before said that these persons had been nicknamed a School of Poets; and I said so, because, if we understand by that term what we do when talking of the Schools of Plato or Raffaelle, it is to all intents and purposes a misnomer. Every one knows that in schools of philosophy and painting the precepts and the manner are scrupulously obeyed and imitated; and when any striking aberration from that standard has occurred, the author of such separation has ever been considered the founder of a new sect or school in his own person. Now whoever is at all acquainted with the writings of the Lake Poets (I use the term at present for conciseness) must have perceived, that, so far from there existing any imitation of, or intimate communion with each other, with respect to the choice of subject-matter, or the manner of treating it in their works, nothing can be more essentially different, in almost all points of importance than they are; and as far as concerns the individual genius of each person, I will venture to say that there do not exist such opposite and strikingly various characters of intellect in any other given number of writers of the present day, whether English or Foreign . . . [attacks the Scottish reviewers]

Wordsworth, Coleridge, and Southey were 'Lake Poets,' and their works of course '*Lakish!*' These Scotchmen were born with the malignity of Caligula, but purloined his wit as usual, and gave a collective name to destroy at once.

Since, however, this consummation so devoutly wished for has not taken place, and the reputation and pervading influence of these bespattered Poets, so far from decreasing to a non-entity under the 'unceasing stowre,' have on the contrary gone on slowly, but steadily widening and deepening, and still continue so to do, it becomes a matter of reasonable curiosity to inquire into the causes which have preserved and invigorated them under this tyranny of abuse, whilst not a few of their contemporaries, who, at their first appearance, were bepraised *ad nauseam* by these same learned Thebans, are now sinking fast, some into neglect, and others into contempt.

Now a Poet, in the highest and strictest sense of that word, is he who is a αοιητὴς, a *Maker*, an *Inventor*, whose Imagination, or Shaping Power, can and does embody the forms of things unknown, and can create realities out of airy nothings . . .

The second accomplishment of an absolute poet, or rather, of Poetry, is Imitation; by which term I mean all efforts of the mind, which are not in a genuine sense *original* and *self-springing*, but are modelled after prototypes existing somewhere in *rerum natura* . . .

That many have been endowed more or less with detached emanations of the Poetical Power, and that more have possessed the auxiliar accomplishments, *without* that Power, is also as certain: but to enter upon that subject would be endless; – it is more my immediate object to show that a large portion of the spirit, and an absolute empire over the dependencies, are in the present day centered in the person of W. Wordsworth.

This object, I imagine, cannot be more effectually attained, and certainly not more expeditiously and delightfully to the reader and myself, than by extracting a few passages of different kinds, containing all the essentials, as before laid down, of genuine Poetry; but which shall not be connected particularly with the Author's more private theory, as it is quite necessary, according to all good reasoning, to show that Wordsworth is *generally* a great Poet, before it can be proved even worth the while to investigate that theory at all. For I acknowledge that there is no intrinsic excellence in Singularity of itself, unless it be grounded on, and spring from, the immutable laws of reason and nature, and be *therefore* singular, simply because it is a straight line exposing the obliquities of a thousand crooked ones.

My first proof is the beginning of the 'Address to H.C. six years old.' [Quotes the first 14 lines of 'Address to H. C. six years old', *PW*, I, p. 247; *Poems 1807*, pp. 71–2:

> O Thou! whose fancies from afar are brought . . .
> For what may be thy lot in future years.]

I make no comments upon this extract, or those which follow; because I really suppose that there can be no lover of poetry in any shape who will not confess this and them to be admirable, and such as neither Milton nor Shakspeare in their highest moments would have been ashamed of.

c. Henry Nelson Coleridge, from his second essay on Wordsworth's poetry, *Etonian*, December 1820, I, 217–25. Signed 'G. M.'

I now come to the latter department of my humble vindication of William Wordsworth's Poems, in which I proposed to myself to take notice of those other ingredients of matter or style, which are, or are supposed to be, peculiarly characteristic of those productions. But before I proceed any farther, I must here remark, that the distinction which I have apparently created between Wordsworth as a Poet generally, and the same as a Poet in a sense peculiar to himself, is in reality little better than imaginary; the whole of his Poems, from the shortest to the longest, from the most humble to the most impassioned, being composed strictly upon the principles of one grand comprehensive system; and consequently the extracts in my first letter being just as thoroughly and genuinely the offsprings of that system as any thing which I may think it right to quote hereafter in this my second. The real foundation of the distinction, if any, is this, that the class of Poetry from which those quotations were made is one, with the external dress of which the world is commonly entertained in the writings of others; whereas a few specimens, which I shall take the liberty of presenting to your readers in this essay, will be either the living impressions produced on the heart and the mind by common incidents and natural objects, or they will be the emanations of impassioned feelings, deep thought, and high imagination, and which imperiously demand from the Reader a corresponding sensibility, and an associated temper of the affections, without which much of the most exalted Poetry in the world must of necessity appear dead and meaningless phraseology, from the simple cause that the Reader is himself not sufficiently *alive* to perceive or be animated by the *life* that is before him. The motto and defence of all original thinkers must be, and ever has been, '*Intelligibilia, non Intellectum fero.*'[1]

Having premised thus much, to guard against misapprehension, I now enter upon the particular subject of this letter, namely, the principles which are the foundation as well as the pervading spirit of Wordsworth's Poems. And here I have to lament the utter impossibility of doing any thing like justice to my cause within the narrow limits which necessity imposes on me; though certainly it is some consolation to remember that even Wordsworth himself, with all the eagerness of an advocate, and all his own nervous and fervid eloquence, has finished an exposition of his system with confessing that he found a full and satisfying development of his principles impracticable within the space allowed him in a Preface. What the Poet himself has left undone, I will not presume to fulfil, but will rather content myself by mentioning one or two of the grand creative articles of his faith, upon which every thing he has written is built up, and which, if duly attended to, will lead us, without fear of wandering, into the hidden and wonderful abysses of his Thoughts, and the treasure-house of his Imagination.

This Poet, then, in the first place, is a lover of Nature; not a blind confounder of the Creator with his own creation – not a soul-less grovelling worshipper of the earth without even the supposition of a Providence; – none of these, – but a genuine, pure, religious lover of the Universe, from an ardent belief that it is the symbol and visible exponent of the immeasurable wisdom, and goodness, and majesty of that Almighty God, who is, and was, and is to come. Penetrated, as he himself says, 'to his heart of hearts,' with this living idea, he can pass by in neglect or contempt no component part of this mysterious whole; he denies not to any being, animate or inanimate, its due share of his love; he recognizes in all and singular of the infinite germs of the Universe, the finger and the impress of a superior Being; in winter or summer, in storm or sunshine, in solitudes or in crowds, in joy or affliction, he is still one and the same; ever extracting from human contingencies their universal essence; ever inspiring, in return, his own passionate and blended sympathies, whilst he chastens, subdues, and purifies every thought and every wish by a spirit of unutterable and boundless love. It follows intimately, from the foregoing convictions, that no natural object or incident (with obvious and manifest exceptions) can be too low or insignificant for Poetry; nay, to carry the principle to its legitimate length, that not seldom in rustic life the passions are more vigorous and decisive, the moving springs of thought and action more simple and unelaborate, and the whole system of society more genuine and unadulterated, than when encumbered and concealed by forms of city ceremonial, and deadened by the depraving habitude of perpetual though unconscious deceit. Low life, therefore, is not destitute of admirable materials for poetry; and this particularly, when it is, as is usually the case, associated with the beautiful and sublime of Nature; but these are only the rude *materials* of poetry; they cannot become Poetry itself, unless they are arranged, and modified, and combined by the Fancy; and, above all, impregnated and shaped by the Imagination of the Poet. To express what I mean more clearly by examples, I would entreat my readers to recall to their minds for a few moments the 'Tam o' Shanter' of Burns, and any of Bloomfield's or Clare's verses, and they will instantly understand and feel the mighty difference with which similar or even humbler subjects may be treated by a Poet and a Verse-maker. Here then it is, that Wordsworth lives and breathes in the full enjoyment of creative observation; and, elevated as that observation must be by the vicinity, and, as it were, relationship of the most noble scenery in England, much of his most interesting poetry is concerned at bottom with the ordinary incidents of humanity . . .

Wordsworth is not a *poetical man*, but always and exclusively a Poet; or, to give you his own words –

> Thanks to the human heart by which we live;
> Thanks to its tenderness, its joys, and fears;
> To me the meanest flower that blows can give
> Thoughts that do often lie too deep for tears.
> ['Ode: Intimations of Immortality', *PW*, IV, p. 285, ll. 201–4]

It would be unfair, however, both to Wordsworth's fame and to my readers also, if I compelled them to take what I have said simply upon credit; and I am sure it is delightful to me when I can claim a proper opportunity of committing the cause to the Poet's own maintaining, by quoting his own words. The three following passages are an eminent proof, in different manners, of his wondrous power of creating and colouring common objects by the intenseness of his Imagination: –
[Quotes *Peter Bell*, *PW*, II, pp. 353–5 in footnote, ll. 491–530:

> He scans the Ass from limb to limb . . .
> And drops, a senseless weight, as if his life were flown!]

Can any thing, especially if read in connexion with the original Poem, be more intensely terrific than this passage? – and yet what is the real cause of the terror?
Again: –
[Quotes *The Waggoner*, *PW*, II, pp. 200–1, Canto IV, ll.102–15:

> And the smoke and respiration . . .
> Him and his enemies between!]

Can any thing, I repeat, be more natural and exquisitely beautiful than this? – and yet what is the object which has become the cause of this beauty?
Now mark, lastly, the miraculous, and almost sylphish fineness of melody and imagination displayed in these lines following: –
[Quotes 'The Kitten and Falling Leaves', *ibid.*, p. 170, ll. 5–16; *Poems 1807*, pp. 58–9, ll. 5–16:

> Withered leaves – one – two – and three – . . .
> In his wavering parachute.]

But it is a pernicious, though a common mistake, to suppose that the largest, or the most important share of Wordsworth's Poems is composed of pieces of the character of those quoted above. Inimitably beautiful as are these workings upon natural incidents, and quite, as I believe, beyond the example of former ages, yet they are as dust in the balance, when brought in contact with those mighty, those painfully mighty, energies and travaillings of the Soul, of which many of his longer Odes and Blank Verse poems are composed. And here it may be a good opportunity to point out one eternal master feeling, which more or less may be traced as either forming the foundation of, or giving a colouring to, almost all his writings. It is an earnest faith in the intrinsic godliness and immortality of the Soul, raised upon the Platonic theory of pre-existence; differing from the sordid system of metempsychosis, in that he believes that Spark within us hath never been sullied or dimmed by mortal incarnation before, but comes, as it were, fresh and original from some unimaginable vision and enjoyment of the Deity. Hence those passionate addresses to infancy; those melancholy retrospects upon what is never to return again; for in our downward course of life we go daily farther from the fountain of our existence, and become more and more 'earthy,' and forgetful of 'that imperial palace whence we came.' But why do I hesitate to give you his own intense and exalted creed in his own matchless numbers?

[Quotes 'Immortality Ode', *PW*, IV, p.281, stanza 5:

> Our birth is but a sleep and a forgetting . . .
> And fade into the light of common day.]

These 'shadowy recollections,' then, 'are the master light of all our seeing;' they 'cherish us – and have power to make

> *Our noisy years seem moments in the being*
> *Of the eternal Silence.*

And then for the retrospect which a meditative and imaginative Mind can exercise: –

[Quotes *ibid.*, p. 284, stanza 9, ll. 162–8:

> Hence, in a season of calm weather . . .
> And hear the mighty waters rolling evermore.]

I am conscious that I have already quoted more than my limits will properly allow; and yet I know not how I can omit showing my favourite in one more, and that probably the most affecting point of view. The following lines are from the poem on 'Revisiting the Wye,' which let no one presume to read without also *thinking*. They are Φωνᾶντα συνετοῖσι· ἐς δὲ τὸ τὰν ἑρμηνέων χατίζει.[2]

[Quotes 'Tintern Abbey', *PW*, II, pp. 260–1, ll. 35–57; *Poems 1807*, pp. 112–3, ll. 35–57:

> Nor less, I trust . . .
> How often has my spirit turned to thee!]

Before I conclude I must take notice of one specious and very common objection to any assertion of the merits of Wordsworth. 'If,' it is said, 'Wordsworth be so great a poet as you would have us believe him to be, why is he not more popular?' I will also ask a question. What is the meaning of the word *popular?* Is it to be the first and eternal requisition at the circulating library? Is it to be praised in the reviews? Is it to be copied in the newspapers? Is it to be the pillow and dear favourite of boarding-school misses, or even (*salvo pudore dixerim*)[3] of desperate harlots? If this be to be *popular,* – and I declare conscientiously I believe it to be the essence of modern popularity, – then the most frantic and impure novels of Lady Morgan or Godwin, then Brutus and the Italians, then Little's Poems, then Hone's ingenious squibs, then Don Juan, are unquestionably the most popular works of the present day! For who or what shall compete with them? It is frightful to know the tremendous and exclusive empire which these, and works like these, hold over the variously intermingled classes of England. *They* are *popular* – and verily, verily, they have their reward.

But I entirely and absolutely deny the validity of the criterion that popularity is the test of merit! It is not so now; it never was in England or any other country. If it had been, then would neither Æschylus, nor Sophocles, nor Euripides, nor Aristophanes, be the first of ancient tragedians and comedians; for they were repeatedly beaten in a contest with rivals, whose works are now as if they had never been, and whose names are only preserved by the grammarians! . . .

EDITOR'S NOTES

1. 'I bring what can be understood, not what is (already) understood'.
2. 'those that speak to the wise, but for the generality need interpreters' (Pindar, *Olympian*, 2, 85–6).
3. 'May I have spoken without offence to modesty'.

Index

Page numbers in **bold** type refer to individual documents.

579, 625, 815, 818, 925, 950–1;
Records of Literature, **176–7**;
revisions, 91; Rickman, **127**;
Robinson, **60**; *Satirist*, **201–4**;
Seward, **129**; Southey, **57**, **58–9**,
60, **65–8**, **107–8**, **120–1**, **161–5**;
Spedding, **59**; Stoddart, **137–43**,
148; Stuart, **84–6**, **159**; 'T.N.',
160–1; Twining, **119**; Warner,
115–16; Wilson, **108–14**; C.
Wordsworth, **55**, **102–3**; D.
Wordsworth, **107**; J. Wordsworth,
95–9; W. Wordsworth, **104–5**,
161–5; s*ee also under individual titles
of poems*
Lysons, Samuel, 254, 255

McArthur, John, 82
Macaulay, Thomas Babington, Lord,
6, 290, **503**
Mackintosh, Sir James, 1, 3, 41, 317
Mackintosh, Lady, 308
'Mad Mother, The', 42, 69, 77, 81, 85,
89, 100, 106, 151, 147, 255, 335,
883
Madge, Rev. Thomas, 316, 317, 318,
493, 497, 498, 504
'Malham Cove', 654
Malthus, T. R., 501
Manning, Thomas, 46, 91–2, 100–2,
103–4, 293
Mant, Richard, *see Simpliciad, The*
Marini, 901
Marlborough, Duke of, 726
Marshall, 669
Marshall, Cordelia, 843, 983
Marshall, Jane, 843, 983
Martial, 1039, 1041
Marvell, Andrew, 224, 356, 924, 925
Massinger, Philip, 397
'Mathetes', 108–9, 287, 299
'Matron of Jedborough and Her
Husband, The', 184
'Mathew', 103, 227
Matthew poems, 91, 103, 140, 150,
226, 464, 808, 830, 832, 978,
1017–18
Mawman, 171

May, John: Southey to, 121
Medwin, Thomas, 291, 909–10, **994**
'Memoir of the Rev. Robert Walker',
772, 777
'Memoir of William Wordsworth',
1025–30
Memorial of a Tour of the Continent, 9
Merivale, John Herman, 56, 171, 327,
437–43
Metaphysical Poets, 365, 444, 561n,
705
metaphysics, 43, 842, 842n
Methodism, *see* religion
'Michael', 52, 89–90, 96, 97, 98, 101,
103, 108, 121, 141, 172, 243, 244,
260–1, 287, 298, 758, 808, 833, 838,
841, 871; 'Sheepfold', 98
Michelangelo, 77, 183, 1011
Mill, John Stuart, 10, 11
Milnes, Richard Monckton, 974
Milton, John, 56, 75, 101, 104, 118,
125, 158, 160, 200, 202, 208, 218,
220, 263, 285, 332, 333, 334, 338,
340, 342, 376, 382, 425, 449, 450,
471, 489, 490, 496, 504, 534, 558,
580, 606, 619, 620, 672, 685, 756,
757, 784, 798, 801, 818, 823, 841,
848, 875, 876, 904, 912, 913, 917,
918, 919n, 920, 925, 929, 932, 937,
1012, 1023, 1044–5, 1062;
'L'Allegro', 753; *Comus*, 879;
History of Britain, 628, 798;
'Hymn on the Morning of Christ's
Nativity', 1051; 'Lycidas', 1051; 'On
the Detraction Which Followed
Upon My Writing Certain
Treatises', 770–1, 772, 1051;
Paradise Lost, 344, 415, 459, 491,
572, 612, 768, 856, 924, 949, 1013,
1015; *Paradise Regained*, 768, 856,
1015; *Samson Agonistes*, 625, 626,
879, 1050, 1051; 'To Sir Henry
Vane the Younger', 879; 'To the
Lord Protector Cromwell', 879;
Wordsworth 'the Milton of our
day', 51, 936, 1036
Mitchelson, Miss, 114
Mitford, Mary Russell, **842–4**

THE CRITICAL HERITAGE SERIES

GENERAL EDITOR: B. C. SOUTHAM

GEORGE ELIOT	David Carroll
HENRY FIELDING	Ronald Paulson and Thomas Lockwood
GEORGE GISSING	Pierre Coustillas and Colin Partridge
OLIVER GOLDSMITH	G. S. Rousseau
THOMAS HARDY	R. G. Cox
GEORGE HERBERT	C. A. Patrides
GERARD MANLEY HOPKINS	Gerald Roberts
SAMUEL JOHNSON	James T. Boulton
BEN JONSON	D. H. Craig
JOHN KEATS	G. M. Matthews
SIR THOMAS MALORY	Marylyn Parins
CHRISTOPHER MARLOWE	Millar MacLure
ANDREW MARVELL	Elizabeth Story Donno
GEORGE MEREDITH	Ioan Williams
JOHN MILTON 1628–1731	John T. Shawcross
JOHN MILTON 1732–1801	John T. Shawcross
WILLIAM MORRIS	Peter Faulkner
WALTER PATER	R. M. Seiler
ALEXANDER POPE	John Barnard
EARL OF ROCHESTER	David Farley-Hills
JOHN RUSKIN	J. L. Bradley
SIR WALTER SCOTT	John O. Hayden
WILLIAM SHAKESPEARE 1623–1692	Brian Vickers
WILLIAM SHAKESPEARE 1693–1733	Brian Vickers
WILLIAM SHAKESPEARE 1733–1752	Brian Vickers
WILLIAM SHAKESPEARE 1753–1765	Brian Vickers
WILLIAM SHAKESPEARE 1765–1774	Brian Vickers
WILLIAM SHAKESPEARE 1774–1801	Brian Vickers
PERCY BYSSHE SHELLEY	James E. Barcus
PHILIP SIDNEY	Martin Garrett
JOHN SKELTON	Anthony S. G. Edwards
TOBIAS SMOLLETT	Lionel Kelly
ROBERT SOUTHEY	Lionel Madden
EDMUND SPENSER	R. M. Cummings
LAWRENCE STERNE	Alan B. Howes

PRAISE FOR

'Anne Holt reveals how truly dark it gets in Scandinavia'

Val McDermid

'Anne Holt is a thriller writer of the highest order'

Liza Marklund

'Lively, unusual and persuasive. Holt writes with the command
we have come to expect from the top Scandinavian writers'

The Times

'It is easy to see why Anne Holt, the former minister of justice
in Norway and its bestselling female crime writer, is rapturously
received in the rest of Europe'   *Guardian*

'Step aside, Stieg Larsson, Holt is the queen of Scandinavian
crime thrillers'   *Red*